A DEBATE

BETWEEN

REV. A. CAMPBELL AND REV. N. L. RICE,

ON THE

ACTION, SUBJECT, DESIGN AND ADMINISTRATOR

OF

CHRISTIAN BAPTISM;

ALSO, ON THE

CHARACTER OF SPIRITUAL INFLUENCE

IN

CONVERSION AND SANCTIFICATION,

AND ON THE

EXPEDIENCY AND TENDENCY

OF

ECCLESIASTIC CREEDS,

AS TERMS OF

UNION AND COMMUNION:

HELD IN LEXINGTON, KY., FROM THE FIFTEENTH OF NOVEMBER TO THE SECOND OF DECEMBER, 1843, A PERIOD OF EIGHTEEN DAYS.

REPORTED

BY MARCUS T. C. GOULD, STENOGRAPHER,

ASSISTED

BY A. EUCLID DRAPIER, STENOGRAPHER,

AND AMANUENSIS

PUBLISHED,

LEXINGTON, KY.: BY A. T. SKILLMAN & SON;

CINCINNATI: J. A. JAMES;—LOUISVILLE: D. S. BURNETT;
NEW YORK: R. CARTER;—PITTSBURG: T. CARTER.

Stereotyped by J. A. James, Cincinnati.

1844.

Stereotyped by J. A. James,
Cincinnati.

CERTIFICATE.

CINCINNATI, March 6th, 1844.

HAVING carefully examined the Report of the within discussion, furnished by Messrs. Gould, of Cincinnati, and Drapier, of Louisville, and compared it with our notes and memoranda; we hesitate not to authenticate it, and to commend it to the public, as a full exhibition of the facts, documents, and arguments used by us on the several questions debated.

A. CAMPBELL.

N. L. RICE.

RELIGIOUS BOOK SERVICE
722 North Payton Road
Indianapolis 19, Indiana

CORRESPONDENCE.

Richmond, Ky, September 19, 1842.

MR. CAMPBELL:

I should have addressed you at an earlier date, but my engagements have been such as to utterly forbid. Upon reflection, I have concluded to leave the questions involved in our contemplated discussion, with other preliminaries, to a committee, which can meet, probably, at an early day in November.

The brethren who will engage in the discussion, so far as the Presbyterian church is concerned, will be selected during the sessions of the synod, which will commence at Maysville on the 13th proximo.

Of how many shall this arranging committee consist—two or three on each side? When and where shall they meet—Lexington? say November any time before the 5th or after the 17th.

This committee will be empowered to fix the time (Lexington being the place agreed upon) of debate, form of questions, rules, moderators, and make arrangements for one or more competent stenographers to take down the debate preparatory to publication, as agreed by the committee.

To shorten our correspondence, I hope you will fix the number of the arranging committee, at either two or three, as you may prefer; also the day of meeting, within the time specified. I hope to receive an answer before I leave for synod, so that all our arrangements and appointments can be made while there. I consider our correspondence as private until consent is given for publicity. Yours, fraternally, JNO. H. BROWN.

Bethany, October 5, 1842.

MR. JOHN H. BROWN:

Dear Sir—Yours of the 19th ult., mailed the 20th, is to hand. From the earnestness with which, while I was in your town, you sought a discussion of certain points at issue between Presbyterians and those christians called Reformers, and from the proposition to address me in writing, soon after my arrival at home, about the end of August, I had promised myself the pleasure of an early communication from you relative to the proposed discussion, and a more ample interval for settling, the propositions for discussion. as well as other preliminaries, before the meeting of the synod. But from your delay, no doubt occasioned by an unavoidable expediency, you now propose, "upon reflection, to leave the questions involved in our contemplated discussion, with all other preliminaries, to a committee, which can meet, probably, at an early day in November."

You then ask me of how many shall this arranging committee consist, &c. &c. To all which I beg leave to respond, that I do not think that any committee, which I could nominate, in conjunction with such a one as you might raise, could so satisfactorily to the parties arrange all these matters, as we ourselves, who enter into. the discussion. I prefer to express my own propositions, in my own words; and in all such matters, where the principals can so easily act, I do not think it expedient to employ attornies or

11

proxies. As to the appointment of moderators and the adoption of the rules of discussion, these are minor matters, compared with the propositions to be discussed; still, they are important, and, while I would not pertinaciously object to any equitable arrangement of such matters, my conscientiousness and my prudence alike forbid the selection of propositions by a committee on which to form an issue, unless after their submission to my consideration and adoption. This would require time, and, probably, occasion a long delay. But it is competent to the synod to select its own propositions, and to propound in its own terms what it wishes. I will therefore suggest what I think will meet your views, as expressed during our interview.

1st. You affirm that the infant of a believing parent is a scriptural subject of baptism. We deny it.

2nd. You affirm that sprinkling water upon any part of an infant or adult is scriptural baptism. We deny it.

3rd. You affirm that there is no indispensable connection between baptism and the remission of sins, in any case. We affirm that there is.

4th. You affirm that the constitution of the Presbyterian church is founded on the New Testament. We deny it.

5th. You affirm that the doctrinal portions of the Westminister confession of faith are founded on the Scriptures of truth. We deny that they all are.

In this form, or by dividing the propositions into affirmatives and negatives, so as to give to each party an equal number, we can soon form a just and honorable issue. In one word, I will defend what I teach and practice, in plain and definite propositions, and on your agreeing to do the same, the whole matter may be arranged in the most satisfactory manner by correspondence, the only alternative that I can at this late period think of.

Very respectfully and fraternally, your obedient servant,

A. CAMPBELL.

Richmond, October 22, 4842.

ELDER A. CAMPBELL:

Dear Sir—Yours of the fifth was received previous to my leaving for synod, also a duplicate copy while at Maysville attending its sessions.

There is evidently a misapprehension, on the part of one of us, as it regards our interview at Richmond, in August last. You seem to intimate that I, with earnestness, sought a discussion of certain points at issue between Presbyterians and those christians called Reformers. Let the facts speak for themselves. They are briefly the following:

At the close of your address in Richmond on the 3rd of August, your friend, Mr. Duncan, approached me and asked my opinion as to the address, which I gave with as much candor as it was sought.

After other interrogatories were propounded and answered, he inquired, if I thought discussion advisable; to which I gave an affirmative reply. He then remarked, that he had engaged to dine with you, and would ascertain your feelings and wishes on the subject.

All this occurred before we left the church. About 4 o'clock in the afternoon Mr. Duncan sought a second interview with me, and requested me to call in company with him at your room, stating that you desired an interview with me on the subject, about which he and I had conversed in the forenoon.

I conformed to his wish, and accompanied him to your room, which ultimated in a mutual agreement to discuss certain points of difference for the edification of the church and the prosperity of the cause of Christ, with a definite and expressed understanding that neither was to be considered the challenging party.

You further intimate that my delay in commencing the correspondence was doubtless "occasioned by an unavoidable expediency." This I consider a very unkind and unfraternal insinuation, and one which I had not expected from your urbanity as developed in our interview, and especially after recognizing me as a " *brother* " in the close of your epistle. It is a plain intimation that the correspondence was procrastinated *solely* on the ground of expediency, when I had expressly placed it on *another* and a *very different* ground.

I also understood it to be *settled*, in case *we* did not agree as to the form of the propositions, that *this*, with all other preliminaries, was to be left to a committee, selected from ten chosen individuals, composed of an equal number from each side. Your reply is evidently a departure from this agreement. You say, no committee could so satisfactorily arrange the propositions as we ourselves could. You add, " I prefer to express my own propositions in my own words ;" " My conscientiousness and my prudence alike forbid the selection of propositions by a committee on which to form an issue, unless after their submission to my consideration and adoption."

You further state, " It is competent to the synod to select its own propositions, and to propound in its own terms what it wishes."

The competency of the synod to express its wishes on this or any other subject, I presume, would not be questioned. But the synod is not a party in this matter, and, *as such*, has no propositions to make. According to our arrangement, they were to be agreed upon by *you and myself*, and, in case of our disagreement as to *their form*, the committee, referred to above, was to arrange the whole matter.

You present five propositions, which " you think will meet my views, as expressed during our interview."

The 1st, 2nd, and 3rd of these propositions embrace points of discussion agreed upon in our interview.

The 4th and 5th not only embrace subjects agreed, but every thing else we, as a denomination, believe and teach. In the 5th, you put us upon the defence of the entire confession of faith. To this I do not object, because of its indefensibleness, but on the ground of its not being one of the agreed points of discussion, and introducing far more than was, at the time, contemplated either by you or myself.

Your 1st proposition, in the following words, " You affirm that the infant of a believing parent is a scriptural subject of baptism," is accepted without any modification or alteration.

Your 2nd, in these words, " Your affirm that sprinkling water upon any part of an infant, or adult, is scriptural baptism," I accept with only a slight verbal alteration, viz : I affirm that sprinkling, or pouring, water on a suitable subject is scriptural baptism. You deny.

I might justly have required you to take the affirmative and prove *immersion only* to be baptism, but I would not pertinaciously stand out for the mere verbiage of a proposition, but only for its substantiality.

Your 3rd proposition is, " You affirm that there is no indispensable connection between baptism and the remission of sins in any case."

Strange as it may be, you make me, in this proposition, affirm a negative. I therefore substitute another, which, while it will in its discussion involve substantially your proposition, presents as the main point, a question on which we differ widely, and one which you urge in your various works as of primary importance. The proposition is as follows :

3rd. You affirm that the new birth, as mentioned in John, third chapter, is a change of state, and not a change of heart. I deny.

I now propose a substitute for your 4th and 5th propositions, covering the agreed points of discussion, and to which you will not object, as they are taken substantially, if not verbally, from your own publications.

4th. You affirm that the use of creeds, or confessions of faith, is contrary to the Scriptures, and destructive of the unity and perpetuity of the church of Christ. We deny.

5th. You affirm that all the converting and sanctifying power of the Holy Spirit is contained in the Divine Word. We deny.

B

Upon these several propositions an equitable issue can be taken, and the whole matter speedily arranged for full and free discussion.

On my part the men are selected:—Brethren Jno. C. Young, R. J. Breckenridge, N. L. Rice, J. F. Price, and myself, will engage in the discussion. Brother Rice and myself have been selected as a committee of arrangement, to meet such committee as may be selected on your part, to settle preliminaries, at some suitable time and place, agreed upon by you and myself. I would suggest Lexington as the place, and the 21st of November next as the time.

In hope that the issue is now made, and that the preliminaries may soon be settled, I subscribe myself, respectfully, yours,

JNO. H. BROWN.

Baltimore, Nov. 17, 1842.

Elder John H. Brown,

Dear Sir—Your favor of the 22nd ult., addressed to me at Bethany, Va., having been, by my orders, copied by my clerk, was duly forwarded to me at this point, and received by me on my arrival here. Such, however, have been my engagements with the public, (having had to deliver a public address for every day during the last three weeks, on a tour in eastern Virginia, and to this city) that I could not find a leisure hour to reply before this date. Of this tour, I gave you some intimation when you proposed to me your views and wishes relative to a public discussion.

To proceed, then, to the contents of your favor, now on my table, allow me to say, that the narrative you now give of the occasion of your soliciting a discussion, is as curious as it is novel and unexpected. The fact of your soliciting a public conference, with no other preamble to me expressed, than "*that once yourself and your brethren had not been friendly to public debates, but that now you have changed your ground, being convinced that the state of society and religious opinion demanded it,*" is all that I thought important to the arrangements proposed, without the details of the mere *occasion* of your personal application to me. As to the definite and express understanding that neither should be regarded as the challenging party, I have no distinct recollection. I do, indeed, remember that you emphatically spoke of your desiring a friendly discussion; and, if the phrase " challenging party," was expressly used, of which I cannot say I have any recollection, it could, in the connection of ideas, by you suggested, intimate no more than that you did not desire to be contemplated in the light of a challenger, but as of one desiring an amicable discussion; to which I fully accorded, as in courtesy bound. Still, however, our respective positions to the fact of a discussion must stand, now and forever, different. You as the originator and propounder of it; I as accepting, and agreeing to, your proposition. No complimentary or courteous disclaimer of the technicalities or usual compellations on such occasions, could possibly change our positions to the fact of a discussion.

I admit the ambiguity of the phrase, at which you demur, in my former communication. to you, viz. " Your delay in reply was, doubtless, occasioned by an unavoidable expediency." But I left it with you to interpret it; and as you now say, the expediency was not of choice but of necessity, I am perfectly willing to accord to you in the case, the most ingenuous conduct. I wonder, however, how you could construe this into a discrepancy with my subscribing myself yours, "*fraternally,*" inasmuch as I have often heard, in synods and councils of your own church, much less complimentary interpretations of actions pass most fraternally amongst the ministry.

You next proceed to say, that you "understand it to be *settled,* in case we do not agree as to the form of the propositions," &c. I, indeed, as you will, I doubt not, remember, stated distinctly, that as our conversation in Richmond was wholly extemporaneous and fugitive, that I would expect from you a written statement of all matters, as you proposed them, on my return, which communication should be regarded as an original document, and as the basis of our correspondence relative to a discussion, and, therefore, I considered nothing as fixed about it, further than, *I did agree to meet at Lexington, Kentucky, in conference, with such persons as the synod of Kentucky would appoint—provided they would select certain persons to meet a delegation to be appointed by our brethren in Kentucky; but that I would agree to debate, not as one of a conference, but with one responsible person only*, and then named President Young, as such a person. You immediately responded, I should have him, as you did not doubt the synod would select him. As for propositions, on my inquiry, you went on to name those concerning baptism, &c. I emphatically say, that I then considered, and now consider, every thing else as open to our future arrangements, not as arranged. True, indeed, as a conference was spoken of, without any distinct understanding of the mode of procedure, or of the topics to be introduced into it, it might have been said, that a committee might arrange such matters; but as to a *personal discussion*, on my part, with any reputable and authorized disputant, I repeatedly said, that I went for single combat; and on premises explicitly stated, propositions clearly and fully expressed, before we met upon the ground. And this is all for which I now feel it my duty to contend. I am happy, indeed, that there appears, on the principal points, named by you, at our interview, so nearly a perfect agreement. I cheerfully accept your amendment to the second proposition, and will agree to place the third in an affirmative form. The three propositions would then read,

1st. The infant of a believing parent, is a scriptural subject of baptism.

2nd. The sprinkling, or pouring water, upon any part of an infant, or adult, is scriptural baptism.

3rd. There is a scriptural connection, of some sort, between baptism and the remission of sins of a believing penitent.

These three cover all the ground of debate between us, on christian baptism. If you insist upon five propositions only, I shall not insist upon any more. One of these would respect the Holy Spirit; the other, human creeds as the causes of schisms among christian professors. Touching your suggestions of a proposition, embracing the difference between us, on special influence, I have not much objection to either of them, as containing, in the connections, and with the modifications, always contemplated by me, a just view of the matter. Still, they cover not the whole ground of debate. We both agree, that the Holy Spirit is given to all who believe and obey the gospel. But, with regard to the influence of the Spirit in converting sinners, there is some discrepancy. We teach, that the Holy Spirit operates on sinners only through the Word, and not without it. Your denomination teaches, *that the Spirit, without the Word, regenerates the sinner*. Thus, the Word contains the converting power—and regeneration is a change of heart and life by the Word. But the 3rd and 5th contemplate a change of state, in reference to the kingdom of heaven, therein referred to. I will then offer two propositions, expressive of our real position.

4th. The Spirit of God regenerates sinners, without the Word.

5th. Human creeds have always occasioned and perpetuated divisions among christians, and are barriers in the way of their union.

To this I would add a 6th—"The celebration of the Lord's death is essential to the sanctification of the Lord's day, by a christian community." Of these six propositions, I affirm three, and you affirm three. You affirm the 1st, 2nd, and 4th. I the 3rd, 5th, and 6th. I will discuss these in single debate with Mr. Young, provided the conference, you contemplate, do not agree on these points.

It will then be necessary for me to have a distinct understanding upon this view of the matter. All the preliminaries, for such a discussion, must be agreed upon before I leave home.   Such as, 1st. The proposition.   2nd. The order of discussion on the affirmative and negative sides.   3rd. The board of moderators.   4th. The stenographer, and the mode of publishing said discussion.   5th. The disposition of the avails of said publication.

I will select for the conference, Elders James Shannon, Dr. James Fishback, Aylett Rains, and John Smith, of Kentucky, as associates in the conference.   The two first shall be my committee of arrangements as to the conference; and as to the debate, they shall be my moderators, to meet two of your choice; these four choosing a president moderator.   If these matters are thus despatched, as aforesaid, I see no great need of delay in securing a stenographer, and in agreeing to bestow the avails of the publication, half and half, to the two Bible Societies.   So soon as I hear from you satisfactorily, I will address Messrs. Shannon and Fishback, on the subject of meeting your committee at Lexington.

Very respectfully, yours fraternally,
A. CAMPBELL.

Richmond, Ky., Dec. 8, 1842.

Elder A. Campbell:

Your favor of the 22nd ult., is now before me.   After the explicit statement, in my last letter, of the circumstances which led to our interview in Richmond, and which resulted in an agreement to have an amicable discussion of the points of difference between us; I deem it unnecessary, at present, to say any thing more on that subject.

In regard to the points to be discussed, I hope we shall be able, without serious difficulty, to make a fair and honorable issue.

You say " I cheerfully accept your amendment to the 2nd proposition," and yet you immediately present it again, without that amendment.   This, I presume, was done through mistake.   The proposition, with my amendment, which you have accepted, reads as follows, " I affirm that sprinkling, or pouring water, on a suitable subject, is scriptural baptism.   You deny."

Concerning the 3rd proposition, as presented in my last, you say nothing, but present another, as follows :

" 3rd. There is a scriptural connection, of some sort, between baptism and the remission of sins of a believing penitent."

This proposition is an exceedingly indefinite sort of thing, and is, therefore, decidedly objectionable.   I can see no possible objection to the following proposition, as already offered you, viz :

" 3rd. You affirm that the new birth, as mentioned in John, 3d chapter, is a change of state, and not a change of heart.   We deny."   With you, baptism is the new birth, so that the proposition, above stated, presents for discussion <i>the design</i> of christian baptism, and this is what we desire to embrace in the proposition.

Your 4th proposition, of which you expect us to maintain the affirmative, is as follows: "The Spirit of God regenerates sinners, without the Word."   This is not the doctrine of the Presbyterian church.   We maintain, that in the conversion of men, there is an operation of the Spirit <i>distinct from the Word,</i> but not in ordinary cases, <i>without the Word.</i>   I propose, as a substitute for your 4th, the following proposition, taken verbatim from your Christianity Restored, p. 350.

" 4th. The Spirit of God puts forth all its converting and sanctifying power, in the words which it fills with its ideas."

The 4th proposition, as contained in my last, is, I think, preferable to your 5th, on the subject of creeds; and mine certainly is not stronger than the language you have on that subject.

The sixth question, which you propose, I think, does not present a difference of such importance, as to make it a point of discussion.   If a 6th question be desirable, (though not embraced in our original agreement) I propose the following :

6th. None, except ordained ministers, are by the Scriptures, authorized to administer baptism.

There is now no probability that Brother Young will be able to enter into the discussion with you. He has, for several weeks, been confined to a sick bed, and, when last heard from, was dangerously ill. Should he recover, the condition of his lungs would not admit of his engaging in a protracted discussion. You shall, however, be met by "a reputable" disputant.

It is my duty, also, to state, that the name of Rev. R. J. Breckenridge, was placed among those selected by me, without his knowledge. He informs me, that he cannot be in Kentucky at the time the discussion will take place. In his place, therefore, I will name the Rev. J. K. Burch.

Rev. N. L. Rice, and myself, will meet your committee of arrangement.

Rev. J. K. Burch, and myself, will be moderators. Other matters, such as the order of discussion, &c., I presume can be settled by the committee of arrangements. If you object to this, you can make, in your next letter, any proposition which you may think important.

I hope to hear from you, at your earliest convenience. If you agree to the propositions for discussion, as now presented, other necessary arrangements can be made, I presume, with little difficulty.

Very respectfully, yours,
JNO. H. BROWN.

Bethany, Va., Dec. 15, 1842.

ELDER BROWN,

My Dear Sir—Yours of the 8th ult., was received yesterday. My acquiescence in the proposition you were pleased to make in August, touching an amicable discussion of points at issue, between our respective denominations, was given with a reference to two great objects. The first, the prospect of having the main topics of difference fairly laid before the community, with the reasons for and against—the second, that the arguments, on both sides, might go to the world with the authority of the denominations, so far as their selection and approval of the debaters were concerned.

Only on these grounds, and with these expectations, could I have been induced to participate at all in any oral discussion, after all that I have written and spoken on these subjects; and, therefore, it is essential to my position and aims in this affair, that the preliminaries be so arranged as to secure these objects. I should think, indeed, that, to you, these points are equally interesting and important.

Allow me, then, to say, that the three great topics which have occupied public attention for some twenty-five years, so far as our purposed reformation is concerned, are,

1st. The ordinances of christianity.

2nd. The essential elements of the gospel itself.

3rd. The influence of human creeds as sources of alienation, schism, and partyism in the church.

Now, in some points, only, of these three categories do we differ from Presbyterians, and other Pedo-baptist professors. These are baptism, the Lord's supper, spiritual influence, as connected with the use of the word "regeneration," and human creeds.

You selected baptism, and I alluded to the others. On baptism we agree, that, both logically and scripturally, there are three distinct propositions. The *action*, the *subject*, and the *design*. On the Lord's supper there is one—on regeneration one, and one on the subject of human creeds. In all six. According to our respective teaching and practice, these six propositions are as follows:

1st. Sprinkling, or pouring water, upon a suitable subject, is scriptural baptism.

2nd. The infant of a believing parent is a scriptural subject of baptism.

2   B 2

3rd. Personal assurance of the remission of past sins, to a believing penitent, is the chief design of baptism, or, if you prefer it, "*Baptism is for the remission of sins.*"

4th. *In all christian communities the Lord's supper should be observed every Lord's day.*

5th. *The Word, as well as the Spirit of God, is, in all cases, essential to regeneration; or, some persons are regenerated by the Spirit, without the Word believed.*

6th. *Human creeds, as bonds of union and communion, are, necessarily, heretical and schismatical; or, human creeds, as bonds of union, are essential to the unity and purity of the church.*

You affirm the 1st and 2nd positions on baptism, and, also, the two last versions of the 5th and 6th. I mean to say, your printed creed and party do so. I affirm the 3rd and 4th, and the 1st version of the 5th and 6th. We can, therefore, easily find each three affirmative propositions, such as we are accustomed to teach and to defend. Now, sir, as I said before, I am prepared and willing to defend what I teach, on my affirmatives. Are your party? If so, then I am not fastidious about a word. I regard the above as a candid and definite expression of our relative positions on these six points: and these involve our whole systems of christian doctrine and teaching. As you have led the way in baptism, I claim as many propositions on the other points at issue. You have extracted some two or three propositions from my writings; and, in return for these, I might select as many from your creed, which is still of higher authority than the writings of any individual—and, although you may believe them, such as some articles on effectual calling and election, yet they are not such propositions as convey all that you would affirm on those themes. This is just my case. These propositions are expounded in their contexts, and they need their contextual adjuncts. I, therefore, prefer independent, clear, and definite expressions of great principles. I have no doubt that you, too, will prefer these, to such passages as those to which I have alluded.

After this full expose of propositions, I have only to advert to the second great object of such a discussion, viz. the *authority* with which it addresses the community. You cannot have forgotten that the express condition of my taking part in any oral debate with your denomination on such topics, was, that the synod, to whose timous meeting you alluded, should select, or approbate, such persons as might be supposed able and competent to enter into such a discussion, to make it as much as possible an end to the controversy. You first alluded to synodical arrangements, and this suggested to me the necessity of stipulating for Mr. Young, president of the Centre College, at Danville, because I regarded him as a gentleman, and a scholar of high standing, who had the double stake of a theological and literary reputation, to stimulate and govern his efforts on the occasion. You immediately rejoined, I should have him. Now, sir, allow me to say, that having consented on this condition, and only on this condition, to attend such a discussion as you proposed, I could not be expected to engage with any other person, unless in one of two events;—that Mr. Young continued to be physically unable to attend in person, within some reasonable term, or, in case of his ultimate inability, that the synod have appointed some person in whose ability the community might confide. It will, therefore, on your part, as well as mine, be expected that I should be assured of the fact, that Mr. Rice, or Mr. Burch, or some other person, has been selected, or approbated, by the synod, to represent the party in the contemplated discussion.

The propositions being agreed upon, and the person with whom I am to contend, selected by the proper authorities, those other matters, as to a stenographer, and the rules of discussion, &c., &c., can be easily arranged. I do hope, then, kind sir, that you will embrace your earliest convenience in responding to such items, in the communication, as may demand your special attention. With the kindest regard, I remain, as ever, yours.

                                                    A. CAMPBELL.

Richmond, Jan. 3, 1843.

ELDER CAMPBELL :

Dear Sir—Yours of the 15th ult., was received on the 22nd, and would have been answered earlier, but protracted religious exercises prevented.

One point *only*, in your last, demands present attention. Until that is understood and agreed, all efforts to settle the questions for discussion, and arrange preliminaries, will be unavailing.

I allude to synodical action. I understand you to take the ground that you will not debate, unless the individual is appointed, or approbated, by synod.

In your first communication you intimated as much. In reply, I stated definitely, that the synod neither was, nor could be, a party in the contemplated discussion. I also stated, that the persons selected, were chosen, *not* by the synod, but in conference, and, that some of them were known and acknowledged to be the most prominent men in our church.

All these facts were before you, yet, in your reply, you do not make a single objection, but pass the whole matter in silence.

Surely, if you intended to object on this ground, *then* was the time, and *there* the correspondence would have terminated.

My understanding was, that the persons engaging in the discussion would be agreed upon at the meeting of synod, not that there would be a synodical appointment.

I well knew that such an appointment, for such an object, was not within the legitimate power of any of our ecclesiastical judicatories.

Even had the synod possessed the power, and exercised it, and appointed the requisite number of men, there appears to have been no appointment by any body of men on your side.

If the appointment, on your side, had been made by a body of men, convoked for the purpose, still, *that* body would sustain to your church no such relation as our synod does to ours, and, therefore, we would not stand on equal footing.

Perfect equality is that for which we will most certainly insist.

If your object be to give importance to the discussion, we will agree to add, 5, 10, or 15, to the number on each side, with the understanding, that the debater, on each side, be selected by them.

We fear not discussion, and are willing to do all that is equal and honorable, but, if you insist on making unequal or impracticable terms of debate, the matter, of course, must terminate. I await your response.

Very respectfully, yours, JNO. H. BROWN.

Bethany, Va., Jan. 13, 1843.

ELDER BROWN:

Dear Sir—Yours of the 4th inst., was received on the 11th ult. My engagements yesterday forbade an immediate reply.

You say one point only demands present attention, viz.—synodical action. The idea of synodical action was suggested by yourself at our interview, and again presented in your first written communication, in the words following, to-wit:—"The brethren, who will engage in the discussion, so far as the Presbyterian church is concerned, will be selected during the sessions of the synod, which will convene at Maysville, on the 13th *proximo.*" This, though strong enough, is not quite so expressive of synodical action in the case, as your original, verbal declarations, in the presence of our mutual friend, Mr. Duncan.

Your next epistle, after the meeting of synod, contained the ambiguous phrase, that the synod were not "to be a *party*" in the debate. I did not then contemplate them in the light of a party; but while I hesitated what such a phrase could mean, after our previous interchange of views and intentions, I concluded, for the moment, to reserve it for future explanation

On learning, from your last, that certain persons were to be withdrawn, and certain new persons were to be appointed in their stead, I ask, what could have been more natural, with all these references to synodical arrangements, before made, than to recur to original propositions, both verbal and written, as to this thing of synodical, or confidential, selection and approval. I have done so, and find your present communication makes new propositions and arrangements, never before contemplated. Really, I was not prepared for this.

My participation in any discussion was asked by you, and stipulated by me, on the assurance that I should have certain persons, some of them then named; and that too, with the concurrence of your church met in synod. Whether the thing was to be transacted *in concione clerum, ex cathedra,* or in various conferences, gave me then no concern; provided it had the concurrent approbation of your church. You positively said, I should have the persons named, and, that you doubted not that the synod would agree to it. Such were the clearly expressed premises on which I assented to be present.

If you have changed your views of the expediency of such an arrangement, or, if the persons, then agreed upon, will not attend, you are at perfect liberty to withdraw your propositions. But I will make no new covenant, the first having been abandoned.

I am perfectly willing to meet the persons named by you, in your first communication after the synod met, at our mutual convenience, believing that they were agreed upon at the meeting of the synod. But I cannot admit of your substitutes for them.

I care not who the Presbyterian church appoints, nor in what form it be done, provided, the persons appointed are known to be the selection of the denomination. The reasons I have always given, for any preference, were, that I desired a final discussion of those litigated points; and such a discussion as would have the highest authority, that our respective denominations could confer upon it.

If our brethren, in Kentucky, prefer any other person to me, I yield the arena in a moment. But, friend Brown, I go not in pretence, but in fact, for *equality.* Let your church sanction, in any way you please, some new man, or give me those you promised, and I am perfectly satisfied.

You say you *fear* not discussion, and are willing to do all that is equal and honorable. This is just what I wish to hear you say. I only ask you to redeem the pledge, and shew your faith by your works. Very respectfully and benevolently, your friend, **A. CAMPBELL.**

Richmond, Madison Co., Ky., March 8, 1843.

Elder A. Campbell:

Serious inflammation of my eyes has prevented me from writing for several days past, but for this your communication would have been answered at an earlier date.

In reply to my last, on the subject of synodical action, you thus remark: " The idea of synodical action, was suggested by yourself at our interview, and again presented in your first written communication."

The language I employed at our first interview, which made the impression of synodical action, I know not. I may have expressed myself incautiously, and, possibly, I employed such language as would authorize such an inference. But, manifestly, the language of my first written communication, quoted in your last, and now before me, does not authorize such a deduction.

Whatever may have been your previous understanding of synodical action, and whatever requisitions you may have been disposed to make, relative to this point, I am gratified to find the whole difficulty obviated by the following declaration in your last, viz. " I am perfectly willing to meet the persons named by you, in your first communication, after the synod met, at our mutual convenience, believing that they were agreed upon at the meeting of the synod. But I cannot admit of your substitutes for them."

Your perfect willingness to meet those individuals, is in *full view* of the fact definitely stated, in my former communication, that *they* were *not appointed by* the synod, but only agreed upon *at* the synod.

In a former communication, I suggested that one of the men selected at synod, lived in a distant state, and, that when written to, he found it utterly impracticable to attend.

You certainly cannot object to *one* being chosen to fill his place, by the other *four*, inasmuch as this plan was agreed upon *at* synod, in case the individual, who was absent, could not come, and, especially so, when the men, on your side, (and you go for equality) have not been selected "*in concione clerum, ex cathedra*, or, in various conferences."

You are aware, also, of the fact, that the synod cannot meet again till next autumn, and, therefore, an individual to fill the vacancy, cannot be chosen *at* synod.

The difficulty you make (surely without the slightest reason) seems equivalent to a declinature of the discussion.

But, if you still object to our selecting an individual to fill the vacancy, then the *four*, who were named in the letter, after the meeting of synod, will meet you and three of the men selected by yourself, and go on with the debate.

The health of brother Young is much improved since I last wrote, and this impediment would, therefore, be removed.

If you agree that the vacancy shall be filled by the *four*, originally appointed, (it being understood at the time that they would exercise this power)—or, if you are willing to proceed with four on each side, then the way will be open for the settlement of the three remaining questions, preparatory to discussion.

I await your response, and shall be governed accordingly.

Respectfully yours,   JNO. H. BROWN.

Bethany, Va., March 17, 1843.

Dear Sir—Yours of the 8th inst. was received on the 15th, and, though not in very good health to-day, I hasten to reply in a few words to the favor before me.

Waiving any comment on your explanations and historic allusions to our correspondence, I hasten to say, that I have no objection to the choice of a fifth person, in room of Mr. Breckenridge, by the four gentlemen agreed upon at synod ; especially, as you say, that it was an understanding at synod, that should any one fail in attendance, the others might elect a substitute.

I sincerely hope, that in all despatch, you may be enabled to respond satisfactorily on the propositions already offered, so that time may be redeemed, especially as now full two months have been consumed in getting an answer to my former letter. Should matters progress so slowly on the propositions, and other details, it will require a full year, at least, to settle the preliminaries. I think, indeed, it is very prudent, nay, absolutely necessary, to have every thing clearly understood, and plainly stated in writing, before commencing, as nothing more directly tends to preserve good temper, and to prevent a mere logomachy, than clear and definite propositions, good rules and equal terms. In this, I feel a very *special* interest, also, as the debate contemplated will, according to our previous understanding, be immediately between Mr. Young and myself, supported, as we shall be, by our respective friends on each side.

Please then afford all facilities for a consummation so devoutly to be wished, and as promptly as possible.

With all respect and benevolence, I remain your friend,
A. CAMPBELL.

Georgetown, April 8, 1843.

ELDER A. CAMPBELL:

Dear Sir—Yours of March 17th, post-marked 20th, is received. You agree that the four individuals, selected *at* synod, may select a fifth in lieu of Rev. R. J. Breckenridge. We, therefore, select Rev. Jas. K. Burch, as before mentioned.

Although the health of brother Young has improved, as stated in my last, so that he can be present as one of the five, there is scarcely any probability that he will be physically able to go through with a debate so protracted as the *one* we have in contemplation.

I did agree, in our first interview, that *he* should be one of the five, but not by any means that he should be the only debater, for I did not at that time, suppose that the discussion would be confined to *two* individuals, but that *all* on each side would take part; however, I will not object to such an arrangement, if you desire it, only reserving the right, in case of physical inability on the part of brother Young, to select *one* from our number to debate with you.

With regard to the questions, I hope we shall have but little further difficulty. As to the mode and subjects of baptism we are agreed.

Your 3d proposition, as stated in your letter of Dec. 15, is objectionable in both of its forms. In the *first* form, because your full ground is not occupied; and, in the *second*, because in scriptural language, concerning which we would probably differ. I must, therefore, insist on *my* 3d, as presented in my communication, of Dec. 8th, viz.

3d. "You affirm that the new birth, as mentioned in John, 3d chapter, is a change of state, and not a change of heart." We deny.

This embraces the difference between us, the *design of baptism;* for *baptism,* is, with you, the new birth. To this proposition you have presented no objection, though you offered another in its place.

Your 4th is as follows, "In all christian communities, the Lord's supper should be observed every Lord's day." This is objectionable, because comparatively unimportant. If any church, or denomination, choose to observe the supper every Lord's day, then be it so. We do not consider it a matter of sufficient importance to demand discussion. We have already suggested a much more important subject, involving the validity of baptism, which we offer as the 4th proposition for discussion, viz.

4th. "None except ordained ministers are, by the scriptures, authorized to administer baptism." We affirm. You deny.

Your 5th proposition is objected to, because it affirms *less* than in your *publications* you have affirmed, and does not fully present the difference between us. We hope you will agree to discuss the proposition already submitted, taken *verbatim* from your Christianity Restored, p. 350, which we present as the 5th proposition.

5th. "The Spirit of God puts forth all its converting and sanctifying power in the words which it fills with its ideas." To this you certainly cannot object. It is in your essay on Divine Influence, *italicised,* and therefore the *cream,* the very *essence* of the whole thing. You can, of course, refer to your writings in illustration of your doctrines.

Your 6th proposition is as follows, "Human creeds, as bonds of union and communion, are necessarily heretical and schismatical." We do not understand *exactly* what you mean by the phrase "*bonds of union and communion*." We, therefore, suggest the following alteration or amendment, viz.

6th. "The using of creeds, except the Scriptures, is necessarily heretical and schismatical." You affirm. We deny.

As soon as we shall agree on these, or other propositions, involving the difference between us, on the agreed points of discussion, brother Rice and myself will meet your committee in Lexington, and arrange preliminaries preparatory to discussion, at our earliest mutual convenience.

Very respectfully,   JNO. H. BROWN.

Bethany, Va., April 24, 1843.

Dear Sir—Yours of the 8th inst., post-marked 10th, arrived here on the 19th inst. Business of much importance, and obligations various and numerous, prevented my careful reading of it till to-day. You inform me that the improvement of Mr. Young's health is not such as to warrant the hope that he will be physically able to endure the fatigue of a protracted discussion. My consent to participate in a public conference, was given upon the solemn pledge on your part, that if single combat should be the result of our interview, I should have Mr. Young. This has again been stated in our correspondence, and fully assented to by yourself. A rumor has more than once or twice reached my ears, that this pledge on your part, was never to be redeemed; and that in the well known policy and style of ecclesiastic diplomacy, in a protracted correspondence, you would manage it to substitute Mr. Rice for Mr. Young; and thus in any issue of the affair, Presbyterianism would stand either upon her reserved learning and talents, or upon the triumphs of the said Mr. Rice. Reluctant though I have been to listen to such a rumor, so discreditable to your candor and christian sincerity, I confess, things begin to wear an aspect somewhat ambiguous, squinting, at least, in that direction.

I am not a man to be managed just in that way, and have replied to madam rumor, that the moment you presented Mr. Rice, you have forfeited every claim upon my attendance; and that unless the denomination, in some way, selected him in preference to Mr. Young in scholarship and discursive talent, I should have nothing to do with the affair. True, indeed, I should not insist upon Mr. Young's presence if he was physically unable—but I am often physically unable myself, to do justice to any subject, in the way of even a single speech, much more to questions of protracted discussion, and, therefore, make my appointments and arrangements accordingly. The time has been so long protracted already, that it will not greatly affect your reputation, should it be made to suit the health and convenience of Mr. Young.

Mr. Rice may be as learned, and as able a disputant, for any thing I know to the contrary, as Mr. Young; but he stands not so high with the community either as a polite gentleman or a scholar; and I presume, is discreetly located at Paris, while Mr. Young *exmerito* presides at Danville. The reasons given by me first and last for taking part in such a discussion, compel me to demand the fulfillment of at least the two essential conditions on which my consent was obtained;—the first, that there should be a full discussion of the main points between us;—the second, that I should have the disputant named, in order to give it authority with the whole community. The moment you recede from this ground, you have released me from every pledge and obligation that I have given. You need not repeat to me that I ask from you conditions which you have not propounded to me, as you have done on a former occasion. We do not meet exactly upon that ground. My presence was *demanded*, even after I had said that Kentucky had talent and learning enough to maintain the reformation cause against every denomination in the state; and it was *promised* on those conditions, AND THOSE CONDITIONS ONLY. If then yourself and your brethren are not willing to meet on the conditions stipulated, you will please so inform me, and the matter ends.

With regard to the propositions, I am not a little surprised at the reluctance you manifest to discuss the *design* of baptism, indubitably one of the main issues and points advanced in the pending reformation controversy. Would you have me and the public to think that you wish to slur and blink that question? If not, why propose such a substitute for the main point of debate? You offer the new birth for the design of baptism!! and then again, bring up spiritual influence and converting power in another proposition. If you do not design to evade the design of baptism altogether, why create the suspicion by such an indirect and ambiguous mode of procedure! This will never do, Mr. Brown. You and your party have assailed our views of the design of baptism a thousand times; and, depend upon it, you must not shrink from it now. I have often told you I must defend what I preach; and as your party oppose my views behind my back, you must in honor, do it now before my face; if not for my sake, at least for your own. Unless then you concede that our views are correct on that subject, you must debate it! As you refuse to take up the whole confession of faith, I cannot but admire your generosity in putting me on the defence of all my writings, and your culling out such insulated and detached sentences as you think most favorable to your intentions. I see you have formed high conceptions of my magnanimity. Still I would have you take care of your own. Do not say, nor even think, that I refuse the examination of those sentences; you can bring them forward under their proper heads. But through respect for the literary character of our discussion at the bar of public opinion, I would not appear as a logician in defence of a sentence or an individual expression, while the whole category to which it belongs is unassailed. Let us prove the genus—or the species—and then we shall not contend about the individual. Your calling a sentence the cream and essence of a whole system, because it is italicised, is an aberration of reason of the same character. Divine influence—creeds, and the ordinances of the supper—are points at which we are at issue. We must have propositions setting forth our respective views on these topics. I deny abstract spiritual influence in conversion and sanctification. You affirm it. The propositions submitted by me, are indicative of our respective views, as I understand them. So of creeds. If you choose to add another proposition, concerning who may administer baptism, I have no objection—rather than substitute any one of these offered by any other you can devise. I will discuss as many more as you please, essential to our respective systems. But the four questions of baptism, regeneration, the Lord's supper, and creeds, are great, essential points of discussion: and the six propositions furnished by you and myself on these topics, must, according to our agreement, be debated, unless you concede some of them.

The time is already past in which this meeting was, according to our Richmond conversation, to have taken place. Our college vacation is in July and August. I do hope then you will accommodate me and the public, so far as to have it either in the end of July or first of August. You may, in a single letter, now settle all these points on fair and honorable principles. It is in your power. We must have stenographers secured as soon as possible, or we must sell the copy-right to some good house in the East, who will send on a stenographer, and so have matters speedily arranged. The propositions, and the main points settled, our committee can soon adjust other matters. Please answer this immediately.

In all benevolence, yours, &c.   A. CAMPBELL.

Richmond, Ky., May 15, 1843.

Elder Campbell:

Yours of the 24th ult. is before me. Its contents present too much evidence of what I have for some time apprehended, that you are resolved to avoid the proposed discussion.

I gave no pledge of any kind, that Mr. Young should be your opponent, but only that he should be one of the five in debate; but if I had, *physical inability* is, I believe, universally admitted to excuse. Mr. Young has for months been in feeble health; and there is no probability of his being able to engage as the *only debatant*, in such a discussion as the one proposed. He is now able to preach only *occasionally*. But when you are informed of this fact, you insult me by speaking of your reluctance to listen to a rumor, "so discreditable to my candor and christian character!" Yet you say, "True, indeed, I should not insist upon Mr. Young's presence if he were physically unable."

Well, sir, he is *physically unable* to go through with such a debate. Still he is able and willing to be present as one of the *five* on our side. If then you are resolved to debate with no other man, the matter is at an end.

Ordinary courtesy, I suppose, would have forbidden the introduction of the name of Mr. Rice, as you have thought proper to introduce it. It would have been quite time enough for such remarks, when his name had been mentioned by me, as the disputant on our side. I do not wonder at your reluctance to meet Mr. Rice. He has health to go through such a discussion, and is accustomed, as well as yourself, to public debate. But it seems his standing in the community "as a polite gentleman," is not high enough for you! With all deference, I beg leave to say, I am not aware that his standing, in this respect, is inferior to Mr. Campbell's. As to his *learning*, it is sufficient that Presbyterians are willing to risk their cause in his hands, even against Mr. Campbell. Whilst it is unnecessary for me to say any thing about the comparative merits of Messrs. Young and Rice, I may smile at the ground on which your opinion is founded, viz. that the one is at Danville, and the other at Paris. I am not aware that the standing of Mr. Campbell "as a polite gentleman," or "a scholar," is much higher since he became President of *his* college, than before. We offer you a Presbyterian minister as your opponent, who shall be selected by us precisely in accordance with the arrangement made AT synod, viz. that we would select one of our number to meet you in debate. Now you have your choice to retreat or accept.

I have manifested no reluctance to discuss the *design* of baptism. I have simply presented it precisely in the form in which you yourself have constantly presented it in your publications. With you baptism is the *new birth*, and it is designed to effect a change of state. This is precisely what we propose to discuss. Yet you seem to be in great wonderment that I should "offer the new birth for the design of baptism!"

But I am not particular as to the precise statement of the question. All I ask is that you take the whole ground in debate, which you have taken in your publications. This you have not ventured to do, and I fear you never will. The moment you do, we shall accede to your proposition.

On the influences of the Spirit, I have offered you a proposition in your own language, and you refuse to discuss it.

When you find a clear proposition in our "Confession of Faith," which we refuse to discuss, you may then proclaim to the world that we have retreated.

The proposition I have offered you is clear and full, embodying avowedly your faith on this point; whilst those you offer us, throw both sides off their true ground. What you mean by "abstract spiritual influence," I do not know; but if you mean spiritual influence *without the word*, you must know, if ever you read our Confession, that we hold no such thing, except in cases where the word cannot be received.

State a proposition containing your real views, and making a fair issue, and it will be accepted. But if you retreat from your own language, the reason will be understood.

In regard to the Lord's supper, we have objected to discussing your proposition, simply because we deem it of minor importance, and because our church, in her confession of faith, neither affirms nor denies. It is silent on that point. We are not, therefore, disposed to discuss such a question. The question concerning the administrator of baptism, is quite as important as either of the others, involving the validity of the ordinance.

Your reluctance to discuss it, is, I fear, another evidence that you have published important things which you would rather not defend.

We are ready for you, just so soon as you are willing to meet a man who is "physically able" to go through with the debate, and to defend your published doctrines. Respectfully yours,   JNO. H. BROWN.

C

Bethany, Va., May 24, 1843.

ELDER BROWN:

Dear Sir—Yours of the 15th, came by to-day's mail. You now say that it "presents too much evidence of what you have for some time apprehended, *that I have resolved to avoid the proposed discussion.*" This conclusion makes me curious to know your premises. Nothing that I have said or done, would seem to me to authorize such an inference. The propositions which constitute your premises, are most likely those which you are now about to offer, at which you thought I would most probably revolt. Circumstances appear to favor this presumption. Hence, ever since you thought of offering them, you have apprehended that I "would avoid the proposed discussion."

When seeking to withdraw the man of my choice, promised by yourself, and to dictate all the terms, propositions, and conditions of debate, it is natural for you to expect, that as an honorable man, I should decline taking any part in such a discussion. I demanded your most gifted, learned, and accomplished man as my opponent, in case of a debate. Nothing mentioned at our personal interview, is more distinctly remembered, nothing is more frequently alluded to in our correspondence, and never contradicted by yourself, than that I should have Mr. Young for my opponent, if it came to single combat, as I then affirmed my convictions, and expressed my desire that it would. You now seem to deny any such pledge, or agreement on your part. Your words are, "You shall have him." If these words do not constitute a pledge, pray what language could be so construed?

Nor is this fact, though deeply engraven on my memory, depending on that alone for its certainty. In my letter of Nov. 16, it is written "I will debate with one person only," and then named president Young as such a person. You immediately responded, "You shall have him, as you did not doubt but the synod would select him." This is freely admitted in your reply of Dec. 8, stating at the same time that "there is now no probability that brother Young will be able to enter into the discussion with you." Do not these words affirm that he was to have "entered into the discussion" with me! Surely you will not stultify yourself. You know the meaning of words too well, to plead ignorance of the import of your own language. But you are even still more explicit in declaring your understanding of the pledge, for you speak of his engaging in a protracted discussion with me, for which you alledged "the state of his lungs would disqualify him." In these words, you admit the pledge, or agreement, which through the treachery of your memory you now seem to deny.

Again, my dear sir, may I not ask why you did not attempt to undeceive me when, in my letter of Dec. 15th, I stated my reasons for preferring Mr. Young; reminding you also of the fact, that you stood pledged to have him for my opponent, and that I could not be expected to engage with any other, unless on conditions then proposed. In your reply to this letter, Jan. 3d, you do not demur at all to this view of the matter in any one particular. You merely inform me that the appointment was not made *by*, but *at* the meeting of synod.

Again, in your letter of March 8th, after quoting my words indicative of my willingness to meet such a conference raised at the synod, you informed me "that brother Young's health is much improved, and that, therefore, this impediment would be removed." Now, after all this, to say that there was no such agreement or pledge, on your part, indicates it not that some of your mental powers have given way, and that you ought to be allowed the benefit of retraction?

Well, but if you did so agree, you may ask—indeed, you have virtually asked, would I insist upon having an opponent physically unable? No, indeed; I want a full grown man, of good natural and acquired ability, and also in good plight. But Mr. Young was such a man last August, and he may be such a man again next August, or soon after. I have long since resolved never to debate with an inferior man when a superior can be had. I prefer to await his perfect recovery, rather than to enter the list with an inferior man.

My object has been so often stated to you, that I deem it almost needless again to say, that neither my own honor nor interest demand this, but the interest of the whole community. That, sir, now calls for the best man in your ranks. True, I am so sensible of the strength of my position, that however inferior I may be in other respects, I am willing to meet the strongest man in Christendom on those points at issue between us.

If, then, I am constrained to refuse your new proposition, it is not because the man offered is so formidable, so mighty and argumentative, but because he is not by the community judged to be equal, much less superior, to the persons named. At least such are my impressions. If, however, in this I am mistaken, I am open to conviction. I say again, sir, I desire your strongest and most accomplished man, whether in Kentucky or out of it. I desire to make an end of the controversy, so far as I am concerned, and, therefore I desire an opponent beyond whom your community cannot look with either desire or expectation.

There are but two ways you may drive me from this discussion. You can, indeed, accomplish your predictions of my avoiding the discussion by one of two expedients. You may offer a disputant of inferior rank, or you may refuse the discussion of the real issue, and offer substitutes that meet not the subject proposed.

You say something of my speaking discourteously of Mr. Rice, and of rather insulting you in my allusions to certain rumors. To each of which inacceptable imputations I desire to plead *not guilty*. If, sir, I should say that lord Brougham is not so courteous a gentleman as sir Robert Peel, do I insult lord Brougham! It is, methinks, somewhat prudish to affect such a sense of honorable courtesy. With me there yet remain three degrees of comparison, but with you it seems there is no comparison at all that is not discourteous. I believe, sir, all Kentucky, in so far as Messrs. Rice and Young are known, will award to the latter a comparative superiority in courtesy, as well as in some other points of comparison. And, sir, as your denomination is to be represented on the occasion, I put it to your good sense, whether a very courteous gentleman be not, other things being equal, a desideratum to you, as well as to me. But as I speak from report, and not from personal acquaintance, I am in this always pervious to new light.

And with regard to the second item in your late bill of indictment, my insulting you by speaking of my reluctance to listen to a rumor discreditable to your candor and christian courtesy, I confess myself so obtuse as not to perceive the precise point that impinges upon your honor in the form of insult. If the report were false there was no insult in alluding to it, and if true, you will admit, on reflection, there could be no insult; because the truth in such a connection, never can be an insult. Would it not, however, be discreditable to your candor and christian character, to believe that you had decided at synod, that Mr. Rice should be the man of your choice, and for almost a year to hold up the words of promise to my ear, that I should have Mr. Young. Nay, farther, would it not be still more discreditable for you to have so designed, and then afterwards nominate and appoint Mr. Rice one of the committee to make out the propositions and details of debate, when you calculated on my not being one of that committee. I shall present you a dilemma for your grave consideration. Either you agreed at synod that Mr. Rice or Mr. Young should be the man; if the latter, then I am right, yourselves being judges, in waiting for him; but if you agreed on Mr. Rice, you are wrong on two accounts. 1st, for holding up Mr. Young at all to my ear, and in the 2nd place, for appointing Mr. Rice one of the committee of arrangement, in this clandestine and cunning way. Extricate yourself if you can!

Or do I insult you by declaring my reluctance to believe another report that has reached me, from various sources, that you never intended a debate with me on the points proposed, but only intended to appear willing and ready for such a discussion, and then, by so managing the matter, as to compel me to back out, or to secure to you such advantages as would sustain your standing with the community. Such reports have almost since the date of your first overtures reached my ear from different sources; and shall I be regarded as insulting you either by mentioning them, or by affirming my reluctance to believe them. Is it not rather kind for me to state them fully, when your proceedings assume a form squinting so much in that direction. It is, methinks, due to you, to allow opportunity for you to take such a course as will thoroughly refute imputations so discreditable' and so usually regarded dishonorable. It was, indeed, as I imagined, kind to apprize you of such reports, and to afford you opportunity to refute them by your actions.

You very politely, on the heels of this double imputation, say, "I do not wonder at your reluctance to meet Mr. Rice. He has health to go through such a discussion, and is *accustomed*, as well as yourself, to public debate." This, of course, is neither discourteous nor insulting!! Why, sir, in thus saying, you have called my attention to Mr. Rice, under a new angle of vision. If I regard your voice as that of the denomination, I have no difficulty as to my course. You have elevated Mr. Rice to a position greatly superior to that occupied by Mr. Young. You cannot but admit that the reputation of Mr. Young, for learning and talent, has not terrified me so as to evince any reluctance to meet him in debate: but in your esteem the fame of Mr. Rice is so superlatively formidable, that I am fearful of encountering him. Convince me, sir, that this is his true position in the denomination, and I at once accept him as your strongest man. I desire, however, at least another witness or two of this fact, especially since reading a letter written by yourself, setting forth your triumphs in a discussion in which you have been engaged not many moons since. From that document, it would seem that your imagination sometimes leads captive your reason, at least in the opinion of many impartial and independent men.

A word or two as to the propositions for discussion. You manifest a singular pertinacity in selecting fragments of my views, and also in imputing to me a reluctance to defend what I have written. Have I thus assailed you? The propositions touching the action and the subject of baptism, are as you would wish them, and have been frequently so discussed by your denomination. The design of baptism is the only one on that subject peculiar to the present controversy. I have offered a proposition that covers the main ground occupied by me in my writings: for which you offer a most ridiculous substitute. "With me," you say, "baptism is the new birth, and it is designed to effect a change of state." If it be the new birth, can the new birth be the *design* of it? That it changes the state, is your own belief, and what controversy is there on this point! I must have a clear enunciation of the *design* of baptism. The propositions offered on that subject are such as to cover the real ground of difference between you and us. I shrink from nothing I have written. You have no reason to say so. You may protract the time, but I will never debate a proposition that does not meet my views. I have just as good a right to select from my writings as you have, and I can select a score on this subject that cover the real ground of debate.

Christian baptism is designed to confer personal assurance of the remission of sins on every legitimate subject. Or, *Christian baptism is for the remission of past sins.* This is my doctrine on the subject: and this I will defend. You may use all that I have written upon the subject, if you please; but such is the concentrated view which I propose.

On the influences of the Spirit—*I teach that in sanctification it operates only through the written word.* You teach that *in some cases, it operates without the word.* I, therefore, affirm that *the Spirit of God operates on sinners and on saint only through the word.* You affirm that it regenerates and sanctifies, in innumerable instances, without the word. Here is the gist of the controversy. All that I have written, and every thing in your creed, comes up under this proposition.

As you admit that our views of the weekly celebration of the Supper are scriptural, so far as your creed affirms, I shall not press that proposition farther upon your attention.

Touching your new proposition, about the administration of baptism, I regard it as a very small affair. I teach that for good order's sake, persons ought to be appointed to baptize, but that baptism by the hand of a layman, as you call him, when no other can be had, is just as valid as that of the pope, or your ministers. You can produce no divine precept nor precedent confining baptism to bishops, or elders—nor of their baptizing *as such.*

That human creeds, added to the Bible, are now and always have been unauthorized by God, roots of bitterness, apples of discord, necessarily tending to schism, and always perpetuating it, I affirm to be a great practical truth, deeply affecting the very existence of pure religion, and essentially obstructing the union of christians.

These are main points of difference between us, and such as we have agreed to discuss—baptism, the work of the Spirit, and creeds. You may, in your reply, settle the whole matter of the propositions, or you may protract the subject for months. I must have some two months interval, after all things are agreed upon, to make preparations for leaving home. Such are my duties and my numerous responsibilities, that I cannot in a few days obtain leave of absence. I intimated to you my desire of having the discussion during our vacation ; but you seem to pass it over without notice. I must make my arrangements in a few days for the vacation, and it will depend upon the promptness and the distinctness of your reply, whether my arrangements can be made to permit my attendance during vacation or after it, sooner than late in September or October. I am pleased to be able to say, from the retrospect of the past, that this long delay in bringing these matters to a close, is neither of my option nor creation.

With all due respect, I remain yours, &c.   A. CAMPBELL.

Elder A. Campbell :—Yours of the 24th has been received. You are anxious to know the premises from which I concluded that you are resolved to avoid this discussion. It is, I believe, universally admitted that a man can give no more unequivocal evidence of his purpose to avoid a contest, than by insisting on extraordinary and unequal terms of fight. This evidence you have abundantly afforded.

You assert that I, in our interview at Richmond, gave a pledge that Mr. Young should be your opponent, in case of a debate occurring. I will disprove this assertion by your own testimony. In your Harbinger for November, you state, that you consented to attend the meeting at Lexington, " provided only, that if we should go into a regular debate, that out of the most respectable of said delegation one be selected whose authority with the people was highest in the state—such as the president of their college at Danville, and with such a person I would go into a regular debate," &c. Is this not singular language in which to express the fact, that you were to debate with president Young, and no other ? Why did you not say " Provided only, that if we should go into a regular debate, I should have the president of their college as my opponent ?" This would have been a totally different thing, for then there could be no *selection* at all, " out of the most respectable of said delegation." But you have recently given a second version of this matter, plainly contradictory of the first. In the Harbinger for April, you say—" And in the event of the conference not coming to an agreement, I would go into single combat with a certain gentleman then named," &c. Now, Mr. Campbell, can you reconcile these two statements ? According to the first, the debater on our side was to be selected out of the most respectable individuals of the delegation; according to the second, there was to be no such selection, but you were to debate with a certain gentleman then named. It is absolutely impossible that both can be true. Your first version is doubtless nearer the truth, and it plainly contradicts your assertion concerning a pledge, that Mr. Young should be your opponent.

The following declarations are certainly marvellous. "In my letter of Nov. 16th, it is written, I will debate with one person only, and then named president Young, as such a person. You immediately responded, you shall have him, as you did not doubt but the synod would select him." Now, Mr. Campbell, the synod met early in October. How then could I have answered your letter of Nov. 16, by saying, I did not doubt that the synod would appoint brother Young, one month after its adjournment? In my letter, Dec. 8th, I stated as a reason why we could not accommodate you in your wish to debate with Mr. Young, that there was at that time, no probability of his being able to engage in such a debate with you, and this you (by what process I cannot imagine) convert into an affirmation that he was to have done so? And you ask why I did not *undeceive* you, when in your letter of December 15th, you brought up this matter! Why, sir, by examination of the Harbinger for November, you could easily undeceive yourself. Besides, in that letter you placed an obstacle in the way, which I supposed would prevent the proposed discussion, and speedily close our correspondence; which was a sufficient reason why I deemed it unnecessary to say any thing about the particular arrangement, until your objection should be withdrawn. In March I informed you, that brother Young's health was much improved, and, therefore, he would be able to be present as one of the five on our side, the only thing I have pledged him to do; and this again is strangely perverted. But your first version of the matter, may stand against what you now say.

But you have, as you imagine, placed me in quite a sad dilemma, and with an air of triumph, you say, "extricate yourself if you can." You begin thus: "Either you agreed at synod that Mr. Rice or Mr. Young should be the man; if the latter —" Stop, Mr. C., we did not agree at synod either that Mr. Rice or Mr. Young should be the man. One of the five selected at synod lived at a distance of several hundred miles, and we did not choose to appoint one of our number to debate without conferring with him. On writing to him, we ascertained that he could not be with us at the proposed discussion; and you objected to our filling his place with another man; we, therefore, could not properly appoint a debater until our number was complete; so your dilemma disappears. To your charge, that I have, for almost a year, held up the word of promise to your ear, that you should have Mr. Young, I plead *not guilty*, and prove that I have done no such thing by Mr. Campbell himself. As early as December 8, yourself being witness, I informed you that there was no probability that you could have him. The man who can convert such a statement into a word of promise, must possess some extraordinary powers.

It is, indeed, amusing to see you insisting upon meeting no man, whom you are not pleased to think, "all Kentucky" considers *the very politest and most accomplished gentleman* in the Presbyterian ranks. With you, it is not enough that your opponent should be regarded by his church as a scholar, a theologian, and a christian gentleman: he must be superlatively polite and accomplished; and we must produce witnesses to prove him such!!! Really, sir, this strikes me as an extraordinary, and, I think, a most ridiculous demand—a demand too, which necessarily implies a claim on *your part*, to be superlatively polite and accomplished. In view of such claims, I presume we must all on our side, retire from the contest, since we claim to be nothing more than christian gentlemen. But if I can understand you, you do not insist now upon meeting Mr. Young—you desire our "strongest and most accomplished man, whether in Kentucky or out of it." Well, are *you* to select the man, or to judge who shall defend our cause; or shall *we?* If you say *you* are to select him, there is an end of the matter. Why, sir, if you will allow me to get your chief men into a discussion, and then select from your body the man whom I may choose to consider eminently polite and accomplished, &c.; I can demolish your cause at any time. I can select a man, as *you* insist on doing, whose want of health makes it impossible for him to do justice to it; or who from some other cause, is inadequate to the work. I have never known a man who had not courage enough to fight, if he might be permitted to select his man. You may very safely propose to wait till Mr. Young's health may enable him to go through such a debate, since he has long been in feeble health, and more than once at death's door; and since there is no probability that at any early day he will be able to encounter such labors. But if you say, *we* are to select the man, who shall defend our cause, we are ready for you.

But you desire " at least another witness or two," that he is our strongest man; and the reason you assign for this wish, may constitute a part of the evidence of the propriety of your claim, to meet no man who is not exquisitely courteous and polite! I cannot so far forget what is due to myself, as to reply to your remarks. But, sir, we are *five* in number, and the gentleman who is ready to debate with you, has been selected by four of us, of whom Mr. Young is one. So you have quite as many witnesses as you desire. If you say, you will not *condescend* to meet the man of our selection, you at once close the correspondence. The matter may as well be settled at once. We have selected the man, to whose hands we think proper to commit the defence of our cause. His standing is well known, both in Kentucky and out of it. We will not select another. You can either debate with him, or retreat from the discussion.

As to the propositions for discussion, whilst we should have been pleased to see you willing to defend your doctrines, as stated by yourself; perhaps, however, we ought to give you some advantages—we will, therefore, accept of your proposition on the *design* of baptism, and on the influences of the Spirit—with a slight verbal alteration of the latter, reserving, of course, the right to explain the meaning of the questions by your publications. The proposition on the *design* of baptism, which we accept, is as follows:

1. *Christian baptism is for the remission of past sins.*

The question on the influence of the Spirit, we accept, as follows:

2. *The Spirit of God operates on persons, only through the Word.*

I hope you will not shrink from the defence of your doctrine, in regard to the administrator of baptism. It involves the validity of the ordinance. How you can consider it as " a very small affair " I do not know. The Presbyterian church certainly regards it as of very great importance. From a remark in my last letter, your deduction relative to the comparative merits of Rev. Mr. Young, if at all allowable, is not such as I intended. Unaccustomed to polemic correspondence, I may have expressed myself ambiguously or incautiously, in many respects. I recognize no man as *his* superior. Tis true, his experience in oral controversy is not equal to some others, yet if his health would justify, the cause of truth could not be committed to abler hands.

You seem in a late publication to congratulate yourself, in view of the fact, that the discussion has not been procrastinated by any delay on your part, (one instance only excepted, and that unavoidable,) but that the delay is wholly attributable to me. I presume the correspondence, (if ever published) will present the facts. However, I do not suppose that even Mr. Campbell himself, would expect *one* who is neither a president, nor the occupant of a point more prominent than *Paris*, but only a *village Pastor*, inexperienced in ecclesiastical polemics, to compete with *him*, either in *despatch*, or *any thing else* involved in such a correspondence. But, sir, if the discussion has not been delayed by you for *this* reason, the community may yet have the opportunity of judging whether *other*, *and more important* reasons, of delay are not attributable to Mr. C. himself.

I do not think it important to reply to your tedious remarks, in defence of your offensive language in a former letter. Perhaps I ought to be amused at your gravely talking about rumors, that I never intended to debate with you. Rumors about what I *intend* ! ! ! I rather think you are pretty thoroughly convinced, that the rumors about my intentions, so far as the debate is concerned, are untrue. Respectfully, JNO. H. BROWN.

Bethany, Va., June 25, 1843.

ELDER J. H. BROWN:

Dear Sir—Yours of the 16th lies before me. Our college examination prevented my reply on the day of its arrival. I hasten, however, to respond before our next mail.

I know not whether the imputation of my insisting on "extraordinary and unequal terms of fight," or the evidence by which you would sustain it, be the more eminently amusing and ridiculous. You cannot, Mr. Brown, make even one Presbyterian in a hundred believe it. That you gave a pledge that I should have Mr. Young for an opponent is just as certain to me as that I saw you in Richmond last August ; and you have not brought, nor can you bring, one particle of evidence to disprove it.

The passages quoted from the November and April Harbinger are most illogically applied. No passage of Scripture, alledged in proof of transubstantiation or infant affusion, was ever more glaringly perverted and misconstrued than those two passages. In the general and passing notice of your call upon me at Richmond, to which you allude in the November number, is it not distinctly stated that I specified Mr. Young as, in my esteem, the most prominent man in your denomination, and named him as a condition of my attendance on the proposed discussion ? And had you quoted in your epistle, evidently designed for the public eye, the whole passage, it would have been an evidence of, and not against, the truth of my present position. The very next sentence says, " To all of which Mr. Brown most readily assented." To have been more definite or precise in such a notice would have been wholly out of place. It seems to me, at least, rather singular, amongst candid and honorable men, that Mr. Brown, while denying the pledge, should so accidentally suppress the sentence that affirms it.

But to make out of this a contradiction from any thing written in my April number, would seem to require the genius and the daring of Ignatius Loyola himself. Without note or comment, the words themselves clearly indicate all that I have constantly affirmed. " And," said I, " in the event of the conference not coming to an agreement, I would go into single combat with a *gentleman then named*." Now I ask every candid man of every party, in what terms could I have more perspicuously affirmed the essential *provision*, that I should have Mr. Young, and your assent to it, than in the words above quoted, in all the circumstances which called them forth ?

The recklessness of these attempts at constructive contradiction is only surpassed by the still more glaring attempt to make my November letter read as though it had been written before the meeting of synod. My statement of what was agreed upon on a prior occasion, is converted into a new proposition then presented ! ! Surely, Mr. Brown, you do great injustice to your own understanding. Why, sir, it looks more like the trick of a schoolboy than the grave and self-respectful product of a Presbyterian clergyman. Yet you are constrained to admit that you suffered the illusion to deceive me till in your March letter, written after full two months' deliberation ! But you get out of the dilemma by breaking its horns : you deny that either Mr. Rice or Mr. Young was selected at the meeting of synod— *absolutely*, you must mean ; for that such was the understanding you will not certainly deny. All reflecting persons will understand how you get out of this dilemma :—It is one thing *absolutely* to say that Mr. Rice or Mr. Young should be the man ; and another, to have an understanding that in a certain event he should be the man. Is not this the truth, Mr. Brown ?

You have been most singularly unfortunate in every attempt, in this most elaborate apologetic epistle, to extricate yourself from the unenviable attitude in which you must appear to stand before a discerning community. Your uncalled for quizzical allusions to the "very politest gentleman" in your ranks, is worthy of the ingenuity that placed allusions to antecedent matters, in my November Harbinger, in the attitude of present history. Every thing else being equal, I do certainly prefer, in an antagonist, a courteous well bred christian gentleman, and I care not who knows it. If such be the character of Mr. Rice, or any one else elected by your church, I shall be happy to meet him. If he be not, you are just as much disgraced as I may be annoyed by his rudeness.

The perfection of your climax of suicidal aberrations, as it seems to me, is your representation of me as seeking a weak man instead of a strong one. Mr. Young must certainly be indebted to you for the new honors you have added to his doctorate. I choose a weak man then, it seems, like a coward, in choosing Mr. Young! and you want to give me a strong man!! As I before said of Mr. Young, if withdrawn on the ground of ill health, I sympathize with him, and am willing to wait his recovery. But recollect, sir, the plea of physical inability will not stand in the presence of a proposition to await his restoration to such health as he enjoyed when first you offered him. The public will no doubt properly estimate the matter.

Well, now, as you have finally tendered your grand *ultimatum*, an unequivocal *sine qua non*, uncommitted and untrammeled as I am, I cannot but feel the responsibility in which you place me. The case, as you now make it, is: Five men were chosen by the ministers of the Presbyterian church of Kentucky, met at synod last October, and these five have chosen one of themselves, by agreement of said ministers at synod, to represent the denomination, supported by themselves, in council assembled, in a discussion of the leading points at issue between Presbyterians and our brethren in that state and elsewhere. And this arrangement, or no discussion, being now tendered, I have to choose between these alternatives. In view of all my responsibilities, I resolve, the Lord willing, to meet said representative of that church and conference, (my brethren in Kentucky so concurring,) to discuss those points at issue, as comprehended in the following six propositions, four of which are now agreed upon, viz.:

I. I affirm that immersion in water, of a proper subject, into the name of the Father, the Son and the Holy Spirit, is the action ordained by Jesus Christ as *the one only christian baptism*. This you deny; affirming that sprinkling or pouring water, on a suitable subject, is scriptural baptism.

II. You affirm that the infant of a believing parent is a scriptural subject of baptism. This I deny; affirming that a professed believer of the gospel is the only proper subject of baptism.

III. I affirm that, to a believing penitent, baptism is for the remission of past sins. This you deny.

IV. You affirm that baptism is to be administered only by a bishop or ordained presbyter. This I deny.

V. I affirm that the Spirit of God, in conversion, operates on persons only through the word of truth.

VI. You affirm that the constitution of the Presbyterian church is the constitution of Christ's church: or, you affirm that a human creed, such as the Westminster, is essential to the existence, unity and peace of the church. Both of these I deny.

Thus, sir, I have conceded to you the proposition concerning the administration of baptism, and have arranged them in the natural and logical order of debate:—1st, the *action*, or thing to be done, in the name of the Lord; 2d, the person *on whom;* 3d, the design *for which;* and 4th, the person *by whom* it may of right be performed. To this order I presume no person can object. I have also, to expedite an issue, conceded another point, viz. the omission of the question about the Lord's supper. I have,

3

in thus drawing them out, supplied the ellipsis, but have not changed a single iota known to me in our respective positions to these great questions.

As the arrangements concerning the taking down of the discussion and the publication of it, are not only important, but may require some time, may I expect a speedy answer to the above. I must moreover decide upon my course of action during vacation in a few days. I therefore earnestly request an immediate answer. If it arrives not in the same space of time occupied by my reply to your last, I cannot possibly attend to the discussion during vacation. Meantime I will write to my brethren in Kentucky, for their acquiescence on the first subject as aforesaid. Other preliminary rules are to be adopted, and arrangements made for conducting the debate with all decorum, which will require some time.

Respectfully, your friend,   A. CAMPBELL.

Richmond, Ky., July 7, 1843.

ELDER CAMPBELL—Yours of June 25th is received. If you should ever be able to reconcile the statement, that of five men, one was to be *selected* to meet you in debate, with your recent declaration, that there was to be no *selection at all*, but that a certain individual then named, was to meet you, I shall be constrained to acknowledge, that you possess some *original powers* of mind! That I agreed that you should have Mr. Young, as one of the five individuals on our side, is not denied; but to prove that, without ever having conferred with him on the subject, I pledged him to go through such a discussion as the one contemplated—a kind of employment in which he had never engaged, and for which his feeble health would, to a great extent, disqualify him—will require more evidence than you will ever be able to produce. When you represent me as intimating or admitting, that in choosing Mr. Young, you chose a " weak man," can you imagine, that any one, on reading this correspondence, will believe what you say? My remarks in previous letters, flatly contradict it; and his reputation makes a defence of his talents and scholarship wholly unnecessary. Your willingness to await his recovery, after what you knew of the state of his health, only proves your disposition *indefinitely to postpone the discussion.*

Since your fancied " dilemma" disappeared upon the statement of the facts, in reference to the selection of Mr. Rice or Mr. Young at synod, you resort to a most singular expedient to sustain your position. You say " That such was the understanding, [that Young or Rice should meet you] you certainly will not deny. Is not this the truth, Mr. Brown?" When a gentleman undertakes to place another in a dilemma, by assuming things to be true of which, in the nature of the case, he can know absolutely nothing, and when, on finding his mistake, he resorts to *catechising* in order to elicit something favorable to his wishes; I rather think, he is, if not in a " dilemma," at least in an unpleasant *predicament!*

I am truly gratified, however, that you have at length felt constrained to withdraw your extraordinary claim *to select your opponent in debate,* and to agree to meet the man of our selection, without further testimonials in regard to his ability, or his *extraordinary politeness!!*

We will endeavor to accommodate you with " a courteous, well-bred, christian gentleman "—one, who we trust and believe, will not mortify us by so far disregarding the established rules of courtesy, as Mr. Campbell has repeatedly done in this correspondence.

In regard to the selection of the individuals on our part, my statements have been so repeated and so distinct, that I cannot imagine any thing more necessary on that point, however objectionable some of your representations may be.

Your 6th proposition, in both forms, is decidedly objectionable. We choose to debate it as presented in your letter of Dec. 15th, viz : " Human creeds, as bonds of union and communion, are necessarily heretical and schismatical "—unless you agree to the modification already suggested, viz: "The using of creeds, except the Scriptures, is necessarily heretical and schismatical." We prefer the modified form of it; but if you object, we will not insist upon it. Then, in order to give an equal number of affirmatives and negatives to each party; the first question can be thrown into the form already agreed upon, viz: "Sprinkling, or pouring water, upon a suitable subject, is scriptural baptism."

Your *fifth* proposition is not quite satisfactory. We are willing to take it as presented in your last letter, with a slight verbal alteration suggested in my reply, and which you have made. Then it will stand thus: "The Spirit of God operates on persons only through the Word."

Now, since you have all the propositions, in almost the precise language chosen by yourself, I hope this matter may be considered as settled.

Brother Rice will withdraw from the committee of arrangements, and brother J. K. Burch and myself will constitute that committee. This change is made in view of remarks made in your letter of May 24th—and in view of the fact, that Mr. Rice will be your opponent in debate. We are prepared to meet your committee, at any time mutually agreed upon, and to make all necessary arrangements. Respectfully, &c.

JNO. H. BROWN.

Bethany, Va., July 13, 1843.

ELDER BROWN:

Your very courteous letter of the 7th inst. lies before me. Your reiteration concerning Mr. Young, and your polite allusion to my reasonable demands for a respectable opponent, I shall hereafter expect as a part of every epistle for the next six months. To these matters I shall hereafter pay no attention. If any testimony is wanting concerning your promises in reference to Mr. Young, I have recently learned that such testimony (living and unexceptionable) to all my allegations can be had.

I have said, for the next *six months;* for it appears nothing is yet fixed. The arrangement of the propositions concerning baptism, it would seem from allusions to the first, found in your letter before me, is yet to be made. In endeavoring to find our relative *positions* to points at issue,—what you affirmed and what I affirmed,—and thus to ascertain the subjects and number of topics, I did not imagine that either the order in which these subjects were named, or the affirmative or negative forms in which they were expressed, was to be that of discussion. Hence, in my last, after hearing all the explanations, statements, amendments and objections, I drew out in order and form the propositions, and our positions to them, which fairly exhibit our standing before the community on these points.

These six propositions were:

I. I affirm that immersion in water, of a proper subject, into the name of the Father, the Son and the Holy Spirit, is the *action* ordained by Jesus Christ as the one only christian baptism.

II. You affirm that the infant of a believing parent is a scriptural subject of baptism.

III. I affirm that, to a believing penitent, baptism is for the remission of past sins.

IV. You affirm that baptism is to be administered only by a bishop or ordained presbyter.

V. I affirm that, in conversion and sanctification, the Spirit of God operates on persons only through the word of truth.

VI. You affirm that the constitution of the Presbyterian church is the constitution of Christ's church.

To the last you object, and prefer an expression of my views of creeds found in former communications. That expression covers not the whole ground of my dissent from creeds ecclesiastic. You will then affirm your views of your creed as essential to the unity, purity and peace of the

church, and I will take the negative. This is the only point undefined between us, so far as the six propositions go. I desire the privilege of affirming what I teach in my own words, and extend the same to you. But on
those points on which we have fully expressed our views,—namely, the first
five propositions,—I think it is time we had done. You need not protract
the time for the sake of any changes in the propositions, since I will sustain my real position and no other. Besides, no committee shall choose
propositions for me, nor the mode of discussing them. You have more than
once offered your *sine qua non*, your grand *ultimatum*: it is time for me to
commence.

As I expect to be in Lexington from the 1st to the 6th of August, I have
no objections to your making Mr. Rice one of the committee to meet myself and another person or two for arrangements of the laws and etiquette
of the debate, as well as the mode of reporting and publishing. This will
save much time in correspondence. Please address me there, to the care of
Mr. Ficklin.

In very much haste, and with all due respect,

A. CAMPBELL.

Richmond, July 29, 1843.

ELDER A. CAMPBELL:

Dear Sir—Your communication of the 13th is now before me. Only the
closing paragraph demands attention. In this you propose that Mr. Rice
be made one of the committee, to meet you, and another person or two, in
Lexington, between the 1st and 6th of August, for the arrangement of preliminaries, preparatory to discussion. To this proposition I am requested
to address you at Lexington, to the care of Mr. Ficklin.

I have postponed a reply, awaiting the return of Mr. Rice from Nashville.
I expected him to have been at my house on the 27th, to assist me in the
services of a protracted meeting; but in this I have been disappointed, his
stay at Nashville having been unexpectedly protracted. I still expect him,
and hope he will arrive to-day. If so, the arrangement you propose will
be acceded to. If not, Mr. Burch and myself will meet your committee at
Lexington, on Friday, the 4th of August, if in accordance with your
wishes. I have postponed a reply to the last hour, expecting the arrival of
Mr. Rice. Time, therefore, will allow me to reply only to this single proposition; other matters in your communication will be attended to at no
very distant day. Please reply by return of mail. Respectfully,

JNO. H. BROWN.

Richmond, July 31, 1843.

ELDER A. CAMPBELL—Since I replied to your last letter, brother Rice
has returned from Nashville, and in accordance with your wish, he will be
added to the committee on our part, and he, Mr. Burch, and myself, will
meet you and your committee in Lexington, on Thursday afternoon, at 3
o'clock, P. M.

Until I received your last letter, I supposed the propositions for discussion
might be considered as settled, since I had accepted them as stated by yourself, with merely slight verbal alterations, to almost all of which you had
agreed. But I am not a little surprised to learn from your last letter, that
you are unwilling to debate *your own propositions!!!* On the *mode* of baptism you proposed the following, which, with a small change, to which you
agreed, was accepted by me, viz: "Sprinkling, or pouring water, upon a
suitable subject, is scriptural baptism." You now, after both parties have
agreed to the above proposition offer another quite different in form. What
does this mean? In relation to the *subject*, the *design*, and the *administrator* of baptism, and the work of the Spirit, we are agreed on the proposition
to be debated.

On the subject of creeds, we have agreed to discuss *your own* proposition, viz: "Human creeds, as bonds of union and communion, are necessarily heretical and schismatical." But you now inform me, that this proposition, stated by yourself for discussion, covers not the whole ground of your dissent from " creeds ecclesiastic," and you propose the following : " You [I] affirm, that the constitution of the Presbyterian church is the constitution of Christ's church." And does this proposition really cover the whole ground of your objection to creeds ecclesiastic ? Is it true that all that you affirmed against creeds, amounts only to this—that the constitution of the Presbyterian church is not the constitution of the church of Christ ? Or have you not gone on a crusade against *all creeds*, because they " supplanted the Bible, made the Word of God of non-effect, were fatal to the intelligence, purity, union, holiness, and happiness of the disciples of Christ, and hostile to the salvation of the world ?"—*Chris. Sys.* p. 9. These and many such things, you have affirmed concerning the use of creeds. You say, " I desire the privilege of affirming what I teach." Now, my dear sir, we have accepted your own proposition, thus affording you the opportunity of *affirming* and *proving*, what you have so constantly, and so loudly, affirmed and taught ; and *mirabile dictu !*—you decline affirming, or attempting to prove it, and desire us to affirm a totally different proposition, not at all covering the ground of your published sentiments ! This procedure does strike me as marvellous in the extreme. You have before declined discussing the doctrine of the influences of the Spirit, as published in one of your most important books ; and now you are unwilling to discuss a proposition of your own forming ! I must insist now, that you defend your own proposition. I cannot accept a totally different one in place of it.

But it seems that all this while we have been engaged, not in settling propositions, as they were to be debated but only in " hearing all the explanations, statements, amendments, and objections." Yet propositions were stated, verbal or other alterations suggested and agreed to. Still, although the precise language of the propositions was agreed upon, you now feel at liberty to begin *de novo*, and restate them in different form ; or to state entirely new propositions ! To this *twisting* and *turning* you must allow me decidedly to object.

In a word, we have accepted your propositions, and we are now prepared to arrange other preliminaries, and to enter upon the discussion at the earliest convenience of the parties concerned.

In regard to the testimony, of which you speak, in reference to your allegation, I will now only say, I am prepared to meet it. Hoping to see you on Thursday next, I remain yours, &c.   J. H. BROWN.

N. B. We will be at the residence of Rev. J. K. Burch, at the hour specified above, and will receive any communication you may deem expedient.

Lexington, Ky., August 2, 1843.

ELDER J. H. BROWN:

Dear Sir—Yours of the 31st ult. is just to hand. I am not unwilling to debate my own propositions. Propositions submitted by me to elicit your position, and to ascertain your views, are not, however, my *own* propositions. Had you been willing that I should have debated my own propositions, a single letter would have been sufficient to settle the whole issue of debate. In the six propositions, so often and so variously propounded to ascertain the true issue, but one of them is exactly my own proposition. True, I have elicited the attitude you wish to maintain, and such as you would desire me to maintain ; but this is a very different thing from my having obtained my own propositions, or my having absolutely agreed to discuss a single proposition, the verbiage of which you have at all interfered with. My approval of any proposition, so far as expressed, has always been prospective of the amicable settlement of the whole issue. I was willing, however, and am still willing, to distribute the four propositions on baptism as expressed in my last, which are in exact accordance

D

with our respective positions as before defined; but I am not willing to give you three affirmative propositions out of four, and even then not have my single affirmative in my own words!!

I confess I was not prepared to expect such exorbitant demands at the hands of my Presbyterian friends, especially after conceding so much to their views of expediency. Called upon for a discussion of my views as opposed to Presbyterianism, and pressed into this debate, as I have been, by your importunities, I was prepared to expect the privilege of propounding my own propositions in my *own* words, and to expect that such chivalrous spirits as the sons of the Solemn League and Covenant would manfully stand up to their own tenets and defend their own true and veritable position before this community, and allow me to defend and assail in regular turn. But what is my disappointment, after one year's diplomatic negotiation, to find them claiming three out of four propositions, and thus refusing me an opportunity to sustain my proper attitude in this long protracted controversy. I never can yield to demands so arbitrary and unequal. If, then, I have given opportunity and latitude to ascertain what advantages would be sought, and how promptly you and your brethren would assume the defence of your own tenets and assail mine, I am not to be understood as agreeing to place myself three times in the mere negative of your tenets on baptism, since I have been summoned by *you* to stand up to the defence of my own teaching. I must affirm my views on at least the two main points in which I have been most assailed by Presbyterians. This is not only *just* and *equal*, but it is my special right, coming into this discussion as I do.

Besides all these considerations, obvious and imperative though they be, I have others, affecting not only these, but the other propositions submitted, which in harmony with our original stipulations, are entitled to your special regard. *You* represent a denomination: so do *I*. *You* have had frequent consultations among yourselves: *I* have not had *one* with my brethren till my arrival in this city. From them I have learned how we, as a denomination, have been assailed, both in Kentucky and Tennessee, by your representative Mr. Rice. From the facts stated, and the representations given, to meet the objects of this discussion, it will also be expedient and necessary that the proposition concerning the Spirit, and that concerning creeds, shall be more full than before propounded. According to the views of such as have conferred with me, it is requisite that your views of Spiritual influence, regeneration, &c., so far as they differ from ours, should be fully developed and discussed. I should, therefore, amplify the proposition already before us, so as to bring all *our* views, and *yours*, fully before the community, thus: *The Spirit of God, without any previous, special, separate, spiritual operation on the mind, illumination, or call, is known, believed, received, and enjoyed, through the word of God; which word is the only and all-sufficient instrument through which sinners attain the knowledge of God, are converted, sanctified, and obtain the true religion* As respects creeds, I affirm that *human, authoritative creeds, superadded to the Bible, are an insult to its Author, unphilosophical in their nature, schismatic in their tendencies, and retard the conversion of the world.* But as you may claim a negative attitude in the discussion of this point, I consent to your framing any proposition that precisely and fully negatives the above.

I should be pleased to add one or two other propositions:—one concerning the weekly observance of the ordinance of the supper; and one concerning the constitution of the Presbyterian church; but leave this matter wholly to your own discretion.

I am sorry to state that the misconstructions and misrepresentations which have reached my ears from various quarters, together with the spirit and details of your letter now lying before me, recommend to me the expediency of settling all the important preliminaries by writing, rather than by a personal interview. I therefore state distinctly, that of the six propositions I claim the 1st, 3d and 5th, as before stated, viz.:

I. That the immersion in water, of a proper subject, into the name of the Father, the Son and the Holy Spirit, is the one only apostolic or christian baptism.

III. That, to a proper subject, baptism is for induction into the christian covenant, or for the remission of sins.

V. "The Spirit," &c., as above expressed.

Should you think proper to place my proposition on creeds before that on the Spirit, and allow me to affirm it, and then select one indicative of your full views on the Spirit expressed in your own words, or in those of your creed, and allow me to negative it, you shall have my consent. As I sincerely desire a frank, candid and friendly interview, I am willing to allow you a full expression of your tenets in the best terms you can select. I only state distinctly, that if there be but six propositions, I shall have three affirmatives, as aforesaid, and that you shall have three. I claim the *action and design of baptism*, and either that on the *Spirit* or *creeds*, as you please. If to these fair and equitable terms you agree, I am prepared to go into other preliminary arrangements immediately. If not, say so, and the matter ends.

I sincerely and solemnly profess to go for *truth*, and not for *victory*,—for truth indeed, and victory,—for the Bible, and its triumph over all rivals. And if you can concur with us in such views and feelings, I think we ought to agree to spend the day antecedent to the commencement of the discussion in prayer and fasting. All of which is respectfully submitted.

Please address me at Mr. Henry Bell's.

With all due respect, yours, &c. **A. CAMPBELL.**

Lexington, August 3, 1843.

ELDER A. CAMPBELL—Yours of the 2nd is before me. It contains information *curious*, if not *instructive*, viz: that propositions submitted for debate by Mr. Campbell, are not *his own* propositions!!! Then, pray, whose are they? But it seems, that you submitted them to elicit my position, &c. Is it true, then, that you submitted for my consideration propositions *which you knew did not correctly present our relative positions*, in order to ascertain my views? If they do correctly represent the ground of difference, why do you now insist on changing them? If they do not, why were they offered? Why did you not offer such propositions as you were willing to discuss? This is, indeed, a new species of military tactics!

But surely your memory fails you; for in your letter of Nov. 17, you state six propositions for debate, and then remark, "*I will discuss these in single debate*," &c. Again, in your letter of Dec. 15, after stating *six* propositions you say, "I regard the above as a candid and definite expression of our relative positions on these six points," &c. And yet you tell us, these are not *your own* propositions; and some of them you refuse to debate! Nay more, we accepted your sixth proposition, in the letter of Dec. 15th, without even insisting on the slightest *verbal* alteration, and then, behold, Mr. C. informs us, "that expression covers not the whole ground of his dissent from creeds ecclesiastic," and proposes to introduce another proposition, wholly different, which does not even touch the question of the lawfulness of creeds!!! Again, in yours of July 13th, you state, that the only point really undefined between us is that concerning creeds, on which we had accepted *your own proposition!*—and then remark, "but on those points on which we have fully expressed our views—namely, the first *five* propositions, I think it is time we had done." But what do I see in your letter now before me? Another proposition on the work of the Spirit, entirely new and wholly unintelligible in its phraseology! Your next epistle will, probably, insist on other propositions, different from all these? Alas for the cause that requires such manœuvring extraordinary to sustain it.

But can we understand you? You tell me you did not absolutely agree to discuss a single proposition, the verbiage of which I have at all interfered with. Of course, then, you are absolutely pledged to discuss those questions, the verbiage of which we have not interfered with, *except with your consent;* for when you accepted proposed amendments, the propositions as amended, were your own—such as you were bound to discuss. Now look at the following:

1. *Sprinkling, or pouring water, upon a suitable subject, is scriptural baptism.* To this proposition, as originally offered by you, we proposed a *verbal* alteration, to which you *cheerfully agreed.* This proposition, therefore, according to your own showing, you are bound to debate.

2. *The infant of a believing parent, is a scriptural subject of baptism.* This was accepted without alteration. Of course, it is settled.

3. *Christian baptism is for the remission of past sins.* This also had been accepted without change—it is settled.

4. *Baptism is to be administered only by a bishop, or ordained Presbyter.* Accepted in your own language, without change—it is settled.

5. *In conversion and sanctification the Spirit of God operates on persons only through the word of truth.* Accepted in the precise language used in your letter of July 13th. This is settled.

6. *Human creeds, as bonds of union and communion, are necessarily heretical and schismatical.* Accepted in the precise language of Mr. Campbell, (see his letter of Dec. 15th) without the slightest change; and that language Mr. Campbell has declared to be "a *candid and definite expression*" of our differences on this point. This, too, is settled. Every proposition has been accepted, either in your precise language, or with slight verbal changes, *to which you have agreed!* Yet Mr. Campbell is not satisfied!!!

But you say, you are not willing to give us three affirmative propositions out of four, on the subject of baptism. Yet, in your letter of Dec. 15th, you say, there are three great topics, which have occupied the public attention for some twenty-five years, so far as your reformation is concerned, viz: the ordinances of christianity, the essential elements of the gospel itself, and the influence of human creeds, &c. On precisely the point relative to baptism, on which your reformation has been most assailed, you have the affirmative. On the 2nd great point, the work of the Spirit, you have the affirmative—and on the 3d great point, creeds, you have the affirmative; yet you are not satisfied with your *affirmatives!!!*

Your reformation does, indeed, call for sympathy, if it cannot sustain itself, even in the hands of Mr. C., without such advantages as he demands.

And, be it observed, the matter in dispute is not merely nor chiefly the affirmative and negative forms of the propositions. In your letter now before me, after having previously stated that on *five points* the propositions were fully agreed on, you refuse to debate them, though proposed by yourself, and present *three* new propositions:—one relative to the Spirit, which no man who wishes the people to understand him would discuss; one relative to the *design* of baptism, making it perfectly ambiguous; and one relative to creeds, which assigns them a place (if your language is intelligible) which no Protestant denomination ever did assign to them. And what has led Mr. Campbell to such an unexpected and unheard of course? Why he has heard how Mr. Rice has assailed his denomination in Kentucky and Tennessee! Ah, what a dangerous man this Mr. Rice must be, that in prospect of meeting him even Mr. C., after stating and re-stating his propositions during twelve months past—propositions containing "*a candid and definite expression* of our relative positions," finds it necessary once more to re-state and mystify them as far as possible!!!

To these new and most extraordinary claims of Mr. C. we cannot accede. We have accepted *his own propositions, in his own language, or slightly modified with his own consent, and in his own order; we having three affirmatives, and he precisely as many; he having affirmatives on the precise points on which his reformation has assailed Protestant Christendom, and on which it has in turn been assailed.* Now, Mr. C. tells us, unless we will let him change his own propositions and his own arrangement, he will not enter into the discussion. If we will not consent to his demands, such as in public debate were never before heard of, "the matter," says he, "*ends*." Well, it is just what we have for some time anticipated. So, after all you have said of the fear of light among "the clergy,"—after all this boasting of the reformation of the nineteenth century,—you, the leader of the host, thus signally retreat!!!

We press the matter no further. If Mr. C. fears to debate *his own propostiions*, we are willing that the matter shall end, and that the world shall know the grand result! But upon Mr. Campbell himself the entire responsibility of its termination must ever rest.

Yours, respectfully,   JNO. H. BROWN.

P. S.—Mr. Campbell is now at liberty, should he think proper, to publish the correspondence.   J. H. B.

Lexington, Ky., August 4, 1843.

MR. BROWN:

Sir—Your letter of last night, though it fulfills the predictions of almost all the prophets that have spoken to me concerning the contemplated discussion, is nevertheless a development which I could not have expected from even Mr. Brown in reply to the epistle I have just addressed to him. I do not exaggerate when I say, that of the scores of persons that have, since my arrival in this state, spoken to me concerning your proposition for a debate, almost all have said, that either I must concede to your party all that you demand, or that I should be quibbled out of a discussion. Nay, some have said, that Mr. Brown himself was actually engaged a few days since in efforts to retract his having solicited and challenged my attendance to debate the points at issue between us and Presbyterians, it was believed with a reference to some immediate publication of our correspondence, in anticipation, I presume, of the license you have now given me to publish the correspondence! Be it so, then. But, before the final adieu, I shall add one letter more, which must first go to the public before the whole correspondence can appear.

I will not be at pains to review the letter lying before me at this time. I have neither the time nor the documents. On leaving home, I forgot to bring with me a single letter of our correspondence, though it had occupied my attention almost at the moment of departing. And to undertake to unfold the perplexities, and to expose the dexterous and ingenious manœuvres and subterfuges with which it seems to abound, without these documents, would be as imprudent, as it is now unnecessary. To enlighten *one* who could confound the *submission* of a proposition with the *approval* of it, or an agreement to discuss a special proposition, as one of an issue, in anticipation of a fair and equitable adjustment of the whole issue, as absolutely binding, whether the issue be as anticipated, or to convict me of dishonorable intentions by such a mode of retreat from a debate solicited by himself, would require more details than at present I have leisure for. Again, to represent one as introducing new propositions, when only changing an affirmative to a negative, or a negative to an affirmative, and to make what he says of *topics* of debate equivalent to what he says of *propositions* of debate, and to make a single word indicating his attitude to a question identical with the question itself, are efforts of ingenuity and dexterity, that require corresponding efforts on the part of him who would expose them, beyond the common limits of an ordinary letter.

The matter then ends here. Presbyterians proposed a discussion, and promised that each party should have an equal chance in defending what it taught. In making out the issue, they assign the representative of the other party just *as many affirmatives and negatives as they please, on what topics they please, and in what order they please!* They tell him: "Sir, every proposition you affirm during the whole correspondence with a refer-

D 2

ence to that issue, must be considered as your own ; and in the end we will choose such of them as we please, arrange them as we please,—and if you will not debate them, we will report and denounce you as a coward, and claim for our party a glorious victory ? !" This is no exaggeration. It is but a fair representation of the case, which, when requisite, I will fully demonstrate.

I again affirm, before heaven and earth, I did not contemplate such a development. As a christian man, I sincerely desired to discuss with christian men what I regarded to be the true and principal points of difference. I sought no advantage ; I desired no advantage. I supremely desired the true issue, and sought for propositions to elicit it. If I have from time to time, during the incidents and labors of a year, in reply to various communications, proposed various forms of expressing the difference, it was purely for the sake of having it clearly, tangibly and fully set forth. I acted as a party in forming a covenant, during the negotiation of which numerous stipulations and re-stipulations are offered, canvassed, accepted, rejected, amended, &c. &c. ; but all in reference to a final agreement. Nothing is binding till the whole understanding is perfect and complete. Precisely so stands this matter with me. The propositions offered yesterday are not new propositions. They are mere amplifications of those already offered, at the suggestion of those who have a right to be represented in this discussion, with a reference especially to this community.

I could not have imagined that intelligent, God-fearing and truth-loving men, sincerely desirous of coming to the light, would seek by quibbles and evasions to dodge the proper issue, or to retreat from the proposed debate, unless every word was so arranged and modified as to suit their party, or to render ambiguous, conceal, or metamorphose the proper issue.

My time of life, business obligations—all forbid the waste of time in engaging in frivolous or mere verbal criticisms. I was pleased to be called upon by a party, for which I have always cherished a high respect, for a full, manly, frank and christian-like discussion of all the great points between us. For this I am prepared ; but not for a mere logomachy—a wrangle—a system of special pleading, for party and sinister ends. If any point were misstated, distorted, or suppressed, I desired to have it disentangled, disintricated, or set forth in its proper colors and proportions. Any thing from you with such intentions would, at any time, have commanded my attention and acquiescence.

But, sir, to come to a close, *you either intended, in the letter before me, to* COMPEL *me to come up to your terms, or have no discussion.* You are preparing for a publication of the correspondence, and to represent *me* as backing out, because, forsooth, of the prodigious champion and defender of the faith, who is to represent your denomination. Do you think, Mr. Brown, *you can make any intelligent Presbyterian in Kentucky believe it?* If you do you are more credulous than I thought.

Having, then, so far committed yourselves, as to avow that you will not debate the propositions, as amplified in my last, and as I introduced no new ground in the effort to present them in a more extended form, I will take, rather than have no debate, the whole six propositions, as drawn up in your letter before me, with the simple change of the first, on the action of baptism, as proposed in my last. Or, if you will not grant that, and take for it the negative form of the proposition on *creeds,* I will propose to take the whole six, as you have quoted them, by changing simply the order of them, which, I presume, you will not pretend to have ever been arranged. Place the proposition on *creeds* first—that on the *Spirit* next—and then the four on *baptism.* I have not, as before intimated, the correspondence with me ; but of two things I feel perfectly certain, that the whole six propositions, as you have stated them, were never all agreed upon as containing the whole issue, nor was there ever an agreement as to the order of the topics of debate. It is then wholly at your own option to do one or the other.

But certainly you will not make the *order of the questions*, nor the change of the form of a proposition, a *sina qua non.*

Please inform me of your determination at as early an hour as suits your convenience.　　　　Respecfully yours,

　　　　　　　　　　　　　　　　A. CAMPBELL.

Lexington, Aug. 5, 1843.

Elder A. Campbell—We were a good deal surprised at receiving from you, on yesterday afternoon, between one and two o'clock, another letter, which is now before me. We were surprised, first, because your previous letter declared positively, that unless we acceded to your *new* propositions, the matter was at an end. We supposed that you meant what you said, and, therefore, as we could not yield to your demands, considered the correspondence closed. We were surprised, secondly, because you had delayed to so late an hour. We were in Lexington by your invitation, to have with you a personal interview. Yet after inviting us to meet you here, you, in palpable violation of ordinary rules of courtesy, refused such interview, throwing out as a reason for your course, some undefined, intangible insinuations. Nevertheless, we sent a reply to your long letter in a few hours after receiving it. ‑ The committee were in Lexington till 1 o'clock, P. M., without hearing a word from you. I then left for Frankfort, expecting, of course, no reply to my last. After tedious delay, however, it came to hand. This fact will account for the delay of my reply.

In regard to the predictions of your " prophets," and the surmises of " the scores of persons " that have spoken to you, together with what " some have said " of me, I hold them all in very low esteem. There always have been men who *prophecied* concerning things of which they were profoundly ignorant; individuals, even " scores " of them, who judge others by themselves, and false acccusers. That such a man as Mr. C. should condescend to retail such trash, can be accounted for only on the supposition, *that he is greatly at a loss.* We stand ready to be judged by our conduct.

A part of your epistle is inimitably confused. A reply to that portion is unnecessary. When you come to sum up the matter, however, the mist disappears; and we think we get your ideas. You tell us, that in making out the issues for this discussion, we assign to you *just as many affirmatives and negatives as we please.* What is the fact? We have precisely as many affirmatives and negatives as Mr. C., and no more! But you say, we assign you the affirmatives and negatives *on what topics* we please. What is the fact? We have three affirmatives on *precisely the topics on which Mr. C. gave them to us.* On the *mode*, the *subject*, and the *administrator* of baptism, you never once offered us a negative, until after we had accepted the whole of your six propositions! Then you began to place new obstacles in the way. You further say, we give such affirmatives and negatives *in what order we please.* What is the fact? We have them precisely in the order in which they were offered us repeatedly by Mr. C! How do these indisputable facts look by the side of your charges!!! No, sir, our offence consists in the fact, that we expect Mr. C. to discuss *his own propositions, with his own affirmatives and negatives, and in his own order;* and when he positively refuses, we charge him with re treating.

You say, " The propositions offered on yesterday, are not new propositions; they are mere amplifications of those already offered." So long as we understand the meaning of words in our own language, it is vain for Mr. C. to tell us, that those propositions are the same as those previously offered. But if they are the same, why *amplify* them? We had thought that it was desirable to have propositions for discussion presented in as few words as would definitely express the difference between the parties.

When you come to close your letter, your remarks are quite as curious as those already noticed. You say, " *You either intended, in the letter before me, to* COMPEL *me to come up to your terms,* or *have no discussion*" Now, sir, look at your letter to which mine was a reply. After stating your new propositions, and making your new demands, you thus remark, " If to these fair and equitable terms (!) you agree, I am prepared to go into other pre-liminary arrangements immediately. *If not, say so, and the matter ends.*" The fact turns out to be, that Mr. C. intended by his letter to force us to *his* terms, or have no debate. We took him at his word, and not choosing to be forced, we supposed the matter at an end. I repeat it, all we ask of Mr. C. is, to debate his own propositions, in his own language and order.

But you now say, " I will take, rather than have no debate, the whole six propositions, as drawn up in your letter before me, with the simple change of the first on the action of baptism, as proposed in my last." In view of the fact, that we have accepted your own propositions in form and order, and in view of the further fact, that you have received none of *our* propositions, we are under no obligation to allow any change whatever. In your letter, of May 24th, you say, " You may, in your reply, settle the whole matter of the propositions, or you may protract the subject for months." How could I settle the whole matter, unless by accepting your propositions then and previously offered? They were accepted; and thus the whole matter, as I had a right to believe, was settled. Now you refuse to abide by the settlement called for by yourself! We will, however, ac-commodate you in this matter. We accept your new proposition, on what you call the *action* of baptism, giving you the affirmative you desire, pro-vided that all the propositions be discussed in the order in which you have repeatedly stated, and we have accepted them, and that the other proposi-tions remain unaltered.

As to the *order* in which the propositions should be debated, we have simply agreed to the order repeatedly presented by yourself. In your letter of June 25th, you present the propositions, perhaps, for the third time, in the order in which we are willing to debate them. And in your letter of July 13th, you say, in reference to that of June 25th, " Hence in my last, after hearing all the explanations, I drew out *in order and form* the propo-sitions," &c. We see no possible reason now for changing the order which heretofore you have uniformly considered the best.

We have now conceded all that we intend to concede in this matter. We have taken your own propositions, in your own order, and we now agree to accommodate you in the change of one of the most important of them. We have been unnecessarily detained by your refusal of a personal interview, to which you invited us. Two of us are obliged to leave Lex-ington this afternoon at 2 o'clock. If you agree to go into the discussion, as now agreed to by us, we shall expect to be informed of your determina-tion before that hour.

Concerning our *motives*, in this whole affair, we choose to say nothing. We are willing to have our conduct indicate them.

Respectfully, &c.

JNO. H. BROWN

Lexington, Ky., August 5, 1843.

ELDER J. H. BROWN:

Sir—It is now within a few minutes of twelve o'clock, and your letter of this morning is just received. You request an answer in two hours; and in the midst of company, and various engagements, I cannot formally reply to all that is in your letter. The complimentary part of it, indeed, especial-ly so much of it as you very courteously devote to my " palpable violation of ordinary rules of politeness," would seem to demand a very special and cor-dial acknowledgment. But as I have not recognized your pretensions to that chair of instruction, and consequently have not placed myself under your special tuition, you will please excuse my further palpable violation of your rules of politeness in not thanking you for the compliment. In our code of good manners, Mr. Brown would have called to see me, especially after my journey of almost four hundred miles to see him. But I excuse him, on the ground that ministers of religion frequently study the theology of the dark ages, and have as good a right to freedom of opinion on this, as on other subjects.

As to those dark and inscrutable portions of my epistle, it seems they have answered their purpose so well, that it would be superfluous now to explain them. Touching one point, however, I must say a word or two, viz. "*the end of the matter*." I presumed that enough had been said on the propositions of debate, and that the matter was never to end, unless I gave you such a letter as that which elicited your throwing the responsibility of no debate on me. This you did in such an urbane, respectful and gentlemanly style, that you constrained me to re-consider the matter, especially as you threw so much light upon the subject from my former letters. But had you not, indeed, produced those documents, and offered me such a responsibility, after the just and honorable issue I had offered, I certainly would not have responded to yours of the 3d inst. You, however, changed my premises, and of course I changed my purposes.

Although, then, I do not cordially approve of the issue, as formed, it not being equal, still, as it is this or nothing, I consent to the discussion of the propositions as you have stated them,—I having the affirmative on the action of baptism, as before stipulated. Touching all the forms of expression in which these propositions have been offered, we shall, in the course of the debate, fully explain ourselves.

I answered your letter of yesterday in about as many hours as you spent on mine. I received it at bed time, and from breakfast to one o'clock, the period spent on mine, furnished a reply.

I am obliged to leave on Monday evening, and will now request it as a favor to have other matters attended to immediately. I shall be glad to see you at four o'clock, if possible, at Mr. Henry Bell's; or I will wait upon you, at any place you may appoint, at that hour, or on Monday morning. Please favor me with an immediate reply, at Dr. Fishback's.

Respectfully,   A. CAMPBELL.

Lexington, Ky., August 5, 1843.

ELDER A. CAMPBELL :—Yours of this date is before me. It is indeed well that we have no written, authoritative code of politeness, as to some whose theology wears a *modern garb*, it might be more intolerable than even creeds. It is well, as it turns out, that I did not call to see Mr. Campbell, since, in his existing state of mind, having just heard divers things terrific, he would have declined a personal interview. Ignorant, however, of all such rumors, I expected, on reaching Lexington, at the hour and the place mentioned in my letter, to receive a note from Mr. C., informing the committee where they might see him. I did receive a letter, declining the interview proposed by himself!

We are quite happy in witnessing the effects of our epistle of the 3d inst. But for that, it seems, we should have had no debate. The propositions, as to language and order, having been agreed upon, we are prepared to attend to other preliminaries. We cannot, however, meet you this afternoon, as two of us have appointments for Sabbath, in order to fill which we must immediately leave Lexington. We will meet you, God permitting, on Monday morning at eleven o'clock, at the house of Dr. Bell, on Hill street, unless you prefer some other place, of which you will of course inform us.

We desire now to suggest the propriety and importance of publishing our correspondence as soon as possible, without note or comment. We deem this course desirable, to prevent the circulation of false rumors, which may be injurious to either party or to both.

Respectfully,   J. H. BROWN.

Lexington, Ky., August 7, 1843.

ELDER BROWN—Your proposition to publish immediately our correspondence touching the contemplated discussion, without note or comment, has been duly considered.

In the first place, it is unusual to publish such correspondence before the debate is published. In the second place, not having the correspondence with me, and believing that the representations in your letter of the 3d inst. are not in exact accordance with it, I could not consent to its publication till I have examined it. And in the third place, that those who may assemble to hear the discussion may hear with candor and impartiality, it is, in my judgment, better that they should not read the correspondence till they have heard the discussion. For the above reasons, I cannot consent to the proposition to publish at this time.

I expect to meet you to-day, at the time and place appointed.

Respectfully,   A. CAMPBELL.

PRELIMINARIES.

REFORMED CHURCH, LEXINGTON, KENTUCKY, }
Wednesday Morning, 10½ *o'clock, Nov.* 15, 1843. }

This being the time and place appointed for a commencement of the discussion between the Rev. Alexander Campbell, of Bethany, Virginia, and the Rev. Nathan L. Rice, of Paris, Kentucky: the president, moderators, debators, stenographers, committees, and an audience of some two thousand persons, having, in pursuance of previous notice, assembled on this interesting occasion; and a copy of the programme, presenting the points at issue, having been placed in the hands of the moderators, the Honorable Henry Clay, president of the board, rose and remarked as follows:

It is presumed that the object for which this assembly is now convened, is known to every person in attendance.

I understand, that the gentlemen who are to discuss the highly interesting topics, embraced in this printed programme, are now prepared to proceed to the discussion. Before they do so, however, on an occasion so grave, so interesting, and one in which there should be perfect order, it is proper to observe, that it is the prevailing usage every where; it is according to the sense of religion, with which this subject is so intimately connected, that there should be no confusion: and I trust, there will be a preservation of order, and undivided attention during the whole progress of the debate. In the mean time, one of the clergymen present is prepared to invoke the blessing of heaven.

Whereupon, the Rev. Joseph Bullock being called upon, arose and prayed as follows:

O, thou Great and Eternal God, who art the Creator, the Preserver, and the Governor of the universe, we desire this morning to look up to thee for thy blessing to rest upon us. We pray that we may be under the guidance of thy Holy Spirit; and that thou wouldst enable us, while assembled together, to give heed to the discussion, which is about to take place in our hearing. We pray that all may have a sincere desire to know the truth: and when the truth is proclaimed, we pray that we may be enabled to receive it in the love of it, and that it may spring up and bring forth fruit unto eternal life.

Our Father, we pray that our meeting may not be in vain, but that much good may be done in the name of thy Son. May the cause of truth, and of righteousness, and of holiness, be advanced. And may the discussion which is now being entered upon, be followed by great and manifold blessings, not only to the assembly now present, but to those who may attend from time to time. Especially, may those engaged in this discussion be guided by that wisdom which cometh down from above; which is first pure, then peaceable, gentle, and easy to be entreated; full of mercy and good fruits; without partiality, and without hypocrisy.

We beseech thee, our Father, to keep us all from error and delusion, and guide us in the right path—in that straight and narrow path which leads to heaven and to God.

Wilt thou be with us all, not only while assembled here, but be our guide and our support through all the journey of life; and when we come to lie down upon our beds of death, grant unto us the unspeakable consolations of thy gospel, and finally receive us all into thy kingdom above, to dwell with thee through ceaseless ages of eternity.

We ask for Christ, our Redeemer's sake. Amen.

RULES OF DISCUSSION.

1. The debate shall commence on Wednesday, 15th November.
2. To be held in the Reform Church.
3. Judge Robertson, selected by Mr. Rice, as moderator. Col. Speed Smith, selected by Mr. Campbell. And agreed that these two shall select a president-moderator. In case of either of the above named gentlemen declining to act, Judge Breck was selected by Mr. Rice, as alternate to Judge Robertson—and Col. Caperton as alternate to Col. Speed Smith.
4. In the opening of each new subject, the affirmant shall occupy one hour, and the respondent the same time; and each thereafter half hour alternately to the termination of each subject. The debate shall commence at 10 o'clock, A. M., and continue until 2 o'clock, P. M., unless hereafter changed.
5. On the final negative no new matter shall be introduced
6. The propositions for discussion are the following:

I. The immersion in water of a proper subject, into the name of the Father, the Son, and the Holy Spirit, is the one, only apostolic or christian baptism. Mr. Campbell affirms—Mr. Rice denies.

II. The infant of a believing parent is a scriptural subject of baptism. Mr. Rice affirms—Mr. Campbell denies.

III. Christian baptism is for the remission of past sins. Mr. Campbell affirms—Mr. Rice denies.

IV. Baptism is to be administered only by a bishop or ordained presbyter. Mr. Rice affirms—Mr. Campbell denies.

V. In conversion and sanctification, the Spirit of God operates on persons only through the word of truth. Mr. Campbell affirms—Mr. Rice denies.

VI. Human creeds, as bonds of union and communion, are necessarily heretical and schismatical. Mr. Campbell affirms—Mr. Rice denies.

6. No question shall be discussed more than three days, unless by agreement of parties.
7. Each debatant shall furnish a stenographer.
8. It shall be the privilege of the debaters to make any verbal or grammatical changes in the stenographer's report, that shall not alter the state of the argument, or change any fact.
9. The nett available amount, resulting from the publication, shall be equally divided between the two American Bible Societies.

10. This discussion shall be conducted in the presence of Dr. Fishback, President Shannon, John Smith, and A. Raines, on the part of the Reformation ; and President Young, James K. Burch, J. F. Price, and John H. Brown, on the part of Presbyterianism.

11. The debatants agree to adopt as " rules of decorum " those found in Hedges' Logic, p. 159, to-wit :

RULE 1. The terms in which the question in debate is expressed, and the point at issue, should be clearly defined, that there could be no misunderstanding respecting them.

RULE 2. The parties should mutually consider each other as standing on a footing of equality, in respect to the subject in debate.   Each should regard the other as possessing equal talents, knowledge, and a desire for truth with himself; and that it is possible, therefore, that he may be in the wrong, and his adversary in the right.

RULE 3. All expressions which are unmeaning, or without effect in regard to the subject in debate, should be strictly avoided.

RULE 4. Personal reflections on an adversary should, in no instance, be indulged.

RULE 5. The consequences of any doctrine are not to be charged on him who maintains it, unless he expressly avows them.

RULE 6. As truth, and not victory, is the professed object of controversy, whatever proofs may be advanced, on either side, should be examined with fairness and candor ; and any attempt to answer an adversary by arts of sophistry, or to lessen the force of his reasoning by wit, cavilling or ridicule, is a violation of the rules of honorable controversy.

[Signed.]   A. CAMPBELL.
              N. L. RICE

DEBATE

ON

CHRISTIAN BAPTISM.

~~~~~~~~~~~~~~~~~~~~~~~~~~~~~~

Wednesday, Nov. 15, 1843—10 *o'clock, A. M.*
[MR. CAMPBELL'S OPENING ADDRESS.]

MR. PRESIDENT,—I feel myself peculiarly happy in being specially called, in the good providence of God, to appear before you, sir, and your honorable associates, in the midst of this great community, to act an humble part in that long-protracted controversy, commenced more than three centuries ago, when the Genius of Protestantism first propounded to Europe and the world the momentous and prolific questions, Is the Bible an intelligent document? Is it a book to be read by all the people? Does it fully contain and clearly reveal the whole duty and happiness of man? The bold and intrepid Luther promptly responded in the affirmative; and immediately a numerous host gave in their adhesion, seconded his efforts, erected their standard, unfurled their banners, and rallied under the sublime motto, The Bible, the whole Bible, and nothing but the Bible is the religion of Protestants.

The pope, his cardinals, and his lordly prelates, heard, with a scornful and indignant smile, this bold and comprehensive declaration of independence. Little did his Roman holiness, Leo X., and the lions around him imagine what mighty revolutions of empire, civil and ecclesiastical, were concealed under those symbols. No one, indeed, then living, comprehended that motto in all its amplitude. None saw that the regeneration of a world was in it. None anticipated the mighty impetus it was about to impart to the human mind, to the cause of human government, to the advancement of civilization, to the eternal redemption of the world from ignorance, error, and crime.

It was not merely a renunciation of popery—of all sorts of popery, ecclesiastical and political; it was not merely a renunciation of despotism, of tyranny, of anarchy, of misrule, of every species of cruelty and oppression on account of opinions, on account of human traditions or political interests; it asserted the rights of man—liberty of thought, liberty of speech, and liberty of action. It asserted that God had no vicegerent on earth, no representative amongst men; that he alone is Lord of the conscience.

From that moment to the present the march of mind has been onward and upward. The mighty spell that had for ages held all Christendom in abject slavery to kings and priests, those demigods of human admiration and worship, began to be broken. Opinions held sacred from times immemorial began to be discussed; learning awoke from the slumber of

4   E   49

centuries; science assumed her proper rank; the arts, both useful and ornamental, began to be cultivated with new vigor; and Protestant society, at least, laid aside the austere sanctimoniousness of a religious grimace, put off the cowl of superstition, and appeared in the more pleasing costume of an open countenance, a smiling face, a generous heart and a more spiritual devotion.

Still, however, all error was not detected, discussed, and repudiated. The human mind, like the human body, takes but one short step at a time; and that step rather indicates the decrepitude and feebleness of age than the vigor and energy of youth. Unfortunately, Protestantism soon obtained favor at court, and immediately mounted the throne of the greatest empire in the world: and in doing this, she had to retain so many of the traditions and doctrines of the fathers as secured the favor of kings and princes, and flattered the pretensions of bishops, archbishops and their dependents, who in affection were wedded to Rome; whilst they abjured her power merely because it eclipsed and diminished their own.

The leaven of popery, sir, still works in both church and state. The hierarchies of England, Scotland, and Protestant Germany, alas! too fully substantiate the allegation. Oxford is not the only university, nor her tracts the only documents which show a professed sympathy with some of the bolder attributes and views of the Papal power. That sympathy is clearly evinced on the continents of Europe and America; and what strange involutions and evolutions may yet farther characterize its movements, the pages of the future alone can disclose.

The power of Protestantism in some important points of view is comparatively feeble—greatly feeble. Its strength lies in the leading truths of the system. Its feebleness is wholly owing to errors long cherished, and still sought to be maintained as fundamental truths, by many of its warmest friends and admirers. These errors make parties. For, while truth is essentially attractive and conservative, error is necessarily repellant and divisive. Numerous as the sects, that have impaired the Protestant influence and power, are the errors that have generated them. Every party has its truth, and, probably, its error too. For, even when truth makes a party, error not only occasions it, but infuses itself into the system. Good and wise men, of all parties, are turning their attention more and more to the causes and occasions of schism; and that, too, from an ardent wish to fathom the occult causes of so much discord amongst brethren; in the hope, too, of discovering some grand scheme of union and fraternal co-operation in the cause of our common christianity.

The last century terminated with the downfall of consolidated Atheism in France, after a reign of terror, the darkest and most desolating on the rolls of time. All Europe stood aghast at the awful spectacle, and saw in it developments of the tendencies of sectarian discords, that suggested to the reflecting and intelligent, the necessity of some very important changes in the social system. One of the results was, that the present century was ushered in with the formation of one grand Bible society, composed of various denominations, cherishing the truly magnanimous and splendid scheme of giving the Bible, without note or comment, to the whole family of man; so that every man might read in his own language the wonderful works of God.

This truly benignant scheme has, in various ways, already contributed greatly to the introduction of a brighter and a better era. The project of divesting the margin of the sacred writings of prophets and apostles of the cumbrous inscriptions of sectarian tenets and traditions—the dogmata of all schism—under the insidious pretence and titles of Notes and Comments on the Sacred Text, has given.a new impulse to the mind, because it has proposed the Bible to mankind in harmony with the great Protestant motto. A new and improved system of Hermaneutics is another happy effect of the attempt to make man, more or less, his own interpreter of the testimonies of God. The improvements in sacred criticism, and in biblical philology in general, have already elevated the present century above the last, as the sixteenth excelled the fifteenth in the grand developments of truth, and of the elementary principles of a new order of things.

No living man can fully estimate the exact momentum of the principles at work in his own time. The objects that obtrude upon his consideration are too near him to be seen in all their just proportions. Time, that great revealer of secrets and infallible exponent of the wisdom of all human schemes, must pass its solemn verdict upon every human enterprise before its proper character can be fully and justly appreciated.

The points of debate on the present occasion may, to some minds not conversant with such matters, appear to embrace points extremely frivolous and unimportant. The question, for example, of baptism, as respects its action, whether it shall be understood to mean sprinkling or immersing, is frequently made to assume no higher importance than that of a mere scuffle about the difference between a large and a small basin of water. It is, indeed, an *elementary* question; yet it may possibly have much of the fortunes of Christendom in its bosom. It stands to the whole christian profession as circumcision to a Jew, as hereditary descent to a British lord, or the elective franchise to an American citizen.

Let no one undervalue the points at issue in the present controversy. Let no one be startled when I affirm the conviction, that, in the questions to be discussed on the present occasion, the fortunes of America, of Europe and the world, are greatly involved. Can that be regarded by the mere politician (to say nothing of the philanthropist or the christian) as a minor matter which gives to the pope of Rome one hundred millions of subjects every three and thirty years; and that, too, without a single thought, volition or action of their own? Can any one regard that as a very unimportant ceremony, which binds forever to the Papal throne so many of our race, by five drops of water and the sign of a cross imposed upon them with their christian name? The omission of an *h* in pronouncing a word became, providentially, the occasion of the slaughter of forty-two thousand Ephraimites in one day; the conversion of an *o* into an *i* divided the ecclesiastic Roman empire into two great parties, which disturbed its peace, fostered internal wars, and exhausted its blood and treasure for a succession of several imperial reigns; and the eating of an apple brought sin and death into our world, and has already swept the earth clean of all its inhabitants more than one hundred times. Let no one, therefore, regard anything in religion or morals as excessively minute, or unworthy of the highest conscientious regard. There is sometimes more in a monosyllable than in a folio. A Yes, or a No has slain millions; while a thousand volumes have been written and read without any visible disaster to any human being.

The greatest debate in the annals of time, so far as consequences were involved, was upon the proper interpretation of a positive precept. The fortunes, not of a single nation, of an empire, or of an age, but of a world were staked upon its decision. The parties consisted of two persons: the word in debate was Die; and because of the misrepresentation of it one of the parties lost paradise, and gained labor, and sorrow, and death. In this world we have great little matters, as well as little great matters. To the former class belongs the affairs of kingdoms, empires and of all time: to the latter, individual purity, holiness, happiness. To infinite space, an atom and a mountain bear the same proportions. In the presence of endless duration, a moment and an age are equal. If, then, by a drop of water and the sign of the cross, Gregory XVI. sits on yonder gorgeous throne in the midst of the vatican, worshiped by more than one hundred millions of human beings; and if the Protestant Pedo-baptist churches in America annually increase more by the touch of a moistened finger than by all the eloquence of their seven thousand ministers; then, I ask, is not so much of the present discussion as pertains to that single rite of transcendent importance to this nation and people, whether contemplated in their ecclesiastical or political character?

In justice to my respondent and his church, I must distinctly state that this community are not at all indebted to me for the present discussion. It originated with our zealous and indefatigable Presbyterian brethren, who have ever been forward in the great and good work of religious controversy; and, as an apostle commands us to render honor to whom honor is due, we must award to them the honor of the present debate and all its happy influences. The present interview, when solicited by Mr. Brown, [Rev. John H. Brown, of Richmond, Ky.,] was indeed acceded to on my part with an express and covenanted understanding, that it was to be a frank, candid, full, and amicable discussion of the great points of difference between us; that each party was to affirm and maintain what it taught, and thus give to our respective communities authentic views of our peculiar tenets, so far as they may materially conflict with each other; and thus furnish the public with a book containing the numerous and various arguments by which our respective tenets may be assailed and defended. That the discussion might have all authority with the people, it was stipulated that, in case of a single combat, one person should be chosen as the oracle of the party, with whom I would enter into a formal debate on all these questions; and that other ministers should be present as helps and counsellors. I am happy in having the assurance that my friend [Mr. Rice] appears here, in consequence of that agreement, as the elect debatant, chosen by his brethren while assembled at synod—being not only one of the five persons chosen at the meeting of the synod, but also the one chosen by the other four, and commended to my acceptance by Mr. Brown, one of his electors, in the words following: " We have selected the man into whose hands we think proper to commit the defence of our cause. His standing is well known in Kentucky and out of it. We will not select another." To add to my satisfaction, he [Mr. Rice,] is also aided and sustained by a learned cohort of divines of high standing in the Presbyterian church; and not by these only, but doubtless by many others, present and absent. Such an array of talent, learning, and piety would seem to authorize the confident expectation that, if those tenets of his party from which we dissent can be convincingly maintained and made acceptable to this community, it will now be done.

In addition to all this, I am now assured that my friend [Mr. Rice] is not compelled into this discussion by the mere authority and importunity of his brethren, but that he enters into the business as one that long and ardently panted to render some distinguished service to the church of his ancestors and of his adoption, and to deliver himself on the great questions now before us. It is our singular good fortune to meet on this arena a gentleman exceedingly zealous for the doctrines and traditions of his church, and who, for one year at least, if not for several years past, has been in habitual preparation for such an occasion as the present. So desirous of merited applause, and so untiring in his zeal and devotion to ancient orthodoxy, he has been in one continued series of conflicts, wrestling with tongue and pen—entering the lists with all sorts of disputants, Baptists and Reformers, old and young, experienced and inexperienced, and, in amicable discussion, breaking numerous lances upon the brazen shields and steel caps of such members of the church militant as either foreordination or contingency threw in his way—and on these very subjects now before us. Neither his devotion to the cause of truth nor his labors of love, have been confined to Kentucky; but, in his pious opposition to heresies and heretics, like one of old, he has pursued them into foreign cities. Nashville yet resounds with the praises of his zeal and the fame of his achievements in the cause of Presbyterianism. If, then, flaw or weakness there be in that series of arguments and evidences that I am prepared to offer on the present occasion, or if my facts and documents are not true and veritable, I have every reason to expect a full and thorough exposition of them. But should they pass the fiery ordeal of the intense genius and vigorous analysis to which they are now to be subjected, may I not, in common with those who espouse them, repose on them as arguments and proofs irrefragably strong and enduring?

The questions to be discussed on the present occasion are, it is conceded on all hands, not only elementary and fundamental, but of vital importance to every saint and sinner in the world. They alike enter into the peculiar essence and living form of the christian religion. Accurate and comprehensive views of them, not only promote the purity and happiness of the individual, but also conduce to the union of christians and the conversion of the world. So long as we have in the christian profession two faiths, two baptisms, and two Spirits, we shall have a plurality of bodies ecclesiastic arrayed in open hostility to each other; and by consequence, the whole train of evils and misfortunes incident to alienated affections and rival interests. I rejoice in the present discussion, because it strikes at the three main roots of modern partyism—the creeds, the baptisms, and the spirits of moral philosophy and human expediency. Before a holier and a happier era, we must resume the original basis of one Lord, one Creed, one Baptism, one Spirit. United on these we stand: divided we fall. These opinions, creeds, baptisms, and spirits must be repudiated. Hence the necessity of discussion. Either there must be a conviction of those errors and a repudiation of them, else an agreement to regard them as matters of opinion, as matters of forbearance, and take no account of them. One of these results is essential to union.

With these views and convictions, and with a supreme desire for holy union, harmony, and love in the truth, and for the truth's sake, with all them that believe, love and obey it, I consent unto the present discussion. The two baptisms, the human and the divine, are first in order. In distributing the subject into its proper parts, four questions arise : What is the action called baptism? who is the subject? what its design? and who may administer it? Without further introduction, I proceed to the first proposition: and may the Spirit of all wisdom and revelation direct our deliberations, subdue all pride of opinion, restrain every illicit desire of human approbation, inspire our souls with the love of truth rather than of victory, lead our investigations to the happiest issue, and give to this discussion an extensive and long-enduring influence in healing divisions, in promoting peace, and in extending the empire of truth over myriads of minds enthralled by error and oppressed with the doctrines and commandments of men!

My proposition is, *That immersion in water, into the name of the Father, and of the Son, and of the Holy Spirit, is the only christian baptism.*

In the commission which the Messiah gave to his apostles for converting the nations, he commanded three things to be done, indicated by three very distinct and intelligible terms, to wit: *matheteusate, baptizontes, didaskontes.* Unfortunately, one of these three Greek words has become a subject of much controversy. While all agree that the first term may be literally and properly rendered "make disciples," and the last "teaching them," the second, not being translated but transferred into our language, is by some understood to mean *sprinkling*, by others *pouring*, by a third class *immersing*, and by a fourth class *purifying* them into the name of the Father, and of the Son, and of the Holy Spirit.

Fortunately, the meaning of any word—Hebrew, Greek, Latin, or English—is a question not of opinion, but a question of fact; and, being a plain question of fact, it is to be ascertained by competent witnesses, or by a sufficient induction of particular occurrences of the word, at different times on various subjects and by different persons. All good dictionaries, in all languages, are made upon a full examination of particular occurrences—upon a sufficient induction of distinct instances—and convey the true meaning of a word at any given period of its history.

The action, then, which Jesus Christ commanded to be done in the word *baptizo*, is to be ascertained in just the same manner as the action enjoined in *matheteuo*, or that commanded in *didasko*, its associates in the commission. We ask no other law or tribunal for ascertaining the meaning of *baptizo* than for ascertaining the sense of *matheteuo* or *didasko*. They are all to be determined philologically, as all other foreign and ancient terms, by the well established canons of interpretation. From a candid, judicious, impartial application of these laws, there is not the least difficulty in the case.

There is, indeed, less difficulty in ascertaining the meaning of the word *baptizo*, than that of either of the other words standing with it in the commission; because it is a word more restricted, more circumscribed and appropriated in its acceptation than either of its companions; because, moreover, it is a word of specification, and not so general and undefined as *matheteuo* or *didasko*—"making disciples," and "teaching them." It indicates an outward and formal action into the awful name of the whole divinity; and consequently, *a priori*, we would be led to regard it as a most specific and well defined term. The action was to be performed by one person upon another person, and in the most solemn manner.

Besides, it is a most peculiar and positive ordinance. All admit that baptism is a positive ordinance, and that positive precepts, as contradistinguished from moral precepts, indicate the special will of a sovereign in some exact and well defined action; the nature, form and necessity of which arise not from our own *a priori* reasonings about utility or expediency, but from the clearly expressed will of the lawgiver. It is farther universally agreed that circumcision was a positive and not a moral institution—made right and obligatory by the mere force of a positive law. It enjoined a specific act upon a specific subject, called for exact obedience, and was therefore definitely set forth by a specific and not by a generic term. This fact will not, I presume, be disputed. Baptism, then, like circumcision, must have the specific action to be performed implied and expressed in it. That baptism is such a term, if it be disputed, the sequel will, we presume, abundantly prove. Meantime, before hearing the witnesses or submitting the induction, it may not be uninteresting to pursue the analogy a little farther, and to show, *a priori*, that such a specific precept is to be expected.

Will it not be conceded by all, that whatever good reason can be given why, not a general but a specific word was chosen by God in commanding circumcision to Abraham and his posterity, the same demands a term as specific and intelligible from the Christian Lawgiver in reference to the institution of baptism? Now, as Jesus Christ must have intended some particular action to be performed by his ministers and submitted to by the people, in the command to baptize them, it follows that he did select such a word, or that he would not or could not do it. This is a dilemma from which escape is not easy. If any one say that he could not, then either the language which he spake or his knowledge of it was defective. If the former, then the language was unfit to be the vehicle of a divine communication to man; if the latter, his divine character and commission are directly assailed and dishonored. Or, if any one say he could have done it but would not, he impeaches either his sincerity or benevolence, or both: his sincerity, in demanding obedience in a particular case, for which he cares nothing; his benevolence, in exacting a particular service in an ambiguous and unintelligible term, which should perplex and confound his consciencious followers in all the ages of the world. Follows it not, then, that he could, that he would find such a word; and that he has done it; and that *baptizo* is that specific word?

Before summoning our most authoritative witnesses to the meaning of this important word, [*baptizo*,] I shall assert a few facts, which, I presume, will not be denied by any one properly acquainted with the orig'-nal language of the New Testament: 1. *Baptizo* is not a radical, but a derivative word; 2. Its root [*bapto*] is never applied to this ordinance; 3. In the Common Version *bapto* is translated both in its simple and compound form, always by the word "dip:" 4. *Baptizo* is never translated by "dye," "stain," or "color;" 5. *Baptizo*, with its derivations, is the only word used in the New Testament to indicate this ordinance; and 6. The word *baptize* has no necessary connection with water, or any liquid whatever.

Now, from these indisputable facts, hereafter to be developed, some corollaries are deduced; such as—*baptizo* indicates a specific action, and consequently, can have but one meaning. For, if a person or thing can be immersed in water, oil, milk, honey, sand, earth, debt, grief, affliction, spirit, light, darkness, &c., it is a word indicating specific action, and specific action only.

Baptizo, confessedly a derivative from *bapto*, derives its specific meaning, as well as its radical and immutable form, from that word. According to the usage of all languages, ancient and modern, derivative words legally inherit the specific, though not necessarily the figurative meaning of their natural progenitors; and never can so far alienate from themselves that peculiar significance as to indicate an action specifically different from that intimated in the parent stock. Indeed, all the inflections of words, with their sometimes numerous and various families of descendants, are but modifications of one and the same generic or specific idea.

We sometimes say, that words generally have both a proper and a figurative sense. I presume we may go farther and affirm, that every word in current use has a strictly proper and a figurative acceptation. Now, in the derivation direct, (for there is a direct and an indirect derivation,) the proper and natural or original meaning of the term is uniformly transmitted. Let us, for example, take the Saxon word *dip* through all its flexions and derivations. Its flexions are, *dip, dips, dippeth, dipped, dipping.* From these are derived but a few words, such as the nouns, *dipping, dipper, dip-chick, dipping-needle.* Now in all the flexions and derivations of this word, is not the root [*dip*] always found in sense as well as in form? Wherever the radical syllable is found, the radical idea is in it. So of the word *sprinkle:* its flexions are, *sprinkle, sprinkleth, sprinkling, sprinkled;* and its derivatives are the nouns *sprinkling* and *sprinkler.* Does not the idea represented in the radical word [*sprinkle*] descend through the whole family? We shall visit a larger family. From the verb *read,* whose flexions are, *reads, readeth, reading;* come the descendants, *reading,* (the noun,) *readable, readableness, readably, reader, readership.* The radical syllable is not more obvious than the uniformity of its sense throughout the whole lineage. Let us now advance to the two Greek representatives of the words *dip* and *sprinkle.* These are ancient families, and much larger than any of the modern. *Bapto,* the root, has some seven hundred flexions, besides numerous derivatives. We shall only take the indicative mood, through one tense and through one person: *Bapto, ebapton, bapso, ebapsa, ebaphon, bapho, bebapha, ebebaphein.* Its derivatives are *baptizo,* and its regular flexions—more than seven hundred, including all its forms of mood, tense, participle, person,' number, gender, case: from which spring *baptismos, baptisma, baptisis, baptistes, baptomai, baptizomai, baptos, baptisterion, bapha, baphikos, bapheis.* These, through their some two thousand flexions and modifications, retain the *bap,* and, as uniformly, the *dip* represented by it. The same holds good of its distant neighbor, *raino,* "I sprinkle." It has as many flexions and nearly as many derivatives as *bapto.* It has *raino, rainomai, rantizo, rantismos, rantisma, ranter, rantis, rantos,* with their some two thousand flexions. These all exhibit the radical syllable *rain* or *ran,* and with it the radical *sprinkle.* Now, as it is philologically impossible to find *bap* in *rain,* or *rain* in *bap;* so impossible is it to find *dip* in *sprinkle,* or *sprinkle* in *dip.* Hence the utter impossibility of either of these words representing both actions. It is difficult to conceive how any man of letters and proper reflection can for a moment suppose, that *bapto* can ever mean "sprinkle," or *raino* "dip."

This my first argument is, I own, a work of supererogation: inasmuch as all admit that *baptizo,* and not *bapto,* is the word that the Messiah chose to represent the action he intended, called baptism; and all the learned admit, that its primary, proper, and unfigurative meaning is,

" to dip." Hence if all that I have said on flexion and derivation were grammatically and philologically heterodox, as well as illogical, my cause loses nothing. I feel so rich in resources, that I can give this and many such arguments for nothing, and still have much more than a competency for life. But, be it all strictly and philologically true and solid, (as I unhesitatingly affirm it,) this single argument establishes my first proposition without farther effort. For, as all allow that *dip* is the primary and proper meaning of *bapto*, and *color, stain, dye, wet*, its figurative or secondary meanings ; and, as all admit that *baptizo* is the word that the Christian Lawgiver consecrated to indicate this ordinance ; and, as it is incontrovertibly derived from *bapto*, and therefore inherits the proper meaning of the *bap*, which is " dip ;" then, is it not irresistibly evident that *baptizo* can never authorize or sanction any other action than dipping, or immersion, as found in Christ's commission ? Such is my first argument ; which, if false, I lose nothing ; which, if true, my proposition is already established.

But we must have arguments and illustrations for the unlearned as well as for the learned. Before we advance to our second argument, founded on *baptizo* itself, I shall, in three English words, selected at random, show that neither number nor variety of derivations from a common stock, can ever nullify the original idea or action suggested. I take a verb, a noun, and a preposition, with their whole families. I open at the verb, *adduce: duce*, (from *duco*, "I lead,") is the root. The family lineage is, *abduce, adduce, conduce, deduce, educe, induce, introduce, obduce, produce, reduce, seduce, traduce, circumduction, deduction, induction*. Next comes the noun, *guard*, from which the verb, *guard, guarding, guarded, guarder, guardly, guardedness, guardship, guardable, guardful, guardage, guardance, guardiant, guardian, guardianess, guardianship, guardianage, guardless*. And finally, we open at the preposition, *up*, whence springs *upon, upper, uppermost, upperest, upward*. Now, can any one for a moment doubt, that, in all these three examples, the radical syllables, *duce, guard*, or *up*, retain the same sense, whatever it may be, generic or specific, through every branch of their respective families ?

Ancient Greek grammarians sometimes arranged their verbs in the form of trees, making the origin of the family the root ; the next in importance the trunk ; the next the larger branches, and so on to the topmost twig. In this way both flexions and derivations were occasionally exhibited. This fact I state, because it suggests to me a new form of presenting this my first argument, to the apprehension of all my hearers. A great majority of our citizens are better read in forests, fields and gardens, than in the schools of philology or ancient languages. Agriculturists, horticulturists, botanists, will fully comprehend me when I say, in all the dominions of vegetable nature, untouched by human art, as the root, so is the stem, and so are all the branches. If the root be oak, the stem cannot be ash, nor the branches cedar. What would you think, Mr. President, of the sanity or veracity of the backwoodsman, who would affirm that he found in a state of nature, a tree whose root was oak, whose stem was cherry, whose boughs were pear, and whose leaves were chestnut ? If these grammarians and philologists have been happy in their analogies drawn from the root and branches of trees, to illustrate the derivation of words, how singularly fantastic the genius that creates a philological tree, whose root is *bapto*, whose stem is *cheo*, whose

branches are *rantizo*, and whose fruit is *katharizo!* Or, if not too ludicrous and preposterous for English ears, whose root is *dip*, whose trunk
is *pour*, whose branches are *sprinkle*, and whose fruit is *purification!*

My first argument, then, is founded on the root, *bapto*, whose proper
signification, all learned men say, is *dip*, and whose main derivative is
baptizo—which, by all the laws of philology, and all the laws of nature,
never can, never did, and never will signify " to pour" or " to sprinkle."

I now proceed to *baptizo* itself—the word pre-ordained by the Messiah,
to indicate his will in this sacred ordinance. Meanwhile, I have not forgotten in this long preamble, that the meaning of *baptizo* as well as *bapto*,
is a question of fact, to be decided by impartial and disinterested witnesses, whose testimony is to be fairly stated, candidly heard, and impartially weighed, before the case is finally adjudicated.

My witnesses are so numerous that I must call them forth in classes,
and hear them in detail. I shall first summon the Greek lexicographers,
the most learned and most competent witnesses in this case, in the world.
These gentlemen are, and of right ought to be, inductive philosophers.
Philology is the most inductive of all sciences. The meaning of a word
is ascertained by the usage of those writers and speakers, whose knowledge and acquirements have made them masters of their own language.
From this class of vouchers we derive most of our knowledge of holy
writ, and of all that remains of Grecian literature and science. We,
indeed, try the dictionaries themselves by the classics, the extant authors
of the language. We prove or disprove them by the same inductive operation, by which we ascertain the facts of any science, mental or physical.
I rely exclusively upon the most ancient, the most impartial, and the most
famous lexicographers. I therefore prefer those on my respondent's
side of the question, to those on my own; and I prefer those who lived
and published before the controversy became so rife, as it has been
during the present century.

1. We shall first hear the venerable Scapula, a foreign lexicographer,
of 1579. On *bapto*, the root, what does this most learned lexicographer
depose? Hear him: " *bapto*—mergo, immergo item tingo (quod sit immergendo,") To translate his Latin—To dip, to immerse; also, to dye,
because that may be done by immersing. Of the passive, *baptomai*, he
says, " Mergor item lavor"—To be immersed, to be washed. Of *baptizo*
—" Mergo seu immergo, item submergo, item abluo, lavo"—To dip, to
immerse; also, to submerge or overwhelm, to wash, to cleanse.

2. Next comes the more ancient Henricus Stephanus, of 1572. *Bapto* and *baptizo*—" Mergo seu immergo, ut quæ tingendi aut abluendi
gratia aqua immergimus"—To dip or immerge, as we dip things for the
purpose of dyeing them, or immerge them in water. He gives the proper and figurative meanings, as Scapula gives them.

3. We shall next hear the Thesaurus of Robertson. My edition was
printed at Cambridge, 1676. It is the most comprehensive dictionary
I have ever seen. It contains eighty thousand words more than the old
Schrevelius. It is indeed, sometimes titled, *Cornelii Schrevelii Lexicon
Manuale Græco Latinum Copirossissimi Auductum.* His definitions
are generally regarded as the most precise and accurate. He defines *baptizo* by only two words—mergo and lavo—one proper and one figurative
meaning—to immerse, to wash.

4. Schleusner, a name revered by orthodox theologians, and of enviable fame, says, (Glasgow Ed. 1824,) " 1st. Proprie, immergo ac intingo,

in aquam immergo. Properly it signifies, I immerse, I dip, I immerse in water. 2d. It signifies, I wash or cleanse by water—(quia haud rare aliquid immergi ac intingi in aquam solet ut lavetur)—because for the most part, a thing must be dipped or plunged into water, that it may be washed." Thus he gives the reason why *baptizo* figuratively means " to wash,"—because it is frequently the effect of immersion.

5. After Schleusner, we shall hear the distinguished Pasor. My copy is the London edition of 1650. " *Bapto* et *baptizo*—mergo, immergo tingo quod sit immergendo, differt a dunai quod est profundum petere est penitus submergi." Again he adds—" Comparantur afflictiones gurgitibus aquaram quibus veluti merguntur qui miseriis et calamitatibus hujus vitæ conflictantur ita, tamen merguntur ut rursus emergant." All of which we translate as follow : " To dip, to immerse, to dye, because it is done by immersing. It differs from *dunai*, which means to sink to the bottom, and to be thoroughly submerged." Metaphorically, in Matthew, afflictions are compared to a flood of waters, in which they seem to be immersed, who are overwhelmed with the misfortunes and miseries of life ; yet only so overwhelmed as to emerge again.

6. After these venerable continental authorities, we shall now introduce a few English lexicographers, both general and special. Parkhurst's lexicon for the New Testament deposes, that *baptizo* first and primarily means to dip, immerse, or plunge in water ; but in the New Testament it occurs not strictly in this sense, unless so far as this is included in " to wash one's self, be washed, wash the hands by immersion, or dipping them in water." Mark vii. 4 ; Luke xi. 38. To immerse in water, or with water, in token of purification from sin, and from spiritual pollution ; figuratively—" to be immersed or plunged into a flood or sea, as it were, of grievous affliction and sufferings." So the Septuagint and Josephus use it. *He anomai me baptizei*—Iniquity plunges me into terror.

7. Next comes Mr. Donnegan, distinguished and popular in England and America. " *Baptizo*—to immerse repeatedly into a liquid, to submerge, to sink thoroughly, to saturate ; metaphorically, to drench with wine, to dip in a vessel and draw. *Baptismos*—immersion, submersion, the act of washing or bathing. *Baptiztes*, (a baptist)—one who immerses, submerges. *Baptisma*—an object immersed, submerged, washed or soaked."

8. Rev. Dr. John Jones, of England, deserves the next place at least in rank. *Bapto*, he defines, " I dip, I stain ;" and *baptizo*, " I plunge, I plunge in water, dip, baptize, bury, overwhelm."

9. Greenfield, editor of the Comprehensive Bible, the Polymicrian New Testament, &c. &c., whose reputation as a New Testament lexicographer is well known, says, " *Baptizo* means to immerse, immerge, submerge, sink,"—" I. N. T.—To wash, to perform ablution, cleanse, to immerse, baptize, and perform the rite of baptism."

10. Two Germans of distinction may be next heard. Professor Rost, whose reputation is equal to that of any other German linguist, in his Standard German Lexicon, defines *bapto* by words indicating to plunge, to immerse, to submerge.

11. Bretschneider, said to be the most critical lexicographer of the New Testament, affirms that " an entire immersion belongs to the nature of baptism." He defines it, " Proprie, sæpius intingo, sæpius lavo," and adds, " This is the meaning of the word : for in *baptizo* is contained

the idea of a complete immersion under water: at least, so is *baptisma* in the New Testament." But more fully he explains as follows : *Baptizo,* in N. T. non dicitur nisi de submersione solemni et sacra qua utebantur Judæi, ut vel ad vitæ emendationem aliquem obstringerent, vel peccatorum ejus culpamedelerent. *Ritu solemni submergo* aquis, *baptizo* (ut patres Latini loquuntur,) et legitur in N. T. *simplicitur* ; activum : *baptizo aliquem,* Jo. i. 25, &c.—passive *immergor in aquas* solemni ritu, *baptismo initior,* Matt. iii. 16; Marc i. 4, &c.; Rom. vi. 2 ; *osoi ebaptisthemen ;* quotquot sacra submersione obstricti sumus Christo, etiam obstricti sumus, ut in consortium mortis ejus veniamus, *i. e.* moriamur peccato, ut ipse pro peccatis mortuus est. *Baptisma, immersio, submersio;* in N. T. tantum de *submersione sacra,* quam patres *baptismum* dicunt. Dicitur de Johannis baptismo, &c. In the New Testament *baptizo* is not used, unless concerning the sacred and solemn submersion which the Jews used, that they might oblige an individual to an amendment of life, or that they might release him from the guilt of his sins. In the New Testament, without any adjunct, it means, I *baptize* in water in the solemn rite, (as the Latin Fathers use it.) Actively, I baptize one— passively, I am immersed into water in the solemn ordinance—I am initiated by baptism. Matt. iii. 16; Mark i. 4 ; Rom. vi. 2. *Baptisma,* immersion, submersion. In N. T. it is used only concerning the sacred submersion, which the Fathers call baptism. It is used concerning John's baptism.

12. Bass, an English lexicographer for the New Testament, gives *baptizo,* "to dip, immerse, plunge in water, to bathe one's self; to be immersed in sufferings or afflictions." If Pickering could be regarded as a new or distinct lexicographer, we should add his testimony, as it is corroborative of the above. He gives " *Baptisma*—immersion, dipping, plunging ; metaphorically, misery or calamity with which one is overwhelmed."

13. I shall conclude this distinguished class of witnesses from the nigh school of lexicography with the testimony of Stokius, who has furnished us with a Greek clavis and a Hebrew clavis—one for the Hebrew and one for the Greek Scriptures. My edition is the Leipsic of 1752. This great master of sacred literature says, " Generatim ac vivi vocis instictionis ac immersionis baptizo notionem obtinet. Speciatim proprie est immergere ac intingere in aquam;" which we translate, " *Baptizo* generally, and by the force of the word, indicates the idea of simply dipping and diving; but properly, it means to dip or immerse in water." He defines *baptisma* in like manner—" It generally denotes immersion and dyeing ; but by the innate force of the term, it properly imports immersion or the dipping of a thing in water, that it may be washed or cleansed." And mark especially, the following frank declaration of this distinguished theologian and critic : " The word is transferred to denote the first sacrament of the New Testament, which they call the sacrament of initiation ; viz : baptism. In which sacrament those to be baptized were anciently immersed in water, as now-a-days they are only sprinkled with water, that they may be washed from the pollution of sin, obtain the remission of it, and be received into the covenant of grace, as heirs of eternal life."

So depose these thirteen great masters on the native, original and proper meaning of the word in debate: to whose testimony I might add that of another thirteen dictionaries, both classical and theological, Greek and Latin ; such as Wilson's Church Dictionary, 1678; Bailey, of 1772 ;

Robertson; Hedericus, 1778; Ash, 1775: Charles Richardson; Calmet; Schœttgenius, 1765; Suicerus; Schilhornius; Cliznetus, 1661;
Leigh's Critica Sacra: and Tromius' Concordance. These all are respectable authorities, and some of them, indeed, rank with those of the
first class. They all concur with Suicerus, in defining *baptizo* as properly denoting immersion or dipping into. But as they are in general
but a mere monotonous repetition of the first thirteen, I shall not quote
them *in extenso.*

But, to sum up this class of evidence, and to show, from the highest
source of American theological authority, that I have neither misquoted
nor misinterpreted the verdict of this illustrious jury of thirteen unchal-
lenged judges, I will quote the words of Prof. Stuart, of the Andover
Theological School: " *Bapto, baptizó,* mean to dip, plunge, or immerse
into any liquid. All lexicographers and critics of any note, are agreed
in this.''—Bib. Repos. 1833, p. 298. Professor Stuart is my American
apostle, standing to this argument, as Paul stood in comparison to the
original twelve—himself the only apostle to the gentiles, though the thirteenth, as respected the original twelve, selected of and for the Jews.

Before dismissing this class of witnesses, it is pertinent to my proposition, that I state distinctly three facts: 1. These lexicographers were not
Baptists, but Pedo-baptists; 2. Not one of them ever translated any of
these terms by the word *sprinkle;* 3. Not any one of them ever translated any of these terms by the word *pour.* Consequently, with all their
prejudices they could find no authority for so doing, else doubtless, they
could have done it.

I hope my hearers will pardon the introduction of so many Greek and
Latin words. The occasion demands it. From the course pursued by
our neighboring denominations, we are compelled to lay the corner-stone
of our superstructure; not only deep in the earth, but upon a solid Greek
basis. The foundation being laid upon a Grecian rock, and the wall
above-ground, our labors will, we hope, be more intelligible, and consequently more agreeable and more interesting to us all.

We have, then, the unanimous testimony of all the lexicographers
known in Europe and America, that the proper and everywhere current
signification of *baptizo,* the word chosen by Jesus Christ in his commission to the apostles, is, to dip, plunge, or immerse; and that any other
meaning is tropical, rhetorical, or fanciful. This being so, then our first
proposition must be undoubtedly true. But, besides these, I have various other classes of witnesses to adduce, in solemn confirmation of the
testimony of this most learned, veritable and venerable class of men.

Before I sit down, permit me to assure you, Mr. President, and through
you, my friend, Mr. Rice, and this great concourse, that it is by constraint,
and not willingly, I have summoned those witnesses whose testimony you
have already heard, and others from whom you are yet to hear in the progress of this discussion. It is our Pedo-baptist friends who have imposed
on us this task. It is they and not we, that are demanding new translations, ingenious and learned criticisms. It is they who call for dictionaries and grammars, for divers versions, for ancient fathers, for the venerable decrees of synods and councils, and for all manner of extrinsic helps
and vouchers.

I have had the misfortune, sir, to be represented times without number,
as desirous of introducing a new version of the New Testament, to favor
my peculiar views and tenets. But, sir, a more unjust and unfounded

F

assertion has rarely been circulated among the American family. So far as my peculiar tenets are involved, the common Testament and common sense are all-sufficient. I ask no other earthly auxiliaries. In proof of this declaration, I now say, in your presence, gentlemen, and in the presence of this great congregation, that if my friend Mr. Rice, dare risk his cause on that version of the Scriptures read in his own church, I will meet him on that book alone, and from its plain grammatical construction, sustain not only the propositions before us, but every other doctrine I believe and teach; and that too without substituting one new reading, change or alteration from what is presented by the authority of Queen Victoria, or the General Assembly of the Scotch and American Presbyterian Church. Now, sir, when it is known, as we presume it will be, before this debate closes, that the Bishops' Bible published in the tenth year of Queen Elizabeth, and on which so much of the present King James' Bible, as appertains to the action of baptism, is especially based, was got up by the present Pedo-baptist authority, at the very crisis when immersion was being repudiated to make way for affusion in both Scotland and England, it will doubtless appear that I make a most liberal offer, when I agree to risk the defence of those propositions touching baptism, exclusively on that version, founding upon it every scriptural argument which I shall offer in the support of each and every one of those propositions. One point, at least, I must gain from this overture, whatever be its reception on the part of my respondent. If he accede to it, I, in common with the audience, will gain much time in coming to a satisfactory issue; if he do not accede to it, I shall never need another argument to prove, whether Reformers or Presbyterians have the greater confidence in, or affection for, the common version, so far at least as the establishment of our respective tenets are concerned. It is now, Mr. President, entirely in the hands and at the option of Mr. Rice, whether before an English audience, we shall exclusively employ an English Bible, and the common version, as the standard of orthodoxy, and the ultimate appeal on every proposition; or whether we shall abandon it as a whole, and only use it in a discretionary way, just as we may regard it favorable to our respective tenets.

I am, however, prepared for any course the gentleman pleases. I have just as many learned authorities, as much documentary evidence of all sorts around me, or at my disposal on the premises, as I desire, or can expect to use in the most protracted discussion. On him then be the entire responsibility, and not on me, for the direction which the present controversy may take.

But while I do, *ex-animo*, adopt the common version, as all-sufficient, and alone sufficient for my use in this debate, I would not be understood, as at all approving of it as the most faithful, correct and intelligible translation of the original Scriptures, which we have or can have, in our vernacular. It is however with much pleasure, that after having more or less examined many versions, and possessing, as I do, some fifteen or twenty varieties of them, I can and do avow my full conviction, that by a candid person, of the most ordinary, or extraordinay attainments, the way of salvation, our whole duty and happiness, can be learned with the greatest certainty and assurance, from the most imperfect version I have ever seen. I am therefore willing, if circumstances should command me, to meet any virtuous man, on any version extant, and maintain all that I now stand pledged to maintain on the present occasion.—[*Time expired.*

Wednesday, Nov. 15—11½ *o'clock, A. M.*

[MR. RICE'S FIRST REPLY.]

MR. PRESIDENT—With regard to the reformation of the sixteenth century and its glorious results, I perfectly agree with my friend, whose address you have just heard. And I am truly happy to appear before this large audience to-day in the defence of the great doctrines and truths elicited by the investigation of those eminent men, who were the honored instruments of rescuing the Scriptures from ecclesiastical despotism, and proclaiming to the world the fundamental truth, that the Bible teaches all that is necessary to be believed, or to be done, to secure eternal life.

I am perfectly aware of the disadvantage under which I attempt to perform this duty, partly from the fact, that I meet in debate one so much my senior, whose arguments and statements may be supposed to have an authority which cannot accompany such as I may offer. Besides, I meet a gentleman who has been engaged for thirty years past in discussing the very points now at issue—one who, if not the originator, is certainly the leading man of a numerous body of professing christians, by whom he is regarded almost as an oracle. In the opinion of many I shall doubtless be chargeable with presumption in venturing, under such circumstances, to become his opponent. But when I consider what multitudes of the wisest and best men, in past ages and in the present, have maintained and do maintain the principles for which I now contend; and when I remember that my friend himself, when perhaps younger than I, ventured to wage war upon the christian world, I think I may justly claim acquittal of the charge.

It is true, as he remarked, that in the Reformation all error was not detected and repudiated; but it will scarcely be denied, that so much of the truth was discovered and embraced as was essential to the existence of the church and the salvation of the soul. And if this be admitted, the doctrine of my worthy friend cannot be sustained; for certain it is, that the Reformers did not ascertain that immersion into water is the only apostolic or christian baptism. If, then, the Scriptures do teach this doctrine, they failed to discover one of the most important features of the christian system; and they and their followers were alike unbaptized, and were aliens from the church of Christ. Nay, if this doctrine be true, there is not now a true church on earth, save the few who have been so happy as to make this remarkable discovery!

A word in regard to the origin of this discussion. We are unwilling to receive any credit not due us, however disposed my friend Mr. C. may be to award it to us. It is more than doubtful whether he has given a correct account of the matter. I will read an extract from the second letter of Rev. Mr. Brown to Mr. Campbell, which places the subject in a very different light. "There is," says Mr. B., "evidently a misapprehension on the part of one of us as it regards our interview at Richmond, in August last. Let the facts speak for themselves. They are briefly the following: At the close of your address at Richmond, on the 3d of August, your friend Mr. Duncan approached me, and asked my opinion as to the address, which I gave with as much candor as it was sought. After other interrogatories were propounded and answered, he inquired if I thought discussion advisable, to which I gave an affirmative reply. He then remarked that he had engaged to dine with you, and would ascertain your feelings and wishes on the subject. All this occurred before we left the church. About four o'clock in the afternoon, Mr. Duncan sought a second interview with me, and requested me to call in company with him at your room, stating that you desired an interview with me on the subject about which he and I had conversed in the forenoon. I conformed to his wish, and accompanied him to your room, which ultimated in a mutual agreement to discuss certain points of difference, for the edification of the church and the prosperity of the cause of Christ, with a definite and expressed understanding that neither was to be considered the challenging party."

From this letter it appears, that the debate originated with Mr. Duncan, Mr. Campbell's friend, and not with Presbyterians. With its origin, it may be proper for me to say, I had nothing to do. It was agreed upon before I heard of it. I was afterwards requested, and consented to be one of *the five* who should undertake to conduct it.

My friend in his address paid me quite an unmerited compliment. I regret that I had not *written* something, as he has done, that might be considered a suitable return. But I am so little accustomed to writing speeches, and withal am so poor a reader of them, that I shall be under the necessity of returning the compliment as well as I can *extemporaneously*.

He has represented me as extremely anxious to press into this discussion. The truth, however, is, that I nominated successively two individuals to manage the debate, both of whom declined. I had had as much public discussion as I desired; but my brethren have thought proper to devolve upon me the duty of defending our views on this occasion. But Mr. C. would have you believe that I am quite a furious warrior—that, like the persecuting Saul, I have pursued the Reformers to strange cities, even as far as Nashville. I have had, it is true, more frequent discussions than most of my brethren, owing chiefly to the peculiar situation in which, in the early part of my ministry, I was placed. Providentially, I was settled where Romanism exerted a prevailing influence. It became necessary for me to engage in a war against that system, which continued for some seven years. During that period, I was employed in defending those great principles of the Reformation on which Protestant Christendom are mainly agreed.

With the followers of Mr. C. I have not sought controversy. The first discussion I ever had with a Reformer, occurred in Stanford, Ky., where, at the close of a sermon I preached on the mode of baptism, a Mr. Kenrick arose and requested the privilege of replying, which was granted. I had previously received from him a challenge to a discussion, of which I took no notice. My second discussion was with President Shannon, who visited Paris—the place of my residence, and made a public attack upon our Confession of Faith; to which, as in duty bound, I responded. This led to a rather informal controversy, which resulted in a written discussion. In Nashville, it is true, I had a discussion with one of Mr. Campbell's friends. I visited that city in fulfillment of a previous promise, to hold a protracted meeting. Whilst there I was requested by a number of the citizens to preach on the subject of baptism. I consented, and the appointment was announced. On the next morning I was called on by four prominent and very respectable Reformers, who gave me a challenge to meet in debate their most prominent man. I informed them, that as I was a stranger in Nashville, having no particular responsibility there, I should leave my friends to determine whether I ought to accept their invitation. My friends decided that it was my duty to accept. I accordingly did so, and, having but four days to remain, engaged in a brief discussion with Mr. Fanning.

These facts show how I have persecuted the Reformers, even to strange cities! Mr. Campbell has published the charge against me of waging furious war against his church; but let facts be known, and the charge is refuted.

This discussion, it should be known, is in no sense an *ecclesiastical* affair. The synod of Kentucky could not become a party to it; nor had that body any authority to appoint a representative to conduct such a discussion. It is, therefore, strictly an *individual* concern. It is true, some of my brethren have devolved upon me the important and difficult task of defending what we believe to be revealed truth; but I claim not the high standing in my church which my friend has been pleased to assign me. Whilst, however, I occupy an humble place amongst the minsters of the Presbyterian church, I have no fears of being unable to sustain the principles in regard to which so great a part of Christendom are agreed.

A large portion of the speech of my friend was occupied with matters in which we are all deeply interested, concerning which he has said much that is true; but certainly those things have no immediate connection with the subject now under discussion. I will, therefore, proceed immediately to the matter in hand.

Let the audience distinctly understand the proposition which Mr. C. affirms. He undertakes to prove, not that immersion is the best mode of administering baptism, nor that in the days of the apostles it was sometimes practiced, but that it is absolutely essential to the validity of the ordinance—that nothing short of the entire submersion of the body in water is apostolic or christian baptism; and consequently, that the whole christian world not thus immersed, are unbaptized, and are out of the church of Christ. It is an arduous undertaking; but my friend has bound himself to sustain this proposition. If this doctrine is true, it is certainly one of the most singular truths discovered in any age of the world. The Bible is, especially on all important points, *a plain book.* This Mr. C. acknowledges. Then how shall we account for the fact, that not more than one in a thousand, from the days of the apostles to the present time, has ascertained that immersion is essential to christian baptism? From a very early period it is certain that different modes were practiced. In the writings of the christian fathers we read of three immersions, and of partial immersions—ter caput mergitare—*to immerse the head thrice.* And it is fact, that as far back as history can take us, pouring and sprinkling were practiced; and baptism thus administered was universally considered valid. Now if those who practiced trine immersion, whose prejudices were all in favor of immersion, and whose vernacular tongue was the Greek, could not see that immersion only is christian baptism; I am obliged to doubt whether Mr. Campbell or any other man at this day will be able to prove it. I cannot believe that he can now make it clear, that the most learned, wise, and good men, who for long years studied the Bible on their knees, have lived and died in the firm belief that they had been baptized and were members of the church of the great Redeemer, when in truth they were unbaptized, and " aliens from the commonwealth of Israel !"

It strikes me, that if all those of whom I have spoken, failed to discover in the Bible this important doctrine, it must be taught, if taught at all, *most obscurely*. If Mr. C. had taken the ground, that it is really taught in the Scriptures, though with much obscurity; there might have been perhaps some plausibility in the declaration, at least a possibility, that he is in the right. But when he asserts, that it lies upon the very surface, that it is so clearly taught, that nothing but folly or perverseness can prevent the discovery of it; we are bound to believe, either that he is wholly mistaken, or that the multitudes of apparently wise and good men of whom I have spoken, were in truth most perversely rebellious or most profoundly stupid! When we read of such men as the celebrated Commentator, Dr. Thomas Scott, (and he is one among hundreds) who for long years carefully searched the Scriptures, that he might know the truth on this subject, coming finally to the clear conclusion that baptism is scripturally performed by pouring or sprinkling; shall we be told, that the Bible most plainly teaches, that nothing short of immersion is christian baptism? I repeat it—this discovery, if indeed it be true, is certainly the most singular of all the discoveries made since the commencement of the christian era!

Three things, and only three, have been commonly regarded as essential to the validity of baptism, viz: 1st. That it be performed in the name of the Father and of the Son and of the Holy Spirit; 2d. That it be administered by an ordained or properly authorized minister of the Gospel; and, 3d. That water be the fluid employed. The precise mode of applying the water has been regarded as essential by only a mere handfull, compared with even Protestant christians. I shall indeed be surprised if Mr. C. should now make it manifest, that they were all deceived in a matter so important as he regards this.

My worthy friend has proposed to take the common translation, (King James',) and rest the whole controversy upon it. But he was careful not to make this proposition, until he had appealed to the Greek lexicons, ancient and modern! But having first adduced these authorities, and having heretofore proclaimed from Dan to Beersheba, that the common version is not a translation, but a gross perversion of the original Greek; he gravely proposes to determine the whole controversy by the English translation! If he had ventured to make this proposition at first, I might with perfect safety have accepted it. But he has appealed to the Greeks, and to the Greeks we will go, though, I think, with less obscurity of criticism than has characterized his remarks.

The evidence in support of his views, he would have us believe, is so abundant, that he has a great deal to spare. I am inclined to think, that he will need it all. Perhaps it would be wise in him not to be too generous.

Much of his criticism I am obliged to consider wholly incorrect. If I can understand him, he maintains, that when a word has in it a leading syllable, as *bap*, in the word *bapto*, it never in any of its inflexions loses the original or radical import—that *bap* expresses *dip*, and consequently, wherever you find *bap*, you find the idea of dipping or immersing. Now it is certain, (and I can prove it by some of the most learned men on his own side of the question,) that there is no such general rule. Take, for example, the English word *prevent*. It is derived from the Latin words *pre* and *venio*, and signifies literally *to come before;* and then *to anticipate,* and in this sense it was first employed in the English language. But is this the sense in which it is now used by correct writers and speakers? The word retains the leading syllable *vent;* but, I ask, has it not entirely lost its original meaning? Is it not now universally employed in a secondary sense, *to hinder?* When Mr. C. was about to give a new translation of the New Testament, he asserted that this word had lost its original meaning, and, to prove it, quoted the passage—"Mine eyes *prevent* the dawning of the morning." And this was one of the evidences of the necessity of a new translation. I agree with him, that this word has lost its original meaning.

Again—what is the literal or radical meaning to the word *conversation?* It signifies *turning about from one thing to another.* Hence it was formerly used to signify *conduct;* and in this sense it is almost uniformly used in our translation of the Bible. But is this its present meaning? Has it not lost its original import and assumed a meaning quite different? It is now certainly used in the sense of *talking*—oral communication.

Mr. Carson, one of the most learned critics who has written in favor of immersion, fully sustains the principle for which I am contending. He asserts, that words very often lose entirely their original signification, and a secondary meaning comes to be the true and proper meaning. It is not true, therefore, that words of any class always retain their original philological import. On the contrary, their meaning is perpetually changing; and *usage only,* as the ablest critics declare, can determine it. But as I shall have occasion to revert to this point, and to read some of Mr. Carson's remarks upon it, I will for the present pass it.

I must not omit to notice a remark of my friend in regard to *new translations.* The Pedo-baptists, he says, and not the immersionists, call for new translations. I had not learned that they have either made or desired a new translation. I knew that Mr. Campbell had made *one,* and that in every case but one he had translated the word *baptizo, to immerse.* I was also aware, that our Baptist brethren had got a translation of their own, in which they rendered the word *to immerse* in all cases except *two.* But I did not know, that the Pedo-baptists desired any change. I had supposed, that they were well satisfied with the common version.

In the further discussion of this subject, allow me to turn your attention to the words *bapto* and *baptizo.* It is admitted on all hands, by immersionists, that the controversy turns mainly on the meaning of these words. The main battle, as they themselves admit, is to be fought on this ground. And let it be particularly remarked, that it is acknowledged by the advocates of immersion, that these two words, so far as *mode* is concerned, have precisely the same meaning, viz: to immerse. So says Mr. Carson.

My friend has appealed to the *lexicons,* as the highest authority, and has quoted a number of them in support of his views. I will appeal to the same lexicons. He attaches great importance to the fact, that some of them are *ancient* lexicons. And yet on another occasion he maintained, that in these latter days we enjoy superior advantages, and have consequently more light on these subjects—that we have all the light possessed by the older critics, with the addition of all the improvements of later times. And he offered this as one of the reasons in favor of a new translation. If this be true, I do not know why the modern critics should possess less authority with the gentleman, than those of more ancient date. But I will appeal to the *ancient*, as well as the modern lexicons. I will commence with

Hedericus, who defines the word *bapto*—Mergo, immergo, (2) Tingo, intingo, (3) Lavo, &c.,—to immerse, to plunge, to dye—*to wash*, &c.

Scapula defines it—Mergo, immergo—Item tingo—inficere, imbuere—Item *lavo*—to immerse, to plunge—also, to stain, dye, color—also, *to wash.*

Coulon—Mergo, tingo, *abluo*—to immerse, to dye, *to cleanse.*

Ursinus—To dip, to dye, *to wash, to sprinkle,* (abluo, aspergo.)

Schrivellius—Mergo, intingo, lavo, haurio, &c., to dip, to dye, *to wash,* to draw water.

Groves—To dip, plunge, immerse, *to wash, to wet, moisten, sprinkle,* to steep, imbue, to dye, &c.

Donnegan—To dip, to plunge into water, to submerge, *to wash,* to dye, to color,—*to wash,* &c.

The lexicons, you will observe, not only define the word *bapto,* to dip, plunge, dye, but also *lavo, to wash.* Now every one at all acquainted with Latin, knows that *lavo* signifies simply to wash, without regard to *mode*—that it never expresses mode. *Scapula* defines this word not only to dip, dye, &c., but *to wash,* (in any mode;) and he is one of the first authorities adduced by Mr. Campbell. Groves goes even further, and defines it to *wet, moisten, sprinkle,* &c. How ignorant he must have been, not to have learned Mr. Campbell's rule, that wherever you find *bap* you find also the idea of *dipping!* How strange that he should have been so unwise as not only to define it to *wash,* but also to *wet;* not only to *wet,* but to *moisten;* not only to *moisten,* but to *sprinkle!* But in due time I will prove that wiser men than Groves have done the same thing.

To wash, every one knows, does not express *mode,* neither do the words *dye, color.* Each of the lexicons just quoted gives several definitions of *bapto;* at least two of which, to wash and to color, exclude the idea of mode; whilst some of them define it to moisten, to sprinkle. I have not seen the tree of which my friend has spoken; but it is certain, unless the lexicographers are all in error, that *bapto* does not uniformly signify to immerse. Even Carson, the great Baptist critic, admits that it does not always express mode. I will read on pages 62, 63, 64:

"A word," says Mr. Carson, "may come to enlarge its meaning, so as to lose sight of its origin. This fact must be obvious to every smatterer in philology. Had it been attended to, Baptists would have found no necessity to prove that *bapto,* when it signifies to dye, always properly signifies to dye by *dipping;* and their opponents would have seen no advantage from proving that it signifies *dying in any manner.*" Again, "*Bapto* signifies, *to dye by sprinkling,* as properly as by *dipping;* though originally it was confined to the latter." Again, "Nor are such applications of the word to be accounted for by metaphor, as Dr. Gale asserts. They are as literal as the primary meaning. It is by extension of literal meaning, and not by figure of any kind, that words come to depart so far from their original signification."

Observe, Carson says, *bapto* originally signified to *dip,* then to dye *by dipping,* and then to dye *in any manner,* even by *sprinkling.* Now if it signifies *to dye* by sprinkling, why can it not signify *to wet* by sprinkling? Is there any rule or principle of interpretation, which teaches that a word may denote the sprinkling of a *colored* fluid, and be incapable of expressing the sprinkling of a *colorless* fluid? If there is, let it be produced. If there is not, *bapto* will express the sprinkling of *water*, as well as of any other fluid. Mr. Carson, moreover, declares that such applications of the word are not to be accounted for by *metaphor* or *figure*, as Dr. Gale, another learned immersionist, maintained, but that they are *as literal as the primary meaning*—that it is by the extension of the *literal meaning*, and not by *figure* of any kind, that words depart so far from their original signification. The word *bapto*, therefore, not only expresses the application of a fluid by *sprinkling*, but this is a *literal* signification. Now Carson, who was a zealous immersionist, did not intend to concede any thing more than candor and truth demanded. We have, therefore, evidence conclusive that *bapto* signifies not only to dip, plunge, &c., but *to wash* and *to sprinkle*.

We will now examine the testimony of the lexicons concerning the word *baptizo*, the word uniformly used in the New Testament to express christian baptism.

Scapula, one of the *old* lexicographers to whom Mr. C. appealed, thus defines the word *baptizo*: "Mergo, seu immergo—Item tingo: ut quæ tingendi aut abluendi gratia aqua immergimus—Item mergo, submergo, obruo aqua—Item abluo, lavo, (Mark 7, Luke 11,) to dip or immerse—also, to dye: as we immerse things for the purpose of coloring or washing them; also, to plunge, submerge, to cover with water; also, *to cleanse, to wash.* (Mark 7, Luke 11.) *Baptismos*, he thus defines: "Mersio, lotio, ablutio, ipse immergendi, item lavandi seu abluendi actus," (Mark 7, &c.) Immersion, *washing, cleansing,* the act itself of immersing; also of *washing,* or *cleansing,*" (Mark 7, &c.)

Hedericus thus defines *baptizo:* "Mergo, immergo, aqua abruo,—(2) Abluo, lavo; (3) Baptizo, significatu sacro"—To dip, immerse, to cover with water; (2) to *cleanse;* to *wash;* (3) to baptize in a sacred sense.

Stephanus defines it thus: " Mergo, seu immergo, ut quæ tingendi aut abluendi gratia aqua immergimus—Mergo, submergo, obruo aqua; *abluo, lavo*"—To dip, immerse, as we immerse things for the purpose of coloring or washing; to merge, submerge, to cover with water—*to cleanse, to wash.*

Schleusner defines *baptizo*, not only to plunge, immerse, but *to cleanse, wash, to purify with water;* (abluo, lavo, aqua purgo.)

Parkhurst defines it: "To immerse in or *wash with water* in token of purification."

Robinson defines it: " To immerse, to sink; for example, spoken of ships, galleys, &c. In the New Testament, *to wash, to cleanse by washing*—*to wash one's self, to bathe, perform ablution,*" &c.

Schrivellius defines it: " Baptizo, mergo, *abluo, lavo*—to baptize, to immerse, *to cleanse, to wash.*"

Groves—" To dip, immerse, immerge, plunge; *to wash, cleanse, purify—Baptizomai*, to wash one's self, bathe," &c.

Bretschneider,—"Propriæ sepius intingo, sepius lavo; deinde (1) lavo, abluo simpliciter—medium, &c.; lavo me, abluo me:" properly often to dip, often to wash; then (1) simply to wash, to cleanse; in the middle voice, " I wash or cleanse myself."

Suidas defines *baptizo*, not only to sink, plunge, immerse, but *to wet, wash, cleanse, purify,* &c., (madefacio, lavo, abluo, purgo, mundo.)

Wahl defines it, first—*to wash, perform ablution, cleanse;* secondly, to immerse, &c.

Greenfield defines it: to immerse, immerge, submerge, sink; and in the New Testament, *to wash, perform ablution, cleanse;* to immerse.

I have now adduced the principal lexicons, ancient and modern ; and it is a fact, that with remarkable unanimity, they testify that the word *baptizo* signifies not only to sink, dip, plunge, &c., but *to wash, to cleanse, to purify.* *Scapula*, the learned lexicographer, to whom Mr. C. appealed with so much confidence, defines it not only to dip, plunge, &c., but *to wash, to cleanse;* and, mark the fact, he refers to the New Testament as the place in which we find the word used in the sense of washing, cleansing.   Now every one at all acquainted with Latin, knows that the words *lavo* and *abluo,—to wash, to cleanse,—*do not express *mode.*   They signify washing and cleansing *in any mode.*

Let me here distinctly remark, that I am not contending that the word *baptizo definitely expresses* pouring or sprinkling.   I maintain that, as used in the Scriptures, it expresses *the thing done*—the application of water to a subject—but not *the mode* of doing it ; that the mode in which baptism was administered cannot be determined by the word, but must be learned from the connection and circumstances, or from other sources.

Hedericus defines the word—first, to immerse or plunge, and secondly, *to wash, cleanse,* without reference to mode.   Schleusner, besides the definition *to plunge*, &c., gives three others, which express the thing done, but not the mode of doing it : viz. abluo, lavo, aqua purgo—to cleanse, to wash, to purify with water.   Parkhurst makes it mean either to immerse in, or wash with water.   Robinson, one of the first lexicographers, first gives the definition to immerse, to sink, &c., but *in the New Testament* the first meaning he finds is *to wash, to cleanse by washing, to perform ablution.*   Bretschneider gives as the general meaning of *baptizo,* " Proprie sepius intingo, sepius lavo"—*properly often to dip, often to wash*—thus putting these two definitions upon a perfect equality with each other.   This is all for which I contend.   But as his is a lexicon of the New Testament ; the *first* meaning he there finds, is " lavo, abluo sempliciter ;" *simply to wash, to cleanse.*   Here, certainly, is no immersing.   I deem the authority of Bretschneider more important, not only because he is one of the most learned lexicographers, but because he was evidently partial to immersion.   Yet, as a scholar, he was constrained to give *lavo, abluo,* to wash, to cleanse, as a *literal* meaning of *baptizo.*   Suidas, one of the oldest lexicographers, as we have seen, defines it not only to plunge, sink, &c., but *to wet, wash, cleanse,* &c. and every one knows that a thing may be *wetted, washed,* or *cleansed,* without being immersed.   Greenfield defines it, as you see, to sink, *to wash,* &c.

Now let it be remarked, that each of these lexicographers, ancient and modern, establishes all for which I contend.   With entire unanimity they declare that the word *baptizo* does *not* signify simply and only to immerse, but that it means also *to wash, cleanse,* &c.   It certainly has these different meanings.   Now if my friend, Mr. C., can prove that the Savior and the inspired writers employed it in the sense of *immersing,* he will have gained his point.   But if he cannot prove that it was used by them in the specific sense of immersing, and not in the general sense of washing, cleansing, he is defeated.   For if it should be true, that they used it in the general sense of washing, &c., how can Mr. C. prove, by the force of the word, the doctrine for which he is contending ?   I maintain that they did use it in the general, and not in the specific sense ; and I expect to prove it by the Scriptures.

My friend says, the ordinance of circumcision required to be expressed

by a specific term.   Now I would like to see any man attempt to determine by the Greek or the Hebrew word employed, what was the precise *modus operandi* of circumcision.   He could not do it.   I should
like to see any one attempt to give those words, as applied to denote
circumcision, a *literal translation.*   Such a translation, I presume, would
appear rather ludicrous.

But mark this fact: a number of washings are commanded in the Old
Testament, the *mode* of performing which is not specified.   The word
employed both in the Hebrew and the Greek Septuagint is a generic
term, signifying simply *to wash.*   The washing, therefore, might be
performed, (and the command obeyed,) in different modes ; because no
particular mode was prescribed.   In these instances the thing to be done
was important, but the mode of doing it was not.

My friend, Mr. C., maintains that the mode of baptism is *essential* to
the ordinance, and that the command to baptize must have been denoted
by a *specific term.*   Let him first prove that it cannot be validly administered but in one particular mode ; for until he has established this position he cannot prove, *a priori,* that the Savior must have used a specific
term.   He might as easily prove, that in appointing the washings of the
Levitical law, just mentioned, Moses must have used a specific term ;
which is contrary to fact.

I do not, however, maintain that the mode in which baptism is to be
administered is *unimportant,* though I do contend that it is not *essential.*
But though the word *baptizo* does not definitely express the mode, it
may be learned from the design of the ordinance, and from the circumstances attending the administration of it; and these evidences are decidedly in favor of pouring or sprinkling.

Let the facts now established be remembered, viz : that the words
bapto and *baptizo* have several meanings—that they are used sometimes
in the sense of dipping, plunging, sinking ; sometimes in the sense of
washing, cleansing, purifying ; sometimes in the sense of pouring,
sprinkling.   In the classics I can prove, that four times in five *baptizo*
expresses *sinking to the bottom.*   Let it be remembered, too, that the
lexicons refer to the Bible for the use of *baptizo* in the general sense of
washing, cleansing.

Perhaps I ought not to anticipate my friend in his argument.   He has
appealed to the lexicons ; and I have now proved that they do not sustain
his doctrine.   I might admit, that the primary or original meaning of
baptizo was to immerse, though it cannot be proved.   I can admit this,
and still prove, that there is not the slightest evidence that such was its
meaning among the Jews, as used to denote their religious washings.

I am willing, at any time, to go with my friend to classic usage, and to
prove that it will not sustain him.   I am also prepared, and it is my purpose, to go to the usage of the word in *the Bible;* and this, according to
the decision of the best critics, must, after all, determine the meaning of
the word.   Thus I expect to make it manifest, that baptism is validly
and scripturally performed by pouring or sprinkling.

I am gratified to learn the estimation in which Mr. C. holds professor
Stuart, whom he styles *his American apostle.*   He tells us, Stuart admits
that all critics and commentators of any note agree in defining *baptizo* to
dip, to plunge.   This is true, but is not the whole truth.   Let us have
the whole testimony of this apostle.   Stuart also says, *baptizo* means to
overwhelm, which certainly is not identical with *dip, plunge.*   He goes

further, and tells us that it signifies *to wash, to cleanse;* and maintains, that there is no satisfactory evidence that, as used among the Jews, it signified to immerse; and he gives several examples in which it evidently has not that meaning, but signifies to wash by applying water to the subject. I am willing to take the testimony of *our American apostle.* He does, indeed, say, that *baptizo* signifies to *dip,* to *plunge;* but he does not admit that such is its ordinary meaning in the Scriptures. Nay, he positively denies that there is in the New Testament a single command to immerse any one, and calls upon those who say there is, to produce it. I will, if it should be necessary, turn to the pages and read the declarations to which I refer.

I am willing, if Mr. C. wishes it, to appeal to critics and learned men; and I will find as many to sustain me, as he can produce against me. Or I am willing to appeal directly to the Bible. But for the present I close my remarks.—[*Time expired.*

Wednesday, Nov. 15—12½ o'clock, P. M.
[MR. CAMPBELL'S SECOND ADDRESS.]

I think it is usual, Mr. President, and a rule in all scholastic discussions, that the respondent shall confine himself to the arguments of the affirmant, on whom the *onus probandi* rests. Till the affirmant has offered all his proofs, it is not usual for the respondent to anticipate him. His duty it is to respond to such arguments as he relies on, rather than to those which he has not brought forward. However, as these introductory speeches are usually more general than special in character, I am willing to overlook the aberrations observable in the desultory remarks of my worthy friend.

It may occasionally become necessary for me to advert to the *comments* of the gentleman upon the arguments which I shall offer as we proceed. He begins by declaring himself, if not relevantly, at least, clearly and forcibly, on the premises. He observes, that large majorities of learned men are against me. I will however show, at the proper time, that every reformer is agreed with us as to the antiquity and propriety of immersion, as well as in the etymology of the terms in debate—his own Calvin, and all the rest. As to the great superiority of numbers on the side of the Pedo-baptists, it is a great mistake. I have been often surprised to find that this groundless opinion should have obtained so generally in this country. Talk about the immense numbers of Pedo-baptists, as contrasted with those who practice immersion! The gentleman must certainly have forgotten his ecclesiastical readings. He ought to know very well, that the great mass of Christendom have always immersed. He speaks in his hyperbolical way, of a thousand to one against the immersionists. I will not be so particular as to state the fractional ratios of all ages, but in the bold style of my friend, I will say that the whole christian world for the first thirteen centuries, and for the last five, at least one half have immersed. I repeat, sir, almost the whole church immersed for the first thirteen hundred years, and at least one half of it for the last five hundred years. So that the gentleman is entirely mistaken in representing us as in a fearful minority. So far as numbers are concerned, we have in all time, a decided and overwhelming majority. But, at present, I lay no stress upon numbers. I have said thus much with reference to the emphasis my friend appeared to place upon the antiquity and universality of his views. His views and practice are neither so ancient nor so universal as ours. I now pledge myself to sustain this assertion at the proper time.

With regard to the origin or occasion of this discussion, it is alledged that my friends had something to do with it, of which I know nothing, and for which, were it so, I am not answerable. I was asked by a friend, while in Richmond, August, 1842, whether I was willing to have an interview with Mr. Brown, should he call upon me touching my sermon delivered in that place? To which I promptly assented.

After an introduction to Mr. Brown, he observed that he desired to know whether I would be willing to go into a discussion of the points of difference between Presbyterians and us. To which I assented on certain conditions. One of the most prominent of which was, that it should have the authority of both parties, and come out under their denominational sanctions. To which he consented.

Mr. Rice has represented this as a mere personal affair. I do not so understand it. I know that in my interview with Mr. Brown, it was proposed that the Presbyterian synod of Kentucky should make the selection of a debatant to meet me in the discussion of these questions. I did not think, at the time, and I presume he did not, that the synod had no authority to select any person to represent the Presbyterian church on such an occasion; that when assembled together in synod, they could not ecclesiastically make such a nomination. I am, however, officially informed, that a *conference* relative to this discussion, was actually held while the synod was in session; that five persons were selected for this occasion, one of which was to be the debatant. I will, however, read the result of this conference in letters received from Mr. Brown.

Under date of January 3d, 1843, Mr. Brown writes as follows:—

"I also stated that the persons selected were chosen, not by the synod, but *in conference*, and that *some* of them were known and acknowledged to be the most prominent men in our church."

Again, under date of the 8th of March, the Rev. Mr. Brown says:— "Your perfect willingness to meet those individuals, is in *full view* of the fact, distinctly stated in my former communication that they were not appointed *by* the synod, but only agreed upon *at* the synod."

With regard to filling vacancies, it was also agreed that any vacancy occurring "should be filled by the *five* originally appointed."

This is again reiterated under date of the 15th of May:—"We offer you a Presbyterian minister as your opponent, who shall be selected by us, precisely in accordance with the arrangements made *at synod*, viz:—that we should select one of our number to meet you in debate. Now you have your choice to retreat or to accept."

Once more, under date of June 16th, 1843: "But, sir, we are *five* in number, and the gentleman who is ready to debate with you has been selected by four of us, of whom Mr. Young is one: so, you have quite as many witnesses as you desire. We have selected the man into whose hands we think proper to commit the defence of our cause. His standing is well known both in Kentucky and out of it. We will not select another; you can either debate with him or retreat from the discussion."

Mr. Rice is then the elect Presbyterian clergyman—elected, not *by*, but *at* synod, in *conference* of the ministry, and that is enough for me. I care not how the ministry elected him; the fact of his election is incontrovertible. It is not therefore a *personal* affair between Mr. Rice and myself.

G

With regard to the lexicographic authorities we have quoted, I am glad to find that the gentleman, [Mr. Rice] has not excepted to one of them. I have proposed a very respectable class of witnesses, but I have not yet begun to descant upon their testimony. I had intended also to have quoted some thirteen other authorities, of the same class, and corroborative of the same position.

[He gives the dates of the imprints of several lexicons, some thirteen, which he might have adduced, and says:]

These all concur with those already quoted: and sustain my criticism on the words *bapto* and *baptizo*. I have examined, in all, some thirty-five authorities of this class, ancient and modern, and, in regard to the whole family of words, they exhibit a concurrence of testimony uniform and perfect as can be found on any other word in the language.

My friend did not seem to understand my criticism on the syllable *bap*. I did not, nor do I argue, that words never change their meaning—never depart from their etymological import. Nay, I have often asserted that an almost infinite variety of changes has occurred, and will occur, in the words of all living tongues. These were substantially my own words, quoted by my friend to show that the meanings of words are constantly undergoing change in the current usage of a living language.

I presume that the gentleman did not intend to misrepresent me in this. I affirmed that the meaning of the radical syllable of a *specific* word remains the same in its various flexions; and also that all words originally specific, never so change their meaning as to lose their original import—that terms expressing specification never change. And I now call upon the gentleman to produce an exception to this rule. That, however, is what I am persuaded he cannot do.

With me, Mr. President, all active verbs indicate either generic or specific action. Generic words are frequently changing their import;—they are such words as informally express active passion or emotion. For all words of *mode*, as Mr. Carson would call them, (thereby improperly admitting, in this case, that there may be a mode of baptism,) have but one meaning. His words of mode are all included in my specific terms; words indicating specific forms of action. It is essential that it be singular, in order to its being specific. If, therefore, I establish the fact, that *baptizo* is a specific word, indicating specific action, then all its other meanings are figurative; and so I shall prove with reference to this word.

Every person who pays attention to the etymology and philology of language, knows that all words are used figuratively. Not even the name of the Deity is exempt from this law of language. The word *God* is transferred to any thing that can be deified—to men's appetites and passions. There is no word so sacred as to be exempted from the possibility of being accommodated in this way. But no specific word, (though it may be used *figuratively*) can be made to have a signification specifically different from the proper idea or action for which it originally stood; for the moment you change it, *it forever loses its first meaning*. For example—if you prove that *baptizo* originally signifies to dip, you cannot by any possibility make it signify to sprinkle or to pour. For were we to make immersion an indictable offence, as it has been, and suppose that A was indicted for having immersed B, but during the trial it appeared in evidence that he only poured a little water upon him, either pouring or immersion must cease to be specific actions, and mean the same thing, or A would be discharged, and the complainant would pay the costs. For that would destroy its specific character—its first meaning; and besides, such a liberty would destroy the precision and utility of speech.

Before entering further into these matters, or bringing it to a close, there are some things of secondary importance bearing upon it, adverted to in the speech which you have just heard, to which I will briefly allude.

The reason I prefer the older lexicons is this: they were made before this controversy had become rife. For example: Mr. Groves, a late lexicographer, or some other person, has foisted the word sprinkle into his Greek and English dictionary, as one of the meanings of *baptizo*, a most daring innovation! Whether Groves or some other person has interpolated it we know not; the person to whom it is attributable is unknown to us. And yet, I dare say, the editor, whoever he was, 'did it conscientiously. I even presume that my friend, [Mr. Rice] were he to make a dictionary of the Greek language, would also insert the word sprinkle as one of its meanings. Such is the force of prejudice and usage on the minds of men, that many good Pedo-baptists, in their preachings, always give the words *pour* and *sprinkle* as meanings of baptizo. I have been astonished at the liberty taken with the older lexicons by some of our modern editors. For example: The lexicon of Schrevellius has passed through seventeen editions; it gave but two meanings to *baptizo*, to wit—*mergo, lavo;* but now, in four recent editions, somebody has presumed to increase the meanings of this word to four. It is on this account that I prefer the earlier lexicons. These give the definition of words as they were used before this controversy began.

With regard to the meaning of the word *baptizo*, I request the particular attention of the audience; for it is on this point, as the gentleman has correctly observed, the controversy must be decided. It shall be my purpose and object then, to establish the fact, that *baptizo* is a specific word, and as such, can have but one proper, original, and literal meaning.

Asserting that the action of baptism is not implied in the word, my friend has said, that no man could learn the action of *circumcision* from the word. Strange indeed! Is not *"cutting round"* its meaning, its specific meaning? Certainly that is as expressive of the action as any word can be. True, the history and precept of the ordinance shows us *on what part* of the body the action was performed. A positive ordinance, binding on the nation of Israel, under the penalty of death, it was expedient and necessary to indicate by a specific term, so plain and so definite that it would be impossible to misunderstand it; and because circumcision is exactly such a term, this is the best and the only reason that can be given for its selection.

Hence, it is reasonable to suppose, that when the Great Lawgiver of the christian religion came to the conclusion that he would institute the ordinance of baptism, he had some specific idea in his mind. Indeed, it is impossible to suppose that he had not. He must have intended some particular thing to be done. He must have had some specific design in his mind; and he could not have been consistent with himself, had he not selected a word expressive of that specific design. How, then, could the author of this institution do otherwise than select a specific word— the best word in human speech to express his design? Having it wholly in his power to select his own term, would it have been consistent, reasoning *a priori*, for him to select the word pouring, when he intended immersion? or the word immersion, when he intended sprinkling? No, reasoning from analogy, evident it is, that the Author of our religion would give a term essentially specific.

But now there are three words submitted to us by our Pedo-baptist brethren, which are alledged to express this design: they are *sprinkle, pour, dip.* These are all specific words. Sprinkling is well defined and understood amongst all men; so is pouring; so is dipping. Is it not impossible to conceive that each of these terms has been chosen to express the same specific idea and design? Could the Messiah, to express and define one action, have selected a word signifying *three* distinct actions? I cannot admit it. No three actions can be more different than sprinkling, dipping, pouring. When we sprinkle an individual, we put something *upon* his person; and when we immerse an individual, we put the person *into* something. In the former case, we change the position of the matter with regard to the person; and in the latter case, we change the position of the person with regard to the matter.

In baptism, we have an inward spiritual intention and transition, or a passing from one state to another; and if the outward action is to exhibit the intention and transition, how, I ask, are we to regard these three terms, sprinkling, pouring and dipping, as expressive of the same intention? They are each specifically different from the others. No one term could express the meaning of these three. Every one of them has its representative in the original.

There is no opposing these lexicons. They universally agree with us in determining the primitive meaning of the word *baptizo.* That the original meaning of the term is to dip, to immerse, is, indeed, a matter hardly to be debated at this day; and I was glad to hear my friend admit, what is universally admitted and agreed to, that this word had but one meaning. Now this being conceded, how comes it to pass, that, in process of time, the word has come to signify a plurality of actions! But I can demonstrate that the term has uniformly meant the same thing, from the earliest ages of the world, in its religious as well as in its classical usage.

In the law of Moses we have an ordinance for cleansing a leper; and I presume that my friend will admit that the cleansing of a leper from his disease, was indicative of the cleansing of a sinner from his sins. Well: this ceremony is solemnly put to record in Lev. xiv.; and it is remarkable, that, in a single sentence of this chapter, the three words which are sometimes called baptism, are brought together in solemn contrast. They are all found in the law for purifying the unclean, and cleansing the leper. Blood was to be sprinkled, oil was to be poured, hysop was to be dipped, and then, after these ceremonies, the unclean was to bathe. In giving a detailed account of these ceremonies, the inspired writer has presented these words in contrast thus: "And the priest shall take some of the log of oil, and pour it into the palm of his own left hand, and shall dip his right finger in the oil that is in his left hand, and shall sprinkle of the oil with his finger seven times before the Lord." In cleansing from the leprosy, the way is prepared by first sprinkling with blood seven times, then the priest was to dip his finger in the olive oil, and sprinkle the olive oil seven times before the Lord. First, blood was sprinkled upon the unclean, then oil was poured upon his head, and afterwards he was commanded to wash his clothes, shave his hair, and *bathe himself* in water, that he might be clean.

This is from the oldest record in the world. We have no writings more ancient than the five books of Moses. These have fixed an ever-lasting contrast between the words *sprinkle, pour*, and *dip*,—so that each must forever indicate a distinct action, fixed among the legal ceremonies of a typical people. Since the time when the leper was cleansed by having blood sprinkled upon him, oil poured upon him, and his flesh bathed in water—from that time till now, these words have been used as distinct in meaning, and as immutable as the law of Moses.

In the case of cleansing an unclean person, made so by the touch of a dead animal, a positive ordinance was got up. It is recorded in the xix. of Numbers.

The manner of preparing the water of separation to be used for such purification is very minutely set forth. The ashes of a red heifer, without spot, and upon which never came yoke, were to be kept for the congregation of the children of Israel for a water of separation; and the text says: "It is a purification for sin." "And for an unclean person they shall take of the ashes of the burnt heifer of purification for sin, and running water shall be put thereto in a vessel; and a clean person shall take hysop and dip it in the water; and the clean person shall sprinkle upon the unclean on the third day and on the seventh day: and on the seventh day he shall purify himself, and wash his clothes, and bathe himself in water, and shall be clean at even." I can conceive of no authority more sacred than this.

Here the individual is commanded to observe three things; and they are to be done in reference to the cleansing of his person from legal impurity, or from a disease that indicates sins. Can any one say that these are not separate and specific actions?

With regard to the translation of the word *baptizo* by the term *sink*, my friend remarked that he could bring many respectable authorities to prove that this was a legitimate and proper meaning of the term: that it means going to the bottom; and hence the person baptized must be sunk to the bottom. It is not true that immersion is such a very general term; and I would remind my fellow-citizens that the question in debate is not whether we shall dip to the bottom, nor whether we shall perform only a partial dipping; it is not whether we ought to dip so far, or so deep, but whether immersion simply, to the bottom or not, is the action commanded.

We have, however, an exemplification at hand, which ought forever to settle this matter. It is a case in which the word baptize is used in a contrast that forbids sinking to the bottom. It is a remarkable passage found in one of the sybilline oracles, a poetic prediction concerning the fortunes of the ancient city of Athens. The poet says: *Askos baptizee dunai de toi ou themis esti*—"Thou mayest be *dipped*, O bladder! but thou art not fated to *sink:*" showing that in ancient times, it was a part of the signification of *baptizo* to emerge again, as well as to immerge, making it equivalent to *katadusis* and *anadusis* combined. Certainly and clearly it is that the word *baptizo* never meant to sink to the bottom, except by chance. *Bapto* may leave the substance some considerable time under water or any liquid: indicating that a change might come upon the substance, and that it might acquire some new matter which it had not before, being put into the liquid. But *baptizo* permits the subject to stay under the water but a very little time, and then emerge again. In the etymology and philology of the Greek language, the word *baptizo* never can be shown to mean going to the bottom and staying there. *Duoo dunai,* and their compounds indicate that.

It would be entirely impertinent, before such an audience as this, to enter into any discussion and criticism upon the meaning of the termination *zo;* a question upon which philologists and critics have written much.

Grammarians and critics have speculated on the termination *zoo* with great freedom. Some make it the symbol of frequent action, and call those verbs so ending, frequentatives: others, of diminished action, and call them, diminutives. They make a few specifications. But they seem not to remember that a change on the end of a word, when agreeable to the ear, soon loses its meaning by being extended to many words, for the sake of euphony. So of the termination *zoo.* I can give as many specifications of rapid action, if required, as can be given of frequent action in words of this ending.

I have a new theory of my own upon this subject, or rather it is a theory adopted from an old one, as it ought to be called. It goes to explain a material fact in the history of *bapto.*

My idea is that the word originally meant, not that the dipping should be performed frequently, but that it indicated the rapidity with which the action was to be performed; that the thing should be done quickly; and for this reason the termination *zo* is never used when the word is employed in connection with the business of dyers and tanners. But the word *baptizo* is always used to express the ordinance of baptism. This is the best reason I can give for the change of the termination into *zoo.*

With regard to the frequent occurrence of this word in the New Testament usage, I said that there might be some good reason given. And that reason is found in the fact that *bapto* means to dip, without regard to continuance long or short, but *baptizo* intimates that the subject of the action is not necessarily long kept under that into which it is immersed. —[*Time expired.*]

Wednesday, Nov. 15—12½ *o'clock, P. M.*
[MR. RICE'S SECOND REPLY.]

MR. PRESIDENT:—I have no objection to the rule suggested by my friend, Mr. C., requiring the respondent to follow the affirmant, provided there be also a rule obliging the latter to *proceed in the argument.* But I must protest against being required to say but little on the subject in hand, because the affirmant has done so.

With regard to the *ecclesiastical character* of this discussion I remark, that there are but two ways in which things of this kind can be done, viz: either by the church as a body, or by individuals. The synod of Kentucky had no authority to select persons for such a purpose. My appointment to conduct this debate, therefore, could not have been made by that body. And if all the elders and ministers of the synod had, as individuals, agreed to select me, it would have been only the act of so many *individuals,* for which the Presbyterian church in Kentucky would have been no more responsible than if it had been done in England. The debate is, therefore, an *individual* affair. It has never been stated by us how many persons were consulted about it, or what number agreed to my appointment to conduct it. Nor does it appear by how many my friend was appointed, or whether he was appointed at all. There is no ecclesiastical body connected with his church, sustaining the same relation to it, which is sustained by the synod of Kentucky to our church.

His appointment, therefore, must have been simply by *individuals*. How many have been concerned in it, or what importance his church may attach to it, I know not. But I am not willing to involve ecclesiastical bodies in matters with which they have nothing to do.

My worthy friend made a statement concerning the early reformers which is calculated to make an impression favorable to his cause. He says that all the early reformers were immersionists, and that the great majority of christians have always practiced immersion; that I must have forgotten my reading. I presume I was understood by the audience. I said, not that nine hundred and ninety-nine in every thousand were *opposed* to immersion, but that they did not believe immersion *essential to the validity* of the ordinance—that they never did make the discovery which my friend has made, that nothing short of immersion is baptism. And if he can name one of the reformers who made the discovery for which he is now contending, that immersion only is christian baptism, I hope he will not fail to do it. In the third and immediately following centuries *trine immersion* was practiced, the subjects being divested of their garments. Yet those who adopted this practice never learned that *baptizo* means *only to immerse*. Gradually again pouring and sprinkling became most common. Yet immersion continued to be very frequently practiced even to the times of Luther; but all conceded the validity of pouring and sprinkling. None disputed what had been so long admitted.

But my friend Mr. C. has said, that as biblical criticism progressed, we have gained more light on such subjects. So it appears, that as more light has been obtained, the great majority of christians have abandoned the defence and the practice of immersion. He cannot, however, point to one reformer, of any considerable standing, who maintained the doctrine for which he is contending. However favorable some of them may have been to the practice of immersion, not one of them ever admitted that our Savior commanded immersion only. They with one consent admitted sprinkling and pouring to be valid baptism; and they regarded themselves as obeying the command of Christ—"Go teach all nations, baptizing them"—when they administered the ordinance by sprinkling or pouring. Having been baptized by sprinkling, they lived and died in the belief that their baptism was valid.

Both modes were anciently practiced. And if our immersionist friends had continued on the ground of the old immersionists—if they had simply maintained that immersion is the *preferable mode*, they might have enjoyed their opinion without controversy. But when they contend that all who have received the ordinance by pouring or sprinkling are unbaptized, and that sprinkling is a human invention, they assume a position occupied by very few; and we are constrained to demur.

Let me revert to the principle advanced by Mr. C., that specific words having a leading syllable, in all their inflections retain their original import. Language, he admits, is always changing; and usage only determines the meaning of words. But the principle he now inculcates is, that specific words retain their original meaning. If, for example, the original idea was *dip*, the word retaining the leading syllable, will retain also this idea, in all its combinations. Now I stand in opposition to this principle. There is no such principle recognized. There are facts (and I will produce them) in the very face of it. For example, the word *bapto*, as Mr.

C. and immersionists generally contend, contained originally the idea only of *immersing*. I now understand him to abandon this ground. He now says, that *literally* it signifies to *dip*, and *figuratively*, to *dye*. For this I should like to see some authority, because Mr. Carson says it signifies to dye as literally as to dip; and he asserts, that the history of a thousand words proves the principle. He gives an example, which I will read. He says, (p. 60,) that " Hyppocrates uses *bapto* to denote dyeing by dropping the dyeing liquid on the thing dyed: ' When it drops upon the garments, (*baptetai*,) they are dyed.' This," says he, " surely is not dyeing by dipping." What is there *figurative* here? There is a *literal* fluid, dropped upon a *literal* garment; and when a thing is dyed by dropping or sprinkling, it is dyed as literally as if done by dipping. I will, if necessary, furnish other examples. On the 61st page Carson gives another—" Nearchus relates, that the Indians (*baptontai*) dye their beards." There are many similar examples. Dr. Gale maintained, that when *bapto* signified *to dye*, it retained the idea of *dipping;* but Mr. Carson differs from him, and says, the history of a thousand words proves that it signifies *to dye by sprinkling* as literally as by *dipping*. Till my worthy friend produces some authority in support of the principle he has advanced, I must beg leave to dissent from it.

Mr. C. says, if he can prove that *baptizo* expresses a *specific action*, he proves that it has but one meaning—and, therefore, that it can never express the act of pouring or sprinkling. Carson maintains, that *bapto* expresses a specific action; and yet he proves, that it has another meaning which is *literal*, viz: to dye by dipping or by sprinkling. And if it expresses the coloring of a thing by dropping or sprinkling, it has certainly not the original idea of dipping.

Let it be remembered, we are not contending that *baptizo* expresses *definitely* the act of pouring or sprinkling. The circumstances and the connection sometimes prove, that *sinking* or *plunging* is the thing done; sometimes that *pouring* or *sprinkling* is the thing done; sometimes that *partial dipping* or *wetting* is meant. It is a universal rule of language, that when a word has several meanings, the connection in which it occurs, must determine, in any given case, which is the true meaning. For example, the word *faith* has in the Scriptures three distinct meanings. It denotes the act of believing, or the exercise of the mind in believing, as in the passage— " By grace are ye saved through faith." It denotes the truth or doctrines believed, as when persons are said to "make shipwreck of the faith." And it signifies fidelity or faithfulness, as when it is said, " What if some did not believe? Shall their unbelief make the faith of God of non-effect?" Now how are we to determine, in any particular case, which of these meanings is the true one? Evidently by the connection. Dr. Geo. Campbell says the word *flesh* has in the Scriptures *six* meanings, not more than one of which is found in any classic writer. How shall we determine, in any particular case, which is the true meaning, but by the connection?

We are not contending that *baptizo never* signifies to immerse, but that it does not *definitely express mode*. It expresses *the thing done;* the circumstances and the context may determine the mode of doing it, though the word itself does not.

It is true, as my friend says, that if a man were indicted for *dipping* a person, and it were proved that he had only *sprinkled* him, the action could not be maintained against him. This, however, only proves what no one denies—that dipping is not sprinkling. But let him prove that *baptizo* signifies *only to immerse*, and I will yield the point. That it is sometimes used in the sense of dipping I admit, and that it is sometimes used in the sense of pouring, or sprinkling, I can prove. That it sometimes signifies simply *to wash*, I can demonstrate by the very highest authority. Each of these statements I will establish in due time.

But I fear my friend, Mr. C., will consider me as anticipating his argument. If he will not again prefer this charge against me, I will state, as I am prepared to prove, that three of the oldest and best versions have rendered the word *bapto* to *sprinkle;* and one of the most learned of the Greek fathers gave it the same signification.

Schrivellius, Mr. C. says, originally gave to the word *baptizo* but two meanings—*mergo* and *lavo*—to *immerse* and to *wash*. Well, this is all I contend for. For if it sometimes signifies to *dip*, and sometimes to *wash*, how shall we determine in any case which is the true meaning? *Mergo* and *lavo* are the Latin words by which it is defined, and we know that *lavo* signifies *to wash in general*, without reference to mode. The most ancient lexicographers, moreover, define *baptizo* to *cleanse*, no matter in what mode it is done. If, then, this word has sometimes one meaning, and sometimes another, how can it be a specific term expressing a definite action? If Mr. C. cannot prove that it is always· used in the definite sense of immersing, he must give up the argument.

It is true, as he says, that the word *circumcision* signifies *cutting round;* but who, I ask, could have understood by this word alone, how the ordinance was to be administered? By the accompanying directions it might be known, but I affirm that no man could determine by the word alone, what precisely was the action to be performed.

Again—take the word *deipnon*, sometimes used to denote the Lord's supper. From this word we could not determine what element should be used, in what quantity it should be received, or in what manner the ordinance should be observed. Yet my friend, Mr. C., labors to prove, that when our Savior employed a particular word to denote an ordinance, it must necessarily express *the mode* in which it is always to be administered and received !

He says, he is glad to hear me express my conviction, that the original meaning of *baptizo* was to *immerse*. I did not say so. I said, I *could* safely admit it, though he could not prove it. Critics are not agreed, whether *to dip* or *to dye* was the original meaning. Professor Stuart expresses the opinion, as far as he can judge, that *to dip* was the original sense, and *to dye* a secondary meaning. Others, however, contend that *to dye* was the primary or original meaning. The word *bapto*, as far back as we can trace it, was used in both senses. It may be true, therefore, that *to dye* or *color* was the original meaning; and *to dip* a secondary meaning. Critics have not determined this question; nor can they prove, that *to immerse* was the original meaning of the word. But, as I before remarked, I *can* concede this point, and yet fully sustain my position. Still Mr. C. cannot prove it, and therefore I shall not admit it.

Mr. C. asks, how could *baptizo*, if it signify specifically *to dip* or *immerse*, come to express an entirely different action? I answer, it does not *definitely* express dipping or immersing. The lexicons, as we have seen, define it *to wash* as well as to immerse. Suppose, then, you direct your son *to wash* his hands, and he has water *poured* on them ; does he not obey your command? Or suppose he *dips* them in water, does he not obey you? He does. You direct him to do a certain thing, but do

6

not prescribe any particular mode in which he must do it. He may, therefore, select any mode he prefers. So the word *baptizo* expresses the application of water to the person or subject; but the precise mode of its application must be determined by the circumstances and the design of the ordinance.

My friend gave us a dissertation on the words *dip, bathe, pour,* and *sprinkle,* as they occur in Leviticus. If he would not consider me as anticipating him, I could prove, that the word *bapto* is used in the Bible in several senses—dipping, partial dipping, wetting or smearing. Thus it is said, the priest shall " dip his finger *from (apo)* the oil," &c. Is it true that he did literally dip his finger *from* it? Does such an expression signify to *dip in?* Or does it not rather mean, as professor Stuart says, *to wet or smear by means* of the oil? There is, properly, no dipping in the case. The priest was simply to moisten or wet his finger with the fluid, so as to sprinkle it. If my friend will not charge me with anticipating him, I will say, that the word *bapto* occurs in the Scriptures again and again in connection with the preposition *apo, from;* and evidently in such cases it does not express *mode.*

There are in the Greek language words that definitely signify to *immerse,* and words which signify to *pour,* and to *sprinkle;* but I deny, that *bapto* or *baptizo* definitely expresses the one or the other of these modes. I can find a Greek word that does uniformly signify *to immerse;* but *baptizo* is not the word. The word *baptisma* is the name of an ordinance instituted by our Savior for the benefit of his church. It denotes the application of water to a proper subject, in the name of the Trinity; but it does not express the precise mode of applying the water.

But Mr. C. has insisted so much on the necessity of employing a specific term, expressing a definite action, to denote a religious ordinance, that I must read a passage in Numbers xix. 19, in which we find mentioned one of the washings to which I have before referred: " And the clean person shall sprinkle upon the unclean on the third day, and on the seventh day; and on the seventh day he shall purify himself, and wash his clothes, and bathe himself in water, and shall be clean at even." Here we find *sprinkling, washing,* and *bathing.* I invite your attention to the phrase—" *he shall bathe himself.*" The Hebrew word translated *bathe,* is *rahats,* which is a generic term signifying simply *to wash ;* and it is translated in the Septuagint by the Greek word *louv,* to wash. Here the unclean person is commanded to do a certain thing— to wash himself; but does the word employed prescribe the *mode* in which he is to do it? It does not. But my friend insists, that the word employed must express a definite action—that it must precisely express the manner in which the ordinance is to be performed. I can find many examples similar to the one just adduced. Now, if his rule requiring a specific term is good in one instance, why not in another? But I can point to other rites, the mode of administering which is not expressed by the word employed.

My friend, Mr. C., admits that *baptizo* may mean *sinking to the bottom;* but he seems disposed to contend, that it more properly implies that the thing immersed is again raised out of the water. And he refers to the language of a Greek writer concerning Athens, which he explains to mean—that Athens might be *overwhelmed,* but not *destroyed.* But if I understand the word *overwhelm,* I should think a city overwhelmed is well nigh *destroyed.* But by an appeal to classic writers, I can prove, that in *four-fifths* of the instances in which it is supposed to favor immersion, it signifies *sinking to the bottom*. Suppose, then, an individual should understand the command to be baptized in the sense of *sinking;* what could be the result? *To sink* is the common meaning of the word in the classics. But if you substitute the word *sink* for *baptize* in every place where *baptizo* occurs in the Scriptures, it makes nonsense.

As to the idea advanced by my friend, that the syllable *zo* in *baptizo* implies that the action is to be performed *quickly*, I know of no evidence whatever that it is true. Dr. Carson (I believe that he is a *doctor,*) says, that *baptizo* denotes the putting of a thing into water; but whether it is raised out again or sinks to the bottom, cannot be ascertained by the *word*, but must be learned from the *circumstances.*

But I should be pleased to seē some few examples adduced from the classics, in which the word *baptizo* expresses the action contended for by Mr. C. as essential to baptism. For I believe there is scarcely an instance in which it expresses the actions he performs in baptizing.[*—Time expired.*

Wednesday, Nov. 15—1½ oclock, P. M.
[MR. CAMPBELL'S THIRD ADDRESS.]

MR. PRESIDENT—An objection to the use we make of the testimony and criticism advanced from Pedo-baptist authority, now offered by my friend, Mr. Rice, reminds me of an objection advanced by some modern sceptics against the arguments generally relied on, in proving the resurrection of the Messiah. They say, your testimony is all one-sided. Produce any one of the ancient sceptics who admitted the fact. Unfortunately your testimony is all on the wrong side. Produce only one witness who was not himself a believer. That is indeed impossible; inasmuch as such an admission would have made the witness a christian. So in the present case. If those *Pedo-baptist* lexicographers and critics adduced, had entertained no excuse for their position, (either in the metaphorical meaning of the word, or in the unimportance of the mode,) they would have been Baptists; and then their testimony would have been more plausibly repudiated, because indeed one-sided.

So much with reference to the remarks made on professor Stuart's testimony, adduced some time ago. Mr. Stuart is a Pedo-baptist, and practices sprinkling; although he has said as much for immersion as any man could say, and yet continue where he is. It is indeed most true, as the gentleman presumes, that he [Prof. Stuart] is wholly indifferent as to the mode. He, in common with many others, says that immersion was the ancient mode; nay, he is compelled to admit that it was almost the universal practice in the ancient church; yet still he thinks with Calvin that mode is of no importance, and that we may alter and amend, according to circumstances, so that we do not make it a new rite. The same is true with regard to all the authorities brought forward by my worthy friend. Their testimony is, indeed, in one sense, *ex parte.* They are all of *his* own party, *not of mine.* Every dictionary he has quoted is a Pedo-baptist dictionary; and yet most of them have said all that is possible to be said by persons not wholly with us; while indeed they all give the true original and proper meaning of the word, they are sure to give a tropical meaning, that squints to their own position. They must do this or abandon their position. They all believed in this practice of sprinkling; while as scholars, in their definitions, they have told the truth, with one or two exceptions. With one consent they all give to dip, or to immerse, as the proper original meaning of the word *baptizo*. Not a single exception. Many of them give the reason for other meanings; such as—to wash, to cleanse, to color. They all concur in this, that such meanings are the *effect*, or the names of the *effects* of immersing. Not one of them says that it means to wash or cleanse *in any mode*, but only as the effect of dipping or immersing. Do they say it means to wash, &c., they immediately add, because it is done by immersing. This fact cannot be made too prominent. But what have we to do with the *effects* of an action, of an ordinance of God, in ascertaining the form or mode of the ordinance itself!! Hence all the learned abjure the rhetorical use of words in expounding laws, statutes, and ordinances, as we shall show in its proper place.

I wish, at this particular crisis of the discussion, to make a single impression, clearly and indelibly, upon the minds of the audience. It is this: *there is not a word in universal speech that is absolutely incapable of a figurative use.* Hence, if we may take the figurative meaning for the true and proper, there is an end to all discussion in ascertaining positive statutes and precepts; for, I repeat it, there is not in universal speech a noun, verb, or adjective, that may not be used figuratively. In verbs, very often, these figurative meanings are the results of specific actions. Hence where dyeing, washing, cleansing, are given as meanings of *bapto* or *baptizo*, lexicographers usually give the reason why a specific word could have such vague and general meanings.

I have said, in my introductory address, that the word *baptizo* has no more reference to water, than it has to oil, or sand, or any thing else; that it has reference to action only, and consequently can have but one meaning, which is most obvious, if the lexicons can be taken as authority. I again say there is neither *water* nor *washing* in the word *baptizo*. Any thing dipped into any thing, and covered over with it, fluid or not, is, in all propriety, said to be baptized, whether in oil, sand, wax, tar, milk or water. Why persons or things are said to be washed or cleansed by being immersed, is because *generally* they are immersed into clean water. Otherwise it could not be said that *baptizo* means to wash or cleanse. It would be as proper to say it means to pollute, to mire, to daub, if persons and things were *generally* immersed in mud, and mire, and unclean fluids. Hence some things dipped are said to be dyed, others colored, others cleansed, others washed, according to the material into which they are immersed. No figure of speech more common than a metonomy of the effect for the cause. Now what relation has the specific action to the effect produced by it? Can one word mean to wash, to mire, to cleanse, to pollute? Such is the logic of that whole school against which we contend.

But the question recurs whether in laws or ordinances we are to take the figurative or the literal meaning of words. This is the great question. I am happy to say that I have the concurrence of all the learned men of the world known to me, who have written on the subject, in the opinion that we are not to take the figurative meaning. All writers on law say, with Blackstone and Montesquieu, that in the interpretation of laws and statutes, terms are not to be taken rhetorically, but literally. Both in the enactment and in the interpretation of laws, the common meaning of words is to be regarded, and not the remote or figurative. A number of distinguished names will, at a more convenient season, be presented in proof of this conclusion.

With regard to the passage quoted from Mr. Carson, if the gentleman had just read a page or two further he would have shown his author was a little more consistent. It is of little consequence to us to argue and reply to conclusions drawn from the figurative use of the word.

It has been already distinctly stated that *baptizo* is the only word used to express the christian ordinance; and that for some reason (most probably the one I have given) it never signifies to *dye*. *Bapto*, however, tropically signifies to dye. Now although Dr. Carson argues that *bapto* means to dye, without regard to mode, he expressly traces the origin of this sense to a *figure*—the effect for the cause. His words are, page 60, "From signifying to *dip* it came to signify to *dye by dipping*, because this was the way in which things were usually dyed." This is my argument concerning both these words. The effect of dipping, for a length of time, is, in some substances, coloring or dyeing; the effect of dipping in clear water, for a short time, is washing, cleansing. Mr. Carson goes farther, it is alledged, and says that *bapto* and its family means *dye* or color, without any regard to the manner in which it was effected. This is then making the figurative the *proper* meaning of the word,—from this I dissent. But if Mr. Rice rely on Carson in this case, why not rely upon him in the case of the word used in the ordinance, which, according to him, signifies to *dip*, and nothing else?

I most readily admit, that, in the language of poetry and of imagination, objects are said to be painted, colored, dyed, not only in this mode, and that mode, but without any mode at all. Thus we have *ornis baptos*, the *colored bird*, of Aristophanes; the *pictæ volucres*, the *painted birds*, of Virgil; and Milton, in describing the wings of Raphael, sings of "colors dyed in heaven." In the same license Homer, in his reputed battle of the frogs and mice, represents a whole lake as tinged with the blood of a mouse. But what does all this prove? That because birds, flowers, clouds, and angels' wings, are said to be colored, dyed, or painted, without reference to any mode, that in the language of narrative, of precept, and of positive law, a person is baptized without any mode at all!! I have only one remark to make on all these cases and usages of *bapto*, that in the *passive form* things are said to be *dyed*, not with respect to the mode in which the process was completed, but with respect to the effect or result of the process; and again, nothing is said to be *dyed*, *painted* or *colored* by *bapto*, in its various forms, that is not, at the time of which it is spoken, covered over with the dye color. This is enough on this subject so far as the root *bap*, or the words *bapto* and *baptizo* are concerned. In all this there is a perfect conformity to the established laws of language in all similar cases.

I wish Mr. Rice had read a little more from Mr. Carson—such as, from the same pages he has quoted, "With regard to the other side, (Pedobaptist) to say nothing of the straining to squeeze out of the word the several meanings of sprinkling, pouring, washing, wetting, &c., for which there is not any even plausible ground, the obvious fact that it signifies dyeing by any process has been uncritically pressed to prove that when it relates to the application of pure water it denotes all modes equally." We may, however, hear Mr. Carson a little further on this subject, (page 59,) "If it be possible," says he, after giving many examples from Hippocrates, "to settle the meaning of a common word, surely this is sufficient to fix the meaning of *bapto* beyond all reasonable controversy. In the words of the Father of Medicine, in which he has occasion to

H

treat of every mode of the application of liquids, and which consists of no less than five hundred and forty-three closely printed folio pages, all the words of mode are applied, and *bapto* invariably is used when he designates immersion."

Other criticisms and reasonings from my friend Mr. Rice, not included in those remarks, shall be taken up in their proper place. We must not forget that we are furnishing a new book on baptism, and other matters connected therewith. We must, therefore, have supreme regard to that as we proceed.

So far as I lead the way, I propose the following method:—On rising I shall attend to so much of my respondent's speeches as are relevant to the premises I have offered. While affirmant, it is my privilege to lead the way. Whatever my respondent advances, relative to my arguments, shall be immediately attended to. Other matters, calling for any special attention, shall be attended to at proper and pertinent seasons. Should any thing of this sort, which Mr. Rice deems important, be overlooked or forgotten, I request him to bring it up to my attention, and I shall give to it all due regard. I shall then immediately proceed with my arguments, in numerical order, to which, of course, I shall expect a particular attention in the same order.

As the matter now stands, my second argument, drawn from the Greek lexicons, is fully stated and considerably illustrated. Not one of my authorities being challenged, I shall hereafter, in the discussion, always take for granted that *baptizo*, the word in debate, does, by consent of all the lexicons offered on the occasion, originally and properly signify to *dip* or *immerse;* that these words, in our language, properly represent it in its primitive and unfigurative import; and that to wash, or cleanse, are accidental and figurative meanings of the word: that *dip* and *immerse* are specific terms, and that, as Carson observes, when any word once signifies to *dip*, it never can signify to *sprinkle* or *pour*, any more than black never can signify white, nor white black, being specific and not general terms. To proceed argumentatively and logically, it now becomes my duty to examine the foundation on which these dictionaries depend.

III. ARG. This, for method's sake, I shall call my *third* argument; for though intimately allied to lexicography, it is nevertheless a separate and distinct argument. Dictionaries being founded on the usage of the best writers in the language of which it is a dictionary, we must look to them for the authority of the lexicons. We shall then appeal to the classic authors, to sacred and biblical usage to sustain the definitions already given. This is going to the proper foundation. Dictionaries are not the highest authority only in so far as they are the exponents of the classic, or most learned and approved use of words—we correct the dictionaries by the classics, and not the classics by the dictionaries. They are therefore the ultimate and supreme tribunal.

Hence the importance of particular attention to the age in which a language was best understood, and to the time and persons which gave us dictionaries. There is one fact of special importance here. Dictionaries frequently give the particular usage of the times of their authors; for example—Webster explains baptism by the word *christen*, because that was a common use at the time he made his dictionary. Hence, the particular age in which a dictionary is made may, more or less, affect the meaning of its words. Now, had it been the object of those who made Greek lexicons to do as Richardson, Johnson, Webster and others have done, that is, to give also the popular meaning or use of their own time, finding persons baptizing by sprinkling or pouring, like Groves, they would have, no doubt, made pouring or sprinkling the sixth or seventh meaning of the word. My preference for the lexicons made before sprinkling became rife will, therefore, be most apparent without further exposition. No Greek lexicon down to the 19th century, ever gave sprinkle or pour for baptism. I will shew the reason of this by a few specimens out of a mighty multitude prepared for this occasion.

I need scarcely add that the Greek is now a dead language. Its words are, therefore, in meaning, all stereotyped in the classics and sacred writings. This usage, therefore, is all we have to inquire into. Take, then, the following instances :

1st. Of the proper meaning of *baptizo :*—

" Lucian, in Timon, the man-hater, makes him say—' If I should see any one floating toward me upon the rapid torrent, and he should, with outstretched hands, beseech me to assist him, I would thrust him from me, *baptizing (baptizonta)* him, until he would rise no more.' "

" Plutarch, vol. x. p. 18, 'Then *plunging (baptizon)* himself into the lake Copais.' "

" Strabo, lib. 6, speaking of a lake near Agrigentum, says—'Things that elsewhere cannot float, *do not sink (baptizesthai.)* In lib. 12, of a certain river he says—'If one shoots an arrow into it, the force of the water resists it so much, that it will scarcely *sink (baptizesthai.)* "

"Polybius, vol. iii. p. 311, ult. applies the word to soldiers passing through water, *immersed (baptizomenoi)* up to the breast."

"The sinner is represented by Porphyry, p. 282., as *baptized (baptizetai)* up to his head in Styx, a celebrated river in hell. Is there any question about the mode of this baptism ?"

"Themistius, Orat. iv. p. 133, as quoted by Dr. Gale, says, 'The pilot cannot tell but he may save one in the voyage that had better be drowned, *(baptisai,)* sunk into the sea.' "

" The Sybilline verse concerning the city of Athens, quoted by Plutarch in his life of Theseus, most exactly determines the meaning of *baptizo*. *Askos baptizee dunai de toi ou themis esti.* "

" Thou mayest be dipped, O bladder ! but thou art not fated to sink."

" For our ship," says Josephus, " having been baptized or immersed in the midst of the Adriatic sea."

" Speaking of the murder of Aristobulus, by command of Herod, he says, ' The boy was sent to Jericho by night, and there by command having been immersed *(baptizomenos)* in a pond by the Galatians, he perished.' The same transaction is related in the Antiquities in these words: 'Pressing him down always, as he was swimming, and *baptizing* him as in sport, they did not give over till they entirely drowned him.' "

" Homer, Od. i. 392: As when a smith *dips* or *plunges (baptei)* a hatchet or huge pole-axe into cold water, viz : to harden them."

" Pindar, Pyth. ii. 139, describes the impotent malice of his enemies, by representing himself to be like the cork upon a net in the sea, which does not sink : As when a net is cast into the sea, the cork swims above, so am I *unplunged (abaptistos:)* on which the Greek scholiast, in commenting, says : ' As the cork *ou dunei, does not sink*, so I am *abaptistos, unplunged, not immersed.* The cork remains *abaptistos*, and swims on the surface of the sea, being of a nature which is *abaptistos ;* in like manner I am *abaptistos.*' In the beginning of this explanation the scholiast says : ' Like the cork of a net in the sea, *ou baptisomai, I am not plunged* or *sunk.*' The frequent repetition of the same words and sentiment, in this scholium, shows, in all probability, that it is compiled from different annotators upon the text. But the sense of *baptizo* in all is too clear to admit of any doubt."

"Aristotle, de Color. c. 4, says: By reason of heat and moisture, the colors enter into the pores of things *dipped into them,* (*tou baptomenou.*) De Anima. iii. c. 12, If a man *dips* (*bapsei*) any thing into wax, it is moved so far as it is dipped. Hist. Animal. viii. c. 2, speaking of certain fish, he says: They cannot endure great changes, such as that, in the summer time, *they should plunge* (*baptosi*) *into cold water*. Ibid. c. 29, he speaks of giving diseased elephants water to drink, and *dipping* (*baptontes*) hay into honey for them."

"Aristophanes, in his comedy of *The Clouds*, Act i. scene 2, represents Socrates as gravely computing how many times the distance between two of its legs, a flea could spring at one leap; and in order to ascertain this, the philosopher first melted a piece of wax, and then taking the flea, he *dipped* or *plunged* (*enebaphes*) two of its feet into it, &c."

"Heraclides Ponticus, a disciple of Aristotle, Allegor. p. 495, says: When a piece of iron is taken red hot from the fire, and *plunged* in the water, (*udati baptizetai,*) the heat, being quenched by the peculiar nature of the water, ceases."

"Herodotus, in Euterpe, speaking of an Egyptian who happens to touch a swine, says: Going to the river [Nile] he *dips* himself (*ebaphe eauton*) with his clothes."

"Aratus, in his Phænom. v. 650, speaks of the constellation Cepheus, as *dipping* (*baptoon*) his head and upper part into the sea. In v. 858 he says: If the sun *dip* (*baptoi*) himself cloudless into the western flood. Again, in v. 951, If the crow has *dipped* (*ebapsato*) his head into the river, &c."

"Xenophon, Anab. ii. 2, 4, describes the Greeks and their enemies as sacrificing a goat, a bull, a wolf, and a ram, and *dipping* (*baptontes*) into a shield [filled with their blood,] the Greeks the sword, the Barbarians the spear, in order to make a treaty that could not be broken."

"Plutarch, Parall. Græc. Rom. p. 545, speaking of the stratagem of a Roman general, in order to insure victory, he says: He set up a trophy, on which, *dipping* his hand into blood, (*eis to aima—baptizas*) he wrote this inscription, &c. In vol. vi. p. 680, (edit. Reiske) he speaks of iron *plunged* (*baptomenon*) viz. into water, in order to harden it. Ibid. page 633, *plunge* (*baptison*) yourself into the sea."

"Heraclides, Allegor. says, When a piece of iron is taken red hot from the fire and *plunged* (*baptizetai*) into water."

"Heliodorus, vi. 4. When midnight had *plunged* (*ebaptizon*) the city in sleep."

FIGURATIVE USE.

"Plutarch. *Overwhelmed* with debts, (*bebaptismenon.*)"

"Chrysostom. *Overwhelmed* (*baptizomenos*) with innumerable cares."

"Lucian iii. page 81. He is like one dizzy and *baptized* or *sunk* (*bebaptismeno*)—viz. into insensibility by drinking."

"Justin Martyr. *Overwhelmed* with sins (*bebaptismenos.*)"

"Aristotle, De Mirabil. Ausc. speaks of a saying among the Phenicians, that there were certain places beyond the pillars of Hercules, which, when it is ebb-tide, are not *overflowed* (*me baptizesthai,*) but at full-tide are *overflowed* (*katakluzesthai;*) which word is here used as an equivalent for *baptizesthai*."

"Plato, Conviv. page 176. I myself am one of those who were *drenched* or *overwhelmed* (*bebaptismenon*) yesterday, viz. with wine. In another place: Having *overwhelmed* (*baptisasa*) Alexander with much wine. Euthydem. p. 267, ed. Heindorf, A youth *overwhelmed* (*baptizomenon*) viz. questions."

"Philo Judæus, vol. p. ii. 478, I know some, who, when they easily become intoxicated, before they are entirely overwhelmed (*printeleos baptisthenai,*) viz. with wine."

"Diodorus Siculus, tom. i. page 107, Most of the land animals that are intercepted by the river [Nile,] perish, being *overwhelmed* (*baptizomena;*) here used in the literal sense. Tom. i. page 191, The river, borne along by a more violent current, *overwhelmed* (*ebaptise*) many; the literal signification. Tom. i. p. 129, And because they [the nobles] have a supply by these means [presents] they do not *overwhelm* their subjects with taxes."

It were easy to increase this list by quotations from other Greek writers, authors, poets, scholiasts, critics and Greek Fathers, all in further proof of the same import of the word in question—such as Anacreon, Moschus, Callimachus, Theocritus, Dionysius Halicarnassus, on the 16th Iliad, v. 333; Demosthenes, Dio Cassius, Lycophron, Sophocles, Esop, Libanius, Pseudo-Didymus, Heliodorus, Aphrodetus, Lactantius, Alcibiades, Josephus, Symmachus, Athenæas, Porphyry, Marcus Anotoninus Pius, Gregory Thaumaturgus, Gregory Nazianzen, Clemens Alexandrinus, Theophylact, Basil, Trypho the Jew, in Justin Martyr, Origen, &c.

I regard it as more pedantic, than necessary, to display so many authorities. I may, however, say that I could read scores of such as you have heard, all in perfect concurrence with those read. We have the entire phalanx of all classic authority—poets, philosophers, orators, historians, metaphysicians, critics, shewing one perfect agreement in their use of *baptizo* and its derivatives.

It has been a question amongst theologians, whether the sacred use, that is, the Jewish and Christian, agrees with the classic use of this word; whether in one sentence the New Testament writers use *baptizo*, as do all other writers of that age; a most singular question in such a class of words—words indicating outward physical specific action. Such words are not the subjects of idiomatic and special law. It would be indeed adopting a very dangerous principle and precedent, that this word means one thing out of the New Testament, and another in it. The usage of the age and the context must in all cases decide the precise meaning of any word—a law of philology which I have published as often as any of my contemporaries, not only in this case, but in all others.

Speakers, by a particular emphasis and tone, are capable of making a particular word mean just what they please. I have known some of this class of persons who could make a word mean what they pleased by emphasis, tone and action. There are, too, writers in every age, who use terms in a sense very remote from the true. But whether the apostles were such men; or whether we, in a grave discussion like this, are to decide upon the meaning of a word by such corruptions, and licences, or whether we shall accept the sense in which a word was used by those who lived contemporaneously with the apostles, will hardly admit of question, or of doubt.

I am one of those who admit, and can prove, the most exact agreement between the classic, the New Testament, and the Septuagint use of this word. These perfectly corroborate each other. All use the word as indicative of the same action, universally expressed by those classic writers adduced.

We have the entire cohort of classic, apostolic, and Jewish writers, as well as the more ancient christian fathers, all concurring in the same view. And now the question is, whether we shall take a meaning universally maintained and admitted, or whether we shall now invent a new one, never found amongst the proper and fixed meanings of the term. Any one who carefully reads the commission—"Go ye into all the world, and preach the Gospel to every creature. He that believeth and

H 2

is baptized, shall be saved; and he that believeth not shall be condemned," might infer from the solemn position of the word baptism, and the emphasis placed on it—from the fact of its intermediate position between faith and salvation—that it is one of the most definite, clear, and intelligible terms in the world.

I solemnly affirm it now, as I have before affirmed it, and, as I believe, already shown it, that there is not now, nor has there ever been, at any past period, a term in universal speech, more definite and more fixed in its meaning than this same specific term baptism, now before us.   And this I further argue from the fact, that no sacred writer has ever defined the word.   Our Savior did not define it; John the Baptist did not define it; the Apostles never defined it.   Must it not therefore have been used by them, in the established meaning of the time in which they lived and taught the christian religion!—[*Time expired.*

[The hour having now arrived for the close of the session, at the suggestion of the presiding moderator, (Hon. H. Clay,) Mr. Rice waived his right of reply till to-morrow morning; and the adjournment was accordingly announced in form.]

Thursday, Nov. 16—10 o'clock, A. M.
[MR. RICE'S THIRD REPLY.]

MR. PRESIDENT—It is exceedingly important in this discussion, that we distinctly understand the point in controversy.   I will again read the proposition, that all may hear it: " The immersion in water of a proper subject, in the name of the Father, the Son, and the Holy Spirit, is the one, only, apostolic and christian baptism."   This Mr. Campbell affirms, and I deny.   I desire the audience to mark distinctly what he undertakes to prove, viz: that the entire submersion of the body in water, is absolutely essential to christian baptism; that nothing short of this is baptism; and, consequently, that all who have received the ordinance in any other mode, are unbaptized, and are not in the church of Christ.

This is the position of my friend.   And, as I remarked on yesterday, so I say again—if this discovery, of recent origin, be real, and not an entire mistake, it is one of the most remarkable discoveries made since the days of the apostles. For I repeat the fact, that nine hundred and ninety-nine in every thousand of those in favor of immersion, as well as of those against it, have failed to see in the Bible this doctrine which Mr. C. says, is so plainly taught, that he that runs may read and understand it !

Mark again *how* he undertakes to prove this important proposition. His main argument is founded on the meaning of the words *bapto* and *baptizo*.   To determine the meaning of these words his first and main appeal has been to the lexicons, as being the highest authority.   Now observe this fact: by the same lexicons to which he has appealed, ancient and modern, I have proved that they have other meanings, essentially different from that which he attaches to them.   He, let it be noted, is bound to prove, that they signify to immerse, and only to immerse; for if they have other meanings, the connection must determine, in any given case, which is the true meaning.   The sense must be determined by the connection, and not simply by the *words.*   But I have proved by the lexicons, ancient and modern, that these words have several distinct meanings.   His argument, therefore, has wholly failed.

I have proved that these words signify to sink, (and the word *sink* is quite different from *immerse*,) to plunge, to dip, to dye, stain, color, to wash, to cleanse, to wet, to moisten, to sprinkle. All these definitions have been found in the different lexicons. And, observe, I have proved this, not by the *modern* lexicons only, which Mr. C. considers of less authority than the ancient, but by *both ancient and modern;* such as Hedericus, Scapula, Stephanus, Suidas, Schleusner, Schrivellius, Bretschneider, Parkhurst, Robinson, Greenfield, Wahl, &c. &c. I have appealed to all these, and every one of them declares, that the words *bapto* and *baptizo* signify not only to *dip*, to *plunge*, &c., but also to *wash*, without reference to mode.

My friend has told you that modern legicographers, such as Groves, add new meanings to Greek words—that Webster, for example, defines the word *baptize* to *christen*. I had supposed that the business of a Greek lexicographer was, to ascertain, not what meanings persons in modern times attach to Greek words, but in what senses they were used by Greek writers. And if so, no modern lexicographer will give to a Greek word a meaning which he does not believe to have been attached to it by Greek authors. Webster was defining an English word; and he gave it such meanings as he found attached to it by those who speak the English language.

Mark again—these lexicographers do not define the words *bapto* and *baptizo* to dye and to wash *only by immersion*. There is not one amongst them who confines them to washing or dyeing by immersion. They generally agree with Bretschneider, who defines *baptizo*, " propr. sepius intingo, sepius lavo"—*properly often to immerse, often to wash;* and in the New Testament, first, " *lavo, abluo simpliciter'*—*simply to wash, to cleanse.* Schrivellius defines it, mergo, abluo, lavo—to immerse, to *cleanse*, to *wash.* They do not, then, say, that these words signify to wash or to dye only by dipping.

Nor, allow me further to remark, do the lexicographers say, that the words in question signify *to wash* FIGURATIVELY. There is not a lexicographer, ancient or modern, on the face of the earth, who says that *baptizo* means to wash figuratively. It would indeed be marvellous to say, that *washing* or *sprinkling* is *figurative immersion.* It is true, these and all other words may have a figurative sense; and I have given an example in which the word *sprinkle* is figuratively used, viz: in the Epistle to the Hebrews: "Having our hearts *sprinkled* from an evil conscience." Here we know the word is employed figuratively, because a literal fluid is not supposed to be used. But when Ezekiel says, " Then will I sprinkle clean water upon you," the word is employed in a literal sense, because literal water is supposed to be used. Every figure must bear some resemblance to the thing of which it is the figure. But what resemblance is there between sprinkling and immersing? or between washing and immersing? Washing may be a *consequence* of immersion, but certainly it cannot be a *figure* of it. *We go for the* LITERAL MEANING ! And all these lexicons define *baptizo*, to wash, cleanse, purify, *in a literal sense.*

I appeal to Carson, one of the most zealous immersionists. He declares, that the word *bapto* signifies *literally* to dye in any manner. (P. 64.) " Nor are such applications of the word *(bapto)* to be accounted for by metaphor, as Dr. Gale asserts. *They are as literal as the primary meaning.* It is by extension of literal meaning, and not by figure of any kind, that words come to depart so far from their original signification."

Professor Stuart has been styled by my friend, Mr. C., his American apostle. Now, let us have the whole testimony of this apostle. Stuart does, indeed, say, that *baptizo* signifies *to dip, to plunge*, as Mr. C. has stated. But let him speak for himself. On page 29, he speaks of the word as used in the New Testament; and the *first* meaning he gives is *to wash*, not *figuratively*, but *literally*—" to wash in a literal sense."

But my friend has told us, that Stuart acknowledges that the *ancient church* immersed. He does say, that the ancient church (in the third century) immersed *three times*, divesting the persons of all their garments. But he does not admit, that Jesus Christ ever commanded any one to be immersed. I will read a paragraph from his work on baptism: (p. 18,) " But we have already seen, in numbers 6, 7, above, respecting classic usage, that *bapto* is employed in the sense of *bathing* the surface of any thing with a fluid, and also of washing it. We have seen in numbers 2, 5, 6, of examples from the Septuagint and Apocrypha, that the word *baptizo* sometimes means *to wash*, and *bapto* to moisten, to wet, or bedew. There is, then, no absolute certainty, from usage, that the word *baptizo*, when applied to designate the rite of baptism, means, of course, to *immerse* or *plunge*. It may mean *washing ;* possibly (but not probably) it may mean *copiously moistening* or *bedewing ;* because words coming from the common root *bap*, are applied in both these senses, as we have seen above." There is Stuart for you. And I can, and, if necessary, will turn to the page where he declares, that there is not in the New Testament a command that persons should be immersed.

Now mark what I have proved; for I intend that every hearer shall understand my arguments on this subject. I have proved, that *bapto* and *baptizo* signify not only to sink, dip, plunge, but to wash, to cleanse, to purify, to wet, to moisten, and even *to sprinkle ;* and I will yet prove, by even higher authority than the lexicons, that they have these meanings. Now the question is—did our Savior and his apostles use the word *baptizo* in the sense of *plunging ?* or did he use it in the sense of *washing, cleansing, purifying ?* If Mr. C. can prove, that he used it in the sense of plunging, he will have gained his point; if he cannot, his argument fails and he is defeated. I defy him to point to one passage in the Scriptures in which it signifies to *plunge* or *immerse*.

We have now gone through with the examination of the lexicons, and we have found them testifying that the word *baptizo* signifies *literally* to wash, to cleanse, as well as to plunge, to dip. Now, my friend, Mr. C., must be in error, or all the lexicographers must have been very stupid. He has told us, that wherever we find *bap*, we find also the idea of dipping. The lexicographers do not say so, and I have proved that it is not true.

He informs us, that he is now going to pursue a regular course in his argument. He appeals to the classics. I also go to the classics, and I will prove that they do not sustain him. But why does he appeal to the classics, unless he wishes to prove the lexicons wrong ? He has admitted, however, that they are correct; and I maintain, that they have correctly defined the words in question. Their definitions are founded upon a careful examination of classic usage ; and if they have all erred, it is scarcely probable that we shall ascertain the truth. But I am prepared to go to the classics.

My friend, Mr. C., admits, that so far as *mode* is concerned, *bapto* and *baptizo* have the same meaning. Now let me quote a sentence from

Hippocrates. He, as we have seen, uses the word *bapto* to denote dyeing a garment by dropping upon it the coloring fluid. " When it drops upon the garments, *(baptetai)* they are dyed," or as perhaps my friend would say, they are *immersed!* Then, when water is *poured* upon an individual, of course he is immersed ; and this is all Mr. C. could ask !

Carson quotes the following sentence from Arrian's Expedition of Alexander the Great: " Nearchus relates, that the Indians *(baptontai)* dye their beards ;" and he remarks—" It will not be contended that they dyed their beards by immersion."—So Mr. Carson is with us again.

Ælian, speaking of an old coxcomb who endeavored to conceal his age by dyeing his hair, says, " He endeavored to conceal the hoariness of his hair, by dyeing it"—*(baphe.)* " *Baphe*," says Carson, " here denotes dyeing in general ; for hair on the head is not dyed by dipping."

Homer, in his Battle of Frogs and Mice, uses the following language : " He breathless fell, and the lake was tinged *(ebapteto)* with blood." Or would you say, the lake was *immersed* in his blood !

Aristophanes says, " Magnes, an old comic actor of Athens, used the Lydian music, shaved his face, and smeared it over *(baptomenos)* with tawny washes." On this passage, Dr. Gale remarks, " He speaks of the homely entertainments of the ancient theatre, where the actors daubed themselves with lees of wine and many odd colors, before Æschylus reformed it, and introduced the use of masks and vizors. Aristophanes expresses this by *baptomenos*, *batracheiois*, not that he supposes they dipped their faces into the color, but rather smeared the color on their faces." *Reflec. on Wall's Hist. of Inf. Bap.*, v. iii. p. 109.

Aristotle speaks of a substance, which, " if it is pressed, dyes *(baptei)* and colors the hand."

I could produce many other examples of the use of *bapto*, where it cannot mean to dip, or immerse ; but it is unnecessary, since Mr. Carson, the learned Baptist critic, admits that it signifies to dye by sprinkling as literally as by dipping. If, then, the words *bapto* and *baptizo* agree in meaning, so far as mode is concerned ; what becomes of the argument of Mr. C. for immersion, derived from the meaning of *baptizo ?*

Let me now turn your attention to the classic usage of the word *baptizo*. And here I repeat what I have before asserted, that, if necessary, I will prove, that in *four-fifths* of the instances in the classics which are supposed to favor immersion, this word signifies sinking to the bottom. *And is that the* ACTION *for which my opponent is contending ?*

But here is a passage in which *baptizo* signifies *moistening* or *wetting*. Plutarch, relating the stratagem of a Roman general a little before he died of his wounds, says: " He set up a trophy, on which, having *baptized (baptisas)* his hand in blood, he wrote this inscription," &c. Did he *immerse* his hand in blood in order to write ? Is not *baptizo* here used simply in the sense of *wetting* or *moistening ?*

Hypocrates directs, concerning a blister plaster, if it be too painful, " to *baptize* or *moisten* it with breast milk or Egyptian ointment." Did he intend, that the plaster should be *immersed* in breast milk ? Is this the direction which physicians are accustomed to give concerning blister plasters ? Evidently, the word is here used in the sense of *moistening*.

Dr. Gale, a learned immersionist, furnishes us with an example in which the word *baptizo* certainly does not express the *action* for which my friend, Mr. C., is contending. Aristotle says, " The Phenicians, who inhabit Cadiz, relate, that sailing beyond Hercules' Pillars, in four days, with the wind at east, they came to a land uninhabited, whose coast was full of sea-weeds, and is not overflowed *(baptizesthai)* at ebb; but when the tide comes in, it is wholly covered." On this passage, Dr. Gale thus remarks: "Besides, the word *baptizo*, perhaps, does not so necessarily express the action of putting under water, as, in general, a thing's being in that condition; no matter how it comes so, whether it is put into the water, or the water comes on it."—*Reflec. on Wall's Hist.* vol. iii., p. 122.

The land, we are told, was not *baptized* at ebb, but was overflowed by the tide. Is the land put into the water, or does the water flow over it? Gale certainly gives up the question; for he says *baptizo* does not so necessarily express the *action* (the very thing my friend is contending for) of putting into water, as in general a thing's being in that state, no matter how it comes so.

We have now gone somewhat into the classics; and I care not to what extent the investigation may be pursued: for, as before remarked, I will, if necessary, prove, that in four-fifths of the instances in which the use of the word is supposed to favor immersion, it occurs in relation to the sinking of ships, the drowning of men, &c. Surely these are not the *actions* for which the gentleman is contending. There are, moreover, as we have just seen, examples in which this word comes far short of immersion.

One of the most serious errors of the gentleman, and of those who agree with him on this subject, is their undue reliance upon classic usage to determine the meaning of words found in the Scriptures. The pagan Greeks are certainly unsafe guides in the exposition of the language of the New Testament; so the best critics declare. And it is on this account, that we have *Lexicons of the New Testament*. To give a single example, Dr. Geo. Campbell says, the word *flesh* has, in the New Testament, *six* meanings, not more than one of which is found in classic authors. The principle holds good in regard to hundreds of words.

I am, therefore, inclined to come to the *Bible usage*—and since our friends (the reformers,) boast of going by *the Book*, I would a little prefer appealing to it. I am prepared to prove by the ablest critics, that the usage of the Bible, and of the Jews in their religious writings, is the only tribunal by which to determine the meaning of words in the New Testament; and, in these writings, I can prove that the word *baptizo* rarely, if ever, signifies to *immerse*.

[Mr. Rice here asks the moderators whether his time has expired; and being informed that he might yet occupy two minutes, he proceeds:]

Before sitting down I will state two facts, which go to prove that classic usage cannot determine the meaning of words used in the New Testament:—

First—*The inspired apostles did not speak or write classic Greek.* They were Jews; and, as critics tell us, they not only could not speak classic Greek, but they could not have understood it.

Second—*The character, manners, habits, customs and religion of the Jews were widely different from those of the pagan Greeks;* hence the usage of the latter cannot determine the meaning of words employed by the former.

It is, moreover, a fact, that the pagan Greeks never employed the word *baptizo* with reference to *religious washings*, but always with reference to things in common life. And it is a fact, that the Jews (except Josephus, who sought to imitate the classic Greek,) never used it in their religious writings, in relation to matters of common life, but always in relation to *religious washings*.   Now, it is a principle of interpretation, that words often have one meaning in matters of common life, and quite a different meaning in matters of religion.   Consequently, even if the word *baptizo* had, in classic usage, the meaning for which my friend (Mr. C.) contends; it would by no means follow, that it has the same meaning in the New Testament.—[*Time expired.*

Thursday, Nov. 16—10½ *o'clock, A. M.*
[MR. CAMPBELL'S FOURTH ADDRESS.]

MR. PRESIDENT—I am much gratified, sir, to observe the improvement in the health and energy of my friend, Mr. Rice.   He seems to have slept profoundly on the work of yesterday, and appears refreshed and invigorated, and eager for the work before him.   His speech this morning is, however, but a reiteration of the developments of yesterday. It amounts to neither more nor less than this; The word *baptizo* sometimes signifies *to wash*.   He talks of other meanings.   They amount, however, to no more than this.

I concur with him, indeed, in the necessity of an occasional recapitulation, and in the propriety of keeping the main question before us.   It is important to have frequent recurrence to the points at issue, and to the progress made.   What then is the question—the main issue?   Not whether we Baptists are right?   That is not the question.   Mr. Rice himself concedes that we are right in the practice of immersion.   Greek and Roman, ancient and modern christians, all sects and parties, agree that immersion is good and valid baptism.   That is not the question, nor the point to be discussed and decided here.   We have a tremendous, an overwhelming majority of those who so believe.   The question is, whether our Pedo-baptist friends are right?   Whether there are two distinct baptisms; one immersing, the other sprinkling or wetting a person by *Divine* authority.   Methinks it would suffice to prove to ordinary minds that immersion is baptism; and then, as there is but *one* baptism, sprinkling cannot be that one baptism.   But let me ask, what are the essentials of baptism?   They are usually said to be four: 1. A proper subject—2. A proper action—3. The Divine formula of words, into the name of the Father, and of the Son, and of the Holy Spirit; and 4. A proper administrator.   These are the sole and necessary requisites.   A failure in any one of these may affect the validity of baptism.

The question now before us concerns the *action*—the thing commanded to be done.   This is, of course, the most important point—the significant and all-absorbing point.   Paul gives it high rank and consequence when he says, "There is one Lord, one faith, one baptism."   There are not two modes of any one of these.   When we have ascertained that one action called baptism, there can be no other.   I said yesterday, and I repeat it this morning, that it is wholly sophistical to talk of two modes of baptism, unless, indeed, it be two ways of immersing a person.   In this sense there may be a plurality of modes.   A person may be immersed backwards or forwards, kneeling or standing.   Other modes than these there cannot be.   Sprinkling is not a mode of immersing; neither is immersion a mode of sprinkling.   If sprinkling, pouring, and immersion be modes of baptism, then, I ask, what is the *thing* called baptism?   Who can explain this?   Of *what* are these three specifically different actions, the mode? If sprinkling be a mode, and pouring a mode, and immersing a mode, then baptism is something *incognito*—something which no philologist, or lexicographer can explain. I pronounce these modes an unmeaning, sophistical jargon, which no one can comprehend.

Baptism is not a *mode*—it is an *action*. The word that represents it is improperly, by Mr. Carson, called a word of *mode*. *It is a specific action;* and the verb that represents it is a verb of specific import; else there is no such verb in Hebrew, Greek, or Latin.

I had the honor of first exposing the sophistry of this word *mode*, and of publicly repudiating it some twenty-three years ago, in a debate on this same question. I showed the superior prowess of the Pedo-baptist in introducing this term. He gained half the controversy by calling immersion a mode of baptism. When the honest and unsuspecting Baptist received the imposition, he was half defeated. He felt that he had but a mode, and the Pedo-baptist had another mode, and they both had baptism! The controversy was then reduced to a question of mere mode; whereas the true and real debate is about a *thing*, an *action*, and not at all about a mode. The Messiah commanded a solemn and most significant action, and not a mode. Since 1820 the word *action* is being substituted for mode.

The gentleman has given you several quotations from classic authors, a number of which I intended to have read, and some of them belong not to the word in debate. For good reasons our Lawgiver chose the word *baptizo*, not *bapto*. The former is therefore found 120 times, in some of its flexions and forms, in the New Testament, while we have the latter only six times. They are both said to be specific words by Mr. Carson; whilst he most singularly, it would seem, gives *bapto* both a specific and generic meaning. It is impossible that any word can be both specific and generic. Dyeing, coloring, staining, and dipping, are not of one class of words. Dyeing may be done many ways; so may coloring, staining; but dipping can be done but one way. Therefore no one word can be specific, which represents them both, in its true and proper meaning.

Our issue, says Mr. Rice, after all, depends upon the lexicographers. They are, no doubt, a proper court of appeal, but they are not the supreme court of appeal. They have themselves to appeal to the classics and approved writers for their authority. They are often wrong. Mr. Carson says they are all wrong in affirming that *wash* is a secondary meaning of *baptizo*. We all appeal from them to the classics. No learned man will ever rest his faith upon dictionaries. He will appeal from them, in very many cases, to their teachers, the classics. They often interpolate their own caprices, and insert their own whims and prejudices. Yet with all their prejudices and caprices, no lexicographer has been produced, nor can there be one now produced, who during 1800 years, (and before that time we have none,) translated *baptizo* by *sprinkle* or *pour;* while they all, without one single exception, have translated the word *immerse*, or *dip*, or *plunge*, or *immerge*, words of one and the same signification. Nor can any classic author be produced in which *baptizo* means to sprinkle or pour. This is full proof of my proposition, let men assert what they please. Many Pedo-baptists think it means to sprinkle, and therefore they so practice. But for this, I again say, they have no authority, classic, lexicographic, or sacred.

After all, this is a question of authority. My friend, Mr. Rice, has his opinion, and other men have their opinions. Every man's opinion is equal to the amount of his intelligence and his honesty. The opinions of lexicographers are to be estimated as other opinions. My opponent says he has proved from the lexicons, ancient and modern, that *baptizo* has several distinct meanings, therefore I have failed in proving that it has but one proper meaning. All this is easily said, and quite as easily repeated. But it is only an opinion, and of course I, as well as many others, am of a different opinion. And we have our reasons for these opinions. I have, indeed, as yet, only offered a portion, a very small portion of my evidence; still from that I opine it is quite obvious that there is no authority for his opinion. I have been quoting all my proofs from Pedo-baptists, from dictionaries made by them, both classical, and also theological. They generally, indeed, give *wash*, or *cleanse*, or some purifying word, after giving the *proper* meaning. They always and universally, however, despite of their prejudices, give *dip* as the proper and native meaning of the word. The other definitions, as we shall still more fully show, are accidental or contingent acceptations, rather than meanings of the word. The difference between our witnesses then is this; Mr. Rice is maintaining his opinions by witnesses selected out of his own Pedo-baptist party, while I am quoting his own witnesses, and never once using any one of my party, ancient or modern. He might as well quote the clergymen in this house, of his own church, as the authors he has already quoted, to maintain his conclusions; and I might as well quote them too, to prove mine, as most of those whom I do quote. If from such testimony I have already adduced an unanswerable phalanx of proof, how strong must be the evidence in favor of our practice! But you shall yet have much more of it.

I yesterday proposed an English discussion for an English audience. Mr. Rice ingeniously refused it, on grounds so transparent that all could see through them. I had read a few lexicon authorities, which would and could have all been withdrawn in a moment. I was willing to rest the whole affair upon the common English version—the Pedo-baptist version of the Old and New Testaments. I presumed, however, that a majority preferred the present method of proceeding, else I might more amply have shown how easily a few lexicographers of his own school might have been disposed of. The excuse was, as all saw, more ingenious than solid; the responsibility, then, rests upon himself.

I shall, therefore, patiently proceed with the various arguments prepared for the occasion. But for the remainder of this address, I shall glance at some things not yet understood by all present. I desire all to see the precise point in this branch of the evidence: In the first place, then, all the lexicons give dip or immerse as the true, proper, primitive and literal meaning of *baptizo*. They give *wash*, *wet*, *moisten*, &c., as the secondary meanings, or the effects of dipping, immersing, &c. Mr. Carson, who in the judgment of Mr. Rice, is a profound critic of the Baptist school, utterly repudiates the idea of *wash*, *wet* or *moisten*, as meanings of a word that has not in it one drop of moisture, fluid, or liquid of any sort. He disdains such lexicography as makes a word of mere mode, as he calls it, mean two things; and, especially, seeing that any thing being immersed or even sprinkled may be polluted by the action. Now that a word can mean to cleanse and to pollute, to wash and to daub, is with him wholly inadmissible. But I am willing to say that metonymically or tropically, *baptizo* sometimes may mean to wash

7   I

or to cleanse; still as that can be no other than an accidental circumstance, it cannot in strict propriety be called a meaning, and by no means a *proper* meaning of the word. But even were it shown to be a fixed meaning of the word, it being so by a figurative, and not by any proper intrinsic force, another question of paramount importance must be established before that would relieve my friend in the least, viz: Has ever a positive ordinance been enacted by the figurative meaning of a word?

Mr. Carson is, indeed, a profound linguist and an able critic; and was himself once a burning and a shining light in the Presbyterian church. He is also well esteemed by the Edinburgh reviewers. He, however, is not the only eminent critic who argues for but one meaning for *baptizo*. It is becoming fashionable among learned men, true philologists, to give to specific verbs but one meaning, and I shall, at a proper time, produce one of America's most distinguished classic scholars, in concurrence with Mr. Carson and myself, on this subject.

But in reason's name, had the Messiah commanded his apostles to *wash* the nations, while converting them; why did he not take the word *louo*, which all the then living world, Jew and Gentile, would have instantly understood? If he had meant *wash the face*, why not have taken *nipto?* If he had meant to *wet*, why not *brecho*—if to *sprinkle*, why not *raino?* These words exactly indicated those meanings—and our friend, Mr. Rice, says that *baptizo* is a word of diverse senses!!

I have examined, one by one, all the passages in the Old and New Testaments in which the words *nipto, pluno, louo, raino, cheo* occur, and have made some valuable discoveries, as to the singular definiteness and precision of the Greek writers, of which I shall hereafter speak. At present I will only say, that when applied to persons *louo*, washes or bathes the whole body; *nipto*, only the face, hands or feet, and *pluno*, invariably cleanses the garments. They are never, in any case, substituted the one for the other. I ask my friend for a single exception in the Bible. They frequently occur in the same line, on the same occasion, in the same verse, and touching the same person, but are never confounded. If, then, three kinds of washing are defined by these words, in laws canonical, how can it be reconciled to the Divine character, and to that of His moral government, to have chosen for *the one baptism* a generic word, that may mean any thing which any one may please to affix to it? Mr. Rice has repeatedly said that *wash* is a meaning of *baptizo*, and that *wash* is certainly not a word of *mode*. But there is no philology in the observation. The effects of a specific action may be very numerous and diverse—dip, for example, may heat or cool, cleanse or pollute, wash or daub a subject:—follows it, then, that these are all specific words of the same significance, because the meanings or effects of one specific action!

But to return to his favorite *louo, wash*. I think I can satisfy even himself, that as a meaning of *baptizo*, wash is so only as an effect of the action. Allow me to prepare the way by the statement of a philological law.

In a logical definition, *the term and its definition* must be convertible. To speak to every person's apprehension—the definition, when substituted for the term expressed, must always make good sense. Philanthropy is the love of man—the love of man is philanthropy—are convertible propositions. So are—man is a rational animal, and a rational animal is a man. *Louo* and *baptizo* must be convertible terms, if the one fully defines the other. But is that the fact? He may find *baptizo* represented by *wash* in some of our dictionaries, but in not one of them can he show wash represented by *bapto* or *baptizo*. I say *not one;* a clear proof that the one is not the definition of the other. Take, however, *dip, immerse,* and he will find *baptizo* representing them in every Greek and English dictionary, but never *wash* and *baptizo!* To those who comprehend it, this is an unanswerable refutation of the assumption that *baptizo* means to wash, or that wash and *baptizo* are convertible terms. I wish my friend, Mr. Rice, would demonstrate a little more and assert a little less, and make an effort to show how immersing a person in mud could cleanse him; or how immersing a person in pure water could color him; or how immersing one in sand could wet him. And yet immersion means washing, and washing means immersion. *Credat Judæus Appella, non Ego.* Yet in baptizing, Mr. R. neither washes nor immerses.

I am told, however, I am not fully understood on the oft repeated and all-important distinction of generic and specific terms. I shall, therefore, once for all, more fully deliver myself on this essential difference—a point in this discussion of no ordinary importance. Tree, for example, is a generic term, because it comprehends under it many species of trees. We have the species oak, hickory, ash, maple, &c., all included under the term tree. Animal is a genus, under which we have the species man, horse, sheep, dog, &c. Now a specific term includes but one class —and not two under it; whereas a generic term may have two or three hundred species under it. To travel is a generic term; because there are various ways of traveling; such as walking, riding, sailing, &c. Now, the reason why specific terms can have but one meaning is apparent from the fact, that a second meaning would destroy the first. For example—if to walk means both to ride and walk, when told that a person was walking, how could we distinguish the action performed?

It is a common observation, that the genus includes the species, but the species does not include the genus. Thus, the word animal includes all manner of quadrupeds, but the word quadruped does not include all manner of animals. Washing is a generic term, under which sprinkling, pouring, dipping, may be specific terms. Not necessarily, but accidentally they may be specific terms; for it depends upon what is *sprinkled* or *poured* upon, or what a thing is dipped into, whether or not it be washed. But suppose they are all three modes of washing, then they are all specific words. And if the Lord chose any one of them in preference to the others, then that, and that only, will be agreeable to his will.

Now that baptism is a specific action, and can be performed acceptably only in one way, methinks will appear very obvious to all candid persons on a little reflection. Jesus, our Savior, must have had all these three actions of sprinkling, pouring, and immersing in his mind before he ordained any one of them. It is impossible to suppose, that of three, or even two, he would have no preference. No rational being can think of any two ways of effecting any object, without preferring the one to the other. Now, the Lord must have preferred one of these actions to the other, and having a specific object and intention, he had not only the will but the authority to demand and enforce it. Well, now it will, it must be conceded, that he chose one, and but one, out of two or three possible ways of accomplishing that end. Suppose, then, the object to have been washing, of which you may suppose there were three practicable ways. Of these, we are constrained to conclude that he preferred one; and that he would and could specify that one, no one can deny. Follows it not, then, that he has chosen and commanded one specific act to be performed in the most solemn manner? Whosoever, then, has not been a subject of that act, is, of course, unbaptized. I see no way of evading this. Will my friend, Mr. Rice, show some way of escape from these conclusions?

He says that washing is a generic term; then these three, sprinkling, pouring, and dipping are specific, himself being judge. If, then, *dip* is specific in English, it is so in Greek; and if *baptizo* means *dip*, as all the world agrees, then follows it not that *baptizo* is a specific word, and has but one meaning? Had the Messiah, in giving the commission, said, "Travel into all nations and preach the gospel," then, this word being generic, his apostles could have obeyed the precept by walking, riding, sailing, or any other mode of traveling. But had he said, "Walk through all the world," &c., he could not have been obeyed by riding.

He, however, gave them specific directions what they should do in executing his will. He made three words pregnant with their whole duties as his functionaries. They were to disciple, baptize, and teach all nations. He gave then the two generic words *matheteuo* and *didasko*, and the one most *specific*, because it required an outward, formal, and well defined action, by which they were to be publicly recognized and known as his followers. True faith and true obedience will always exact a literal compliance with this divine institution.—[*Time expired.*

Thursday, Nov. 16—11 o'clock, A. M.
[MR. RICE'S FOURTH REPLY.]

MR. PRESIDENT—I am happy to return the compliment of my worthy friend. I conclude that he has slept as soundly as myself. For I must acknowledge, I was somewhat disappointed in the display he made on yesterday. But I am happy to see him coming to the work this morning with so much energy. I desire to get into the heat of the battle—the warmer the better, provided we have the *suaviter in modo, fortiter in re*—soft words and hard arguments.

He is certainly mistaken when he represents us as admitting that immersionists are *in the right*. We do admit the *validity* of baptism by immersion; but we admit it, only because we do not believe the *mode* of administering it *essential* to the ordinance. If he will convince me, that the mode is essential, I will promptly deny the validity of immersion. But when we, for such a reason, admit that baptism by immersion is *valid*, we certainly do not thereby acknowledge that it is performed in the *right* mode. On the contrary, we contend that the scriptural mode of administering baptism is by pouring or sprinkling.

The gentleman tells us, the question is, whether there are *two baptisms;* and he thinks it enough for him to prove that immersion is valid baptism. But if, as he maintains, the precise mode is essential to the ordinance, he will find it difficult, if not impossible, to prove that immersion is baptism. Precisely on this point he will fail. He *assumes* the position, that the mode, or as he expresses it, the *action* is essential to the validity of the ordinance. This is one of the points he came here to prove. He tells us, the phrase *mode of baptism* is a perfect sophism—perfect gibberish; that it is as absurd as to talk of the *mode of sprinkling*. He takes for granted the precise point in debate, viz: that the word *baptizo* signifies simply and only *to immerse*. But that is to be proved; and it is precisely what he cannot prove. We are as much disposed as he, and those who agree with him, to obey the command of our Savior to be baptized; but we differ from them as to the mode of applying the water.

Now if, as the lexicographers declare, *baptizo* means to *wash*, to *cleanse*, and if the Savior used it in this sense, there is no absurdity in speaking of the *mode of baptism*. Are there not different modes of *washing?* May I not wash my hands by pouring water on them, or by dipping them into water? Let the gentleman first prove that the *mode* is essential to the ordinance, and that *baptizo* means only to immerse, and then he may pronounce the mode of baptism a sophism, unmeaning "gibberish."

The gentleman passes over my quotations from the classics, by saying they are *irrelevant;* that *bapto* is not the word in debate. He has, from the commencement of this discussion, admitted that *bapto* and *baptizo* have the same meaning, so far as *mode* is concerned; that these words express the same *specific action*. Now, when I prove by reference to the classics, that *bapto* is not a specific term—that it does not definitely signify to *immerse;* he replies, that *bapto* is not the word in debate! This assuming a position, and then retreating from it, strikes me as rather singular, particularly in so old a warrior! Really I was not prepared to expect this. I supposed that when he put his foot down, he would stand firmly. But when I prove that the dyeing of a garment, by dropping upon it a coloring fluid, is expressed by the word *bapto;* and that the dyeing of the hair or beard, or the smearing of the face, is denoted by the same word; what is his reply? O, says he, *bapto* is not the word in dispute—the references to the classics are all irrelevant !!!

But he cannot so easily escape the difficulty; for both Dr. Gale and Carson, learned and zealous immersionists, maintain that, so far as *mode* is concerned, *bapto* and *baptizo* have precisely the same meaning. Mr. Carson says—"The learned Dr. Gale, in his Reflections on Mr. Wall's History of Infant Baptism, after giving a copious list of quotations, in which *bapto* and *baptizo* are used, says: "I think it is plain, from the instances already mentioned, that they are (*isodunamai*) exactly the same as to signification." "As far," says Carson, "as respects an increase or diminution of the action of the verb, I perfectly agree with the writer. That the one is more or less than the other, as to mode or frequency, is a perfectly groundless conceit;" p. 12. Now, if these learned immersionists are correct, when I prove that *bapto* is employed by the Greeks to express the dropping of a fluid upon a garment, I have also proved that *baptizo*, which has the same meaning, does not definitely signify *to immerse*.

Dr. Gale contended, that in all cases in which *bapto* signifies to *dye*, it retains the idea of dyeing by *dipping;* but Mr. Carson contradicts this position, and maintains, that it means *to dye by sprinkling as literally as by dipping*. Thus these learned immersionists, while they come to the same conclusion, cross each other's path in reaching it. Indeed, Carson charges Gale with giving up the question! So far, however, as relates to an increase or diminution in the *action* of these words, they are perfectly agreed. They agree in affirming that these words express the same *specific action*. What, I ask, was the specific action in the dropping of a coloring fluid upon a garment? or in coloring the beard, or the hair? or in smearing the face with tawny washes? Carson asserts, that *bapto* means literally to dye by sprinkling. Then why may it not mean to *wet* by sprinkling? Where is the rule of language which teaches that a word may express the sprinkling of a colored fluid, and yet be incapable of expressing the sprinkling of a colorless fluid?

But my friend (Mr. C.) was mistaken, when he told you, that in all my examples from the classics, *bapto* and not *baptizo* was the word used. I adduced several examples of the use of *baptizo* where evidently it does not mean to *immerse*. I referred you to the case of the Roman general mentioned by Plutarch, who, when dying of his wounds, *baptized (baptisas)* his hand in blood and wrote on a trophy. I read to you the direction of Hippocrates, that the blister-plaster should be *baptized (baptizein)* with breast-milk and Egyptian ointment; and I asked my friend (Mr. C.) whether he supposed, that the plaster was to be *plunged into* breast-milk and the ointment? Does not the word *baptizo*, in these cases, express a *partial wetting* or *moistening*? I produced an example from Aristotle, in which it is impossible that this word could express a specific action. And I proved, that Dr. Gale, one of the most learned and zealous immersionists, admitted that it does not, perhaps, so necessarily express *the action* of putting under water, as in general a thing's being in that state, no matter how it comes so. But *the action* of putting under is the very thing my friend (Mr. Campbell) is laboring to prove by this word. Now, which of these Doctors shall we believe? [a laugh] No! my friends, the classics do not sustain him.

But what about the lexicons? They, it seems, are all wrong to-day; though yesterday my friend told you, they were the very highest authority! And he mustered so many of them, that they appeared quite formidable enough to terrify a small man like myself. But I took up the very weapons with which he expected to overwhelm me, and turned them against him! I proved that the *old* lexicons, of whose authority he boasted, define the word *baptizo* by the generic terms *lavo, abluo*—to *wash*, to *cleanse*. Mr. Campbell replied, that they gave to *wash*, to *cleanse*, as *figurative* meanings of the word. This allegation was immediately disproved. I proved to you, that the learned Bretschneider defines *baptizo*, "*propr. sepius intingo, sepius lavo*"—*properly, often to dip, often to wash;* and in the New Testament, first, "*lavo,* abluo simpliciter*"—*simply* to *wash*, to *cleanse*. What reply does he make to these facts? Why, he abandons the lexicons, and says, they are wrong; and he abandons the word *bapto*. So far, so good! We are making encouraging progress. Two of the strongest positions are abandoned!

My friend (Mr. C.) has told you, that no lexicographer has defined the word *baptizo*, to *sprinkle*. But some of them have defined *bapto* to sprinkle, as we have seen; and I am prepared to prove, that some eminently learned men, who lived hundreds of years before the oldest lexicons extant were made, did the same thing. They lived and wrote when the Greek was a living language, spoken all around them. Surely they had the means of ascertaining whether *bapto* was ever used by Greek writers and speakers in the sense of sprinkling.

I am not much alarmed at the host of Pedo-baptists with whose concessions my friend (Mr. Campbell) threatens me. I know something of them. It ought to be known, that many Pedo-baptists have been, in their views, decided immersionists. A Pedo-baptist is one who believes in the *baptism of infants*. Yet in the minds of many persons the name of Pedo-baptist is inseparably associated with the idea of sprinkling; and the declarations of those Pedo-baptists who are decidedly favorable to immersion, are often paraded before the public as the concessions of the advocates of pouring and sprinkling, which their candor or their regard for their reputation forced them to make! But I will be with the gentleman when he brings up this formidable host. I have something to say concerning them.

He tells us, that the lexicographers are all Pedo-baptists. I have not taken the trouble to inquire to what denomination they belonged, or whether they were all professors of religion. But if the fact be as he states it, I can account for it only on the supposition, that there has always been more learning amongst the Pedo-baptists, than amongst their opponents. If it were otherwise, surely we should have had *some one* or *two* lexicons by immersionists. It strikes me, however, as very remarkable, that on a subject such as this, the *unlearned* should always have been in the right, and the *learned* always in error! But it matters not to what denomination of christians the lexicographers may have been attached. They had a reputation to sustain; and they risked it upon the correctness of their definitions. Public sentiment has sustained them; and their lexicons have become *standard works*. Their reputation is established; and no criticisms of my worthy friend can bring them down from the eminence on which an enlightened public have placed them.

But I have not relied exclusively upon Pedo-baptist authorities. I have adduced, against my friend, (Mr. Campbell,) the authority of immersionists; and I have shown you how immersionists, in discussing this subject, came into collision with each other.

Mr. Campbell repeats the statement, that he was willing to have risked the decision of this controversy upon the English version of the Bible. Why did he not sooner make this proposition? He first attempts to overwhelm us with the abundance of his Greek, and then gravely says to us, please now to confine yourself to the English version! This is, indeed, a singular manœuvre. I cannot believe, that the gentleman expected me, after his appeal to Greek, to accede to his proposition.

He thinks, Mr. Carson did not intend to admit, that *all* the lexicographers and commentators were against him in his views of the word *baptizo*. Carson's language is as follows:—"My position is, THAT IT [*baptizo*] ALWAYS SIGNIFIES TO DIP; NEVER EXPRESSING ANY THING BUT MODE. Now, *as I have all the lexicographers and commentators against me in this opinion*, it will be necessary to say a word or two with respect to the authority of the lexicons," p. 79. Yes—all the lexicographers, ancient and modern, were against him! I leave this intelligent audience to determine, whether it is not far more probable, that Mr. Carson, a man zealously laboring to establish a favorite tenet, is in error on this subject, than that all the lexicographers and commentators should have failed to learn the meaning of this word. My friend (Mr. C.) threatens to bring forward a *very learned* gentleman, who sustains Mr. Carson in his position. We will attend to him when he is brought up. We have heard the voice of distant thunder before.

He asks, why did not our Savior use the word *louo*, which every body knew meant *to wash?* or *nipto*, which means to wash the hands, &c.? I answer, the reasons are obvious. *Louo* was a word in constant use in reference to *ordinary washings*. *Baptizo* had been long in use among the Jews to express their *religious washings* of all kinds. Our Savior found it thus employed, and therefore selected it to denote the ordinance of baptism. He did not use *nipto*, because the water was to be applied to the *person*. Baptism is not the washing of the hands or feet; it is the consecration of the *person* to the service of God. But I am not concerned to answer such inquiries, though these reasons are abundantly sufficient. Let Mr. Campbell, if he can, disprove the facts I have established concerning the word *baptizo*.

Did I correctly understand the gentleman as saying, that the word *lavo* never expresses the washing of the *whole body?* [Mr. Campbell: No sir—I said *nipto* signifies a partial washing.] Oh, I have not the least use for *nipto*. [a laugh.]

To prove that *baptizo* does not properly mean *to wash*, Mr. Campbell asserts, that the word *louo, to wash,* is never defined by *baptizo;* and, therefore, they are not synonymous. The reason is perfectly obvious. *Baptizo* means more than *louo*. It signifies *to wash, (louo;)* but it has also other meanings. It is, of course, not allowable, in defining a word, to employ another word of more extensive meaning than the one to be defined.

But, says Mr. C., *baptizo* cannot properly mean *to wash;* because it does not necessarily imply the use of *water*—it may be used with equal correctness with reference to any other fluid. But let it be remembered, that the question under discussion is not concerning the use of any particular fluid, but concerning *the mode of applying it*. When the Roman general baptized his hand in his blood, and wrote on a trophy; the hand or writing instrument was not immersed in blood, but only moistened or wetted with it. And, besides, Virgil uses the Latin *lavo*, which certainly does mean *to wash*, to denote smearing with blood.

Mr. Campbell thinks the Savior must have preferred some one mode of baptism. So I think; and I am prepared to show what that mode was. I am not, however, disposed to enter upon the proof just now. I am, at present, clearing away the rubbish; for a large amount of Greek rubbish has been thrown around this subject. When I shall have removed it, I shall be prepared to sprinkle my friend in English [laughter.] I will give him a plain English argument, untrammeled with Greek words; and, I think, I can make it so plain, that all will understand it.

Yet I do not admit the correctness of the logic by which he attempts to prove, that our Savior must have preferred some particular mode. For I have already proved, that in the Levitical law, (Num. xix. 19,) a washing is commanded, and no mode specified. If my friend had lived in the time of Moses, perhaps he would have proved that *rahatz*, the Hebrew word used in this passage, meant *to dip*, though it is uniformly used in the general sense of *washing*. For he would have insisted, that the Lord must have preferred some one mode, and that mode must have been expressed by the word employed!

I have now answered the arguments of my friend as far as he has gone. Perhaps I may as well now produce some further evidence of the incorrectness of his exposition of the words *bapto* and *baptizo*. Before I do this, however, allow me to refer to one or two authors to prove, that the classic Greek is an unsafe guide in expounding the Greek of the New Testament.

I will read from Ernesti, as published with notes by Professor Stuart, p. 14:—

"The question as to the idiom of the New Testament, turns on the use of such words and phrases as designate those objects that the Greeks are accustomed to designate; and the question here must be whether such words in the New Testament are used in the *same* sense which the Greeks attach to them; and whether phrases not only have the same *syntax* as that of the classic Greek, but also the same sense as in the Greek authors: for this is essential to the purity of language," &c.

"The question being thus stated and defined, we deny without hesitation, that the diction of the New Testament is pure Greek, and contend that it is modelled after the Hebrew, not only in single words, phrases, and figures of speech ; but in the general texture of the language. This can be established by clear examples, more numerous than those who agree with us in opinion have supposed," &c.

"It is no small argument for the Hebraistic style of the New Testament, that many parts of it can be more easily translated into Hebrew, than into any other language; as Erasmus Schmidius confesses, though a strenuous defender of the classic purity of the New Testament. Nay, many parts of the New Testament can be explained in no other way than by means of the Hebrew. Moreover, in many passages there would arise an absurd and ridiculous meaning, if they should be interpreted according to a pure Greek idiom ; as appears from the examples produced by Werenfels," &c.—*Ernesti*, pp. 56, 57.

If this author is worthy of credit, they spoke an idiom of the Greek language different from that spoken by the pagan Greeks. Dr. George Campbell, whom my friend considers as a very learned critic, also confirms the testimony of Ernesti. He says:

"But, with the greatest justice it is denominated a peculiar idiom, being not only Hebrew and Chaldaic phrases put in Greek words, but even single Greek words used in senses in which they never occur in the writings of profane authors, and which can be learned only from the extent of signification given to Hebrew or Chaldaic words corresponding to the Greek in its primitive and most ordinary sense."—*Prelim. Dissert.* vol. i. p. 32.

"It is true, that as the New Testament is written in Greek, it must be of consequence that we be able to enter critically into the ordinary import of the words of that tongue, by being familiarized to the genius and character of the people who spake it. But from what has been observed it is evident, that, though in several cases this knowledge may be eminently useful, it will not suffice ; nay, in many cases it will be of little or no significancy. Those words, in particular, which have been in most familiar use with the old interpreters, and have been current in the explanations given in the Hellenistical synagogues and schools, have, with their naturalization among the Israelites, acquired in the Jewish uses, if I may be allowed the expression, "an infusion of the national spirit." "Classical use, both in the Greek and in the Latin, is not only in this study sometimes unavailable, but may even mislead. The sacred use and the classical are often very different." *Ibid.* pp. 57, 58.

Prof. Stuart, also, agrees with Ernesti and Campbell.

If, then, the Jews and inspired writers did not speak and write classic Greek; if they used words in a sense not found in any classic author; how can it be certain, that they attached to the word *baptizo* the same meaning it had among the pagan Greeks? Are we to be told, that it is certain, that words, used by two different nations, speaking different idioms of the same language, of different manners, habits, customs, and religion, have precisely the same meaning! The Greeks, it is admitted, never used the word *baptizo* in a *religious sense:* the Jews never used it in any other than a religious sense. The only way satisfactorily to determine the meaning of the word, is to examine into its use amongst the Jews, as applied to their religious washings, and by the inspired writers, previous to the time and at the time our Savior appropriated it to the ordinance of baptism.

I am prepared to come to "*the Book*," and to prove clearly, as I think, that there is not an instance from Genesis to Revelation, in which *baptizo* can be proved to mean *to immerse.*—[*Time expired.*

Thursday, Nov. 16—11½ *o'clock, A. M.*
[MR. CAMPBELL'S FIFTH ADDRESS.]

MR. PRESIDENT—As we are in quest of more light on this great subject, and as an increase of light is desirable not only for ourselves but also for others, we sincerely wish Mr. Rice all possible success in his endeavors to acquire and communicate it; and certainly he will afford us new light, when he proves his last assumption, that *baptizo* never means to immerse in all the Bible.

In this attempt, he will have to conflict not only with us and all Baptists, but with the most enlightened and distinguished men of his own denomination, and of all the Pedo-baptist world. True, like Mr. Stuart, whom I have allegorically called my American apostle, and to whom I take pleasure in giving rank and honor, though I swear to the words of no master, and, like Calvin, also, while admitting both the true meaning of the word, and the antiquity, and generality, if not universality of the practice, they considering *mode*, as they call it, a thing of no consequence, said as much as they could in favor of sprinkling, but have never presumed to say that *baptizo* did not signify *immerse* in all the Bible. That Mr. Stuart sometimes errs—that he has been guilty of oversights and omissions, and that especially in his article on baptism, I, in common with others, have noted and recorded. But neither he nor any reputable writer has ever gone this far.

Mr. Rice seems not to appreciate nor comprehend the ground on which I stand, both as respects the lexicons and the difference between *bapto* and *baptizo*. He would represent me as retreating from the positions which I assumed on yesterday. Is this candid? Does any gentleman present understand me as taking back a single word or position assumed or uttered on the whole premises before us? I sincerely think, not one. Nor does Mr. Rice really believe it. Does not the gentleman distinguish between accepting a witness as evidence and authority in a question of fact, without endorsing for all his views and opinions. Why should I, sir, object to the lexicons? They are all with me in asserting the true and proper meaning of the words *bapto* and *baptizo*. Not one of them asserts that *to wash, to cleanse*, is either a proper or a primitive meaning of these words. Perceiving, however, as I thought, that the gentleman was seeking to impair the testimony of the classics by aggrandizing that of the lexicons, I desire to give to both, as two separate classes of witnesses, their proper weight and authority.

I adopted the lexicons as my first class of witnesses because, indeed, they are supposed to be the exponents of the meaning of the classics. I did not, as Mr. Rice says, represent them *" as the highest authority."* No sir. In *my first speech* I held them subject to the classics! I regard the authors of classic literature as second in order of *interrogation*, but as *first* in point of *authority. They are both with me.* In other words, I assert what they both depose. I say the dictionaries are sometimes wrong, and that I can prove. So say all philologists and critics of eminence. The lexicons frequently contradict each other on various points. I therefore, in common with all philologists, constitute the classics the supreme court of appeal.

But I have also retracted my position on *bapto!* Does the gentleman intend to annoy me, and retard my progress? I suspect it. What have I retracted? Have I said that it is not the root of *baptizo?* that it does not signify to *dip?* that it is not a *specific* word? that it has more *proper*

meanings than one? or that wherever we find *bap*, there we shall find
dip? No sir. If I had, I should be desirous to hear by what force,
argument, or evidence I did so! Does the gentleman assume that he has
compelled me?

I am glad that in my work on baptism, now partly printed, though not
yet published, I have fully expressed the very sentiments delivered here.
I will frequently cite from it in the discussion. It will protect me from
such imputations, as well as save time and protracted discussion.

To express myself fully and once for all on these words, I repeat, that
bapto, metonymically, means to dye—*baptizo*, never. This is the difference asserted in my first speech. The reason for this difference, as it
appears to me, I have given. It is expressed in the form of the two
words—the former indicates such an immersion as, from *its continuance*
under water or any fluid, may give color; the latter indicates rapidity of
action, and, therefore, produces not the effect of dyeing. This is my own
criticism, be it *true* or *false*. I will hereafter give specifications. But
nothing depends upon it here. The classics never give *dye* or *color* to
baptizo. The dictionaries sometimes do. Again, *bapto* is never used
in any case connected with christian baptism! There is some reason for
this. There is then a difference of some sort between the words—and
this difference occasions a considerable variety of figurative use. Hence
all figures of color came from *bapto;* generally those of cleansing from
baptizo. But, sir, I do differ from Mr. Carson in some of his remarks on
bapto. With him, and Dr. Gale, and with me also, it is a *specific* word—
and as such, with me and Dr. Gale, it can have but one proper meaning.
I trust my friend, Mr. R., will not again cause me to consume so much
of my time in replying to assertions made by him without any authority
whatever. I will not soon again reply to any such unfair imputations—a
simple denial is all the honor I shall confer on them.

As to Gale and Carson crossing each other's path, I think the sequel
will show that they are not the only eminent men in the world that have
crossed each other's path, and sometimes their own. This is a common
sin amongst the most eminent Pedo-baptists. It comes with an exceedingly ill grace, from Mr. Rice, to accuse Baptists of this sin, in arriving
at diverse conclusions, sometimes from the same, and sometimes from different premises. There are not two respectable writers on infant baptism, or affusion, that agree either in the topics of *debate*, of argument, or
in the mode of reasoning from them. I am acquainted, more or less, perhaps, with some fifty writers on infant sprinkling, and at present I do
not know any two of them that agree more fully than Drs. Gale and Carson. And notwithstanding the hundreds of tracts, and the scores of volumes, and the countless hosts of pleaders for infant *rantism*, or *baptism*,
that have written on the subject, every new year gives us a new book on
the subject. Taylor's new work, a part of which I thoroughly refuted
in my McCalla debate, just came to my hand a few days ago, fresh from
the New York press—a new work and a new tract unoccupied by any
previous writer. It is indeed a whimsical affair, and looks as if the
cause, or the author, was in a state of dotage.

But Mr. Rice, with dauntless boldness, reasserts that *baptizo* is not a
specific word, that it is even more general than *louo*, an assertion never
before made, and quotes the classics to prove that it does even signify to
dip, among them!! He adduces examples, the strongest of which, in
appearance, is Plutarch's Roman general, who, when dying of his

wounds, dipped his hand or finger in his blood and wrote on a trophy, &c., and something, I know not what, from Hippocrates. If then I dispose of this, the strongest case in appearance, I may be presumed to have answered all the subalterns. I will then take the general's case—and in it, despatch them all. I shall dispose of them by one *canon* of criticism, a principle universally conceded by all critics—viz: certain words of current and accommodated use, are often employed without their regimen—(i. e. the word they govern;) in all such cases the whole object on which they terminate is understood; when any special object is denoted, it is expressed: for example—we say a person *bathed*, without adding the word, *himself;* but if it is not taken in its whole objective sense, the limitation is defined: for example, he *bathed* his feet, his head, &c. Every one comprehends this. So in the case cited. The general dipped, not himself, but his hand or finger in blood, and wrote, &c. Can the gentleman have forgotten this!

He is refuting himself in saying that *baptizo* is not specific. He has said that dip is a specific word, and he admits that *baptizo* is its Greek representative. Why then make the same action specific in one language and general in another!

But to make an end of all his special pleading—for various and numerous meanings and acceptations of words—I shall at once summon a few umpires, judges of the highest legal, literary, and theological eminence, and leave them in the hands of my opponent and this community. I have only to shew that *baptizo, generally,* not *universally*, means to dip, according to them, to gain my cause before this tribunal.

"It is with the proper and unfigurative, and not with the fanciful and rhetorical meaning of words, we have to do in all positive institutions. Sir William Blackstone has truly said, (and who is higher authority than he?) —'The words of a law are generally to be understood in their USUAL AND MOST KNOWN SIGNIFICATION ; not so much regarding the propriety of grammar, as their *general* and *popular* use: but when words bear either none or a very absurd signification, if literally understood, we must a little deviate from the received sense of them.'* Bishop Taylor has also well said, 'In all things where the precept is given in the proper style of laws, he that takes the first sense is the likeliest to be well guided. In the interpretation of the laws of Christ the strict sense is to be followed.' Dr. Jonathan Edwards, the greatest of American Presbyterian theologians, has truly said, 'In words capable of two senses, the natural and proper is the primary; and therefore *ought*, in the first place, and chiefly to be regarded.'

A greater still, Vitringa, has said, 'This is accounted by all a constant and undoubted rule of approved interpretation, that the ordinary and most usual signification of words must not be deserted except for sufficient reasons.' To similar effect declare Sherlock, Waterland, Owen, and Dr. Cumming, as quoted in Booth's Defence of his Pedo-baptism Examined, vol. iii., London, 1792, pp. 253—256.

Before dismissing this subject we must yet hear Turretine, the systematic standard theologian of the orthodox schools of Presbyterianism. He has stood on my shelf for more than thirty years. His words fairly translated are, 'It is acknowledged by all that we should never depart from the proper and native signification of words, except for the weightiest and most urgent reasons.'† We shall conclude with Dr. Benson, another favorite :— 'What can be more absurd than to imagine that the doctrines or rules of practice which relate to men's everlasting salvation, should be delivered in

---

* Com. vol. i. sect. 2.   † De Satisfactione Christi, part 1, sect 23.

such ambiguous terms as to be capable of many meanings.' Well does the English Pirie say, ' Law requires words and phrases of the most ascertained and unequivocal sense.'

If seven such names as here given are not valid authority on the proper interpretation of laws and positive institutions, to whom shall we hearken? Their testimony being admitted, and the plain and unanimous testimony of the lexicographical jury above given, on the proper, current, and popular use and meaning of *baptizo*, can any one show reason why we should not, a second time, regard my first proposition as fully proved? All the dictionaries give *dip* or *immerse* as the proper, common, and current use of *baptizo*, and all our quotations from numerous classic authors, as well as the canonical Greek Scriptures of the Old Testament, sustain them in so doing. And that the proper, common, and current use of words is to be always preferred and adopted in the interpretation of laws and ordinances, is attested by a host of witnesses of the highest authority, and sustained by Horne and Ernesti in their canons of interpretation. I repeat—must we not then conclude that immersion, and immersion only, is christian baptism, according to the mind and will of our Lawgiver and Judge?"

Before stating my fourth argument, I must anticipate, that as Mr. R. has not yet given any special preference to any "*mode* of baptism," immersion with him being valid only because water is *applied*, it is presumed *sprinkling* and *pouring* may be valid for the same reason. Still as *wash* is generic, yet included in *dip*, (*baptizo* being with him *generic*, and *louo* specific!!) we are not certain, in his particular case, which he may choose. We think it likely he will go for the Illinois, (Dr. Beecher's) theory of purification. He, benevolent man, makes us all right, Baptists, Presbyterians, &c. though we seem ungrateful to him, and contend that there cannot be two right ways of obeying a positive command. I will request, then, Mr. Rice to shew how the precept of Christ is to be obeyed—if he meant and said wash the nations into the name—purify them into the name of the Father, &c. I opine such a precept could not be obeyed without a special form accompanying.

Again, as there are but three kinds of uncleanness, from which any one can be purified—*physical, legal, moral*—by what symbolic or figurative term, shall purification from these be properly indicated? Did any one ever wash away physical impurity by sprinkling or merely wetting the unclean part? Has legal or ceremonial uncleanness ever been removed in this way? *Never*, I say again, NEVER. *Since time began its career, no Divine Lawgiver, Jewish or Christian, ever commanded any priest, Levite, or minister to cleanse, wash, or purify any one from any sort of impurity by pouring or sprinkling water upon him!* From which fact I yet intend to deduce an argument, in this discussion, and therefore wish Mr. R. to be prepared for it by opposing facts and documents. It may, indeed, be the first time this fact has been publicly announced in discussion; therefore I desire to have it thoroughly tested. If true, I need not say that it alone nullifies the logic of all the sprinklers, pourers, and wetters of faces in Christendom.

I am now prepared to state my fourth argument. My second argument, deduced from all authoritative lexicons down to the present century, is, that they all, without one single exception, give dip, immerse, sink or plunge, synonymously expressive of the true, proper, and primary signification of *baptizo*; not one of them giving sprinkle or pour as a meaning of it or any of its family.

My third argument has been drawn from the classic use of the word. They sustain the lexicons except in one point. They never give to

K

baptizo the sense of dyeing, &c. They never use it either to represent the actions of sprinkling or pouring. Every attempt to make out, by construction, a single instance of this sort, has been a total failure.

IV. ARGUMENT. My fourth argument is deduced from the ancient, and especially from the modern versions of the New Testament. Before stating it, I must premise a few words—Mr. Rice alledges a difference between sacred and classic use, to which I have paid little attention. Under this argument it is fully met and refuted by the highest authority. In some instances there is a difference in idiom, in particular phrases, and words. But such differences never occur in words indicating common physical actions. There may be many good reasons why the words *flesh, faith, law,* &c., should differ in Jewish and Gentile style; but none why to *walk,* to *eat,* to *drink,* to *dip,* to *pour,* to *sprinkle,* &c., should differ. I accord with all that you have heard from Ernesti and Campbell—Campbell's version, and all the versions made by the canons of Horne. Ernesti and Campbell thoroughly refute the imputation, that any one of them ever regarded *baptizo* as a word of private interpretation.

These translators well understood all these matters; therefore their practice is worth many a splendid controversial theory. I have studied the difference between sacred and classic usage, under these great masters, and I can solemnly say, that in the words at issue here, the difference between them is just nothing at all; save that *baptisma,* in the sacred Scriptures, always represents immersion into the Lord.

We are making a book for the illumination of a portion of the community; and, consequently, what I say here, is said very solemnly and publicly, and under the conviction of all my responsibility. I affirm, that so far as the ancient versions are understood by me, through the medium of learned controversy on the question, and so far as I have had time and leisure to examine the moderns, especially those in our mother tongue, they all agree on this general predicate. None of them has ever translated *baptizo* by the word sprinkle, pour, or purify. We have here a critical exhibit of some fifty of them on this very word; and, if we may believe the greatest masters in these ancient languages and criticisms, they have generally selected a word that intimates immersion; or, if they have not, they certainly either have adopted the Greek or Latin names, or never used a word intimating the idea of sprinkling or pouring. Of these the oldest is the Peshito Syriac version, supposed to have been completed early in the second century, if not at the close of the first. Dr. Henderson, a learned Pedo-baptist, gives it as his opinion, that when the Lord gave the commission to baptize, being himself a Syro-Chaldæic, he used the word *amad.* But we shall first give an exhibit of them all.

VERSION.	DATE.	WORD EMPLOYED.	MEANING.
SYRIAC:			
Peshito,	2d cent.	*amad.*	*immerse.*
Philoxenian,	6th cent.	*amad.*	*immerse.*
ARABIC:			
Polyglott,	7th cent.	*amada* 47 times.	*immerse.*
Propaganda,	1671	*amada*	*immerse.*
Sabat,	1816	*amada.*	*immerse.*
PERSIC;	8th cent.	*shustan & shuyidan.*	*wash.*
ETHIOPIC:	4th cent.	*shustan.*	*immerse.*
Amharic,	1822	*shustan.*	*immerse.*
EGYPTIAN.			
Coptic,	3d cent.	*tamaka.*	{ *immerse* { *plunge.*

VERSION.	DATE.	WORD EMPLOYED.	MEANING.
Sahidic,	2d cent.	} baptizo.	immerse.
Basmuric,	3d cent.		
ARMENIAN :	5th cent.	mogridil.	immerse.
SLAVONIC :	9th cent.	krestiti.	cross *
Russian,	1519		
Polish,	1585		
Bohemian,	1593		
Lithuanian,	1660	} same root.	"
Livonian or Lettish,	1685		
Dorpat Esthonian, &c. &c.	1727		
GOTHIC :	4th cent.	daupjan.	dip.
German,	1522	taufen,	dip.
Danish,	1524	dobe.	dip.
Sweedish,	1534	dopa.	dip.
Dutch, &c. &c.	1560	doopen.	dip.
Icelandic,	1584	skira.	cleanse.
ANGLO-SAXON :	8th cent.	dyppan, fullian,	{ dip, cleanse.
LATIN :			
Of the early Fathers,	8th cent.	tingo.	immerse.
Ante-Hieronymian,	3d cent.	baptizo.	
Vulgate,	4th cent.	baptizo.	
French,	1535	baptiser.	
Spanish,	1556	baptizar.	
Italian, &c. &c.	1562	bapttezzare.	
English : Wicklif,	1380	wash, christen, baptize.	
Tindal,	1526	baptize.	
Welsh,	1567	bedyddio.	bathe.
Irish,	1602	baisdim.	
Gaelic,	1650	baisdeam.	

Here, then, we have sixteen ancient versions, six of them in the 2d and 3d centuries, and ten of them completed before the close of the 9th, indicative of immersion—one, from the sign made in baptism by the Romanists, is rendered *cross*. From the 9th century we have twenty more, all indicative of the same fact. In all these we have thirty-six foreign, and many of them ancient versions, in proof of our first proposition.

In all these it is not once rendered by the word *sprinkle* or *pour*. The investigation of Mr. Gotch goes to show, moreover, that the notion of either transferring the original word into translations, or of manufacturing new words, has no countenance from these thirty-six ancient and modern versions. He very justly observes :

" Our investigation, then, shows that it has not been the practice of translators, until in quite recent times, to adopt the plan of 'transference' in respect to the word *baptizo*. The word has been translated, in most instances, by a term strictly native; or where the term has been derived from the Greek, it appears to have become naturalized in the respective languages before the translation was made. There is no instance, until of late years, in which it can be shown that the translators *made* the word ; and it well deserves the consideration of all who are engaged in translating, or disseminating translations of the word of God, how far such a plan is justifiable.

" It may, indeed, be said, that though the word *baptizo* has not been thus transferred, other words have ; and that thereby the *principle* of transference is countenanced by former translators. It is certain that such words as proper names, and designations of things which are not known, and

---

* The Slavonians have adopted the word *Cross*, to designate the ordinance of baptism, from the fact, that whenever they receive baptism they always cross themselves, &c.

therefore have no word by which they can be expressed, must be so rendered: but what proof is there of translators, in general, carrying transference further than this? Let it be remembered, that the Greek language was closely united to the Latin, to which the appeal has been frequently made; and that on this account Greek words were continually naturalized in it. Such words we may expect to meet with; but to prove that translators *transferred* words in the modern sense of the term, it must be shown that words, the meaning of which might have been expressed in the language, were given, not only by terms derived from the Greek, but without meaning—being made for the occasion, and purposely left without definition. It will not surely be said that the word *baptizo* has no meaning —that a command involving, as most christians believe, a thing to be done by or for every disciple, yet conveys no definite idea of what is to be done. We are not now inquiring what that meaning is; every one who attempts to translate the word of God, is bound to judge for himself on that point. Let him so judge, and give the result of his judgment."

To all which we cheerfully assent.

Now, inasmuch as some branch of this family of words occurs one hundred and twenty times in the New Testament, is it not an overwhelming argument against sprinkling and pouring, that in no one instance any of these thirty-six versions should ever have translated any one of them by the words sprinkle or pour, if that was at all the sense of the original?—[*Time expired.*]

Thursday, Nov. 16—12 *o'clock.*
[MR. RICE'S FIFTH REPLY.]

Mr. President—My worthy friend seems disposed to keep us in terror of that host of Pedo-baptists, whose concessions he threatens to bring forward. I know them, and, therefore, am not at all alarmed. When he produces them they will be attended to. In the meantime I feel quite at ease. If he can find any two of them who sustain the doctrine for which he is contending, I will acknowledge that I had not heard of them. But I pledge myself to give him the concessions of immersionists in return—of *Greek* immersionists, who well understood the language.

The gentleman says, he has not taken back one single assertion he has made. This I am not so well able to understand. In the early part of this discussion he told us, that specific words, retaining the leading syllable, never lose their original meaning; that whenever you find *bap*, (as in *bapto*,) you find the action of *dipping*. I produced several examples from the classics, in which *bapto* is used, where, in the nature of the case, there could be no dipping. What was his reply? These examples he said, were *irrelevant*, because *bapto* is not the word in debate. This appeared to me very much like giving up the argument from *bapto*. Yet he says he has not changed his ground.

He, at first, informed us, that the *lexicons* were the highest authority by which the meaning of the words in controversy could be determined; and now he is going to prove that they are all wrong! Well, if he should prove that all the lexicographers have erred, he will do a great work! I still believe they have defined the words correctly; and I have proved, not only by the modern lexicons, but by the most ancient, of whose authority my friend spoke so highly, that *baptizo* signifies to *wash, cleanse,* as well as to *sink, plunge,* &c.

But if Mr. C. has not given up the argument from the word *bapto,* why has he not attempted to reply to the argument against his position, founded on several quotations from the classics? "When the coloring fluid drops upon the garments, (*baptetai*) they are dyed." Here is the *bap,* but where is the *dip?* Will my friend say, when the fluid drops upon the garments, they are immersed? Where was the immersion when the Indians dyed their beards?

Mr. Campbell thinks the termination *zo*, in the word *baptizo*, expresses *the rapidity* of the action; and he supposes that the Savior selected this word, in preference to *bapto*, for that particular reason; that *bapto* may signify *sinking to the bottom*, and hence *baptizo*, expressing the idea of *raising out* of the water, was preferred. But Carson admits, that *baptizo* does not express the raising of the thing immersed out of the water. "The word" says he, "has no reference to what follows the immersion; and whether the thing immersed lies at the bottom, or is taken up, cannot be learned from the word, but from the connection and circumstances," p. 91. That it *is* constantly used by the classics in the sense of sinking to the bottom, I am prepared to prove. I will give a few examples:

Diodorus Siculus, speaking of the sinking of animals in water, says: "When the water overflows, many of the land animals, (*baptizomena*) *sunk* in the river, perish."

Strabo, speaking of the lake near Agrigentum, says: "Things which otherwise will not swim, do not *sink* (*baptizesthai*) in the water of the lake, but float like wood." Again, speaking of the lake Sirbon, he says: "If a man goes into it, he cannot *sink* (*baptizesthai*,) but is forcibly kept above." I might quote many other examples, but really I deem it unnecessary. Josephus, who sought to imitate the classic Greek, uses the word repeatedly to signify the sinking of ships, the drowning of persons, &c.

It is, then, certain that *baptizo* is constantly used by the classics in the sense of *sinking*—that this, in the examples supposed to favor immersion, is its common meaning. It is not true, therefore, that the Savior selected this word, because it expressed putting in and taking out of the water quickly; for it does not at all express the action of raising out of the water. Yet this is as essential to baptism by immersion as the putting under—the latter being supposed to represent the burial of Christ, and the former, his resurrection.

The gentleman tells us, that according to an established rule of language, the definition, if substituted for the word defined, will make good sense. Let us apply this rule, substituting the word *sink*, the common classical meaning, for the word *baptizo*. "John did *sink* in the wilderness, and preach the *sinking* of repentance." "He that believeth and is *sunk*, shall be saved." Or, as our friends say, *baptizo* means to *plunge*, perhaps Mr. C. would prefer that word. "John did *plunge* in the wilderness, and preach the *plunging* of repentance." "He that believeth and is *plunged*, shall be saved." You see, my friends, the substitution of these words for *baptizo* makes the Scriptures speak nonsense. So, according to my friend's own rule, it is impossible that *baptizo*, as used to denote christian baptism, can mean to *sink* or *plunge*. Yet these are some of its classical meanings. His own rule, therefore, destroys his argument. *Baptizo*, as used in the Bible, is a *generic term;* and it will not answer to subtitute a specific term in its place.

There is no great difference, my friend would have us believe, between the baptism of the Roman general's hand in order to write on a trophy, and immersion. Well, if I, in baptizing an individual, come as near immersing him as the general did immersing his hand in his blood; will Mr. Campbell consider him *baptized?* He will not; and yet he has brought forward this very example to prove, that *baptizo* always means to immerse!

8   K 2

He did not, however, attempt to immerse the blister-plaster in breast-milk and Egyptian ointment.   And it was well he did not; for all the Doctors would have risen up against him.   [A laugh.]

The gentleman read Blackstone to prove, that the "usual and most known signification" of words should be preferred.   To this rule I by no means object; but I contend, that the usual and most known meaning of *baptizo*, as used among the Jews in relation to their religious rites, is, *to wash, to cleanse*.   But we are told, that all the lexicographers prefer *immerse*, as the primary and literal meaning.   Now let me turn your attention to Robinson.   He gives its general meaning to *immerse, sink*, spoken of ships, galleys, &c.; but the *very first* meaning he gives it in the New Testament, is *to wash, to cleanse by washing*.   Bretschneider gives the general meaning—"sepius intingo, sepius lavo"—*often to dip, often to wash;* and the *first* meaning he gives it as used in the New Testament, is "lavo, abluo simpliciter"—*simply to wash, to cleanse*.   Greenfield defines it in the same way.   Now my friend says, *all* the lexicographers prefer *immerse* as the primary meaning of this word.   Will he please to produce *one* who gives *immerse* as its primary meaning, as it was used by the Jews, or as it is used in the Bible?   I am for taking the primary and literal meaning of the word, as employed by the people amongst whom and for whom the ordinance was instituted, not the common meaning as used by another people, speaking a different idiom, in relation to entirely different subjects.   And in this I am sustained by all the best critics.

There is no rule which requires us to take the *original* meaning of a word in preference to every other.   *Etymology*, as Ernesti says, is an uncertain guide.   Language is perpetually changing, and words are constantly acquiring new meanings.   I might admit, that the *original* meaning of *baptizo* was to *immerse*, and then prove, that before the time when it was applied by our Savior to the ordinance of baptism, it had amongst the Jews acquired a different meaning.   The word *prevent*, as I have before remarked, originally meant to *come before;* but now it means *to hinder*.   It is the meaning in common use at the time when the ordinance was appointed—as Blackstone says, "the *general* and *popular* use"—that is to be taken in preference to any other.   I perfectly agree, therefore, with Blackstone, Vitringa and Turretin, as quoted by my friend (Mr. C.)

We come now to the *translators*, ancient and modern.   The gentleman has greatly magnified their authority.   I hope he will not hereafter fall out with them.   They, he tells us, knew the difference between the Jewish and classic usage.   I am happy to see the translations brought forward; for I am prepared to prove, that they, (at least the great majority of them) did not translate the word *baptizo*, to immerse.   Possibly some two or three may have done so; but certainly the most ancient and valuable, as well as the most respectable of modern date, did not.   I have examined a goodly number of these translations; and I am prepared to prove what I affirm.

I will begin with the old *Peshito Syriac*, the oldest and one of the best translations in the world.   The gentleman asserts, and has repeatedly published, that no translator, ancient or modern, ever translated *baptizo*, or any of that family of words, by the word *sprinkle*.   This I deny, and am prepared to disprove.

By the way, the gentleman told you, that I would very probably give you Dr. Beecher's dissertation on *purification*.   Unfortunately I have never read it. I sent for the work, but failed to procure it; so I must forego the pleasure of giving you Beecher's dissertation.

But let us briefly examine into the truth of this bold assertion of my friend. He says, no translator, ancient or modern, ever rendered *baptizo* or any of that family, by the word *sprinkle*. Now, the old Peshito Syriac, of which he has spoken so favorably, has translated *bapto* to *sprinkle*. Here is the book itself: it looks old and venerable. I will give the translation by Schaaf and Leusden, whose edition I have, as the audience could not understand the Syriac. Rev. xix. 13. "Et amictus veste quæ *aspersa* (Greek, *bebammenon*) sanguine." *And he was clothed with a garment* SPRINKLED *with blood*. The Vulgate, translated by Jerom, who, I presume, immersed thrice in baptizing, translates the passage in the same manner: "Et vestitus erat veste aspersa sanguine. He was clothed with a vesture sprinkled with blood." The passage, doubtless, has reference to the 63d chapter of Isaiah's prophecy, in which Christ is represented going forth as a mighty Conqueror against his enemies. "For," says he, "I will tread them in mine anger, and trample them in my fury; and their blood shall be *sprinkled* upon my garments, and I will stain all my raiment," v. 3. Here we have two of the oldest and most valuable translations in the world translating the word *bapto* just as my friend (Mr. C.) asserts that no one ever did translate it.

Origen, too, the most learned of the Greek fathers, was unwise enough to fall into the same error, if indeed it be an error. He, as Dr. Gale in his Reflections on Wall's History of Infant Baptism informs us, in quoting the passage in Rev. xix. 13, almost verbatim, puts *rantizo* for *bapto*. How ignorant of the Greek language Origen must have been, if the views of Mr. Campbell are correct! From the fact that these old and valuable versions translate *bapto* to *sprinkle*, in this passage, and from the fact that Origen, giving the substance of the passage, substitutes *rantizo* for *bapto*, Dr. Gale concludes, that there must have been a different reading, and that those men had a copy of the New Testament having *rantizo* instead of *bapto*. Mr. Carson, however, differs from him decidedly on this subject. After stating Dr. Gale's reasons for supposing there was a different reading, he remarks—"These reasons, however, do not in the least bring the common reading into suspicion in my mind; *and I never will adopt a reading to serve a purpose*. [This is a noble resolution.] Misapprehension of the meaning of the passage, it is much more likely, has substituted *errantismen*on for *bebammenon*," p. 37. So it would seem, according to Mr. Carson, Origen, the learned Greek father, did not understand his vernacular tongue! And those learned translators, (who did the very thing my friend said, no one ever did,) could not ascertain the meaning of the word *bapto*, though the Greek was then a living language, spoken all around them!!! Unless we can believe, that they were ignorant of the meaning of *bapto*, we are obliged to believe, that in their day it was used in the sense of *sprinkling*. It has not been my object to prove, that *bapto* and *baptizo* definitely express the idea of sprinkling or pouring. I maintain, that, as used in the Bible and in the religious writings of the Jews, it expresses the *thing done*—the application of water to a subject; but the connection and circumstances must determine the precise *mode* of doing it, whether by pouring, sprinkling or dipping.

I am prepared to meet my friend on the translations, and to prove, that they are by no means favorable to the doctrine for which he is contending.

I have said as much as I intended in reply to his argument. I will now turn your attention to the meaning of *bapto* and *baptizo*, as they are used in the Bible, and in the religious writings of the Jews.

Bapto, as used in the Bible, sometimes expresses a *partial dipping* or *wetting*, as in Leviticus xiv. 6, 7, where the priest was directed to kill a bird, and then take a living bird, and cedar-wood, and scarlet, and hysop, and *dip* them in the blood of the bird that was killed over running water. *Bapto* is here used; and every one knows, that it was impossible to *immerse* these things into the blood of one bird. It evidently here signifies a partial dipping or wetting. Indeed, in all the instances in which *bapto* occurs in the Bible, there are not more than four or five where it expresses an immersion! It generally expresses a partial dipping, a wetting or smearing.

In Exod. xii. 22, it signifies *wetting* or *smearing*—"And ye shall take a bunch of hysop, and dip it in the blood that is in the basin, and strike the lintel and the two side posts, with the blood that is in the basin." This may answer as a specimen. I will produce other passages, if necessary. In this passage the Septuagint has the expression *bapscte apo*—ye shall *dip from*, or, more properly, *wet by means* of the blood. A similar expression occurs in Lev. xiv. 17: "And the priest shall dip his finger in some of the blood, and sprinkle it seven times before the Lord." And in verse 16, "The priest shall dip his right finger in the oil that is in his left hand," &c. In both these passages the expression is *bapsei apo*—he shall *dip from*. Does my friend immerse *from* the water? The meaning of the word here evidently is, *to wet* or *smear* by means of the fluid. If a dipping or immersion had been intended, the writer would have used the preposition *eis*—into, instead of *apo*, from.

Bapto signifies simply *to wet* or *bedew*, as is evident from Dan. iv. 33: "The same hour was the thing fulfilled upon Nebuchadnezzar: and he was driven from men and did eat grass as oxen, and his body was wet (*ebaphe*) with the dew of heaven." Precisely the same expression occurs in the following chapter, verse 21. Now every body knows how this baptism was performed. His body was *wet from (ebaphe apo)* the dew. Or will my friend say, his body was *immersed from* dew?! Dr. Gale attempted to escape the difficulty by saying, Nebuchadnezzar *was as wet as if he had been immersed*. Dr. Cox, another learned immersionist, took the same ground. But Mr. Carson charges them both with having given up the question. And he insists, that it does express *mode* in this passage, and ought to have been translated *immersed!* He makes it a *figurative* immersion! Our immersionist friends have a great deal of ingenuity. If they cannot get Nebuchadnezzar immersed, they will have him as wet as if he had been immersed. Or if they cannot have him immersed *literally*, they will immerse him *figuratively!* They are resolved on having him immersed in some way. My friend, (Mr. C.) in his debate with Mr. McCalla, maintained that Nebuchadnezzar was *overwhelmed* in dew! This, one might be tempted to think, is something new under the sun. A man *overwhelmed in dew!!!*

I have already turned your attention to Rev. xix. 13, where *bapto* has been translated by the word sprinkle. But I omitted to state one important fact, viz: that not only the Syriac and Latin Vulgate, but the Ethiopic, one of the most ancient and valuable versions, as Gale informs us, translates *bapto*, in this passage, to *sprinkle*. So carefully has my friend (Mr. C.) examined the old translations on this point!—(*Time expired*

Thursday, Nov. 16—12½ *o'clock, P. M.*

[MR. CAMPBELL'S SIXTH ADDRESS.]

MR. PRESIDENT—Were the positiveness of the gentleman's assertions any assurance, either of their strength or their verity, we might well fear for the issue of our cause. But we have learned to estimate their strength in the inverse ratio of the confidence with which they are uttered. Greater and more numerous aberrations from propriety, and more palpable perversion of fact and argument within one half hour, have seldom fallen under my observation than during the last. If, however, my fellow-citizens, you will patiently lend me your ears, I will endeavor to set these matters before you in their proper light.

I do not ascribe to my worthy friend, sinister motives, willful aberrations, or any fixedness of purpose to pervert the truth. I presume, however, I may say of him, as professor Stuart once said of the famous Beza, " that he was so mad against the Anabaptists, that it drove him out of his reason." Few of us, however, on this side of the ocean can see the force of the professor's remark if we have had nothing before us but Beza's criticisms on *baptizo.* I shall place this man Beza in contrast with my friend, by quoting one passage from his comment on Mark vii. 4 :

" Christ commanded us to be baptized, by which word, IT IS CERTAIN *immersion* is signified. *Baptizesthai,* in this place, is more than *niptein;* because *that* seems to respect the whole body, *this* only the hands. Nor does *baptizein* signify to *wash,* except by consequence: for it properly signifies to immerse for the sake of dyeing. To be baptized in water signifies no other than to be immersed in water, which is the external ceremony of baptism. *Baptizo* differs from the verb *dunai,* which signifies to plunge in the deep, and to drown."

So thought, and so wrote, next to Calvin, the strongest Presbyterian of that age, the translator of the New Testament from Greek to Latin ! But he was *wrong,* because I agree with him in every word of the above, and because he refutes every main position of his brother Rice on this occasion, and especially some of his recent remarks. Whether he or Mr. Rice is most worthy of your confidence judge, my fellow-citizens, for yourselves.

But to return with the gentleman to *bapto* again. With Beza, I say it means to dye or to wash *by consequence,* not *vi termini,* not by the force of the word. It is then a metonymy—the name of the effect produced. This, then, explodes the whole speech, so far as the gentleman will have Hippocrates, whom he quotes from Carson, representing garments as dyed by dropping the coloring matter upon them. Now the question, the plain, common sense, and critical question, too, is, does the dying relate to the dropping of the color, or to the garment when colored. The original phrase is—*epeidan epistaxee epi ta himatia baptetai.* And when the coloring matter has dropped upon the garment *it* (the garment) is colored. In the passive voice, the effect of an action, and not the mode of an action, is generally expressed. Nothing is more evident, then, than that the coloring has respect, not to the process, but to the effect of it. Nearchus' narrative of the Indians dyeing their beards, is also an exemplification of the same mode of speech. Thus, Nebuchadnezzar was wet with dew ; not by the manner of its falling, but in the effect. Thus, as Mr. Carson says, a man gets soaked and dipped, in common parlance, under a heavy shower.

Nay, the poets go farther. Milton sings of Raphael's wings as exhibiting " colors dipped in heaven." Was there any sprinkling, pouring, or dipping in that figure ? I have already sufficiently exposed the frailty of that logic which would impress upon you the mode, or the process, for the effect of it—the thing done. Daniel, as well as the poets, and all the Jewish prophets, delight in poetic imagery. To be immersed in dew, to paint the flowers, to have colors dipped in heaven, or painted birds or clouds baptized in gold, are all of the same poetic license. In such beautiful allusions, never the process, or modus operandi, but the thing itself is described.

The gentleman sought to be witty, and to provoke your smiles in his eloquent dissertation upon *sinking*. One thing you all must have observed, the sense is good, although he would make you smile at his pronunciation and action. They were, indeed, ridiculous. This, however, is both a grave and solemn subject, and demands of me, at least, both dignity and gravity. While in the amplitude of my generosity, I am willing to say, that *baptizo* may be translated *sink*, as well as *dip*, or *plunge*, or *immerse;* still *sink* is not its strictly proper meaning, as all the learned, with Beza, admit. But it does not at all mean *to sink to the bottom!*

It may, indeed, so happen, that in immersing persons, they sometimes go to the bottom. That, however, is an accident, for which the word *baptizo* is never chargeable—or should a ship at sea be ingulfed, and go to the bottom, *baptizo* is not blamed for it. Mr. Rice says this is a very sinking subject; if so, the fault is his, not that of the question in debate. The consequences of any act are not always denominated by the same word—nor are the different words declarative of the effects of any specific action, equivalent to each other. Mr. Rice will have them synonymous. He will have dipping, pouring, and the effect produced, equivalents. Should a person be wholly covered with any substance that may be sprinkled or poured upon him, then sprinkling and covering are the same actions.

Take another exposition of the fallacy of his mode of expounding terms; in the word killed—this term indicates an *effect*. The modes of killing a person are innumerable—he may be shot, stabbed, poisoned, hung, drowned, &c., &c. Now, is the word kill or killed synonymous with all these !! Is to shoot, or to kill, or to stab, synonymous words !! It is preposterous to suppose that a word must be responsible for all the various applications of it. Then dipping must be responsible for the most contradictory results. We heat water and cool iron by dipping a heated bar into it. Is dipping equivalent to both cooling and heating !!

But my friend, Mr. Rice, will now have it that the dictionaries give *wash* as the first meaning of *baptizo*. He *cannot show one!* I say, again, *he cannot show one* that does so. He may, under some particular application of the word, find *wash* its first meaning, but that is nothing—and very different from showing that what is the first of a *special* class, is first as a *proper* meaning !! I call for any general or classic dictionary of the Greek language, presenting *wash* as the proper, primitive, or first meaning of *baptizo*.

But what a fearful array of evidence does the gentleman, all at once, oppose to my third argument. I was startled, at the moment, to hear him assail, with such vehemence and with such an air of demolition, my oft published declaration, that no translator of the New Testament, had ever translated the word, in debate, by either *pour* or *sprinkle*. I began to reflect, with no little wonder, were it possible that such an occurrence, as that which, with so much air of triumph, he displayed before you, had, in truth, escaped my notice. But no sooner had the gentleman named the text, than I felt myself in full possession of my premises; and he only anticipated me, in stating an apparent exception to my sweeping affirmation. I am now glad of the opportunity afforded me, of sustaining the eminence, upon which I have long sought to stand before the community, viz: that, when I affirm any great fact or general principle, I do it advisedly; not rashly, not wantonly, not at the impulse of the moment. I have, in my edition of the New Testament, and elsewhere, affirmed the fact constituting my third argument, so far as English versions of the New Testament are concerned. And, till the last half hour, I never heard it called in question. True, my printed affirmations respected *modern* versions, and of these, primarily, the English versions. But the proposition, now before us, embraces the ancient as well as the modern, on the word *baptizo*.

The case alledged as an objection (and it is the only single objection, which, in all ages, can be brought against my third argument,) is this. That the word *bebammenon*, a passive participle of *bapto*, not of *baptizo*, in the common Testament rendered *dipped*, as it ought to be, but in the Syriac, Ethiopic, and Vulgate is rendered sprinkled. We have, then, out of all versions ever made, but three; and these three all one and the same word, in one and the same verse, which, in the first place, is rather a suspicious circumstance, and goes to confirm, in my mind, the views of Dr. Gale, a very learned Baptist of his day, in England.

Origen, who flourished early in the second century, quotes this passage and its context, from verse 11 to 16—and for *bebammenon* reads *errantismenon*, a participle passive from *rantizo*, which signifies to *sprinkle*. Now the probability is, that Origen quoted from another reading, or a more ancient copy; and if the Syriac copy alluded to was before Origen's time, it would corroborate that conclusion. The fact, also, that Jerom, the real author of the Vulgate, has it, he having been the translator of Origen's Greek works into Latin, still more confirms a different reading. Unless, then, it can be proved that they had the present reading before them, it is wholly idle to urge this solitary verse as an exception to the universal practice of the whole christian world, in all time.

The words of Gale are—"Origen's writings are older than any copies of the New Testament we can boast of, and, therefore, what he transcribed from ancient copies must be more considerable than any we have. However, I should not think the single authority of Origen sufficient to justify my altering the word; but I have likewise observed that in the Syriac and Ethiopic versions, which, from their antiquity, must be thought as valuable and authentic as the original itself, being made from primitive copies, in or very near the time of the apostles, and rendering the passage by words which signify to sprinkle, must greatly confirm Origen's reading of the place, and very strongly argue that he has preserved the same word which was in the *autographa*."

The gentleman quoted one or two passages from Leviticus, yesterday, to which I did not respond. He has revived my recollection of them by calling them up to day. Really this is a species of little criticism, which I did not expect. The passages are Levit. iv. 17—xiv. 16; Ex. xii. 22. "And the priest shall dip his right finger in the blood of the bullock," *apo tou aimatos*. True, indeed, Professor Stuart has hence suggested the notion of *smearing with blood*—because of *apo*, meaning *by* or *from*. This escape from dipping is not sustainable by Messrs. Stuart, Rice, or any one else. We have three occurrences of this construction—*apo tou elaiou*, in the oil. This is neither the time nor place for either Greek or Hebrew criticism on particles. But men as learned as any American scholars, or critics, understand the Hebrew particle *men*, translated into Greek by *apo*, and into English by *from*, as a preposition *partitive*, equivalent to *some of*. Gesenius, in his Hebrew lexicon, renders it *some of the blood*. To "*dip from*," however, taking it literally, is in good taste and good sense. I write a letter *from* Lexington to Philadelphia. I strictly write it *in* the city, yet we say I write *from*. So the priest dips *from* the oil, or dips *from* the blood. Or if we will follow the Hebrew idiom, we read—"He shall dip *some of* the blood; *some of* the oil," &c. There is, then, no necessity for any "*smearing* with blood," or "*smearing* with oil" in the case; especially in a country in which we are accustomed to talk of dipping water *from* the well, and of writing *from home*.

But we must return to the old versions. If we are to examine and decide upon the thirty-six versions, read here by our own scholarship, in all those languages, we shall never decide the matter. No one in this house, or country, is prepared for such a work. We decide the matter by the testimony of the best witnesses we can summon, and not by our particular scholarship in the Syriac, Ethiopic, and Coptic, &c. &c. We take the lexicons; and to advert to the first of these, the Syriac *amad*, which is found in both the Syriac versions, and essentially adopted in three other versions, we shall hear Dr. Henderson and the lexicons, as quoted by Mr. Grotch, A. B., of Trinity college, Dublin:—

"There is every reason to believe that he employed the identical word found in the Peshito Syriac version. That the word for *baptizo* is *amad*, which this aforesaid Dr. Henderson maintains etymologically, signifies "*stand up*," "*stand erect*." If this be the original word used by the Savior in his native Syro-Chaldaic language, then *baptizo*, found in our Greek copies, must be a translation of *amad*; and, in the judgment of the Greek translators of Matthew, equivalent to it. But who of the Pedo-baptist school will presume to say that *baptizo* means to *stand up* or *stand straight*? The fact, then, is, Dr. Henderson is wrong either in his construction of *amad*, or our Lord could not have used *amad*, inasmuch as all copies have *baptizo* in the commission 'according to Matthew; and no man, now-a-days, will argue that *baptizo* means to stand up, or that the Syriac *amad* means to sprinkle, pour, or purify."

One might argue that as baptism has a resurrection in it as well as a burial, it might be no more figurative or improper to call it a rising up to a new life, than a laying down, or putting off of an old one—an emersion as well as an immersion. If, indeed, as some Pedo-baptists suppose, it etymologically means to "stand up," or "rise up," rather than to be buried, it makes nothing at all against our views, while it certainly does against infant sprinkling: for who could make an infant stand up, or stand erect, to receive a drop of water, or the sign of a cross?"

But what say the lexicons?

"Castel, and his editor, Michaelis, Buxtorf, and Schaaf, are all unanimous. The first gives the following meanings: 'Ablutu est, baptizatus est. *Aphel*, immersit, baptizavit.' Buxtorf gives, 'Baptizari, intingi, ablui, abluere se. *Ethp*. Idem. *Aphel*, baptizare.' Schaaf: 'Ablui se, ablutus, intinctus, immersus in aquam, baptizatus est. *Ethpeel*, Idem *quod Peal*. *Aphel*, immersit, baptizavit.' Gutbier, in the small lexicon affixed to his addition of the Syriac Testament, gives the meanings, 'Baptizavit, baptizatus, est. *It*. sustentavit;' but without any reference to support the last meaning; and it is apparently introduced simply for the purpose of deducing from the verb the noun *columna*. With this exception, the authority of the lexicons referred to, is altogether against any such meaning as ' to stand.' "

These three great authorities give to *amad* the very same meanings which our twelve Greek lexicons give to *baptizo* and its family—to immerse, dip, or plunge, and figuratively to wash or cleanse.

But to go no farther than our own English translators. We argue, from concessions and declarations made by many of them, that, from their knowledge of the original tongues and their own conclusions of right, they could not so translate any word of this family.

Let us, for illustration and confirmation, hear a few of them. We shall hear first the oldest of our English translators—the martyred but immortal William Tyndale:

" *The plunging into water* signifieth that we die and are buried into Christ, as concerning the old life of sin, which is Adam; and the *pulling out again* signifieth that we rise again, with Christ, to a new life."

I need not quote Beza again. He speaks almost in my own language on the whole proposition as amplified in this discussion. He says the word *baptizo* does not mean to *wash*. Doddridge says, on Acts viii. 38—" Baptism was generally administered by immersion, though I see no proof that it was essential to the institution." That is, as I would say, immersion is not essential to immersion, or we may immerse a person without immersing him. Still we must hear him out on this passage. " It would be very unnatural to suppose that they went down to the water, merely that Philip might take up a little water in his hand to pour upon the eunuch. A person of his dignity had, no doubt, many vessels with him in his baggage on such a journey through a desert country; a precaution absolutely necesssary for travelers in these parts, and never omitted by them." On Romans vi. 4, Doddridge repeats the same views, saying: " It seems the part of candor to confess that here is an allusion to the manner of baptizing by immersion, as most usual in these early times."

McKnight also, not only in his Epistles, but in his Harmony of the 4 Gospels, says, Mark vii. 4: " For when they come from market, except they dip themselves, they eat not." He also translates the diverse washings of Hebrews ix.—" *diverse immersions*." He did not then believe that *washing* was the proper meaning of *baptisma*. But on Rom. vi. 4, and Col. ii., and 1 Peter iii., he speaks still more forcibly.

" In baptism, the rite of initiation into the christian church, the baptized person is buried under the water, as one put to death with Christ on account of sin, in order that he may be strongly impressed with a sense of the malignity of sin, and excited to hate it as the greatest of evils, ver. 3. Moreover, in the same rite, the baptized person being raised up out of the water, after being washed, he is thereby taught that he shall be raised from the dead with Christ, by the power of the Father, to live with him forever in heaven, provided he is prepared for that life by true holiness, ver. 4, 5.—Farther, by their baptism, believers are laid under the strongest obligations to holiness, because it represents their *old man*, their old corrupt nature, as crucified with Christ, to teach them that their body, which sin claimed as its property, being put to death, was no longer to serve sin as its slave."

" Christ's baptism was not the baptism of repentance; for he never committed any sin: but, as was observed, Prelim. Ess. 1, at the beginning, he submitted to be baptized, that is, to be *buried under the water*, by John, and to be raised out of it again, as an emblem of his future death and resurrection. In like manner the baptism of believers is emblematical of

L

their own death, burial and resurrection. See Col. ii. 12. note 1. Perhaps also it is a commemoration of Christ's baptism.

"He tells the Romans, that since they were *planted together in the likeness of his death*, namely, when they were baptized, *they shall be also planted together in the likeness of his resurrection*, by being raised to a new life in the body at the last day."

"The burying of Christ and of believers, first in the water of baptism, and afterwards in the earth, is fitly enough compared to the planting of seeds in the earth, because the effect in both cases is a reviviscence to a state of greater perfection."

Dr. George Campbell need scarcely be named in this place, inasmuch as his views of *baptizo* and *baptisma* are so clearly, fully and repeatedly declared. A single passage from him is all that we shall quote at present:

"'Undergo an immersion like that which I must undergo,' *to baptisma ho ego baptizomai baptisthenai*. English translation: To be baptized with the baptism that I am to be baptized with. The primitive signification of *baptisma* is *immersion;* of *baptizein*, to *immerse, plunge*, or *overwhelm*. The noun ought never to be rendered *baptism*, nor the verb *to baptize*, but when employed in relation to a religious ceremony. The verb *baptizein* sometimes, and *baptein*, which is synonymous, often occurs in the Septuagint and Apocryphal writings, and is always rendered in the common version by one or other of these words, *to dip, to wash, to plunge*. When the original expression, therefore, is rendered in familiar language, there appears nothing harsh or extraordinary in the metaphor. Phrases like these, to be overwhelmed with grief, to be immersed in affliction, will be found common in most languages."—*Campbell's Dissert.* vol. iv. pp. 128, 24.— [*Time expired.*

Thursday, Nov. 16—1 *o'clock, P. M.*
[MR. RICE'S SIXTH REPLY.]

MR. PRESIDENT—If it be true, as my friend (Mr. C.) charges, that I have made bold *assertions*, I am certainly in good company; for he has abounded in that species of argument. Perhaps it may be fair to put assertion against assertion.

The gentleman would have you believe, that I am furiously mad against the Baptists. I am not, however, so mad, but that I can recognize evangelical Baptists as constituting a part of the church of God—as christian brethren; but he, in his zeal, excommunicates every church on earth but his own and those who adopt his views of immersion! I leave the audience to judge which is most prejudiced—I, who acknowledge immersionists as disciples of Christ, or Mr. Campbell, who excommunicates all who differ from him.

The word *baptizo* is likely to become very troublesome to my friend. He told us on yesterday, that *bapto* and *baptizo* retain the idea of *dipping* through all their flexions—that as the root, the trunk, and the branches of a tree are all the same kind of wood, so these and similar words retain in all their branches the radical idea of dipping. I produced from the classics, as well as from the Bible, abundant evidence that such is not the fact. I proved, that *bapto* is used to express dyeing by dropping the coloring fluid on the thing dyed; that it is used to denote the coloring of the beard, the hair, the face, the staining of the hands, &c. He is now forced to admit, that *bapto* does not always express dipping. He tells us, that it expresses not the *dropping* of the fluid on the garment, but *the effect*. The effect of what? of dropping? If it express the effect of dropping, where is the immersion? But this, he says, is a *figurative* use of the word. Is there any thing figurative in the dropping of a fluid on a garment? Is the fluid a figure? Is the garment a figure? Is the dropping a figure? What is there figurative about it? Can dropping or sprinkling be the figure of immersion? Surely this is a modern discovery in rhetoric.

But I will again produce the authority of that *shrewd critic*, Mr. Carson, against the gentleman. He asserts, that *bapto* signifies to dye by sprinkling as properly as by dipping. And if it means to dye by sprinkling as *properly* as by dipping, the former is not a figurative meaning. But, says Carson, " Nor are such applications of the word to be accounted for by metaphor"—they are not figurative. "They are," says he, "as literal as the primary meaning. It is by the extension of the literal meaning, and not by figure of any kind, that words come to depart so from their primary meaning." So my friend is still in difficulty about *bapto*.

I prove, that the word *bapto* signifies *to wet*, from the passage in Dan. iv. 33, in which it is said of Nebuchadnezzar, "his body *(ebaphe apo)* was wet with or from the dew of heaven." But the gentleman tells us, that by a beautiful figure of speech Daniel represents the king as *dipped* in dew; and he quotes the language of Milton—" A cold shuddering dew *dips* me all o'er." It is not denied that such license may be allowed to *poets,* who, writing under the influence of the excitement so essential to that species of composition, are expected to abound in the boldest figures. But does it follow, that such figures are to be expected in simple and sober narrative? Are we to expound the language of plain history by the imaginative flights of poets? Johnson, however, gives as a second meaning of the word *dip, to wet, moisten,* and quotes the passage from Milton as an example of this secondary sense.

The language, says my friend, is *figurative.* Is literal water descending upon a man, a figure? Where is the figure? Of what is it a figure? If it be figurative, it must have relation to something literal. If the wetting with dew is the *figure,* what is the *letter?* Here is a baptism, the mode of which every one understands. It is certain, that in this instance *bapto* expresses something even less than copious sprinkling.

My friend (Mr. C.) told us, that according to an important rule of language, the definition of a word might be substituted for the word defined, and would make good sense. I applied his rule. To prove by his own rule, that *baptizo* does not definitely express mode, as applied to the ordinance of baptism, I substituted the word *sink*—its most common classical meaning, and the word *plunge*, in its stead. He gives me a gentle reproof for treating grave subjects with too much levity. I was but following a direction given by himself, as he will see, if he will take the trouble to read an article in the Millenial Harbinger, in which he gives an argument for young christians against the advocates of sprinkling. I did not design making any one laugh, unless he felt like it. Mr. Carson himself repeatedly translates *baptizo* to sink. I will give one or two examples. He says—"Diodorus Siculus, speaking of the sinking of animals in water, says, that when the water overflows, many of the land animals *(baptizomena) sunk* in the river, perish." Again—Strabo, speaking of the like near Agrigentum, says, " Things which otherwise will not swim, do not *sink (baptizesthai,)* in the water of the lake," &c. In a number of other instances, Mr. Carson translates the word to *sink.*

But the sinking of the ship, says my friend (Mr. Campbell), is merely accidental. And so, if we are to believe Mr. Carson, is the raising the person out of water. For he says, whether the thing goes to the bottom or is raised out of the water, cannot be learned from the word *baptizo.* But,

I ask, is not the raising of the person out of water an essential part of his baptism? The gentleman, however, dips them by the *word*, and raises them out of the water by *accident!*

He says, no *classical* lexicon gives *to wash* as the primary meaning of the word *baptizo.* He at first asserted, that *all* the lexicons prefer immersion as the primary meaning. I proved, that several of the best of them give *to wash* as its primary meaning in the Scriptures. He now calls for a classical lexicon that thus defines it. But I have proved, that the Jews (and the inspired writers were Jews) did not speak or write classic Greek. This he does not deny. Why, then, call for a classical lexicon to define a word as used by the Jews? If the classical lexicons correctly define Greek words as used by the Jews and inspired writers, why have we *lexicons of the New Testament?* His call for a classic lexicon is a mere evasion.

But he tells us, no classic lexicon gives *to wash* as the primary and *original* meaning of the word. I have proved, that the *original* meaning is not to be taken in preference to other meanings—that the word *prevent*, for example, originally meant *to come before*, but now it means literally *to hinder.* USAGE, as all critics agree, must determine the meaning of words.

Let me briefly notice the remarks of my friend concerning *bapto*, which, as I have proved, is translated, to *sprinkle*, by three of the oldest and most valuable versions: the Peshito Syriac, the Ethiopic and the Vulgate. He has repeatedly asserted and published, that no translator, ancient or modern, Jew, Christian, or Turk, ever did so translate any of this family of words. I have proved, not only that the three versions just mentioned have so translated *bapto*, but that Origen, the most learned of the christian fathers, in giving the substance of the passage in Rev. xix. 13, substituted *rantizo*, to sprinkle, for *bapto.*

How does the gentleman attempt to escape this difficulty? Why, he supposes there must have been a different reading—some copy of the book of Revelation having the word *rantizo* instead of *bapto ;* and he would have us believe that Origen gives a different reading. But where is the evidence that there was any such reading? He may *guess* that there was ; but there is no evidence of it whatever. And if he may be permitted to alter the Bible by mere conjecture, there is no difficulty from which he may not escape. Origen does *not* give a different reading of the passage. He did not quote it *verbatim*, as Dr. Gale admits, but only gave the sense or meaning of it. In doing so he substituted *rantizo* for *bapto.* But those learned men did not translate *bapto* to suit my friend, Mr. C., and therefore he presumes, without the least evidence, that they had before them a different reading.

Mr. Carson, on this as on some other points, is against my friend That shrewd critic, as he considers him, says, as I have already proved : "These reasons, however, do not in the least bring the common reading into suspicion in my mind ; and I will never adopt a reading to serve a purpose. Misapprehension of the meaning of the passage, it is much more likely, has substituted *errantismenon* for *bebammenon.*" What are these reasons, of which Mr. Carson speaks? Why, the Syriac and the Ethiopic versions translate the word (Rev. xix. 13.) to sprinkle, and Origen, in giving the substance of the passage, substitutes *rantizo*, to sprinkle. Are these reasons sufficient to alter a passage in the word of God? Why, Mr Campbell himself, in his translation, has retained the very reading he would now reject. Griesback saw no evidence in favor of a new reading. Carson, though a zealous and learned immersionist, saw not the least reason to suspect the common reading; and he says, he will never adopt a reading to serve a purpose. He thinks, however, that Origen, though a very learned Greek, did not understand the meaning of the word !!! Well, if those learned translators and Origen failed to ascertain the meaning of *bapto*, it is scarcely probable that we shall discover it. What, then, are we to think of the bold assertion of Mr. C., that no translator had ever rendered any of this family of words by the word *sprinkle!*

The Peshito-Syriac version has been appealed to by Mr. Campbell, as one that translates *baptizo* to *immerse.* It does not so translate it, as I am prepared to prove. I have Schaaf's Syriac lexicon, which is one of the best in the world. I will read his definition of the word by which *baptizo* is uniformly rendered. The word is *amad,* and is thus defined : "Ábluit se, ablutus, intinctus, immersus in aquam; baptizatus est."—*He washed himself, was washed, stained, immersed in water, was baptized.* Schaaf refers to every place in the New Testament where this word is used, and he finds not one in which it means *immerse ;* and in the Old Testament he finds *but one* passage in which he supposes it to have this meaning, viz: (Numb. xxxi. 23.) " Every thing that may abide the fire, ye shall make it go through the fire, and it shall be clean, &c.; and all that abideth not the fire, ye shall make go through the water." In this passage there is no evidence that the word means *immerse.* To *pass through* the fire does not mean to *dip into* fire. Neither the Hebrew, nor the Greek word here employed, signifies to *immerse.* Where, then, is the evidence that the Syriac word by which the Hebrew word is translated, has that meaning? The meaning of the passage evidently is this : That which cannot be purified by fire, must be purified by water. There is, therefore, not a solitary example in the Bible of the use of the word *amad* in the sense of *immerse.*

The Syriac language has a word (*tzeva*) which properly signifies *to dip.* And this word is used in every instance where *dip* occurs in the New Testament; but it is never employed to translate *baptizo.*

I have all the lexicographers against my friend in regard to the meaning of the word *amad.* Mr. Gotch, who has published an article in which he attempts to prove that the Syriac version favors immersion, states that the lexicographers, " Castel and his editor, Michaelis, Buxtorf, and Schaaf, are all unanimous" in defining it. They, of course, all agree to the definitions I have read from Schaaf; and no one of them, it seems, could find in the Bible an example, except the one already noticed, in which *amad* means to immerse.

The primary or original meaning of this word, as Mr. Gotch admits, is *to stand.* He says—"The word *amad,* has been generally and perhaps correctly referred to the same root as the Hebrew *amad,* (found also in the Arabic and Ethiopic,) the general meaning of which is undoubtedly *to stand. "—Appendix to the Bible Questions,* p. 156. Some have supposed that this word was chosen to denote christian baptism, from the fact that it was common for persons, in receiving baptism, to stand in water and have it poured on them. Others suppose it to have been used in the sense of *confirmation,* as baptism was supposed to be a confirmatory rite. But in whatever way the use of the word may be accounted for, its original meaning evidently was *to stand.* It is not likely, therefore, that it so changed its meaning as to signify immerse. But let not the *fact* be forgotten, that in the Bible there is not an instance in which the connection shows that it has that meaning. The old Peshito Syriac must be given up; it does not favor the doctrine of my friend, (Mr. Campbell.)

The LATIN VULGATE in not a single instance translates *baptizo* to immerse. The learned Jerom, the author of this translation, lived in the fourth century; and, I presume, was accustomed in baptizing persons to immerse them three times. Yet, with all his prejudice in favor of immersion, he never did translate *baptizo* by the Latin word *immergo*—a word which, converted into English, has become so great a favorite with my friend, Mr. C. In every instance, except one, he *transferred* the word, (Latinizing it,) as our translators did. And it is worthy of remark, that in that one instance, the only one in which he ever translated the word, he rendered it by *lavo*, a generic word, which means simply *to wash*: "Descendit, et *lavit* in Jordane, septies juxta sermonem viri Dei"—*He descended and* WASHED *seven times in Jordan, according to the word of the man of God.*—2 Kings v. 14.

The OLD ITALIC VERSION, which was in general use in the western church before Jerom translated the Vulgate, did not translate *baptizo* to immerse, but transferred it, as Jerom afterwards did.

Here, then, we have three of the most ancient and valuable versions, neither of which translates *baptizo* to immerse. I am prepared to examine others, whenever the gentleman undertakes to prove that they favor his views. He has said, that Luther translated *baptizo*, by a German word, signifying to immerse. That this statement is incorrect, is evident from Luther's translation of Matth. iii. 11—"I, indeed, baptize you *mit wasser—with* water, [not *in* water.] He shall baptize you *with (mit)* the Holy Ghost and *with (mit)* fire." Can any one believe that Luther so translated this passage, as to make John the Baptist say—"I *immerse* you *with* water?" Luther, and the German ministers who used his translation, practiced baptizing by pouring or sprinkling. Did they render themselves perfectly ridiculous by standing up and saying— "I *immerse* thee," &c., and then sprinkling water on the person? It is absolutely incredible. No sensible man would act such a farce.

That Luther did not understand *baptizo* as meaning always to immerse, is evident, from the fact, that in those passages, where it is not used to denote the ordinance of baptism, he translates it by a generic term, signifying simply *to wash*. He thus renders it in Mark vii. 4, 8, and Luke xi. 38. These remarks apply with full force to the Dutch, Danish, and Swedish translations. Not one of these versions translates the word *immerse;* and the people who read them, it is well known, have never practiced immersion. I shall be with my friend, when he undertakes to support immersion by these translations.

The gentleman has spoken of Tyndale's translation. I happen to have that work. Tyndale transfers the word where it is used with reference to the ordinance of baptism. When it is not so used, as in Mark vii. 4, 8, and Luke xi. 38, he translates it by the word *wash*—"Except they *wash*—the *washing* of cups," &c. Tyndale, I believe, was favorable to immersion; though, my friend says, he quotes only the advocates of sprinkling. Why, then, did not he translate *baptizo* to immerse, instead of to wash? Why did he not say—"When they come from the market, except they *immerse* themselves, they eat not?" Why did he not put the *immersion* of cups, &c., instead of *washing?*

The gentleman quoted Beza. Well, does Beza translate *baptizo* to immerse? He does not. He transfers it when it is used in relation to the ordinance; and in other cases translates it *to wash*.

My friend is not quite consistent in his mode of reasoning. At one time he tells us, that the *old critics* were not so well versed in the science of criticism as those of modern times—that great improvements have been made of late days. But when he thinks the old critics favorable to his views, he magnifies their authority. There seems to be a kind of twisting and turning to escape difficulties.

He has brought forward Doddridge's remarks on the baptism of the eunuch—going *into* the water. At the commencement of this discussion he agreed, that the controversy turned mainly on the meaning of the word *baptizo*. He is now running from it to the *prepositions* and other arguments. I am disposed to proceed in the discussion with some regard to system. I hope the gentleman will return to the word.

Campbell and McKnight, to whom he has referred, were both favorable to immersion. For sometime after the Reformation, immersion was generally practiced in England. Gradually it fell into disuse, though many were anxious to have it restored. They were Pedo-baptists—believed in infant baptism—but they were immersionists. These concessions are not, therefore, to be regarded as the concessions of the advocates of sprinkling. Yet, neither Campbell, nor McKnight, nor Doddridge, believed the doctrine for which Mr. C. contends. They all admitted the validity of baptism by pouring or sprinkling—thus differing essentially from him.

If, however, this question is to be determined by the opinions of learned men instead of argument, I will count learned men with my friend. I will produce as long and as learned a list who deny that *baptizo* definitely expresses the act of immersing, as he can find to maintain the contrary. Nay, I will prove that those Greek and Latin fathers who practiced trine immersion, still admitted the validity of baptism by pouring and sprinkling. And if their concessions do not prove him in error, how do the partial concessions of a few Pedo-baptists prove that I am in error?—[*Time expired.*

Thursday, Nov. 17—1½ *o'clock, P. M.*

[MR. CAMPBELL'S SEVENTH ADDRESS.]

MR. PRESIDENT—I will travel over the ground again with my friend. The gentleman says that he has consulted these authors. His consultations, then, do not secure him against error; for he certainly has mistaken me, touching my quotations from Tyndale, Doddridge, Beza, Campbell, McKnight, &c. He has generally evinced a disposition to anticipate me, and now, instead of offering pertinent replies, he would represent me as forsaking the ground I have taken, and on which I have said the whole controversy must ultimately rest, viz: the proper meaning of the precept *baptize*. We both admit that all depends upon the meaning of a single word. If, then, I offer a thousand arguments, facts, and observations, their ultimate and grand object is, to ascertain the meaning of *baptizo*, as used by the Christian Lawgiver.

The gentleman, indeed, has repeatedly told us that professor Stuart has never admitted that Jesus Christ commanded his apostles to immerse. That, however, would have made the professor a Baptist, and then his testimony to us would have been worth nothing. Does any one think that he would say the Lord commanded his apostles exclusively to immerse, and himself proceeded with his sprinkling! But thousands, as learned as he, have said, that it *does* signify immerse. I as firmly believe that Jesus Christ commanded his apostles to immerse, as I believe that he was the true Messiah. Now that is equivalent to saying that he commanded them to immerse only. I presume not to say how Mr. Stuart came to that conclusion; for he not only, as Mr. Rice says, admits immersion in the third century, *but in the apostolic age.* He says, indeed, that "*baptizo, in the New Testament,* does, *in all probability,* involve the idea that *the rite* WAS *usually performed by immersion,* but not ALWAYS." The only difference between him and me is in the word *always.* I say *always,* he says "*usually.*"

But the gentleman, in his own imagination, has compelled me by his force of logic, to admit that *bapto* does not always mean *to dip.* How others may have felt I know not—but I have neither seen nor felt any thing stronger than his force of action. I have always admitted that *bapto,* not only in the active voice, indicates to dip, but also in the passive, indicates the effect of any action which literally or figuratively immerses, or covers, or conceals the thing. In the case before us it intimates the effect produced by dropping, but most certainly does not mean dropping, for that is expressed by another word! And as for Mr. Carson's rule of "the exclusion of literal meaning by" use, I do not admit it in specific words, but in general words. It is neither, then, an argument *ad rem,* nor *ad hominem.*

I have then abandoned no position touching verbs, nouns, facts, or canons of criticism assumed in the discussion. Why should I? What has the gentleman done to compel such a surrender? I ask what has he done? Asserted, re-asserted, and re-affirmed. I am proceeding in a regular inductive train of argumentation; and I hope, notwithstanding my frequent interruptions by his assertions, and sometimes impertinent readings and comments, that I will, by a regular cumulative process of inductive argumentation and proof, carry conviction to many minds of the certain truth and sublime importance of my conclusions.

The quotations just made from these translators, to which others of a similar character may be added, were read to demonstrate the impossibility, or strong improbability, that persons avowing such opinions could afterwards translate these terms by *pour* or *sprinkle.* They are then pertinent to the argument on hand.

While on the subject of translations, we must, for a moment, honor father Jerom and the Vulgate with a passing notice. Jerom, the father and the founder of the Vulgate, did not, as Mr. Rice affirms, ever translate *baptizo* by the word *immerse.* He retained the word *baptizo* in every instance where the rite is named or alluded to. He once, and only once, translated it by *lavo,* to wash; and that was in a case which he presumed of difficult import, and then he assumed the *commentator,* and laid aside the character of the *translator.* There is not then, one grain of argument, or any relevancy in Mr. R.'s assertion concerning the Vulgate and St. Jerom. The custom then was to call every thing by its proper name.

At that time, or till then, the Greek church and Greek language controlled Christendom. The Jews first, the Greeks next, gave laws, and usages, and style, to the christian community. Hence all the ecclesiastic terms are Greek. In my debate with Bishop Purcell, I deduced an argument against the Roman Catholic pretension of being the mother and mistress of churches, from the fact that the Greeks gave the whole church nomenclature, and not the Latins. A pithy argument too. This startling fact also accompanied it, viz : That in all the councils of some four or five centuries, there were present 2200 Greek bishops, and only some 28 or 30 Roman bishops. This immense preponderance in the early church and councils, baptized into Greek all official names, honors, offices, ordinances, &c., and explains the mystery why Jerom retained this Greek word, in common with a host of kindred names. The church vocabularly is almost all Greek : for example—bishop, deacon, evangelist, presbytery, synod, baptism, eucharist, ecclesiastic, &c. &c. Hence, as Dr. Campbell well observes, Jerom adopted rather than translated *baptizo*. And as Jerom's version reigned for a thousand years, the word *baptizo* pervaded and pervades almost all Christendom down to the present day, even when, as Dr. Campbell has shown, they could have found the Latin *immersio*, which as exactly corresponds with *baptisma*, as does *circumcisio* correspond with the Greek *peritomee*.

Mr. Rice, it seems, is a great admirer of Dr. Carson. I wish he would take him for his guide, and lean upon his authority throughout. I have often wished that some able hand had written a dissertation or a volume on quoting authors ; showing, amongst other matters, what difference ought to be made in their testimony when it is for us, and when it is against us. Mr. Rice believes Mr. Carson when he supposes he wounds the Baptists ; but always disbelieves him when he wounds the Pedo-baptists. Now, when I consent to receive any man as a witness in any case of importance, I take his whole testimony in questions of fact, so far as he clearly and fully expresses himself.

As respects the quotation from Daniel, Mr. Carson, indeed, concurs with me in regarding it as rhetorically, poetically, or if you please, symbolically, picturesque and graphic. "And they shall immerse thee in the dews of heaven till seven times pass over thee."

Our great English bard, the immortal Milton, seems to have caught his bold and beautiful flight from this passage, in which he sings,

"A cold shuddering dew, dips me all over."

I shall not speak of the Asiatic dews, nor of those most profuse around Babylon and through all the valleys of the Tigris and the Euphrates. Any one, well read in the geography of that country, and acquainted with the reports of Asiatic tourists, will appreciate the correctness as well as the beauty of this passage.

In interpreting positive precepts, and in commenting upon poetic or symbolic effusions, we do not proceed upon the same principles, so far as the acceptation of words is concerned. In positive statutes and laws we look for perspicuity and precision in the selection and use of words. In poetry and symbolic narratives and descriptions, we expect a free, rich and luxuriant style. Moses the lawgiver, and Isaiah the prophet, John the evangelist, and John the prophet, in his apocalyptic visions and descriptions, are not to be interpreted in the same strict and grammatical way. In describing nature, providence, redemption, and in proclaiming a law, enacting an ordinance, or issuing a commission, men think, and feel, and speak in different words and images.

But I object not in this case to the word *wet*. He was covered with dews, and, consequently, as an effect, he was wet. Even we, in the far west of time and of the globe, say he was drenched or soaked with wine. So sang the Greek and Roman poets, and so speak the Americans.

9

Mr. R. asks for some manuscript copy having *errantismenon* in it. I might ask him for a manuscript of the Vulgate, or the Ethiopic. He ought to know that the Alexandrian manuscript, the oldest known on earth, is hundreds of years after Origen, from whom we quote the reading. If this is not an *ad captandum* argument, wherefore appears it here!

Mr. Rice has not read all that Dr. Gale has said. That distinguished man does not found his conclusion simply on the passages in Origen. He argues from the Ethiopic and Syriac versions, as you have heard from me. And the fact that these, together with the Vulgate, should have only in one and the same instance, departed from universal usage, is of itself enough to induce the suspicion of some different reading, without even Origen's reading. Only reflect upon it, fellow-citizens; in eighteen hundred years, in a hundred versions, in a hundred languages and dialects, and in a word occurring one hundred and twenty times in the New Testament, we should find in only three versions, only in one and the same verse, and in the same word, a single exception! Has the like ever before occurred!! I challenge all the volumes of criticism to furnish a similar instance.

Mr. Carson's explanation of the matter—or his opinion concerning the reading of Origen, has no authority. His solution of the difficulty is, however, no relief to Mr. Rice. He supposes, that these old translators mistook the meaning of the word.

Does that satisfy my friend, Mr. Rice! Then, according to Messrs. Rice, Carson, and Gale, there is no exception to the universality of the fact—that no translator into any language, in any age, *who knew the meaning of the word*, did ever translate a single member of the family of *baptizo* by the words *pour* or *sprinkle*, which is the point in my third argument.

Mr. Carson is a learned, acute, and candid critic, and an honest man—for whom I entertain a high respect and esteem. He wrote a work, some years since, on the Inspiration of the Scriptures, in which he goes so far as to contend for the inspiration of the language, as well as of the ideas. He does not, however, contend for the inspiration of the translators, copyists, and printers of the letter. Still I am not sure but that his views of inspiration, somewhat ultra, as I presume, may have influenced him to oppose the presumption that we have lost a single autographic reading. This, however, by the way.

But we must have something of *baptizo* or *bapto* in every speech. The gentleman has reiterated his favorite *sink*, and for no reason that I can see but for a laugh; and yet where is the laugh unless at his own expense? The sense is as good as the translation. Wherever *sink* is a fair version, it is good sense; so is *plunge* always. But you can neither *pour* a man nor *sprinkle* him into drops! therefore, they cannot be a translation at all: but both sink and plunge may be, for they make sense.

But, notwithstanding we are told that *sink* is, in classic use, as four to one against immerse, I feel constrained to say, that *sink* and *dip* are not more diverse in English than *baptizo* and *deuo*, or *dunai*, are in Greek; and although, sometimes, to dip is to sink, and to sink to the bottom, yet no classic scholar will affirm that *baptizo* means to sink more than to drown. It is wholly accidental, and what is accidental never can be the meaning of a word. This is certainly as great an *ad captandum* as to give *prevent* as an offset to *baptizo* in the case of the change of meaning of words. The radical *vent* still means to *come*. It has never changed any more than *bap*. Though it might have changed, and yet the rule be true; for the rule is not for words of *generic*, but of *specific*, meaning. To come in one's way, or to come before one, is to hinder, as well as to anticipate. But in no sense has the *vent* changed.

This *sinking* argument, and this *preventing* argument, and this *washing* argument, are of the same category. From general lexicons, he has got down to some Pedo-baptist lexicons upon the New Testament, and they only give *wash*, as in their opinion, the first of New Testament meanings. Still it is not true that any one of them gives *wash* as the *first meaning* of the word. It is said without authority. Neither Robinson nor Bretschneider have made *wash* a primary meaning of *bapto* or *baptizo*. I still say, that all the lexicons, general and special, make *immerse* the primary and proper—*wash* only a secondary and accidental meaning. As often as Mr. R. asserts, we shall assert on these premises.

But we must again resume the ancient translations. Mr. Rice will allow us only some of these translators—a very few. He would even take from us Luther, whom all the world knows to have argued that all should, "according to the meaning of the word *taufe*, be *dipped* all over in water, and again raised up." He will not allow us Jerom, because he Latinized *baptizo*. Now, as our most learned critics allow that the adopting of any word, at a particular time, into any language, indicates the current usage of that time, and that the word adopted is to signify whatever was the usage, at that time, in the language wherein adopted, we must regard Jerom as rendering it immerse; for all the world knows, that was the universal custom in the fourth century. But I shall read a passage or two farther, with a few remarks on the subject of these translations.

We have already heard that Castel, Michaelis, Buxtorf, and Schaaf, are all unanimous in defining *amad*. *Schaaf*, of whom Mr. R. speaks with so much approbation, translates it by—*immersus in aquam, immersed into water*. Buxtorf gives *intingo*, to be dipped—and *baptozari*, to be baptized. Castel, in the active form, gives it *immergo, baptizo*; making it not only mean to immerse, but making *immerse* and *baptizo* synonymous. These all are against the notion of *standing* as the meaning of this important word. The Syriac translation could not indicate any thing else by that word; if, as Dr. Henderson, a learned Pedo-baptist, argues, it was the word used in the commission by our Lord, who spoke that language—for, as that word was translated by *baptizo*, which word no man construes by *stand*, certain it is that it has the meaning assigned to it by those lexicons and critics already quoted.

But to enter into a dissertation upon all these words, were we all profoundly learned in these languages, would be wholly inexpedient and unprofitable; inasmuch as it is admitted that some of them clearly give immersion, and not one of them *sprinkling* or *pouring*. I shall give the sense, or the conclusions of no mean man, Mr. Gotch, who, after a laborious research, gives the following conclusion of the whole matter:

"The conclusions to which the investigation leads us, are—

1. With regard to the ancient versions, in all of them, with three exceptions, (viz. the Latin from the third century, and the Sahidic and Basmuric,) the word *baptizo* is *translated* by words purely native; and the three excepted versions adopted the Greek word, not by way of transference, but in consequence of the term having become current in the languages.

Of native words employed, the Syriac, Arabic, Ethiopic, Coptic, Armenian, Gothic, and earliest Latin, all signify to *immerse;* the Anglo-Saxon, both to *immerse* and to *cleanse;* the Persic, to *wash;* and the Slavonic to *cross.* The meaning of the word adopted from the Greek, in Sahidic, Basmuric, and Latin, being also to *immerse.*

2. With regard to the modern versions examined, the Eastern generally adhere to the ancient Eastern versions, and translate by words signifying to *immerse.* Most of the Gothic dialects, viz. the German, Swedish, Dutch, Danish, &c., employ altered forms of the Gothic word signifying to *dip.* The Icelandic uses a word meaning *cleanse.* The Slavic dialects follow the ancient Slavonic; and the languages formed from the Latin, including the English, adopt the word *baptizo;* though, with respect to the English, the words *wash* and *christen* were formerly used, as well as *baptize.*"

But I have yet a moment to notice the alarming fact that Mr. Rice, backed by Mr. Carson, too, teaches us that the word immerse, and its Greek representative, will put us under the water or sink us to the bottom, without affording us any prospect of ever getting out. This makes it a more alarming affair. I will say, with Mr. Carson, that *absolutely, baptizo* means to immerse, without the idea of emersion; but yet, in the currency of all usage, classic, Jewish, and Christian, to dip and to immerse, differ from *dunai* and other words in this, that it has connected with it, if not *vi termini,* by intrinsic force, the hope of getting out. To dip, nine times in ten, implies lifting up as well as putting down. And in sacred use, immersion and emersion are like shadow and substance connected.

Perhaps, however, this will help my friend to explain why the Syriac version chose *amad,* which some translate like the Hebrew *amad, to stand,* "to stand erect." A resurrection out of the water, rather than a going down into it, might have been more persuasive to obedience. This would be giving a name to the rite from the more pleasing portion of the symbol.—[*Adjourned till* 9½ *to-morrow morning.*

Friday, Nov. 17—9½ *o'clock, A. M.*
[MR. RICE'S SEVENTH REPLY.]

MR. PRESIDENT—I shall, to-day, proceed in the discussion more leisurely than I had intended; inasmuch as my friend, Mr. C., desires to occupy another day on this subject.

Let the audience keep in mind what the gentleman has undertaken to prove, viz: that the entire submersion of the body in water is essential to christian baptism.

We agree that the Bible, especially on all important points, is a *plain* book. We agree, also, that baptism is an important ordinance; and my friend ascribes to it more efficacy than I do. He must, therefore, admit that, if the entire submersion of the body in water is essential to the ordinance, the Scriptures teach this truth with great clearness. And if they do, is it not marvellous that, during a discussion of two days' continuance, he has made so little progress in proving it? If this doctrine is indeed true, we may well doubt whether the Bible is a revelation from God. For it is incredible that a truth, so essential to the very existence of the church, should be left in such obscurity, that multitudes, of the wisest and best men, have never been able to discover it. And my friend himself finds it extremely difficult to make it apparent to the minds of this audience. It is not in the Bible; or, occupying so important a place in the christian system, it would have been taught with greater clearness.

All, I think, must admit, that the doctrine of exclusive immersion ought to be most unequivocally proved, before its advocates venture to excommunicate all who refuse to embrace it. And these exclusive views, let it be remarked, are not peculiar to Mr. Campbell and his church; they are common to immersionists.

My friend, Mr. C., has labored to sustain his views, mainly by the force of the words *bapto* and *baptizo*. To determine the meaning of these words, he first appealed to the lexicons, ancient and modern. I appealed to the same lexicons, and proved that they define these words not only to sink, dip, plunge, but to wash, to cleanse, &c. He then told us, that the lexicons were wrong, and he could prove it. It is truly singular that they should all have erred in defining these particular words! He still insisted, however, that they all preferred *immerse* as the primary and literal meaning of the word. I proved that Bretschneider, Robinson, Greenfield and others, give to *wash*, *cleanse*, as the *first* meaning of *baptizo*, as it is used in the Bible. He called for a *classical* lexicon that gave to *wash* as its primary meaning. This I exposed, by proving that the Jews did not speak nor write classical Greek; that we have lexicons of the New Testament, designed to explain the Greek, as it was spoken by the Jewish people. The gentleman still insists, that neither Robinson nor Bretschneider gives wash as a primary meaning of *baptizo*. Bretschneider, as we have seen, gives its general meaning, " sepius intingo, sepius lavo "—*often to dip, often to wash*. And the very first meaning assigned to the word by these lexicons, (as it is found in the Bible,) is simply to wash, to cleanse. If then, as the gentleman will not venture to deny, the Jews and inspired writers spoke a widely different idiom of the Greek, from that found in classic authors; and if the Jews always used it in reference to their religious washings, and the pagan Greeks in reference to matters of common life; we must take the definitions of the lexicons of the Jewish Greek, in preference to those of classic Greek. Can he produce a lexicon that gives *to immerse* as the literal and proper meaning of this word, as used in the Scriptures or among the Jews?

The second appeal of my friend was to *classic* usage. I also appealed to classic usage, and proved, that Greek authors give the words in question the same variety of meaning attached to them by the lexicons. We find them using *bapto* to express the coloring of garments by the dropping of the coloring fluid; the dyeing of the hair and the beard, the staining of the hands or the face, &c. &c. We find *baptizo* used to signify the wetting of the hand with blood, the moistening of a blister-plaster with breastmilk and Egyptian ointment. We find Dr. Gale, though a zealous and learned immersionist, admitting that *baptizo* does not necessarily express *the action* of putting under water. And yet the *action* is the very thing for which Mr. Campbell is contending, as definitely expressed by it! So two of his main sources of evidence have failed him.

His third appeal was to the *translations*. He began with the Peshito Syriac; but I proved, that the lexicographers, Schaaf, Castel, Michaelis and Buxtorf, give to the Syriac word *(amad)* employed to translate *baptizo*, the general meaning—*abluit se*—he washed himself, and that they find but one instance in the whole Bible, where they suppose it to mean *immerse*. And even in that instance, neither the Hebrew word nor the Greek word used by the Septuagint has that meaning. I am, therefore, prepared to prove, that there is no example in the Bible of the use of the Syriac word for baptism in the sense of immersion. Yet I might admit, that there is *one* example of the kind, and still prove all for which I contend.

M

But I will now prove by Mr. Gotch, the gentleman's own witness, that the Syriac word does not definitely signify to *immerse*. Mr. Gotch, it should be remembered, is laboring to prove the Syriac version favorable to immersion. Mr. Gotch says—"We are, moreover, warranted in concluding, that though the term was peculiarly appropriated to the rite of christian baptism, as is manifest from its being used as the translation of *photisthentes*, it was, nevertheless, regarded by the Syriac translator as synonymous with *baptizo* in *all the senses* in which that word is used in the New Testament, and not as simply expressive of the christian rite ' see *e. g.* Mark vii. 4, and Luke xi. 38, where the word is used in reference to Jewish ablutions." * * * But the fact seems clear, that it had acquired in the time of the Syriac translator the meaning which the lexicons give, "*abluit se.*" *Append. to Bib. Question*, pp. 164, 165.

Now observe, Mr. Campbell is laboring to prove, that *baptizo* has but one meaning, viz: to immerse. To prove this, he appeals to the Syriac version. But Gotch, his own witness, admits that *baptizo* has in the New Testament *several meanings*, and asserts, that the Syriac word by which it is translated, was synonymous with it in all those senses! Is this the evidence that *baptizo* signifies definitely to immerse? This is not all. Mr. Gotch says, it is clear, that the Syriac word, when the translation was made, had acquired the meaning which the lexicons give it, viz: "*abluit se*"—*he washed himself*. My friend, Mr. C., knows perfectly well, that the word *abluo* is a generic term, and does not express *mode*. If, then, the Syriac word had acquired this meaning when the translation was made, it is certain that the Syriac translator understood *baptizo* in the general sense of *washing*, *cleansing*. The oldest and best translation, then, is against the gentleman, according to the testimony of his own prejudiced witness.

The Vulgate, too, and the old Italic which preceded it, it is acknowledged, transferred the word, and never translated it *immerse*. The Latin language has several words which signify definitely to immerse, as mergo, immergo, submergo, mergito. Is it not most unaccountable, if the literal and proper meaning of *baptizo* is to immerse, that Jerom and the author or authors of the old Italic version, never once translated it by any one of these words? Is it not passing strange, that in the only instance in which Jerom translated it, he rendered it by the generic term *lavo*, to wash? These versions were made, when the Greek was a living language; the authors of them had the best possible opportunity to ascertain the prevailing usage in regard to this word; and certainly Jerom was not prejudiced in favor of sprinkling. Why, then, did he not, at least in some few instances, translate it by some one of the words just mentioned?

But Mr. Campbell tells us, the word *baptizo* was then so well understood, that it was as definite as any Latin word that could be found; and therefore it was transferred. This, however, is a great mistake. Cyprian, one of the most celebrated of the christian fathers, who lived in the early part of the third century, certainly did not know, that *baptizo* meant simply to immerse. The question was propounded to him by a certain country minister, whether those who had received baptism by pouring or sprinkling were validly baptized. This question Cyprian (and there were sixty-six bishops in council with him,) answered in the affirmative. His language is as follows:

"You inquire also, dear son, what I think of such as obtain the grace in time of their sickness and infirmity; whether they are to be accounted lawful christians, because they are not washed all over with the water of salvation, but have only some of it poured on them. In which matter, I would use so much modesty and humility, as not to prescribe so positively but that every one should have the freedom of his own thoughts, and do as he thinks best. I do, according to the best of my mean capacity, judge thus; that the divine favors are not maimed or weakened, so as that any thing less than the whole of them is conveyed, where the benefit of them is received with a full and complete faith, both of the giver and receiver."—*Wall's Hist. of Inf. Bap.*, v. ii., pp. 357, 358.

" And no man need, therefore, think otherwise, because these sick people, when they receive the grace of our Lord, have nothing but an affusion or sprinkling ; when as the Holy Scriptures, by the propnet Ezekiel, says, *Then will I sprinkle clean water upon you, and ye shall be clean*," &c. He quotes to the same purpose, Numbers xix. 13, and viii. 7, &c. And having applied them, says, a little after, " If any one think they obtain no benefit, as having only an affusion of the water of salvation, do not let him mistake so far, as that the parties, if they recover of their sickness, should be baptized again."—*Ibid.*, pp. 386, 387.

Cyprian, you perceive, did not know that *baptizo* meant only to immerse. If he had so believed, he never could have answered the question propounded to him as he did. He declares those who had received baptism by sprinkling, as truly and validly baptized as those immersed ; and he says, " If any one think they obtain no benefit, as having only an affusion of the water of salvation, do not let him mistake so far as that the parties, if they recover from their sickness, should be *baptized again.*" Did he mean to say, let them not be *immersed again ?* This would imply, that they had been immersed by *pouring!* But Cyprian believed, that *baptizo* meant to *sprinkle* as well as to immerse. Hence, in giving the answer to the question, he proves its correctness by reference to Ezekiel xxxvi. 25 : " Then will I *sprinkle* clean water upon you," &c.

It is, moreover, a fact, that at the time, and before the time when Jerom made his translation, many believed that John baptized by *pouring*. Aurelius Prudentius, who wrote A. D. 390, speaking of John's baptism, says, " *Perfundit fluvio* "—he poured water on them in the river. Paulinus, bishop of Nola, a few years later, says—" He [John] washes away the sins of believers," *infusis lymphis*—by the pouring of water. Bernard, speaking of the baptism of our Lord by John, says, " *Infundit aquam capiti Creatoris creatura* "—the creature poured water upon the head of the Creator. Lactantius says, Christ received baptism " that he might save the gentiles by baptism; that is, *(purifici roris perfusione,)* by the distilling of the purifying dew." See *Pond on Baptism*, pp. 33, 34. These and similar evidences force us to the conclusion, that the word *baptizo* was not, in Jerom's day, understood to mean simply to immerse. My friend's reason, therefore, why he did not translate it by a Latin word having that meaning, is proved incorrect. *He will be obliged to give up the old Italic and the Vulgate!*

The Arabic version, which is of greatest authority, translates *baptizo* by a word of the same form and the same meaning as the Syriac word *amad*. This version, of course, does not sustain Mr. Campbell.

The Persic version, as Mr. Gotch admits, translates *baptizo* by a word signifying *to wash ;* and since it was translated from the Syriac, it affords additional evidence that the Syriac word *amad*, of which we have already spoken, means *to wash*, and not to immerse.

The Ethiopic version, according to Mr. Gotch, uses a word which signifies *ablution* as well as *immersion*. It cannot, of course, sustain Mr. Campbell.

The Sahidic and Basmuric versions transfer the word as our translators did. The Arminian used a word which, according to Mr. Gotch, "undoubtedly signifies, in one instance, to *dip;* in others, at least, to *bathe*, or *perform ablution.*" The one instance to which he refers, is the case of Naaman, 2 Kings, v. 14, where the word *baptizo*, as we have seen, is by Jerom translated by *lavo*, to wash in general. It cannot, therefore, be proved, in that instance, to mean *dip*. But he says, the Arminian word means to *bathe, to perform ablution ;* and we know a person may bathe or perform ablution without being immersed. The German version, as we have proved, does not sustain Mr. Campbell. Luther uses the expression, "I baptize you *mit wasser*, (with water,) which is inconsistent with immersion ; and, in other passages, translates the word by the generic term to wash. The same remarks apply to the Dutch, Danish, and Swedish translations. And it is an important fact, that the people who use these versions have always practiced pouring or sprinkling. The Anglo-Saxon translation uses a word which means *to cleanse*. So says Mr. Gotch, my friend's learned witness. The Geneva Bible, (French) the common French version, the Italic, Arias Montanus, Tyndale, all either transfer the word *baptizo*, or translate it by a generic term, signifying *to wash, to cleanse*.

Here, then, we have *nineteen* of the most important translations of the Scriptures, not one of which translates *baptizo* by a word definitely signifying to immerse. *My friend must abandon the translations!*

We have made considerable progress. We have taken three of the gentleman's strong fortresses—the lexicons, the classics, and the translations !

I have appealed to Bible usage in regard to the words in controversy ; and I have proved that *bapto* is used in a number of instances where an *immersion* is impossible. Indeed, as I have before stated, there are not more than four or five instances in the Bible in which it means to immerse. It signifies a partial dipping or wetting, as in the case where the living bird, the cedar wood, the scarlet and the hysop, were to be dipped in, or wetted in, the blood of the slain bird. That it, in several instances, means merely wetting, or, as professor Stuart says, smearing, is evident from the use of the preposition *apo* (from) in connection with it. The priest was to dip or wet his finger *from* the blood or oil.

I was amused at the criticism of the gentleman on this expression. He tells us, the expression *to dip* water *from* a vessel is very common. This would answer very well, if Moses had said, the priest shall dip oil or blood from the hand ; but most unfortunately for this criticism, he says, the priest shall *dip his finger from the oil!* Is it common to speak of dipping a vessel from water? Who ever heard of such an expression? The simple direction was, that the priest should get on his finger so much of the fluid as that he could sprinkle it. The preposition *apo*, which is here used, nèver signifies *in*, but always *from*.

Once more I revert to the passage in Dan. iv. 33, where it is said, Nebuchadnezzar's body was *wet from* (*ebaphe apo*) the dew of heaven. This, my friend will insist, is a very poetic effusion of the prophet. I knew that Isaiah was a poet of the first order, but I was not aware that Daniel had any pretensions of the kind. In both instances where this expression occurs, he is giving a very plain and simple narrative. " The same hour was the thing fulfilled upon Nebuchadnezzar ; and he was driven from men, and did eat grass as oxen, and his body was wet with (*ebaphe apo*) the dew of heaven." What evidence do you see of poetic effusion here? Milton, it is true, said—" A cold shuddering dew *dips* me all o'er." But, I again ask, are we to go to the flights and bold figures of poets, in order to understand a word used of simple narrative? Besides, as I before remarked, Johnson gives *to wet, to moisten,* as a second meaning of dip. It is impossible to immerse Nebuchadnezzar in dew !

I must once more briefly notice the effort of the gentleman to sustain his assertion, that no translator, ancient or modern, ever translated *baptizo*, or any of that family of words, to *sprinkle.* I have proved, that three of the oldest and most valuable versions, the Syriac, the Ethiopic, and the Vulgate, did so translate *bapto ;* and that Origen, the most learned of the christian fathers, did, in giving the sense of a passage of Scripture, substitute *rantizo*, to sprinkle, for *bapto.* But the gentleman insists, that there *must* have been a different reading. Why? Is there in existence a manuscript copy of the New Testament which gives a different reading? This is not pretended. But Origen's writings, we are told, are older than any manuscript now extant. *Does Origen give a different reading?* He does not. Dr. Gale himself admits, that he does not quote the passage *verbatim*, but only "*almost* verbatim." Why, then, must there have been a different reading? Only because the claims of immersion are ruined, if it be admitted that *bapto*, sometimes, means to *sprinkle.*

I have quoted Carson, who says, there is no evidence that there was a different reading. But the gentleman thinks, I ought either not to quote Carson, or take all he says. I do take his testimony as to the matter of fact, especially when it is against himself; but when he expresses the opinion, that Origen, and those learned translators, did not understand the meaning of *bapto*, I must beg leave to dissent. But why did Mr. Campbell quote Doddridge and McKnight? He gave us, not their testimony as to matters of fact, but their *opinion.* Will he, then, adopt *all* their views on this subject? If he will, our controversy may at once terminate.

I have now examined the usage of the word *bapto*, as found in the Bible, sufficiently to prove, that it will not sustain the claims of immersion. I will next examine the usage of *baptizo*, and will endeavor to prove, that, in no one instance in the Bible, or in the religious writings of the Jews, the Apocryphal books, can it be proved to mean to *immerse.* It occurs, first, in 2 Kings v. 10—14. Elisha, the prophet, directed Naaman, the Syrian leper, to go and wash in Jordan seven times.—[*Time expired.*

Friday, Nov. 17—10 *o'clock, A. M.*
[MR. CAMPBELL'S EIGHTH ADDRESS.]

Mr. President—It is transcendently important, sir, that every man having reason and conscience of his own to appreciate his probable destiny and solemn responsibilities in this universe, should judge for himself, on every question involving present duty, and future happiness. Were it only necessary to wait upon the decision of others, and implicitly receive their assertions as infallible oracles, we should all be justified in giving up our understanding, conscience and destiny into the hands of my friend, Mr. Rice. He has kindly undertaken for us, and with great authority, much sincerity and unfeigned benevolence, informed us that he has proved every

M 2

position he assumed, and that in every point we have utterly failed. This, indeed, is a discovery which none of us would likely have made in an age, if left to ourselves to ponder upon the premises before us. Nevertheless it is so; for the gentleman has said so, and that should satisfy every prudent and reflecting man!

There is, however, two sides to every question; and, unfortunately, we have different ways of speaking and reasoning, and consequently we sometimes arrive at different conclusions. Allow me then to review the past, retrace our course, and also give my opinion. Still, however, it is but an opinion which I shall give; and, therefore, you must hear both sides and judge for yourselves.

I cannot but approve the course of my friend in one particular. It is a rule which I have prescribed to myself, and recommended to others. It is, to make every day a critic upon the past. I shall therefore carry out this principle, follow the good example before me, and take a summary retrospect of our progress hitherto.

No person has ever been much more prodigal in debate than I have been on the present occasion, in the way of submitting and managing universal propositions. The affirmative of any proposition is always a laborious affair compared with the negative; but the affirmative of a universal proposition is superlatively onerous and dangerous. The reason of this liberality on my part I will candidly give you. I feel myself exceedingly rich in resources of evidence, on a very grave and important question, vital to the interests of the church, which ought to have been decided long since; and perfectly fearless as to the issue, determined to turn a very broad side to the enemy, to speak in the style of naval engagements, that all might see the invulnerability and strength of the ship in which we have embarked upon the high seas in this stormy and tempestuous season.

Now that this is a work of supererogation on our part, will appear to all who know that in almost every department of life's employments, we act on probable evidence, and, at best, upon general rules. Apart from the laws of nature, we have but few universal laws or rules of action. Still we have one great advantage in affirming a universal proposition, that we may sometimes fail by one or two exceptions, and then we have so general a law that all may be justified in conforming to its requisitions. My first universal proposition is founded upon a well established fact, in language—viz: that all verbs indicating action are either *generic* or *specific*. From this postulate I proceeded to form my first universal proposition, viz:

That the specific idea expressed in the original root, of any *specific* word, continues through all the branches of that word in its various flexions and deviations. Where, then, we have the radical word or syllable, we have the original idea. In the case before us, as respects *bapto*, no exception has been found. The gentleman offered two, viz: *prevent* and *conversation*, taken from my preface to a new version of the New Testament, indicative of the change to which some words are incident in lapse of time, losing much of their etymological meaning. But these are *generic* words, and come not under the rule—and even they have not changed in their radical significance. He has instanced *bapto* itself; but it meant dip in the days of Homer, and still means dip. It is, therefore, no exception. In the investigation of this general prefatory universal proposition, several important developments have occurred, such as:—all words *at first* have but one meaning. 2d. That specific words always retain it, while other terms may lose it. 3d. That, as the effects of any specific action may be both numerous and various, there may be many figurative or rhetorical uses of the original word because of its connection with these effects which it may have produced. Hence the results of the simple specific action, dip, are numerous and various. By a dip, a thing may be stained, colored, dyed, cleansed, washed, warmed, cooled, polluted, purified, &c. &c. Now, while the dip is immutably the same action, the effects may be numerous and diverse, and consequently expressed by very different terms. I have as yet called in vain upon my friend for an exemplification of the falsity of this law. I observed at the commencement, that I laid no great stress upon it; hence, if disproved, I could lose nothing, but if not, my cause triumphed.

My second universal proposition is, that all the lexicons down to the present century have given one and the same proper and primitive meaning to *baptizo*, the word in dispute; and that it never has been translated by either *sprinkle* or *pour*, by any lexicographer for 1800 years. This is the all-important word, because selected by the Holy Spirit to indicate the ordinance which our Savior enacted. If ever any word was definite and precise, it ought to be this one on which so much emphasis is laid in the New Testament. And I have shewn that our Savior *would* and *could*, and *did* select just such a term, to which no reply has been made.

But the gentleman will have it that I have been in the brush for two days. No doubt of it, for he has sought to hide in it. But we shall get out of the brush, by and by. Well; but I have proved nothing in two days! As much at least, I presume, as he proved in a seven years' war with the Roman Catholics of Bardstown. I never heard of his converting any of them. I am, indeed, in a way which he seems not very well to comprehend, establishing facts and affording inductions which must demonstrate to others, if not to him, the barrenness of his soil and the luxuriant fertility of ours.

I have also affirmed another still more overwhelming and grand universal proposition. After having shewn that the Greek classics amply sustain the dictionaries in their definitions of *baptizo*, by as liberal an induction as can be adduced in any word in the language, I advanced to one of the most convincing positions that could be taken on our premises, viz:— that of all the versions, ancient and modern, not one had ever translated *baptizo* by the words *sprinkle* or *pour*, but that some of them had used words equivalent to *immerse*. This is the more remarkable as respects the moderns, especially that all these versions appealed to were made by those practicing sprinkling—and yet, though meeting with this family of words one hundred and twenty times, not one of them had ever translated it by either of the words sprinkle or pour; the words, too, indicative of their own practice. This is also a universal proposition, and of course a single translation produced, so rendering the word, would negative it, and reduce it to a general proposition. I have called upon the gentleman to produce one man, living or dead, who has ever so rendered it, as to accord with the practice of his church. He has not produced the semblance of one. But he alledges that in the case of *bapto* he has found one— *and only one*, be it observed; of course, then, should he sustain that one! he has made my universal law, minus one—a general law. I am under no necessity to sustain any one of these three universal laws. The cause requires it not at my hand. No one ever before me, known to me, has taken such high ground. But still I do it, believing that I can sustain it.

And certainly if I do, the cause of sprinkling in this community has received an incurable wound.

Let us, then, calmly and dispassionately weigh the objection. I desire to give this solitary example a fair hearing, and to treat it with as much courtesy as though it were backed by a thousand. He found in the baptist Gale, and in the baptist Carson's works, an instance in the 19th chapter of the Apocalypse, where the perfect participle passive of *bapto*—*bebammenon*, is now found, and where we find in the Latin Vulgate of Jerom, and in the almost contemporaneous Ethiopic, and in the more ancient Syriac version, a rendering equivalent to our word, *sprinkling*, and this being the true reading, and a true version of it, he finds a single exception to our universal proposition. We shall then give a summary of our reasons against the alledged case.

The old Syriac is supposed to have been completed early in the second century. Origen flourished about the middle of the third. In one of his homilies on John, he quotes from the 11th to the 16th verses of the 19th of the Apocalypse, almost as we read, in every particular substituting *errantismenon* for *bebammenon*, as we have before explained—a word which is justly rendered *sprinkled*. The presumption is, from the singularity of the case, no other being found in universal sacred literature, that this quotation in Origen is from another reading, another and older version, different from the common one. This is my candid conviction, and I will set forth my reasons in order before you.

1. It is exceedingly improbable that these three versions could have all selected one and the same word, upon which to differ, from the universal custom of all other translators, and that, too, on its last occurrence in the book, having nothing special calling for it.

2. We know that there were numerous differences in the ancient versions in point of diverse readings, and that these differences were sometimes corrected by quotations found in the primitive fathers.

3. That Jerom should have followed Origen, is again most probable from the fact that he had long been employed in translating his Greek works into Latin, and although differing from him on some points, still his great admirer, and to such a degree that the ancients said that Jerom had studied Origen with so much admiration, that he had copied his errors and imperfections as well as his beauties. Now what could be more probable than, in having been so conversant with his Greek writings, and having such a veneration for his great parts and learning, he would have followed him in this version, especially as Origen was acquainted with the Syriac and all the then existing manuscript copies.

4. But I have another and a highly corroborating argument, deduced from a fact which occurred in the Baptismal Controversy. Dr. Wall, the greatest and most learned of the Pedo-baptist party, in the defence of this rite, wrote this great work you see in my hands (four large octavos;) one of them, indeed, the work of this said Dr. Gale, to whose book he has devoted one of these volumes, in the form of a particular answer. For this truly learned treatise in defence of the Church of England practice, this said Dr. Wall received the unanimous thanks of a whole consistory of the clergy. Now the question is, how did he dispose of Dr. Gale's remarks on this passage? Perhaps I ought to ask, first, how did these parties stand to each other? I will briefly state the facts:—Dr. Gale occupied my precise ground on this question. He argued for immersion only as the christian institution, and took the same view of the

disputed passage, though he did not argue the translations uniformly as I now do. Still he was a thorough immersionist, and went for immersion only. Now on this word *only* he was, in this question, opposed by Dr. Wall; for he, too, believed and taught that apostles taught and practiced immersion, but like Stuart of Andover, thought they did not do so *always*. The question then was about the word always. It then lay upon the Doctor to seize this same occurrence in the Apocalypse, especially as Dr. Gale had brought it before him. How, then, did he dispose of it? He conceded it—so far as passing it by in silence was concerned. He makes no objection to it, but passes it in silence. Certainly Mr. Rice knows this fact, and if so, why not state and explain it upon his principles.

5. I have, however, yet remaining another argument, and with that I shall, for the present, dismiss the subject. I have not time to read the sixty-third of Isaiah. I must, however, quote a few verses to shew that both Isaiah, and John in the 19th of the Apocalypse, had the same scene before them, and that they are describing the same person returning from the same battle, covered with the blood of his slain enemies. He breaks out in the most sublime strains on seeing the king return—"Who is this that cometh from Edom with *dyed* garments from Bozrah, this who is glorious in his apparel, traveling in the greatness of her strength? I," responds he, "that speak in righteousness, mighty to save. Wherefore red in thine apparel, and thy garments like him that treadeth in the wine vat." Again, he responds, almost in the words of Rev. xix. 13: "I have trodden the wine press alone; and of the people there was none with me: for I will tread them in mine anger, and trample them in my fury; and their blood shall *be sprinkled* upon my garments, and I will stain all my raiment." Now, that the idea of sprinkled blood should have, with the other parts of the same imagery, passed into the Apocalyptic scene, is, I think, most natural, and justifies still more strongly the reading quoted from Origen. From all these considerations, is there not almost a moral certainty that there was a different reading, and that that reading was the same both in Isaiah and the Apocalypse— or as quoted by Origen? But be this case construed as it may, one thing must be done according to the laws of evidence, as I interpret them, before an exception can be legally sustained. In the face of such evidence as I have given in favor of a different reading, it is incumbent on him who would constitute an exception, to shew that *bebammenon* and not *errantismenon* was the reading before the unknown author of the Syriac, and before Frumentius, the author of the Ethiopic, and before Jerom, the author of the Vulgate. This is now essential to constitute an exception; it must be first proved that *bebammenon* was *in the text*, before it can be proved that it was *translated* by sprinkled. This not being done, and being impossible, we now strongly re-affirm our third universal proposition, viz: *that no translator of the New Testament, in any language, ancient or modern, has ever translated baptism, by sprinkling or pouring*.

This being so, or were it with even a single exception so, in the case of *bapto*, how can the practice stand, having these universal propositions against it?

The two propositions combined in one, take away all lawful authority for the practice of either affusion or sprinkling. When it is fully established, as we now candidly must regard it, that no dictionary, during eighteen hundred years, no translation, of either Old or New Testament, during the same time, has ever rendered *baptizo*, or any one of its family, by either *sprinkle* or *pour ;* how can unprejudiced persons consider the practice as commanded by the Lord ? If Baptists had done all this some excuse might be for it ; but as it is wholly the work of Pedo-baptists, so far as English versions are concerned, we know not how the practice can be reconciled to their conscience and views of human responsibility.

As to the reputation of Mr. Gotch, from whom I have read some extracts, Mr. Rice having introduced him here, it was expected that he would have given us the proper information ; I can say that Mr. Gotch is a graduate of Trinity college, and, I can moreover say, that degrees conferred at Trinity college, Dublin, are always merited, and a worthy passport to public confidence.

He has given so much evidence, and bestowed so much attention to the subject, as to authorize him to say, that all those translators, that have translated by native words in their own language, have chosen words signifying to *immerse,* with the exception of some three or five, that have chosen such words as moisten, wash, cleanse.

I have yet a fourth universal proposition, but I perceive my time has expired.

Friday, Nov. 17—10½ *o'clock, A. M.*
[MR. RICE'S EIGHTH REPLY.]

MR. PRESIDENT—I think, all who have heard us on this occasion will admit, that my friend, Mr. C., has taken very high ground—the highest, he thinks, that ever has been taken. And this fact presents an important reason for suspecting that he is in error. Is it true, that he has risen, in learning, so far above the wise men of earth, that he may assume positions from which they all shrink ? Has he made discoveries in criticism to which none who have preceded him could attain ? Is it not more than probable that he is in error ?

I have a remark or two to make concerning his oft-repeated rule, that specific words, having a leading syllable, always retain their original idea. He calls on me to find a solitary exception to this rule. I have found an exception in the word *bapto* itself, if, indeed, it ever was a specific word, as he contends. I have repeatedly produced examples of its use from the classics, as well as from the Bible, in which the common sense of every unprejudiced individual, will enable him to perceive, that there could be no dipping. Where was the dipping, when the coloring fluid dropped on the garments and dyed them ? or when the coloring substance, being pressed, stained the hand ? Is this, as the gentleman pretends, the effect of *dipping ?*

I gave him, as an exception to his rule, the English word *prevent.* But this, he tells us, is a *generic term,* and, after all, has not changed its radical meaning. The word is derived from two Latin words—*pre* and *venio,* to come before. That it now generally means to *hinder,* cannot be denied. Was this always its meaning ? Every boy, who has read Cæsar, knows, that originally it meant simply to *come before.* It is used in this sense in 1 Thess. iv. 15, " For this we say unto you, by the word of the Lord, that we which are alive and remain unto the coming of the Lord, shall not *prevent* [ascend before] them which are asleep." Does it mean to hinder here ? Originally it meant to come before ; then, to anticipate ; then, to hinder ; and the third meaning has now become the literal, uniform meaning. The original syllable *(vent)* remains ; but the original idea *(to come)* is lost. This word was, primarily, as specific in its meaning as ever *bapto* was.

But I will again deliver the gentleman into the hands of his shrewd critic, Mr. Carson. He says, "Nothing in the history of words is more common than to enlarge or diminish their signification. Ideas, not originally included in them, are often affixed to some words, while others drop ideas originally asserted in their application. In this way *bapto*, from signifying mere mode, came to be applied to a certain operation usually performed in that mode. From signifying *to dip*, it came to signify *to dye by dipping*; because this was the way in which things usually were dyed. And afterwards, from dyeing by dipping, it came to denote *dyeing in any manner*. A LIKE PROCESS MIGHT BE SHOWN IN THE HISTORY OF A THOUSAND WORDS;" p. 60. Again, he says—"A word may come to enlarge its meaning, so as to lose sight of its origin. This fact must be obvious to every smatterer in philology. Had it been attended to, Baptists would have found no necessity to prove that *bapto*, when it signifies to dye, always properly signifies to *dye by dipping*, and their opponents would have seen no advantage from proving that it signifies *dyeing in any manner;*" pp. 62, 63.

But Mr. Campbell tell us, the meanings of the word, except *dip*, are figurative, rhetorical, &c. Mr. Carson, however, says, this is wholly incorrect. "They are," says he, "as literal as the primary meaning;" p. 64. And he tells us, a *thousand* examples could be produced confirming these principles.

The gentleman asserts, that all the lexicons, *before the present century*, have given *immerse* as the proper and primitive meaning of *baptizo*. *If he* has made great improvements in the science of criticism, as he professes to have done, I hope he will allow modern lexicographers the credit of having done the same. I, however, have found no ancient lexicographer who gives *immerse* as the literal and proper meaning of this word, *as used amongst the Jews in relation to their religious washings*. Can he produce one?

He attempts to excuse his failure thus far to prove any thing, by telling you, that though I was for seven years engaged in controversy with the Papists, he has heard of no conversions made. I think it probable, that many things have happened in this world of which he has not heard. I have, more than once, satisfied the minds of persons on that subject in a very short time.

The gentleman labors hard to prove, that our Bible ought to be changed—that, at any rate, Origen had a copy of the Apocalypse, in which, in Rev. xix. 13, the word *rantizo* was used instead of *bapto*, and that the same is true of the translators of the Syriac and Ethiopic versions. If Origen had quoted the passage verbatim, with the exception of that word, there might have been some plausibility in the conjecture of Mr. Campbell and Dr. Gale. But it is admitted, that he did not quote verbatim—but only "*almost* verbatim." When a man attempts simply to give the sense of a passage, nothing is more common than to employ, to some extent, words different from those in the text. But it is not, perhaps, surprising, that men who can immerse a man in dew, or immerse a garment by dropping a liquid on it, should, to save their cause, indulge in such conjectures.

But we are told, that Jerom was a great admirer of Origen, and that in translating the Vulgate, he probably followed the reading in Origen's writings. Is it credible that Jerom would alter the Bible for no better reason, than that Origen, in giving the sense of a passage, not quoting it verbatim, had used a word not in the text? Who ever heard of a critic who would venture, on grounds so perfectly flimsy, to change the text of God's word? There is no passage in the Bible, the purity of which might not be brought into doubt, if such guesses may be allowed. But I am not aware that Jerom was a great admirer of Origen. On the contrary, he was greatly prejudiced against his peculiar doctrines. There can, therefore, be no probability that he altered a passage of the Bible on any such grounds.

But here the gentleman presents, what appears to him, conclusive evidence, that there must have been another reading. Dr. Wall, he tells you, wrote a large volume in reply to Gale; and yet he did not attempt to answer Gale's remarks about this passage. But he did not tell you that Wall was avowedly writing on infant baptism, not on the mode; and that he declares his determination not to attempt an answer, at any length, to Gale's remarks on the mode. The truth is, Wall was himself a decided immersionist, and only contended that baptism, by pouring, was lawful in cases of necessity. The impression the gentleman made on the audience, I presume, was, that the large volume, he held up before you, was written on the *mode* of baptism; whereas, perhaps, not more than a tenth part of it is on that subject. When a man avows his determination not to answer a particular class of arguments, because they do not belong to the subject he is discussing; is it fair, is it true to say he *cannot* answer them?

Alas! for the criticism that would take a word out of the Bible and put another in place of it, where there is not a solitary manuscript or copy authorizing it! The cause must be sorely pressed that requires the word of God to be changed before it can be sustained!

My friend has read, in support of his statements concerning the translation, from Mr. Gotch, whom he considers quite a learned man, because he graduated at the Royal College of Dublin; where, he tells us, diplomas are given to none who are not learned. I know not how they manage such matters there; but, in this country, I know a diploma is no very certain evidence that the bearer is learned. He may be a very learned man, but, I believe, his fame has not yet reached this country, except among the advocates of immersion. But I have proved, by Gotch, that the Syriac and several other of the most important versions are against Mr. Campbell—that they did not translate *baptizo* to immerse.

The gentleman would have you believe that the translations are with him. How are they with him? Do they translate *baptizo* by words signifying to immerse? They do not. He has not proved that any one of them so translates it. I have proved that some nineteen of the most valuable do not translate it to suit him, but they employ generic terms signifying to wash, cleanse, &c. Immersion can gain no aid from the translations.

I will now return to the Bible usage of this word; for, after all, the usage of the Jews in their religious writings, as all the best critics agree, must determine its meaning, as applied to denote the ordinance of christian baptism. The first instance in which *baptizo* occurs, is in 2 Kings v. 14. In the tenth verse we are told, that "Elisha sent a messenger unto him, (Naaman) saying, go and wash in Jordan seven times, and thy flesh shall come again to thee," &c. And in verse fourteenth we learn, that "he went down and baptized *(baptizo)* himself seven times in Jordan, according to the saying of the man of God." Did he *immerse* himself?

He was told simply *to wash, (louo;)* and he obeyed the direction. *Baptizo* appears to be used as synonymous with *louo,* which all admit to be a generic term, signifying simply to wash, without reference to mode. Jerom, the author of the Vulgate, translates *baptizo,* in this passage, by the Latin word *lavo,* a generic term, signifying to wash. His words are—" Descendit, et *lavit* in Jordane septies juxta sermonem viri Dei." "He went down and *washed* in Jordan seven times, according to the word of the man of God." This, it is worthy of remark, is the only instance where Jerom translates the word at all. There certainly is no evidence that Naaman immersed himself.

The word *baptizo* occurs again in the book of Judith, an Apochryphal book, ch. xii. 7, "And she went out in the night, into the valley of Bethulia, and *baptized* herself at *(epi)* a fountain of water." Here is a baptism which the language employed and the attending circumstances prove, not to have been an immersion. She baptized or washed herself, not *into,* but *at* a fountain. It was a *fountain,* a spring, not a large stream. Did she immerse herself *at* a *spring ?* But she was in the military camp of Holophernes, where regard to decency forbid her immersing herself. Mr. Carson admits, that she did not immerse herself in the spring ; but he thinks, perhaps, there was a stone trough there, and that she got into it ! Our friends, when pressed, are good at guessing. But, as I have said, the language and the circumstances alike forbid us to believe, that she immersed herself. Here, then, is a clear example of the use of the word to denote washing by the application of water to the body—by *pouring.*

Baptizo occurs in Sirach or Ecclesiasticus, ch. xxxiv. 25, as follows : " He that is baptized after touching a dead body, *(baptizomenos apo nekrou,)* if he touch it again, what is he profited by his washing? *(loutro.")* Here is a baptism which is expressly called a *washing.* *Baptizomenos* is used as synonymous with *loutron*—a washing. By turning to Num. xix. 16, and the following verses, we can ascertain how this baptism was performed : " And whosoever toucheth one that is slain with a sword in the open field, or a dead body, or a bone of a man, or a grave, shall be unclean seven days. And for an unclean person they shall take of the ashes of the burnt heifer of purification for sin, and running water shall be put thereto in a vessel : and a clean person shall take hysop, and dip in the water, and sprinkle it upon the tent, and upon all the vessels, and upon the persons that were there, and upon him that toucheth a bone, or one slain, or one dead, or a grave ; and the clean person shall sprinkle upon the unclean, on the third day, and on the seventh day : and on the seventh day he shall purify himself, and wash his clothes, and bathe himself in water, and shall be clean at even."

Now, it is certain that *sprinkling* constituted a part of this baptism ; and it is equally certain, that no immersion was required. The word translated *bathe,* in this passage, is *rahatz*—the generic Hebrew word for *washing,* translated in the Septuagint by *louo*—the generic Greek term for washing. The sprinkling, moreover, is the most important part of this baptism, as the twentieth verse clearly proves: " But the man that shall be unclean, and shall not purify himself, that soul shall be cut off from among the congregation, because he hath defiled the sanctuary of the Lord : *the water of separation hath not been sprinkled upon him ; he is unclean.*" Here, then, we have a baptism without an immersion, the most important part of which is sprinkling.

10   N

These two passages I regard as of great importance in this discussion; because they show the sense in which the word *baptizo* was understood by the Jews, in relation to their religious washings. This word, let it be remembered, had long been in use among the Jews, before our Savior appropriated it to the ordinance of christian baptism. He, doubtless, used it nearly in the same sense in which he found it employed in relation to these religious washings. When, therefore, I prove that the Jews used it to express the application of water to the person by pouring or sprinkling, I have given conclusive evidence that our Savior used it in that sense.

I come now to the New Testament. The first instance in which we find it used in a literal sense, and not in relation to the ordinance of baptism, is in Mark vii. 4. I will read from the first verse: "Then came together unto him the Pharisees and certain of the Scribes, which came from Jerusalem. And when they saw some of his disciples eat bread with defiled (that is to say, with unwashen) hands, they found fault. For the Pharisees and all the Jews, except they wash their hands oft, eat not, holding the tradition of the elders. And when they come from the market, except they wash, *(baptizo)* they eat not. And many other things there be, which they have received to hold, as the washing *(baptisms)* of cups, and pots, and brazen vessels, and tables."

Now, the question presents itself, Were the Pharisees and all the Jews accustomed, when they came from the market or public places, always to immerse themselves before eating? Observe, the only charge ever made against our Savior and his disciples on this particular subject, was, not that they did not immerse themselves, but that they ate with *defiled or unwashen hands*. Nor did they charge them with not washing their hands by *dipping them*. The Jews certainly were not accustomed to immerse themselves before eating. We do not find in the Bible, nor elsewhere, a trace of any such general practice. Surely, if such a custom had existed, there would have been some reference to it—some evidence of a practice so remarkable. Besides, it must have been almost impossible that such a custom could exist. Even in our well-watered country, we should find it extremely difficult and inconvenient to immerse ourselves every time we return from a public place; and in the dry country inhabited by the Jews, it must have been far more difficult. If any one can believe that they not only immersed themselves on such occasions, but their tables or couches also, let him believe it. I cannot believe things so utterly improbable, without even the shadow of evidence.

But let us examine the translation of my worthy friend. He has followed Dr. George Campbell, who, though a Presbyterian, was an immersionist. It reads thus, "For the Pharisees, and indeed all the Jews, who observed the tradition of the elders, eat not except they have washed their hands *by pouring a little water on them*, and if they be come from the market, *by dipping them*." By what authority the phrase, "by pouring a little water on them," is here introduced, I know not. Can it be, that the little adverb *pugme* contains all this? If so, it is certainly the most remarkable adverb I have ever seen! I assert that this is no translation at all—it is not akin to a translation. In the original Greek the expression, "they eat not," occurs twice. One of these expressions the gentleman has thrown out in order to get in the phrase, "by dipping them!" for if he had not rejected part of the Greek, he could not have thus translated the passage. Having got part of the Greek out of his way, he makes a most singular reading of what remains! The Greek phrase, *ean me baptizontai*, (literally, unless they baptize) he translates, " by dipping them." That is, he takes a Greek *conjunction*, an *adverb*, and a *verb* in the third person, plural number, and translates them by a preposition *by*, a participle *dipping*, and adds the word *them*, which is not in the Greek !! Such a translation, or rather such a perversion of Scripture I do not remember ever to have seen—and all to sustain the claims of immersion !

Baptizo occurs again in Luke xi. 38. A certain Pharisee asked the Savior to dine with him ; and he went and sat at table. " And when the Pharisee saw it, he marvelled that he had not first washed *(baptized)* before dinner." Did the Pharisee wonder that the Savior had not gone and *immersed* himself before dinner? As I have already remarked, we find no such custom prevailing, and the only charge preferred against him was that he did not *wash his hands*. But let me read Mr. Campbell's translation of this passage ; for I intend, if he pleases, to have him help me in this discussion. His translation is as follows : " But the Pharisee was surprised to observe that he *used no washing* before dinner." Although the gentleman set out with the purpose of uniformly translating *baptizo* to immerse, he could not, in this instance, venture to do so. It would have looked too badly. He was forced to give it its true meaning, *to wash*. The Baptist translation, it is worthy of remark, renders the word in this passage and in Mark vii. 4, to *bathe*. Although the authors had intended to give the word a *literal* translation, they could not venture to render it *immerse* in these passages. In both these instances it is evident that it is used to express the washing of the hands, which among the Jews, we know was commonly done by pouring water on them.

This word occurs once more in a literal sense in Heb. ix. 10, where the apostle says of the ceremonial law, "which stood in meats and drinks, and divers washings *(baptisms)* and carnal ordinances." Or as Mr. Campbell's translation runs : " Only with meats and drinks, and divers immersions— ordinances concerning the flesh," &c.

I have no objection to this general construction, which is that of Knapp's Testament. The word *baptism* here evidently includes all the religious washings of the ceremonial law. And it is a fact, that all those washings, the *mode* of which was prescribed, were by *sprinkling*. It is also a fact, that there is not a *personal* immersion required in the law of Moses. Many sprinklings were enjoined, but not an important immersion. And in this same chapter some of those sprinklings are mentioned. The divers baptisms, then, included all the sprinklings, pourings and washings of the law. The word, therefore, does not signify *immersion*. But this is not the only evidence I have to offer on this subject.—[*Time expired.*

Friday, Nov. 17—*12 o'clock.*
[MR. CAMPBELL'S NINTH ADDRESS.]

MR. PRESIDENT—Mr. Rice is so far in advance of me, that I cannot hope soon to overtake him. Before resuming my argument, I shall briefly advert to so many of his remarks, as have any special reference to the matters introduced by myself. The other and foreign matters, when they come fairly in my path, may probably be noticed.

He certainly does me too much honor, when he supposes, or pretends to suppose, that I am sorely pressed, with one apparent exception, out of at least ten thousand occurrences. Even suppose he had made out one case, if I were to multiply all the versions by one hundred and twenty, the number of occurrences of this word, I should then have more than ten thousand to one. How fearful, then, is a single exception in his eyes! But, as we have shown that he has not yet made out one exception, we shall proceed to other remarks until he find one.

I am not so much gratified with following the lead of others, right or wrong, as my friend would make me say Jerom was in making a Bible. Had I been led by Mr. Rice through all his meanderings, we should have been wading through many foreign matters, such as his oft-related readings on various versions, with which this age is every where replete—all of which are as irrelevant here as St. Cyprian's disclosures of African learning in the third century.

Probably Jerom had before him the Ethiopic as well as the Syriac version then extant, and as many judged the latter equal to the original, Jerom, not merely from his esteem and admiration of Origen's learning, may have followed it. All the use I made of Origen's quotations from the Apocalypse, was to shew that Jerom from that source alone could not but have known the different reading, and that Origen's testimony was to him a confirmation of the Syriac reading—if, indeed, such was the ancient Syriac.

The gentleman, in good keeping with other assertions, affirms that the translations make no more for me, than for him. His vision, or his art of making assertions, is of a rare character. He admits, then, they make nothing for him! Well, be it so! But for me it is far otherwise.

To make out his assumption, he should have proved that the translations have, but *in one instance*, translated it immerse. Then there would have been some slight appearance of truth in the assertion. But what are the facts? Even suppose he could have tortured Mr. Gotch, whom he first introduced into this discussion, into an ambiguity, and rendered even doubtful the old Vulgate and Italic, the Arabic and the Persic, the Ethiopic, &c. &c., and could have made even John the Baptist pour water upon the head of the Messiah, as the pictures do, what would all this prove! Are these all the versions? Not the half of them. And these, too, Mr. Gotch, with him many others of equal learning, have proved to be on our side. But as I will not go into a warfare in all the languages of the world, I again ask, where are all the other translators? Has one of them named *sprinkling* or *pouring?* No: not one! The facts, the solemn and irrefragable facts are:—many of them have always used words expressive of immersion, all of them have sometimes translated it by the word *dip*, or its equivalent; and some of the moderns are not only with me in the fact of having translated *baptizo*, by immerse, but like McKnight and Campbell, in approving and commending it. The last named two, were Presbyterians of the highest fame. Dr. McKnight was prolocutor or chairman of the whole general assembly of the Kirk of Scotland; and Dr. Campbell was some time president of the Mavischal College of Aberdeen, and Regius professor of Scotch Presbyterian theology, and the most profound critic and translator in his day. Besides these, all the twenty English versions, public and private, to which I have referred, a majority of which I have in my possession, in their translations, notes and comments, are decidedly with us and against him. Some of these, like McKnight, in translating the "diverse washings" of the Hebrews, by "diverse *immersion*," and the passage in Mark, "except they wash (into, except they *immerse*) they eat not," have taken from the

Pedo-baptists the cases of "*washing*" on which they rely. McKnight has not left, then, a single pin on which to hang up an objection. There is a great difference between these two propositions ;—the translations are all sometimes with us ; many of them often with us, some of them affirming that it ought always to have been *immerse*—and the proposition ;—not one of them is ever with Mr. Rice, many of them openly against him, and some of them reproaching the ancients for not having translated it immerse. Such are the facts of the two cases—from which this community may always judge how much reliance is to be placed on my worthy friend's assertions.

There is only one other point upon this subject to which I must again recur. The gentleman will, by the force of reiteration of the same assumptions, keep these topics on hand as long as possible. He will yet have pouring, sprinkling, immersion, *modes* of baptism. If each of these be a mode, I again ask what is the substance of which they are *modes ?* They are not the thing itself. If, for example, sprinkling be the action Jesus Christ commanded, how can immersion be a mode of sprinkling, or how can sprinkling be a mode of immersion ? Will the gentleman deliver himself clearly and definitely on this important point ? Surely there must be some great action of which these are but mere modes. Mr. Rice will not, cannot, dare not, say that these three terms in our language are not specific. He has, indeed, if I mistake not, admitted that sprinkling is a specific word, and consequently all the others. It does, to me at least, seem very strange and inexplicable, that some persons cannot learn that specific words can have but one meaning, and that at all times. Take again the words *walk, ride, sail*, each a specific mode of traveling. *Travel* is a generic word, and includes them all. Not one of them includes *travel*, while travel includes them all. Men can travel other ways than by walking, therefore the former is general and the latter special. Now does not every one perceive that to walk, means one specific action ; to ride, another ; to sail, another ? If, for example, to ride means to walk, suppose you were told that A B walked to town, could you know how he came, whether on foot or on horseback ? Two meanings, pardon the incongruity, two meanings to a specific word wholly destroy its sense, effectually make it meaningless. Does not every stripling in the congregation perceive that this is so ; and, therefore, assent to that all-important law of language, that *specific words* can have but one meaning. Let any one who wishes to convince the stupid or the incredulous, select a few specific words—such as *reading, writing, talking*—and placing one in another room, say of him that he is *writing ;* and on the hypothesis that specific words have two or three meanings, can any one who is told that he is writing, know what he is doing ? It is impossible, utterly impossible. Am I not now understood and believed by every one in the assembly ? I shall hereafter presume, that I am universally understood on this highly important, though I am sorry to say much neglected branch of criticism, so vital to the question now in debate.

Now, as Mr. Rice admits that sprinkling, pouring, and dipping, are just as specifically different as reading, writing, talking, walking, riding, sailing, flying, &c., I ask, in the name of reason and consistency, must not their representatives in other languages be specific too !! Why should *dip* be specific in English and not in Greek ? Or will he assume the all-confounding position that a word in one language can represent both generic and specific terms in another ? This would be still more preposterous. This law of language, as I shall call it, will certainly settle this controversy one day, with all scholars; with persons of real learning and unprejudiced minds. I am glad of the occasion of delivering myself, even partially upon it; and that it is about to be stereotyped. I am willing to risk upon it, with an intelligent community, what little reputation I have for discrimination in the use and application of language.

I have before said that from specific acts many effects may follow. A person may, for example, be dipped in, or sprinkled with, a hundred substances, each of which will, of course, produce a different effect; such as fire, water, milk, honey, wine, tar, sand, mire, &c. How absurd would it be to make all these effects the meaning of the word *dip*. I own that in consequence of the original fewness of words in all languages, by the figure metalepsis, or metonymy, or metaphor, or synecdoche, &c. words were used rhetorically and figuratively to represent different things; and therefore, the most common effects of actions in dictionaries are sometimes wisely, and sometimes not wisely, but very unwisely appended to words. Hence the law and the usage of reprobating the figurative meanings of words, because unsafe and always changing, in the passing of laws and ordinances. *Baptizo* therefore, has but one proper meaning, and every effect ascribed to it in books is to be received as every one pleases, but *dip* must be received by all.

I hope I may be excused in these efforts to establish a great principle, not before, as far as I know, developed or applied in this controversy. I know the distinction between specific and generic words is as old as Aristotle; but the full development of the distinction, and its importance in language, and especially in this controversy, have not, so far as known to me, at all received a proper attention. I honestly consider it of more importance than all the display of words and specifications of examples adduced on this occasion. They indeed, generally, go to the establishment of the law; but beyond that they effect but little.

It would be well to canvass this law of language to the bottom. I am prepared for it, and am willing to stake the whole question of the action of baptism upon its truth and validity. Will my respondent please discuss this point, and, in his own style, develop to us the specific action, of which his sprinkling and pouring are modes?

In my rich resources of evidence, and in my exuberant liberality, I feel disposed, just at this point, to tender to my friend, Mr. R., another universal proposition. I have, indeed, taken upon myself a work of supererogation, a task wholly gratuitous and uncalled for, the labor of sustaining four universal propositions. Has any one ever before presumed so much upon the strength of his cause, as thus, in the very commencement, to take to himself such a labor, and give to his antagonist such an easy task as only to make out one single exception: for one well established exception will reduce a universal proposition to a general one. If any word in Greek, Latin, or English, will allow any man to be so liberal and generous—*baptizo* is that word. The master knew well what he said, and what he did, when he issued the precept "BAPTIZE THEM." I say, I am prepared to risk another universal proposition, which attacks another department, a main post on the negative side of the question. I will then expose another side to the assaults of my opponent.

I affirm, then, that all the *sprinklings* and *pourings* of the law, from Moses to Christ, required something more than water to effect any legal ceremonial, or typical cleansing. By an induction of all the cases on record, it will appear most evident, that, to give any efficacy or value to sprinkling, something more than water was required. Hence the addition of blood, or its substitute, the ashes of a blood-red heifer, was essential to every purgation in which water was sprinkled. To give to this proposition another form, and that Mr. R. may easily disprove it, I assert, that from the creation till now, in all time, the great Lawgiver of the universe *never commanded any thing to be sprinkled with water alone*, in order to its legal, ceremonial, or moral purification, or cleansing; a fact which can be disproved by a single instance, and which, if true, most significantly and solemnly inhibits the Papistical custom of sprinkling water, though, I believe, except in baptism, the Romanists generally use holy water. A single example from Moses or the prophets; from the Messiah or his apostles, of the pouring or sprinkling of water, *per se*, of water unmixed with some purifying ingredient, will be accepted on my part as a full refutation of this, my fourth universal proposition. Unless, however, some such precept be produced, or some example be offered, of some person (I care not who—man, woman, or child,) having had water poured, or sprinkled, upon him by divine authority, the cause of rantism, or of affusion, with water alone and unmixed, is sunk forever. When I say Mr. Rice cannot do this, I would not be understood as at all disparaging his acquaintance with the Bible. I have just as much confidence in his ability to do this, as in any minister of that portion of the Presbyterian church, which he represents on the present occasion. I know, indeed, that no man can do it. Therefore my proposition will stand till the christian dispensation ends. If a fair impersonation of the Biblical learning of the Presbyterian church of Kentucky, a highly respectable community, cannot do this, I am sure that this congregation will acquiesce with me in opinion, that no other branch of the church of denominations can do it. This proposition, also, as far as known to me, has never been affirmed in any discussion of this question; I therefore solicit for it a thorough examination, and refutation, if possible.

Leaving, then, these, my four universal propositions, in the hands of my friend, to be disposed of as, in his judgment, best he can, I shall proceed in my regular line of march in the maintenance of the proposition before us; reminding him, however, that not in my opinion only, but I presume (so much upon my knowledge of the human mind, and of this community especially, to say) in public opinion also, that if only one of the four stands erect, sprinkling and pouring, as baptism, must fall to the ground. How impossible to hold it up if they all stand?

I shall finish my present address by reading a few extracts from my yet unpublished book on baptism; a portion only, and but a small portion of its documents can, I perceive, find admission into this discussion. It is, indeed, a volume more of facts and documents than any thing else. For, when these are laid before the public, not much argument will be needed. The two or three extracts yet to be read, are from the translators, in farther proof of my fourth argument founded on them. I open this venerable volume, 280 years lodged within this cover, reaching back almost to the age of Calvin and Beza. It is the celebrated and learned Latin version of the Old Testament, by Junius and Tremmelius, and the New Testament by Beza—from whom, in addition to another reading, I shall only now read his note on Rom. vi. 4—"We are buried with him by baptism into death," &c. *The allusion here is to the ancient manner of baptizing.* This is, then, a clear testimony from this translator, that, in the apostolic age, immersion was understood to be the meaning of *baptisma*. Almost in the same words speaks John Wesley.

I shall conclude this argument by two short extracts from our American apostle, Stuart of Andover. He closed my first argument, and he shall close my fourth.

"That the Greek fathers, and the Latin ones who were familiar with the Greek, understood the usual import of the word *baptizo*, would hardly seem to be capable of a denial. That they might be confirmed in their view of the import of this word, by common usage among the Greek classic authors, we have seen in the first part of this dissertation.

"For myself, then, I cheerfully admit that *baptizo*, in the New Testament, when applied to the rite of baptism, does in all probability invole the idea, that this rite was *usually* performed by immersion, but not always."— *Biblical Repository*, vol. iii. p. 362.

I leave my friend, Mr. Stuart, to explain his "*not always*," as best he can ; his *usually* is enough for me. And, so long as one of our greatest American Biblical scholars and Pedo-baptists has said, that the apostles *usually* immersed, or that such is the New Testament acceptation of the word, I care not should Mr. R. a thousand times say, that there is neither in philology, nor in history, proof that *baptizo* means to *immerse*.

V. My fifth argument and fourth class of witnesses, in support of my first proposition, shall consist of the testimony of Reformers, Annotators, Paraphrasts, and Critics, on the meaning of the word *baptism*, selected, not from amongst the Baptists, but from amongst the Pedo-baptist writers, who have regarded sprinkling a more convenient, comfortable, and polite usage. I place at the head of the list, the reformer and translator, Martin Luther. In the fifth of the Smialcald articles, drawn up by Luther, he says—"Baptism is nothing else than the word of God with immersion in water."

"Baptism is a Greek word, and may be translated *immersion*, as when we immerse something in water, that it may be wholly covered. And although it is almost wholly abolished, (for they do not *dip* the whole children, but only pour a little water on them) they ought nevertheless to be wholly immersed, and then immediately drawn out ; for that *the etymology of the word seems to demand*." "Washing of sins is attributed to baptism ; it is truly, indeed, attributed, but the signification is softer and slower than it can express baptism, which is rather a sign both of death and resurrection. Being moved by this reason, I would have those that are to be baptized, to be altogether dipt into the water, as the word doth sound, and the mystery doth signify."—*Op*. vol. i. 336.

Calvin : "The word *baptizo* signifies to immerse, and it is certain that immersion was the practice of the ancient church."—*Instit*. b. iv. s. 15.

Grotius : The great Grotius says, "That this rite was wont to be performed by immersion, and not by perfusion, appears both by the propriety of the word and the places chosen for its administration, John iii. 23, Acts viii. 38, and by the many allusions of the apostles, which cannot be referred to sprinkling, Rom. vi. 3, 4, Col. ii. 12. The custom of perfusion or aspersion seems to have obtained some time after, in favor of such who, lying dangerously ill, were desirous to dedicate themselves to Christ. These were called *Clinics* by other christians. See Cyprian's epistle to Magnus to this purpose. Nor should we wonder that the old Latin fathers used *tingere* for *baptizare*, seeing the Latin word *tingo* does properly and generally signify the same as *mersare*, to immerse or plunge."—*Matt*. iii. 6. *Gale*.

Dionysius Petavius : "And indeed," says he, "immersion is properly styled *baptismos*, though at present we content ourselves with pouring water on the head, which in Greek is called *perixusis*, that is perichysm, if I may so anglicise, but not baptism."

Casaubon: "For the manner of baptizing," says he, "was to plunge or dip them into the water, as even the word *baptizein* itself plainly enough shows, which, as it does not signify *dunein*, to sink down and perish, neither certainly does it signify *epipolazein*, to swim or float a-top; these three words, *epipelazein*, *baptizein*, *dunein*, being very different."

Vitringa: "The act of *baptizing* is the immersion of believers in water. This expresses the force of the word."—*Aphor. Sanc. Theol. Aphoris.* 884.

Salmasius: "*Baptism* is immersion, and was administered in former times according to the force and meaning of the word."—*De Cæsarie Virorum*, p. 669.

Hospinianus: "Christ commanded us to be baptized; by which it is certain immersion is signified."—*Hist. Sactram.* 1. ii. c. i. 30.

Zanchius: "The proper signification of *baptize* is to immerse, plunge under, to overwhelm in water."

Alstedius: "To *baptize* signifies only to immerse; not to wash, except by consequence."

Witsius: "It cannot be denied that the native signification of the words *baptein* and *baptizein*, is to plunge, to dip."—*In. His. Ecc.* p. 138.

Gurtlerus: "To *baptize*, among the Greeks, is undoubtedly to immerse, to dip; and baptism is immersion, dipping. *Baptismos en Pneumati hagio*, baptism in the Holy Spirit, is immersion into the pure waters of the Holy Spirit; for he on whom the Holy Spirit is poured out, is, as it were, immersed into him. *Baptismos en puri*, 'baptism in fire,' is a figurative expression, and signifies casting into a flame, which, like water, flows far and wide; such as the flame that consumed Jerusalem. The thing commanded by the Lord is baptism, immersion into water."—*Institut. Theo.* cap. xxxiii. § 108, 109, 110, 115.

Buddaeus: "The words *baptizein* and *baptismos*, are not to be interpreted of aspersions, but always of immersion."—*Theolog. Dogmat.* 1. v. c. i. § 5.

Ewing, of Glasgow: "*Baptizo*, in its primary and radical sense, I cover with water. It is used to denote, 1st. I plunge, or sink completely under water."

Leigh: "The native and proper signification of it [*baptize*] is, to dip into water, or to plunge under water."

Bossuet: "To baptize signifies to plunge, as is granted by all the world."

Vossius, as quoted by Gale: "The great Vossius speaks exactly to the same purpose, and indeed almost in the same words; for without ever taking the least notice of *lavo*, or the like, he expressly says, that *bapto* and *baptizo* are rendered by *mergo*, or *mergito*, and *tingo*, yet they properly signify *mergo*; and *tingo* only by a metalepsis, i. e. as *tingo* implies *mergo*; and therefore he adds, tinging follows immersion, and is done by it."

Venema: "The word *baptizein*, to baptize, is nowhere used in the Scripture for sprinkling."—V. p. 5.

Bloomfield: "There is here [Rom. vi. 4,] plainly a reference to the ancient mode of baptism by immersion; and I agree with Koppe and Rosenmuller, that there is reason to regret it should have been abandoned in most christian churches, especially as it has so evident a reference to the mystic sense of baptism."

Scholz, on Matt. iii. 6: "Baptism consists in the immersion of the whole body in water."

Augusti: "The word, baptism, according to the etymology and usage, signifies to immerse, submerge, &c., and the choice of the word betrays an age in which the later custom of sprinkling had not been introduced."

Buttmann, in his Larger Grammar, simply puts down, "*bapto*, to immerse."

Edinburgh Reviewers of Carson's work: "They tell me, (says Mr. Carson,) that it was unnecessary to bring forward any of the examples to prove that the word signifies *to dip*—that I might have commenced with this as a FIXED POINT UNIVERSALLY ADMITTED."—[*Time expired.*

Friday, Nov. 17—11½ *o'clock.*
[MR. RICE'S NINTH REPLY.]

It is true, Mr. President, I have got ahead of the gentleman; and I am apprehensive he will not overtake me. I presume my cause is somewhat easier to manage than his. He, doubtless, could travel as fast, perhaps faster than I, if he had no heavier burden to bear. When a *giant* travels so slowly that even a small man can get ahead of him, there is pretty conclusive evidence that he has a heavy burden.

He tells you that I have found but one passage in which *bapto* is translated to *sprinkle*, and that he has thousands of others to sustain his position. This is a mistake. I have produced a number, and can produce many more from the classics, where there could be no dipping; where the fluid must have been applied to the subject, not the subject dipped into the fluid. I have produced several examples from the Bible of the same kind; and I have stated the fact, which he has not ventured to deny, that though *bapto* occurs some twenty times or more, in the Old and New Testaments, there are not more than four or five instances in which it expresses an immersion. I quoted the passage relative to Nebuchadnezzar's baptism in dew, to show that in this instance, *bapto* means even less than sprinkling. Jerom, the author of the Vulgate, though favorable to immersion, did not translate the word *immerse*, in this instance. The Geneva Bible translates it *bedewed*—" his body was bedewed with dew." I have produced three of the most valuable ancient versions in which *bapto* is translated by the word *sprinkle*.

The gentleman guesses that Jerom had the Syriac version before him, when he translated it to sprinkle. But did not Jerom know the meaning of *bapto?* The Greek was then a living language, which he constantly read and heard spoken; and if he could not ascertain its meaning, we shall scarcely succeed in learning it. But the Syriac is itself a translation from the Greek. There is no escape for my friend.

The English translations, the gentleman says, are with him, and he refers particularly to Campbell's and McKnight's. But neither of these men ventured uniformly or commonly to translate *baptizo* to immerse. And if they had, who, I ask, has ever adopted their translations instead of the common version? Both of these men, though Presbyterians, were favorable to immersion. We do not excommunicate men for such an opinion. Hence we have had, from time to time, in the Presbyterian church, men who were in some sense immersionists. Still none of them could ever see the truth of Mr. C's. doctrine, that our Savior commanded specifically immersion as the only valid baptism. But let the gentleman, if he can, produce one respectable English translation, that renders *baptizo* to immerse. I believe he cannot find one, good or bad, except his own and that recently published by the Baptists, that will sustain him. The whole of the English translators, so far as I know, translate the word by a *generic term.*

My friend again criticises the expression *mode* of baptism. He asks, if sprinkling, pouring, and immersion are *modes*, what is the substance? And I ask him, if sprinkling, pouring and dipping are modes of *washing*, what is the substance? As I have repeatedly said, washing, cleansing may be performed in different modes. So water, as an emblem of cleansing, may be applied in different ways. You tell your son to wash his hands. May he not obey you, either by dipping them into water, or by pouring water on them? The substance of baptism is the application of water to a suitable subject by an authorized minister, in the name of the Trinity. I hope this will be satisfactory.

If *baptizo* is a specific word, the gentleman argues, it never can become *generic*. This cannot be proved. But I deny that *baptizo* is a specific word. I have proved by the best lexicons, ancient and modern, that it has several distinct meanings. Consequently, according to a universal rule of language, the connection must determine in any particular case, which meaning is to be attached to it.

Mr. C. has told us, that all the lexicons prefer *immerse* as the proper and literal meaning of *baptizo*. I have called on him to produce one lexicon of the New Testament, that gives immerse as its first meaning. He has not produced one.

He tells you he has in his conscious strength presented his broadside to the enemy, so as to give the fairest opportunity to fire into him. True, his broadside is toward the enemy. A vessel at sea sometimes gets into such a predicament, that it cannot avoid presenting its broadside. The sails and rigging are cut away, it becomes unmanageable, and is obliged to receive the enemy's shot. In such cases it is better, perhaps, to make a virtue of necessity, and to appear to have taken such a position as matter of choice.

My friend, Mr. C., has made a broad assertion, which he seems to consider of great importance, viz: that pouring or sprinkling water alone was never commanded, as a mode of purification. I will suggest to him a single passage, which will destroy the whole force of his *universal* assertion, if indeed it has any force. Ezekiel says, " Then will I sprinkle clean water upon you, and ye shall be clean: from all your filthiness and from all your idols will I cleanse you." Will the gentleman, in view of this passage, deny that the sprinkling of clean water is a suitable emblem of purification? This passage will answer for the present. I think it will appear, as we progress, that he, with his broadside exposed, frequently makes very positive assertions, which cannot be of service to his cause, whilst he fails to prove positions absolutely essential to save it from ruin.

He told us, he would ere long get out of the brush; and I had hoped to see him in the Bible, for he boasts of going by *the Book*. But I begin to fear, that he will not reach it. The best works he can get to sustain his cause, it would seem, are sixteen hundred years too late for inspiration. He appeals to Beza, Calvin, and divers other learned men. Beza was a learned man; and so were Luther and Calvin. But men in the midst of such a revolution as that in which they were destined to act so prominent a part, were not likely to turn their attention very particularly to such a subject as we are now discussing. They had themselves but just emerged from the midnight darkness of Popery; they found it necessary to lay anew the very foundation of christian doctrine; in doing which their lives were often in danger. Is it likely, that men under such circumstances would thoroughly investigate the mode of baptism—a subject which then excited little or no interest? Calvin considered it a matter of entire indifference. And is it common for men to investigate, at any great length, subjects in which they feel no interest? Calvin wrote a system of theology, which, I believe, contains about *four lines* on the mode of baptism; and in these lines he declared his opinion, that it is a matter of indifference. He had enough to do without discussing modes and forms.

Beza differs from bòth Mr. C. and myself. He makes *baptizo* mean *immerse,* and also to wash; and to dip for the purpose of dyeing. In this last particular, my friend says, he was wrong; and yet he would have me think he is, as to immersion, in the right!

Luther, as I have before remarked, seems to have been favorable to immersion; and yet he did not translate *baptizo* to immerse. I have his translation of the New Testament, in which, as I have repeatedly stated, he makes John the Baptist say—" I baptize you *with* water, (*mit* wasser) He shall baptize you *with (mit)* the Holy Ghost;" and in which he translates the word in Mark vii. 4, 8, and Luke xi. 38, by a generic term, meaning to *wash*. Now, since he was favorable to immersion, why did he not do as my friend Mr. C. has done—translate *baptizo* to *immerse?* Why did he not make John say, "I baptize you *in* water"? Evidently he was not convinced that such was definitely its meaning.

But the gentleman quotes John Wesley as sustaining immersion. Let us hear Wesley speak for himself. He says—

" The *matter* of this sacrament is water, which, as it has a natural power of cleansing, is the more fit for this symbolical use. Baptism is performed by *washing*, *dipping*, or *sprinkling* the person in the name of the Father, Son, and Holy Ghost, who is hereby devoted to the ever blessed Trinity. I say, by *washing*, *sprinkling*, or *dipping;* because it is not determined in Scripture in which of these ways it shall be done, neither by any express *precept*, nor by any such example as clearly proves it; nor by the force or meaning of the word baptism."—*Wesley*, p. 144.

Wesley says the word cannot prove immersion, nor is there any thing in the Bible that does prove it.

It is true, Stuart has admitted too much; and it is equally true, that he has not admitted half enough for my friend. He expresses his firm conviction that immersion was *not* always practiced by the apostles. The gentleman tells you that Stuart has admitted that the ancient church practiced immersion. He does say that the ancient church immersed *three times*, divesting the persons of all their garments. I will read on p. 97 of Stuart on Baptism.

" I go farther with this argument. If you take your stand on the ancient practice of the churches, in the days of the early christian fathers, and charge me with departure from this; in my turn, I have the like charge to make against you. It is notorious and admits of no contradiction, that baptism in those days of immersion, was administered to men, women, and children, *in puris naturalibus*, naked as Adam and Eve, before their fall. The most tender, delicate and modest females, young and old, could obtain no exception, where immersion must be practiced. The practice was pleaded for and insisted upon, because it was thought to be apostolic. At all events it began very early in the christian church."

If this is the mode of baptizing for which the gentleman is contending, I will not oppose him! But if he will not follow the example of the ancient church, why does he plead its authority.

Witsius was a learned man. He, as quoted by Mr. C., says, the *native* signification of *baptizo* is, to immerse. This, as I have repeatedly said, I could admit without injury to my cause. Very few words retain their native or original signification. Therefore critics tell us, that etymology, which teaches the native meaning of words, is a very uncertain guide in interpretation. The question before us is, not what the word *baptizo* meant, when first used by pagan Greeks, but what was its meaning amongst the Jews in the days of Christ and the apostles.

But if the controversy is to be determined by the opinions of learned men, I will sustain my position by as great an array of learning and talent, as the gentleman can produce in his favor.

Dr. Owen is admitted to have been one of the greatest and most learned men. He says:

"*Baptizo* signifies *to wash;* as instances out of all authors may be given, Suidas, Hesychius, Julius Pollux, Phavorinus, and Eustachius. It is first used in the Scripture, Mark i. 8, John i. 33, and to the same purpose in Acts i. 5. In every place it either signifies to pour, or the expression is equivocal. "I baptize you with water, but he shall baptize you with the Holy Ghost;" which is the accomplishment of that promise, 'that the Holy Ghost shall be poured on them.'" Again—"No one place can be given in the Scriptures, wherein *baptizo* doth necessarily signify either *to dip* or *plunge.*" Again—"In this sense, as it expresseth baptism, it denotes *to wash* only, and not *to dip* at all : for so it is expounded, Tit. iii. 5," &c. Again—"Wherefore in this sense, as the word is applied unto the ordinance, the sense of dipping is utterly excluded."—*Owen's Works,* vol. xxi. p. 557.

Dr. George Hill, principal of St. Mary's College, St. Andrews, was an eminently learned man. He says—"Both *sprinkling* and *immersion* are implied in the word *baptizo;* both were used in the religious ceremonies of the Jews, and both may be considered as significant of the purpose of baptism," &c.—*Hill's Divinity,* p. 659.

Dr. John Dick, Professor of Theology to the United Session Church, was a learned man; and his system of Theology is a standard work. He says, concerning *bapto :* "Examples, however, have been produced, from which it appears, that the idea sometimes conveyed even by this verb, which it is commonly admitted signifies *to dip,* is that of *sprinkling,* rather than of dipping." Concerning *baptizo* he says—"We here see that nothing certain as to mode can be learned from the original term *baptizo,* because it has different meanings, signifying sometimes *to immerse,* and sometimes *to wash,*" &c.—*Divinity,* pp. 470, 471.

Dr. Adam Clarke is admitted to have been an eminent linguist. In his Commentary on Matt. iii. 6, he says—"In what form baptism was originally administered, has been deemed a subject worthy of serious dispute, Were the people *dipped or sprinkled? for it is certain* BAPTO *and* BAPTIZO *mean both.*"

Dr. Thomas Scott, the commentator, is admitted to have been a learned man. He quotes Leighton as saying—"It [*baptizo*] is taken more largely for any kind of washing, rinsing, or cleansing, even when there is no dipping at all"—then remarks—"The word was adopted from the Greek authors, and a sense put upon it by the inspired writers, according to the style of Scripture, to signify the use of water in the sacrament of baptism, and in many things of a spiritual nature, which stood related to it. Some indeed contend zealously, that *baptism* always signifies *immersion;* but the use of the words *baptize* and *baptism* in the New Testament, cannot accord with this exclusive interpretation." This he gives as a conclusion resulting from "many years' consideration and study."

Dr. Dwight is admitted to have been one of the most learned men in the United States. He says—"I have examined almost one hundred instances, in which the word *baptizo* and its derivatives are used in the New Testament, and four in the Septuagint : and these, so far as I have observed, being all the instances contained in both. By this examination, it is to my apprehension evident, that the following things are true—That the primary meaning of these terms is cleansing; the effect, not the mode of washing—That the mode is usually referred to *incidentally,* wherever these words are mentioned, and that this is always the case, wherever the ordinance of baptism is mentioned, and a reference made, at the same time, to the mode of administration—That these words, although often capable of denoting any mode of washing, whether by affusion, sprinkling, or immersion, (since cleansing was familiarly accomplished by the Jews in all these ways) yet, in many instances, cannot, without obvious impropriety, be made to signify immersion; and in others cannot signify it at all."—*Theology*, v. 5, p. 331.

I might add the opinion of Dr. Wall, who, though decidedly favorable to immersion, maintains that "the word *baptizo*, in Scripture, signifies to *wash* in general, without determining the sense to this or that sort of washing."

But I must return to the Bible argument. I was proving, when I closed my last address, that the word *baptisms* in Heb. ix. 10, comprehends all the washings of the Levitical law, which, in all cases where the mode was prescribed, were to be performed by *sprinkling*. The Levitical law, the apostle says, consisted in "meats and drinks, and divers baptisms or washings;" and he immediately mentions some of those ablutions—verses 13, 19: "For if the blood of bulls and of goats, and the ashes of an heifer *sprinkling* the unclean, sanctifieth to the purifying of the flesh," &c. Again: "For when Moses had spoken every precept to all the people, according to the law, he took the blood of calves and of goats, with water, and scarlet wool, and hysop, and *sprinkled* both the book and all the people," &c.

I have now examined every passage in the Bible and in the Apochryphal writings of the Jews, where the word *baptizo* is used in a literal sense, without reference to the ordinance of christian baptism; and my clear conviction is, that there is not one instance in which it can be proved to mean *immerse;* that in every instance except, perhaps, one which may be doubtful, it can be, and has been, proved to express the application of water to the person or thing, by pouring or sprinkling. The usage of the Jews and of the Bible, in regard to this word, is, therefore, evidently against Mr. Campbell; and if so, his cause is lost. For, as I have proved, the Jews and inspired writers did not speak classic Greek; and consequently, the Bible and Jewish usage, as the best crules agree, must determine its meaning as appropriated to the ordinance of christian baptism.

I wish now to invite the attention of the audience to the usage of this word amongst the Greek and Roman christians. This is a very important branch of evidence; for certainly the Greek fathers, and the Latins, who lived when the Greek was a spoken language, understood the meaning of the word in debate.

I have already given my friend considerable trouble by quoting Origen, the most learned of the christian fathers; and, I presume, difficulties are likely to increase upon him. Origen, as we have seen, substituted *rantizo*, to sprinkle, for *bapto ;* and this same father used *baptizo* in the sense of *pouring*. His authority, it will be admitted, is worth more than that of Beza, and Calvin, and Luther, and half a dozen lexicons besides. His language is as follows:

"How came you to think that Elias, when he should come, would baptize, who did not, in Ahab's time, baptize the wood upon the altar, which was to be washed before it was burnt, by the Lord's appearing in fire? But he ordered the priests to do that; not once only, but says, Do it the second time: and they did it the second time: and, Do it the third time; and they did it the third time. He, therefore, that did not himself baptize then, but assigned that work to others, how was he likely to baptize, when he, according to Malachi's prophecy, should come."—*Wall's Hist. of Inf. Bap.*, vol. ii. p. 332.

Now by turning to 1 Kings xviii. 33, any one can, in a moment, see how this baptism was performed: "And he put the wood in order, and cut the bullock in pieces, and laid him on the wood, and said, Fill four barrels with water, and POUR it on the burnt sacrifice, and on the wood," &c. Origen says, the altar was baptized, (*baptizo* is the word he uses ;) and the Bible tells us *how* it was baptized, viz. by *pouring* several barrels of water upon it. If the altar was baptized when water was poured on it, is not a person baptized when water is poured on him? If *baptizo* expresses the pouring of water upon the altar, surely it may express the pouring of water on a person. Did Origen understand his native tongue? If he did, this word means to wash or wet by pouring, as well as by dipping. This single authority is worth more to show us in what sense it was used amongst Jews (for Origen was writing to the Jews) and christians, than all the classical lexicons. But the lexicons, as we have seen, are not against us.

Other learned Greeks used this word in a similar sense. Clemens Alexandrinus, speaking of a backslider whom John the Apostle was the means of reclaiming, says " he was baptized a second time with tears." Athanasius reckons up eight several baptisms : 1. that of the flood; 2. that of Moses in the sea; 3. the legal baptism of the Jews after uncleanness ; 4. that of John the Baptist; 5. that of Jesus ; 6. that of tears ; 7. of martyrdom; and 8. of eternal fire. Gregory Nazianzen says, " I know of a fourth baptism, that by martyrdom and blood ; and I know of a fifth, that of tears." " Bassil tells us of a martyr that was baptized into Christ with his own blood."—*Pond on Bap.*, p. 34.

Did these learned fathers understand the Greek language—their vernacular tongue? If they did, the pouring of water on the altar, the flowing of tears of a penitent over his face, and the flowing of the martyr's blood over his body, are all properly expressed by the words *baptizo* and *baptisma*. Was the altar immersed? Was the penitent backslider immersed in tears? Were the martyrs immersed in their own blood?

The Latin fathers used this word just as did the Greeks. Lactantius says, that Christ received baptism " that he might save the gentiles by baptism, that is, (purifici roris perfusione,) by the distilling of the purifying dew." Cyprian and the sixty-six bishops, as we have seen, declared persons truly baptized by sprinkling, and quoted Ezekiel xxxvi. 25, to prove it.—[*Time expired.*

Friday, Nov. 17—12 *o'clock, M.*
[MR. CAMPBELL'S TENTH ADDRESS.]

MR. PRESIDENT—Mr. Rice complains of me on various occasions and in various manners, and more especially because I have not yet got into the Bible. 'Tis hard to please him. The sequel may, perhaps, show which of us does most homage to that volume. Facts can be better trusted than predictions. He gets into the Bible and out of it too often for my taste. When I get into the Bible I do not like soon to get out of it. I am preparing the way to understand what is in it. Indeed, I am always in the Bible while discussing the meaning of its language, to ascertain its institutions.

He speaks of sundry translations, of which I know nothing. Among them is a Baptist Bible, translated for that society. I know of no such Bible. There is, indeed, a new or improved version, having some very plain and obvious improvements in style, which some Baptists read ; and there is another new version which some of us read. We avail ourselves of all means of better understanding the good book. But no one amongst us, or of the Baptists, so far as I know, substitutes this for the commonly

received king James' version. No community submits to them as umpires in any case of controversy. In such cases we all appeal to the
common version; not because it is better, but because it has authority
with all the people. We waive all denominational advantages for the
sake of having a common text. I maintain no point of doctrine, I hold
no article of faith, which I cannot fairly prove from the common version,
with all its faults and imperfections on its head, and these are neither few
nor small. I have a copy of the Baptist Bible, for which I paid five dollars in Philadelphia. I find it contains various improvements worthy of
the age, and every Baptist ought to have it in his house. In no respect,
however, does the version interfere with the authority of the king's Bible.

I am glad, even at this late period, to hear my friend, Mr. Rice, distinctly
declare himself on the subject of washing. We understand him now to
say, that sprinkling, pouring, and immersing are so many modes of
washing. If, then, our Redeemer has appointed one of these modes in
preference to all others, we should observe that mode. It is essentially
important that we should conform to it exclusively.

This assumption, if I mistake not, comes from Dr. Owen, who wrote
some two and twenty volumes of theology, and who has furnished full
six or eight pages on the subject of baptism. He seems, indeed, to have
been in a very bad humor when writing this large treatise on baptism.
"I must say," says he, "and I will make it good, that no honest man,
who understands Greek, can deny that the word *baptizo* signifies *to
wash* as well as *to dip*. This is, after all, conceding that the version dip
is by far the most clear and universal representative of the word."

I have another remark on these *modes* of washing. You must have
observed the great caution of my friend, who has, sage-like, informed us
that one may wash his hands by dipping them in water. He has even
gone so far as to say that one may wash his hands by pouring water
upon them. But why so cautious to proceed? why always stop there?
why not add, and one can wash his hands by *sprinkling* water upon
them? Yet this last is his spiritual, his favorite washing. Any one may
conceive of washing one's hands by dipping them in water, or by pouring
water upon them; but who has ever seen any one wash his hands by
sprinkling water upon them. As sprinkling or moistening has long been
the almost exclusive practice of his church, it is expected that he would
throw all his logic and rhetoric about "*that mode of washing!*"

Now, as observed yesterday, there are three kinds of pollution—physical, legal, and moral. Of course, there are but three kinds of cleansing.
And, as cleansing is always an important operation, in a moral or religious sense it is superlatively so. Hence, the various divine ordinances
connected with that service. But, as before observed, he never, in the
age of types and symbols, he never authorized any sort of cleansing,
natural, moral, or ceremonial, to be performed or consummated by sprinkling common water. Neither the leper nor any other unclean person
was ever so cleansed. Water and blood united, or water and the ashes
of a blood-red heifer combined, were the only waters of cleansing ever
authorized by God, or ordained by Moses. Nor even in the age of ceremonies did the sprinkling of clean or cleansing water upon any one effect
his ceremonial purification. Neither the sprinkling of water and blood,
nor the sprinkling of blood and ashes, nor the subsequent anointing with
oil, did ever cleanse any leper or unclean person. He must finally be
washed, he must *bathe himself* in water.

As to sprinkling, then, being a "*mode of washing*," is it not an ideal-ism? Who ever saw a man, a garment, a house, washed by sprinkling? John Calvin reduced the Roman *pouring* down to the mildest affusion! to wetting a fore-finger and laying it gently on an infant's brow—or by scattering a gentle spray all over its face. If then the mere touch of a man's finger will perform ablution, is not the operation of cleansing re-duced down to a thing of nothing? I propound it to the good sense of the community, if, as we are now informed, baptism is a " washing with water," whether there ought not to be such a change in the mode as would shew some resemblance to a washing.

As to the sprinkling of clean water so often alluded to, found in Ezekiel, as expressed in the following words, a remark or two will be expedient and necessary. The words are: " Then will I sprinkle clean water upon you, and you shall be clean: from all your filthiness, and from all your idols will I cleanse you." The question is, what means here the phrase *clean* water. It is common water, free from all physical impuri-ties! As this is a point of some importance, from the frequent citations of Pedo-baptists, I hope I may be permitted to enter somewhat fully into its exposition; for which purpose I must dip a little into the law of Moses. No person ever has understood, indeed no person can fully understand the christian institution, without a thorough knowledge of the five books of Moses, as well as of the five historical books of the New Testament.

The writings of Moses constitute the great font of evangelical types and symbols. In the Jewish ritual there was so much use of blood, fresh from the veins of the victim, in all the offerings and sacrifices of that in-stitution, that there was danger of a very serious error, viz : that the cleansing and atoning virtue of blood was only present while it was warm and fresh from the sacrifice. Blood was constantly sprinkled both upon persons and things, mingled sometimes with water, but in the former case, indeed in any case, it could only be sprinkled while warm. It was necessary, too, that it should be sprinkled, because many were to partake of its benefit. Now to prevent the aforesaid error, as well as for other reasons, it became necessary to place in this font of types, one that would prevent, or correct an error of such dangerous tendency. For this pur-pose it was ordained that a *blood-red heifer*, without a parti-colored hair from the horn to the hoof, should be obtained, and that she, together with her blood, and all her appurtenances, should be burned to ashes in a clean place without the camp. It was commanded that her ashes should be carefully gathered, and deposited in an urn, or some vessel, for future use.

Ascending to the traditions of the Rabbins, it sometimes happened that hundreds of years revolved without affording a heifer exactly fulfilling the description in the law. Now, according to a Divine provision, it was or-dained, that the smallest quantity of these ashes, infused into a quantity of water from a running stream, imparted to it the virtue of cleansing from all legal and ceremonial impurity; thus imparting to it the efficacy of blood. This beautiful type clearly taught that the virtue of sacrificial blood, whether for atonement or for purification, was not confined to the time of its being shed, or to its freshness; but long after the death of the victim, nay, indefinitely, retained all the power it originally possessed, for the accomplishment of these most sacred and important purposes.

The water was sometimes called *katharon hudoor*, clean water, and sometimes *hudoor rantismou*, the water of separation; the effect being put metonymically for the cause. This water of purification was to be used for one class of pollutions—a species of offences or pollutions artificially created, as it were, to complete the type. Any one who should at all touch the bone of a dead man, a dead body, a grave, or a couch upon which a corpse had been laid, was to be constituted unclean for seven days; and if, in that case, he presumed to come into the tabernacle of the Lord, he was to be cut off from the congregation of Israel. Thus a neglect of this institution became as fatal as moral transgressions of the deepest malignity. It was important to make this ceremonial uncleanness as similar as possible to moral turpitude, that it might, in all the parts of the type, correspond to actual transgression, by affording to the clean water the efficacy of blood in taking it away. How, then, was the polluted person to be cleansed? A priest appears. He takes the clean water, and sprinkles it upon him, on the third day, and again on the seventh, dipping (but not sinking) a bunch of hysop into the preparation. In some cases the water of purification was used by the unclean person himself. But in all cases, finally, he must bathe his whole person in water, for even sprinkling clean water, without a subsequent immersion, could not take away this legal impurity.

Louo, the word used in this case, is the word used amongst the Greeks to indicate *bathing*. Such, also, is its use amongst the Jews. Pharaoh's daughter is said to have *bathed* herself in the Nile. This bathing is represented by the word here used; and, therefore, indicates that the person put himself under the water in order to the consummation of the process of cleansing. Thus, after having this water of purification sprinkled upon them, like Judith of the Apocrypha, who washed herself in the camp at a fountain of water, he bathes himself, and washes off the clean water, mingled with ashes, and is now fit to enter the sanctuary of the Lord. Such, then, is the clean water, and such the ceremony of purification. The passage, in Ezekiel, is always misapplied, except when quoted in the true technical sense of the law, which has given to it its proper signification. The history of the case in Ezekiel is this—the Jews had profaned the name of the Lord, and polluted themselves among the heathen. The Lord said, not for their sake, but for his own honor, he would bring them out and restore them to their own land, and as they had, by contact with the heathen, polluted themselves, he, speaking in their own national and appropriate sense of the phrase, said, he would cleanse them by sprinkling clean water upon them, a symbol of the sanctification externally, and that he would also put his spirit within them; a passage which has no more to do with the sprinkling of common water for baptism, than any other ceremony in the law. Does any one suppose that the clean water here spoken of, or in the epistle to the Hebrews, is water free from mud?

As all arts, sciences, and callings have, what may be called, their technical terms, so has religion its technical terms. Clean water literally means, in religious technicality, a red heifer's ashes mixed with running water, as the antitype of the blood of Christ in its sanctifying power. Water, indeed, is sometimes the symbol of God's spirit. To the Samaritan woman Jesus said—"I will give a fountain of water, springing up within him to eternal life, to the man who drinketh of my water." This water denoted the spirit, as elsewhere explained, but it is never called clean water. The water of baptism may, in one case in Paul's style, be compared with this clean water, but in that case it is not sprinkled, but contrasted with sprinkling. The words are—"Having your hearts sprinkled," (by Christ's blood,) from a guilty conscience, and your bodies bathed, washed with pure or clean water.

I expected to hear this verse often quoted by my friend. It is a great favorite amongst all *sprinklers*. It has been quoted by them a thousand times—it chimes with another of great celebrity in the baptismal controversy—" I will pour water upon the thirsty, and floods upon the dry ground." But all these poetic and prophetic allusions to spiritual things had better be applied with more caution and prudence, than to seize them because of the words sprinkle and pour, which happen to be in them. Some preachers use these verses in their sermons as a chorus in music.

I think I have already said—if I have not, I will now say, that the sprinkling, pouring, and bathing, in the law are, indeed, indicative of a beautiful series, or order of things, in the evangelical economy. In effecting a cure blood was sprinkled upon the leper ; oil was poured upon him, and his person was bathed in water. Under the gospel the moral leper has the blood of sprinkling in its antitypical character, applied through faith to his conscience—he has his soul enlightened and sanctified by the spirit poured out, for christians have an *unction* from the Holy One, and understand all things in the gospel—and they have also had their bodies bathed in the water of cleansing. But of these we may have occasion more fully to speak hereafter. I have, at present, a few words to say upon the opinions of Mr. R. in reference to the allusions to Doddridge and Carson. The quoting of authors is rather a delicate point. I have expressed my desires for a dissertation on that subject. To quote them, as we have sometimes heard them quoted, is rather a very licentious affair. We can prove things the most antipodal by the same author. I argue that justice and consistency alike demand of us that, if we quote a man's opinions as authority, we ought to take all his opinions ; if we only quote him as a witness of facts transpiring in his time, or coming under his cognizance, we ought to take his whole testimony, and not just so much of his opinions, and just so much of his testimony as suits our prejudices or our interests. I plead for some system in quoting authors. If I quote Blackstone as authority in law, in one case, I quote him in all cases. I will admit the testimony of Doddridge, but not his opinions. So of Luther and of Calvin.

I do, indeed, especially quote the concessions of Pedo-baptists and other opponents, with considerable deference to their judgment in such matters, as are against their practice and against their interests ; for men seldom make such concessions unless the force of evidence is very strong and overwhelming. The testimony of reformers, annotators, and critics in favor of immersion, themselves having been not only sprinklers, but enemies of the *Anabaptists* and Baptists, is exceedingly strong and irresistible. Twenty such men witnessing for us, are worth two hundred of our own party. They have, too, more weight with their own party than our testimony.

The Greek and Latin fathers generally were very weak men compared with the modern. Some of them were mere visionaries, mystics, and fond of old wives' fables. But I regard them as faithful witnesses of facts. I receive their testimony as honest men, but I will neither receive their inferences from their own facts and premises, nor their opinions, farther than the rationale of them is obvious to myself. In this way I receive evidence and use it.

I have not much time for my regular argument. The succeeding remarks will, however, explain sundry matters, and either obviate or answer objections.

In relation to the baptizing of the wood and the altar, made out of Origen's critique by construction, I have a remark or two to offer.   I neither believe in constructive treason, nor in constructive baptism.   Twelve barrels of water poured upon the altar, and filling up the trench, might, indeed, thoroughly soak and even overwhelm the sacrifice.   But one thing I know, that neither Origen nor any Greek ever called any pouring an immersion, though the effect of pouring out the water might be an immersion of the altar and the offering too.   We are all in the habit of carrying figures too far, and of violating propriety, as well as Origen.

If Mr. Rice proposes to go ahead and introduce new matters, rather than to discuss the arguments I have submitted, I award to him perfect liberty.   I may perhaps get ahead of him before we are through.   I have already said there is no need of argument concerning Jewish idioms on this question at all.   I admit and teach the necessity of regarding it on such subjects as are affected by it.   But in specific words, expressing physical action, there is neither Jewish nor gentile idiom.   To eat, drink, sleep, talk, walk, dip, pour, sprinkle, &c., are the same physical acts in all lands, languages, and idioms.   We find shades of difference in many points, and then we expound by the current usage.   Unless we interpret the words of Paul and Peter by the currency of the age in which they lived and wrote, by what system are we to ascertain their meaning?   Do not John the Baptist and Josephus use these words as Paul and Peter, and the other apostles did?   We admire the wisdom of our Heavenly Father in causing the Greek language to cease to be a living tongue after the canon was closed and translated into one or two languages.   By that means the sense of its words changes no more ; and we have a fixed language of immutable meaning and of all authority, preserving and perpetuating the will of God to all ages and for all nations.—[*Time expired.*

Friday, Nov. 17—12½ *o'clock, P. M.*
[MR. RICE'S TENTH REPLY.]

MR. PRESIDENT—My friend (Mr. Campbell) says, I complain of his mode of discussing this subject.   Not at all : I am well satisfied with it. I cannot find it in my heart to fall out with him for failing to sustain his doctrine.   But he says, if he is not in the Bible, he is in the *portico*.   It must be an immense portico—extending from the days of the apostles to the time of Calvin, Beza and Grotius!   I should think he is a great way from the Bible—at least sixteen hundred years.   I have chosen not to remain in the portico.   I have now examined every passage in the Bible, in which *baptizo* is used in a literal sense ; and I have found no evidence that it is used in the sense of *immerse*.   On the contrary, I have found evidence conclusive, that in the Bible and Jewish writings it is used, with almost, if not entire uniformity, in the sense of applying water to the person or thing by pouring or sprinkling.   He thinks it probable, that when I shall be in the affirmative, he will get ahead of me.   If he should, I will give him credit for it.

He tells us that he is not aware of the existence of a *Baptist Bible ;* and yet he is aware, that there is a translation made by Baptists !   It certainly is not a Pedo-baptist Bible.   Then what is it ?   I did not say it was made by the Baptists as a denomination, but by individuals who are Baptists.   And it is well known, that our Baptist friends, in all their translations made for the heathen, do uniformly translate *baptizo* by words meaning to *immerse*. They are thus chargeable with the inconsistency of insisting or giving the heathen a pure translation, whilst they are contented to leave the people of this country in the dark. But the gentleman has himself made a new translation. Or, speaking more properly, he has taken some three old ones, and by selecting from one or the other of these as best suited him, and adding various emendations of his own, he has succeeded in getting up a translation which, I think, must in justice be called *Campbell's translation*. One very prominent object of this translation evidently was, to render the words *baptizo* and *baptisma*, immerse and immersion. To accomplish this, the gentleman, as I have proved, gave a translation of a passage, which is in truth no translation at all, but a gross perversion.

The treatise of Dr. Owen on baptism, he says, is very small, and was written when he was very mad against the Anabaptists. Certainly he never manifested greater opposition to the Anabaptists, than my worthy friend has evinced towards Pedo-baptists. If, then, his criticisms are to be undervalued for such a reason, on the same principle great allowance must be made in estimating the worth of Mr. C's criticisms, for his exclusive views and feelings. He represents Owen as admitting, that *immerse* was the most common meaning of *baptizo*. Let us hear Owen speak for himself. After stating, that instances out of all authors prove, that it signifies to *wash*, he remarks—" It is first used in Scripture, Mark i. 8, and John i. 33, and to the same purpose, Acts i. 5. In every place it either signifies to pour, or the expression is equivocal. ' I baptize you with water, but he shall baptize you with the Holy Ghost;' which is the accomplishment of that promise, that the Holy Ghost should be poured on them. For the other places, Mark vii. 3, 4, *nipto* and *baptizo* is precisely the same; both, to wash, Luke xi. 38, the same with Mark vii. 3. *No one instance can be given in the Scriptures wherein* BAPTIZO *doth necessarily signify either 'to dip' or 'to plunge!'* " Such is the declaration of one of the greatest men who has lived.

The gentleman attaches great importance to his discovery, that the sprinkling of pure water was never commanded in order to purification. I am gratified that he gave us his dissertation on the preparation of the water of purification; it will aid me in my argument. The ashes of the heifer, he tells us, were to be put into water, to show that blood had a permanent efficacy, not only when warm, but afterwards. Very well. Christian baptism is designed to represent the cleansing of the soul from sin by virtue of the blood of Christ and by the influence of the Holy Spirit. If, then, the water, after having the ashes of the heifer put to it, was to be sprinkled upon the unclean, as an emblem of purification; certainly the water of baptism should, for the same reason, be *sprinkled* on the person baptized. There is special propriety in this, inasmuch as the blood of Christ is called "*the blood of sprinkling.*"

But, says the gentleman, *washing* cannot be performed by sprinkling. Christian baptism, he certainly knows, is not intended to be a literal washing of the body. It is an *emblematic* washing—the application of water to the person, as an emblem of spiritual purification. Is the sprinkling of clean water a suitable emblem of such cleansing? Ezekiel the inspired prophet, certainly thought so; and therefore he said, or rather God said through him—" Then will I sprinkle clean water upon you, *and ye shall be clean,*" &c. Ezekiel was doubtless in the right, and my friend, Mr. C., is in the wrong.

But, let it be remembered, we are not now contending about the *quantity* of water to be used in baptism, but only about the mode of applying it to the person. I am willing to pour as much water, as may be desired —even as much as was poured on the altar which Origen says, was baptized by pouring. I presume the gentleman will not deny, that washing or cleansing may be performed by *pouring*. His remarks, therefore, concerning the inefficacy of sprinkling to cleanse, are entirely without force.

The sprinkling required in the Levitical law, he tells us, did not wholly cleanse the person. Ezekiel certainly represents the sprinkling of clean water, as a complete emblem of purification. But, says my friend, the unclean person was required to go and wash, after he had been sprinkled. He was to *wash* himself; but who does not know, that a man may wash himself in different modes. There are *shower-baths*, where the water falls on the person, as well as baths of a different kind; and he is as truly said to bathe when the water is poured upon him, as when he gets into it. The Hebrew word, however, as I have before stated, is *rahats*, which means simply *to wash*, without regard to mode. The unclean person, therefore, when directed *to wash*, would never imagine, that any particular mode was prescribed—that he was required to *plunge* himself into water.

The gentleman says, we have in the law, dipping, pouring and sprinkling; and so in the Gospel we have immersion, pouring out of the Spirit, and sprinkling of the blood of Christ. But the truth is, there is not one personal immersion required in the law of Moses. There are many sprinklings commanded, but not one important immersion. If there is, let it be produced. So in the Gospel we have sprinkling of the blood of Christ, pouring out of the Spirit, and pouring or sprinkling of water in the ordinance of baptism !

My friend, Mr. C., seems to be considerably annoyed by my quotations from learned authors; and he would have the audience believe, that I ascribe to them more learning than they possessed. I am not aware, that I have given any one of them a higher place than public sentiment has assigned him. If I have, let it be shown. I do not know whether we should be much wiser by having a book written, as he suggests, on the subject of quoting authors; unless the writer could put us on a plan of weighing their talents and learning. When an author is appealed to in proof of a fact, doubtless fairness requires, that his whole testimony on that point be stated. Mr. C. gave us a *part* only, of the testimony of his "American apostle"—Stuart, in regard to the meaning of *bapto* and *baptizo*, thus evidently doing his author injustice. I quoted Mr. Carson to establish a fact, viz: that there is no evidence to prove a different reading, for which Dr. Gale and my friend contend, in Rev. xix. 13; but I did not feel bound to adopt his opinion, that Origen did not understand the meaning of *bapto*.

I have a word to say about the Jewish idiom of the Greek language. The gentleman would persuade you, that in the meaning of Greek words in classic authors and in the New Testament there is very little difference. I have quoted Dr. George Campbell, one of his favorite critics, who says, that although a knowledge of the classic Greek may be of service in interpreting the New Testament, it will very often entirely mislead. I have quoted Ernesti, one of the most celebrated writers on interpretation, who says, that in interpreting the language of a people, respect must be had to their manners, customs, and religion; that the New Testament is written in "Hebrew-Greek," not in classic Greek; and that in many instances it would make ridiculous nonsense to give words in the New Testament their classic meaning. It is, indeed, a matter of which any one can form a correct judgment. What would you think of a man who should insist upon explaining the language of a Dutch settlement, speaking the English quite imperfectly, by the dictionary of Walker or Webster?—especially when they used English words in relation to things they had never amongst us been employed to denote?

I prefer going to the Bible itself, and then to Greek christians who knew in what sense *baptizo* was understood, when used in relation to religious rites. I have appealed to them, and have proved, that they used it to express the pouring of water on an altar, the flowing of tears over the face, the flowing of a martyr's blood over his body. Every one can see, that in such examples there could be no immersion; that the word expresses the application of a fluid in small quantities, smaller than is usually employed in baptizing by sprinkling.

It is worthy of special remark, that when immersion came to be generally practiced, the Greek christians, when they wished definitely to express that mode, used another word—*kataduo*. On this subject professor Stuart says—" Subsequent ages make the practice of the church still plainer, if indeed this can be done. The Greek words *kataduo* and *katadusis* were employed as expressive of *baptizing* and *baptism;* and these words mean *going down into the water*, or *immerging*. So in the following examples: Chrysostom, Homil. xl. 1 Cor. 1, "To be baptized and to submerge (*kataduesthai*,) then to emerge (*ananeuein*,) is a symbol of descent to the grave, and of ascent from it." Basil De Spiritu. c. 15, " By three immersions (*en trisi katadusesi*) and by the like number of invocations, the great mystery of baptism is completed." Damascenus Orthodox, Fides iv. 10, " Baptism is a type of the death of Christ; for by three immersions (*kataduseon*) baptism signifies," &c. So the Apostolical Constitutions (probably written in the fourth century) Lib. iii. ch. 17, "Immersion (*katadusis*) denotes dying with him (Christ:) emersion (*anadusis*,) a resurrection with Christ." Photius (apud Œcumenicum) on Rom. vi. "The three immersions and emersions (*kataduseis kai anaduseis*) of baptism signify death and resurrection." Quest. apud Athanasium, Qu. 94, "To immerse (*katadusai*) a child three times in the bath (or pool,) and to *emerse* him (*anadusai:*) this shows the death," &c. Chrysostom in Cap. 3, Johannis, "We, as in a sepulchre, immersing (*kataduonton*) our heads in the water, the old man is buried, and *sinking down* (*katadus kato*) the whole is concealed at once; then as we emerge, the new man again rises," pp. 73, 74. Gregory Thaumaturgus, speaking of Christ's baptism, represents him as saying to John, "*kataduson me tois Jordanou reithrois*"—Plunge me in the river of Jordan. Cyril, of Jerusalem, uses this language: " Plunge them (*kaduete*) down thrice into the water, and raise them up again." *See Gale's Reflec. on Wall*, v. 3, pp. 202, 203.

Now, if it be true, as Mr. C. contends, that *baptizo* is a specific term, signifying definitely to *immerse;* why did the Greek fathers, when they wished to express the idea of immersing, select *kataduo* instead of *baptizo*, the word used in the Bible? But suppose we take one of these passages from the Greeks, and translate *baptisma*, immersion, as Mr. C. does. Photius: "The three immersions and emersions of immersion (*baptisma-*

tos) signify," &c.! How does this sound? The truth evidently is, that *baptisma* denotes the ordinance, and *katadusis*, the mode in which, at that time, it was commonly administered. Hence the Greeks used *baptisma* in relation to the ordinance, when administered by pouring or sprinkling, as well as by dipping.

The Latins, like the Greeks, when immersion became prevalent, selected other words, such as mergo, mergito, immergo, to express definitely their mode of administering the ordinance. Cyprian, as I have proved, presiding over a council of sixty-six bishops, expressed the decided belief that baptism administered by sprinkling is valid, and, in proof of it, quoted Ezekiel xxxvi. 25: "Then will I sprinkle clean water upon you," &c. The Latins certainly had the very best opportunity of understanding the meaning of *baptizo*, as it was used among the Greeks; for the Greek was then a living language. Yet with them *baptizo* denoted the ordinance, and tingo, mergo, mergito, &c., the mode of administering it, by immersion. If, as Mr. C. has said, *baptizo* was universally understood by the Latins to mean immerse, why did they, when they would definitely express immersion, select some other word? The truth doubtless is, that both Greeks and Latins understood the word to express washing, cleansing, whether by pouring, sprinkling or immersing. They, therefore, with great unanimity, recognized the validity of baptism administered in either of these modes. This is the more remarkable, inasmuch as their prejudices at the period referred to, were generally in favor of *trine immersion*.

But I am getting so far before the gentleman in the argument, that I ought perhaps to wait for him! And yet he is one speech ahead of me!

I will, however, proceed to state that the *places* where baptism was administered, do not prove immersion to have been practiced by the apostles. John baptized in or about Jordan, and in Enon, near Salim, "because there was much water there." But it cannot be proved that John was literally in the water of Jordan. We read in one place that he baptized *in (en)* Jordan; and in John i. 28, it is said—"These things were done in Bethabara, *beyond* Jordan, where John was baptizing." Bethabara was probably a small village near the Jordan. How, then, could John baptize literally in Jordan and *in* Bethabara *beyond* Jordan? The preposition *en*, I presume, here, as in many other places, signifies *near to*. Thus both passages are reconciled. Dr. Geo. Campbell himself, though so decidedly favorable to immersion, admits, that but little stress can be laid on this preposition, inasmuch as it is used with the same latitude of meaning as the Hebrew *baith*, which signifies *at* as well as *in*. Mr. Carson does not think John was literally *in* Jordan; though he supposes that he put the people in.

I presume the gentleman will not urge an argument from the expression concerning our Savior, that after his baptism "he went up straightway *out of* the water." He will scarcely deny that the common meaning of *apo*, the preposition used in the passage, is simply *from*, not *out of*. Justin Martyr speaks of Christ as going to *(epi)* Jordan to be baptized.

But from the fact that John went where there was *much water*, and baptized, our immersionist friends *infer* that he baptized by immersion. But is there any certainty that this inference is correct? The multitudes who resorted to John often remained together for several days. They were Jews, and they could not have been prevailed on to remain where they could not attend to their ablutions. They would not even eat without wasning; and if, as some immersionists contend, they were in the habit of immersing themselves before eating, there must have been a great many immersions daily, besides such as John might perform! It is, however, certain that they wanted water for the religious washings of their law, and for ordinary purposes; but can it be proved that John wanted "much water" for the purpose of baptizing? If my friend, Mr. C., will prove it, he will have gained his point; if he cannot, his argument, so far as this source of evidence is concerned, must be abandoned. It will not do to make such an ordinance depend upon vague inferences.

I have several facts to state, which, I think, will satisfy every unprejudiced mind, that the apostles baptized by pouring or sprinkling. I do not design, however, to enter just now upon the argument in proof of this mode. I can promise the audience that it will be brief. I design giving you a plain argument in English. It requires no labored criticism to sustain our practice. Thus far I have not attempted an argument directly in favor of pouring and sprinkling. I have been removing the rubbish out of the way. In the mean time, I hope my worthy friend will endeavor to extricate himself from the brush, and get, at least, into my neighborhood.

In regard to the *history* of the mode of baptism, I do not know that it is necessary for me to add any thing more to what I have presented. I will, however, state an important fact which cannot be disproved, viz.—No one can find any account of the practice of immersion before the *third century;* and then we find *trine immersion*, accompanied with various superstitions and some indecencies—the divesting of the candidates for baptism of their garments, the sign of the cross, the use of honey, oil, spittle, &c. And I pledge myself to find pouring or sprinkling practiced and admitted to be valid baptism as early, and even earlier, than immersion can be found. The history of the mode is against the exclusive claims of immersion.—[*Time expired.*

Friday, Nov. 17—1 o'clock, P. M.
[MR. CAMPBELL'S ELEVENTH ADDRESS.]

MR. PRESIDENT—Neither yourself nor this attentive audience can complain of the want of variety and digression in our discussion. My friend sows broadcast, and with a liberal hand, and gives you dissertations numerous and diversified. You have been treated to a part of the Pedo-baptist natural history of prepositions. The celebrated *eis*, and his comrades *en, ek, apo, kata,* and old *deuo*, &c. have run the gauntlet, and paid the usual compliments to *baptizo.* But in the history of this venerable family, my friend has been rather precipitate. He has brought them before us before we had time to pay them a respectful attention. But he is pleased with the license given him, and is determined, if possible, to lead, rather than to follow us. He has ceased to be respondent, and assumed the affirmant. Touching Baptists, Anabaptists, and their translations, what have they to do with this discussion? The Baptists have *a* new translation, but it is not *the* Baptist Bible. The gentleman, I think, has no occasion, then, to speak of them.

Dr. Owen, it seems, has said that *baptizo* and *nipto* are used synonymously. Neither Dr. Owen nor any other man can prove it. On yesterday I said something on the subject; and I will now say, that, in the Greek scriptures we find *nipto* thirty-four times; *pluno* seventeen times; *louo* thirty-five times. I also asserted then, that though *nipto* was so

P

often found, it was, when applied to persons, universally confined to the washing of face, hands, and feet; and never to the whole person, nor to apparel. *Louo* is applied to the whole body, and to certain parts of the body; but never to the cleansing of garments, nor as interchangeable with *nipto*. And *pluno* is never applied to the washing of the person at all, but always to garments. What stronger evidence, ask we, of the precision of the Greek tongue than this fact? The Greeks never confounded these terms. Their minds seem to have been cast in moulds of precision. I, in common with many others, have been astonished at this singular precision in the use of words connected with the use of water. Even though frequently occurring in the same verses, these terms are never confounded.

As to *kata duo*, and its whole family, I can, in a few words, give its history. There is an old fashioned Greek verb found, I believe, in Hesiod, Homer, and other still more modern writers. It is *dupto*, from which, in the old English style of changing *u* into *y*, we have the word *dyp*. Again, in the Anglo-Saxon style of transmutation *dyp* is changed into *dyph*, and that again into *dive*. Now of this whole family *duo* is the remote ancestor, and consequently without the *kata*, itself signifies to *dip* or *dive*. The *kata duo*, and the *anaduo*, and the *katadusis* and *anadusis*, are merely special forms from the same common fountain. It is highly improper to perplex the uneducated part of the community with the learned sophistry which would make these words separately equivalent to *baptisma*, because sometimes used, not in the New Testament, but in the fathers, as a substitute for it. The practice of the third century has nothing at all to do with the New Testament style.

Dr. Beecher, of Illinois, has dealt largely in this species of sophistry, in his essays on *baptism* for purification. He has writtten a book which virtually goes to prove *that words representing the same thing are identically synonymous.* I have heard that professor Stuart of Andover has said of it, that he never saw a more learned and splendid essay founded on a more gratuitous assumption.

Mr. Rice says that there never was an instance of personal immersion required under the law of Moses. Well, what of it, if it were so? But the gentleman must have observed, that so perfectly associated with *louo* was the idea of bathing and of immersion too; and that all leprous persons were enjoined to be immersed, or to immerse themselves, that when the Assyrian leper was commanded by the prophet to go and *wash*, or bathe (*louo* is the word) in Jordan; he having learned how leprous persons were to be cleansed from the leprosy, according to Jewish custom, as indicated in the word *louo*, went and *dipped* himself seven times in the Jordan. I ask on what principle of abstract reasoning could he have come to the conclusion to immerse himself in the Jordan seven times by the word *louo*, if he had not understood that to be its Jewish acceptation? This is, in my judgment, an unanswerable argument, that by the word *louo* the Jews were accustomed to immerse themselves by the received sense of the term, and hence personal immersion was commanded in the law.

I shall now proceed with my authorities under my fifth argument: and, in the first place, we shall listen to Dr. Campbell affirming both the classic and the Jewish acceptation of this term—*baptizo;* than whom, we have no higher Presbyterian authority.

" The word *baptizein*, both in sacred authors and classical, signifies *to dip*.

to plunge, to immerse; and was rendered by Tertullian, the oldest of the Latin fathers, *tingere,* the term used for dyeing cloth, which was by immersion. It is always construed suitably to this meaning. Thus it is, *ea hudati, en to Jordane.* But I should not lay much stress on the preposition *en,* which, answering to the Hebrew *beth,* may denote *with* as well as *in,* did not the whole phraseology, in regard to this ceremony, concur in evincing the same thing. Accordingly, the baptized are said *ana bainein*—to *arise, emerge,* or *ascend;* Matt. iii. 16, *apo tou udatos;* and Acts viii. 39, *ek tou udatos,* from or out of the water. Let it be observed further, that the verbs *raino* and *rantizo,* used in Scripture for *sprinkling,* are never construed in this manner. *I will sprinkle you with clean water,* is, in the Septuagint, *Raino eph umas katharon hudor;* and not as *baptizo* is always rendered, *Raino umas en katharo udati.* See also Eze. xxvi. 21; Lev. vi. 27—xvi. 14. Had *baptizo* here been employed in the sense of *raino,* *I sprinkle,* (which, as far as I know, it never is, in any case, sacred or classical,) the expression would doubtless have been, Ego *baptizo eph umas udor,* or *apo tou udatou,* agreeably to the examples referred to. When, therefore, the Greek word *baptizo* is adopted, I may say, rather than translated, into modern languages, the mode of construction ought to be preserved so far as may conduce to suggest its original import. It is to be regretted that we have so much evidence that even good and learned men allow their judgments to be warped by the sentiments and customs of the sect which they prefer. The true partisan, of whatever denomination, always inclines to correct the diction of the Spirit by that of the party."—*Campbell's Dissertations,* vol. iv. p. 128, and p. 24.

The great Selden has said—

"In England, of late years, I ever thought the parson baptized his own fingers rather than the child.—*Works,* vol. vi., Col. 2008.

Before submitting my next argument on this proposition, I beg leave to introduce the special testimony of one of America's most eminent classic scholars. I believe I only accord with enlightened public opinion, when I introduce professor Charles Anthon, of Columbia College, New York, as one of the most distinguished Greek scholars in the Union. His long devotion to the study and teaching of this language, is not the only reason of this superiority. His laborious researches in ancient literature, his critical collation of copies, various readings, marginal notes, general criticisms, as editor of so many of the classics already in our colleges, and his excellent classical dictionary, have obtained for him this high reputation.

Professor Charles Anthon being addressed by Dr. Parmly, of New York, on the subject of this proposition, last spring, he favored him with the following answer. I shall quote the correspondence, that the subject may come fairly before the reader.

"*No.* 1, *Bond Street, N. Y., March* 23, 1843.

PROFESSOR CHARLES ANTHON,

In conversation with Dr. Spring, last evening, he stated that, in the original, the word baptism, which we find in the New Testament, has no definite or distinct meaning; that it means to immerse, sprinkle, pour, and has a variety of other meanings—as much the one as the other, and that every scholar knows it; that it was the only word that could have been selected by our Savior, having such a variety, as to suit every one's views and purposes. May I ask you, if your knowledge of the language, from which the word was taken, has led you to the same conclusion? And may I beg of you to let the deep interest I take in the subject plead my apology.

I have the honor to be, with great respect, most respectfully yours,

E. PARMLY."

" Columbia College, March 27, 1843.

DR. PARMLY,

My Dear Sir—There is no authority, whatever, for the singular remark, made by the Rev. Dr. Spring, relative to the force of *baptizo*. The primary meaning of the word is to dip, or immerse; and its secondary meaning, *if ever it had any*, all refer, in some way or other, to the same leading idea. Sprinkling, &c., are entirely out of the question. I have delayed answering your letter in the hope that you would call and favor me with a visit, when we might talk the matter over at our leisure. I presume, however, that what I have here written will answer your purpose. Yours, truly,

CHARLES ANTHON."

To these I could have added, from one and the same divinity school, Philip Lemborch, John Le Clerc, Episcopius, Stephen Curcellæus, who, with Vossius, succeeded each other in the same professor's chair at Amsterdam, a Pedo-baptist school. For them all, and expressive of their views, I shall quote the words of the first named of them, the famous Lemborch, who filled that chair from 1664 to 1712, a period of 48 years. His words on *baptisma* are—" Baptism is that ceremony or rite, wherein the faithful, by *immersion into water*, as by a sacred pledge, are assured of the favor of God, remission of sins, and eternal life; and by which they engage themselves to an amendment of life and an obedience to the divine commands." In another place he says, " Baptism consists in washing, or rather in immersing the whole body into water, as was customary in the primitive times."—Blish. p. 79.

With this mere specimen of Pedo-baptist authorities, I must conclude my fifth argument, and proceed to my sixth. Before stating it, I desire again to say, that our arguments are not multiplied because we suppose any one of them is insufficient by itself. With me, it has almost passed into a maxim, *that one good sound logical argument is enough to sustain any proposition in the universe;* inasmuch as all the mind in the universe cannot annihilate one good argument. But although one good argument is all-sufficient to prove any one proposition; and although, in various departments of his works and ways, the great Author of nature has used but one argument; yet, reasoning from the philosophy of the human mind, I have thought it expedient, on the present occasion, to introduce various arguments deduced from different sources and classes of evidence; rather, indeed, after all, as parts of one great argument, in support of the apostolic and divine ordinance. Not, however, I repeat, because of any supposed inadequacy in any one of them, but because we have so many ways of reasoning—so many modes of thinking; no two minds reasoning alike in all respects, no two eyes seeing alike, no two ears hearing alike, we have to approach the human understanding by various avenues, one particular argument carrying conviction to one mind, while another, and perhaps a weaker argument, carrying conviction to another mind.

My plan on the proposition, it being merely a question of fact, is to bring up my evidences in the character of witnesses, and to classify them by some one general idea. Each individual is, in fact, a witness and an argument in himself. I summon none but witnesses of high rank, of acknowledged eminence; and hence, not one of them has been challenged; not one of them can be. My witnesses are all renowned in some department of society, either as lexicographers, classical teachers, critics, historians, reformers, commentators, translators, or theologians, &c., &c We shall, therefore, still call them up in classes.

VI. My sixth ARGUMENT shall consist of a few witnesses selected from English lexicons and encyclopœdias. These, too, like the former, are of the school opposed to us on the question. Not that I disparage my Baptist friends, nor their men of renown. They, too, have some names of renown ; their Gills, and Gales, and Booths, and Fullers, and Halls, &c. We are, indeed, without many theological schools, and, till recently, without many colleges and distinguished Rabbis. Yet still, the Baptists in America, the land of free discussion, are much more numerous than any learned denomination in it. Societies with a learned ministry, are not, unless aided by a secular arm, greatly prolific. Hence the Baptists, despite of the ignorance among their teachers, and it is by no means, in numerous instances, inconsiderable ; despite of their want of theological schools and colleges, and a well disciplined clerical corps of leaders, have, to the great annoyance of their more learned, shrewd, and well marshaled competitors in the field, spread, like the locusts of Egypt, through all ranks of the community, and are likely not to leave one green thing in the pastures of their better educated brethren. They spring up in the country and in the city, and spread themselves over the whole face of the earth, as though they rose by magic. The reason is, they have a plain story to tell, and a plain book from which they read it ; and it strikes the ear with a mighty force, as if it came from heaven. It has, moreover, a powerful ally, called common sense ; which, although not always eloquently, yet always efficiently pleads for it, not only in the person of the preacher, but in that of the hearer. Whenever they secure a reading of the book, a candid examination of the evidences, without note or comment, in nine cases out of ten, the work is done.

I shall place the learned and profound Richardson at the head of this class of witnesses. He defines the word "to dip or merge frequently, to sink, to plunge, to immerge." He concludes a long list of quotations in support of his definition from ancient English literature, with a few lines from Cowper—

> Philosophy baptized
> In the pure fountain of eternal love,
> Has eyes, indeed, and viewing all she sees
> As meant to indicate a God to man,
> Gives him his praise and forfeits not her own.
> *Cowper's Task*, book ii.

Dr. Johnson, in his dictionary, says, " to baptize is to sprinkle, to administer the sacrament of baptism to one. Baptism, an external ablution of the body with a certain form of words." He speaks this as a member of the church of England; but where he speaks *ex cathedra*, he is thus quoted by Boswell, as follows :

" Dr. Johnson argued in defence of some of the peculiar tenets of the church of Rome. As to giving the bread only to the laity, he said, ' they may think that, in what is merely ritual, deviations from the primitive mode may be admitted on the ground of convenience : and I think they are as well warranted to make this alteration, as we are to substitute *sprinkling* in the room of the *ancient baptism*.' "

I wish you now to hear what the Monthly Reviews of England have said on the baptism of Nebuchadnezzar, and on the baptism of the lake in the Battle of the Frogs and Mice—a most ludicrous affair, both on the part of the poet, and of the critics, who make the coloring of a wave with the blood of a mouse, the sprinkling, or the pouring, or the immersion of a lake ! !

" We acknowledge there are many authorities to support it [immersion] among the ancients.   The word *baptize* doth certainly signify immersion, absolute and total immersion, in Josephus and other Greek writers.'   *   * *   ' The examples produced, however, do not exactly serve the cause of those who think that a few drops of water sprinkled on the forehead of a child, constitute the essence of baptism.   In the Septuagint it is said that Nebuchadnezzar was baptized with the dew of heaven: and in a poem attributed to Homer, called The Battle of the Frogs and Mice, it is said that a certain lake was baptized with the blood of a wounded combatant—(*Ebapteto d aimati limne porpureo.*)   A question has arisen, in what sense the word baptize can be used in this passage.   Doth it signfy immersion, *properly* so called?   Certainly not: neither can it signify a partial sprinkling.   A body wholly surrounded with a mist; wholly made humid with dew; or a piece of water so tinged with and discolored by blood, that if it had been a solid body and dipped into it, it could not have received a more sanguine appearance, is a very different thing from that partial application which in modern times is supposed sufficient to constitute full and explicit baptism. The accommodation of the word *baptism* to the instances we have referred to, is not unnatural, though highly metaphorical ; and may be resolved into a trope or figure of speech, in which, though the primary idea is maintained, yet the mode of expression is altered, and the word itself is to be understood rather *allusively* than *really;* rather *relatively* than *absolutely.*   If a body had been baptized or *immersed,* it could not have been more wet than Nebuchadnezzar's ; if a lake had been *dipped* in blood, it could not have put on a more bloody appearance.

" Hitherto the Antipedobaptists [or Baptists] seem to have had the *best* of the argument on the mode of administering the ordinance.   The most explicit authorities are on their side.   Their opponents have chiefly availed themselves of *inference, analogy,* and *doubtful construction.* "

It is due to our opponents, that when we quote their special pleaders, we ought to give their testimony on both sides.

Chambers' Cyclopedia, or Dictionary of Arts and Sciences: London, 1786. " Baptism, in Theology ; formed from the Greek *baptizo,* of *bapto—I dip* or *plunge,* a rite or ceremony by which persons are initiated into the profession of the christian religion.

" The practice of the Western church is, to sprinkle the water on the head or face of the person to be baptized, except in the church of Milan, in whose ritual it is ordered, that the head of the infant be plunged three times into the water; the minister at the same time pronouncing the words, ' I baptize thee in the name of the Father, the Son, and the Holy Ghost '— importing that by this ceremony the person baptized is received among the professors of that religion, which God, the Father of all, revealed to mankind by the ministry of his Son, and confirmed by the miracles of his Spirit. A triple immersion was first used, and continued for a long time: this was to signify either the three days that our Saviour lay in the grave, or the three persons in the Trinity.   But it was afterwards laid aside, because the Arians used it: it was thought proper to plunge but once.   Some are of opinion, that sprinkling in *baptism* was begun in cold countries.   It was introduced into England about the beginning of the ninth century.   At the council of Celchyth, in 816, it was ordered that the priest should not only sprinkle the holy water upon the head of the infant, but likewise plunge it in the bason.   There are abundance of ceremonies delivered by ecclesiastical writers, as used in baptism, which are now disused ; as the giving milk and honey to the baptized, in the east ; wine and milk in the west, &c.

" The opinion of the necessity of baptism in order to salvation, is grounded on these two sayings of our Savior : ' He that believeth and is baptized, shall be saved ;' and, ' Except a man be born of water and of the Spirit, he cannot enter into the kingdom of God.'" —[*Time expired.*

Friday, Nov. 17—1½ o'clock, P. M.
[MR. RICE'S ELEVENTH REPLY.]

MR. PRESIDENT—The gentleman says, he would have said nothing about the Baptist translation, if I had not called it *the Baptist Bible.* I certainly did not intimate, that is was sanctioned by the Baptists as a denomination. There was, therefore, no necessity that he should defend them.

The word *nipto*, he tells us, signifies the washing of the *hands*, and therefore it cannot be synonymous with *baptizo*, in Mark vii. 3, 4, as Dr. Owen supposed. But certainly the gentleman himself agrees with Owen on this point; for his own translation makes *baptizo* denote the washing of the hands. It is as follows:—"For the Pharisees, and indeed all the Jews who observe the tradition of the elders, eat not until they have washed their hands by pouring a little water upon them; and if they be come from the market, *by dipping them*," *(baptizontai.)* According to his own translation, *nipto* denotes the washing of the hands; and *baptizo* means the same thing, only in a particular mode. If, then, baptizing the hands is baptizing the person, surely baptizing the face would be at least equally so.

I am not able to understand what Dr. Beecher's sophistry has to do with our discussion. His work on baptism, the gentleman considers very sophistical. Having never seen it, I cannot say whether it is so or not; but I heard an immersionist of high standing pronounce it unanswerable! I presume he did not consider it very sophistical. I do not know whether professor Stuart ever spoke of it slightingly, as Mr. C. has heard he did; but from my knowledge of the character of that gentleman, I am induced, very seriously, to doubt whether he used such language concerning Dr. Beecher. It is far better, I think, not to introduce these flying reports into such a discussion. They are absolutely worthless.

I have asserted that not a single personal immersion was required in the law of Moses. The gentleman is disposed to dispute the correctness of the statement. He tells us, the leper was required to be immersed; that the idea of dipping was so fixed in the minds of the Jews, that the Hebrew words *rahatz* and the Greek *louo* readily suggested it. But this is an assertion that cannot be proved. Where is the evidence? There is absolutely none. He asks, how came Naaman so to understand the command *to wash?* Let him first prove that he did so understand it, and his question will be proper. I suppose he did not understand the prophet to command him to immerse himself; and, in this opinion, I am sustained by Jerom, the translator of the Vulgate. He, with all his prejudice in favor of trine immersion, translated *baptizo*, in this instance, by *lavo*, a generic term, signifying *to wash*. I repeat the declaration—there is not in the law of Moses a personal immersion required. If there is, let it be produced.

The gentleman appeals to the authority of Dr. Geo. Campbell. Dr. Campbell, though a Presbyterian, was decidedly favorable to immersion; yet he did not believe, with my friend, that immersion is the one only apostolic or christian baptism. He was undoubtedly a man of considerable learning; but I am more than doubtful whether, as a critic and translator, he ought to be placed in the first rank. I think, a careful examination of his translation will prove, that he falls far short of that accuracy and that simplicity of style, which should characterize a translator. An instance of his want of simplicity of style just now occurs to me. He thus translates Matth v. 1—"Jesus, seeing so great a confluence, repaired to a mountain," &c. The word "confluence" is sometimes used to signify a multitude of people; but certainly this is not its most common meaning. How much more simple as well as literal is our common version—"Jesus, seeing the multitudes," *(tous ochlous,)* &c. But this by the way.

Dr. Campbell, like other men, was somewhat under the influence of his feelings; and it is, to my mind, evident that his partiality for immersion induced him sometimes to speak unguardedly. For example, he states it as a fact, that the Syriac version, in translating Matth. iii. 11, uses the word *in*, not *with*—"I baptize you *in* water." Now any one who will carefully examine the passage as it is found in the Syriac Testament, will see that he was in an error. The preposition used is *baith*, which, like the Hebrew *baith*, is very frequently employed in the sense of *with*. This preposition is used in Rev. xix. 13, where the sense requires it to be translated *with*—"He was clothed with a vesture sprinkled *with (baith)* blood." The passage in Matth. iii. 11, is thus translated from the Syriac into Latin by Schaaf and Leusden, whose edition I have —"Ego baptizo vos aqua [not *in* aqua] ad conversionem—ipse baptizabit vos Spiritu sancto et igne "—*I baptize you* WITH *water to conversion—He shall baptize you* WITH *the Holy Ghost and* WITH *fire.*

I will oppose to the authority of Luther, who admitted that the original or etymological meaning of *baptizo* is to immerse, the testimony of Ernesti, one of the ablest writers on interpretation, who pronounces *etymology* an uncertain and an unsafe guide in ascertaining the meaning of words. To the authority of Tertullian, who is mentioned as having translated the word by *tingo*, I will oppose that of Cyprian and the sixty-six bishops, who used it in the sense of pouring and sprinkling.

Dr. Anthon, I presume, is a classical scholar; but I have abundantly proved, that an acquaintance with classic Greek will not qualify a man to expound the language of the New Testament, which is written in "Hebrew Greek," The classic usage, as Ernesti, and Dr. Campbell, and Prof. Stuart affirm, will, if followed, in many cases entirely mislead the interpreter of the New Testament. I would attach very little importance, therefore, to the opinion of a classical scholar concerning an important word in the New Testament, unless I knew he had studied the idiom of the Greek spoken by the Jews and inspired writers. Dr. Anthon, says my friend, decided that Dr. Spring was in error concerning this word. But I venture to say, that Dr. Spring is quite as well known as a scholar, as the gentleman who sat in judgment upon him. Dr. Spring is one of the first men in our country; and it will not do to attempt to put down the views he may have expressed, merely by the *ipse dixit* of Dr. Anthon. Dr. Clark will, perhaps, be admitted to have been equal as a classical scholar, at least so far as *languages* are concerned, to Dr. Anthon; and he says, it is certain that *baptizo* means both to dip *and to sprinkle.* Perhaps Dr. Dwight will be admitted to have been superior in Biblical criticism to Dr. Anthon; and he, after a thorough examination of the subject, came fully to the conclusion, that in the Scriptures *baptizo* does not at all mean to *immerse*. Dr. Scott, the learned commentator, was of a similar opinion. I will put the authority of such men as these against that of Anthon, and of Bloomfield, (who is admitted to be a learned man,) if indeed his opinion has been correctly represented by my friend, Mr. Campbell. To what extent the Edinburgh Reviewers made themselves acquainted with this subject, before expressing the opinion quoted by the gentleman, I know not. They thought, it seems, that Mr. Carson had put himself to needless trouble in maintaining his position. Mr. Carson, of course, thought differently; and probably he was the better judge in the case.

But really, this species of argument is worth very little. My friend has told us, that *one* good argument is sufficient to establish a point. He seems, however, thus far to have failed to produce even one. The lexicons have failed him; the classics cannot prove the *action* he seeks to find in *baptizo;* the translations will not sustain him; and his learned authorities have been met by names equally learned, if not more so. Where, then, is the evidence, proving that immersion is the only apostolic or christian baptism?

The opinion of Calvin, on any subject, I will admit is of more weight by far, than mine or that of my friend. But when he himself says, that in regard to any particular subject he is wholly indifferent; I cannot attach much importance to his opinion about it, unless I learn from him, that he has examined its merits. For we all know, that men are not accustomed extensively to investigate subjects that do not interest them.

But the gentleman boasts of the number of immersionists in the United States, and of the rapid increase of his own church. I noticed in his Harbinger, some time since, an article in which he spoke of the rapid increase of Presbyterians and Old Baptists during the year preceding; and I remember, he consoled himself by saying, that error very commonly spreads faster than truth. When his own denomination goes ahead, it affords cheering evidence, that his principles are true; but when others increase, he says, Ah, error will outrun truth any how. [A laugh.] But let us make a fair calculation. Count the Methodists, the Presbyterians, the Congregationalists, the Episcopalians, &c.—and we can out-number immersionists three times over. The gentleman gains nothing by counting numbers.

I have now noticed his remark, so far as necessary. He is yet " in the portico." I hope he will ere long venture into the good Book. In the meantime, lest in the Bible argument I should get too far ahead of him, I will turn your attention more particularly to the *history* of this subject.

I have said, and I will repeat it, that immersion cannot be found in the history of the church earlier than the *third century.* The first writer who mentions it, is Tertullian, who flourished in the beginning of the third century; and he informs us, that the practice then was *trine immersion,* accompanied with sign of the cross, the use of honey, oil, and the indecent custom of entirely disrobing the persons, male and female! Will my friend take Tertullian as his witness? If so, I hope he will agree to take his whole testimony, not a small part of it. In courts of justice, when a man calls in a witness, I believe he is obliged to take his entire testimony—he cannot select just so much as may suit him. Will the gentleman, then, agree to practice the trine immersion of Tertullian, with the accompanying ceremonies? No—he must cut off two immersions, the sign of the cross, and divers other things then practiced. So he will reject some three-fourths or four-fifths of the testimony of his own witness. He cuts it down, till it suits him. Very well: let me have the same privilege. Let me cut off a little more; and it will suit me. And in doing so, I only act upon the principle which he adopts—I follow his example.

12

The truth is—this witness proves too much for either of us. When we first find immersion, we find it attended with much superstition. The question arises—how much of the practice in the third century is superstition; and how much is truth? My friend says, two immersions, the disrobing, the use of honey, the sign of the cross. But may there not be a little more superstition, than he admits? Evidently the ordinance was greatly corrupted; and it is impossible to separate the pure from the vile, except by going to the Bible itself. It is worthy of remark, that Justin Martyr, the earliest writer on baptism, speaks of it as a *washing* (*loutron*,) but not as an immersion. Tertullian, as I have said, is the first who speaks of immersion.

But it is an important fact, that we find pouring and sprinkling practiced and universally admitted to be valid and scriptural, quite as early as we find immersion. Cyprian, who lived early in the third century, and the sixty-six bishops united with him in council, were unanimously of that opinion. And it is worthy of special remark, that not a voice was raised against their decision in favor of the validity and scripturality (if I may coin a word) of baptism by sprinkling. So far as we can learn, there was not a word of controversy on the subject, as certainly there must have been, if it had been considered an innovation. Both Greeks and Latins were united in regarding baptism by sprinkling or pouring as valid and scriptural.

But I can find sprinkling rather earlier than this. Walker, an English writer, who studied this subject with great care, in his book on baptism, mentions the case of a man, some sixty or seventy years after the apostles, who, whilst on a journey, was taken dangerously ill, professed christianity, and desired baptism. As water could not be obtained, the place being desert, he was sprinkled thrice with *sand*. He recovered; and his case being reported to the bishop, he decided that he was baptized "if only water were poured (*perfunderetur*) on him." Here is an instance of baptism by pouring, earlier than any account of immersion, so far as I know, can be found.—*See Pond.* p. 45.

It has been asserted, that baptism by pouring and sprinkling was, at the period of which we are speaking, deemed so doubtful as to its validity, that persons so baptized were not permitted to bear the ministerial office. This, however, is not true. There was a rule, as we learn from the council of Neoceserea, that persons who made profession of religion on a sick bed, should not enter the ministry, unless they afterwards gave decided evidence of piety. The difficulty arose, not from any doubt entertained of the validity of their baptism, but from the doubtful character of their piety. This will be proved, if disputed. The christians of that day certainly gave the most unequivocal evidence of their entire confidence in the scriptural character of such baptisms; for although the prevailing belief was, that persons dying unbaptized would go to perdition, they had no scruples about baptizing the sick by pouring; nor did they ever rebaptize such as had received the ordinance in this manner. They, therefore, risked the salvation of the soul upon the validity of such baptisms.

Indeed it is certain, that many of the ancients entertained the belief, that John baptized by pouring. The proof of this fact I have already produced; and it is scarcely necessary to repeat it. Aurelius Prudentius (A. D. 390) represents him as pouring water on the persons in the river—"*perfundit fluvio.*" Paulinus, bishop of Nola, about the same time, represents him as baptizing "*infusis lymphis*"—by pouring water. Bernard, speaking of the baptism of our Savior by John, says—"Infundit aquam capiti Creatoris creatura"—*the creature poured water on the head of the Creator.* Lactantius speaks of baptism performed "*purifici roris perfusione*"—by the distilling of the purifying dew. In the 5th century it was very common in many places to baptize by pouring.

I might safely agree to decide this controversy by the testimony of the early Greek and Latin fathers; for, to a man, they believed that baptism, by pouring or sprinkling, was true christian baptism. They furnish us with concessions of immersionists that are worth something. They, it will not be denied, understood the Greek language. They certainly knew whether *baptizo* signified only to immerse. And it will not be pretended, that they were prejudiced in favor of our mode. Our immersionist friends love to claim them as genuine advocates of theirs. Yet with all their knowledge of the Greek, and with all their strong partialities for immersion, they did not know, they did not believe, that immersion is the only apostolic or christian baptism. Here we have concessions that will outweigh all the Pedo-baptist concessions that can be produced. These concessions are fatal to the doctrine of my friend, Mr. Campbell; whilst the concessions of Pedo-baptists touch not the validity and scriptural character of our baptism.

Whether, therefore, we regard the testimony of the lexicons, or the usage of the classics, or the authority of the translations, or the usage of the Jewish writings and of the Bible, or the opinions and practice of the ancient churches, or all of these together; we stand on a firm foundation. With one voice they testify, that *baptizo* does not mean simply to immerse. With almost irresistible evidence they establish the validity of our mode of baptism.

Let not the fact be forgotten, that when the Greeks would definitely express immersion, they used *kataduo;* and when the Latins spoke of that mode of baptism, they used tingo, mergo, immergo, mergito. But when they spoke simply of the ordinance, they all used *baptizo.* How are we to account for this fact? How can it be explained, on the principles for which the gentleman is contending?

I will put the testimony of Origen, the learned Greek father, against the opinion of Anthon and Johnson. Origen says, Elisha had the altar baptized; and the Bible tells us how that baptism was administered. The water was *poured* upon it. The altar was not put down into the water. None of your classical scholars can say that Origen did not understand his vernacular tongue. Athanasius, Gregory Nazianzen, Clemens Alexandrinus, and Basil, understood the Greek, and they all used the word to express the application of a fluid, even in small quantities, to a subject. The testimony of such men, concerning a Greek word in the New Testament, is worth more than all the lexicons and classics, even if they were against us.

I think it unnecessary to pursue the subject further to-day. I have it precisely in the position in which I wish it. On to-morrow, if spared, I will make an argument directly in favor of baptism by pouring or sprinkling.—[*Time expired.*

Saturday, Nov. 18—10 *o'clock, A. M.*
[MR. CAMPBELL'S TWELFTH ADDRESS.]

It is important, my fellow-citizens, that we always have before us the precise point at issue, in every department of this debate. Various minor points will come up in the discussion of any great question. But, how-

ever numerous these points may be, they should always be considered
with reference to the great point. Their relevancy, pertinency, and
power, should be regarded with special reference to it.

That great point now before us, is to ascertain, if we can, from the
Scriptures of truth, and from ancient learning, what is the precise precept
of Jesus Christ in the commission. As we said before, he doubtless intended some one definite action to be performed. He had but one design,
one aim, and he gave one plain precept clearly indicative of it. What
that precept was, we cannot mistake ; for he said, " BAPTIZE." By this,
he certainly meant some one well-defined action; not any action which
every one pleases. Is not this perfectly plain ? I care not what that one
action may be. It is acceptable to me because it is his will. Had he
said wash, or purify, without respect to any mode, I would be pleased
with any mode whatever, provided it were indeed *washing* or purifying
the whole person. But even then, it must be the whole person. His
will is always my pleasure. Were I to consult flesh and blood, I had
much rather be with than against Mr. Rice. His mode is certainly the
easier of the two, and we all love easy and comfortable services. It is
also the most convenient ; and there is no cross about it. And no one likes
to carry a cross if he can help it. It is also said to be more polite and
genteel, and that is a good argument. Flesh and blood, then—and they
are eloquent pleaders—are with him and against me. But when reason,
and conscience, and the love of the Savior mount the throne, we feel and
know that he has commanded some one action to be performed, and we
must understand it, if possible, and just do that action, and no other; for
nothing else will please him. This is the fact and the law, both in
heaven and earth. The reason is, his will is always wise and benevolent.

I have presented this subject in various forms, that it may be apprehended. When God speaks and legislates in human language, he uses
our words in their most precise, proper, and correct meaning at the time
in which he speaks ; and, therefore, in interpreting them, we have only
to bring them to the same tribunal and to the same code of laws to which
we appeal in any other case of the same time, country, language, &c.
We ask no special tribunal, no special laws in the case. The tribunal
to which we appeal, and the laws by which we would be tried, are universally admitted in all the commonwealth of learning and of law.

We have first appealed to the great law, defining the meaning of words,
as general and specific.

We have in the next place, opened the dictionaries of that language in
which the christian laws were written by inspired apostles. The whole
host of lexicographers depose that dip, immerse, or plunge, is the proper,
primitive and current meaning of *baptizo*. In this point there is no
discrepancy—all other uses and acceptations of this word are figurative
and rhetorical.

The gentleman [Mr. Rice,] has frequently told you what he has proved, and what he has refuted. I envy no man the talent, the peculiar faculty of strongly and repeatedly affirming his conviction, or imagination,
that he has proved, conclusively and irrefragably proved, himself right,
and his opponent wrong. He that imagines that his bold, simple, unsup-
ported assertion will pass with the community for proof, " strong as holy
writ," conceives not of his audience as I do, nor as I wish to do. With
me, a man's saying that he has proved a proposition, and repeating it a
thousand times, passes for nothing. And thus I judge of my audience.

They ask me not to judge for them—but they ask me for light, for evidence, for proof. I give it to them, and then leave the forming of conclusions to themselves. I seek to treat them as I would wish them to treat me. I ask no man to tell me what he has proved; he may give me his opinion on that subject, if he pleases, and I will then examine his opinion.

The gentleman says, he has proved from lexicons—what? He has nothing to prove! He may find exceptions, or objections, but he has nothing to prove—except that the authorities I offer are either not truly alledged, or that they are irrelevant, or that they are defective. Has he done so? In what instance? Has he proved that *baptizo* is not a specific word, or that it is generic? At one time he said that *baptizo* comprehended more than to wash; and, at another time, that dipping, the proper and first meaning of the word, is only a *mode* of washing—thus making it generic or specific, as the case requires. Has he produced a lexicon, of the eighteen centuries past, giving *sprinkle* or *pour* as the *proper*, or as the *figurative* meaning of *baptizo?* How often must I contradict and repel such an assumption? How, then, has he sustained the practice of his church? Let him adduce any modern dictionary, English, French, Spanish, German, &c., thus expounding the Greek words, *bapto* or *baptizo*.

And the translations are all with him too! And why not add all the world also! He has not produced a version of the Bible of his own church, or of ours, ancient or modern, in any language, that ever did translate *baptizo*, in one single instance, by any word that justifies the practice of his church. What, in the ear of reason and of truth, are assertions worth, not only unsustained by a single fact, but opposed by thousands? Have I not shown that they are with me? That so far as any of them has introduced any word for baptism, it has sometimes, nay often, substituted immerse, or its equivalent; and never, on any occasion, a word that sustains the Presbyterian practice? His proofs, such as they are, are all *exparte.* Suppose I were to quote Baptist authorities, (and many of them are as authoritative, rational, and veritable, as any in the world,) what would he have then asserted! Yes, if he thus asserts now, when I give him all my proofs out of the Pedo-baptist church, what would he say if I had done as he has done—quote all my authorities from those with me?

Let him adduce any Baptist dictionary, commentator, annotator, or critic, that has ever conceded to him sprinkling, or pouring, or wetting, as thousands of his party have done, and been constrained to do to us, in the case of immersion!

He says he can bring book for book, name for name, dictionary for dictionary, ad infinitum! Then they are like some twenty authorities which he has quoted, in anticipation of me, marked out by me as evidences—not one of them asserting his practice; all of them, either directly or indirectly, vindicating mine. Thus he gets before me in time, and place, and books, if not in argument. But does any one of these books, or authorities, say for him what he teaches and practices? Not one. If such methods of argument, assertion, and proof, will pass for evidence with this community, I must say, I have greatly mistaken its character.

I did not expect, nor intend, to bring the discussion of this proposition to a close to-day. I am compelled, however, to gallop through it in the

Q

best way I can.   We are, indeed, to have a night session of three hours, in order to make out the time agreed upon: for, were we to close at two o'clock, we should then have had but sixteen hours, instead of eighteen, on this proposition.   I did, indeed, expect that, by intrenching somewhat on the time allotted other propositions, of less comprehensive proof, I would have been allowed to go through this question more deliberately and fully.   In hasting over such a field, I shall frequently be obliged merely to state some principles, and topics, from which I would have argued at much greater length.

My friend, Mr. R., in his concluding remarks on yesterday, spoke of some peculiar license afforded him from Ernesti.   That distinguished writer on *hermeneutics*, has given him no such license as that for which he pleads. Ernesti, Horn, Stuart, and all that school, with which I profess to be tolerably well acquainted, affirm that we are never to depart from the common and well established meaning of words, without a clear and well established necessity.   They try the meaning of words by contemporary writers, by the currency of usage, country, people.   Had we the space of a long summer's day to discuss these principles of interpretation, I would demonstrate that I am pursuing the course commended by Morus, Ernesti, Horn, Stuart, and all of them.   Mr. R. has no authority for claiming for *baptizo* a special court, a special code, or in any way to exempt it from the common rules of interpretation.   It is not a word of idiom, as I have frequently observed.   To dip, to sprinkle, to pour, like other outward, physical, and well defined actions, are not effected by any national peculiarity.   Men performed these actions in all ages, languages, and countries, in the same manner.   Ernesti has given him no law any more than Gregory X. to interpret the word in dispute, in any shade of sense differing from Josephus, the Septuagint, or the Greek classics.   They all perfectly agree on the subject.   He must not get a dispensation or a bull for trying *baptizo*, as a heretic is tried.   Let him show reasons why he would plead for a special law in the case.   When such reasons are offered, and not till then, they shall be examined.   We need no special pleading, and we cannot allow it in so plain a case.

Before proceeding to my next argument, there yet remain two other documents to be heard from in conclusion of my sixth argument.   There is a short extract from Calmet, and a still shorter one from the Edinburgh Encyclopedia.

Taylor's Calmet.   " Baptism is taken in Scripture for sufferings, ' Can ye drink of the cup that I drink of, and be baptized with the baptism which I am baptized with?' Mark x. 38.   And Luke xii. 50, ' I have a baptism to be baptized with, and how am I straitened till it be accomplished?'   We find traces of similar phraseology in the Old Testament, (Ps. lxix. 2, 3.) where waters often denote tribulations; and where, to be swallowed up by the waters, to pass through great waters, &c., signifies to be overwhelmed by misfortunes.

" There is a very sudden turn of metaphor used by the apostle Paul, in Rom. vi. 3–5, ' Know ye not that so many of us as were *baptized* into Jesus Christ were *baptized into his death?* therefore we are *buried with him by baptism into his death*—that we should walk in newness of life.   For if we have been *planted together* [with him] *in the likeness of his death*, we shall be also planted in the likeness of his resurrection.'   Now what has *baptism* to do with *planting?*   Wherein consists their similarity, so as to justify the resemblance here implied?   In 1 Peter iii. 21, we find the apostle speaking of baptism, figuratively, as ' saving us;' and alluding to Noah, who long lay buried in the ark, as corn long lies buried in the earth.   Now, as after having died to his former course of life in being baptized, a convert was considered as rising to a renewed life, so after having been separated from his former connections, his seed-bed as it were, after having died in being planted, he was considered as rising to renewed life also."

Edinburgh Ency.—" In the time of the apostles the form of baptism was very simple. The person to be baptized was dipped in a river or vessel, with the words which Christ had ordered, and to express more fully his change of character, generally assumed a new name. The immersion of the whole body was omitted only in the case of the sick, who could not leave their beds. In this case sprinkling was substituted, which was called *clinic baptism.* The Greek church, as well as the schismatics in the east, retained the custom of immersing the whole body ; but the Western church adopted, in the thirteenth century, the mode of baptism by sprinkling, which has been continued by the Protestants, Baptists only excepted."

I am sorry to dip into the Greek again ; and, therefore, for the sake of condensing, I prefer to read my seventh argument and its developments as derived from the words used in construction with *baptizo,* as I have sketched it in my book on baptism. I will pass over it as rapidly as possible.

VII. Our seventh argument, in development and confirmation of the true meaning of *baptizo,* is derived from the words used in construction with it, as contra-distinguished from all its rivals, *raino, cheo, louo ;* and the prepositions *epi, en, eis, ek, apo,* used in construction with them.

We shall commence with *epi,* the word essential to the use of *raino, rantizo,* and that family, For the reasons already given we are obliged, in positive laws and precepts, to take all the words in their primitive, proper, or common, and not in their figurative and peculiar significations. *Epi* frequently signifies *on* or *upon ; en,* generally in ; *eis,* into ; *ek,* of, out of, or from ; and *apo,* from. But we have a shorter and more satisfactory way of ascertaining the use and import of these prepositions, than the more common method of comparing all the occurrences. We take them and their principals together. For, in this way, there is less room for false and inconclusive reasoning, and the most illiterate may thus comprehend them. We shall illustrate this by taking *raino* and its compounds, *perir, raino* and *epi* together, and *bapto* and *baptizo,* with *en* and *eis,* as they are found in common usage. I assert, then, that for some reason *raino* and *epi* agree together ; *baptizo* and *en* also agree together. But *raino* and *en,* or *baptizo* and *epi,* so perfectly disagree, as never to be found construed in amity in any Greek author, sacred or profane.

1. *Peri-raino epi ton katharisthenta*—sprinkle the blood upon him to be cleansed, Lev. xiv. 7 ; 2. *Perir-ranei epi teen oikian*—sprinkle upon the house, Lev. xiv. 51 ; 3. *Ranei epi hilasterion*—he shall sprinkle it upon the mercy-seat, Lev. xvi. 14. This phrase occurs a second time in the same verse—*Peri-ranei epi ton oikon*—he shall sprinkle it upon the house ; *epi ta skeua ; epi tas psuchas,* upon the persons. The same idiom is here found three times in one verse, Num. xix. 18 ; again, in the 19th verse, *Perir-ranei epi ton akatharton*—he shall sprinkle it upon the unclean ; again, Eze. xxxvi. 25, *Raina epi humas katharon hudoor* —I will sprinkle upon you clean water. In construction, then, with the person upon whom water is sprinkled, the verb *raino* is followed by *epi ;* never by *en* or *eis.* *A* sprinkles water, blood, oil, dust, or ashes *upon B ;* but never sprinkles B *in* blood, oil, dust, &c. : whereas *baptizo,* in such cases is followed by *en* or *eis,* never by *epi.* *A* immerses *B,* not *upon,*

or *with*, but *in* water.   This is a most convincing fact, that *baptizo*, occurring eighty times in the New Testament, is never construed with *epi*, nor *raino* with *en* or *eis*.   *Baptizo* is frequently construed with *en* and *eis*, and *raino* with *epi*; but they never interchange their particles.   A shadow does not more naturally accompany an object standing in the sunshine, in this latitude, than does *epi* accompany *raino*, and *en*, *baptizo*, in the cases described.

All this is equally true in the case of *cheo*, to pour.   The object on which water or anything is poured, is designated by *epi*, never by *en*. The thing poured or sprinkled always follows the verb to pour or sprinkle; the person is always preceded by upon.   Neither of these facts ever occurs in the case of *baptizo*.   In that case the person always follows the verb; and the material in which the action is performed, is always preceded by *en*, expressed or understood.   Hence the uniform construction in the one case is, " I immerse *B in water;* " in the other case the construction is, " I pour or sprinkle water *upon B*."   Not more clearly different are these two constructions in English than they are in Greek. Indeed, the object immersed is never governed by a preposition—the object sprinkled or poured is always governed by a preposition.   The actions, then, in the original are just as distinct as the words *baptizo*, *cheo*, *raino*, and their respective constructions.

Louo, to wash, is by some supposed to be identical with *baptizo*. They imagine, that because *baptizo* is metaphorically rendered by *louo*, to wash, in a few instances, they must be identical in meaning.   But such is not the fact.   *Baptizo* is sometimes figuratively rendered by *louo*; but *louo* is never rendered by *baptizo!*   Hence, and I wish I could read this with the most imposing emphasis, *louo* and *baptizo*, and their representatives, to wash, and to baptize, are not convertible terms.   But, in the definition of words, the word defined and the definition must, in all cases, be convertible, if the definition be a correct one.   Hence *baptizo* does not mean to wash, except by accident, metonymically.   To one accustomed to read the New Testament with a critical eye, these are facts which clearly forbid such an assumption.   For instance, *louo* and *baptizo* occur in the same sentence, and sometimes in the same clause of a sentence, in direct contra-distinction.   Thus in the case of the jailor, Acts xvi., " He *washed* their stripes and was *baptized*,"—and Ananias said to Paul, " Arise, be *baptized* and *wash* away thy sins."

It is not said, Be washed and then wash away thy sins.   It does not say, He washed their stripes, and was washed himself and all his family. These examples most satisfactorily demonstrate that the apostles never used *baptizo* and *louo*, or immerse and wash as convertible or equivalent terms.   Baptism is, therefore, not washing, nor washing baptism; in virtue of the meaning of the original terms.   *Rantizo* and *louo* are as inimical as *baptizo* and *louo*; for we find them standing in the same clause together.   Thus Paul says, " Having your hearts *sprinkled* from an evil conscience, and your bodies *washed* with pure water."   Sprinkling and washing are, therefore, as inconvertible as immersion and washing.   *   *   *   *

The congruity of things, therefore, calls for certain prepositions in construction with verbs of action, and these go very far to settle any thing doubtful in the acceptation of the principal word in any given passage.   Now as *baptizo* has frequently both *en* and *eis* construed with the liquid or material used in the ordinance, and *raino* and *cheo* never; follows it not that these prepositions demonstrate a meaning in these words wholly incompatible with each other, so far as action is concerned?

It is as impossible either to pour or sprinkle a man *into* or *in* a river, as it is to immerse him upon it, or to immerse water upon him. It is, therefore, offering the grossest violence to all the laws of congruous construction to attempt to translate *baptizo* by sprinkle, pour, or purify; or *raino* and *cheo* by immerse, plunge, or overwhelm. The best lexicography, both of the principals and their usual retinue of particles and circumstances, peremptorily forbids such liberties. Concerning *ek* and *apo*, we shall say something in our next argument.

VIII. Our eighth argument is derived from the places where the ordinance of baptism was anciently administered; which will still farther develope the force of the prepositions in construction with *baptizo*.

Baptism was first administered in rivers. The first Baptist, during his public ministry, spent much of his time on the banks of the Jordan. Thither resorted to him "all Judea and Jerusalem, and were baptized of him in the Jordan, confessing their sins." They were not baptized *upon* Jordan, nor were they baptized *with* Jordan, nor was Jordan baptized *upon* them; but they were baptized *in* Jordan. Our English *in* is but the adoption of the Greek *en*. The Romans borrowed their *in* from the Greeks, and we borrowed our *in* from the Romans; and all these *ins* are of one and the same signification and construction. *In* is neither *at*, *with*, nor *by*; except by figure. It is literally *in*. In the house, is not *at* the house, *with* the house, nor *by* the house; but in the house.

Now, as *epi* does not bring the Jordan upon them, and as *eis* and *en* place them in the river, the meaning of *ek* and *apo* is by necessity established as assisting the baptized to emerge out of the river.

If the liberty which Pedo-baptists have taken with these prepositions, in the heat of controversy, has called forth the admiration and reproofs of their own most learned and sober-minded men, why should it be thought strange that we should be astounded at the recklessness of such men as Dr. Miller of Princeton, and others, who, in defiance of their own reputation for learning and good sense, have contradicted, in express terms, all our lexicographers, translators, reformers, historians and distinguished critics, for the sake of the papal dogma of infant rantism, consecrated by John Calvin, John Knox, Theodore Beza, and their adherents.

On counting the actual occurrences of *en* in the New Testament I find it is found 2660 times. Of this immense number of times, though these learned doctors tell you of its two-and-twenty meanings, it is translated in your common Testament 2045 times by *in*. Yet such critics as Dr. Miller, when they put on their Pedo-baptist spectacles, will have it *with* always when baptism is alluded to. John baptizes *with* water; but, when the phrase comes, *en to Jordanee*, he passes it by. He does not say he baptized them with Jordan; but, passing it by, he says that *eis* means *at* or *to*, in such cases. Well, not having time to count over the whole book, I found in the four gospels that *eis* occurs 795 times. Of these, it is translated by *into* 372 times, and by *to*, for *into*, more than one hundred times; for to the house, to the temple, to the city, to Jerusalem, Bethany, Nazareth, &c., means into; and of 273 times *unto*, it might have been very often into; thus making, in all, 500 out of 795 occurrences.

As for *ek* and *apo*, frequently rendered *out of* and *from*, it is, on two accounts, unnecessary to speak particularly; because, first, whether they are more commonly rendered by *from*, or *out of*, avails nothing, seeing that *from*, nine times in ten, is out of, in sense. For example, from heaven, from the temple, from the city, from the grave, means out of these places, and not from the boundaries of them. In the second place, it being evident that *baptizo*, with *en* and *eis*, most certainly places the subject *in* the pool, *in* the river, or *in* the bath, *ek* and *apo* must bring them out of it.

Fancy or taste may increase indefinitely the figurative meaning of words;

but the number of figurative meanings is of no philological account in fixing the common or proper meaning of any word, still less the mere connectives of speech.

The partial and one-sided mode of interpretation is nowhere more apparent than in the cavils about these prepositions. We shall produce but a single example: *Epi* and *en* will illustrate the matter. After *raino* or *cheo*, *epi* is always translated *upon*, without one demurrer in all the Pedo-baptist ranks; yet *epi*, out of 920 times in the New Testament, is translated by *upon* only 158 times, that is, about once in six times; whereas, *en* is translated four times in every five by *in*. Yet to *sprinkle upon* is never cavilled at by a Pedo-baptist; while to baptize, or *immerse in*, is always repudiated as an unwarrantable license on the part of a Baptist!!

But the reason given why John baptized at Enon, one would think, ought to silence every doubt or cavil on that question. But, alas! for frail human nature! it will not always be persuaded, though one rose from the dead. Hence, although we are expressly told that John baptized at Enon, *because there was much water there;* the spirit of the sectary sets about to prove that there was not much water there, but only a few rivulets. And, if at last he is constrained to admit, that even many pools might be collected from many rivulets, he sets about finding some other use for the many rivulets and pools than for the performance of baptism. In his heated imagination, he sees all the dromedaries and camels of Arabia carrying the people to John's tent, and, that these thirsty animals, coming off their long journey, might have something to drink, the humane John, who always kept a bason and a squirt upon his table for the purpose of baptizing, pitched his tent near to Enon for the sake, not of baptizing, but of watering the caravans that flocked to his baptism. *Credat Judæus Appela, non ego.* To argue against imagination, is like arguing against love or our instinctive appetites. Still we must remark, that *polla hudata* signifies much water, and that John the apostle uses the phrase in his writings no less than *five* times; the other instances, too, all requiring much water. The mystic mother of papal Rome sits on "many waters." Are these little rivulets, indeed! The voice of God, too, is compared to the sound of many waters! Can these be rivulets?

John, in the Hebrew and Greek style, uses *polla hudata*, in the plural form, for much water. I believe we never have *hudor* in the singular number in all the Septuagint; hence, we are confirmed in the belief that, in Jewish style, the plural form indicates much water, just as the word always indicates to us.

But does not the sentence itself refute the presumptuous construction sometimes imposed on it. Reads it not, that John *baptized* at Enon for a given reason? He did not encamp or lodge there for that reason; but he baptized there for that reason. Hence, the baptizing and the reason, *much water*, must fairly and honorably go together. John baptized at Enon for no other reason than that there was much water there.

Suppose, for example, we were told that a celebrated mill-wright had located on a certain creek because it contained much water, who would more honor his own understanding, he that affirms he located there for the sake of watering his stock—or he who says, for the sake of erecting mills?

As to the location of Enon, whether it were north of John's first location, some fifty miles up the river Jordan, or whether it was a stream issuing from a fountain called "*Ainyon, Doves-eye Spring,*" or whether it was a *sun*-fountain, near Salim, venerated by the old Canaanites, are questions I have neither leisure nor inclination to discuss. Robinson, in his History of Baptism, discusses such questions at great length. I refer the curious to him, and will only give a short extract from his work on the use of the words *polla hutata:*

"It is observable, that the rivers Euphrates at Babylon, Tiber at Rome, and Jordan in Palestine, are all described by *polla hudata.* Jeremiah speaks of the first, and, addressing Babylon says, O thou that dwellest upon *many waters,* thine end is come ; for Babylon was situated on what the Jews called *the* river, the *great* river Euphrates. The Evangelist John describes Rome, which was built on the Tiber, by saying, The great harlot, the great city which reigneth over the kings of the earth, sitteth upon *many waters.* Ezekiel describes Judea and Jordan, by saying to the princes of Israel, Your mother is a lionness, her whelps devour men, she was fruitful by reason of *many waters;* an evident allusion to the lions that lay in the thickets of Jordan. The thunder which agitates clouds, charged with floods, is called the voice of the Lord upon *many waters;* and the attachment that no mortification can annihilate, is a love which *many waters* cannot quench, neither can the *floods* drown. How it comes to pass that a mode of speaking, which on every other occasion signifies *much,* should in the case of baptism signify *little,* is a question easy to answer."

To an unsosphisticated mind, this passage, together with the various locations of John along the Jordan, sometimes on this side, and sometimes on that side, methinks, independent of every other argument, would refute the notion of sprinkling. But how much more when the meaning of the word and the laws of construction, already established, assert that John's disciples were immersed in the Jordan, confessing their sins."

My worthy friend says that he has got ahead of me—but by this being ahead he cannot mean ahead in argument, but in place. He goes in advance : he leaves the matter upon my hands unanswered. In this way, he goes ahead of me. He was going to Biblical usage ; but instead of that, he brings up Tertullian to disprove in advance what he supposes I will present. But I will pursue, as I have done, my regular course of argument, not regarding his witticisms, but the convictions of the understandings and hearts of the audience.—[*Time expired.*

Saturday, Nov. 18—10½ *o'clock, A. M.*
[MR. RICE'S TWELFTH REPLY.]

MR. PRESIDENT—I had expected that my friend, Mr. C., would to-day make a furious assault upon the citadel of the sprinklers. It had been supposed by many, that he was holding in reserve his most destructive fire, and that to-day we should hear the roar of his great guns, and witness the destruction of our strong fortress. Such being our anticipations, we really did not expect to see him come and *read* us an argument ! It is truly marvellous, that one of the greatest debaters of the age—one who has, for the last thirty years, been engaged in this species of controversy, should find it necessary to *read* his arguments ! Is it true, that he had his defence of immersion prepared, " cut and dried," before the discussion commenced, to be read to the audience ? Cannot my friend sustain his cause by any other means ? I never heard of but one man reading a speech in Congress ; and I believe every body laughed at him.

My friend, however, finds himself in the situation of a certain lawyer, who had with great care, written and memorized a speech in defence of a cause he had undertaken. In the progress of things, the aspect of the case was considerably changed, some portions of his testimony being rejected. The lawyer commenced his speech, but was soon interrupted by the judge, as bringing in irrelevant matters. He again attempted to proceed, and was again interrupted. He became impatient, and replied with great emphasis, " May it please your Honor, it is in my speech, and I *must* speak it." [Laughing.] So it is in the gentleman's book, and he must *read* it. [Continued laughter.]

For three days the gentleman has been out of the Bible. On yesterday, he told us he was in the portico, and he is in the portico still. I know not how to account for his movements. According to our rules, we debate no question more than *three days*, except by consent of parties; though I informed him that I would continue the debate as many hours, each day, as he pleased. I have given him a fourth day to bring up his argument; and yet he tells me he has not time enough. I am apprehensive he never will have time enough to sustain his cause. I have, however, agreed to continue the discussion of the present subject this evening.

I have a remark or two to make concerning the *action* of baptism. The Savior commanded the observance of an *ordinance*. Baptism is not an *action*, but an *ordinance*. The gentleman was, however, not quite fortunate in one of his illustrations. He mentioned the word *ride* as an example of a specific term. Now I had supposed that we could ride in several different ways; on horseback, in stage, steam car, or boat. Perhaps I might admit, that *baptizo* is as specific as the word *ride;* for we can ride in about as many ways as we can *wash*. But let it be distinctly understood, that *baptizo* denotes, in the New Testament, an *ordinance*, not an *action*. And I have proved, contrary to the reasonings of my friend, that in the Old Testament, several washings or ordinances were appointed, the *mode* of which was not prescribed, neither by the word used, nor even in any other way. Let this fact stand as an unanswerable refutation of all his efforts to prove the necessity of a specific word to denote the ordinance of baptism.

He professes to believe, that, in consequence of the greater labor and exposure attending the practice of immersion, it would be his interest to believe and practice as we do. This affords some pretty good evidence that we are in the right, for it is scarcely credible, that our Savior would have appointed an ordinance, at all times inconvenient, and often dangerous and impracticable. Some, indeed, plead these very difficulties in favor of immersion. In being plunged under water they consider themselves as *bearing the cross!* I read in the Bible of no cross, but that which is found in denying ourselves of all ungodliness and worldly lusts, and living soberly, righteously and godly in this present evil world. My friend has told us, in his Harbinger, that Paul was too small to be able to baptize! Still, it would seem, he managed to baptize some few. Since, however, the practice of immersion is difficult for all, and particularly so for small men like myself; I think it would be wise in my friend to adopt a mode requiring less labor and exposure—to aim more at securing purity of heart—the great thing—and less at putting the cross in bodily endurance.

I must briefly reply to what the gentleman has said about the lexicons. As to my *assertions*, of which he complains, the difference between him and myself, I think, is—that I make assertions and *prove* them; he makes assertions and *leaves* them. Whenever my statements are called in question, they will be proved. I have asserted and proved, that the lexicons, ancient and modern, with entire unanimity define *baptizo, to wash, to cleanse,* as well as to *sink, plunge,* &c. I have asserted and proved, that they give *to wash, to cleanse,* as the *first* and leading meaning of the word in the Bible. I have called upon the gentleman to produce *one* lexicon that gives *immerse* as its leading signification in the New Testament. He has not done it; and I presume, he cannot. Where is there a lexicon, ancient or modern, that defines this word as a specific term, having but one meaning? I verily believe, the gentleman cannot produce more than one, if he can find one. Where is the lexicon, that gives *immerse* as its leading meaning, as it is used in the Bible and religious writings of the Jews? Yet he would persuade the audience, that the lexicons sustain him in the position that *baptizo*, as appropriated to the ordinance of christian baptism, is a specific term, meaning only to immerse!!! Mr. Carson candidly acknowledged, that all the lexicographers and commentators were against him. I have before read this acknowledgment, and I will read it again. " My position," says he, "is that it *(baptizo)* always signifies to dip; never expressing any thing but mode. *Now as I have all the lexicographers and commentators against me in this opinion*, it will be necessary to say a word or two with respect to the authority of lexicons."—P. 79.

The gentleman tells the audience, that I am in the habit of quoting authors on my own side of the question; whilst he is sustaining his cause by those opposed to him. Do you remember what trouble I gave him with Dr. Gale, one of the most learned and zealous immersionists? Dr. Gale, as I have proved, admitted that *baptizo* does not so necessarily express the *action* of putting under water, as it expresses something else. Yet the very thing he has, throughout this discussion, labored to prove, is that *baptizo* does express definitely and necessarily the *action* of putting under water. The concession of Gale, therefore, is destructive to his argument. And have I not brought against him Carson, another most zealous immersionist, whom he admits to be a profound linguist? He has earnestly contended, that *bapto* is a specific term, and that it means *to dye* only in a *figurative* sense. Mr. Carson most positively denies, and most unanswerably refutes this principle, proving that it means to *dye by sprinkling as literally as by dipping*. I have not brought forward immersionists, as he has adduced Pedo-baptists, who avowed themselves wholly *indifferent* on the subject; but I have appealed to the most zealous advocates of exclusive immersion—men laboring most earnestly to defend their favorite dogma.

But I have not appealed only to Gale and Carson; I have brought against the gentleman the Greek and Latin fathers,—men who, however superstitious they may have been, understood the Greek, and whose prejudices were all in favor of immersion—men whom my friend loves to count on his side. I proved that Origen, the most learned of them, in giving the sense of Rev. xix. 13, substituted *rantizo*, to sprinkle, for *bapto*, and that Mr. Carson could escape the force of this fact only by concluding that Origen did not understand the meaning of the word! And although Mr. Campbell has said and published, that no translator, ancient or modern, ever rendered any of this family of words to *sprinkle*, I have proved that the translators of the venerable Syriac, the old Ethiopic and the Vulgate, (all of whom, according to him, were immersionists,) did so translate *bapto*. But he says, there must have been a different reading. Where is the evidence? Is there any one copy of the New Testament found in all the searching for old manuscripts, which presents a different reading? *There is not one.* Why, then, contend for a different reading? Simply and only because the claims of immersion demand it!!! If, on such a pretence, one passage of the Bible may be changed, it may all be rendered doubtful.

I have appealed to the Greek and Latin fathers, and amongst them Jerom, the learned translator of the Vulgate. These were immersionists of the *old school;* and they, with unbroken unanimity, use *baptizo* to denote the ordinance administered by pouring or sprinkling, and pronounce baptism thus administered valid and good. The gentleman forgets, when he represents me as having appealed almost exclusively to authorities on my own side of the question; but a man's recollection sometimes fails him remarkably, when he is sorely pressed.

The gentleman made a broad assertion concerning a principle inculcated by Ernesti; but unfortunately, he read not a word from that author. I admit, that in all ordinary cases we are to adhere to the *common acceptation* of words *amongst the people whose language we are interpreting.* And hence it is, that I have appealed to the usage of *baptizo* amongst the Jewish writers. I read to you the declaration of Ernesti and of Dr. George Campbell, that the Greek of the New Testament is not classic Greek, and that the classics are very unsafe guides in interpreting the language of that book, applied, as it is, to new subjects and new ordinances. My friend makes assertions, but fails to prove them; I make assertions and prove them. This is the difference between us. Perhaps, however, I ought to give the authority of his "American apostle," professor Stuart; for he admits him to be a very learned critic. He says:

" New Testament usage of the word, in cases not relevant to this rite, clearly does not entitle you [immersionists] to such a conclusion with any confidence. If you say, ' The classical usage of the word abundantly justifies the construction I put upon it ;' my reply is, that classical usage can never be very certain in respect to the meaning of a word in the New Testament. Who does not know, that a multitude of Greek words here receive their coloring and particular meaning from the Hebrew, and not from the Greek classics? Does *theos,* (God,) *ouranos,* (heaven,) *sarx,* (flesh,) *pistis,* (faith,) *dikaiosuna,* (righteousness,) and other words almost without number, exhibit meanings which conform to the Greek classics; or which, in several respects, can even be illustrated by them? Not at all. Then how can you be over confident in the application of the classical meaning of *baptizo,* where the word is employed in relation to a rite that is purely christian? *Such a confidence is indeed common; but it is not the more rational, nor the more becoming on that account.*"

Such is the language of one of the first critics in America. And here let me remark, Stuart notices a very important peculiarity in the language of the New Testament in connection with *baptizo.* He states, that when *baptizo* occurs in the classics in the sense of immersing, it is generally followed by the preposition *eis,* as *baptizo eis;* but in the New Testament this expression occurs in but a single instance. There we find *baptizo* with the dative case simply, or with the preposition *en*—the very form of expression employed by the classics to denote the fluid *with* which baptism is performed. If the inspired writers spoke and wrote in regard to this word, as the classics did, as Mr. Campbell contends, and if they designed to express the action of immersing; why, I emphatically ask, did they so uniformly avoid the phraseology employed by the classics to express that idea, and adopt precisely the phraseology which in classical authors does not express it?

But the gentleman insists, that *lavo, to wash,* is only a *figurative* meaning of *baptizo.* Where is the evidence of the truth of this oft-repeated assertion? Let him, if he can, produce one lexicon, that gives *to wash* as only a figurative meaning of *baptizo.* I venture to say, he cannot do it. But he tells us, that the two words *louo* and *baptizo,* so far from meaning the same thing, are presented in the Bible in *contrast,*

I do not say, that *louo (to wash)* has the same meaning precisely as *baptizo.* There is just this difference: *louo* means *any kind* of washing; *baptizo* is in the Bible uniformly used in relation to *religious washings*—the use of water, and of water *only,* in the sense, or for the purpose of purification. Yet christian baptism, as Mr. C. will not deny, is constantly spoken of as a *washing,* and *louo* and *loutron* are the words used in such passages. Thus, Paul says to the Corinthians, "And such were some of you; but ye are *washed, (apelousasthe,)* but ye are sanctified," &c. 1 Cor. vi. 11. And writing to Titus—"According to his mercy he saved us by the *washing* of regeneration *(loutron)* and the renewing of the Holy Ghost," &c. In these passages the gentleman himself believes the apostle had reference to baptism, and called it a *washing;* and yet he tells us, the Greek word which signifies to *wash,* stands in *contrast* with *baptizo!!!* Justin Martyr, the first of the christian fathers who, so far as we know, wrote on this subject, speaks of baptism as a *washing,* as I have before stated. My friend gives us some rare specimens of criticism!

He has at length reached the Bible, and is aiming to get into Jordan. I might very safely admit, though it cannot be proved, that John went literally *into* Jordan. But the question is, what did he do, after he got in? Mr. C. *infers,* that he immersed the people. But where is the proof? He thinks John could not have gone into the water, except for the purpose of immersing. Is there, however, any certainty that his *inference* (for it is but an inference) is legitimate? There are many ancient pictures which represent persons standing in a stream, and the minister pouring water on their heads. There are several of very ancient date, that represent John baptizing our Savior in this mode; and, as I have proved, many of the ancients believed, that John did uniformly thus baptize. On what evidence, then, can it be asserted, that if John went into the water, he must have immersed? It is one thing to go *into* water, and quite another, to plunge *under* the water.

But observe, it is said, as I have already proved, that John was baptizing in Bethabara *beyond* Jordan. John i. 28, "These things were done in Bethabara beyond Jordan, where John was baptizing." If John baptized *in* Bethabara *beyond* Jordan, how could he have baptized literally *in* Jordan? It cannot be proved, that John went *into* the Jordan; and if it could, there is no evidence that he went in for the purpose of immersing. The gentleman's argument, therefore, is without force.

In reply to the very disparaging remarks made by Mr. C. concerning the venerable Dr. Miller, I will only say, that his reputation is too well established to need any defence from me. It will require something far more potent, than the denunciation of the gentleman, to bring him down from the eminence which as a great and good man he occupies.

My friend, Mr. C., has quoted Bloomfield as sustaining his views. I beg leave now to read Bloomfield, and to prove, that he is with us. On the passage in Matth. iii. 11, "I indeed baptize you with water," &c. he thus remarks:

"*En hudadi* [with water.] The *en* is thought redundant; and commentators adduce examples from classical writers. It rather, however, denotes the *instrument,* as Luke xiv. 34, and often." If, then, *en* denotes the instrument, the expression, *en hudat,* means *with* water, not *in* water. Mr. Bloomfield, then, would not read "I immerse you *in* water," but "I baptize you *with* water."

Mr. C. appeals to the account of the baptism of the eunuch, as proving immersion. "And they went down both *into* (*eis*) the water, both Philip and the eunuch; and he baptized him. And when they were come *up out of* (*ek*) the water," &c. But has he produced one lexicon, that says, *eis* uniformly or commonly means *into?* He has not; and if he had, I could appeal to a number of the very best, ancient and modern, which deny it. Scapula, one of the gentleman's favorite authorities, gives as the first meaning of *eis*, *ad*, *to*. Bretschneider, whom he admits to be one of the most critical lexicographers, gives *to* (*ad*) as its first and leading meaning; and Stuart agrees with him. Buttman, whose large Greek grammar is a standard work, gives its leading signification, *to*, *into*. Other authorities will be produced, if necessary. I will even make the gentleman himself my witness. In his translation of the New Testament he has, in very many instances, translated it *to*, not *into*. In a number of places where, in the common version, it is translated *into*, he renders it *to*. I will, if he desire it, refer to the passages.

The rule observed by the Greeks in relation to the preposition *eis*, is this: when they wished *by force of the words* definitely to express the idea of going *into*, they prefixed the preposition to the verb, as *eiserchomai eis*, or *embaino eis*. If Mr. C. will tell us, how many times the prepositions *eis* and *en* precede the verb, where in our version *eis* is translated *into;* we will venture to compare numbers with him. In some cases, the connection shows that it means *into;* in other cases, that it means simply *to.*

But, for the sake of argument, I will admit, though it cannot be proved, that Philip and the eunuch went literally *into* the water. The question then arises, what did Philip do after they got in? Did he immerse the eunuch? My friend says, yes; but where is the evidence? He *infers*, that the eunuch was immersed, from the fact of their going into the water. The inference, however, is not certainly legitimate; for he might have gone into water and had it poured on him. Besides, there are strong reasons for believing, that he was not immersed. The place was *desert;* and it is not at all probable, that they found sufficient water there for an immersion. Moreover, it is not probable, either that the eunuch undressed in the public road; or that he traveled on with his garments perfectly wet. The same remarks may be made concerning the people baptized by John. Did the multitudes, male and female, continue dressed in their dripping garments? Regard to health and to decency would forbid it. Yet we read nothing of changes of raiment, or of accommodations for changing, even if they had with them other garments. But at a later day, when immersion prevailed, we find baptisteries, napkins, towels, changes of garments, &c. Since, however, we read of no such things in the days of John, or of the apostles, we conclude they did not practice immersion.

But let me again turn to Bloomfield, whom my friend quoted as in favor of immersion. Commenting on Acts viii. 38 he says:

" *Ebaptizen auton* (he baptized him)—no doubt, with the use of the proper form ; but whether by immersion or by sprinkling is not clear. Doddridge maintains the *former;* but Lardner ap Newc. the *latter* view ; *and I conceive, more rightly.* On both having descended into the water, Philip seems to have taken up water with his hands, *and poured it copiously on the eunuch's head.*"

Bloomfield was with my friend yesterday ; but he seems to have been converted, for he is with us to-day. My friend has referred to *but one*

example of christian baptism, which seems to favor immersion; and this will not sustain him.

John, it is true, was baptizing in Enon near Salim, because there was much water there. But did he want much water to baptize in; or did he want it for other purposes? As I have already stated, multitudes of the Jews who resorted to him, remained together several days at a time. They must observe their daily ablutions. For these and for ordinary purposes they needed much water; but it cannot be proved that John wanted the water for the purpose of baptizing.

The expression, "*much water*," moreover, literally translated, is *many waters (polla hudata.)* I will read the remarks of Prof. Stuart on this expression. After narrating the facts, he remarks:

"Now John was baptizing IN (or *at*) Enon, near Salim, *hoti hudata polla en ekei*, for there was MUCH WATER there; or (more literally,) there were MANY WATERS there. The question is whether John baptized at Enon, near Salim, because the waters there were abundant and deep, so as to afford convenient means of immersion, or whether the writer meant merely to say, that John made choice of Enon, because there was an abundant supply of water there for the accommodation of those who visited him for the sake of being baptized, and hearing the powerful addresses he made to the Jews. The former statement makes the *much waters*, or *many waters* necessary, or at least convenient and desirable, for the purposes of the baptismal rite; the latter, for supplying the wants of the multitudes who attended the preaching of John. It has always seemed to me a very singular mode of expression, if the sacred writer meant to designate the former idea, to say *hoti hudata polla en ekei*. Why not say, because the water was deep or abundant simply? A single brook of very small capacity, but a living stream, might, with scooping out a small place in the sand, answer most abundantly all the purposes of baptism, in case it were performed by immersion, and answer them just as well as *many waters* could do. But, on the other hand, a single brook would not suffice for the accommodation of the great multitudes who flocked to John. The sacred writer tells us that "there went out to him Jerusalem, and all Judea, and all the region of Jordan," Matt. iii. 5; and that they were baptized by him. Of course, there must have been a great multitude of people. Nothing could be more natural than for John to choose a place that was watered by many streams, where all could be accommodated.

"The circumstances of the case, then, would seem to favor the interpretation which refers the mention of the *many waters* to the wants of the people who flocked to hear John."—*Stuart on the Mode of Baptism*, pp. 37, 38.

He gives from the Old Testament an example of the use of *polla hudata* to signify many springs or streams of water. When the country was invaded, and Jerusalem was likely to be besieged, it is said—"So there was gathered much people together, who stopped all the fountains, and the brook that ran through the midst of the land, saying, why should the king of Assyria come, and find *much* water?" (*polla hudata.*) 2 Chron. xxii. 4. Here evidently the expression means *many* fountains or small streams, not *deep* water.

But my friend, Mr. C., *infers*, that John immersed, because he went where there was much water. Is this inference legitimate? Is there any certainty that he wanted much water for the purpose of baptizing? I think it is by no means certain, and, when all the circumstances are considered, by no means probable.

I have now, I think, without having had the opportunity to *write* a speech, met the arguments of the gentleman, and showed their weakness. I have wished, and the audience, I think, have desired to see him enter the Bible. I am gratified to see, that there is some prospect of his doing so. I design, to-day, making an argument directly in favor of pouring and sprinkling. I should have done so on yesterday, but my friend was too far behind. I have met and answered his arguments, and kept ahead of him; and, unless he shall hereafter travel faster, I apprehend that he will remain quite in the rear.—[*Time expired.*

Saturday, Nov. 18—11 o'clock, A. M.
[MR. CAMPBELL'S THIRTEENTH ADDRESS.]

MR. PRESIDENT—Were I to touch on so many topics, and have them so singularly assorted as those which you have just now heard from Mr. Rice, in one short speech, I should expect to make but little progress through the day. My reading, it seems, is a great annoyance to my friend. The more concentrated arguments, exhibited in that form, require a more special attention than, as yet, he has bestowed on any thing I have advanced; for, indeed, the gentleman asserts much more than reasons, and affirms more than he proves. His gifts are rather of that order. I have no preference for reading, as all who know me, I presume, will admit. But I cannot, at present, indicate my course farther than to say, that one great reason of my presenting some of these arguments in this form is, that they abound in criticisms and matters somewhat minute, requiring great accuracy, and which no stenographer in Christendom could rationally be expected to report accurately. To take down so many foreign words, pronounced so rapidly, and to place them in their proper order, in such a disquisition, is, I think, impossible. For this reason, I prefer to read a few items of critical analysis. I am neither to be allured nor driven from my course, to suit the convenience of my worthy friend. He knows full well how his desultory and incoherent mode of speaking will appear in print, especially upon subjects demanding a close and neat analytic and sometimes synthetic arrangement. He had better, however, attend to the argument, and he shall have speaking to satiety, in proper time and place. I am one of those who can afford to read; I fear he cannot.

I do not fully comprehend some of his allusions to myself, or my method, or both; especially his remark that I "have imposed myself upon you by my reading." I do not comprehend this. He is certainly doing himself great injustice, if, indeed, he have anything better to offer, especially in the reckless and unauthorized assertions which he has made; provided, only, that there be either philosophy or good sense in the following remarks, which I will read for his especial benefit, from that eminent Presbyterian doctor and critic, Dr. George Campbell:

"I have heard a disputant, in defiance of etymology and use, maintain that the word rendered in the New Testament, *baptizo*, means more properly to sprinkle than to plunge; and, *in defiance of all antiquity*, that the former was the earliest, and—the most general practice in baptizing. One who argues in this manner, never fails, with persons of knowledge, *to betray the cause he would defend:* and though, with respect to the vulgar, bold assertions generally succeed as well as argument, and sometimes better; yet, a candid mind will always *disdain to take the help of falsehood*, even in the support of truth."

So speaks Dr. Campbell. How pertinent these remarks are to the whole case before us, methinks requires neither note nor comment. I must, it seems, again refer to the word *specific*. It is not at all incompatible with the special character of an action, that it must be always performed in the same way. That there are various ways of *reading*, militates not with the fact that reading is a specific action. The pronunciation, tone, time, cadence, &c., may vary; still, reading is neither singing, nor speaking, nor writing. So of dipping, sprinkling, pouring. These actions may all be performed different ways : still, they retain their peculiar and incommunicable difference. No one with whom it has been my good fortune to discuss any question, appears to have made more proficiency in the art of making, perhaps sometimes inadvertently, false issues. I am now, according to him, proving that *baptizo* is only used in one acceptation—that it is not used figuratively. I am not affirming nor proving that *baptizo* never means anything but dip, in any acceptation of usage. It has this only as its literal, natural, original, and proper meaning ; and never means any thing, even figuratively or in a secondary sense, incompatible with this sense. All our most learned lexicographers say this. With Mr. Anthon, they say, *if it ever have any other sense than dip*, it is one analagous to, or compatible with this, its proper and perpetual meaning. Even "wash and cleanse" are noted as its figurative meaning in some of our best lexicons. Have I not said that any specific action may yield a thousand results ? Has the gentleman forgotten the instances given in reference to the word kill?

Mr. R. either forgets or misquotes the lexicons. He says some of them give *wash* and *cleanse* as the *proper* or *literal* meaning of *baptizo*. Now I have frequently controverted this, and shown that some of them positively declare that it is a figurative meaning. Schleusner represents *washing* as the effect of dipping ; and Bretschneider does not say that " it *simply* means to wash, to cleanse," in the New Testament—that is a particular case. No dictionary has ever said, what I have sometimes heard from my friend, that it signifies " *to wash in any mode.*" Have I not read from Beza and others, that it so signifies only by *consequence?* Such, indeed, is the definition of the distinguished Schleusner, in his lexicon. His words are, *jam quia haud raro aliquid immergo* ac intingi in aquam solet ut lavetur. *Because it frequently occurs that a thing is to be immersed or dipped into water that it may be washed.* I therefore speak in harmony with all the dictionaries, when I say that cleansing, washing, &c., is the *effect* of the action baptism, and not *the act* itself.

He would, in his paradoxical mood, this morning, have it, also, that he had quoted Baptist authority against me ! If, indeed, he had, what then ? They are not infallible ! But who are they ? Dr. Carson, and who else ? There is no discrepancy between Messrs. Gale, Carson, or any other Baptist, and myself, on the action of baptism. They all subscribe, *examimo*, to the proposition I am sustaining. They all affirm the solemn conviction, that immersion is the only christian baptism. They have no more faith in sprinkling, or pouring, or wetting the face, than·they have in the salt, and spittle, and sign of the cross, formerly attached to the ceremony? They all say that *baptizo* means dip, *immerse*, and that only in its true, and proper, and christian, and Jewish, and classic acceptation. We are all of one heart and soul on this proposition. Messrs. Gale, and Carson, and myself may differ on some critical matters. I certainly dissent in some matters of that sort. But these do not, in the least, affect the issue here, any more than an Indian mound affects the sphericity of the earth. Better, too, that Mr. R. had quoted Baptist writers against me, than that I had quoted them in my favor.

Mr. Rice spends his strength on matters as frivolous as the Apocryphal cases of Judith and Sirach—as *when* the former immersed herself; and how an unclean person was cleansed from contact with the dead! matters as intelligible as the laws of purification, so often explained, as if his inability to find the precise place where Judith went into the water, must change the meaning of the word!! These matters have been disposed of a thousand times!

"Mr. Carson says the dictionaries are all wrong," and proves, by the classics, that they are so in his view of the secondary meaning of this word. He also will extend the meaning of *bapto* without the interposition a of metonymy. I differ from him in this particular. But that avails not one atom in the great conclusion to which we have come. I agree with him, that we have just as good right to judge the dictionaries by the classics, as the makers of them had to judge the classics.

With regard to the Syriac, the Ethiopic, and the Vulgate, and some other ancient versions, on which my friend, Mr. Rice, loves to dwell, I have time to make only a remark or two. In these days it is easy to fill a volume with dissertations on such learned matters, for the benefit of common people. I have many volumes of this kind of learning at my disposal—but what avail such disquisitions here? I have, indeed, affirmed that none of all these versions has ever translated *baptizo* to favor Pedo-baptist practice. I examined them carefully enough to come to this conclusion. Now, after all that has been said by Mr. Rice on some dozen of them, has he even pretended to quote one instance of any one of them ever translating it by any word averring his practice? We might speak for a week upon them—upon the Hebrew *tabel* and *rahaz*, upon the Syriac *amad*, and the Arabic *amada*, &c. &c., but inasmuch as he cannot adduce one such instance, what would be the advantage?

His apology for Dr. Wall's neglect of replying to Dr. Gale, is wholly unsatisfactory. He says, he did not intend to reply to Dr. Gale on the *action* of baptism! Why then did he write a considerable portion of this volume on that subject, if he did not intend to reply? He has indeed replied to him on many points; on all points of importance *save this one*. But of *it* he took no notice whatever!! And yet the very point on which they were pre-eminently in collision.

In the same style of response, my friend accuses me of seeking to interpret Rev. xix. 13, for the sake of my criticism! This is doubtless very candid and magnanimous. I have no need of that. We have the same scene described in Isaiah, just as I presume John wrote it. And, in the case of the present versions, we have it "dipped in blood," and on that account have nothing to complain of. I have logically and legally, as I conceive, shown that Mr. R. must prove that the word *bebammenon* was in the Greek text, from which these versions were made, before he can make out the first case of an exception to my universal proposition. That he will not attempt, and, therefore, that point is fairly and fully settled.

I quoted from Ernesti, the other day, from memory. I shall now read a few periods from him on the proper method of interpretation. From these sentences you may judge of the correctness of the quotations and comments which you have heard from him.

"§ 21. From what has already been said, in this chapter, about the use of words, we may discover the ground of all the certainty which attends the interpretation of language. For there can be no certainty at all in respect to the interpretation of any passage, unless a kind of necessity compel us to affix a particular sense to a word; which sense, as I have said before, must be *one;* and unless there are special reasons for a tropical meaning, it must be the literal sense." (Morus, p. 47. xi.)—*Ernesti,* p. 10.

" § 31. *The principles of interpretation are common to sacred and profane writings.* Of course the Scriptures are to be investigated by the same rules as other books. These fanatics, therefore, are not to be regarded, who, despising literature and the study of the languages, refer every thing merely to the influence of the Spirit. Not that we doubt the influence of the Spirit; or that men truly pious, and desirous of knowing the truth, are assisted by it in their researches, especially in those things that pertain to faith and practice." (Morus, p. 69. xix.)

" If the Scriptures be a revelation to men, then are they to be read and understood by men. If the same laws of language are not observed in this *revelation,* as are common to men, then they have no guide to the right understanding of the Scriptures; and an *interpreter* needs *inspiration* as much as the original writer. It follows, of course, that the Scriptures would be no revelation in themselves; nor of any use, except to those who are inspired. But such a book the Scriptures are NOT; and nothing is more evident than that, ' when God has spoken to men, he has spoken in the language of men; for he has spoken by men, and for men.'" (Note by professor Stuart.) —*Ernesti,* pp. 15, 16.

A word or two on *baptizo eis* and *baptizo en,* as commented on by professor Stuart. On infant sprinkling Mr. Stuart is a partizan. Though he is a very candid one, still he is sectarian on this subject. But, quoting with approbation the following words of Calvin, he gives in his adhesion to sprinkling on other grounds than the meaning of the word. Calvin had not only said that the church had "from the beginning taken to herself the right to change the ordinances somewhat, excepting the substance;" but in another place spake in this wise: "It is of no consequence at all whether the person baptized is wholly immersed, or whether he is merely sprinkled by an affusion of water. This should be a matter of choice to the churches in different regions, although the word *baptizo* signifies to *immerse,* and *the rite of immersion was practiced by the ancient church.*" The first I quote from memory; the second I quote, I think, almost verbatim from the Institutes, iv. c. xv. sec. 19. To these last words, adds Mr. Stuart: "To this opinion I do most fully and heartily subscribe." Of course, Mr. Stuart is not quite so easily satisfied with the identity of the sense of baptizo *eis* and baptizo *en.* In one place he says that *baptizo eis* would more certainly prove immersion in the Jordan than *baptizo en.* But yet when *baptizo eis,* the very phrase found in Mark i. 9, comes to be reconsidered by him, it becomes so doubtful, that even this most common classic use is discarded. Persons, however, so generous as he and Calvin, I think, could not be convicted by all the laws of the Greek language on this subject! There is no cure for such obliquities, but the grace of God. To reason with such prejudices and early predilections, is as hopeless as to reason against the animal instincts, or the fiercer passions of our nature. I can sympathize with my friend, Mr. Rice, and such liberal spirits as professor Stuart.

I was once a Presbyterian, fully imbued with all the doctrines of the church. Its catechisms were as familiar as household words. My understanding, my conscience, my affections were all baptized in the font of pure orthodox Presbyterianism. I experimentally knew the struggle, the inward conflict, of calling in question any of its sage decisions. I traveled over all the ground more than thirty years ago. I gathered all the Pedo-baptist authorities around me, when infant baptism began to totter in my mind. I did not wish to read any Baptist books; I sent to booksellers for a whole suit of Pedo-baptist authors. But the more earnestly I sought argument and evidence and proof in them, the less I found. The more I read, the more I doubted. I became even angry that they could not give me proof of infant baptism. I finally threw them from me with disgust—Edwards, the last hope, proved himself fallacious, despite of all my wishes. His argument was, what logicians call, *a begging of the question*, from beginning to end. I seized the Greek Testament. Six months most fervent examination of the pure text wrought a full conviction, that *infant affusion had no more footing in the Bible than infant communion, than praying to the saints, or auricular confession.*

But to give up Pedo-baptism and Presbyterianism was to immolate my prospects, my influence and my earliest and long cherished ecclesiastic partialities and associations. Truth and conscience finally triumphed. I yielded to the light. I have never since regretted it. The Lord led me by a way I knew not of, and cared not to go. I say, then, I can sympathize with many good and well meaning men, whose minds and feelings are, or may be, where mine were some thirty years ago.

Mr. Rice and his brethren turn logical Unitarians and Universalists in all debates on baptism. I had a long protracted controversy with one of those Rabbis of Universalism, some years since. I know their tactics well. Take, for example, the words, *aioon, aioonion, aidios.* They are constrained to admit that these words do mean, *eternal, everlasting, unending*, sometimes. Nay, that in all etymological import and grammatical, that is, literal propriety, they certainly do mean duration without end; that no other words in universal language do more fully, more precisely, intimate that which is unending; but, yes, *but*, say they, in all cases where punishment, the punishment of the wicked is spoken of, *there* they do not mean literally *everlasting*—any more than when applied to hills and mountains, &c. Then they find a number of special cases; and by an interminable talk about these special cases, and by every sort of mystification, false issues, and special pleading, they induce thousands to believe that *aioon, aioonion, aidios*, and all that family, when applied to future punishment, mean not eternal, unending. Nay; when you remind them that these words represent the state of future felicity— they retort just as you have heard on immersion—they believe in eternal happines—but not because *aioon*, &c. so intimate in this case. I have never observed a more full and perfect parallelism than in this present case, and my argument with the Universalist.

Again, in the case of the Unitarians; take the words, *Lord, God, Jehovah*, and they admit, at once, that these terms do, in their *literal, proper*, and pure grammatical construction, mean the Supreme, Eternal, and Un-originated God; one that always was, and is, and evermore shall be. But, say they, words have many meanings, and the context must decide the meaning. Now, the word *God* is applied to magistrates, rulers, angels, &c. and used in a subordinate sense times without number. They make out a number of examples, reason speciously about them, and finally conclude that in all cases when applied to the son of Mary they are used not in their literal, proper, and primary sense; but is a rather figurative and special sense. Precisely, and without one shade of variation, manage they their cause of special pleading, as my friend, Mr. Rice, has done all through this question. Their system of philology, criticism, modes of quotation are identically the same as his. The only difference is, that the word is baptism, and not *theos, deus,* or *Jehovah.*

So of *eis, en, ek, apo—eis* signifies *into,* and is so translated more than two thousand times in the common version—often by *unto,* and to, where it ought to be into—but although it takes saints *into* heaven, and sends the wicked *into* hell, it must never mean *into* when baptism is spoken of. It can lead us *into* any place but *into* the water. So with all the prepositions connected with baptism. Not one of them will either help us *into* the Jordan or *out of* it. They will bring us *to* it, but not *into* it; and if by accident we get *into* it, they will not bring us *out of* it !! It is all of the same category with Unitarian and Universalian logic and tactics.

Doddridge says, " That man is the best commentator and the safest expositor of Scripture, and always most likely to arrive at its true meaning who follows common sense, and takes the words of the New Testament in their most common and usual signification,"—or in words to that effect. When so read, it annually converts thousands of Pedo-baptists into Baptists.

Mr. Rice, as you have often noticed, has a very powerful argument— he says, by way of chorus, " It won't do; no, it won't do." [A laugh.] Why? because it does not suit his side of the question. But I must resume my line of argument.

X. My tenth argument shall be deduced from those passages which Pedo-baptists usually urge against *baptizo* and *baptisma,* as not indicating immersion. The very passages which they quote against our views, together with their efforts at explaining them away, greatly confirm and establish our conclusions. We shall commence with Mark vii. 3, 4, and Luke xi. 38. (The Jews,) " Except they wash their hands oft, eat not. And when they come from market, except they wash, [*baptisoontai,*] they eat not. And many such things they hold, as the *washings,* [*baptismous,*] of cups, pots, brazen vessels, and beds," [or couches.] Luke xi. 38. " The Pharisees wondered that Jesus had not washed [*ebaptisthe*] before dinner."

I wish to make a remark: I am never for ascribing to any man motives for his conduct—motives very far-fetched—other than the plain sense of the case would indicate. The gentleman has told you, that I was obliged once to translate *baptizo* by the word *wash.* How he knows that I was obliged to do it—how he knows that I was so perplexed, is a matter which he can probably explain. The case, however, is this: In setting up the New Testament from Dr. Campbell's Gospels, the compositor followed the copy which was placed before him, it not being corrected in this passage; and the mistake thus passed through several editions without being noticed; and as nothing is depending upon it, it so stands. Besides, as I have before said, there is nothing improper in so using it as a figurative representation of the word. I have no objection to using the word occasionally as a metonymy—as the effect for the cause. I have some curious remarks to make on this fact by and by, but I will not make them now.

" These washings before dinner, reported by Mark and Luke, contain the only two instances in which any part of *baptizo* is ever translated by *wash* in the New Testament. And, fortunately, the antithesis between the washings here mentioned, indicated by the words employed in the original and the facts stated, not only do not sustain the common version in translating both words by the same word, *wash ;* but clearly intimate that the latter term, *baptizo,* ought here to have been rendered immerse. In verse 3d, it is *nipto* with *pugmee,* a word already shown to mean washing the hands, face, or feet, always when applied to the human person. This is true in every case in the Bible. Moreover, it has *pugmee,* the fist, in construction with it ; that is, as Lightfoot and others interpret it, to the fist, or so far as the fist extends. When the hand is shut, says Pollux, as quoted by Carson, the outside is called *pugmee.* Now, as this limits the first washing, the second, being expressed by *baptizo,* and having no part of the body mentioned as its peculiar regimen, according to the usage of the Greeks, (and the Romans, in the case of *lavo,*) the whole body is meant. Hence, they dip or bathe themselves after being to market, whereas, ordinarily, they wash their hands only up to the wrist.

" Both Campbell and McKnight translated the word in this passage, immerse. Some of our lexicons, such as Schleusner's, Scapula's, Stokius', &c., quote this passage in proof that washing is sometimes the effect of immersion. The meaning of *baptisoontai,* here, as in Luke xi. 38, being thus clearly indicated, (for Luke speaks of the same custom as Mark,) we have, then, found *baptizo,* in its eighty occurrences in the New Testament, uniformly signifying immersion ; and never sprinkling nor pouring.

" *Baptismos* is also translated washing in Heb. ix. 2, as well as in Mark vii. 4. The diverse washings of cups, pots, brazen vessels, tables, couches, persons, and things mentioned among the traditions of the elders and the institutions of the law, were for ceremonial cleansing. Hence, all by immersion ; inasmuch as nothing was ever cleansed, since the world began, by sprinkling water upon it. Meantime, I assume this fact, but I will hereafter demonstrate it :—McKnight and Campbell were much more learned in the true meaning of this word than the whole college of the king's translators. McKnight translates the " *diverse washings*" of the common version by " *diverse immersions,*" Heb. ix. 2.

" *Baptismos* is never applied to the christian ordinance—*baptisma* generally ; and, therefore, our translators never translated the latter but by baptism, and *baptismos* three times by washing. We have, then, in the one hundred and twenty occurrences of *baptizo, baptismos, baptisma,* and *baptistees,* not found a single exception.

" But we find *bapto,* in Daniel, in some of its flexions, twice translated *wet ;* and that, too, by the dew of heaven ! It was, then, a general wetting—profuse as immersion ; and this metonymy of the effect for the cause, clearly indicates that in the days of the Septuagint, the idea of sprinkling was never associated with *bapto.* Dews are more wetting in this country, much more so in Asia, in the environs of the Euphrates—than any Pedobaptist sprinkling since the council of Ravenna. Soaking, wetting, dyeing, coloring and even washing, it has always been conceded, are frequent meanings of *bapto ;* because, as all the dictionaries explain, these processes are accomplished by immersing. Indeed, these metaphors all go to show that immersion was the proper and fixed meaning of the term ; for, unless things were covered in some way, they could neither be dyed, colored, washed, soaked, or even thoroughly wet."—[*Time expired.*

Saturday, Nov. 18—11½, *A. M.*
[MR. RICE'S THIRTEENTH REPLY.]

MR. PRESIDENT—I will commence my remarks (though it may be rather out of the regular order) by noticing the statement of the gentleman concerning Schleusner, viz : that he gives to *wash* as a *figurative* meaning of *baptizo.* Schleusner does first define it to immerse, and to wash by immersing ; but he gives, as the *second* meaning, not as a *figurative* meaning, *abluo, lavo, aqua pingo*—to cleanse, to wash, to purify with water ; and for examples of this second meaning he refers to the New

Testament, particularly Mark vii. 4, "And when they come from the market, except they wash, (*baptizontai*) they eat not. Were not these *literal* washings? Is not *baptizo* here used in a literal sense? The gentleman's own lexicon is against him; and so are all the others. When I make assertions, I will certainly prove them. The gentleman may rest assured of that.

I think he is getting a little warm in debate. So much the better. Let us hear something to waken up our energies. I regret, however, that he does not get on faster with his reading.

He tells us, he has not attempted to prove, that *baptizo* means *only* to *immerse*, but that this is its *native, original* and *proper* meaning. But if he would read Ernesti, (and he speaks highly of him,) he would discover, that in proving this, he really proves nothing in favor of immersion. On page 52 of Ernesti, we read as follows:

"*Etymology, an uncertain guide.* The fluctuating use of words, which prevails in every language, gives rise to frequent changes in their meaning. *There are but few words in any language, which always retain their radical and primary meaning.* Great care, therefore, is necessary in the interpreter, to guard against rash etymological exegesis, which is often very fallacious. Etymology often belongs rather to the history of language, than to the illustration of its present meaning; *and rarely does it exhibit any thing more than a specious illustration.*"

Suppose then, the gentleman could demonstrate, that the *native, original* meaning of *baptizo*, was to sink or to plunge; of what advantage would this be to his cause? I could admit it, though it cannot be certainly proved; for it would still remain extremely doubtful, whether, as used some centuries afterward, by a people speaking a peculiar idiom of the Greek, and in relation to matters foreign to its first usage, it retained the same meaning. Ernesti, you observe, who is admitted to be one of the ablest writers on interpretation, tells us, that but few words in any language (even when still used by the same people) always retain their radical and primary meaning. I have furnished you with some examples (and they might be multiplied indefinitely) in which English words, in the space of two centuries, have entirely lost their original meaning; and the gentleman himself has pointed out several examples of the kind in his new translation. Within two hundred years the English language has, in regard to multitudes of its words, undergone a radical change; and shall we be told, that words in the Greek retained their primary meaning unchanged during the long period of its existence before the advent of our Savior, and even when transferred to another nation and to new subjects? He must either prove, that *baptizo*, at the time when, and amongst the people for whom christian baptism was instituted, meant only, or, at least, commonly to immerse; or he must fail to sustain his cause.

It is true, as he says, that Dr. Gale is with him in advocating the exclusive claims of immersion; and therefore it is that I have quoted him to refute his arguments. True, our immersionist critics all come to the same conclusion, though by different and contradictory modes of reasoning. Both Gale and Cox, according to Carson, gave up the question, at least so far as *bapto* is concerned; and I have proved that Gale has given it up, so far as *baptizo* is concerned. So they travel on, fighting by the way, but arriving finally at the same place. But, mark it, the Pedo-baptists are, *en masse*, against the gentleman. If a very few admit, that immersion was the apostolic practice; I can only say, they have admitted too much. Against their concessions, however, I have adduced the testimony of the old Greek and Latin fathers, who immersed three times, in favor of the validity and scriptural character of our baptism.

Carson, my friend thinks, had no need to contradict the lexicons, though he can prove them wrong. Thus far, however, he has failed to produce a lexicon that makes to *wash* a figurative meaning of *baptizo*. Nor has he been able to produce one, though repeatedly urged to do it, that gives *immerse* as the primary or proper meaning of the word, as used amongst the Jews, and in the Bible.

I have proved, that Origen used *bapto* in the sense of sprinkling; and he, it is presumed, understood the Greek as well as my friend. On the shoulders of such a giant, even though I were a Lilliputian, I would not fear the assaults of Mr. C., whom I am bound to consider a mighty man, since he contradicts Origen and all the lexicons! He held up before you a volume of Wall in reply to Gale, and triumphantly asserted, that he did not venture to reply to Gale's speculations about a different reading in Rev. xix. 13. He did not, however, tell you that Wall was himself an immersionist, contending for pouring only in case of necessity; and that he was writing almost exclusively on infant baptism. No—he would leave on your minds the impression, that the whole volume was written in defence of pouring or sprinkling, when the truth is, that probably not a tenth of it is on that subject. He will gain nothing by this mode of warfare.

The gentleman tells us that Prof. Stuart quotes Calvin, as claiming for the church the right to change the ordinances, except the substance. Stuart has not quoted such a remark from Calvin. Neither Stuart nor Calvin ever claimed for the church any such authority. On the contrary, Calvin, in his commentary on Acts viii. 38, says, as regards the ceremony of baptism, in so far as it was delivered to us by Christ, it were a hundred times better to be slain by the sword, than that we should allow it to be taken from us. But he believed that the Savior did not prescribe any particular mode of administering the ordinance; and therefore the church had from the beginning freely practiced different modes, as immersion, trine immersion, partial immersion, pouring and sprinkling. Stuart takes the same view of the subject, denying most positively, that the New Testament contains a command to practice immersion, and calling upon any one who asserts the contrary, to produce such a command, It is not true, then, to say, that either of these men claimed for the church the right to change the ordinances of God's house. They maintained, that the mode of administering baptism is indifferent, because not, in their opinion, prescribed by the Savior.

My friend labors to get Philip and the eunuch *into* the water by the force of the preposition *eis*, maintaining that its proper meaning is *into*. The audience will remember that I quoted Buttman's Greek grammar, a standard work, as defining it *to*, *into*, in answer to *whither*, that is, *to* (not *into*) what place? Its leading meaning, therefore, according to Buttman, (whose authority I must, with all deference, consider higher than that of my friend,) is simply *to*. Precisely so it is defined by Scapula, "*ad, in*"—*to, into*. Hedericus defines it, *in*, (2) *ad*, (3) *erga; into, to, towards*. Donnegan thus defines it: general signification, *to, into*, with verbs of motion. Robertson gives, as the primary or original meaning— "*into*, then *to, towards*, &c., after verbs of motion," &c. Bretschneider, as I have already said, gives *to* as its first and leading meaning, Schrivellius defines it, *ad, in; item, erga*—*to, into;* also *towards*. Not one of these lexicons, nor any other known to me, says, that *eis* generally means *into;* but several of the best of them gives *to* as its leading meaning.

The gentleman charges Pedo-baptists with adopting the principles of interpretation by which Universalists and Unitarians seek to sustain their tenets. Is this charge true? Have I not, throughout this discussion, been contending for the ordinary and proper meaning of words, as they are used by the people whose language we are expounding? But I pledge myself to prove, before the close of this discussion, that he has much more affinity with Unitarians and Universalists than I.

But let me read a few passages of Scripture, translating the word *eis, into,* and *ek, out of*—as the gentleman wishes; that the audience may judge of the soundness of his criticisms: 2 Kings vi. 4, "When they came *into (eis)* Jordan, they cut down wood." Did the persons go literally *into* Jordan in order to cut wood? Isa. xxxvi. 2, "And the king of Assyria sent Rabshekeh *out of (ek)* Lachesh *into (eis)* Jerusalem, unto Hezekiah with a great army." John vi. 23, "Howbeit, there came other boats *out of (ek)* Tiberias." John viii. 23, "And he said unto them, ye are *out of (ek)* beneath; I am *out of (ek)* above: ye are *out of (ek)* this world; I am not *out of (ek)* this world." Ch. ix. 1, "And as Jesus passed by, he saw a man blind *out of (ek)* his birth." Verse 7, "And [Jesus] said unto him, go wash *into (eis)* the pool of Siloam." Verse 11, "And [Jesus] said unto me, go *into (eis)* the pool of Siloam and wash." Ch. xi. 31, "She goeth *into (eis)* the grave to weep there." Verse 38, "Jesus cometh *into (eis)* the grave. It was a cave and a stone lay upon it."

I will read another passage or two from John xx., for the gentleman seems to consider this an important point. "The first day of the week cometh Mary Magdalene early, when it was yet dark, *into (eis)* the sepulchre, and seeth the stone taken away *out of (ek)* the sepulchre, &c. Peter therefore went forth, and that other disciple, and came *into (eis)* the sepulchre. So they ran both together: and the other disciple did outrun Peter, and came first *into (eis)* the sepulchre. And he stooping down, and looking in, saw the linen clothes lying; yet went he not in," &c.

The unlearned hearer can at once perceive, that by translating these prepositions *into* and *out of*, without regard to the connection, we make the Scriptures speak nonsense and contradictions. But the gentleman thinks, that in many passages where these words are translated *to* and *from,* the real meaning is *into* and *out of;* as we speak of *sending* a letter *from* Lexington *to* Philadelphia. In all such cases, however, the idea expressed is that of going from one *point* to another point. Hence, we should laugh at a man who would speak of going *out of* Lexington *into* Philadelphia! He parades before us with triumph the number of instances in which in the New Testament *eis* is translated *into.* But will he please to tell the audience in how many of those cases the verb is preceded by the preposition? The general rule in this subject, I have already presented. In some cases the connection and the sense show, that *eis* means *into,* and *ek, out of.* Then they should be so translated. In other cases, such as I have just read in your hearing, the connection and the sense prove that these prepositions mean *to* and *from.* But in cases where the connection does not determine their meaning, as in Acts viii. 38, the Greeks, if they wished definitely to express the action of going *into* or coming *out of,* prefixed a preposition to the verb, as *eiserchomai eis,* I go into; *ekporeuomai ek,* I go *out of.* In the case under consideration, however, these definite expressions are not employed; and since to go down *to* the water, makes as good sense as to go down *into*, it cannot be proved that Philip and the eunuch went down *into* the water.

In thus reasoning, however, I am doing a work of supererogation; for I can safely admit, as already remarked, that they did go literally *into* the water. And I defy any man then to prove, that Philip immersed the eunuch. What advantage, then, is gained by the labor to prove, that they did go in?

My friend says, he can sympathise with me; for he has been a Presbyterian, and knows what it is to be under the unhappy influence of such a system. I am obliged to him; but I am so little sensible of my need of his sympathies, that I am quite unable fully to appreciate his kindness. I even find myself doubting, whether he ever was a *bona fide* Presbyterian. Presbyterianism I once heard, very appropriately, compared to a kind of grass that grows in some parts of the South, which is said to be very valuable, but if once it becomes fairly set, there is no such thing as rooting it out. [A laugh.] If a man ever becomes a genuine Presbyterian, it will stick by him, living and dying. [Laughter.] I really doubt whether the gentleman ever was the *true blue.*—[Continued laughter.]

But he tells us, he has examined, thoroughly, this whole subject—discovered and repudiated the errors of Pedo-baptism. Peter Edwards, I believe, was once a good Baptist; but upon careful examination of the whole ground, he came over to the side of truth, and wrote one of the ablest works I have seen in favor of Pedo-baptism. Dr. Thomas Scott, the commentator, for a time, had difficulties on this subject; but on thorough examination of the evidence in the case, he, too, settled down in the firm conviction that the Bible teaches the doctrines for which I am now contending. In company with such men, I cannot realize my need of the sympathy of the gentleman.

He tells you, that the common English version of the Scriptures is making immersionists quite rapidly. Then why did he not let it alone? Why has he made a new translation, if the old one was doing the work so effectually? And why have immersionists (and he amongst them) so liberally bestowed their censures upon it? Why has the gentleman, and those who agree with him, been writing and preaching so long and so constantly on this very plain subject, so clearly presented in the common Bible? Ah, I seriously doubt, whether he has not felt great dissatisfaction with our excellent translation, on this very subject.

I will briefly notice the remarks of the gentleman on Mark vii. 4, and Luke xi. 38. In the former passage we read—that "the Pharisees, and all the Jews, except they wash their hands oft, eat not, &c. And when they come from the market, except they wash [Greek—except they *baptize*,] they eat not." Now the question is—did the Pharisees, and all the Jews, *immerse* themselves before eating, whenever they came from the market or public place? Mr. C. does not venture to say, that they did. He adds the pronoun *them*, referring to the hands—"by dipping them." But there is no such word in the Greek, and he has no right to supply it. Mr. Carson, speaking of the very translation adopted by the gentleman, pronounces it nothing more than "an ingenious conceit;" and he states, that in such connection, where no part of the body is mentioned, or excepted, the whole body is meant. So he would make the Jews literally immerse themselves before eating; though there is not the least evidence of the prevalence of any such custom, and it is almost incredible that it could have existed. But the cause of immersion demands the belief of great improbabilities.

The translation, given by Mr. Campbell, I have said, and I repeat it, is no translation at all. He makes one little Greek adverb contain the whole phrase, "*by pouring a little water on them;*" and then he drops some two of the Greek words out of the text, and translates the phrase, *ean me baptizontai*, (literally, unless they baptize,) by the preposition *by*, and the participle *dipping*, and supplies the word *them*, referring to the hands!! Such a translation I do not remember ever to have seen.

The only charge ever made against Christ and his disciples, connected with this subject, was, that they neglected to *wash their hands* before eating. The baptism here spoken of, therefore, was a washing of the hands, which, as it was a religious washing, is represented as baptizing the person; and, it is certain, that the Jews were accustomed to have water poured *on* their hands. So universal was this custom, that a servant was described as one who poured water on the hands of his master. "Here is Elisha-ben-shaphat, *who poured water on the hands of Elijah.*" The word *baptizo* in this passage, therefore, denotes the partial application of water.

But I proved, that in one instance Mr. Campbell himself had translated *baptizo*, to wash or *use washing*, (Luke xi. 38.) He tells us, however, that this was by a mistake of the compositor, which, in the reading of the proof-sheets, was overlooked. I, of course, cannot contradict this statement; but I am constrained to consider it one of the most remarkable blunders that ever fell under my observation. I cannot but wonder, that a man so sharp-sighted as Mr. C., publishing edition after edition of a new translation, one prominent object of which was to translate that very word, should at last have stereotyped such an error undiscovered!!! The meaning of the word in the passage under consideration, is sufficiently clear. It is scarcely credible, that the Pharisee should have wondered that our Savior had not immersed himself before dinner. His surprise evidently arose from the fact that he had not washed his hands. The new Baptist translation labors under the same difficulty I had supposed my friend to feel, in regard to this passage, and also Mark vii. 4. In both cases, they translate *baptizo* by the word *bathe;* which every body knows does not express either *mode* or *specific action*. The translators were zealous immersionists; and they set out with the purpose of translating this word correctly. But they could not venture, in these two cases, to translate it *immerse:* it would have looked *too badly!*

I see not why Mr. C. should make so much ado about his momentous fact, that God never commanded purification to be effected by sprinkling unmixed water on a person. I have called on him to show one instance in the law of Moses, where a person was ever commanded to be immersed in water, pure or mixed; and he has not been able to do it. His attempt to prove immersion by *louo*, a word which is universally admitted to be generic, and to mean simply *to wash*, shows how he feels the difficulty. Let the fact, then, be known, that the Old Testament requires a number of purifications by sprinkling water, but not one immersion. I am unwilling to anticipate the argument of my friend from the burial of Christ, as mentioned in Rom. vi.; and yet I have nothing particularly to do, unless I do still run ahead of him. I have replied to his arguments, besides offering many to which, as yet, he has attempted no answer. I will, then, introduce my argument directly in favor of baptism by pouring or sprinkling.

S

My first remark on this point is this : *Baptism is a significant ordi-*
nance.   Man is a sinful being ; and when baptized with water, the universal purifier—he is taught, at once, this truth, that he is polluted, and that
he must be cleansed from sin by the Holy Spirit.   The water of baptism
is, then, an emblem of spiritual cleansing—of sanctification.   Hence it is
so frequently in the New Testament mentioned as a *washing*.   The gentleman, I presume, will not deny, that baptism is a significant ordinance,
an emblem of sanctification.   I need not, therefore, multiply evidence to
prove it.

I have now several important *facts* to state, which, I think, clearly
establish the doctrine for which I am contending, viz : that baptism is
scripturally performed by pouring or sprinkling ; the first of which is this :
All the personal ablutions of the Old Testament, the mode of which is
prescribed, were required to be performed by sprinkling.   The gentleman has boasted of his universal affirmations.   Now I affirm the fact just
stated to be true, without exception.   There is not a washing of the Levitical law, having respect to persons, nor an important washing of any
kind, the mode of which, if there is any mode commanded, is not sprinkling.   By turning to Leviticus, ch. xiv. you will find particular directions
concerning the cleansing of the leper.—[*Time expired.*

Saturday, Nov. 18—12 *o'clock, P. M.*
[MR. CAMPBELL'S FOURTEENTH ADDRESS.]
Before entering upon my address, I will ask Mr. Rice, Did you, sir,
ever see this lexicon I now hold in my hand—Stokius on the New
Testament ?

Mr. Rice.   No, sir.

Mr. Campbell.   Mr. Rice acknowledges that he has never seen this
lexicon.   Did he not, then, I am constrained to ask, speak too hastily
when he said, that there is not a dictionary in the world that says, to
wash, to cleanse, are figurative meanings of *baptizo?*

Mr. Rice.   If the gentleman will allow me to explain.

Mr. Campbell.   Certainly.

Mr. Rice.   I said that I never heard of such a dictionary, and I called
upon my friend to produce one.   And as he had not produced it, I, giving
him full credit for his learning, supposed and took it for granted, that
there was not one on earth.

Mr. Campbell.   This is not perfectly satisfactory.   It might have been
so but for the fact that in his third speech, when making his first formal
effort to sustain wash, he strongly affirmed that " there is not a lexicographer, ancient or modern, on the face of the earth, who says that
baptizo means to wash, figuratively."   I noted the words.   Since then,
too, he has had other opportunities of knowing that Stokius is not the
only one who says so.   He is only one of a considerable number, who
affirms that wash, cleanse, wet, &c., are, *by consequence,* or tropically, or
metonymically, meanings of baptism.   Stokius, one of the most learned
Rabbis in the school and learning of orthodoxy, deposes as follows :
1. Generatim, ac vi vocis intinctionis ac immersionis notionem obtinct.
2. Speciatim (A) *proprie* est immergere ac intingere in aquam.   3. (B)
Tropice, per metalepsin est lavire abluere, quia aliquid intingi ac immergi solet in aquam ut lavetur vel abluatur.   Which I translate :—
Generally it obtains the sense of dipping or immersing.   Without
respect to water or any liquid whatever.   2. *Specially, and in its proper*

signification, it signifies to dip or immerse in water. This is its New Testament sense.   3. Tropically, and by a metalepsis, it means to wash, to cleanse, because a thing is usually dipped or immersed in water that it may be washed, that it may be cleansed. Its general sense is to dip. Its proper sense, to dip in water. Its figurative sense, to wash, to cleanse. This is a true version of this great author; and it is exactly what I believe and have taught from the beginning. Have I not, then, in my own time and way, after giving him full space to develop himself and his argument, clearly shown that he has misconceived, mistated and greatly misrepresented the Greek lexicons, and especially those on the New Testament. He has often vauntingly asked for a New Testament lexicon, that gives immerse as the proper and primary meaning of baptizo. He has got it now ! Indeed, they all do so, that define its proper meaning.

Mr. Rice. I will fix that directly.

Mr. Campbell. I wish to have it explained now, or *fixed*, as the gentleman says. I pause for a reply.

Mr. Rice. I will shew from Ernesti, that tropical words sometimes become proper ones, and a secondary meaning is used for the first :

" But there are several different points of light in which tropical words are to be viewed. For, *first*, the primitive or proper signification, strictly understood, often becomes obsolete, and ceases for a long period to be used. *In this case, the secondary sense, which originally would have been the* TROPICAL *one, becomes the* PROPER *one.* This applies especially to the names of things. Hence there are many words which at present never have their original and proper sense, such as etymology would assign them, but only the *secondary* sense, which may in each case, be called the *proper* sense ; e. g. in English, tragedy, comedy, villain, pagan, knave, &c.

" Secondly, *in like manner, the* TROPICAL SENSE *of certain words has become so common by usage, that it is better understood than the original sense. In this case, too, we call the sense* PROPER ; *although strictly and technically speaking, one might insist on its being called* TROPICAL. If one should, by his last will, give a library [*bibliothecam*] to another, we should not call the use of *bibliotheca* tropical ; although, strictly speaking, it is so ; for bibliotheca originally meant the *shelves*, or *place* where books are deposited."— *Ernesti*, pp. 23, 24.

Mr. Campbell. I am sorry that my confidence in the candor of my friend is somewhat diminished by this manouvre.

Mr. Rice. Tropical words, with the critics, are not figurative words.

Mr. Campbell. I should like to refer the decision of the translations which I have given, to classical gentlemen present. Mr. Rice says, a tropical word, or, as I understand it, a word used TROPICALLY, is not a figurative word with the critics. This is a new doctrine in the schools. Whence comes the word that indicates figurative use ? Comes it not from *tropos*, and that from *trepo*, to turn ? To turn a word from its proper signification, is to make it a trope ; and that is what we call a figure. There is no dictionary of credit that otherwise explains and defines these words, or that distinguishes tropical from figurative language, as used in the schools of logic and rhetoric. But this is not mere inference or conjecture in this particular case. Stokius gives the name of the figure. He calls it a *metalepsis*. So the matter is ended with him as respects Ernesti—Ernesti's remarks and the question before us, belong not to the same class. They are wholly misapplied. They belong to another subject.

But why this excitement about Stokius ? He is only a little plainer

than some of the others.   He goes no farther than Schleusner and Bretschneider.   He gives the name of the figure, and calls it a *metalepsis*, which
transfers the name of an effect to its cause.   They explain it *as a figure*
or trope, without naming it.   My ear has been pained—repeatedly
pained, with the manner that some dictionaries are quoted by my friend.
I do not like to go into expositions of this sort ; nor into debates about
foreign languages before a popular assembly.   But really, I am obliged
to say, that Schleusner and Bretschnieder are as much with me as Stokius, and as much mystified by my respondent.

Hear Schleusner's own words.   The question is, when and how
comes baptizo to mean *wash*, cleanse?   He says : 1. *Jam quia haud raro
aliquid immergi ac intingi in aquam solet, ut lavetur hinc.*   2. *Abluo lavo aqua pergo notat.*   Because a thing must be dipped or immersed
into water that it may be washed.   Hence comes the sense, I wash, I
cleanse.   Now he might as well have called it a metonymy ; for he describes the figure without calling its name, while Stokius does not.

The gentleman also knows, that Bretschneider so understands it.   He
knows that he defines *baptisma*, in the New Testament, to mean nothing
but "immersion, or submersion;" and why he should so often quote a
special clause, "*lavo aluo simpliciter*," in direct contravention of this
definition, is of the same category with the two still more venerable
names of Schleusner and Stokius.   Now these are all New Testament
lexicographers, well acquainted with the Jewish idiom of which Mr. R.
speaks so sensitively, and they are still more decidedly with us, *though
Pedo-baptists*, than any one, or all of the classic dictionaries.

This is the first and the only time, since our commencement, that we
have had any debate; and it is upon the real gist of the whole controversy.   I stake the whole cause of immersion on this single point, for
this is just the point on which the whole baptismal controversy turns.   I
am willing, then, to give it all the conspicuity it deserves—to open up the
case, and place it fairly before the community.   Mr. Rice has been constrained to admit, on the testimony of three New Testament lexicons, as
well as upon that of many others, that *baptizo* properly, originally, and
primarily signifies *to dip ;* but he also contends that it properly, primarily,
and originally signifies *to wash.*   He will not, indeed, say, that it means
to sprinkle, or pour.   It *properly*, however, signifies to wash.   Now
this wash, he says, is a generic word, as we all admit.   Next he has got
three *modes of washing ;* he will take sprinkling, and give us dipping,
on condition that we say that his is baptism.   This is a fair narrative of
the case, as he will admit.   Well then, of course this word *wash* is the
struggle.   The whole battle is about *wash.*   He says it is the *proper*,
primary, and *original* meaning—at all events, he sometimes, rather
in a faltering tone, says, it is certainly a *proper* meaning of the word.
Now, then, we have got the great New Testament lexicons, as well as
some other great authorities, deposing *that it does not at all properly
mean to wash*, but only so by *accident*, by trope or figure ; and that,
too, only as an effect of immersion.

I contend, before Christendom, that the question is now decided.   That
plainer proof cannot be afforded on any literary question now before the
schools.   This is just what ought to be.   The debate is now brought
down to one clear, tangible, appreciable point, which all may see and all
may comprehend.

If the Savior spoke plainly upon a point which involves the salvation of the world, we ought to speak plainly upon every thing connected with it. I ask all persons of reflection, if the Savior spoke tropically or figuratively, when giving laws, involving the salvation of the world, when he should have spoken plainly, and without a figure? Do men, in dictating or in writing their last wills and testaments, speak figuratively and rhetorically? Surely, then, we cannot take shelter in a trope, in a metaphor, or figure of speech, when discussing the most sacred and solemn of ordinances was enacted by the Savior of men.

To leave this matter for a moment, I have been invited by my friend, to pay more attention to the Jewish use of this word than to the classical; as if I had not given it the first part of my attention; or as if there were some real, undefined difference between the Jewish and classical style. I would not care to write a book on such questions, for those who might have leisure, or taste, to read it; but, really, to throw dust in the eyes of a plain and unsophisticated popular assembly, by such verbose and interminable jargon, I could not endure.

Did I not, however, begin with Jewish use? Did I not take the types in the law, and shew from the Septuagint how dip, sprinkle, and pour were contrasted, at the very fountain head of precision?

But my prudent and calculating friend would not wait for me. He gave us Josephus in anticipation. At least he concurred with the learned Wall, and the more learned Stuart, that Josephus wrote Greek very classically; but then, the misfortune is, that this proves nothing for us; for the cunning, artful Josephus imitates the Greeks, for the sake of gaining Gentile favor! Instead of using his Hebrew Greek style, the shrewd Jew laid it aside, and, it seems, preferred to mimic the Gentiles. There is no conquering such logicians. They *will* have the advantage. Josephus, and all the Greeks contemporary with the apostolic age, used this word just as Stokius, Schleusner, and Bretschneider use it; as Wall, Campbell, McKnight, and a thousand others have contended that it should be used. All the difference, according to Stuart, is, that the Jews did not, in one book, the Bible, use *bapto* and *baptizo* in as many acceptations as can be found in all the classics. He found no new or special use of the word in the Bible. Not one. He thought that the Jews used wash more frequently than the Greeks. But that was only an opinion. Dr. Wall found no difference. But then Mr. Rice says he was an immersionist! He did not like to oppose Dr. Gale on that subject. He only gave one tenth of his book to immersion, and nine-tenths to the babes! How singularly men's prejudices pervert their optics! But I could have brought many passages from Josephus, who, in fifty places probably uses the word, and always uses it to signify immerse, as Stuart, Carson, and Ewing have shewn. But this would be in vain. If I say Josephus lived contemporary with the apostles, that he was well acquainted with both Hebrew and Greek, and that it is certain he used the word just as the Greeks always used it—I am anticipated. I am told by Mr. Rice, that this was through his affectation of Grecian learning!! I repeat it, no one could prove to such men that which they are determined not to believe. Did not Stokius, Schleusner, Bretschneider, McKnight, Wall, Campbell, &c., understand the Jewish idiom?

But to return to the New Testament lexicons. I have said that Stokius is not alone in his definitions. Take a little specimen. [Here Mr. Campbell, taking up Dr. Wall's work in answer to Dr. Gale, and inserting his fingers between the leaves.] Here is just the one-tenth of the

14   s 2

book, according to the optics of my friend. If, my fellow-citizens, this be one-tenth of the whole, do apply the same doctrine of ratios to the assertions and reasonings of my friend, Mr. Rice. [A laugh.] Mr. Rice says, by way of apology for the strong and honest sayings of Wall, Campbell, McKnight, Bretschneider, that they were immersionists; he does not mean Baptists, but only theoretically with us. This is one of my friend's ingenious arts of getting ahead of me. He took Josephus, Judith, and Naaman, and now he will take all these great christian Rabbis by some manœuvre. I could bring scores from the Presbyterian and Episcopal churches, all concurring with these; but my quoting them, or even his apprehension that I am about to quote them, will instantly convert them into immersionists! Should he admit the true meaning of a word in the Koran, would that constitute him a Turk? Their philological, ex cathedra admissions and concessions do not convert them into Baptists. With me, a christian is one who practices Christ's precepts, and an immersionist is either an immersed man, or one who immerses others.

Calvin, Stuart, Wall, Campbell, McKnight, and many such distinguished men, thought it an enlargement of soul, a generous and magnanimous liberality not to be so scrupulously exact as to contend for a strict obedience to all matters of clear theological accuracy, reposing upon the easy couch that the church, from the beginning, assumed to herself, "the right of changing the ordinances somewhat, excepting the substance." But I must risk the charge of illiberality in avowing my conviction, that there is nothing within human power so terrific and appaling, as any attempt to touch the ark of the Lord, by accommodating any of Christ's ordinances to the pride, the caprice, the vanity, or apathy of any man or set of men. There is one sentence in the sermon on the mount that keeps tingling in my ears when I hear men talk so—Jesus said, "Whosoever shall violate one of the least of these my commandments, and shall teach others to do so, shall be of no account in the kingdom of heaven." In my esteem the highest style, and honor, and dignity of man, is to know, to teach, and to practice the institutions of Jesus Christ. I am zealous for the letter; for although a man may have the letter and the form without the spirit, he cannot have the spirit without the letter and the form of godliness. To neglect, to disparage, or corrupt the ordinances of God never were, in any age, small matters in the sight of God. Isaiah, in his twenty-fourth chapter, saith—"The land shall be emptied and utterly spoiled—the earth mourneth—the world languisheth and fadeth away—the haughty do languish—the earth is defiled under the inhabitants thereof; because they have *transgressed the laws*, CHANGED THE ORDINANCE, broken the everlasting covenant." This is enough for one lesson on the solemnity of the ordinances.

My friend, Mr. Rice, gives me no reason to hope favorably in his case. He does not say, yet indicates as much as, that he will never suffer himself to change, and that I never knew any one of his class to change. This is dangerous ground. Popes have changed. Liberius changed four times during his life, yet was always infallible. I would not for this commonwealth say that I will never change. God gave us two ears, Mr. President, and he put one on each side of our heads. I move, sir, that we keep them there, and do not put them both on one side. I believe, sir, that we should not only hear on both sides, but that we ought to hear both sides, and whenever enlightened, act.

The passage from Ernesti is just to my taste—I wish the gentleman had read a little farther. He would have given us two sayings of much pith. Melancthon said—"The Scripture cannot be understood *theologically* unless it be understood *grammatically.*" Luther also said, "A certain knowledge of the sense of Scripture depends solely on the words." No one, I will add, is at liberty to plead for a special law or tribunal in any case of scriptural investigation.

And, once more, I will say that to talk of Greek, and Hebrew, and Roman idiom, and peculiarity, in expounding words indicated by outward bodily actions, seems as visionary and eccentric as to argue that eating, drinking, sleeping, walking, riding, &c., are subject to the changes of political opinion, religious belief, or geographical lines.—[*Time expired.*

Saturday, Nov. 18—12½ *o'clock, P. M.*
[MR. RICE'S FOURTEENTH REPLY.]

MR. PRESIDENT—My friend, Mr. C., I discover, is becoming extremely uneasy. He seems to feel, that unless he can succeed in diverting the minds of the audience from the subject in debate to something personal, his cause is lost. I regret to see him so sorely pressed, that he feels it necessary to attempt to injure me by making the impression, that I misstated a fact in regard to Wall's reply to Gale. It is so little a thing to come from a great man. Without having counted the pages, I made the remark, that not more than a tenth of it is occupied in replying to Gale on the *mode* of baptism. He holds up before you the first part of the volume, to show you, that it is much more than a tenth of it; but he does not inform you, that a number of pages in this division are an introduction to the work, and not a reply to Gale on the mode! I still believe, that not more than about a tenth is occupied on that particular point. As before remarked, Wall declared his purpose not to answer at length the arguments of Gale on the mode of baptism. But this is a very small matter. I can sustain my cause without descending to such trifles.

The gentleman thinks he has, at length, found a lexicon that gives *wash* as a *figurative* meaning of *baptizo.* With quite an air of triumph he brings forward Stokius; and he attempts to make a great deal of capital of my declaration, that no Greek lexicon so defined this word. But I will make the blow aimed at me recoil on his own head. Suppose he had even succeeded in finding *one* lexicon that gives *wash* as a figurative meaning of *baptizo;* he would only have put me in company with himself. For he has asserted, and repeatedly published, that no translator, ancient or modern, Christian, Jew, or Turk, ever rendered *bapto,* or any of that family of words, *to sprinkle.* I have proved the fact indisputably, that the ancient Syriac, the Ethiopic and the Vulgate do so translate *bapto,* and that Origen did substantially the same thing. Yet whilst I have convicted him of having repeatedly asserted what is wholly untrue, he labors to make capital of the fact, (which is indeed not a fact) that I made a general statement, to which he has found *one* exception amongst all the lexicons, ancient and modern ! ! !

By the way, he has spoken of a change of views as a mark of wisdom. I will prove, before the close of this discussion, that he has changed again and again, until he has got almost back to " Babylon," from which, some years since, he fled in such haste.

But, after all, what says Stokius ? He gives *immerse* as the *origina* meaning of *baptizo,* and *wash* as its *tropical* meaning. Have I not repeatedly stated, that I could admit, without injury to my cause, that *im-*

merse was the *original* meaning? But the gentleman insists, that a *trope* is a figure, and that the tropical meaning of a word, is a figurative meaning. It is true, that with rhetoricians *tropes* are figures; but with critics the tropical meaning of a word is simply a *secondary* meaning. But let us again hear Ernesti on the tropical meaning of words:

"But, there are several different points of light in which tropical words are to be viewed. For, *first*, the primitive or proper signification, strictly understood, often becomes obsolete, and ceases for a long period to be used. *In this case, the secondary sense, which originally would have been the* TRO-PICAL *one, becomes the* PROPER *one*. This applies especially to the names of things. Hence, there are many words which, at present, never have their original and proper sense, such as etymology would assign them, but only the *secondary* senses, which may in such cases be called the *proper* sense; e. g. in English, tragedy, comedy, villain, pagan, knave, &c.

"Secondly, *in like manner, the* TROPICAL SENSE *of certain words has become so common, by usage, that it is better understood than the original sense. In this case, too, we call the sense* PROPER; *although strictly and technically speaking, one might insist on its being called* TROPICAL. If one should, by his last will, give a library [*bibliothecam*] to another, we should not call the use of *bibliotheca* tropical; although strictly speaking it is so, for bibliotheca originally meant the *shelves* or *place* where books are deposited."—*Ernesti,* pp. 23, 24.

I have now clearly proved, that the secondary or *tropical* meaning of words often becomes the common and the *proper* meaning. And are we not seeking for the common—the proper meaning of *baptizo?* But I will read a note by professor Stuart on the same subject. He says:

"The literal sense [of words] is the same as the *primitive* or *original* sense; or, *at least, it is equivalent to that sense which has usurped the place of the original one.* For example, the *original* sense of the word *tragedy* has long ceased to be current, and the *literal sense of this word now, is that which has taken the place of the original.*"—*Ernesti,* page 8.

According to the principle presented by Stuart, the *literal* meaning of a word is either the original meaning, or that which has usurped the place of it. Now what have I been, from the beginning, contending for? Why, that the Jews, who never used *baptizo,* as did the pagan Greeks, in reference to things in common life, but always in relation to religious washings, employed it in the sense of washing, cleansing, which Stokius considers a secondary sense—that as thus used by the Jews, it never had the sense of plunging, immersing. It was to illustrate this principle, proved by Ernesti and Stuart, that I gave, as one example, the English word *prevent.* The original meaning of this word, as I have repeatedly stated, was to *come before.* The *tropical* meaning, which is now the *proper* and *literal* meaning, is *to hinder.* What would you think of a professed critic who should now insist, that the word *prevent* means, *literally,* to *come before*—that *to hinder* is a *figurative* meaning; and that, in reading authors of the present day, we must understand the word in its original sense? You see, at a glance, the perfect absurdity of such criticism; and yet, such precisely is the criticism of Mr. Campbell! Even Carson, his own *profound linguist,* as I have repeatedly proved, is against him; for he says, that these secondary meanings are as literal as the original. In company with such men as Ernesti, Stuart, and Carson, I have no fear that my reputation, as a scholar or a man of candor, will suffer, before such an audience as I now address. Indeed, Stuart has given *to wash* as a literal meaning of *baptizo;* and so have the lexicons. That *to wash* is a literal meaning of this word, must be obvious to every unprejudiced mind. What does the Latin word *lavo,* or the English word *wash* mean? It denotes the literal application of water to a person or thing. I have, once or twice, given an example of the literal and of the figurative use of the word *sprinkle,* which fully illustrates this point. When the Scriptures speak of the sprinkling of clean water, the word is used literally; but when they speak of sprinkling the heart from an evil conscience, it is used figuratively. But to say, that either washing or sprinkling is a figure of immersion, would be to outrage all rules of sound criticism. Stokius gives *to wash* as the *secondary* meaning of the word; for, in this sense, the word *tropical* is used. And I contend, and expect fully to prove, that, as it was used amongst the Jews and by the inspired writers, *wash* or *cleanse* is the proper and literal meaning. He is welcome to make the most of Stokius.

The gentleman tells you, that the fact that I have nothing to do, may account for my doing nothing. I will only reply, that I have done enough to make his friends tremble for their cause, unless I greatly mistake appearances, and am misinformed concerning remarks made in various quarters.

I have said, that Josephus sought to imitate the classic Greek writers. Mr. C. seems disposed to dispute this, and to call for the evidence. The evidence depends not simply on the declarations of critics, but is found in the fact, that Josephus, in every instance but one, used *baptizo* in relation to matters in *common life,* as did the classics uniformly; whilst the Jews and inspired writers always employed it in relation to *religious washings.* The gentleman says, Josephus used the word *fifty times.* I presume he spoke hyperbolically; for I have seen not more than some twelve or fifteen examples from his writings; and I suppose Gale and Carson, whose works I have examined, have collected as many, at least, as were favorable to immersion.

Mr. C. has repeatedly referred to Calvin, as having claimed for the church the right to *change* the ordinances instituted by our Savior. I wish he would give us Calvin's words. I am anxious to see the quotation. I have examined it, and I desire the audience to hear Calvin speak for himself. He tells us, Stuart quotes from Calvin the passage in which he prefers this claim. [Mr. Campbell, without rising, was understood to say, that his words were, not that Stuart had quoted Calvin, but that he had given something like a quotation.] No—Stuart quotes no such sentiment from Calvin, nor anything like it. He quotes from Calvin nothing intimating a claim to change the ordinances of God's house.

My friend, Mr. C., has, at last, given us a quotation from Ernesti, and I subscribe to every word of it most cordially. Ernesti says, the meaning of words is to be determined by *usage;* and so say I. And I am doing the precise thing which he directs—I am inquiring into the *usage* of *baptizo* by the very people amongst whom the ordinance was instituted. I am apprehensive, that I shall lose confidence in the learning of the gentleman quite as fast as he loses confidence in my candor.

But he tells us, that words indicating *physical action,* never change their meaning. Can he produce any respectable authority to sustain him in such an assertion! Where can he find it? We cannot any longer rely upon his declarations on these subjects. I call for some higher authority. The word *prevent,* which I have so repeatedly mentioned, is itself a refutation of his assertion; for this word does express a physical action (coming before;) and yet it has lost its original meaning. In the

commencement of this discussion he told us, as a general rule, that wherever you find the syllable *bap*, as in *bapto*, you find also the action of
dipping.   But I showed you *bap* where there was the dropping of a
fluid, the dyeing of the beard, the hair, the face; the staining of the hand
by pressing the coloring substance : and I gave examples where the
expression *bapto apo*, (to wet by means of) occurred ; where a man was
wet from (*ebaphe apo*) the dew, &c.   I find, however, that the gentleman
possesses great ingenuity.   He can immerse by dropping, immerse *from*
oil, and even *from dew !!!*   He can get into water by almost any of the
prepositions !   He has, indeed, great difficulty in sustaining his principles.

I did not say, that Dr. Scott ever was a Baptist.   I said he had difficulties on that subject, which led him to a careful and thorough examination of it ; and that it resulted in the firm belief of the correctness of the
views for which I am now contending.   Of the hundreds who have abandoned these views and become immersionists, I am acquainted with but
few.   But I venture to say, that a greater number have apostatized from
this gentleman's church to the world, than have become immersionists
from our ranks.   So the world has as good reason to boast as he.   As
to the increase of members of which he boasts, there are many places
where, a few years ago, there were no Presbyterians, in which now there
are numbers of them ; and in many places, the Methodists have multiplied rapidly where, until recently, they had no churches.   The gentleman's argument, therefore, (if it deserves to be called an argument) would
prove both Presbyterians and Methodists to be in the right !   In regard
to his *prediction*, I may truly say, he is neither a prophet nor the son of a
prophet.   The signs of the times, at any rate, do not indicate its fulfillment.   If for thirteen hundred years, almost the whole christian world,
as he says, practiced immersion, there has certainly been a wonderful
falling away from the ranks.

He desires me to produce my arguments for pouring and sprinkling.
Well, he shall have a fair sweep at them.   He sometimes complains of
me for going ahead of him, and, at other times, for going too slowly.   I
fear, I shall not be able to please him in any way.   I will, however, proceed to state the facts and arguments ; and if he can refute them, he shall
be welcome to do so.

I. My first fact, which I have already stated, is—*That all the washings of the Old Testament, the mode of which was prescribed, were required to be performed by sprinkling*.   The only possible exception was
in regard to *vessels*.   In Levit. xiv. we find directions concerning the
ceremonial cleansing of lepers ; and they require them to be *sprinkled*
seven times, to wash their clothes, and *wash* themselves in water.   But
the *mode* of the washing is not prescribed—no immersion is required.
Again, Num. xix. 17—20, " And for an unclean person, they shall take of
the ashes of the burnt heifer of purification from sin, and running water shall be put thereto in a vessel ; and a clean person shall take hysop,
and dip it in the water, and *sprinkle* it upon the tent, and upon all the vessels, and upon the persons that were there, and upon him that touched a
bone, or one slain, or a grave : and the clean person shall *sprinkle* upon
the unclean on the third day, and on the seventh day : and on the seventh
day he shall purify himself, and wash his clothes, and bathe (Hebrew—
wash) himself in water, and shall be clean at even.   But the man that
shall be unclean, and shall not purify himself, that soul shall be cut off
from the congregation, because he hath defiled the sanctuary of the Lord :

the water of separation hath not been *sprinkled* upon him," &c. Here, you observe, sprinkling is particularly required; but immersion is not. The unclean person was to *wash* himself; but the *mode* of the washing is not prescribed. So you will find it throughout the Old Testament.

All those washings were emblematic of *spiritual cleansing*—of *sanctification*. This is evident from the language of David in Ps. li. 7, "Purge me with hysop, and I shall be clean: wash me, and I shall be whiter than snow." Here is evident reference to Levit. xiv. 1, where the priest is directed to take hysop, and cedar-wood, and scarlet, and *sprinkle* the unclean seven times. David prays, that God would grant him that inward cleansing of which the sprinkling with hysop was an emblem. Hence he adds—"Create in me a *clean heart*," v. 10.

Now, I presume, it will not be denied, that when God selected a mode of representing emblematically inward purification or sanctification, *he selected the most appropriate, significant and impressive mode*. But it is a fact, that he chose *sprinkling*. If, then, sprinkling was once the most appropriate, significant and impressive mode of representing purification; can any man give a reason why it is not so still? How has it come to pass, that a mode selected by God himself, has become so ridiculous as immersionists would make sprinkling; whilst a mode (immersion) never selected by him, has become so very appropriate?

II. My second fact is—*That the inspired writers never in a solitary instance represent sanctification by dipping a person into water, either literally or figuratively.* From Genesis to Revelation you cannot find an example of the kind. Why did they never speak of immersing a person as a mode of cleansing? The reason, I presume, was, that they did not regard it as an appropriate and impressive mode. And if it was not so then, how has it become so since?

III. *The inspired writers did constantly represent sanctification by sprinkling and pouring.* This is my third fact. Indeed, so commonly was sprinkling employed, as the mode of purification, that the lexicons give to *purify* as the metaphorical meaning of the Greek word *rantizo*. I will read the passage already so repeatedly quoted, in Ezekiel xxxvi. 25—"Then will I sprinkle clean water upon you, and ye shall be clean: from all your filthiness and from all your idols will I cleanse you. A new heart also will I give you; and a new spirit will I put within you," &c. Here we find the emblem and the thing signified. The thing signified is a new heart and a new spirit—sanctification. The emblem is the sprinkling of clean water. Well, christian baptism is designed to be an emblem of spiritual cleansing. If, then, Ezekiel was right in representing sanctification by sprinkling; how can I be wrong in doing the very same thing?

My friend helped me to an argument by his remarks on yesterday, concerning the putting of the ashes of the heifer into the water of purification. He told us, the ashes were intended to teach, that blood had a permanent virtue to atone for sin, and therefore they were put into the water to be sprinkled on the unclean. So christian baptism is designed to represent the cleansing of the soul from the guilt and pollution of sin by the blood of Christ and by the Holy Spirit. The blood of Christ is called "the blood of sprinkling;" and the Spirit is represented as *poured out, shed forth.* If, then, it was proper to sprinkle on the unclean the water containing the ashes of the heifer; surely it is proper to sprinkle upon the sinner the water which represents the efficacy of the blood of

Christ. Did not Ezekiel consider the sprinkling of clean water a suitable and impressive emblem of sanctification? Most assuredly he did. Did he not prophecy, that the Jews, when converted to God, under the new dispensation, should have clean water sprinkled on them? I think my friend understands his language as a prediction to be fulfilled under the Gospel. When will it be fulfilled! But whether it is a prophecy to be fulfilled under the gospel dispensation or not, certain it is, that sprinkling was then deemed a suitable mode of representing sanctification. Why is it not equally so now? Can my friend give a reason?

Again—Isaiah, speaking of the advent and work of our Savior, says, "So shall he *sprinkle* many nations," lii. 15. The meaning of which is, so shall he cleanse, purify from all sin, many nations. I know the Septuagint translates it, so shall he *astonish* many nations. But we are not to correct the Hebrew, in which Isaiah wrote, by an imperfect translation. In every instance where the Hebrew word here translated *sprinkle*, occurs in the Bible, it evidently has this meaning. There is, therefore, no room to doubt, that this is the correct translation of Isaiah's language.

Now, did not Isaiah consider sprinkling an appropriate mode of representing purification from sin? Most assuredly. This is not all. Here is a *prediction*, the fulfillment of which certainly belongs to the new dispensation, for it relates to "many nations." If, then, the Savior represent the cleansing of all nations by *sprinkling*, how can I be wrong in doing the same thing? And if all christians should be *immersed*, when will this prophecy be fulfilled?

IV. My *fourth* fact is this: *The work of the Holy Spirit, of which the baptismal water is an emblem, is called a* BAPTISM. 1 Cor. xii. 13, "For by one Spirit are we all baptized into one body, whether we be Jews or Gentiles, whether we be bond or free," &c. Now what is the *mode* selected by God of representing this spiritual baptism? The Holy Spirit is uniformly represented as *poured out, shed forth:* "I will pour out in those days of my Spirit."—"He hath shed forth this which ye now see and hear," Acts ii. 18, 33. But it may be said, this language is *figurative.* I admit it; but God employs figures correctly. Then why did he never represent men as *immersed* into the Spirit? Why was such language never used even figuratively? The obvious and only conclusion is—that *pouring* is the most appropriate mode. If, then, the baptism of the Spirit is represented by pouring, why should not water baptism, the emblem, be administered by pouring or sprinkling?

On the day of Pentecost there was a baptism of the Spirit, but there was no immersion. John had said, "I indeed baptize you with water— He shall baptize you with the Holy Ghost and with fire." Matt. iii. 11. On the day of Pentecost this promise was fulfilled. "And suddenly there came a sound from heaven, as of a rushing mighty wind, and it filled all the house where they were sitting. And there appeared unto them cloven tongues, like as of fire, and it sat upon each of them," Acts ii. 2, 3. This has always been a difficult passage for immersionists. They have sometimes said, the Spirit filled the room, and thus the people were immersed. But the Bible says no such thing; and, moreover, such a baptism as that would be, was not promised by John. Others have said, the *wind* filled the room, and they were immersed in it. But Luke does not say so. He says, there came a sound *as of* a rushing mighty wind; but he does not say, there was *a wind.* And if he had, the promise was not of a baptism in wind.

Our friends have been in great difficulty, too, to find an immersion *in fire.* My friend, Mr. C., has adopted an opinion advanced by some of the old immersionists, that there is in the passage a promise and a threat, and that *some* were to be baptized with the Spirit, others to be immersed *into hell, or into severe sufferings!* But look at the passage: " I indeed baptize *you* with water—He shall baptize *you* (the same persons) with the Holy Ghost and with fire." Would you understand by such language, that some were to receive the Spirit, and others to be plunged into hell? No—there was no immersion into fire. Spiritual baptism, then, is represented by *pouring;* water baptism, the emblem, should, of course, be performed by pouring.

V. My *fifth* fact is this: *From the time that christian baptism was instituted, no apostle or christian minister, so far as the New Testament informs us, ever went one step out of his way in search of water for the purpose of baptizing.* The case of Philip and the eunuch is the only possible exception; and they were not going after water, but came to it, as they were journeying. This is a most unaccountable fact, if the doctrine of immersion is true. If Luke was so careful to tell us where John baptized, is it not marvellous, that in all the accounts he has recorded of christian baptism, he never dropped one remark from which it could be inferred, that the apostles and christian ministers ever went after water?

On the day of Pentecost *three thousand* were baptized. These were the first who ever received christian baptism. An example was now to be set—a precedent to be established, to be followed by all future ages. Is it not, then, passing strange, if immersion was so essential, that Luke gives no intimation, not even the slightest, that they went after water?

In reading the Christian Baptist we find Paul and Ananias represented as going after water; but Luke is silent on that subject. In recording the baptism of the three thousand, he mentions no delay, and gives no intimation that the apostles found any difficulty in obtaining water enough, or in administering baptism to them all. Luke wrote like a Pedo-baptist. Were I to record the baptism of three thousand persons, I should not think of telling where the water was obtained; for it would not require a great deal. But our immersionist friends do not write thus. In looking over the Millenial Harbinger, I find Mr. Campbell giving an account of a sermon he preached in Bowling Green, under which one old gentleman was induced to come forward and desire baptism. But he tells us, as the weather was inclement, and the river at some little distance, his baptism was deferred till the next morning. The apostles had to baptize three thousand persons in a city where there was no considerable stream of water, and no conveniences for immersing. Yet the inspired historian does not intimate that there was any delay; nor that they even left the temple, where they were converted, in search of water!

This apparent defect in inspired history would not appear so strange, if the necessary information were given in any other part of it. But the defect, if it be a defect, runs through the entire history. Not long after the conversion of the three thousand, we read of a large number of conversions in Samaria, and we read that they were baptized; but not a word is said about going after water. How can this be accounted for?

Well, we come to the conversion of the jailor and his family; and we learn, that they were baptized at midnight in a prison. Surely now we may expect to find something about going after water. But, no—not

T

a word is said on the subject. How shall we account for such omissions, if indeed the apostles held the doctrine of my friend, Mr. Campbell?

This is an important argument; for it is safer to go to the apostles to learn the mode of christian baptism. Mr. Campbell agrees with me, that John's was not christian baptism, but belonged to the old dispensation. John went where there was " much water;" but where do we ever find an apostle going after water?

We come now to consider Paul's baptism.—[*Time expired.*

Saturday, Nov. 18—1 *o'clock, P. M.*
[MR. CAMPBELL'S FIFTEENTH ADDRESS.]

MR. PRESIDENT—Little matters become great matters when there is great use made of them, or when they involve great events. I have said, during this discussion, that forty-two thousand men were slain in one day, because in pronouncing a single word they left out the letter *h.* We also stated that the difference between an *o* and an *i,* in the spelling of a word, so changed its meaning, in the case of *homoousios* and *homoiousios,* as to divide the church for ages, and to rend the Roman empire with internal wars and commotions. When any matter, however minute, involves principle, or character, it ceases to be an unimportant affair. Had not the gentleman attempted to disparage a strong argument, by an allusion to the little attention Dr. Wall bestowed upon that question, I should not have held up this volume in refutation of his allegations. The subject of Dr. Gale's book is baptism—*action and subject.* He wrote six letters on the mode. To these six, Dr. Wall replied in about the same number of pages, and you have seen the space occupied in the reply. His not replying to Dr. Gale, in this particular, must have been, because he could not; and not for the want of room. The gentleman admits he had room enough. Why then does he not reply? I say, because he could not.

As respects the tropical and literal use of *baptizo,* as defined by Stokius and Schleusner, I presume it will have to be referred. I am weary of continual assertions and re-assertions No lexicon has ever given *wash* as the *literal* or *proper* meaning of *baptizo.* Many of them represent it as secondary, consequential, or tropical; I therefore prefer to refer the question at once, whether or not, as I have read it, *wash, cleanse,* &c., be given as the *literal, proper,* or grammatical meaning of *baptizo,* or only its *tropical, figurative,* and accidental meaning. Let the matter be decided at once—for on this pivot turns the whole philological controversy. I understand there are several professors of the languages here. Here is professor McCown, of the Transylvania University, a Methodist minister; and here is professor Farnum, of the Georgetown College; I know not what his religious views are. Neither of these gentlemen are of my views. I am willing to settle this question by a reference to them. Is my respondent, Mr. Rice, willing to refer the matter to them?

Mr. Rice. I will reply when I rise, or now.

[*Rising*] I remark, that with one of the gentlemen I have lately had a controversy upon one branch of these criticisms, and therefore it would not be proper for me to abide his decision.

[Mr. Rice said to Mr. Campbell, I will agree to refer it to two professors, if you will also refer the case of *bebammenon* to the same. To which Mr. Campbell immediately responded, *certainly.*]

Mr. Campbell. I re-affirm, then, all that I have said on these lexicons, and am willing to stake my reputation upon the correctness and impartiality of my quotations, and translations from them; and solemnly affirm the conviction that the gentleman is totally mistaken, and that he has committed a great error in so positively affirming that these lexicons are not fully, and to the letter, with me.

It will not do for the gentleman to seek to balance this unfounded assertion, concerning the sacred use of this term in the judgment of New Testament lexicographers, with the allegation concerning the single case of *bapto*, found, as he *assumes*, once translated to sprinkle. Let him first prove that *bebammenon* was there; let him first prove that *bapto* was translated *sprinkle* by any translator, before he proposes such an adjustment of this palpable mis-statement. I will not admit that I have either stated a false fact, or made a false criticism, on the entire premises before us. I am willing to let all my statements be stereotyped, and sent to the world. In the case of *erantismenon* and *bebammenon*, on which so much has been said, he must first prove, both in logic and in law, that the latter was *in the text*, before I have to apologize for the translation.

I again say, it would be a most singular and unprecedented fact, if *baptizo*, or any of its family, did truly signify to *pour*, *sprinkle*, or *purify;* that in so many translations, public and private, into so many languages, made by so many hundreds of learned men, during eighteen hundred years—on a family of words so numerous, occurring more than 120 times, in no one single case it should be so translated. As marvellous and mysterious this, as why the Syriac, Ethiopic, and Vulgate should have selected *bapto* in the same verse, and have once, and only once, translated it *sprinkle*. Does it not amount to a demonstration that they had another reading, different from that in common use; not a single authenticated instance having ever been proved of such a translation? a fact without any parallel in universal criticism, if, indeed, sprinkle, pour, or purify be a true meaning of *bapto*. May I not then say that I am sustained in every capital point, and in this grand result, as now clearly set forth by all the distinguished lexicographers, translators, ancient and modern, by an overwhelming majority of the most learned and distinguished scholiasts, reformers, annotators, and critics of all classes, parties, and denominations!

I presume not to speak with infallible accuracy of the number of times the terms *bapto* and *baptizo* are found in Josephus. They are found often. It is of common occurrence, and is quoted often by Carson, Stuart, and sometimes by Ewing. It always signifies immerse in the "Hebrew-Greek," or "sacred style." Mr. R. cannot shew any Jewish usage of the word, different from the classic. Indeed, all the great Bible critics, and Jewish doctors, are against his assumption. His Jewish use of *baptizo*, after Josephus and the New Testament are subtracted, amounts to four occurrences—two in the Apocrypha, and two in the Old Testament, and they have never been translated sprinkle, or pour, in any work known in the annals of criticism.

Next to Josephus, Hippocrates is good authority, on account of his frequent use of the word in medical prescriptions, which, of course, require precision. He has been fully proved, by Mr. Carson, to be strictly conformable, in all instances, to the laws and usages of interpretation, propounded by me in this discussion. Mr. Rice often tells us of a garment colored with matter dropped upon it. Now had it been the *pro-*

cess of dripping that was said to be colored or dyed, there would have been relevancy; but as it is, there is none whatever in the case. How often shall I have to respond to such puerility! It is not the dripping, but the garment, that is dyed.

The philosophy of the whole subject is this: when any thing is dyed, it is covered with something. The thing is not seen. The covering of it, called the dye, the tint or the color only is seen. Hence, the metaphorical use of *bapto*. I have sometimes said, whenever I see the word *bapto* or any of its progeny, the first impression is the *dip*. But whether the thing dips, or is dipped, depends upon the active or passive voice; and whether the thing is wet or dried, heated or cooled, colored or discolored, improved or injured, is a matter of after thought and consideration, as well as the selection of a name to represent it. Whether, then, it shall be called literal or figurative, or whether it must be understood grammatically, or rhetorically, depends entirely upon contextual views and circumstances—wherever there is *bap*, there is *dip*, in fact or in figure.

The gentleman made some allusion to physical action in the word *louo*, which I do not well understand. I am understood when I say that we perform both mental and physical actions. The latter, especially, are free from the control of special idiomatic arrangements, because they are similar, outward, visible, corporeal acts, which all men perform in the same specific manner. As to the specifications so often submitted, methinks there can be no further controversy. Mental acts—or acts involving theory, principle, moral or religious,—and terms denoting *states*, may, indeed, be subject to peculiar idioms, because of the almost infinite varieties of them; often, too, the effect of education, national and state, association, &c. Hence, the word *faith*, or the word *flesh*, or the word *spirit*, &c. may have peculiar, national, or sectarian meanings and acceptations, which require the knowledge of various peculiarities before such can be well defined. But walking, talking, writing, eating, sleeping, rising, &c. &c. and the words in debate are not governed by any national or provincial or sectarian code. So that it is all a mere phantasy to seek for a special meaning of such terms in the laws, manners, customs, or other peculiarities of nations and religions.

I concur with Dr. Campbell, McKnight, Horne, Ernesti, &c. on all they say on idiomatic expressions and peculiarities. And I agree with the former two, and many such, in translating *baptizo* immerse, in the New Testament. These great masters of sacred criticism, are, almost to a man, with me in translating this much debated word, according to its common classic usage, wherever they do translate it. No man but a special pleader has ever argued for any other than a classic meaning of it in the New Testament.

But Mr. R. goes for sprinkling, theologically, as a symbol of sanctification and purification. His argument here is built on two assumptions: 1st. That *baptism is for sanctification*, and 2d. That sanctification was, in the law, performed by sprinkling water alone! When these are proved, and not till then, is his argument entitled to any consideration. No person, as I have already shewn, was ever sanctified by the pouring or sprinkling of water, from any sort of pollution whatever. My fourth universal proposition fully disposes of his argument for sprinkling water. But who believes that any subject of sprinkling is thereby sanctified by the Spirit? Sprinkling unholy water upon unholy persons, in order to make them morally, legally, and ecclesiastically clean!! When, where, and by whose hands did God ever so command Gentile, Jew, or Christian? Romanists make *holy* water by a recipe obtained from Pagan Divinity, an African or an Asiatic lustration. Protestants do not understand the manufacture, and, therefore, they sanctify by common water!

There is some radical mistake about this sprinkling, or pouring, as an emblem of spiritual sanctification, without a subsequent immersion. Mr. R. believes that the clean water of Ezekiel is common water here literally sprinkled, or to be sprinkled in baptismal sanctification! Has he forgotten that those sprinkled with the ancient water of purification had afterwards to be immersed in water, before cleansed, according to the law of types? We have yet another passage in Isaiah, relied on, to prove sprinkling— both on baptism, and on sanctification. It would be both a curious and interesting disquisition to expound, in the light of their respective ages, dispensations, and contextual circumstances, those passages of Scripture, which by a sort of sectarian conscription have been pressed into the maintenance and support of the ecclesiastical potentates, theories and shib-boleths of this our age of hoary and venerable traditions. Still theologi-ans will put passages, side by side, spoken thousands of years apart; un-der different dispensations, by kings, prophets, and apostles, on subjects, too, as diverse as their names, times, employments and languages.

" So shall he sprinkle many nations," Isa. lii. like the " pouring out" and " baptism of the Spirit," has often appeared in company with, " I will sprinkle clean water upon you," to support an usage ordained at Ravenna, in France, by the pope, in the year 1311, A. D. It was then and there authority was given to sprinkle many nations by him whose fame it has been to change times and laws.

I presume I may again open this venerable volume of Junius and Tre-mellius, who in 1580 printed this memorable work, replete with many valuable and profound notes and exegetical dissertations. Not so fond of sprinkling water, as we now-a-days seem to be, it not being then so much in fashion with learned Pedo-baptists, as in Kentucky, these learned translators, though of that school, give the following note—

It is the beautiful passage which we have in Isaiah lii. speaking of the Messiah : " Behold, thy servant shall deal prudently, he shall be ex-alted and extolled, and be very high. As many were astonished at thee, (his visage was so marred, more than any man, and his form more than the sons of men;) so shall he sprinkle many nations," &c. Junius and Tremellius, in their Latin versions lying before me, (London ed. 1581,) thus render it : "*Ito perspergat stupore gentes multas*—" So shall he astonish (sprinkle with astonishment) many nations." The Septuagint uses *thaumasontai*—" So shall he astonish many nations." Adam Clarke observes, on this passage—" I retain the common rendering, though I am by no means satisfied with it. *Yazzeh*, frequent in the law, means only to sprinkle : but the water sprinkled is the accusative case, the thing on which has *al* or *el*. *Thaumasontai* makes the best *apodosis*." So think I. The connection would be more consistent: " So shall he astonish many nations." But Lowth has it, " So shall he sprinkle with his blood many nations." So far as my position is concerned, either translation is equal.

I was myself a great admirer of Dr. Scott. I read his whole com-mentary through, when I was a student of theology, from beginning to end. He was before my eyes for three or four years. I also read his

Force of Truth, his communications and correspondence with the celebrated John Newton.

I am just now informed that Dr. Scott's son states, in the history of
his life, that so long as his father read the Bible, he came well nigh to
the conclusion that the Baptists were right; but that when he studied the
controversies on the subject, he admitted that baptism came in the room
of circumcision, and was satisfied with this foundation for his future
practice. I am thankful to the gentleman who has put me in possession
of this fact. In this way, then, Scott changed!

I return now to give you that cluster of Pedo-baptist grapes that I was
opening upon when I sat down. It is not necessary now to tell you the
dimensions of the pool of Bethesda—some hundred and twenty yards in
length, and eight feet deep, to find water to baptize three thousand: the
matter was so plain, so evident, so common, the knowledge was in the
possession of every living man. They all understood it, insomuch that
it would have been ridiculous in this instance to tell where they got water
to baptize, or how they performed the ordinance. But these are merely
thrown up as difficulties. To any one who makes himself acquainted
with the travels in Asia, Jerusalem and the Holy Land, it would be easy
to refute every hypothesis of that sort.

I find a rich cluster of these Pedo-baptist grapes, just ready to my hand,
in Booth's reply to Dr. Williams, and I will just transfer it, leaves and all,
to my page.

" Gurtlerus: ' *Baptism in the Holy Sprit*, is immersion into the pure waters of the Holy Spirit; or a rich and abundant communication of his
gifts. For he on whom the Holy Spirit is poured out, is as it were immersed into him.'

" Bp. Reynolds: 'The Spirit, under the gospel, is compared—to water;
and that not a little measure, to *sprinkle*, or *bedew*, but to BAPTIZE the faithful in: (Matth. iii. 11, Acts i. 5,) and that not in a font, or vessel, which
grows less and less, but in a spring, or living river.'

" Ikenius: ' The Greek word, *baptismos*, denotes the immersion of a thing
or a person *into* something. Here, also, (Matth. iii. 11, compared with
Luke iii. 16,) the *baptism of fire*, or that which is performed *in fire*, must
signify, according to the same simplicity of the letter, an *immission*, or *immersion*, into fire—and this the rather, because here, *to baptize in the Spirit,
and in fire*, are not only connected, but also opposed to being baptized *in
water*.'

" Le Clerc: ' *He shall baptize you in the Holy Spirit*. As I plunge you in
water, he shall plunge you, so to speak, *in* the Holy Spirit.'

" Casaubon: ' To baptize, is to immerse—and in this sense the apostles
are truly said to be baptized; for the house in which this was done was filled
with the Holy Ghost, so that the apostles seemed to be plunged into it 'as
into a fishpool.'

" Grotius: ' To be baptized here, is not to be slightly sprinkled, but to have
the Holy Spirit abundantly poured upon them.'

" Mr. Leigh: ' Baptized; that is, drown you all over, dip you into the
ocean of his grace; opposite to the sprinkling which was in the law.'

" Abp. Tillotson: ' *It* [the sound from heaven, Acts ii. 2,] *filled all the
house*. This is that which our Savior calls baptizing with the Holy Ghost.
So that they who sat in the house were, as it were, immersed in the Holy
Ghost, as they who were buried with water, were overwhelmed and covered
all over with water, which is the proper notion of baptism.'

" Bp. Hopkins: ' Those that are baptized with the Spirit, are as it were
plunged into that heavenly flame, whose searching energy devours all their
dross, tin, and base alloy.'

" Mr. H. Dodwell: 'The words of our Savior were made good, Ye shall be baptized (plunged or covered) with the Holy Spirit, as John baptized with water, without it.'

" Thus modern Pedo-baptists, who practiced pouring or sprinkling. Let us now hear one of the ancients, who wrote in the Greek language, and practiced immersion. Cyril, of Jerusalem, who lived in the fourth century, speaks in the following manner—' As he who is plunged in water and baptized, is encompassed by the water on every side ; so are they that are wholly baptized by the Spirit : *There* [under the Mosaic economy] the servants of God were partakers of the Holy Spirit ; but *here* they were perfectly baptized, or immersed, of him.' These testimonies are quite sufficient, one would imagine, to vindicate our sense of the term, *baptize*, when used allusively with reference to the gifts and influences of the Holy Spirit."

If, then, so many learned Pedo-baptists can themselves reconcile this style to immersion, why should any of them complain of our so attempting! One question more. If baptism be *pouring*, why do they *sprinkle?* Are pouring and sprinkling the same action ?

But I have yet another objection from which an argument may be drawn—"Arise and be baptized, Saul, said Ananias ; and Saul arose and was baptized,"—a clear proof that Paul was baptized standing ; consequently, not immersed ! !

In Luke's writings alone, we have this idiom eight times—*Anastas*, with an imperative immediately following, and without a conjunction or a comma, is found in Luke xviii. 10 ; xxii. 46 ; Acts ix. 11 ; x. 13, 20 ; xi. 7 ; xxii. 10, 16. In every instance, it indicates a divine command from the Lord in person, or from a supernatural agent acting for him. Nothing expressed by the term *rise*, different from the action to be performed. In no instance does the precept *arise*, terminate the action. It never means two actions in any one case. It is not arise *and* be baptized. It is an idiom of expressing one immediate action.

The idiom always changes when an action different from rising up is intended. Another imperative form with a copulative of some kind, intimates two actions—Acts viii. 26 ; ix. 6, 34 ; xxvi. 16. In all these it is *anasteethi*, followed by a copulative, rise *and* stand upon thy feet ; rise *and* go into the city, &c. In these last cases there is something more than mere earnestness and authority expressed. There are two distinct imperatives. Do this *and* do that. But *anastas poreuouo* is quite a different idiom. In this case rising is no more than an adjunct. It is not a distinct precept ; therefore, it is never rendered " stand up."

Almost every orator, indeed, in a persuasive and exhortatory address in our language, uses the term *rise*, when an erect position, or a mere change of position, is never thought of. In this way it is used ten times for one in any other sense, especially in warm and ardent appeals : Rise, citizens ! rise, sinners ! rise, men ! and let us do our duty. In this common-sense import of the term, did Ananias address Paul.

From the whole premises, I argue, that if Ananias intended to sprinkle Paul, he would not have commanded him to rise and be baptized. For immersion, he must go to the water ; for sprinkling, the water could have been brought to him. The efforts made by some Pedo-baptists to make it appear from this passage, that Paul was baptized standing up, are alike indicative of their humble attainments in Greek literature, as well as of the inveteracy of their prejudices. No man, so far as known to me, of any eminence for Greek literature, has ever made such an attempt. When all the objections against immersion are considered, one by one, we may conclude with professor Stuart : " For myself, then, I cheerfully admit, that *baptizo* in the New Testament, when applied to the rite of baptism, does, in all probability, involve the idea that this rite was usually performed by immersion, but not always." Not in the third century, as Mr. Rice interprets him, but in the first century.

These three last words, " *but not always,*" founded on such passages as I have examined, are built upon too slender a basis for so strong a man.

XI. My eleventh ARGUMENT shall be drawn from a fact already several times stated, and which, from what has already been said upon it, I shall not now amplify any farther than to state it fully and in a proper form. If it receive no other reply than the notice already taken of it, I shall go no farther into the proof of it. It is this : Sprinkling and pouring mere water on any person or thing, for any moral, ceremonial, or religious use, was never performed by the authority of God, under any antecedent dispensation of religion, and not being commanded in the New, is without any authority, patriarchal, Jewish, or christian. Let no one be startled at the novelty of this announcement. I am aware that it has been overlooked in all the books upon the subject, and in all the discussions that have ever fallen under my observation. It is, however, on that account, no less true and no less important.—[*Time expired.*

Saturday, Nov. 18—1½ *o'clock, P. M.*
[MR. RICE'S FIFTEENTH REPLY.]

MR. PRESIDENT—A single remark in regard to the small affair of Wall's reply to Gale. A good brother has just counted the pages, and informs me that between a *seventh and an eighth* of the volume is on the mode of baptism. I guessed pretty well.

I have adduced the authority of two of the most celebrated critics, proving that the *tropical* often becomes the *proper* and *literal* meaning of words. The gentleman proposes to *refer* the question. Have we here scholars who better understand the rules of interpretation than they? Even his own ancient lexicons, on which he has so much relied, give *lavo* and *abluo*—to wash, to cleanse, as *literal* meanings of *baptizo*. Bretschneider, as we have seen, gives its general meanings—"sepius intingo, sepius lavo—*often to dip, often to wash.* He speaks not of *lavo* as a *tropical* meaning. In company with such men as Ernesti, Bretschneider, and Stuart, I can consent to be represented as ignorant of the Greek language. To one of the gentlemen named, however, I have no objection ; and my reason for objecting to the other, will be appreciated. I will, however, as I have said, cheerfully refer the matter to any two impartial linguists, provided the gentleman will also refer the question, whether *bapto* has ever been translated *sprinkle.*

In my remarks on the question, whether any translator has rendered the word *bapto*, to sprinkle, I shall, for the sake of the audience, be brief. Gale, as I have repeatedly stated, admits that Origen did not quote the passage in Rev. xix. 13, verbatim, but *almost* verbatim. Would there not, then, be as much propriety in rejecting any other word in the text which differs from Origen's language, as the one in question ? It is impossible for the gentleman to escape the difficulty. If he will prove, that *bapto* is not the true reading in the passage under consideration, I will prove the same thing in regard to every word he will mention in the Bible.

It is very strange indeed, he would have us think, that in this one instance the word should be translated in a manner so singular. But singular as he considers the translation, Carson, who was equally interested with himself in defending immersion, could see no evidence of another reading. And, after all, the translation is not so singular; as the various examples I have adduced from the classics and from the Bible, prove. The baptism of Nebuchadnezzar with dew, was certainly something even less than sprinkling. The French version translates the word in that place *bedewed.*

But my friend says, I must prove that Origen and the translators of these ancient versions had *not* another reading before them! Really I had supposed it to be his business, since he maintains that they had another reading, to prove it. He does not deny, that the word *bapto* is found in all existing copies and manuscripts of the New Testament; and if any man call in question the reading in any passage of Scripture, what more proof can be given or desired, than the fact, that all the copies have the same reading? Surely no man could ask more, unless, like my friend, he were resolved to sustain his doctines by *all means.* This is not the only instance in which he has evinced extraordinary zeal for immersion. I pointed to a passage in the gospel by Mark, which he has strangely perverted for the sake of his cause—giving as a translation what is not even akin to a translation of it. Does immersion require the word of God to be thus tortured and wrested, in order to sustain it?

Whether the water to which Ezekiel and Isaiah had reference in the passages I quoted, was simply clean water, is of little importance in this discussion; since the question before us relates exclusively to the *mode* of applying it; and that mode was certainly *sprinkling.* This point, however, has been sufficiently explained. The gentleman says, I make baptism nothing more than an *emblem.* I have not so represented it. I have said, baptism is a significant ordinance—that the water is an emblem of spiritual cleansing; but I have not said, that it answers no other purposes. It is a door of admission into the church, or an ordinance for the recognition of membership; it is a seal of God's covenant; and it is a significant ordinance. If the gentleman desires proof of this last point, I refer him to Acts xxii. 16, "Arise and be baptized, and *wash* away thy sins." Now, we know perfectly well, that the application of water to the body, does not really cleanse from sin. It must, therefore, be an emblem of purification.

The gentleman has just learned by a paper handed him, that Dr. Scott, whilst he read the Bible, thought the Baptists were right; but when he read the commentators, he thought baptism came in the room of circumcision! So far as the present discussion is concerned, I care not whether this incredible story be true or false. We are not now discussing the question, whether baptism came in the room of circumcision. We are inquiring whether *immersion* is the only apostolic or christian baptism. I would not give a farthing for such papers, coming from we know not whom. Give us *facts* and *documents.* But let Dr. Scott speak for himself. I read from his Commentary on Matth. iii. " It [*baptizo*] seems to be a word borrowed from the Greek authors, signifying to plunge in, or bedew with water, without any exact distinction; (which, being a diminutive from *bapto*, to dip, it might do according to the analogy of language) and it was adopted into the style of Scripture in a peculiar sense, to signify the use of water in this ordinance, and various spiritual matters,

15

which have a relation to it.   *   *   *   Some, indeed, contend zealously, that *baptism* always signifies *immersion;* and learned men, who have regarded Jewish traditions more than either the language of Scripture, or the Greek idiom, are very decided in this respect; but the use of the words *baptize* and *baptism* in the New Testament, cannot accord with this exclusive interpretation." Such was the opinion of Scott, as he says, "after many years consideration and study."

Isaiah, as I have proved, speaking of the work of Christ, says—"So shall he *sprinkle* many nations. The gentleman produces the authority of the Septuagint as edited by Junius and Tremellius, to prove that it should be translated—so shall he *astonish* many nations. That is, as they understand it, so shall he astonish many nations by *sprinkling them!* Well, I suppose, since he could overwhelm Nebuchadnezzar with *dew,* it is not wonderful that he should talk of astonishing the nations by sprinkling!

But the fact is stated by the Rev. A. Barnes, after careful examination of all the places in which the Hebrew word translated *sprinkle,* occurs in the Bible, that in every instance it means to sprinkle. The Septuagint is only a translation, an *imperfect* translation of the Old Testament. Some parts of it are more correct; others less so. Are we, then, to correct the Hebrew Scriptures by such a translation? The very idea is absurd. The passage, then, must stand as it is, affording clear evidence that the sprinkling of water is an appropriate and impressive emblem of purification.

I have stated an important fact, which the gentleman does not venture to deny, viz: that from the time when christian baptism was instituted, we never read of any apostle going out of his way for water for the purposes of baptism. But he tells us, it was so universally understood, that baptism was immersion, that it was unnecessary to mention it. This, however, is *assuming* the question in debate. Let him prove that immersion was then universally practiced, and he will have gained his point.

But, if it was universally known, that immersion only was christian baptism; why were the inspired writers careful to mention the fact, that John the Baptist went to Jordan, and to Enon near Salim, where there was much water? If it was important to record these facts in regard to John's baptism, was it not much more important, that the church should know, that the apostles went after water to immerse christians? Ah! the cause of my friend is sorely pressed.

The matter, I think, is easily explained. John the Baptist needed much water for other purposes. Multitudes flocked to hear him, and remained together for several days without dispersing. They could not have been kept together where water for ordinary purposes and for their ablutions could not be obtained. It was absolutely necessary, therefore, especially in a dry country, such as that inhabited by the Jews, that John should select places for preaching and baptizing, where there was much water.

The *apostles* did not collect crowds that remained for days together. They had no need, therefore, to see that their hearers were furnished with water for ordinary purposes or for Jewish washings. They, therefore, never went after water. One of two things, I conclude then, is true, viz: *either John wanted much water, not for administering baptism, but for other purposes; or, the apostles did not baptize in the mode practiced by him.* From the fact, that John went where there was much water, immersionists *infer*, that he practiced immersion. Suppose we admit the inference to be legitimate. Then from the fact that the apostles never did go after much water, I infer that they did *not* practice immersion. And I think my inference is decidedly the stronger; for certainly John *might* have gone where there was much water, and still have practiced pouring or sprinkling; but the apostles could not have immersed the thousands converted under their ministry, without going where there was much water. Inasmuch, then, as they could not have practiced immersion without much water; and inasmuch as we never find them going after water, the conclusion seems inevitable, that they did not immerse.

But the gentleman tells us, that when John baptized the multitudes it was necessary that he should go to Jordan ; and therefore, he concludes he must have immersed. Then, how happened it, that on the day of Pentecost water was so plenty in Jerusalem ? John, it seems, could not find water to baptize in, without going to Jordan ; but the apostles, despised and persecuted as they were, could find water in great abundance on the day of Pentecost and afterwards ! Was Jordan brought to Jerusalem? Where did they find water in such abundance, that without delay or difficulty they could immerse three thousand persons in a day ? Is it not passing strange, that Luke, the inspired historian, should have failed to throw any light on this subject ! Error is generally contradictory. In one breath, we are told that it was necessary for John to go to Jordan to baptize ; and in the next, we are informed that the apostles found water plenty in Jerusalem !

The gentleman again attempts to sustain himself by Pedo-baptist consession. Who is a Pedo-Baptist? One who believes in the baptism of infants. Many Pedo-baptists are immersionists ; and yet the concessions of such are paraded before the people, as the concessions of the advocates of sprinkling. Amongst those advocates of sprinkling the gentleman has quoted Cyril, of Jerusalem, who was really an advocate of trine immersion of persons *in puris naturalibus*—divested of their clothing ! Grotius, though entirely disposed to favor immersion, speaks of the Holy Spirit as *poured* on the people on the day of Pentecost; thus admitting that the baptism of the Spirit is properly represented by pouring. Tillotson, if the gentleman has correctly represented him, says, they were, *as it were*, plunged into the Spirit ! How singularly would the promise read, if we were to supply that clause—"I indeed baptize you with water— He shall, *as it were*, baptize you with the Holy Spirit ! " Are these the expositions of Scripture, by which the cause of immersion is to be sustained ? Let it not be forgotten, that in the church of England, immersion was, for a length of time, the almost universal practice. Pouring was only allowed in cases of necessity. Gradually immersion fell into disuse ; but many of the clergy were anxious for the general restoration of the practice. Those men, decided immersionists, are the authors of most of the Pedo-baptist concessions, of which the gentleman, and those who agree with him, are in the habit of boasting ! They never were advocates of sprinkling.

I now invite your attention to the baptism of Paul. In the twenty-second chapter of the Acts of the Apostles we read, that Ananias came to Paul, and, having first delivered his message, said, " Arise, (Greek, *anastas ;* having risen to your feet,) be baptized ; " and Luke, the Evangelist, says, " He received sight forthwith, and arose *(anastas)* and was baptized." Compare chapters twenty-six and nine. Here we find Paul in the city of Damascus, in a private dwelling. He had been blind, and had eaten nothing for three days. Ananias comes to him and says—what? Arise, stand up, and be baptized; and what did he do? He arose, stood up, and was baptized. The plain and obvious meaning of this language is, that Paul immediately stood up in the house, and received baptism.

But some of our immersionist friends have fine imaginations, and can easily supply what may be defective in sacred history! A worthy old Baptist father, in an article on this subject, copied into the Mllenial Harbinger, indulges in the following strain :—

"See what a heavenly hurry Saul was in, though weakened down by a distressing fast; behold him, with great weakness of body, and load of his guilt, staggering along to the water. I almost fancy that I see the dear little man (he was afterwards called Paul, which signifies little,) hanging on the shoulders of Ananias, and hurrying him up, with his right arm around him; and, as they walked on, saying, Be of good cheer, brother Saul; when you are baptized, your sins, or the guilt of them, shall be washed away."

There it is to the life. The good old father saw them on their way to some pond or stream. The vision was as clear as day !

[Here Mr. Campbell inquired for the name of the writer quoted.] His name was Taylor; an excellent man; for I knew him well.

My friend, Mr. C., has evidently less poetry in his composition than the old father; but he, too, draws on his imagination to supply the facts that Luke omitted to state, as we shall see by reference to the Christian Baptist, p. 422.

"Had any person met Paul and Ananias, *when on their way to the water*, and asked Paul for what he was going to be immersed; what answer could he have given, if he believed the words of Ananias, other than, I am going to be immersed for the purpose of washing away my sins? Or had he been accosted *on his return from the water*," &c.

Mr. Campbell gave the history, and farther Taylor made the poetry! Both were enabled to see Paul and Ananias going to some stream or pond, where Paul could be immersed! But, the misfortune is, we read not a word of all this in the Bible. Luke tells us, that Paul was in Damascus, in a private house, in a very feeble state; and he tells us, that Ananias came and baptized him. But, instead of informing us that they went forth in search of water, he simply relates, that Ananias told Paul to arise and be baptized; and he arose and was baptized! In such matters I prefer to go by the *Book*. I care not even for any criticism on the language; I am willing to take it as it stands in the English Bible; for the clear and obvious meaning is, that Paul was baptized standing up in the house. The Greek, however, makes the argument, if possible, clearer than the translation. I will quote a few passages in which we find *anastas*, the word employed by Ananias and Luke, to express Paul's rising to his feet. Matth. xxvi. 62, "And the high priest arose *(anastas)* and said unto him, answerest thou nothing?" Did not the priest stand on his feet and speak? Mark xiv. 57, "And there arose *(anastantes)* certain, and bare false witness against him." Acts i. 15, "And in those days Peter stood up *(anastas)* in the midst of the disciples, and said," &c. Acts xiii. 16, "Then Paul stood up, *(anastas)* and beckoning with his hand, said," &c. Acts xv. 7, "And when there had been much disputing, Peter rose up *(anastas)* and said unto them," &c. Ch. xi. 28, "And there stood up *(anastas)* one of them named Agabas, and signified," &c.

These passages, to which many others might be added, show the common usage of the New Testament in regard to the word *anastas*. It is constantly used to express the act of rising to the feet. And, you observe, the language conveys the idea, that the baptism was administered immediately on his rising to his feet. *Anastas*, having risen up, he was baptized. Not an intimation is given that there was a moment's delay, or that they left the house. If Ananias had but said to Paul, Arise, and let us go to a pond, or a stream, that you may be baptized; there would have been no necessity that father Taylor and Mr. Campbell should have supplied, from their imagination, the imperfect account of this interesting occurrence. But, as in all the passages I have just read, *anastas* expresses the action of rising to the feet, and the action expressed by the following verb, followed immediately and was performed in a standing position; so, here, Paul rose to his feet and was immediately baptized. This looks exceedingly like Pedo-baptist practice—very much indeed! And it is very unlike the practice of our immersionist friends. If a Pedo-baptist were giving a particular account of a baptism, he would write just as Luke did; but our immersionist friends constantly speak and write of going to ponds and streams.

Let us now, for a moment, recur to the *facts* I have established. I have stated it as an indisputable fact, that when God originally selected a mode of representing sanctification, *sprinkling* was the mode. This fact has not been denied, and it cannot be disproved. I have stated as a second fact, that the inspired writers never, in any one instance, represented spiritual cleansing by immersing persons into water, speaking figuratively or literally. I have stated as a third fact, that they did constantly represent it by sprinkling and pouring. Neither of these facts has been or can be disputed. I have stated a fourth fact, that from the time when christian baptism was instituted, not an instance is recorded of the apostles, or any of them, or of those ministers associated with them, going one step out of their way after water for the purpose of baptizing. This fact has not been denied, and it cannot be. The apostles, as I have said, always baptized persons whenever and wherever they professed faith in Christ—in the crowded city, in the country, in the desert, in private houses, in prison, day or night—there was no delay for lack of conveniences to baptize either many or few. But in the accounts given of the administration of baptism by our immersionist friends we find frequent delays mentioned, either because they have not sufficient water, or from some other difficulty peculiar to immersion. In the Millenial Harbinger, as I have already stated, I find a delay in administering baptism to *one individual;* and in the same work I find other accounts of a similar character. Yet the country in which christian baptism was first practiced, was by no means so well watered as ours. How, then, shall we account for the fact, that the apostles, at all times and under all circumstances, could administer baptism to any number of converts; whilst our immersionist friends find it necessary so often to delay? We, like the apostles, can administer baptism to any number of converts, at any time, and in almost any place. Whose practice, I ask, most resembles that of the apostles?

I have stated a *fifth* fact—that the work of the Holy Spirit is called a baptism; and the baptism of the Spirit is represented by pouring and sprinkling. The Holy Spirit is said to be *poured out—shed forth, to fall upon the people.* Christian baptism is designed to be a significant ordinance, in which the water is the emblem of purification of heart. If,

U

then, the Lord has chosen to represent the work of his Spirit—the baptism of the Spirit, by pouring and shedding forth, water-baptism should be administered in that way.

I might safely leave the audience to determine, in view of these indisputable facts, whether baptism administered by pouring or sprinkling is not scriptural and valid. I have, however, another important argument to introduce; but perhaps I have not time now to present it. I will, however, briefly introduce it.

John, the apostle, says—" There are three that bear record in heaven," &c.—" And there are three that bear witness in earth, the Spirit, and the water, and the blood: and these three agree in one," 1 John v. 7, 8. These three witnesses agree in their testimony. In what, then, do they agree? The *blood* of Christ, we know, cleanses from the guilt of sin. The saints in heaven are represented as having " washed their robes, and made them white in the blood of the Lamb," Rev. vii. 14. The Holy Spirit cleanses the soul from the *pollution* of sin, Titus iii. 5, 6. We have, then, the testimony of two of the witnesses; and they agree in the cleansing of the soul from the guilt and pollution of sin. The water, the third witness, of course, points to the same thing. The blood of Christ is the procuring cause of purification from sin; the Holy Spirit is the efficient agent in imparting holiness of heart; and the water applied in baptism is the symbol and seal of spiritual blessings.

But the blood of Christ is called " *the blood of sprinkling*." Paul says—" Ye are come to—the blood of sprinkling, that speaketh better things than the blood of Abel," Heb. xii. 24. Peter speaks of believers as "Elect according to the foreknowledge of God the Father, through sanctification of the Spirit, unto obedience and *sprinkling* of the blood of Christ," 1 Pet. i. 2. The Spirit of God, as I have already remarked, is constantly represented as *poured* out, *shed forth*, &c. How, then, would you apply the *water?* The sprinkling of the blood of Christ, and the pouring out of the Spirit, and *immersion* in water, would not make a very striking agreement. But if the blood be sprinkled, the Spirit poured out, and water poured or sprinkled, is not the agreement of the witnesses most strikingly exhibited?—[*Time expired.*

Saturday, Nov. 18—6 *o' clock, P. M.*
[MR. CAMPBELL'S SIXTEENTH ADDRESS.]

MR. PRESIDENT—As we have just heard from you, sir, the meeting of this evening, and all our meetings on this occasion, are solemn matters. In this sectarian and schismatic age, we have assembled for the purpose of discovering, if possible, the roots of discord and the seeds of schism which have unhappily alienated and estranged us from each other; that we may, peradventure, find some remedy for those wounds and grievances which have so disgraced our holy faith, marred its beauty, and impeded its progress in the world. It is not for the purpose of carrying a favorite point, of maintaining a sectarian tenet, that we have assembled; but that we may clear away the rubbish of human tradition, and then lay a deep, a broad, and an enduring foundation, upon which christians may meet and harmonize their discords; shake hands, bury the tomahawk and scalping knife of partizan wars, and unite in one solid and fraternal phalanx, for the civilization of the world—for the illumination, reformation, and the redemption of mankind. I humbly hope, sir, that we shall all remember that this is our supreme object, and conduct ourselves in a manner worthy of an occasion so grave, so responsible, and so solemn as the present.

In opening the discussion of this evening, I have a remark or two to make on the topics before us during the latter part of the afternoon. My friend, Mr. R., in his last speech, attempted to reply to my remarks on that passage in the Acts of the Apostles, in which Paul is commanded by Ananias, to " arise and be baptized, and wash away his sins." He did not apprehend the point of my criticisms, or if he did, he forgot it. Consequently, his response was wholly wide of the mark. I specified all the passages in which this idiom of Luke was preserved. His specifications were of a different character, not falling under the idiom adduced, and consequently were wholly irrelevant. We have time only to state the fact, and proceed to weightier matters.

The water of separation was ordained for a specific purpose. It was to consummate the symbols of the law, and to give a full view of some of the virtues of the christian atonement. Mr. R. professed to be pleased with it, because, he said it afforded him a new argument for his favorite sprinkling of common water!! He observed, that we have water mixed with blood, as the ashes of a red heifer were mixed with water, and that the water of sprinkling was a sort of antitype of that symbol. The gentleman has forgotten the fact, that we can no more have a type of a type in theology, than a shadow of a shade in nature. Nothing but substances make shadows. This fact reduces his argument, as it presents itself to my vision, to a shadow. If he make the sprinkling of clean water not the type of sprinkling Christ's blood, in sanctification, but the type of sprinkling baptismal water, then he must make the pouring of oil, not the type of the unction of the Holy Spirit, but of pouring out water ; and then I ask, of what was the immersion of the whole flesh of the leper a type of ? Immersion in the water of baptism, of course!! Then it was all water!! Three things occurred under the law in cleansing a leper: 1st. The water of purification was sprinkled ; 2d. The oil of olive was poured upon the head ; and 3d. The whole person of the leper or polluted person, was bathed in common water.

If, then, Mr. R. can find for the first and for the second, an antitype in the New Testament, he must also find one for the third ; and that, of course, would be immersion ! He has repeatedly stated the utter impossibility of finding any language in that book, to authorize the putting of a person under water. These identical words, indeed, cannot be found, because the book is written in Greek ; but whenever *baptizo en hudati* is translated by a competent linguist of an unprejudiced mind, we shall find the precept in English as well as in Greek.

The innate force of *eis*, he admits, may bring us *to*, and sometimes *into* the water ; but, alas, when there, we must come out for the want of a word informing us what to do. It has then, at last, been discovered, in this enlightened age, that one capital precept in the commission cannot be understood, consequently, that it cannot be obeyed ; that it means nothing definite or intelligible, because of the incompetency of the Greek language, or the unskillfulness of our clergy to interpret it. But what other word more perspicuous and specific might have been selected, neither he nor any other person has, as yet, informed us.

According to his philology, no one could prove that the disciples ever eat the Lord's supper in Jerusalem. Yet the terms used in the institution, and in the report of it, seem to be quite definite and precise. It is said they sat down, and did eat, &c. According to the philology of Mr. Rice, no ordinary man could satisfactorily prove either that the Messiah commanded the mystic loaf to be eaten, or that his apostles eat it after the last passover. To common minds, the language appears perspicuous and satisfactory; but to learned men, like my respondent, it is peculiarly mysterious and unintelligible. He would admit that they went into an upper room—that they sat down—that there was a table, having upon it a loaf of bread and a flagon of wine. All that, says he, is incontrovertible. But then comes the precept, after the benediction of the loaf—Take, *eat*, this is my body. Here, says he, is the difficulty. The term *eat* is a generic term, and has many meanings. I own, says he, it sometimes means to take a substance into the mouth and masticate it; but is it not applied to *acids* also? They are said to eat up various substances. Again; is not a cancer said to eat up a person's flesh? Sometimes, also, we read of words eating as a cancer; zeal, too, is said to have eaten up the Savior—"The zeal of thy house has eaten me up." A person, moreover, who treasures up revelation in his mind, is said to eat it. David says, I found thy word, and I did *eat* it. And who has not heard of interest eating up money as a moth? To go no farther, here are seven meanings of the word *eat*. Which shall we take? The Quaker takes the sixth; the plain, unsophisticated man of common sense, takes the first; but Mr. R., by the mere force of the word, could not decide which of the seven. Tradition and the primitive fathers, or the customs of the Church, or something else, but the word itself would never satisfy his mind. Now, that *baptizo*, to dip, is as plain as *phago*, to eat, every unprejudiced Jew and gentile on earth, knows. What a glorious uncertainty a person of a little ingenuity and learning may throw around the christian law!

Other matters, in the afternoon discourse, and in some other previous speeches, on which we cannot now find time to descant, will come up as pertinently under the *design* of baptism; and as we must at least give an outline of the whole argument, I shall hasten to another point.

XII. We shall now state our twelfth argument. For the special benefit of the more uneducated, I shall deduce an argument for immersion from the first precept of the decalogue of philology. That precept, according to my copy, reads thus: *The definition of a word and the word itself, are always convertible terms.* For example—*a law is a rule of action*—is equivalent to saying, *a rule of action is a law. Philanthropy is the love of man*—is equivalent to saying, *the love of man is philanthropy.* Now, if a definition, or translation, (which is the same thing,) be correct, the definition, if substituted for the term defined, will always make good sense, and be congruous with all the words in construction.

In order, then, to test the correctness of any definition or translation, we have only to substitute it in the place of the original word defined or translated. If in all places the definition makes good sense, that is, if it be convertible with the word defined, it is correct; if not, it is incorrect. Let any one unacquainted with Greek take a New Testament, beginning with the first occurrence of *baptizo*, or any of its family, and always substitute for it the definition or translation given, and if it be the correct one, it will make sense; good, intelligible sense, in every instance.

We, then, read:—"In those days, the Jews of Jerusalem and Judea went out to John, and were sprinkled by him in the Jordan, confessing their sins." To perceive the impossibility of such an occurrence, it is only necessary to know that the word sprinkle is always followed by the substance sprinkled, and next by the object. We can sprinkle ashes, dust, water, or blood, &c. because the particles can be severed with ease; but can we sprinkle a man! We may sprinkle something *upon him;* but it is impossible for any man to sprinkle another in a river; and it is equally so to sprinkle the river upon him. The same reasoning will apply to *pour.* This verb is also to be followed by the substance poured. Now, was it not impossible to pour the Jews in the Jordan, or any where else? And to pour the Jordan upon them would be as inacceptable to them as it would have been impossible for the Baptist. It remains, then, that we try the word immerse. That, too, is followed by the substance to be immersed. Now a man can be immersed in water, in oil, in sand, in grief, in debt, or in the Spirit, though it is impossible to pour him into any one of these. Having, then, subjected these three to the same law of trial; two are condemned and reprobate: one only is possible, desirable, and reasonable.

This test will hold to the end of the volume; even where the association may appear strange and uncouth in style, it will always be not only practicable in fact, but good in meaning. For example: Jesus was to baptize in the Holy Spirit. The influence of the Spirit poured out fills some place; into that persons may be immersed; as we are said to be immersed in debt, in affliction, in any special trouble; but a person cannot be sprinkled into these. Such an operation is always impossible, under any view, literal or figurative.

Let it be carefully noted, in this most useful test, that the three words are all to be subjected to the same laws. 1st. The material is always to follow the verb. 2nd. The place, or thing, or relation into which the action is to be performed, is to follow the material. In baptism, the material is a man; the element, water. Now, as John cannot pour the material James, neither can he sprinkle him; but he can immerse him in a river, in debt, in grief, &c. It is highly improper and ungrammatical to use such a phrase, unless by special agreement of the parties present.

Some persons, accustomed to a very loose style, see no impropriety in the phrase, "sprinkle him—pour him," because of the supplement in their own minds. They think of the material which is sprinkled or poured *upon* him, and, for brevity's sake, say, sprinkle him; that is, sprinkle dust or water upon him. But in testing the propriety of such phrases, the ellipsis must be supplied. There is no ellipsis in "*immerse him;*" but there is always in *sprinkle* or *pour him.* The material is suppressed, because it is supposed to be understood, as in the case—sprinkle *clean water* upon him. Now, while the abbreviation may be tolerated, so far as time is concerned, it is intolerable in physical and grammatical propriety; because it is physically impossible to scatter a man into particles like dust, or to pour him out like water; and it is grammatically improper to suppress the proper object of the verb, and to place after it a word not governed by it.

Others, again, with Mr. Williams and Dr. Beecher, become so captivated with a peculiar theory, that they neither see nor feel any thing repulsive in such sayings as—"Jesus made and purified more disciples than John; though Jesus purified not himself, but his disciples." "I have a purification to be purified with, and how am I straitened till it be accomplished." "He that believeth and is purified shall be saved." "We are buried with him by purification into death." "Christ sent me not to purify, says Paul, but to preach!!" What further witness need we, that when a man is captivated with his own inventions, he may be reconciled to any thing, however incongruous and absurd in the eye of reason, and contrary to the dictates of that learned doctor, *Common Sense.* To cap the climax, Dr. Beecher ends his quotations with " The like figure whereunto purification doth also now save us."

As Mr. Rice has elaborated *wash* with persevering assiduity, as his great favorite, it is due to him, as complimentary to his good taste, and as a reward for his labor, that I should fairly, if not fully, test the propriety and pertinency of his definition by a few select examples. He contends that it is a *proper* meaning of *baptizo.* It will, therefore, be convertible with *baptizo,* and always make good sense, substituted for it, in every passage in which it is found, according to the law and argument now before us. To proceed—we shall give a few specimens and try it in a few cases. Jesus says, Matth. xx. 33, I have a *washing* to undergo, and how am I straitened till it be accomplished! Again, Rom. vi. We are buried with him by a washing into death. Acts i. and v., John verily washed in water, but you shall be washed in the Holy Spirit not many days hence. 1 Cor. xii. 13, For by one Spirit we have all been washed, poured, or sprinkled into one body, &c. To cap the climax, John said, Matth. iii. and xi., I indeed wash you in water unto repentance—but he shall wash you in the Holy Spirit, and he shall wash you in fire!! Needs any one a clearer refutation of the assumption that washing is the proper representation of *baptizo,* in our language! When ever men can be washed in fire, then, and not till then, can I believe that *baptizo* properly, or literally means to wash.

As before said, in every passage in the Bible, where *baptizo* is proved, *dip* or *immerse* will make good sense, but not so *sprinkle, pour, wash, purify.* In this way persons, not acquainted with the original tongues, may always arrive at the most satisfactory certainty of the proper interpretation of a word.

XI. I hasten to my eleventh argument. It is one that I hoped to have had an hour to develop and illustrate. It is drawn from the apostolic allusions to baptism, such as Rom. vi. 4., where it is compared to a *burial* and *resurrection;* also to a *planting* of seeds in the earth. This occurs, also, in the second chapter of Colossians, and again, by Peter, it is compared to Noah's salvation by water in the ark, &c. The first passage quoted, Romans vi. 4, is "Therefore we are buried with him by baptism into death; that like as Christ was raised up from the dead by the glory of the Father, we also should walk in newness of life." Again, Col. ii. 15, " Buried with him in baptism, wherein also you are risen with him through the faith of the operation of God, who raised him from the dead."

Baptism, as administered by the primitive church, was a monumental evidence of the three great facts of man's redemption from sin, death, and the grave, by the death, burial, and resurrection of Christ. On presenting himself, the candidate confessed judgment against himself by admitting his desert of death for sin, and promising to die unto it; while confessing that Jesus died for our sins, was buried, and rose again for our justification. His immersion in water, and emersion out of it, was a beautiful commemorative institution indicative of the burial and resurrection of the Messiah. All the world comprehends this definition of *baptizo.* It has done more than a thousand volumes to break down the Papal institution of sprinkling. It is only recently, sorely pressed by its immense weight, that any one presumed to spiritualize it away. As I shall not have time to argue it at length, I shall let a few of the great and learned of the infant sprinklers be heard on the occasion. They will accomplish two point, viz: 1. Establish the fact of the resemblance; and 2. Somewhat illustrate the meaning of these passages. We shall, as usual, begin with Calvin.

Calvin: " *Are you ignorant!*—The apostle proves that Christ destroys sin in his people from the effect of baptism, by which we are initiated into the faith of the Messiah. For we, without controversy, put on Christ in baptism, and are baptized on this condition, that we may be one with him. Paul thus assumes another principle, that we may then truly grow into the body of Christ when his death produces its own fruit in us who believe. Nay, he teaches us that this fellowship of his death is chiefly to be regarded in baptism, for washing alone is not proposed in this initiatory ordinance, but mortification, and the death of the old man; whence the efficacy of Christ's death shows itself from the moment we are received into his grace."

Barnes: " *Therefore, we are buried, &c.* It is altogether probable that the apostle in this place had allusion to the custom of baptizing by immersion. This cannot, indeed, be *proved,* so as to be liable to no objection; but I presume that this is the idea that would strike the great mass of unprejudiced readers."

Locke: " We did own some kind of death by being buried under the water, which, being buried with him, *i. e.* in conformity to his burial, as a confession of our being dead, was to signify, that as Christ was raised up from the dead into a glorious life with his Father, even so we, being raised from our typical death and burial in baptism, should lead a new sort of life, wholly different from our former, in some approaches towards that heavenly life that Christ is risen to."

Wall: " As to the manner of baptism then generally used, the texts produced by every one that speaks of these matters, John iii. 23, Mark i. 5, Acts viii. 38, are undeniable proofs that the baptized person went ordinarily into the water, and sometimes the baptist too. We should not know from these accounts, whether the whole body of the baptized was put under water, head and all, were it not for two later proofs, which seem to me to PUT IT OUT OF QUESTION : *one,* that St. Paul does twice, in an allusive way of speaking, call baptism a burial; *the other,* the customs of the christians, in the near succeeding times, which, being more largely and particularly delivered in books, is known to have been generally, or ordinarily, a total immersion."

Archbishop Tillotson: " Anciently, those who were baptized, were immersed and buried in the water, to represent their death to sin; and then did rise up out of the water, to signify their entrance upon a new life. And to these customs the apostle alludes, Rom. vi. 2—5."

Archbishop Seeker: " Burying, as it were, the person baptized in the water, and raising him out again, without question, was anciently the more usual method; on account of which St. Paul speaks of baptism as representing both the death, burial, and resurrection of Christ, and what is grounded on them,—our being dead and buried to sin, and our rising again to walk in newness of life."

Sam. Clarke : " *We are buried with Christ by baptism, &c.* In primitive times, the manner of baptizing was by immersion, or dipping the whole body into the water. And this manner of doing it was a very significant emblem of the dying and rising again, referred to by St. Paul, in the above mentioned similitude."

Wells: " St. Paul here alludes to immersion, or dipping the whole body under water in baptism; which, he intimates, did typify the death and burial (of the person baptized) to sin, and his rising up out of the water did typify his resurrection to newness of life."

Bishop Nicholson: "In the grave with Christ we went not; for our bodies were not, could not be buried with his; but *in baptism,* by a kind of analogy or resemblance, while our bodies are under the water, we may be said to be buried with him."

Doddridge: "*Buried with him in baptism.* It seems the part of candor to confess, that here is an allusion to the manner of baptizing by immersion."

George Whitefield: "It is certain that in the words of our text, Rom. vi. 3, 4, there is an allusion to the manner of baptism, which was by immersion, which is what our own church allows," &c.

John Wesley: "*Buried with him*—alluding to the ancient manner of baptizing by immersion."

Whitby: "It being so expressly declared here, Rom. vi. 4, and Col. ii. 12, that we are buried with Christ in baptism, by being buried under water; and the argument to oblige us to a conformity to his death, by dying to sin, being taken hence; and this immersion being religiously observed by all christians for thirteen centuries, and approved by our church, and the change of it into sprinkling, even without any allowance from the author of this institution, or any licence from any council of the church, being that which the Romanist still urges to justify his refusal of the cup to the laity; it were to be wished that this custom might be again of general use, and aspersion only permitted, as of old, in case of the Clinici, or in present danger of death."

Assembly of Divines: "*If we have been planted together,* &c. By this elegant similitude the apostle represents to us, that as a plant that is set in the earth lieth as dead and immoveable for a time, but after springs up and flourishes, so Christ's body lay dead for a while in the grave, but sprung up and flourished in his resurrection; and we also, when we are baptized, are *buried,* as it were, in the water for a time, but after are raised up to newness of life."

I cannot find room for the witnesses I could accumulate on this point. Concurrent with these are Grotius, Beza, Bloomfield, Koppe, Rosenmuller, McKnight, &c. &c. I will conclude this venerable, learned, and highly authoritative list, with the most distinguished Presbyterian preacher now living. In his recent "Lectures on the Epistle to the Romans," the justly honored Thomas Chalmers, D. D. and LL. D., boldly and independently thus expresses himself.—[*Time expired.*

Saturday, Nov. 18—6½*, P. M.*
[MR. RICE'S SIXTEENTH REPLY.]

MR. PRESIDENT—I am happy to discover, that my friend is getting along. Three days was the length of time we expected to spend on this subject; but I have given him seven hours more, because he had fallen almost two days behind in his argument. I intend that all shall see, that the clergy are not so much afraid of the light as he has represented them.

Baptism by pouring or sprinkling, the gentleman has represented as a very ridiculous affair—a thing which will not bear investigation, even for an hour; and yet, he has been *four days* laboring most faithfully to sustain the claims of immersion, and is yet calling for more time!!! One good argument, he says, is sufficient to prove any point; but he has not yet found even one; and I presume, he will not.

I think it would have been wise in him to have passed in silence Paul's baptism: it is so obviously unfavorable to immersion. He talks about a peculiar idiom in the expressions used on that occasion. But what is there peculiar about it? Ananias said to him, "Arise (stand up) and be baptized; and he arose and was baptized." I see nothing peculiar in the expression. Are they not precisely like those quoted to show the meaning of *anastas?* "In those days Peter stood up (*anastas*) in the midst of the brethren, and said," &c. "Then Paul stood up (*anastas*) and beckoning with his hand, said," &c. I am unable to discover the slightest peculiarity of idiom. The plain, unsophisticated meaning is, that Paul stood up in the house, and was (not immersed, but) baptized—a very different operation. A person may indeed be baptized by immersion; yet immersion and baptism are by no means identical.

I expressed myself as well pleased with the gentleman's dissertation on the ashes of the burnt heifer, put into water to show that blood had a permanent virtue to atone for sin; because, since the water in baptism is a symbol of the cleansing of the soul from sin by the blood of Christ and by the Holy Spirit, it should be sprinkled upon the morally unclean, as the ashes of the heifer were sprinkled upon those ceremonially unclean. But he now represents me as making the sprinkling under the Old Dispensation a *type* of baptism. I said nothing about types: I did not use the word *type* at all. I said, that when the Lord chose a *mode* of representing purification, sprinkling was the mode selected; and I argued, that if it was once an impressive and significant mode, it must be so yet. I had no occasion to speak of types; I spoke only of the mode of applying water as an emblem of purification. Formerly sprinkling was certainly the best mode, or God would not have selected it; but now, if we are to believe the gentleman, it will not answer at all! Why not? Can any one give a reason why it is not now as appropriate an emblem of spiritual cleansing as formerly? I presume, it would be difficult to do.

Mr. Campbell says, I admit, that *eis* will take a man *to* or *into* the water; but maintain, that *baptizo* will not put him *under;* and he asks, what Greek word will express the action of putting under. I have already given the word which would definitely express the idea of putting under; and it is not a word of my selection. It was selected by the Greek fathers of the third and fourth centuries. When immersion became the general practice among them, they employed *baptizo* to denote the ordinance; but when they wished definitely to express the mode of administering it by immersion, they used *kataduo.* Thus Photius speaks of the three immersions and emersions (*treis kataduseis kai anaduseis*) of baptism. Now to translate the word *baptisma*, immersion, in this passage, as Mr. C. does, would make perfect nonsense. It would read thus: *the three immersions and emersions of immersion (baptismatos!)* What sense would this make? It is evident, that the Greeks employed *baptizo* and *baptisma* to denote the *ordinance* of baptism, and *kataduo*, to express the *mode* of administering it by immersion; for when a person was baptized on a sick bed by pouring or sprinkling, they spoke of him as *baptized.* Dr. Gale, as I have already proved, quotes the Greek fathers, using *kataduo*, and represents it as properly expressing immersion. "*Kataduson me*—plunge me into Jordan." I ask again, how came it to pass, that when immersion prevailed among the Greeks, they selected another word instead of *baptizo*, to express the mode of administering baptism? *Why did they drop the word uniformly used in the Bible, and take another, if, as Mr. C. insists,* BAPTIZO *is precisely the word to express the specific action of immersing?*

Again, when immersion prevailed amongst the Latins, they, too, found other words by which to express that mode. *Baptizo* and *baptismus*, transferred as in our Bible, expressed the ordinance of baptism; but intingo, mergo, mergito, &c. expressed the mode of administering it by immersion. The Latin fathers, I presume, understood the Greek better than I or my friend. Why, then, did they select other words instead of *baptizo*, to denote immersion? The only possible reason was, that *baptizo* did not definitely express immersion.

The gentleman tells you, that according to my logic, it would be impossible for men to ascertain their duty. For example, we could not know whether in partaking of the Lord's supper the apostles did really eat bread; for *acids* are said to eat divers things! Why, I presume, there would be no great difficulty about it, if we could only ascertain whether the apostles were acids!!! Men, I believe, are not in the habit of consuming things by means of acidity. The gentleman, however, contends for the original meaning of words; and he tells us, *eat* means to *chew*. Of course, he should contend that acids chew! It is amusing to see him running to objections so perfectly flimsy, in order to sustain immersion.

We have now come to my friend's *eleventh* argument, designed for his *unlearned* hearers. His method of *reading* his arguments, I think, is not adapted to please either the learned or unlearned—certainly not the latter. But he proposes to substitute the definition for the word defined; and he tries *sprinkle* and *pour* instead of baptism—thus: they were sprinkled in Jordan, or poured in Jordan, &c. If it be true, that *baptizo* definitely expresses *immersing*, it is easy to show the absurdity of substituting for it words expressing different modes; but this is precisely the point to be established. I can *travel* by walking or riding; but it would not do to substitute walking or riding for the word *travel*. For this word expresses the *thing done;* but walking or riding denotes the *mode* of doing it. If I were to say, I saw a man *laboring* to-day; would you deem it correct to substitute *ploughing* for the word laboring? Certainly not; for the word *labor* expresses more than ploughing. There are many ways in which a man may labor. I can *wash* my hands either by pouring water on them, or by dipping them into water; but you would not consider it correct to say to your child, go, *pour* your hands, or, go, *dip* your hands; though if he should either have water poured on them, or dip them, he might obey your command to *wash* them. So *baptizo* expresses the *thing done*, the application of water to a person or thing; but it does not express the *mode* of doing it.

The gentleman, however, tries the word *wash*, and the word *purify;* and he thinks *baptizo* cannot mean either the one or the other. The Lord's supper is taken by *eating* and *drinking;* but if you would substitute eat or drink for *deipnon*, the word sometimes used to denote that ordinance, it would make nonsense; and Mr. Campbell might thus prove, according to his logic, that the supper is not to be taken by eating and drinking! I think it probable, if he had lived in Paul's day, he would have ridiculed the apostle; for he calls baptism a *washing*. He says, God saves us "by the *washing* of regeneration, and renewing of the Holy Ghost," Tit. iii. 5. Again, speaking of the wicked, he says "And such were some of you; but ye are *washed*, but ye are sanctified," &c. 1 Cor. vi. 11. In these and similar passages the gentleman admits, that Paul spoke of baptism. He, therefore, is forced to admit, that baptism is a washing. And if it is not, Paul was evidently in an error; but if baptism is a washing, then it means washing.

I should be happy to hear from my friend, a dissertation on the word *deipnon,* showing, from the primary or original meaning of the word, the manner in which the Lord's supper should be administered and received. Could he determine from the word alone what elements should be used, and in what quantity? Could he learn from it any thing more than that something was to be eaten? He could not. We must go to the institution of the ordinance, and learn its nature and design, before we can determine the manner of receiving it. And so we must go to the institution of baptism, and learn its nature and design, in order to understand how it should be administered.

But the gentleman would put *immerse* in place of *baptize;* and this, he supposes, would make excellent sense. But in strictness of language *immerse* does not express all for which he is contending. A man may be *immersed,* without being *submersed.* He is contending for the entire submersion of the body in water. Some have thought the word *plunge* a fair definition of *baptizo.* Let us try it. "John the plunger did plunge in the wilderness, and preached the plunging of repentance!" Some prefer the word *dip.* Let us try it. "John the dipper did dip in the wilderness, and preached the dipping of repentance," &c. Such language sounds very curiously. [A laugh.]

Mr. Campbell told you, that circumcision signifies *cutting round.* Now put the definition in place of the word, as applied to a religious rite. Let us now read in Gen. xvii. "This is my covenant, which ye shall keep between me and you, and thy seed after thee: every man child among you shall be circumcised (cut around.) And he that is eight days old shall be circumcised (cut around.) And the uncircumcised (uncut around) man child." My friends, you see it wont do. My friend does not like the expression; but I must say, *it wont do!* [A laugh.]

The truth is, *baptism* is the word appropriated to denote a religious ordinance; and it will not do to substitute in its place any word which expresses merely the *mode* of its administration. The ordinance is one thing; the mode of administering it is another. The principle, therefore, on which the gentleman reasons, is wholly unsound, and will prove quite fatal to plunging or submersion, as to pouring or sprinkling.

Mr. Campbell has, at length, reached his argument founded on the burial spoken of in Rom. vi. 1. I discover, however, that instead of making an argument from the passage, he contents himself with reading the opinions of others. Almost any one could do as much. These opinions have been published and republished for the thousandth time, and are found in almost every little book that has been published in favor of immersion.

Calvin is brought forward as one of his authorities; but I am disposed to think, the gentleman has done Calvin injustice. For in looking over his commentary on Rom. vi., I saw no allusion to immersion.

Rev. A. Barnes is another whose opinion is adduced. Mr. Barnes is a man, doubtless, of considerable learning; but I will bring against him the authority of Prof. Stuart, an older and abler critic, who has proved with great clearness, that there is in the passage no allusion to immersion. I will also present the authority of Dr. Hodge, of Princeton, who is one of the ablest critical writers.

Dr. Wall was quoted; he was notoriously an immersionist of the *old school.* He was for allowing pouring only in cases of necessity. Dr. Clarke was also quoted; but I apprehend, that he was not treated quite fairly. In his comment on the 6th of Romans, he distinctly says, it cannot be certainly proved, that the apostle alluded to immersion, and in his remarks on Matth. iii. 6, he says, it is certain that *baptizo* means both to *dip* and to *sprinkle*. John Wesley was a man of learning; but he was not on the side of my friend. As already quoted, he says:

"The *matter* of this sacrament is water, which, as it has a natural power of cleansing, is the more fit for this symbolical use. Baptism is performed by *washing, dipping*, or *sprinkling* the person in the name of the Father, Son, and Holy Ghost, who is hereby devoted to the ever blessed Trinity. I say, by *washing, sprinkling*, or *dipping;* because it is not determined in Scripture in which of these ways it shall be done, neither by any express *precept*, nor by any such example as clearly proves it; nor by the force or meaning of the word baptism."—*Wesley*, p. 144.

Whitefield is another of the gentleman's authorities. He was a great preacher; but I never heard that he was considered a learned critic. He spent a considerable part of his life in going from place to place, and from country to country, preaching the Gospel to thousands and tens of thousands. It is not to be presumed, therefore, that his critical knowledge was very extensive.

Dr. Whitby was one of the clergy of the church of England who lived not long after immersion had generally ceased to be practiced in that church, and who were very solicitous to have it restored, except in cases of necessity. Like Wall, he was a decided immersionist. McKnight belonged to the same general class.

The gentleman quoted the Assembly of Divines. I presume, he is aware that the Notes which bear their name, were not really the work of that body, but only of a few individuals. He has, however, repeatedly published the statement, that in that Assembly the resolution in favor of sprinkling was carried by only one of a majority—that there were twenty-four for immersion, and twenty-four for sprinkling, and Dr. Lightfoot gave the casting vote. I happen to have the account of that matter, as given by Lightfoot himself, from which I will read an extract or two : Dr. Lightfoot says :

"Then fell we upon the work of the day, which was about baptizing of the child, whether to dip him or sprinkle. And this proposition : "It is lawful and sufficient to besprinkle the child," had been canvassed before our adjourning, and was ready now to vote; but I spake against it as being very unfit to vote—that it was lawful to sprinkle when every one grants it. Whereupon, it was fallen upon, sprinkling being granted, whether dipping should be tolerated with it," &c. "After a long dispute it was at last put to the question, whether the Directory should run thus : 'The minister shall take water and sprinkle, or pour it with his hand, upon the face or forehead of the child ; and it was voted so indifferently, that we were glad to count names twice, for so many were unwilling to have dipping excluded, that the votes came to an equality within one—for the one side was twenty-four, and the other twenty-five ; the twenty-four for the reserving of dipping, and the twenty-five against it; and there grew a great heat upon it; and when we had done all, we concluded nothing in it, but the business was recommitted.' * * * * But it was first thought fit to go through the business by degrees, and so it was first put to the vote, and voted thus affirmatively : 'That pouring on of water, or sprinkling of it in the administration of baptism, is lawful and sufficient.' But I excepted at the word 'lawful,' as too poor, for that it was as if we should put this query—whether it be lawful to administer the Lord's supper in bread and wine? And I moved that it might be expressed thus : 'It is not only lawful, but also sufficient;' and it was done so accordingly. But as for the dispute itself about dipping, it was thought fit and most safe to let it alone, and to express it thus in our Directory—

' He is to baptize the child with water, which for the manner of doing is not only lawful, but also sufficient and most expedient to be by pouring or sprinkling water on the face of the child, without any other ceremony.' But this cost a great deal of time about the wording it."—*Pittman & Light-foot's Works*, vol. xiii. pp. 300-1.

This is the account given by Pittman and Lightfoot, and the gentleman is welcome to their testimony. It shows how impartially he has recorded historical facts!

Dr. Chalmers is a learned and great man. But in immediate connection with the passage quoted by Mr. Campbell he says, that he regards the mode of baptism as a matter of entire indifference; and, as I have repeatedly remarked, no man is likely to go through a thorough investigation of a subject in regard to which he is perfectly indifferent. If a man express himself as perfectly indifferent concerning any political question which agitates the public mind, you at once conclude that he has not given himself much trouble to investigate it; and so it is on religious subjects. But, as before remarked, I will balance his great names with others equally great; for it appears that the controversy is to be determined by celebrated names, not by argument. I have already given you the concessions of the Greek and Latin christians, who practiced generally *trine immersion*, and who, with one voice, pronounce pouring and sprinkling valid and scriptural baptism.

But let us examine the passage in question; and this, I believe, is the last strong-hold of immersion. I will read the passage : " What shall we say then? shall we continue in sin that grace may abound? God forbid. How shall we, that are dead to sin, live any longer therein? Know ye not, that so many of us as were baptized into Jesus Christ, were baptized into his death? Therefore we are buried with him by baptism into death; that like as Christ was raised up from the dead by the glory of the father, even so we also should walk in newness of life. For if we have been planted together in the likeness of his death, we shall be also in the likeness of his resurrection: Knowing this, that our old man is crucified with him, that the body of sin might be destroyed, that henceforth we should not serve sin," Rom. vi. 1—6.

The first question that naturally presents itself in view of this passage, is this: what is the subject on which the apostle is writing? what is he aiming to prove? He had, in the previous part of the epistle, proved the doctrine of justification by faith, without the deeds of the law. He now anticipates and answers an objection urged by some against this doctrine, viz : that its tendency is to induce men to commit sin; and he proves that, so far from having any such tendency, this doctrine necessarily results in a holy life in the case of all who sincerely embrace it. He is not at all speaking of the mode of baptism; his single aim is to expose this Jewish cavil, and to prove that christianity, from its very nature, leads those who embrace it to a holy life. Having now learned the main object of his argument, we are prepared to understand his language.

We find in the passage before us, some five expressions figuratively employed, viz : death, burial, resurrection, planting, crucifixion. These figurative expressions must, of course, be interpreted consistently with each other. If, then, we can ascertain the meaning of the *death* and the *resurrection* of which he speaks, we shall easily understand the *burial*. The death is certainly spiritual—a death to sin: " How shall we that *are dead to sin*, live any longer therein?" verse 2. The resurrection is also

16   X

spiritual—a resurrection to a new life. "Therefore we are buried with him by baptism into death; that like as Christ was raised from the dead by the glory of the Father, *even so we also should walk in newness of life*," verse 4. The death is spiritual, the resurrection is spiritual, and the burial, must it not also be spiritual? Would you so interpret the passage as to have a spiritual death, a spiritual resurrection, and a *physical* burial of the body under water?! Would these three things be consistent? The simple meaning is, that the old man (our corrupt nature) is dead and buried; and the new man (our renewed nature) is risen to live a new life. Christ died *for* sin, that is, to deliver us from sin; so they who are baptized into his death, profess their desire and purpose to die *unto* sin—to enjoy the benefits arising from his death. Christ arose literally for our justification; so they who are baptized into Christ, rise spiritually and live a new, a holy life. Baptism, therefore, is that ordinance by which we become publicly and visibly identified with Christ in his death and resurrection. The same idea is presented in the *planting* and the *crucifixion* of the *old man*, verses 5, 6. If the burial is immersion, what is the planting, (or engrafting, as some render it)? Are we accustomed to plant seed in water? The meaning (if *planted* is the correct rendering of the word) is this: The seed is put into the earth, and it dies; but a new stalk springs up from it. So the old man is put, as it were, into the earth; and the new man rises up, like a new stalk, to live a new life. But if both burial and planting express the mode of baptism; what mode is indicated by *crucifixion*, which we find used in the same connection to express the same idea? It will not answer to select one of the figures to express mode, and exclude the others.

What, then, are we to understand by the death, burial, resurrection and crucifixion? The death to sin, and resurrection to a newness of life, certainly signify the change of heart and life from sin to holiness, that is, sanctification. The planting and the crucifixion of the old man, "that the body of sin might be destroyed," evidently express precisely the same idea. Whether, therefore, we look at the design of the apostle's argument, or at the language employed, we cannot but see that he spoke of sanctification, holiness of heart and life, as secured by christianity. We then inquire, in what way does God generally represent sanctification or purification from sin? Does he represent it by immersing into water? *He never does.* Does he not uniformly represent it by *pouring* or *sprinkling?* He does, both in the Old and in the New Testament. In what way, then, should christian baptism, the emblem of spiritual cleansing, be administered? Evidently by pouring or sprinkling. Whilst, therefore, this passage contains not a word about the *mode* of baptism, but speaks only of its *design;* when correctly understood, it is decidedly favorable to pouring or sprinkling as the proper mode.

That I have given the true exposition of this passage, will be still more manifest by comparing with it Colossians ii. 11, 12: "In whom [Christ] also ye are circumcised with the circumcision made without hands, in putting off the body of the sins of the flesh, by the circumcision of Christ: buried with him in baptism, wherein also ye are risen with him through the faith of the operation of God, who hath raised him from the dead." Here we find distinctly presented the *spiritual nature* of this burial and resurrection.—[*Time expired.*

Saturday, Nov. 18—7 *o'clock, P. M.*
[MR. CAMPBELL'S SEVENTEENTH ADDRESS.]

MR. PRESIDENT—Can you, sir, or can you, my fellow-citizens, withhold your admiration of the liberality and benevolence of Mr. Rice, in allowing me so much more time than stipulated, for the affirmation of the first proposition! Would you believe it? he has vouchsafed me just *one half hour* over the stipulated time. It was propounded, and solemnly agreed upon, that I should have the establishment of the number of hours per diem. The minimum was set down at four hours—the extension beyond that was left to me. On Wednesday, I informed Mr. Rice that I found myself in such health as to justify six hour sessions. Some of the moderators, however, preferring four hour sessions, I consented, upon the assurance from Mr. Rice, that I should have the time made up in number of days equal to three days of six hours each. At nine o'clock this evening, I shall have had nine hours and one-half for the affirmative, that is one half hour more than our stipulation. I asked, but could not obtain, another day, to be refunded by the subtraction of a day from some other proposition, not extending over so large a field of investigation. I have asked a day, and obtained half an hour! My friend claims other honors besides that of a magnanimous generosity, on grounds quite as slender as those on which he would now claim your admiration.

Another proof of the exemplary generosity of Mr. Rice, you have in the fact, that I have had two affirmative propositions assigned me for his one. I always asked, from the beginning, an equal number of affirmatives and negatives. My friend, as I begin to see, knew on which side his strength lay, and therefore refused me any better terms than two to one. It was this, or no debate at all. He is good in denying. He admirably suits the negative side. Besides, he has secured to himself two closing speeches for my one. With some, the last word and the last speech is a great matter, and therefore he wisely secured that also; for, even when the four affirmatives were given me, he would not change the position of them, so as to allow me the final closing speech. This may be good generalship, but who will call it generosity, equality, or equity!! Still, I feared not to give the Presbyterian church these fearful odds; especially, as without them, we should never have met here. The affirmative, according to the usages of our courts of law, and of the civilized world, has the opening and the closing speech. But in this case I would not have asked it, if the number of affirmatives had been equal.

I regret, my fellow-citizens, exceedingly regret, that while discussing a question of this magnitude, a question more or less involving the world's destiny, a question of the utmost gravity and solemnity, there should have been any indications of levity, especially such as occurred during the last speech. While thus ascertaining the meaning of Messiah's commission; that commission which contains the gospel of an eternal salvation; a commission embracing in its sublime philanthropy, all the nations of the earth and all the ages of time; I say, while thus arguing the cause of eternal truth and righteousness before heaven and earth, I feel myself not only standing in the midst of you, in the midst of this great assembly, but in the midst of a mighty host, an innumerable multitude of high intellectual and spiritual beings, who, though they are unseen by us, I am not, nor are you, my fellow-citizens, unseen by them. I hope, then, to feel my responsibilities, both to God and man, and to act faithfully in accordance with them, while I retain your attention to the point before us.

In the even tenor of my way, without turning aside to vain jangling, or
to respond to matters designed to provoke a laugh rather than conviction,
I shall proceed in the exhibition of documents and arguments addressed
to your understanding and your consciences, before the searcher of all
hearts, and in reference to your eternal destiny. The ordinances of
christianity are its greatest solemnities. They are a divine embodiment
of its salutary, life-giving, and sanctifying power, and should, therefore,
be examined in a frame of mind, and with a devotional spirit, consenta-
neous with their transcendent importance.

I have been contemplating christian baptism in its sublime allusions to
the death, burial, and resurrection of the Messiah, as a public, living,
standing, convincing monument, erected by the great benefactor of our
race, to be repeated upon every occasion of the nativity of a new member
of his redeemed family, for his grand purposes—one peculiar to the subject, and one extending to all the spectators. To him, it is a solemn
pledge of his interests in a crucified and living Redeemer ; a significant,
memorable, and honorable commencement of his christian race ; while
to the world around, it proclaims that Messiah died, shed his blood as an
expiation for the sins of the world, went down into the dark and desolate
mansions of the dead, and triumphantly rose again, opening the gates of
life and immortality to a benighted, condemned, and ruined world. An
ordinance of such significance, solemnity, and grandeur, ought to be discussed with the most profound devotion and solemn reverence for its
great author. This discussion, on my part, was not undertaken for any
momentary effect. It was not undertaken for the citizens of this city or
of this commonwealth, especially or exclusively. It was undertaken for
the whole community ; for the honor of God, the glory of the Messiah,
and the good of suffering humanity. It was, therefore, to be stereotyped
and sent on a glorious mission all round the land. Its object is to collect,
combine, arrange and exhibit, facts, documents and arguments, for all sorts
of readers, for all classes of men. Such were, and such are my views,
intentions, and aims in the whole affair. I desire to remember, to feel,
and to rejoice, that whatever of truth, of fact, of argument, I may offer,
is taken down by competent stenographers, and to be engraved upon metal.
But still, I am more influenced, and cheered, and awed, by the reflection
that there is another recording angel of an ethereal constitution, of a celestial temper, and of more than earthly competency, dignity, and grandeur, from whose pen not one iota escapes, and who writes what is
spoken here, not to be read on earth, but in heaven—not for a few days,
but through a vast, a boundless eternity. I have no use at all, then, for
any of those violent gesticulations, those theatrical attitudes, to catch
your attention, to provoke your smiles, or to hide from your observance
the inapplicability or impertinences of my arguments.

The occasion of these remarks, I doubt not, you all comprehend, and,
therefore, I shall only briefly respond to one or two of those *ad captandum*
efforts, adapted more to the facetiousness of boys than to the gravity and
dignity of men. I propounded, in my last speech, a useful law of interpretation, of more use to the uneducated and unlearned of the community,
than to those acquainted with the etymology of those languages through
which we have received the revelation of God. *Every sound grammatical and logical definition or translation of a word is convertible
with the word defined*, and therefore, we sometimes test a definition by
placing it in all places in which we find the word it defines. If it always

make good sense, it is a correct definition; if it does not, it is incorrect and to be reprobated.

To turn away your attention from this most useful and incontrovertible law, the gentleman made an effort to create a laugh, for an argument, made more ridiculous by his pantomimic gesticulation and pronunciation than by the word adduced. "In those days came John the *plunger*, *plunging* in the wilderness and preaching the *plunging* of repentance for the remission of sins." Well, now the Messiah himself was laughed at under an old scarlet cloak ! Still there was nothing ridiculous in the cloak, in itself, nor in him. It was the association, and the laugh was in the minds of the spectators.

There is not any thing grammatically, logically, scripturally, or religiously amiss in the word *plunge*. It was in the ridiculous association and manner. It is good sense; while washing in fire is nonsense. John, the dipper, or John, the immerser, or John, the plunger, or John the Baptist, are all good sense, good language, good definition and beyond censure. The principle is sound, and the sense is good : and the laugh is only in the vacuity or folly of those who are tickled by it.

So nigh the close of this proposition, I should not occupy a moment unnecessarily with such a matter; for, perhaps, this was the intention of the affair; but for the sake of all public discussions of religious questions, I am constrained to say that there is a very bad, irreligious, and pernicious taste of this sort to which disputants, too generally, cater. All christian men, and especially ministers, should set their faces against it.

By the way, while on this unworthy theme, I shall request my friend, Mr. Rice, when next he assumes the mountebank or pantomimic style, to take a little more room for it—to keep his arms a little farther from my face, and figure more within the bounds of the stage allotted him. Thus my speculations and meditations will not be quite so much incommoded. I shall demand this not so much as a favor, as a right due to me.

I shall now resume my reading of documentary proofs under my 12th argument. I promised to add only a single quotation from a most distinguished Presbyterian minister, now living. I wish you to place him in the scale against Mr. Rice, as they likely are quite antipodal on the subject. In his recent lecture on the Romans and on the passage before us, Dr. Chalmers says—

"The original meaning of the word baptisma, is *immersion*, and though we regard it as a point of indifference, whether the ordinance so named be performed in this way, or by sprinkling; yet we doubt not that the prevalent style of the administration, in the apostles' days, was by an *actual* SUBMERGING *of the whole body under water*. We advert to this for the purpose of throwing light on the analogy that is instituted in these verses. Jesus Christ, by death, underwent this sort of baptism, by an immersion under the ground, whence he soon emerged again by his resurrection."

Am I not, then, in the very best of company, when I reprobate Mr. R's. use of *kataduo*—when I say that no word could be more inappropriate ? The Dr. continues :

"We, being baptized into his death, are conceived to have made a similar translation. In the act of *descending under the water* of baptism, to have resigned an old life, and in the act of *ascending*, to emerge into the second or new life, along the course of which it is our part to maintain a strenuous avoidance of that sin, which as good as expunged the being which we had formerly, and a strenuous prosecution of that holiness which should begin with the first moments that we are ushered into our present being, and be perpetuated and made progress toward the perfection of full and ripened immortality."   x 2

It is exceedingly painful for me to read on such an occasion. I have had so much to do with facts, that I have been compelled to it: and I prefer to read from those not with us, rather than from those on our own side. This, indeed, is not so much a question of reason, as a question of fact. I averred at the commencement, that the whole matter and burthen of this proposition is a question of fact and to be decided as all such questions are. Our witnesses are lexicographers, translators, annotators, critics, commentators, historians, &c. We concluded this last class with Chalmers. He candidly, truthfully, and independently, affirms that *immersion* is the meaning of the term in sacred usage, that it was the custom of the apostolic age, and what more do we ask? He thinks sprinkling will do, in Scotland, and in the 19th century. Regarding it, however, as a matter of indifference, he affirms, like a full grown man, as he is, that the Greek and the apostolic practice are both against him; but, then, Mr. Rice says " it wont do." Chalmers is wrong and he is right. Well then, I leave it for Presbyterians to prefer their man—their leader, Dr. Chalmers, or Mr. Rice. But were Mr. R. to make himself as facetious as any comedian that ever walked the stage, he can neither talk down nor laugh down Dr. Chalmers and that mighty host, the glory of Episcopalianism and Presbyterianism, that have candidly declared for us, while taking it upon themselves to act upon their own responsibility.

I neither need special witnesses, nor special pleading on my side of the question. Therefore I have given you more witnesses, more facts than reasonings, and thrown upon my audience the responsibility of acting for themselves. When the case is a clear one, it is frequently given to the jury without much argument. The more special pleading, always the more doubtful the case, and the more precarious the testimony. My witnesses are all borrowed from the party that opposes me. You are all witnesses that I have not quoted from Dr. Gill, down to any living doctor of the Baptist church, one single sentence as argument or authority. You have now a mighty host of witnesses before you, and yet they are not the half; I might say not more than a tithe of all that might be adduced. I have chosen names well known to fame, and of unquestionable learning and authority in the several Pedo-baptist parties. It is then for you to decide whether the mere *ipse dixit* of my respondent, or a thousand like him, ought to outweigh the facts, concessions, and affirmations which I have given you.

Need I ask whether special pleadings, opinions, and mere reasonings, without the proper data of appropriate facts, will be an offset, or rather a counterbalance against such authorities? If a person possessed the highest powers of ratiocination, could he, think you, fellow-citizens, annihilate such an array of facts and authorities! I should have much less respect for the good sense and mental character of this community; of the whole American family, indeed, than what I do entertain, if I could think it behooved me, on the present occasion, to show cause and reason why you should prefer the hosts of witnesses, (many of them indeed, individually, like Chalmers, a host himself) to the opinions or dogmatic assertions of any special pleader, living or dead.

As usual, the gentleman introduces matters, and makes reference to others to which, according to the laws of discussion, I am not obliged to respond. Whatever is advanced in reply to my arguments offered, or to my facts and documents submitted, I am bound to notice. Other matters, introduced by him, are only entitled to a mere complimentary notice. It is optional, with the affirmant, how much of such matters, or whether any of them, shall be at all noticed. Several matters of this sort have received no formal attention. Some of them have, and one or two of them will come up more in my way on the third proposition. If a person were to be obliged to advert to every thing which his respondent may please to throw in his way, he would travel very slowly indeed. One person may throw out as many facts and assertions in one period, as might occupy another a week, or a month, to refute.

A fallacy to which Mr. Rice is frequently addicted, and to which the author of the Essay on Purification is no less so, is that of assuming that, if one thing be represented by two names, or two words, these words are synonymous from the circumstance of their being thus appled. For instance, suppose *washing* be applied to baptism in one case, and conversion in another—will that make washing and conversion synonymous! Baptism anciently, in the second century, was called *illumination, regeneration, the gift, sanctification, conversion,* &c. Now, because all these terms were applied to baptism, does that make baptism and any one of them synonymous; or will that make any two of them synonymous! Because baptism is called, as he alledges, the *loutron phalingenesias,* the washing of regeneration, therefore, washing and baptism are the same thing!

Before dismissing the argument, found in these allusions, to a burial, allow me to remark, that, of all the comments in the world upon baptism, this is the best. Few men know much about philology, about criticism and the etymology of words. But all men understand the meaning of the word burial. When a person is covered in the earth he is *buried,* and not till then. Now as respects baptism, being so compared, there can be no reasonable doubt. And that fact established, as all the learned, Roman Catholics and Protestants, of every name and of every party, agree, there is a burial of all doubt on this subject. Even the commentary of the Assembly of Divines so gives it. This is truly a common sense argument, as some of our greatest critics have called it. For if seeds planted in the earth, if Noah in his ark, and a man buried in the earth, are compared to baptism, or rather if baptism be compared to them, then all doubts must cease in all minds who admit the mere fact of the analogy having the sanction of the apostles. Like Calvin, or Stuart, or Chalmers, they may, indeed, suppose it a matter of indifferency, and rest satisfied that the church has a right to modify and change these institutions. But few men, comparatively, not long hackneyed in the way of clerical accommodation, will be satisfied with such a decision.

Now, inasmuch as all denominations of christians, Romanists and Protestants, orthodox and heterodox, admit that baptism is called a burial, it is at once, and as if by acclamation, confirming all our philological dissertations on the subject. The discussion properly ends, and is sanctioned here. If Jesus Christ was buried, was covered with the earth, then were the first christians all buried in baptism, or by an immersion into water.

XIII. Next to this, in plainness and strength, is the argument drawn from history. History is a very authoritative commentator on language, as well as on men and manners. It sometimes enters into the philosophy and the philology of language, and decides the proper interpretation of words, by shewing, in matter of fact details, how these words were understood in days of yore. The historians tell us what the ancients did under the name, baptism. They record certain acts and then call them by this word. They are, then, stronger proof, to the great mass of society, than dictionaries, grammars, classics, translators, or any thing in the form of mere language. History is now the favorite, the growing favorite in all departments of philosophy. The history of nature is philosophy, the history of plants is botany, the history of animals is zoology, the history of man is anthropography, and the history of the church is christianity. I mean the whole church, primitive, ancient, and modern. The history of baptism is, therefore, the philology of the word. It is the history of the human mind on that subject—of all men, of all nations, and of all ages of the church. Whenever the history of baptism is fully read, and by whomsoever, there will not remain one doubt on the meaning of *baptizo*. I affirm, without fear of successful contradiction, that all Christendom, Hebrew, Greek, Roman, and modern, down to quite a comparatively recent period, *practiced* immersion. I have given you, already, the testimony of the justly celebrated Dr. Whitby, of the church of England, affirming that immersion was religiously observed FROM THE BEGINNING, for *thirteen hundred years*, without any exception by authority, except in the case of sick and dying persons. That it was changed into *sprinkling* without any allowance by Jesus Christ, without any license from any council of the church—and that the Romanists refuse the sacramental cup to the laity, on the ground of the indulgence claimed in changing immersion into sprinkling. This being an indisputable fact, what need have we of all this controversy about the meaning of words? This fact is worth all the languages, dictionaries, commentators, and critics, of two thousand years.

The gentleman tells you of the trine immersion of Tertullian, and of their baptizing persons, not only once into each of the names of the Divinity, but also undressed! And what have we to do with these excentricities! It only makes the argument stronger; for, if they thus submitted to three immersions instead of one, how strong their faith in immersion. The gospel commands one immersion, but, it seems, they got to three.

I again ask, if the whole world, from the days of the apostles, as Calvin, Chalmers, and Whitby admit, and as all the ancient historians declare, practiced immersion—none excepted but the sick and dying, (and their baptism was not for ages regarded valid) why presumes any man to innovate and adopt another! I have here ancient copies of Eusebius, and of Scholasticus, Evagrius, and other ecclesiastical historians; Du Pin, Mosheim, Milner, Waddington, down to the last, the living Neander, and, with one consent, they confirm the affirmation of Whitby. Indeed, we can give the name of the person who first had water poured all over him in a bed. Eusebius tells the story, p. 120. This memorable case occurred in 252 or 253—and, when told by Eusebius, he adds, "if that can be called baptism." Novatian, from this copious affusion, however, recovered; but when candidate for the see of Rome, for the episcopate of the imperial city, he lost it—as some say, because of the invalidity of his baptism. The presumption is, he might have been pope of Rome, because of his distinguished parts and great learning, but for this unfortunate affusion instead of immersion. Certain it is, it did not satisfy the church, and was a cause of his reprobation.—[*Time expired.*

Saturday, Nov. 18—7 *o'clock, P M.*

[MR. RICE'S SEVENTEENTH REPLY.]

MR. PRESIDENT—Before entering upon the question before us, I wish to read an extract of a letter of Mr. Campbell to Rev. J. H. Brown. I am astonished to hear the gentleman state, that he had been forced to take *four* affirmative propositions, or have no debate.   I wish to prove by his own letter, that, so far from his statement being correct, he himself refused to debate, unless we would allow him a fourth affirmative. The truth is, we had agreed to discuss the six propositions, each party having three affirmatives and three negatives ; but when he came to Lexington in August last, to make final arrangements as to other preliminaries, he positively refused to go into a discussion, unless we would give him another affirmative proposition on baptism.   His language is the following :

" I never can yield to demands so arbitrary and unequal   If then I have given opportunity and latitude to ascertain what advantages would be sought, and how promptly you and your brethren would assume the defence of your own tenets and assail mine, *I am not to be understood as agreeing to place myself three times in the mere negative of your tenets on baptism.* Since I have been summoned by *you* to stand up to the defence of my own teaching, I must affirm my views on, at least, the two main points in which I have been most assailed by Presbyterians.   This is not only *just* and *equal*, but it is my special right, coming into this discussion as I do."

The gentleman, you perceive, here complains, that he is *thrice* in the negative on baptism, and demands, as a right, to have another affirmative. " Since I have been summoned by *you* to stand up in defence of my own teaching, I *must affirm* my views on, at least, the two main points in which I have been most assailed," &c.   Before we received this letter, the proposition we are now discussing stood thus : " Sprinkling or pouring water on a suitable subject is scriptural baptism."   In this form we had agreed to debate it ; but the gentleman insisted that he was in the negative too often, and demanded to have the proposition so worded, as to place him in the affirmative.   We accommodated him ; and now, after refusing positively to debate, unless we would give him the affirmative, he tells the audience that four affirmatives were forced on him, and that we would not enter into the discussion on any other terms ! ! !   We urged the immediate publication of the correspondence, inasmuch as the debate was so long deferred, that the public might correctly understand our relative positions, but the gentleman positively refused to permit it !

I am unable to determine whether he compliments me or the audience, when he represents me as " a pantomime," making antique gesticulations and playing off fantastic tricks for their amusement, and reproves them for allowing themselves to be thus amused.   My gestures, it seems, disturb his reflections very much ; and he desires that I should turn away from him in future.   *Aye, it is the* ARGUMENT *that so much disconcerts him.*   I am quite willing that he shall gesticulate as much as he pleases, and in his own way ; and he must allow me to make gestures as I may feel inclined.   But I wont look at him, since I thus disturb his reflections !   Oh, no.   If the gentleman had not attempted to brow-beat and confuse me this morning, I should probably not have disturbed him by exciting the risibles of the audience at his expense.

But he has repeatedly told you, that he is not speaking for *present effect ;* he is making a book, which, when read by the intelligent and learned, is to have a tremendous effect.   Does he intend to intimate, that this intelligent audience cannot comprehend his profound investigations? I have never learned that a speech which, when spoken, produces little effect, will, when read, become overwhelming. I go for present effect and for future effect. I am not afraid, that that which now produces a powerful effect, will, when printed, become perfectly powerless.

I will make a few remarks in reference to the *burial by baptism*. Dr. Chalmers, I have said, is a learned man and a great man: but against his opinion I will place the authority of Scott, Clarke, Calvin, Stuart and Hodge. Perhaps these men, thrown into the opposite scale, will outweigh Dr. C.

By the way, I was amused to hear the gentleman so confidently express his opinion, that the audience could not resist the authorities—the opinions of learned men, he has adduced in support of immersion. Such remarks appear most singular, coming from a man who has discarded all human authority, and made war upon the whole christian world. He claims to think for himself, to reject all authority; but he seems to think his hearers will not venture to do so! Of all men, it would seem, he is one of the last who ought to make such an appeal. Why, he has started a reformation *de novo!* I am quite willing to give to the opinions of the learned due weight; but I must then be permitted to make my final appeal to the word of God.

In the passsge under consideration, (Rom. vi. 1—6) Paul, as I have shown, was not speaking of the *mode* of baptism, but was proving that the Gospel, whilst it teaches the doctrine of justification by grace, without the deeds of the law, necessarily leads to holiness, and not to sin. The *death* of which he speaks, I proved to be a death to sin, and the resurrection, a resurrection to a new and holy life. If, then, the death is spiritual, and the resurrection spiritual, is not the burial also spiritual? According to my interpretation, the passage is expounded consistently; for there is spiritual death, spiritual burial, and spiritual resurrection. But if the burial is immersion, as Mr. C. contends, we have spiritual death, spiritual resurrection, and *physical* burial! Does not every one see the inconsistency of such an interpretation?

But, I again ask, if the burial expresses the mode of baptism, what mean the *planting* and the *crucifixion?* These figures are all used in the same connection, to illustrate the same great truth. The seed planted dies, and a new stalk springs up; the man crucified is dead, and so our old sinful nature is by the grace of God overcome, and we cease to sin, and live a holy life. Christ was crucified, died for sin, was buried, and rose again for the justification of his people. They who are baptized into Christ profess and, if sincere, feel an ardent desire to be identified with him in his death, burial, and resurrection—to die *to* sin as he died *for* it; to have " the old man," the sinful nature, crucified, dead, and buried, as Christ was buried; to rise to a new and holy life, as he rose from the grave to die no more. Christian baptism is the ordinance by which we become visibly identified with Christ, receive the benefits of his death, and are bound more strongly to a life of holiness. Such appears to me to be the clear meaning of the passage; and, as before remarked, since the apostle is speaking of holiness of heart and of life secured by the gospel, and since sanctification is in the Bible constantly represented by pouring and sprinkling; this portion of Scripture, correctly understood, is decidedly favorable to this mode of administering baptism.

The gentleman is disposed to make an argument for immersion from the fact of the burial of our Savior in the earth. But I ask, was he put *under ground?* Never, never. A place was cut in a rock, in which he was laid, and a stone rolled against the entrance. When persons in our country and in our day read of a burial, they at once think of a place dug in the earth, into which the dead are put and covered with earth. But this was not the mode of burial among the Jews. And the Romans, to whom the epistle was directed, did not thus bury their dead. They were accustomed to *burn* the bodies of the dead, and to gather the ashes into an urn. Hence, every one accustomed to read Latin writers, is familiar with the expression, *ashes of the dead.* Indeed, this mode of expression has been transferred, in a figurative sense, to our own language.

What idea, then, I ask, would be conveyed to the Roman christians by the language in the passage under consideration? The expression, "buried by baptism," certainly never would have suggested to their minds the idea of plunging persons under water. And this is the correct method to determine the meaning of the language. If we would correctly interpret an ancient book, we must go to those by whom, and those for whom it was written, and inquire into their manners, customs, and opinions. Many are led into error, by taking it for granted that the manners and customs of ancient nations were similar to ours.

Let it be remembered, too, that the mere fact of the burial of our Savior is never mentioned in the Bible as a matter of primary importance. His death, the shedding of his blood, and his resurrection from the dead, are presented to our minds as laying the foundation of our hopes; but the mere fact, that his friends laid him in a tomb, is not so presented. It is not probable, therefore, inasmuch as the supper commemorates his death, that the other sacrament, baptism, is designed to commemorate his resurrection *out of a tomb.*

I must proceed without much system, until I get through my reply to the gentleman's speech. He has brought forward what he considers an irresistible weight of authority to prove the proposition he is affirming. He has quoted amongst the Pedo-baptists who have made concessions, old Cyril, who believed in trine immersion; and Wall, who was very solicitous to have immersion practiced, except in cases where it was impracticable; and Whitby, who was of the same mind! But the misfortune is, not one of those Pedo-baptists immersionists (for many of those quoted were such) sustains his proposition. He may appeal to the old Greek and Latin immersionists of the third and fourth centuries, and to all those of a later day; but of all the learned authors he has quoted, or can quote, he can find not one, save the Anabaptists, who believed the the doctrine for which he is contending to be true! Their knowledge of the Greek, and the strong prejudices of multitudes of them in favor of immersion, even of *trine immersion,* did not enable them to see in the Scriptures, what he sees with the clearness of light itself!!! If the gentleman, and those who on this subject agree with him, had only occupied the ground of the old immersionists, or of those more modern writers, whose learning he extols, and of whose authority he boasts; there need not have been any controversy on the subject. They might quietly have enjoyed their preferences for immersion; and we would have enjoyed ours for pouring or sprinkling, without exciting controversy and divisions of the church of Christ. But when they assume to know more about the Greek than the Greeks themselves, more than all antiquity and the great body of the learned of modern times; and when on this assumption of superior knowledge, they undertake to excommunicate all who cannot see with their eyes; we are constrained to demur.

We are not discussing the question, whether the church, in any period of her history, has generally practiced immersion; nor even whether it was sometimes practiced in the days of the apostles; *but whether the submersion of the person in water is essential to christian baptism.* And let it be remarked, not one of the gentleman's learned authorities has sustained him in affirming this proposition. Not an individual of them believed submersion in water to be the only apostolic or christian baptism. Yet, whilst himself differing from almost the whole world, he seems to suppose that the audience cannot resist these multiplied authorities, every one of whom falls far short of sustaining him; every one of whom lived and died in the firm persuasion, that baptism, by pouring or sprinkling, is valid and scriptural! I cannot help thinking he had better try to prove his doctrine by argument, for his authorities fail him essentially.

But, says the gentleman, suppose it is true that baptism is called a *washing;* does this prove that *baptizo* means to *wash?* Certainly, I should think, if baptism is a washing, as the Scriptures so repeatedly teach, *baptizo* must mean to *wash*, and *baptisma*, a washing. So thought the lexicographers; for they all define *baptizo* to *wash, cleanse, purify.* This they give as a literal meaning of the word; and I have no doubt they are in the right. That the word, as appropriated to the ordinance of baptism, is employed in the general sense of washing, is clear from the fact that baptism is so frequently spoken of as a *washing*, not as a *dipping* or *plunging.*

We are informed, however, by Mr. Campbell, that the concurrent voice of all Christendom says, that baptism is a *burial.* This is a wide mistake. Many of the ablest commentators and writers have denied that baptism is a burial, that is, that it is a putting the body under water. Indeed, the concurrent voice of Christendom denies that it is a burial in this sense; for the great majority, at this day, do not practice immersion; and yet they regard themselves as truly baptized; and since the ancients admitted baptism to be valid, when performed by pouring or sprinkling, they could not have considered it necessarily a burial.

All Christendom, the gentleman repeats, practiced immersion for thirteen hundred years. This, too, is a mistake; or, at least, it cannot be proved true. For, as I have already proved, we find not a word about immersion from any respectable writer for the first two hundred years of the christian era. The first writer of any standing who speaks of immersion is Tertullian, in the beginning of the third century; and he says, the practice then was trine immersion, with sign of the cross, oil, spittle, &c. Will Mr. Campbell practice baptizing according to the custom of the church at that period? No—he rejects two of the immersions, the sign of the cross, the oil, &c.; and yet he appeals to the authority of the ancient church! In those days they objected to *one* immersion as decidedly as to pouring or sprinkling. Indeed, they considered it a matter of such importance, that in one of the early councils, as Dr. Gale informs us, it was decreed, that a bishop should be deposed if he ventured to baptize a person by *one* immersion only! The ancient church considered his practice quite as heretical as ours and even more so, for they universally admitted the validity of our mode. If, then, the gentleman claims the ancient church in support of immersion, I insist, that he ought to immerse three times, having the persons entirely disrobed. It will not answer to call in witnesses, and then reject four-fifths of their testimony. But, in the fourth century, as I have proved, immersion was, by no means, universally practiced; and from that period the practice of pouring and sprinkling became more and more common. And let it be remembered, I have found pouring or sprinkling universally admitted to be valid and scriptural, even earlier than the gentleman can find immersion. Such was the decision of the bishop concerning the Jew taken ill in the desert, and sprinkled with sand—and such the decision of Cyprian, and sixty-six bishops, in the early part of the third century. Where the gentleman finds immersion, he finds it connected with much that he is not willing to practice. He rejects so much of the testimony of the old immersionists as he dislikes. I hope, then, he will allow me the same right, unless he is disposed to claim peculiar privileges for the cause of immersion.

In the fifth century baptism was, in many parts of the church, very commonly administered by pouring or sprinkling; and this practice became more and more common till the period of the glorious Reformation, in the sixteenth century. And it is not a little remarkable, that since the Reformation restored the Bible to the people, and since it has been made the study of so many of the wise and the good, the overwhelming mass of the christian church—the Bible reading people—have entirely abandoned the practice of immersion, and now baptize by pouring and sprinkling. Those who contend for immersion alone are a mere handfull; making, perhaps, one in fifty of protestant Christendom. Moreover, in the ranks of those who practice pouring and sprinkling are to be found the great majority of eminently learned expounders of the Scriptures! History can afford little aid to sustain the exclusive claims of immersion. The Greeks and Latins, the ancients and the moderns, however prejudiced multitudes of them were in favor of immersion, have, with wonderful unanimity, proclaimed our baptism valid and scriptural, and the doctrine of Mr. C. untrue! If, then, this controversy is to be determined by the authority of the learned, of those who best understood the Greek language; he must yield the question. For all his Pedo-baptist concessions I will give him, in return, the concessions of immersionists, whose vernacular tongue was the Greek, or who lived when it was a living language.

I wish now to review the argument on the whole question before us. Let us, then, have distinctly before our minds the proposition he has undertaken to establish: viz. *that immersion of the person in water is the one only apostolic or christian baptism;* and consequently all who have received the ordinance in any other mode are unbaptized, and are "aliens from the commonwealth of Israel!" This sweeping proposition he has sought to prove, mainly by the words *bapto* and *baptizo*. The whole controversy, as he admits, turns chiefly on the meaning of these words. To prove that they are specific terms, expressing definitely the *action* of immersing, he appealed—

1st. To the lexicons, ancient and modern, of which he quoted a large number. But mark the fact: I appealed to the same lexicons, and proved, that with almost entire unanimity, they define these words to *wash, cleanse, purify,* as well as to plunge, sink, &c. Some of them, both ancient and modern, defined them to *wet, moisten, sprinkle.* Now all admit that these words—*wash, cleanse,* &c. are generic terms, expressing *the thing done,* but not the *mode of doing it.* If then, it be true, as all the lexicons, ancient and modern, declare, that these words mean to wash,

Y

cleanse, &c,, how is it possible for the gentleman, by them, to prove immersion? Every one knows that washing, cleansing, purifying, may be performed in different modes. So the lexicons, instead of proving these words to be specific in their meaning, definitely expressing the action of immersing, prove just the opposite—that they are often used as generic terms, expressing washing, cleansing, purifying *in any mode*.

But the gentleman told us, *bapto* and *baptizo* meant to wash, to cleanse, &c., not in a proper or literal, but only in a *figurative* sense; and he labored faithfully to find *one lexicon* to sustain him in this position. He brought forward Stokius, who says, *baptizo* means to wash *tropically;* but unfortunately for him I immediately proved, by Ernesti and Stuart, that the *tropical* or *secondary* meaning of words is, in a great many instances, their *proper* and *literal* meaning; that very few words in any language retain their original meaning, much the larger number of them acquiring tropical or secondary meanings, which become proper and literal. Carson, whom the gentleman admits to be a profound linguist, also asserts, that the secondary meaning of *bapto*, (*to dye by sprinkling*,) is as literal as the primary meaning. And the lexicons, *en masse*, give to wash, cleanse, as *literal* meanings of *baptizo*.

Mr. Campbell has insisted, that *immerse* is the *primary*, *original*, and *proper* meaning of *baptizo*. But unfortunately again I proved, that the meaning of words is constantly changing—that few words retain their primary or original meanings. Moreover, the lexicons do give *to wash*, *to cleanse*, as the *first*, the *primary* meaning of *baptizo*, as used by the Jews and inspired writers. The lexicons, therefore, though he so much relied on them, have all failed him. But, he says, they were all Pedobaptists, and were often in error! Right or wrong, they give to these words precisely the definition for which I contend. *They are with me!*

2nd. His second appeal was to the *classics*. He had very learnedly taught us, that all specific words, having a leading syllable, retain their original idea, and therefore wherever we should find *bap*, as in *bapto*, we would also find the idea of *dipping*. He was again unfortunate. I turned to a few passages in the classics, and found *bapto* used to express the dyeing of a garment by the dropping of the coloring fluid, the dyeing of the beard, the hair, the coloring of the face, the staining of the hands, the coloring of a lake, &c., all by the application of the fluid to the person or thing, not by dipping. In all these instances, and others, we found the syllable *bap*, and even *bapto* itself, where there was no dipping, no immersing.

But, said the gentleman, *bapto*, in these instances, expresses not the dropping, smearing, &c., but the *effect*. The *effect!* The effect of what? The effect of dipping, immersing? No; for there was no dipping, no immersing in the case. It must, then, express the effect of *dropping*, *wetting*, *smearing*. Then where is the immersing? And if *bapto* will express the effect of the dropping of a coloring fluid, why not also the effect of a colorless fluid—wetting? Mr. C. responds again, these are *figurative* meanings of the word. No, says Mr. Carson, his profound linguist; they are as literal as the primary meaning. So that the classical usage of *bapto* cannot help the cause of immersion; and since *bapto* and *baptizo* are admitted to have the same meaning, at least so far as mode is concerned, *baptizo* must also be given up.

I, however, went with my friend to the classics to ascertain their usage in regard to *baptizo*. I found it, in four-fifths of the instances supposed to favor immersion, meaning *to sink*, and so translated by Mr. Carson, Dr. Gale, and by the gentleman himself! I found it constantly used to signify the sinking of ships, the sinking of animals and men under water, the flowing of water over land; and I proved that Dr. Gale, one of the most learned and zealous immersionists, whilst commenting on one of these difficult passages in the classics, admitted that *baptizo* did not necessarily express the *action* of putting under water—*the very thing and the only thing Mr. Campbell was laboring to prove by it!!!* The Doctor had found a place in which *baptizo* was employed, where it was perfectly certain there could be no *action* of dipping, or of any other kind. I produced a passage from Plutarch, in which he spoke of a Roman general who, when dying of his wounds, baptized (*baptisas*) his hand with his blood, and wrote on a trophy. In this instance every one sees, at once, there could be no immersion—nothing more than a *wetting* of a finger or writing instrument. Yet the hand was baptized. I produced also a quotation from Hippocrates, where he directed, concerning a blister-plaster, that it should be baptized (*baptizein*) with breast-milk and Egyptian ointment. The gentleman did not attempt to remove the blister-plaster. It has been on him now some two days, and I have serious apprehensions that it has drawn too much! He could not immerse it in breast-milk, as the doctor directed, so I fear it has drawn very severely. [A laugh.] The classics will not sustain him; they must be given up.

3d. The gentleman's third appeal was to the *translations;* and he informed us, they were almost, if not quite all, in favor of immersion. If I am not mistaken, he relied for his proof exclusively on a little essay of a few pages, written by a Mr. Gotch, of Dublin, whose fame has never crossed the waters, except amongst immersionists! I was not a little surprised to see Mr. Campbell relying for the support of his cause on evidence so slender!

He commenced with the venerable old Peshito Syriac, the oldest and one of the best translations in the world, made, if our immersionist friends are to be believed, before pouring and sprinkling were known. I happened to have the Syriac Testament and Schaaf's lexicon. I proved, that Schaaf defined *amad*, (the Syriac word by which *baptizo* is translated,) by the Latin phrase *abluit se*—he washed himself; and all admit, that *abluo* is a *generic term*, signifying to *wash*, to *cleanse in any mode*. I further proved, that Schaaf, Castel, Michaelis and Buxtorf could find not one instance in the New Testament, where *amad* means to *immerse*, and but one in the Old Testament; and even in that neither the Hebrew word nor the Greek of the Septuagint has that meaning. I proved by Mr. Gotch himself, the gentleman's own witness, that *amad* is used in the Bible in the general sense of washing—*abluit se*. I also stated, (and it has not been, and will not be denied) that the Syriac language has a word (*tzeva*) which properly means *to dip*, but which is never used with reference to christian baptism. *The old Syriac is with us, translating* BAPTIZO, *not to immerse, but to* WASH, CLEANSE *without regard to mode.*

I then turned your attention to the *old Italic version*, and the *Vulgate*, translated by the learned Jerom; and in both these venerable versions we found the word baptizo not translated by the Latin words *mergo, immergo*, &c., but *transferred*, just as in our English version. In the only instance where Jerom translated the word, he translated it by *lavo*, to wash—a generic term. Mr. Campbell told us, that *baptizo* was understood by the Latins to mean *immerse*, and therefore was not translated. This was immediately disproved by showing, that they frequently baptized by pour-ing and sprinkling, and with entire unanimity regarded baptism thus per-formed as valid and scriptural—nay, that many really believed, that John the Baptist administered baptism by pouring. *The old Italic and Vul-gate, therefore, must be abandoned.*

I then turned your attention to the Arabic version, of highest authority, and stated, (and it has not been denied) that it employs in translating *bap-tizo*, the same word in form and signification as the Syriac. I appealed to the Persic version, which is admitted to have translated *baptizo* by a word meaning *to wash.* I further appealed to the Ethiopic, the Sahidic, the Basmuric, the Arminian, the German, the Swedish, the Danish, the Anglo-Saxon, Arias Montanus, the Geneva Bible, the French, the Span-ish, Tyndale's translation, proving by Mr. Gotch, the gentleman's own witness, that a number of them translated *baptizo* by generic terms, signi-fying *washing, ablution,* and declaring myself prepared to produce the others, and to prove that they do not countenance the idea, that it means definitely *to immerse. And now I ask, has the gentleman given evi-dence that any one respectable translation, ancient or modern, translates this word* TO IMMERSE? No, and I venture to say, he cannot. THE TRANSLATIONS MUST BE GIVEN UP. His third strong-hold has been taken!

4th. He was very slow, indeed, in getting into the Bible, and thus far, has passed over it very superficially. In regard to *bapto*, I stated the fact, that although it occurs in the Bible *more than twenty times*, it does not express an immersion in more than four or five instances. *This fact Mr. C. has not denied.* I have produced examples in which it means a partial dipping, wetting, smearing;—examples also in which it is used in con-nection with *apo* (*from,*) and of necessity signifies *to wet or moisten by means of.* I turned to the passage in Dan. iv. 33, where Nebuchadnez-zar was said to have been *wet from* (*ebaphe apo*) the dew of heaven. The gentleman, however, will have it, that by some strange figure of speech he was *immersed from* the dew!!! I turned to Rev. xix. 13, and proved, in the face of the repeated assertions of my friend, that *bapto* was here translated *to sprinkle* by the old Syriac, the Ethiopic and the Vul-gate versions, and that the learned Origen, in giving the sense of the pas-sage, substituted *rantizo* for *bapto.* But the gentleman guessed, that there was another reading. What evidence does he furnish? Is there any copy of the New Testament having another reading? No. Does Origen give another? No—he only gives the meaning of the passage. There is absolutely no evidence. Still the Bible itself must be altered to sustain immersion! This same Origen, moreover, used *baptizo* in the sense of *pouring.* The altar, he said, was baptized when water was *poured* upon it by the order of Elisha. *This is high authority.*—[*Time expired.*

Saturday, Nov. 18—7 o'clock, P. M.

[MR. CAMPBELL'S CLOSING ADDRESS.]

MR. PRESIDENT—This is the last time that I am to address you, sir, on this proposition. Numerous topics yet demand attention, and therefore, we must notice the most important of them with despatch. The version of the previous correspondence which you have heard is not correct. This shall be shewn at a proper time. Indeed it will appear with the debate *in extenso*, and will then speak for itself. I am glad that it is all written, and to be published without note or comment.

It is not a fact that the proposition which I sustain differs from every other proposition on the action of baptism. In one or two words it may differ, but all Baptists maintain it as fully as I do. It is not true, that no former writers on this same subject have taken the same view of it. Multitudes in all ages have believed that immersion is the only christian baptism. All Pedo-baptist writers do indeed dissent from it, for they believe in a plurality of modes of baptism. I believe there are not two Lords, two faiths, nor two baptisms. When I prove that immersion is baptism, there being but one baptism, I have then proved that immersion is the only christian baptism.

This is the ground on which I stand. Before heaven and earth I affirm the full conviction that there is but one true Lord, one true faith, one true baptism; and *that* baptism is immersion. I care not, so far as my popularity is concerned, how unpopular the affirmation may be. I most benevolently, honestly, and conscientiously avow my conviction, that he who has not been immersed in water, into the name of Father, Son, and Holy Spirit, has never received christian baptism. All Baptists believe thus.

There is a true and a false charity; the former is a virtue, the latter a vice. I care not if it were written over the whole earth and through all the heavens, that I have said so. I declare this conviction, not from the impulse of the moment; but after many years calm, devout, and concentrated attention to the subject. Many are the treatises examined, many the authors read on the opposite side of this question; but after full thirty years reflection on the subject, I am the more deeply penetrated with the solemn and important truth of the proposition which I have been sustaining. The renunciation of my traditional belief cost me many a severe trial, and subjected me to a life of labors equal, I presume, to those of any other man of my age in this community. But for that change of views, and a concomitant desire in all other things to follow the consecrated and divinely approbated model of the primitive faith, worship, and manners, I might have led as easy a life, as pertains to the present, as any of my preaching brethren, whose sails are filled with the popular breeze of admiring multitudes, and who, upon a smooth sea, are gently sailing to a better country. Before attempting to enumerate the arguments offered on the present occasion, I must again recur to the only proper issue formed, and the only real discussion had, between myself and my respondent on the present proposition. Assertions are cheap commodities, but arguments based on facts, are stubborn things. The gist of the whole debate has, so far as language is concerned, turned upon the *proper*, *grammatical*, or *litere' ~ ning* of *baptizo*. Various words, such as *dip*, *immerse*, *merge*, *immerge*, *plunge*—all indicative of one and the same action, have been submitted by me, as its one, only, proper meaning. Mr. Rice has offered wash, cleanse, sink, wet, as other meanings equally *proper*—both agreeing that the proper meanings is the true meaning here. These meanings resolved ultimately into *wash*. He has all along sought to make it the primitive, proper, and literal meaning of the word. That question was fully decided to-day in the final verdict of the New Testament Pedobaptist lexicons. I have never witnessed greater confusion in any controversy in which I have been engaged, or indeed, at which I have been present, than displayed by Mr. Rice, on the occasion of taking from him this grand and fallacious assumption. Wash was demonstrated to be merely a circumstantial, accidental, or *casual* meaning of the word, and not at all its proper meaning. His confusion was such, after a refusal to refer the matter, that he threw himself headlong into Ernesti; forgot, or lost the point of discussion, and went on to read that in some cases words wholly lose their proper meaning, and that a *tropical* meaning becomes the proper one ; at the same moment denying with all his energy, that wash was a *tropical* meaning !!   He opened Ernesti to prove that tropical meanings became proper, while denying that wash was a tropical meaning ; and finally, again attempted to prove that tropes were not figures, and that a figurative and a tropical meaning are quite different matters !!   A victory more complete in a question of philology could neither be wished nor expected by any one conversant with all the difficulties attendant on Greek philology and criticism, in the presence of an ordinary English assembly.   The gentleman's assertions upon these subjects, I am sorry to say, appear to me throughout superlatively reckless ; but they are now matters of record and I must commend them to the cautious acceptance of those into whose hands they may fall.

To resume the argument from history, the gentleman will have Tertullian to be a sort of cotemporary with the origin of immersion.   Trine immersion he ought to have said ; for trine immersion and *katadusis*, as a favorite word with one or two Greek fathers, were indeed cotemporaries ; but Tertullian denies that *three* immersions (not one immersion) had an ancient origin.   Sprinkling was never heard of till A. D. 251.   I am truly astonished at such assertions, in the face of all our ecclesiastical writers.   I cannot, however, regret to hear them from Mr. Rice, just at this moment.   They will serve as cautions to all, touching that confidence due to all his assertions on such matters.   The gentleman has even asserted that I have admitted that *bapto* in the Old Testament, does not always mean to dip !

And I have said, according to him, that the lexicons are all wrong ! And what have I not said that suited his purpose to make me say !! One thing, however, I now say, that I have neither now, nor at any former period, heard one objection to my views on this question, or an argument in favor of anything different from immersion, that, in my candid judgment, weighed as much as one atom in counterpoise with a mountain.   Much more than we have now heard, lies spread over the pages of Pedo-baptism, and is often received by Baptists without any other emotion than sympathy for the prejudices of its authors.

But I could read from Barnabas, the shepherd of Hermas ; and Justin Martyr, who, next to the apostles, stand on the page of ecclesiastical history.   I can now only read a sentence, however, from Barnabas : "Considering," says Barnabas, "how he has joined both the cross and the water together ; for this he saith : Blessed are they who, putting their trust in the cross, *descend into* the water."   Again: "*We go down into the water* full of sin and pollutions, but come up again, bringing forth fruit, having in our hearts the fear and the hope which is in Jesus."   This is plain enough immersion and emersion.   I could read you several such passages, from the highest authority, to the same effect.   Not only Mosheim, Neander, but *all the historians*, as well as professor Stuart, trace trine immersion to the times of the apostles.   Stuart, indeed, in commenting on Justin Martyr's Apology, admits that it is decidedly in favor of immersion ; and concerning the Oriental church, he avows a full conviction that it *has always immersed.*   To quote only one passage from him on this subject, he says :

Stuart : "The mode of baptism by immersion, the Oriental church has always continued to preserve, even down to the present time : see Allatii de

Eccles. Orient. et Occident. lib. iii. ch. 12. sec. 4; Acta et Script. Theol.
Wirtemb. et Patriarch. Constant. Jer. p. 63, p. 238 sq. Christ. Angeli
Enchirid. de Statu hodierno Græcor. ch. 24: Augusti, Denkwurd. vii. p.
226. sq. The members of this church are accustomed to call the members
of the western churches *sprinkled christians*, by way of ridicule and contempt: Walch's Einleit. in die relig. Streitigkeiten, Th. V. pp. 476—481.
They maintain that *baptizo* can mean nothing but immerge ; and that *baptism by sprinkling* is as great a solecism as *immersion* by *aspersion* ; and they
claim to themselves the honor of having preserved the ancient sacred rite of
the church free from change and from corruption, which would destroy its
significancy : see Alex. de Stourdza, Considerations sur la Doctrine el l'Es-
prit de l'Eglise Orthodoxe, Stutt. 1816, pp. 83—89.

F. Brenner, a Roman Catholic writer, has recently published a learned
work, which contains a copious history of usages in respect to the baptismal
rite : viz. Geschichtliche Darstellung der Verrichtung der Taufe, etc. 1818.
I have not seen the work ; but it is spoken of highly, on account of the diligence and learning which the author has exhibited in his historical details.
The result of them respecting the point before us, I present, as given by
Augusti, Denkwurd. vii. p. 68.

" Thirteen hundred years was baptism generally and ordinarily performed
by the immersion of a man under water ; and only in extraordinary cases,
was sprinkling or affusion permitted. These latter methods of baptism
were called in question, and even prohibited." Brenner adds, " For fifteen
hundred years was the person to be baptized, either by immersion, or affusion, entirely divested of his garments."

These results will serve to show, what a Roman Catholic writer feels
himself forced by historical facts to allow, in direct contradiction to the
present practice of his own church ; which no where pratices immersion,
except in the churches of Milan ; it being every where else even forbidden.

In the work of John Floyer on cold bathing, page 50, it is mentioned
that the English church practiced *immersion* down to the beginning of the
seventeenth century ; when a change to the method of sprinkling gradually
took place. As a confirmation of this, it may be mentioned, that the first
liturgy in 1547 enjoins a *trine immersion*, in case the child is not sickly :
Augusti, ut sup. page 229."

My readings from Whitby give the same representations. Out of
documents that would require a day's discussion, I can read but a short
extract from the Edinburgh Encyclopædia :

" The first law for sprinkling was obtained in the following manner :
Pope Stephen II. being driven from Rome by Adolphus, king of the Lom-
bards in 753, fled to Pepin, who, a short time before, had usurped the crown
of France. Whilst he remained there, the monks of Cressy, in Brittany,
consulted him whether in case of necessity, baptism poured on the head of
the infant would be lawful. Stephen replied that it would. But though
the truth of this fact be allowed—which, however, some Catholics deny—
yet pouring, or sprinkling, was admitted only in *cases of necessity*. It was
not till the year 1311 that the legislature, in a council held at Ravenna,
declared immersion or sprinkling to be indifferent. In Scotland, however,
sprinkling was never practiced in ordinary cases, till after the reformation
(about the middle of the sixteenth century.) From Scotland, it made its
way into England, in the reign of Elizabeth, but was not authorized in the
established church."—*Art. Baptism.*

So the more intelligent and candid Pedo-baptists concur in fixing the
origin of sprinkling according to law, in the council of Ravenna, and in
the year 1311. Sprinkling is, indeed, traced to one of the darkest periods in church history ; yet, in the face of these facts, Mr. Rice asserts
that it was the custom of the primitive church, till about the time of

Tertullian, and that the church degenerated from sprinkling to immersion!! Such was the antiquity and universality of immersion, and such was the origin and authority of sprinkling. The facts are, therefore, as before stated. The whole church, oriental and occidental, practiced immersion for 1300 years. The eastern half still continues the practice—the western half took the benefit of the Pope's indulgence only gradually. England, as Erasmus sportively said, not so tractable as the Dutch, still holds on to immersion. The English Protestant church was a Baptist church for a considerable time. The first Protestant king, Edward the sixth, was immersed. The first Protestant queen, Elizabeth, was immersed. It was, through Calvin's influence, introduced into Scotland; and in the course of half a century, generally prevailed. All the adults brought, by conquest, into the Roman empire, and others migratory into it, on profession of the faith, were immersed, as well as infants ; so that there has been always an immense majority of immersionists or Baptists. Affusion, never, till the last two or three hundred years, fully satisfied any portion of Christendom. Clinics, or unimmersed persons, were inhibited holy orders, by the twelfth canon of the council of Neocesarea, and consequently, were ineligible to sacerdotal functions. With regard to the relative proportions of *immersed* and *sprinkled* persons, in all time, I will read another short extract from my book on baptism :

" Now, allow an average of one hundred millions every third of a century to have been baptized, which is certainly within the limits of the actual number, (but it will show the ratios just as well as the true number,) then we have for eighteen centuries, in all, five thousand five hundred millions ; of this number, four thousand millions were immersed during the first thirteen centuries. Then we have the one-half of five centuries, which is seven hundred and fifty millions, added to four thousand millions,—giving an aggregate of four thousand seven hundred and fifty millions immersed, for seven hundred and fifty millions sprinkled, during all the ages of christianity ; that is in the ratio of seven immersed to one sprinkled. In making this estimate, we have given all that have been immersed in the western half of Christendom for the last five hundred years, to compensate for all the clinics that were sprinkled during the first thirteen centuries. After making the most reasonable deductions which can be demanded, we have an immense majority of immersed professors, compared with the sprinkled. This argument is not urged in proof of the truth of our position, but as a refutation of those who would represent immersion as a small affair, in the esteem of all ages, compared with sprinkling."

This estimate, or any other based on any aggregate population, distributed as above, will give, in all time, SEVEN TO ONE. So that the question is not, where shall we find a Baptist church in every century ? but, where shall we find a church of sprinkled christians ?

I shall now attempt a very rapid and brief recapitulation. I have not time, however, more than to name the items. I could, in imitation of my boastful friend, assert in wholesale style, and tell of all that I have proved, and all that he has not proved ; as from what is past, I will prognosticate he will do. But, fellow-citizens, you must judge for yourselves, at last, and not from our imaginations or assertions of what we have proved.

If, then, I have not miscounted, I have offered in all thirteen distinct arguments in proof of the first proposition.

I. I argued from the law of specific words, to which class *bapto* and *baptizo* belongs—showing from the philosophy of words indicative of *specific* action and from usage, that while such words retain their radical form, they retain the radical idea. Thus in the case of *baptizo*, while ever we retain the *bap* we have the dip in *fact* or in *figure*. No proper exception was found to this rule.

II. *Baptizo*, according to *all the lexicons* of eighteen hundred years, signifies to dip, immerse, plunge, as its literal, proper, original meaning; and is *never found* translated by *sprinkle* or *pour* in any dictionary from the christian era down to the present century. No example was given contrary to this fact. The gentleman labored to construct exceptions from casual meanings, but found not one such rendering in all those lexicons.

III. The classics were copiously alledged in proof of all that argued from the lexicons. No instance was adduced from them subversive of the facts alledged from the dictionaries.

IV. All the translations, ancient and modern, were appealed to in confirmation of the above facts. From a very liberal induction of the ancient and modern versions, it did not appear that in any one case any translator had ever translated *baptizo* by the words sprinkle or pour; but that it had been frequently translated dip, immerse, &c. Of modern translations, I have examined many, and though this word occurs one hundred and twenty times, it is *never* translated by the words preferred by the Pedobaptists.

V. My fifth class of evidence offered, consisted of the testimonies of reformers, annotators, paraphrasts, and critics, respecting the meaning of *baptizo*; selected, too, as under every branch of evidence, from the ranks of those whose practice was contrary to ours. This whole class, amongst whom were Luther, Calvin, Grotius, Witsius, Vossius, Vitringeo, &c., declare that in the New Testament use of the word, it means to immerse, and some of them say, in so many words, " *never to sprinkle.*"

VI. Our sixth argument consisted of the testimony of English lexicographers, encyclopœdias and reviews, whose testimony sustains that of the reformers, annotators, and critics.

VII. Our seventh argument was an exhibit of the words in construction with *baptizo—raino* and *cheo*—showing a very peculiar uniformity never lost sight of in a single instance; shewing that to sprinkle and pour have necessarily *upon* and never *in* after them: while *baptizo* has *in* or *into* after it, and never *upon;* an argument to which Mr. Rice made no reply whatever, and, indeed, no response to it could be given. It is, indeed, as I conceive, the clearest and most convincing argument in the department of philology, because it groups in one view the whole controversy on all the prepositions and verbs in debate. I believe it to be unanswerable.

VIII. Our eighth argument was deduced from the places mentioned in the Bible, intimating that much water was necessary. There is not one intimation in the Bible of ever bringing water to the candidates; but there are intimations of taking them out to rivers, and places of much water. Mr. R. could give no reason for going to the Jordan to wet one's fingers, or out of doors to baptize any one, if sprinkling had been the practice.

IX. The ninth argument was deduced from the first law of the decalogue of philology—which makes all true definitions and translations of terms convertible. Which, when applied to *baptizo*, clearly proves that in the New Testament it cannot possibly signify to sprinkle, pour, wash, or purify.

X. Our tenth argument was drawn from the principal objections of Pedo-baptists, showing that in these very objections there is farther evidence in demonstration of immersion.

XI. The eleventh argument asserted the overwhelming fact, that sprinkling common water, or pouring it on any person or thing, was never commanded by God under any dispensation of religion, for any purpose whatever. This unanswered argument is fatal to the whole plan of sprinkling advanced by Mr. Rice.

XII. Our twelfth evidence consisted of the allusions used by inspired men in reference to baptism; their comparing it to a *burial* and *resurrection*, to a planting of seed, and in making it a sort of antitype of water and the ark during the deluge. To this last argument, admitted by all the great founders and luminaries of Protestant parties, Mr. Rice has instituted a recent discovery, made, I think, at Andover, New England; which in effect says, that baptism is not compared to a burial. The gentleman, if I understand him, denies the proper burial of Greeks, Romans, and Jews, and even of the Messiah, to get rid of this figure. It exceedingly annoys him. I do not wonder at it; though I wonder at his temerity in speaking of the Messiah's burial as a thing of "no consequence any how." I say I do not wonder at his opposition to the fact of a real common sense burial; for that admitted, and he must say, with Chalmers and all enlightened men, that certainly, in the apostolic age, they immersed, they buried men in water. Cannot a person be buried in a rock? Is a rock not earth? Is not a grave cut into a rock, a grave as much as if dug out of sand or earth? If a grave of one or two rooms, such as the sepulchres of the rich, be cut into a rock on the side, or even summit of a hill, and a corpse laid in it, and the door closed; is not the person covered in the earth? Jesus, according to him, lay not like Jonah three days and nights in the heart of the earth. If there was no burial, there may be a revival, but no resurrection. I wonder no more at his freedom with Greek philology—Greek verbs, and translations, and declensions—if the facts of the literal and proper burial and resurrection of the Messiah must be set at nought, to find for him an escape from christian immersion. Fellow-citizens—my Presbyterian friends, are you prepared for this? Do you reject the burial of Jesus, to get rid of being "buried with him by an immersion into death;" as many of your own doctors translate, and you should read it. Are you prepared to say, that the ancient Jews, Abraham, Isaac, Jacob, Joseph, Moses, and David, were not buried? or that Jesus did not rise and come forth from the earth? Ah me! methinks it matters not what have been the forms of graves, the rites of sepulture, the formalities of interment, at any time or in any country. The earth has opened its mouth and devoured all. All came from the dust, and all return to it again; youth and old age, beauty and deformity, rich and poor, noble and ignoble, all go down *into* the earth. Jesus, who is the resurrection and the life, went down with them into the bosom of the earth, that he might open for them a way out of it. What more fitting, then, in making the christian profession, than that we should die to sin and earth; and being buried with our Lord in water, rising out of it in token of our being born again, to live a new and holy life; that being raised with Christ, we may place our affections on things above!

XIII. My thirteenth, or last argument, the history of baptism and of sprinkling, you have just now heard. You have heard that all the Greek and Latin fathers from the very earliest antiquity—from the very age of the

apostles, according to our historians ;—and indeed the oriental church always—and the western church, for thirteen centuries, practiced immersion-
What further evidence can any one desire! Now, as I have already stated,
*if only one of these thirteen arguments be true and valid, immersion, and
immersion only, is established forever beyond a rational doubt or contradiction.* Any one of them is enough! How irresistible, then, to the candid mind, the accumulated evidence of them all! In addition to the maintenance of these positions, I believe I have noted and replied to every argument, (if not to notice every specification,) advanced by my opponent.

In view of all those learned Rabbis, lexicographers, translators, reformers, annotators, critics, historians, theologians, and scholars, do I not
stand in the midst of a respectable and honorable band, when I plead for
immersion merely in a literary and philosophical point of view! But
when we contemplate it as a solemn ordinance of Jesus Christ, the great
Law-giver and King of Zion, and think of the multitude of ancient worthies, those martyred hosts of ancient confessors, those mighty spirits that
loved not their lives even unto death, but gave them up a voluntary sacrifice at the shrine of eternal truth and everlasting love, who washed their
robes and made them white in the blood of the Lamb; who went down
into the water and were buried with the Lord in holy immersion ;—feeling ourselves surrounded with such a pure, elevated, venerable, sacramental host of elect spirits; may we not feel strong, courageous, joyful, triumphant ;—able to endure all the reproaches, scoffs, derisions, contume-
lies, anathemas, and persecutions of earth and hell, should they all con-
spire against us, and seek our destruction, because of our loyalty and allegiance to heaven's rightful sovereign, our great and glorious Lord Messiah! Could we not suffer an immersion in the dark, deep waters of
earth's most bitter trials, for the sake of being enrolled and classed with
such a noble band of illustrious men and women! Methinks, one could
almost wish for persecution in the maintenance of this creed—for the
sake of the honor of standing, as in some humble degree I feel myself, in
the midst of Hebrew saints, Greek worthies, Latin fathers, (not of the pa-
pacy,) illustrious advocates of the christian faith; pillars of the church,
both in the oriental and western sections of the christian profession.

When I see such a crowd of earth's great ones—the philanthropists,
public benefactors, men of high intellectual and moral eminence, standing
on the banks of rivers, in the midst of pools—around the ancient baptisteries, bowing their heads and their hearts to immersion—cheerfully going
down into the mystic waters, and there covered with the glories of the
Father, and of the Son, and of the Holy Spirit—immersed into the faith
and hope of eternal life, methinks there is no trials too grievous to be
borne, no opposition too great to endure, for the sake of participating with
them in these high honors and heavenly ecstacies. Thus they showed their
faith in him, and gratitude to him who came down from heaven, not to do
his own will, but the will of him that sent him, and to offer up his life a
ransom for many. So must we, so would we partake of their joys on earth,
their triumphs in death, and their eternal honors in the world to come.

Pure, primitive, Bible christianity has had to fight its way down to us
through hosts of opponents. We are indebted to the zeal, and courage,
to the firm, unyielding integrity, and persevering devotion of myriads of
choice spirits, for all that we know, and all that we enjoy, of the hope of
eternal life. It is our duty to imitate our benefactors and to transmit the
same blessings to posterity. But our time is almost expended.

Mr. Rice, as his manner is, will no doubt tell you I have proved nothing; that he has proved everything; that we have converted no one; that parties remain as they were. Were this indeed the fact, we should then be no more unfortunate than thousands, who confirmed their testimony at the stake without converting any one. We are not to judge of the force of argument, nor of the weight of evidence, by its immediate effect upon a partizan and super-excited population. The blood of the martyrs ultimately became the seed of the church. We sow now and reap again.

But as the soundness, or plainness, or importance of a doctrine is not always a passport to immediate, or to general favor; neither is the absurdity of any tenet, or practice, a guarantee that it is speedily to be demolished and driven from society. Were that so, transubstantiation would long since have been exploded. It has, however, survived Luther and Calvin almost three centuries. *Eckius*, the celebrated antagonist of Luther, laughed and manœuvred down all the logic and rhetoric of Luther and his companions, on auricular confessions, transubstantiation, and purgatory. Like my worthy antagonist, he always proved his theses—demolished his antagonist, and proclaimed victory for the ancient, venerable, apostolic doctrine of the pope, and the holy see of Rome.

Lutheranism, however, had many lives. It was often killed, but soon revived again; gained a triumph in every defeat, while Eckius and popery were prostrated by their triumphs.

Protestantism could not be put down by such a policy, nor by such opponents. Its principles, so far as they deserved to triumph, have triumphed amidst all opposition. So do the principles for which we contend. During some five and twenty years they have been publicly opposed in every form, and what has been the result! Often defeated, as our opponents say, while *they* always prove their positions, still they spread continually. They triumph every where, amongst all who give them a candid hearing—and they will continue to triumph till all partyism cease—till the whole christian world shall bow together in one spacious temple; till, in one grand concert, they shall raise their grateful hosannas and joyful hallelujahs to the King of Zion; till the redeemed, of all nations, and languages, and people, shall meet and worship around one altar; confessing one Lord, one faith, and one immersion.—[*Time expired.*

Saturday evening, Nov. 18—8 *o'clock, P. M.*
[MR. RICE'S CLOSING REPLY.]

MR. PRESIDENT—From the remarks of my worthy friend, you would be induced to suppose that he and his immersionist friends are the only people in the world who believe there is but *one baptism.* But, sir, all Pedo-baptists maintain this doctrine. Who ever imagined that there are two or more baptisms? The Scriptures teach that there is one baptism; but the gentleman would make an important addition to their language: he would say, there is but one *mode,* or one *action* of baptism. But does the Bible so teach? It certainly uses no such language. This one baptism is an ordinance administered with water, in the name of the Father, and of the Son, and of the Holy Spirit, by an ordained minister of the gospel.

The gentleman tells you, I was amazed and confounded to-day, when he produced that terrific author, Stokius; that I was quite frightened out of my senses, and, in my confusion, turned and read a passage which condemned the position I had assumed! I will simply remark, that the fear of Mr. Campbell has never been before my eyes, neither to-day, nor heretofore. I have been in war of this kind before to-day; and I have seen big books, and heard wind-guns fired, without doing much execution. And, pray, what was it that so alarmed me? Why, Stokius says, *baptizo* means, *tropically*, to wash. But does not Mr. Carson, his profound critic, fully sustain me in all I have said? I have asserted, that *bapto* and *baptizo* signify not only to sink, plunge, &c., but also to dye, to wash, to cleanse in a *literal sense*. Mr. Campbell maintains, that these last meanings are *figurative*. But what says Carson? He asserts, most positively, as I have repeatedly proved, that *bapto* means *to dye*, in any manner, even by sprinkling, and that *this meaning is as literal as the primary meaning.* "Nor," says he, "are such applications of the word to be accounted for by metaphor, as Dr. Gale asserts." (And Dr. Gale contended for the very principle now urged by Mr. Campbell.) "It is by extension of the *literal meaning*, and not by figure of any kind, that words come to depart so far from their primary meaning." I have asserted, that, even admitting these meanings to be secondary, or tropical, they became, by usage, particularly among the Jews, the proper and literal meanings of the words. Carson, whom the gentleman considers a profound linguist, asserts the very principle for which I have contended. Why, then, should I have been confounded, with the gentleman's learned critic standing by me and defending me from his assaults?

But he tells you, that, in my great alarm, I turned and read a passage from Ernesti that directly condemned me, and was not aware of it! Let me read the passage again; and the audience will be able to determine whether he or I ought to be most confounded. Stokius gives *to wash* as a *tropical* meaning of *baptizo;* and Mr. C. asserts, that the tropical meaning of words is always *figurative.* Now hear the language of Ernesti:

"But, there are several different points of light in which tropical words are to be viewed. For, *first*, the primitive or proper signification, strictly understood, often becomes obsolete, and ceases for a long period to be used. *In this case, the secondary sense, which originally would have been the* TROPICAL *one, becomes the* PROPER *one.* This applies especially to the names of things. Hence, there are many words which, at present, never have their original and proper sense, such as etymology would assign them, but only the *secondary* senses, which may in such cases be called the *proper* sense; e. g. in English, tragedy, comedy, villain, pagan, knave, &c.

"Secondly, *in like manner, the* TROPICAL SENSE *of certain words has become so common, by usage, that it is better understood than the original sense. In this case, too, we call the sense* PROPER *; although strictly and technically speaking, one might insist on its being called* TROPICAL. If one should, by his last will, give a library [*bibliothecam*] to another, we should not call the use of *bibliotheca* tropical; although strictly speaking it is so, for bibliotheca originally meant the *shelves* or *place* where books are deposited."—*Ernesti,* pp. 23, 24.

Sustained by such authorities, I have felt as cool and as deliberate as if I were eating my dinner.

To prove, that immersion was practiced, at a very early period in the christian church, Mr. C. quotes Barnabas and the Shepherd of Hermas. I reply to this testimony by reading a paragraph from Mosheim's Church History.

"*The Epistle of Barnabas* was the production of some Jew, who, most probably, lived in this century, and whose mean abilities, and superstitious

Z

attachments to Jewish fables, show, notwithstanding the uprightness of his intentions, that he must have been a very different person from the true Barnabas, who was St. Paul's companion. The work, which is entitled *The Shepherd of Hermas*, because the angel, who bears the principal part in it, is represented in the form and habit of a shepherd, was composed in the second century by Hermas, who was brother to Pius, bishop of Rome. This whimsical and visionary writer has taken the liberty to invent several dialogues, or conversations, between God and the angels, in order to insinuate, in a more easy and agreeable manner, the precepts which he thought useful and salutary, into the minds of his readers. But, indeed, the discourse which he puts into the mouths of these celestial beings, is more insipid and senseless than what we commonly hear among the meanest of the multitude."—*Mosheim's Ch. His.* vol. ii. part ii. ch. 21.

These are his witnesses. If they were the authors of the works quoted, he is welcome to their testimony.

Stuart, the gentleman tells us, admits, that the Oriental church has practiced immersion *from the beginning*. It is true, Stuart admits, that from an early period the Oriental church practiced *trine immersion*, as the Greek church still does; but he does not admit that such was the apostolic practice. But let him speak for himself. He says:

"I have now examined all those passages in the New Testament, in which the circumstances related or implied, would seem to have a bearing on the question before us, viz: *Whether the mode of baptism is determined by the sacred writers?* I am unable to find in them any thing which settles this question. I find none, I am quite ready to concede, which seem absolutely to determine that immersion was not practiced. But are there not some, which have been cited above, that serve to render it improbable that immersion was always practiced, to say the least? I can only say that such is my persuasion. The reader has the evidence before him, and can judge for himself. He will indulge me, I hope, in the same liberty. I do consider it as quite plain, that none of the circumstantial evidence thus far, proves immersion to have been exclusively the mode of christian baptism, or even that of John. Indeed, I consider this point so far made out, that I can hardly suppress the conviction, that if any one maintains the contrary, it must be either because he is unable rightly to estimate the nature or power of the Greek language; or because he is influenced in some measure by party feeling; or else because he has looked at the subject in only a partial manner, without examining it fully and thoroughly."—*Stuart*, pp. 53, 54.

Such was the conclusion of Stuart, whose learning and candor the gentleman has frequently applauded. Every one must see that, if correct, it is fatal to the exclusive claims of immersion—destructive of the very position Mr. C. is laboring to establish.

He has made an important statement concerning those baptized by pouring or sprinkling, in the ancient church; viz. that of so doubtful character was their baptism considered, that they were not permitted to enter the Gospel ministry. I will prove to you that this statement is wholly incorrect. The council of Neocesarea, which met some eighty years after Cyprian and the council of sixty-six bishops had declared their belief, that baptism by sprinkling or pouring is valid and scriptural, uses the following language:

"He that is baptized when he is sick, ought not to be made a priest, (*for his coming to the faith is not voluntary, but from necessity,*) *unless his diligence and faith do prove commendable, or the scarcity of men fit for the office do require it.*"

Mr. Campbell. [Addressing the Moderators.] I wish to have the second rule of this debate now read.

Mr. Moderator (Judge Robertson) then read as follows; "Rule 2. On the final negative, no new matter shall be introduced."

Mr. Campbell. I now appeal to the president whether the gentleman is not now out of order. I submit the question, whether he is not now introducing new matter?

Mr. Rice. And I submit whether Mr. Campbell did not, in his last speech, introduce the matter to which I am now replying?

Mr. Moderator (Col. Speed Smith.) The respondent has certainly the right to answer all the arguments adduced in the last speech of the affirmant.

Mr. Rice. The Moderators have decided correctly, that I have the right to answer his last speech. It is to be regretted that my friend has sought to protect his argument by an appeal to the Moderators.

You perceive, that no doubt whatever was entertained of the *validity* of such baptisms. The persons thus baptized were debarred from the ministry, until they had afforded clear evidence of piety, because it was believed that sick-bed repentance was of a suspicious character.

Mr. C. is quite sanguine in the belief, that immersion will, ere long, be universally practiced. Yet, he tells us, that until the thirteenth century all Christendom immersed. Then there has certainly been a wonderful falling away from the primitive practice. On what evidence he founds his confident anticipation of the prevalence of immersion, I know not. "The signs of the times," I think, do not indicate such a change. Nevertheless, his faith is quite strong enough to utter the prediction. Well, we must wait and see whether it will be fulfilled!

He asks, why was it necessary to go where there was *much water*, if baptism was not performed originally by immersion? This question has already been fully answered. John, we know, needed much water, even if he practiced pouring or sprinkling; because multitudes, attending his ministry, remained together for several days at a time, and they must have had much water for ordinary purposes, and for their ablutions. But the apostles (the fact is remarkable,) never, in a solitary instance, went after water for the purpose of baptizing any number of converts, at any time or place! If they had been immersionists, they would doubtless been found going to ponds or streams of water; and Mr. C., and father Taylor, would not have found it necessary to draw so largely on their imaginations to supply the defect in sacred history.

He is quite astonished at my saying, that our Savior was not buried in the earth; and he tells us, christianity is founded on the fact, that he was buried and rose again. I did not say, he was not buried. We are discussing the *mode* of baptism; and I said, he was not put under ground, so that the plunging of persons under water could be a representation of his burial; and so I still say. I have also said, (and I now repeat it) that the mere fact of our Savior's being put *into a tomb*, is not, in the Scriptures, presented as a matter of fundamental importance. There are different modes of burying the dead; and our Savior would have risen from the dead, wherever his body might have been placed. The matter of greatest moment to us and to all men is, that he died for our sins, shed his blood for us, and rose from *the dead*. It is not, therefore, to be supposed that the ordinance of baptism is intended as a representation of his burial.

My friend is certainly right in determining not to be laughed out of his religion, and in meekly bearing all the persecution that may come upon

him. Why, one would think, judging from his last speech, that he is
a martyr among martyrs!—that he is one of that "sacramental
host," of whom he has spoken so eloquently! I really supposed that the
reformers persecuted us quite as much as we persecute them. Every
body, I believe, is disposed to allow them quietly to enjoy their own
opinions. We have not excommunicated immersionists because they
prefer a particular mode of baptism; but they have excommunicated us,
and pronounced us unbaptized, and out of the church of Christ. We
are the persons who should complain of reproach. But he feels himself
in company with the sacramental host of God's elect, the immersionists
of olden time. They, however, did not believe the doctrine for which
he is now contending. They recognized the validity of baptism as administered by us; and we rejoice to acknowledge them as a portion of
the family of our Heavenly Father.

But the gentleman himself, though he has appealed to your sympathy,
as one that is suffering reproach and persecution for conscience' sake,
rejects from the church of Christ, such men as Luther, and Calvin, and
Zuinglius, and Cranmer, and Wesley, and Whitefield, and the whole of
the Pedo-baptists. Aye, and his faith puts them out of heaven! For
if his doctrine concerning the importance and efficacy of immersion be
true, they have failed of reaching heaven. I know, he has expressed the
opinion, that some unimmersed persons may be saved; but if his doctrine is true, his opinion is false. We might, perhaps, with some show
of reason, appeal to sympathy; but we will not. I leave the audience to
determine whether Mr. C. or I more resemble Eckius, the popish priest.
In the mean time, I will proceed to review the arguments I have offered.

Having reviewed the arguments from the lexicons, the classics, and
the translations, I was presenting that from Bible usage. *Bapto*, as
I have proved, as used in the Bible, rarely expresses an immersion, generally a partial dipping, wetting, moistening or sprinkling. If, then, *baptizo* has the same meaning, as to mode, the argument for immersion must
fail.

I have also examined the Bible and Jewish usage of *baptizo*. It occurs first in 2 Kings v. 10—14, where Naaman, the leper, was directed to go and *wash* seven times in Jordan; and he went and *baptized*
seven times, as the prophet directed. The command was to *wash*, not to
immerse; and he obeyed it. Accordingly Jerom, notwithstanding his
prejudices in favor of immersion, here translated *baptizo* by *lavo*—a
generic term, signifying *to wash*, without reference to mode. In this
instance the word cannot be proved to mean *immerse.*

Baptizo occurs also in Judith xii. 7. She went out in the night, in a
military camp, and *baptized* herself *at (epi)* a *fountain* [or spring] of
water. Both the language and the circumstances here prove that she
did not immerse herself, but applied the water to her person by pouring
or sprinkling.

It occurs again in Ecclesiasticus, where a man is said to be *baptized*
from the dead, or after touching a dead body; and the question is asked,
what will his *washing* profit him, if he touch it again? We examined
the law relative to this cleansing, and found *sprinkling* commanded, as
the most important part of it, but no immersion required. The gentleman could not find time to reply to these arguments! Here we have two
clear examples of the use of *baptizo*, in the sense of cleansing by pouring or sprinkling. These examples are particularly important, as show-

ing the sense in which the word was employed by the Jews, in relation
to their religious washings.

Baptizo occurs again, in a literal sense, in Mark vii. 4, 8, where the
Jews are said to have baptized themselves *(baptisontai)* when they came
from the market. Mr. Campbell's translation of this passage, I have
proved not to be a translation, but a strange perversion of the original
Greek. He throws out some two Greek words, translates a conjunction,
an adverb, and a verb in the third person, plural number, by a preposition
by, a participle *dipping*, and adds the word *them*, (referring to the hands,)
which is not in the original! And he makes the little adverb *pugme*
mean "*by pouring a little water upon them!*" But the gentleman has
not found time to defend his translation, or to attempt to prove that the
Jews immersed themselves, their hands, or their couches! But let it be
understood, that in the stereotyped edition of his New Testament, *baptizo*
is made to mean the washing of *the hands*. If the washing of the *hands*
is baptizing the *person*, (for such is the meaning of *baptisontai*,) surely
the application of water to the *face*, through which the soul looks out,
may be regarded as a baptism.

Baptizo again occurs in Luke xi. 38; and here I find it in Mr. C.'s
translation, rendered "*used washing*." This, however, we are told,
happened by a mistake of the compositor, and the error having escaped
notice through several successive editions, is now *stereotyped!* It was
truly a remarkable oversight! But the gentleman has not attempted to
prove that the Pharisee wondered that the Savior had not *immersed* himself before dinner! Here, then, we have some four examples of the
use of the word in the sense of *washing the hands*, (which, amongst
the Jews, we know, was generally done by pouring water on them,) and
of purifying tables or couches, which was doubtless performed in the
same way.

The last example of the use of the word, in a literal sense, not in relation to christian baptism, is in Hebrews ix. 10, where the ceremonial
law is said to consist in "meats, and drinks, and divers *baptisms*." There
are in the law, divers *baptisms*; but there are not divers *immersions*. I
have repeatedly asserted, that in not one instance was personal immersion required by the Levitical law; and I called on the gentleman to show
one. He has not done it. In this passage, the word *baptism* evidently
includes all the ablutions of the Jews, the most important of which were
required to be performed by *sprinkling*.

After a careful examination of all the passages in the Bible, where
baptizo is used in a literal sense, not in relation to christian baptism, we
have found no one instance in which it can be proved to mean *immerse;*
indeed, in every case but one, which might be considered doubtful, it is
evidently used to signify washing or purification, *by pouring or sprinkling*. The conclusion is not only fair, but most obvious, that as appropriated to the ordinance of christian baptism, it has the same meaning.

5th. I have appealed to the usage of the Greek and Latin christians, in
regard to *baptizo*. We have seen that Origen, the most learned of them,
speaking of the altar on which Elisha directed the priests to POUR several
barrels of water, says, it was *baptized*. Here is a baptism, the *mode* of
which we can all understand. We know that the water was *poured* on
the altar; and we know that Origen says, it was *baptized*. And if an
altar was *baptized* by *pouring*, why may not a *person* be baptized in the
same way? This is high authority. Origen was a native Greek; he

z 2

was a christian; and he was an eminently learned man. Yet he certainly uses the word *baptizo* to signify the pouring of water on the altar. The gentleman did not find time to tell us how this altar was immersed! I think he did intimate that Origen did not employ *figures* very correctly!! But it will not answer to make a figure of twelve barrels of *literal* water, poured on a *literal* altar. If this was not a literal baptism, where will you find one?

Origen, let it be remembered, is the same man who substituted *rantizo* for *bapto*. If he understood his vernacular tongue, (of which, however, Mr. Carson expresses a doubt!) it is certain that *baptizo* expresses the application of water by *pouring*.

But Origen does not stand alone in thus using this word. I have proved that Athanasius, Gregory Nazianzen, Basil, and others, employed it to express the flowing of the tears over the face, and of a martyr's blood over his body. My friend has been profoundly silent concerning all these quotations! If the Greek fathers understood their vernacular tongue, *baptizo* means pouring and sprinkling, as well as dipping.

I have also appealed to the Latins, and have proved, that Cyprian and sixty-six bishops, early in the third century, declared baptism administered by sprinkling or pouring, valid and scriptural, and to prove it, appealed to Ezekiel xxxvi. 25, "Then will I *sprinkle* clean water upon you," &c. Did they not believe, that *baptizo* expressed the application of water by sprinkling? If they had not, they would not have appealed to Ezekiel, nor have decided as they did. Observe, they said, let not those who have received baptism by pouring, so far mistake as to be *baptized again*. *The usage of the word baptizo by the Greek and Latin fathers sustains my position, and refutes that of Mr. Campbell.*

6th. I have proved another important fact, viz: that when immersion came to prevail among the Greeks and Latins, they employed *baptizo* to denote the ordinance, and selected other words to express the mode of performing it by immersion. The Greeks used *kataduo* and *katadusis;* and the Latins, *tingo, intingo, mergo, immergo,* &c. If *baptizo* expressed definitely the *action* of immersing, as Mr. Campbell contends; how shall we account for the indisputable fact, that they selected other words to express that action, and employed *baptizo*, when no such action was performed? *I have the authority of the Greek and Latin christians against my friend, Mr. Campbell.*

7th. I have appealed to the *history* of baptism, and proved that the first writer of any respectability who mentions immersion, is Tertullian, in the beginning of the third century; and he speaks of trine immersion, with sign of the cross and other superstitions. The gentleman will not practice according to Tertullian, but subtracts from his testimony, till it suits him. On the same principle I may subtract a little more from it, and it will suit me. But I have found sprinkling practiced and universally admitted to be valid and scriptural baptism, earlier than immersion can be found. I mentioned the case of the Jew who fell sick in a desert, and, having no water convenient, was sprinkled with sand. The bishop decided, that he was truly baptized, if only water was poured on him *(perfunderetur.)* *The history of the ordinance sustains us.* For if, as history teaches, our baptism is valid and scriptural; if it has ever been so recognized from the earliest ages of christianity; the doctrine for which the gentleman is contending is proved, so far as history is worthy of consideration, to be false. And if so, there is not only sin in excommunicating all who do not practice immersion, but something like a profanation of the ordinance by a repetition of it in case of such as have been validly baptized. The Pedo-baptist concessions of which he boasts, do not touch the validity of our baptism; but the concessions of the old Greek and Latin immersionists place him in an unenviable position.

I must close this discussion by stating *the facts* which more directly prove, that baptism by pouring or sprinkling is valid and scriptural.

1st. Christian baptism is a significant ordinance, in which water is used as an emblem of spiritual cleansing—of sanctification. Hence it is frequently called a *washing*, as I have abundantly proved.

2d. When God first selected a mode of representing spiritual cleansing, he selected *sprinkling*. The ablutions of the Levitical law, the mode of which was prescribed, were required to be performed by *sprinkling*. No personal immersion was required. This fact cannot be disproved. If, then, sprinkling was once the most appropriate mode of representing spiritual purification; why is it not so still? Can a reason be given?

3d. The inspired writers never did represent spiritual cleansing or sanctification by putting a person under water, either figuratively or literally. No exception can be produced. If, then, immersion was not then a suitable mode of representing sanctification; how can it be so now?

4th. The inspired writers did constantly represent sanctification by pouring and sprinkling. "Then will I sprinkle clean water upon you, and ye shall be clean. A new heart also will I give you," &c. Here the prophet represents a new heart by sprinkling. We do the same thing in administering christian baptism. The apostles used the same mode of expression, "Having our hearts *sprinkled* from an evil conscience, and our bodies washed with pure water." If you would represent emblematically the sprinkling of the heart; would you not sprinkle water?

5th. I have stated another very important fact—that from the time when christian baptism was instituted, we find not one instance on record of the apostles going after water for the purpose of baptizing. Philip and the eunuch were not going in search of water, but came to it, on their journey. Tens of thousands were baptized by the apostles in a country, having few streams of water of any considerable depth; yet they were always able to baptize the many or the few without delay, whenever and wherever they professed faith—in the crowded city, in the country, in the desert, in the prison, night or day. And in no one instance is it recorded, that they went one step out of their way after water! This is indeed most unaccountable, if immersion was then practiced; but if the apostles baptized as we do, the history of their baptisms is just such as we should have expected.

6th. Paul, I have said, according to the obvious meaning of the language employed, was baptized in a city, in a private house, standing up. Ananias came and found him blind and enfeebled, and said, "Arise (stand up) and be baptized;" "and he arose and was baptized." Just so Pedo-baptists, who practice pouring or sprinkling, write; and thus our immersionist friends do not write. We certainly write as Luke wrote, whether we practice as he did or not; and immersionists do not write as he wrote, It is indeed remarkable, that those who write as he did, differ from him in practice; whilst those who do not write as he did, do yet imitate his example!

7th. I derive an argument for our practice from the three witnesses, the water, the Spirit and the blood, 1 John v. 8. The blood of Christ cleanses from all sin. The Spirit sanctifies the heart. The blood is called " the blood of sprinkling;" the Spirit is represented as *poured out, shed forth* and the water, the emblem of spiritual cleansing—how should it be applied? Surely by pouring or sprinkling. Thus these three witnesses most strikingly agree; and the scriptural representation is uniform and constant.

The argument is before the audience. I now ask you, my friends, has my opponent produced evidence to satisfy your minds, that immersion is the only valid and scriptural baptism; and that all who have received the ordinance in any other form, are really unbaptized and out of the church of Christ? Look at his arguments and the indisputable facts I have stated and proved, and determine for yourselves. All true christians have one God and one Savior, and are going to the same bright and glorious habitation. It is no trifling matter to divide the church and excommunicate multitudes of its most pious and worthy members. Has the gentleman produced evidence, in view of which you are prepared to take such a step? My decided conviction is, that he has not,—that, on the contrary, I have clearly proved, that baptism should always be performed by pouring or sprinkling. I cheerfully leave you to judge of the weight of my arguments; and pray, that God will in his mercy lead us to the truth.

[END OF THE FIRST PROPOSITION.]

PROPOSITION SECOND.

The Infant of a Believing Parent is a Scriptural Subject of Christian Baptism. Mr. Rice affirms. Mr. Campbell denies.

Monday, Nov. 20—10 o'clock, A. M.

[MR. RICE'S OPENING ADDRESS.]

MR. PRESIDENT—The subject of discussion, this morning, is *the baptism of infants;* and the proposition which I undertake to establish, is the following: *The infant of a believing parent is a scriptural subject of christian baptism.*

I am constrained to regard this subject as one of greater practical importance than that of which we have just disposed. For it involves, in no inconsiderable degree, the interests, present and future, of our children. In the mind of every affectionate parent, therefore, it must excite a deep and tender interest: for what is more natural than the strong desire, in the bosom of the parent, to secure for his offspring all the blessings, temporal and spiritual, which God, in his boundless condescension and mercy, has offered? It becomes us, then, to give this subject, if possible, even a more candid and thorough examination than that which has preceded it; for, in regard to this, we are called to act for those who are incapable of acting for themselves.

Allow me here to remark, (and the fact is worthy of special consideration,) that whether this doctrine is taught in the Scriptures or not, it certainly has commanded the belief, the firm belief, of almost the whole of Christendom, in all ages; not of the ignorant and superstitious only, or chiefly, but of the wise and good—of those who have taken the Bible as their only infallible rule of faith and practice. The overwhelming majority of those who have diligently sought to know their duty, as connected with this interesting subject, have understood the Scriptures to teach, that the children of believing parents ought to be baptized in the name of the Father, and of the Son, and of the Holy Spirit. The exceptions, I may venture to say, are as one to a thousand. The opposers of this doctrine, compared with even Protestant Christendom, are a mere handfull.

My worthy friend, Mr. C., agrees with me, that the Bible is a plain book, easily understood on all important points. This being admitted, we have the very strongest presumptive evidence of the truth of the doctrine for which I contend. For, if it be the absurd and ridiculous thing it is often represented—nay, if it be not true, how shall we be able to account for the almost universal belief of it amongst the pious readers of the Bible? How unaccountable has been the infatuation of almost the whole christian world, on the supposition that this doctrine is false and absurd!

In support of the proposition before us, I appeal to the word of God. And I am happy to be able to say, that on this subject there will be but little necessity for dry criticism. The doctrine of the baptism of infants can be defended in plain English.

18

I commence my argument by reading the commission given by our Savior to his apostles. Matt. xxviii. 18—20, "And Jesus came and spake unto them, saying, All power is given unto me in heaven and in earth. Go ye, therefore, and teach all nations, baptizing them in the name of the Father, and of the Son, and of the Holy Ghost: teaching them to observe all things whatsoever I have commanded you: and, lo, I am with you alway, even unto the end of the world. Amen."

Such is the high and momentous commission under which the twelve apostles went forth, to proclaim to a dying world "the unsearchable riches of Christ." That we may understand its import, so far as the present subject is concerned, I will state a few facts.

1. *This is not a commission to organize a church.* As it is recorded by Mark, it required the apostles to go and preach the gospel to every creature. But in neither case does it contain even an intimation, that a new church was to be organized; nor do we learn from the Acts of the Apostles, that they ever did organize the christian church. God had long had a church on earth, and long had the gospel substantially been preached. But hitherto the blessings and privileges of his church had been confined to the Jewish nation. A gentile could enjoy them only by becoming a Jew, and submitting to all the forms and ceremonies of the Levitical law. But the period had now arrived, when the privileges of the church, and the blessings of the gospel, were to be extended to all nations; when, as Paul says, God "would justify the heathen through faith." To this happy day Isaiah was enabled to look forward, when, comforting God's afflicted church, he pointed her to a brighter period in her future history, when the gentiles should become fellow heirs with the pious Jews, and exclaimed—"Sing, O barren, thou that didst not bear; break forth into singing, and cry aloud, thou that didst not travail with child: for more are the children of the desolate than the children of the married wife, saith the Lord. Enlarge the place of thy tent, and let them stretch forth the curtains of thy habitation: spare not, lengthen thy cord, and strengthen thy stakes. For thou shall break forth on the right hand, and on the left; and thy seed shall inherit the gentiles, and make the desolate cities to be inhabited." The gentiles were to be admitted into a church already in existence, not into a church then to be organized.

2. The second fact I state, is this: the commission specifies neither infants nor believers as proper subjects of baptism. "Go, teach all nations, baptizing *them*"—the nations. Or, as Mark gives it, "Go ye into all the world, and preach the gospel to every creature. He that believeth and is baptized, shall be saved; but he that believeth not shall be damned." In the commission, as given by Mark, the Savior informs us who shall be *saved*, but not who shall be *baptized*. It may be said, the expression— "He that believeth and is baptized"—necessarily confines baptism to believers, since infants cannot exercise faith. I answer, if you thus exclude infants from baptism, you must also exclude them from *heaven*; for the commission also says, he that believeth not shall be *damned*; and infants cannot believe. The Savior's language was to be addressed and is applicable only to those capable of understanding and believing; and it neither excludes infants from heaven nor from the church.

3. I state a third fact: the apostles were to make disciples (for such is the meaning of *matheteuo*) by *baptizing and teaching*. This is man's part of the work. A more important part belongs to God. Mr. Campbell and I are agreed, that disciples were to be made by baptizing and teaching.

4. I wish distinctly to state a fourth fact : the commission does not say, that, in all cases, teaching must precede baptizing ; nor does it say, that in any case, it must precede.   This must be determined from other sources of evidence.   In the case of adults it is necessary to teach both before and after baptism.   Infants are taught after baptism.   If you would induce an adult to enter your school as a pupil, you must first convince him that it is his interest to do so ; but children may be placed in the school by their parents.   In both cases you speak of them as *scholars* or *disciples*.   Adults must enter the church voluntarily, as they receive all instruction voluntarily ; but parents are to " train up their children in the nurture and admonition of the Lord."   Since, then, the Savior has not said, that teaching must always precede baptism ; no man has the right to say so.

The question, then, arises—who or what characters are, according to the law of Christ, to receive christian baptism ?   I think, the gentleman will agree with me, that all who have a right to be in the church of God, ought to receive baptism.   All admit, that now (whatever may have been the case under the old dispensation) no one can enjoy membership in the church of Christ, until he is baptized.   A man may be pious before he is baptized ; but he cannot be a member of the visible church of Christ, entitled to its privileges and bound by its rules.   It will not be denied, that all to whom Christ has given the privilege of membership in his church, ought to be baptized ; since, whatever other purposes baptism may answer, it is certainly the initiatory rite of the church.

This being admitted, the great and most important inquiry is this : *who or what characters are, according to the law of God, to enjoy membership in his church?*   The answer to this question will necessarily determine to whom baptism is to be administered ; for if we can ascertain, that certain persons have a right to enter a house, it follows that they have a right to enter by the door.

Now let us inquire, where shall we look for the law of membership in the church of Christ ?   Or when would the question concerning the right of membership necessarily be determined ?   I answer, when the church was first properly organized.   You cannot organize a society of any kind, even a little debating society, without determining who shall be admitted to membership.   When a society is organized, the constitution, of course, determines the question concerning membership.   If, therefore, we would ascertain who has the privilege of a place in the church of God, we must go to the organization of the church.

We are thus brought to another very important inquiry, viz : *when and where was the church organized ?*   I do not learn, that the apostles were directed to organize the church ; nor do I find, that they did so.   I am obliged, therefore, to look elsewhere for the correct answer to this question.

I maintain, then, *that the church was organized in the days and in the family of Abraham ;* when God entered into a covenant with the father of the faithful to be a God to him and to his seed.   Before proceeding to the proof of this proposition, allow me to give a definition—or, if you please, a description of the church of Christ.   *The church is a body of people separated from the world for the service of God, with ordinances of divine appointment, and a door of entrance, or a rite by which membership shall be recognized.*   The correctness of this definition or description, I think, will not be called in question.   What is the church of Christ now, but a body of people separated from the world for the service of God, with ordinances of divine appointment, and a door of admission? Whenever I find such a body of people, I find a church of God. Let us now inquire whether such a people are to be found in the family of Abraham.

In the 12th chapter of Genesis, we are informed, that the Lord spoke to Abraham in the following language: " Get thee out of thy country, and from thy kindred, and from thy father's house, unto a land that I will shew thee: and I will make of thee a great nation, and I will bless thee, and make thy name great; and thou shalt be a blessing: and I will bless them that bless thee, and curse him that curseth thee; and in thee shall all the families of the earth be blessed." And in the 7th verse—"And the Lord appeared unto Abraham, and said, Unto thy seed will I give this land." Here we find promises of blessings, both temporal and spiritual, to Abraham and his seed. The same promises substantially were afterwards repeated, as recorded in Gen. xv., and again, some years after, re-iterated and ratified by the sign of circumcision; of which we read in Gen. xvii. 1—14.

According to the tenor of this covenant Abraham and his family were circumcised, and thus became a people separated from the world for the service of God, with ordinances of divine appointment, and a door of entrance—a rite which distinguished them from all other people, as in covenant with God. Here we find the church of God organized. Of circumcision the great Baptist writer, Andrew Fuller, says, it distinguished Abraham and his family from others, as in covenant with God, and bound them to his service. Is not this true of christian baptism? I care not, however, so far as this discussion is concerned, whether baptism came in the place of circumcision or not.

From this time God spoke of Abraham and his descendants through Isaac and Jacob, as *his people.* He directed Moses thus to speak to Pharoah, king of Egypt: "Thus saith the Lord, let *my people* go, that they may serve me," Exod. viii. 1 and ix. 1. Again—"Thus saith the Lord, *My people* went down aforetime into Egypt, to sojourn there," &c. Isa. lii. 4. They are also repeatedly called *the church,* Acts vii. 38. " This is he that was in *the church* in the wilderness, with the angel which spoke to him in Mount Sinai," &c.

Here, then, we find the church of God organized. Whether it is identical with the christian church, we shall inquire in due time. We are now prepared to inquire, *to whom did God give the privilege of membership in this church?* We are at no loss for an answer; for it is absolutely certain, that he by positive enactment made believers and their children members. Abraham, who was the father of believers, and his children and family, constituted the church. Some, perhaps, may object, that Abraham's adult servants were also circumcised. It is, however, a fact—an important fact—which I am prepared to prove, that adults were never permitted, according to the divine law, to receive circumcision, but upon profession of faith in the true God. It cannot be proved, that any of Abraham's servants were unbelievers. Professed believers and their children, therefore, were, by positive law of God, constituted members of his church. This fact cannot be successfully controverted.

Let me now state another important fact, viz: From the organization of the church, to the moment when the commission was given to the apostles, believers and their children enjoyed together the privilege of membership. This fact cannot be disputed.

In view of these facts I will now state an important principle. Since the children of believers were put into the church *by positive law of God ;* they can be put out only by positive law of God. Inferences will not answer the purpose. You cannot *infer* men out of their political rights. Men do not reason so conclusively that we may safely trust our rights and privileges to their deductions and inferences. I enjoy the rights of a citizen of these United States by the plain letter of the constitution. If you wish to deprive me of these rights, you must prove, that the constitution has been so altered as to exclude me. You must, in order to deprive me of my political rights, find law as positive, and of as high authority as that which originally conferred them. The principle holds good in ecclesiastical matters. If I prove that God put certain persons into his church, you cannot exclude them, unless you can point to the law authorising you so to do. God did put the children of believers into his church by clear and positive enactment; and you may as lawfully exclude believers from the church, as their children, unless you can produce a *"Thus saith the Lord"* for excluding the latter. This principle is so perfectly understood, that I need not spend time either in proving or illustrating it.

I wish now to state one more important fact, viz : *The commission given the apostles, does not exclude the children of believers.* As already remarked, it specifies neither believers nor their children, as proper subjects of baptism. It says, " Go, make disciples of all nations, baptizing *them*"—the nations.

But you ask : Does dot the Savior say, He that believeth and is baptized shall be saved ? and can infants believe ? And I ask, does he not also say, He that believeth not shall be damned ? Then infants must be damned, if you apply this language to them. If my friend will take that ground, very well. Our Savior, in this language, has told us who were to go to heaven, but not who were to be baptized. He that believeth and is baptized, shall be *saved.* Did Matthew give the commission complete ? Certainly. But did he say that children should be excluded ? He did not.

Here, then, we find the children of believers put into the church by positive law, and remaining in the church for long successive ages without interruption. They entered by the same door with the parents, and had the same seal of God's covenant upon them. We find them there till the Savior gave this commission, and it does not exclude them. Indeed, it would have been marvellous if it had; for it was a privilege expressly granted to Abraham, to have his children in covenant with the Lord. If it had not been a privilege, the Lord would not have required it. And, if it were a favor to the Jews to have their children in the church, why is it not to christians ?

Did Jesus Christ, the Great Immanuel, come to take away privileges which had been enjoyed for so many centuries ? Believers had, from the days of Abraham, enjoyed the privilege of having their children embraced in God's covenant. Did the Messiah come to deprive his people of their privileges ? No : he came rather to enlarge than to diminish them.

Here, then, we find the children of believers put into the church by positive law, and remaining in the church to the moment of the giving of the great commission; and the commission does not exclude them. *Where, then, I ask, is the law for excluding them?* I have found a law, clear and positive, for putting them in. Can Mr. Campbell find the law for putting them out ?

But it is urged as an objection, that the baptism of infants is not directly mentioned in the New Testament. Suppose it is not. Infants are in the church by positive law; and it will not do to *infer* them out, on the ground, that the baptism of such is not in so many words mentioned. You have the rights of a citizen of this commonwealth by the plain letter of the constitution; and you, therefore, have the right to a vote in the election of public officers. But many legislatures have met, and many changes have been made in our laws, since the adoption of the constitution. Suppose, now, some one should attempt to deprive you of the right to vote; would you not at once appeal to the constitution? But he might say, there have been many changes in our laws since that constitution was adopted; and in these changes, not a word is said about your right to vote. Would you not demand of him to prove, that the constitution had ever been so altered as to exclude you? Just so we find the children of believers put in the church at its first organization, and the right of membership secured to them by the highest authority in the universe. My friend, Mr. C., and those who agree with him, are anxious to put them out. *We call for the law.* But they, instead of producing any thing remotely resembling such a law, tell us, infant-membership is not directly mentioned in the New Testament; and thus they would put them out by an *inference!* an inference, too, by no means legitimate! No—neither believers nor infants can be despoiled of their privileges in this way.

I have said, the Savior in giving the commission, gave no intimation of a purpose to exclude the children of believers from his church—not even *a hint* that he designed to make any change in the law of membership. I desire the audience particularly to remark the strength of the argument for infant-membership, founded on this fact. It was extremely important, if he purposed to make any such change, that it should have been very distinctly stated. The apostles had grown up under a system of religion which embraced in the church not only believers, but their children. All their prejudices, therefore, would incline them to believe, that children were still to occupy a place in the church. And, let it be remarked, their Jewish prejudices were exceedingly strong—so strong, that although the Savior commanded them to go into all the world and preach the gospel to *every creature;* they still did not understand that it was to be preached to the gentiles. They seem to have understood only that they were to go and preach the gospel to the Jews dispersed among the surrounding nations; and so strong was this impression, that it was removed only by a miracle and a special revelation. The family of Cornelius (Acts x.) was the first gentile family to whom the gospel was preached; and Peter was the first of the apostles who ventured to offer salvation to the gentiles; and he was induced to do so only by a special revelation from God. So far were the other apostles from doing any such thing, that they called Peter to an account for what he had done.

Now look at the language of the commission—" Go, teach *all nations*"—" Preach the gospel to *every creature.*" Is it not perfectly clear? Yet the apostles, for a length of time, did not understand it. Is it not, then, most marvellous, if whilst they did not understand what was so plainly spoken in regard to preaching the gospel to the gentiles, they did so readily understand what was not at all expressed—that henceforth children were to be excluded from the church? Their Jewish prejudices, it would seem, prevented them from understanding what was most plainly commanded; and yet, notwithstanding those prejudices, they at once inferred what was not stated—that there was now to be a radical change of the law of membership in the church! Is it credible, that whilst, in the face of the express language of the Savior, they believed that the kingdom of God was to be confined to the Jews; they so readily inferred a change as to the right of membership which was not specified, and which almost the whole christian world have failed to see? Can any one believe it? Surely the very prejudice which would prevent their perceiving the extent of the commission, would also prevent them from discovering, unless it were most unequivocally stated, that a change of the law of membership was designed; and having always been accustomed to see believers and their children side by side in the church, they would still have received both.

Under such circumstances, if our Savior had purposed to exclude children from the church; he certainly would have said so as distinctly as he commanded the apostles to preach the gospel to all nations. Even then it would not have been wonderful, if they had been as slow to understand him on this point as they were on the other.

This is not all. The Savior not only did not give the slightest intimation of a purpose to exclude children from the church, but he employed such language as must have left on the minds of the apostles, the distinct impression, that no change of the kind was to be made. When little children were brought to him, that he might lay his hands on them and pray, the disciples rebuked those who brought them. What was his reply? "Suffer little children, and forbid them not, to come unto me; *for of such is the kingdom of heaven,*"—Matth. xix. 13, 14. Mr. Campbell will not deny, that by the phrase "kingdom of heaven," in this passage, is meant the church of Christ. If he does not admit it, Dr. Gill, the Baptist commentator, does. Now, consider the character and religious views of the persons whom the Savior addressed. They had always been accustomed to regard the children of professed believers as entitled to a place in God's church. They had never known a church constituted on any other principles. When, therefore, the Savior said to them, "Suffer little children to come unto me," &c.—"for *of such* is the kingdom of heaven "—THE CHURCH; would not the impression be made most distinctly, on their minds, that the children of believers were still to constitute a part of his visible church?

It is, then, clear that the children of believers were put into the church by positive law of God; that they remained in the church to the moment when our Savior gave to the apostles, the commission to preach the gospel; that he gave not the slightest intimation of a purpose to exclude them; that the strong Jewish prejudices of the apostles would induce them, unless explicitly forbidden, still to receive into the church believers and their children; that the Savior had employed language which would naturally induce them to believe that children were not to be excluded. Do not these facts, not one of which can be disproved, establish the doctrine of infant-membership in the church of Christ? I might here close my argument; for I have put the children of believing parents into the church by clear and positive law. It is the business of the gentleman to produce a law equally clear and positive for excluding them. If he cannot do this, (and I am certain that he cannot,) they must be permitted to remain. It is, moreover, a fact which cannot be denied, *that infants and adults entered the church by the same door—the same rite was ad-*

ministered to both. Since, then, both infants and adults still have a right to a place in the church, they must still enter by the same door. Circumcision was, at first, the initiatory rite ; and both adults and infants were circumcised. Baptism is now the initiatory rite ; and both must receive baptism.

But it may be objected, that only *male* children received circumcision ; and therefore the argument would prove, that only males ought to be baptized. I answer, that under the old dispensation, females, both infants and adults, enjoyed the privilege of membership in the church without any initiatory rite being administered to them. They enjoyed these privileges by virtue of their connection with the males of the family. Under that dispensation, ministers were not sent forth to proselyte the nations. When proselytes were made from the gentiles, they came as *families ;* and the males being circumcised, the whole family, males and females, were admitted to all the privileges of the church ; Exodus xii. 48. Under the gospel dispensation, all are invited and commanded to enter the church ; and nothing is more common than to see the females of a family enter without the males. Hence it became proper, under the new dispensation, to appoint an initiatory rite equally applicable to males and females. Under the former dispensation, both adult and infant females entered the church without receiving any initiatory ordinance ; and under the present dispensation, both enter by the same rite which is administered to males.

The argument, as it appears to me, is conclusive. It is an indisputable fact, that the children of believers were put into the church by positive law of God. It is a fact, that for many centuries, believing parents enjoyed the privilege of having their children with them in the church. It is a fact, that our Savior and his apostles never excluded them : no law of the kind can be produced. The conclusion appears inevitable, that they still have the right to be in the church, and of course, to enter by the door—christian baptism.

I do not wish to hasten through the investigation of this subject, as I have three days within which to establish the proposition before me. I will, however, make some remarks on another very important point.

It will, doubtless, be said, that my whole argument is inconclusive, inasmuch as the church into which children were put, and the christian church, are two entirely distinct organizations ; and, therefore, it does not follow, that because infants were put into the former, they are to be admitted into the latter.

The question now presents itself—*Is the christian church the same into which children were, by divine authority, admitted ? I affirm that it is ;* and I now undertake to prove the identity of the church of God, under the Jewish and christian dispensations ; to make it evident that Christ has had but one church on the earth. Will you give me your close and candid attention, whilst I proceed to state a number of important principles and facts, which, as I believe, establish this point incontrovertibly.

Let the fact already stated, be kept in view, that the commission given to the apostles did not authorize them to organize a *new church.* Hitherto the privileges of the church of God had been confined to the Jews. The time had come when those privileges were to be extended to *all nations.* The burthensome ceremonies of the Levitical law, which rendered it impossible that the church should embrace the gentile nations, were now passed away, and fewer and simpler ceremonies substituted for them. And now the apostles were commissioned to go forth and offer to all nations the blessings which had been confined to the Jews. They were not to organize a new church, but to extend the boundaries of the existing church.

That we may be enabled correctly to weigh the facts and arguments to be offered on this point, it is essential that we distinctly understand in what consists *ecclesiastical identity*. What are we to understand by *the identity* or *sameness* of the church? Perhaps I shall be able more satisfactorily to answer this question, and to illustrate the point before us, by reference to a subject with which we are all, to some extent, familiar—I mean *political identity*.

In what, then, does political identity consist? If I were to ask you, whether the commonwealth of Kentucky is the same political body which existed under this name forty years ago, you would unhesitatingly say, it is. But suppose I were to deny that it is the same, how would you undertake to prove its identity? I could truly say, that it is not composed of the same *persons ;* for the greater part of them are gone. With equal truth I could affirm, that it is not governed by *the same laws ;* for, year after year, the legislatures have repealed, altered, amended and added to them. How, then, would you prove, that notwithstanding all these changes, the commonwealth is the same political body? You would tell me, that although it is not composed of the same persons, nor governed by the same laws precisely, it is the same political body ; because the constitution is, in all its important features, the same ; and the same power, " the sovereign people," reigns. We find, then, that political identity consists in these two things, viz; *the identity of the governing power, and the sameness of the constitution, at least, in its essential features.* For if, within the last forty years, the constitution of this commonwealth had been radically changed, and a monarchical or kingly goverment established, its identity must have been lost. So long, however, as it retains these two great characteristics, although every individual of whom it was originally constituted, may die, and although the legislature continue annually to repeal, alter, amend, and add to the laws, it will continue to be the same political body.

These principles are so obviously correct, that I am sure they will not be controverted. Let us apply them to *ecclesiastical identity*. And I venture the assertion, that if you can prove the commonwealth of Kentucky, or these United States, to be the same political body which existed under the name forty years ago, I can produce three times the amount of evidence to prove that the christian church is the same ecclesiastical body which was organized in the family of Abraham, of which believers and their children were constituted members. My evidence shall consist chiefly of INDISPUTABLE FACTS—the best of all arguments.

1st. It is a fact, that under both dispensations the same King reigns. The same glorious God, the God of Abraham, Isaac, and Jacob, is acknowledged, worshiped, and obeyed, as the only true God, the only object of religious worship, the only Legislator, whose all-wise laws are binding on the consciences of all men. The world does not acknowledge, worship, and serve him, and, therefore, cannot constitute a part of his church or kingdom, This fact will not be denied.

2nd. The same moral law is received and obeyed under both dispensations. This law, briefly presented in the ten commandments, is admitted to be as binding on the Christian as on the Jew. Some, it is true, object to the *fourth* commandment, as not obligatory on the christian church; but although I believe it can be unanswerably proved to be still in force, I might admit that one commandment out of ten has been abolished, and still prove all for which I am contending. For the constitution of this commonwealth might be changed in a number of its features, without destroying the identity of the political body. I need not enter into an argument to prove that the moral law is obligatory on the christian church, and has ever been so recognized. Was it the duty of the Jew to obey the command, "Thou shalt have no other Gods before me?" It is equally the duty of the christian to worship the one living and true God. Was the Jew forbidden to make any similitude of any thing in heaven or in earth, through which to worship God? It is equally the duty of the christian to worship God " in spirit and in truth." Was the Jew forbidden to take the name of God in vain? It is equally the duty of the christian to hallow the name of the great God. I need not go further into particulars. It will not be denied, that the moral law is obligatory upon Jew and Christian, and that, under both dispensations, it has been acknowledged and obeyed as the rule of right and wrong. This law may be considered, in an important sense, *the constitution of God's moral government;* for it defines the duties of the subjects to the great King, and their rights, duties, and responsibilities toward each other. Under both dispensations, therefore, we find the same King reigning, and the same great moral constitution existing.

3d. Under both dispensations the same *gospel* is received and rested upon for salvation. In proof of this fact, the language of inspiration is so perfectly clear, that I cannot believe that it will be disputed. Paul says—"And the Scripture, foreseeing that God would justify the heathen through faith, preached before *the gospel unto Abraham*, saying—In thee shall all nations be blessed. So then they which be of faith are blessed with faithful Abraham," Gal. iii. 8, 9. Here we find the gospel preached to Abraham, in the very covenant on which I have said the church was organized. It was substantially contained in the promise, "In thee shall all nations be blessed." Accordingly our Savior said to the Jews—"Your father Abraham rejoiced to see my day: and he saw it and was glad," John viii. 56. Abraham, in the light of this promise, looked forward, saw the advent and work of the Messiah, and rested on Christ crucified for the salvation of his soul. The same gospel, therefore, is received and trusted in for salvation, by the church, under both dispensations. This fact is further confirmed by the language of the apostle, in Hebrews iv. 2, where, speaking of the Jews in the wilderness, he says: " For unto us the gospel was preached, as well as unto them; but the word preached did not profit them, not being mixed with faith in them that heard it." The Jews in the wilderness had the gospel as well as we; and it did profit those who received it by faith. This important fact is incontrovertibly established; yet it is susceptible of being, if possible, even more convincingly proved. The gospel consists of a number of parts or doctrines, and it is easy to prove, that in all its most important features, it is presented in the Old Testament, that every one of its fundamental doctrines is there taught. Let us look at a few facts on this point.

1st. Under both dispensations the church had the same *Mediator*, the Lord Jesus Christ. The saints of the Old Testament, and of the New, alike trust in Christ, his atonement and intercession, for eternal life. The *ministry* of the church has been somewhat different; but the great Mediator has been the same. This we are taught in many parts of God's word. Heb. ix. 15—"And for this cause he is the Mediator of the New Testament, that by means of death, *for the redemption of the transgressions that were under the first Testament*, they which are called might receive the promise of eternal inheritance." Here, you observe, the death of Christ atoned for the sins of those under the old dispensation, as well as of those under the new. The same truth is taught in Rom. iii. 25, which, if necessary, I will quote. Isaiah, presenting the same general truth, teaches that the church has, under both dispensations, the same *foundation*. "Therefore, thus saith the Lord God—Behold, I lay in Zion, for a foundation, a stone, a tried stone, a precious corner-stone, a sure foundation : he that believeth shall not make haste," ch. xxviii. 16. And the fifty-third chapter of his prophecy contains a most clear and lucid exhibition of the death of Christ, and the doctrine of the atonement.

2d. The great doctrine of *justification by faith*, is also taught in the Old Testament, as well as in the New. In Rom. iv. 1, Paul proves and illustrates this doctrine by quotations from the Old Testament—"For if Abraham were justified by works, he hath whereof to glory; but not before God. For what saith the Scripture? Abraham believed God, and it was counted to him for righteousness. Now to him that worketh is the reward not reckoned of grace, but of debt. But to him that worketh not, but believeth on him that justifieth the ungodly, his faith is counted for righteousness. Even as David also describeth the blessedness of the man to whom God imputeth righteousness without works."

3d. The doctrine of *sanctification* by the Holy Spirit, is clearly taught in the Old Testament. Thus Ezekiel says—"A new heart will I also give you, and a new spirit will I put within you : and I will take away the stony heart out of your flesh, and I will give you an heart of flesh. And I will put my Spirit within you, and cause you to walk in my statutes," &c. And David prays—"Create in me a clean heart, and renew a right spirit within me," Ps. li. 10. Did not David believe in the doctrine of sanctification by the Holy Spirit?

4th. The *resurrection of the dead* is taught in the Old Testament as well as in the New. Paul, writing to the Corinthians, says—"For I delivered unto you first of all that which I also received, how that Christ died for our sins according to the Scriptures, [Old Testament;] and that he was buried, and that he rose again the third day, *according to the Scriptures.*" And, in presenting the glorious doctrine of the resurrection of the just, he says—"So when this corruptible shall have put on incorruption, and this mortal shall have put on immortality, then shall be brought to pass the saying that is written, [in the Old Testament,] death is swallowed up in victory," 1 Cor. xv. 3, 4, 54.

5th. The doctrine of the eternal happiness of the righteous, and the eternal punishment of the wicked, and the doctrine of a general judgment, are also taught in the Old Testament. In the 50th Psalm, we find an awful and sublime description of that great day, to which the world is looking forward, when the Judge of the living and the dead, shall ascend his throne, and fix, by an unchangeable decree, the destiny of the righteous and of the wicked.

6th. The Old Testament presents the same conditions of salvation that are found in the New.' What are the conditions of salvation under the present dispensation? Paul tells us, that he preached, as conditions of eternal life, "repentance toward God, and faith toward our Lord Jesus Christ." And, in the eleventh chapter to the Hebrews, we find a long catalogue of worthies, who walked *by faith*, looked for a city whose maker and builder is God, eternal in the heavens, overcame the world, died *in faith*, and were received to eternal glory. These saints lived under the Jewish and patriarchal dispensations. The doctrine of *repentance* is taught with equal clearness. Thus David, in that penitential Psalm, (the 51st,) says, "The sacrifices of God are a broken spirit: a broken and a contrite heart, O God, thou wilt not despise." It is clear, that under the Old, as under the New Testament, the conditions of salvation were faith, repentance, and consequent reformation, or obedience to existing laws and ordinances. They are all included in the following exhortation by the prophet Isaiah: "Let the wicked forsake his way, and the unrighteous man his thoughts, and let him return unto the Lord, and he will have mercy upon him: and to our God, for he will abundantly pardon;" ch. lv. 6.

7th. *The qualifications for church-membership* are the same under both dispensations. I assert again, and am prepared to prove, that no adult, according to the law of God, could enter the Jewish church, without professing his faith in the God of the Bible, and his purpose to serve him. No gentile could enter into it, without renouncing his idol gods, and professing his faith in the God of Abraham, Isaac, and Jacob. Under the Old Testament, then, adults must profess faith, repentance, and reformation, before they could, lawfully, enter the church; and then, it was their privilege, and duty, to bring their infant children with them. And so it is under the New Testament. The proof that, under both dispensations, the church did receive, and expect salvation by, the same gospel, is absolutely unanswerable and irresistible.

If, then, under both dispensations, the church worshiped and served the same God and King, received and obeyed the same moral law, and received and trusted in the same gospel, the same plan of salvation, I ask, is not the church the same ecclesiastical body under both?

But what is the chief and only important difference between the two dispensations? Under the former, there was a code of ceremonial and civil laws, adapted to the existing state of the church; which, after the death of Christ, gave place to a few more simple ordinances, adapted to the church, as about to be extended in her boundaries to all nations. This is the simple and only difference, so far as the present discussion is concerned.

The civil and ceremonial laws were appointed by God for a *specific purpose* and *for a limited* time. So Paul teaches in Galatians iii. 19, "Wherefore then serveth the law? *It was added, because of transgressions, till the seed should come to whom the promise was made.*" It was added, because of transgressions—it was designed to keep the Jews entirely distinct and separate from the pagans, that they might not be drawn away from their allegiance to God; and it was to continue in force only till Christ, the seed to whom the promise was made, should come. Consequently, when Christ came and died on the cross, the civil and ceremonial law of the Jews, having accomplished the purposes for which it was enacted, expired by virtue of its own limitation; and, of course, the priests and other officers appointed to administer it, so long as it was in force, went out of office. And now, instead of those burdensome laws and ceremonies, new and simpler ordinances were instituted, and proper officers appointed to administer them and to preach the word.

But even the ceremonial law proclaimed the gospel in types and shadows. Its bloody sacrifices pointed to the cross of Christ, which was also the constant theme of prophecy; and its ablutions pointed to the sanctification of the heart by the Holy Spirit. The apostle teaches "that the law had a *shadow* of the good things to come;" Heb. x. 1.

Now I ask, did the passing away of those laws and ceremonies by virtue of their own limitation—the disappearing of those shadows to give place to the substance;—did this destroy the identity of the church? Was its identity destroyed by the fact, that the officers appointed to execute those temporary laws, went out of office when the laws had answered the purpose for which they were enacted? I think every one must see, in a moment, that the passing away of those civil and ceremonial laws could not affect the existence of the church.

Suppose the legislature of Kentucky should enact a number of laws (say fifty) to answer a specific purpose, to continue in force for twenty years; and should also appoint a number of officers to carry into execution these laws. At the termination of the twenty years, the laws would cease to be in force by virtue of their limitation; and all the offices growing out of their provisions would cease to exist, and those filling them would go out of office. Now what would you think of the wisdom of the man, who should insist that the passing away of those laws had destroyed the identity of the commonwealth, and that it is no longer the same political body? And what would you think of him, if he should go further and say, the fact that you were a citizen of the commonwealth of Kentucky and had a right to vote before the expiration of the supposed code of laws, affords no evidence, that since that time you are entitled to such privileges? I presume, you would smile at the absurdity of such sentiments.

No less absurdly do they reason, who contend that the passing away of a number of ceremonial and civil laws, enacted for the benefit of a previously existing church, to answer a specific purpose, and to be in force only for a limited period, really annihilates the church!!! No—the church still existed, after the passing away of its types and shadows, worshiping and serving the same God, obeying the same moral law, receiving and rejoicing in the same glorious gospel, (taught in all its essential features under both dispensations,) and having substantially the same conditions of membership, and (as I will prove) the same covenant.

The church, then, is the same under the Jewish and Christian dispensations—the same into which God did, by positive law, put believers and their children.

I have already exhibited more evidence of the identity of the church, than can be produced to show the identity of the commonwealth of Kentucky during the last forty years. But I have much more yet to produce. —[*Time expired.*

[MR. CAMPBELL'S FIRST REPLY.]
Monday, Nov. 20—11 o'clock, A. M.

MR. PRESIDENT—You doubtless perceive a great difference in the positions we occupy this morning. The laboring oar has at length fallen into the hands of my former respondent. He has something to prove to-day; and that, too, before an English audience and in the English language.

The jury are therefore more competent to decide on the issue, the arguments, and the proof, than when the subject was partially, at least, enveloped in the mists of Greek and Latin dissertations.

It was fortunate for my friend, that his hour had almost expired when he sat down. Ten minutes more, sir, and we should have heard every argument, save one or two, which we may expect to hear from him on this proposition. If we have been able to separate them, he has already given the materials of some fifteen or twenty, such as they are. There remains but one or two more to be heard from. I predict, we shall have little more that will be new to the end of this question.

It is all important, sir, as you well know, to make few points, to concentrate the mind upon them, and to fortify them well with documentary proof. A multiplicity of matters confusedly thrown together, is neither so edifying nor so convincing as a few well selected and digested arguments properly arranged and fully elaborated. Without a distinct and methodical arrangement, we might argue for years and prove nothing satisfactorily.

I feel particularly happy, that I stand in the midst of more than a hundred ministers who appreciate what I now say, and whose experience proves the importance, nay, the indispensable necessity, of fixing the mind upon one subject at a time, and prosecuting it till fully discussed, before a final dismissal of it.

He first informed us, that this was a more important proposition than that which we have just discussed. I do not compare atoms with the universe, nor moments with eternity. All things commanded by God are equally important to be observed, so far as Divine authority is regarded; for he that said, " thou shalt not kill," " thou shalt not steal," said also, " repent and be baptized, every one of you." The authority of the language, being contemplated, he that keeps the whole law, omitting one point, is guilty of disparaging the whole law. He is, therefore, said to be guilty of all. A proper regard to the subjects of baptism, humanly speaking, is more important to the church; inasmuch as the introduction of infant baptism has served greatly to corrupt it by admitting all the world into it. The operation and tendency of infant baptism, is to bring all that are born of the flesh, without being born of the Spirit, into the church; consequently, to make the doors of the church as wide as the doors of the world. Indeed, for hundreds of years, it has in many nations brought the whole population nominally into the church; and has, therefore, obliterated all the land-marks between the church of Christ and the kingdom of Satan. The visible and nominal church of Christ, as it is sometimes designated, is thus filled with a mass of ignorance, a mere assemblage of flesh, and blood, and bones. It was in this view of the matter, this introduction of the uncircumcised in heart and life into the professed family of God, that gave to Daniel those fearful types of its corruption—the savage monsters, true symbols, indeed, of Babylon, the great mother of harlotry and abominations. Nothing, I presume, tended more effectually to mix up the church and the world, to confound the spiritual with the natural, than the introduction of millions of babes into it, by the operation of the regenerating process of infant baptism.

The gentleman told you of a majority of a thousand to one, that were, as he supposed, at one time with him on his side of the former question. He is now about to show you how he got that majority. The true majority was, however, fearfully against him. But he has a majority with him on this question, I confess—a great majority. But you will see how he has got that majority—just as the ancient Jews and modern Turks obtain a majority for circumcision. Truth with me is truth, whether believed by one or one million. The largest majority on earth would not make transubstantiation true, nor any other falsehood in the universe. In religious affairs, the majority of mankind, since the days of Noah, has always been wrong. I never quote a majority as a test of truth. With me they are but an *argumentum ad hominem*—an argument to them who go for majorities. The majority of the world, with shame be it spoken to christians—the majority of the world are pagans: I had the majority on the former question, he will have the majority on this. The argument was as good on the last as on the present proposition, and no better. So far, then, the truth must rest upon other evidence than the suffrage of an untaught, unthinking, fickle multitude—a multitude that to-day would make Jesus a king, and to-morrow would crucify him.

To the law and to the testimony, then, we go. We will take with us in this case also, the Presbyterian confession of faith, so far as the capital truth is stated,—" Baptism is a sacrament (ordinance we call it) of the New Testament." To the New Testament, then, we must look for a precept, or a precedent, for infant baptism. But who ever saw one there! Comes it not, then, with an awkward grace, from a Presbyterian, after affirming so important a truth, to abandon the New Testament in the debate, and to haste away to Moses and father Abraham for proof of a " sacrament of the New Testament!" I, however, affirm, with the confession, that it is a *New Testament ordinance*, and consequently, to the New Testament I am disposed to go to look for it.

In a very complimentary way, indeed, Mr. Rice read you the commission given for converting the nations : but after a very obscure remark or two upon "discipling them," he very soon abandoned it and fled away into the wilderness and to Mesopotamia, to Abraham and the law. I regret that he did not break the seal of the commission ; that he was pleased to read the envelope, and hand it over to me. I expected an hour, at least, upon the commission, especially as that was the only document relied on from the New Testament. He said, indeed, what we all know, that Jesus commanded his apostles to make disciples, baptizing them. He expected me to assent to this view of the matter. Certainly, I do ; but not with his emendation added to it, by ONLY baptizing them. Do I understand him as intimating that baptizing them resembles marking or branding sheep or cattle? From all the development he has yet given, I would suppose this to be his meaning. He makes disciples first, and teaches them afterwards—that is, he baptizes them in his way, before they have one idea, and then enlightens them. St. Xavier seems to have been his beau-ideal of an enlightened minister, acting under the sanction of the commission. In order to replenish the church of Rome, by way of compensation for the loss sustained by the Lutheran defection, he became a missionary to Central America. He chose the Mexican Indians for the special field of his benevolent operations. And, like my friend, anxious to disciple the Indians, he had them sometimes allured and sometimes driven up into large companies, and by some kind of a squirt or huge sprinkler, dipped into a large basin of holy water, he scattered it over hundreds in a group, in the name of the Trinity. In this way he discipled about a million of them in the space of a few years, at least he so reported the matter to the pope ; and for the great travels, and labors,

and eminent success in discipling the American Indians, he was canonized
St. Peter's, and is known among the worthies as *Saint* Xavier.   Mr.
Rice, then, and the Saint, it seems, concur in opinion on the proper im-
port of the words *disciple them.*

I should wish to begin with my friend somewhere, if I could only find
him, either in the commission or in some other place ; but he treads so
lightly upon the ashes as if he feared the embers, that I know not where
to find him.   There appeared some policy in the scattering remarks which
he gave us.   It seems he designed to plunge into the olden times of the
Abrahamic covenants, and yet he wished to say something about the New
Testament for the sake of appearances.   He needed a mark or a sign, to
inscribe on his banners, and found it, at last, in the fleshly mark of circumcision.   Well, so let it be.   Every one in this free country, has a
right to choose his mode of defence.   Circumcision was a door into the
Abrahamic church ; and hence we must have doors into all churches and
dispensations.

I must, however, demur at his commencement of the church at so late
a period.   Abraham was born, according to the Old Testament Hebrew
chronology, in the year of the world 2008, and was called out of Urr of
Chaldea in the year 2083, and circumcision was not given till twenty-
five years later—till 2108.   Now the question which I propound to the
audience, and to Mr. R. especially, in accordance, I presume, with a common sense of propriety, is—*Was there no church of God, in his sense
of the phrase, during the first* 2108 *years of the world ; and if so,
what was the door into it ?*   I shall expect an explicit answer to this
question.   If the church of God, as he argues, was virtually the same in
all ages, were infants members of it for the first 2000 years ? and if so,
by what door did they enter?

He seems to touch circumcision very delicately.   I wonder not at this.
Light has gone forth on that subject, and Pedo-baptists know it is a delicate point.   Yet, still it is indispensable to the plea.   Take that away,
and infant baptism is immediately defunct.   He must have, therefore,
circumcision somewhere in the argument.   I hope, indeed, to drive it
wholly out of his head, and yours, my fellow-citizens, if it have any
lodgment there, before we close this discussion.

There are three prominent grounds of defence of infant baptism : 1st.
The Romanish ground of oral ecclesiastic tradition ; 2d. The proselyte
baptism of the Jews ; and 3d. Circumcision, or the identity of the Jewish commonwealth and the church of Christ.   The first is the foundation
of infant baptism.   The Roman bishop of Philadelphia, in a recent work,
in which he does me some honor, fully sustains the ground of papal tradition.   The church of England, according to Dr. Wall, frequently founds
it upon Jewish proselyte baptism, one of the most baseless figments in
Christendom, born in the Mishna, or rather, the Talmuds, since the
christian era.   John Calvin took the ground of circumcision, and has
been closely followed by the Scotch Presbyterians and their liege American sons.

Bishop Kendrick, in his work on baptism, ably sustains his position—
ecclesiastic tradition.   He candidly concedes that infant baptism, or infant
affusion, is not found in the apostolic writings.   It has not one word
of authority from the New Testament.   But the primitive fathers got it
orally from St. Papias, or St. Somebody, who had heard some other St.
Somebody say that he heard one, who had heard the apostles declare it.

The pope and his councils have sanctioned the affair, and that is plenipotentiary authority to satisfy every sound, liege, unthinking Romanist in the four quarters of the world.

Dr. Wall had rather make a god-father out of some of the Jews, than of any auditor of the apostles, and strongly makes it appear, that not from heaven, but from men came infant baptism. A learned Pedo-baptist, not a hundred miles from this house, has taken it into his head to give a new volume on baptism, and he, (Rev. W. Hendricks,) I think, has followed Wall in his phantasies about Jewish washings of proselytes. Mr. Rice, however, has read Stuart, and with him, it seems, makes no account of proselyte baptism. He takes circumcision—*alias, the identity* of something called the Jewish church, with the Christian. Still he does not wish to appear as though he leaned much on circumcision. That is, however, his whole basis; because of what account is identity, unless what he calls Jewish infant-membership, is not the plea for christian infant-membership!! Without farther preamble, then, I must follow the gentleman, not all at once, indeed, into all the amplitude of his *comprehensive* speech, but into the essence and main point of it. I shall then begin where he began, and trace his remarks upon the Abrahamic institution. While, with brevity, I shall attempt this, I hope not to sacrifice perspicuity in my attempts to condense my views and reasonings on so large a field. I shall only farther premise, that no man can well understand the New Testament who is not profoundly read in the five books of Moses. Certainly, without that knowledge, he is not fit to be a teacher of the christian religion. Before the gospels and the Acts of the apostles were written, the five books of Moses were the most valuable documents on earth. Had I to choose between them and all the books of the most hoary antiquity; nay, between them and all the writings of the whole pagan world, in all time, and all other records of all past times, I would not hesitate a moment in seizing Moses in preference to them all. No man (I am sorry to have to make the remark) who understands the pentateuch, will apply any portions of it as you have heard this morning.

Allow me, then, to give a brief sketch of the whole scheme of the Abrahamic institution :—When God called Abraham, he gave him *two promises* of an essentially different import and character. The first was personal and familiar; the second, spiritual and universal ; in other words—the first had respect to Abraham and his natural descendants, according to the flesh; the latter had respect to the Messiah and all his people. Two covenants, sometimes called two testaments, old and new, and two schemes of Divine government and special providence, are founded on these two promises. The whole Bible grows out of these two promises ; and is but a development of them. The whole Jewish nation, with all its peculiarities, grew out of the first; the whole christian church, out of the second. The words are as follows—" I will make of thee a great nation, and I will bless thee, and make thy name great, and thou shalt be a blessing ; and I will bless them that bless thee, and I will curse him that curseth thee." So reads the first promise, personal and familiar ; that is, a promise of a nation in his own family, to be placed under a peculiar providence, extending so far as to bless and curse individuals and nations for their treatment of Abraham's people. The second promise is—" And in thee shall all the families of the earth be blessed." This blessing is spiritual and eternal. Paul regarded it as the gospel in embryo. He preached the gospel to the descendants of Abraham, saying—" In thee, or in thy seed, shall all the families (i. e. nations) of the earth be blessed." These two promises, one for a nation, and one for all nations ;—one for fleshly, and one for spiritual blessings—one for a time, the other for all time and for eternity too, embrace within them the entire destinies of humanity. The universal history of man is but a development of the import of these two most sublimely comprehensive promises. They are the fountains of two streams of promises, prophecies, and histories, which, from that moment, began to flow, and whose waters meander through all ages, and disembogue themselves at last into the vast ocean of eternity. Never were so many promises uttered, so many prophecies sketched, so many histories written in one short period, since language was instituted, as are couched in those momentous words, pregnant with the fates and fortunes of all time.

From that moment a single family of two branches constitutes the meridian line of all revelation, of all developments. I shall endeavor to keep these two from becoming one—from being confounded, in this discussion. By keeping these two, the Bible is all intelligible ; by making them one, no man can understand the Old Testament or New. By this key of interpretation, all covenants, promises, laws, ordinances, principles, promises, dispensations, &c. &c. are to be interpreted, understood and applied. Emanating from these, the fleshly and the spiritual, the temporal and the eternal, the rational and the animal, the earthly and the heavenly, all Biblical matters are easily adjusted and reconciled.

The distinction of Jew and Gentile is conceived in these two premises. The Jew stands for Abraham's nation. The Gentile is always a cosmopolite—a citizen of any nation. The *Gentiles*, or the nations, on the one side, and the Jews on the other, are here first placed in comparison and contrast. But, after being, for a time, severed by a special providence, a portion of both meet in the Messiah, by a mystic tie, and become one in him ; in whom " there is neither Jew nor Gentile, bond nor free, male nor female "—we are all one in the ONE SEED of Abraham. For, says Paul, " He speaks not of *seeds* as of many, but as of one ; that is, the *Messiah*." I earnestly hope that my Presbyterian friends, for whom I entertain a very high respect for the sake of old times, will give due attention to these considerations ; for indeed, I doubt not, should I be permitted in this discussion to draw that grand line as I ought, all persons of candor and intelligence will approve and admire the grandeur of the developments emanating from so simple, yet so comprehensive a conception.

That these two grand germs of blessings, planted in the person of Abraham, have grown up into different covenants and dispensations, still retaining the original characteristic idea, is clearly stated and propounded to us by prophets and apostles. Paul, to the Romans, says, chap. ix. 4, " To the Israelites pertain the adoption, and the glory, and the *covenants*, and the giving of the law, and the service of God, and the *promises*." There are, then, a plurality of covenants with Abraham, and a plurality of covenants with the seed of Abraham. The two grand covenants, however, one from Sinai and one from Jerusalem, or the old covenant and the new, are the two complete developments of the promises made ; Gen. xii. 3, before quoted.

Comprehensive and concentrated views of the great principles of things, are regarded as the most felicitous developments of mind. Hence minds are sometimes graduated upon the scale of their ability to attain a comprehensive simplicity, both in conception and expression. The Bible abounds with examples of this sort, and we ought to acquire, as far as possible, a taste for them, and a proficiency in the application of them. The great masters of modern science have devoted themselves to this work of simplification and classification; and to their successful labors are we chiefly indebted for the great improvement and advancement of the sciences of the present day. We need a simpler application of mind to the things of revelation; not to the origination of a new nomenclature, or a new classification, but to the discovery, development, and application of that, furnished us by the inspired authors of the Bible. We shall, then, in the first place, take up the first promise to Abraham, and briefly trace the covenants growing out of it.

The first is developed in the 15th of Genesis. It is a covenant concerning the inheritance of Canaan. Sometime after these two promises, given to Abraham while yet in Chaldea—when he was in the land of Canaan, at Moreh, the Lord appeared to him and promised him that land. Some years after, on a certain occasion, Abraham asked the Lord, whereby shall I know (be assured,) that I shall inherit this land. The Lord commanded him to prepare a splendid sacrifice of all clean birds and quadrupeds, and at even the Lord met with him at the altar, and while a burning lamp passed between the severed animals, the Lord revealed the fortunes of his family for the next four hundred years; and made a covenant with him, securing to him and his fleshly seed, the whole land from the borders of the Nile to the Euphrates—a district of country then possessed by some ten nations. The details of this whole transaction are recorded, Gen. xv., in the words following: "Take me an heifer of three years old, and a she goat of three years old, and a ram of three years old, and a turtle dove, and a young pigeon. And he took unto him all these, and divided them in the midst, and laid each piece one against another; but the birds divided he not. And it came to pass that, when the sun went down, and it was dark, behold, a smoking furnace, and a burning lamp that passed between those pieces." Then the Lord solemnly grants, in passing between the parts of the sacrifice, to Abraham and his seed, the inheritance of the land—saying, "Unto thy seed have I given this land, from the river of Egypt unto the great river—the river Euphrates."

Not long after these transactions, Abraham having, at Sarah's bidding, taken to wife Hagar, an Egyptian maid, her slave, had a son by her called Ishmael. This slave-wife of Abraham, and her slave-son, Ishmael, become allegoric characters in after times, and it is important that we notice them here. But the time drawing nigh, when the promised son by Sarah, the free woman and wife proper of Abraham, should be born, in order that this issue by Sarah might be contradistinguished from that by Hagar, God was pleased to command Abraham to prepare for another covenant. This next covenant, growing out of the first promise, is made especially for the sake of ascertaining, by a fleshly mark, the natural offspring of Abraham, and guarantying to them the parental blessings, conveyed to Abraham by the covenant concerning the inheritance, and also as to the time of its institution, one year before the birth of Isaac: it occasioned a remarkable difference between Ishmael and Isaac, though sons of the same parent—the former being the son of his uncircumcision, the latter of his circumcision; though both circumcised themselves, Ishmael in his thirteenth year, and Isaac on the eighth day. This cove-

nant has in it no new specification. In the preamble to it, God reminds
Abraham of all that he had promised and covenanted to him, concerning
his own special family. He calls him *Abraham*, instead of Abram ; for
a " Father of many nations have I made thee, and I will make thee exceedingly fruitful, and I will make nations of thee, and kings shall come out
of thee. And I will establish my covenant between thee and me, and thy
seed after thee in their generations, for an everlasting covenant, to be a
God unto thee, and to thy seed after thee; and I will give unto thee, and
to thy seed after thee, the land wherein thou art a stranger—all the land
of Canaan for an everlasting possession, and I will be their God." Then
he proceeds on these promises to enact, what Stephen calls " The covenant of circumcision."   " 'Thou shalt keep my covenant, therefore, thou
and thy seed after thee, in their generations. Every man-child among
you shall be circumcised, and you shall circumcise the flesh of your fore-
skins, and it shall be a *token of the covenant* between me and you. He
that is eight days old, &c., every man-child born in thy house, or bought
with thy money, must needs be circumcised ; and my covenant shall be
in your flesh for an everlasting covenant. And the uncircumcised man-
child, whose flesh of his foreskin is not circumcised, that soul shall be
cut off from his people. *He hath broken my covenant.*" In this covenant, then, is a further development of the second promise concerning the
natural descendants of Abraham.

The second promise concerning the Messiah is no farther developed
during the whole Jewish dispensation. It is, indeed, repeated to Isaac,
and to Jacob, and confirmed by an oath at the virtual sacrifice of Isaac—
and is called by Paul "*the covenant confirmed by God (eis) concerning
the Christ,* made four hundred and thirty years before the giving of the
law."

We have now got the covenant concerning Christ, and two covenants
based on the first promise. There is yet wanting a third covenant, or the
fuller development and engrossment of all that is contained in the first
promise, Gen. xii., as drawn out in that concerning the inheritance, and
in that concerning circumcision. This is not done till after the Exodus ;
till the giving of the law, four hundred and thirty years after the calling
of Abraham. Then it is 'all proposed to the twelve tribes, amounting to
about three millions, having six hundred thousand men of war. It is
now, with certain developments, thrown into a new form, proposed to the
people, accepted by them, and ratified with bloody sacrifices.

To sum up the whole, *the two promises* tendered to Abraham at the
time of his being called, while he was yet in Urr, of Chaldea, and depending on which he consented to leave his own country, and become a
voluntary pilgrim for life, constitute the basis of *two great institutions.*
The first promise is developed in the covenant concerning the inheritance,
some ten or twelve years after he had become a pilgrim. The covenant
of circumcision was instituted twenty-four years after—and the Sinai
covenant, or great national development, embracing all these other developments, was sealed four hundred and thirty years after the time of these
two promises.

The second promise, containing the spiritual blessing of the gentiles
of all nations in Christ, is denominated by Paul, Gal. iii., "The covenant
confirmed by God concerning Christ, four hundred and thirty years before
the law." They are then *dated* as well as *named.* They are arranged as follows—The covenant concerning Christ was confirmed Anno

Mundi 2183, in the seventy-fifth year of Abraham. That concerning
circumcision, Anno Mundi 2107, in the ninety-ninth of Abraham. The
covenant at Sinai was ratified immediately after the Exodus, Anno Mundi 2513. Now, these facts being indisputably true, the christian covenant, which was developed according to the prophecy of Jer. xxxi. 31,
re-written Heb. viii. 8—13, was not based upon, nor is it identical with,
either the covenant of circumcision, nor with the old covenant made
with all Israel at Horeb.

That the national covenant and organization at Sinai, grew out of
the preceding covenants, appears from the following testimonies—and as
much depends on the clear understanding of this matter, we shall read a
passage from Exodus vi. 4—8 : " I have established my covenant with
Abraham, Isaac and Jacob, to give them the land of Canaan, the land of
their pilgrimage, wherein they were strangers. I have also heard the
groaning of the children of Israel, whom the Egyptians keep in bondage,
and I have remembered my covenant. Wherefore, say unto the children
of Israel, I am the Lord, and I will bring you out from under the bondage of the Egyptians—and *I will take you unto me for a people*, and
I will be to you a God—and I will bring you unto the land, concerning
which I did swear to give it to Abraham, Isaac, and Jacob, and I will give
it to you for an heritage. I am the Lord."

Mr. Rice will have the covenant at Sinai, and the proceedings thereupon, *a church organization;* although, in the whole transaction, there
is not one word about the Messiah, or the blessing of the nations in him.
Nay, indeed, Paul contrasts the whole affair with the ministration of the
Gospel and the christian church, 2 Cor. iii. But of this again. Meantime, after all the solemn preparations recorded in Exod. xix. and xx..
the nation was organized, and immediately was added to the covenant,
written and engraven on stones, a judicial law, for the management of
their national affairs, with a symbolic ceremonial, prospective of a better
covenant and a more spiritual dispensation.

It is important to observe, that circumcision was appended to the institution, and incorporated with it. It was taken, as it were, from the hand
of Abraham, and put into the hands of Moses. It becomes a national
from a patriarchal affair. Our Lord says, " Moses gave you not circumcision ; yet you circumcise a child on the Sabbath day, (part of the law
of Moses,) that the law of Moses may not be broken ; that is, that circumcision may be performed according to the law." But again, Ex.
xiii. 48, speaking of the law of the passover, it is enacted that circumcision be imposed upon all persons identifying themselves with the Jewish
nation, in order to a participation of the ordinances commemorative of a
national salvation. " One law, says the Lord," concerning the institution
of circumcision, "shall be to him that is home born, and to the stranger
that sojourneth among you." Here, then, is circumcision, as enacted by
Moses. But if any one want still fuller and clearer legislation on this subject, he may find it in Leviticus xii. 3, " And in the eighth day the flesh
of his foreskin shall be circumcised." Indeed the New Testament contemplates it as a part of the Jewish law. Acts xv. 1. " And certain men came
down from Judea, and taught the brethren : Except ye be circumcised
after the manner of Moses, you cannot be saved." Evident then, it is,
that circumcision had become a part of this ceremonial of Moses, and
was identified with his institution, as much part and parcel of it, as was
the passover that also occurred before the organization at Mount Sinai.

That covenant, need I add, was sealed with the blood of sin-offerings. " For as," Paul says, " when Moses had spoken every precept to the people, according to the law, he took the blood of bulls and of goats, with water, and scarlet wool, and hysop, saying; this is the blood of the covenant which God has enjoined upon you." Of that national institution, not circumcision, but the blood of sin-offerings, was the seal.

Thus was consummated the national organization, and the promises to Abraham, Isaac, and Jacob, concerning this inheritance, and also the blessings in the first promise, were now engrossed in it. God was now known not only as the God of Abraham, Isaac, and Jacob; but the "God of the Hebrews" also. Let me observe, emphatically, that from that day to the destruction of Jerusalem and the repudiation of that nation, no other compact, covenant, or law, was given them; and all the special favors of having God for their God were manifested while they kept his law.

Jeremiah promised a new covenant, as aforesaid, having in it *four spiritual blessings*, comprehensive of the whole evangelical dispensation of mercy. To show that this is the only contrast of the first covenant, and that the first general covenant was that at Mount Sinai; the preamble to the new evidently demonstrates—" I will make a new covenant with the house of Israel, and with the house of Judah, saith the Lord. Not like that which I made with their fathers, when I took them by the hand to lead them out of the land of Egypt," &c. The second promise, or the " covenant confirmed by God, concerning Christ, is, then, developed in the new covenant, while that contained in the first promise was fully developed in the old covenant. And Paul says, " In that he saith a *new* covenant, he maketh the first *old*. Now that which decayeth and waxeth old, is ready to vanish away." We have, then, in this simple narrative of these all-important transactions, fully, as we conceive, set forth the whole scope and meaning of these two promises, with all the covenants germinating from them. From which facts most important conclusions are deducible, wholly subversive of the Pedo-baptist assumptions.

Nothing can be plainer in sacred history than that there are two general covenants, growing out of two promises to Abraham. God's nation built upon the one, and Christ's church upon the other. The one guarantying all manner of temporal benefits, under a special providence; the other, guarantying all spiritual and eternal blessings, under a mediatorial interposition. The one founded on *flesh*, the other on *spirit;* the one received by *sight* and *sense*, the other by *faith* and *hope*.

Before we descend into the particular details of the subject, I desire your attention specially to the precept of circumcision, as commented on by Paul, Rom. iv. With this great master, in our Israel, circumcision, in the person of Abraham, differed from circumcision in the person of every other man. In his case it was both a *sign* and a *seal*. The language is so peculiar, that no grammarian can misconceive it. And, says Paul, he received THE *sign* of circumcision, A *seal* of *the righteousness* of the faith which he had, being yet uncircumcised. Circumcision was not *a* sign, but *the* sign—it was not *the* seal, but *a* seal. The former style denotes a thing well defined and established—the latter, a special occurrence. To all the Jews it was *the* sign; to Abraham it was *a* seal—a seal of what? Of something which he had before circumcision. I challenge a discussion of this point. It is the gist of the controversy about circumcision.

If there be not a demonstrable difference between " *the righteousness of faith*," and " the righteousness of *the faith which he had* "—then there is no appreciable difference between any two propositions on the whole subject of faith. Circumcision was but the *sign* of a covenant to the whole Jewish nation. It was the *seal* of the peculiar excellency, of the extraordinary faith vouchsafed to Abraham. On this point I may, perhaps, anticipate, in my turn, Mr. Rice. I do it, however, not in the way of retaliation, but to apprise him of my course, that he may prepare for a defence, on this much litigated case. I have never seen it fully cleared up in any discussion. I hope we shall satisfactorily dispose of it on the present occasion. I desire him, most sincerely, to make the best effort that he can. I could, for public utility and satisfaction, wish that my opponent possessed the most discursive and argumentative powers, and the largest amount of information on the whole premises—that he had all learning—all talents of this sort—that he might give the highest satisfaction, and demonstrate that he neither needs nor calculates upon quibbling, manœuvring, or any expedients incompatible with conscious strength, and christian dignity, and decorum. I concur with him, that a more important question can scarcely be discussed in the present age. It is of the utmost importance to humanity. I am astonished that any one can contemplate the subject with indifference, or seek to slur it over from public inspection and examination. It is the duty of all men to understand this subject. It concerns the church, the state, the whole world, to know what is true on a question that affects millions, by imposing on them a religion, without a deed, or thought, or volition of their own. Besides, if we could only root out this root of partyism, how much would be achieved for the cause of suffering christianity ! What advances towards a harmonious concert and co-operation !

I have some fifteen or sixteen facts on the subject of circumcision, indicative of its general repugnance to any accommodation with Pedo-baptist assumptions. They put it, methinks, wholly out of debate, as to the feasibility of baptism coming in the room, or standing in the stead of circumcision. I never heard so egregious a turn given to a phrase, as that given to a clause of a sentence, in my first address on the last proposition. I had, in speaking of its prominence in the christian system, observed that baptism stands in importance " as circumcision to a Jew, hereditary descent to an English nobleman, or the elective franchise to an American citizen." This, Mr. Rice, in his sometimes left-handed and infelicitous ingenuity, converted into a proof that I held baptism as coming in the room of circumcision ! ! Why did he not put it also in room of the elective franchise, or hereditary descent to a nobleman ! ! I wonder not at some comments on the new version, and on my other writings, by this gentleman, who could in my presence commit so palpable an error. I shall now proceed with my specifications.

1. *Males* only were the subjects of circumcision. All females were excluded from the blessings, if blessings they were, in the sign of whose flesh a man was clothed. I argue that there were no spiritual blessings in circumcision, else females had not been at all excluded. The God of Abraham never would, by a covenant seal, exclude *them* from spiritual blessings—from any thing tending to their sanctification and salvation. Baptism certainly has not come in the room of circumcision in this particular.

2. Adults circumcised themselves, at any age, whenever they took it

into their heads to become Jews. Do children baptize themselves? To circumcise one's self was a very general practice on sundry occasions.

3. Infant males were to be circumcised the eighth day. Do they baptize infants on the eighth day?

4. Infants were circumcised by either parent, as the case may be. You all remember the case of Zipporah! Why then employ ministers to baptize, if these are both seals of the same spiritual church covenant, and if the churches, Jewish and Christian, be identical?

5. A Jew's property in a man or child constrained his circumcision. Abraham's servants, adults and all, *because his property*, were circumcised. Three hundred and eighteen warriors belonged at one time to his household. Why do not Presbyterians baptize all a man's slaves when he joins the church, on the principle of identity?

6. Circumcision was not the door into any church or religious institution. It was no initiatory rite to any moral institution. The Ishmaelites, and Edomites, and many other nations by Keturah, were circumcised. Into what church did they enter? The Jews were members of the politico-ecclesiastico church by natural birth. Circumcision was no initiatory rite or door to them. But none can enter Christ's church unless " born again," " born from above." How then are the two churches identical?

7. The qualification for circumcision was *flesh*. Is that the qualification for baptism? for admission into Christ's church?

8. Circumcision was not a dedicatory rite. Pedo-baptists talk much and often about dedicating their infant offspring to the Lord. Now under the law, females were never dedicated, and of males *none but the first born!* How righteous, over much, in dedicating both male and female! The Lord never asked this much from the Jews. But Pedo-baptist dedication is only *nominal*. Among the Jews it was *real—bona fide* dedication. Jesus Christ, being the *first born*, was dedicated. He was also circumcised and baptized; circumcised the eighth day at home, dedicated the fortieth day in the temple, and baptized when thirty years old in the Jordan. Are the churches identical here? What singular identity!

9. Circumcision, requiring no moral qualification, communicated no spiritual blessings. Ishmael, Esau, and all the servants of the Jewish nation, were circumcised on the *faith of their masters*.

10. Idiots were circumcised—for not even reason, intellect, or sanity were qualifications—flesh only! It was a covenant *in the flesh*, and went for preserving the flesh till the Messiah was made of the seed of Abraham and of David, according to the flesh.

11. It was a visible, appreciable mark, as all signs and seals are. Is sprinkling so, or any use of water?

12. It was binding on parents and not on children. The commandment was, "Circumcise your children." But the christian word is, "Be baptized every one of you." No one ever found a precept in the New Testament, commanding parents to baptize their children. Where there is no law, there is no transgression: and where there is no precept, there can be no obedience. There is, therefore, no transgression in the neglect, nor obedience in the performance, of infant baptism.

13. The right to circumcision in no case depended upon the faith, the piety, or the morality of parents. The infant of the most impious Jew, had just as good a right to circumcision as the son of Abraham, David, or Daniel. Why, then, do Pedo-baptists suspend the right to baptism upon

the faith of a father or grandfather, or some kinsman of the infant? Does their practice look like their faith in the substitution of baptism for circumcision, or in the identity of the two churches, the Jewish and the christian?

14. Circumcision, say our Pedo-baptist friends, guarantied certain temporal blessings to the Jews. Query—What temporal blessings does baptism secure to infants?

15. It was not to be performed into the name of any being whatever, neither in heaven nor on earth. Why, then, baptize or sprinkle into any name, if the latter fills the place of the former?

16. The subject of circumcision, was a debtor to keep the law of Moses in all its institutions : for, says Paul, "Whosoever among you is circumcised is a debtor to do the whole law," of which, as before shown, circumcision was a part. Query—Are those infants baptized, debtors to keep all the Jewish ordinances? If not, how does baptism fill the place of circumcision?

These sixteen indisputable facts show—that circumcision was peculiar in its nature, character, and designs—that it was the sign of a national covenant—that it was *the sign* of the same privilege to all its subjects; and, consequently, never the sign of any spiritual blessing in Christ to any one of them.

That the covenant of which it was a sign was not the covenant of the christian church, will appear most evident from a fact which I will just now state, viz : that some eight hundred years after its establishment, Jeremiah foretold that it should be abolished, and that God would make a *new* covenant, and instead of writing his new laws upon marble or upon parchment, he would write them upon the hearts of his people. The words are :—"Behold the days come, saith the Lord, that I will make a new covenant with the house of Israel, and with the house of Judah. *Not according to the covenant* which I made with their fathers in the day that I took them by the hand to lead them out of the land of Egypt. (Which my covenant they break, although I was a husband to them, saith the Lord.) But this shall be the covenant which I will make with the house of Israel. *After those days*, I will put my law in their inward parts, and write it in their hearts, and will be their God and they shall be my people. And they shall teach no more every man his neighbor, and every man his brother, saying, Know the Lord; for all shall know me, from the least to the greatest of them, saith the Lord; for I will forgive their iniquity and remember their sins no more."—[*Time expired.*

Monday, Nov. 20—11½ *o'clock, A. M.*
[MR. RICE'S SECOND ADDRESS.]

MR. PRESIDENT—I have no objection to holding the laboring oar, or to have something to prove. Many very intelligent persons thought that I proved something, even when the laboring oar was in the gentleman's hand ; and, perhaps, I may now accomplish even more than before. I despair, however, of pleasing him. I find it impossible to travel at a gait that will suit him : I am always either too fast or too slow—generally too fast. I must be permitted, in this matter, to pursue my own course ; and I shall cheerfully leave him to pursue his. If, however, I should still be far in advance of him, I will often return to pay him my compliments. I venture to say, that I shall be with him as often as he wishes to see me. When I passed on before him in the argument on the mode, he gave me warning, that he should probably soon have the same advantage of me; but at the very outset, he is again complaining. Well, I cannot help it.

Infant baptism, the gentleman believes, has done more to corrupt the church, than all things else. Did you not hear on Saturday evening, how eloquently he spoke of "the sacramental host"—the innumerable multitudes of immersionists of olden time, in whose footsteps he was journeying on to a better world? Alas! the great majority of them were baptized in infancy! From the earliest period to which the history of the church can take us back, infant baptism prevailed universally. If we subtract from the immersionist ranks, all who experienced the sad consequences of being baptized in infancy, his sacramental host dwindles to a very small company. On the other evening, whilst he contemplated them as immersionists, they seemed to his imagination a host of saints and martyrs; but now they are with us most fully, and they appear, in his eyes, sadly, deplorably corrupt!!!

But it is vain to reason against *indisputable facts.* The baptism of infants has been practiced in our country by Congregationalists, Presbyterians and others, for more than two centuries; and during a much longer period in Scotland and other countries. Now, I ask this intelligent audience, are not the Pedo-baptist churches, that take the Bible as their only rule of faith, as moral, as upright, as virtuous, as pure in their lives, and, so far as man can judge, as pious, as those of the anti-Pedo-baptists? Where is the corruption which, according to the gentleman's logic, must have flowed like a torrent into our churches? I am more than willing to compare the Presbyterian church with his; and in the comparison, his would have this great advantage; that, being only about *sixteen years of age,* (!) it has had scarcely time to lose its first love, or to lose any portion of the virtue originally belonging to it. And now I assert, (and those who hear me will bear me witness,) that the Presbyterian church, and the other Pedo-baptist churches that take the Scriptures as their infallible guide, are as moral, as religious, in every respect as pure and pious, as any anti-Pedo-baptist church on earth. Where, then, is the corruption of which the baptism of infants is the prolific cause? The *cause* has been operating in our own country more than two centuries; but the *effect* has not appeared. Is it not, then, evident that the gentleman, under the influence of strong prejudices, has fallen into the error so common among men, of ascribing to things they dislike, tendencies which they do not possess?

You heard, whilst we were discussing the mode of baptism, with what pleasure the gentleman counted the number of immersionists. To-day, however, he has quite a distaste for that mode of reasoning! Eckius, the Roman priest, he tells us, boasted of number whilst the world was against Luther. The comparison, however, is unfortunate; for, in the first place, it was not true that the whole christian world was with Eckius. During the first five centuries of the christian era, the church, though becoming gradually corrupt, did not become papists; and in the second place, the assertion of Eckius was true only of those who did not search the Scriptures, and take them as their infallible guide. Luther was an instrument in the hands of God, in commencing a glorious reformation, at a period when it might be emphatically said, "darkness covered the earth, and gross darkness the people;" when the Bible was almost unknown, and the people were not permitted to read it for themselves. It is the peculiar prerogative of Mr. Campbell to have commenced a radical reformation, at a time when the Bible, untrammeled by note or comment, is in the hands of the people, and to proclaim to vast multitudes of the most devout readers and students of that plain 'book, that they have utterly failed to understand its fundamental doctrines ! ! ! This reformation, methinks, will hereafter be regarded as one of the most singular in its character, and the most absurd in its pretensions, that history records—a general, radical reformation of churches, whose ministers and members make the Bible their daily and prayerful study, and who, in their lives, exhibit the spirit of that blessed book quite as fully, to say the least, as they who would reform them !

The gentleman tells us, that we cannot understand the New Testament without consulting the Old ; and yet he finds fault with me because I have appealed to it ! Baptism, it is true, is a sacrament of the New Testament ; but connected with the subject before us, there are two distinct questions, viz : 1. What persons are entitled to membership in the church of Christ ? and, 2. By what ordinance must they be introduced ? I do not go to the Old Testament to ascertain, whether persons are to enter the church by circumcision or by baptism. I appeal to the Old Testament, in part, to ascertain who has a right to membership in the church ; and I appeal to the New Testament to determine by what ordinance they are to be recognized as members. If you wish to ascertain to whom the rights of citizenship in these United States, belong ; you do not go to the transactions of the last congress. You go back to the organization of the government and the adoption of the constitution ; and if the last or any preceding congress has changed the forms of recognizing those rights, you will appeal to the latest enactments on that subject to learn what those forms are. And so I go to the organization of the church—the period when the law of membership was passed—to ascertain who are to be admitted as members, and to the new dispensation to learn by what rite or ordinance they are to enter. If in this there is any absurdity, .the gentleman is welcome to expose it.

He agrees with me, that the commission required the apostles to go and make disciples by baptizing and teaching ; but he insists, that he does not make disciples as I do. That is likely enough ; but I make them, so far as human instrumentality is concerned, *by baptizing and teaching ;* and if he makes them in any other way, he does not act according to the commission. With the errors and superstitions of Xavier we have no concern.

He tells the audience, that I went back to Abraham only to get the *mark.* This is a mistake. I went to Abraham, as every intelligent and attentive hearer saw, for the purpose of finding the church and the law of membership. I care not, so far as the defence of infant-baptism is concerned, whether baptism did, or did not come in the place of circumcision. His fifteen arguments I may notice in passing. I had informed him, that I cared not whether baptism came instead of circumcision ; and I will show the audience, that my argument does not at all depend upon establishing that fact. I prove, that infants have the right to a place in the church ; and the conclusion is inevitable, that they have a right to enter by the door. Whether it is in the same side of the building as formerly, is of little importance. But his fifteen arguments were in his speech, and, like the lawyer, he must speak them !

The papists, he informs us, do not profess tó find infant-baptism in the Bible ; and he quotes a certain popish writer to that effect. The church of Rome, however, does not make this admission. I have several sermons delivered on the subject of infant-baptism by bishop Kenrick, of Philadelphia, and published with the approbation of bishop Flaget, of Louisville, in which the doctrine is defended at considerable length by the Scriptures.

Dr. Wall, too, he informs us, does not undertake to prove this doctrine by the Scriptures, but relies for its defence on Jewish proselyte baptism. Dr. Wall undertook simply to write the *history* of infant-baptism, not to go at length into the Bible argument in support of it. Yet he did very repeatedly appeal to the Scriptures in the progress of his history, as clearly teaching the doctrine. As to the Jewish proselyte baptism, I am not particularly concerned about it. I can and will prove the doctrine for which I am contending, independently of that source of evidence. Yet it will require, I think, something more than the mere assertion of the gentleman to disprove a fact which has so generally commanded the belief of the most learned men.

He repeats the declaration, that Calvin claimed the right *to change* the ordinances of the church. I regret, that he cannot be induced to give us Calvin's language—to let him speak for himself. Until he will do so, I shall pass his assertions without particular notice.

We come now to notice the main point in his speech. He tells us, that God made to Abraham two promises, and formed with him two covenants. I am curious to know where he finds in the Scriptures a plurality of covenants with Abraham. I read of *the covenant* with Abraham; but I find no mention of *the covenants* (in the plural.) It is true, Paul, in the Epistle to the Romans, speaks of "the covenants of promise;" but unfortunately for the gentleman, he does not say, that these covenants were made *with Abraham.* It is admitted, that God made to Abraham several promises; but this affords no evidence of a plurality of covenants; for who does not know, that one covenant may embrace a number of distinct promises? The gospel contains a number of promises; and if there must be a distinct covenant for every promise, it contains quite a number of covenants! When the gentleman proves, that God made with Abraham two covenants; I will prove, that our Savior has made with his church *half a dozen!*

In the 12th chapter of Genesis, we find several promises made to Abraham, but not ratified in the form of a covenant. In the 15th, we find the promises repeated, but still not ratified by any seal to be applied to Abraham and his posterity. In the 17th, we find the same promises again repeated, and ratified in the form of a covenant, of which circumcision was the seal to be administered to Abraham and his seed in succeeding generations. "And when Abram was ninety years old and nine, the Lord appeared to Abram, and said unto him, I am the Almighty God: walk before me and be thou perfect. And I will make my covenant [one covenant only] between me and thee, and will multiply thee exceedingly. And Abram fell on his face: and God talked with him, saying, As for me, behold my covenant is with thee, and thou shalt be a father of many nations. Neither shall thy name any more be called Abram; but thy name shall be Abraham: for a father of many nations have I made thee. And I will make thee exceeding fruitful, and I will make nations of thee, and kings shall come out of thee. And I will establish my covenant between me and thee, and thy seed after thee, in their generations, for an everlasting covenant, to be a God unto thee, and to thy seed after thee.

And I will give unto thee, and to thy seed after thee, the land wherein thou art a stranger, all the land of Canaan, for an everlasting possession: and I will be their God. This is my covenant, which ye shall keep, between me and you, and thy seed after thee. Every man child among you shall be circumcised," chap. xvii. 1—10.

Here is the covenant upon which the church was organized. It contains three distinct promises; 1. A promise of a numerous natural seed, which has been fulfilled; 2. That his natural seed should possess the land of Canaan, which has also been fulfilled; 3. That he should be a father of many nations; that in his seed all the families of the earth should be blessed. This is the great promise of the covenant, the promise of spiritual blessings to all nations through Jesus Christ, the promised seed, and is now being fulfilled. This covenant containing these three promises, the same that are recorded in the 12th and 15th chapters, was ratified and sealed by circumcision. With Abraham, therefore, God made but *one covenant*. My friend may, if he pleases, insist on three covenants, each containing the same promises; but it is all apocryphal—it is absurd. There is not a passage in the Bible that speaks of more than one.

With the organization of *the nation* which he supposes to have taken place at Sinai, I have nothing to do, so far as the present discussion is concerned. I am concerned only to find the organization of the *church*, and to ascertain the law of membership in it.

But the gentleman tells us, that when the nation was organized, circumcision passed out of the hands of Abraham into the hands of Moses. To prove this most singular declaration he refers to John vii. 23, "If a man on the Sabbath day receive circumcision, that the *law of Moses* should not be broken," &c. But it is most manifest, that his construction of this passage is wholly incorrect. It is flatly contradictory of the teaching of Paul, Rom. iv. 11, "And he [Abraham] received the sign of circumcision; a seal of the righteousness of the faith which he had, yet being uncircumcised; that he might be the father of all them that believe, though they be not circumcised; that righteousness might be imputed unto them also: and the father of circumcision to them who are not of the circumcision only, but who also walk in the steps of that faith of our father Abraham, which he had, being yet uncircumcised." Now if, as the gentleman contends, circumcision passed from the hands of Abraham to Moses; how could circumcision make Abraham the father of all believers in all time to come?

The first five books of the Old Testament were written chiefly by Moses, and were, therefore, commonly called *the law of Moses*, (2 Kings xxiii. 25; Daniel ix. 11; John vii. 19.) Indeed the Old Testament was divided into the Law, the Prophets and the Psalms, or the Law and the Prophets. It was on this account that circumcision was said to be administered, that the *law of Moses* might not be broken, not because it had in some incomprehensible sense been transferred from Abraham to Moses. The law which was given at Sinai, was a temporary *addition* to the Abrahamic covenant, designed to answer a particular purpose, for a limited time; and therefore circumcision, the seal of the Abrahamic covenant, embraced and sealed those additions to it, made for the purpose of carrying out its provisions. So Paul teaches in Galatians iii. 19, "Wherefore then serveth the law? It was ADDED [of course, to the Abrahamic covenant] till the seed should come," &c. The law at Sinai, was not,

2 C

therefore, another covenant entirely distinct from that made with Abraham, but was only an *addition* to it.

The gentleman informs us, that circumcision was a *seal* only in the case of Abraham—that to his posterity it was a *sign*, but not a *seal*. That is, he makes this ordinance one thing to Abraham, and quite another to his posterity and to all others who received it! Well, if he will be good enough to point us to the Scripture which so teaches, I will believe it. And it is particularly proper, that he should do this; for he commenced his reformation with the avowed purpose of having a " thus saith the Lord " for every item of faith and practice. I now call upon him to produce the passage of Scripture which sustains his assertion.

My acknowledgments are due to him for his benevolent wish, that I possessed very great powers, in order to sift to the bottom this important subject. But feeble as my powers are, they were sufficient, in the opinion of very many intelligent persons, to give him great trouble last week. When we see a great man, like my friend—a man standing at the head of a reformation of extraordinary pretensions in the nineteenth century, in such difficulty, so puzzled to meet the arguments of one of the small men of the Presbyterian church; we are obliged to think, he has a difficult cause to plead. It affords strong presumptive evidence, that truth is on the side of the small man. Under such circumstances I incline to the opinion, that he ought to be satisfied with my powers.

But I must very briefly pay my respects to the gentleman's fifteen arguments, designed to prove that baptism did not come in place of circumcision. As I have before stated, I care not, so far as the defence of infant baptism is concerned, whether it did or not. I can, however, easily prove that it did. What do we mean when we say that baptism came in place of circumcision? We mean simply this; *that baptism answers the same purposes to the church under the new dispensation, that circumcision answered under the old.* Circumcision was the door of entrance into the church under the former dispensation; baptism is the door under the present dispensation. Circumcision was the sign and seal of God's covenant with his people, the mark which distinguished them from those not in covenant with God; and baptism is now the ordinance which distinguishes his people from the world, and which seals to them his promised grace. Circumcision was a significant ordinance, pointing to the sanctification of the heart by the Holy Spirit; and hence the wicked were called *uncircumcised in heart,* and were exhorted to *circumcise the foreskin of their hearts.* Baptism is a significant ordinance, pointing emblematically to the same thing. These statements, I am prepared to prove, if indeed they require proof; and these things being true, it is certain that baptism came in place of circumcision—that it answers the same ends in the church now, that were answered by circumcision under the former dispensation. But I am not at all concerned to prove this point. The whole of his fifteen arguments are based on the false assumption, that the substitute must be, in all respects, like the thing for which it is substituted, regardless of difference of circumstances!

But I will answer the gentleman's question. He inquires whether I acknowledge the existence of a church before the days of Abraham—and if so, how infants entered it? I will, for argument's sake, admit the existence of a church before the organization in Abraham's family; and now, if he will tell us how *adults* entered it, I pledge myself to show how infants were received. This certainly is a fair proposition.

He asks a second question, (and I like to answer questions,) viz. what spiritual blessing was conveyed by circumcision to the Ishmaelites and Edomites? He labors to prove, that circumcision conveyed to those who received it, no spiritual blessing. I will answer his question by asking another, viz. What spiritual blessing does *immersion* convey to the *Mormons?* If many were circumcised who did not receive any spiritual blessing; have not many (and the Mormons among them,) been immersed without receiving such blessings? Yet the gentleman firmly believes, that immersion conveys spiritual blessings.

But I am truly surprised, that any one who has carefully read the Old Testament and the New, should assert, that *piety* was not required of adults, in order to membership in the Jewish church. God entered into covenant with the Jewish church. He represents himself as *married* to her. Did he, I emphatically ask, enter into covenant with men, without requiring them to obey him? And could they truly obey him without possessing true piety? It would, indeed, have been most marvellous, if God had entered into covenant with the Jews, promising to them blessings not bestowed on any other nation, and yet left it optional with them whether they would serve him! But the gentleman's assertion is in direct contradiction of the Bible. Paul, writing to the Galatians, says: "I testify again to every man that is circumcised, that he is a debtor to do the whole law," chap. v. 3. Could any one keep the whole law, which was given to the Jewish church, without possessing piety? That law required them to love God with the whole heart. Could they do this without piety? Why, Paul teaches us, that circumcision, without true piety, was absolutely worthless, "For circumcision verily profiteth, if thou keep the law; but if thou be a breaker of the law, thy circumcision is made uncircumcision," Rom. ii. 25. Now, can a man keep the law, the moral law, of which, as the connection shows, he is speaking, without piety? Every one must see that it is impossible. Circumcision, therefore, did require piety, and no one could be a worthy member of the Jewish church, without possessing it.

Let us now place before our minds the real state of the argument. The gentleman complains that I travel too rapidly, that I present too many points; but I discover that the audience can easily keep up with me. He, however, is not speaking for *present effect.* He is elaborating from this Book, which he professes to believe quite plain, ideas too profound to be appreciated by this audience. *He is making a book*—a book for *posterity!* He does not speak for the multitude. I go for present effect and for future effect; and I think I shall be understood, and my arguments will be appreciated by those who hear me.

I have said, and Mr. Campbell has not disputed it, that all who are entitled to membership in the church of God, ought to be baptized. I have defined the church to be a body of people separated from the world for the service of God, with ordinances of divine appointment, and a door of admission—a rite for the recognition of membership. He has not disputed the correctness of this definition. I have found such a body—a church organized, in the family of Abraham. I have proved that believers *and their children* were put into this church by positive law of God, and my friend has found no law for putting out the one or the other. I have proved the identity of the church under both dispensations. The conclusion follows inevitably, that the children of believers are still entitled to a place in the church, and, of course, to baptism, the initiatory rite.

The great Baptist writer, Andrew Fuller, comments on the twelfth and seventeenth chapters of Genesis, as follows:

Fuller, vol. v. p. 115. "This promise has been fulfilling ever since. All the true blessedness which the world is now, or shall hereafter be possessed of, is owing to Abram and his posterity. Through them we have a Bible, a Savior, and a gospel. They are the stock on which the christian church is grafted."

Ibid. p. 153. "The first promise in this covenant is, that he shall be *the father of many nations;* and as a token of it, his name in future is to be called ABRAHAM. He had the name of a *high*, or eminent *father*, from the beginning; but now it shall be more comprehensive, indicating a very large progeny. By the exposition given of this promise in the New Testament, (Rom. iv. 16, 17,) we are directed to understand it, not only of those who sprang from Abraham's body, though these were many nations; but also of all that should be *of the faith of Abraham*. It went to make him the father of the church of God in all future ages, or, as the apostle calls him, *the heir of the world*. In this view, he is the father of many, even of *a multitude of nations*. All that the christian world enjoys, or ever will enjoy, it is indebted for it to Abraham and his seed. A high honor this, to be the father of the faithful, the stock from which the Messiah should spring, and on which the church of God should grow."

Fuller, you observe, though a decided anti-Pedo-baptist, did not believe that God made with Abraham more than one covenant. Observe, too, he believed that the covenant of circumcision, recorded in Gen. xvii., constituted him the father of the church of God in all future ages; and he says, the christian world is indebted to Abraham, and his seed, for all they now enjoy, or ever will enjoy. I will put Fuller, who was both a great and a good man, against Mr. Campbell.—[*Time expired.*

Monday, Nov. 20—12½ o'clock, A. M.
[MR. CAMPBELL'S SECOND REPLY.]

MR. PRESIDENT—To condescend, sir, from the dignity of rational and grave argument upon divine ordinances, connected with man's sanctification and salvation, to the *ad captandum* statements of my politic opponent, is by no means gratifying to my taste, nor to my feelings. I have already suffer d many instances of this species of rhetoric to pass without any notice, hoping that a proper sense of the dignity of the church he represents, would elevate him above such unworthy modes of defending a religious proposition. Being disappointed in these hopes, I am constrained, for once, to notice his course. Had the subject of his valorous achievements last week been the question of debate, or were the display of a captious temper his supreme aim, then, indeed, there would have been much more pertinency and propriety in the speech which you have just now heard.

A person so sensitive of praise, and so much devoted to his own dear self, as to be always talking of himself in such a style, had better turn his attention to the proverbs of Solomon, on the ways and means of promoting his own glory. Solomon delivers some sage remarks on that subject, which I would commend to him as a beautiful text for a useful sermon. It is happily expressed in the following apposite terms: "Let another praise thee, and not thine own mouth; a stranger, and not thine own lips."

There is something, too, in this invidious comparison of churches and communities, which savors a little of the same ruling passion—and which neither christian morality, nor a high sense of christian courtesy, commends. I have not made one allusion to the comparative attainments, virtues, or excellencies, personal or social, in our respective communities. I have never contrasted Presbyterians and Disciples, in any one point of view, in this discussion. In speaking of the great mass of uneducated mind—mere flesh and blood, brought into a community by the operation of infant affusion, I had no special reference to Presbyterians, more than to Congregationalists, Methodists, or Episcopalians. ,Nay, indeed, I had especial reference to that great mother of ignorance and superstition, who annually brings under her priesthood some three millions of speechless babes, by the operation of a few drops of water, and the sign of the cross.

Any one who desires to appreciate the truth of these remarks, I commend to the history of Old Spain and New Spain, of Italy and Portugal, lands not much imbued with the spirit of Protestantism A more beautiful sky spreads not itself over a more polluted land than that which looks down upon Italy, the very home of infant rantism; and the sink of European pollutions. Any one who desires to know what have been the operations of the unhallowed alliance of church and state, and of infant membership, the main pillar of it, had better make himself master of Italian, Spanish, and Portuguese history. But to ascertain its operations at home, we have documentary evidence enough to show, that it tends rather to the carnalizing and secularizing, than to the purification or elevation of the church's character. Of the multitudes of baptized members of the Presbyterian church, how few ever approach the Lord's table! How many baptized infidels are there in the bounds of all the Pedo-baptist communities! Of the nominal members of the christian profession, perhaps one half are the veriest sinners in Christendom. And does not Pedo-baptism claim its own children, initiated and dedicated by this rite? does she not claim them, I say, as members of her churches!! Now, I admit, that of those who make the christian confession, on their own responsibility, some apostatize and return to the world. But what is their number, compared with the sprinkled myriads all over the land, that are living without God, without Christ, and without hope—and, consequently, without either righteousness or holiness! Only think, one branch of the Pedo-baptist church baptizes, as she calls it, one hundred millions every three and thirty years! The "mother church," as she calls herself, the mother church of this church of Pedo-baptist communities, gains more by infant baptism, in making members, than all the other parties combined. The whole Lutheran community, the largest branch of Protestantism, sprinkles only thirty millions in thirty-three years. The Greek church immerses very many millions in the same time. All these are made members of *Christ's church* by this rite, in the esteem of the respective communities that practice it. What an immense weight of carnality, sensuality, and of varied wickedness, would be severed from the christian profession by the annihilation of this rite of infant initiation!

Luther, no doubt, intended an entire reformation of the church, but was prevented. Eckius withstood him—and, as the pope's representative, opposed the incipient reformation. No living man can now say how far these efforts retarded that glorious revolution. The case was as I represented it—Luther aimed at the reformation of the church from all errors. Eckius used the same logic and rhetoric against him, as you have heard urged against me by my too imitative opponent; and to a good degree prevented the progress of that soul-redeeming principle, that questions every thing but the Bible.

He would make capital out of that sacramental host to whom I alluded the other evening; as if it was chiefly or wholly composed of Pedo-baptists! The gentleman, it seems, knows of no church but the Pedo-baptist. There were no persecuted ones in the valleys between the mountains of Europe in those days of proscription! No Piedmontese—no Waldenses—no Albigenses—no Vaudois—no Cathari—no remonstrants against popery—no church but that of Rome or of Constantinople ! !

But Mr. R. says I blamed him for going ahead! No; I blame him rather for not going into the argument. What is the point? What does he mean! Already he begins to speak of circumcision and the arguments formerly drawn from circumcision, and, of course, from the covenants— as a matter for which he does not care, to quote his own elegant style, " a single straw." Do I understand the gentleman or not! Has he really abandoned circumcision; or does he only desire to appear to place no emphasis upon it, for the sake of effect; or of turning my attention away from the main stay of the whole theory of infant-membership! What does it mean! If Jewish proselyte baptism is abandoned; if the tradition of the church is abandoned; and if circumcision is about being abandoned, too, I shall have easy work of it—and infant-membership will, indeed, hang upon "a straw !" I cannot think that he will abandon father Calvin, the great founder of Presbyterian infant affusion.

But I blame him, too, for going into the Old Testament! Not at all. I blame no man for going into the Old Testament. I wish he would go into it thoroughly. I only blame him for abandoning the New, and going into the Old to find what his creed calls " a sacrament of the New Testament."

Unless to kill time, I know not why the gentleman deals so much in this kind of logic. But instead of proving that God made but one covenant with Abraham, or of disposing of my argument already delivered, he is now asking me to prove again that there were two covenants made with father Abraham. Well, then, I must tell him the story a second time. Paul to the Romans, 9 chap. says—"To the Israelites pertain the adoption, and the glory, and the covenants, and the giving of the law, and the service of God, and the promises." There was, then, besides the law and the promises, a *plurality* of covenants given to Israel. This only proves a plurality of covenants. And to find out the amount of this plurality I go into the history of the Jews, beginning, of course, with the founder of the religion, or the father of the faithful. God made but one covenant with all Israel, at Horeb; therefore, that being also named, and *covenants* besides, we are obliged to look for a history of those transactions in the Abrahamic family, designated by that name. I have, then, clearly distinguished and documented with proof no less than *three* covenants, made with Abraham;—two, based on the first promise, and one, on the second. The one on the second, is that which concerns us, because Paul calls it " *the gospel*, in its origin," and the first indication of gentile justification—Galatians iii. 8. This is the gospel covenant, called, by the same apostle and in the same epistle, " *the covenant concerning Christ*." The covenant is made out, denominated, and even *dated* by the same apostle. He says it was made four hundred and thirty years before the law—chap. iii. 15. He says—"Brethren, I speak after the manner of men ; though it be but a man's covenant, yet if it *be confirmed*, no man disannuleth, or addeth thereto. Now to Abraham and his seed were the promises made. He saith not, And to seeds, as of many ; but as of one, even to *thy seed*, which is the Christ." Now then, I say, that the covenant that was confirmed before of God, in Christ, *the law*, which was *four hundred and thirty years after*, cannot disannul, that it should make *the promise* of non-effect. Nothing can be more clearly expressed. Here is a covenant named, described, dated. We can have its date most accurately traced. Abraham was seventy-five years old when the two promises were given him; one, concerning the Messiah, as aforesaid—and one, concerning his own family, with a reference thereunto. He was one hundred years old when Isaac was born. Isaac was sixty when Jacob was born, and Jacob told Pharaoh, when he went down into Egypt with his family, that he was one hundred and thirty years old. Now add these respective sums of 25+60+130=215. Now, sir Isaac Newton's chronology, arch-bishop Usher's, the commonly received chronology, make the whole sojourning in Egypt 215 years—which two sums exactly make 430 years, from the covenant concerning the Messiah—the gospel covenant, to have transpired before the giving of the law, as Paul expressly declares.

We have, then, one covenant indisputably made out and dated. We shall now look for a second. This we find amply delineated in the 18th chapter of Genesis, about ten, or twelve years at most, after the former. This covenant, as I have already stated, had respect to the promised inheritance. It was made to define, and secure the patrimony of the sons of Abraham in the line of the promised seed. While confirming it over sacrifice, the Lord informed the patriarch, that his posterity should be sojourners, strangers and oppressed, for four hundred years. In the fourth generation they shall come to this land again, for the cup of the Amorites is not yet full. "In that same day," says Moses, "the Lord made a *covenant* with Abraham, saying, Unto thy seed have I given this land, from the river of Egypt unto the great river, the river Euphrates." Can any language more definitely designate the making of a covenant on a certain day than this? Examine Gen. xv. 7—21. I have fixed this covenant in the 86th year of Abraham; because immediately after it we are informed of the birth of Ishmael, who was thirteen years old at the date of the covenant of circumcision; to which I next invite your attention.

It will require no proof, I presume, to any one acquainted with ancient patriarchal history, that the covenant styled by Stephen, "the covenant of circumcision," was made one year before the birth of Isaac, and in the ninety-ninth year of Abraham, twenty-four or twenty-five years after the "covenant concerning Christ." We have all the dates given, the covenants detailed in the 17th of Genesis, and even down to Acts vii. 8, denominated as follows: "And he gave him the covenant of circumcision, and then Abraham begat Isaac, and circumcised him the eighth day." We have, then, delineated three distinct covenants made with Abraham during the period of five and twenty years; and no man can convert these three into one covenant. The parties were always the same, but the stipulations, pledges, seals, objects, and dates, are just as different as any three transactions ever made between one and the same two persons. I trust my friend will more seriously and religiously approach the subject. Let us have some argument, some demonstration; let him take some other time to trifle. He now represents the dignity, gravity, purity, and learning of the Presbyterian church. I respect and treat him in that character; otherwise we should not have condescended to this discussion.

He has said the Mormons immerse! What a profound discovery!

What does it prove! Romanists sprinkle as well as Presbyterians! And what does that prove? Better meet my proposition. Better discuss the question whether circumcision conveyed spiritual blessings, or was the sign, or the seal, of a gospel covenant. I am prepared to reason with him on such a subject, on any thing relevant to the points on hand. I have said that circumcision was neither the conveyance, the sign, or the seal of any spiritual privilege, to those who were its *proper* subjects— mark me, its *proper* subjects. What did circumcision convey to its proper subject? Of what was it the sign to him? How adroitly does the gentleman get out of the difficulty! He might as logically have invited you to examine the first chapter of the Maccabees, as to have asked what does immersion convey to a Mormon? Is a man with a new Bible in his hand, a proper subject of christian immersion! He might as well ask me, what would immersion convey to an unenlightened Indian? Will his brethren feel proud of this defence of their infant baptism? When asked what scriptural blessings circumcision conveyed to a proper subject, such as Ishmael, Esau, and all the household of Abraham, men, boys, and children of eight days, his sage and shrewd response is—What does immersion convey to a Mormon! Thus making a Mormon, believing the lying tales of an infamous imposter, as proper a subject of immersion as was any son of Abraham. I ask again, were not the Ishmaelites, the Edomites, and all that nation that died in the wilderness, and that which perished in Jerusalem—were they not all fit subjects of circumcision?

I have never said, nor intended to say, nor, by any fair construction, could be made to say, that God ever " entered into covenant with impiety." I am ashamed at this gentleman's recklessness of assertion. Did any one, in this great concourse, save Mr. Rice, hear me say any thing that could, by fair construction, be so interpreted? (I fear I shall have to descend to an exposition of my friend, as the best means of exposing his arguments.) I said that God made a covenant with Abraham *concerning his flesh.* That Abraham's flesh was precious to him, no matter who wore it for the sake of *the seed,* the blessing of the nations that was in it. God approved the faith of Abraham; constituted it the model faith; and to seal it, gave him the *sign of circumcision.* But that was a " covenant *in his flesh,*" till out of it should come the seed of David, according to the flesh: " In thy seed shall all the families of the earth be blessed." This promise suggested circumcision, not before Ishmael, but just before Isaac was born. God is determined to identify and preserve this flesh; commanding fathers to brand their sons before they knew any thing about it, while they were yet as passive as a stone; that the world might recognize it, and know that God keepeth covenant and mercy forever; and that his word standeth fast for a thousand generations.

There is no Pedo-baptist, as it appears to me, that has written or spoken with much light or discrimination, on this great fact in the Jews' religion, viz: *That flesh, and neither faith nor piety, qualified, not only for membership, but for every holy office in the Jews' religion.* Of Levi, with whom was the URIM and the THUMMIM, Jacob said: " Cursed be his anger, for it was fierce, and his wrath, for it was cruel. I will scatter him in Jacob and divide him in Israel." And of him Moses said; " The sons of Levi shall teach Jacob thy judgments and Israel thy law: they shall put incense before them, and whole burnt offerings on their altar." There was no tribe of the twelve that had less piety than the Levites (a good type of the great mass of the priesthood, who count after the Levitical order.) But there was neither moral nor spiritual qualifications necessary to any office. Aaron's first born son, if he had a complete animal body and a reasonable soul, though he were as wicked as Hophne and Phineas, as Annas or Caiaphas, might legitimately officiate in that institution. Priests were the sons of priests. High priests were the sons of high priests, as were Levites the sons of Levites. What clearer or more convincing demonstration, that *flesh*, and neither faith nor piety, was contemplated in the Jews' religion? The Spirit of God, too, occasionally attended their ministry. Even the wicked Caiaphas was visited with an oracle. The Spirit came upon him, and " he prophesied, being high priest that year." He was, then, a good high priest, though a wicked man. The genius of that dispensation allowed such a state of things. When Joseph, or Nicodemus, was pleading the cause of the Messiah in the council that condemned him, Caiaphas, we learn, admitted the plea of his innocence, and replied, " It is better, [notwithstanding innocent he be,] that one man should perish, and not that the whole nation should be destroyed." This he said because high priest that year, and it intimated that he should die, not to save the Jewish nation only, but the Gentiles also. No wonder that John the Baptist and the Messiah preached a new religion, a new repentance, a new birth, and that flesh must give place to faith, and blood to piety. In Christ's kingdom, "To as many as received him, gave he privilege to become the sons of God ; even to them that believed on his name: born not of flesh, nor of blood, nor of the will of man, but of God."

" God entered into covenant with impiety !! " What an unfounded imputation ! If the gentleman, in my presence, and in your hearing, can thus pervert language, misconstrue and misinterpret my words, what confidence can any one repose in him, as a commentator upon the arguments of those whom he opposes ? If in my presence, much more in my absence, might I not expect my arguments and sayings to be tortured into whatever his cause or his party may religiously require at his hands ; I say again, God made three covenants with Abraham, one all spirit, one all flesh, and one all property. The flesh and the land went together. The spirit reaches beyond flesh—beyond land—beyond time—to an inheritance incorruptible, and undefiled, and that endureth forever. All nations, by faith, inherit the latter ; while to the Jews alone belonged both the flesh of Abraham and the soil of Canaan.

The gentleman has introduced Andrew Fuller. He is fond of the Baptists. Well, he makes good selections. Gale was Arminian, Carson is Calvinian, and Fuller was mediator. I am much pleased with them all. I agree, probably, as much with him as with the others. The gentleman may read as much as he pleases from them all. I hear all, but vow to none. Still his reading from Fuller will be quite as acceptable to me as any thing he can himself say.

My friend, Mr. R., too often adverts to the business of last Saturday evening. Calvin's words are quoted in my debate with McCalla ; I have not with me his treatise on the Acts. The words are—" The church did grant liberty to herself, since the beginning, to change the rites somewhat, excepting the substance." Does Mr. Rice say that these are not the words of Calvin " in our language ? "

I have lost too much time in noticing minor matters. Still I have responded to every thing of any weight or importance in the evidence adduced in favor of infant subjects. He leads the way—I follow. While he affords any thing better, I will not respond to trifles. The public, I doubt not, will understand this argument, and ultimately come to proper conclusions. I have brought down the history of covenants, so far as to contradistinguish the old and the new. The covenant of flesh, and the covenant of spirit, the law and the gospel, the constitution of the Jewish church, and the constitution of the christian.

I said, in my last speech, no person was made a member of the Jewish state by circumcision—or, in other words, that circumcision was not the door into it. Mr. R. says it was. Has he proved it? Proselytes came in partially that way. But the question is about the family of Abraham. Was circumcision to *them* the door? By no means. There was no Jewish church till four hundred years after the institution of circumcision. Consequently the door would have been of no use. The advocates of circumcision as the *door*, are mechanically and theologically at fault. They have a door reared up without a wall, standing by itself, without a house attached to it, for four hundred years; and they have all the seed of Abraham born in the house, and yet coming in by the door! !

I do hope my friend will concentrate his mind upon some main point of argument, after he has disposed of the objections and reasons I have offered against his assumption.—[*Time expired.*

Monday, Nov. 20—1 o'clock, P. M.
[MR. RICE'S THIRD ADDRESS.]

MR. PRESIDENT—The manner of my speaking must be a very mysterious affair. There is something in my *ad captandum* style so difficult of comprehension, that the gentleman thinks it will be necessary for him to *explain* it to the audience! They, it would seem, are incapable of forming a correct judgment concerning it! It requires as much explanation as the Bible! In this debate the gentleman cannot excite me; though he continue his efforts till the going down of the sun. I always conduct such discussions in good temper. I can even argue, and occasionally smile; but I cannot so forget what is due to this audience, nor so far disregard the rules of courtesy, as to charge the gentleman with "licentiousness of the tongue." I have no occasion to use language of this character. He is an older man than I, and I can permit him to indulge his feelings in this manner.

I do not, in this discussion, represent any denomination of christians, in an *ecclesiastical* sense. So far as a minister of the gospel is a representative of the church by which he is sent forth to defend the truth, I appear here as a representative, but no further. And, thus far, I am happy to know, that my brethren are not ashamed of my defence of their views. I am perfectly aware of the existence and of the propriety of Solomon's admonition, to which the gentleman refers; and I am also aware that there are some occasions which require a man to speak in self-defence. I should not have made the remarks which have given him offence, if he and his friends had not proclaimed it over the land, that I must be *endorsed* before he would condescend to meet me in debate. It looks rather badly, I should think, that the gentleman who called for endorsers of his opponent, has made so unsuccessful a defence of his principles!

He did not intend, he says, to draw a contrast between Presbyterians and Immersionists, but had allusion to the corruptions of popery. But I deny, that infant baptism caused any of the corruptions of popery. He has ascribed certain effects to a certain cause. How did I reply to him? I proved that the cause has existed in divers places for centuries without producing the effects. He asserts, that infant baptism is the cause of the corruptions which have overrun large portions of the church of Christ; but I proved, (and he does not deny it,) that infant baptism has long existed in the Pedo-baptist churches of this and other countries, and has produced no such evil effects. I have instituted no invidious comparisons; but I have proved, that he has egregiously erred in seeking the true cause of the corruptions of the church.

Infant baptism does not, as the gentleman strangely imagines, give the pope his power over the human mind. If Gregory XVI. were now to send forth his decree, that no infant should hereafter be baptized in his spiritual dominions; would he not retain his despotic power over them all? Would not Italy, Spain, Portugal and Austria still prostrate themselves before the chair of St. Peter? So long as his claim to infallibility, and the keys of the kingdom of heaven is credited, so long will he wield an unlimited power over the intellects and consciences of parents, and, of course, over those of the rising generation. No—infant baptism never introduced one error into the church. The secret of the pope's power is not in infant baptism, but in his claim to be infallible, to interpret God's will to man as he may choose, to impose human tradition as articles of faith, to open and shut the gates of heaven. These, not infant baptism, are the true sources of the tyrannical power of Rome.

The gentleman, by the way, speaks of Calvin as the *founder* of Presbyterianism. I venture to assert, that Calvin never did exercise in the Presbyterian church a power so extensive as Mr. Campbell exerts over his. Calvin was a great and good man, but the Presbyterian church has never adopted all his views. I presume it would not be difficult to prove, that Presbyterianism, at least in all its important features, is much older than Calvin.

He does not find fault with me, he says, for going to the Old Testament, but for appealing to it improperly—for going contrary to the Westminster assembly of divines, who say, that baptism is a sacrament of the New Testament. There are, as I have before stated, two distinct questions connected with the subject under discussion, viz: 1. What characters are entitled to membership in the church of Christ? 2. By what ordinance shall they be introduced into its fellowship? The Westminster divines never did say, that to find an answer to the first, we are to confine ourselves to the New Testament. They do say, that the New Testament gives the answer to the second. Precisely in accordance with their teaching, I go to the Old Testament, to the organization of the church, to find the law of membership, and to the New to ascertain the ordinance by which membership shall be recognized. The gentleman has told us, that he was once a Presbyterian, and that he did with great care and labor examine this whole subject; and yet he evidently does not understand some of the most prominent doctrines of the Confession of Faith! He is charging me with going contrary to its teachings, when, as every well-instructed Presbyterian knows, I am defending precisely the principles it inculcates!!! I told you, a day or two since, that I doubted whether he ever was a genuine Presbyterian; and now my doubts are confirmed.

He has labored to prove, that God made with Abraham two covenants, and that the covenant of circumcision is a mere *national* transaction. I called upon him to point to the passage of Scripture that speaks of two covenants with Abraham. He has appealed to Rom. ix. 4, "Who are Israelites, to whom pertaineth the adoption, and the glory, and the covenants, and the giving of the law, and the service of God, and the promises." I have replied, that Paul does not say, these covenants were made *with Abraham*. The gentleman says, the covenants are distinct from the giving of the law at Sinai; and, of course, they were made with Abraham. But are not the covenants in this passage as distinct from the *promises*, as from the giving of the law? So he would succeed in proving, according to his logic, that God made with Abraham covenants without promises, and that he made to the Israelites promises without a covenant! Can you conceive of a covenant without a promise?

But let us turn again to the chapter of Genesis, where he imagines that he finds two covenants. In the twelfth chapter we find three distinct promises, viz. 1st. A promise of a numerous natural offspring: "And I will make of thee a great nation, and I will bless thee, and make thy name great." 2nd. A promise of the land of Canaan to him and his seed: "Get thee out of thy country, and from thy kindred, and from thy father's house, *unto a land that I will show thee.*" "And (verse 7) the Lord appeared unto Abram, and said, Unto thy seed will I give this land." 3rd. A promise of spiritual blessings through the Messiah: "And in thee shall all the families of the earth be blessed." This promise, Paul the apostle says, contains the gospel, Gal. iii. 8. In the fifteenth chapter we find precisely the same promises repeated. In the fourth verse is the promise of a son, Isaac; and the fifth reads thus: "And he brought him forth abroad, and said, Look now toward heaven, and tell the stars, if thou be able to number them. And he said unto him, so shall thy seed be." This promise includes both his natural and his spiritual seed; and the seventh verse contains the promise of the land of Canaan. In the seventeenth chapter we find precisely the same promises very distinctly reiterated, and sealed to Abraham and his seed by circumcision. 1. The promise of a numerous natural seed is found in verses 2 and 6; 2. The promise of the land of Canaan is found in verse 8; and 3. The promise of a numerous spiritual seed, through Christ, in the 5th verse. So Paul explains it in Rom. iv. 16.

Now observe, in the 12th chapter we find these promises first made; but no *sign* or *seal* was appointed. In the 15th we find them repeated; but still no *seal* is affixed to them. In the 17th, the very same promises are reiterated, ratified, and *sealed* by circumcision, appointed to be the sign and seal of the covenant. Now, can you believe that God made two covenants with Abraham, each embracing *precisely the same promises?*

You make a bargain to-day, for example, with your neighbor, selling him a farm. The next week the bargain is again talked over, and the week following writings are drawn, and a deed is given. Would it be true to say, that you had made *three* contracts? Precisely so God made certain promises to Abraham: then, a few years after, repeated them; and still a few years later, reiterated and sealed the very same promises. Will any one believe, with these facts before him, that God made with Abraham more than one covenant?

I have said, that in the Scriptures we never read of *covenants* (in the plural) made with Abraham, but of the *covenant*. In confirmation of this assertion, let me read 1 Chron. xvi. 15—17, "Be ye mindful always of his covenant, the word which he commanded to a thousand generations; even the covenant which he made with Abraham, and of his oath unto Isaac; and hath confirmed the same to Jacob, for a law, and to Israel for an everlasting covenant," &c. Evidently the inspired writer knew of but *one* covenant with Abraham. There is not a passage in the Bible which speaks of more than one.

The gentleman is quite dissatisfied at my answer to his question concerning the circumcision of the Ishmaelites and Edomites. He inquired, by way of proving that circumcision conveyed no spiritual blessing, what blessing it conveyed to those descendants of Abraham. I inquired of him, what spiritual blessing was conveyed by immersion to the Mormons. But he says, he asked what spiritual blessing was conveyed to those who were *proper subjects* of circumcision. The Edomites and Ishmaelites were as truly apostates, as are the Mormons. They did not pretend to keep covenant with God, and were, therefore, never recognized as a people in covenant with him. Is it, then, surprising, that circumcision, though strictly a religious ordinance, conveyed no spiritual blessing to *apostates?* Does christian baptism impart spiritual blessings to such persons? My reply to the gentleman's query was, then, appropriate and conclusive.

He tells us, he did not say, that God entered into covenant with wicked persons, but that he entered into a covenant with Abraham, which did not require piety in his decendants or those embraced in it. But the difficulty is not to be escaped in this way, for God said to Abraham—"And I will establish my covenant between me and thee, *and thy seed after thee, in their generations,* for an everlasting covenant, to be a God unto thee, and to thy seed after thee. And God said unto Abraham, Thou shalt keep my covenant, therefore, thou *and thy seed after thee,* in their generations," Gen. xvii. So it appears, that not only Abraham, but his posterity, were embraced in the covenant, and were all required, as truly as was Abraham, to keep covenant with God. *Could they do this without piety?* And who has not read in the Scriptures, that the Jews were repeatedly punished and finally sent in captivity to Babylon, because they broke God's covenant? If, as the gentleman strangely asserts, the covenant of circumcision did not require piety; how happened it that for their *impiety* the Jews were so sorely punished? Do you not remember how frequently, in the Old Testament, God represents himself as the *husband* of the Jewish church, and their rebellion as the unfaithfulness of a wife who abandons her lawful husband, and disregards her marriage vows?

But the apostle Paul, in his Epistle to the Romans, has forever settled this question. He not only declares, as I have proved, that without true piety circumcision is worthless, but he further says: "For he is not a Jew, which is one outwardly; neither is that circumcision which is outward in the flesh; but he is a Jew which is one inwardly; and circumcision is that of the heart, in the spirit, and not in the letter; whose praise is not of men, but of God." Now if Judaism was nothing but a *national* affair, and circumcision only a *national* mark; how could Paul say, he is not a Jew, who is one *outwardly?* And if circumcision did not require piety, how could he say, that that is not circumcision which is outward in the flesh? Could a Jew possess that circumcision of the heart, in the spirit, whose praise is not of man, but of God, and yet have no piety?

2 D

Just here, then, is a striking analogy between baptism and circumcision. For he is not a christian who is one outwardly; and baptism is not the mere application of water. The outward profession and the external ordinance are worthless without the inward baptism of the heart. The gentleman will admit the propriety of this reasoning from circumcision to baptism; since he has himself done so in his Millennial Harbinger. When some of his friends complained of him for admitting that there might be christians among " the sects ;" he replied; "As the same apostle reasons on circumcision, so we would reason on baptism: 'Circumcision,' says the learned apostle, 'is not that which is outward in the flesh;' that is, as we apprehend the apostle, it is not that which is outward in the flesh; but 'circumcision is that of the heart, in the spirit, and not in the letter, [only,] whose praise is of God, and not of man,' So is baptism. It is not outward in the flesh only, but in the spirit also. We argue for the outward and the inward—the outward for men, including ourselves—the inward for God; but both the outward and the inward for the praise both of God and of a man." *New Series*, vol. i. p. 507.

There was, then, an outward and an inward circumcision, as there is an outward and an inward baptism; and circumcision as positively required holiness, as does baptism. Hence the exhortation to the Jews, " Circumcise the foreskin of your hearts. " Unconverted Jews, like unconverted professors of christianity, had the outward sign, but had not the inward grace—the thing signified.

The gentleman even goes so far as to say, that Caiaphas, the high priest, was a worthy member of the Jewish church; the very man who sustained the office of high priest, and in God's name condemned the glorious Messiah who was promised in the Abrahamic covenant ! ! ! How does he prove this startling proposition? Why, he tells us, Caiaphas spoke on a certain occasion by inspiration. But did not Balaam, the wicked prophet, do the very same thing, when, instead of cursing God's people as he designed for the sake of money, he was constrained by the Spirit of God to bless them? And did this prove, that he was worthy of a place in the Jewish church? No more did the prophecy undesignedly uttered by the wicked Caiaphas, prove him a worthy member of the Jewish church. The truth is, the whole Jewish nation was excommunicated by God for the sin of unbelief, and were scattered abroad to the ends of the earth. So untrue is the declaration, that piety was not required in order to membership in the Jewish church.

Mr. Campbell denies that circumcision was a door of entrance into the Jewish church, and tells us that the Jews were born in the church. This he presents as quite a difficulty; since, if infants were born in the church, they could not enter it by circumcision or by baptism. He will not, I presume, deny that circumcision was a door of entrance to proselytes; for the law says—" And when a stranger shall sojourn with thee, and will keep the passover to the Lord, let all his males be circumcised, and then let him come near and keep it ; and he shall be as one that is born in the land: for no uncircumcised person shall eat thereof. One law shall be to him that is home-born, and unto the stranger that sojourneth among you," Exod. xii. 48, 49. So, I presume, we shall have *three circumcisions ;* for the gentleman makes circumcision one thing to Abraham—another to his posterity, and yet another to proselytes ! To Abraham, he says, it was a *sign* and *seal ;* to his posterity only a *sign,* not a *seal ;* and to the proselyte it was a door of entrance—a rite for the recognition of membership! If this is not making three circumcisions, it looks very much like it.

The truth is, that circumcision was, both to Abraham and to his posterity, a sign and seal—a mark which distinguished them from others as in covenant with God, and a seal of that covenant. The children of the Jews were, by birth, entitled to a place in the church—they were members *by right;* but they were not members *in propria forma*—formally, until circumcised. So when an adult is received, on profession of his faith, by the proper officers of the church, he is a member of the church *by right;* but, until baptized, he is not a member *in form*—entitled to all the privileges of the church. If a man be elected to the presidency of these United States, the voice of the people gives him a right to the office; but he cannot enter upon its duties until he is formally inaugurated. Just so the children of believing parents have, by birth, a right to membership in the church; but that membership must be recognized by the appointed ordinance.

I do not admit that the covenant of circumcision made with Abraham related merely to the *flesh;* for it made him the father of all believers. Nor, so far as the requirement of true piety is concerned, was there more of flesh under the Old, than under the New Testament. Let us now review the argument, and see what progress we have made. I have given you a definition of the church, to which Mr. C. does not object. I have proved that it was organized in Abraham's family; that God, by positive law, made the children of believers members of it; that our Savior did not exclude them, and the New Testament contains no law for depriving them of their membership. The gentleman has not found any such law. I have proved that God has had but one church on the earth—that under both dispensations it is the same ecclesiastical body. This argument was based on principles which cannot be successfully controverted, and on facts that cannot be disputed. Since, then, God put the children of believers into the church by positive law, and never excluded them, they must be permitted to remain.

The gentleman is very much mistaken in supposing that I am almost through with my evidence. I have a great deal more, a part of which I will now present. Having proved that, under both dispensations, the church worshiped and served the same God, obeyed the same moral law, and received and trusted for salvation in the same gospel—I proceed to remark:

5. That, under both dispensations, the church enjoys her blessings by virtue of the same *covenant*—the covenant with Abraham. We have already seen that the Abrahamic covenant contains some three distinct promises viz:—1st. Of a numerous natural seed; 2d. Of the land of Canaan; 3d. That in Abraham's seed all the families of the earth should be blessed. The two first have been fulfilled. The third is now being fulfilled; but, as all the families of the earth have not yet been blessed in Christ, the promise is not entirely fulfilled. Of course the covenant cannot be abrogated, till all the promises contained in it are fulfilled.

For example, I purchase a farm, and give the vendor my note, binding myself to pay him in three instalments. When the first payment is made I am credited by the amount; but he holds the note. The second is made and I am credited; but he yet holds the note until the last payment is made, and the whole debt cancelled. So of the three promises contained in the Abrahamic covenant, two are fulfilled; but the third is fulfilled only in part. The covenant must, therefore, remain till the period of its entire fulfillment, which will not be until all the families of the earth shall be blessed—till time shall end.

The perpetuity of the Abrahamic covenant is further evident, from the fact, that it was *confirmed in Christ.* So teaches Paul in Gal. iii. 17: "And this I say, that the covenant, that was confirmed before of God, *in Christ,* the law, which was four hundred and thirty years after, cannot disannul, that it should make the promise of none effect." Again: this covenant contained *the gospel.* "And the Scripture, foreseeing that God would justify the heathen through faith, preached before *the gospel* unto Abraham, saying, In thee shall all nations be blessed," Gal. iii. 8. Now, I ask, what more can be said of the *new covenant,* as it is called, than that it is confirmed in Christ, and contains the gospel?

Again: justification, according to the Abrahamic covenant, is gospel justification. "So then, they which be of faith, are blessed with faithful Abraham;" Gal. iii. 9. Paul teaches the same doctrine in Romans iv. 1—.

Finally—it is because of the perpetuity of the Abrahamic covenant, that believers are now called *Abraham's seed.* "And if ye be Christ's, then are ye Abraham's seed, and heirs according to the promise," Gal. iii. 29. Christians are never called Noah's seed, or Enoch's seed, or David's seed; but they are called Abraham's seed. Is it not, then, evident that they sustain a relation to Abraham, which they do not sustain to any other man that ever lived? But if the Abrahamic covenant is no longer in existence, where is the link that binds us to Abraham? And how can it be true, as Paul teaches, that that covenant constituted him the father of all believers, Jews and Gentiles?

Now mark this fact: the Abrahamic covenant originally embraced professed believers and their children; and since it has never been altered, it includes them still, and they have the right to its seal—baptism.

But I will suppose, for the sake of argument, that the Abrahamic covenant has passed away; *though it is a most important fact, that in the Scriptures it is never called an* OLD COVENANT, *nor is it ever said* TO HAVE PASSED AWAY. But admitting, for argument's sake, that it has passed away, I will prove the identity of the church under the old and new dispensations, upon this admission. The apostle, writing to the Hebrews, says, "For finding fault with them, he saith, Behold, the days come, saith the Lord, when I will make a new covenant with the house of Israel, and with the house of Judah; not according to the covenant that I made with their fathers in the day when I took them by the hand to lead them out of the land of Egypt," &c. Now, supposing this to be, *literally,* a new covenant, and not, as I believe, new in its mode of administration, with whom was it made? With a *new church?* No, but with *the* OLD CHURCH—*the house of Israel and the house of Judah.* So take either view of the subject, *the church is the same.*

Now observe, it is a fact, that into this church God did put the children of believers; and it is a fact, that he has never excluded them. They, therefore, have still a right to membership; and, of course, to baptism, the initiatory rite.—[*Time expired.*]

Monday, Nov. 20—1½ o'clock, P. M.
[MR. CAMPBELL'S THIRD REPLY.]

MR. PRESIDENT—I have not said that the covenant with Abraham has become old. The ultimate and final development of that covenant, in its national form, at Mount Sinai, has become old and vanished away. But the covenant, pregnant with blessings to the gentiles, through Christ, yet lives.

I do not feel it either my duty, or my honor, to violate the rules of decorum, because Mr. Rice assumes to himself the right to dispense with them; because of the inalienable rights and immunities of orthodoxy. I shall, however, occasionally take notice of these indications for the benefit of society; and will only endeavor that by this device he will not escape from his frequent embarrassments, without your observation also. Why all this tirade and declamation which you have just now heard! Has not his cause hitherto been characterized by details a little too egotistic for this meridian? Few men have displayed higher talents in the science of boasting, than the specimens the gentleman gave us on Saturday evening.

I did this morning speak of the corrupting influence of infant baptism. This has been a prolific theme for the gentleman, and he would rather expatiate on this, because it suits his peculiar taste, than prove the truth of his proposition. He would have it, however, that this is not the great cause of corruption in Pedo-baptist churches. How, then, have the Pedo-baptist churches of former times become so corrupt? How does the gentleman explain this matter? We all want light on this subject.

The system of Pedo-baptism has operated in this way. Take, for example, the oldest of Pedo-baptist churches. An infant is presented to the priest. It is sprinkled, anointed, and crossed. It is said to be christened. It is understood by the parents that they are now more solemnly bound to teach it the faith and traditions of the church, and to save it from heresy, by all possible means. The child, soon as it is capable of learning, is taught that it is in Christ's true church, in which there is salvation for all, and out of which there is salvation for none. It grows up in this belief, and feels itself secure of reprobation, while it continues in a church, in which accident, and not choice, directs its destiny.

I need not attempt to describe the character of such members of the church. They differ in no respect from surrounding society. This is as true of many thousands of sprinkled Protestants, as it is of sprinkled Romanists. True, the Romanists generally instil their principles with more assiduity and success, than do the Protestants. They impart less light, encourage more credulity, and speak with more authority.

A gentleman of the west told me that a Catholic boy, of some seven or eight years old, had been specially entrusted to his care, in Baltimore, to conduct him to Wheeling. His attention to the boy had so won his affections, that as they were approaching Wheeling, the lad, accosting him, said,—Are you a Protestant, sir? Yes, replied the gentleman, I am a Protestant. I am very sorry for that, replied the child. When you die you will go to hell. Why do you say so, asked the gentleman. Both my mother and the priest say that all Protestants will go to hell—was the reason given. This may be regarded as a strong case, but it is a true one, and demonstrates the tendency of the system. It may not always work so successfully or so fatally; but, more or less, it works mischievously in innumerable instances. Catholic parents do their work more faithfully than most of the Protestants; and the consequence is, it is generally more difficult to convert a Romanist to any Protestant profession, than a Protestant to the Roman persuasion.

The gentleman did not precisely quote the passage from the ninth of

2 D 2

the Romans, on which he says I rely for a plurality of covenants. That he evaded the point in the passage, must have been clear to the conviction of every person in this house who has ever examined the passage. He acknowledges that there were three promises, and that these promises were often repeated. But Paul speaks both of *covenants* and promises— and if the gentleman will go to Gen. xii. 3, he will not find in that transaction one word about land. When God covenanted with Abraham, in Urr, of Chaldea, he never mentioned inheritance or land of promise, to him. The gentleman cannot find but two promises in that whole affair, as reported by Moses. The promise of Canaan was made in Canaan, and a covenant was confirmed over dead bodies in Canaan in ratification of its provisions. This is incontrovertibly fatal to my friend's assumptions. The case, he honors, by comparing it to two men making a bargain. They often meet together and talk about it a little now and then, and after a long time of stipulation and re-stipulation, they finally agree upon several items. They then write it out, call witnesses, sign, seal, and deliver it. But can the gentleman shew any indications of such a policy between God and Abraham? No. God says, and it is done. He promises, and Abraham believes. He stipulates, and Abraham acquiesces. Abraham left Urr, of Chaldea, on two promises. God gave him another in Canaan—and after twenty-four years travels he gave him another. All these are called *covenants* by inspiration. And, indeed, all God's promises are covenants, to be acquiesced in by those to whom they are tendered. Some, however, are emphatically so called. The covenant concerning the Messiah, based on the second promise, was confirmed by an oath. The covenant concerning the inheritance, by sacrifices. The covenant of circumcision, consisted in the act of recognition. The third covenant is marked by every circumstance common to those transactions of a public and general character amongst men. There were parties, stipulations, re-stipulations, seals and confirmation. God propounded it; Moses negotiated it; the chosen tribes acceded to it. It was publicly read—fairly transcribed, witnessed to, and ratified by blood, visibly and audibly. Can any one suppose that the cases of the Edomites and the Ishmaelites, as brought forward by me, were either inapposite or irrelevant? Though thus cast out at last, were not Ishmael and Esau and their sons lawfully circumcised, and were they not proper subjects? It cannot be successfully denied. What spiritual blessings, I must yet ask, were bestowed on them through their circumcision?

Why now seek to off-set these cases, fairly and legitimately brought forward, by allusions to Mormons, and apostates of every grade and character? Is it not, obviously, unfair to bring up cases essentially dissimilar to those adduced by us? I have brought up true and legal subjects of circumcision—persons possessing all the qualifications the law required. I have, indeed, instanced by name, a few persons well known to us by fame, to whom I might add all the sons of Keturah. What covenant was sealed to all these? Were these similar to Mormons and apostates? If millions apostatized from the Jewish religion, that is nothing to the fact of their having been proper subjects of circumcision, at the time of their circumcision. The persons named by Mr. Rice were never proper subjects of baptism. He cannot, then, escape from the difficulty by this attempt.

His next effort is to show, that circumcision becomes uncircumcision, if the circumcised persons do not keep the law; but what does that prove in this case? No one denies the necessity of keeping the law, and no one believes that circumcision, or any other observance, will profit the person who does not conform to the requisitions in the case. But the question, *what spiritual blessings did circumcision convey?* is yet unanswered. The gentleman has not yet named one. He cannot.

But there is the "circumcision of the heart." To this he flies for succor. But is that a spiritual blessing, belonging to circumcision, promised to all the subjects of it? He cannot avow such an opinion. Words soon become figurative. The cutting off of a small piece of flesh, soon came to indicate the separation of fleshly lusts and passions from the heart. This circumcision of the heart is what was promised by the prophets, and what is enjoyed under the gospel. "Christians," says Paul, "are the true circumcision;" the anti-type of the fleshly or typical circumcision. "They worship God in the spirit, rejoice in Christ Jesus, and have no confidence in the flesh." But who will say that such were the spiritual blessings connected with Jewish circumcision?

Baptism passed into a metaphor in a few years. Jesus said "I have a baptism to be baptized with, and how am I straitened till it be accomplished." Was this the spiritual meaning of baptism? There was also the "baptism of the Holy Spirit;" was that the spiritual blessing of baptism, or is it not another metaphor? What popular term is it that we do not, now-a-days, to say nothing of the ancients, immediately turn into metaphor. Even proper names are not exempted from this law of language. We have even Macadamized roads, Washington republicans, and political Swartouters. How many metaphors are found in the New Testament taken from the death of the Messiah?—*Crucify* the flesh, *crucified* with Christ, *buried* with him, *risen* with him, &c.

But in ascertaining the literal rite of circumcision, and the benefits thereby conferred, why bring up the spiritual and allegorical sense? What is the question before us? Spiritual or literal baptism? Spiritual or literal circumcision? Why confound them; or why suppose that because two words have been used figuratively to represent certain states or privileges, that the things properly and unfiguratively represented by those terms, are the same in substance or in effect? That some resemblance between these two ordinances exists, as well as between every thing Jewish and Christian, all men of sense and information admit. But that admission involves not the consequence that the one has come in the place of another, or occupies the same ground, or secures the same results. We also use the same epithets in speaking of different institutions, without involving any such substantial or consequential identity. We say the true circumcision, the true baptism, the outward and the inward baptism, circumcision, the true Jew and the true christian, the true passover and the true Canaan, &c., without involving identity.

I have asked for specifications of the spiritual blessings connected with the circumcision of a Jew—but I have asked in vain. I have solicited a discussion of the only reference to this subject yet submitted, viz. "The seal of the righteousness of faith." The gentleman too well understands the difference between this phrase and the one in the book, to hazard an investigation of it. Any one who reflects on the sentence—"a seal of the righteousness of *the* faith which *he* had, before he was circumcised;" and the general phrase, "*the seal of the righteousness of faith*," cannot possibly but appreciate the sophism, passed upon a community, by the substitution of the latter for the former.

Suppose, for example, it were said by an historian, that Gen. Washington received the presidency of the United States, a seal of the patriotism which he displayed in the revolutionary war; and some commentator should thence argue, or represent the presidency of the United States as a seal of the patriotism displayed in the revolutionary war by every incumbent; would any one say he was a sound, logical commentator? As logical and sound as he who says, that circumcision is to any one, or to every one, what it was to Abraham. But to apply this to infants shocks all common sense.

I have challenged Mr. Rice to prove, that the *seal* of circumcision, so called, is ever spoken of but once in the Bible; or ever so applied, except in the solitary case of Abraham. Mark Paul's singular style in this instance: "He received *the sign* of circumcision." Did he say, "A *seal of righteousness*," or of "*the righteousness of faith?*" No, he did not. He said, "it was a seal of (a special righteousness,) *the* righteousness of THE faith which *he* (Abraham) had while yet uncircumcised.

Abraham had a very singular and exalted faith. It was a model faith, and of transcendent value. To confirm that faith, and stamp upon it the Divine approval, God's own *probatum est*, it was expedient to make him a grand covenantee—to give him the "covenant of circumcision," and make him the spiritual father of all believers, in attestation of the value of the faith which he had while in uncircumcision. Circumcision was, then, a solemn seal or approval of this special faith—setting it forth as a model faith, stamped by the Divine signet. It was, then, a Divine mark. *To the descendants of Abraham* IT NEVER WAS A SEAL—*it was but a sign.*

In adverting to the case of Caiaphas, Mr. R. makes the wrong issue again. I said that it was as high priest he prophecied; but he will have him to prophecy as Balaam did, or as Balaam's ass, probably—(for it might have introduced the ass, in this connection of things, with as much pertinency as Mr. R. has introduced many other things.) Did Balaam prophecy because he was high priest? He spake by the Spirit, for another reason and for another purpose. The New Testament gives the reason why and how he uttered the oracle—"This he said not of himself, but being *high priest that year*, he prophecied that Jesus should die for that nation, and not for that nation only." Loud as a voice from heaven these words demonstrate that the office was as sacred as ever—though the officer was instigated by Satan.

I am sorry to be doomed, in the prosecution of any argument, to have to notice so many matters, so irrelevant, and so little interesting. I may pass over something, nay, I must pass in silence various such matters. I might spend a month in this way, and then not reply formally to every thing the gentleman may throw out. I will keep my eye on all matters that may affect the real issue. Others may stand for what they are worth.

The gentleman has, then, so far utterly failed to point out any spiritual privilege connected with circumcision—and, I presume, will indeed be as much perplexed and embarrassed, to show that his infant baptism secures any thing more to its subjects, than did circumcision secure to Jacob or Esau, Isaac or Ishmael.

But he says, that probably they had faith before they were circumcised. Grant that sometimes they had—the fathers of proselyte families for example. What then? Was circumcision a seal from God in *illustration of the peculiar character of the faith of each individual prose-*

lyte? Who ever heard such logic? What does the term *seal* mean? A confirmative mark, or a mark approbatory? We have seals to bonds, and we have seals to diplomas and credentials. Surely the gentleman does not properly understand the word *seal* in this case, if he make it represent to every proselyte that God gives this as a proof of the genuineness and excellency of his faith!! Will Mr. Rice say, that circumcision was to each believing proselyte, a mark approbatory of his particular belief?

Again—the logic is still more evidently at fault in another particular. It is a sophism of the most palpable character to argue from a special to a general law or fact. And would it not be arguing from a special to a general law or fact, to say that circumcision was to a thousand, what it was to one individual of a thousand? In the Jewish history, the number of proselytes, it is presumed, in all time, did not average one to a thousand born within the covenant. Now, who would reason on any other subject in this way? Who would affirm that circumcision, as a Divine institution, took its character from one subject in a thousand, rather than from the nine hundred and ninty-nine? Such, however, is the logic of all Pedo-baptists that found their usage on Calvin's assumption. Better take the Roman Catholic, or the Episcopalian, or any other ground than this; for, as it appears to me, this is superlatively the most untenable of them all.

It behooves my friend to pay more attention to the fact, that circumcision was not the door into the Jewish church; that Jews brought forth Jews; that natural, and not supernatural, birth was the wide door into the Jewish church. Why then call baptism the door? The palpable fact already suggested, is unanswered and unanswerable, viz: that circumcision was administered to Jewish infants, not to bring them into the church of Abraham, but because they were in it. How then could it be a door? Is not the gentleman now obliged to give up circumcision, or to affirm that we are born members of Christ's church, just as we are born into the world? And whence comes the necessity of the second or new birth? When my friend shall have proved, that circumcision was a door into a house four hundred years before the house was built; that when the house was built, and the children born in it, they still had to come in by the door of the house, he will have gained a victory over reason and palpable fact, hitherto unachieved by all his predecessors. This, too, is the main gist of his discussion of baptism in room of circumcision!

The radical misconception of all Pedo-baptists is, that the Jewish commonwealth and the christian church are built on the same principle; and that that principle is FLESH. That if faith be at all necessary, it is not *personal* faith, nor personal conviction—it is hereditary faith. And yet they cannot see, that circumcision is at war with them on one side, while they imagine it favorable on the other. It shows that the nature of the necessity of parental faith, or immediate ancestral belief, is a perfect dream. No child descended from a Jew, was ever inhibited from circumcision because his parents were both reprobates. Not one instance can be shown. There is some policy on the part of my friend, in seeming to disparage circumcision, while, nevertheless, building on it. In Judaism rights to ordinances were *hereditary;* in christianity they are *personal.* It is now, therefore, *faith* and not *flesh;* then it was *flesh* and not *faith.* When shall my Pedo-baptist friends learn this lesson?—christianity is a *per-*

21

sonal affair. Those called sons of God, are all born again. The sons of Abraham were born of the flesh, and therefore, only once born. Christians are born of the Spirit after they are born of the flesh. Will my friend pay no attention to such declarations as these. To as many as (and to no more than) received him, he gave the privilege of becoming the sons of God; to them that believe on his name who were born not of blood, nor of the will of the flesh, nor of the will of man, but of God." Why should not these words of the Messiah, along with those spoken to Nicodemus, decide this subject forever? Did he not say to the ruler of Israel, " *You must be born again?*" You cannot enter into my church, or the kingdom of heaven, of which I speak, Nicodemus, unless you are "born from above, born of water and of Spirit." Nicodemus, " THAT WHICH IS BORN OF THE FLESH IS FLESH, AND THAT WHICH IS BORN OF THE SPIRIT IS SPIRIT." *You must be born again.* Mr. Rice says, you need not be born again to get into the church; but you may be born again after you get into it! But unfortunately for you, my friends, Mr. Rice is but a mere professor of the faith, and neither a lawgiver nor king in Israel. He can never dispose of this case of Nicodemus. No one can imagine two societies founded upon more opposite principles than faith and flesh, or spirit and flesh. Now when we look at two societies, pure and unmixed, built upon the two principles, we shall see a very different result. In the one, " all know the Lord, from the least to the greatest;" all have God's law written in their hearts; all enjoy his favor and protection; all rejoice in hope of the glory of God. In the other, it is a kingdom like Spain, Portugal, Italy, France—every thing that liveth and moveth upon the face of the earth! Allow the members in each to be sincere in their profession, when existing and contemplated apart from each other, the difference is no less striking; because the great majority in every Pedo-baptist community are necessarily unconverted persons.

My friend has several times called for help this morning, in the form of a request to furnish some evidence from the Bible, that the old Jewish state of things has been done away, and substituted by another. I shall certainly attend to this request as a matter of generosity. It is his place to show that christianity is but a continued and improved form of Judaism, and not a *new* institution, built upon a new and better foundation than the mere flesh, blood, and bones of father Abraham.

Before I set down, I shall advert for a moment to the two institutions. Paul contrasts them in good style, 2 Cor. 3d chapter. The one that is "done away," and the one "that remaineth;" the letter and the spirit; the law and the gospel. The Jewish institute was necessarily temporary and preparatory. It was confined to one nation and people. Its proper boundaries were Palestine. Judea, Jerusalem, and its temple, were the theatre of all its glories. Christianity is the religion of humanity. It was intended for the whole human race. It excludes neither Jew nor Greek, barbarian, Scythian, bond nor free. It throws the wide arms of its philanthropy around the whole human race. It embraces with equal cordiality, " the frozen Icelander and the sun-burned Moor." It pays no homage to sceptered royalty, to ancient heraldry, to castes, ranks, or conditions of men. It invites all, makes provisions for all, and tenders the same conditions to all. It addresses every man as responsible for himself. It recognizes the most perfect free agency and responsibility. It proposes the same conditions to the prince and the beggar. It demands from all, faith, repentence, and unreserved obedience. It must have the same voluntary devotion to God, as was manifested in the free and voluntary devotion of the Messiah to the salvation of man. He freely came down from heaven to earth, and we must freely ascend from earth to heaven. A christian people are essentially a free people: they are, indeed, the only free people. The son of God makes men free indeed. No one can be physically or metaphysically brought into, or cast out of, Christ's church. We must know the Messiah, believe in him, acquiesce in his mission, reverence his official fullness and glory, and adore his person as GOD WITH US. We must solemnly bow to his authority, submit to his government, walk in his ways, and follow his example. Then, and only then, can we claim the honor of the christian name, and of a place in the church of the living God, "the pillar and the support of the truth." There is, too, an inexpressible pleasure in acting for one's self in making the christian profession. The feeling of our own responsibility, and of our coming, under a sense of it, into a new and an everlasting relation to God, to angels, and to men. We feel a thousand times more awful pleasure and high dignity, treating in our own person with our Redeemer, without any interfering earthly mediator or negotiator. It is the highest enjoyment of personal liberty ever attained by mortal man, to have the privilege of signing the covenant with his own hand, and vowing with his own lips, eternal allegiance to him that has redeemed him, and tendered to him an everlasting life, through his death, by a patient continuance in well doing, seeking for glory, honor, and immortality.—[*Time expired.*

Tuesday, Nov. 21—10 o'clock, A. M.
[MR. RICE'S FOURTH ADDRESS.]

MR. PRESIDENT—Before proceeding immediately to the subject under discussion, I wish to read from Calvin the passage to which Mr. Campbell has so repeatedly referred, in which he represents him as having claimed the right to *change* the ordinances appointed by Christ. He read, from his Debate with McCalla, the following passage, taken professedly from Calvin's Commentary on the eighth chapter of the Acts of the Apostles: " *The church did grant liberty to herself, since the beginning,* TO CHANGE THE RITES SOMEWHAT, *excepting the substance.*" And he called on me to say, whether these are not the words of Calvin. I answer, *they are not.* He has quoted from Calvin only *a part* of a sentence, without its connection; and he has given a very incorrect translation even of this fragment. I have here Calvin's Commentary on the Acts, from which I take leave to read the whole sentence, with its connection. After admitting what I, of course, do not admit, that immersion was the general practice in the apostolic age, he thus remarks:

" Cæterum, non tanti esse nobis debet tantillum ceremoniæ discrimen ut Ecclesiam propterea scindamus, vel rixis turbemus. Pro ipsa quidem baptismi ceremonia, quatenus nobis a Christo tradita est, centies potius ad mortem usque digladiandum, quum ut eam nobis eripi sinamus: sed quum in aquæ symbolo testimonium habemus tam ablutionis nostræ, quam novæ vitæ : quam in aqua, velut in speculo, sanguinem nobis suum Christus repræsentat, ut munditiem inde nostram petamus: quum docet nos Spiritu suo refingi, ut mortui peccato, justitiæ vivamus ; nihil quod ad baptismi substantiam faciat, deesse nobis certum est. Quare ab initio libere sibi permisit ecclesia, extra hanc substantiam, ritus habere paululum dissimiles : nam alii ter, alii autem semel tantum mergebant,' " &c.—*Com. on Acts* viii.

" But so small a difference of the ceremony ought not to be considered by us of so great moment, that on that account we should divide the church, or disturb it with dissensions. As to the ceremony itself of baptism, in so far as it was delivered to us by Christ, it were a hundred times better that we perish by the sword, than permit it to be taken from us: but when in the symbol of water we have the testimony as well of our cleansing as of our new life: when in water, as in a mirror, Christ represents to us his blood, that thence we may seek purification: when he teaches us to be renewed by his Spirit; that being dead to sin, we may live to righteousness: it is certain that we lack nothing which appertains to the substance of baptism. Wherefore from the beginning the church has freely allowed herself beyond [extra] this substance *to have rites a little dissimilar:* for some immersed thrice, but others only once. Wherefore there is no reason why, in things not really essential, we should be too illiberal: only let them not pollute the simple institution of Christ by adventitious pomp."

You perceive that, though Calvin admits what I think is not true, he does not claim for the church any power to *change* what Christ has determined concerning the ordinances. On the contrary, he maintained, as I have before stated, that our Savior did not prescribe any particular mode of baptizing, but left that matter to be determined by circumstances. Whilst I do not agree with Calvin in all he has said on this subject, I am unwilling to have misrepresentations, so injurious to the reputation of a great and good man, pass uncorrected. I have no doubt, that this piece of a sentence, incorrectly translated and published by Mr. Campbell, has made many false impressions. I have a Baptist author who refers to the same passage, thus: " The church (that is, Presbyterianism,) hath granted to herself the liberty to change the ordinances, except the substance, that is, the words!" I think I have given the precise words of the author. This is a specimen of the perversions of authors which often are imposed on the public.

I wish to present to the minds of the audience the ground over which we have passed. As a strong presumptive evidence in favor of infant baptism, I have stated that the overwhelming majority of the wise and the good, of all ages, have believed that it is taught in the Scriptures. And since the Bible is a plain book, especially on important points, it is not probable that such immense multitudes have misunderstood its teachings on a subject so essential to the very existence of the visible church.

I turned to the commission, and showed that it is not a commission to commence a new organization, but to extend the limits and privileges of the existing church; that it specifies, as proper subjects of baptism, neither adults nor infants; that disciples were to be made by baptizing and teaching; and that it does not say that teaching must, in all cases, precede baptism. It is admitted, that all who are entitled to membership in the church, ought to receive baptism. The great question, then, is, who, according to the law of God, are entitled to membership in the church of Christ? To determine this question, we go to the organization of the church.

A church I defined to be a body of people, called out from the world, for the service of God, with ordinances of divine appointment, and a door of admission, or a rite by which membership may be recognized. This, it is not denied, is a correct definition of the church of Christ. We find in the family of Abraham, precisely such a people—a people separated from the world, for the service of the true God; with ordinances of divine appointment, and an initiatory rite, to wit: circumcision—distinguishing them from all other people, as being in covenant with God. From

that time onward, God speaks of them as " My people." Believers and
their children, were put into this church by positive law, and there they
remained till the time of giving the commission by our Savior. There is
no law excluding them. Since, then, we have put them in by positive
law, I call upon my friend to put them out by a law as clear and positive.

I have shown, most conclusively, that the church of Christ is the same
which was organized in the family of Abraham. You remember the illustration of the principle of identity, drawn from the commonwealth of
Kentucky. Now, I will produce three times as much evidence to prove
that the christian church is the same body that was organized in the
family of Abraham, as can be produced to prove that the commonwealth
of Kentucky is the same political body that existed under that name forty
years ago. Under both dispensations, the church serves the same God,
obeys the same moral law, and trusts for salvation in the same gospel;
all the prominent doctrines of which are contained in the Old Testament.
The christian church, I have proved, is enjoying her blessings under the
same covenant, of which two promises have been fulfilled; but the great
promise is yet only in part fulfilled—a covenant *confirmed in Christ* and
containing the gospel; a covenant which is never called *old*, and which,
in the Scriptures, is never said *to pass away;* a covenant which makes
Abraham the father of all believers. It is new only in the mode of its
administration.

But, I might go even as far as my friend desires, and admit that the
Abrahamic covenant has passed away, and yet sustain my argument: for
I have shown from the epistle to the Hebrews, (ch. viii.) that a new
covenant (even if literally new) was to be made with *the same people*—
THE SAME CHURCH.

Now, believers and their children were put into this church by positive
law, and there is no law to exclude the one or the other. There is, therefore,
just as much authority for excluding believers, as for excluding children.

I wish now to notice some few objections, urged by my worthy friend,
in his last speech on yesterday. I must confess, however, that I was at
a loss to know what he was trying to prove.

He attempted to show that there were several covenants made with
Abraham. To this, I replied, that the Bible speaks of but *one covenant*
with Abraham. The following passages are conclusive on this point:—
Exodus ii. 24: " And God heard their groaning, and God remembered
his covenant with Abraham, with Isaac, and with Jacob," &c. Acts of
the Apostles iii. 25: " Ye are the children of the prophets, and of *the
covenant* which God made with our fathers, saying unto Abraham, And
in thy seed shall all the kindreds of the earth be blessed."

Here the word *covenant* is used in the singular number; and there is
not a passage in the Bible which speaks of more than one covenant with
Abraham. The same promises, as we have seen, were contained in the
12th, 15th, and 17th chapters of Genesis. The promises first made in
the 12th and 15th, were ratified and sealed by circumcision, as recorded
in the 17th. Now, to have three covenants, and the same promises in
each, would be marvellous indeed! It is true, my friend said, there was
no *land* promised in the 12th chapter; but what says the first verse?—
" Get thee out of thy country, and from thy kindred, and from thy
father's house, *unto a land* that I will show thee." And when he reached the land, the promise was repeated, so that in each of these three
chapters we find the same promises.

2 E

But I do not care, so far as my argument is concerned, if my friend finds half a dozen covenants with Abraham; for the covenant of circumcision contains *the promise of spiritual blessings*, which was the great promise. I will read a few verses in the seventeenth chapter, which, I think, will convince every one that such is the fact: "I will make my covenant between me and thee, and will multiply thee exceedingly." Again, in the fifth verse: "Neither shall thy name any more be called Abram, but thy name shall be Abraham; for a father of many nations have I made thee." With this last verse we will compare the language of Paul, in Rom. iv. 16, 17: "Therefore, it is of faith, that it might be of grace; to the end the promise might be sure to all the seed: not to that only which is of the law, but to that also which is of the faith of Abraham, who is the father of us all, (as it is written, I have made thee a father of many nations.") Here, you observe, the apostle refers to the covenant of circumcision, as containing the promise of spiritual blessings to the gentiles as well as Jews. Again, Gen. xvii. 7: "I will establish my covenant between me and thee, and thy seed after thee—to be a God unto thee, and to thy seed after thee." What more do we want, than that he should be our God, and the God of our seed? and that we should be the children of Abraham, and be blessed with him? We have, then, the promise of spiritual blessings in the covenant of circumcision. We are, therefore, under the same covenant, which was sealed by circumcision, and which made Abraham the father of all believers. Take away that covenant, and how is Abraham my father any more than Enoch or Noah?

The second objection was, that circumcision was not a door of entrance into the church. Now, I will read to you the language of the great Andrew Fuller upon this subject—a man who did not intend to favor our views,—vol. v. p. 155:

"This ordinance was the mark by which they [Abraham and his seed] were distinguished as a people in covenant with Jehovah, and which bound them by a special obligation to obey him. Like almost all other positive institutions, it was also pre-figurative of mental purity, 'or putting off the body of the sins of the flesh.'"—*Lecture on Gen.* xvii.

What is baptism? Is it not the ordinance which distinguishes christians as a people in covenant with Jehovah? by which they are bound to him, and obliged to obey him? All who received circumcision were peculiarly bound to serve God; and so are all who receive christian baptism. I remark again; in Ex. xii. 48, we are particularly informed how gentile proselytes might enter the church, if they wished to partake of the passover. All the males of the family were required first to be circumcised. Compare this with Gal. v. 3: "For I testify again to every man that is circumcised, that he is a debtor to do the whole law." He has all the privileges, and he is bound to perform all the duties of the law; and that is door enough for me.

But my friend's next objection is, that the church was not organized till the Israelites arrived at Mount Sinai. To prove this, he quotes the language of Stephen, in Acts vii. 38: "This is he that was in the church in the wilderness, with the angel which spake to him," &c. Stephen, it is true, speaks of the church in the wilderness; but he does not intimate that it was *organized* in the wilderness. His argument is, therefore, wholly without force.

But the gentleman has told us, that a constitution was adopted, and that all were called upon to vote for it; and this was the national organization.

Paul, however, teaches a very different doctrine. He says, " Wherefore then serveth the law ? It was *added*, because of transgression," &c. Paul does not represent the law as the constitution, nor does he say any thing of an organization of *the church*. He says, " The law was *added*." To what was it added ? Of course, to the Abrahamic covenant ; for it could be added to nothing else. The law at Sinai was an additional enactment for the benefit of a church already organized, designed to answer a specific purpose, till Christ should come.

Circumcision, the gentleman insists, did not require piety in those who received it. Then did God enter into covenant with wicked men without requiring them to abandon their sins ! It will not do to confine the covenant to Abraham ; for it is certain that God entered into covenant with him *and his seed in their generations.* If, then, those who were circumcised, were not required to be pious ; the conclusion is inevitable, that God made a covenant with the wicked, and did not require them to serve him ! Believe it who can ! Paul, as I have proved, says, " Circumcision profiteth, if thou keep the law," but not otherwise. The law, as expounded by our Savior, requires man to love God with all his heart. soul, mind and strength, and his neighbor as himself. Could the Jews observe such a law, and yet possess no piety?

But the gentleman talks about *figurative* circumcision, and appeals to the corruption of the Jewish church at the advent of our Savior and afterwards, to sustain his untenable position. It is true, the Jewish church was, to a great extent, apostate, when our Savior appeared on earth. Yet there were some pious souls, here and there an aged Simeon and an Anna, who waited for " the consolation of Israel ;" and they received him with open arms. And notwithstanding the corruption of the mass, he still granted to those who received him, the privileges of sons. But if the Jewish church became very corrupt, is it not also true that the christian church has been almost inundated with error and impiety? You might as logically maintain, therefore, that baptism does not require piety, as that circumcision did not.

The gentleman has mustered in fearful array *fifteen* arguments, to prove that baptism did not come in place of circumcision. On that subject, as I have repeatedly said, I feel very little concern. I will now, I think, satisfy the audience, that the defence of infant baptism does not require me to prove, that baptism came instead of circumcision. I have proved that the children of believers have a right to membership in the church ; that God did, at the organization of his church, put believers and their children in together. This point is settled. It is also an indisputable fact, that under the Old Testament adults and infants, parents and children, entered the church by the same door—had their membership recognized by the *same ordinance.* If children have still the right to a place in the church, it is certain that they have the right to enter by the door. Under the former dispensation there was but one door, through which all entered. Under the present dispensation there is but one ; and all who have a right to membership, must, of course, enter through it. You may tell me the door is not now precisely where it was formerly. Very well : I care not whether it is on this side of the house, or on that. Children have the right to enter ; and if you will find a door for adults, I will find one for their children ; for they have always entered by the door. Whilst, therefore, I can prove, that baptism answers the same ends under the new dispensation, that were answered by circumcision under the old ; I am not concerned to do it; for the defence of infant baptism requires it not.

There is only one more point in the gentleman's speech which I wish to notice. He has told us how much infant baptism tends to corrupt the church; but I have appealed to the *fact*, which he will not dispute, that the Pedo-baptist churches that have long practiced the baptism of infants, are quite as pure as the purest Anti-pedo-baptist churches. He has represented infant baptism as the secret of the pope's tyrannical power; but he has not proved, nor can he prove, that such is the truth. He told us an anecdote of a little Romish boy, who, whilst on a journey, became greatly attached to a gentleman to whose care he was committed; but on ascertaining that he was a Protestant, he told him, he would certainly go to hell. When asked how he knew; he replied that his mother told him so. And this occurrence is held up before the audience as demonstrative of the horrors of infant baptism! It is, of course, clear as light to the gentleman's mind, that the Popish mother never would have instilled such errors into the mind of her child, if he had not been baptized!! The water of baptism produced this sad effect!!! It is a little remarkable, that sometimes apparently opposite courses of conduct seem to lead to the same results. I recently heard of a little girl belonging to the gentleman's church, who made to an old lady of another church just such a remark as fell from the lips of the Romish boy! Shall we hold up this case and say, behold the fruits of *immersion?* The simple truth is, that children very naturally imbibe the errors of parents, whether baptized or not. Such anecdotes are poor arguments—very poor.

The audience must now judge for themselves, whether Mr. Campbell has answered any one of my arguments. I have put children into the church by positive law; and I have called upon him, so far in vain, to produce the law for putting them out—for depriving parents and children of privileges which God in his mercy has given them. If he can produce a "thus saith the Lord" for it, I will agree to put them out; but I must protest against the attempt to exclude them by far-fetched *inferences*, contrary to every principle of law.

I have several more arguments, which demonstrate yet more fully the identity of the church under the Jewish and christian dispensations; but I shall have quite sufficient time to present them. The only difference, so far as this discussion is concerned, is to be found in the passing away of the civil and ceremonial laws of the Jews, added to the Abrahamic covenant, for a particular end, and for a limited time. And as no man in his senses would maintain, that the commonwealth of Kentucky is not the same political body, because certain temporary laws expired at the end of the period to which they were limited; so no man can consistently contend, that the passing away of the civil and ceremonial laws of the old dispensation, annihilated the church of God. He might as well assert, that I am not the same man, because I have put on a new coat!

The truth is, that God has never inculcated but one religion. The religion of the heart—the great matter, after all—was the same in Abraham's day as now. External ordinances have changed, but the church is the same—true piety is unchanged. The religious exercises of Abraham, of David, and of all the saints of the Old Testament, correspond substantially with the experience of all christians. The saints of the former dispensation looked forward through prophecies and sacrifices to a Savior to come. The saints, under the new dispensation, look back through inspired history, and the sacraments, to a Savior who has come. The eyes of all have been fixed upon the same glorious object; and, through him, upon the same blessed heaven. Ordinances have been changed; but the conditions of salvation—faith, repentance, and holy living, have been to all the conditions of salvation.

Having now put the children of believers in the church, by clear and positive law, I shall wait for the gentleman to produce the law for excluding them.—[*Time expired.*]

Tuesday, Nov. 21—10½ o'clock, A. M.

[MR. CAMPBELL'S FOURTH REPLY.]

MR. PRESIDENT—I have often had occasion to observe and remark, that a man can assert and deny more in half an hour, than he can prove in a whole year. To review in special detail the points which my friend *says* he *has* proved, and those which he *means* to prove, as now stated, it will require more time than has been allotted to the discussion of this proposition. All that was said yesterday, has been repeated this morning. Indeed, I believe that all that has been said now, was said by my friend in his first speech. It is not to be expected, therefore, that I will merely reiterate as well as he, especially as I have much new matter yet to offer. It is necessary to advance into the main points of evidence and argument, upon which ultimately this subject must rest in the minds of this community.

My friend began by reading to you a passage out of Calvin, and *his* translation of it; to which I will first advert, lest my silence be construed into an admission that I did not read the whole section, but suppressed some part of it from improper motives. I did not, nor do I usually in debate, read the whole section or passage from which I may quote a fact or an argument; but what I do read, I read in the full light of its own context, and intend that it shall fully contain a fair and honest representation of the mind of the writer. In this instance, I contend that I have done so to the letter. I will put the question—I will ask, whether what was read this morning does, in the part quoted or in the whole, in the least change the sense of what I read on yesterday? This manœuvre seems to be intended for effect—to make you believe that I left out something of great importance, or changed the sense. If the gentleman will give me the book from which he has translated this passage, I will show that there is not in it a single idea repugnant to what I have read. Calvin does claim that the church has taken this liberty, *extra* the substance. No Presbyterian supposed that the church is bound to walk by the exact letter, but may change and modify the ordinances according to expediency. In my view, indeed, the Presbyterians have always done so; and in some instances much more grossly than in the case now before us. They have rites "a little dissimilar," as Mr. Rice reads it. It is not necessary that I should read the whole page from an author, when a shorter extract will give the whole spirit and force of his argument.

My friend says he has "put children" into the church, according to law. I suppose he means *infants;* for we are all *children.* He certainly believes that *infants* ought to be in the church with their parents. We all believe that *children* ought to be in the church as soon as they know the Lord. But that is not the argument. It is, Are the offspring of professing parents, *soon as born,* by virtue of their parentage,—because of their being of the same flesh and blood, entitled to be in the church? Is the

2 E 2

infant born of a Presbyterian father or mother, by virtue of that natural birth, that accident, necessarily, and by Divine authority, a member of the church of Christ?

The gentleman is certainly throwing dust in your eyes. Who denies that *children* should be in the church? The question is as to whether the infant progeny are born members of Christ's church, because their parents were professors of the faith? If he should speak, as he has been speaking, through a thousand years, or through as many volumes as composes the Vatican library, it would not reach this question at all. I ask him to show, by one single passage, where infants are placed in Christ's church? He cannot do it. There is not in the Old Testament nor in the New, one single passage indicating any such thing.

As I intend to occupy a part of this day in answering minor matters, having nothing else, indeed, to answer, I will now, in order that you may have the whole subject before you, read a passage from Gal. iii. accompanied with a remark or two. I do it rather to exhibit the unfortunate obliquities in the reasoning of my opponent, than because of the validity of the argument, or the importance of the point in issue; for I had rather charge it to an unhappy obliquity, than to any disposition on his part to sophisticate or interpolate the sacred text. My friend says "the law was added to the covenant." But the apostle does not happen to say so. It is not so written in the Old Testament or in the New. I have the Bible before me, and I say the law was not added to the *covenant*. "It was added to the *promise*." Now this promise had reference to a single point—that of possessing the land of Canaan. It was not added to the covenant, for that would be to add the law to itself, or a covenant to itself. The argument proves this beyond a doubt. Need I show that the Jews never inherited Canaan by, or in consequence of, their own works? They were on their way to the promised inheritance before the law was promulged. Therefore, the law has nothing to do with the inheritance. The law, indeed, was added to the promise, concerning the inheritance. It was solemnly covenanted to Abraham's family four hundred years before the law was given. Hence, the addition of the law gave no additional right to the inheritance. "For if the inheritance came by the law," says Paul, "it is no more of promise." But God gave it to Abraham by promise. The addition of the law was, therefore, for a different purpose, for reasons stated by the apostle.

I now design requesting your especial attention to a passage in Gal. iv.; I shall read it: "My little children, of whom I travail in birth again until Christ be formed in you, I desire to be present with you now, and to change my voice; for I stand in doubt of you. Tell me, ye that desire to be under the law, do ye not hear the law? For it is written, that Abraham had two sons, the one by a bond-maid, the other by a free woman. But he who was of the bond-woman was born after the flesh." My friend asks for a repudiation of the old covenant, and infant membership. I intend to assist him with an argument from this passage. Here is the first point in the argument: "But he who was born of the free woman was by promise." Here, then, are two births; the one by virtue of the flesh, the other by virtue of a promise. Now, says Paul, these things are an allegory. "For these are the two covenants; the one from the Mount Sinai, which gendereth to bondage, which is Agar; for this Agar is Mount Sinai in Arabia, and answereth to Jerusalem which now is, and is in bondage with her children. But Jerusalem, which is above, is free, which is the mother of us all. For it is written, "Rejoice, thou barren, that bearest not; break forth and cry, thou that travailest not; for the desolate hath many more children than she which hath an husband. Now we, brethren, as Isaac was, are the children of promise. But as, then, he that was born after the flesh, persecuted him that was born after the spirit, even so it is now. Nevertheless, what saith the Scripture? Cast out the bond-woman and her son; for the son of the bond-woman shall not be heir with the son of the free woman. So then, brethren, we are not children of the bond-woman, but of the free."

That I may place the precept of repudiation fairly before you, and conclusively show that the children of the flesh are no longer "counted for *the seed*," I shall require your particular attention to an analysis of this much neglected passage. The four principal tropes in this allegory are Hagar, Ishmael, Sarah, Isaac, a sort of *dramatis personæ*, were it a scenetic representation. These two *women* represent *two covenants*—the consummated covenants of which I have spoken; the one from Horeb, the other from Jerusalem. The two *sons* of one father, Abraham, represent *the children* of the two covenants; Ishmael the Jews, and Isaac the christians. Now, the question is, in how many points do the two women represent the two covenants, and the two sons the two kinds of children under these institutions? They represent them in the four following particulars: 1. In the conception of their offspring. Hagar's was *natural*, Sarah's was *supernatural*. Hagar was a young woman, Sarah was superannuated; and, as Paul says, as "*good as dead*." Hence the births, or offspring, were essentially different. That of Hagar was according to the *flesh*, that of Sarah according to the *spirit*. The birth of Ishmael was *natural*, that of Isaac was as much above nature, as the conception of the Messiah, on the part of Mary, was *supernatural*, in one point of view.

2. In the condition of their offspring. Hagar was a slave, and Sarah a free woman. Now the issue always follows the mother, when contemplated according to property. If the mother be *free* the offspring is free—if a *slave*, her offspring is a slave. Hence Ishmael was a slave, and Isaac was free born.

3. In the *spirit* of their offspring. Not only in personal freedom, as respected condition, but in the spirit of freedom. There is a free, generous, noble, and magnanimous spirit; and there is a slavish, low, and mean spirit, which is homogenous with the condition. Isaac was docile, pious, and elevated above the flesh—a spiritual man. Ishmael was selfish, envious, and rude—an animal man.

4. In the inheritance of their offspring. Hagar had no property, not being the proper wife of Abraham. She had only a slave's portion—bread and water. Hence a loaf of bread and a bottle of water constituted her whole fortune, and Ishmael's inheritance. But Isaac was an only son of his mother, and also in the marriage covenant. He was the only child of Abraham by Sarah, and the rightful heir of his vast estate. But in one point of comparison, under the allegory, the contrast is most striking, viz. the casting out of the bond-woman and her son, and the perpetual enjoyment of the inheritance at home, by Isaac.

We now have sufficient specifications and dates, not only to give a clear and unambiguous precept of that precise meaning, sought after by Mr. Rice, but also to sanction, as well as to illustrate, and even farther develop, the views and conceptions given on this proposition. There are, then, two church covenants. The two women, says Paul, are *the "two cove-nants."* These, then, are well defined covenants. The one is from Mount Sinai—"Agar in Arabia," the Jewish church covenant beyond a doubt; the other is from "Jerusalem above," the new christian constitution or covenant, first promulged and sealed in Jerusalem. "This is the new covenant in my blood," said Jesus in Jerusalem. Hence the "word of the Lord went forth from Jerusalem" to all the world. The christian church is married to the Lord, through this new covenant, as certainly as the Jewish church was by the former covenant. "I was an husband to you," says the Lord.

Need I farther show, that the children of Israel, compared to Ishmael, were, as *church members*, only *"born of the flesh?"* Is it not indisputable? Paul says, the first covenant children were born *"after the* FLESH," and the second covenant children are born *"after the Spirit."* This single passage, this most graphic allegory, these most appropriate tropes and images, it seems, go all the length and breadth of my views of the proposition now before us. While we have, in our Testaments, this illustration of the objects of the two institutions, Jewish and Christian, my friend's notions of church identity and infant membership, founded on ancient covenants, have not one inch of ground, Old Testament or New.

The two principles of *flesh* and *Spirit*, natural and supernatural birth, are now clearly shown to be the differential character of the two institutions. We have, then, two communities, under two very distinct constitutions, of very different spirit, character, and circumstances. On these we have no time to expatiate. He that was born after the flesh persecuted him that was born after the Spirit, is, however, a point so prominently characteristic of the two communities, as to be worthy of notice. It occasioned the rejection of Ishmael from the privileges of Abraham's family, and elicited that identical precept for which Mr. R. inquires— "CAST OUT THE BOND-WOMAN AND HER SON," "for the son of the bond-woman shall not inherit with the son of the free woman." "So then," says Paul, "brethren, we are children, not of the bond-woman, but of the free." Christians are under a new covenant, have a new spirit, and are heirs of a better inheritance than that of the old covenant.

Abraham, the prince and distinguished patriarch, was called upon, by Divine authority, to hearken to Sarah and cast out the bond-woman and her son. That a king, so rich in gold and silver, in flocks, and herds, and servants; so generous too, should have given her no more for herself and her son, than one loaf of bread and one bottle of water, is not to be explained upon any other principle than that God intended it to be an allegoric representation of the difference between these two covenants; two births, two spirits, two characters, two inheritances, as well as a solemn warning to those who will cleave to the letter rather than to the Spirit—to the Old Testament rather than to the New.

Let him, then, who will be under that covenant, follow Hagar into the desert. Let him contemplate her, poor and homeless, parched with thirst, without bread, her son almost dying under a shrub for lack of the comforts of life—let him listen to her complaints, and survey her wretched condition, and ask why all this suffering, almost under the eye of Abraham. And when he learns that all this happened for an example to those who will cleave to the old order of things rather than to the new, and seek to confound and identify things which God has separated, let him at once desist from a course of action so dishonorable to the Divine wisdom, and so fatal to himself.

The gentleman has now the precept sought, and I feel that my pledge is redeemed. And should he ask for a second, he shall have it as soon as he shall have disposed of this allegory, and the argument deduced from it. I presume, however, that this will be so satisfactory to him, that he will not ask for another, pending the present proposition.

I wish the gentleman would dipense with the sowing of assertions in this broad-cast style, and make an issue upon some point or other. He may have the allegory, or the covenants, or the identity, if he will only debate them. I will risk my cause upon such an issue. In this way of scattering assertions, no opportunity is afforded to test or decide any thing. A person of very little address can assert more in half an hour, than he can prove in an age.

Mr. R. argues that the Jewish and christian churches are identical. But he seems to confound similarity and identity. They are, indeed, very different predicaments. There is some similarity between a man and a tree—but much more between a man and a monkey, yet they are not identical, [a laugh.] He argues for the identity of the church, and its rights of membership in all ages. But when I asked him for the door by which infants entered during the first 2000 years, he could not tell, but concluded that if I should tell how adults entered he might then find a door for infants. Well, I will now try. Adults entered God's church, so far as he had any on earth, during the first 4000 years, by faith and obedience, or if he prefer the phrase, by an active and operative belief of God's testimonies and promises.

A beautiful passage in Isaiah, in prospect of the calling of the gentiles, seems clearly to refer to this transaction. It was designed to show that finally the children of Sarah would greatly outnumber those of Hagar: that is, that the spiritual children of Sarah and Abraham would incomparably transcend their fleshly progeny. I shall paraphrase as I read it. It immediately follows the sufferings of Christ, foretold in the fifty-third chapter of Isaiah, and is here quoted and applied by Paul to the offspring of Sarah. " Rejoice, thou barren, (Sarah) that bearest not ; break forth and cry, thou that travailest not, for the desolate (deserted for Hagar) has many more children than she (Hagar) who had a (Sarah's) husband." Hence we boast of Sarah, the mother of us all.

I will give you a sample of his argument for identity. He says that the Jewish and Christian churches are the same, because they have the same moral code. Massachusetts colony for a time adopted the law of Moses for her law. Was Massachusetts and the Jewish church, therefore, identical? They have, also, adopted the same code of morality in Kentucky : but is this commonwealth and the christian church identical? Upon that principle, Free Masonry and Christianity are identical ; because they have adopted something in common.

But again—the same God reigns over both churches. Does not the same God reign over Kentucky and Jerusalem ? The same God reigns over the Ottoman empire and the United States ; are they, therefore, the same people ? He also argues the identity of the ancient and modern churches, because they have the same gospel. But this is not strictly true : they have not the same gospel, unless upon the principle, that France and England have the same language, because they have the same alphabet. The christian gospel is not that *the Messiah is to come;* yet that was the Jewish gospel. Paul calls the promise concerning Canaan, a gospel—so says Dr. McKnight—just as we have a gospel concerning a rest in heaven. We have, then, two gospels: the one earthly, fleshly; the other, heavenly. My friend says that both churches have the same ordinances. I should like to see him attempt to prove that the Jewish and Christian ordinances are the same. Is baptism and circumcision identical? Is the passover and Lord's supper identical? He says they have the same king. Not exactly the same king! Messiah is now king. All power and authority in this universe, is now in his hands. It was not so in the Jewish church. There was a change in the government when the Messiah was exalted. Who was it that placed the crown upon the head of the exalted Messiah? Who placed him upon the throne, and said, "Reign in the midst of thine enemies?" It was that God that governed the Jews—the God of Abraham, of Isaac, and of Jacob. But he made Jesus Christ the rightful Sovereign over heaven and earth; over all authorities, principalities, and powers. Peter said, "Let all the house of Israel know that Jesus is Lord and Christ." Therefore, it is not strictly true, that the government is in the same person, and in the same hands now, that administered it during the Jewish theocracy. Jesus was not then born, much less king. My friend says, the Mediator is the same. Moses was the mediator between God and the people. Gal. iii. 19, "Wherefore then serveth the law? It was added because of transgressions, till the seed should come to whom the promise was made; and it was ordained by angels in the hand of a mediator." In the hand of the mediator, Moses. Is Moses and the Messiah the same? Paul to the Hebrews, says, "Having obtained a more excellent ministry than Moses and Aaron, he is the mediator of a better covenant."

Christ's church is a spiritual community—a community of persons intelligent, believing, loving, fearing and serving God in the hope of eternal life. They are possessed, every one, of God's Spirit, else they are not his. The church is the temple, the house of the living God, the dwelling place of the Most High. It is not a community of speechless babes and carnal, sensual men. Its members are all born again, born of the Spirit, born of God.

I have one question to ask, itself a full refutation of the assumed identity of the two institutions, the Jewish and the Christian. Was not Nicodemus a proper, an honorable, an official member of Mr. Rice's *Jewish identical christian church?* And did not the Master say to him—Nicodemus, unless you, sir, "are born again"—or from above, "you cannot enter into my kingdom, or church, as almost universally understood? Did not John the Baptist come preaching the necessity of faith, repentance, and baptism, to the Jewish people; even to prepare them for admission into the kingdom of God? Did not John tell the Jews that Abrahamic descent would now profit nothing; that they must not think that, having Abraham to be their father, would avail any thing, without a new faith, a real reformation—a new birth?

I have shown that some six or seven of his points have no identity. I would be willing to rest the whole controversy upon his ability to make them out points of identity. If, now, he will stake the whole case upon a thorough syllogistic canvassing of identity, I will meet him upon that single question. I predict that he will not do it.

As I have said before, I am willing to take any number of points. It is his method to say that he *has* proved, or will prove so and so; but there is not much light, conviction, or evidence in such promises and assertions. I will show, at the proper time, as I have already in part, that the churches are not at all identical, even in his own specifications ; that in his examples, he has failed to prove any identity ; nay, I have showed that they had not the same constitution ; that they had not the same laws, same subjects, same observances, same promises, &c. &c.

How much better is Presbyterian flesh and blood than Jewish—than Roman Catholic flesh and blood ? Why should Protestants demand for their flesh and blood, what they would not extend to a Jew, a Mussulman, or a pagan ? "God has made of one blood all nations of men." Why prefer one child of the flesh to another—baptize one and repudiate another ! !

It is a remarkable fact, that the New Testament begins with a repudiation of national and fleshly descent, of all family aristocracies in religion. "Think not, men of Israel, to say that you have a covenanted father Abraham !" A proclamation of repentance is made to all men. Did they not baptize all the circumcised Jews that repented ? What comes of circumcision as the door now ? Two doors into Christ's house ! ! one by circumcision and one by baptism. This is an insuperable argument against identity. No man can dispose of it.

There is, indeed, but one door into the world, and but one door into Christ's church. There is no back nor side door into either. Men cannot cut doors into Christ's house just when and where they please. Remember, the King himself has said, " Ye must be born of water and of the Spirit." You must repent, and bring forth fruits worthy of repentance. You must come to him, believe on him, receive him, or he will not give you the privilege of becoming children of God. So John the Harbinger, the Messiah himself, and his apostles, preached to the Jewish church, to the lost sheep of the house of Israel.—[*Time expired.*

Tuesday, Nov. 21—11 o'clock, A. M
[MR. RICE'S FIFTH ADDRESS.]

MR. PRESIDENT—I decidedly object to Mr. Campbell's quotation from Calvin, for two important reasons. 1st. He has given part of a sentence without its connection ; and 2d. The part he has given is very incorrectly translated, so as to make the impression that Calvin claims for the church the authority to *change* the ordinances appointed by Christ ; when in truth he only maintains that *the mode was not prescribed.*

So far as the gentleman's side of the question is concerned, it may be true, that there has been no debating. Such is certainly the fact, if by debating be understood the making of a fair issue on the points in controversy. I think it likely that many will be of opinion that he has left my most important arguments untouched. He would fain have me confine myself to some few points. It would, no doubt, be of great service to his cause, if he could exclude a large portion of the evidence bearing on the question. I prefer, however, concentrating, as far as possible, the whole teaching of the Scriptures relative to it, and if he fails to answer my arguments, I cannot help it.

He tells you that I am throwing dust in your eyes, by using the word *children* instead of *infants*. Does he really believe that any one, even the most ignorant, misunderstood me ? The gentleman, who does not speak for *present effect*, seems to think that the audience cannot understand me. I am, however, disposed to presume somewhat upon their intelligence.

He calls on me to show where the children of believers were put into the church under the new dispensation. But I call on him to prove that the new dispensation has put them out. I have put them into the only church that ever did exist on the earth ; and let him prove, if he can, that the passing away of the ceremonial law did put them out. If he cannot do this, (and I say, he cannot,) he must let them still enjoy their privileges.

The law, my friend says, was not added to the Abrahamic covenant ; but to the promise with reference to the land of Canaan. Yesterday I thought he had three covenants, and that this was one of them. Let me turn to the Scripture (Gal. iii.) which he read upon the subject. The fact is, that Paul does not mention the land of Canaan in this whole chapter. He is writing against false teachers, who sought to be justified by *the deeds of law ;* and he proves that even Abraham did not pretend to be justified by the law, but by faith ; that he is introducing no new doctrine, but is teaching that which was believed by the father of the faithful himself. Gal. iii. 11 : " But that no man is justified by the law, in the sight of God, is evident ; for the just shall live by faith. And the law is not of faith ; but the man that doeth them [the deeds of the law] shall live in them." Verse 13 : " Christ hath redeemed us from the curse of the law ; being made a curse for us : for it is written, Cursed is every one that hangeth on a tree : that the blessing of Abraham might come on the Gentiles through Jesus Christ, that we might receive the promise of the Spirit through faith." Does this prove that Paul was speaking of the land of Canaan ? So far from it, the apostle is teaching, that we receive not only justification, but a promise of the Spirit, through faith in the Lord Jesus, according to the Abrahamic covenant. But I will read a little farther : verse 15 : " Brethren, I speak after the manner of men ; though it be but a man's covenant, yet if it be confirmed, no man disannulleth or addeth thereto." Again, verse 16 : " Now to Abraham and his seed were the promises made. He saith not, And to seeds, as of many ; but as of one, And to thy seed, which is Christ." Compare with this the declaration of the apostle in the Heb. xi. 8 : " By faith, Abraham when he was called to go out into a place which he should after receive for an inheritance, obeyed ; and he went out, not knowing whither he went. By faith he sojourned in the land of promise, as in a strange country, dwelling in tabernacles with Isaac and Jacob, the heirs with him of the same promise : for he looked for a city which hath foundations, whose builder and maker is God." This was the bright inheritance to which Abraham and his children were looking. Again, Gal. iii. 19 : " Wherefore, then, serveth the law ? it was *added* because of transgressions ; till the seed [Christ] should come to whom the promise was made." The law was added—added to the Abrahamic covenant, which is the subject of Paul's whole discourse. The land of Canaan is not once mentioned in the epistle. The law at Sinai was, therefore, neither the constitution of the Jewish church, nor an addition, simply, to the promise of the land of Canaan ; but an addition to the Abrahamic covenant, made for a specific purpose, till Christ should come.

I am quite pleased, that the gentleman has introduced the passage in the fourth chapter of the epistle to the Galatians ; for it establishes most conclusively the very doctrine for which I am contending. I will read from the twentieth verse :

" I desire to be present with you now, and to change my voice ; for I stand in doubt of you. Tell me, ye that desire to be under the law, do ye not hear the law? For it is written, that Abraham had two sons; the one by a bond-maid, the other by a free woman. But he who was born of the bond-woman was born after the flesh; but he of the free woman was by promise. Which things are an allegory; for these are the two covenants; the one from the Mount Sinai, which gendereth to bondage, which is Agar. For this Agar is Mount Sinai in Arabia, and answereth to Jerusalem which now is, and is in bondage with her children. But Jerusalem which is from above is free, which is the mother of us all. For it is written, Rejoice thou barren that bearest not; break forth and cry, thou that travailest not: for the desolate hath many more children than she which hath a husband. Now we, brethren, as Isaac was, are the children of promise. But as then he that was born after the flesh persecuted him that was born after the Spirit, even so it is now. Nevertheless, what saith the Scripture? Cast out the bond-woman and her son: for the son of the bond-woman shall not be heir with the son of the free woman. So then, brethren, we are not children of the bond-woman, but of the free."

Here we have distinctly presented, the two covenants; the one with Abraham, which is represented by Sarah and Isaac; and the other at Sinai, represented by Agar and Ishmael. The Jews who clung to the law given at Sinai, as a temporary addition to the Abrahamic covenant, and rejected the Messiah promised in that covenant, were in bondage. Christ " came to his own, and his own received him not." The glorious Redeemer, the seed promised to Abraham, had appeared in Judea; but the great body of the Jews rejected him, and turned to seek justification and salvation in the types and shadows of the Levitical law. They, in consequence of their apostasy from the Abrahamic covenant, were in bondage. Yet the promised Messiah was not rejected by all the Jews. The olive-tree still had some living branches. The great majority were broken off because of unbelief; but many who received the Divine Savior, remained. Those who despised him and trusted in the law, were cut off; as Agar and Ishmael were removed from Abraham's family. Those who received him, still constituted his church, the Jerusalem which is from above, the mother of us all.

That such is the true meaning of the passage, is made perfectly clear by the quotation given by the apostle from Isaiah liv. 1. I will read several verses, that the connection may be understood:—" Sing, O barren, thou that didst not bear; break forth into singing, and cry aloud, thou that didst not travail with child: for more are the children of the desolate, than the children of the married wife, saith the Lord. Enlarge the place of thy tent, and let them stretch forth the curtains of thine habitations: spare not, lengthen thy cords, and strengthen thy stakes: for thou shalt break forth on the right hand and on the left; and thy seed shall inherit the gentiles, and make the desolate cities to be inhabited. Fear not, for thou shalt not be ashamed: neither be thou confounded, for thou shalt not be put to shame: for thou shalt forget the shame of thy youth, and shalt not remember the reproach of thy widowhood any more."

I was somewhat amused to hear the gentleman quote this prophecy as an address to Sarah—Rejoice, O barren Sarah! Whence he derives his authority for this singular interpretation, I know not, unless he considers Sarah *the church.* God did not represent himself as the husband of Sarah, but as the husband of the church.

This prophecy is certainly addressed to the church under the old dispensation. It was intended to comfort her in a period of prevailing wickedness, and approaching calamity, by pointing her to a brighter day

22   2 F

in her future history—a day when her children should be greatly multiplied, *and she should inherit the gentiles.*

Here is an unanswerable argument for the identity of the church under the Jewish and christian dispensations. For if, as Mr. Campbell contends, the Jewish church ceased to exist as the church of God, at the commencement of the new dispensation; I call on him to tell us when these promises were fulfilled. When did the Jewish church, to which they were addressed, lengthen her cords and strengthen her stakes? *When did she inherit the gentiles?* When did she rejoice in the multitude of her children? It is certain that these promises were never fulfilled under the old dispensation; and if the christian church is not the same church under another dispensation, *they never have been, and never can be fulfilled!* When the apostles went forth to proclaim to the gentiles "the unsearchable riches of Christ;" when "the middle wall of partition" was broken down; then it was that the church, which had for centuries been oppressed and afflicted, began to lengthen her cords and strengthen her stakes, and to receive the gentiles as her children. I am gratified that the gentleman turned our attention to this most interesting portion of Scripture. We here find promises, great and precious, made to the church in the days of Isaiah, which received their fulfillment under the new dispensation. Thus we have evidence, the most conclusive, that the church is the same under both dispensations.

The identity of the church under the Jewish and christian dispensations, is also clearly proved by the prophecies, in the 60th chapter of Isaiah: "Arise, shine, for thy light is come, and the glory of the Lord is risen upon thee. For, behold, the darkness shall cover the earth, and gross darkness the people: but the Lord shall arise upon thee, and his glory shall be seen upon thee. And the gentiles shall come to thy light, and kings to the brightness of thy rising."

When did the gentiles come to the light of the Jewish church? When did kings come to the brightness of her rising? Was it under the old dispensation? No: it was when the gospel went forth in triumph and glory, from nation to nation, and gathered its thousands into the church of the Redeemer. Then it was that the gentiles came to the brightness of her rising. Then kings shut their mouths, for that which they had not heard, was told them.

Again, ver. 4: "Lift up thine eyes round about and see: all they gather themselves together, they come to thee: thy sons shall come from far, and thy daughters shall be nursed at thy side. Then thou shalt see, and flow together, and thy heart shall fear, and be enlarged; because the abundance of the sea shall be converted unto thee, the forces of the gentiles shall come unto thee."

Now, when was the abundance of the sea converted to the Jewish church? and when did the gentiles pour into it? Here are promises that could not be fulfilled under the Old Testament. The christian church, therefore, is the same which received the promises; or if not, God made promises that never were and never can be fulfilled!

I might read the whole of this chapter; but allow me only to read the verse 10: "And the sons of strangers shall build up thy walls, and their kings shall minister unto thee: for in my wrath I smote thee, but in my favor have I had mercy on thee." Did the sons of *strangers* (gentiles) ever build up the walls of Jerusalem? Were these promises ever fulfilled to the church? Never, never: unless the christian church is identical with the Jewish. And certainly it will not be denied, that the church which received the promises, lived to see their fulfillment. My friend has told us, that Christ's church is a *spiritual church.* I admit that it is a spiritual church, and so was the Jewish church intended to be spiritual. Hence no adult ever entered into it, according to God's law, without professing to be a believer ; and its members were required to worship God in spirit and in truth. Nicodemus was not a worthy member of that church.

My friend says, that before the new dispensation, repentance was not preached. David said, " A broken and a contrite heart, O God, thou wilt not despise." God, speaking by Isaiah, said, " To this man will I look, even to him that is poor and of a contrite spirit, and trembleth at my word." What did Isaiah say—54th chapter ? " Let the wicked forsake his way, and the unrighteous man his thoughts : and let him return unto the Lord, and he will have mercy upon him ; and to our God, for he will abundantly pardon." Were not repentance and reformation then taught as conditions of salvation ?

I will answer, very briefly, if I have time, some of my friend's further remarks. In relation to the church for two thousand years before Abraham, he asks, if there was a church, how did infants get in ? He asserts that adults entered *by faith.* I desire the proof of this : I call for the proof that faith, before the days of Abraham, ever constituted an individual a member of the visible church. That there were many pious people, and that they exercised faith, is certainly true ; but did faith constitute them members of a visible church ? The gentleman cannot find a church of God, in which the children of believers did not enjoy the same privileges granted to believers, so far as they were capable. If he will show how adults entered a visible church, before the time of Abraham, *by the Bible,* and not by *assertion,* I will attend to his arguments.

I have proved that the church is the same, under both dispensations, from the fact, that she receives and obeys the same *moral law.* My friend replies, that the state of Kentucky has adopted the code of laws taught by Moses. I did not know it; and I very much doubt whether the state of Kentucky professes to receive and obey Moses' law. I knew that she had borrowed a great deal from the Bible ; but that she had adopted the moral law of God, and professed to be governed by it, is one of the things that I did not know. I am equally ignorant of the fact, if it be a fact, that Massachusetts ever adopted *the moral law* as a rule of action. If it were true, however, it would prove that there is a sameness in one point.

But, the gentleman says, if I had maintained that the Jewish and Christian churches were, in many respects, *similar,* he would have admitted it. I said precisely what I meant, and what is literally true. Under both dispensations the church worships and serves the *same* God—not a *similar* God. She obeys the *same* (not a *similar)* moral law. She receives the *same* (not a *similar)* gospel ; and she enjoys her blessings under the *same* (not a *similar)* covenant. I am not speaking of *similarities,* but of *identity.*

The Free Masons, the gentleman tells us, have adopted the moral law. If he will prove that there are as many and as important points of sameness between the Masons and the christian church, as I have shown between the church under the old dispensation, and under the new, I will recognize them as a part of the church of Christ. But he will not attempt it.

In reply to the fact I have stated, that under both dispensations the church worships and serves the same God, he says—the same God reigns over Kentucky and over Jerusalem! Can he see no difference between a revolted province and a people obedient to the laws of their sovereign? I did not say, simply, that the same God controls all things, under both the Old and the New Testaments, *but that the church does, in fact, worship and serve the same God.* Do not all the nations that acknowledge the queen of England as their sovereign, and obey the laws of Great Britain, constitute one kingdom, even though oceans roll between them? And so the church which has, in all ages, worshiped the same God, constitutes one spiritual kingdom.

Mr. Campbell, strangely indeed, denies that the Jewish church had the same gospel, any more than France and England, because they have the same alphabet, have the same language! Thus he flatly contradicts Paul, who says, the gospel was preached to Abraham, Gal. iii. 8. Again, in Hebrews iv. 2, he says: "For unto us was *the gospel* preached, as well as unto them"—that is, the Jews in the wilderness. But, he says, the gospel that was preached to them was the *promise of Canaan.* LET HIM PROVE IT. The Greek word is the same which, throughout the New Testament, is used to denote the gospel of Christ; and, therefore, it devolves upon him to prove, that in this instance, it has an uncommon meaning—a meaning it has not in another instance in the New Testament.

He tells you, that I say, the church has the same *ordinances* under the Old and New Testaments. *I did not say so.* On the contrary, I said precisely the opposite—that the ceremonial law, with all its ordinances, has passed away, and given place to a few simple ordinances, adapted to the extension of the church over the world. What could he have been thinking of?

He denies that the church under both dispensations has the same *King!* I thought there was but one true God, the Father, the Son, and the Holy Spirit! He denies, too, that under both dispensations the church had the same *Mediator!* and he tells us, Moses was mediator under the Old Testament. In what respect was he mediator? In giving the law Moses acted as a daysman between God and the people. In what sense was Christ the mediator? He stepped between offended God and offending man; and, in due time, laid down his life for all his people, in all ages, past and future. Accordingly Isaiah says: "All WE, like sheep, have gone astray; we have turned every one to his own way; and the Lord hath laid on him the iniquity of us ALL." Christ died to atone for the sins of those who lived before, as well as of those who should live after his advent. This I have already proved, by the plain declarations of Paul, in Rom. iii. 25, and Heb. ix. 15. Hence, in the book of Revelation, he is spoken of as "The Lamb slain from the foundation of the world." It is, therefore, worse than vain for the gentleman to deny, that under both dispensations the church has worshiped and served the same God, obeyed the same moral law, and received the same glorious gospel.

Not a Jew, the gentleman tells us, ever passed into the church of Christ because of his connection with Abraham. But adults have always entered the church on a profession of faith. I desire, however, if he pleases, to be informed *when the apostles received christian baptism.* I do not find in the New Testament, that any one of them except Paul, who was converted at a later period, was baptized. Mr. Campbell admits that John's baptism was not christian baptism; and our Savior, we are informed by John the apostle, did not baptize. Then by whom were they baptized?

They were a portion of the branches of the good olive-tree, that were not broken off because of unbelief. They were in the church, and were never excluded. It was, therefore, unnecessary that they should be grafted in again. They formed, as it were, the connecting link between the two dispensations, showing the identity of the church under both. If there is any part of inspired history that mentions their baptism, I have overlooked it.

It is true, as the gentleman says, that the kingdom of Christ is a spiritual kingdom, and so it has ever been. He quotes John i. 11—13, to prove, that whilst the kingdom of Christ is spiritual, the Jewish church was fleshly. " He came to his own, and his own received him not. But as many as received him, to them gave he power to become the sons of God, even to them that believe on his name : which were born, not of blood, nor of the will of the flesh, nor of the will of man, but of God." Now what is the simple truth on this subject? Christ came to *his own ;* his *own people,* HIS CHURCH : but the great majority of them had become apostates, and they rejected him. But, amid all the error and corruption that prevailed, there were still some who were born, not of the flesh, but of God. Such were the aged Simeon, and Anna the prophetess, and many others. Those who were born of God, possessed true piety—received him with open arms ; and, notwithstanding the defection of others, he gave to them the privileges of children. The new dispensation was not yet introduced ; and yet there were persons who were born of God. This passage is decidedly in favor of the doctrine for which I am contending. For if Christ had no church till the new dispensation, how could it be said, " he came to *his own,* and *his own* received him not?"

I have now answered the gentleman's arguments, so far as he has offered arguments, and have presented a greater number in favor of our views, than he is willing to examine. He does not forget frequently to charge me with making bold assertions ; and he does not neglect to make many such, without offering the slightest proof. He asserted, that before the days of Abraham, adults entered a visible church simply *by faith.* I called upon him for some little evidence. Has he produced any? No—and he never will. When I make a statement, I hold myself bound, especially if it is questioned, to produce the proof. Whether the evidence adduced is conclusive, the audience must judge.—[*Time expired.*

Tuesday, Nov. 21—11 *o'clock, A. M.*
[MR. CAMPBELL'S FIFTH REPLY.]

MR. PRESIDENT—The gentleman errs in stating, that I proposed to explain the whole subject of casting out the Jewish church and the covenant from the relation which they once sustained to Abraham's God. That is just as unnecessary to my argument, as my friend's disquisition upon Sarah, as the barren woman of Isaiah. His is the rare art of evading arguments, by extraneous matters and false issues. What I have said of Sarah and her progeny, from Isaiah, as quoted by Paul, is no part of my argument, nor at all necessary to it. It is, however, a view full of consolation, that Sarah has become the mother of many millions more than all the children of the flesh, born of Hagar ; and that Abraham's spiritual progeny bids fair greatly to out-number the children of his flesh. Mr. Rice has prudently substituted certain declarations and declamations concerning the calling

2 F 2

of the gentiles and the enlargement of the church, for a discussion of the allegory, or the precept for casting out the bond-woman and her son. I presumed he would find the allegory and reasonings of Paul upon it, unanswerable, and certainly, his passing it, without a single remark, shows that I have not been mistaken.

Not having been furnished with a copy of Calvin's commentary, I cannot say whether the version we have had of it, is *literatim et punctuatim*, according to the text. I read from the English version. I know the gentleman quotes Scripture with freedom, and I presume he quotes Calvin in the same manner. But my representation of Calvin's views on that subject is not, *in the sense*, at all impaired by even his free translation of the passage, nor has it any thing at all to do with the question now before us. "The church," he says, "has freely allowed herself to have rites a little dissimilar *extra* the substance." Now what is the difference?

I spake of a plurality of covenants with Abraham. I gave chapter and verse. He has not by quotation, or argument, attempted a refutation of these views. They stand unanswered, and I presume he considers them unanswerable. The gentleman made some effort to quote Rom. ix. 4, but failed to give the verse as found in either the original or the common version. Paul does not make the last word of this verse exegetical of all the items in it. The verse gives a series of honors and emoluments belonging to the Jews. "To them pertained the adoption, and the glory, and the covenants, and the giving of the law and the promises—whose are the fathers, and of whom as respects *the flesh* the Messiah came—who is over all God blessed forever." This method of putting in some words and leaving out others, I cannot approve—nor do I approve of the transposition of words, when critically quoting a verse or a sentence from the sacred Scriptures. The *covenants* are different from the giving of the law, and from the promises. Now the Jews, besides the law, had no *covenants* but the Abrahamic. Therefore, I properly quote the verse to prove a *plurality of covenants* with Abraham.

He also read a passage from Gal. iii. in order to prove that the law was added to the covenant. And to what covenant was it added? The law was itself a covenant, and is so called. The very ark that held the two tables on which it is written, is called "the ark of *the covenant*," and the tables themselves are called the "two tables of the covenant." The law added to the covenant! The covenant added to the covenant! What does the gentleman mean!! The old covenant, or the law, was, indeed, added to an antecedent promise concerning Canaan,—and it was added to the promise concerning the Messiah. But the question is: what is THE *promise* alluded to Gal. iii. 18? The Messiah or the *inheritance* in Canaan, emblem of the rest in heaven! Not the Messiah: for Paul immediately adds, "God gave the *inheritance* to Abraham by a promise," consequently, not by a law of works; for, as the same writer says to the Romans—"The promise to Abraham, that he should be the heir of the world, (the heir of Canaan,) was not after, or through the law, but through the righteousness (or obedience) of faith. Now the facts are, as every one who has carefully read the history remembers:—God promised Canaan to Abraham at a very early period, probably soon after his arrival in it. Certainly, however, he confirmed it by a covenant before Ishmael was born. Ishmael was fourteen years old when Isaac was born—making the covenant aforesaid date some ten to twelve years after the call of Abraham. If the gentleman means, then, that the law was added to the covenant, concerning the inheritance, he may have it so for any thing our debate cares, or is interested in the discussion. The plurality of covenants with Abraham stands as erect as ever.

By a singular freak of imagination, the gentleman was borne away to heaven and the eternal inheritance, and was found, if not like Philip at Azotus, at least in the 11th of the Hebrews—and, by expatiating on the heavenly inheritance, has lost himself and the subject so far as not to hear Paul in the same passage loudly speaking—" These all (Abraham, Isaac, Jacob, Sarah, just now named) died in faith, not having received *the promises* concerning Canaan, but having seen them afar off (400 years,) were persuaded of them and embraced them, and confessed that they were pilgrims and strangers in the earth," (the land promised them for an inheritance,) all of which, indeed, was a *type* of heaven. The gentleman, no doubt, found this flight to the eternal inheritance, an happy escape from the difficulties which environed him. But all this is his proof " that the infant of a believing parent, is a proper subject of christian baptism !" He has a right to prove this point just as he pleases.

You will please to remember, however, that there was an earthly inheritance, actually and formally added to the promise. The very boundaries of which, northward, and southward, and westward, and eastward, are given by the Lord himself to Abraham. Which, however, being a type of the future and boundless inheritance of heaven, was to be inherited, not by works of law, but by the righteousness of faith. Hence, faith and grace were in the Abrahamic family anterior to law—the only point we are careful now to maintain.

It was important, in a typical institution, that there should be an exact correspondence between the typical scenes, and the things adumbrated by them. What is not true in the letter could not be true in the type, nor in the anti-type. Moses represented the law; Israel the elect of all nations; their bondage in Egypt, man's slavery in sin; their redemption by the first-born of Egypt, and the blood of the slain lamb, the christian ransom; their escape through the red waters, their eating the manna, their drinking from the rock, their journey through the wilderness, their passing Jordan, &c. Abraham's walking by faith in a land not his own, and dwelling in tents, with his co-heirs, on a soil deeded to him by the Lord of the whole earth. And the grace, and the promises, and the richness of the inheritance, all were unique; and literally, typically, and antitypically true. He, then, that confounds one letter, one type, in this primer of Divine knowledge, inflicts a great misfortune upon those who desire to understand the glorious scheme of deliverance, originated, developed, and consummated by the grace of God.

I shall not reiterate my labors of yesterday, in fixing the chronological dates of those three Abrahamic covenants, consummated at last in the old church, or national covenant, ratified and confirmed at Horeb, 430 years after the original promise concerning the Messiah, the seed of all spiritual blessings. The matter appears to be, satisfactorily or unsatisfactorily, established beyond controversy. When assaulted, I shall be forthcoming with new resources. The time, place, and circumstance of any transaction is, of all sorts of proof, the best.

If I understood Mr. Rice's account of these affairs, he compares the three covenants to one great bond, having three distinct instalments; one concerned the covenant at Horeb, due in 430 years—or perhaps the land of Canaan; one concerning the flesh of the Messiah, payable at some indefinite future period; and one to be paid in the millenial dispensations. Now, if any inspired apostle had said so, I should have had no objection to it; yet even then it would have been unintelligible to any one who either understands the doctrine of the Bible, or the laws of bonds. For each one of these transactions is positively called a covenant *per se*, and independent of any other one; and one of them has respect to blessings not found in either Canaan, or the flesh of the Messiah, or the latter-day glory. Not one of these has the gospel in it. The new triune or triple bond has no gospel in it for Jew or gentile. Where now is the identity of the two churches?

But finding only two promises, and no land of promise, in this covenant of Gen. xii. 3, on reflection, my friend perceived that to cover the whole ground of subsequent development, he must get some land into it. And what was the expedient? On turning over to Gen. xii., and reading down a few verses, he meets with a promise made to Abraham, in the plains of Moreh, in the land of Canaan—no one knows how long after—concerning the country in which Abraham was now residing. This promise concerning the land of Canaan, was, in truth, a promise of the inheritance But strange to tell, the gentleman has forgotten that " *the covenant confirmed of God, concerning Christ*," and reported in the third verse of Gen. xii., was given to Abraham, *not in Canaan* at all; but in Urr of Chaldea! and so the fourth and fifth verses plainly declare; " So Abraham departed (from Urr of Chaldea) as the Lord *had* spoken to him, and Lot with him; and Abraham was seventy-five years old when he departed out of Haran." Some time after this he arrived in Canaan, and from place to place had removed, till he came to Moreh. The Lord appeared to him, and said, "*Unto thy seed will I give this land.*" What, sir, could not be proved from the Bible by such a licence of interpolation, transposition, and annihilation of times and places !! I have never heard a more glaring, nor a weaker effort, to interpolate a new provision on an old transaction. I shall not farther expose this attempt; believing that there is no intelligent or attentive person present who does not thoroughly comprehend the failure of my ingenious and resolute friend. But my duty to the whole community commands me to make a remark, I could wish not to have been constrained to make in the presence of this assembly. It is this: If a commentator or teacher can thus foist into a solemn covenant, a provision so different in time, place, and significance, under the influence of partizan prejudice or feelings, how shall we confide in his judgment and discretion, in other cases, as a biblical expositor?

I may again remark, that, in matters of such high magnitude, it is all-important that we be governed by those lines of separation so essential to correct interpretation, those geographical and chronological metes and boundaries, which are providentially introduced, and from which, sometimes, arguments are deduced, even by inspired writers themselves. In one verse we are told that Abraham was seventy-five years old when he left Haran. Fortunate too, it seems to me, was it, that when father Jacob appeared before Pharaoh, the monarch asked him for his age. For from the answer made by the patriarch to the king, we ascertain the period of the sojourn, both in Canaan and in Egypt. The venerable Jacob responded in the most apposite terms, saying; " The days of the years of the life of my pilgrimage are one hundred and thirty years." From these dates of the call of Abraham, of the birth of Isaac, of the birth of Jacob and Esau, of

Jacob's descent into Egypt, we are able to make out the items of those 430 years from the covenant of the Messiah to the giving of the law. The three grand transactions are forever permanently fixed—the covenant in Chaldea, the covenant of circumcision, the covenant at Horeb. The first 25 years before the second, and the second 405 years before the third; the three together occupying, in all, four hundred and thirty years. Paul founds two important arguments against the Judaizers on these dates. To the Romans, he proves that circumcision had nothing to do with justification; because Abraham was justified twenty-five years before he was circumcised, as they knew, and that the promise of blessing the gentiles, through faith, could not be vacated or disannulled by the law of works, he proves to the Galatians, from the fact that the covenant, promising to bless the gentiles, was confirmed, and immutably too, four hundred and thirty years before the giving of the covenant of peculiarity to the Jews. It is not in the power of any man to refute this argument. These are plain historical and chronological facts and documents, which are as indestructible as the universe, and shall stand for ever. To confound these transactions is to confound law and gospel—the covenant concerning the blessing of us gentiles, with the circumcision and the Canaan provisions for the Jews. That circumcision that was contrary to us, Jesus Christ took out of our way, as a religious solemnity, nailing it to his cross.

Mr. Rice has taken the ground of the *identity* of these two institutions as the main basis of his argument. It is the most untenable ground in creation. It is worse than proselyte baptism, or tradition. Circumcision has been thought most plausible, and now we have it transmuted into identity. He must, then, tear up all these land-marks by the root. He must annul dates and places. He must confound law and gospel, Jew and Gentile, flesh and Spirit. It is a hard task. And, in arguments of this kind, the proof extends to every single point of comparison; for a case of identity is the most difficult case in law, in gospel, in ecclesiastics, in physics, and in metaphysics. Similarity, the gentleman knows, will never do. He is right—he must prove identity; and that is impossible.

Some imagine, and amongst them, I believe, is Mr. Rice, that the promise "I will be a God unto thee, and to thy seed after thee," implies spiritual blessings; and if so, then there is one provision in the covenant of circumcision, indicative of spiritual blessings: for in Gen. xvii., "The Lord said to Abraham, I will be a God unto thee, and to thy seed after thee." Well, it is so written, and so we read Gen. xvii. 7. Whether, however, it is in that place to be regarded as a mere preamble to the covenant of circumcision, or as a provision in it, is questionable—highly questionable. But I shall not question it at this place, nor in this discussion. That God intended, in these words, to take the twelve tribes under his special protection and providence, is admitted; and that, as their God, he would bless them with corn, and wine, and oil, and all earthly good—giving them a delightful land, flowing with milk and honey, is universally understood and admitted. But that, beyond this, anything more was intended or implied in these words, is not inferrible from any thing in the Old Testament—nor from the words themselves. Indeed, the palpable fact that God found fault with them and that institution, promising in the next to convey spiritual blessings—to write his laws upon their hearts—and to make them know him, from the least to the greatest of them, is itself enough to show, indeed to prove, to all persons of reflection, that the blessings of the former were temporal, and those of the latter, spiritual. Here, however, I am reminded of a complaint made against me by my sensitive friend, for calling God the husband of Israel, or of Sarah. It will be, I hope, but a venal offence in the esteem of those who have noticed that God himself first used the endearing appellation. "I was," said he, "an husband unto them;" yet they broke the marriage covenant. And more than this, all their apostasies are set forth under the imagery of an unfaithful wife, that has broken her covenant with her husband. Jesus, indeed, calls himself the bridegroom, and Paul espoused the church, and desired to present her a chaste virgin to the Lord. And has not God promised to be an husband to the widow, as well as a father to the fatherless? There is nothing, then, so heinous, nor so reprehensible in my allusions to God as an husband to Sarah.

Such matters as these, however, fill up the time and save the resources of Mr. R., which I presume he is reserving to a more convenient season, when we may expect him to prove his position by a formidable array of New Testament arguments.

But, by way of an offset to my remarks on the opening of the New Testament with the preaching and baptism of repentance, for remission of sins, he asks, was not repentance preached to the Jews? Now, what does this mean? I said, (in order to prove that the Jewish and Christian institutions were not the same identical church,) that, before a man, who was a good member of the Jewish church, could be admitted into the Christian church, he must repent of his sins and be baptized. Moreover, I asked him to show a single instance of a son of Abraham entering into the Christian church, without repentance and baptism, on the ground of former membership. I challenge him again to produce a single case. He cannot do it. It is, therefore, idle to talk of preaching repentance under the old dispensation—we sometimes preach repentance to those in the church. This is a position which no man denies. But it seems to evince the extreme sterility and barrenness of his side of the question, in point of argument.

I have endeavored to show, that, whatever the door into the Jewish church might have been, it was a door that suffered them to carry in too much flesh; and, therefore, another and a straiter door was required. Jesus has spoken something of the straitness of the gate of life, and of the narrowness of the way leading to it.

The gentleman has again adverted to my remarks upon the corrupting influence of infant membership. Does he wish for more evidence? He can have it to satiety. What would corrupt the church more, than to bring all the world into it without a change of heart? And will, or can Mr. R. show that this is not his aim, or the tendency of the views he inculcates? Suppose, for illustration, that Mr. Rice's views of the necessity of infant baptism universally obtained; what would the consequences be, but the introduction of the whole community into the church? It would cause the church to throw her arms all round the earth, and take into her bosom every thing born of the flesh. Such is the design and tendency of the doctrine. It would make the doors of the church wide as the doors of the world. But that is not all. It goes in this way to make void the commandment of the Lord.

The Messiah brought this as a serious charge against certain contemporaries, scribes and pharisees, doctors and public leaders. You, said he, make void the commandments of God by your traditions.

The law of God says: " Honor thy father and thy mother;" but you say, "Whoever shall say to his father or his mother, This that you need I call a *gift*, and devote it to the Lord, and honors not his father or mother, he shall be free." Now, what is the difference in principle, where parents prevent their children from honoring their Heavenly Father, by taking from them the opportunity and the right of obeying his precept, " Be baptized every one of you." A parent can neither believe, nor repent, nor be baptized for his child. Nor has he any authority from God to take away from his child the exquisite pleasure of believing, repenting, and of being baptized for himself. Parents, you rob your children of their highest honor—that of being buried with their Lord, on their own clear conviction, firm belief, and joyful acquiescence.

Neither can you dedicate your infants to the Lord in baptism. Your notions of dedication are most unscriptural, if you think so. Whatever is dedicated to the Lord, is given wholly to him, to be exclusively employed in his service. Samuel was thus taken to the sanctuary and left there. But that was a free-will offering. If you go for dedication, according to law, you can only give your first-born son. The Lord asks for neither son nor daughter besides. Again; there is a special ordinance for this purpose, Exodus xiii. 2—12; Levit. xii. 6—8. Our Lord was dedicated according to law; for he was the first-born son. Now, Jesus was circumcised the eighth day, and dedicated on the fortieth, and was not baptized till his thirtieth year.

You see how idle it is to attempt to blend and confound these ordinances, when the great Master himself, the great Lawgiver of the universe, was first circumcised at eight days old, dedicated at forty days, and received the baptism of John at thirty years: at the age of perfect maturity, he came forward; (though not in need of baptism for the remission of sins;) but it became him to honor every divine institution. Is not this the duty of all his followers ?

My friend has asked me to show the passage which speaks of the baptism of the apostles. He knows there is no account of it. But its not being recorded is no evidence that it did not take place. He asks me to tell when each of the apostles was baptized, as if it were requisite to give the time, place, and circumstances. They were baptized with John's baptism; no other was instituted during their first discipleship. Between John's baptism and that ordained by the Messiah himself, there was, in this respect, little difference. When the time came for their baptism, they were believing adults, and were immersed in the Jordan, confessing their sins. They made a public profession and confession. They voluntarily came forward and were immersed.

Christian baptism did not commence till at the Pentecost in Jerusalem, and after that Paul, like any other convert, was immersed. There was then no necessity for proving their previous baptism, any more than that of John's.

I have yet time to state another objection to the identity of the two institutions. Jesus said to Peter that he would build his church upon a certain rock. Now, as the rock was then, for the first time, displayed, upon which the church of Christ was to be founded, can we either scripturally or rationally conclude, that the Jewish church had stood upon that same foundation for 1500 years ? If the foundation laid by Moses, or by God, in the Abrahamic family, was Jesus Christ, or the confession of faith in him as the Messiah of God how could Jesus say, I will lay a new foundation ? or, On this rock will I build my church, and the gates of hades shall not prevail against it ?—[*Time expired.*

Tuesday, Nov. 21—12 o'clock, M.

[MR. RICE'S SIXTH ADDRESS.]

MR. PRESIDENT—In my last address I offered some additional arguments from the prophecies, proving the identity of the church of Christ under the old and new dispensations. To these arguments, the only reply of the gentleman is, that they are entirely irrelevant, that they have nothing to do with the question. That is, he would have you believe, that the fact that certain most important promises were made to the church under the old dispensation and fulfilled under the new, does not prove the church to be the same under both!—does not prove, that the church lived to enjoy the fulfillment of the promises! He might as well say, the fact that an infallible promise made to a man ten years since, and now fulfilled to him, does not prove that he is the same individual!!! He will doubtless better serve his cause by making positive assertions and attempting no reply; for then those who may consider him infallible, will suppose that all is right. This mode of interpreting, or rather of slighting prophecy, is, I will not say "licentious," (for this is an offensive word,) but most unwarranted.

As to the plurality of covenants with Abraham, I have said (and I repeat it) that I care not, so far as infant baptism is concerned, if the gentleman could find half a dozen. I have proved every thing that is necessary to the defence of it, viz: that the covenant of circumcision contains the great promise of spiritual blessings through Christ. I have fully proved, that in Genesis xii., xv., and xvii. the very same promises are made, repeated and sealed by circumcision; but it is an indisputable fact, proved by the apostle Paul, (Rom. iv.) that the great promise sealed by circumcision, was of spiritual blessings to all the nations of the earth, through Christ. This is the covenant and this the promise on which the church was organized.

The gentleman tells you, that I did not fully and correctly read the passage in Romans ix., on which he had commented. I read every word of it. He had maintained, that inasmuch as the giving of the law was mentioned in addition to the covenants, there must have been some three covenants with Abraham. I replied, that the *promises* are given as distinct from the covenants also; and that according to his logic, there were covenants without promises and promises without a covenant! I am apprehensive that he hears badly. I have repeatedly called on him to produce the passage of Scripture that speaks of a plurality of covenants with Abraham; but he has not done it. It is quite unfortunate for him, that the inspired writers did not ascertain that there was a plurality of covenants with Abraham. In the ninth chapter to the Romans we read of covenants, but not of *covenants with Abraham;* and what, I ask, does the gentleman expect to gain by proving that with the Jews several covenants were made ?

The gentleman will have it, that the law, mentioned in Galatians iii. 19, was an addition to the single promise of the land of Canaan; that this was the inheritance spoken of, which was by promise. I ask him, whether the land of Canaan is once mentioned, directly or indirectly, in the chapter? Is it mentioned in the connection, or even in the epistle to the Galations? There is not a word about Canaan in the epistle! If there is, I have overlooked it. As I have already proved, the apostle's object in the connection, and the prominent design of the whole epistle, is to prove the doctrine of justification by faith, without the deeds of the law—justification by faith in the great promise contained in the Abrahamic covenant.

This is not all. Let me turn to Romans, chap. iv., where we may learn something about this inheritance; for Paul, in this chapter, speaking of circumcision, (11th to 17th verses,) says :—" And he received the sign of circumcision, a seal of the righteousness of the faith which he had, yet being uncircumcised; that he might be the father of all them that believe, though they be not circumcised; that righteousness might be imputed unto them also : and the father of circumcision to them who are not of the circumcision only : but who also walk in the steps of that faith of our father Abraham, which he had, being yet uncircumcised. For the promise that he should be the heir of the world, was not to Abraham, or to his seed, through the law, but through the righteousness of faith. For if they which are of the law be heirs, faith is made void, and the promise made of none effect : because the law worketh wrath : for where there is no law, there is no transgression. Therefore it is of faith, that it might be by grace : to the end the promise might be sure to all the seed : not to that only which is of the law, but to that also which is of the faith of Abraham, who is the father of us all, (as it is written, I have made thee a father of many nations,)" &c.

Here Paul was quoting from the seventeenth chapter of Genesis, and proving that by the covenant of circumcision Abraham was made the *father of many nations*—the heir of the world in a spiritual sense, the father of all believers.

My friend asks why I fly off to heaven? I desire to fly that way very often. Why was Paul, when speaking of the same covenant, disposed to fly off in that direction? Heb. xi. 8, " By faith Abraham, when he was called to go out into a place which he should afterwards receive for an inheritance, obeyed : And he went out, not knowing whither he went. For he looked for a city which hath foundations, whose builder and maker is God." 13th verse, " These all died in faith, not having received the promises, but having seen them afar off, and were persuaded of them, and embraced them, and confessed that they were strangers and pilgrims on the earth. For they that say such things declare plainly that they seek a country." They were strangers and pilgrims on their way to a heavenly city, of which, in that covenant, they had the promise.

As for his chronological dates, they affect not my argument. I have already proved to demonstration, that the promises recorded in Gen. 12th, are precisely the same which are in the 17th, ratified and sealed by circumcision—that the covenant sealed by circumcision contains the spiritual promise which made Abraham the father of the church of God in all ages. He has affirmed, that in the 12th chapter, the land of Canaan was not promised; but the very first verse is a refutation of the assertion—" The Lord said unto Abraham, get thee out of thy country, and from thy kindred, and from thy father's house, *unto a land that I will shew thee.*" Did not God command him to leave his native country for the express purpose of giving him the land to which he would direct him? And yet the gentleman asserts, that in this covenant there was no promise of Canaan—that we find nothing of the kind, till Abraham reached that country! I am not in the habit, as he intimates, of throwing out arguments or of making quotations *loosely.* I generally look all around them, before

2 G

they are presented. The promises were first made, as recorded in Gen. xii. ; and from this period Paul dates the existence of the covenant. The same promises substantially were repeated in Gen. xv. ; but no *seal* was appointed. They were again repeated in the 17th, and sealed by circumcision.

The gentleman makes a vain effort to justify himself in representing God as the husband of Sarah ! He has represented himself as the husband of the *church;* but never do the Scriptures speak of him as the husband of any individual—never.

He tells you, that if the Calvinistic doctrine of election be true, the Jewish church were not God's people; for then they never could have fallen away. I have had occasion since the commencement of this discussion, to remark, that he never was a genuine Presbyterian. At any rate, he seems to have very imperfect acquaintance with the doctrines of the Presbyterian church. For who does not know, that a church may gradually become corrupt, because the pious die, and the rising generation are not converted; and yet not one who was truly pious, may fall away ? But whether this doctrine is true or false, I will not now inquire; because it has nothing to do with the subject under discussion, from which I will not allow myself to be diverted.

The gentleman insists, that the terms of membership in the Jewish and in the Christian church are not the same; and he tells us, that Nicodemus was a worthy member of the former, but could not enter the latter, unless he were born again. But I deny that Nicodemus was a *worthy* member of the Jewish church. At the time of our Savior's advent, the church, as all must know, had become extremely corrupt, and was filled with unworthy and ungodly members. The mere fact, that at such a time Nicodemus was a member, affords no evidence whatever that he possessed the qualifications for membership required by the law of God. Indeed he was reproved by the Savior, because, whilst he was professedly a teacher in Israel, he was ignorant of one of the fundamental doctrines of the Old Testament. Let him prove that Nicodemus was a worthy member ; and I will be prepared to respond.

He challenges me to show, that any individual ever entered the christian church without professing *faith* and *repentance*. And I challenge him to prove, that any adult ever entered the Jewish church, *according to the law of God*, without professing faith in the God of Abraham, Isaac and Jacob, and a purpose to obey the law of Moses. So I will put my challenge against his ; and I shall be prepared to.meet them both, whenever he chooses to bring them forward.

By way of showing the corrupting influence of infant baptism on the church, Mr. Campbell tells us, that if all parents would have their children baptized, the whole world would be introduced into the church. True enough ; and if all the parents in this world were truly pious, what a glorious world this would be ! I am prepared, as I have repeatedly said, to compare any Pedo-baptist church, that take the Bible as their only infallible guide, with any anti-Pedo-baptist church, and to prove, that they are as moral, as benevolent, as pious, as exemplary christians, as they who eschew the baptism of infants. Yes—if all parents were truly pious, and would give their children to Christ in the ordinance of baptism, solemnly promising to train them up in the nurture and admonition of the Lord, and humbly claiming the promised blessing; this would be a happy world ! Methinks, the song would be heard around the throne of God—" Alleluia ; for the Lord God omnipotent reigneth."

But the gentleman adduces another sweeping argument against our doctrine, viz: that it makes void the command of Christ, that all shall be baptized; for if all were baptized in infancy, he supposes that none could obey this command. This argument is very conclusive, on the supposition that the doctrine of infant baptism is false; but it is of no force whatever *to prove* it false. If we take it as granted, that Christ commanded only *adults* to be baptized; it is clear, that those baptized in infancy do not obey this command. But if it be true, as we contend, that he commanded believers and their children to be baptized; infant baptism, instead of making void the command, really obeys it. But he *assumes* that the doctrine is false; and then on that assumption triumphantly proves, that it is untrue!!! Let him prove, that our Savior commanded all to be baptized at adult age; and I will give up the question.

Another objection is presented, viz.: If children are members of the church, they ought to enjoy all its privileges, and of course to commune at the Lord's table. But are not our children citizens of this commonwealth and of these United States, in such a sense that they enjoy the protection of the government and all the privileges of which they are capable? Yet you will not allow them to vote till they are twenty-one years of age, nor to become members of the legislature till they are yet older. Precisely so the children of believers enjoy all the privileges of the church to which they are by the law of God entitled. As the constitution of our government determines at what age and with what qualifications our children shall enjoy all the privileges belonging to it; so does the law of Christ determine what qualifications are necessary for a worthy participation of the Lord's supper. And so soon as our children have "faith to discern the Lord's body," they are permitted to commune.

I must say, I was not a little surprised to hear the gentleman derive an argument against infant baptism from the baptism of our Savior. He told us, that Christ was circumcised and dedicated; but it was also necessary that he should be baptized. *But did our Savior receive* CHRISTIAN BAPTISM? Mr. Campbell has himself published the declaration, that he did not. Yet he argues, that because the Savior submitted to a certain ordinance, his disciples must receive one that is radically different! This is indeed singular reasoning. The Savior was not baptized till he was thirty years of age; and if his example in this matter is to be followed, none should be baptized till they arrive at the same age.

I called on Mr. Campbell to tell us, where the apostles, except Paul, received christian baptism. He admits, that we have no account of their baptism; but maintains, that the absence of any record is no proof that they were not baptized. But here is the difficulty: they could not possibly have received the ordinance. It is said, in so many words, that our Savior did not baptize; (John iv. 2.) and they could not baptize themselves, unless indeed they did as certain immersionists in Rhode Island. Two individuals, it is said, desiring to be immersed, and not being able to find any immersed person to plunge them, determined to immerse each other. This mode of doing things might answer for them; but it will not square with the word of God. But Christ did not baptize the apostles, and they could not baptize each other. By whom, then, were they baptized? The truth is, as I before remarked, they were in the church, and were never broken off because of unbelief. They therefore formed the connecting link between the two dispensations; proving demonstrably that under both the church is the same. They were the officers appointed to introduce the new dispensation, and to administer to converts the newly appointed ordinance of baptism. If the church is not the same under both dispensations, the apostles were not at all in the christian church.

But Mr. Campbell says, they received John's baptism, which he represents as differing very little from christian baptism. Now, I have the *Christian Baptist*, of which he was the editor, which teaches that there was *a great difference*. ["Read it," says Mr. Campbell.] He is proving, by several arguments, that John's baptism is not christian baptism, as follows:

" 1. 'He [John] immersed in the name, or by the authority of God, and not in the name, or by the authority of the Lord. * * * * 2. He immersed *into* no name. * * * * 3. But in the third place, he did not immerse into the christian faith. * * * * 4. In the fourth place, John's immersion brought no man into the kingdom of heaven.'"

By which my friend understands *the church of Christ*. Then it did not bring the apostles into the church of Christ! They did not receive christian baptism; and John's baptism left them out. I desire him then to show how they got in. Let me read further:

" The reason is obvious: no person could come into a kingdom which was not set up, &c. The state in which John's immersion left his disciples, was a state of *preparation* for the kingdom of heaven, which at *first* must be gradually developed, and progressively exhibited to the world. But the state in which christian immersion leaves the disciples of Jesus, is the kingdom of heaven—a state of righteousness, peace, joy, and possessed of the Holy Spirit of adoption into the family of God. They are pardoned, justified, glorified, with the title, rank, and spirit of sons and daughters of the Lord God Almighty. Such are the prominent points of dissimilarity between the immersion of John and that of the New Institution. *Hence, we never read of any person being exempted from christian immersion, because of his having been immersed by John.* But, though all Judea and Jerusalem turned out and were immersed in the Jordan, confessing their sins, and receiving absolution from John, yet when the reign of heaven was experienced in Pentecost, of all the myriads immersed into John's immersion, not one refused or was exempted from christian immersion. We read, however, of the immersion of some of John's disciples into Jesus Christ, who had been immersed. See Acts xix. I know to what tortures the passage has been subjected by such cold, cloudy, and sickening commentators as John Gill. But no man can, with any regard to the grammar of language, or the import of the most definite words, make Luke say, that when those twelve men heard Paul declare the design of immersion, they were not baptized into the name of the Lord Jesus. Nothing but the bewildering influence of some phantasy, of some blind adoration, of some favorite speculation, could so far be-cloud any man's mind as to make him suppose for a moment, that those twelve persons were not *immersed into* the name of the Lord Jesus. Luke says literally, 'Hearing this, or upon hearing this, they were immersed into the name of the Lord Jesus.' Then after they were immersed into the name of the Lord Jesus, Paul laid his hands upon them, and the Holy Ghost fell upon them. Nothing can more fully exhibit the pernicious influence of favorite dogmas, than to see how many of the Baptists have been Gillized, or Fullerized, into the notion that these twelve men were not baptized into the name of the Lord Jesus, when they heard Paul expound to them the design and meaning of John's immersion."—*Christian Baptist*, pp. 647, 648.

It is extremely difficult for a man to be consistent, unless he hold *the truth*. Error is always contradictory, and, therefore, he who has embraced it, is almost certain to cross his own track. Such is the predicament of the gentleman here, as in many other parts of his writings. In the *Christian Baptist* he makes an essential difference between John's baptism and christian baptism; but in this discussion he makes them almost identical! The fact is, the apostles never received christian baptism; and unless the church was the same under both dispensations, they entered not the christian church. They were the branches of the olive-tree, not broken off.

I must now advert to the gentleman's last argument against the identity of the church. It is founded on the language of our Savior to Peter: "Thou art Peter, and on this rock will I build my church." From this language he argues, that the Savior had not yet begun to build it. But is this the Savior's meaning? God said, long before, by the prophet Isaiah, "Behold, I lay in Zion for a foundation, a stone, a tried stone, a precious corner-stone, a sure foundation: he that believeth shall not make haste," chap. xxviii. 16. Again—"All *we*, like sheep, have gone astray; we have turned, every one, to his own way; and the Lord hath laid on him the iniquity of *us all*." This foundation was a matter of as much interest to the Jewish church, as to the christian church. The foundation of the church is *Christ crucified*. On the foundation, as it was presented in prophecy and in types, did all the ancient prophets and servants of God build. It is, therefore, called "the foundation of the apostles *and prophets*." The foundation, viz. the doctrine of salvation, through the death of the Son of God, had been laid, and the building commenced; and on this foundation the Savior declares his determination to complete the building; and the head-stone shall be brought forth with shoutings of "*Grace, grace unto it*."

This is the foundation promised in the covenant with Abraham, the father of believers; and it will not answer to have the father in one church, and his children in one of a radically different character; or the prophets in one, and the apostles in another. The church is the same. Into it I put the children of believers, by positive law of God. Where, I again ask, is the law for excluding them?

I will now further prove the identity of the church, by the *olive-tree*, to which I have repeatedly alluded. Eleven of its branches, as we have seen, were not broken off.—[*Time expired.*

Tuesday, Nov. 21—12½ o'clock, P. M.
[MR. CAMPBELL'S SIXTH REPLY.]

MR. PRESIDENT—My worthy friend has to prove a certain proposition: I have only to show that he does not prove it. If he wishes to spend his time with trifles, he is at perfect liberty to do so; I have no right to complain: I shall, therefore, pass on. He may think that I am anticipating him; but as he is about to make a circumlocutory defence of his thesis, I shall glance at several things of which he has just spoken, and proceed to make objections, by way of opposing arguments.

The gentleman says he cannot believe there was a plurality of covenants with Abraham, unless I can produce the very identical phrase, "There were covenants with Abraham." Now, this is a new principle in criticism—a new law of interpretation. Henceforth, a person who affirms any proposition, must find that proposition in so many identical words, written in the book, or it must be repudiated as false doctrine.

I will state the whole case to this audience. Suppose I bring up three distinct and different transactions, concerning different subjects, made at

23　　　2 G 2

different times, each one ratified in a different manner, and *each one called a covenant*, and not only circumstantially, but formally show, that each of them is so denominated by the spirit of wisdom; must I be told that all this must pass for nothing, unless they are somewhere called, in so many words, "*the covenants with Abraham?*" Was there ever such a principle of interpretation heard of? I have thrice produced the Bible words, indicative of three distinct covenant transactions : one called "*the covenant of circumcision;*" one called "the covenant concerning Christ;" and one called a covenant—which had respect to the inheritance alone. And my friend says, unless you can produce a verse that will say just so much, in so many words, it must all pass for nothing.

Again; my friend says, I have not got one concerning the land of Canaan—a mere reiteration of the same objection: I must produce the very phrase; and unless I produce it by that name, it must be repudiated, though promised and confirmed, as I have before shown, in Genesis xv. 18 : "In that same day, *the Lord made a covenant with Abraham, saying, Unto thy seed have I given this land.*"

Again; I am asked, how did this covenant make Abraham the father of many nations? Was there any covenant made specifically for that purpose? Have I not shown, that in the fullness of time, the covenant of circumcision, and that concerning the inheritance, were engrossed and given to the posterity of Abraham by Isaac, in one great national institution at Sinai? And have I not shown, that the "covenant concerning the Messiah," as developed by Jeremiah, became the covenant of "the many nations," or of all those who inherit the faith of Abraham in his seed; and is now called "the *new*" and "*better* covenant," by Paul to the Hebrews and the Galatians? Have not these facts already been matters of record? Certainly they have. I will, therefore, not spend time in now repeating them. If Mr. Rice cannot comprehend this subject, others can and will.

The gentleman sometimes makes much of a little matter; and again, little of a great matter. His is the rare art of magnifying mole-hills into mountains, and of reducing mountains to mole-hills, just as he pleases. He also occasionally assumes an ironical air, when arguments are scarce; and seeks to accomplish by a wise look or an action, what he fails to achieve by an argument. In these rare excellencies, he does not, however, seem to be highly endowed, either by nature or art. He would rather descant upon my representing Sarah as under the guardianship of a divine husband, than supplying us with proofs of his proposition. To represent a state under the figure of a female, is one of the most common, and the most appropriate images in classical literature. To make Hagar and Sarah the symbols of two states, or nations, or classes of people, is most apposite, beautiful, and instructive. But why, says he, should God be called the husband of Sarah? and I ask, why should he be called the "father of the fatherless?" He thus condescends to speak in harmony with the feelings of our nature, and the exigencies of our condition.

Nicodemus, he says, was a very bad man, and not fit to be selected as an example. Well, in so saying, he admits the reasoning to be just, only demurring at the case brought forward. Is it not strange, that his believing in Christ, should have made him worse than the rest of the Jews!!

Does it not appear surpassing strange, that a ruler of Israel, who believed in Jesus, should, on that account, be considered worse than the great mass of the nation! It is singular that my friend can comment so phantastically on men and things! Show me, says he, one case, of an

adult getting into the Jewish church, without a profession of faith in Abraham's God; and then, adds he, I will show you a similar case in the Christian church. I accept the challenge and will hold him to his promise.

Abraham had three hundred and seventeen warrior-men, who were all circumcised the same day with himself. He had a great many more. All the male servants of his house were circumcised on *his* faith, merely *as his property.* These, and all other servants, the property of proselytes, were introduced into the Jewish state—not on account of their own faith, but of that of their masters; or, from the principle of *property* alone. For the law, in such cases, asked only for property. Hence the Jewish polity threw its arms around multitudes of unbelieving men.

So far as we know, says my friend, they had faith. If so, let him prove it. Let him show that they were not taken in by the faith of Abraham and as his *property*, but each upon his own faith. I hope he will redeem his pledge. But if so, he has annulled the law of circumcision. That law commanded servants to be circumcised, not on the principle of faith, but of property.

The next item in my friend's remarks, was the purity of the sects—Congregational, Presbyterian, Baptist, and all other people, except my unfortunate brethren. He has brought us up as the *beau ideal* of a reformed state of society. I will not draw invidious comparisons. I will give the Pedo-baptists full credit for all their virtues, and I do wish before heaven that they were a thousand times more virtuous than they are. But are all the baptized in infancy, by Methodists, Presbyterians, Episcopalians, &c., to be classed among the virtuous and pious? No: the one half, probably, of all the persons thus made members of the church, in infancy, are now amongst the sceptics, infidels, or worldlings of the present day. Were you to explore drinking-houses, gambling-houses, theatres, and other vicious haunts of dissipation, profligacy and crime, you would find them filled with hundreds and thousands of these baptized members of the Presbyterian, Episcopalian, Congregational, and Methodist churches. Among these vast multitudes, how many are there who do not even believe in the truths of the religion of their fathers, nor in that Lord to whom they have been so solemnly dedicated in infancy. Not half, I say, not one half—I might say not one third—that have been sprinkled, ever sit down at the Lord's table. I should be glad to be informed that even one half had become *bona fide* communicants, or moral members of their own churches in which they were baptized.

My friend says, that my argument about making void the commandments of God, does not apply to this case. If he produces a command to baptize infants, then, and only then, will it be inapplicable. Let him produce such a command, and I will withdraw it. Till he does so, I cannot. Without such a precept, in view of the subject, there is no proof that can authorize such a thing to be done. But we have a command to baptize him that believeth : "Go ye into all the world, baptize them that are taught." Here is a command to baptize believing proselytes. Let him show a command to baptize infants and speechless babes. Let him produce only one precept for it, or one example of its having been practiced by the apostles.

With regard to all this matter, which he has read from the Christian Baptist, I have only to say, I stand up to every word of it—to the very letter. I am glad to hear so much of it read with approbation, on the present occasion. But what, as respects this question, does it amount to? Who says that John's baptism is identical with christian baptism? Who teaches so? They are, indeed, much more nearly identical than the Jewish and Christian religions. They are, however, precisely identical in two or three grand points. First—the action in both is *immersion in water*. Second—the subject of both is a *professed* believer and reformer. Third—in the intention of the subject—his reformation of life, his subordination to law—in all these they are similar, nay, identical. There are some points, however, in which they are not identical. John's baptism was not administered in the name of the Father, Son, and Holy Spirit. This revelation was not yet given; nor were the facts believed in both cases the same. The Messiah and his kingdom were coming in the first. They have come in the second.

My friend asks me who baptized those in the previous, the intercalary dispensation? Who baptized John? who baptized the first Baptist? Should I not be able to show who baptized these, what then? What will the gentleman infer from our ignorance in this case? Are we to infer that they never were baptized? What does that prove or disprove? No person who, in any age, sets up an institution, was himself a subject of it. An executor was to be appointed. When a person is appointed by God to set up an institution, he is not himself to be regarded as a subject of that institution. In the style of Mr. B., we might ask who consecrated Moses? who put the mitre upon the head of Aaron? who poured the consecrating oil upon his head? who anointed Melchisedek? What a sage question! Who married Adam? The gentleman will find a satisfactory answer to his difficulties in these cases.

Who baptized John? God bade him baptize. My friend asks, was he in the christian church? No: because there was no christian church at that time. The Messiah was not yet slain—the corner-stone was not yet laid. Meantime, I ask, what was John to do? what was Jesus to do? what were the holy twelve to do? They were to prepare a people for the new institution; some stones must be quarried out; some materials for the building must be gathered. The proper time and place for erecting the building was ordained by God himself. The twelve were baptized by John: they were amongst those prepared for the Messiah's kingdom. Some one must commence the institution—there must be some one to commence christian baptism; that could not be done till Jesus had died, was buried, and rose again : because christians are said to be baptized into his death, they are said to be buried with him, and to rise with him. This could not be the case till Jesus died, was buried, and rose again. Christian baptism could not be anticipated. Its facts must first transpire.

They began to immerse into Christ on the day of Pentecost. Those prepared for the kingdom of heaven, and commissioned by the Messiah, had the same authority to administer baptism, that John the Baptist had; the same divine warrant from the Great King. Read the commission—will not that suffice?

The gentleman, in vain, remonstrates against my objection to his theory, drawn from Christ's laying the corner-stone, the glorious corner-stone of the new building, promised through the evangelical Isaiah. Does he argue that this promise has been fulfilled, and the corner-stone laid? Did Isaiah write history rather than prophecy? Is intention and execution identical? According to him, many things in prophecy, because spoken of in the past tense, have transpired. I will make his own grammar, and logic, and rhetoric reverberate upon himself in a much more fundamental matter. His theory would prove that the Messiah was slain before he was born. Most preposterous, indeed, though it appear, it is nevertheless true, on the principle of escape, that my friend employs. Does not Isaiah say, " He was oppressed, and he was afflicted, yet he opened not his mouth? He is brought as a lamb to the slaughter; and as a sheep before her shearers is dumb, so openeth he not his mouth." Is that not in the past tense? and does that prove that Messiah was slain seven hundred years before he was born? " He was taken from prison and from judgment. He was cut off: He has made his soul an offering for sin," &c. What, then, is the use of quoting phrases of this sort, to prove that the foundation of the church was laid by Moses? They have been used, it appears, to give strong interest to the prophetic themes—to make things pass before us in bold relief—to stand out upon the canvass in that vivid form which will most powerfully impress us. That the corner-stone of Christ's church was not laid before he rose from the dead, is as evident as any other fact in the Bible.

I have now glanced at every thing that I have noted in my friend's last address; the remainder of my time I will employ in prosecution of the subject upon which I was descanting when I sat down. The materials for the new building were being got out of the quarry, by all the workmen in the field; vast multitudes were being baptized by John, and by other Baptists with him. *Not a single Jew was excepted from his baptism, because of his circumcision.* Why should not the circumcised Jew be excepted, if circumcision and baptism be identical. Most evident, then, it is, that neither circumcision nor the Jewish church was at all in the way of John's baptism.

Do not all agree that the very best of the remnant of the twelve tribes, were the people prepared for the Lord? These were the elect of the Jewish state. Yet even these persons, notwithstanding their Jewish church membership, were constrained to be baptized by John. Is it not, then, strong evidence, that John's baptism was entirely independent of circumcision? that they are not identical in any sense of the word whatever? But I must ask a still more confounding question: By whom were the first three thousand baptized, by the authority of the Lord? *They were circumcised persons.* Every single man of them had been circumcised! They were all Jews! not a gentile was converted that day. Now these three thousand Jews, first immersed in the name of the Divinity, were immediately added to one hundred and twenty disciples in Jerusalem. These were the nucleus of the new institution—the mother church. They entered by believing, repenting, and being baptized: therefore their circumcision did not stand in the way. It was void, as respects christianity. The new church began entirely upon new principles. This significant and momentous fact, alone, will render forever abortive all the policy, wisdom, learning, and eloquence of Pedo-baptists to establish identity.

I have seldom been more startled than when the gentleman, in his opening speech, observed, that "no command was ever given to the apostles to organize a new church." In the boldest flights of imagination which have been called forth in support of infant baptism, I have never yet seen or heard any declaration more glaringly baseless and startling than this one. I know, indeed, it has been asked—where is the command given to Moses to organize the Jewish church? and, perhaps, with more philosophy! But, fellow-citizens, is it true that Jesus, being about to leave this world; about to establish and ordain a new bond of union—a new society; having chosen men, and brought them into his own school; teaching them for three years, and explaining to them in parable after parable; saying, the kingdom of heaven is like this—like that—and teaching them concerning the kingdom of God, for forty days after he rose from the dead; and yet had no intention at all of giving to them authority to organize his church!! It is a most singular and hazardous position, on which Mr. Rice places his defence of infant baptism. A position superlatively hazardous indeed. A scheme which involves in it much contradiction of plain common sense, and of the most plain and interesting portions of the sacred Scriptures. Go and convert the world. What means these words? Instruct, baptize, and teach them my laws and ordinances. Did he not give them a kingdom to manage? Did he not make them his ministers, ambassadors, plenipotentiaries, and say to them, "As my father sent me, so send I you?" Did he not place them on thrones of government, and make them ministers of the new covenant? Shall we hear Paul: "As a wise master-builder, I have laid the foundation of the church in Corinth. Let every man take heed how he builds upon it." The apostles were commissioned to build a new church; and as you see at once, they rejected the Jews by thousands. They would not receive a single man upon Jewish pretensions. "Do not think to say in your hearts that you have Abraham to your father: you must bring forth fruits of your own, worthy of repentance." This was as much the doctrine of the apostles as of John.

It is as clear as the sun, that in the commencement, the first members of the christian church were all Jews, and that their former rights availed them nothing at all.

The history of the first fifteen years of christianity is a perfect and complete refutation of the whole Pedo-baptist assumptions. The word of the Lord was proclaimed, and myriads of Jews believed and were baptized. The Samaritans—mongrel Jews, who had all been circumcised— also received the word of the Lord. Many of them believed, repented, and were baptized. The Samaritans were received into the new kingdom just as others. Their Mount Gerizim availed them no more than the temple worship of the Jews. The new kingdom was thrown open to all men. The Jew and the Samaritan met in it.

After six or seven years of laborious preaching; setting the church in order; giving laws and ordinances; God says, I will make of Jews, Samaritans and pagans a new institution. Go to the gentiles, Peter. He went, and preached the same gospel successfully to the gentiles, preached to them the same faith, repentance and baptism. Peter had the keys of the kingdom of heaven. Jesus gave them to him in the singular number. I took this ground at the beginning of this controversy. I now find it is occupied by some of the greatest ecclesiastic dignitaries. Archbishop Whateley has recently come out, affirming every principle assumed in the Christian Baptist upon the organization of the church, as I shall show in its proper place. Those principles, which have been so often repudiated on this continent during the last few years, have become the very ground now assumed by archbishop Whateley. We are now standing in much higher association and communion in the old and new world, in Europe and in America, than when these views were first promulged.

While on this subject, and although my friend has been, on several occasions, inclined to insinuate a want of soundness in the doctrine of the divinity of the great Author of our religion; if put to the proof of it,—I say it solemnly and dispassionately,—that if I am any judge of what Presbyterianism is, or what are the doctrinal views of the so-called evangelical professors of this country, I am decidedly more evangelical than the Presbyterians of Kentucky, not only on this point, but on every single point connected with it, in the whole remedial system. I say it now, that I am willing to bring up the old Scotch church, and the evangelical Independents, and their symbols; and if I am not, in every point of evangelical religion, more orthodox than they are, I am ignorant of the involutions and evolutions of the church in this community for the last thirty years.

I stand, then, on high and elevated ground. I am sustained in affirming, that the christian church is a new organization, of a more spiritual, celestial and divine character, originated by the Messiah in person, and committed to his apostles, to be by them developed and established in the world.

I had gone down to the house of Cornelius. I will return to it. When they heard and believed the same gospel, what was the door of faith and communion opened for them? I call it *the door of faith;* and find myself in excellent company. I have high and venerable authority for so denominating it. The proper door into the society of the saints, for two thousand years, was faith. It was constituted, in all ages, the redeeming principle; without it, it was always impossible to please God. It is, however, but a door of access to God; and when by it brought near to him, it prompts to all conformity to his will, and qualifies for cordial, unreserved and universal obedience.—[*Time expired.*

Tuesday, Nov. 21—1 o'clock, P. M.
[MR. RICE'S SEVENTH ADDRESS.]

MR. PRESIDENT—I was particularly pleased with the last remarks of the gentleman; because they disprove a considerable part of what he has written concerning his reformation! Faith he now makes the door into the church; and if this be true, every believer is, of course, in the church. Yet the doctrine for which he has long contended is—that persons are not in the church, nor even partakers of the blessings of Christ's kingdom, till they are immersed. If he will prove, that faith alone ever constituted an individual a member of the visible church of God; I will admit, that infants are excluded from it! The gentleman is running a tilt against his own doctrine.

He complains, because I call on him for the passage of Scripture that speaks of a plurality of covenants with Abraham. I thought it was the glory of his reformation, that it demands a "thus saith the Lord" for every thing in faith and practice. No one has more magnified the evils brought on the church by the *inferences* of men, than he. Certainly, then, he ought not to complain, when I call on him to act on the fundamental principle of his reformation, and prove by a "thus saith the Lord," the truth of his assertion, that God made with Abraham *three* covenants. I do not demand of him any particular *words*, but a passage which by fair construction will sustain his assertion. The difficulty in which he has involved himself, is this: the inspired writers, whenever they speak of the promises of God to Abraham, use the word *covenant* in the *singular number*. They never speak, as does Mr. Campbell, of *covenants* (in the plural) with Abraham. And when they write *covenant*, no man has the right to add an *s* to the word.

But he tells us, there were three *transactions*, and of course three covenants; yet before he proceeded far, he had " *engrossed*" them and made only two ! Then why not go a little further, and engross them in *one ?* If by this process (which I think is original) he can so engross *three* covenants as to reduce them to *two ;* by a little more engrossing he might reduce the *two* to *one ;* and then he would be precisely with the Bible.

The law at Sinai, I have said, was only a temporary *addition* to the Abrahamic covenant. Mr. C. contends, that it was an addition to the single promise of the land of Canaan. Yet it is a fact, that Canaan is not mentioned in the whole epistle in which the law is spoken of as an addition. The apostle is proving by the great promise in the Abrahamic covenant, the doctrine of justification and salvation by faith. By such perversions of the Bible as that which introduces Canaan where it is not mentioned, I can prove any position, however absurd.

The passage from Isaiah's prophecy, quoted by Paul in Galatians iv. was applied by Mr. C. to Sarah; though evidently it was an address to the church. If he chooses to call the church *Sarah*, I shall not object! I have said, that God is represented as the husband of the church, but not of any individual. In a certain sense, it may be allowable to call him the widow's husband, as he is the Father of the fatherless; though the Scriptures, I believe, do not use such language.

The gentleman will have Nicodemus a worthy member of the Jewish church; and he asks, how did his being a believer in Christ make him worse than others? He believed that Christ was a teacher come from God; but his faith seems to have extended no further. Did he acknowledge him as the Son of God—the Savior of the world ? He did not. He acknowledged him as a teacher come from God; but he was wholly ignorant of one of the fundamental doctrines of religion, which is clearly taught in the Old Testament, as well as in the New—the doctrine of the *new birth*. The Savior, therefore, reproved him for his ignorance—" Art thou a master [teacher] of Israel, and knowest not these things ?" John iii. 10. Nicodemus was not a true believer, nor a worthy member of the Jewish church.

I challenge the gentleman to prove, that an adult ever entered the Jewish church according to the law of God, without professing faith in the God of Abraham. He gives as an instance the servants of Abraham, who were circumcised. But were they unbelievers ? Can he prove, that they were ? We have no particular account concerning any of them but one; and he was an eminently pious man. It was he who was sent to obtain a wife for Isaac. The gentleman calls on me to prove, that they were believers. This is truly a singular mode of reasoning. He asserts, that the Jewish church is not the same as the Christian, because unbelieving adults were admitted to be members of it. I call upon him to prove this fact; and he brings forward the servants of Abraham. I ask him, does he know, that they were unbelievers? He must admit, that he does not. Then what is his argument worth ? The strong probability, aside from the evidence afforded by the nature and design of circumcision, is—that they were professed believers. It is, at least, not likely that Abraham had in his family men who did not acknowledge the true God; nor is it probable, that any part of them, seeing him erect an altar and

worship God wherever he journeyed, and knowing of the frequent revelations made to him, would persist in refusing to acknowledge his God.
If, however, Mr. C. will produce evidence, that any one of them was not
a believer, I will give up the point.

But it is enough for me, that Paul the apostle says, circumcision profited those to whom it was administered, only when they kept the law;
that he is not a Jew who is one outwardly, neither is that circumcision
which is outward in the flesh. For if circumcision had been, as Mr. C.
contends, a mere national mark, he would have been a Jew who was one
outwardly, and circumcision would have been only that which was outward in the flesh. But according to Paul, circumcision, like baptism,
was worthless without the religion of the heart. The gentleman is only
plunging deeper into the mire, whenever he touches this subject.

He magnifies the numbers of those baptized in infancy, who become
gamblers, drunkards, and the like; and he asks, have *one half* of them
become members of the church? I cannot, of course, give the precise
proportion who become truly pious; but I rejoice to say, from observation and from information gathered from other sources, the large majority
of those whose parents consecrate them to God, and who regard faithfully
their promise to train them up for God, do give cheering evidence of conversion. Often have I, and others older in the ministry, remarked, that in
many of the most interesting and powerful revivals, there are not a great
many baptisms to be administered. Of those who enjoy the blessing, the
large majority are very frequently the children of the church, who turn
from their evil ways, and say to their rejoicing parents, as Ruth to Nao-
mi, " thy people shall be my people, and thy God my God." Many, it
is true, through the unfaithfulness of parents, and from other causes, remain in impenitency, and some even become drunkards. But how many,
I ask, of those *immersed at adult age,* (to say nothing of their children,)
do apostatize, and become drunkards or gamblers? Multitudes of the
members of the gentleman's own church have apostatized; insomuch that
one of his brother ministers—not an enemy—wrote to him, stating, that
he knew a number of churches which, a few years since, were large and
flourishing, but are now almost dead. [*Mr. Campbell.* " Read the passage."] The gentleman desires me to read the passage. I have it not
here at present; but it shall be forthcoming on to-morrow. The statement is contained in a letter written by a Mr. Gates to Mr. Campbell,
and published in the *Millenial Harbinger,* with remarks by himself.
When I state facts, I will prove them.

He calls on me to produce the command to baptize infants. The commission, he says, requires the baptism of *disciples.* I deny that it requires any such thing. The command is, " Go, make disciples of all
nations." How? By baptizing and teaching. The gentleman himself
gives the passage this construction; and yet, in palpable inconsistency,
he insists on first making disciples, and then baptizing them? I choose
to go by the Bible; and it does not say, that in all cases teaching must
precede baptism. As to the *order* of the words, if it were of any importance, baptizing comes before teaching. The commission, as I have repeatedly stated, requires all to be baptized who have a right to membership in the church.

John's baptism, the gentleman admits, was not christian baptism; and
he is obliged to admit, that the apostles were not introduced into the
church by christian baptism. But he seems now disposed to maintain,

2 H

that they might be introduced *without baptism;* and he asks, *who baptized John?* I answer, John was not setting up a new church, as Mr. Campbell says the apostles were. He was a priest; and in that office he had the right to administer any of the "divers washings" of the Jewish law, or any other that God might appoint for the benefit of his church. John neither entered, nor introduced others into, a new church. The gentleman has asserted, that none were permitted to pass from the Jewish into the christian church without receiving christian baptism; but here is a stubborn fact in the face of his assertion. The apostles were the branches of the olive-tree, never broken off, and therefore not graffed in again by baptism. *The church under both dispensations is the same.*

If I should attempt much system in my argument, I should not be able to follow my friend in his wanderings; and I wish fairly to meet and answer all his arguments against the baptism of infants.

He states, as an important fact, that the best of the Jews became christians and were baptized. Three thousand, he tells us, were *immersed* on the day of Pentecost. I have no doubt they were baptized; but that they were *immersed* I do not believe. But if they were in the church already by circumcision, why, he asks, were they baptized? The answer to this inquiry is found in Rom. xi. 20: "Because of unbelief they were broken off." Our Savior "came to his own, and his own received him not." The great majority of the Jews were *unbelievers,* and were therefore broken off—excommunicated. If a limb has been broken from a tree, and you wish to restore it to its place, do you not graff it in? The great body of the Jews were broken off—solemnly excommunicated, when our Savior, standing on the Mount of Olives, exclaimed weeping: " O Jerusalem! Jerusalem! thou that killest the prophets and stonest them that are sent unto thee, how often would I have gathered thy children together, even as a hen gathereth her chickens under her wings, and ye would not. Behold, your house is left unto you desolate." But on the day of Pentecost three thousand of them returned, and professed faith in Christ. Christian baptism had now been appointed as the initiatory rite—the door into the church; and they entered by the existing door. No government employs two seals at the same time. To avoid confusion, as well as to distinguish believing Jews from those who were apostate, all who returned to their forsaken Redeemer were received by the newly appointed ordinance. But the apostles, having never been broken off because of unbelief, were not introduced by baptism.

The gentleman, I perceive, has a great facility of becoming astonished. He is quite astonished, that I should venture upon the *bold and reckless* assertion, that the apostles were not commissioned to *organize a church.* And yet he knows, if he is at all acquainted with the controversy, that in making this bold assertion, I am saying only what all Pedo-baptists say! Do they not all maintain the identity of the church under the old and new dispensations? Have they not so believed for near two thousand years? Yet, whilst he professes to be very familiar with the principles of Presbyterianism, he is expressing great surprise that I should assume positions which Presbyterians have ever maintained!

As for his pretensions to be nearer the old Scotch Presbyterians, than the Presbyterians of this country, it may pass for a jest; but if he means that we shall consider him serious in the remark, it is a wide mistake, a total mistake. I profess to have some little acquaintance with Scotch Presbyterianism.

Whether his principles are like to prevail, as he imagines, admits of serious doubt. It may be well for him, however, to be sanguine, even when his cause is sinking. Not having seen bishop Whateley's work, I can say nothing concerning it; nor is it necessary that I should, so far as this argument is concerned.

But when and where was the christian church organized? The gentleman has attempted to prove, that it was set up at the commencement of the new dispensation, from the language of our Savior to Peter: "Thou art Peter; and on this rock will I build my church." But the Savior did not say, he would lay the foundation of his church at that time. Peter had boldly acknowledged him to be the Son of God; and he replied, "Thou art Peter; (perhaps indicating by his name his firmness of purpose,) and on this rock (viz: the truth Peter had acknowledged) will I build my church." But was it a new doctrine, that Christ is the Son of God, the Savior of men? Had it not long been proclaimed in prophecy, and in types and sacrifices? Did dot Abraham look forward to his advent, and rejoice? And did he not ascend to heaven through faith in this glorious foundation? The foundation was laid in the first promise to Adam; and, therefore, Christ is represented as "the Lamb, slain from the foundation of the world." The blessed *effects* of his death extended back to the first believer; and, from the beginning, the church was built on this foundation.

Peter laid the foundation, in one sense, when on the day of Pentecost he preached salvation through Christ crucified; but years afterwards, Paul, writing to the church at Corinth, could say, "I, as a wise masterbuilder, have laid the foundation;" 1 Cor iii. So now, when a minister of Christ proclaims his gospel to those who have not heard it, he lays the foundation. But all this does not prove, that it has never been laid before. Paul laid the foundation at Corinth; but the prophets had laid the same foundation long before he lived; and, centuries before, the building had been going up.

Mr. Campbell attempted to prove, that the christian church is not identical with the church of the Old Testament, by the expression in Eph. ii. 15, "For to make in himself of twain *one new man;*" that is, as he understands it, *one new church*. I will read several verses in connection with this passage. Eph. ii. 13: "But now in Christ Jesus, ye who sometime were far off, are made nigh by the blood of Christ. For he is our peace, who hath made both one, and hath broken down the middle wall of partition between us; having abolished in his flesh the enmity, even the law of commandments contained in ordinances; for to make in himself of twain one new man, (my friend read it body,) so making peace; and that he might reconcile both unto God in one body by the cross, having slain the enmity thereby; and came and preached peace to them that were afar off, and to them that were nigh. For through him we both have access by one Spirit unto the Father. Now therefore ye are no more strangers and foreigners, but fellow-citizens with the saints, and of the household of God; and are built upon the foundation of the apostles and prophets, Jesus Christ himself being the chief corner-stone; in whom all the building, fitly framed together, groweth unto an holy temple in the Lord: in whom ye also are builded together for an habitation of God through the Spirit."

On this portion of Scripture I will make a few remarks. 1. The *middle wall of partion* between Jews and gentiles was broken down.

The apostle does not say, the building was destroyed, nor that a new building was erected ; but the middle wall, the ceremonial law which with its burdensome rites made it impossible for the gentiles to enter the church, was taken away, that both Jews and gentiles might dwell together in the same building.   But Mr. Campbell will have the building destroyed, and an entirely new one erected !   2. This building, which is represented as a temple, is built on the foundation of the *apostles and prophets.*   They both laid the same foundation, and, of course, contributed to build the same temple—the same church.   It is *new* only in its ordinances and forms of worship.   So the gentleman has helped me to another argument to prove the identity of the church, as he had previously turned my attention to the 4th chapter of Galatians.   I am likely to become quite his debtor.

Let us now examine the evidence of the identity of the church, afforded by Rom. xi. 16.   The apostle, speaking of the rejection of the great body of the Jews, says:—" For if the first fruit be holy, the lump is also holy; and if the root be holy, so are the branches.   And if some of the branches be broken off, and thou, being a wild olive-tree, wert graffed in among them, and with them partakest of the root and fatness of the olive-tree; boast not against the branches ; but if thou boast, thou bearest not the root, but the root thee.   Thou wilt say then, The branches were broken off that I might be graffed in.   Well, because of unbelief they were broken off ; and thou standest by faith.   Be not high-minded, but fear.   For if God spared not the natural branches, take heed lest he also spare not thee.   And they also, if they bide not still in unbelief, shall be graffed in ; for God is also able to graff them in again.   For if thou wert cut out of the olive-tree, which is wild by nature, and wert graffed contrary to nature into a good olive-tree; how much more shall these, which be the natural branches, be graffed into their own olive-tree ? "

The first question that arises in view of this passage is—what are we to understand by the *olive-tree ?*   Dr. Gill, the learned Baptist commentator, who never for a moment forgot to oppose Pedo-baptism, says, that the olive-tree is the *gospel church-state.*   Now, observe, the Jews who were rejected, are here twice denominated the *natural branches* of this tree ; and it is called *their own olive-tree.*   But how could the Jews be the natural branches of this tree, the members of the gospel church ?   And how could it be their own olive-tree—their own church ?   The only possible answer, as I think, is—that the christian church is the same which existed before the new dispensation, and of which the Jews were members.

Again. The Jews are represented as having been broken off from the good olive-tree—excommunicated from the church because of unbelief. But how could they have been broken off, or excommunicated from the gospel church, unless they had been in it ?   And how could they have been in it, unless it is the same ecclesiastical body which previously existed ?

Again ; the gentiles were graffed into the same tree from which the Jews were broken off.   But it is certain that gentiles were introduced into the christian church.   It is, therefore, the same church which before existed, to which the Jews belonged.

Observe again ; the Jews, when converted to christianity, are to be again graffed into their own olive-tree ; they are to be received into the same church from which they were excluded.   But into what church are converted Jews received? Into the gospel church. Then it is the same from which they were excluded. If the identity of the church under both dispensations is not here taught, I cannot conceive of any language in which it could be expressed. What possible exposition can be given of this interesting chapter, to make it consistent with Mr. Campbell's doctrine?

He would fain induce the audience to believe that I offer no argument in support of infant baptism. Let us, however, look at the position of the argument, and judge whether it has any force. In regard to the commission given to the apostles, several important facts have been established:—1. That it is not a commission to organize a new church, but to extend the blessings and privileges of an existing church. 2. That it does not specify adults or infants as proper subjects of baptism. 3. That it requires disciples to be made by baptizing and teaching. 4. That it does not say that in all cases teaching must precede baptizing. 5. That the commission requires all to be baptized who are entitled to a standing in the church.

6. To determine who are to be members of the church, I went to its organization, and proved that, by positive law of God, believers and their children were constituted members. 7. I stated, and it is not denied, that they occupied their place in the church unmolested, till the moment when the commission was given. 8. I proved that the commission does not exclude them, and that the Savior gave not the slightest intimation of a purpose to make a change in the law of membership, but used such language as was calculated to make the impression that no change was contemplated. 9. I have proved, by facts and principles incontrovertible, the identity of the church. I have put children into the church by positive law; and the gentleman cannot *infer* them out. I have called for the law that excludes them. He has not produced it, and he cannot. Then believing parents and their children must still remain in the visible church; and still, till time shall end, they shall rejoice to acknowledge the faithfulness and the mercy of the *covenant-keeping God.*—[*Time expired.*

Tuesday, Nov. 21—1½ *o'clock, P. M.*
[MR. CAMPBELL'S SEVENTH REPLY.]

MR. PRESIDENT—Before adverting to the last point, I must recapitulate the last speech. The gentleman said, on rising, that he was glad that I had conceded, at last, that faith was the door into the christian church. Did I say so? I did not say that faith was the door of admission into the christian church. The question was about the Patriarchal church from Adam to Moses—from the foundation of the world till the calling of Abraham. He says there was a *church* during that period. I have conceded that there was some religious society, and the whole christian world admits that there was a church *state of some sort,* during that period, though *no public worshiping assemblies.* As to religions, the world may be divided into three great periods: the patriarchal, continuing about two thousand years; the Jewish, from Abraham, about two thousand; and the christian, almost two thousand.

With regard to the first, the door by which men were admitted into its enjoyments, was faith, without which it was always impossible to please God. When Paul brings up the mighty host of illustrious heroes, witnesses of the power and piety of this principle, Abel stands the first on that renowned list of worthies, who shone with such transcendent splendor dur-

ing the antediluvian age. Still, it was a very different thing from christianity. It was a state in which men enjoyed communion with God by
faith, prayer, and sacrifice, in social acts of religious worship. Let him
now show how their infants got into that "church state!" I presume he
will never satisfy you or himself on that subject; he will not be able to
give any information. He is contending that there was a church, and that
infants were always members of it, from the beginning of the world. His
mode of development and proof is rather singular and phantastic. With
Abraham, he commences his infant membership by natural birth. Before
Abraham, it was *faith*, after him, *flesh*, that opened the door. It behooves
him to show why he begins then and there. Is it not because he first
meets circumcision there? And yet, when pressed, there is no church
door in it!

The gentleman could not be serious, when he said that we began with
a " *Thus saith the Lord.*" And now he has called upon me for a Thus
saith the Lord. I do, indeed, teach that we ought to have a " Thus saith
the Lord," for what we believe and teach in his name; but I do not teach
that I must have a Thus saith the Lord for the caricature that Mr. Rice
has exhibited. He drew the picture, and I am not obliged to produce any
proof of it. If any man asks me for the christian covenant, I show it to
him; and I show it sealed and ratified by various institutions. And if it
cannot be made plain and evident, I know not what matter of fact can be
established beyond the power of contradiction.

He wishes me to engross the covenants into one. I said they were
engrossed into two covenants, and still there are two in the Bible unnoticed and unexplained by him; and I am sorry to see that he still passes
them without argument or inquiry. They are engrossed by Paul into
two grand institutions, represented by two women. I have also produced
the positive precept for casting out part of Abraham's family; but the
gentleman seems not to hear it. It stands, like the mountains, unmoved
and immovable. He has never attempted so much as to explain away the precept, though it is now full two hours since I offered it. With regard to these
believing adults, he must have forgotten the principle which we recognize.
We say, inasmuch as the law made it obligatory upon every master, to
have every one of his servants, if he had thousands of them, circumcised
on the day and at the hour in which he professed to obey the law himself,
their faith could have nothing to do with his obedience. It behooves every
soul to have the males of his household circumcised, nolens volens, on
that day. It is impossible to make adult circumcision, on the part of
masters, a duty, and then place it on the faith of servants. Faith, indeed,
*was never a condition of circumcision, in master or servant, since the
world began.* We have the law and the testimony. Here they are.
Let the gentleman give an example. If the ordinance does not require faith
in the infant, why demand faith in the adult? When there was no moral
qualification required in the million, why ask it in the hundred? Why
raise objections of this sort? What the law never asked for, it is not our
duty to require.

If the law of Christ had commanded a master in this commonwealth to
baptize his whole stock of servants, I question if one in ten good Presbyterians, if depending upon Mr. Rice for development, would observe it; and
if they did, there would certainly be a great number of unbelievers in their
church. There are a thousand difficulties in his way, which neither Mr.
Rice nor any other man can dispose of. The case is so plain, I am sur-

prised that he should not respect his own intellect more than to put me
to the necessity of reiterating it.

Had I never read Dr. Wall, on Baptism, I would have supposed Mr.
Rice was one of the greatest lovers of paradoxes I had met with. But in
this instance, as in most others, he is rather led than leads. Still I had
hoped, that in this age of improvement and advancement on the past, no
one could be found so servilely in love with the past, as to make the commission read—"Go, convert the nations, by first enrolling them as scholars,
then baptize them, and finally teach them the christian religion." Now,
preposterous though it be, it is nevertheless true, that Dr. Wall, and after
him, my friend, Mr. Rice, will have *matheteuo* to mean, in this place,
"make disciples simply by the act of baptizing them, without any previous teaching;" and then commence some few years afterwards to teach
them ! It is no exaggeration, sir—no hyperbole. It is the simple truth !

The argument, illustration, and proof is here. A school-master makes
up his school, by simply getting scholars enrolled ; and when his school
is made up, he goes to teaching them. But there, indeed, is still one
difference existing in favor of the schoolmaster. He commences teaching
when he gets the school made up ; but our preacher, after he makes up a
school of baptized infants, has to wait some ten years before he gives
them the first lessons. St. Xavier done better with the Indians, for he
taught some of them to repeat the Lord's prayer, and to say "Hail Virgin Mary !"

I will count out this family of words—I mean this *matheteuo*, a family
amounting in the New Testament to 272 individual occurrences ; and if
any one, of any learning, can show that in any one instance it means
such a scholar, or such a discipline, I will, at once, give up the matter.
In three other cases only, it is found in somewhat a similar predicament
as in the passage in the commission, but in these no one would presume
to contend that it means enrollment. The great Grotius, in his simplicity, distinguished *matheteuo*, the first word in the commission, as distinguished from *didasco* the last; both translated *teach* in this common
version, thus : *Matheteuo*, says he, "means to communicate the first, or
elementary principles ; then after baptizing those who receive these rudimental views, teach or introduce them as persons initiated into the higher
branches of christian doctrine." This is my view of the passage ; and, certainly, it is the etymological and well received meaning of the word, all the
world over ; excepting a few Pedo-baptists, partizans in the superlative degree. But, methinks, even amongst intelligent and sober-minded Pedo-
baptists, this licence of fixing upon a word, a meaning nowhere else found,
in all sacred, and, I might say also, in classic use—a meaning got up just
for the emergency, can never find any, certainly not much favor. In an
essay on *baptizing*, then, as the consummating act of discipline, I have
argued, and still argue, that it indicates the concluding act of the process;
that is, we make disciples in the sense of the commission, by first teaching them the rudimental principles, and, on their receiving these, we then
baptize them, and the process of bringing them into the school of Christ
is completed. They are afterwards to be taught the whole way of the
Lord more perfectly.

I am glad that we have at last got upon the commission again. From
it, indeed, Mr. R. ought never to have gone till it had been fully discussed.
I have been always willing to stand upon the commission alone. Certainly it is a clear, intelligible, as it most certainly is a superlatively au-

thoritative document. It comes from the King of kings. Now I will stake the whole cause for which now I plead, upon a fair grammatical and logical construction of this single document. There are three things to be done. The nations are to be taught *what to believe;* they are, when taught what to believe, of course, *believers;* and to be baptized—and then they are to be taught *what to do.* Not merely the grammatical arrangement of the words, but the nature of the case itself implies this order. Faith is necessarily first in order; consequently, the principles or facts to be believed must first be propounded. Then obedience, or the precepts to be obeyed, follow most naturally. The order then is—the nations are to be taught the facts, then baptized, then inducted into the whole practice of the christian religion.

On these plain, grammatical and logical principles, I therefore take this ground; that all laws and commissions are not only inclusive of all the persons and things specified in them, but exclusive of all other persons and things not therein mentioned. For example:—Suppose that a law is passed in this commonwealth, requiring all male persons, from sixteen to forty-five, of sound and perfect bodies, to muster three days each year. Follows it not, as evidently, by the universal construction of all mankind, that no other persons but males within those ages, and of such qualifications, are required to attend, as that the person so described shall perform the services so enacted? Or take another example:—Suppose a law regulating the right of suffrage, should say that all free-holders, house-holders, and heads of families citizens of the state, from twenty-one years old and upwards, shall have the right of suffrage; does not this arrangement exclude from the polls all persons not possessed of those qualifications? Are they not positively and by law excluded?

When, then, the commission says—Preach the gospel to the nations; baptize them that believe, and teach them to obey my precepts—does it not exclude from baptism those that are not first taught the gospel, as well as exclude from the ordinances designed for the faithful, those who have not been baptized?

When, according to Mark, Jesus says, "Go you into all the world, preach the gospel to every creature: he that believeth, and is baptized, shall be saved;" follows it not that the gospel is to be first preached to every creature, and also to be believed before any one ought to be baptized? I see Mr. Rice is taking down a note just at this point. He need not write that I exclude all from salvation who do not hear, believe, and are baptized. That is not the reading, the fair grammatical reading, of the commission. It reads thus, when the proper ellipsis is supplied:— "Preach the gospel to every creature. He that hears the gospel, believes the gospel, and is baptized, shall be saved; but he that hears the gospel and disbelieves the gospel, and is not consequently baptized, shall be condemned." That is the true reading; therefore, the gospel threatens damnation, in the commission, to those only who hear the gospel, disbelieve, and reject it. Such is its true exegetical exposition. According to the commission, no one can be damned who does not hear, in his own language, in intelligible words, the gospel, or so have it within his reach, that the not hearing of it shall be voluntary. I am now willing even to appeal to my opponent whether such is not the fair grammatical and exegetical exposition of the words of the commission. If, in the Celtic language, the gospel was preached to the Chinese, they not understanding a word of it, could they be justified in believing, or condemned for not believing and obeying it, by either God or man? And simply, because their not hearing it in intelligible words, was not hearing it at all. Like Saint Anthony, we might just as well preach to the fish, as to any community, unless we speak to it in their own language, and in terms which they can understand. For this reason, God bestowed tongues upon the first promulgers of it, that they might speak it intelligibly, and that those who hear it, believe it, and are baptized, might be saved.

Touching infants, their case comes not into the commission. The Lamb of God, who took away the sin of the world, has rendered it possible and consistent with our heavenly Father, to extend to those, dying without actual transgression, salvation—without faith, without repentance, and without baptism. I state this opinion to save time, (unless Mr. R. desires more time than to-morrow,) as I perceive a disposition on his part to debate any thing but the question before us.

The commission is a vital matter. All depends upon it. It is most unprecedented and inexplicable, upon any other principle than a consciousness of its affording no help to his views, that for two days we have heard so little about it from Mr. Rice. You would think the Abrahamic covenants had imposed baptism on Christ's commission in every word of them, were we to judge of their importance by the attention paid to them by Mr. Rice. Can he not give one instance of infant sprinkling in the whole Bible? or can he show no word of the Lord, apostle, or prophet commanding it, or alluding to it! As he makes *sprinkling* a means of sanctification, and regards the affusion of water as the most scriptural method, can he not, in all the thousands of additions to the church, and in all the conversions recorded in the New Testament, afford one solitary instance of infant sprinkling? Stranger still that the Father of Mercies should make the sprinkling of water a means of sanctification to infants—as baptism, in all cases, is, (according to his theory of sanctification,) and make no provision by hint of any sort, precept, or promise, that it should be so done. If I thought that the affusion of water on the face of a babe, was the means of its sanctification from the pollution of sin, I would stand in the high-ways, and public places, and publish it to all parents and persons whatsoever; and yet the Lord, who is incomparably more humane and merciful than any of us, has not commanded it to be promulged by any apostle or prophet. He has left the splendid affair at hap-hazard; and should the parent be a Quaker, a non-professor, or a sceptic, his whole offspring are debarred from the gospel means of sanctification! It is all, it seems, left to a mere contingency. But kind parents regret not this seeming neglect on the part of the Messiah. He blessed babes—and said, "of such was the kingdom of heaven;" and yet he never once sprinkled, nor commanded to have water sprinkled upon them. From all which we may infer, there is no necessity for it. You see no difference between the babes sprinkled and unsprinkled. We Baptists generally have as many children raised to manhood, as beautiful, as healthful, as happy—and as many of them at the Lord's table, (especially when we do our duty,) as have any branch of those communities that believe, or practice sprinkling for sanctification. If, indeed, the virtue of one drop of this water of sanctification, can, after so many years sinning, make the adult son of a Pedobaptist holy—if its virtues are so potent and enduring, it were well to have it. But as, from the testimony of our senses, we see no difference in their faces, or in their characters—no difference in their health,

24

growth, or vigor—as it leaves no mark, physical, intellectual, or moral, in their history, with regard to this life, we shall presume it is equally impotent beyond the grave; and I will reserve the further notice of this point for a speech by itself.

I believe I have answered all the gentleman has said for two days; and you will find on the docket a number of important matters, to which he has not answered. But it is for himself and not for me, to point out the course which he ought to pursue. If the infants of professing parents are to be baptized, the proof lies upon him, and he ought to show it. Of course he has taken what he considers the best ground. He has repudiated the ground usually before taken. He does not value at the price of a single straw, the law of circumcision, formerly relied on; which, after all, is still the base of the whole matter. He does not, seemingly, use this argument in support of his cause. Well, now, I know that he must advocate the identity of the two churches, and that, too, for the sake of circumcision. For this reason, I go on to show that the principle is not recognized in all the New Testament.

I had pursued the history of baptism down to Cornelius. After he and his friends were converted by hearing Peter preach the gospel, as soon as they gave intimation of their conviction, Peter said, " Can any man forbid water, that these should not be baptized, seeing they have received the Holy Spirit as well as we?" Certain christian Jews, standing by his side, who had never yet seen such a thing before, as a proof that there was no proselyte baptism in their heads, looking around at these gentiles who had just received the Holy Spirit, he said, Can any one of you forbid water that these persons should be baptized as well as we? They were all silent. He therefore commanded them to be baptized by the authority of the Lord. Making their qualification a reason for their bap tism, he asked, Can any one forbid water that these persons *who have received the Holy Spirit, and have thus been qualified, should* not be baptized as well as we?

In the very commencement, then, of the gospel ministry, you will perceive, that the apostles required a moral qualification,—a belief in one Lord, one gospel, one baptism; *as in one case, so in all cases.* Hence, whatever was necessary to constitute a qualification in one man, is necessary in every other man. Can any one give one reason, why there should be a moral qualification in one case and not in another?

I have now showed, that in Judea, Samaria, and every place baptism was practiced, and that without any regard to circumcision more than to uncircumcision. Personal qualifications were always, and in all cases, required.

Take another instance from Ethiopia—an individual case, marked, indeed, by prominent incidents. An Ethiopian officer, under queen Candace, had been to Jerusalem to worship, was very much interested in what he read, and in returning home to his own country, carried with him a copy of the prophecy of Isaiah. As he read, the Spirit of God suggested to Philip that he should go and join himself to the chariot. He did so. Presenting himself to the officer, he invited him into the carriage; and Philip addressing him, said, Understandest thou what thou readest? How could I, he replied, unless some one should guide me? He read on, and Philip interpreted. Beginning at the same passage, he preached unto him the Lord Jesus. The eunuch heard him with great attention; and as soon as they came to a proper close, they happened to come to a *certain water.* How much, or how large, or of what kind,—whether a pond, a lake, or stream, is not material; but they came to a certain water. Immediately the officer said, What does hinder me from being baptized? That was the time to declare the law, the whole law, and nothing but the law. Eunuch was going into a new part of the world. Ethiopia was stretching out her hands to God. It was very important that he should have a clear version of the whole matter, and understand all about it, as it respects both Jews and Gentiles. The question was asked, formally, (I suppose,) "If thou believest with all thy heart, thou mayest." I admit that this is a little involved in the various Greek texts and translations. Still the connection shows that it was virtually implied in asking the question. It shows that he must have faith, and that it was necessary to receive him upon a confession of it; or as it reads—"If thou believest with all thy heart, thou mayest. I believe that Jesus is the Messiah, the Son of the living God." This is the faith which Peter confessed to Jesus, and of which he said, the foundation of the church shall rest upon this faith.

When they had closed their reading, they went down into the water, both Philip and the officer; and when they went down into the water, he baptized him. You all know what that word means by this time. They went down into the water before he began to perform the ceremony, and when they had descended into the water, he baptized him.—[*Time expired.*

Wednesday, Nov. 22—10 o'clock, A. M.

[MR. RICE'S EIGHTH ADDRESS.]

MR. PRESIDENT—It will be remembered by those who heard the discussion yesterday, that in reply to Mr. Campbell's remarks on the tendency of infant baptism to corrupt the church, I stated that many of the members of his own church had also apostatized; and therefore his argument proved as much against adult baptism, as against the baptism of infants. In confirmation of the statement I referred to a letter written by a Mr. Gates, one of his own ministers, and published in the Millenial Harbinger. The reading of the letter was called for by the gentleman. I will now, according to promise, read an extract from it. After some preliminary remarks, Mr. Gale says:

"I could instance churches, within a few years, which have had scores of converts added to them that are now scarcely alive, that have very few active members, other than those who were such, previous to excitements, which resulted in such large accessions to their numbers."—*Mill. Har.* vol. vi. no. viii. p. 325.

This letter is published with some remarks by my friend. He does not call in question the statements it contains, but says:

"I have neither time nor space at present for much comment on the above; *I am aware that there is much ground for complaint on account of the errors alluded to by brother Gates. He is not the only complainant on such accounts.* Thousands affirm the conviction that the making of disciples is a work of far inferior importance to that of saving those that are made. And certain it is, that the teaching and discipline of all the disciples is in all the apostolic writings the great object. Without bishops and well accomplished teachers, there is little or no importance to be attached to the work of baptizing. *Not a tithe of the baptized can enter the kingdom of heaven.*"—*Ibid.* p. 327.

If, then, the children of believers sometimes go astray, great numbers of the gentleman's immersed believers do no better.

He informed you, on yesterday, that I had not attempted to find in the New Testament a precept for baptizing infants; but every attentive hearer must know, that such is not the fact. From the commencement of my argument, I have maintained that the commission given the apostles, properly understood, requires the baptism of the children of believers. Our Savior did not say, go and baptize adults, nor go and baptize infants; but, go and *make disciples of all nations.* How were they to make disciples? By baptizing and teaching. He did not say, teach first, and then baptize. I said, (and the gentleman has not ventured to controvert the position,) that the commission requires the baptism of all who are entitled to membership in the church of Christ. If, then, I prove that the children of believers are entitled to a place in the church, the school of Christ, I prove, conclusively, that the commission requires the initiatory rite, baptism, to be administered to them.

And although the gentleman has labored to make the impression, that I abandoned the commission with scarcely a passing notice, and have been wandering in all directions; the truth is, my whole argument has been directed to a single point, viz. *to prove that the children of believers are entitled to membership in the church, and that, therefore, the commission is, itself, a command to baptize them!* But he has evidently resorted to an artifice often practiced by adroit lawyers, when pleading a bad cause. If they can succeed in convincing the court and the jury, that all the evidence adduced by their opponents, is illegal or irrelevant, their point is gained. His efforts, however, to divert the attention of the audience from the point in debate, will not succeed; for every intelligent hearer can see the immediate bearing of all the arguments I have adduced. The scattering has all been on the side of my opponent.

In another respect, also, he exhibits something of the tact of an artful lawyer. When arguments are urged, to which he cannot reply, he becomes suddenly astonished—amazed, that any one should venture on positions so rash, so reckless! For example, when I stated the simple and obvious fact, that the commission given the apostles did not direct them to organize a new church, he was quite astounded; and yet, I presume, he is perfectly aware, that all Pedo-baptists take this ground. Again, when he supposed that I expounded the commission as Dr. Wall and many others did, he was amazed, that I should agree with many of the ablest critics! Well, there is policy in all this. He may induce some, who allow him to think for them, to believe, that it is just as he says, and to be astonished because he seems to be astonished!

But let us look a little more particularly at the commission. Instead of taking Dr. Wall's view of it, I agreed with Mr. Campbell, and, it seems, have driven him from the views for which he has heretofore contended. What says the commission? "Go, make disciples of all nations!" The gentleman agrees, that such is the meaning of the language. But how are they to be made? By baptizing and teaching. This is precisely the construction for which he has contended. In the Christian Baptist, (p. 630) he writes to one of his correspondents as follows:

"Have you, my dear brother, ever adverted to the import of the participle in the commission, Matth. xxviii. 'Disciple or convert the nations, immersing them?' I need not tell you that this is the exact translation. Let me ask you, then, does not the active participle always, when connected with the imperative mood, express the manner in which the thing commanded is to be performed? Cleanse the room, washing it; clean the floor, sweeping it; cultivate the field, ploughing it; sustain the hungry, feeding them; furnish the soldiers, arming them; convert the nations, baptizing them, are exactly the same forms of speech. No person, I presume, will controvert this. If so, then no man could be called a disciple or a convert; no man could be said to he discipled, or converted, until he was immersed."

Here he maintains that the meaning of the commission is—Go, make disciples by baptizing and teaching them; but now he abandons this construction, and agrees with Grotius, who says, that *matheteuo* (make disciples) means to *teach them the first principles of christianity,* then baptize them, and afterward go on instructing. But how does this interpretation of the commission agree with what I have just read from the Christian Baptist? He now says, the phrase, make disciples, baptizing them and teaching them, means, teach them in part, then baptize and continue to teach. Now look at his own illustration in the passage just quoted from his writings: " Cleanse the room, washing it," that is, get it partly clean, and then wash it ! " Clean the floor, sweeping it," that is, get it partly clean, and then sweep! " Sustain the hungry, feeding them," that is, sustain them in part, and then feed them ! " Furnish the soldiers, arming them," that is, partly furnish them, and then arm them ! "Cultivate the field, ploughing it," that is, cultivate it in part, and then plough it ! Evidently the construction he now attempts to put on the commission, is in flat contradiction of that he has heretofore defended. The Savior commanded the apostles to make disciples by baptizing and teaching; but did he say they must, in all cases, first be taught the rudiments of christianity, then baptized, and afterwards taught other parts of divine truth ? He did not; and no man has authority to say so. In the case of adults, teaching must necessarily both precede and follow baptism; but when infants are first baptized and then taught, they are made disciples just as our Savior directed—by baptizing and teaching.

But the gentleman insists that the word *matheteuo,* which is employed by Christ, (in the common version translated *teach)* means to teach *the first principles* of christianity. *Can he find one instance in the Bible in which it is used in this sense?* I venture to say he cannot. By what authority, then, does he confine its meaning to *first principles.* A *disciple,* in the scriptural sense, is a true follower of Christ, whether instructed only in first principles, or in all the principles of christianity; and such disciples are made, so far as human instrumentality is concerned, by baptizing and teaching. I hope the gentleman will not fall out with me for agreeing with him, and that he will not attempt to escape from a difficulty by retreating from his own principles of interpretation, as, on yesterday, he did in regard to John's baptism.

But he told us, the other day, that *wise* men sometimes change, but fools never. If, then, changes of opinion are evidences of wisdom, it may be supposed that the more rapid the changes, the greater the manifestation of wisdom ! It has, indeed, been said, to the praise of one of the most eminent politicians and statesmen now living, that in the course of a long life he has scarcely ever been known to change his views of any great political principle. But this, according to the logic of my friend, would only prove his weakness and his folly !

Infants, says he, cannot be made disciples. But I will prove to you that they can do things quite as difficult. In the book of Numbers, xxiii. 28, we read as follows: " In the number of all the *males, from a month old* and upward, were eight thousand and six hundred, *keeping the charge of the sanctuary.*" If children of a month old could keep the charge

2 I

of the sanctuary, I should think they might be *disciples*. You see here how inspired writers were accustomed to speak concerning children. The gentleman seems to imagine that the commission requires disciples to be made as in the twinkling of an eye! True, infants of a month old could not be taught; but they might be disciples as early as those of whom I have just read, could keep charge of the sanctuary. And as the latter were enrolled, as those who were to keep the sanctuary afterwards, so may children be in the school of Christ. Again—Deut. xxix. 10; "Ye," says Moses, "stand this day, all of you before the Lord your God; your captains of your tribes; your elders, and your officers, with all the men of Israel, YOUR LITTLE ONES, your wives, and the stranger that is in thy camp, from the hewer of thy wood unto the drawer of thy water, that thou shouldest enter into covenant with the Lord thy God, and into his oath, which the Lord thy God maketh with thee this day." If their *little ones* could enter into covenant, they might also be *disciples*. Again; when, in the days of the apostles, the question was agitated whether the gentile christians should be required to keep the law of Moses, whether they must be circumcised; Peter said: "Now, therefore, why tempt ye God, to put a yoke upon the neck of the *disciples*, which neither our fathers nor we were able to bear?" Acts xv. Now suppose the decision had been that circumcision should be observed in the christian church, does not every body know that it must have been administered to *the children* of believers, on the eighth day? Yet Peter speaks of it as a yoke put upon the neck of the *disciples*. If it was proper for the inspired writers to speak of children as keeping charge of the sanctuary, because they were to do it as soon as capable; as entering into covenant, when their parents only did so; and if circumcision was spoken of as connected with *disciples;* why may not the children of christians, and the ordinance of baptism, be spoken of in the same way? Certainly, such is the manner in which the inspired writers constantly spoke and wrote.

I would like to ask Mr. Campbell one important question: *When did God ever enter into covenant with parents without including their children?* Is there a solitary example of the kind in the Bible?

He has commented at length on the baptism of the eunuch by Philip, and of Cornelius, and others; and he has certainly proved conclusively, that, in the case of *adults*, faith was required in order to baptism; but I am not aware, that this is denied by any one! When, however, he infers from this fact that *infants* must be excluded from baptism, because they cannot believe; there is certainly no connection between his premises and his conclusion. By precisely the same kind of reasoning, I can prove that infants cannot go *to heaven*. For I can easily prove, that faith is positively required of adults as a condition of salvation: and from this fact, the inference that infants cannot go to heaven, because incapable of believing, will follow quite as legitimately as that which deprives them of baptism.

But he thought he had guarded against this difficulty, when he observed me noting his remarks, by expounding the commission thus:— "He that *heareth*, and believeth, and is baptized, shall be saved." But this construction does not help him; for then the other clause of the passage must read, "He that heareth not, and believeth not, shall be damned;" and it is certain that infants cannot hear understandingly, nor believe. If, therefore, the gentleman can *infer* them out of the *church*, because they cannot believe; I can quite as logically infer them out of *heaven* for the very same reason! He cannot make the commission exclude them from the church, without at the same time keeping them out of heaven. By the way, he seems quite dissatisfied with his argument on the *mode* of baptism. Hence he could not let the opportunity pass to give us something about *going down into the water!*

I was a little surprised to hear him assert, that if infant baptism is so important, it ought not to be left to parents to have it administered. Is not their religious instruction of great moment? and is it not left to the parents? May they not greatly neglect it, and thus seriously injure their children in time and in eternity?

But, as a sweeping argument against the doctrine, he says, the children that are baptized in infancy are no better than others. I wish to inquire of the gentleman, *whether he has not published it in the Millenial Harbinger as his decided opinion, that there is a greater probability of salvation to the children of Presbyterians, than to those of the Baptists?* I am prepared to prove that he has! Now, let it be remembered, that he attaches very great importance to *immersion;* that he considers it necessary to the remission of sins; and yet he has said, that it is more likely that the children of Presbyterians, who practice sprinkling, will be pious, and will be saved, than that the same will be true of the children of Baptists who practice immersion!!! And yet he tells us, that the children that are baptized by pious parents are no better than others!

It is not difficult to see the good that must result from the doctrine of infant baptism. We do not, indeed, believe that an infant dying would be lost because it had not received baptism. We do, however, know perfectly well how prone parents are to neglect these solemn and momentous duties to their children. Now if you see a friend of yours neglecting some important duty, do you not feel that you have done him great service when you have induced him solemnly to promise that he will neglect it no longer? Has not the temperance reformation proceeded and spread its blessings over the land on this very principle? And shall we be told that no good will result from the most solemn promise of parents to God, that they will train up their children for his service? And will not the effect be still greater, if, in addition to their promise, they are also encouraged to perform their duties by a promise from God of special blessing upon their efforts?

The gentleman has repeatedly charged me with making bold and reckless assertions. I must now present a brief catalogue of his unproved and unscriptural assertions. They may serve to show into what difficulties he is still thrown, though so long accustomed to discuss the subject before us.

First. He says adults entered the visible church, before Abraham's time, *by faith.* He professes to go by the *Book.* I have called for the passage which so teaches, and it is not to be found. The Bible mentions neither a visible church nor the mode of getting into it.

Secondly. He asserted that there were three distinct covenants with Abraham; but the *same promises* are embraced in each of them, and the inspired writers always put the word *covenant* in the singular—never speaking of more than one with Abraham.

Third. He said, these covenants were afterwards engrossed in *two;* but the Bible says nothing about engrossing.

Fourth. He asserted that the Jewish church was organized at Sinai;

and the law of Moses was the constitution ; but Paul says, the law was a *temporary addition* to a previously existing covenant.

Fifth. He asserted that the law was added to the promise of the land of Canaan ; though Canaan is not mentioned in that connection, nor in the epistle.

Sixth. He told you that circumcision did not require piety ; yet Paul says it was of no avail without piety ; " Circumcision verily profiteth if thou keep the law ; but if thou be a breaker of the law, thy circumcision is made uncircumcision." Yes, he says, circumcision required no piety ; yet Paul says, it required that a man should keep *the whole law of God.* Then the whole law of God can be kept without piety !

Seventh. The apostles, he at first maintained, did receive christian baptism, though we have no record of the fact ; or, at least, they received John's baptism, which, he said, differed but little from it. But it was proved, that they could not have received christian baptism, and that the gentleman himself had maintained, that John's baptism was *radically* different ; leaving its subjects out of the kingdom of Christ ! Then he was inclined to assert, that it was wholly unnecessary that they should have received christian baptism ; that no one appointed to introduce an ordinance, had been required to submit to it. Yet Abraham, though appointed to introduce circumcision, was circumcised ! Thus he *turned* and *twisted* to escape insuperable difficulties.

Eighth. I called on him to produce a law for excluding children of believers from the church. He promised to do it ; and, behold, he triumphantly adduced a law for excluding *apostates !* He pointed us to the fourth chapter to the Galatians : " Cast out the bond-woman and her son." But who are the bond-woman and her son ? The apostle himself answers the question : " Jerusalem which now is, and is in bondage with her children "—the Jewish people who have rejected the promised seed, and clung to the covenant or law of Sinai. I called for a law for excluding *the children of believers ;* and he boastfully produces a law for excluding *adult apostates and their children !!* And this is the only law he can find to sustain him ! He cannot produce a law for excluding children, which does not also exclude their parents. Alas ! for the cause that cannot be sustained by any thing better than this.

I now invite your attention to the argument founded on *household or family baptisms.* I will examine only one case ; and the remarks I shall make with regard to it, may apply to the other family baptisms recorded in the New Testament. I cite the case of Lydia and her family, Acts xvi. 14, 15 : " And a certain woman named Lydia, a seller of purple, of the city of Thyatira, which worshiped God, heard us ; whose heart the Lord opened, that she attended unto the things which were spoken of Paul. And when she was baptized, and *her household,* she besought us, saying, If ye have judged me to be faithful to the Lord, come into my house, and abide there." Lydia, it is distinctly said, became a believer ; her heart was opened by the Lord, so that she received the preached word ; and she was baptized. But the account does not stop here. Her household, also, were baptized. Now, observe the peculiarity of this history. The inspired writer is particular in stating that Lydia believed, and that she and her family were baptized, *but not an intimation is given that her family believed.* Precisely so Pedo-baptists are accustomed to write in giving accounts of accessions to their churches : but anti-Pedo-baptists do not so write. Some years ago, whilst I was editor of a religious paper, having some discussion on this subject with two editors of prominent

Baptist papers, I called on them to find one example in which Baptists, in giving a history of additions to their churches, had written as Luke did in this instance. They found some accounts of the baptism of whole families; but in every case, the writer had been so unfortunate as to say, that all of them were believers. They were not able to produce one example in which Baptists had written as Luke wrote—had mentioned the conversion of the heads of the family and the baptism of all the family, without intimating that all believed! One thing is certain: we *write* as Luke wrote, and our anti-Pedo-baptist friends do not. They neither talk nor write as he did. Would it not be truly wonderful, should it turn out to be true, that those who *write* like Luke, do not *act* like him; whilst those who do not *write* like him, are the very persons who *act* like him?

There is a passage in 1 Cor. vii. 14, which has been almost universally understood to authorize the baptism of the children of believers: " For the unbelieving husband is sanctified by the wife, and the unbelieving wife is sanctified by the husband: else were your children unclean, but now are they holy." The words *holy* and *clean* have in the Bible two prominent meanings. 1. They are used in the sense of *consecration*. Thus the temple and all its vessels were holy or clean; and the priests were holy, in the same sense. 2. They signify *moral purity*. Now what does Paul mean by saying, that when one of the parents is a *believer*, the children are holy; and when both are unbelievers, they are unclean? He cannot mean, that they possess moral purity, more than others. The obvious meaning, then, seems to be, that they are holy in such sense, that they are proper subjects to be set apart by baptism, and trained up for the service of God. Dr. Gill, the Baptist commentator, understands the words *holy* and *unclean* in the sense of *legitimacy!* This, however, only shows how difficult it is to give the passage even a plausible interpretation which will not involve the doctrine of infant baptism; for every careful reader of the Bible knows, that these words have no such meaning in the Scriptures. Besides, it is not true, that when both parents are unbelievers, their children are *illegitimate*.

A strong and unanswerable argument for the identity of the church, and, consequently, for the membership of children, is derived from such parables, as we find in Matthew viii. 11, 12. When a certain centurion had manifested remarkable faith, the Savior said—" And I say unto you, that many shall come from the east and west, and shall sit down with Abraham, and Isaac, and Jacob, in the kingdom of heaven: but the children of the kingdom shall be cast out," &c. The kingdom of heaven in the parables of our Savior, is admitted to mean the church under the new dispensation. The covenant-breaking Jews, who, clinging to the shadows of Sinai, had rejected the Savior promised in the Abrahamic covenant, were now to be cast out of the church—deprived of its privileges; and the gentiles, from east, west, north and south, were to come and set down *in the same church* with Abraham, Isaac, and Jacob.

We have now seen, that by positive law the children of believers were put into the church, that there is no law for excluding them, and that the apostles were in the habit of baptizing whole families, of which only the heads are mentioned as believers. But it is asked, why was infant baptism never particularly mentioned in the New Testament? I will answer the gentleman in his own way. When I asked how it happened, if immersion was practiced by the apostles, that there is no intimation of their ever having gone after water; he replied, it was so well understood, that it was not necessary to mention it. He must, then, admit the pertinency of my reply, when I say, it was so universally understood, that children were to be received with their parents, that it was unnecessary to mention it. There is, indeed, far more propriety and pertinency in my reply, than in his; for we know, that the strong prejudices of the Jewish christians were in favor of infant-membership. We know, too, that there was much controversy as to whether circumcision, which was to be administered to children, should be retained in the church. Is it not, then, passing strange, that the Jewish christians, while so much inclined to circumcision, should yet submit without a solitary word of complaint, to have their children excluded from privileges they had ever enjoyed? If infants had been excluded from the christian church; is there not the strongest reason to believe, that there would have been some controversy on the subject— at least some call for an explanation of the matter ?—[*Time expired.*

Wednesday, Nov. 22—10½ *o'clock, A. M.*
[MR. CAMPBELL'S EIGHTH REPLY.]

MR. PRESIDENT—Were you, sir, to judge of the progress and success of Mr. Rice by the number of topics introduced and disposed of in a single speech, you would doubtless conclude that the volume that reports this discussion will not only contain a great variety of subjects, but also an immense fund of knowledge upon them. Unfortunately, however, there is more of reiteration and repetition than of novelty in most of the speeches you have heard from him, on this question as well as on the former. How little variation in the speech now uttered from the details of yesterday !

Were I to respond to all these same matters as often as he repeats them, then, indeed, not only would you be fatigued in listening to them, but you could not possibly acquire a comprehensive view of our respective premises nor of the real issue. Still I must, to a certain extent, follow the course which he prescribes, inasmuch as the burden of proof lies upon him; consequently, he has a right to choose his own arguments. If, then, he thus occupy his time with the approbation of his denomination, I cannot object to it; but I must remind my audience that the main question of discussion has' not been contemplated in what we have heard, except in his effort to sustain himself on the commission.

For the last two days the gentleman has, at intervals, been proving the identity of the Jewish and Christian churches; yet who has seen or felt any evidence of identity ? We have seen some points of similarity. But who does not perceive that my friend is all the time confounding similarity with identity?

Have I not shown, that in every single specification the proof comes not up to the proposition? But suppose it did: so far as he has shown, there are yet so many points remaining as' to nullify his argument. To dispose, then, of the argument at once, and to make way for something better, if he have it; for neither in truth nor in logic, does it affect the real issue—admit that he has proved the commonwealth and the church to be identical in every point he claims, nothing would be gained on his own showing. He admits that the state of Kentucky, or any other state, may frequently change important parts of the fundamental law or constitution, as frequently happens, and yet the state remain legally, and, in the common sense of the community, one and the same identical state, community, or body politic. But suppose Kentucky, Virginia, or any other state, should undertake to revise its constitution and change some part of its fundamental law—the right of suffrage, for example. Does it follow that the community is changed, or that its identity is lost? In Kentucky and some other states, the right of suffrage is almost universal, so that every young man, as soon as he arrives at the age of twenty-one, is, on the single and simple virtue of nativity, invested with that most responsible political right. Suppose, however, as it not unfrequently happens, in the actual details of human experience, that the usage is not so commendable as the theory; that it does not work quite so well as was expected, and that the law ought to be either repealed or new modified ! A convention is called, the constitution is revised, and a new provision introduced; thenceforth adding to nativity a property or freehold qualification. It then becomes the law of the land. Has the state of Kentucky lost its identity ? If it has not, neither would the commonwealth of Israel, nor the church of Christ lose its identity, by changing the right to any ordinance from simple natural birth to faith, or any other qualification. So, then, the gentleman's argument on *identity*, in the comparisons and illustrations given by himself, even was it all made out, is of no value or applicability whatever in the case. But he never can establish identity between the commonwealth of Israel and the christian church: although Stephen called the congregation in the wilderness, once the assembly, or the church, or the congregation, just as we please to render the word. Call it, however, a church, if any one pleases, and call circumcision the sign and seal of membership. Then, as in the illustration taken from the right of suffrage in Kentucky, has the right of membership been changed; and yet the church is identical. A new qualification has been enacted—" *If thou believest with all thy heart, thou mayest.*" The commission given to the apostles (not to enlarge the Jewish church, as my friend most imaginatively asserts,) but to organize Christ's church, has actually required both faith and baptism before admission. The church, however, is still identical, according to the logic of Mr. Rice, and therefore his argument for identity is most singularly illogical and inconclusive. The church may be the same, and yet the constitution so modified, as he himself has repeatedly shown—if not in his arguments, in his illustrations—as to change one of the most important usages. Let me again say, it is all labor in vain to prove identity. It requires hundreds of items to make out identity, and were it proved in the gross and wholesale way which he attempts, it amounts to nothing. No one can deny that faith has been required in order to baptism, and *what is essential in one case to any ordinance of God, is essential in all cases.* The commission itself, as we have shown, enjoins three things to be done, not two. I shall, therefore, for the present, leave it with the good sense and candor of the audience to decide how far we have succeeded on this point, and proceed to notice some other points introduced this morning.

With regard to this letter of Mr. Gates, it is a very small matter indeed ; and I should not have called for the reading of it at all, only that the gentleman used such ambiguous, ominous, and tremendous words, indicative of the apostasy of vast multitudes. And now, what does the whole affair amount to ? The fact is, that a certain disaffected brother, wrote such a letter as you have now heard. You have also heard the length and breadth of my admission. And have I not admitted, as I always feel bound to admit, that mistakes, and errors, and faults do exist amongst some of our brethren as well as in some other communities. And do I not attempt to

reform them in our own community as I do, nay, more than I do, those
of other communities? I would reprove my brethren even more severely than other professors; and do I not stand in the best company in the
world in so doing? Many, said Paul, "walk disorderly, of whom I have
told you before, and now tell you weeping, that they are the enemies of
the cross, making their appetites their god, and minding earthly things,"
&c. But was that a proof that christianity was of human device? Because he published that some individuals had deserted his people, or dishonored their profession, can any one say, that such an occurrence dishonors or discredits the whole profession!! Yet such is the offset, and the
only offset which the gentleman has been able to present against the fact
that I stated in the beginning—the fact that, bringing the whole world
into the church had corrupted christianity. I care not for a thousand off-
sets and arguments of this sort. It is a self-evident proposition. If the
whole world were in the church, there would be no world out of it. It
would be all church, bearing upon its head all the faults, imperfections,
and vices of sinful and degenerate men.

As to the quotation from the Christian Baptist, I am glad my friend
read it; and in relation to the whole subject and his remarks upon it, I
have nothing to take back. I wish he had read the whole essay. I was
speaking of universal usage. The argument is this: I said that there are
certain acts in all processes, which are called consummating acts—the
last act; and to this act all men occasionally give the name of the whole
process. I have heard farmers frequently say, when a good shower
would come just at a proper crisis, that shower has *made* the corn. No
one, however, understands them to intimate that nothing before had been
done favorable to such a result. The same style obtains in most of the
mechanical processes. We say of leather, it is tanned, when the last act
of the process is completed; and of cloth, that it is fulled—not when the
coloring matter is put upon it, but when it is perfectly dressed. So a
person is proselyted, converted, discipled when the last act is completed,
and not till then.

It is well that we have different versions of the commission. They
explain each other. According to Matthew, they were to "disciple all
nations." According to Mark, they were to "preach the gospel to every
creature." According to Luke, "repentance and remission of sins" were
to be preached to all nations. These were to be first performed. Hence
Luke says, that "daily in the temple, and from house to house, they
ceased not to *preach* and to *teach* Jesus Christ." This is the uniform
order. He did not command them to baptize first, and *preach* afterwards,
nor to baptize first and teach afterwards. They all explain each other
without any contrariety. There is not a passage in the book that at all
intimates that any one ever was *discipled* without being first taught; and
no one was considered discipled until baptized.

As to the import of the word, if it were worthy of a critical analysis,
or if, with any kind of propriety, it could be debated, I could give doctors by the scores. Indeed, Gale has done it; showing that both *disci-
pulus* in Latin, and *matheteuo* in Greek, and the verbs and families to
which they severally belong, never mean to write down one's name and
enroll himself, or any other person, as a *scholar* or a *learner*. We would
smile at the simplicity of the teacher who would say he had made twenty
scholars, when he had got their parents to write down their names. To
what most singular and phantastic extremes are Pedo-baptists driven, to

get rid of such plain and positive injunctions, as those uttered by the great teacher and his apostles. It requires an immense labor and waste of ingenuity and learning, to make the New Testament an obscure and unintelligible book. I have no language adequate to express my astonishment, that now, in the nineteenth century, any christian minister would take the ground, to carry any point whatever, that our Lord gave instructions to his apostles, to baptize the world—all nations—every creature—first, and then teach or instruct them in the doctrine of Christ, and seek to convert them to his religion.

I might have brought a great variety of authority to show it. I happen, however, to have one before me, which I will read—the distinguished Pedo-baptist, Mr. Baxter. Recollect, this is not the Baptist Gale, or Fuller, this is Mr. Baxter.

" *Matheteuo* means to preach the gospel to all nations, and to engage them to believe it, in order to their profession of that faith by baptism. I desire any one to tell me, how the apostles could make a disciple of an heathen or an unbelieving Jew, without becoming teachers of them, whether they were men sent to preach to those who could hear, and to teach them to whom they preached, that Jesus was the Christ, and only to baptize them when they did believe this? This is so absolutely necessary in the nature of the thing, till a christian church among the heathens or the Jews was founded—and so expressly said by Justin Martyr, to have been the practice of the first ages of the church, that to deny what is confirmed by such evidence of reason and church history, would be to prejudice a cause, which in my poor judgment, needs not this interpretation of the word *matheteuo* ; nor needs it be asserted that infants are made *disciples*, any more than they are made *believers*, by baptism ! !

Again, by the first teaching, or making disciples, that must go before baptism is to be meant, the convincing of the world that Jesus is the Christ, the true Messiah, anointed of God with fullness of grace, and of the Spirit without measure, and sent to be the Savior and Redeemer of the world ; and when any were brought to acknowledge this, then they were to baptize them, to initiate them to this religion," &c.—pp. 91, 92.

The gentleman presumes that he has found an exception to *matheteuo* as always indicating one that is actually taught, or a learner. I have said there is no instance of its having been applied to a babe. He says it is so used, Acts xv., " Why tempt you God to put a yoke upon the neck of the disciples, which neither we nor our fathers were able to bear." That yoke he supposes to be circumcision ; and, as children were circumcised, he infers that an infant of eight days old was called a disciple ! Profound logic ! But unfortunately circumcision was not the yoke, but *the keeping of the law*, which was to be connected with it. For the Judaizers said that it was necessary that the gentiles be circumcised *and keep the law*, in order to salvation ; consequently, as infants eight days old could not keep the law, they had no yoke to bear, and were not amongst the number of disciples.

I have expressed my astonishment once and again, that the gentleman should say that Jesus Christ commissioned twelve men to disciple the nations, and still gave them no authority to organize a church. McCalla in debate—though he did not, in the same bold and unqualified terms, insist that the apostles had not the power to organize a church—said there was no organization necessary ; if so, the Lord would have given distinct authority to organize a church. With regard to this question of identity, the best argument I have heard, was that made by Mr. McCalla. It has been introduced by Mr. Rice, but it has not been carried out with the same order and efficiency. I will give a specimen of Mr. McCalla's scheme of argument.

"In proving the truth of this proposition, I will observe the following method. I will prove, *First.* That they had the same religion.

Second. That they had the same inspired names.

Third. That they had the same covenant.

These, we conceive, to be the grand essential properties which constitute religious societies, one and the same in all primary points. Any two religious societies, that possess the same theology and morality, that are called by all the same names and appellations, and that exist under the same grand constitution or covenant, form but one and the same social compact, and are called, in the legitimate and proper use of the word, *one and the same church.*"—*McCalla Debate*, p. 129.

"Thus we have seen that the Jewish society before Christ, and the christian society after Christ, have had the *same religion* in profession, in ordinances, in forms of worship, in requirements, in doctrine, in promises, in discipline, in government, and in members.

I now proceed to shew, in the second place, that they had the same inspired names."—*Ibid.* p. 141.

To which arguments I then responded:

"To affirm that the Jewish and christian religions are one and the same religion, is not only a logical error, for no *two* things *are one* and the *same*, but it is a theological error, that shocks all common sense. To say that the Jewish circumcision, altars, priests, sacrifices, oblations, tabernacles, festivals, holidays, new-moons, tithes, lents, temples, timbrels, harps, cornets, vestments, views, feelings, prayers, praises, &c. &c. constitute one and the same religion with christian faith, hope, charity, baptism, and the supper, is as absurd as to say that the human body and the soul are *one* and the same thing. To say this, because they were types of the christian religion, therefore they are one and the same, is similar to saying, that because Canaan was a type of heaven, and Jerusalem a type of the heavenly city, therefore Canaan and heaven are one and the same place, and the Jerusalem in Canaan and the *heavenly Jerusalem*, are one and the same city.

And to affirm, as Mr. McCalla does, that they were different in some respects, destroys his whole argument: for if different in some respects, we then say they were different in this: that baptism and circumcision were different in their *nature, manner of operation, subjects* and *design;* and so at last, the whole argument is lost, and comes down to a controversy on this one point: for if I should admit they were similar in all other respects, but different in this, then he has lost all his pains, and is obliged to dispute this one point. So that his plan is as injudicious as his arguments are inconclusive."—*Ibid.* pp. 154, 155.

With regard to the remarks made of those children, of a month old, having charge of the sanctuary: a certain tribe of the twelve tribes was set apart to the service of the sanctuary; all the males of that tribe were set apart to do the service of the tabernacle. They were some twenty-two thousand; every child was counted belonging to the class from a month old and upward. That these children were to perform any of the services of the temple, no one here can believe. These are profoundly learned arguments.

I believe that I have now touched upon all the minor matters in the last speech, and shall proceed to some greater points not yet disposed of. As this is the last day set apart for this branch of the discussion, or upon this proposition, we must redeem the time. I have asked Mr. Rice whether he will require any more time than to-day. He responded in the negative.

He has, then, but three speeches more to make, and I have but three replies.

The gentleman has waived all the main points; and I presume it is a good omen. He says he does not care a straw about the argument founded upon baptism in the place of circumcision; he does not care a straw about Jewish proselyte baptism: and now, for the first time, he has faintly glanced at household baptism. He also mentions some portions of New Testament scripture—one is, "Suffer little children to come unto me and forbid them not, for of such is the kingdom of heaven." This is always quoted in all books upon this subject. "Suffer little children to come unto me,"—why were they brought to Jesus Christ? was it for the purpose of being baptized? No one pretends to think so: they were brought to him to be blessed. There are some who argue that these little children were believers. John speaks of some little children as believers. The Savior also says, "Unless you humble yourselves and become as little children, ye cannot enter into the kingdom of heaven. And whosoever shall offend one of these little ones that believe on me." These little children, many think, may have been of that very class. He, however, says, "Let them *come* unto me." Whatever the character of these little children may have been, they came to him, or were brought, to obtain a *blessing*, not *baptism*. He was always willing to bless all that came to him, old or young, babes and their sires.

But, does he say, the kingdom of heaven is composed of babes and little children? No: but of those that are like them; "Of *such* is the kingdom of heaven." It is not composed of children, but of those who are like them in docility, humility and meekness. Besides, at this time christian baptism was not instituted. This passage, then, cannot possibly allude to baptism; and certainly that cause must be extremely destitute of scriptural proof, that seizes passages of Scripture, spoken on other subjects, even before the commission prescribing baptism was uttered or written. Yet, indeed, I presume this is one of the best proofs that can be found, merely because the word children is in it—a most convincing proof of christian infant affusion.

But next comes a few words from Paul to the Corinthians, 1 Epis., 7th chapter, 14th verse—"For the unbelieving husband is sanctified by the wife, and the unbelieving wife is sanctified by the husband, else were your children unclean, but now are they holy."

Mr. Barnes, a distinguished Presbyterian in Philadelphia, and a prolific writer in that church, whose works are popular, and whose commentary now lies before me, says—that the passage can possibly have no allusion to baptism whatever. Yet from the days of Peter Edwards till now, it has been allowed to be a strong proof of Pedo-baptism. I find, however, that as Biblical and true philology and general criticism are cultivated, the strongholds of infant membership are being surrendered one by one into our hands. Mr. Rice very modestly alludes "to household baptism." Mr. Taylor, some twenty years ago, made it an overwhelming proof. Mr. Barnes gave up 1 Cor. vii. Mr. Rice does not care a straw for circumcision, nor Jewish proselyte baptism; and, I think, before long, will care as little about "*identity*." I have seen a great change within thirty years on this subject.

But, in the mean time, I intend to show that 1 Corinthians vii. 14, is also decidedly against infant baptism. I think it may be made evident to all intelligent and candid persons, from this passage, that infant membership was never thought of during the apostolic age. I only wonder why Baptists have not generally made more use of it in all the discussions of this question. Most commentators and learned men, among whom are Dr. Gale, Dr. McKnight, and many Baptists and Pedo-baptists, have, in their dissertations on this passage, wholly mistaken the most prominent point in it, which would have decided the whole matter: even Barnes himself has mistaken its meaning. They have supposed that Paul here, to illustrate his meaning of the words *holy* and *clean*, and their contraries, *unsanctified* and *unclean*, referred to the children of persons intermarried with unbelievers, and not to the children of the whole church. In one word, they make Paul say, " else were *their* children unclean," instead of " else were *your* children unclean," but now are they *holy*. This mistake most evidently led them astray.

The case is this—a question arose, in Corinth, whether persons intermarried, one party a christian, the other a pagan, ought to continue as husband and wife, and still live together. It was referred to Paul. He takes up the matter, and using the words *clean*, *sanctified*, and *unclean*, in the current ecclesiastic and Jewish sense, affirms that " The unbelieving wife is sanctified to the believing husband, and the unbelieving husband to the believing wife; otherwise *your* children were unclean, but now are they holy." As our food is said, by Paul, to be " *sanctified* by the word of God and prayer," so he uses the word here, not to denote *real* holiness, but that kind of lawfulness or holiness in the use of persons and things, authorizing such use of them, and an intimate civil connection with them. It is not, then, *legitimacy* of wives, husbands, and *their* children; but whether believing and unbelieving parties might, according to the law of Christ, continue together. Paul's response is briefly this: They may live together—they are sanctified or clean persons, as to one another, in this relation. If you may not do so, you must put away your children also—for all your children stand to you as do those unbelieving, unholy persons. If you must reject your unchristian, unprofessing husbands and wives, you must, for the same reason, reject all your unprofessing, unbelieving children. Does not this passage, then, conclusively prove that infant membership and infant baptism had never occurred to any one in Corinth? for in that case Paul's proof would have been taken from him by one remark, such as—No, Paul, we may retain our children, for they have been baptized, and are not at all like our unbaptized and unsanctified wives and husbands. I do, sir, then contend that in 1 Cor. vii. and 14th verse, we have, at length, found a clear and invincible evidence that infant sanctification, or dedication, or affusion, or immersion, or baptism, had never entered the mind of Jew or gentile, that all the children of the members of the church in Corinth, stood in the same *ecclesiastic* relation to the church as did their unbelieving, unsanctified, unbaptized fathers and mothers. Paul does, most indisputably, place all the infant children of the church in a state of such cleanness as unbelieving parents occupy towards believers. This passage, I have no doubt, in the great fact involved in it, will go farther than a thousand lectures to displace this superstitious usage from the church.

The usual argument from this passage is, indeed, a very good one: That if the relative holiness of the child gives it a right to baptism, then the relative holiness of the unbelieving father or mother would also give them a right to this ordinance. But that is an argument not *ad rem*, but *ad hominem*. It is an argument designed not for the question, but for the party.

To recapitulate this argument, let it be observed that the main question

turns upon *your* children, and *their*, the parties' children. That the children of all the members of the church in Corinth, stood in the same relation
to the church as did their unbelieving parents—and that if it would be lawful to baptize the children upon the faith of one of the parents, because
of being sanctified to their parents; then it would be equally right to baptize the unbelieving party on the faith of the other, or because sanctified
in, to, or by the other.

I hope the gentleman will not slur this matter over, as too often he
does such palpable points. I say to him that I lay much stress upon it,
and that I regard it as amounting to a demonstration, that infant membership was unheard of in the apostolic age, because unknown to Paul, and
unthought of at Corinth in the year sixty-four.—[*Time expired.*

Wednesday, Nov. 22—11 o'clock, A. M.
[MR. RICE'S NINTH ADDRESS.]

MR. PRESIDENT—The gentleman has utterly failed to answer the arguments and facts by which I have proved the identity of the church under the Jewish and christian dispensations. But he says, that admitting
the church to be the same, it does not follow that children are entitled to
membership in it; that a state, for example, may so change its constitution, as to take the right of suffrage from persons who have previously
enjoyed it. This is all true; and now all that I ask, or have asked of
him, is to prove, that the law of membership in the church of Christ has
been so changed, as to deprive the children of believers of privileges they
had previously enjoyed. Where is the evidence that our Savior made
any such alteration? Suppose the state of Kentucky should call a convention, and in several particulars change the constitution. The year following, you come forward to vote as formerly; but an individual objects to
your exercising this right, and informs you that the constitution has been
altered. Would you not ask him, in what respect has it been altered?
and would you not demand of him to prove, that the alterations were such
as deprived you of rights hitherto enjoyed? All that I ask of the gentle-
tleman is, to show the clause of the law of Christ, the Head of the
church, which says, that whereas the children of believers have hitherto
enjoyed the rights of membership in the church, it is now determined
that they shall henceforth be excluded. So soon as he shall produce the
law, I will agree to abandon the baptism of infants; but so long as he
cannot do it, his own illustration affords a conclusive argument against
him.

In reply to what I read from Mr. Gates, the gentleman says, he was a
disaffected brother. I presume he was disaffected by the disorders, the
confusion, and the apostasies he witnessed in this *pure* church of the 19th
century; for he has found his way back to the old Baptists. He would
have you believe, that I exaggerated the number of apostasies from his
church; but if one minister knew of a number of churches that had, in a
short time, almost ceased to exist; what numbers there must be, in the
length and breadth of the land, who have returned to the world!

But if Mr. Gates was a "disaffected brother," Mr. Campbell did not
intimate that he had slandered the church. On the contrary, he confirmed
and strengthened his testimony. He says: "I have neither time nor
space, at present, for much comment on the above. I am aware that
there is much ground for complaint, on account of the errors alluded to
by brother Gates. He is not the only complainant on such accounts.

25   2 K

Thousands affirm the conviction, that the making of disciples is a work of far inferior importance to that of saving those that are made. * * * * Without bishops and well-accomplished teachers, there is little or no importance to be attached to the work of baptizing: *not a tithe of the baptized can enter into the kingdom of heaven!*"

I should not have introduced these unpleasant facts, but to meet the gentleman's oft-repeated argument derived from the fact, that all baptized children do not evince piety. It is intended to be *argumentum ad hominem*. What Paul said about the disorders in his day, will not help Mr. C.'s argument against baptizing infants. The argument proves as much against the baptism of adults, as of infants.

I will make one or two remarks further, concerning the commission. I am sorry that my friend will not allow me to agree with him. I proved to you, that, to escape a difficulty, he had abandoned his own construction of the commission. But he tells us, that *matheteuo* means to teach first principles, and baptizing is the concluding act: as, for example, farmers say, a shower is the *making of a crop*. I am not aware that human instrumentality, in making a crop, can be thus illustrated. When you command your servant to cultivate the ground, ploughing it; according to Mr. Campbell's own construction, he is not first to cultivate it in part, and then plough it; but he is to cultivate it *by ploughing*. So disciples are to be made by baptizing and teaching, not first made in all cases, and then baptized and taught.

The words *matheteuo* and *mathetes*, the former of which is employed in the commission, occur, I think he said, two hundred times, or more, in the New Testament. I have called upon him to point out one instance in which it signifies teaching simply the *first principles of christianity*— the meaning he insists on giving it. He cannot show even one. On the contrary, christians are called *disciples*, (*mathetai*) as long as they live.

The gentleman says, it is preposterous to talk of making disciples, by throwing water in their faces. He certainly knows, that such language is offensive. I could speak quite as contemptuously of making disciples by *dipping* or *plunging* them, as he can of sprinkling; but my cause does not require me to attempt to wound the feelings of those from whom I may differ. I think he must see the impropriety of using such expressions.

We do not contend, that disciples are made *simply by baptism;* although so far as the force of the word *matheteuo* is concerned, I might say, that all are disciples who have been introduced into the school of Christ, for the purpose of being taught. If you enter a school-room on the first morning of the session, before any instruction has been given, and ask the teacher how many *scholars* or *disciples* he has; he will answer, by giving you the entire number of those who are engaged as pupils; and he will speak correctly. We do not, however, contend for this view of the subject. A disciple, in the scriptural sense of the word, is a true convert—a follower of Christ, made, so far as human instrumentality is concerned, by baptizing and teaching. Baptizing alone does not make a disciple; but it is one of the things to be done in making disciples. Many have been baptized and taught, and still were not true disciples, because they were not truly converted. The commission does not require teaching, in all cases, to precede baptizing; and, therefore, it does not, and cannot, exclude the children of believers.

The gentleman has brought against me Mr. Baxter's exposition of the commission. But suppose I should, on this point, differ from Mr. Baxter, and agree with Mr. Campbell. He ought not to fall out with me for it. Baxter seems to have considered the language of the commission as having direct reference to those who were capable of hearing the gospel; but still he deemed it proper to baptize the children of believers under that commission, and, therefore, did not understand it as excluding them.

I have invited the gentleman to show us when and where the christian church was organized. If the previously existing church had ceased to exist, and a new one was organized; it was a most important event. Surely we should expect to find in the Acts of the Apostles, or somewhere in the New Testament, an account of it. He has not found the chapter; but he expresses great astonishment, that any one could imagine, that the Savior sent his apostles to establish a *new religion*, and yet gave them no authority to organize a church. I deny, that he sent them to teach a religion that, in any proper sense, can be called *new*. God has never taught on earth more than *one religion*. Enoch walked with God by faith. Abraham was justified by faith. True religion has always consisted in holiness of heart and of life; of repentance, faith and obedience.

But Mr. Campbell is astonished, that it should be doubted whether the Savior authorized his apostles to organize a new church. He had long had a church on earth; and it was yet living. Why, then, organize another? James, the inspired apostle, has told us what they were authorized to do. Acts xv. 13—17, "And after they had held their peace, James answered, saying, Men and brethren, hearken unto me. Simeon hath declared how God at the first did visit the gentiles, to take out of them a people for his name. And to this agree the words of the prophets; as it is written, After this I will return, and will build again the tabernacle of David, which is fallen down; and I will build again the ruins thereof; and I will set it up: that the residue of men might seek after the Lord, and all the gentiles upon whom my name is called, saith the Lord, who doeth all these things." James here quotes from the prophecy of Amos a prediction concerning the christian church. What was to be done? Was a new church to be organized? No; but the tabernacle of David, which had fallen down, was again to be set up. The church, overrun with corruption and overwhelmed by calamity, was like a tabernacle that had fallen into ruins. The Lord sends his servants to raise it up and repair it, and to call the gentiles to come and worship in it. This passage affords another unanswerable argument to prove, that the church under the new dispensation is the same which existed under the old; and that the apostles did not organize a new church.

The gentleman tells us, that Mr. McCalla, in the debate some twenty years since, presented more points of argument, than I have. Yet he complained of me, at first, for making too many. He was anxious to have me confine myself to a few. I cannot now engage in a defence of brother McCalla. I presume, he does not stand in need of a defence from me. It is, however, often easier to answer the arguments of an absent man, than of one who is present. Some years since, the Roman clergy of Bardstown made such attacks upon Protestantism, that I considered it my duty to reply. One of their champions, getting weary of the war, averred that he was not in controversy with me, but rather with Calvin and Beza! I replied, that he doubtless found it easier to war with dead men, than with the living. So my friend succeeds better in answering an absent opponent!

I have not abandoned the doctrine, that baptism came in place of circumcision. I have showed, that it answers the same purposes to the church under the new dispensation, that circumcision answered under the old. But I have attached no considerable importance to it; because I have arguments enough without it. I do not need more. The gentleman has told us truly, that one good argument is enough to prove any point. I have given him a number of them. Certainly, then, he has no occasion to complain.

I have said, that our Savior more than intimated to his disciples that the children of believers were to remain in his church; when he said, "Suffer little children, and forbid them not, to come unto me; for of such is the kingdom of heaven." The gentleman thinks they were, at least, old enough *to walk.* But Mark, speaking of the same event, says, "They brought *young children* to him, that he should touch them. And he took them up in his arms," chapter x. 13, 16. I presume they were *infants;* at any rate they were not old enough to be believers. Mr. C. thinks, the expression "*of such*," means persons in some respects resembling little children. This interpretation is not only unauthorized by the common usage of the language, but it makes our Savior employ most singular reasoning. Little children are brought to him that he may bless them; that he may lay his hands on them and pray. The disciples forbid them; and the Savior, according to this exposition, is made to say, Suffer little children to come to me, that I may lay my hands on them and pray ; *because the church is composed of persons in some respects resembling them!* I cannot believe, that he ever reasoned in this way. The interpretation we adopt, makes his reasoning clear and forcible— Suffer little children to come unto me, that I may bless them; because to such belong the privileges and blessings of my church. It is true, as Mr. C. says, they were not baptized; for christian baptism was not yet instituted. But certainly the language of the Savior implied, that they were still to enjoy the privilege of a place in his school, of membership in his church.

Mr. Campbell's exposition of 1 Corinthians vii. 14, is, I think, so novel, that it behooves him to adduce some little proof that it is correct, before he can expect the public to receive it. It is scarcely credible, that the meaning of this passage has been so long concealed from the christian world.

He quotes Barnes as admitting that it does not teach infant baptism, yet he himself pronounces Barnes' explanation of it incorrect. Does he, then, expect us to receive it? But I will bring against Mr. Barnes such men as Scott, Doddridge, Whitby, and others, who, after thorough investigation, were convinced that the words *unclean* and *holy* are employed in relation to the baptism of infants. I will meet *authority* with *authority.*

Having now answered the remarks of the gentleman, I will proceed with the argument. I do not ask any more than the stipulated time for the defence of the doctrine of infant baptism. I think I shall succeed in making it clear to the unprejudiced, before the three days expire.

I now invite the attention of the audience to the evidence furnished by *history;* which, as it appears to me, is conclusive. I expect to prove the fact, that at the earliest period of the christian era, to which history can take us back, infant baptism was universally practiced, and was believed to be of Divine authority. My first witness shall be IRENEUS, who wrote about eighty years after the apostolic age. He wrote as follows: (I read from Wall's Hist. of Inf. Bap. vol. i. p. 72.)

" Therefore, as he was a Master, he had also the age of a Master. Not disdaining nor going in a way above human nature, nor breaking in his own person, the law which he had set for mankind: but sanctifying every several age by the likeness that it has to him. For he came to save all persons by himself: all, I mean, who by him are regenerated [or baptized] unto God, infants and little ones, and children and youths, and elder persons. Therefore, he went through the several ages; for infants being made an infant, sanctifying infants: to little ones, he was made a little one, sanctifying those of that age: and also giving them an example of godliness, justice, and dutifulness: to youths he was a youth," &c.

The value of the testimony of Ireneus depends upon a single expression, viz: *regenerated unto God.* If, as Dr. Wall asserts, he used this expression to signify *baptism*, his testimony is clear in favor of infant baptism: for Christ, he says, came to save all " who by him are regenerated into God, [or baptized,] *infants* and *little ones*," &c.   Mr. Campbell admits, that by this expression Ireneus meant baptism. In his debate with McCalla he disputed this; but he tells us he has since gained more light on the subject, and has ascertained that he did use the expression to mean baptism. He must, therefore, admit the full weight of the testimony of Ireneus in favor of the baptism of infants.

The testimony of this writer is extremely important, for he wrote the work from which this quotation is made, only about *eighty years* after the apostolic age; and he was then a very old man. He was a disciple of Polycarp, who was a disciple of the apostle John; so that there was but a single individual between Ireneus and John. Ireneus says, he often heard Polycarp relate how he sat under the ministry of John, and many interesting circumstances which then occurred.

This venerable writer, it is important to remark, speaks not of the baptism of infants as a novelty, as a practice recently introduced, *but as a thing universally understood and admitted.* His manner of introducing it, shows that he considered it as much a known and admitted truth, as adult baptism.

Now the question is—had Ireneus the opportunity to know the fact concerning which he testifies? *For, let it be distinctly understood, I appeal to the early christian fathers, not for their* OPINIONS, *but I call them up* AS WITNESSES TO A MATTER OF FACT, *viz: that in their day, and, so far as they knew, to the days of the apostles, the baptism of infants was universally practiced.* The indirect, yet clear testimony of Ireneus, so near to the apostle John, goes very far indeed to prove, not only that it was generally practiced, but that it was of divine authority.

CLEMENS ALEXANDRINUS, who lived about *ninety* years after the apostles, also testifies of its prevalence in his day. But as I can read only a part of the testimony on this subject, I will pass to that of TER-TULLIAN, who flourished about two hundred years after the apostles. He says:

" But they, whose duty it is to administer baptism, are to know that it is not to be given rashly. *Give to every one that asketh thee,* has its proper subject, and relates to alms-giving: but that command rather is here to be considered, *Give not that which is holy to dogs, neither cast your pearls before swine:* and that, *Lay hands suddenly on no man, neither be partakers of other men's faults.* * * * Therefore, according to every one's condition and disposition, and also their age, the delaying of baptism is more profitable, especially in the case of little children. For what need is there that the godfathers should be brought into danger? because they may either fail of their promises by death, or they may be mistaken by a child's proving of a wicked disposition. Our Lord says, indeed, *Do not forbid them to come to me*. Therefore, let them come when they are grown up; let them come when they understand; when they are instructed whither it is they come; let them be made christians when they know Christ. What need their guiltless age make such haste to the forgiveness of sins? Men will proceed more warily in wordly things; and he that should not have earthly goods committed to him, yet shall he have heavenly? Let them know how to desire this salvation, that you may appear to have given to one that asketh.

For no less reason, unmarried persons ought to be kept off, who are likely to come into temptation, as well as those that were never married, upon the account of their coming to ripeness, as those in widowhood, for the miss of their partner: until they either marry or be confirmed in continence. They that understand the weight of baptism, will rather dread the receiving it, than the delaying of it. An entire faith is secure of salvation."—*Wall*, vol. i. pp. 93, 94.

On this testimony I wish to make two or three remarks: 1. Tertullian, you perceive, expresses himself as averse to infant baptism; but his very opposition to it, proves that it was practiced at that time. 2. He does not oppose it as *unscriptural*, or as an *innovation*. He, however, gives his opinion that it is better to delay the baptism of little children. But, since he was opposed to it, he was certainly inclined to offer against it the strongest arguments he could command. If he could have said, that it was unscriptural; and if he could have pronounced it an innovation, contrary to the faith and the practice of the church; these would have been the most effective arguments against it. The very fact, therefore, that, whilst he opposed the practice, he did not venture to pronounce it either unscriptural or an innovation, affords evidence conclusive, that, generally, so far as he knew, the church had been accustomed to baptize infants, and regarded the doctrine as scriptural. 3. He opposed not only the baptism of infants, but of young and unmarried persons. "For no less reason," he says, they should delay receiving baptism. If, therefore, his testimony proves, that the baptism of infants was not universally practiced in his day, it proves equally, that young and unmarried persons were not generally baptized; which will not be pretended. The truth is—Tertullian advised the delay of baptism, because of a superstitious belief, that sins, committed after baptism, were *peculiarly dangerous*. I consider him one of the very best witnesses for the apostolic doctrine of infant baptism; because, although he was opposed to it, and was, of course, inclined to produce the strongest arguments against it, he did not venture to condemn it either as unscriptural, or as contrary to the faith and the practice of the church.

Robinson, a learned anti-Pedo-baptist writer, attempted to evade the force of this testimony, by asserting, that Tertullian spoke not of *infants*, but of children capable of asking baptism. To make out this position, he gave a gross mis-translation of the language of that author. Few anti-Pedo-baptists, however, I believe, have been disposed to adopt his notion.

I now invite your attention to the testimony of ORIGEN, one of the most learned of the early christian fathers. In his Homily on Leviticus, he says:

"Hear David speaking. I *was*, says he, *conceived in* iniquity, and in sin did my mother bring me forth: shewing that every soul that is born in the flesh, is polluted with the filth of sin and iniquity; and, that therefore, that was said, which we mentioned before, that *none is clear from pollution, though his life be but the length of one day*. Besides all this, let it be considered, what is the reason that, wheieas, *the baptism of the church is given for the forgiveness of sins, infants also, are, by the usage of the church, baptized;* when, if there were nothing in infants that wanted forgiveness and mercy, the grace of baptism would be needless to them."

Again, in his Homily on Luke :

" Having occasion given in this place, I will mention a thing that causes frequent inquiries among the brethren. Infants are baptized for the forgiveness of sins. Of what sins ? or when have they sinned ? or how can any reason of the law in their case hold good, but according to that sense we mentioned even now, none are free from pollution, though his life be but of the length of one day upon the earth ? And it is for that reason, because by the sacrament of baptism the pollution of our birth is taken away, that infants are baptized."

Again, in his Commentary on Romans :

" For this also it was, that the church had from the apostles, a tradition [or order] to give baptism even to infants. For they to whom the divine mysteries were committed, knew that there is in all persons the natural pollution of sin, which must be done away by water and the Spirit; by reason of which, the body itself is called the body of sin."—*Wall,* vol. i. pp. 104, 105, 106.

Now, the question arises—what is the testimony of this witness worth ? Let it be remembered, I am not concerned about his theological *opinions.* I bring him forward *only as a witness to a simple matter of fact.* The fact to which he testifies, is—that, in his day, the " baptism of the church" was given to infants, and that it was done by command of the apostles. What means had Origen of being informed concerning the faith and practice of the church ? He was a man of eminent learning, and of very extensive information. That I may not seem to exalt him unduly, I will read the following testimony of Mr. Jones, the Baptist historian.

" But the name of Origen is too important to be passed over in a history of the christian church, with only a casual or incidental mention. 'He was a man,' says Dr. Priestly, 'so remarkable for his piety, genius, and application, that he must be considered an honor to christianity and to human nature.' Even Jerom, his great adversary, admits that he was a great man from his infancy."—*Church Hist.* p. 147. Even Jerom, though a great adversary of Origen, [Mr. Campbell represented him as quite an admirer,] admitted him to have been a very great man.

Origen was descended from a christian ancestry. His father was a martyr, and his grandfather and great grandfather were christians. He traveled very extensively. He resided in Alexandria, in Palestine, and in Rome. He found it necessary repeatedly to fly from persecution. His learning and his fame caused him to be consulted, doubtless, on all important questions relative to the interests of religion. If there was, in that day, a man in the world who was qualified to give correct information concerning the universal practice of the church, Origen was that man. What does he testify ? That *the church*—not a portion of it—gave baptism to infants, and believed the doctrine to be apostolical. Can we, at this late day, expect to gain more correct information than Origen possessed, who lived in the third century, and whose pious ancestors reached back to the very days of the apostles ? His testimony settles this question, so far as history or the most credible uninspired testimony can settle it.

I will now give you the testimony of another very important witness ;

or rather the testimony of about *sixty-seven* bishops, who met in council at Carthage, only *one hundred and fifty years* after the apostles. Cyprian, whom Jones, the Baptist historian, admits to have been an eminent man, presided in the council; and the question was proposed to them, not whether infants should be baptized, (for about that there was no controversy;) but whether it was proper to baptize them *before the eighth day.* I will read their decision, contained in a letter written by Cyprian, to the minister who presented the inquiry:

Cyprian, and the sixty-six bishops, thus write:

"We read your letter, most dear brother, in which you write of one Victor, a priest," &c.   * * *   "But as to the case of infants, whereas you judge that they must not be baptized within two or three days after they are born; and that the rite of circumcision is to be observed, so that none should be baptized and sanctified before the eighth day after he is born; we are all in our assembly of the contrary opinion. For, as for what you thought fitting to be done, there was not one of your mind, but all of us, on the contrary, judged that the grace and mercy of God is to be denied to no person that is born. For whereas our Lord, in his gospel, says, *The Son of Man came not to destroy men's souls,* [or lives] *but to save them;* as far as lies in us, no soul, if possible, is to be lost."—*Wall,* vol i. p. 129.

I need not read the whole of this long epistle, setting forth various reasons for their decision. They determined unanimously, that it was not necessary to delay baptism until the eighth day. And, so far as history can inform us, their decision called forth not one word of controversy; which proves conclusively, that there was no difference in the faith and practice of the church on this subject. This council met, as I stated, about the year A, D. 250; and Cyprian was, at the time of its meeting, advanced in age. Of course, he must have lived within one hundred and fifty years of the apostles.

The testimony of these witnesses is, in substance, that infant baptism was universally practiced in their day, and had been practiced so far back as they could gain information. This testimony, added to that of Origen, Tertullian, and Ireneus, becomes almost irresistible. To these may be added Gregory Nazianzen, St. Ambrose, Chrysostom, bishop of Constantinople, Jerom, Augustine, Pelagius, &c., some of whom I will bring forward in my next speech; although it seems a work of supererogation to attempt to add to the testimony of those who lived so near the apostles, and who enjoyed such opportunities to know the faith and practice of the churches.—[*Time expired.*

Wednesday, Nov. 22—11½ o'clock, A. M.
[MR. CAMPBELL'S NINTH REPLY.]

MR. PRESIDENT—It is important always to keep before us the main issue. It should never be lost sight of. I have complained of what I call *false* issues, and of irrelevant issues; that is, making matters of great moment out of matters casually or subordinately introduced, and thus expending a large portion of a speech upon matters not at all at issue, while the main points are greatly neglected. My friend has not yet abandoned this course; though I am gratified to observe that he has in some small degree reformed in that particular. He has, however, again made a false issue this morning. He says I complain of my brethren for want of attention to their children, and that I say, from the superior attention paid to the education of children in Presbyterian families, their children have made superior attainments in piety. It always gives me pleasure to commend virtue wherever I see it; still I must give to Romanists more praise, in this respect, than to most Protestants. It is, indeed, a very great shame to Protestants that they do not give that attention to family culture, so far as religion is concerned, that is generally exhibited by the Catholics, who have it in their power; so that it is by no means so easy to convert them from what they receive as good and wholesome instruction from their parents, as it is for them to proselyte Protestants. Now observe, the issue which Mr. Rice manufactures out of this, is: that I ascribe these superior benefits to sprinkling, and to sprinkled children, who, as a matter of course, are therefore more intelligent than the children of Baptists, or of our brethren.

Again: with regard to the quotations from the Christian Baptist. I am not only willing but gratified and pleased that my friend should read so much from my writings. I should be pleased if he would spend more of his time in reading such portions as these you have now heard. He could not do me a greater honor. He shows that I am willing to hold up the defects of my own brethren, while I acknowledge even the *appearance* of virtues in his. I hope that I may never be so blinded by partiality as not to be able to see the faults of my own brethren, or my own. I will hold up every thing of the kind to public attention, so far as I deem it expedient or necessary, that it may stir them up to reformation. I may have occasion hereafter to speak more fully of this matter.

The gentleman often alludes to my changing. But if I change for the better it seems to grieve him; if for the worse, to please him; and if I do not change at all, it is yet worse than either. Well, I confess, I am changing a little every day—I am always learning something. I am wiser to-day than yesterday, and I hope to be wiser to-morrow than to-day. But of all the great principles that I have advocated in this commonwealth for twenty years, and in other communities for a longer period, in which of them have I changed, and how far? I have, indeed, changed, or been changed once—very essentially changed indeed: I gave up with all my hereditary faith in human creeds, and formulas—my hereditary faith in every branch of *Pedo-baptism*—subject, action and design, and in all its aspects and tendencies, in all its influences and bearings on the christian system, and the christian religion; and they are neither few in number, nor minute in character. I have experienced one great change of views, thereby giving up an hereditary faith for one obtained from the Bible, by my own personal instrumentality, through the favor of God. But on baptism I advocate, on this occasion, precisely the same views—in action, subject, and design—sustained in my debate with Mr. McCalla twenty years ago. Mr. Rice, however, has never changed it seems, nor has been changed in his faith.

Well, I am pleased to hear him commend the style of Luke, and the propriety of using it, as well as to hear of the high regard which his brethren entertain for this same style of Luke. I profess to be an admirer of it too. Suppose then we take a sally into Luke's style, and try which of us speaks most like it. Take one case directly bearing on the question before us. Luke never confounds the Jewish and christian religions. He always speaks of Jews and christians, or disciples, as not only a distinct people, but having a different religion. He reports the speeches of Paul when he tells of his "conversation in the *Jews' religion*;" how Paul "profited in the Jews' religion;" how, "after the strictest sect of OUR (Jews) RELIGION, he lived a pharisee!"

There is sometimes a volume of sense in a single sentence, as there are some whole volumes without one good idea. "The Jews' religion," commended by Luke—"our religion" too. Yet, this amateur of Luke and his fine style, will contend that the Jewish church and the christian, had "*one and the same religion;*" that is, the Jews' religion and the christian and the christian religion, are just one and the same religion!! Yet Paul positively, directly, and literally places them in opposition. Hear him say: "You have heard of my behavior in the *Jews' religion*, how that, beyond measure, I persecuted *the church of God*, and wasted it." Here is the most explicit contradiction of Mr. Rice and his theory of identity, than can be imagined. Here is "the church of God" and the "Jews' religion," directly, formally, literally contrasted; and that, too, by the most learned apostle, and the greatest teacher of christianity the world ever saw, or ever will see. Which of us now, fellow-citizens, pays the greater deference to the sacred style? I state this fact, that in the year of our Lord 58, when Paul wrote to the Galatians on the difference between the law, the covenant, and all the dispensations of redemption, he then spake of "the church of God" and the "Jews' religion," in direct and positive contrast. No one can, in my humble opinion, dispose of this fact and argument against this assumed identity. Yet, Mr. Rice argues, that the Jews' religion and Christ's religion are one and the same religion!!

I hope the gentleman will give this up, with the argument formally based on the 14th verse of the 7th chapter 1 Corinthians. He must perceive and feel the weight of these arguments. I have too much respect for his sagacity and discrimination, to think that he does both see and feel that they are insuperable objections to his system. I am bold to say, he never can dispose of them.

As to the novelty of the view of 1 Cor. vii. 14, I am not wholly singular or alone in it. I do not claim a patent-right for it; a few others entertain nearly the same view of it. It is, however, a clear and satisfactory exposition of the whole passage. Paul teaches, that all the children of christians, in their unconverted state, were just as ecclesiastically unclean as those unsanctified, unbelieving husbands and wives; and if the believing party may not, in civil life and in the same family, live with an unbelieving and ecclesiastically unclean partner, they must, for the same reason, *put away their children?* Answer this who can: Pedobaptists cannot!

My friend says, he was glad that I touched household baptism so lightly. I have seen a new work from the New York press, 1843, mainly based upon household baptism, in favor of baptizing infants. My friend has, doubtless, seen it; and has not yet seen fit to bring it forward in this controversy. It is from the pen of a gentleman no less distinguished than the author of Calmet's dictionary of the Bible, [Mr. Taylor.] It was published in England some thirty years ago, and lately in the city of New York. It is, to the minds of the English, an unanswerable performance.

In my debate with Mr. McCalla, he introduced some extracts from this work, and brought them up in proof of infants in households. My friend has read that debate, and knows full well how I disposed of them twenty years ago. It is little else than a collection of palpable sophisms. Still, the English think and represent it unanswered and unanswerable. They have given them all up, except the solitary case of Lydia: and how many assumptions are there in this case of Lydia!

Mr. Rice assumes, that Lydia was a married lady ; in the second place, he assumes that she had children ; in the third place, he assumes that she had infant children ; and in the fourth place, that those infants were baptized on her faith. Give me four assumptions like these, and what can I not prove? Now, Lydia's case is the most plausible one in the New Testament; and that, no doubt, is the reason why the gentleman passed over all the others, and perched upon this one. I discover there is some poetry and romance in the constitution of my friend, Mr. Rice, as well as there was in our old friend, John Taylor, with whom he amused us the other day. He made Ananias and Paul pass along in mutual embraces, on their way to the water, holding a very fanciful conversation. But now, all at once, my friend, Mr. Rice, is inspired with the same gift of poetic imagination. He sees Mrs. Lydia and her handmaids, carrying along with them her little children down to the oratory on the bank of the river, near to the city of Philippi, [a laugh.] She carries an infant in her bosom into the house of prayer ; Paul arrives, begins to preach,—Lydia listens—her heart is opened. She comes forward—makes the good confession. They return to the river for baptism—she and all her little ones. Mr. Rice sees some one going down to the river for a cup full of water ; and instantly he observes the apostle dipping his fingers into it, and sprinkling first mother Lydia and all her dear little children, one by one. But in the noise and screaming of the little ones, he cannot be certain whether Paul baptized any of the young ladies that belonged to her household. If they were, however, he infers they must have been upon her faith too, according to the text : for Lydia's heart is the only one said to have been opened on that occasion ! Well, now, to my taste, the fancy of John Taylor is in just as good taste and keeping as that of Mr. Rice.

Here is the late ecclesiastic history of Niander, fresh from a German press. It has passed through the ordeal of Pedo-baptist learning, both European and American. He is a Pedo-baptist. Hear him :

" It is certain that Christ did not ordain infant baptism; he left, indeed, much that was not needful for salvation, to the free development of the christian spirit, without here appointing binding laws. We cannot prove that the apostles ordained infant baptism, from those places where the baptism of whole families is mentioned, as in Acts xvi. 33, 1 Cor. i. 16. *We can draw no such conclusion,* because the inquiry is still to be made, whether there were any children in these families of such an age, that they were not capable of any intelligent reception of christianity ; for this is the only point on which the case turns."—*Neander's Church Hist.* p. 198, Philad. edit., 1843.

I think my friend must have heard this passage : " IT IS CERTAIN THAT CHRIST DID NOT ORDAIN INFANT BAPTISM." He left much that was not needful to salvation. One such learned and dignified author, in this age of improvement and strict research—one such witness, most profoundly read in church history, is worth a thousand special pleaders, and their ephemeral productions, got up at the impulse of the moment, for sectarian purposes. This gentleman writes for posterity. His researches into the highest antiquity are said to have been more ample than those of any other historian living.

There is another question upon this subject of identity, which we have not forgotten nor given up. Infants, he says, " *are born in the church.*" Presbyterian infants are born members of the Presbyterian church—they are therefore in it. Yet he has spoken of baptism as a *door.* Now if they are born in the church, the question is, through what door do they enter into the church? or rather what is the use of a door? I should be glad to be informed, since children are born in the church, what need have they of a door? The Jews were born in the church, and circumcised because they were born in it. Presbyterians, and all other Pedo-baptists, are born in the church. According to the doctrine of identity, I should like to know why, then, it is necessary to have a door at all, unless to turn them out. I hope the gentleman will answer this most interesting question at his earliest convenience.

I shall now advance to some other points. I have not yet done with the Bible. I will leave church history for a time, but I may read from it, more, perhaps, than my friend would like to hear. I have a passage lying before me, to which I must now beg your attention. It is found in Rom. iv. " I have made thee a father of many nations." The Jews, as it now appears, received the sign of circumcision, to show that they were of the elect nation.

To father Abraham, that renowned friend of God, as I stated at the commencement, were two distinct promises made. One constituting him the father of many nations, according to the flesh; the other constituting him the father of many nations, according to the spirit. It has been proved that he was the father of the Jews, the Edomites, the Ishmaelites, and other descendants of Keturah. But he asked me to show an instance where circumcision was administered to adults without faith. Has he shewn a precept requiring faith, or connecting faith with circumcision? I gave the adult slaves of Abraham, who were circumcised, as his *property* merely, and consequently, that fact precludes faith altogether as a pre-requisite. But if that will not suffice, he may have a stronger case— that of the Shechemites, as detailed Gen. xxxiv. Certainly he must admit, that no faith was either propounded or professed, in that case.

Why does this case of adult circumcision, as property, without faith, give him so much pain! On his new doctrine of substitutes, avowed the other day, there is no need for identity, or even similarity. I gave some fifteen or sixteen points of dissimilarity. But, he says, I am wrong for supposing that any such identity or similarity belongs to the subject!! It is enough that the one supplies the place of the other!! In what single point, then, must there be identity? His doctrine of substitutes is fatal to identity. But to return again to the covenants of promise. It has been observed that the covenants with Abraham, which alone could be called the "*covenants of promises,*" (for as yet the nation was not,) were engrossed at Sinai into one national covenant, with the exception of the one *concerning the Messiah,* given to them merely on deposit. They had the use of this promise concerning the Messiah, and all their saints believed and hoped in it. Still they had it only on deposit. It was not theirs only in common with the nations for whose benefit they held it. Their chief advantage from circumcision, or their national peculiarity, was, that " unto them were committed the oracles of God." If, then, I might compare them to a great bank, to speak in our own style, they had a capital stock of their own, in the charter given them at Mount Sinai. Besides that, there was a much greater sum left in their vaults on deposit. They had the use of that sum for fifteen hundred years, *without interest,* just for preserving it for those of their own issue, and of other nations, for whose benefit it was then laid up. It was no part of the Jewish capital. It was not in the company's charter, but simply placed in their hands for safe keeping. But he was not only the father of the Jews, in a literal sense; but the *spiritual father* of all the Jews that believe. He was the spiritual father of those persons, in 'all nations, who walk in the steps of that faith, which he had while he was yet uncircumcised. By virtue of these two promises, he is constituted the father of multitudes. By one, he became the natural ancestor of many nations; by the other, he is the father of all that believe, in every age and nation. Thus, you see, that the two promises made to Abraham, were prolific of blessings, numerous and various.

Mr. Rice, on yesterday, did not advert to the covenants with Abraham in the plural form. I brought up only one passage representing plurality of covenants. The gentleman seems to regard it as a solitary case. But, while he can quote passages speaking of covenant in the singular number, we must give him instances in the plural form. Paul, then, tells the gentiles, at Ephesus, that they had been, formerly, strangers to the *covenants* of promise. Let him note this. The gentiles were, indeed, interested in those covenants, though no party to them. Abraham's seed, then, was Christ, so far as the gentiles were interested. Through that seed Abraham became the father of all believers in his seed; therefore, if we gentiles are in THE SEED of Abraham, or *in Christ*, we are Abraham's children, or seed, and heirs according to *the promise*—not the promises— but the promise; that is, the promise of blessing all nations (spiritually and eternally,) in his seed, which is the Messiah. They who are *of the faith*, then, Jews or Gentiles, are blessed with believing Abraham. All the promises concerning spiritual blessedness, made to Abraham, when taken in detail, are now in Christ, " *Yea and Amen.*" When, then, we have the word covenant in the singular form, in the New Testament, it either refers to this, or the new covenant—that dispensation of mercy, righteousness, and life, through Jesus Christ. Of this, however, still more hereafter.

Next comes the olive-tree. Our Pedo-baptist friends ought not to quote this passage. It is all against them. Our Lord, at one time, told the Jews, that the seed, and all the blessings—or rather the kingdom of God and its blessings, should be taken from them and given to a people bringing forth the fruits of it. While they had that relation to God, "salvation was of the Jews;" as the Messiah said to the Samaritans. But God now gives salvation to the gentiles. A portion of the Jews believed— they became the nucleus of the new dispensation. They are "the *first fruits*, and the *root* of the christian church." They hold by *faith*, and not by flesh, all the spiritual blessings promised Abraham. Paul compares them to a good olive-tree of which, in one sense, Abraham was the root—standing as a spiritual father to the believing Jews, and as containing in the covenant, made with him concerning Christ, all these blessings. On Abraham's account, then, the believing Jews were *first*—dear to God on two accounts, both *in the flesh*, for the sake of Abraham, his friend, and also *for the sake of the Lord*, his and Abraham's son. Hence the Jew is always *first* with Paul, and the Greek second.

But to the point, the single point, now before us. Paul says, You gentiles must not mistake God's dealings with this people—"for if the first fruit be holy the mass is also holy, and if the *root* be holy so are the *branches.*" Well, now, the Gentiles were grafted in among the believing Jews. On the same old identical principle? No: truly!—not on the same principle, at all, on which the Jews stood naturally related to

2 L

Abraham. Both enter the new covenant by *faith*, and both *stand by faith* in it, and whosoever has not faith, is broken off and cast away.

There is, then, clearly a repudiation of the fleshly principle. Because of unbelief, the Jews were broken off; because of faith, the nations were grafted in: and now faith in the Messiah is the principle and bond of union—so that there is not an atom of identity in the *connecting principle* and *covenant* of the new institution. I will concede, if the gentleman pleases, all he assumes concerning Abraham as the *holy root*. He admits that a great change has taken place; that all the seed of Abraham, but those who have the holy faith that made him holy, are rejected; that the believing gentiles, or those gentiles made holy by faith, are never engrafted with the holy seed of Abraham, and both make A NEW BODY STANDING BY FAITH. And this, therefore, is a perfect and complete annihilation of his imaginary identity. *Faith* and not *flesh*, is now the only bond of union to Christ and among christians. So the matter ends.

The two promises, one concerning the natural, and one concerning the spiritual seed of Abraham, have, then, been fully developed. The covenant concerning Canaan, and the covenant of circumcision, were ultimately engrossed into one great national institution. The latter promise was, under Christ, developed and made the constitution of a "*new man*," a new body, a new community—and thus, with Paul, we arrive at the place of beginning, in the allegory, of the two covenants, the two seeds, the two nations, the two inheritances, and the casting out of the one to make room for the other.

On yesterday, the gentleman said, if I understood him, that the moral law was the constitution of the christian church; thus making it a legal institution. Paul, on this point as well as on many others, essentially differs from my friend. He compares the new and old constitutions, (vulgarly called testaments,) and contrasts them in his second epistle to the Corinthians, third chapter, in some four points. The law, or old constitution, he calls "*letter*," "*the ministration of death written and engraven on stone*;" "*the ministration of condemnation*," and "*to be done away*." The new constitution, in contrast with the former, he called "the Spirit," "the ministration of the Spirit," "the ministration of righteousness," and "that which remaineth." I know, indeed, that the comparison takes in the two institutions, and their introduction or ministration; and although the first was "glorious," as Moses' face indicated, the second "excelled in glory." *Letter, condemnation* and *death*, define the former in its nature and operation—*Spirit, righteousness*, and *life*, the latter in its nature and operation. Mr. Rice's christian church is organized under the former; and that in which I believe, was organized under the latter.

Can any one imagine a more clearly marked contrast than that depicted by our apostle when speaking of the difference of Moses and the apostles—as employed, the one in organizing the old institution, the other in introducing the new? It is the first time in my life that I have ever heard any one say that the christian church was founded upon the moral law as its constitution. The moral law, indeed, in its two grand abstractions, of love to God and our fellows, is the foundation of all governments —celestial, terrestrial, patriarchal, Mosaic, christian, angelic, human, temporal, eternal—but that it is specially or properly the constitution of the christian church in the hands of a Mediator, is without reason and without proof. Paul's contrasts between the two testaments, his face and that of Moses, with all that written in the aforesaid chapter, concerning *letter* and *spirit*, *righteousness* and *condemnation*, is at variance with such an hypothesis. The moral universe is all one church, if the moral principles be its constitution.

The method pursued on this proposition is rather singular, methinks. Instead of furnishing us with New Testament facts, precepts, examples or promises, in development and proof of his proposition; he is all the while hiding in the remote questions of patriarchal and Jewish institutions—listening to Moses and the prophets, rather than to the Messiah and his apostles; and all this for an identity which is impossible to prove; and which, if it were proved, avails nothing, so long as circumcision is a substitute for baptism: for here identity fails with the law of baptism. But he has made the admission, that invalidates his own argument! Why then prosecute it farther?—[*Time expired.*

Wednesday, Nov. 22—12 *o'clock, M.*
[MR. RICE'S TENTH ADDRESS.]

MR. PRESIDENT—It is a little remarkable, that I am always charged with making false issues, when I adduce arguments which precisely match those of Mr. Campbell! He urges, as an argument against infant baptism, that many baptized children live and die unconverted. I answer his exaggerated statement by proving, that large numbers of adults immersed into his own church, have apostatized and become worse than before. And this is making "false issues!" It is somewhat singular, too, that I am rarely ever diverted from the subject under discussion, except when I am in pursuit of him!

The gentleman is obliged to admit, that he has expressed the opinion, that there is more probability of the salvation of the children of Presbyterians, than of the children of Baptists; but he does not ascribe this difference to the virtue of sprinkling. I, however, do ascribe it to the fact, that Presbyterian parents have solemnly covenanted with God to train up their children in the nurture and admonition of the Lord; and whilst they had applied to them the seal of the covenant, have been encouraged in their difficult duties by the soul-cheering promise—"I will be a God to thee and to thy seed after thee." Is nothing gained, when an individual, who is disposed to neglect an important duty, is induced honestly and solemnly to promise to neglect it no more? Is he not more likely to persevere in the effort to accomplish it, if he have assurance of the assistance he needs? If human nature can be affected by the most solemn promises, or encouraged by the prospect of needed help; much, very much is gained by the baptism of infants. It was not the mere act of circumcising a child in Abraham's family, that secured the blessing. It was the covenant with God, of which circumcision was the seal, which bound him more strongly, and more encouraged him to command his household after him, that they might enjoy the blessing of the covenant-keeping God. The gentleman's own acknowledgment, drawn from him in spite of his prejudices, is proof conclusive of the value of infant baptism.

I have said, that there has been, properly speaking, but one *true religion* on earth, and that the Savior did not send his apostles to establish a new one. Mr. C. insists that this cannot be true, because Paul says, that before his conversion to christianity he profited in *the Jews' religion.* But at the time when Paul was converted, the Jews' religion was false.

The prophecies, and the sacrifices of the Old Testament pointed them to the Messiah, as the Savior of men. They, in their blindness rejected the glorious substance, and clung to the shadow. They had rejected the Savior, and were unbelievers—apostates. Their religion, therefore, was false. But does this prove, that the piety of Paul, as a christian, was essentially different from the piety of Abraham, the father of believers? or from that of Daniel, or Isaiah, or Jeremiah, or other devout servants of God, under the former dispensation?

The gentleman would fain induce you to believe, that I have abandoned the argument from 1 Cor. vii. 14. How have I abandoned it? By putting the learning of Scott, Doddridge, Whitby, Woods and other eminent men against the assertion of Mr. Campbell! He affirms, that they have all entirely mistaken the apostle's design; and he calls on me to prove, that they have not. They evidently thought that they understood something about the meaning of the passage; and so long as he deals in bold assertions without proof, I am content to throw his learning into the one scale, and theirs into the other. I have said, that the word *holy* and *clean* have in the Bible *two meanings ;* and, in the passage under consideration, they can mean nothing but consecration to God. If the gentleman can show that these words have other meanings, let him do it; but it is vain for him to put forth his *assertions* against the views of such men as those just named.

He is quite pleased that I touched household baptisms so lightly, and that I have not brought forward the argument on which Mr. Taylor relies. We are rich in resources on this subject. I did not design to offer all the arguments by which infant baptism can be proved. The gentleman says, one good argument is enough to establish a point. I have given him several, which he has not been able to answer. Were I to bring forward Mr. Taylor's argument, I think it very doubtful whether he could answer it; but I do not need it. It is true, I remarked on but one case of household baptism, for the very good reason, that the remarks made concerning that, will apply to the others. I remember, not long since, reading a critique of the gentleman on an argument in brother Hendrick's book on Baptism. The author gave, perhaps, *nineteen* instances in which the Greek preposition precedes the verb, where the idea of going *into* is designed to be definitely expressed. Mr. Campbell decided very critically, that the nineteen examples, being just alike, amounted to only *one!* But when I give, as an example, one household baptism, he is quite amused, that the subject is touched so lightly!

I have, he says, assumed that Lydia had a husband and children, &c. I have assumed nothing. I have no occasion to draw upon my imagination, as did Mr. Campbell and father Taylor, to supply the defects of sacred history. I state simple, indisputable facts—that the Evangelist states that Lydia believed, and that she and her family were baptized ; but he did not say that her family believed. I say, we write as Luke wrote ; and anti-Pedo-baptists do not thus write. I cheerfully leave the audience to decide, in view of these facts, whether we, or the gentleman and those who agree with him, practice as Luke and the apostles did.

Mr. Campbell quotes Dr. Neander's opinion, that Christ did not ordain infant baptism, and also a statement concerning the history of it. Dr. Neander lives at too late a period to be admitted as a *witness*, only as he gives authority for his statements. We are not, however, discussing the question, whether Christ *ordained infant baptism.* That he instituted the ordinance of baptism, all admit. But the question arises, viz. *to whom is baptism to be administered?* We prove, at least to our own satisfaction, that adult believers and their children, are scriptural subjects of this ordinance. Our Savior did not ordain *female communion.* He did, however, appoint his supper to be observed in all future time ; and, although there is no precept for admitting females to commune, it can be proved to be their privilege and their duty. And so it is with infant baptism.

Dr. Neander, though a great man, does not always reason as conclusively as he might, as we may see by an extract which I will read from his history of the church:

" But immediately after Ireneus, in the latter years of the second century, Tertullian appeared as a zealous opponent of infant baptism, a proof that it was not then usually considered as an apostolic ordinance, for in that case he would hardly have ventured to speak so strongly against it."—*Ch. Hist.* p. 199.

According to his logic, infant baptism could not have been usually considered an apostolical ordinance ; or Tertullian would not have ventured to speak so strongly against it. But did he not speak as strongly against the baptism of young and unmarried persons? And are we thence to conclude, that the baptism of such persons was not usually considered as of divine authority? The reasoning would be quite as conclusive in the one case as in the other.

The children of believers, the gentleman tells us, are, according to Presbyterian doctrine, born in the church ; and, therefore, baptism cannot be to them a door of entrance. I am not at all tenacious about the particular word *door,* which, however, when figuratively used in regard to the church, is correct. Baptism is a rite by which membership in the church of Christ is recognized. The children of Jews were, by birth, entitled to membership in the church ; but they could not partake of the passover nor enjoy the privileges of the church, till circumcised. Precisely so the children of believers cannot enjoy the privileges of the church, until their membership is recognized by baptism.

By the way, the gentleman says, he has more to say on the *history* of infant baptism, than I will be inclined to hear. I am prepared to listen patiently to all the history he can produce ; and I will be with him whenever he chooses to enter upon it.

He is again descanting on the covenants with Abraham. He found fault with me for going to the Old Testament in support of infant membership ; and yet admitted that the New Testament could not be understood without the Old. Still, however, though he has continued *to* wander through the Old Testament, he fails to find more than one covenant with Abraham. And if he could find half a dozen, my argument would not be affected by the discovery ; since it is certain that the covenant sealed by circumcision, *contains the promise of spiritual blessings,* and, as Andrew Fuller says, constituted him the father of the church of God in future ages.

I have repeatedly called on the gentleman to prove, that any adult ever entered the Jewish church, according to God's law, without professing faith in the God of Abraham. He failed to produce an example ; but he thinks he has found one to-day. My friend will rally sometimes. He has brought forward the case of the Shechemites, whom two of Jacob's sons induced to be circumcised, that they might murder them, because of an insult offered their sister by a son of the prince! And this ungodly trick, resorted to by two wicked young men, for purposes of revenge, and severely condemned by Jacob, is brought up by Mr. Campbell, as an example of the scriptural administration of circumcision; to show that adults, without professing faith, might be circumcised according to the law of God!!! His cause is surely laboring under great difficulties, or he would not have attempted to sustain it by such means. Let him show, if he can, that the Shechemites were circumcised *according to God's law.*

The kingdom of heaven, the gentleman says, was to be taken from the Jews and given to the gentiles. But, if it be true, as he contends, that a *new religion* was given to the gentiles, and a *new church* established among them, what, I ask, was taken from the Jews, and given to the gentiles? The kingdom of Christ—the church, with its privileges and blessings, was taken from the former, and given to the latter; and this adds strength to the argument, proving the identity of the church.

It is vain for Mr. Campbell to attempt to evade the force of the argument afforded by the *olive-tree*, (Rom. xi. 16—.) He cannot deny that, by the olive-tree, is meant the christian church; but he says, the *first fruit*, of which the apostle speaks, were the *first converts* to christianity. If this be true, how is it that the unbelieving Jews were *broken off* from it, as the apostle declares? Were they broken off from the first converts to christianity?! The olive-tree is the church, from which the Jewish nation (so far as they rejected Christ) were broken off; into which the believing gentiles were grafted, and into which the Jews, when converted to christianity, shall be again introduced. The conclusion is inevitable, that the church to which the Jews belong, is the same into which the gentiles were brought, and to which the converted Jews, with their children, shall return. I wish the gentleman would have told us how the unbelieving Jews were broken off from the first converts to christianity; but he seemed to forget to remove this difficulty!

He says, I stated, that the moral law is *the constitution of the christian church.* I did not say so. I said, the moral law may be considered, in a sense, the *constitution of God's moral government ;* inasmuch as it defines the duties of the subjects to the great King, and their duties, rights, and privileges relative to each other. So he is again mistaken, and has spent some time in disproving what I never thought of affirming.

I will now resume the argument for infant baptism, derived from history. I have quoted Ireneus, the disciple of Polycarp, who was the disciple of John the apostle, and have proved that he speaks of infant baptism, so as to make the clear impression, that, at that very early period, it was universally believed and practiced, as of divine institution. That, by the language he used, he meant baptism, I can prove by Mr. Campbell himself and by Dr. Neander, whom he has quoted as a very learned man.

I have also given the testimony of Clemens Alexandrinus, of Tertullian, Origen, and of Cyprian and the council of *sixty-six* bishops. I will now give you the testimony of Augustin and Jerom, two of the most learned of the christian fathers, who flourished in the latter part of the 4th and beginning of the 5th centuries; and who speak of infant baptism, not only as in their day universally practiced by the whole church, but as having ever been regarded as of divine authority.

I will first quote a passage from the writings of Jerom.

" This is said of those that have understanding of such as he was, of whom it is written in the gospel, *He is of age, let him speak for himself.* But he that is a child, and thinks as a child, (till such time as he come to years of discretion—and Pythagoras' letter (Y) do bring to the place where the road parts into two,) his good deeds, as well as his evil deeds, are imputed to his parents. Unless you will think the children of christians are themselves only under the guilt of the sin, if they do not receive baptism; and that the wickedness is not imputed to those also who would not give it them, especially at that time when they that were to receive it, could make no opposition against the receiving of it," &c.—[*Epist. ad Letam.*] *Wall.* vol. i. p. 240.

Augustine thus comments on 1 Cor. vii. 14:

" *For an unbelieving husband has been sanctified by his believing wife, and an unbelieving wife by her believing husband.*

I suppose it had then happened that several wives had been brought to the faith by their believing husbands, and husbands by their believing wives. And though he does not mention their names, yet he makes use of their example to confirm his advice.

Else were your children unclean, but now are they holy.

For there were then christian infants that were sanctified, [or made holy, i. e. that were baptized] some by the authority of one of their parents, some by the consent of both; which would not be, if as soon as one party believed, the marriage were dissolved," &c.—*De Sermone Domini in Monte.*

Again,—p. 251:

" So that many persons, increasing in knowledge, after their baptism, and especially those who have been baptized either when they were infants, or when they were youths; as their understanding is cleared and enlightened, and their inward man renewed day by day, do themselves deride, and with abhorrence and confession renounce their former opinions which they had of God, when they were imposed on by their imaginations. And yet they are not, therefore, accounted either not to have received baptism, or to have received a baptism of that nature that their error was," &c.

Again—p. 254:

" And as the thief, who by necessity went without baptism, was saved; because by his piety he had it spiritually : so where baptism is had, though the party by necessity go without that [faith] which the thief had, yet he is saved. Which the whole body of the church holds, as delivered to them, in the case of little infants baptized : who certainly cannot yet believe with the heart to righteousness, or confess with the mouth to salvation, as the thief could," &c. * * * " And if any one do ask for divine authority in this matter: though that which the whole church practices, and which has not been instituted by councils, but was ever in use, is very reasonably believed to be no other than a thing delivered [or ordered] by authority of the apostles: yet we may besides take a true estimate, how much the sacrament of baptism does avail infants, by the circumcision which God's former people received."—*De Baptismo cont. Donatistas.*

Augustine, you observe, states, that the *whole church* practiced infant baptism, and that it was never instituted by councils. I will read one or two more extracts, (pp. 382, 383.) Having quoted some passages from the writings of Jerome, he remarks as follows:

" And now some people, by the boldness of I know not what disputing humor, go about to represent that as uncertain which our ancestors made use of as a most certain thing, whereby to resolve some things that seemed uncertain. For, when this began first to be disputed, I know not : but this I know, that holy Hierome, whose pains and fame for excellent learning in ecclesiastical matters is at this day so great, does also make use of this as a thing most certain, to resolve some questions in his books," &c.

Then having quoted some passages out of St. Hierome on Jonah, he proceeds:

" If we could with convenience come to ask that most learned man, how many writers of christian dissertations and interpreters of holy scripture in both languages could he recount, who from the time that Christ's church has been founded, have held no otherwise, have received no other doctrine from their predecessors, nor left any other to their successors? For my part, (though my reading is much less than his,) I do not remember that I ever heard any other thing from any christians that received the Old and New Testament, *non solum in Catholica ecclesia verum etiam in qualibet hæresi vel schismate constitutis:* neither from such as were of the Catholic church, nor from such as belonged to any sect or schism. *Nom memini me aliud legisse,* &c. I do not remember that I ever read otherwise in any writer that I could ever find treating of these matters, that followed the canonical Scriptures, or did mean or did pretend to do so."

Such is the testimony of two of the most eminent fathers of the christian church. There not only was, in their day, no controversy on the subject of infant baptism, but they declare that there never had been any difference of opinion in regard to it.

I now invite your attention to the testimony of PELAGIUS. And let it be remarked, his testimony is peculiarly valuable, not only because he was a man of extensive learning, but especially because the doctrine of infant baptism was plainly inconsistent with the fundamental doctrine of his system—the denial of original sin; and with this difficulty he was constantly pressed by his opposers. He had, therefore, every motive to deny the doctrine, and to prove it an innovation in the church. But hear what he says:

" Men slander me as if I denied the sacrament of baptism to infants, or did promise the kingdom of heaven to some persons without the redemption of Christ: which is a thing that I never heard, no not even any wicked heretic say. For who is there so ignorant of that which is read in the gospel, as (I need not say to affirm this, but) in any heedless way to say such a thing, or even have such a thought," &c.—*Wall,* vol. i. p. 450.

Now look at the strength of this testimony. I began with Ireneus, almost in sight of the apostle John. Then came Tertullian and Origen, a few years later; then Cyprian and the sixty-six bishops; then, at a later period, Jerom and Augustine; and, finally, Pelagius—all testifying to the universal prevalence of infant baptism. Now, if any fact can be established by history, it is the fact, that this practice prevailed from the days of the apostles themselves.

I have another interesting portion of history, which I will present for your consideration. Mr. Campbell, and other anti-Pedo-baptists, have claimed the Waldenses and Albigenses, (those witnesses for God and the truth, in the dark ages, when christianity seemed almost lost from the earth,) as anti-Pedo-baptists. This claim is set up by Mr. Jones, the Baptist historian, of whose history Mr. Campbell has spoken in the highest terms; yet in his account of the Waldenses, though quoting avowedly from Perrin's history, he left out every thing that squinted at infant baptism! Perrin was a descendant from these people, and he took the pains to visit them, and obtained their confessions of faith, and other books and documents, from which he wrote their history. Their enemies, (the Roman priests,) did charge them with denying the baptism of infants; and Mr. Jones published the charge as if it were undoubtedly true. In reply to it John Paul Perrin, their historian, thus remarks:—(Book i. ch. iv. p. 15.)

" The fourth calumnie was touching baptisme, which, it is said, they [Waldenses] denied to little infants: but from this imputation they quit themselves as followeth :—The time and place of those that are to be baptized is not ordained, but the charitie and edification of the church and congregation must serve for a rule therein, &c.; and therefore, they to whom the children were nearest allied, brought their infants to be baptized, as their parents, or any other whom God hath made charitable in that kind."

Again : (Perrin, book i. chap. vi. pp. 30, 31.)

" King Lewis XII, having been informed by the enemies of the Waldenses, dwelling in Provence, of many grievous crimes, which were imposed [charged] upon them, sent to make inquisition in those places, the lord Adam Fumee, Maister of Requests, and a doctor of Sorbon, called Parne, who was his confessor. They visited all the parishes and temples, and found neither images, nor so much as the least show of any ornaments belonging to their masses and ceremonies of the church of Rome, much lesse any such crimes as were imposed [charged] upon them ; but rather that they kept their Sabbathes duely, causing their children to be baptized according to the order of the primitive church, teaching them the articles of the christian faith and the commandments of God."

Now let us see how faithfully the historian, Mr. Jones, who has been recommended by my friend, has quoted Perrin: (Church Hist. p. 348.)

" Louis XII, king of France, being informed by the enemies of the Waldenses, inhabiting a part of the province of Provence, that several crimes were laid to their account, sent the Master of Requests and a certain doctor of the Sorbonne, who was confessor to his majesty, to make inquiry into the matter. On their return, they reported that they had visited all the parishes where they dwelt, had inspected their places of worship, but that they had found there no images, nor signs of the ornaments belonging to the mass, nor any of the ceremonies of the Romish church ; much less could they discover any traces of those crimes with which they were charged. On the contrary, they kept the Sabbath day, *observed the ordinance of baptism according to the primitive church,* instructed their children in the articles of the christian faith, and the commandments of God."—*Joachim Camerarius,* in his History, p. 352, quoted by Perrin, book i. chap. v.

Here Mr. Jones, when he came to *infant baptism,* wholly omitted it ; and instead of saying, as did the author he quoted—" causing their children to be baptized "—he says, " observed the ordinance of baptism according to the primitive church ! ! !" Thus the Waldenses are proved to be anti-Pedo-baptists, by concealing their testimony. A more glaring falsification of history I never saw ! I have a great deal more testimony upon the same point, only part of which I can present ; I will read some passages from their confessions of faith.

Perrin, book ii. chap. iv. pp. 60, 61 :

" Touching the matter of the sacraments, it hath been concluded by the Holy Scriptures, that we have but two sacramental signes, the which Christ Jesus hath left unto us ; the one is baptisme, the other the eucharist, which wee receive to shew what our perseverance in the faith is, as wee have promised when wee were baptized, being little infants : as also in remembrance of that great benefit, which Jesus Christ hath done unto us, when hee died for our redemption, washing us with his most precious blood."—*Conf. of Faith, Art.* 17.

" Amongst others there appeared a poore, simple, laboring man, whom the president commanded to cause his child to be re-baptized, which had lately been baptized by the minister of Saint John, neere Angrongne. This poore man requested so much respite, as that hee might pray unto God before hee answered him, which being granted with some laughter, he fell downe upon his knees in the presence of all that were there, and his prayer being ended, he said to the president, that hee would cause his childe to be re-baptized, upon condition, that the said president would discharge him by a bill signed with his owne hand, of the sinne which hee should commit in causing it to be re-baptized, and beare one day before God, the punishment and condemnation which should befall him, taking this iniquity upon him and his. Which the president understanding, hee commanded him out of his presence, not pressing him any farther."—*Perrin,* book ii. p. 64.

Doctrine of the Waldenses and Albigenses, book i. ch. vi. p. 43.—"Now this baptisme is visible and materiall, which maketh the partie neither good nor evill, as it appeareth in the Scripture, by Simon Magus and Saint Paul. And whereas baptisme is administered in a full congregation of the faithfull, it is to the end that hee that is received into the church, should be reputed and held of all for a christian brother, and that all the congregation might pray for him, that he may be a christian. And for this cause it is, that wee present our children in baptisme; which they ought to doe, to whom the children are neerest, as their parents, and they to whom God had given this charitie."

"The things that are not necessary in the administration of baptisme, are the exorcismes, breathings, the signe of the crosse upon the forehead and breast of the infant, the salt put into his mouth, spittle into his eares and nostrills, the anoynting of the breast," &c.—*Book* iii. ch. iv. p. 99.

The Waldenses and Albigenses, whilst they boldly and fearlessly testified against all the corruptions of popery, still contended for the scripture doctrine of infant baptism.

We have now a connected chain of evidence in favor of this doctrine, extending from the Waldenses and Albigenses, up through Pelagius, Augustin, Jerom, Origen, Cyprian and the council at Carthage, and Tertullian, to Ireneus; between whom and the apostle John there was but a single individual.

I will now read to the audience the conclusion to which Dr. Wall, after long and careful examination, was induced to come.—[*Time expired.*

Wednesday, Nov. 22—12½ *o'clock, P. M.*
[MR. CAMPBELL'S TENTH REPLY.]

MR. PRESIDENT—Mr. Rice has to address us but once more on this proposition. It is, therefore, incumbent on me to give him all the points on which I rely. I will premise on the identity question, and on some one or two other matters, a few items, that he may be prepared to respond in his next speech. He commenced, and he seems disposed to conclude, his defence of infant affusion by an appeal to maternal tenderness, or that it some way takes hold of the conscience and obliges parents to do for their offspring more than either nature or the precepts of christianity would or could possibly accomplish. Thus he infuses into infant sprinkling a moral power of constraining parental affection, or obliging parents to do for their children what, without these vows and protestations, they could not otherwise be induced to do. Well, now, the first question is— Is this fact? I shall make my appeal at once to christian mothers. I put the question to every christian mother, whether her maternal affections for her own offspring, and her christian obligations to the Lord, growing out of his love and authority, commanding and enjoining her to bring up her children in the nurture and admonition of the Lord, can be augmented and enhanced by a promise extorted from her without any authority for it in the Bible, to do what the Divine impulses, the motherly instincts, which the God of love and sympathy has planted with his own hand in her bosom; and the pure, and holy, and authoritative precepts of the Savior that bought her, cannot accomplish? I have no doubt of the issue of such

an appeal.   Nature is stronger than the artificial vows appended to the
rite of initiation—and so reads the history of the world, so far as it details
the experience of all ages and nations.   You cannot exercise maternal
affection if you would lead every mother to the altar and make her swear
seven times to do her duty to her children, after you have laid before her
the precepts of Christ.

Why did my friend stop with the case of Lydia?   Why went he not
round all the other households, as usual?   Why did he not, when asked,
produce the case of Stephanus and his house, of Cornelius and his house,
of the jailor and his house?   He thought it enough to try the strongest
case, and failing in that, despaired of the others.   He makes so many
assumptions, he has not time to defend them.   He would, in Parthian
style, say, as he moves along, that there is no precept for female communion.   This objection is a surrendering of the plea for any authority preceptive of infant baptism; and then by way of reprisals, to gain concession, says—You have no precept nor example for female communion!
Well, as there is neither male nor female communion, but *christian* communion—proving the latter, we prove both male and female.   But as he
will not ask for proof on that point, I will refer him especially to Acts,
1st and 2d chapters.   He will find that one hundred and twenty men
and women were in communion in Jerusalem, before the first Pentecost.
He will, also, find that three thousand were added to them on that day;
and he will next find that these three thousand one hundred and twenty
disciples, *male and female*, continued in all *christian* communion, and
among the rest, in *breaking the loaf*.   Here is a Divine warrant for male
and female communion in the loaf.   Give only one such case of infant
baptism—we ask no more!

Well, we have gained another point of some importance.   He now
says that baptism is not the *door*.   I congratulate him in giving that up.
He has no use for a door in getting into his church.   He rather needs one to
get out of it.   Indeed, none of us imagines that there is any thing in the form
of a door into a Christian or Jewish community.   We use the term metaphorically.   By *initiation, entrance,* and *door*, we mean the same thing.
Infant baptism, then, does not initiate into the christian church on the
principle of identity, for circumcision did not initiate.   No initiation, no
door.   So that matter is also settled.   If he should ever speak of baptism
as a door or an initiation, I will again request him to tell us *into what*
does it initiate a child; or *into what* is it a door?

I might advert to the new version of the commission, given from Mark,
though he has not replied to the other versions—Mark's version and
Luke's version.   What does Mark say: "Go ye into all the world, and
preach the gospel to every creature; he that believeth and is baptized
shall be saved, and he that believeth not shall be condemned."   Luke is
still more clear.   Here the Savior commands that "repentance or reformation and remission of sins should be preached in his name among all
nations, beginning at Jerusalem."   That single word, *reformation*, includes the whole—among all nations.   Faith, first; repentance, next,
and baptism next.   These versions we plead in explanation of the words,
disciple them.

With regard to the Schechemites—I know it was an ugly affair; but if
circumcision had required a confession of faith, I am persuaded that the
whole clan never could have been prevailed upon to submit to the rite.   It
could not be supposed that advantage was taken of their ignorance.   No

one ever thought of such a thing as professing faith in order to circumcision. Can the gentleman name any one who was ever called to make profession of faith in order to circumcision? There is the breadth of the heavens of difference between circumcision and baptism; otherwise, there would be some passage found, or some precept, saying—"*Believe, and be circumcised.*"

The gentleman *did* say that we are under the same moral law; for I wrote it down as he uttered it, and I have company in this assertion. I have others with me who heard the same. I said in replication, that Massachusetts and Kentucky had the same moral law. It is so written out in so many words in my notes, and I am particular in writing down every important matter.

As to Mr. Jones and this accusation, I have nothing to say at this moment. He is an honest historian, as I believe, though he does not agree with me in some matters. His reputation as an historian stands very high. The gentleman might have saved himself the trouble of quoting many authorities in favor of infant baptism.

Against his doctrine of identity I offer the following arguments, already hinted, though not fully developed. The Savior has positively said, "The law and the prophets were (in authority, or were public instructors) your teachers till John came. Since that time the kingdom of God is preached, and all men press *into it*," Luke xvi. 16. What language could be more clearly expressive of the cessation or withdrawal of one class of teachers, and the introduction of a new institution? The law and prophets were the Old Testament; but now a new institution *into* which, *out of* some other one, all the conscientious press. The Jews' religion was corrupted, the gentleman says; but so has been the christian. The Jews' religion was once reformed, so has the christian, nominally, been reformed at sundry times. But this is more than reformation; it is the kingdom of God that is preached, and men are now leaving the law and the prophets, and that institution, and pressing into it. There were many pious Jews amongst that people, like Simeon and Anna, Zacharias and Elizabeth—and even Saul of Tarsus, who was so pious and zealous for the religion of his fathers, and of the law and the prophets, that he persecuted the christians, because they had got up, as he understood it, a new religion. It would be impossible to conceive of one so learned as Paul, and so discriminating, as not to have seen that christianity was only *reformed Judaism*, if that were its real character.

Again, the church is said to be "built on the foundation of the apostles and prophets, Jesus Christ himself being the chief corner-stone." Were these the foundation of the Jewish church? Was it built on this foundation? Did Jesus Christ live cotemporary with Moses, and the ancients who prophecied of him!! Into what wild extremes are we driven, in avoiding the truth, whether the evasion be voluntary or involuntary!

Another proof I have always deduced from Daniel. This most celebrated of Jewish prophets foretold, that in the time of the Romans, the God of heaven would set up a kingdom, a new institution of course; for who SETS UP an old institution already existing? How could that kingdom be set up, while that of Moses was standing? Will God have two kingdoms on earth at the same time? Messiah, the prince, then, was to come first, and then his kingdom. Certainly Daniel foretold a new institution—a kingdom of God. Who can plausibly show that the kingdom of God, to be set up, was the identical Jewish church? in its national and wordly form, too, for that was an essential element of its constitution! Isaiah, also, is indisputably with us. He says, or rather the Lord says by him, chap. xxviii., Thus saith the Lord God, "Behold I lay in Zion, *for a foundation stone*, a tried stone, a precious corner-stone, a sure foundation." This is the foundation of all those brilliant passages, read from the prophets, in proof of identity. Every bright scene of the future glory of the *true Israel of God*, is drawn from the visions of the Messiah and his saints, then in the flesh, of the Jewish ceremonial. All the bright scenes are, by the apostles, applied, in this way, to Him who, at first, was a stone of stumbling, and a rock of offence.

I need not say, for no one will debate it, that this passage is quoted and applied by the apostles to Jesus Christ, who appeared in the days of the Cæsars; consequently it must be conceded, that the *foundation* of the new institution was not laid, while, as yet, the Mosaic was standing.

Evident, then, it is, that the kingdom of the Messiah is radically, essentially, and formally different from the Jewish theocracy, from the patriarchal, and every other religious institution on the earth. It was to be builded on an entirely new foundation, and to consist of a spiritual people, whose nativity should be spiritual and heavenly. Since the world began there never was, till the day of Pentecost, a society of men who met together, purely upon spiritual grounds; never a church of God, in the New Testament acceptation of that most abused word. On that commenced a new society, who met together purely on the ground of a spiritual faith, hope, and love. These were believers in Christ, converted men. No such a separate society was ever before convened. The family religion of the patriarchal age had natural bonds of association, and was necessarily mixed in its character. The Jewish religion was national, and therefore mixed in its very nature and constitution. But the church is neither *natural* nor *national;* but supernatural, spiritual, and divine. That there were saints among Jews and patriarchs, by myriads, I believe and hope. But there was no church, such as christianity contemplates, at all. Nothing like it. If Christ's church be a continuation of the Jewish, then it must be *national!*

Defection and corruption, alas, follow men every where on earth—in paradise and out of it; under all dispensations and administrations. Outside of the New Testament there is no church authority whatever; no christian authority. The arguments heard are no earlier than the third century—for, indeed there is no vestige of infant baptism till in the third—Tertullian is the first person that names it. But suppose it were found in the second century, evident as any other historical fact whatever, what then? It is, in the judgment of the most learned Presbyterian doctors now living, of no value or authority whatever. You shall now have these words fully confirmed, by one of the most virulent opponents of the Baptists now living; one of the greatest devotees to Presbyterianism, and one who has, for his opportunities, said and written as bitter things against myself, as any other doctor of divinity in that church; I mean Dr. Miller, of Princeton Theological school, and professor of ecclesiastic history, and, of course, he ought to know what such evidence as you have just heard from Mr. Rice is worth. I am sorry I have not time to read so much from him as I could wish.

Dr. Miller says : (Letters on Epis. pp. 290, 291.)

" We are accustomed to look back to the first ages of the church with a veneration nearly bordering on superstition. *It answered the purpose of*

2 M

popery, to refer all their corruptions to primitive times, and to represent those times as exhibiting the models of all excellence. But every representation of this kind must be received with distrust. The christian church, during the apostolic age, and for half a century, did indeed present a venerable aspect. Persecuted by the world on every side, she was favored in an uncommon measure with the presence of the Spirit of her divine Head, and exhibited a degree of simplicity and purity, which has, perhaps, never since been equalled. But before the close of the *second century*, the scene began to change; and before *the commencement of the fourth*, a deplorable corruption of doctrine, discipline, and morals, had crept into the church, and disfigured the body of Christ. Hegesippus, an ecclesiastical historian, declares that the " virgin purity of the church was confined to the days of the apostles."

" I shall not now stay to ascertain what degree of respect is due to the writings of the fathers in general. It is my *duty*, however, to state, that we do not refer to them, *in any wise, as a rule either of faith or practice.* We acknowledge the *Scriptures alone* to be such rule. By this rule the fathers themselves are to be *tried;* and of course they cannot be considered *as the christian's authority for any thing.* It is agreed, on all hands, that they are not infallible guides : and it is perfectly well known to all who are acquainted with their writings, that many of them are inconsistent, both with themselves and with one another. We protest, therefore, utterly against any appeal to them on this subject. Though they, or an angel from heaven, should bring us any doctrine, as essential to the order and well-being of the church, which is not to be found in the word of God, we are bound by the command of our Master to reject them."

Dr. Miller, in his Letters on Epis. pages 164 and 149, says :

" Even supposing you had found such declarations in SOME or ALL of the early fathers; what then ? Historic fact is not divine institution."

Once more :

" Suffer me, my brethren, again to remind you of the principle on which we proceed, in this part of our inquiry. If it could be demonstrated from the writings of the fathers, that in one hundred, or even in fifty years, [in four years, or four centuries, he remarks in another place,] after the death of the last apostle, the system of diocesan episcopacy had been generally adopted in the church, it would be nothing to the purpose. As long as *no traces of this fact* can be found in the *Bible*, but *much of a directly opposite nature*, we should stand on a secure and immovable foundation. To all reasonings, *then*, derived from the *fathers*, I answer with the venerable Augustine, who, when pressed with the authority of Cyprian, replied, ' His writings I hold not to be canonical, but examine them by the canonical writings : and in them, what agreeth with the authority of divine Scripture, I accept, with his praise ; what agreeth not, I reject with his leave.' "

I have a liberal set of extracts from Taylor's Ancient Christianity here, prepared for this place ; but I have not time to read nor comment on them. Those of Mr. Miller, then, must suffice for the present. And the words of no man in America can be read with more acceptance, I presume, by Mr. Rice.

I must treat you to a word or two from that St. Cyprian, of whom you heard so much in commendation from Mr. Rice, who, in his council of sixty-six African bishops, decided in favor of infant baptism. He was one also of Mr. Rice's learned men, that decided that sprinkling water or sand made good valid christian baptism. He was an advocate for infant communion, and for many other such human traditions. I am sorry that I can read but one such extract as the following, for every ten that I might read, and that ought to be read, with notes and comments, especially adapted to the ears of Pedo-baptists. I admit, that from St. Cyprian's time, infant baptism and infant communion were very common; for they began about the same time, and continued for centuries, as true and faithful companions. But let us hear this saint. I quote from Wall's History of Infant Baptism, vol. ii. pages 482–3:

"St. Cyprian says: I will tell you what happened in my own presence. The parents of a certain little girl, running out of town in a fright, had forgot to take any care of their child, whom they had left in the keeping of a nurse. The nurse had carried her to the magistrates: they, because she was too little to eat the flesh, gave her to eat before the idol some of the bread, mixed with wine, which had been left of the sacrifice of those wretches. Since that time her mother took her home. But she was no more capable of declaring and telling the crime committed, than she had been before of understanding or of hindering it. So it happened that once when I was administering, her mother, ignorant of what had been done, brought her along with her. But the girl, being among the saints, could not with any quietness hear the prayers said; but sometimes fell into weeping, and sometimes into convulsions, with the uneasiness of her mind: and her ignorant soul, as under a rack, declared by such tokens as it could, the conscience of the fact in those tender years. And when the service was ended, and the deacon went to give the cup to those that were present, and the others received it, and her turn came, the girl by a divine instinct turned away her face, shut her mouth, and refused the cup. But yet the deacon persisted; and put into her mouth, though she refused it, some of the sacrament of the cup. Then followed retchings and vomiting. The eucharist could not stay in her polluted mouth and body; the drink consecrated in our Lord's blood burst out again from her defiled bowels. Such is the power, such the majesty of our Lord: the secrets of darkness were discovered by its light: even unknown sins could not deceive the priest of God. This happened in the case of an infant, who was by reason of her age incapable of declaring the crime which another had acted on her."

From such teachers and doctors, who, in the name of reason, would expect to find any authority to influence christians in the performance of the most solemn acts of religion—the administration of baptism, and the supper!

That infant communion was as common as infant baptism, I say again, can be fully proved, as Mr. Rice very well knows, or ought to know—and that from the same sources, too. I must give one or two short extracts:—

"St. Austin says: The christians of Africa do well call baptism itself, one's salvation; and the sacrament of Christ body one's life. From whence is this, but, as I suppose, from that ancient and apostolical tradition, by which the churches of Christ do naturally hold, that without baptism and partaking of the Lord's table, none can come either to the kingdom of God, or to salvation and eternal life? For the Scripture, as I shewed before, says the same. For what other thing do they hold, that call baptism salvation, than that which is said, 'He saved us by the washing of regeneration:' and that which Peter says, 'The like figure whereunto, even baptism, doth now save us?' And what other thing do they hold, that call the sacrament of the Lord's table, life, than that which is said, I am the bread of life, &c. and The bread which I will give is my flesh, which I will give for the life of the world; and, Except ye eat the flesh of the Son of Man, and drink his blood, ye have no life in you? If then, as so many divine testimonies do agree neither *salvation* nor *eternal life* is to be hoped for by any without baptism, and the body and blood of our Lord; it is in vain promised to infants without them."—*Wall*, pp. 485, 486.

"Innocent I., Bishop of Rome, does indeed, A. D. 417, plainly and positively say, that infants cannot be saved without receiving the eucharist:

and that in a synodical epistle written to the fathers of the Milevetian council. The council had represented to him the mischief of that tenet of the Pelagians, that unbaptized infants, though they cannot go to heaven, yet may have eternal life; which the Pelagians maintained on this pretence: that our Savior, though he said, '*He that is not born of water cannot enter the kingdom*,' yet had not said *he cannot have eternal life*. To this, Innocent's words are—'That which your brotherhood says that they teach, that infants may without the grace of baptism have eternal life,' is very absurd. Since, ' Except they eat of the flesh of the Son of man, and drink his blood, they have no life in them.' His meaning is plainly this : they can have no eternal life without receiving the communion; and they cannot do that, till they be baptized.' *   *   *   And it is true what Mr. Daille urges, ' That St. Austin says the same thing eight or ten times over, in several places of his books.' And some of these books are dated a little before the letter of Innocent."—*Wall*, vol. i. p. 484.

 " It is a brave thing to be infallible. Such men may do what they will, and it shall be true. What is a contradiction in other men's mouths, is none in theirs. Pope Innocent, in a synodical letter sent to the council of Milevetia, says—" If infants do not eat of the flesh of the Son of Man, and drink his blood, [meaning the sacrament,] they have no life in them.' Pope Pius, in confirming the council of Trent, says, ' If any man say so, let him be anathema."—*Wall*, vol. i. p. 489.

 I have one fact to state, that says more than a hundred volumes can say, against placing any confidence whatever in any document outside of the New Testament, so far as countenance, support, or authority is regarded, for any tenet, practice, or tradition, not found endorsed by some one or more of the apostolic school. It is a fact, clear and indisputable, that in less than fifteen years after the ascension of the Messiah, circumcision would have been imposed on the gentile christians, by a large and respectable number of ministers and others, even from the mother church and city of Jerusalem too, had the apostles been then dead.   The case is this : certain men came down from Judea to Antioch, in Syria, a very large and respectable church, and there, in the presence of Paul and Barnabas, boldly debated, and for some time with considerable warmth disputed with them, in support of the proposition that—*The gentile brethren who had been baptized must be circumcised, and keep the law of Moses, on peril of damnation*. One thing is as clear as the sun from this fact ; *that not yet in Judea, nor Jerusalem, nor Antioch, was the notion that baptism came in the room of circumcision*, else such a question never could have arisen ; or if it had, could have been very easily decided.   It seems that the church in Antioch was not fully satisfied on hearing the whole debate between these great men, but sent Paul and Barnabas, and others with them, up to Jerusalem, to have a grand conference on the question, in the presence of apostles, elders, and the whole church assembled.   There was a meeting held for the purpose, and a considerable debate, in which Peter, Paul, and James distinguished themselves.   It was decided that those brethren from Judea, that had gone down to Antioch, were wrong.   Yet it called for a general epistle, dictated by James, and borne by chosen messengers, to disabuse the churches of this mistake.   From this whole incident, and the transactions thereupon, I learn two important facts :—

 1st. That either the idea of baptism in room of circumcision had not yet been born, or if it had, the whole assembly in Jerusalem, apostles and all, were miserable debaters, for it would have at once settled the dispute, had Paul or any other apostle stood up and said : " Brethren, do you not know that baptism now stands in the place of circumcision; and, therefore, it is preposterous to circumcise those persons who have received it already in the christian form?" Circumcision is done away, and baptism has just come to fill its place in the new institution. Every man of any intelligence or reflection will feel this argument, and feel, too, that it is a triumphant refutation of that notion.

In writing the letter to the Greek churches, would it not have occurred to some of the twelve apostles, or those present, to say: Brethren, do you not know that as many of you as have been baptized into Christ, have also been spiritually circumcised? for circumcision is now substituted by christian baptism.

But the second and most important inference before us now, is—that there is no authority to be placed in the very highest antiquity—I will say, not in any document only five years after the apostolic age; for if, while the apostles, with a single exception, were all living, and their personal converts settled in myriads all over Judea, Samaria, and Syria, &c., &c., a new institution was brought in, by persons of so much learning and influence as to call forth such an array of wisdom and learning, who will confide in any tradition not evidently apostolic, because we can find distinguished names advocating it in the first and second centuries?

I have yet one argument, out of many more not stated, which I hope to have time to state before my time expires. It is, that circumcision never was done away by any apostolic word or action. *The Jews practiced both circumcision and baptism in their families during the apostolic age* —a matter which would have been intolerable, had the one been divinely ordered in lieu of the other. The proof of this fact which I have to offer, is from Acts xxi. It is full, clear, and, to my mind, perfectly conclusive. Paul, after an absence of fourteen years, visits Jerusalem, after having been in the apostleship to the gentiles seventeen years. On his arrival, he was waited upon by a portion of the brethren, who accosted him with the following words: " Thou seest, brother, how many thousands of the Jews believe, and they are all zealous of the law; and they are informed of thee, that thou teachest all the Jews which are among the gentiles to forsake Moses, saying that they ought not to circumcise their children, nor to walk after the customs. What is it therefore? The multitude will that thou art come," &c. They proceed to request Paul to take upon him a vow—to purify himself, to shave his head, and to be at charges with some others; and all this for the purpose of showing to the Jews, that all that they had heard was nothing, (not true,) but that he walked after the customs. They also added, that, as " for the gentiles who believe, we have written to them that *they* observe no such things." Here, then, it is declared that the gentiles, but not the Jews, had been discharged from such observances. Now, either Paul falsified, or he had not taught the Jews who believed, to cease from circumcising their children—and not Paul only falsified, but all the brethren who advised this course. They all conspired to deceive the church in Jerusalem, touching Paul's customs, or he had not interfered with the circumcision of the children of believing Jews. The proof, then, that circumcision was not done away by any apostolic enactment or teaching, is irresistible ; and, therefore, it cannot be believed that the apostles either believed or taught that baptism had taken the place of circumcision among the Jews. These two arguments, adduced from Acts, 15th and 21st chapters, are alone sufficient, in my humble opinion, to settle this question with every one who can understand them. I hazard nothing in avowing my belief that they will never be answered.

I have now attended to all the prominent points of Mr. Rice's argument, and have given him a few new ones, by way of objections to his propositions, that he may have an opportunity to answer them in his last speech. I call his attention to these most prominent and palpable facts, any one of which is fatal to his assumptions. I hope he will also explain the appendages to infant baptism, the meaning of the exorcism, chrism, and holy salt and spittle, and the opening of the ears, so early associated with infant baptism. I would have been pleased to read from Mr. Taylor some of the copious evidence he affords, that the papal system originated in its elementary principles about the time that infant baptism came into being. The authors of the papal system, according to this most deservedly distinguished opponent of the Oxford tracts, and of infant baptism, if not the same identical persons, were certainly their cotemporaries. But my time is expired.

Wednesday, Nov. 22—1 o'clock, P. M.
[MR. RICE'S CLOSING ADDRESS.]

MR. PRESIDENT—When I sat down, I was about to read to you a kind of epitome of the leading facts in the history of infant baptism, embodying Dr. Wall's conclusions, founded on long and thorough examination. It is as follows:

Wall, vol ii. ch. x. p. 501.—" Lastly, as these evidences are for the first four hundred years, in which there appears one man, Tertullian, that advised the delay of infant baptism in some cases; and one Gregory that did, perhaps, practice such delay in the case of his children, but no society of men so thinking, or so practicing; nor no one man saying it was unlawful to baptize infants: so in the next seven hundred years, there is not so much as one man to be found, that either spoke for, or practiced any such delay. But all the contrary. And when, about the year 1130, one sect among the Albigenses declared against the baptizing of infants, *as being incapable of salvation,* the main body of that people rejected their opinion; and they of them that held that opinion, quickly dwindled away and disappeared; there being no more heard of holding that tenet, till the rising of the German anti-Pedo-baptists, anno, 1522."

Such, briefly, is the testimony of faithful history. There were some remarks and statements in the gentleman's last speech, which, when fairly exposed, must astonish this audience. I shall notice them presently.

Infant baptism, he tells us, cannot increase *maternal affection,* and therefore, there can be no necessity that mothers shall solemnly covenant with God to train their children for his service. Why, then, I ask, does he, in his writings, put forth so many complaints that parents do greatly neglect the religious training of their children, and so repeated exhortations to greater fidelity? Will his complaints and exhortations have greater influence with parents, than a solemn promise to God to do their duty, and the encouragement derived from his promise of the needed assistance? Why, according to his logic, it was wholly unnecessary that God should ever have made a covenant with men. For it certainly is their interest to serve him; and self-love cannot be increased by a promise or a covenant! But the truth is, that neither parental affection in the one case, nor self-interest in the other, is sufficient to induce the regular and faithful discharge of difficult duties.·

In regard to female communion, I will only remark, that if the gentleman will point out to us the passage of Scripture which either directly commands it, or records a clear example of it, I will be prepared to attend to it.

He tells you, I admitted that baptism is not a *door* into the church. I admitted no such thing. I said, that I was not at all strenuous about the use of that particular word; though I did not admit that it had been incorrectly employed. Baptism, I have repeatedly said, is a rite for the recognition of membership in the church of Christ. Whether the word *door* is correctly employed in regard to it, is a very unimportant matter.

The circumcision of the Shechemites by Jacob's sons, brought forward by Mr. Campbell to prove that this ordinance did not require of adults, a profession of faith, he acknowledges, was a *very ugly affair.* Still, he is strongly disposed to urge, that it was scripturally done! He cannot bring himself to believe, that those young men, with hearts burning with revenge, would have circumcised the Shechemites in order to be able to kill them, if they had known that faith was a pre-requisite to its reception!!! And this is the only instance he has been able to produce to sustain his assertion, that circumcision did not require piety in adult persons—an assertion, as I have proved, directly contradictory to the teachings of the inspired Paul. Paul says, " Circumcision verily profiteth, *if thou keep the law;* but if thou be a breaker of the law, thy circumcision is made uncircumcision." Again; he teaches, contrary to the doctrine of Mr. C., that " he is not a Jew which is one outwardly; neither is that circumcision which is outward in the flesh; but he is a Jew which is one inwardly; and circumcision is that of the heart, in the Spirit; whose praise is not of men, but of God." The clear meaning of this language is, that the external rite was worth nothing without the inward grace—true piety. But the gentleman (who finds many curious *figures*) told us, circumcision was here used *figuratively.* But when Paul said, " circumcision verily profiteth, *if thou keep the law,*" did he mean *figurative circumcision?* How the cause of my friend labors !

He says, I certainly asserted that the christian church was under the moral law. I certainly said, that the moral law is obligatory on the church—that under both dispensations, it has been received and obeyed. But he charged me with having said, that the moral law IS THE CONSTITUTION OF THE CHRISTIAN CHURCH. Can he see no difference between its being obligatory on the church, and its being the *constitution* of the church? I should, indeed, be astonished if he were so blind.

To disprove the identity of the church under the old and new dispensations, Mr. Campbell quotes the passage: " The law and the prophets were until John: since that time the kingdom of God is preached, and every man presseth into it," Luke xvi. 16. But has not he published it as his faith, that the christian church, which he seems here to understand by the kingdom of God, was not set up till after Christ had risen from the dead? How, then, could men press into it before it existed? So the gentleman is obliged to cross his own track, and to twist and turn in all directions to keep his head above water, fond as he is of water.—[A laugh.]

The phrase " kingdom of heaven," which commonly has the same meaning as the kingdom of God in this passage, is translated by him, " the *reign of heaven;*" and he has told us that a *reign* is one thing, and a *kingdom* quite another. The expressions " kingdom of heaven," or " kingdom of God;" are frequently employed with reference to the more spiritual modes of worship under the new dispensation.

I am quite pleased to hear him quote the passage from Daniel's prophecy : " And in the days of these kings shall the God of heaven *set up* a kingdom which shall never be destroyed." I was looking for him to bring forward this passage ; for I had read his debate with McCalla, and had seen the words " *set up* " printed in capitals. He was careful, however, to pay no attention to the inspired explanation of the expression which I had previously read. In the council at Jerusalem James said : " And to this agree the words of the prophets ; as it is written, after this I will return, and will build again the tabernacle of David, which is fallen down ; and I will build again the ruins thereof, and I will set it up ; that the residue of men might seek after the Lord, and all the gentiles, upon whom my name is called, saith the Lord, who doeth all these things," Acts xv. Here we learn that the tabernacle which had fallen down was to be re-built. Does this look like building a *new tabernacle ?* It is worthy of remark that the Hebrew word used by Amos, in the passage quoted by James, the Chaldaic word used by Daniel, and the Septuagint translation, all have the same meaning, viz. : *to cause to stand.* The meaning of the passage then is : that God would raise up and establish his church which had been so long oppressed and down-trodden.

Mr. Campbell has made a most violent attack upon the *old fathers*. I will not quote Dr. Miller ; though I am confident that his views were misrepresented. I will read, however, from another author of very high authority with my friend : I mean Mr. Campbell himself :

Testimony of Christian Fathers.—" Though no article of christian faith, nor item of christian practice can, legitimately, rest upon any testimony, reasoning, or authority out of the sacred writings of the apostles, were it only one day after their decease ; *yet the views and practices of those who were the contemporaries, or the pupils of the apostles and their immediate successors, may be adduced as corroborating evidence of the truths taught, and the practices enjoined by the apostles ; and as such may be cited ;* still bearing in mind, that, where the testimony of the apostles ends, christian faith necessarily terminates."—*Christian System*, p. 227.

This is not all. Mr. Campbell has actually introduced, as a good and competent witness, Origen, one of those " old wives," whose testimony he now contemns. He says : " *Origen, though so great a visionary, is, nevertheless, a competent witness in any question of fact.*"—*Ibid.* p. 233. And did not I introduce him simply as a witness to prove a matter of fact ? Cyprian, too, whom he now pronounces so great a simpleton, is one of the important witnesses introduced by Mr. Campbell to prove his doctrine of *baptismal regeneration !* These fathers were excellent witnesses when he could make capital of their testimony ; but now it is not worth a straw !

I am not through with Mr. Campbell yet. In the Milennial Harbinger, vol. ii. Extra pp. 37, 38, he reproves a Mr. Broaddus for discrediting the testimony of these very fathers, in the following style :—

" But would it not have been more in accordance with reason, and more satisfactory to his readers, to have adduced, or attempted to have adduced, some contradictory testimony, or some document to set aside or impair my eleventh proposition ? Is all antiquity so silent on the views of my opponent, as not to furnish one document. hint, or allusion in vindication of his views of the point at issue ? [*Argumentum ad hominem.*]

My eleventh proposition is in the following words : ' All the apostolical fathers, as they are called, all the pupils of the apostles, and all the ecclesiastical writers of note, of the first four centuries, whose writings have come down to us, allude to and speak of christian immersion, &c. as the regeneration and remission of sins spoken of in the New Testament.' This proposition I have sustained, Andrew Broaddus himself being judge: for he has not brought a shadow of proof to the contrary. But there is a paragraph preceding this proposition in the Extra, which I must transcribe for the sake of those who may not have it to refer to. It explains the use, the *sole use*, we make of the numerous and decisive witnesses we summon to sustain this proposition. It reads thus—" [Already quoted.]

To discredit the testimony of these VENERABLE ANCIENTS, *as they are called, my friend alledges their* OPINIONS *on other matters, showing how whimsical they were in some things.* Grant it: and what then? Does any man's private opinion discredit his testimony on any question of fact? If so, how do we receive the canonical books of the New Testament? Upon the very testimony here adduced, so far as we regard human testimony at all. Andrew does not see where his imputations terminate. [Nor my friend, Mr. Campbell, neither!] But he admits them to be competent witnesses of facts, and would take them out of our hands by this question, ' When Origen testifies that infants were baptized for the remission of sins, does he not as clearly testify that infants were baptized, as that they were baptized for the remission of sins?' I say, yes: and who says, no? And have I not always admitted that in Origen's time, infants were immersed? have I not affirmed, upon the testimony of Tertullian and Origen, that in Tertullian's time, infants, in some cases, began to be immersed?! How impertinant to the subject are these allegations against the *formidable host of witnesses during four hundred years!* And is this all that can be offered upon or against my eleventh proposition?"

Here we have Mr. Campbell directly against Mr. Campbell! I am amazed to see such a man as Mr. Campbell place himself in such a predicament as this! It is most astonishing indeed!

The gentleman has told us, that, but for the opposition of the apostles, circumcision would have been introduced into the christian church, within fifteen years from the day of Pentecost; and he thinks, if baptism came in place of circumcision, certainly the apostles, assembled at Jerusalem to determine the question concerning circumcising the gentile believers, would have so stated. It was wholly unnecessary that they should say so. They decided, that circumcision, the old seal, was no longer binding—that only baptism, the new seal, was now obligatory. But, as I have repeatedly said, I might admit that baptism did not come precisely in place of circumcision, and yet triumphantly defend the doctrine for which I am contending.

My friend, Mr. C., says, he could defend the reputation of Mr. Jones, as a faithful historian. No man, I assert, can successfully defend him from the charge of having most grossly garbled the testimony of Perrin. It is absolutely certain, as I have proved, that he, in quoting that author, omitted infant baptism, and supplied " baptism according to the primitive church;" in order to conceal the fact, that the Waldenses were Pedobaptists! An attempt to defend such conduct, would very nearly make the gentleman himself *particeps criminis.*

I will now close my address by a brief recapitulation of the argument. *First*—As strong presumptive evidence in favor of the doctrine of infant baptism, I stated the fact, admitted by Mr. Campbell, that the overwhelming majority of Christendom, in all ages, so far back as history can inform us, not of the ignorant and superstitious only, or chiefly, but of the wise and the good, have firmly believed it to be taught in the Bible. The Bible, as Mr. C. admits, is, on all important points, a plain book. The fact, then, that it has been so universally understood by those who have

27

carefully studied it, to teach this doctrine, is very strong presumptive evidence in its favor.

Second—Concerning the commission given the apostles, I have stated several facts. 1. That it is not a commission *to organize a new church*, but to extend the boundaries of one already in existence. 2. That it does not specify infants or adults as proper subjects of baptism, but says, "Go make disciples of *all nations*—baptizing them—the nations." 3. That it does not say, that in all cases, or in any case, teaching must precede baptizing; and, therefore, this question must be determined from other sources of evidence. 4. That it does require all to be baptized who are, by God's law, entitled to membership in the church. This Mr. C. does not deny.

The great question, then, is—who, or what characters are entitled to membership in the church? To find an answer to this question we went to its organization. The church I defined to be a body of people, separated from the world, for the service of God, with ordinances of divine appointment, and a door of entrance, or rite, for the recognition of membership. To this definition, or description, Mr. C. has not objected. Now consider the following facts:

1. It is a fact, that we find such a body organized in the family of Abraham, the father of believers. From the time of this organization, God spoke of them as "*my people;*" and the inspired writers call them the *church.* 2. It is a fact, indisputable, that believers, and their children, were constituted members of this church. 3. It is a fact, that they remained together in the church to the moment when our Savior gave the commission to the apostles to preach the gospel to every creature. 4. It is a fact, that the commission does not exclude the children of believers. This is an important fact; because we know, that the apostles had grown up in a church which embraced the children of professed believers; and we know, that their Jewish prejudices were exceedingly strong. Yet, notwithstanding their prejudices, which must have inclined them still to retain children in the church, our Savior gave not the slightest intimation of a purpose to alter the law of membership. I have found a positive law for putting the children of believers into the church. *Where, I ask, is the law for excluding them?* The gentleman has not produced such a law; and he cannot. Consequently, they still are entitled to membership; and, of course, to baptism—the initiatory ordinance.

I have proved, that the christian church is the same into which God did put the children of believers. What do we understand by *ecclesiastical identity?* I illustrated this point by the principles of *political identity.* How do we know that the commonwealth of Kentucky is the same political body that existed under this name forty years ago? Because "the sovereign people" still reign; and the constitution, in all its essential features, is the same. Apply the same principles to the identity of the church. Let me again state the incontrovertible FACTS which prove the church to be the same under the Jewish and Christian dispensations:

1. It is a fact, that, under both dispensations, the church worships and serves the same God.

2. It is a fact, that she receives and obeys the same moral law.

3. It is a fact, that, under both dispensations, the church receives and trusts in the same gospel. Paul teaches, that the Gospel was preached

to Abraham, (Gal. iii. 8,) and to the Jews in the wilderness, (Heb. iv. 2.) And it is a fact, that all the prominent doctrines of the gospel are taught in the Old Testament—such as the divinity and humanity of Christ, the fall and depravity of man, the atonement, sanctification by the Holy Spirit, future rewards and punishments, the resurrection; repentance, faith and reformation, as conditions of salvation. Every important doctrine of the gospel is taught in the Old Testament.

4. The conditions of membership in the church are the same under both dispensations. Adults, as I have proved, were required to profess faith in the true God, and a purpose to serve him, before they could be circumcised; and then they brought their children into the church with them. Precisely so it is in the christian church.

5. I have proved, that the christian church enjoys her spiritual blessings under the covenant made with Abraham. This I proved by several incontrovertible *facts:* 1st. The covenant with Abraham was *confirmed in Christ;* (Gal. iii. 17.) 2d. It contained *the gospel;* (Gal. iii. 8.) 3d. It constituted Abraham the *father of all believers*—the father of the christian church; (Gal. iii. 29.) 4th. It is never in the Scriptures called *old*, and never said to have *passed away.* The covenant at Sinai, the temporary addition to it, is called old; because, as Paul says, it "decayeth and waxeth old," and "is ready to vanish away;" Heb. viii. 13. But the Abrahamic covenant is never represented as vanishing away. This covenant originally embraced believers and their children; and, of course, it embraces them still.

6. I turned to the prophecies, and proved, that promises great and precious were made to the church under the old dispensation, to comfort her in her affliction, which never were, nor could be fulfilled until the new dispensation was introduced. And if, as Mr. Campbell contends, the Jewish church ceased to exist as the church of God, at the commencement of the new dispensation; those promises never were, and never can be fulfilled! The only reply the gentleman has made to this unanswerable argument, is—that these prophecies are irrelevant!!!

7. I proved the identity of the church unanswerably by the 11th chapter of the Epistle to the Romans. The olive-tree, it is admitted, means the christian church. Now it is a fact, that from this church the unbelieving Jews were broken off—excommunicated; and the believing gentiles were grafted into the same tree—introduced into the same church. And when the Jews shall be converted, they are to be again grafted into *their own olive-tree*, of which they were *the natural branches*—into *their own church*, from which they were expelled. *The church under both dispensations is the same.*

I have now produced much more evidence to prove the identity of the church under the two dispensations, than can be brought forward to establish the identity of the commonwealth of Kentucky during the last forty years.

Now mark the fact—BELIEVERS AND THEIR CHILDREN WERE PUT INTO THIS CHURCH BY POSITIVE LAW OF GOD. There is no law for excluding either the one or the other. The children of believers, therefore, still are entitled to membership in the church, and consequently to baptism, the initiatory ordinance. *The commission requires their baptism.*

The only difference between the two dispensations, so far as the present discussion is concerned, is—that the civil and ceremonial laws of the old dispensation have passed away, and given place to a few simple ordinances, adapted to the extension of the church to all nations. Those laws, as I have proved, were *added* to the Abrahamic covenant for a *specific purpose*—"because of transgression"—and for *a limited time*—till the promised seed should come. When Christ came and died on the cross, the civil and ceremonial laws of the church expired by virtue of their own limitation; and the officers appointed to execute them, went out of office. Just so the legislature of Kentucky might enact a number of laws to meet a particular exigency, to be in force twenty years. At the end of that period those laws would cease to be binding, having answered the purposes for which they were enacted; and all officers appointed to carry them into effect, would go out of office. But no man in his senses would pretend, that the expiration of those temporary enactments could destroy the identity of the commonwealth. No more could the passing away of the ceremonial laws of the old dispensation, affect the identity of the church. The evidence is, therefore, most conclusive, that the church of Christ is the same church into which believers and their children were introduced by God, and from which neither have ever been excluded.

I have invited your attention to household or family baptisms. I confined my remarks to the family of Lydia. The inspired historian says, that Lydia believed, and that she and her household were baptized; but he does not say, that the household believed. We write like Luke, whether we *act* like him or not. Our opponents do not write like him; and the conclusion is obvious, that they do not practice as he and the apostles did.

I have proved by the history of the church, that for fifteen hundred years after the death of Christ, not a writer can be found maintaining, that the baptism of infants was unscriptural, excepting, perhaps, a small sect called Petrobrussians. IRENEUS, the disciple of Polycarp, the disciple of the apostle John, speaks of it as a matter universally understood and admitted. Tertullian, in the beginning of the third century, opposes it, but does not venture to pronounce it either unscriptural, or contrary to the universal practice of the church. His opposition, therefore, makes him a more important witness to us; for certainly he would oppose it with the strongest arguments he could command.

Origen, a few years later, whose talents, learning and piety are so highly commended by Jones, my friend's favorite historian, testifies that the whole church, from the time of the apostles, and by their direction, did practice infant baptism. No man could have possessed more fully the qualifications necessary to give weight to his testimony. He had traveled extensively, had resided in Alexandria, in Rome, and in Palestine; he was a man of great learning and great celebrity. If any man in that day knew what had been the practice of the church, he was the man. And my friend himself admits, that as to matters of fact, he was a competent witness.

Cyprian, and the council at Carthage, Jerom, Augustine, Pelagius, and many others, bear similar testimony. They tell us they never heard of any controversy about it, or of a contrary practice. Pelagius, though a denial of the doctrine would have relieved him from serious embarrassments, was constrained to testify that he had never known even the most impious heretic to deny it.

The WALDENSES and ALBIGENSES—those eminent witnesses for the truth in the dark ages—complete the chain of testimony from the apostles to the Reformation of the 16th century. With the exception of the insignificant sect called Petrobrusaians, all admitted infant baptism to be according to the Scriptures.

Here is evidence conclusive from the Scriptures and from history. I have omitted much that might have been introduced, because I conceived it unnecessary to multiply arguments. One good argument my friend has told us is enough. I have given many.

In conclusion, I offer one more argument. It is this—if it should turn out that infant baptism is unscriptural, and that Mr. Campbell's views of immersion as the only valid baptism, are true ; *we are forced to the conclusion, that for several centuries there was no church of Christ on earth!* From a very early period the great body of christian ministers received baptism in infancy, and, of course, were unbaptized. As we descend in the history of the church, infant baptism becomes the only baptism administered. Dr. Gill, I think, has admitted that for several centuries there were no adult baptisms ; and it is not denied that from the thirteenth century *baptism* was very commonly administered by pouring and sprinkling. So that, by the prevalence of infant baptism, and of pouring and sprinkling, christian baptism was lost, if the doctrine of Mr. C. be true, and there was on earth no church of Christ. We are, then, obliged to believe that the Savior's promise has failed ; and " the gates of hell " did prevail against his church!!! Robertson, the celebrated anti-Pedo-baptist historian, says : " Baptism rose pure in the east, rolled westward, obscured in lustre, and was finally *lost* amongst attenuated particles, shades, nonentities, and monsters ! " I think I have given his words exactly.

Mr. Campbell will say that the Greek church has always immersed, and has preserved scriptural baptism. But if his doctrine be true, the Greek church is not a true church, for she has always practiced the baptism of infants. The conclusion, then, returns upon us, that for centuries there was not a church of Christ on earth ; and the promise of the Savior has failed !

In the *Milennial Harbinger* I observe, that Mr. Campbell proves, that there are some christians among " the sects" by this very argument. For, he argues, if there are not, the church of Christ has ceased to exist ; which, he says, it will not do to admit. Now, he informs us, that he has proved immersion to be the only apostolic or christian baptism, and infant baptism to be a human tradition. Then he has proved, that the ordinance of baptism has been lost. And who, I ask, had the authority to restore it? An unbaptized person certainly is not authorized to administer baptism.

The gentleman has labored faithfully to destroy the validity of his own baptism ! If baptism by pouring or sprinkling is not valid, and if infant baptism is worthless, his own baptism is not worth a straw ; for it has descended from infant baptism and from pouring. If the fountain be corrupt, is not the stream equally so ? So it would seem, he has succeeded in demonstrating, that our Savior has failed to fulfill his promise, and that he himself and all his church are unbaptized ! If he maintains, that an unbaptized man may administer baptism, I call for the passage of Scripture that authorizes it ; and he professes always to give a " Thus saith the Lord," for his faith and his practice.

I now cheerfully leave the audience to judge of the force of the facts and arguments I have presented, and to decide, in view of their responsibility to God, whether I have proved that the infant of a believing parent is a scriptural subject of baptism.—[*Time expired.*

2 N

Wednesday, Nov. 22—1½ *o'clock, P. M.*
[MR. CAMPBELL'S CLOSING REPLY.]

MR. PRESIDENT—I am peculiarly gratified to hear so much read from the Christian System and Milennial Harbinger. I did not expect to hear so much from these works, in such ample and perfect confirmation of what I am now endeavoring to sustain, The gentleman will, I hope, frequently assist our efforts in this way.

I have, occasionally, to complain of his singular talent and proficiency in the art of forming false issues. What, sir, was the issue formed on the extracts read from Miller, Cyprian, and others?—that their testimony on matters of fact transpiring in their times, is *in*credible !! Mr. Rice has been laboring to prove that their testimony *is* credible. Is that the issue ? No, sir; you know, and this audience and Mr. Rice know, that I admit their testimony, when fairly made out, on questions of fact. There is no issue—no controversy, on that subject, at all. In all my debates, with infidels, Romanists, and sectarians, I have admitted their testimony on questions of fact. Was there any other fact in the extract from St. Cyprian, but that he was a dupe of the most visionary and romantic character !

Mr. Rice. Allow me to ask a question. Did not I say, distinctly, that I introduced these fathers as witnesses to facts?

Mr. Campbell. If the gentleman did so, I do not oppose them as such. I oppose them as authorities for opinions or religious institutions; and for this purpose, and no other, read I the extracts from Dr. Miller, all of which went to prove, that, outside of the Bible, of the New Testament, there is no dependence to be put in them, for any of their opinions, customs, usages, ordinances, ceremonies whatever. I will receive the solemn affirmation of a Quaker, in support of a fact which he saw, despite of all his visions and imaginations in matters of religion. But, neither St. Cyprian, nor any of the fathers, can depose to facts that happened in other countries, or before they were born : therefore we have no issue of that sort before us.

I contend that infant baptism, like infant communion, grew out of the reasonings, or inferences, or dreams of such men. No one testifies that he saw an apostle baptize an infant. No one, for two hundred years after Christ's birth, has even named *infant baptism.* There is not a book on earth that can be produced—no Greek or Latin father of that period, that has recorded the words, "*infant baptism,*" or ever used baptism with allusion to an infant. Tertullian, Mr. Rice says, was opposed to it. He is the first writer in all the annals of the church that has named it ; and no one can tell whether he meant babes or boys. Pelagius, who lived two hundred years after Tertullian, is frequently quoted by Pedobaptists, with approbation of his great talents and great learning, as deposing that he never heard of any one, that he never knew any one, who denied infant baptism. If so, then he proves himself ignorant of church history : for Tertullian opposed it, as Mr. Rice says, and as I affirm.

No one can explain the institution of the catechumens, trained in the early christian churches, for baptism, on the ground of the practice of infant baptism. But when I hear Mr. Rice and others talking about the probable high antiquity of infant baptism, tracing it up to Ireneus' or Tertullian's time, I am struck with the singular illusion that flits before their fancy. They speak of one or two hundred years as a period of short duration—as if, in so short a time after Christ, any great errors, or apostasies, or innovations could have occurred !   What a delusion !—two hundred years !   Why, sir, our federal government, our very national existence, is less than the life of one man ; and what changes !—what innovations !—what departures from first principles !—what corruptions ! —how many political castes, sects, parties, shibboleths !—and what constructions, and interpretations, and debates about the meaning of some parts of the constitution, the bills of rights, and even our declaration of independence !   How few men could now relate, from his memory or his own reading, the great political events of this period—the public assemblies, conventions, and changes !   And yet we live in an age of books, pamphlets, magazines, newspapers, issuing from all sorts of printing presses, and in such numbers and sizes that Kentucky might all be carpeted with the millions of sheets that issue in almost one year from the American press.   When to this we add our canals, rivers, rail-roads, steam-boats, and steam-ships, (by which we have reduced time and space to the mere tythe of other times and spaces,) and contrast all these advantages with an age of a few books and parchments, without printing offices, post-offices, post-roads, &c., &c., what shall we think of the mental hallucination of those who talk of one, two, or three hundred years after Christ, as necessarily a more enlightened, pure, and incorrupt period of christianity, than the present !   It is a monstrous delusion.   Taylor and others have shown that all the abominations of popery were hatched in the second century ; and Paul, of still higher authority and greater learning, says, " even *already* the MYSTERY OF INIQUITY *inwardly works!!*"

The gentleman has at length responded something to the question about the door : but yet the mystery remains !   I still ask—but I ask in vain—If Presbyterian infants are born in Christ's church, by virtue of the flesh of one of their parents ; and if baptism be still regarded substantially as a door, *into what does it introduce them?*"   Whenever he answers this, he will have annihilated at least one half of all his logic and rhetoric upon this question.   This is an *argumentum ad hominem.*   It is, in this case, as will probably appear in my next proposition, however, a good and valid argument.

Mr. Rice assumes the identity of " the commonwealth of Israel" and the christian church as one church of God, one and the same ecclesiastical institution, on which to found the right of infants of a certain class of parents to baptism ; and proceeds to prove that identity by sundry arguments, such as :—

1st. That the same God reigns over the Jewish and Christian communities.   This, if true, we showed, constitutes no proof of the identity of any two communities or their institutions : because it proves too much. The same God reigns over Massachusetts, Kentucky, and old England ; and does that prove that these communities are one and the same institution ?   But we do not admit, and have demonstrated that they have not the same identical king : for Jesus Christ was born to be a king, and was not a king before he was born—John xviii. 37.   God himself was king over Israel, as the God of the Hebrews ; but his Son is now made king— made Lord and King.   It is not abstract Divinity, nor Trinity, but Jesus the Messiah, that is king of the church.   All authority was given to him for this purpose.

2. But they have the same moral law, or fundamental code.   This, if admitted, is as true of the patriarchs, New Englanders, and Pennsylvanians.   They acknowledge the same great principles, and are obliged by

them; but that does not make these all one and the same body politic, the same identical, political communities.

3. But the Jews and Christians have the same gospel. Few men dare make such an assertion. The patriarchs, Jews and Christians, have one gospel: as England and France have one alphabet, but not one and the same language. The ceremonial of the Jews had the *types* of our gospel. But the christian gospel is based on three facts which transpired at the end of the Jewish dispensation! These are the death, burial, and resurrection of Christ. "And in the end of the Jewish age did the Messiah put away sin by the sacrifice of himself." We have had various gospels in the history of religion. The Jews' gospel, as preached to the Jews in the wilderness, Paul shows, Heb. iv., was the rest in Canaan. Ours is the antitype of Canaan, and so throughout. Having the same gospel does not, however, make the communities one; for then England, the United States, patriarch and Jews, are one community.

But the gentleman descends into special points of resemblance, from which he next seeks to prove the churches identical. He obviously needs something more specific than these three vague generalities. He alledges:

1. The Jews and Christians have the same mediator. Is this true? Moses mediated that covenant; but Paul says, "Jesus is the mediator of a better covenant, established upon better promises." Neither was Aaron the high-priest and standing mediator between Israel and God, the same identical mediator with the high-priest of our religion. Jesus is a better high-priest, lawgiver, and mediator, than Moses, Aaron and his sons. If Mr. R. looks beyond the Jewish dispensation for his idea of a mediator, it will prove too much: for then, patriarchs, Jews, and Christians are identically the same community.

He then instances, in his second and third items, the same doctrine of justification, and the same doctrine of sanctification—but these extend through all dispensations, so far as there is any identity, and would make them all one and the same community. And certainly the apostles give us quite a dissertation on the difference between the righteousness of the law and the righteousness of faith. He will also add to his list of identity, the resurrection of the dead and eternal life, with all the same conditions of salvation!! Until, indeed, he has falsified the sayings of Paul and the other apostles, who teach that we have a "*better covenant,*" "*better promises,*" a "*better mediator,*" a better high-priest, a better inheritance, better sacrifices, better altars, and *a new institution.* Yet, with Mr. Rice, they are all identically the same!!

Paul, moreover, argues from the change in the christian priesthood, being such as it is, there must also be a change in the law and constitution of acceptance. He establishes this not only in the seventh chapter, but throughout all the epistle to the Hebrews. Can any one conversant with the doctrines taught by John the Baptist in preparing the way for Christ's religion, and the contrasts drawn by Jesus himself between the teachings of former times and his own, and the glorious developments of the apostles after they received the promised gift of the Holy Spirit— that the Old Testament presents the same conditions of salvation as the New. Could any one be saved now, who disdains the christian ordinances—and are these the same as the Jewish?

But, chief of all, the gentleman appeared to rely upon the assumed fact, that they have the same covenant or constitution. This is, indeed, the main point—for if all other points of similarity and coincidence were the same, a change here will be fatal; and this is just the very point in which he, and all others on his side of the question, have always pre-eminently failed. I think it of no consequence to trace other matters of alledged similarity or identity. It is here the work of refutation is always complete, and to all minds intelligible. God found fault with the Jewish institution and the people under it, and solemnly promised to make a *new* constitution seven hundred years before the christian era. Now all the logic and rhetoric in the world will not prove that a *new* and an *old* constitution are identically the same thing. *In every single pro-vision of the New, it is a perfect contrast,* as we have shown, *with all the provisions of the old.* It has even changed the very names "*Isra-el* " and "*the children of Abraham,*" so far as to make the former and the latter indicate a spiritual people, believing Jews and gentiles, for "*the children of the flesh* are no longer counted for the seed.*" It is, then, a *new* covenant, *new* promises, a new people, new institutions, new laws, new terms of communion, a new inheritance; " All old things," indeed, " have passed away, and, behold, all things have become new:" for a Jew in Christ is just as new a creation, as a gentile in him. But of this, more in the sequel.

Knowing, however, that the design of the argument for identity was to establish an identity of infant church-membership, as they call it, on the alledged identity of circumcision and baptism, I especially labored that point. For here is the whole true issue of the question of identity. All intelligent Pedo-baptists know it, and multitudes of them candidly ac-knowledge it: for this very reason, Calvin took this ground. I, therefore, drew out in extenso, no less than sixteen points of essential difference between circumcision and baptism, in the faith and practice of even Pedo-baptists themselves. And, to my no little surprise, the gentleman waived this, the main issue of the whole matter, and contented himself with some few vague generalities, which, were they all true and veritable, fall short, by a hundred particulars, in making out the case of identity. These es-sential points of dissimilarity, you will remember, are:

1. Only males were subjects of circumcision. It belonged, then, to but half the Jewish church.

2. Infant males were circumcised the eighth day.

3. Adult males circumcised themselves.

4. Infant males were circumcised by their own parents.

5. Infant and adult servants were circumcised neither on *flesh* nor *faith*, but *as property.* A point, this, which Mr. Rice strangely overlooked.

6. Circumcision was not the door into the Jewish church. It was four hundred years older than the Jewish church, and introduced neither Isaac, Ishmael, Jacob, or Esau into any Jewish or patriarchal church. It never was to a Jew, its proper subject, an initiatory rite.

7. The qualifications for circumcision were *flesh* and *property.* Faith was never propounded, in any case, to a Jew or his servants.

8. Circumcision was not a dedicatory rite. The rites of the dedica-tion of a first-born son, were different in all respects.

9. Circumcision requiring no moral qualification, neither could nor did communicate any spiritual blessing. No person ever put on Christ, or professed faith in circumcision.

10. Idiots were circumcised; for neither intellect itself, nor any exer-cise of it, was necessary to a covenant *in the flesh.*

11. It was a visible, appreciable mark, as all signs are, and such was its main design.

12. It was binding on parents, and not on children. *Circumcise your children.*

13. The right of a child to circumcision, in no case depended upon the faith, the piety, or the morality of parents.

14. Circumcision was a guarantee of certain temporal benefits to a Jew.

15. It was not to be performed in the name of God, nor into the name of any being, in heaven or on earth.

16. The subject of circumcision was a debtor to do the whole law.

These *sixteen* indisputable facts, are truly distinct and demonstrable attributes and properties of circumcision ; each of which differs ; and, of course, the aggregate differs from baptism as now administered by Romanists and Protestants.   Had we deemed it at all important, we could as easily have, in all the other alledged points of identity, made out lists of specifications, either more or less numerous than the preceding.   But that being only to multiply words to no profit, I am content to annihilate infant church-membership, as founded upon the identity of signs and seals. A thousand vague generalities are worth nothing—absolutely worth nothing in a question of *identity.*

Circumcision conferred no spiritual benefit on the Jew, as Paul himself declares ; inasmuch as he makes its chief benefit, that *" unto the nations were committed the oracles of God."*   " What profit is there in circumcision ?" was the question which Paul propounded to himself, and answered, " Chiefly *because they had the oracles of God."*   This was the best thing Paul *could* say : certain it is, it was the best thing he *did* say of circumcision and the Jews' religion.   Salvation was *in* the Jews' religion, *in its ceremonial,* and in *prophecy :* but not really nor truly.   In christianity, salvation is literally, substantively, and truly.   Its civil advantages were numerous.   Its direct benefits were all temporal and earthly. Suppose, for example, A induces B to migrate from the mountains of Kentucky into Lexington, to superintend his business, and promises him a thousand dollars a year for so doing ; but adds, as a further inducement, the social benefits, the literary, scientific, and moral advantages he may enjoy in this Athens of Kentucky.   Would not the actual remuneration, temporal and financial, be the direct and main inducement to his migration and change of residence ?   Just so the direct and immediate advantages to the Jew were all fleshly and temporal ; the spiritual benefits derived to any were altogether exclusive of the covenant and its circumcision, and were derived from the " *good things to come,"* of which it was but a faint, a very faint *shadow,* and not even, as Paul says, " *an exact image."*

It is scarcely necessary again to allude to the conflict we have had about his capital assumption concerning one only, Abrahamic covenant ; which, next to circumcision is, indeed, the main point in this discussion. His view is one covenant with Abraham, and that an ecclesiastic one, having the *seal* of circumcision !   He thus puts infants into the church, and now he asks for a precept to put them out.   That there were three distinct covenants made with Abraham, based on *three* promises—two made in Urr of Chaldea, primary and all-comprehensive, and one in Canaan— has been fully proved.   These three covenants are different in *name, time, place,* and circumstances, recorded in Gen. 12th, 15th, and 17th chapters, commented on by Paul to the Romans, Galatians, and Hebrews.   These covenants were not made with all Israel as a national covenant ; but a national covenant based on two of them was developed, proclaimed, acceded to, and ratified with all Israel at Horeb. Therefore, all the other covenants belonging to the seed of Abraham, besides this one with all Israel, are properly called covenants made with Abraham, covenants of promise, as denominated by Paul to the Romans and the Ephesians. These covenants were severally made with Abraham in the 75th, 86th, and 99th year of his life ; the first of them 430 years before the law or national covenant at Horeb, to which circumcision and the passover were finally added with the law of dedication.

In his last speech the gentleman has made another effort to sustain his position, that the Jews and christians have the same moral law, *as a constitution.* That the moral principles contained in the decalogue are immutable principles, and that they are, and have always been, the supreme law of mind, in every portion of God's moral creation, I, in common with all intelligent christians, have not only admitted, but always plead. But that they are, as promulged by Moses, and incorporated on Mount Sinai with other enactments and ordinances, the special constitution of Christ's church, as they were then of the commonwealth of Israel, is what he seeks to maintain, and what I deny. This is the only issue in the case; because they were, as principles of piety and humanity, as much the law of paradise, or of the patriarchal institution, as of the Jewish or christian. The gentleman's argument would prove the identity of all dispensations, as well as that of the Jewish and christian.

And with him, too, the doctrine of eternal life, and a future state of rewards and punishments, was identically the same among Jews and christians. There is no greater mistake in all his assumptions than this one: Moses has not incorporated one expression, in all the Jewish institution, on the subject of a future state. It is neither named, nor alluded to, from the Exodus to the last word of Deuteronomy. Bishop Warburton, than whom, in his day, the church of England had no man of superior learning or talents, the greatest antiquarian and archæologist amongst English prelates, in his truly learned treatise on the divine legation of Moses, a work which every student of theology ought to read, has, I do not say how logically constructed, an argument, in proof that God sent Moses ; merely, from the fact, that in all the Jewish institution proper, as given by Moses, there is not one word about a future state. The fact is true, but whether his argument be true is another question. The knowledge of a future life the Jews had; but not from their covenant nor from Moses, but from the patriarchs. Enoch prophesied of the final judgment. The patriarchs and christians are rather more identical in the fact, though not in the development of it, than the Jews and christians.

I am taught by my friend, Mr. Rice, to omit nothing in a general recapitulation, at least of his failures to notice my issues and arguments. Many present will recollect the capital he made out of my omission to notice a few specifications of *baptizo* in his concluding speech on Saturday night. My not showing to his satisfaction how Judith, in the Apocrypha, bathed in the camp, at a fountain of water; and of how little profit a bath was to Sirach's legally unclean person, if afterwards he touched a dead body ; and how a plaster could be dipped in breast-milk, in the days of Hippocrates, who also commanded the same preparation to be dipped in white Egyptian oil, and flies into the oil of roses ! Because I omitted to honor these, and some other matters equally minute and insignificant, with a

formal notice and refutation, a matter to which a school-boy is competent,
the gentleman mustered them in his final cloud of witnesses, of his triumphant refutation of immersion! I do not say, however, that I shall
follow his example, in attending to matters *equally minute* and irrelevant,
when I state the fact, that in no one case in the discussion of this proposition, would the gentleman meet me on any issue tendered by me—such
as circumcision a *seal* to Abraham ; the holy children of parents not both
in the church; household baptism ; baptism in room of circumcision ;
and most of all remarkable, the precept for rejecting, or casting out from
a church relation, the children of the flesh. After so many demands and
vauntings on that subject, that the gentleman should have been so perfectly confounded with the case of Hagar and Ishmael, and the precept
" TO CAST OUT THE OLD COVENANT, AND THE CHILDREN UNDER IT," as
never to presume to reply to it, is really no ordinary occurrence in debate. Had he made any pretence to answer it, it would not have been
quite so singular. But to have passed it in total silence, must have no
little surprised you all. The fact was, in this case, most triumphantly
established ; viz. *that those born merely of the flesh, shall not associate
nor inherit with those born of the Spirit.* This is the law of the christian dispensation.

But I was not content to show that his attempt to make out identity
was abortive in the aggregate and in the detail; that his logic proved too
much for him in all cases. But I gave an induction of particular proofs,
that the christian church is a new institution.

Amongst those proofs were the following:

1. According to the last chapter of Malachi, and the ministry of John
the Baptist, " the law and the prophets," or the Jewish institution, was
to continue only till the preaching of John. " The law and the prophets
were your instructors until John," said Jesus, " but now *the kingdom of
God* is preached, and every man presseth into it," Matt. xi., Luke
xvi. 16.

2. God promised, through Isaiah, chap. xxviii. 16, to lay a new foundation for that glorious church, which, according to the predictions read
from the prophets by Mr. Rice, God was to bring out of the seed, the
nucleus, in the Jewish kingdom. That promise is " Behold I lay in
Zion, *for a foundation*, a stone, a tried stone, a precious corner-stone, a
sure foundation. He that believeth shall not make haste." The gentleman cannot see that all the glorious things spoken by the prophets
concerning the building of the church, and the calling of the gentiles,
that the enlargement of the church of which he spoke, all these splendid things have their foundation intimated here and in other similar passages. The foundation stone of this new institution God would bring
out of the old Zion. So says Daniel.

3. In the days of the Roman empire, or of its kings, according to Daniel, God promised to SET UP a kingdom. " In those days," said he,
" shall the God of heaven set up a kingdom." Of course it could not
be the Jewish; for that had been set up nine hundred years before Daniel was born.

4. On hearing Peter's confession, Matt. xvi., Jesus promised he would
build his church upon it. This was the foundation laid in Zion, on
which the christian church was then about to commence. How the gentleman slurred over, and passed by these great arguments, you have, doubtless, all observed.

5. Paul says, the church is "builded on the foundation of apostles and prophets." Who were the apostles, and who the prophets on which the Jewish church was builded? Is not this as clear as demonstration itself, that the Jewish institution and the Christian church are not identical?

6. Paul taught the Ephesians, and other christians, that Jesus Christ was then making a *new man*, a new body; by uniting believing Jews and Gentiles in one grand association. This was, itself, a reason for changing the covenant of peculiarity, and instituting a new initiation, if I may so speak, for believing Jews and Gentiles.

7. Hence, the New Testament commences with the proclamation of a new institution—a new church; "The kingdom of heaven is at hand." Was this the Mosaic institution that was now coming! As before shown, we must conclude, that " The church of Jesus Christ is a society of faithful men and women, compactly united as one body in Christ Jesus—having one Lord, one faith, one baptism, one spirit, one hope, one and the same God and Father;" a new society that began on the day of Pentecost, and never before.

8. I have also shown, from the 11th Romans, from the figure of the olive-tree, that the manner of incorporation, or bond of union, in the christian church, is radically and essentially new; that faith is substituted for flesh, and that the natural branches are broken off—every one broken off; and that Gentiles and Jews are now grafted by faith, and both stand by faith.

9. But not to be tedious on this head—we farther demonstrated, that, if the two institutions had been, as they certainly are not, identical, still it was compatible with Mr. Rice's own notions of political and ecclesiastic identity to change the right of suffrage, the whole law of naturalization.

10. Was it not shown, from Acts xv., that the idea of baptism coming in room of circumcision was never thought of in the apostolic age?

11. And was it not fully demonstrated, from Acts xxi., that the Jews, with apostolic approbation, continued to circumcise their children during the apostolic age? A fact that flatly contradicts and nullifies the whole Pedo-baptist assumption, that "circumcision is done away, and baptism come in room of it." To these last facts Mr. Rice prudently made no response.

But to conclude, as I have not time to recapitulate and notice every thing, when urged that none were to be baptized but *disciples*, Mr. Rice found an *infant* disciple, of eight days old, in the fact, that Peter asked the Judaizers why they should "tempt God to put a yoke upon the necks of the disciples;" this yoke Mr. R. supposed to be circumcision, although we are told, Acts xv. 5., it was "the law of Moses." The law of Moses was the yoke, and not circumcision, which neither they nor their fathers, as *men*, and not as *babes*, could endure. In refutation of all such fallacious hypothesis, from the commission itself it was shown, that infants are positively prohibited from baptism, inasmuch as all commissions, laws, and statutes, specifying qualifications for any office or privilege, positively exclude all persons not so possessed: as, for example, the law requiring a property qualification in order to suffrage, by making such a requisition, prohibits all persons from that right not possessed of such qualifications. Faith, then, being, in any case, required in order to baptism, not only according to a fair construction of the commission, as reported by all the evangelists, but also in particular cases—as in the case of the eunuch—positively inhibits infants and untaught persons from christian baptism. Not having, then, precept or precedent for infant baptism, nor any fact to support it, may we not conclude with Neander, that—"It is certain Jesus Christ did not ordain infant baptism?"

Had I time, I should have spoken a few things on the degrading and enslaving tendencies of infant baptism, as respects the subject of it in after life; but I see my time is more than expired.

Mr. Rice. May I be permitted to ask a question?

Mr. Campbell. Certainly.

Mr. Rice. I wish to ask, whether my friend has not published that Ireneus means *baptism* when he uses the word *regeneration?*

Mr. Campbell. I believe that the word *regeneration* was used both before and after Ireneus, as equivalent to *baptism;* but whether, in this case, it does certainly so mean, it would be impossible to prove. Still, that the fathers, as they are called, both Greek and Latin, did generally so use the word, I believe. Tertullian, however, who lived after Ireneus, some twenty years, is the first person known on earth who ever mentioned infant baptism.

[By permission of Mr. Campbell, Mr. Rice now read the following extract from the Milennial Harbinger, vol. ii. Extra, pp. 28, 29.]

" In my debate with Mr. Walker and Mr. McCalla, I objected to the substitution of the word *regenerated* for *immerse*, in the extract from IRENEUS, and other of the primitive fathers, as they are called, on the ground of their not being exactly representatives of the same ideas universally. I admitted that sometimes they used the word regenerated for baptized, but not always; and, indeed, not at all, *in the popular sense* of regenerated. Well, now it comes to pass, that I represent ALL the primitive fathers as using the term *regenerated* as equivalent to the term *baptized*. All this is true; and what then? Why, at that time I used the word regenerated as expressive of a *spiritual change*, and found that these fathers spoke of a *spiritual change* as well as we. I could not therefore reconcile this to the exclusive application of the term *regenerated* to the act of immersion; *but on a more accurate and strict examination of their writings, and of the use of this term in the New Testament, I AM ASSURED that they used the term regenerated as equivalent to immersion, and spoke of the spiritual change under other terms and modes of speech,"* &c.

Mr. Rice, my friends, will have the last word; affirmative or negative, he must have the last word. Now this is all for effect. There is nothing in it whatever. Suppose I admit that all the fathers, from Justin Martyr down to Theodoret, 423, used baptism and regeneration as synonymous, and Ireneus generally with the others, though he lived A. D. 178; what does it prove in the case before us? That infant baptism is a Divine institution; because it is *probable*, even *certain*, that Ireneus referred to it, under another name, at the close of the second century!—
[*Time expired.*

[END OF THE SECOND PROPOSITION.]

PROPOSITION THIRD.

Christian Baptism is for the Remission of Past Sins. Mr. Campbell *affirms.* Mr. Rice *denies.*

Thursday, Nov. 23—10 o'clock, A. M.

[MR. CAMPBELL'S OPENING ADDRESS.]

MR. PRESIDENT—and fellow-citizens: the subject before us this morning, I regard as the most important of any that has yet occupied our attention: it is the *design* of baptism. It must be obvious to all, on the slightest reflection, that the importance of right views on the *action* and on the *subject* of baptism, depends wholly on the *design* and meaning of the ordinance: but still, in order to secure its great and manifold advantages, it behooves all, as accountable agents, to proceed intelligently, with reference both to its action, subject and design. Having seen the action of christian baptism in immersion; the subject of it, in the penitent believer; we shall proceed to consider its design, which, we say, *is for the remission of past sins.* These are the terms of the proposition before us, to which we respectfully invite your attention.

Baptism is a divine institution; and, like all other divine institutions, it is both wise and good. It is wise; because it secures some end which could not have been secured so well without it. It is good; because it tends to human happiness. These two attributes must belong to baptism, because they belong to the institution of christianity, which is both wise and good in the aggregate, and consequently, in all its parts. But these attributes belong to all divine institutions. Nature, in all its innumerable systems—in all its primary and secondary ordinances—is one vast system of benevolent and wise adaptations, the supreme end of which is the happiness of sentient, intelligent and moral beings.

It is the part of wisdom to gain the greatest and best results in the shortest possible time, and by the fewest and most simple means. This, and this only, is wisdom. It is the part of benevolence to diffuse as much good over the largest field of existence, and for the longest duration possible, and compatible with the fountain whence it emanates. We must, therefore, regard every means employed, or every ordinance of God (for all means are ordinances, and all ordinances are means) as an essential part of the system, without which it would have been deficient—consequently imperfect.

Our mundane system needs a moon as well as a sun. It needs the companionship of six planets, to give it, not merely the number of perfection, but the perfection of adaptation. Destroy any one of these, and philosophy with her ten thousand tongues would proclaim the extinction of our race. Take away the atmosphere, the water, the light, the caloric, the electricity—take away any of these, and leave all the others, and who of all mankind would live to report the disastrous consequences!

431

From all the realms of nature, then, we must infer that there is no redundancy, no superfluity in any divine system, and especially in the moral and spiritual, which is the highest and best of all. Baptism is, therefore, as essential to christianity, as the moon is to our earth, or as the ocean is, to the vegetable and animal kingdoms. In saying that any one ordinance is essential to the perfection of any one system, as some other ordinance is to the perfection of some other system, we do not, however, mean to say, that these ordinances severally occupy exactly the same place in their respective systems : only that they are each equally indispensible to the system of which they are each an integral part. Baptism is therefore essential to christianity, were we to reason only from the analogies of all the systems that comprise one grand universe. But the precept of Jesus Christ alone, gives it essentiality, authority, and value, without any other consideration whatever. He has solemnly and explicitly commanded faith, repentance and baptism to be preached, in his name, to all nations, beginning at Jerusalem.

He has commanded it [baptism] to be preached for some specific end. That end is clearly stated, and often alluded to, in the gospel of the kingdom over which Jesus reigns, and in which alone the hope of immortality flourishes. We have but three, or perhaps at most four, authentic records of the commission authorising this institution. We shall compare them, and compare them in the order in which they stand.

Matthew reports only the things to be done by the apostles, in establishing the church. " Go, disciple all nations, baptizing them into the name of the Father, and of the Son, and of the Holy Spirit, teaching them to observe all things whatsoever I have commanded you." The things commanded them to teach are not developed here ; nor is the end of any one of the duties prescribed so much as named.

Mark expresses it differently: " Go you into all the world, preach the gospel to every creature." This does not indicate what the elements of the gospel are. It, however, adds, that the reception of it will save every one. The reception of the gospel is thus expressed: " He that believeth and is baptized shall be saved." Unbelief, or a rejection of it, secures condemnation. A belief of it, and baptism into it, secures salvation. So the Evangelist Mark represents it.

Luke gives the substance of the commission in his own words. He mentions neither gospel, nor faith, nor baptism, but simply says, " He commanded repentance and remission of sins to be preached, in his name, among all nations, beginning at Jerusalem." Repentance and remission of sins, with him, then, stand for the whole gospel—for the faith and baptism of the Evangelist Mark. Repentance is, however, but the adjunct of faith, as the remission of sins is of baptism. In preaching repentance and remission, according to Luke, the apostle must therefore have preached faith, repentance, baptism, and remission; for all these terms, or their equivalents, are found in the three versions of the commission now quoted.

There remains yet the testimony of John the apostle. It is more concentrated and laconic than any of the preceding. I shall read the whole passage. John xx. 21—23: On one occasion, Jesus (after he arose from the dead) said to the apostles, "Peace be to you : as my Father commissioned me, so I commission you." Having spoken these words, he immediately breathed on them, saying, " Receive the Holy Spirit." Then he added, " Whose sins soever you remit, they are remitted; and whose sins soever you retain, they are retained." They were, then, evangelically to remit sins and to retain them. How this was done, the history of the apostles, after the descent of the Holy Spirit, must explain.

Guided, then, by the four evangelists, as they have placed the commission before us, we shall open the Acts of Apostles, and attempt a special analysis of the first gospel sermon, reported by Doctor Luke in his Acts of the Apostles.

Before proceeding to the analysis, with a special reference to this grand commission, amplified and spread out before us verbally, by these inspired promulgers of the christian system, we are called upon to state the reason why so much stress ought to be placed upon the second chapter of the Acts—upon the day of Pentecost—upon Peter's sermon—and upon the other scenes and transactions of that day. This is all important to the due appreciation of the argument to be deduced from this portion of the inspired documents which constitute our premises in this argument.

The three divine institutions, of nature, of law, and of gospel, have each a commencement homogeneous with itself. To commence any institution, and to continue it, are very different manifestations of divinity. Creation and Providence, are, therefore, different developments of the divine Father. Hence, the glory of God as Creator, Lawgiver, and Redeemer, appears in perfect harmony with the institutions of nature, of law, and of gospel. From nature we learn wisdom, power and goodness; from law, justice, truth and holiness; from gospel, mercy, condescension, and love; from all these, the eternity, immutability, and infinity of God. The brightest display of each class of perfections was seen in the setting up of these three grand dispensations.

The morning stars sang together, and the sons of God shouted for joy on witnessing the first. Mount Sinai, the theatre of the second, surrounded by three millions of Jews, displayed the fearful grandeur and awful majesty of the second. Jerusalem, filled with the pentecostal convention of the world, with the little family of Christ hailing the resurrection morn, saw the superlative displays of the spirit of holiness and of grace on opening the new administration of the remedial system.

Jesus himself inhibited the removal of the apostles from their own metropolis—from the scenes of his humiliation and death—till they were endowed with power from on high—till, baptized in the Holy Spirit, and endowed with all manner of supernatural aids, they could, in good keeping with the genius and character of the reign of grace, set forth the superlative excellencies and claims of the evangelical administration.

The time when, the place where, and the persons by whom this new and transcendantly glorious display of the whole divinity should be developed, had been the subject of prophecy, both verbal and typical. The clear and luminous Micah, the evangelical Isaiah, had, some seven centuries before Messiah was born, explicitly declared, in immediate reference to his time, "That out of Zion shall go forth the law, and the word of the Lord from Jerusalem." That these predictions, (uttered Isa. ii., Mic. iv.,) had respect to the commencement of the new reign, Jesus himself, the great Expositor, clearly intimates in his conversation after his resurrection. "Thus," says he, "it is written, (in the prophets already alluded to,) and thus it behooved the Messiah to suffer, and to rise from the dead the third day, and that repentance and remission of sins should be preached in his name among all nations, *beginning at Jerusalem.*"

Jerusalem was then the place where the new law was to commence. And as to the time, it was to be in the last days of the Jewish state, as the same prophets declare. The interval between the passover and the giving of the Jewish law, is more especially prophetic of the precise time of the promulgation of the new law. The passover was certainly a type of Christ's death. So the apostles distinctly represented it. The giving of the Jewish law succeeded that sacrifice on the fortieth day. The Lord descended on that day to Mount Sinai, and spake in mortal ears all the words of that law of piety and morality which became the covenant, or constitution, of the typical nation. The promulgation of that law occasioned the death of three thousand persons. Now, Jesus died at the time of the passover sacrifice : he arose on the third day ; he ascended on the forty-third day ; and in one week, and on the first day of that week, the Spirit descended and spake the new law before the world—which occasioned the salvation from death of three thousand persons. No typical prophecy in the Bible, received a more exact accomplishment in its antitype than this one. Besides, Jesus himself foretold, before he left the earth, that in a few days he would send the Spirit down and introduce the new kingdom.

The person by whom this new age was to be introduced was undoubtedly Peter. The Messiah, to sanction his confession of faith, and to communicate it to all men in all ages, promised to him the keys of the kingdom of heaven, that he should open it, and remit and retain sins with all authority. His words are, (Matt. xvi.) " He saith unto them, But who say ye that I am ? And Simon Peter answered and said, Thou art the Christ, the Son of the living God. And Jesus answered and said unto him, Blessed art thou, Simon Bar-jonah : for flesh and blood hath not revealed this unto you, but my father which is in heaven. And I say unto you, that thou art Peter, and upon this rock I will build my church, and the gates of hell shall not prevail against it. And I will give unto you the keys of the kingdom of heaven ; and whatsoever you shall bind on earth shall be bound in heaven, and whatsoever you shall loose on earth shall be loosed in heaven." Again—Jesus makes another promise indicative of the same commencement of his kingdom. (Acts i.) " You shall receive power after the Holy Spirit is come upon you ; and you shall be witnesses for me in Jerusalem, and in Judea, and in Samaria, and to the uttermost parts of the earth." Are we not, therefore, by the highest authority, constrained to look to Jerusalem, to the day of Pentecost, to the apostle Peter, to understand what the new law is ; what the gospel means ; and how sins are to be remitted to men of all nations during the present administration ? No wonder, then, that we have given a new emphasis to the second chapter of the Acts of the Apostles, inasmuch as the Messiah and his prophets send us to Jerusalem, to Pentecost, and to Peter for the law of remission. Can we, then, possibly err in regarding Peter's sermon as the opening speech of the gospel age ? We must, then, examine it with the greatest care. The synopsis given of it by Luke is very brief, yet it gives the great points. These are the death of the Messiah, his resurrection, ascension, and glorification, with the descent of the Holy Spirit. These five points are all set in a clear, distinct and authoritative form before the great assembly. By the revelations of that day, three thousand are convinced of sin, righteousness and judgment ; and, with the most intense and agonizing interest and feeling, inquire what they shall do under the new aspects opened to their consideration. The answer given is such a one as would have been given to the whole world, had it been present and united in the all-engrossing question propounded. It is the gospel in its preceptive form, with its promises annexed. Having already believed the facts stated—the testimony of the Holy Twelve, sustained by the demonstration of the Holy Spirit—the imperatives uttered by Peter, fore-ordained to open the new reign, indicate all that was necessary to be done to secure the benefits of Christ's death and resurrection—pardon, justification, and the Holy Spirit. The answer, given by Peter, (Oh that it were written in all languages, and proclaimed in every human ear, with all the authority of apostles and prophets,) was in these words: " REFORM AND BE IMMERSED, EVERY ONE OF YOU, IN THE NAME OF THE LORD JESUS, FOR THE REMISSION OF SINS, AND YOU SHALL RECEIVE THE GIFT OF THE HOLY SPIRIT." To encourage them, he adds, " For the promise is unto you and to your posterity, and to all that are afar off, even to as many as the Lord our God shall call." This is, when fully and intelligently considered, a synopsis of the whole evangelical economy. It is based on three facts which transpired on earth—the death, burial, and resurrection of the Messiah; and on three facts which transpired afterwards—his ascension, coronation, and reception of the Holy Spirit, for the consummation of the objects of his reign. The precepts are also three—believe, repent, and be baptized. The promises are three—remission of sins, the Holy Spirit, and eternal life. This classification is not merely to assist the memory, (though in that point of view it is invaluable,) but simply and clearly to set forth the facts, the precepts, and the promises of the evangelical system. It is, therefore, an admirable opening speech. I only wonder that a thousand volumes, in this book-making age, have not been written upon it. " With many other words," indeed, than those written here, we are informed that Peter " testified and exhorted, saying, Save yourselves from this untoward generation."

A precept in this discourse is the subject of my proposition—"*Be baptized for the remission of sins.*" We, of course, presume that the person so commanded, has believed and repented. Peter connects these two in the precept—Repent and be baptized, every one of you, for the remission of sins. Hence I argue, that, what God has joined together, man ought not to separate. If, upon any other subject in the world, a precept of this plainness were promulged, all men, methinks, would interpret it as I have done. Were a physician asked by a rheumatic invalid, What shall I do to be healed? and the physician should answer, Go to the Virginia White Sulphur Springs, drink of the waters and bathe in them, for the removal of your pains, and you shall enjoy a renovated constitution; would not such a patient rationally conclude that it were necessary not only to drink the water, but to bathe also, in order to the enjoyment of the remission of his pains, and that the reception of a renovated constitution would be the consequence of his obedience? Some of our ardent opponents, indeed, in the blindness of their zeal, have said, that it ought to be read, because your sins are remitted. But, in the case before us, would not the people laugh the doctor to scorn, who should say to the aforesaid invalid, Go to the White Sulphur Springs and drink the water, and bathe in it, because your pains are remitted? But, perhaps my respondent may devise some better way of disposing of the difficulty, and I shall not anticipate him.

Peter, then, as we conclude, like an honest man, spake just as the Spirit gave him utterance; and expressed, in a plain, unfigurative style, such as a popular audience of several thousand could comprehend, what ought to be done by those that heard him declare the glorious fact, that

God had raised the crucified Messiah to the throne of the universe. He commanded them to repent, and be baptized, in the name of the Lord, for the remission of sins. This single passage, when duly estimated, is, of itself, enough to establish the affirmation I have made of the design of baptism. I am sustained by the identical words of holy writ. True, I have inserted one word, and but one, among the words that Peter spake; but that word was not inserted to obviate a mistake. Some have affirmed, that, like John Calvin, the founder of Presbyterianism, we preached baptism for the remission of future sins, as well as for the remission of past sins. That I might not, then, be regarded as a genuine Presbyterian, of the pure, primitive, Calvinistic school, I inserted the word *past.* My learned Calvinian opponent has taken the negative in some sense; or, perhaps, he only means to advocate pure, ancient, uncorrupted Calvinism, by denying that the virtue of baptism is only retrospective—he affirming that baptism is for the remission of all sins, past, present, and future.

He [Mr. Rice] can, as a christian man, only demur at the word *past;* for, if that word were expunged, my proposition is then expressed in the identical words of the king's own version—a version completed by forty-seven good, learned, pious, Episcopalians. We command inquiring penitents, in the very words of Peter, "Be baptized, every one of you, in the name of the Lord Jesus, for the remission of sins:" in doing which, we exactly conform to the very words of inspiration. Our proposition, then, is incontrovertibly true; provided only, Peter knew what he said, and said what he meant.

My *second* argument is deduced from Mark's version of the commission—"He that believeth and is baptized, shall be saved"—taken in connection with Peter's response to the thousands in Jerusalem. These passages mutually explain each other. Here is given to baptism a most imposing character. Along with faith, and as the adjunct of faith, it saves penitents. That it has power to save one from any thing else than sins, is not to be imagined: inasmuch as we have three distinct salvations expressed in the Bible—the first, a salvation of the body from the ills and evils, the accidents and dangers of this life; the second, a salvation of the soul, from the guilt and pollution of sin; the third, a salvation of both body and soul—of the whole man in heaven forever.

Now, the salvation of the soul being distinguished from the salvation of the body, and from the eternal salvation of the whole man, must simply indicate the remission of sin, its guilt and its pollution. And so it would seem that Peter and Mark must have been guided by the same spirit, in expressing the mind of Christ under the remedial economy: the latter, by connecting it with salvation, and the other, with remission of sins. This harmonizing of the two witnesses, teaches the true doctrine of christianity, to wit: that a saved man is one whose sins are pardoned. To say, then, that a sinner is saved, is equivalent to saying that he is pardoned. He that is pardoned, is saved; and he that is saved, is pardoned. But, whether the saved person shall hold fast his begun confidence unshaken to the end, and finally obtain the salvation to be revealed when the Lord comes, depends not upon faith, repentance, or baptism, but upon "yielding the fruits of holiness, and thus having the end everlasting life." Luke so used the word *saved*, when closing the narration of the christian Pentecost. "And," says he, "the Lord added daily the saved to the congregated." The *saved* were those who had confessed their sins, had repented, and were baptized.

My *third* argument is derived from the fact, that the baptism of John, as well as that of the Messiah, was connected with the remission of sins. So reads the divine testimony—" In these days came John the Baptist— preaching the baptism of repentance for the remission of sins." Nor is this the peculiar style of John Mark. Luke, also, speaks of the design of John's baptism in almost identical words. He says, " And he came into the country bordering on the Jordan, preaching the baptism of repentance for the remission of sins," (iii. 3.) Again; that John's baptism had special reference to remission, appears from the fact recorded by Matthew, " All Judea and Jerusalem were baptized by him, *confessing their sins.*" The confession of sins amongst the Jews was necessary to remission; and generally enjoined with special reference to it. When the administrator baptized for the remission of sins, and the subject received baptism confessing his sins, have we not reason to believe that sins were pardoned in the act of baptism?

A certain prediction concerning this extraordinary minister, uttered by his father about the time of his circumcision, is, of itself, sufficient to warrant the conclusion, that the ministry of John had peculiar reference to some new doctrine of remission. What could be more pointedly said to communicate that impression, than the following words? " And thou, child, shalt be called the Prophet of the Highest; for thou shalt go before the Lord to prepare his way—to give knowledge of salvation to his people *in* the remission of their sins." Literally, it reads—the knowledge of salvation *in* the remission of their sins. That this refers to baptism is not only evident to my mind, from my own reasoning, but it is the judgment of our most profound critics and authors, of marginal readings and references. Mill and Wetsten on these words refer to Mark i. 4; and to Luke iii. 3, which we have before quoted. So do various versions having references.

In this way John's baptism prepared the way for that of the Messiah. Again; this is the peculiar distinction between the new salvation, and the ancient salvations, most usual among the sons of Abraham. Their deliverance was from temporal grievances, and from the tyranny of oppressive enemies; but the new salvation of the gospel is a salvation consisting primarily of the actual, real, and personal remission of sins. Hence, John's baptism was for the remission of sins. That there should be a more sensible, evident, and satisfactory remission of sins under the new dispensation, and that baptism is an ordinance especially designed for that purpose, will appear still farther evident from other declarations found in the first discourses on the opening of the new reign of grace. From the exposition of the transactions which occurred in heaven immediately after the ascension, we therefore deduce

Our *fourth* argument.—On entering the heavens, Jesus was constituted Lord and Christ. This was the last act in the sublime drama of man's deliverance; so far as the means of his redemption from sin and death are contemplated. Hence, this same Peter, when opening and announcing the reign of the Messiah, repeatedly alludes to this glorious consummation of the gospel facts. On the day of Pentecost he said, " Let all the house of Israel know, that God has made that same Jesus, whom you crucified, both Lord and Christ." Again: in his second sermon, reported in the next chapter, he says to the believing thousands, " Repent and be converted, that your sins may be blotted out, so that seasons of refreshment may come from the presence of the Lord; and he will send Jesus Christ, who was before preached unto you, whom the heavens must retain until the times of the restitution of all things." And again, and still more strikingly illustrative and confirmatory of the fact before us, is the annunciation made to the council of the nation, with the high-priest in the chair : " God hath exalted this Jesus to his right hand, a prince and a Savior, to give repentance to Israel, and forgiveness of sins." Princes, when exalted, dispense favors with a more munificent hand than during their minority, or before their accession to a throne. Jesus being constituted Lord as well as Christ ; being invested with universal riches, power, and glory, opens his reign by forgiving, through faith, repentance, and baptism, three thousand rebels, many of whom had thirsted for his blood—"Of whom," said Peter, " you have been the betrayers and murderers." His exaltation to the throne of the universe, is declared to be with a special reference to the dispensation of repentance and remission. Of course, then, these go hand in hand, and are dispensed under new conditions, and in a new, more striking, vivid, and soul-exhilarating manner than formerly. Hence the superabundant joy of the new converts, compared with that of the old saints. There was not merely a freshness and a beauty in those brighter displays of divine philanthropy ; but there was a more substantive and real blessedness imparted, in having an institution dispensed to them, that permitted them to be buried in Christ, and to rise in him, as well as with him, and to receive a personal, plenary, and sensible remission, by and through their faith, repentance, and baptism. There are, then, in the new dispensation of the better covenant, established upon richer and better promises, good reasons why those who now submit to Jesus, the great and mighty Savior, should formally and really receive a purification from sin, unknown in its amplitude and assurance to those under former dispensations. Paul to the Hebrews, argues its superiority in sundry points of view, but most clearly and convincingly by reference to remission. The conscience was never made perfect in any remission of sins, dispensed through Jewish ordinances ; for the worshipers, though often cleansed, still had a consciousness of sins ; which consciousness of sins is thoroughly removed in those who truly understand, and cordially embrace the gospel of the glorified Messiah. These, indeed, have their hearts sprinkled from an evil conscience, and their bodies washed in the clean water of christian purification. From the stress laid upon the exaltation and coronation of the Messiah, and the new dispensation of favor entrusted to him, we are led to expect such change in the conditions and forms of remission, as are indicated in these three words—faith in Jesus as the Messiah, repentance, and baptism.

The order and the change of words in Acts iii. " Repent and turn to God, or be converted, that your sins may be blotted out," &c., is merely exegetical, or farther declarative of the answer given a few days before, on the opening of the new kingdom. Repent and be baptized for the remission of sins, is now expressed—" Repent and be converted, that your sins may be blotted out." I hope my respondent will make an effort to show, that these words can be otherwise understood than as precisely equivalent to Acts ii. 38.

Our *fifth* argument shall be deduced from the fact already assumed and demonstrated in the case of circumcision ; that, whatever circumcision was to any one of the descendants of Abraham, whether infant or adult, it was of the same importance and significance to all. This is a point of great consideration on the subject of all divine institutions. It was true

of all the patriarchal and Jewish ordinances. To every proper subject of
any one of them, the observance secured the same advantages.

This is equally true of all the christian ordinances. To him who is a
proper candidate for baptism, for the Lord's supper, or for any christian
institution, the ordinance conveys the same blessings. This being so,
whatever baptism was to the three thousand Pentecostan converts, to
Saul of Tarsus, to Cornelius, or to any believing penitent in the age of
the apostles, it is to every human being at the present time.

Paul assures us that there is but one christian immersion—" one Lord,
one faith, *one baptism*." Now, if our baptism is for any other end or
purpose than that to which Paul submitted, it is another baptism, as
much as bathing for health is different from a Jewish ablution for legal
uncleanness or impurity. The action has a meaning and a design; and
it must be received in that meaning and for that design, else it is another
baptism.

Our *sixth* argument is drawn from the words uttered in the ears of
Paul, by a messenger specially called and sent to him from the Lord.
Paul was now a believing penitent, a proper subject of the grace of baptism : for baptism has its peculiar grace, as well as prayer or fasting.
Paul had inquired of the Lord, what he should do. The Lord commissioned Ananias to inform him. He went to Paul's room, and proved his
mission by restoring him to sight : and instantly commanded him to rise,
be baptized, and wash away his sins, calling upon the name of the Lord.
Now, the washing away of his sins was certainly to be accomplished
through the water of baptism, according to the language of the highest
authority in the universe. Jesus Christ had so commanded. Neither his
faith nor his repentance had washed away his sins, in the sense of the
precept of the Messiah. In any other case, the literary world would interpret this phrase as I have done. In circumcising adult proselytes,
when connecting themselves with the Jewish nation, it was usual for
them to wash off the blood occasioned by the performance of the rite.
From which fact, some of the Rabbis, one thousand years ago, got up
the notion of Jewish baptism, as before intimated on another question.
Suppose, then, an Hebrew should address a newly circumcised Pagan in
these words : " Arise, sir, go to the bath and wash away your blood,"
would not the whole world understand it, not merely as a necessary precept, but that the washing away of the blood was not in the act of rising
nor of going to the bath, but in the bathing ? But when we place this
saying of Ananias to the penitent Saul of Tarsus, along with that of Peter to the penitent Pentecostans, " Be baptized for the remission of sins ;"
" Be baptized and wash away your sins ;" although spoken by different
persons, at different and considerable intervals, what reasonable doubt
can remain, that all the apostles taught, and all the christians believed, that
the remission of sins was through faith, repentance, and baptism ? On
this remarkable passage, Calvin observes, " That you may be *assured*,
Paul, that your sins are remitted, be baptized ; for the Lord promises remission of sins in baptism : receive it and be assured." (Inst. 4, sec. 15,
De Baptism.) This is the answer that Calvin gives to the question :
" Why did Ananias tell Paul to wash away his sins by baptism, if sins
are not washed away by virtue of baptism ?" This is scarcely modest
enough ! Bucer, the great reformer, " the very learned, judicious, and
pious Bucer," as bishop Burnet calls him, the amiable companion of Melancthon, the student of Luther, the associate of Zuinglius, whose body

the bloody Mary had dug up and burned five years after his death; the man whose very bones were a terror to a Catholic queen, said of this passage, " In those words, then, there is ascribed to baptism the effect of remitting or washing of sins."—(Bucer in loco.)   Not to quote all the ancients, Tertullian, Chrysostom, Augustine, &c., &c., I shall only add, from Wesley's Notes, Acts xxii. 16: " Baptism, administered to a real penitent, is both a means and a seal of pardon.   Nor did God ordinarily, in the primitive church, bestow this on any, unless through this means." It calls for a greater than Wesley to prove that he acts otherwise in the modern church !

My *seventh* argument is deduced from the conversion of Cornelius and his gentile friends.   His excellent moral character and his great devotion to prayer and alms-deeds, had not yet *saved* him.   The message received from God directed him to send for the man who had the keys of the kingdom of heaven, who could " tell him *words* by which he and his family and friends *might be saved*."   I need not relate the whole story, as it is represented in the tenth and eleventh chapters of Acts.   Peter, in relating the matter afterwards, as reported in the eleventh chapter, develops more fully the intention of the mission, and details some of the incidents more at length.   Particularly, in the fourteenth verse, he gives an account of the necessity of his sermon—as " words whereby Cornelius and all his family might be saved."   He also states, that, as he began to speak these words—as soon as he got to remission of sins through the name of the Lord Jesus—at that moment, the Spirit, in its miraculous attestations, fell upon all the gentiles present, as it had done in the baptism of the Jews on Pentecost.   Cornelius and his friends of the gentile world, as the one hundred and twenty Jewish friends (assembled on Pentecost) of the Jewish world, were best prepared for the coming of the new reign—a people prepared for the Lord—it pleased God to admit them both by the same glorious, sensible and visible displays of his grace in the gift of tongues.   Soon, then, as Peter saw all this, he asked the believing Jews, who had accompanied him from Joppa, whether they could, on any account, refuse them the grace of baptism.   No demurrer having been instituted, he commanded them to be baptized *in the name of the Lord*.   Thus, also, were the gentiles saved by faith, repentance and baptism.

Seven such arguments as these are enough for one speech.   The first, indeed, is itself alone sufficient, so far as authority goes, to command and enforce the institution upon the attention and observance of all.   The others, besides their individual weight, explain its meaning and importance, and go to shew what its true construction is.   The authority of Him, in whose name believing penitents are to be baptized, is not susceptible of augmentation by the suffrages of an universe, nor by the addition of all the names amongst the celestial and terrestrial hierarchies.   He alone is the peerless One, by whom kings reign and princes decree justice.   It was he who first marshaled the morning stars, and gave to them laws which they have never transgressed, during all the contingencies of untold ages, and the movements of all the agencies of creation. It was his fiat that made darkness the parent of light, and that caused nothing to become the origin of all things.   When made Head and Lawgiver of the Church ; when constituted both Lord and Christ; when exalted a Prince and a Savior, after sending down his Spirit from his throne, and animating his apostles by his presence and power, the first

precept given to the first inquiring penitents was, " Repent and be baptized, every one of you, in the name of the Lord Jesus, for the remission
of your sins." On that precept the first church acted with joyful haste
and implicit confidence. On that precept the Jerusalem church was
founded : and no good reason can ever be given by any man, why the
same precept should not be given to every inquiring penitent now,
henceforth, and till the Lord shall come again.

Thus far I had prepared my opening address. My time, however, not
yet being expired, I shall proceed to another argument. One clause of
the commission, not commented on during our discussion of the previous
proposition, now demands a few remarks as the basis of a new argument,
in support of the present proposition, which, of course, I shall call my
eighth argument.

8. " Baptizing them *into the name of the Father, and of the Son, and
of the Holy Spirit.*" No language could more clearly indicate a change
of state than the phrase just now read. The prominent design of baptism
is thus fully expressed by the transition spoken of in the words, " baptizing
into the name." The *subject* is here represented as in some way entering *into the name,* or *into the persons* represented by the Father, Son
and Holy Spirit. This may be supposed to resemble the act of naturalization, in the fact that a person in that process is inducted into the possession of the rights of citizenship under a political institution. So Christ
commanded the candidates to be immersed into the name of the whole
Divinity ; that is, into the privileges and immunities of the new kingdom
over which the Messiah now presides, by the authority of the Father
through the Holy Spirit. It is, then, a solemn and sacred enfranchisement of a believer with all the rights and privileges of Christ's kingdom.

This argument rests on the authority of the new version of *eis* by *into.*
When I published my edition of the New Testament, (which many persist in calling my translation,) feeling myself authorized by the original,
and the style of the New Testament, I departed, in this instance, as well
as in several others, from Dr. Campbell, and all other translations then
known to me. This, indeed, was but a verbal matter. Yet, when the
whole world, Catholic and Protestant, were following Jerom's vulgate, it
was a great innovation, on my part, and so regarded by others. Since
that time, however, I have ascertained that in one of T. Dwight's sermons
on the commission, he took the same view of it, and contended that it
ought to have been so rendered. And still more recently, and with more
authority, archbishop Whateley, of the province of Dublin, both in his
logic, and also in a recent work on the kingdom of Christ, has not only
sanctioned this version, but defended it with zeal. These two names are
as authoritative as any other two names which could be selected in Europe or America.

The new version of this passage will certainly grow into fashion at no
very distant day. I find other distinguished names in favor of it. All
feel the difference between " *in the name of the Lord,*" and " *into Christ.*"
The former denotes *authority,* alone—the latter intimates union and relation. " *In the name of the commonwealth,*" is very different from being
inducted into the commonwealth. *Into* always denotes change of position ; a transition from one state to another. It marks boundaries. A
person enters *into,* not *in,* matrimony. A person is baptized in water,
into Moses, into Christ, or into his death, &c.

This solemn and significant moral change or transition out of the world into Christ, is consummated in the following manner:—The gospel is proclaimed to them without the kingdom. Men have it, believe it, become penitent, and are "baptized *in water, into the name of the Father, the Son, and the Holy Spirit.*" They have then put on Christ, are baptized into Christ, and are henceforth *in* him a new creation.

Baptism, my fellow-citizens, is no mere rite, no unmeaning ceremony, I assure you. It is a most intellectual, spiritual and sublime transition out of a sinful and condemned state, into a spiritual and holy state. It is a change of relation, not as respects the flesh, but the spirit. It is an introduction into the mystical body of Christ, by which he necessarily obtains the remission of his sins.

No one can understand or enjoy the sublime and awful import of a burial with Christ; of a baptism into death, who does not feel that he is passing through a most solemn initiation into a new family; high and holy relations to the Father, as his Father and his God—to the Son, as his Lord and his Messiah—to the Holy Spirit, as his sanctifier and comforter. He puts off his old relations to the world, the flesh, and Satan. Consequently, that moment he is adopted into the family of God, and is personally invested with all the rights of a citizen of the kingdom of heaven.

But this ordinance is *monumental* also. It is always a monument and an attestation of the burial and resurrection of the Lord. No one can sensibly contemplate one exhibition of it, without remembering the burial of the Messiah, and his glorious resurrection, by the power of his Father; for it is the administrator that raises from the watery grave the buried saint. With the vividness of a sensible demonstration it strikes not only the *eye*, but the *heart*, of an intelligent spectator. It is not only a commemorative institution, but also it is prospective of our future destiny in the new relation; that when we die, and are buried in the earth—when the Administrator of the new and everlasting institution revisits our earth, he will raise from their graves all his dear brethren, and glorify them with his own immortal beauty and loveliness. How appropriate the symbol of the new birth, this washing of regeneration! How kind that the precept, on which man's enjoyment of salvation rests, should commemorate the Lord's burial and resurrection, should prospectively anticipate our own, while it inducts us *into Christ* and invests us with all the privileges of citizenship in his kingdom!—[*Time expired.*

Thursday, Nov. 23—11 o'clock, A. M.
[MR. RICE'S FIRST REPLY.]

MR. PRESIDENT—In the previous part of this discussion, it has been my business to advocate views in regard to which we differ from some of our christian brethren of evangelical churches. I am happy, this morning, to take my stand on the broad ground on which the great body of Protestant christians are united. The discussion on which we now enter, is designed, on my part, to present the great doctrines of the cross in their proper relation to each other, and to exhibit the ordinances connected with them in their true nature and design.

I regret that my friend, Mr. Campbell, did not, in his address, more distinctly state the point at issue. It is, however, a common misfortune of those who *write* speeches, to give rather more attention to the formation of beautiful sentences and well-turned periods, than to the clear presentation of the subject under investigation. In the discussion of the subject before us, as indeed of all others, it is of the first importance that the audience understand distinctly wherein we differ, and what is the precise point in dispute. The proposition is as follows: " CHRISTIAN BAPTISM IS FOR THE REMISSION OF PAST SINS." This Mr. C. affirms, and I deny.

That the audience may distinctly see the point in debate, it is important to remark, that we are not discussing the question, whether one who contemns, or wilfully neglects, the ordinance of baptism, can have evidence that his sins are remitted. We all agree, that he who despises, or designedly neglects, any one command of Christ, gives clear evidence that he is destitute of true piety, and, consequently, is not pardoned. But the question is, whether a *penitent believer* is unpardoned until he is baptized, or, as my friend would say, *immersed:* whether an individual who to-day becomes truly penitent, and believes on Christ with all his heart, but has no opportunity to be baptized till the next week, is, till the next week, condemned, and is pardoned only in the act of receiving baptism—or whether, if he have no opportunity to be baptized the next week, or if he never have such opportunity, he must live and die unforgiven—or whether, if he have mistaken something else for baptism, and thus substituted a human tradition in its stead, he must die condemned and be lost. In a word, the question is, *whether a penitent believer is, under all circumstances, or under any circumstances, unpardoned, until he is baptized?* To this question, Mr. C. would give an affirmative answer. He maintains, that the sins of a penitent believer are forgiven, not before baptism, but in the very act of being baptized. That I may be certain of representing his views correctly, I will read from his *Christian Baptist*, pp. 416, 417:

" In the third place, I proceed to show that we have the most explicit proof that God forgives sins for the name's sake of his Son, or when the name of Jesus Christ is named upon us in immersion :—*that in, and by, the act of immersion, so soon as our bodies are put under water, at that very instant our former, or 'old sins,' are all washed away; provided only, that we are true believers.* This was the view and the expectation of every one who was immersed in the apostolic age : and it was a consciousness of having received this blessing that caused them to rejoice in the Lord, and, like the eunuch, to 'go on their way rejoicing.' When Jesus commanded reformation and forgiveness of sins to be announced in his name to all nations, he commanded men to receive immersion to the confirmation of this promise. Thus we find that when the gospel was announced on Pentecost, and when Peter opened the kingdom of heaven to the Jews, he commanded them to be immersed for the remission of sins. This is quite sufficient, if we had not another word on the subject. I say, it is quite sufficient to shew that the forgiveness of sins and christian immersion were, in their first proclamation by the holy apostles, inseparably connected together. Peter, to whom was committed the keys, opened the kingdom of heaven in this manner ; and made repentance, or reformation, and immersion, equally necessary to forgiveness. * * * I am bold, therefore, to affirm, that every one of them who, in the belief of what the apostle spoke, was immersed, *did, in the very instant in which he was put under water, receive the forgiveness of his sins,* and the gift of the holy Spirit. If so, then, who will not concur with me in saying, that christian immersion is the gospel in water ?"—*Editor.*

Such is the doctrine of my friend. I will now read a passage or two from his *Christianity Restored*, in which he avows the same doctrine. I read on pages 196, 197:

" A thousand analogies might be adduced, to shew that though a change of state often, nay, generally results from a change of feelings, and this from a change of views ; yet a change of state does not necessarily follow, and is something quite different from, and cannot be identified with, a change of heart. So in religion, a man may change his views of Jesus, and his heart may also be changed towards him ; *but unless a change of state ensues, he is still unpardoned, unjustified, unsanctified, unreconciled, unadopted, and lost to all christian life and enjoyment.* For it has been proved that these terms represent states and not feelings, condition and not character : and that a change of views, or of heart, is not a change of state. To change a state is to pass into a new relation, and relation is not sentiment, nor feeling. *Some act, then, constitutional, by stipulation proposed, sensible, and manifest, must be performed by one or both the parties before such a change can be accomplished.*

Again ; whatever the act of faith may be, it necessarily becomes the line of discrimination between the two states before described. *On this side or on that, mankind are in quite different states. On the one side, they are pardoned, justified, sanctified, reconciled, adopted, and saved: On the other, they are in a state of condemnation. This act is sometimes called immersion, regeneration, conversion,"* &c.

Here, then, you have distinctly stated the doctrine of my friend, against which I protest. He maintains, that the sins of penitent believers are remitted *in the act of immersion*—never before ; that all who have not been immersed, however pious and holy, are still unpardoned ; and living and dying without immersion, they live and die unforgiven and are lost. Here I join issue with him.

So far as his remarks bear upon the question before us, I shall notice them as I pass. He has said some things that are true, and others that, as I suppose, are not true ; but as they have no immediate bearing on the question in debate, I do not deem it proper to reply to them.

Before stating my objections to his doctrine, it is important to remark, *that the Bible is consistent with itself.* This the gentleman will not deny. If, then, his interpretation of Peter's sermon be found directly to contradict other portions of the Scriptures ; it will appear, to the satisfaction of all, that it is entirely erroneous, and that we must look for a different exposition. I, then, offer the following objections to his doctrine and to his interpretation of Peter's sermon :

First: It flatly contradicts the express declarations of Christ and the apostles. I refer you to John iii. 18—the very chapter in which we find the new birth, on which Mr. C. has so largely commented in his writings. Let us hear John speak ; or rather, let us hear our Lord speak in language so perfectly clear, that no difficulty can be felt in ascertaining his meaning, and no criticism can evade it : " He that believeth on him is not condemned." The meaning of this declaration evidently is, that every believer in Christ is pardoned ; for to say he is not condemned, is the same as to say he is pardoned—his sins are remitted. But my friend says, he that believes and is *immersed*, is not condemned ; if not immersed, he is condemned ! Here is a flat contradiction of the Savior ; for he says as plainly as language can express it, concerning every believer, he is not condemned. Again, verse 36, " He that believeth on the Son, hath everlasting life." The Savior does not say, he that believeth may or shall have life, if he will be *immersed;* but he HATH everlasting life—*he has it now in actual possession.* Look now at the predicament in which Mr. Campbell is placed. He asserts, that, until immersed, the believer is condemned, and, of course, has *not* everlasting life. What says our Lord ? " He that *believeth*, HATH everlasting life." My friend will not immerse an individual till he professes to believe. He asks him the question, do you believe that Jesus Christ is the Son of God? He answers in the affirmative. Now if he has told the truth, he *has* everlasting life, and his sins are remitted. My friend cannot, on his hypothesis, get him to the water until his sins are forgiven, and he is in the actual possession of life everlasting. The passage calls for no criticism—it is perfectly plain.

Again, I read, chap. vi. 29, " Jesus answered and said unto them, This is the work of God, that ye *believe* on him whom he hath sent." This is *the* work. Every thing else follows, when faith is exercised. Faith produces good works ; and he who has the princple in him, will be found walking in obedience to the commandments of God.

Again, verses 35, 40: " And Jesus said unto them, I am the bread of life : he that cometh to me, shall never hunger ; and he that believeth on me, shall never thirst. * * * And this is the will of him that sent me, that every one which seeth the Son, and believeth on him, may have everlasting life : and I will raise him up at the last day." Could language be more perfectly unambiguous? Is it possible to express more clearly and strongly the truth, that every true believer is pardoned and accepted of God? He that believes, shall never *thirst*—he shall ever drink of the water of life. It is the will of God that he have everlasting life ; and Christ will raise him up at the last day. Nay, he is now in the actual possession of eternal life. Then are not the sins of all such persons pardoned?

It will not be denied that there have lived multitudes of believers who were never immersed ; and yet, according to the teaching of our Lord, they are in possession of eternal life. I read once more, verse 47 : " Verily, verily, I say unto you, he that believeth on me, hath everlasting life"—is in the actual possession of it, baptized or not, immersed or not. It is wholly unnecessary to go to critics, to interpret language as clear as the light of the sun.

I will now turn to the third chapter of the epistle to the Romans. Here we find the doctrine of *justification* very fully exhibited. The apostle's object was, to teach men how they might certainly obtain the remission of their sins and acceptance with God : and it is a remarkable fact, that baptism is not mentioned, nor even alluded to, in the whole connection. " Therefore, by the deeds of the law there shall no flesh be justified in his sight : for by the law is the knowledge of sin. But now the righteousness of God without the law, is manifested, being witnessed by the law and the prophets : even the righteousness of God, which is by faith of Jesus Christ, unto all and upon all them that believe : for there is no difference. For all have sinned, and come short of the glory of God ; being justified freely by his grace, through the redemption that is in Christ Jesus * * * Therefore we conclude that a man is justified by faith, without the deeds of the law."—*Verses* 20—24, 28. In this and the two following chapters, we have an argument clear and complete, designed to explain the doctrine of justification, to teach men how their sins may be remitted ; and yet baptism is not mentioned, till the apostle reaches the sixth chapter, and then only by way of answering a Jewish objection to the doctrine he was teaching. But while he is explaining the doctrine of justification, he does not even allude to baptism. He teaches, that the righteousness of God by faith is *unto and upon all them that believe;* and again, that a man is *justified by faith.* He does not say, as Mr. Campbell does, that a man is justified by faith *and baptism.* No—bap-

2 P

tism is not even alluded to. If, then, his doctrine is true, Paul must
have practiced an awful deception upon those whom he professed to teach
the way of life ! It is, then, most evident, that baptism does not secure
the remission of sins ; and that it is not a pre-requisite to pardon,

Secondly. My second objection to Mr. Campbell's doctrine is derived from the *fact, that all persons who are* BEGOTTEN *of God, do enjoy
remission of sins.* He, let it be understood, maintains that all believers
are begotten of God, whether they have been *immersed* or not; though,
until immersed, he would say, they are not *born again.* Now, I assert
it as a fact, which I will prove by the plainest declarations of the Scriptures, that every one who is *begotten* of God, is a child of God, and, consequently, enjoys the remission of sins. In the Bible, none but true christians are ever said to be begotten of God. This is proved by the following passages, 1 Pet. i. 3 : " Blessed be the God and Father of our Lord
Jesus Christ, which according to his abundant mercy hath *begotten us
again* into a lively hope, by the resurrection of Jesus Christ from the
dead, to an inheritance incorruptible," &c. Observe, those here spoken
of were begotten *unto a lively hope ;* and the object of that hope is " an
inheritance incorruptible, undefiled, and that fadeth not away, reserved in
heaven for them." They were true christians. Again, James i. 18 : " Of
his own will *begat* he us with the word of truth, that we should be a kind
of first fruits of his creatures."

Indeed, the word *begotten* is the word usually employed in the Scriptures, where reference is made to the *father* of children. Thus in Genesis we read, that such a man lived so long, and *begat* sons and daughters.
And our Savior is called " the only-begotten of the Father." The word
is ordinarily used to express the idea, that in some sense the child derives
its nature and its life from its father.

In the following passages I shall use the word *begotten,* instead of
born, not because I consider it more correct, but because Mr. C. prefers
it. *I intend to disprove his doctrine by his own translation.*

I read, 1 John iii. 9, " Whosoever is begotten of God doth not commit sin ; for his seed remaineth in him : and he cannot sin, because he is
begotten of God." But if a man cannot commit sin, he is a holy man;
and I will leave my friend to prove, that holy men may be condemned
and eternally lost ! Again, *(verse* 10) " In this the children of God are
manifest, and the children of the devil : whosoever doeth not righteousness
is not of God, neither he that loveth not his brother." Here observe,
they who are, in the 9th verse, said to be begotten of God, and are,
therefore, holy, are, in the 10th, called *the children of God;* and they
are distinguished by their righteousness from the children of the devil.
If a man is a child of God, are not his sins remitted ? John found but
two classes among men—the children of God and the children of the
devil. Surely Mr. C. will not venture to say that they who are begotten,
of God, can be the children of the devil ! John most clearly teaches us,
that all who are begotten of God, are his children ; and " if children,
then heirs," says Paul, " heirs of God, and joint-heirs with Jesus Christ,"
Rom. viii. 17.

Let us read again, 1 John iv. 7, " Beloved, let us love one another;
for love is of God : and every one that loveth is begotten of God, and
knoweth God." Compare this with the gospel by John, chap. xvii. 3,
" And this is life eternal, that they *might know* thee the only true God,
and Jesus Christ, whom thou hast sent." Now observe, every one who

loves, *is begotten* of God; every one who is begotten of God, *knows* God; and to know God is to possess eternal life. And who are they that on the day of judgment will be condemned? Paul the apostle answers the question—" The Lord Jesus shall be revealed from heaven with his mighty angels, in flaming fire, *taking vengeance on them* THAT KNOW NOT GOD, and that obey not the Gospel of our Lord Jesus Christ." 2 Thess. i. 7, 8. They who know God, obey the Gospel, and have eternal life. They cannot be condemned. Since, then, all who are *begotten* of God, do *know* God; is it not clear that their sins are remitted?

We will now notice what is said in the 5th chapter of this epistle, concerning those who are *begotten of God.* " Whosoever believeth that Jesus is the Christ, is begotten of God: and every one that loveth him that begat, loveth him also that is begotten of him. By this we know that we love *the children* of God," &c. The obvious meaning of which is, that every believer is a child of God, and loves all God's children. Again, " Whosoever is begotten of God *overcometh* the world." Now what has our Savior promised those who *overcome* the world? " He that hath an ear, let him hear what the Spirit saith unto the churches : to him that *overcometh*, will I give to eat of the tree of life, which is in the midst of the paradise of God," Rev. ii. 7. Again, (verse 11) " He that *overcometh*, shall not be hurt of the second death." Again, (verse 17) " To him that *overcometh*, will I give to eat of the hidden manna, and will give him a white stone, and in the stone a new name written, which no man knoweth, save he that receiveth it." Now mark the fact : every one that is begotten of God, overcometh the world ; and to every one that overcometh, our Lord has promised that he shall eat of the tree of life in the paradise of God ; that he shall not be hurt of the second death ; in a word, that he shall possess eternal happiness in heaven. Are not the sins of such remitted?

I am not quite through with this argument. In the 18th verse of the same chapter, John says, " We know that whosoever is begotten of God sinneth not, but he that is begotten of God keepeth himself, and that wicked one toucheth him not." Every one who is begotten of God, ceases to sin, and keeps himself, so that the devil does not touch him. Are such persons condemned? All must say, they are not—their sins are remitted.

Now you see the insuperable difficulty in which Mr. Campbell's doctrine involves him. He will baptize none but *believers ;* and all believers, he admits, are begotten of God—" Whosoever believeth that Jesus is the Christ, is begotten of God." They are begotten before he can baptize them by pouring, sprinkling or dipping. And if begotten, they are God's children, have ceased to sin, have overcome the world, and, therefore, have the promise of eternal blessedness in heaven. He admits, that they are begotten before they are to be baptized; and these scriptures abundantly prove, that they are God's children and heirs of eternal glory, and, consequently, that they do, before baptism, enjoy remission of sins. His doctrine, therefore, does most manifestly contradict a large number of the plainest declarations of our Savior and his apostles.

Thirdly. My third objection to the doctrine of Mr. Campbell is founded on the *fact, that those who are* BORN OF GOD, *enjoy the remission of sins.* The Scriptures teach us, that the new birth is not connected with baptism, but many are born again before being baptized. The new birth is first mentioned by the apostle John, ch. i. 11—13, " He

came unto his own, and his own received him not. But as many as re
ceived him, to them gave he power to become the sons of God, even to
them that believed on his name : which were born, not of blood, nor of
the will of the flesh, nor of the will of man, but of God." It is important here to notice the difference between *birth* and *adoption*. By our
birth we derive from our parents our *life* and *human nature*—we are like
them. By *adoption*, *privileges* are secured, to which the adopted person
was not before entitled. Birth has relation to life and nature : adoption
to privileges. Now observe, John says, that all who received Christ, or
believed on him, *were* born of God, not *might be* born. They were born
of God, had their hearts renewed, had the disposition of children ; and,
therefore, they received Christ. And to all who, in the exercise of the
disposition or spirit of children, received him, he gave *the privileges* of
children, the blessings of adoption.

I will now prove by a number of facts, that persons are born of God,
before they are baptized, or independently of baptism—that the new birth
is not at all essentially connected with baptism.

1. In the passage in the gospel by John, just now read, where the new
birth is first mentioned, not a word it said about *water*, or about *baptism*.
It is simply stated, that they who received Christ, were *born of God*
Now if the water of baptism had been essential to the new birth, would
it not have been mentioned, when first the birth is spoken of?

2. It is a fact, admitted by Mr. Campbell, that where the conversation
occurred between our Savior and Nicodemus, when the subject is again
presented ; *christian baptism was not in existence*, (John iii. 1—12.)
The first remark he made to Nicodemus, was, " Verily, verily, I say
unto thee, except a man be *born again*, he cannot see the kingdom of
God." Nicodemus did not understand his meaning. He explained,
" Except a man be *born of water and of the Spirit*, he cannot enter into
the kingdom of God." Now the question is, whether, by *the water*, the
Savior meant christian baptism. It is an admitted fact, that at this time,
christian baptism had not been instituted. Now we are certainly safe in
presuming, that the Savior intended that Nicodemus should understand
him. But if he alluded to an ordinance, not then in existence, and of
which Nicodemus could know nothing, how was it possible that he
could understand him? and how could he consistently reprove him for
not understanding him? For,

3. It is a fact, that our Lord did reprove Nicodemus for his ignorance
of this doctrine. " Jesus answered and said unto him, Art thou a master
[teacher] of Israel, and knowest not these things?" v. 10. He seems to
remark it as a strange inconsistency, that Nicodemus should be a teacher,
an expounder of the Old Testament, and yet be ignorant of this doctrine.
It is, then, certain that the doctrine here taught by the Savior, is taught
in the Old Testament. Baptism, in order to the remission of sins, is not
found there ; but the necessity and nature of a change of heart, of regeneration, is. Ezekiel said, " A new heart also will I give you, and a new
spirit will I put within you ; and I will take away the stony heart out of
your flesh, and I will give you an heart of flesh," &c. ch. xxxvi. 26.
Again, David prayed, " Create in me a clean heart, O God, and renew a
right spirit within me," Ps. li. 10. It is evident that the Savoir did not
allude to baptism for the remission of sins, which is not taught in the Old
Testament, but that he spoke of the renewing of the heart by the Holy
Spirit, which is here taught.

4. It is a fact, that after christian baptism was instituted, it never was by the inspired writers called *a birth*. Not an example of the kind can be found. And if our Lord and his apostles never did speak of it as a birth, we cannot safely so denominate it.

5. The reason assigned by the Savior, why the new birth is necessary, proves unanswerably, that it is simply a change of the heart—a change from sinfulness to holiness. It is this: "That which is born of the flesh is flesh; and that which is born of the Spirit is spirit." We must be born again, born of the Spirit, because we were born of the flesh. What are we to understand by the word *flesh*, in this passage? The answer to this question is found in Galatians v. 19, 20, 21, "Now the works of the flesh are manifest, which are these: adultery, fornication, uncleanness, lasciviousness, idolatry, witchcraft, hatred, variance, emulations, wrath, strife, seditions, heresies, envyings, murder, drunkenness, revellings, and such like." Again, Roman viii. 8, 9, "So then they that are *in the flesh*, cannot please God. But ye are not in the flesh, but in the Spirit, if so be that the Spirit of God dwell in you." The word *flesh*, when used with reference to moral character, is constantly employed, as these and other scriptures abundantly prove, in the sense of *depravity, moral corruption*. The meaning of our Savior's language, therefore, is, that they who are born of corrupt or sinful parents, are themselves sinful: and they who are born of the Holy Spirit, are holy. By the natural birth, we are like our parents, sinful; by the spiritual birth, we are like the Spirit, holy. The new birth is, therefore, a change of heart from sinfulness to holiness, not as Mr. C. contends, a change of *state*, affected by baptism, from condemnation to justification. The fact that a man is *condemned*, is a good reason why his *state* or *condition* should be changed; but the fact that he is *sinful*, is a good reason why his *heart*, his *moral nature*, should be changed. The fact that a man is *diseased*, is the reason why he needs medicine; and, of course, the medicine is intended to heal his disease. If then, the necessity of the new birth, as our Lord teaches, arises from the fact of our being depraved, the new birth must be designed to remove that depravity. It is, then, simply a change of heart, from sinfulness to holiness, by the Spirit of God; and, therefore, it is not essentially, or at all, connected with baptism.

6. The *mystery* connected with the new birth, confirms the view of it which I have just presented: "The wind bloweth where it listeth, and thou hearest the sound thereof, but canst not tell whence it cometh, and whither it goeth: so is every one that is born of the Spirit;" *vs.* 8. What is the meaning of this language? The Savior had presented to Nicodemus the doctrine of the new birth. He objects, that it is very mysterious. The Savior admits that it is mysterious, but proves that this is no valid objection against it; for the works of nature are full of mysteries. We know, that the wind blows, for we can see and feel its effects; but *how* it blows, "whence it cometh, and whither it goeth," we do not know—it is mysterious. So the fact, that the Holy Spirit renews the heart, we know, for we experience the effects of the change, and witness them in others; but *how* the Spirit operates on the mind we know not—it is mysterious.

But if the doctrine of Mr. Campbell is true, this allusion to the blowing of the wind, as mysterious, was altogether out of place. For, if God should declare his purpose to remit the sins of every one who, upon evidence, would believe that Jesus Christ is his son, and be immersed, there would be nothing mysterious about it. It would be one of the simplest things imaginable. But if the views, which I have presented, be true, the allusion to the blowing of the wind was peculiarly appropriate. It was a complete answer to the objection offered by Nicodemus. The evidence is thus strengthened, that the new birth is a change of heart.

7. That our Savior had no allusion to christian baptism as essential to the new birth, is further evident from the fact, that water is mentioned but *once*, and then dropped. The inspired writers were constantly in the habit, in speaking of spiritual things, of connecting the *emblem* and the *thing signified*, or of substituting the former for the latter, as illustrating its nature. Thus Ezekiel, in the passage repeatedly quoted—"Then will I sprinkle clean water upon you, and ye shall be clean: from all your filthiness and from all your idols will I cleanse you. A new heart also will I give you, and a new spirit will I put within you," &c., chap. xxxvi. 25, 26. Isaiah, when he would express the idea, that Christ would purify many nations from sin, says, "So shall he *sprinkle* many nations;" chap. lii. 15. So Paul, writing to the Hebrews—"Having our hearts sprinkled from an evil conscience, and our bodies washed with pure water;"chap x. 22. In each of these cases we find water, the emblem of spiritual cleansing, connected with the thing signified. Our Savior was conversing with a Jew. He did not understand his doctrine. How could he better make his meaning clear to a Jew, than by connecting *water*, the emblem of spiritual cleansing, with the Spirit. By the word *birth*, Nicodemus would understand him to speak of a change which would constitute men the children of God; and by the *water* he would, if not amazingly blind, understand, that the change was spiritual purification.

Accordingly, so soon as *water* is once employed as an illustration of the nature of the new birth, it is dropped, whilst the birth itself is still the subject of discourse. Thus, in verse 6th—"For that which is born of the flesh is flesh; and that which is born of the Spirit is spirit." He does not say, that which is born of *water* and of the Spirit is spirit; yet if water were as essential to the birth as the Spirit, he must have retained it. Again, "The wind bloweth where it listeth, &c.—so is every one that is born of the Spirit," not of *water* and the Spirit. It is, then, evident, that the birth of the spirit is the great subject of our Savior's remarks; and that he spoke of water just as did Ezekiel, Isaiah, and Paul, as illustrating the nature of the change.

8. I find yet further confirmation of these views in the scriptural evidences of the new birth. By the natural birth men are sinful; by the spiritual birth they are holy. How, then, is an individual to know that he is a child of God? By the fact that he has been *immersed?* By no means. Paul says, "For as many as are led by the Spirit of God, they are the sons of God." And again, "The Spirit itself beareth witness with our spirits, that we are the children of God;" Rom. viii. 14, 16. That is, when the heart is changed from the love and practice of sin to the love and practice of holiness; when our feelings and our lives correspond with the teachings and the influences of the Holy Spirit; when the Spirit of Christ dwells in us, then we have scriptural evidence that we are born of God. They who love God, and delight in his service, are children of God; and, "if children, then heirs—heirs of God, and joint heirs with Christ."

These facts prove unanswerably, that the new birth is, in no sense, connected essentially with baptism, and, consequently, that we may be, and that many are, children of God, and enjoy the remission of sins, before being baptized. It is, therefore, clear, that Mr. Campbell's exposition of Peter's sermon is false : because it flatly contradicts many plain declarations of the Scriptures. And if a man attempt to establish a tenet by giving a passage of Scripture a particular interpretation, I have most completely refuted it, when I have proved his interpretation contradictory to other plain and unambiguous passages, unless he is prepared to say, the Bible contradicts itself.

I purpose, however, to reply particularly to the gentleman's speech; to analyze the passages on which he chiefly relies; and to prove that his interpretation of them is not sustained by correct principles of language. He has, indeed, read us a pretty speech, but his doctrine is, nevertheless, directly contradictory of the repeated and various declarations of inspired writers. [Here Mr. Rice inquired how much time he had, and was informed that he had 15 minutes.] I will then proceed to answer some of the arguments of my friend.

To prove that baptism is necessary to secure the remission of sins, he appeals to Peter's discourse on the day of Pentecost: "Then Peter said unto them, repent, and be baptized, every one of you, in the name of Jesus Christ, for the remission of sins ;" or, as Mr. C. incorrectly translates the passage, " *reform* and be *immersed.*" The word translated *repent*, is *metanoco*, which signifies, literally, to change the mind. Reformation, as the word is commonly used, expresses the *effect* or consequence of *metanoia*, the change of mind. The former expresses an operation of the *mind;* the latter the conduct consequent upon it. His translation is here, I think, as in many other places, incorrect. This, however, by the way.

That Mr. C.'s exposition of the passage is incorrect, is clear, as already shown, from the fact, that it contradicts many other passages, the meaning of which is perfectly clear. But let us examine Peter's language: " Repent and be baptized, every one of you, in the name of the Lord Jesus, (*eis*) for, (or, as Mr. C. understands it, in order that you may secure) the remission of sins." We will compare with this, Matt. iii. 11, the language of which, in the original, is precisely similar ; " I, indeed, baptize you with water (*eis*) unto repentance," &c. The preposition *eis* is employed in both passages, precisely in the same manner. Peter said, " Repent and be baptized (*eis*) for the remission of sins ;" and John said, " I baptize you (*eis*) for or unto repentance." Will my friend maintain, that John baptized the Jews, *in order* that they might repent— to cause them to repent of their sins ! If he will not, how can he maintain that Peter commanded baptism, *in order* to the remission of sins? The mode of expression in both cases is precisely the same. The Jews came to John, confessing their sins and professing repentance ; and into that profession John did baptize them. But if the gentleman will explain to us the meaning of John's language, I will then be prepared to explain that of Peter's. If he cannot maintain that John baptized the Jews, in order to repentance, he cannot prove that Peter baptized those on the day of pentecost, *in order* to the remission of sins.

He informed us, that John preached the doctrine of *baptism for the remission of sins.* This, however, is not precisely correct. John preached " the baptism of *repentance* for the remission of sins," Mark i. 4. Repentance secured the remission of sins; and on profession of repentance the Jews were baptized. This is, I suppose, the meaning of the passage.

But if we were to admit, that the phrase in Peter's discourse *eis aphesin amartion*, means *in order* to the remission of sins; the question would be, whether repentance or baptism secured remission, or whether, as Mr. C. contends, both were equally necessary. As we have already seen, it was very common with the inspired writers to connect the external ordinance with the inward grace, or with the blessings of which it was the sign and pledge. Ezekiel said, "Then will I sprinkle clean water upon you, and you shall be clean; from all your filthiness and from all your idols will I cleanse you." By taking this passage out of its connection, I can prove, that the sprinkling of clean water upon persons will purify them from idolatry, and from all sin; a doctrine which none of us believe. Just so Ananias said to Paul, "be baptized, and *wash away* thy sins." The water was the external sign and pledge of deliverance from sin.

That repentance without baptism secures remission of sins, I can prove by several passages of Scripture; particularly by Peter's second discourse, recorded in Acts iii. 19: "Repent ye, therefore, and be converted, that your sins may be blotted out, when the times of refreshing shall come from the presence of the Lord." In this instance, you observe, Peter, though directing inquirers what they must do to be saved, omitted baptism. This he certainly would not have done, if he had regarded it as necessary to the remission of sins. But he said, "Repent and *be converted*." Did he preach contradictory doctrines? By no means. Repentance and conversion are both necessary to remission, but the former necessarily implies the latter. It is impossible that a man should *repent*, and not be *converted*. Repentance is a change of mind, a change of views and feelings; and can a man have new views, and new feelings and affections, and not be converted—turned from his former course to a new one? It is equally impossible that a man should be converted without repenting. Conversion is turning from one course to another; but no one radically changes his course of conduct, unless his mind is first changed. Inasmuch, therefore, as repentance and conversion mutually imply each other, as cause and effect, Peter might mention one or both, as he chose. So in his first discourse he mentioned repentance, which implies conversion; and in the second he mentions both repentance and conversion.

But can it be said, with truth, that baptism (and especially *immersion*) is necessarily implied in repentance, or in repentance and conversion? Certainly it cannot be denied, that multitudes do repent and turn to God, and live lives of exemplary piety, who never receive what Mr. C. calls baptism. If, then, baptism had been as necessary to remission of sins as repentance, surely Peter could not have omitted so to state the matter to those inquirers.

The argument is confirmed by the preaching of Paul to the jailor, Acts xvi. He came, trembling, and asked, "What must I do to be saved?" The answer was, "Believe on the Lord Jesus Christ, and thou shalt be saved." Here, neither repentance, conversion, nor baptism is mentioned, and yet Paul preached the same doctrine that had been preached by Peter; for faith necessarily implies conversion. I need not delay to prove, that every one who repents does also believe; and every one who repents and believes, is converted. These thing mutually imply each other, and are never found separated. Hence it is, that remission of sins, and salvation, are promised to those who repent; for wherever we find repentance, we find also faith and conversion. But does repentance, conversion, or faith, or all of them, necessarily imply baptism or immersion. Do not many repent, believe, and turn to God, who never can be baptized, or never will be immersed? How do you imagine the gentleman endeavors to escape from these difficulties? Why, he tells us, that the word *convert* means *immerse!* that the Jews, soon after Pentecost, knew that the disciples called the immersed *'converted;'* and that the time intervening between Peter's first and second discourses was long enough to familiarize this style in the metropolis, so that when a christian used the word *convert*, every Jew knew he meant *immerse!* The unbelieving Jews must have been very apt learners, to have become, in a few days, so familiar with the entirely new meanings of words in the christian dialect! But that the gentleman's conjecture is a wide mistake, is evident from one or two considerations :

1st. No two words in any language are more radically different in their etymological meaning, than *baptize* and *convert*. No lexicon can be found, that assigns to them the same, or even similar meanings.

2nd. In their usage they are as different as in their original meanings. The word *convert* had been long in use amongst the Jews, before the New Testament was written; and its meaning was well understood. A few passages, from the Old and New Testaments, will show what is its meaning in the Scriptures. Psalm li. 13, "Then will I teach transgressors thy ways; and sinners shall be *converted* unto thee." Isaiah vi. 10, "Make the heart of this people fat, &c., lest they see with their eyes, and hear with their ears, and understand with their heart, and *convert*, and be healed." Matt. xviii. 3, "Verily I say unto you, except ye be *converted*, and become as little children, ye shall not enter into the kingdom of heaven." In these passages, the meaning of the word *convert* cannot be misunderstood. It certainly expresses a radical moral change in the heart and in the life—a change of disposition to child-like simplicity and humility. It is used in the same sense in Acts xxvi. 18, where Christ sends Paul to the gentiles, " to open their eyes, and to turn [*convert*] them from darkness to light, and from the power of Satan unto God." Or, as I suppose my friend would read it, to *immerse* them from darkness to light! The truth is, there is not an example in the whole Bible, where the words *conversion* and *baptism* are used synonymously. The former is uniformly used to express a change of heart, and a corresponding change of conduct, particularly the latter. In this sense it was employed, with regard to those who had previously been baptized. Thus James says, " Brethren, if any of you do err from the truth, and one *convert* him, let him know that he which *converteth* the sinner from the error of his way, shall save a soul from death, and shall hide a multitude of sins," chap. v. 19, 20.

No two words, as these and other passages abundantly prove, are more radically different in meaning, than the words *baptism* and *conversion*— the one denoting a moral change; the other, an external ordinance. The gentleman, however, is forced to the glaring error of making them synonymous, in order to sustain his unscriptural doctrine, that baptism is necessary to the remission of sins. It is clear, that Peter, in his second discourse, omitted to mention baptism, as a condition of remission of sins, because he did not regard it in that light.

This is not all. Peter also preached the gospel to Cornelius and his family. He was directed by revelation from God to go and preach the gospel to this gentile family; and when he had heard from Cornelius how God had sent an angel and directed him to send for him, he "opened his mouth, and said, Of a truth I perceive that God is no respecter of persons: but in every nation he that feareth him, and worketh righteousness, is accepted with him," Acts x. 34, 35. Every one that fears God and works righteousness is accepted, whether he have been previously baptized or not. Cornelius had the best possible evidence of his acceptance; for his prayers had been heard, and his alms remembered. Did God hear the prayers of an unpardoned man, and send an angel to visit him, whilst yet he granted him not the burden of his heart's desire—the remission of his sins?

But Peter was sent to tell Cornelius words by which he and his family might be *saved*. He was, of course, to preach the gospel fully—to present very clearly the conditions of pardon and salvation. Did he preach to them baptism in order that their sins might be remitted? Cornelius was acquainted with the Old Testament, and was truly a pious man—a faithful servant of God; but he was not *saved*, in the full sense of this word. He needed all the truths and ordinances of the gospel to aid him in preparation for a holy heaven. But, according to Mr. Campbell's doctrine, here was one of the most godly men—a man who loved God and served him, a man who had received the miraculous gifts of the Holy Spirit; who was yet in a state of condemnation! For, let it be remembered, the Spirit descended upon him and his family *before they were baptized*.

I ask again—did Peter tell Cornelius, that he must be baptized in order to secure the remission of sins? He certainly did not; if Luke has faithfully recorded what he said. And let it be remarked, it was particularly important that this doctrine, if true, should have been preached on this occasion; for the gospel was now, for the first time, preached to the gentiles; and they had not heard of his discourses at Jerusalem. But Peter did not inform Cornelius, that though his prayers had been answered, his alms remembered, an angel sent to visit him, and the Holy Spirit poured out on him, his sins could not be forgiven, except in the act of receiving baptism! The conclusion is unavoidable, that baptism is not necessary in order to the remission of sins.

The correctness of this conclusion is confirmed by the answer given by Paul to the trembling jailor, already mentioned—"Believe on the Lord Jesus Christ, and thou shalt be saved." The apostle seems to have said not a word about baptism *in order to* remission of sins. Doubtless he commanded him to be baptized and to do many other things; but he certainly did not tell him, as Mr. C. tells those who ask him the same question, that his sins could be pardoned only *in the act* of receiving baptism. On the contrary, the language of Paul conveys the idea most distinctly, that so soon as he believed on the Lord Jesus Christ, his sins would be remitted, and his soul would be in safety. Salvation was offered to him on the single condition of faith; and, of course, all that is necessary to salvation, is implied in faith.

But it is not difficult to prove, that repentance does secure remission of sins. Indeed, repentance and remission are constantly associated in the writings of the apostles, as well as in the language of our Savior. A proof of this is found in Luke xxiv. 46, 47, "Thus it is written, and thus it behooved Christ to suffer, and to rise from the dead the third day:

and that *repentance and remission of sins* should be preached in his name, among all nations, beginning at Jerusalem." Did not our Savior connect together repentance and remission? He did not say—that repentance, *baptism* and remission of sins should be preached. Here the gentleman's doctrine labors. He is obliged to make *remission* mean *immersion!* Really, I am apprehensive, that he will convert the whole gospel into water. *Conversion*, we are told, means *immersion;* and *remission* means *immersion!* It is necessary, in order to sustain his doctrine, to make almost every thing mean immersion. Most evident it is, however, that our Savior taught, that true repentance secures the remission of sins. Every true penitent is also a believer; and every penitent believer is truly converted. Consequently, in the New Testament we find remission of sins promised sometimes to repentance, sometimes to conversion, and sometimes to faith.—[*Time expired.*

Wednesday, Nov. 23—12 o'clock, P. M.
[MR. CAMPBELL'S SECOND ADDRESS.]

MR. PRESIDENT—I certainly have a very singular opponent—one of his own class. He presumes not to respond to a single argument that I offer, in any of the usual forms of debate. There is nothing more generally established in the literary world than that, in all discussions in the form of debate, there should be a proposition, parties, an affirmant and a respondent; and that there are duties which devolve upon these parties as they severally stand, to the thesis to be discussed. In all schools, not merely in ordinary debating schools, but in all the high schools and colleges, one law obtains: the proof lies upon the affirmant, and the disproof upon the negative. Whatever arguments, therefore, are adduced by the affirmant, it is the duty of the negative to respond to them in some way or other. If they are weak, irrelevant, or inconclusive, he should expose them and refute them. If they are good, and relevant, and conclusive, he should acknowledge it and yield to them; but not to notice them at all, is at once to confess inability.

I have had some little experience in debates: but not in the person of Romanist, Protestant or infidel, have I found one who, after presenting to his special attention some seven arguments arranged in numerical order, in proof of a specific proposition, would then take up neither the first nor the last, nor any one of them; but immediately put out to sea, and talk of every thing else but the proposition or its proof. Such seems to be, in general terms, and in general practice, the peculiar accomplishments of my friend, Mr. Rice. He has again made a circuit through the Bible, and finally made up a new and a false issue. He has said many things that are true—things that every one admits; some that are not true; and some that, whether true or false, have no more point or bearing than the first verse of the first chapter of the first book of Chronicles, which, if I remember right, reads, "Adam, Seth, Enosh." He might have spoken in such style seven hours or seventy, and no one could know the proper issue. The issue is not about being begotten or born, not about believe, nor repent, nor reform, nor about baptism in general terms; but, is baptism *for the remission of sins*, or is it not? I have adduced seven arguments in proof of the affirmative. Not one of them has been answered. I shall therefore consider them unanswerable by Mr. Rice, and proceed to consider what he has advanced in the light of objections—or of casual remarks and declamations.

Mr. R. seems to have forgotten his obligations to teach the doctrines of his own church, set forth in that confession to which he has solemnly sworn, as containing " *the system* of truth taught in the Scriptures." He now seems to have either forgotten, or to have recanted so much of the Confession of Faith as declares the design of baptism. The confession declares that " baptism is for a sign and seal of the remission of sins." This is his own creed, and in its own words. Now I believe this, and he does not, if I properly understand him ; and, therefore, I am, as I before told you, more evangelically orthodox than he, according to his own confession.

You have heard him on John iii. 5. He says that baptism is not intended there. Jesus said, a person must be born of water and of the Spirit, else he cannot enter into the kingdom of heaven ! Now, I concur with the authors of the Confession of Faith, and with all the Greek and Latin fathers, without one single exception, in so understanding them. And you have heard what confidence the gentleman reposes in all these. They are all with me in this particular, and against him. If the gentleman, after solemnly avowing his full faith in that confession, as aforesaid, can thus set up his single judgment against the Westminster divines, the Greek and Latin fathers, and declare them all wrong, all mistaken, and refuse now to teach the doctrine, nay, *does actually now oppose his own church and confession*, how shall we bind him to any thing ! If neither the Bible, nor the confession, nor the Greek and Latin fathers, are to be understood nor believed, when affirming that baptism is for the remission of sins, what kind of evidence could satisfy him ?

I care nothing for triumphing over Mr. Rice or any other mortal. It is no pleasure to expose human weakness or human folly, only in so far as the cause of the truth and mission of the Messiah, and the interests of humanity may require it. There is a higher tribunal, in my eye, than human approbation, or the plaudits of my poor fellow-mortals. I sincerely ask, to what tribunal are we to bring this discussion?—to the Bible, the Confession of Faith, the catechisms, the Greek or Latin fathers ! They are all with me, but then—they are all wrong ! they are all mistaken !

I used the word *preposterous* the other day. My friend thought it discourteous to him. I did not intend it. He must have taken it in some improper acceptation. It only means to place first what ought to be last, as its etymology indicates. It means, of course, any absurd or palpably wrong course of either reasoning or acting. Now I must say, that in the plain, unsophisticated meaning of the word, his course at this time does truly appear to me somewhat preposterous. For, why at once abjure the creed and the assemblies' interpretation of John iii. 5, and the fathers whom he has, till just now, so highly revered, and raise quibbles about such phrases as these : " He that believeth on the Son of God hath eternal life"—" He that believeth on him is not condemned"—" He that believeth on him is justified from all things," &c.

The gentleman sees, in these passages, and many such, a refutation of my views, as he supposes, and of the confession, and the fathers, and the commentators, &c. He sees in such words as these, arguments strong and irrefragable. I wish he would show us where their great strength lies. I will take one of them for a sample—for the whole category to which it belongs, and lay it open to your consideration: "He that hath the Son, hath eternal life." Now this " having the Son," means believing on him, receiving him, confiding in him, as, I presume, you have all been taught. Now I will use the Scripture to explain and open the Scripture. Jesus says to his Father, in the intercessory prayer, " All thine are *mine*," and " 'That they may see the glory which *thou hast given me.*" Again—Paul says, " We have nothing, and yet possess all things." Now, while our Savior could say, " he had not where to lay his head," he could also say, " all thine are mine ;" all things that God had were his, and yet he had nothing. Does not every one, then, perceive that there are two ways of having things—in grant, or in right, and in actual possession. Here is a lad who has an immense landed estate, but is not yet possessed of a foot of it. He has it, however, in right of his father's will. Now he that believeth *is* justified, *is* pardoned, *has* eternal life, possesses all things, although he is a poor frail mortal. By faith he has them in hope, in anticipation ; he has them in grant, in right, according to the will of God. Is Mr. Rice the only one in this assembly that does not so understand this ? In this sense only could Jesus have the universe, when he had not a penny. In this way only had Paul all things, when he had nothing. And in this way a poor, frail, dying christian has eternal life, and a sinner righteousness, sanctification, and redemption.

If Mr. Rice did not design all this talk about faith, &c., &c., for an *ad captandum* argument, it is clearly one of that class : but not of such high elegance and plausibility as to inveigle any one of much mental comprehension and perspicacity. All things, then, are possible to him that believes. Faith is the great principle. It is, however, but a *principle*— by which we may secure righteousness, holiness, redemption, riches, glory, immortality. But such a faith *works*, works mightily, constantly, and always *by love.*

Before I dismiss this—objection, shall I call it ? for argument it is not, only in so far as it is an objection—may I add, in illustration, that we speak in this community just in the same style as the men of Judea spake two thousand years ago. We say of a naturalized foreigner, he has the rights of an American citizen. He has the right of suffrage, of the protection of our government, of being a representative in congress ; provided only, he properly exercise the rights conferred upon him in his enfranchisement. Still his enjoyments of any of them must, more or less, always depend upon himself. He has them only as the father of a prodigal son once said to his first born—" Son, thou art ever with me, and all that I have is *thine.*"

I would not say, that Mr. Rice has been sporting with the credulity of the audience in his dissertations upon *begotten* and *born.* Far be it. Yet really it looks more like an attempt of that sort, than at any grave argument. Whether we shall read, "He that believeth that Jesus is the Messiah, is born of God," or is begotten of God, must depend upon the taste and discrimination of the translator, as the word is the same in the original text. In all such cases, faith is spoken of as a reality—not as a pretence or a profession—and such a faith will always have in it the germ of universal obedience. But he that regards a person as possessing all this at the moment he believes, errs just as much as he that should take the words of the father of the prodigal son, to indicate that he had actually nothing, because he had told his son that all that he had was his.

But, let me ask, what is the real issue ? Is it faith, repentance, or baptism ? An issue has been agreed upon, and I have come up to it; but I have no opponent. I have, Mr. President, no respondent. My intro-

ductory speech is not now being discussed.   No point made in it is logically, or formally, or in any way directly assailed.

I will state what the true and proper issue is, in another form.   It is
this :   He contends that baptism is a purification or washing; *that* he has
elaborated at great length.   He says it is a purification of some sort—it
is a purification from sin.   He told you, that he goes for washing, cleansing, purifying.   He has baptismal purification, baptismal cleansing, baptismal washing, &c.   He says I agree with him so far.   But what is the
issue ?   I go for baptismal purification *through faith :* he goes for it
without faith.   I will stand to it before the world, that this, according to
him, is the real issue.   He will have infants, without faith, purified by
water, the baptismal purifier—whether it be applied by sprinkling, pouring, or dipping.   According to my friend, every infant that is baptized,
no matter how the ceremony is performed, is baptismally purified; and,
consequently, without faith; and, therefore, his purification is without
faith.   I believe that this baptismal purification comes through faith only.
Hence faith is the vital principle, without which it is impossible to please
God.   According to my views, a person believes, repents, and is baptized, in order to purification.   According to his views, he is purified,
sanctified, adopted, if an adult, by faith alone ; but if an infant, by sprinkling alone, without faith or intelligence.   An adult, with him, if he have
faith he has every thing—pardon, justification, sanctification ; he is a
child of God, he is begotten of God, he is born of God, has every thing.
There is no use for baptism or the Lord's supper ; all means and ordinances, according to his position, are mere superfluities, so far as these
benefits are implied.   But we plead for faith, because without it we cannot please God ; but not for faith alone.

But, my fellow-citizens, to excite the antipathies of religious parties
against us, if not to make us most odiously uncharitable, in the current
style of the present century it has been often said, and said during this
discussion, that with us it is—no baptism, no pardon, no salvation.   Now,
there is, in one point of view, nothing in this peculiar to us.   All professors
of christianity, I mean all parties, make baptism, *under certain conditions*,
essential to salvation.   Roman Catholics believe so.   Protestants say,
that any one who knows that it is a christian ordinance, and wilfully disdains or neglects it, cannot be saved.   I have never written or spoken any
thing stronger than that.   And yet, how often have the pulpits and the
presses proclaimed that we, *in all cases*, make baptism absolutely essential to salvation—that we suspend the eternal destiny of mankind upon the
presence of a certain quantity of water.   Nay, we have been gravely
asked the question, a hundred times, should a person die on his way to
the water, would he be lost forever, because he failed in getting into it !
This, I have always said, is a *non sequitur ;* a consequence that follows
not from any tenet or saying of ours.   Indeed, both in old England and
in New England, this was once the current and standing abuse of the
Baptists—of all immersionists.   But they have survived it.   So will we.
I have said that such views are not a fair consequence of any thing we
have either said or written on this subject.   Still the question, whether
the Lord would suspend, in any way, the salvation of any human being
upon the contingency of the presence of water, savors much more of
ignorance and scepticism on the part of the propounders, than of error on
the part of him to whom such a question is propounded.   Suppose we
ask, for illustration, what portion of the world enjoys the Bible ?   I

am told, not one-half. Now, I presume Mr. Rice makes the possession of the Bible essential to salvation. And what is the material of which the Bible is composed? In one point of view, may we not say, it is composed of rags, oil, and lamp-black? It might, then, in one point of view, be said, that the salvation of the world depends upon the contingency of a certain quantity of rags, oil, and lamp-black? and that we must make such a contingency essential to the salvation of the world? If, then, as one may say, the destiny of half the world be suspended upon such a contingency, ought he, on his own principles, to demur at the state of the case which he himself presents? There is neither wit nor reason in the objection, abstractly considered; nor is there any pertinency whatever in its relevancy to us. We do not hold faith, repentance, or baptism essential to salvation, in all cases. And yet, if water were to be made the most essential of them all, it would, on the principle of the caviler himself, seem most of all consistent, inasmuch as water is infinitely more common than either faith or repentance—three-fourths of the terraqueous globe being covered with it. In responding to this oft-repeated calumny, I have answered many of his arguments and objections, both on the former propositions and in the speech which we have just now heard. For, indeed, this has been incorporated with many of them, or rather the spirit that has animated a majority of them.

Instead of discussing the argument founded on Peter's response to the three thousand, Mr. Rice would make it a matter of importance, that Peter should always have used the very same words on every occasion, and given, identically, the same answer to every querist—as if our Lord, or any of the apostles, had always used the same words, speaking of faith, repentance, or any thing else!! If Peter had never spoken these identical words a second time, " Repent and be baptized, every one of you, in the name of the Lord Jesus, for the remission of sins," after having, on the day of Pentecost, opened the kingdom of heaven with them, the other apostles speaking them in all languages at the same time—the Holy Spirit manifestly present, dictating and authenticating them—methinks it is enough forever. To have used the same words as a *formula*, on all occasions, would have been supremely eccentric. To have told us on every occasion, that every new convert believed, repented, and was baptized, before he entered the church, would not have been more ridiculous, than to have answered every human being in the same number and arrangement of words. We are, but once told, " that they who gladly received the word were baptized"—but never are those identical words used on any other occasion. Then we must infer, that no other persons ever gladly received the word—if we must conclude that Peter never again used exactly the same words!! It is said, " thé Lord added daily the saved to the church," but it is not said that they believed, or repented, or were baptized! Must we then infer they were not? Yet such is the learned logic of Mr. Rice.

Yet in the very next discourse of Peter, at which an immense multitude were converted, in Solomon's portico, we find a similar, if not an identical address. His words are, " Repent and be converted, every one of you, that your sins may be blotted out." Now, " *the blotting* out of sins," according to Mr. Rice, is an innovation. It ought to have been, "for the remission of sins." So is the imperative "*be converted*," instead of " *be baptized.*" Now, as " *be baptized*," on the former occasion, meant " be converted," so " *be converted*," on the present occasion means " be baptized," inasmuch as it just occupies the same portion in both sermons. It stands between "repent," and "for the remission of sins," in the former; and between "repent," and "that your sins may be blotted out," in the latter. In commenting on these words, Mr. Rice represents me as using emersion, and baptism, as synonymous. I have not said so. It would be a sophism, of which I am not guilty, to say, that words that represent the same thing are synonymous. Circumstances do make words represent the same thing that do not mean the same thing. Different persons frequently report the result of a certain meeting in different terms. For example: A says, " ten persons were *baptized* yesterday at such a meeting." B, however, says, " ten persons were *converted* at the meeting yesterday ;" and C says, " ten *joined* yesterday." Now, what philologist will say, that the three words, *baptized, converted, joined,* are synonymous—because circumstances have made them all represent the same thing ! Yet such is the discrimination of my respondent.

Such special pleading is as inconsistent with sound logic, as it is with christian candor. My views of christianity constrain me to place such an estimate on the latter as is favorable to the proper exercise of the former, and protects me from the necessity of having to sustain any point by a course of special reasonings. Mr. Rice has sought to make you smile at his ingenuity in sporting with the word *reformation,* as a substitute for repentance. He did not succeed, however, very well. Dr. Campbell's preference for *reformation,* rather than *repentance,* is sustained, not only by the mere philologists, but by the most distinguished biblical scholars. But now let us look again at the phrase—I baptize you into reformation. Persons are always immersed *into* something, as well as *in* something; and they are baptized *for* that *into which* they are baptized, and not for that *in which* they are baptized. Now John preached not *repentance,* but *reformation ;* for the last word includes the former, while the former does not include the latter. Many repent who do not reform, but no one can reform who does not.repent. John calls for fruits worthy of a professed repentance, fruits indicative of repentance. He, therefore, immersed men on profession of penitence, or while confessing their sins, that they might reform. Hence he baptized men in order to, or for the sake of, reformation. I baptize you *in* water that you may reform, said the Baptist—hence his was the baptism of reformation for the remission of sins. Better the gentleman had discoursed upon some one of the arguments adduced, than to have occupied his time on such frivolous matters. Having now noticed every thing that seems to demand my attention—as well as some matters which I sincerely think do not merit it—I will proceed to some further documentary proof of the proposition before us.

I must introduce the great reformer himself, and let the immortal Luther declare what his views of the design of this institution are. His Commentary on the Galatians, it is believed, was his master performance, so far as its power in establishing justification in opposition to Roman penances and works of merit is regarded. (Luther on Galatians : Philad. 1801, 8vo. p. 302.)

" This is not done by changing of a garment, or by any laws or works, but by a new birth, and by the renewing of the inward man, which is done in baptism, as Paul saith, ' All ye that are baptized have put on Christ.' Also, ' According to his mercy he saved us by the washing of regeneration, and renewing of the Holy Ghost.' Tit. iii. 5. For besides that they who are baptized, are regenerated and renewed by the Holy Ghost to a heavenly righteousness, and to eternal life, there riseth in them also a new light and a new flame; there riseth in them new and holy affections, as the fear of God, true faith, and assured hopes, &c. There beginneth in them also a new will. And this is to put on Christ truly and according to the gospel.

Therefore the righteousness of the law, or of our own works, is not given unto us in baptism; but Christ himself is our garment. Now Christ is no law, no law-giver, no works, but a divine and an inestimable gift, whom God hath given unto us, that he might be our justifier, our Savior, and our Redeemer. Wherefore to be appareled with Christ according to the gospel, is not to be appareled with the law or with works, but with an incomparable gift; that is, with remission of sins, righteousness, peace, consolation, joy of spirit, salvation, life, and Christ himself.

This is diligently to be noted, because of the fond and fantastical spirits, who go about to deface the majesty of baptism, and speak wickedly of it. Paul contrariwise commendeth and setteth it forth with honorable titles, calling it ' the washing of regeneration, and renewing of the Holy Ghost,' Tit. iii. 5. And here also he saith, that all they who are baptized, have put on Christ. As if he said, ye are carried out of the law into a new birth, which is wrought in baptism. Therefore ye are not now any longer under the law, but ye are clothed with a new garment; viz. with the righteousness of Christ. Wherefore it is a thing of great force and efficacy. Now, when we are appareled with Christ, as with the robe of righteousness and salvation, then we must put on Christ also as the apparel of imitation and example. These things I have handled more largely in another place, therefore I here briefly pass them over."

To this I will add two extracts from the Westminster Confession, indicative of remarkable harmony with the master spirit of protestantism. (Page 337.)

" *Q.* 165. What is baptism?

A. Baptism is a sacrament of the New Testament, wherein Christ hath ordained the washing with water in the name of the Father, and of the Son, and of the Holy Ghost, to be a sign and seal of ingrafting into himself; of remission of sins by his blood, and regeneration by his Spirit; of adoption, and resurrection unto everlasting life: and whereby the parties baptized are solemnly admitted into the visible church, and enter into an open and professed engagement to be wholly and only the Lord's."

The doctrine of the Confession is more fully declared in chap. 28. sec. 1 ;—to which we invite attention. It is in the words following, to wit :

" Baptism is a sacrament of the New Testament, ordained by Jesus Christ, not only for the solemn admission of the party baptized into the visible church; but also to be unto him a sign and seal of the covenant of grace, of his ingrafting into Christ, of regeneration, of remission of sins, and of his giving up unto God, through Jesus Christ, to walk in newness of life: which sacrament is, by Christ's own appointment, to be continued in his church until the end of the world."

A sign and seal, then, it is, of remission of sins! Past or future? Of past sins! Then the confession of faith clearly and amply proves my proposition. In every important point it is with me and against Mr. Rice. It makes baptism for admission into the church; Mr. Rice is for baptism to them in the church, and it is for making it a sacrament of the New Testament. I desire no more ample proof of my views on this subject, than the confession of faith and the proof-texts at the foot of the page. I am, then, in this particular, certainly more conformed to the confession of faith than Mr. Rice.

Fellow-citizens, I know of no respectable ecclesiastic writer, who has not taken this view of the subject, if he have gravely considered the matter at all. But the grand reason why so many cannot comprehend the meaning of this institution is, they have got infant church membership so much in their heads; and, as infants cannot be justified by faith, and as they cannot obtain remission of *sins* in baptism, being only implicated in one sin, of one Adam, they cannot understand what the Bible, the creed, or the catechism mean, when they talk of baptism being "a sign and a seal of the remission of sins." They have to say, these articles, in the confession, speak of believers' baptism. This is generally the way of escape. Where then shall we find an account of unbelievers' baptism? The Pedo-baptist party, through the bewildering influence of two baptisms, one for babes and one for believing persons, are now, and forever will be, while they retain these two baptisms, unable to comprehend the subject, and to reconcile to themselves, or to one another, the prophets and the apostles of the Messiah.—[*Time expired.*

Thursday, Nov. 23—12½ *o'clock, A. M.*
[MR. RICE'S SECOND REPLY.]

MR. PRESIDENT—I had not the most distant expectation, when I agreed to conduct this discussion, that I should please my friend, Mr. Campbell, either as an affirmant, or as a respondent. If I had expected to please him, I should not have become his opponent. He would, doubtless, be extremely happy, could he induce me to pursue such a course, so to follow him in his meanderings, as to give him a triumph; but I am not disposed to gratify him. He informs the audience, that I never directly answer his arguments. It is necessary that he should give them this information, or they, in their simplicity, will not discern it! He must repeat the declaration that I have not answered him, every time he rises to speak, or the audience will be sure to believe the contrary! Indeed, I very much question, whether his assertions will prevent them from believing that his arguments have been fully exposed.

How any man, so much accustomed to public debate as he, can affirm, that the respondent is bound to follow precisely in the track of the affirmant, I am at a loss to understand. I profess also to have had some little experience in such discussions, and I do not admit the existence of any such rule. When a man sets forth a doctrine, founded on a particular interpretation of certain texts of Scripture, I have the right to answer him in either of two ways: I may take up those passages, and prove, by the admitted principles of language, that his interpretation is incorrect; or I may prove that it contradicts other plain, and unambiguous declarations of Scripture, and, therefore, is incorrect. In either case, I have fairly answered him; for we both maintain, that the Bible does not contradict itself. When, therefore, I have proved, that the interpretation of certain passages of Scripture, upon which the gentleman's doctrine is based, is contradictory of the clear and repeated declarations of Christ and the apostles, I have triumphantly refuted his doctrine. He may tell you five hundred times, that my arguments are irrelevant; but in so doing he only shows how much his cause requires him to act the part of a cunning lawyer, who is obliged, without evidence, to plead against evidence. He will save himself much trouble and exposure, if only he can induce the audience to believe, that the arguments against his views, are all irrelevant. It will, however, be found extremely difficult, if not impossible, to convince reflecting persons, that an interpretation, which contradicts Christ, can be correct. The contradictions I have pointed out, are so perfectly clear and palpable, they must satisfy every unprejudiced mind, that his doctrine is untrue. It contradicts Christ and his apostles, and that is enough.

But the gentleman, who is quite anxious to appear familiar with Presbyterianism, charges me with having departed from the confession of faith. After all, however, he seems to have a very imperfect knowledge of the system. Of this he has already given us repeated evidences.

Does our confession say, that the passage in John iii. 5, means christian baptism? It does not. I subscribe most cordially to the doctrine of that book, in regard to the ordinance of baptism. It teaches, that it is a sacrament appointed by Christ, to be a sign and seal of our engrafting into Christ, of remission of sins, &c. It is true, the confession, in the chapter on baptism, refers to John iii. 5, as an example of the use of water, as an emblem of spiritual cleansing; but it also refers to circumcision, as the gentleman will see (I have not the book at this moment) by turning to it. So he would prove, that according to our confession, circumcision is baptism! But he certainly ought to know, that in adopting the confession of faith, we do not affirm that every reference to Scripture is appropriate; so that if it were even true, as it may be, that those who made the reference in question, believed the passage to refer to baptism, I might deny it, without being charged with heresy. The reference, nevertheless, is perfectly proper, because, as water was the emblem of purification under the old dispensation, so it is under the new. As the ablution of the Jews pointed to the cleansing of the soul from the guilt and pollution of sin, so does baptism now. I go for the confession of faith; and I think I understand it.

The gentleman tells us, he has not entered into this discussion for a *temporary triumph.* I am quite willing that he shall gain a triumph if he can. I hope he will bring all his powers to bear. I call for no quarters.

His last speech has taught me something new. He has informed us, that when the Savior said, "He that believeth on the Son, *hath* everlasting life;" he did not mean just what he said, but only that he has life *at his offer—he may* have it! Our Savior, the gentleman would have us believe, did not mean what he said; but Peter meant precisely what he said! True, words may be understood in a figurative sense, when the connection requires it; but when Christ says, he that believeth, *hath* everlasting life, the language is perfectly plain, and the meaning most obvious. I must, therefore, believe it. To say, that a man has a thousand dollars, and that to say that he *may get* a thousand dollars, are very different propositions.

One of his illustrations of this new meaning of the word *hath,* was particularly unfortunate. It was this: a man, when naturalized, *has* the rights and immunities of a citizen; but whether he will improve them, depends on himself. Very well. So when a man believes, he is naturalized, and *has* all the blessings of Christ's kingdom, of which one of the most important is remission of sins; but still he must persevere unto death. This, I should consider a very unhappy illustration of his doctrine, that a man is not naturalized in the kingdom of Christ, and enjoys none of its blessings, until he is baptized. But Mr. C. used another illustration, which I think is no better than the one just noticed. He quoted the passage, "The foxes have holes, and the birds of the air have nests; but the Son of Man hath not where to lay his head." How this passage proves, that the word *hath* means *may have*, I am unable to see. The foxes *have* holes. Does this mean, they *may have* holes?—there are holes into which they *may* run? The birds of the air *have* nests—that is, according to the gentleman's logic, they *may have* nests—there are nests into which they *may* go?!! The Son of Man hath not where to lay his head; that is, he *may not* have where to lay his head! The passage confirms all that I have said. The birds have—are in possession of, nests. So he that believeth, *hath*—is in possession of, eternal life. The expressions are precisely similar.

But this is not all. The argument does not depend on this single expression, though it is perfectly clear. The Savior stated the same truth in another form; "He that believeth on the Son, *is not condemned*," John iii. 18. But Mr. C. says, he that believeth *is condemned*, unless he have been immersed!—a flat contradiction. For he does not deny, that a great many have believed on the Son, who never were immersed; and all such, according to his faith, are condemned. I cannot see how he could more directly contradict our Lord. I hope he will consider this an answer to his argument, sufficiently *direct*.

I was gratified to hear him admit, that the word translated *begotten*, is the same which is translated *born*. I used the former word, because he had done so in his translation; and I intended, as I said, to disprove his doctrine by his own translation. I will now, in view of his admission, put the word *born* instead of *begotten*, 1 John v. 1, "Whosoever believeth that Jesus is the Christ, is *born* of God." Now, my friend will not immerse a man, till he professes to believe that Jesus is the Christ; and John the apostle says, he that believeth *is born of God*. He is born —is a child of God, before he can get him to the water; and if he is born of God—if he is a child, then he is an heir of God, (Rom. viii. 17) and his sins are, of course, remitted. I am quite pleased, that my friend has admitted so much of the truth. I will, however, take either translation, *begotten* or *born*, and prove, that his doctrine of baptism in order to the remission of sins, directly contradicts the Savior and the apostles.

But the gentleman, who would have us believe that he never makes false issues, has told us, that the issue is this: that *I* believe in baptismal purification *without* faith; and he believes in baptismal purification *by* faith! I have said not a word about baptismal purification. What is the proposition before us? The question is, whether baptism is necessary in order to secure the remission of sins. I discover, he is disposed to divert our attention from the subject in hand, to something as distant from it as the poles from each other.

He is evidently anxious to say something more on infant baptism. I know, he is not well satisfied with his defence of his views on that subject; or he would not injure himself by thrusting it into the discussion of a different subject. He feels that he is involved in serious difficulties. Well, if he is not satisfied, I cannot help it.

According to my doctrine, he says, faith secures to us every thing; and there is no need of prayer, baptism, or any thing else. He is quite mistaken. I hold, that by faith alone we receive the Lord Jesus Christ, as our "wisdom, righteousness, sanctification and redemption;" and as soon as we receive him, our sins are pardoned, and we are accepted of God. But we are not yet perfectly holy. The good work is commenced, but not completed. We still need to pray, as did David, "Create in me a clean heart, O God, and renew a right spirit within me." Thus, Paul prayed for the Ephesian christians, whose sins had certainly been for-given, that God would grant them " according to the riches of his glory, to be strengthened with might by his Spirit in the inner man," ch. iii. 16. And he prayed for the Philippians, because he was confident " that He which had begun a good work in them, would perform it until the day of Jesus Christ," ch. i. 6. The believer, though his sins are remitted, needs baptism, the Lord's supper, and all the appointed means of grace, as helps to him in his weakness, as means in the use of which God has promised to bless him.

True faith, moreover, always produces good works. That faith which results not in good works, as James teaches, is dead, being alone : it cannot secure the remission of sins. The faith of the gospel answers two important purposes in the plan of salvation. It receives Christ as the Savior, through whose righteousness only men can be justified ; and it overcomes the world. " For whatsoever is born of God, overcometh the world ; and this is the victory that overcometh the world, *even our faith*," 1 John v. 4. Such is the faith for which we plead—a faith that receives Christ, and, through him, immediate remission of sins, and pre-sents before the mind all the motives which God offers to enable us to rise above the temptations of earth. Infant baptism, as well as that of adults, becomes a means of grace ; for when they who are baptized in infancy arrive at years of discretion, they, under the influence of divine grace, acknowledge the obligations assumed by their believing parents in connection with their baptism, and seek the blessings sealed by that ordinance.

We, then, do not plead for *faith alone*, but for faith, repentance, and conversion, which are inseparably connected—for faith, and the good works to which it prompts.

My friend said something about the difficulty under which his doc-trine labors, from the fact, that it sends to hell many who, though entirely disposed to obey God, had not the opportunity to be baptized ; and he expressed the opinion, that under certain circumstances, unbaptized per-sons may get to heaven. But if his *opinion* is true, his *doctrine* is false ; and if his doctrine is true, his opinion is false. His doctrine is, that baptism is necessary in order to the remission of sins.

The pagans, he seems to think, are sent to hell for a very small mat-ter ; only because they have not rags, oil, and lamp-black ! I had sup-posed, that they were pretty well furnished with rags, and perhaps with oil and lamp-black. I have never heard any complaint on that score. [A laugh.] But if the gentleman says they have not, I have nothing to say. [Continued laughter.] If he chooses to represent the Bible as only rags, lamp-black, and oil, let him do so. The pagans, however, are responsi-ble only for the light they have.

He attaches considerable importance to the expression, baptizing *into* the name of the Father, &c. I have no particular objection to that trans-lation of the word *eis*. It does not, however, seem to me to have any direct bearing on the question before us. Faith unites us spiritually to Christ, and gives us an interest in the plan of salvation ; baptism is the external ordinance by which we become visibly united to him, and bound to devote ourselves to his service. Baptism is the external sign. faith is the internal grace. The latter unites us to Christ *really*, the former con-nects with him *formally ;* but the piety of the heart is, in the Word of God, always represented as the *great matter*.

30

In reply to the fact stated by me, that in Peter's second discourse baptism was not mentioned as a condition of pardon; Mr. Campbell says, Peter's having taught a doctrine once, is sufficient—it is not necessarry that he shall repeat it in every discourse. Yes—if he will prove, that in one instance Peter taught that baptism is necessary to the remission of sins, we will give up the question. But I have proved, that his interpretation of Peter's language contradicts many other declarations of Scripture; and therefore Peter could not have said, that baptism is a prerequisite to the remission of sins. He said, repent and be baptized for the remission of sins; and in other portions of Scripture, we learn that repentance does secure the blessing, of which baptism is the outward sign and seal. The difficulty, therefore, is not that we claim a repetition of Peter's teaching before we will believe it, but that the gentleman makes Peter contradict the Savior and the other apostles; whilst the exposition for which we contend, is perfectly consistent with the uniform teaching of the Scriptures.

True, as he says, it is not necessary to preach the same truth in every discourse. But if I to-day preach to a company of ignorant persons in answer to the question, what must we do to be saved? I am bound to tell them all that is necessary to be done that they may be saved. Then if, on to-morrow, I preach to another company twenty miles distant, in answer to the same inquiry, I am obliged to teach them precisely the same truths. But suppose I should, in directing these last inquirers, omit one of the most important conditions of pardon; and when inquired of concerning the matter, should justify myself by saying, I mentioned that to the people in Lexington, and it is unnecessary always to say the same thing; would any one regard me as a faithful minister? A company of emigrants come to our country from Europe, and inquire what course they must pursue in order to be naturalized. You give them all necessary information. Another company comes and ask the same question. You omit, in your reply, one of the things absolutely necessary to be done; and excuse yourself, because you gave full information to the preceding company! I profess not to see the consistency of the gentleman's reasoning.

The truth is, the apostles, whenever they stated to inquiring minds the conditions of salvation, told them all that was really necessary; and inasmuch as Peter did not mention baptism as a condition of remission, either in his second discourse, or in his third at the house of Cornelius; and as Paul, in answering the same momentous inquiry made by the jailor, omitted to do it; it is clear that Mr. Campbell's doctrine is not true.

I was truly surprised to hear the gentleman assert, that he had never said, that *conversion* and *baptism*, as used by the apostles, mean the same thing. I have read his writings with some care; and, if I do not greatly err, he has so said. I will read from his *Christianity Restored*, (pp. 201, 202,) where he is laboring to prove that Peter, in his second discourse, (Acts iii.) preached baptism for the remission of sins, as in the first. He says:—

"The unbelieving Jews, soon after Pentecost, knew that the disciples called the *immersed* 'CONVERTED;' and immersion being the act of faith, which drew the line of demarcation between Christians and Jews, nothing could be more natural than to call the act of immersion the converting of a Jew. The time intervening between these discourses was long enough to introduce and familiarize this style in the metropolis; so that when a Christian said, 'Be converted,' or, 'Turn to God,' every Jew knew the act of putting on the Messiah to be that intended. After the immersion of some gentiles into the faith, in the house and neighborhood of Cornelius, it reported that the gentiles were converted to God. Thus the apostles, in passing through the country, gave great joy to the disciples from among the Jews, ' telling them of the *conversion*,' or *immersion* of the gentiles."

Again:

" One reason why we would arrest the attention of the reader *to the substitution of the terms* CONVERT *and* CONVERSION *for* IMMERSE *and* IMMERSION, *in the apostolic discourses, and in the sacred writings*, is not so much for the purpose of proving," &c.

Now, I ask, does he not make these two words mean the same thing? Does he not assert that *convert* and *conversion* were, by the inspired writers, substituted for *immerse* and *immersion?* When Peter said, " Repent and be converted," he meant, according to Mr. Campbell, reform and be *immersed!* And yet there are not two words in the Bible more widely different in their meaning.

In translating the word *metanoia* reformation, instead of repentance, he says he is sustained by the most learned men now living, or that have ever lived. This I am disposed to dispute. We want the proof. It is truly remarkable, that in starting a new reformation, which makes war upon all the christian world, the gentleman has, on almost every point, all the most learned men with him !!! All are wrong; yet all are with him! I am not disposed to take his broad assertions, without proof. The literal meaning of the word *metanoia*, as he has admitted, is a *change of mind;* and such being its meaning, how can it be correctly translated *reformation*—a word which, in common use, refers more immediately to the external conduct?

The expressions used in Peter's first discourse and in Matt. iii. 11, are, as I have remarked, precisely similar; and I asked Mr. C., whether, as he made Peter say, be baptized *(eis)* in order to obtain remission of sins, he also understood John to say, I baptize you *(eis)* in order that you may repent. He says, John baptized the Jews, *in order to* REFORMATION. But there are very serious difficulties in the way of this rendering; for Peter required reformation (if this be a correct translation) *in order to baptism;* and John baptized *in order to reformation!* How is it that he makes these inspired teachers thus contradict each other? He must be in error; for they did not thus cross each other's path.

But there is another difficulty in his way. John, he says, baptized in order to *reformation.* Now let us turn to Peter's second discourse, Acts iii. 19 : " Reform ye, therefore, [I give Mr. C.'s translation,] and be converted, that your sins may be blotted out," &c. Reform and be converted. Will he please to tell us the difference between *reformation* and *conversion?* *To be converted*, is to turn from sin to holiness—from the service of Satan to the service of God; and to *reform* is precisely the same thing. So that he makes Peter say to those whom he addressed, *reform* and *reform!* or, *convert* and be *converted!* The common translation labors under no such difficulty; neither does our doctrine. Repentance is a change of mind—a change of views and feelings; and conversion is the effect or consequence of that change. The former has direct reference to a change of mind; the other to a change of life. But the gentleman's doctrine forces him into these absurdities. The Bible contains no such contradictions, and no such tautology.

You see the inextricable difficulty in which the doctrine of my friend is involved. To sustain his interpretation of Peter's language, he must either make John baptize the Jews in order to make them *repent*, or in order that they might *reform*. In either case he makes John contradict Peter, who required repentance or reformation in order to baptism!

He quotes Luther as favoring his views of this doctrine. It may be possible that Luther attached an undue importance and efficacy to baptism. In regard to the Lord's supper he differed from the other reformers, rejecting *tran*substantiation, but holding the almost equally unreasonable doctrine of *con*substantiation. It would not be surprising, if a man so much in error in regard to one of the sacraments, should attach an unscriptural efficacy to the other. The Protestant world have rejected Luther's dogma of consubstantiation. I have not particularly examined his views concerning the doctrine now under discussion; and, therefore, shall for the present pass them.

The gentleman seeks to obtain from the Confession of Faith—a book I love to defend—some countenance for his doctrine. Where it teaches that baptism is a sign and seal of our ingrafting into Christ, he makes it mean, that none are in Christ, until baptized. I have repeatedly told you, that he does not understand Presbyterianism. Baptism, according to the confession, is a sign and seal of our ingrafting into Christ. Is the *sign* of a thing the thing itself? Is the sign necessary to the thing? The seal fixed to a document—is it not designed to give it notoriety? It is first written and confirmed; then sealed. There is a vast difference between the sign and seal of regeneration, and regeneration itself; and between the sign and seal of remission, and remission itself. The believer is first pardoned, and then receives the sign and seal. Baptism is a pledge, so to speak, that God will forgive the sins of those who comply with the conditions set forth in his Word. But the sign or seal is not the thing or document, nor essential to it.—[*Time expired.*

Thursday, Nov. 23—1 o'clock, P. M.
[MR. CAMPBELL'S THIRD ADDRESS.]

MR. PRESIDENT—It is always an unpleasant task to expose any thing which is incompatible with the genius and character of honorable discussion, and especially in matters of religion; for if there be any subject under the canopy of heaven, which men ought to discuss with superlative candor, and with supreme regard to the principles of truth and honor, it is the subject of religion. It is, therefore, with no pleasure, but with much pain, that I am constrained to notice the very unfair and ungenerous conduct of my reverend respondent. There is not a soul in this house, who did not understand me to say, that the Bible, as to the *materials* of which the book is made, and in that point of view alone, consists of rags, lamp-black, and oil. I ask, then, how Mr. Rice, a professed christian minister, could, in your presence, represent the Bible, with special reference to my remarks, as nothing but rags, lamp-black, and oil! What, sir, are we to expect from other men, in the private walks of life, if, on this stage, and in the presence of this great assembly, when I brought up his own argument, what signifies *water?* what avails any material thing, or any ordinance consisting of sensible materials, in order to remission of sins, or any spiritual blessings? I said he might also speak of the Bible, the word of life, in the same style, and thus depreciate its indispensable importance. I record this, as an exhibit of the manner of spirit with whom I have to contend for the ordinances of Christ. He represents me as saying the Bible was mere rags! and disdainfully asks if the pagans have no rags, oil, or lamp-black? If, in representing even a portion of a community, so respectable as the Presbyterian church, such morality and logic, meet its conscientious approbation, and obtain its admiration, I must say I am greatly mistaken. I dislike to waste my time in adverting to matters so unworthy of the occasion, and so utterly incompatible with the subject and the argument before us. If I do not again allude to matters of this sort, it will not be because I do not observe them, but because my time is too precious to be thus squandered away on an occasion so solemn and important.

In looking over my notes, the next thing that occurs is another false issue. I said it was not necessary for the apostles to preach the same sermon, in the same words, on all occasions. My special friend then makes out a special case—a new ship-load of immigrants arrives in a new country—and now I am represented as forbidding the same identical words to be uttered to them! Nay, worse than that; I am made to argue that the same gospel which was preached to the first ship-load, should not be preached to the second. Then, to meet his views, one sermon should have been cast in the same identical words, and but one gospel sermon ever preached!! I have preached faith, repentance, and baptism, times innumerable; and I am sure that I have never made two sermons on the subject that were not more dissimilar than that recorded in Acts ii., and that pronounced in Acts iii. I presume many of us here could tell the same story, and yet we all preach the proposition which I now defend! But such is the gentleman's way of responding to my arguments.

But I am setting one apostle against another, and the same apostle against himself, because of my remark on the phrase, " He that believeth, hath eternal life," &c. My remarks on "*hath*" and "*is*," on "*hath* eternal life," and "*is* not condemned," &c. have called forth a reiteration of the former assertions. But without at all impairing the force of the critique offered, I need only exemplify the principle a little farther; the argument, it appears, cannot be weakened. The position is, that in Scripture, and even in common style, we often hear persons speaking of themselves, or spoken of, as *having* what they have not in actual possession, but in promise, in expectation, in grant, or in hope. Hence, persons are said, at one time, to have that which they are seeking for at another. Take an example: Jesus, as already quoted, said, " He that believeth on Him that sent me, *hath* everlasting life—*is* passed from death to life." Again he says, " Whosoever believeth on him *hath* eternal life," &c. Now these same believers are, in other portions of Scripture, represented as not yet having it; but seeking and *looking* for it, and as about hereafter to have it. Paul, Rom. ii. says, " To them, who by a patient continuance in well-doing, are seeking for glory, honor, and immortality, he will bestow eternal life!" Now had these persons, in grant, or in possession, eternal life?

Again, he says to Titus, we are made heirs " according to the hope of eternal life." What a man *hath*, why doth he yet hope for! We are said to be " looking for eternal life." What a man seeth, why doth he yet look for! I shall henceforth regard this point as settled.

I have another remark to make on such passages as these: " He that believeth in him, is justified," &c. In all these instances the Savior, who spoke before the new institution was set up, as well as the apostles afterwards, speak of a true, real, active faith, which would always lead to obedience. These are *actual* believers, who will do what they are bid.

I did not say that the whole learned world agree with me. I wish the gentleman would reply to what I *do* say, and not spend our time so much in replying to what I *do not say*. But I do say, and the gentleman knows I can prove it, that I have not only such men as Luther, and Calvin, and Witsius, but *all the Greek and Latin fathers, for the first four centuries*, concurring with me in my views of John iii. 5., and Titus iii. 5., as well as the Westminster Assembly; and, besides, a mighty host of the reformers, in their individual capacity, avowing the proposition which I am now sustaining. Here is a volume from one of the most learned men (of Oxford, in England,) in the world, in the primitive fathers' Greek and Latin, who is, now, an overmatch for any other individual man in Great Britain, on this question, for whose opinions I by no means endorse, but for whose immense researches and exact knowledge I do—Dr. Pusey is his name. And here is one volume of the Oxford tracts, giving the views of the *design* of baptism, held by the whole ancient church; and, although I am very far from being a Puseyite, nevertheless I must respect the accumulated testimony collected here, a considerable portion of which I have used for years, and so has this same Dr. Wall, but all of which I have never seen before collected together. And what is the sum of it? That in this one thing of the action of baptism and the design of it, there was but one opinion, from the day of Pentecost down to St. Athanasius—down to the fifth century. But we must hear Calvin, the great reformer. Mr. Rice says, that Luther believed in consubstantiation. I will let you hear Calvin, chap. xv. I will read the context:

"Baptism is a sign of initiation by which we are admitted into the society of the church, in order that being incorporated into Christ, we may be numbered among the children of God. Now it has been given to us by God, for these ends, which I have shewn to be common to all sacraments; first, to promote our faith towards him; secondly, to testify our confession before men. We shall treat of both these ends of its institution in order.

To begin with the first:—From baptism our faith derives three advantages, which require to be distinctly considered. The first is, that it is proposed to us by the Lord, as a symbol and token of our purification; or to express my meaning more fully, it resembles a legal instrument properly attested, by which he assures us that all our sins are cancelled, effaced, and obliterated, so that they will never appear in his sight, or come into his remembrance, or be imputed to us. *For he commands all who believe to be baptized for the remission of their sins.* Therefore those who have imagined that baptism is nothing more than a mark or sign by which we profess our religion before men, as soldiers wear the insignia of their sovereign as a mark of their profession, have not considered that which was the principal thing in baptism; which is, that we ought to receive it with this promise, 'He that believeth and is baptized, shall be saved,' Mark xvi. 16.

2d. In this sense we are to understand what is said by Paul, that Christ sanctifieth and cleanseth the church 'with the washing of the water by the word,' Ephes. v. 26; and in another place, that 'according to his mercy he saved us, by the washing of regeneration, and renewing of the Holy Ghost,' Tit. iii. 5; and by Peter, that 'baptism doth save us,' 1 Pet. iii. 21. For it was not the intention of Paul to signify that our ablution and salvation are completed by the water, or that water contains in itself the virtue to purify, regenerate and renew; nor did Peter mean that it was the cause of salvation, but only that the knowledge and assurance of it is received in this sacrament: which is sufficiently evident from the words they have used. For Paul connects together the 'word of life' and 'the baptism of water;' as if he had said, that our ablution and sanctification are announced to us by the gospel, and by baptism this message is confirmed. And Peter, after having said that 'baptism doth save us,' immediately adds, that it is 'not the putting away of the filth of the flesh, but the answer of a good conscience towards God,' which proceeds from faith. But on the contrary, baptism promises us no other purification than by the sprinkling of the blood of Christ; which is emblematically represented by water, on account of its resemblance to washing and cleansing. Who, then, can pretend that we are cleansed by that water, which clearly testifies the blood of Christ to be our true and only ablution? So that, to refer the error of those who refer all to the virtue of the water, no better argument could be found, than in the signification of baptism itself, which abstracts us, as well from that visible element, which is placed before our eyes, as from all other means of salvation, that it may fix our minds on Christ alone.

3d. Nor must it be supposed that baptism is administered only for the time past, so that for sins into which we fall after baptism, it would be necessary to seek other new remedies of expiation in I know not what other sacraments, as if the virtue of baptism were become obsolete. In consequence of this error, it happened in former ages, that some persons would not be baptized except at the close of their life, and almost in the moment of their death, so that they might obtain pardon for their whole life; a preposterous caution, which is frequently censured in the writings of the ancient bishops. But we ought to conclude, that at whatever time we are baptized, we are washed and purified for the whole of life. Whenever we have fallen, therefore, we must recur to the remembrance of baptism, and arm our minds with the consideration of it, that we may be always certified and assured of the remission of our sins. For though, when it has been once administered, it appears to be past, yet it is not abolished by subsequent sins. For the purity of Christ is offered to us in it; and that always retains its virtue, is never overcome by any blemishes, but purifies and obliterates all our defilements."

I am in good company in the use of the word preposterous, notwithstanding Mr. Rice's objections to the word. I am more of a Calvinian than he is. I certainly am in good company when I have Luther on my right hand and Calvin on my left, on the design of baptism.

I have not yet done with the confession of faith. It does not refer to circumcision, either in the first, second, or third sections. But observe, the confession of faith says, "It is a confirmative mark of regeneration—of remission of sins, a mark confirmative." Can any language be more conclusive? The confession of faith represents baptism as a confirmative mark, a confirmative, too, of our pardon and admission into the family of God. I have never spoken more clearly, or more forcibly, on baptism for the remission of sins, than did the great founder of Presbyterianism. I have the two greatest names in Protestant Christendom affirming my proposition.

Let it be remembered, then, that, in addition to the arguments offered from the Scriptures, we have all the Greek and Latin fathers, without one exception, the two great founders of Protestantism, the Westminster divines, and the Scotch Confession of Faith, down to the present century. The present century is really retrograding in the understanding and veneration of the ordinances, both of the communion and of the rite of initiation. America is behind the age, behind Christendom on this subject. The reason is, Baptist views are so prevailing here, that Pedo-baptists are always seeking to defend themselves, and not candidly and perseveringly searching the Scriptures.

Dr. Chalmers, of Scotland, is a century ahead of American Presbyterians. The English and the Germans are leaving us behind. The greatest ecclesiastic historian living, Neander, and the most eminent philologists in Germany, are greatly in advance of any American Pedo-baptist theologians, philologists, historians, and critics, both on the nature and design of baptism.

If we go back to the old creeds, the Nicene and the Athanasian, they put us to shame. The Nicene was a symbol and exponent of the faith of the whole world at the beginning of the fourth century. It says: "We believe in one baptism for the remission of sins." The Athanasian, on which the Roman and English hierarchy rested for so long a time, says: "We confess one baptism for the remission of sins." The church of England still has in her Common Prayer the Nicene and the Athanasian; while her American daughter, more rationally has expunged the Athanasian, because of a more doubtful ancestry. But, Mr. President, not any of these authorities, nor all of them combined, led me to the belief of the true meaning and design of baptism.

I studied under greater masters than any of these. Some twenty years ago, when preparing for a debate with Mr. McCalla, I put myself under the special instruction of four Evangelists, and one Paul, of distinguished apostolic rank and dignity. I had for some time before that discussion, been often impressed with such passages as Acts ii. 38; and that providential call to discuss the subject with Mr. McCalla, compelled me to decide the matter to my entire satisfaction. Believe me, sir, then I had forgotten my earlier readings upon the subject; and upon the simple testimony of the Book itself, I came to a conclusion alledged in that debate, and proved only by the Bible, which now appears, from a thousand sources, to have been the catholic and truly ancient and primitive faith of the whole church. It was in this commonwealth that this doctrine was first publicly promulged in modern times; and, sir, it has now spread over this continent, and with singular success, is now returning to Europe, and the land of our fathers. My faith in it, sir, rests, however, neither upon the traditions of the church, nor upon any merely inferential reasonings of my own, nor those of any other man; but upon the explicit and often repeated declarations and explanations of the prophets and the apostles.

In maintaining this all-important position, however, I build neither upon the ancients nor the moderns; neither upon creeds, synods, councils, nor fathers. If it be not found within the limits of the Book, let it perish from our memory and from our hearts. With pleasure, I can place human authority against human authority, writer against writer, and council against council. They neutralize, correct or annihilate one another. But we stand on the Bible, the whole Bible, and nothing but the Bible, in our faith and in the evidences that support it. Here, sir, we have the blood-sealed charter of immortality to man. " He that believeth and is baptized, shall be saved. The young, the old, the middle aged—the young athletic sinner, and the hoary chief in the ranks of infidelity—have felt the heart-stirring, soul-subduing, transporting efficacy and attractiveness of this message of philanthropy to a bewildered, lost, and ruined world, and have gladly and humbly bowed to Prince Messiah, and gone down into the mystic waters of holy baptism for remission, and have risen to lead a new, an elevated, a heaven-directed life of purity and humanity. Thousands, sir, tens of thousands have been brought into the fold of God, through the instrumentality of this glorious development of ancient christianity. Many are our fellow-laborers and helpers and fellow soldiers in this great work, and wide-extended field of labor. Around me are a host of men, fired with the ancient enthusiasm of converting myriads by the pure, original gospel of the apostolic ministry. Our success, in comparison with any other experiment in the memory of living men, is truly wonderful and animating.

Here is the Presbyterian church with its eighty ministers, its eight thousand and less members, after the labors of more than half a century. In one third of that time the cause we plead, notwithstanding our feebleness, and all the errors and accidents incident to a new commencement, and without colleges and schools of learning, without the aids of hoary veterans in policy, prudence and sage experience—by the force of this simple story of God's Messiah, and his love, depicted in this mighty Pentecostan gospel, and under the star of Jacob; led, guided, aided and blessed, from nothing have, in less than twenty years, outnumbered this old, learned, and well-disciplined host, some five to one. And what is the cause? It is not talent, learning, and an efficient general organization. It is truth, sir, God's mighty truth, that has gone forth like a river and overflowed this land like a wave from the ocean! What argues all this, fellow-citizens! That its destiny is to go forward in its glorious career, building on Divine facts, precepts, and promises—appealing to reason, conscience, the affections, and conquering myriads by its rich, full, free, efficacious grace. The doctrine works well. It is wisdom, righteousness, holiness, and redemption to all that believe it. Those who plead this cause in ancient times, I call, a sacramental host. And may those who now plead it, guided, strengthened, animated by the strength of Jacob, the Lord of hosts, go on conquering and to conquer!

But what is baptism? The Westminsters say—It is a sacrament, a sign of regeneration, a seal of engrafting into Christ—the covenant of grace, of remission of sins—an engagement to be the Lord's. What a rich cluster of blessings are hanging upon baptism, then, according to the creed! Is this true of all, of any infant subject? Are these blessings all sealed to them by it? Then let them have it by all means. But first be assured that this is the fact, else you delude and ruin them, and plant in your own bosoms an everlasting agony. If its design is thus to signify and seal their engrafting into Christ, the Living Vine, what a blessing! But that it is not so, fathers, mothers, sons, and daughters, I appeal to your own experience—I address myself to your common sense, your own observations. Surely you will say it is not so!

Do you teach this catechism to your children? Teach them the Scriptures—the book that God has written. Let their minds be early and deeply imbued with these holy lessons. They came from God's love, and they open and sanctify the heart. Your children cannot digest such crude, indigestible and unhealthy viands; the stale, metaphisical abstrusities of old quaint divinity. Give them God's own Book. Let them learn the lesson there, that GOD IS LOVE—and when they understand it, and believe it, then put his holy name upon them, and let them feel that they, and not you, believe for themselves, the gospel of salvation.

This book so read, so learned, and so believed, will accomplish for them a glorious disenthralment from evil passions. They will feel that it is a soul-illuminating, reviving, redeeming, and exhilarating volume, full of grace and full of truth. By it they will be prepared for all earth's fortunes, good or bad, prosperous or adverse. They will rise above vulgar prejudices and errors, and will pant after the fruition of the sweet and holy communion of heaven's purest, holiest, happiest, and most exalted intelligences. A deep, heartfelt conviction that such are its tendencies, is one of our most urgent reasons for contending, with so much zeal, for its ordinances, its precepts, and its promises as God gave them; believing that it is able to make us all wise unto salvation—useful, honorable, and happy on earth, and prepared for the seraphic intimacies and friendships, among the favored circles of heaven.—[*Time expired.*

Thursday, Nov. 23—1½ o'clock, P. M.
[MR. RICE'S THIRD REPLY.]

MR. PRESIDENT—I will not violate the rules by which we have bound ourselves to be governed in this discussion, by speaking of the gentleman's "obliquities," as he has so repeatedly done. If he choose to disregard the rules of decorum, I will not imitate his example. He tells you, I have greatly misrepresented him in the matter of the rags, oil and lamp-black. The Bible, he now says, is, in one view of the subject, only oil, rags, &c. So his meaning would be, that pagans are ruined because *in one view of the subject*, they cannot get those articles! My reply was, I think, just such as his illustration merited.

It is not necessary, he repeats, that Peter and Paul should continue saying over and over the same thing. But the difficulty is this—Peter, on the day of Pentecost, taught a number of anxious inquirers what they must do to be saved; and he said, "Repent, and be baptized, every one of you, in the name of the Lord Jesus, for the remission of sins." Now if, as Mr. C. contends, baptism is a prerequisite to the remission of sins, Peter must, of course, so present it when he preached to another company of inquirers. The fact, however, is, that in his second discourse, in which he certainly did give correctly and fully the conditions of remission, he did not mention baptism. It is, moreover, a fact, that when he preached to Cornelius and his family, who were gentiles, he did not direct them to be baptized in order to the remission of sins. These facts afford evidence conclusive, that Peter did not regard baptism as necessary to secure remission. If Mr. Campbell's interpretation of Peter's first discourse be correct, he did not always preach the same doctrine; but if ours be the correct exposition, he was perfectly consistent, presenting in each discourse the same conditions of pardon. Repentance necessarily implies conversion, and repentance and conversion necessarily imply faith. So that in each of his discourses he presented to the minds of his hearers, directly or impliedly, all that was necessary to secure remission of sins. But, according to Mr. C.'s views, he omitted, in two of them, what was as important as repentance or faith, viz. baptism. This, then, is the difference between Mr. C. and myself. He makes Peter inconsistent and unfaithful; I make him a consistent and faithful minister of Christ.

He labors in vain to evade the force of the perfectly clear and unequivocal language of Christ—"He that believeth on the Son *hath* everlasting life." He says, the christian is represented as looking for eternal life. Let us have chapter and verse, and I will attend to it. It is admitted, that believers are looking and hoping for eternal happiness; and so long as there is an eternity before us, we shall continue to look forward. But does this prove, that we may not here have the commencement of that life? When our Savior says the believer *hath* eternal life, Mr. C. understands him to mean, that although he is yet condemned, eternal life is offered to him. There is no principle of criticism that will allow such liberties to be taken with Scripture language. Nothing short of a cause most indefensible, could induce a man of the clear intellect possessed by my friend, to maintain that *hath* means *may have*; and that when our Savior says, all believers have eternal life, they may nevertheless be in a state of condemnation.

But to the other declaration—"He that believeth on the Son, *is not condemned*," he attempted no reply, for he saw that it left no room for evasion. This single passage is sufficient to overturn his whole theory of baptism in order to remission. It can mean nothing less than that every believer is actually pardoned.

But, says Mr. Campbell, Christ contemplated a believer as one who would do his whole duty. To this I reply: 1st. A believer cannot baptize himself, and persons are often placed in circumstances in which they cannot be baptized by others. Even in Georgetown, where water is very plentiful, there was, as I learn from the *Harbinger*, a delay for several days of the baptism of some persons who, it was said, had made the good confession. It not unfrequently happens, that believers, who are disposed to do their whole duty, find it impossible to receive baptism for days, weeks, or even months. Are such persons still in a state of condemnation? For example—I am to-day a believer, but I am a hundred or a thousand miles distant from any one who is authorized to baptize me. Am I still condemned because a duty is required, which I have it not in my power to perform? 2d. I maintain, that God did not make my salvation depend upon an act which, however inclined, I cannot perform for myself, and which I may not be able to have performed by others. There is not a word in the Bible that intimates, that any true believer is condemned and exposed to eternal ruin, because he cannot receive an external ordinance. The Bible doctrine is, that every one who truly believes on Jesus Christ, is immediately pardoned and has everlasting life. But according to the doctrine of Mr. Campbell, none are pardoned who have not been *immersed*—no matter why. 3d. But many persons who are disposed to obey every command of Christ, do err as to what baptism is—so says Mr. Campbell. He admits that some, at least, sincerely believe in baptism by sprinkling, which, he says, is not baptism. He admits, moreover, that theirs is an error of the *head*, not of the *heart*. Yet this error of the head, in regard to an external ordinance, keeps them in a state of condemnation, living and dying! They love Christ and desire to obey him; but they, through mistake, suppose themselves to be baptized, when in truth they have not submitted to the ordinance. Now, according to Mr. Campbell's doctrine, such persons must be lost; for he maintains that repentance and immersion are "*equally necessary to forgiveness!*"

He tells us, that Calvin agrees with him on this subject; and he read an extract from his Institutes to prove it. But he has evidently snatched up hastily a few words which seemed to favor his views, without examining the connection. Calvin not only does not sustain him, but does not even approximate his ground. I will read from his Institutes, book iv. chap. xv. sec. 1:

"Baptism is a sign of initiation, by which we are admitted into the society of the church, in order that being incorporated into Christ, we may be numbered among the children of God. Now, it has been given to us by God for these ends, which I have shown to be common to all the sacraments: first, to promote our faith toward him; secondly, to testify our confession before men. We shall treat of both these ends of this institution in order To begin with the first:—from baptism our faith derives three advantages, which require to be distinctly considered. The first is, that it is proposed to us by the Lord, as a symbol and token of our purification ; or, to express my meaning more fully, it resembles a legal instrument properly attested, by which he assures us that all our sins are canceled, effaced, and obliterated, so that they will never appear in his sight, or come into his remembrance, or be imputed to us," &c.

Such precisely is the doctrine of our confession of faith, and the doctrine for which I contend. But I will read another passage from this same chapter, which the gentleman seems not to have noticed, and which proves conclusively that Calvin did not teach the doctrine for which he contends. Sec. 14 :

" We may see this exemplified in Cornelius the centurion, WHO, AFTER HAVING RECEIVED THE REMISSION OF HIS SINS AND THE VISIBLE GRACE OF THE HOLY SPIRIT, WAS BAPTIZED ; *not with a view to obtain by baptism a more ample remission of sins, but a stronger exercise of faith, and an increase of confidence from that pledge.*"

Now the audience will remark, Calvin says, Cornelius, after having received remission of sins, was baptized. He first received remission, then the sign and seal. Is this the doctrine of my friend, Mr. C. ? If it is, we may shake hands, and close this part of the discussion. We can have *christian union* at once ! But he seems not to have read Calvin's remarks on the baptism of Cornelius. Calvin says, just what we say— first remission of sins, by faith in Christ, and then the sign and seal. So teaches our confession of faith. I believe, that baptism is a sign and seal of our engrafting into Christ, of remission of sins, &c. : but faith secures remission, and the sign and seal are added. The document is first written, then the seal is applied. Did not Abraham receive the righteousness, or justification by faith, before he received the seal of circumcision ? Mr. Campbell maintains, that the sins of believers are forgiven *in* baptism. Calvin maintained that they are forgiven when faith is exercised *before* baptism. Calvin differed from his views still more widely ; for he maintained, that baptism is not only a sign and seal of the remission of *past sins*, but that it is equally efficacious through life— that it is a seal of the covenant of God, securing to the believing penitent the remission of sins at all times, and encouraging him to hope in God's mercy, and to persevere to the end.

We now see how carefully my friend reads authors, and how he gets such numbers on his side on these questions. He catches up some expressions, which, taken out of their connection, seem to favor his views, and looks no further. Thus he persuaded himself that Calvin's views accorded with his ; when, if he had read the chapter through, he would have found him directly against them. I will admit, if he pleases, that the whole world is as nearly with him, as he is with Calvin ; that is, they are precisely against him. He might, with some more plausibility, claim Luther, with his notions of *consubstantiation*, than John Calvin.

The gentleman is still on *infant baptism*. He is certainly conscious of having failed to sustain himself on that subject. If not, why does he return to it so repeatedly ? He cannot be satisfied with his previous efforts on this subject. But if he will show us the propriety of circumcising infants, when they could not possibly understand the design of the ordinance, I will pledge myself to show the propriety of baptizing them. Circumcision was the sign and seal of God's covenant ; and, as a significant ordinance, it pointed to the renewal of the heart. Infants could not understand its nature and design, and yet God commanded that it should be administered to them. There is just as much propriety in baptizing infants now, as there was in circumcising them then. I hope, however, that my friend will now acknowledge, that he has done the best he could against infant baptism, and leave it.

He appeals to the Greek and Latin fathers of the four first centuries, as sustaining his doctrine of baptism, in order to remission. Do you remember how he abused them yesterday? and what a reproof he administered to me for calling up such witnesses as they?!! I knew he would need their authority to-day. On yesterday they were grossly ignorant, and amazingly superstitious, great dupes, and their testimony was most worthless. But to-day they have risen surprisingly in his estimation! They are quite enlightened!!!

Yet every unprejudiced mind can see, that their testimony is far more conclusive on the other subject than on this. The difference is this: I brought them forward as witnesses to a plain matter of fact. Any one can tell whether, in the church where he worships, children are baptized, and whether such had long been the custom. But Mr. C. appeals to them for their opinions concerning the nature and design of baptism. This is a matter in regard to which I appeal not to them; for we know, they entertained erroneous opinions on this and many other subjects. Still, however, I do not admit, that the christian fathers held his views on this subject. They held to baptismal regeneration; but they did not mean by regeneration what he means by it. They seem to have believed, that the heart was renewed when baptism was administered, and, therefore, the sins were remitted at the same time; while he holds to no such inward change in connection with the ordinance, but only to a change of *state*, from condemnation to justification. But he is welcome to appeal to them in matters of *opinion*, or as commentators on the Scriptures. I am perfectly willing to receive their testimony as to matters of fact, but not as to their exposition of the Bible. As commentators, it is pretty generally admitted, that they were not very skillful. I will not dispute with him about the Nicene and Athanasian creeds. On this point they are not testifying to facts, but expounding scripture. Their authority, therefore, is not very considerable.

Well, if the gentleman cannot prove his doctrine true, he can, at least, boast of the increasing numbers in his church. What this has to do with the subject under discussion, I am not able to see. I think, he would as well give a dissertation upon the mountains in the moon. Or does he reason thus: Reformers are increasing more rapidly than Presbyterians; therefore, sins are remitted only in baptism! His views on this subject are of a very accommodating character. In noticing, in his Harbinger, the rapid increase of Presbyterians and old Baptists, one year, he consoled himself by the soothing reflection, that error runs faster than truth; but, when his numbers increase, then truth outruns error! So his argument will always prove, that truth is with him, and all others are in error!

But what is the character of this church of whose increase he so much boasts? We are perfectly willing to compare churches with him; and he shall give the character of his own church. In his Harbinger he has informed us, that, in his church, all sorts of doctrine have been preached by all sorts of men!!! He tells us, moreover, that it is in great confusion; and for two years past he has labored faithfully to get up an organization, to save it from perfect anarchy; but, alas! to this day, he has entirely failed to accomplish the object. And I venture to predict, that he will never secure an organization; for the moment he attempts to exclude his ignorant and unworthy preachers, and to fix some standard of ministerial qualification, his church will break into half a dozen fragments. So much for his increase of numbers, which, however, has nothing to do with the question under discussion.

Let us now endeavor to ascertain the state of the argument. The gentleman undertook to prove, that baptism is necessary in order to secure the remission of sins; that the sins of penitent believers are remitted only in the act of being immersed. But I have proved, that this doctrine contradicts the repeated declarations of our Savior—that "he that believeth on the Son, is not condemned—hath everlasting life." I have proved, that it is false, from the fact, that all who are begotten of God, do enjoy remission of sins; and Mr. C., himself, admits that believers are begotten before they are baptized. All such, as the apostle John teaches, cease from sin, live a holy life, overcome the world, and have eternal life. I have also proved, that the new birth is not dependent on baptism, but occurs often before it; and that all who are born of God, baptized or not, immersed or not, enjoy remission. If these things are so, (and the gentleman has made no attempt to disprove most of them,) his doctrine is false.

I have examined the expression in Peter's discourse, on which he relies chiefly for the support of his theory, and have shown, that his interpretation of it makes Peter contradict John the Baptist, and act inconsistently. The expression in Matt. iii. 11, as I have proved, is precisely similar to that employed by Peter; and, if John did not baptize the Jews in order to make them repent, Peter did not baptize in order to remission of sins. The erroneousness of Mr. Campbell's doctrine I proved further, by the fact, that, in Peter's second discourse, baptism is not mentioned as a condition of remission; but he said, "Repent and be *converted*, that your sins may be blotted out." It is certain, that persons may repent and be converted, and yet not be immersed, or even baptized in any way. Conversion is turning to God; and, it will not be denied, that many have turned to God, who were never immersed. But, according to Peter's doctrine, all who repented and turned to God, were pardoned. Peter's second discourse, therefore, contradicts the doctrine of my friend.

When he preached the gospel to Cornelius, he did not teach him, that his sins could not be forgiven, except in the act of immersion. But when the Holy Spirit had descended upon him and his family, proving that they were accepted of God, he commanded them to be baptized, but not in order to remission of sins. So far from it, he preached a doctrine wholly inconsistent with this. I will read a passage from this discourse of Peter, which, I observe, was triumphantly urged against Mr. Campbell by our friend Dr. Fishback. For although these gentlemen are in the same church, they have had considerable controversy on this very subject. By this, amongst other arguments, the doctor proved conclusively, that baptism is not necessary to the remission of sins; and Mr. Campbell has not been able to answer it to this day. The passage is, Acts x. 43, " To him [Christ] give all the prophets witness, that through his name, whosoever believeth in him shall receive remission of sins." Observe, he said, *whosoever* believeth, shall receive remission. Have not multitudes believed on Christ, who never were baptized, according to Mr. C.'s views of baptism? The gentleman tried to find immersion in the expression " through his name." If he will show the least authority for such a sentiment, I will surrender. But with him almost every thing means immersion. If the remission of his sins depended on answering Dr. Fishback's argument from this passage of Scripture, I believe they would never be remitted, [a laugh.] His doctrine is truly in a sad predicament; for either it is false, or we must conclude that Peter did not preach the whole truth to Cornelius, nor Paul, to the jailor.

If I have time, I will present another argument against Mr. C.'s doctrine, viz. *If it be true, multitudes of the most pious, godly persons do live and die condemned, and go to perdition.* That I am not misrepresenting his views will appear from the following declarations in his *Christianity Restored*, pp. 197. 199 :

" Whatever the act of faith may be, it necessarily becomes the line of discrimination between the two states before described. *On this side, and on that, mankind are in quite different states. On the one side, they are pardoned, justified, sanctified, reconciled, adopted, and saved : on the other, they are in a state of condemnation. This act is sometimes called* IMMERSION, *regeneration, conversion;* and that this may appear obvious to all, we shall be at some pains to confirm and illustrate it."

Again :

" The apostle Peter, when first publishing the gospel to the Jews, taught them that they were not forgiven their sins by faith ; but by an act of faith, by a believing immersion into the Lord Jesus. That this may appear evident to all, we shall examine his pentecostan address, and his pentecostan hearers. Peter now holding the keys of the kingdom of Jesus, and speaking under the commission for converting the world, and by the authority of the Lord Jesus, guided, inspired, and accompanied by the Spirit—may be expected to speak the truth, the whole truth, plainly and intelligibly, to his brethren the Jews. He had that day declared the gospel facts, and proved the resurrection and ascension of Jesus to the conviction of thousands. They believed and repented—believed that Jesus was the Messiah, had died as a sin-offering, was risen from the dead, and crowned Lord of all. Being full of this faith, they inquired of Peter and the other apostles what they ought to do to obtain remission. *They were informed, that though they now believed and repented, they were not pardoned;* but must ' reform and be immersed for the remission of sins.' Immersion for the forgiveness of sins, was the command addressed to these believers, to these penitents, in answer to the most earnest question ; and by one of the most sincere, candid, and honest speakers ever heard. This act of faith was presented, as that act by which a change in their state could be effected ; OR, IN OTHER WORDS, BY WHICH ALONE THEY COULD BE PARDONED. They who ' gladly received this word were that day immersed ;' or, in other words, that same day were converted, or regenerated, or obeyed the gospel. These expressions, in the apostles' style, when applied to persons coming into the kingdom, denote the same act ; as will be perceived from the various passages in the writings of Luke and Paul."

In the *Christian Baptist*, the gentleman speaks of three salvations— [*Time expired.*

Friday, Nov. 24—10 o'clock, A. M.
[MR. CAMPBELL'S FOURTH ADDRESS.]

MR. PRESIDENT—I cannot, sir, in one speech this morning, review the various positions of my respondent's replies, delivered yesterday, not yet noticed. In order, therefore, as far as possible to preserve a connection in the arguments by me submitted, before attempting to review, I will proceed in an argumentative way to add a few more evidences to those already before you.

In my introductory speech, I delivered eight consecutive arguments; one, indeed, was not fully developed, the object of which was to shew, that in baptism there is a real transition from one state to another, clearly indicated by the phrase "*into* the name," &c. The outward transition of the body, from one element into another, indicates an inward transition of the mind, from one state into another; from some of our relations to Adam, the first, to certain new relations to Adam, the second.   This is consummated by the words "I immerse thee into the name of the Father, and of the Son, and of the Holy Spirit."   Words so solemn and significant as these, are not to be expressed without a most intelligent consideration, and proper preparation on the part of the penitent.

My ninth argument is based on John iii. 5, 6.   This passage has already become very familiar. It occupied rather a prominent place in the addresses of my friend on Monday.

The great topic of debate between the Messiah and his cotemporaries was his kingdom, and the mistakes concerning himself, his person, offices, and character as relating to it.   This remarkable development of his kingdom to Nicodemus, and of the way into it, extorted no little marvel from this distinguished ruler of Israel, and called forth some new discoveries, never before recorded by any of the other evangelists of Jesus Christ. It is not necessary here to debate in anticipation, whether our Lord's discourse respected developments to be made hereafter, or then; whether that kingdom was hereafter to be entered into, or at the time of this colloquy between him and Nicodemus.   The abstract question is, *how are men to enter the kingdom of Jesus Christ* in this world, in its present, temporal, and earthly character and position?

It was altogether apposite that the king of Israel and the ruler of the Jews should freely communicate upon matters of royalty and empire. The time-serving policy, and the official timidity of the rabbi, are overcome by the curiosity of the man, to inquire into these matters ; yet flesh and blood must be heard, so far as to dictate a visit by night.   The Messiah intuitively perceived the thoughts and intents of his heart ; and with an awful and divine solemnity, said, "Nicodemus, you must be born again," else you cannot see, or understand, this kingdom of which I speak.   Nay ; unless born of water and of the Spirit, you cannot enter into the kingdom of God.   "That which is born of the flesh, is flesh ; and that which is born of the Spirit, is spirit."

Observe, the Savior is speaking of his own kingdom ; not of the eternal kingdom of God in the world to come.   One prolific cause of error on this entire subject, has been a notion that not the church, but the ultimate kingdom of glory was spoken of.   Hence came the Romanist notions of no infant baptism, no salvation.   Protestants, too, have, in some instances, adopted that notion ; hence, the haste, the shameful precipitancy with which, in many instances, babes have been sprinkled lest they should die unbaptized.   No baptism, no salvation, became for a time a proverb in the Pedo-baptist church of Rome.

They made it necessary to take away original sin.   Hence, they commissioned all persons, men and women, to administer baptism in extreme cases, without the presence of a priest.   The discovery that the kingdom of God here indicated the church of Christ on earth, relieved many from this morbid sensibility on the subject of baptism, immediately after birth. Amongst most Protestants it has died away.

Since we began to plead for the ordinances of Christ, a new method of evading the force of this passage has been discovered, and very extensively adopted. It is, to make it half literal and half spiritual. Water, say they, means the Spirit, and the Spirit means the Spirit. But might not any one say, if water means Spirit, Spirit means water—and thus make it all water, and no Spirit. Certainly this is as rational as to make water mean Spirit, and thus make it all Spirit. But the great teacher neither said the one nor the other. He did not say, Ye must be born of Spirit and of the Spirit; nor did he say, You must be born of water, and of the water—but of water and Spirit.

When I referred to all antiquity, I did not mean to say, that I had read all antiquity for four thousand years. I quoted the fathers as corroborative evidence, but by no means as the foundation of my faith. This is neither an interpretation of my own, nor of modern times; but if ever there was a catholic—not Roman catholic or Greek catholic—but if ever there was a catholic interpretation, it is the interpretation which I have given; for all agree to it, both ancient and modern.

I have a few scraps here, giving the words of two of our most distinguished theologians, to wit: Timothy Dwight, president of Yale, who said, "To be born of water here means baptism, and in my view it is as necessary to our admission into the visible church; as to be born of the Spirit is to our admission into the invisible kingdom." "It is to be observed, that he who understands the authority of this institution, and refuses to obey it, will never enter into either the visible or the invisible kingdom."

I have been blamed for being uncharitable in my views of the importance of this institution; but I have never said any thing which, in the judgment of the intelligent, is more uncharitable than the above language of the good Presbyterian doctor, Timothy Dwight. I have said, and I am sustained by one greater than Dwight, (and Edwards excepted, there is no name among American theologians greater than that of president Dwight,) that no man, understanding this saying, and refusing to submit to this ordinance, will ever enter the true visible church, or kingdom, of Jesus Christ.

My friend has called up Dr. Scott. I believe I have read every line of Scott's commentary in my youth. In answer to another question, not so precisely to this point, to wit:

"'Men and brethren, what shall we do?'—To this the apostle replied, by exhorting them to repent of all their sins, and openly to avow their firm belief that Jesus was indeed the Messiah, *by being baptized in his name.* In *thus* professing their faith in him, all who truly believed would receive a full remission of their sins for his sake, as well as a participation of the sanctifying and comforting graces of the Holy Spirit."—*Scott's Commentary* on Acts ii. 38.

I have not only this, but all the Catholic authorities, in addition to the confessions of faith. It is, then, clearly established, that the Savior said, in substance, Unless ye be baptized, ye cannot enter into the christian church. A man may get into some other church without baptism, but into Christ's church he cannot come.

My *tenth* argument shall consist of an induction of all the conversions reported by Luke, in his Acts of the Apostles. It will, therefore, be a highly important argument. It will be, I hope, a satisfactory answer to Mr. R.'s objection on yesterday, viz. that we have the solemn precept, "Repent and be baptized for the remission of sins," only once, in the same identical words. We have, indeed, shown, that if this precept

31   2 S

never had been repeated, still the circumstances under which it was first spoken, give it a meaning and an importance paramount to a thousand repetitions. It was made the opening speech of the gospel age; sanctioned by the holy twelve; confirmed, as well as suggested by the Holy Spirit; most solemnly sealed and authenticated by the conversion of 3000 men in one day, who gladly received the word, and were that same day baptized. That fact, in justification of our interpretation, gives the passage pre-eminent weight in the minds of all conscientious persons.

My opponent said that it was a solitary passage; and he objected to it, because the same verbiage is not preserved in other places. I shall go into an investigation of every single conversion. I shall, however, attempt it with great rapidity. The second sermon and conversion, reported in Acts, chap. iii., says, "Repent and be converted, that your sins may be blotted out; and that seasons of refreshment may come from the presence of the Lord."

Since the gentleman has, himself, decided, in his comments on the commission, that *convert* means to baptize, if I may, without any offence, refer to the discussion of infant baptism, even as a matter of history, (to which, it seems, he is not very partial,) I can quote words, but you doubtless remember them, affirming that Jesus commanded persons to be converted, or discipled, merely by the act of baptizing them. Consequently, according to Mr. Rice, when Peter said " Repent and be converted, every one of you," he said just what he had said on Pentecost—" Repent and be baptized, every one of you, that your sins may be blotted out." So far as infants are concerned, Mr. Rice will say it is good sound criticism. Convert, that is, baptize them, and then teach them. Baptizing, says Mr. Rice, is the main matter; but the act of baptizing, in his system, is equivalent to the term convert. Therefore, Peter meant in the temple, that which he meant on Pentecost.

But the conversion was accomplished in this case, as in the former. They heard the gospel, believed it, and were baptized. The fact is the same, whatever the phraseology may have been. The gentleman says, that *born* is not the word here used by Peter, and therefore " born of water " is not intended. Again—he says, " be baptized " is not found in the second sermon; consequently, that could not be the meaning. Let us try his logic in some other cases, and then unfold its virtues. It is simply this:—That as Peter, in his second sermon, did not say, " *be born of water*," and as he did not say " *be baptized*," but " *be converted*," he must not be supposed to mean, by this word *convert*, either of the other two; and, therefore, there was neither baptism, nor the birth of water, connected with his idea of salvation. I believe I have fairly stated his logic. Let us now return to the first sermon, and reason by his rules. In the first sermon Peter said, " be baptized," but did not once use the words " be converted," nor did he use the words " be born of the Spirit;" consequently, he did not mean either " *be converted*," or " be born of the Spirit," with reference to the remission of sins: for, according to Mr. Rice, he always meant, in such cases, no more than the simple import of the term used. Hence, it must follow, that of the three thousand converted on the day of Pentecost, not one of them believed; not one of them was " born of the Spirit;" not one of them was " converted;" for the plain and evident reason, that Peter did not use one of these words. So much for the profound logic of my worthy friend.

But in the second sermon Peter did not mention faith nor the Holy

Spirit—he only said, Repent and be converted. Now, unless the word conversion mean faith, mean the Holy Spirit, or stand connected with these words, then there was neither faith nor Holy Spirit in Peter's second sermon. But why spend time in the exposition of assumptions and positions never before assumed by any person pretending to philological attainments! I will dismiss this subject by observing, that when *conversion*, or *faith*, or *repentance*, or *baptism*, is once interpreted, it is always used to represent one and the same thing, when applied to the same subject.

I might, indeed, before dismissing the objection to laying much emphasis upon a single occurrence, ask my friend, Mr. Rice, why he lays so much stress upon the formula of baptizing into the name of the Father, Son, and Holy Spirit? especially as we never read that it was so done in those very words in any one instance. If, then, all the world build their practice, on one single occurrence, and if we had but one example, which is not the fact, why blame us for so adhering to Peter—Acts ii.

I will now read a passage from Acts viii. 12; and make a few passing remarks as I proceed, to show how the same rules of interpretation apply in all cases:

" When the Samaritans believed Philip, preaching concerning the kingdom of God and the name of Jesus Christ, they were baptized, both men and women." But it is not said that they repented, nor that they were converted, nor that they were born of water, nor of the Spirit. Shall we therein infer that they only believed, and neither repented, nor were converted, nor born of the Spirit, nor of water? The Bible would have been a singular volume, if every time it related a conversion, it must tell the whole story over. We should soon have been as wearied as we are in reading the preambles to the acts of our legislative enactments. If Luke had said, the Samaritans heard the whole gospel preached, they were all enlightened by the Holy Spirit, they were all penetrated with a sense of sin, they all believed, they all repented, they all were regenerated, they were all born of the water, they were all born of the Spirit, they were all truly converted, they were all baptized, they were all justified, sanctified, saved, and they were all added to the church. This being told over a hundred times in the Acts of the Apostles, would become very interesting!! What a singular book the Bible would have been, had it been formed after the taste of some good orthodox people!!

My next case is that of Cornelius. The gentleman brought up this case with a great deal of emphasis: I design, therefore, to pause a little longer upon it than upon the others. We find a summary of it in Acts xi. 45: " But Peter rehearsed the matter from the beginning, and expounded it in order unto them, saying, I was in the city of Joppa praying: and in a trance I saw a vision, a certain vessel descend, as it had been a great sheet, let down from heaven by four corners; and it came even to me: upon the which, when I had fastened mine eyes, I considered, and saw four-footed beasts of the earth, and wild beasts, and creeping things, and fowls of the air. And I heard a voice saying unto me, Arise, Peter; slay and eat. But I said, Not so, Lord: for nothing common or unclean hath at any time entered my mouth. But the voice answered me again from heaven, What God hath cleansed, that call thou not common. And this was done three times, and all were drawn up again into heaven. And behold, there were three men already come unto the house where I was, sent from Cesarea unto me. And the Spirit bade me go with them, no thing doubting. Moreover, these six brethren accompanied me, and we entered into the man's house. And he showed us how he had seen an angel in his house, which stood and said unto him, Send men to Joppa, and call for Simon, whose surname is Peter; who shall tell thee words whereby thee and all thy house shall be saved."

This good Cornelius gave much alms, and prayed to God always. He was a truly excellent, pious, benevolent man; much better than one half of the best professors in Kentucky; yet he was not a christian, nor even a Jew, nor a Jewish proselyte. A pure gentile, enlightened by portions of the law, he was serving God instantly, day and night; yet he was not evangelically *saved*. But some men will say—had this good man died, would he have gone to perdition? would he have been forever lost?— and such other questions as grow out of these. To which we are bound to give no answer. All we know is, that he was not saved in this world, whatever he might have been, had he been taken out of it by God. Recollect, the angel said, Send for Peter, and " he will tell thee *words* by which thou and all thy house shall be saved." Of course, then, these words and precepts which were promised him, were words essential to his evangelical salvation. For christian salvation is a range much higher than Jewish, patriarchal, gentile, proselyte, and even sectarian salvation. It is a full, perfect, and complete salvation from sin. Cornelius is a very fine specimen of the high excellences to which a person might attain, without a saving knowledge of the only name, given under heaven, by which any man can be saved. His excellences may have been one reason why the Lord chose to make him and his family the first fruits of the gentile world.

I need not further detail the incidents of this case. Peter was sent for to Joppa—and why send for Peter? Let Peter tell the story. "The Lord," said he, "made choice among us apostles, that the gentiles, by my mouth, should hear the word of the Lord, and believe." The keys of the kingdom of heaven had been committed to Peter—this same kingdom of God, into which no man now-a-days can enter, but through a birth of water and of the Spirit. This was the reason, then, that Peter must be sent for.

Peter had a reason, too, just at this crisis. He saw the gentiles in this sheet full of reptiles sent down from heaven. He was slow to learn this before taught. Finally, however, he was prepared to go with the three pious soldiers that were sent for him. Six brethren accompanied him to witness the glorious scene. He arrived, was received with the honors due to one so honored by the Lord. He began to speak. The hearers were already well prepared. The fallow-ground had been broken up by these providences. They drank it down as the thirsty ox drinketh the water. While the porter, Peter, was well nigh the gate of heaven in his discourse, the Spirit fell from heaven directly upon them all, as it had done on the believers on the day of Pentecost; and like them they began to speak with tongues, and to glorify God.

They were all overwhelmed. It was a second Pentecost, and the only second Pentecost the world ever saw. After it became evident that this was the baptism of the Holy Spirit foretold and promised by the Messiah to the first fruits of the Jews, Peter, gathering thence that the gates of the city should be opened, said, Can any man forbid water, that these persons, welcomed as we have been by the Holy Spirit should not be baptized?

All being silent, he commanded them to be baptized, by the authority of the Lord.

Concerning this gift of the Holy Spirit, and that bestowed on Pentecost, there is a very popular and common error abroad. It is supposed to have fallen (on Pentecost) upon the audience—the unbelieving multitude. This is a grand mistake. After the Holy Spirit had been poured out (on Pentecost) on the brethren, not to produce faith, for faith they had, the apostles addressed them, appealing to what they saw and heard, not to what they felt.

So in the present case, the Spirit fell on believing gentiles, to welcome them into the kingdom, as God had received the Jewish converts. He made no difference between the first fruits of the gentiles and the first fruits of the Jews. These again were miraculous gifts, for signs and tokens, and not the ordinary influences of that divine agent which christians ordinarily enjoy.

Peter feeling himself authorized to admit them into the kingdom, as we have heard, commanded their baptism, and thus they too were inducted into the family of God, and united with the Jews in the same fold. But we are not told that they believed, that they repented, that they were converted. Nor are we even told that they were baptized. We only learn that Peter commanded them to be baptized. We presume, of course, they were. The whole affair is, however, afterwards called "*the conversion* of the gentiles." Now we infer, they were baptized, obtained the remission of sins, and received the consolations and joys that make up the christian religion. Cornelius and his household were now *saved*.

I next allude to the case of Lydia. We are told that a certain woman named Lydia, and her household, whose heart the Lord opened, attended to Paul's preachings, and was baptized. Now there is not one word about her believing, repenting, or being converted, nor that she was born of the Spirit, pardoned, or added to the church.

The same also is true of the jailor, whose conversion is reported on the next page, and in the same chapter. Not one word is said about his believing before baptism, or his repenting, or his conversion, or his having received the Spirit. Does not this show that neither the preacher thought it necessary to tell, nor the historian to record, in any case after the commencement, what was preached, nor what the effects on them that heard and obeyed? They always preached the same things substantially; they commanded all men every where to do the same things—to believe, repent, and be baptized for remission.

Again, Acts xviii. 5. In the case of Crispus and the Corinthians. Crispus believed, and all his house. Hearing, he believed, and was baptized, and all his house. Here, we are not told that they repented, or were converted: and why not, if my friend's reasoning be correct?

In chapter xix., we read of baptism in the name of the Lord Jesus Christ, but not one word is said of the conversion, &c., of the individuals.

I have one case more. It is the case of Saul of Tarsus. Ananias was sent to him: presenting himself to him, he said, "Arise, brother Saul, and be baptized, and wash away thy sins, calling on the name of the Lord," Acts xx. 16.

In this last instance, there is a reiteration of what had been promised at Pentecost. The case of Paul was a remarkable one. Like other

Jews in that day, he was guilty of persecuting the christians. His conversion was very extraordinary. The Lord appeared to him on the way : not to convert him, but to make him an apostle, that he might say to the world, he had seen the Messiah and heard his voice. The Spirit sent Ananias to tell this man what he ought to do for his own personal conversion. He says to him, " Arise, brother Saul, be baptized, and wash away thy sins." Nothing, however, is reported of his believing, repenting, or being converted.

Thus, in nine instances given, there is no uniformity in representing this matter. Sometimes faith, or repentance, or conversion, is mentioned —sometimes none of them. Sometimes remission of sins, blotting out of sins, washing away of sins, is spoken of; and sometimes not : sometimes baptism itself is not mentioned. From all which, the conclusion is inevitable, that when any one of the adjuncts of conversation or salvation is named, all the rest are understood to have accompanied.

To take any other view of the matter, would lead to the most absurd consequences.

We should have to admit, that a person was baptized sometimes without faith, without repentance, without conversion, without remission of sins. We are, then, compelled by an insuperable logical necessity, to conclude that in every instance the same adjuncts and accompaniments were present. Hence the doctrine preached on Pentecost was always preached, and baptism was in every instance *"for remission of sins."* [*Time expired.*

Friday, Nov. 24—10½ o'clock, A. M.
[MR. RICE'S FOURTH REPLY.]

MR. PRESIDENT—Inasmuch as, at the suggestion of my friend, we shall continue the discussion to-night, a couple of hours, I shall proceed more leisurely in following him, and shall answer everything of any importance that he may offer. I have a remark to make in regard to the expression *baptize* INTO *the name of the Father, Son, and Holy Ghost.* This expression, Mr. C. says, is indicative of entering into a new spiritual relation. Of course, the person baptized into the name of the Trinity, has no such connection with the Trinity before that event. Now, it happens that we have precisely the same expression in Paul's first Epistle to the Corinthians, chap. x. 2 : " Moreover, brethren, I would not that ye should be ignorant how that all our fathers were under the cloud, and all passed through the sea ; and were all baptized unto (Greek— *into*) Moses, in the cloud and in the sea ; and did all eat the same spiritual meat, and did all drink the same spiritual drink." The expression in both cases is the same. They were baptized *into* Moses in the cloud and in the sea. Now, the question is this : What new relation was constituted by the baptism of the Jews *into* Moses in the cloud and in the sea? Did they sustain any relation to Moses afterwards, which had not existed previously ? Was he not their leader before this baptism ? Had he not led them out from Egyptian bondage ? Was there any new relation now constituted? There was a *recognition* of an existing relation, and a *confirmation* of it. Their passing through the sea, and being baptized, was a public recognition of Moses as their leader, and an expression of their determination still to follow him. So, in being baptized into the name of the Father, Son, and Holy Ghost, the existing relation, formed by faith in the Trinity, and in Christ as our Savior, is recognized and confirmed, but no new relation to God is constituted. It is a happy circumstance that we have the same expressions in these two passages, that we may not mistake the meaning of God's word.

I have a remark or two to make concerning the *new birth*. The Savior says—"Except a man be born again, he cannot see the kingdom of God." And again, when Nicodemus did not understand his meaning, he said—"Except a man be born of water and of the Spirit, he cannot enter into the kingdom of God."

Now, my friend tells us the meaning of this language is—Unless a man be born of water and of the Spirit, he cannot enter into *the church*. I presume this is not the true meaning. It cannot be so ; for multitudes who are not born of the Spirit, do enter into the church. Observe, the Savior says, that they must be born of water and *the Spirit*. Now, the fact is undeniable, that many enter the church who are not born of the Spirit, as their conduct afterwards abundantly proves. The expression *"Kingdom of God,"* may, perhaps, sometimes in the New Testament mean the church ; but such is not its most common signification. It is commonly used, more particularly with reference to the spiritual kingdom established in the hearts of God's people, which, Paul says, " is not meat and drink, but righteousness, and peace, and joy in the Holy Ghost." Sometimes it has reference particularly to the kingdom of glory. The idea which the Savior intended to convey, is, that a man must be born again, or he cannot possess the blessings, present and future, of his kingdom. He cannot enjoy pardon, salvation, and eternal life, unless he experience the new birth, in a change of heart.

But, it is a little remarkable, that Mr. Campbell does not undertake to answer the facts and arguments by which I proved that the new birth is not essentially connected with baptism. But he says, he will produce the great Presbyterian, Dr. Dwight, to sustain his views. My friend gets his authors very singularly misplaced. In his translation of the New Testament, he published Doddridge as a Presbyterian doctor, though he never was a Presbyterian, but an Independent. And now he calls Dr. Dwight a Presbyterian ; and in his Harbinger he represents him as the Rabbi of American Presbyterianism, though he was a Congregationalist, and never a Presbyterian. He is certainly not as careful as he might be in quoting authorities. But I will agree to take Dr. Dwight—I will subscribe to every sentiment he expresses, so far as this argument is concerned. For he says, that, in order to enter the spiritual kingdom of God—to be a true member, we must be born of the Spirit, by which he understands the renewal of the heart. But Mr. Campbell regards the new birth, not as a change of heart, but a change of *state*—a passing from a state of condemnation to a state of justification. Dr. Dwight does indeed say, that, in order to enter the *visible church*, a man must be baptized ; and I never heard this denied, except by Quakers. But, we are not speaking of the manner of entering into the church ; we are inquiring how sins are to be remitted. To prove that baptism is necessary to the remission of sins, Mr. C. appeals to a man who says, you cannot get into the visible church without baptism. He might as well quote what Dr. Dwight says about the truth of the Bible. But Dwight, he tells us, says, that a man cannot be saved who refuses to submit to the ordinance of baptism. Did I not tell you, on yesterday, that he who refuses deliberately to obey any command of God, cannot be forgiven ? that he is not a pious man ? If a man should say, " I will not *pray ;*" he would prove most conclusively that he has no piety. But the question before us is not whether a man who refuses to be baptized, or who is resolved not to obey any one of Christ's commands, can be saved; but whether a *penitent believer* is pardoned before he is baptized?

My friend appeals to the ancient fathers. But I will not receive them as judicious expounders of God's word; for it is admitted, that they entertained many erroneous opinions concerning the meaning of the Scriptures, and greatly perverted their meaning. I called them up to testify to *a fact*. I simply asked them, whether in their day, and as far back as their information extended, infant baptism was universally practiced by the church. They answered in the affirmative. But now my friend calls them up as *theologians*. I will not admit their opinions as evidence. Yet I deny that the old fathers held the views for which he contends. He maintains, that baptism into the name of the Father, Son, and Holy Spirit, is designed to effect a change of *state*, to secure pardon of sins; but they believed that there was connected with the ordinance of baptism a change of *heart*. This idea they made very prominent; and they connected it with the remission of sins. They believed that regeneration and baptism were connected; though by regeneration they understood not what Mr. C. understands by it. But I will agree, for the sake of argument, that they did entertain the views for which Mr. Campbell contends; and then I will say, as he has said, that they are poor theologians!

But he also appeals to popish authorities. I will show you, before I sit down, that his views are quite in accordance with those of the pope; that his language is almost precisely the language of the council of Trent. If he relies on the authority of the pope, I can show that he does agree with him; but I do not consider this a recommendation of his doctrine.

But he understands the Savior to say, that, if we are not baptized, we cannot become members of his church. But does the Savior say, we cannot be pardoned? Instead of proving, by the language of Christ, the doctrine for which he contends, my friend is diverting you from the subject. I admit that we cannot get into the visible church without baptism; but I will not agree that we cannot be pardoned before baptism.

My friend, in speaking of the commission, tells you that I agreed that disciples were made by baptizing and teaching, and that I made baptism the principle thing. I represented it only as an ordinance to be received before individuals can be recognized as disciples, or learners, in the school of Christ. They cannot be recognized as members, nor entitled to the privileges, of the church, till they receive the initiatory rite. But I did not say, that the mere initiation was the main thing in making disciples. It is important, but still it is not the great thing; the most important matter is the teaching.

I will follow the gentleman in his arguments from the Acts of the Apostles. I did so yesterday, but I will do so again to-day, as I have abundance of time.

With reference to Peter's discourse, I have taken this position:— When he said, "Repent, and be baptized, every one of you, in the name of Jesus Christ, for the remission of sins," he did not mean to say that repentance and baptism were *equally* necessary. The language of John, as I have remarked, in Matt. iii. 11, is precisely similar to that here employed by Peter. When Peter says, repent and be baptized into *(eis)* the remission of sins, Mr. C. insists that the meaning is, be baptized in order that your sins may be remitted—that their sins could be pardoned only in baptism. Then I insist, that when John said, "I baptize you with water *(eis) into* repentance," he must have baptized the Jews in order that they might repent—to cause them to feel godly sorrow for their sins! and they could not repent before baptism! Let the audience get the idea distinctly. Peter, according to Mr. C., commanded baptism, in order to remission of sins; but the language of John is precisely similar, and, of course, he must have baptized the Jews in order to repentance! This, indeed, would be a singular doctrine—immerse persons into water, to cause them to repent of their sins!

But, says Mr. Campbell, John baptized the Jews into *reformation*—in order that they might reform. But this rendering of the passage only involves him in another difficulty: for, how came John to baptize, to cause persons to reform, when Peter required them to reform in order that they might be baptized? John, according to this construction, baptized men, in order to reformation; but Peter required them to reform, in order to baptism! Thus the doctrine of Peter is a flat contradiction to that preached by John? Interpretations so inconsistent will not do. John baptized, on profession of repentance; and Peter baptized, on a profession of faith in the doctrine of remission of sins through the Lord Jesus Christ. The baptism of the three thousand on the day of Pentecost, was a public profession of their firm persuasion that Christ was able to save them from their sins. It was a recognition of a previous relation, constituted by their faith in him as their only Savior. Their sins were pardoned; and they received the sign and seal of remission.

I turned to Peter's second sermon: and what did he say? He is again preaching to many anxious inquirers; and he says, "Repent and be converted, that your sins may be blotted out." Then, according to the obvious meaning of his language, every man that repented, and was converted or turned to God, had his sins blotted out.

My friend says, it was not necessary to mention baptism in every discourse, and he has referred us to instances where persons were added to the church; and yet it is not said by the inspired historian, that they believed, or repented, or were converted. The cases, however, are not at all parallel. When I undertake to instruct ignorant and anxious inquirers, concerning the plan of salvation, I must tell them every thing that is necessary, that they may receive remission of sins. If I omit any thing essential, I am a false or unfaithful teacher. Suppose I preach a sermon to this congregation to-day, and state to them all that they must do to be saved; but next week I preach a sermon to another congregation of inquirers, and I neglect to state to them one of the most important conditions of pardon and salvation: am I not justly chargeable with being an unfaithful minister? In view of my responsibility to God, am I not solemnly bound to present to both congregations, the same conditions of salvation?

But when I undertake to write a *history* of the church, I am not obliged, every time I record a number of conversions, to state, that they all repented, believed, and were converted. In such a history, one distinct and full statement of the conditions of admission to the church, is sufficient. But Peter was instructing anxious and ignorant minds concerning the way to be saved; and he was obliged to tell them all that was necessary, in order that their sins might be remitted, &c. He did so; but he did not mention baptism as a condition of remission. Consequently, baptism, in order to the remission of sins, was not part of his doctrine: with him, repentance and conversion were the conditions.

Peter, it is true, did not mention *conversion* in the first discourse. But this objection was fully answered on yesterday. I ask any man of common sense, can a man repent, and not be converted? What is repentance? My friend agrees with me, that it is a change of mind—of views and feelings. Would you believe a man who should profess that his mind is changed, and yet continue to pursue the same course of conduct? If there is a change of mind, there must be change of conduct. If a man repent, he is grieved because of his sins. And will not such a change of mind produce a corresponding change in his conduct? "Make the tree good," said our Savior, "and the fruit will be good." Let the heart be changed, and the conduct will be right. If, then, a man repent, will he not turn? Does not repentance imply conversion? Peter might, therefore, either mention repentance only, or repentance and conversion—the *cause* only, or *cause and effect*. When I speak of a cause, which universally produces a certain effect, I may mention the cause alone, or the cause and the effect. I may, therefore, mention repentance, or repentance and conversion both. Repentance, conversion, and faith, are never separated in any human bosom. You cannot find a man with faith and not repentance. You cannot find a man that has repentance without conversion. The three things go together, as much as the heaving of the lungs and the beating of the pulse. Hence, I may tell any man on earth, if you repent, your sins will be pardoned. Or, I may say to him, if you are converted, they will be blotted out. For no man was ever converted without faith and repentance. These three things are always found associated. This common sense view of the subject will remove one half of the difficulties my friend has presented.

He asks, why do we baptize in the name of the Father, Son, and Holy Spirit, since we can find no example of baptism thus administered? If the one command of our Savior is sufficient to justify and to require it to be so administered, the authority of Peter in one sermon, he argues, is as good. We are disputing, not as to whether Peter's doctrine is true, but about what Peter did say. I agree that what he said is true; but I deny that Mr. Campbell's construction of his language is correct. So his argument or illustration does not touch the question.

The Samaritans heard the gospel preached to them; and it is not said that they repented or were converted; but it is said, that they *believed*. But could they have faith, and not have repentance and conversion? "This is the victory," says John, "that overcometh the world, even our faith." The gentleman will not pretend, that a man can be a true believer, and yet be impenitent. Hence it is that the Savior promised eternal life to every believer, without mentioning repentance or conversion.

My friend pointed us to the baptism of the eunuch. Here, he told us, faith is mentioned, but not conversion. The eunuch said, "I believe that Jesus Christ is the Son of God." There is faith. I ask again, can faith exist without conversion? If it can, then faith is not, as John represents it, the "victory that overcometh the world."

The case of Cornelius was brought forward. He, we were told, was a good man, but not *evangelically saved*. I believe that is the phraseology used by the gentleman; though I do not find such language in the Scriptures. My friend, after all his reforming, retains a good deal of "the language of Ashdod." If he was saved at all, I presume he was saved *evangelically*. If he was saved, his sins were pardoned. Look at the history of Cornelius, and determine in the light of divine truth, whether he was yet unpardoned. When Peter reached the house, and Cornelius reported to him the revelation which God had made to him, then Peter said, " Of a truth, I perceive that God is no respecter of persons ; but in every nation, he that feareth God and worketh righteousness, is accepted of him." Now, Cornelius was *accepted*. A man accepted of God, and not pardoned! Moreover, Peter did not say one word about baptism, in order to *the remission of sins*. He ought to have taught Cornelius this doctrine, if it were true. What did Peter say? Instead of saying, be baptized for the remission of sins, he said, " To him give all the prophets witness, that through his name, *whosoever believeth* on him, shall receive remission of sins."

Now my friend is obliged to grant, that thousands do believe, who never will be immersed.

But again—Peter said, " Can any man forbid water, that these should not be baptized, which have received the Holy Ghost as well as we ?" What did Peter say? Be baptized, that you may receive the Holy Ghost? No—the Spirit is poured out before baptism. Cornelius was not only a good man, a pious man, but he had received the miraculous influences of the Holy Spirit *before baptism*. Here, then, if Mr. Campbell's doctrine is true, we find a good man, a pious man, having received the miraculous influences of the Spirit, and still he is a condemned man ! ! His sins are yet upon him ; and he is in danger of being lost !

My friend has told you about three salvations, viz: of the body, of the soul, and the salvation in heaven. If we admit that there are three, Cornelius, it is true, had not the *third ;* but most assuredly he had the second—the remission of sins. And with great propriety it might be said, Peter told him words whereby he might be *saved ;* because no man can be said to be saved, in the highest sense of this word, till he gets to heaven. I presume the gentleman has not gained much for his cause by introducing the case of Cornelius. He will find it difficult to convince any enlightened mind, that a good man, whose prayers God has heard, who has been honored by a visit from an angel from heaven ; and upon whom he has poured out the miraculous gifts of his Spirit, is yet in a state of condemnation, and cannot be pardoned until he is immersed ! We have higher ideas of the grace and mercy of God, than to believe, that he has bound himself not to pardon a penitent believer, until an external ordinance can be administered to him.—[*Time expired.*

Friday, Nov. 24—11 o'clock, A. M.
[MR. CAMPBELL'S FIFTH ADDRESS.]

MR. PRESIDENT—It is, perhaps, expedient, that I now attend to some objections made to my arguments. As yet, indeed, we have had no direct reply to any one of them—no debate whatever, as doubtless you all perceive. Ten arguments have now been submitted, and not a direct issue formed on any one of them. But the gentleman throws out observations, and asserts other positions, which he presumes will answer the purpose as well as any response which he could make. He has asked the question, " Into what new relation is a person baptized?" He admits there is a new relation, and assumes that baptism is a mere recognition of it. Such, indeed, is his use of baptism—for such, he has argued, was the use of circumcision ; it recognized a previously existing relation. Well, baptism recognizes that an infant is *in* Christ already ! ! His design of baptism is very simple. It merely recognizes a relation already formed. Such, however, was not the apostles' view of the matter. The gentleman can find no text in the Bible that says so. The apostles taught that "as many as were baptized into Christ, had put on Christ; that they were baptized into Christ." The name of the Father, Son, and Holy Spirit, was, in baptism, put upon them; and hence a new relation was now formed. Is marriage, or is naturalization, a mere recognition of a previously existing relation? I ask, also, in what previously existing relation do infants stand to the Father, Son, and Holy Spirit, in respect to baptism? and in what new relation do these infant disciples stand to Father, Son, and Holy Spirit, after baptism?

Was there not some change in the relations of Moses, and the children of Israel, after their baptism *into* Moses in the cloud and in the sea? Moses, with considerable difficulty, constrained them to prepare for a journey from Egypt. Forty years before that time, when he offered his services, they were rejected, and his life endangered. Remembering their unkind treatment of him, it was with great reluctance he undertook the new mission. He did not know how to address them. "Who shall I tell them sent me?" was his own response to God, when about receiving his commission. He knew the reluctance of the king to let them go, and their reluctance to leave Egypt; and between these, Moses felt it would be a labor and a toil insuperable, without some aids, supernatural and Divine. The Lord promised these, and gave him a sign of the power which should accompany him in this great work of redeeming that people. I need not relate the means employed, nor the difficulties encountered and overcome, in making both parties willing—Israel to depart, and Pharaoh willing to let them go. At last they encamped near the Red sea. But when they found themselves encamped between defiles of mountains on right and left, the Red sea before them, and Pharaoh, with his chariots and horsemen, behind them, their spirits sunk within them. They repented that they had left their former masters, and had detached themselves from slavery. Their faith in Moses was not sealed. They desponded— they murmured. He saw himself in the midst of perils. His faith failed not, though theirs did. He threw oil upon the troubled waters. Stretching out his hand, with the rod of God in it, over the Red sea, he said "Stand still, and see the salvation of God." The waters were instantly divided. As though congealed, they stood like walls of adamant—a splendid defile on the right and left. The channel of the Red sea was their pavement. The chariot cloud of the Redeemer of Israel arched it over. Moses marched. He gave the solemn signal, and they obeyed. He led the way, and they followed him. Soon as the millions of Israel were all in the channel of the sea, the cloud of glory covered them. They were, indeed, baptized *into* Moses in the cloud and in the sea. They now, in *fact*, assumed him as their leader, *practically* confided in him, and *united their fortunes with his* from that moment. So with the discipled into Christ. They enter into a covenant, in their hearts, with the Lord. They solemnly give themselves away, and vow an everlasting homage to him practically, actually, and formally, in their burial with Christ, and a formal assumption of his venerable, holy, and beloved name.

The gentleman would have you think that I committed a great error in prefixing the word *Presbyterian* before the name of Dr. Timothy Dwight. Pedo-baptists are so sub-divided, and even Calvinists and Presbyterians so frittered into parties, and the nice shades that designate them so metaphysical, I confess I frequently err in this way. In the old world, in my youth, we called the *Congregationalists*, English Presbyterians—sometimes Puritans. But, inasmuch as Dr. Dwight was a Pedo-baptist, there is no injury done either truth or religion, by placing him under a wrong label. In this country, indeed, it now seems this error has been sanctioned by high authority; for the General Assembly of the Presbyterian church has, within a few years, thrown out of her bosom many thousands of those Presbyterian Congregationalists. The difference, until recently, hurt no man's conscience, except a very few of the deepest shade of true-blueism. Dwight, then, we shall all remember, was a Presbyterian in doctrine, and a Congregationalist in ecclesiastic politics, or government. What an important point we have now decided!

My opponent is, I think, the only man in this house who could so have misconceived me, on the meaning of John iii. 5. When I spoke of " *born of water* and of the Spirit," did any other person imagine that I spoke of a mere outward relation to something called a visible church? No. That is, perhaps, a Pedo-baptist idea; but it is no conception of mine. If it does not indicate more than a nominal outward profession and adhesion to a particular community, it is, indeed, a matter of very little importance. Have I to enlighten my friend upon this subject? It seems as though he were in the dark, on the spirituality of baptism, and the church or kingdom of Christ. With me, union with Christ is not mere union with a creed, and a party built upon it. The kingdom of God is no party, no one party on earth. It is a spiritual kingdom, and is in the hearts of men: consisting not in meats, drinks, creeds, and covenants, " but in righteousness, peace, and joy in the Holy Spirit." Into this no one can enter without faith, and the Spirit of God. *Baptism into Christ*, the effect of faith, is a sensible introduction into this spiritual state, and outwardly unites us with the public profession; but when properly understood, spiritually, sometimes called mystically, or under the symbol, inducts into an intimate, near, and holy union with the Savior of the world, by his Spirit. The outward act, then, is but the symbol of the transition, *inward and spiritual,* by which our souls are bathed in that ocean of love, which purifies our persons, and makes them one with the Lord. Without this, being born of water, or being connected with a church, is nothing—worse than nothing. Hence, without previous knowledge, faith, and repentance, immersion into the name, &c., is a mere outward and unprofitable ceremony. Hence my opposition to infant baptism; and hence my opposition to adult baptism, without a previous knowledge of the gospel.

All outward ordinances, *(and all ordinances are outward,)* prayer, praise, the Lord's day, the breaking of the loaf, fasting, &c., have each a peculiar grace or intercommunion with Christ in them. Like the ordinances of nature—sun, moon, stars, planets, atmospheric clouds, water, &c., &c., each has some peculiar influence of its own which can never be substituted by another. Each of these is a symbol of something more spiritual than itself. Prayer is but the embodiment of something more inward than the heart. But without these symbols, spiritual life, health, comfort can never be enjoyed. Hence, to enter into the sanctum sanctorum, the inner temple of spiritual enjoyment and christian life, baptism is essentially necessary, preceded by a vigorous faith, and genuine penitence, and fixed resolves of obeying from the heart the mandates of the Great King.

Among other grievous and revolting errors and imperfections which
2 T

my very devoted friend, Mr. Rice, detects in me, he says I agree with the pope in my views on baptism. What a misfortune! that the pope should be right in any thing! Has Mr. Rice become so hyperprotestant as not to agree with the pope in any thing? Yes, verily, he agrees with the pope in many truths, such as the death and resurrection, I do not say *burial*, of the Messiah; in his ascension into heaven, in his divinity, in his coming again, &c., &c. I hope these truths are nothing the worse because the pope believes them. But Mr. Rice agrees with the pope in other matters, in which I agree with neither. Even in baptism itself, he and the pope agree much more intimately. In two of three of the points before us on baptism, he and the pope are together; so that, in this case, he is twice as papistical as I.

But the gentleman desires to take from us *eis*, as indicating *into*, in the case before us. In this, he and the pope may be against us. It signifies *for* and *into :* but both are modes of expressing the same idea. Whether I do this *for, into, unto,* or *in order to,* the sense is the same. These are different suits for the same idea. All critics know and admit this. It is, as before shown by me, more than five times to one translated *into* in the New Testament. In reference to baptism, the Pedo-baptist translators of the common version, have generally translated it *into* or *unto ;* as I have, on other occasions, showed at considerable length. They were baptized "*into* Moses" or *unto* Moses, "*into* Christ," "*into* his death," "*into* John's baptism ;" and, if any one prefer it, "*into* repentance," "*into* remission of sins," "*into* one body," &c. In every instance there is a *transition* from one state, profession, or place, into another. The person has suffered an immersion for something, into the possession or enjoyment of which he now enters, or enters into more fully than before.

The gentleman sports with John's "baptism" into repentance—into reformation. He prefers "*in order to,*" to make it ridiculous. He would have it "*because* of reformation," or I know not what. Well, John baptizes those confessing their sins, in order to an amendment of life; and where is the wit? It is good sense, and good English, and a fair version. Many matters of this sort I pass without criticism, without exposition; believing that if I attend to the weightier matters, any one can appreciate these.

Touching baptism for remission of sins, it is lamentable to observe the waste of ingenuity, to speak of nothing worse, displayed on the part of some very zealous and somewhat learned opponents. They have said, like Mr. Rice, that we are only once commanded to be baptized for the remission of sins; but, unfortunately for this sage remark, we are commanded to be baptized into the name of the Father, Son, and Holy Spirit but once in all the New Testament. And as all Christendom follow that one occurrence, why not also this? The gentleman makes many little points, to which I never reply, not because I cannot, but because I will not. They are sometimes so irrelevant as to have no bearing; at other times so palpably defective, as his infant disciples, that all the world shrinks from his logic. But in this case I must, though it be minute, remark, that we have baptism for remission of sins, in the identical same words, three times in the New Testament; and that, too, always in connection with *metanoia, reformation.* Mark i. 4, Luke iv. 3, Acts ii. 38 :—John the Baptist came *kerussoon baptisma metanoias eis aphesian toon amartioon*—preaching the baptism of reformation for the remission of sins.

This identical phrase is used once in each of these evangelists, at the commencement, to indicate the design of his baptism, but never repeated again.   In like manner and form, Acts ii. **38**, Peter *preached*, saying, *Metanoeesate, kai baptistheetoo eis aphesin amartioon.*   Three, then, of the five historical books of the New Testament open in the same style. And what is worthy of special remark is, that when our Lord gave the symbolic cup of blessings into the hands of the apostles, for the first time, he adopts the same phrase exactly, consecrates and fixes its meaning: " This is the blood of the new covenant shed *for (eis aphisin toon amartioon,)* the remission of the sins of many." In no instance, of these four cases, is there one particle of change in the original expression. Even the article *teen,* is never inserted by Matthew, Mark, or Luke, before *aphesin;* a very singular uniformity.   The meaning of *for* or *eis,* is fixed by the last occurrence, beyond controversy.   Baptism *for* the remission of sins, is the only baptism of which the New Testament knows any thing.   There never was any other ordained by God—John's baptism or Christ's baptism—THERE IS NO OTHER.   Mr. Rice will not form an issue on these phrases, I strongly suspect.   He labors irrelevant points, weak points, false issues, or issues of no pertinency.   But he will tell you, this is all a matter of policy on my part to exaggerate or to depreciate topics, arguments, and issues, as suits my cause or my strength. I do not think it worth my denial or refutation.   I know no person of discrimination will believe it.   I only feel mortified that I have not something to do worthy of the occasion.

But we must have a word or two on *metanoia*, which, with George Campbell and others, I prefer to *repent.*   It is not, as often insinuated, because I have any objection to repentance, properly so called; for, with me, repentance, or a change of mind, or regret for the past, must always precede reformation.   *Reformation* both presupposes or comprehends penitence in its biblical acceptation.   I desire to see the broken and the contrite heart as the prelude of effectual repentance ; that is, reformation of behavior.   The reason of my preference is, the inspired writers had two words at command, *metamelomai* and *metanoeoo,* and their verbals. The first indicates a change of mind, accompanied with sorrow and regret, and painful reminiscences of the past.   The latter expresses a change of views, feelings, and purposes ; issuing in a new course of action, not from merely sorrow or regret, though these may, and always in conversion do, accompany this change; but it also includes the discernment, appreciation, or admiration of new, sublime, and excellent principles which constrain to a new course of action.   I could easily document these definitions by a display of quotations from classic and sacred Greek ; but as I have a very fixed dislike to such displays before a popular assembly, I shall only give a few instances from the New Testament, confirmatory of these remarks, and pass on.   We have *metamelomai* only some six or seven times in the New Testament.   It is chosen to represent the repentance of Judas, Matt. xxvii. 3.   He repented, and went and hanged himself.   *Metanoeoo* would not have suited there, for there was no change for the better in the mind of Judas.   Paul says to the Corinthians, 2d epistle vii. 7, 8, " I do not repent that I made you *sorry* by my letter, though I did repent;" for again " Godly sorrow worketh *repentance to salvation*, not to be repented of."   Here is the best illustration in contrast, not only in the New Testament, but perhaps in all classic usage ; for here we have a repentance to salvation expressed by *meta-*

noia, and a repentance not to salvation by *metamelomai*. Surely, then, having two words so different in the original, we ought to have two equally different in our language. This is my reason, then, for prefering reformation to the more doubtful and badly defined something called penitence, or penance. To do better, is a repentance to salvation; this is *reformation*. To be sorry, to regret, and inefficiently to repent our past actions, without reformation, is mere *repentance*.

Having now paid, as I conceive, a very courteous attention to some of my friend's minor matters, I shall advance again toward the field of argument. I was sorry that Mr. R. should have preferred to reply to some one else, on the case of Cornelius, rather than respond to me. Ought it not to satisfy us all, fellow-citizens, that an angel commanded Cornelius to send to Joppa for *words* that would *save* him and his family; and that when these words were being uttered, the Spirit of God descended to confirm them, and to signalize that congregation, making them on their faith a proper first-fruits of the gentile world, and thus sanctioning their baptism and admission into Christ's kingdom?

It seems as if Mr. Rice had found a most delicious theme in my alledged illiberality. He glories in an assumed liberality. I desire no invidious comparisons. Still I hesitate not to say, that, truly and sincerely, on the proper meaning of the word, were our respective views, feelings, and actions thoroughly dissected, I am incomparably more liberal than he: for I suppose there are many conscientious, religious, moral, and christian Presbyterians; and that, although our Savior has no Presbyterian church in heaven, or earth, yet I doubt not but that he has had many, very many, that loved and honored him in that worldly church, whom he will honor in the world to come. So has he in other Protestant communities in this cloudy and dark day. They call themselves *branches* of Christ's church: I wonder where the stem is! In their own esteem they are but *branches*. Now, the Bible knows neither the word nor the thing, branch church. I presume, when I was a Presbyterian, nay, indeed, I recollect perfectly well, that I used to look over my church as the almost exclusive boundary of the elect. Salvation was of us, and a few like us. But since I became a man, I have put away childish things. I thank my Lord that my charities extend far beyond the contents of that little book lying on the table [pointing to the constitution of the Presbyterian church.] Yes, sir, while I go for only one true catholic, apostolic church, and while I cannot find it in any of these Pedo-baptist "*branches*," I can find christian people among them all! There is as much truth as wit in the saying—there are christians without a church, and there is a church without christians.

I wish to add a few words on evangelical holiness and evangelical salvation. Mr. R. seems to censure me for not using certain words, and then blames me for using them. One thing is very obvious, he and I have not been taught in one and the same school. Cornelius was a *good man*, as we sometimes say, but no *saint*. He did not know the Lord Jesus, consequently was not a christian; he had, therefore, no evangelical, no gospel holiness. Peter rehearsed to him John's mission, Christ's mission and character, and opened his credentials, and proved all his sayings and doings by the prophets. He heard, believed, rejoiced, and put on Christ, by a baptism into his death. He is now pardoned, sanctified, saved, adopted, and filled with all blessings of the Spirit of holiness, of heavenly peace and love. Any one that can comprehend how a new dispensation or change in a government affects society, may easily understand how John's mission obliged the good to separate themselves and please God by receiving baptism. The people that heard him, and the publicans, justified God, being baptized with the baptism of John. But the pharisees and lawyers rejected the counsel of God against themselves, being not baptized of him. Now, as no one could please God and obtain salvation by adhering to any former institution, after that a new one was introduced, so it behooved all men, however virtuous and excellent their character, to submit to the christian religion immediately after its introduction. And not only this—christianity was as far above all former manifestations of God's love and dispensations of religion, as the "heavens are higher than the earth." The privileges it communicated to all, were superior to the greatest blessings enjoyed by patriarchs, kings, or prophets of the olden time. On these topics, the New Testament is replete with light. Now, although Cornelius would have been saved, in all probability, under a former dispensation, or had he died without any opportunity of the words brought from Joppa; still, in the christian sense of the word *saved,* he neither was saved, nor could have been saved, without all that Peter did for him. Calvin and Cornelius we shall reserve to another speech, and will return to my series of argumentation.

My *eleventh* argument is based on Eph. v. 25, 26:—"Christ loved the church and gave himself for it, that he may sanctify and cleanse it with the washing of water by the word."

That the *washing of water* here spoken of has reference to baptism, is admitted almost universally. The Westminster divines, and all the commentators of note known to me, concur in this view of it. Now as Mr. R. will have the action of baptism to be a "religious washing with water," he cannot, of course, object to this application of the passage. The only difference here of importance between him and me in this case is—that the apostle is speaking of the cleansing effect of baptism, and not of the action proper to the institution. Just as Ananias once said to the author of this epistle, "Arise, and be baptized, and" as a consequence, "*wash* away thy sins." So here the apostle, in allusion not only to baptism, as some affirm, but also to the eastern custom of brides, to whom the law of matrimony had assigned numerous washings, or baths, before their nuptials, I would say, rather comparing "this bath of water," as McKnight renders it, to baptism, that the apostle here not only connects purification with baptism, purification from sin, but also combines that with the word, and of course, with faith in that word. Now, appears it not evident, that the water and the word here sustain to each other just the same relation intimated by the Messiah, when he speaks of being "born of water, and of the Spirit?" I cannot, then, separate these two, so firmly seated in the minds of those inspired with all wisdom. They are intimately connected in the work of remission, Ephesians v. 26; being corroborated by John iii. 5, furnishes another argument in proof of the all-important evangelical fact, that baptism is for cleansing, for remission of sins. Mr. Rice believes in baptism for purification, though I think he has not satisfactorily defined his position. Still he believes in water as an emblem of sanctification. We differ, indeed, in one essential point just here. He has more faith in water than I have; for he believes that water alone, even a few drops, a mere spray, without faith in the word, purifies from sin, or some way cleanses and sanctifies a person. I do not comprehend the notion of purification, as aforesaid. Justification and sanctification with me are always associated. Paul associated them to the Corinthians; he said, "You are washed; you are justified; you are sanctified, in the name of the Lord Jesus, and by the Spirit of our God." Here, then, justification precedes in position, if not in terms, sanctification. Mr. R. must believe in baptism for remission of sins, if he believes in baptism for purification, for none are purified, who are not first pardoned. God cleanses the guilt of sin, before, or at least simultaneously with sanctification. I hope Mr. Rice will explain his baptismal purification—I mean his infant baptismal purification. Nothing will make it so acceptable as to show its utility. We have never seen any use in infant affusion; but if the gentleman will show that it purifies from sin, that is, of course, both from its guilt and its pollution, he will have done more to procure it a favorable hearing and acceptance, than all the Pedo-baptists, living or dead.

My *twelfth* argument is drawn from Col. ii. 12—15: "Buried with him in baptism, whence also ye are risen with him through the faith of the operation of God, who hath raised him from the dead. And you, being dead in your sins, and the uncircumcision of your flesh, hath he quickened, together with him, having forgiven you all trespasses; blotting out the handwriting of ordinances that was against us, which was contrary to us, and took it out of the way, nailing it to his cross."

Speaking of the design of baptism, it is impossible not to look at and regard both the subject and the action of baptism; because you cannot show the design, without remembering how, in ancient times, it was attended to.

Paul says: "We put off the body of the sins of the flesh." Now this is the most beautiful allusion to circumcision imaginable. Here were those who still hankered after circumcision. To them the apostle says, "You are complete in Christ; you need not to be circumcised with a circumcision made with hand." The old fleshly circumcision only took off a mere atom of flesh; but the spiritual circumcision, which we have in being crucified with Christ, in being buried with him in baptism, cuts off, without a knife, and without a hand, the whole body of the sins of the flesh. This is Christ's way of circumcising now-a-days. So that, instead of baptism for circumcision, we have a circumcision of all our sins, for the old circumcision of a mere particle of flesh. The whole body of sins, the mighty mass, is now cut off through our faith and baptism into Christ, with whom we have risen through the faith of the mighty operation, the operation of God, who raised him from the dead. If such witnesses as these do not prove that baptism is for the remission of sins, I ask what proof would be sufficient to establish it?—[*Time expired.*

Friday, Nov. 24—11½ o'clock, A. M.
[MR. RICE'S FIFTH REPLY.]

MR. PRESIDENT—I will follow my worthy friend (as he desires to be followed,) so far as it may be necessary to answer what he has now advanced. You remember, one of his arguments, to prove that baptism is necessary to the remission of sins, was founded on the expression—baptizing *into* the name of the Father, &c. which proves, as he supposes, that baptism introduces the subject of it into a new relation to God; or, as he now expresses it, a new *state*. In reply, I referred to a precisely similar expression, in 1 Cor. x. 2, where it is said, the Jews were all baptized *into*, (or unto,) Moses. I stated, that he had been previously their leader and deliverer; that there was, therefore, no new relation constituted; that they passed into no new state; that their baptism was only a recognition of an existing relation. It could not constitute a new one.

But my friend has no little ingenuity in escaping from difficulties. He asks, what previously existing relation is recognized when infants are baptized? I have repeatedly stated, that they are, by birth, entitled to membership in the church, and that their baptism is the recognition of their relation to God's covenant, and to his people. They are born with the right to be included in God's covenant—to be introduced into the school of Christ. Baptism is the rite, divinely appointed, by which their relation to the church is recognized. When they are thus recognized, they have all the privileges in the church of Christ, of which they are capable. For illustration, a man is entitled to the presidency of the United States, when the people have elected him to that office; but he is not recognized as the president, nor can he enter upon the duties of the office, till he is *inaugurated;* yet the ceremony of inauguration does not confer upon him the office. The vote of the people places him in a new relation to them, and to the government; and the ceremony of inauguration is but the proper recognition and confirmation of that relation.

But Mr. Campbell, in order to prove, that the baptism of the children of Israel unto Moses, constituted a new relation, or introduced them into a new state, went into Egypt, and informed us, with what difficulty Moses induced the people to follow him; and how, by divers miracles, especially at the Red sea, their faith was confirmed, and they resolved to adhere to him as their leader, &c. But, unfortunately, we find in this history no new relation constituted. The Jews had been induced to acknowledge Moses as their leader, by the miracles he wrought in Egypt; and those miracles may be said to have caused the relation. They approached the Red sea, and saw their enemies behind them—their confidence in their leader was shaken; but it was restored and confirmed by the wonderful miracles there wrought. These confirmed their wavering purposes; and their baptism, as they passed through the sea, was, so to speak, a public recognition and confirmation of the relation which had been constituted in Egypt, when they agreed to take him as their leader. So christian baptism is a sign and seal of that intimate relation to Christ, constituted by faith, and of remission of sins; and it tends greatly to confirm our faith. But who ever before heard, that, by the baptism at the Red sea, the Jews were made to sustain to Moses a new relation; or, that they entered into a new *state?* The gentleman will be obliged to abandon this argument.

His mistake, in speaking of Dwight as a Presbyterian doctor, it is true, is a small matter; but it shows his accuracy in quoting authors. We should have been by no means unwilling to own Dwight, if he had been a Presbyterian; nor do I dissent from his views of this subject. Still Presbyterians and Congregationalists are two distinct denominations—although their doctrines are nearly the same, and they differ chiefly in their form of church government. I alluded to this circumstance only to show, that he was not very accurate in quoting authors.

My friend says, he does not agree with the pope on the subject under discussion; I will read a passage, at the proper time, from his debate with McCalla, in which he asserts, that the baptized person, when he emerges from the water, is *as pure as an angel.* The pope says, the person baptized is " pure, and guiltless, and beloved of God." Their doctrines are so precisely similar, in this respect, that it would require a

skillful metaphysician to show the difference.   It is true, as he says, that
I agree with papists in some items of faith, but I never appeal to them,
as authority, to sustain my principles, as he has done.   Should I ever do
so, his reply will be pertinent.

   I will now read you a quotation from the Millenial Harbinger, vol. iii.
pp. 301, 302.   It is a letter, from Prof. Stuart to Dr. Fishback, upon this
point.   My friend, Dr. Fishback, says :

   " From my great anxiety to possess the true meaning of Acts ii. 38, and
to be able to reconcile the apparent discrepancy between what was said by
Peter to the pentecostal Jews, in reference to baptism and the remission of
sin, as it appears in our common translation, and in your new one, with
what occurred at the introduction of the gospel to the gentiles in Acts x.
and as explained in chapter xi. in relation to the same subject ; I wrote to
professor Stuart to favor me with his interpretation of the Greek preposition *eis*, as it is connected with, and follows baptism.   He was kind and
obliging enough to comply with my request, and sent me his remarks, which
I now present to you, and hope that they will conduce much to unite our
views on the subject of discussion between us.   He observes : ' The word
baptize may be followed by a person or a thing, (doctrine) which has *eis* before it.   In the first case, when it is followed by a person, it means, " by
the sacred rite of baptism to bind one's self to be a disciple or follower of a
person, to receive or obey his doctrines or laws,"—*e. g.* 1 Cor. x. 2, " and
were baptized into (*eis*) Moses." Gal. iii. 27, " For as many of you as have
been baptized into (*eis*) Christ, having put on Christ." Rom. vi. 3, " Know
ye not that so many of us as were baptized into (*eis*) Christ, were baptized
into (*eis*) his death ?"   1 Cor. i. 13, " Were ye baptized into (*eis*) the name
of Paul ?" v. 14, 15, " I thank God that I baptized none of you but Crispus
and Gaius, lest any should say that I had baptized into (*eis*) mine own
name."   Or it means, to acknowledge him as Sovereign, Lord, and Sanctifier,—*e. g.* Matt. xxviii. 19, " Baptized them into (*eis*) the name of the Father, and of the Son, and of the Holy Ghost." Acts viii. 16, " Only they
were baptized into (*eis*) the name of the Lord." Acts xix. 5, " When they
heard this, they were baptized into (*eis*) the name of the Lord." '

   That *name* is used after *eis*, as it is in some of the above cases, makes no
difference in the sense.   In Hebrew, ' the name of the God of Jacob defend
thee,' is just the same as ' the God of Jacob defend thee.'

   2. A person may be baptized into a thing, (doctrine.) So in Matt. iii. 11,
' I baptize you with water into (*eis*) repentance ;' *i. e.* into the profession
and belief of the reality and necessity of repentance, involving the idea that
themselves professed to be the subjects of it.   In Acts xix. 3, we have ' into
(*eis*) one body,' all in the like sense, viz. by baptism the public acknowledgment is expressed of believing in, and belonging to, a doctrine, or one body.
So in Acts ii. 38, ' Baptized on account of Jesus Christ into (*eis*) the remission of sins ;' that is, into the belief and reception of this doctrine ; in other
words, by baptism and profession, an acknowledgement of this doctrine, on
account of Jesus Christ, was made.

   Professor Stuart has rendered the word *eis* INTO in Acts ii. 38, as it is
done in other places when connected with the ordinance of baptism ; and as
you have rendered the same word in Matt. xxviii. 19, in the new version,
and which you have justified by the authority of Dr. Dwight."

   Now what are we to understand by being baptized *into* the remission
of sins ?   Mr. Campbell makes it mean, *in order to* the remission of
sins ; but Stuart, whose learning he admires, tells us it is, to be baptized
into the belief and reception of the doctrine of remission through Christ ;
as to be baptized *into* repentance, is to be baptized upon a profession of
repentance.   The expressions in both cases are precisely similar.   The
Scripture doctrine evidently is, that repentance, not baptism, secures re-

mission; and hence it is, that repentance and remission are so repeatedly connected together by our Savior and his apostles.

Mr. C. insists, that *eis* means *in order to*, in Peter's discourse; and to be consistent, he is obliged to translate Matt. iii. 11, "I baptize you *in order to reformation.*" But, as I have proved, this rendering makes the doctrine of Peter contradict that of John. Moreover, it makes Peter, in his second discourse, speak very singularly. It represents him as saying to his hearers, *reform and be converted.* I have asked the gentleman, (and he has not attempted to answer the question) what is the difference between *reformation* and *conversion?* Reformation certainly is turning from an evil to a righteous course; and conversion is the same thing. So he would, in effect, make Peter say to the Jews, *reform and be reformed,* or *convert* and *be converted!!!*

Metanoia, the word commonly translated repentance, in our Bible, is used to denote that repentance which is acceptable to God. It signifies a change of mind—a change of views and feelings—terminating in sorrow for sin, and leading to conversion, or turning to God. The gentleman, by his translation, confounds cause and effect, and thus makes the inspired apostle speak the most singular tautology. Such are the inextricable difficulties of his doctrine.

In using the phrase "evangelical salvation," with reference to Cornelius, he says, he used my own phraseology. I do not remember to have used the phrase, or even to have heard it from others. I have heard of evangelical *faith ;* but I was not aware that there were so many kinds of salvation. I have always thought, when a man was saved, he was saved. When Paul says, "By grace are ye saved through faith," I suppose, he speaks of salvation from sin and hell, and elevation to the enjoyment of heaven and eternal life. I thought that the word *salvation* comprehended all the blessings promised in the gospel. "He that believeth and is baptized, shall be saved." Here the word comprehends both the present and the future blessings of the gospel. Cornelius had the present, but he needed the future. Hence, Peter is said to have told him words by which he should be *saved.* But the fact is indisputable, that Peter, when he for the first time preached the gospel to the gentiles, did not preach baptism in order to the remission of sins. He did not mention it as one of the conditions of pardon—it was not even a prominent topic in his discourse. Such being the facts, no one has a right to assume that he preached this doctrine.

The gentleman has greatly magnified his charity and liberality; but I am prepared to prove, that Dr. Fishback, his friend and brother, has pronounced his doctrine "the most exclusive, sectarian and uncharitable," in the world!!! And his opinion must be very nearly correct; for he is well acquainted with Mr. Campbell's real views; and is not under the influence of prejudice against him.

The greatness of his charity and liberality are strikingly exhibited, in the following sentence, in his *Christianity Restored:* "Infants, idiots, deaf and dumb persons, innocent pagans, wherever they can be found, with all the pious Pedo-baptists, we commend to the mercy of God," p. 240. In the exuberance of his charity, he has put all pious Pedo-baptists with infants, idiots, and pagans, and commended them to the mercy of God!!!

To sustain his doctrine, making baptism necessary to remission, the gentleman has appealed to Ephesians v. 25, 26, "Husbands, love your wives, even as Christ also loved the church, and gave himself for it; that he might sanctify and cleanse it with the washing of water by the word." Does this passage prove that sins are remitted only in baptism? Let us compare this with a passage in the Old Testament, to which I have repeatedly referred: Eze. xxxvi. 25, "Then will I sprinkle clean water upon you, and you shall be clean; from all your filthiness, and from all your idols will I cleanse you. A new heart also will I give you, and a new spirit will I put within you. And I will take away the stony heart out of your flesh, and I will give you an heart of flesh. And I will put my Spirit within you, and cause you to walk in my statutes."

Now, it is here proved, according to Mr. Campbell's mode of interpreting language, that sprinkling clean water upon persons will cleanse them from all moral filthiness, and from idolatry. Yet he has not the least faith in the efficacy of sprinkling clean water. The language, too, you observe, is very similar to that employed by Ananias, when he baptized Paul. For he said, "Arise and be baptized, and wash away thy sins." So, Ezekiel said, "I will sprinkle clean water upon you, and you shall be clean." If, then, these passages prove that baptism secures remission of sins; that in Ezekiel will prove, with equal clearness, that the sprinkling of clean water upon persons, would cleanse them from moral pollution and idolatry! But what is the truth on this subject? It is, that Ezekiel connects together the emblem and the thing signified. The sprinkling of clean water is the emblem; and the new heart is the thing signified.

We turn now to Ps. li. "Purge me with hysop, and I shall be clean: wash me, and I shall be whiter than snow." What is the meaning of this prayer of David? According to my friend's principles of exposition, sprinkling a person with hysop, would make him white as snow—as pure as an angel. But by turning to Leviticus xiv. we learn that the ceremonially unclean were cleansed by sprinkling blood upon them, with hysop, cedar-wood, and scarlet. In reference to this ceremony, David prayed that God would grant him the inward purity, of which it was the emblem. Thus the prophets and inspired writers were accustomed to connect water with the Spirit. Another striking example of this kind is found in the prophecy of Isaiah, chapter xliv. 3: "For I will pour water upon him that is thirsty, and floods upon the dry ground: I will pour my Spirit upon thy seed, and my blessing upon thine offspring: and they shall spring up as among the grass, as willows by the water-courses." Here the outpouring of the Spirit upon the hearts of men is beautifully represented by the falling of copious showers on the thirsty ground. Epistle to Titus, he says, "He saved us by the washing of regeneration cleansing of the church from sin. Washing is the emblem, and the Spirit is the divine agent in purifying the church from all sin. Thus, in the So Paul employs water, the emblem of purification, to express the entire and renewing of the Holy Ghost." And just so Ezekiel says, "I will sprinkle clean water upon you, and a new heart also will I give you." Such was the custom of the Jewish writers; and Paul was a Jew, and wrote acording to their manner.

The gentleman finally appeals to Col. ii. 10, 11: "And ye are complete in him which is the head of all principality and power: in whom also ye are circumcised with the circumcision made without hands, in putting off the body of the sins of the flesh, by the circumcision of Christ: buried with him in baptism, wherein also ye are risen with him through the

faith of the operation of God, who hath raised him from the dead." Now,
let us inquire, what is the circumcision made without hands? It evidently signifies the renovation of the heart, of which circumcision was
the sign. Hence the exhortation, "Circumcise the fore-skin of your
hearts." Spiritual circumcision is a new heart—a sanctified nature; and,
as circumcision formerly signified the renewal of the heart, so does baptism now. Therefore, Paul puts them in immediate connection, and save
to christians—You have not the external circumcision, but you have the
grace of which it was the sign, the circumcision of the heart. You are
holy in heart; buried with Christ in baptism, and risen with him through
faith of the operation of God. As you have the spiritual circumcision,
so you have the spiritual baptism. You are identified with Christ in his
death and resurrection. I find in this passage not a word about remission of sins. The apostle is speaking of sanctification of heart, a very
different subject.

I have now answered what my friend has advanced in support of his
doctrine. In reply to his remarks on baptismal purification, it is sufficient to say—that I believe in the entire cleansing of the soul from sin,
by the blood of Jesus Christ, as the *procuring cause;* and by the Holy
Spirit, as the *efficient agent,* of which water baptism is the significant
emblem. But we are not now discussing the doctrine of sanctification,
but the doctrine of remission of sins; and I am not to be diverted from
this important point.

I was, on yesterday, proving, that, according to Mr. Campbell's doctrine, multitudes of the most godly persons, live and die unpardoned, and
go to hell. He has, indeed, expressed some opinions quite inconsistent
with his doctrine; but we have now to deal, not with his opinions, but
with his doctrine. That I am not misrepresenting him, is clear from
the fact that he makes *repentance* and *immersion* "*equally necessary*" to
the remission of sins. See Christian Baptist, p. 416, 417, and Christianity Restored, p. 240; already quoted. Here my friend commends infants, idiots, pagans, and *pious Pedo-baptists* to the mercy of God!
He has nothing to say, as to whether they can be saved! In another
place, he expresses the opinion that some of them *may be saved;* but
his opinions are inconsistent with his doctrine. For, if repentance and
immersion be *equally necessary* to the remission of sins, how can unimmersed persons be saved? In view, then, of the fact, that Mr. Campbell
maintains that baptism is an essential pre-requisite to remission does it
not follow that all unbaptized persons must be forever lost? By the
way, he says he must use the English word *immersion,* for baptism.
That it was English, I really did not know—I had thought that it was
Latin. He is pleased to use the Latin word *immersion;* but does not
like the Greek word *baptism!* But, as I was remarking, if, as the gentleman teaches, immersion be an essential pre-requisite to the remission
of sins, then every unimmersed person is unpardoned *through life.* Are
any pardoned *after death?* I have never found the passage that intimates, that any who die unforgiven, will be pardoned in the next world.
I have read, "He that is filthy, let him be filthy still; and he that is holy,
let him be holy still." He who is not pardoned here, cannot be pardoned
hereafter.

I ask, where in the Bible is the doctrine taught, that the righteous shall
be turned into hell? I do not bring this argument to awaken prejudice
against my friend; but, I am constrained to ask, *where is it said, that*

any but the wicked shall be turned into hell? We read, that the *wicked* shall be lost; but, if his doctrine be true, hell will be full of *good men!* Multitudes of pious, godly people will be found, lifting up their eyes in hell, being in torment!

The next argument which I will adduce against my friend, is, that his doctrine *ascribes an unscriptural importance and efficacy to an external ordinance.* The Scriptures uniformly represent the religion of the heart as the great and only essential matter. It was one of the radical errors of the Jews, that they made religion consist, almost exclusively, in attendance upon external rites and ceremonies. And how often did our Savior find it necessary to repeat to them, " I will have *mercy* and not *sacrifice*"—the religion of the heart, not external forms? When Saul brought back a great many oxen and sheep, from the spoils of the Amalekites, and excused himself by saying, he intended to offer them a sacrifice to God, the inspired Samuel proclaimed to him a glorious truth, which characterizes the whole Bible : " Behold, to obey is better than sacrifice, and to hearken, than the fat of rams ;" 1 Sam. xv. 22. David, in that penitential psalm, (li.,) gives utterance to the same great truth? " For thou desirest not sacrifice, else would I give it: thou delightest not in burn-offering. The sacrifices of God are a broken spirit: a broken and a contrite heart, O God, thou wilt not despise." Yet, according to the doctrine of Mr. C., he would despise the broken heart, unless immersed! Every where, from Genesis to Revelation, the religion of the heart is declared to be *the one thing needful.* The remission of sins was never connected, inseparably, with any external ordinance.

Circumcision was omitted for forty years by the Jews, while they were passing from Egypt to Canaan; and, in Joshua v., we read, that Joshua circumcised the whole company after they arrived in Canaan. Now, if this rite had been essential, they would not have omitted its observance for forty years. So Paul teaches, that " if the uncircumcision keep the righteousness of the law, their uncircumcision shall be counted for circumcision ;" Rom. ii. Now circumcision was as important to the Jews, as baptism is to christians.

By the way, I was surprised to hear the assertion made by Mr. C., that the blessings, promised under the old dispensation, were all of a temporal character. There never was an assertion more unfounded. " By faith Moses, when he came to years, refused to be called the son of Pharaoh's daughter, esteeming the reproach of Christ greater riches than the treasures in Egypt. For he had respect to the recompense of the reward." He gave up the earthly crown for a brighter crown in heaven. So it is said of all the pious, under the former dispensation, that they sought a city whose maker and builder is God. Hence David prayed in Ps. li., " Restore unto me the joy of thy *salvation.*"

No external ordinance was regarded as essential to salvation, under the old dispensation, when forms and ceremonies had more importance attached to them than under the christian dispensation.—[*Time expired.*

Friday, Nov. 24—12 o'clock, M.
[MR. CAMPBELL'S SIXTH ADDRESS.]

MR. PRESIDENT—It cannot have escaped your notice before to-day, how often my polite friend has made attempts to draw me off to debate with him about the new version, and other foreign matters. He has made numerous allusions to it, and almost challenged me to the task.

He is not the person, nor this the occasion, for such a discussion. I have, therefore, paid little or no attention to his efforts to entangle the subject, or to draw me off from the proposition before us. He sought to have me defend Dr. Campbell's version of Mark vii. 3, by a most violent assault upon it; as though it were my own work, or as if I had agreed to debate with him such questions. I understand his policy. I am prepared, at a proper time and place, and with a proper person, to defend all that I have written, or said, on those subjects. I have always succeeded pretty well in that department, my opponents themselves being judges. But these are not the questions now before us, and I will not attend to foreign and irrelevant subjects introduced for such a purpose.

Again, the gentleman has sought to entangle this subject, by making out inconsistencies between my present views and my former writings. Whenever the time comes, that it becomes my duty to defend myself on that account, I shall be forthcoming, I hope. One thing I can say, in all conscience, that I feel myself prepared to sustain every prominent view that I ever published on the subject of the christian religion. Here lies a volume before me upon the christian system. I do not call it, as insinuated here, "*the Christian System*," but that system "*in reference to the union of christians.*" In it there is a long article on the remission of sins. It has been written many years ago. It is quite pertinent to the subject now before us. If the gentleman pleases, I shall engross the whole of it as evidence on this proposition. In it there are many scriptural arguments, many authorities from the creeds and concessions of distinguished men, Catholic and Protestant. All of which are in good place and time here. I am ready to sustain every position taken there. I am sorry that I cannot introduce all those facts and documents here.

In his *ad captandum* tactics, my friend, who certainly deserves a diploma for his proficiency in that science, though I think he has almost run himself down by his too frequent attempts at it, seems to quote the pope and Catholic authorities in such a way, as to insinuate that I had, in the use of the term *catholic*, alluded to Roman authorities—to universities at Rome or at Constantinople. Not so, however. My Catholic authorities are neither Grecian, nor Roman, nor German, nor English—they are *catholic*, and all others are *particular*.

But in order to respond to my propositions, failing in other modes of reply, he now takes up some essays and communications between my friend and brother, Fishback, and myself, written some years ago, touching our views on some points bearing on this question. Whatever differences of opinion or of inferential reasonings there may be, between brother Fishback and myself, or any other brother here, is nothing to the purpose, any more than a passage in my debate with Robert Owen. I neither know nor care what are the present opinions of Dr. Fishback on all these topics. He is now with us in practice. Our bond of union is not opinion, nor unity of opinion. It is one Lord, one faith, one baptism, one Spirit, one hope, one God and Father of all. These we all preach and teach. We have no standard opinions amongst us. We have no patented form of sound words drawn up by human art and man's device, to which all must vow eternal fidelity. It is our peculiar felicity, and, perhaps, it may be our honor, too, that we have been able to discover a ground so common, so sacred, so divinely approbated, so perfectly catholic and enduring, on which every man, who loves our Lord Jesus Christ sincerely, may unite, and commune, and harmonize, and co-ope-

2 U

rate in all the works of faith, in all the labors of love, and in all the perseverance of hope. In this age of insular theology, this age of proscription, ecclesiastic dictation, and supercilious orthodoxy, it is like an oasis in the desert, to find an asylum, a sanctuary in which we can all worship, an altar around which all christian men may meet, and on which they may offer up their united praises, petitions and thanksgivings to the Father of all mercies, through the common Savior of all that believe. It is, Mr. President, our honor to have given to the world the first example in modern times, of a great community, made up of accessions from all communities, meeting on the Bible alone; and while aiming at one faith, (for there is but one true faith,) bearing with each other's opinions and views, and still making out to "maintain unity of spirit in the bonds of peace."

It gives me any thing but pleasure, sir, to have so often to turn aside to respond to so many very little things. I shall now turn my face to the argument, and endeavor to find where we are. I stand, sir, for the defence of truth—God's own soul-redeeming truth. It is for what is written in this book, I stand up here. When convicted of any error or false position, which I may have assumed, I will, sir, gladly retreat from it. I fight not for victory. I plead for truth. I would a thousand times rather, were it possible, be vanquished with the truth, than to triumph with error. Before heaven and earth I lift up my voice for the truth of this holy Book. I will stand by it, that it may stand by me; for that alone can strengthen man in the day of trial.

In his last effort to sustain his views, commenting on the second of the Colossians, the gentleman has spiritualized himself far beyond the precincts of the whole church of Scotland. He has made war against his own orthodox divines of Westminster, and a majority of all the reputable commentators known to me. The church of England, of Scotland, with the continental churches, from which I have heard, are, to a man, with me, in expounding this passage as referring to the ancient action of baptism, and to its design. I agree with the authors of the confession of faith, in all their references to this passage, so far as I now remember them, affirming that we do " put off *the body of the sins of the flesh* by the circumcision of Christ (being) buried with him in baptism." The language is most evidently with us, without either note or comment. Whatever is done, or reported as being done in the 11th verse, is said to be done in the 12th, in or by the fact that we have been buried with him, and risen with him in baptism. But we must hasten to another argument, (our *thirteenth*,) in farther confirmation of the preceding :—

I will read Tit. iii. 5, " Not by works of righteousness which we have done, but according to his mercy, he saved us, by the washing of regeneration, and renewing of the Holy Ghost; which he shed on us abundantly, through Jesus Christ our Savior : that being justified by his grace, we might be made heirs according to the hope of eternal life." The introduction to this luminous and most impressive development is sublimely beautiful and captivating in the composition of the original terms. As though he had said—' After that the starlight, moonlight, and twilight ages of the world had passed—after that the PHILANTHROPY of God our Savior, like the rising sun, full-orbed, shone forth, in all the splendor of the heavens, " he saved us in a way divinely simple and supremely kind—not by works of righteousness,"' &c. I have again the concurrent testimony of antiquity—of the Greek, Roman, and Protestant churches,—Westminster theologians, commentators, and paraphrasts, universally applying these words to baptism. I presume it will not be debated. Who, then, can withhold admiration when comparing John iii. 5, Ep. v. 26, Titus iii. 5, and Acts ii. 38, at the singular, yet unstudied similarity of arrangement of the two ideas of water and Spirit in the minds of the Messiah, Peter, and Paul. Jesus said—" born of water and of the Spirit." Peter said— " be baptized and receive the Holy Spirit." Paul said—" he sanctified the church through a bath of water and the Word." And again, he says to Titus, " He saved us through the washing of regeneration and renewing of the Holy Spirit." Here, then, we have the water and the Spirit, or the water and the Word; and the water and renewing of the Holy Spirit; and baptism in water and receiving the Holy Spirit, inseparably associated. Who, then, so indiscriminating as not to see, that there is a fixed connection in the christian dispensation between water and the Spirit! Remission of sins and sanctification are, therefore, inseparably connected with each other in the christian economy.

These facts, thus laid before us by apostolic authority, show how necessary it was in the law to adumbrate that *water alone* could, when sprinkled, or poured, cleanse no person from either legal or moral pollution. That something else must be added to the water, is clearly and firmly established. Faith, the Word, the Spirit, in some form expressed, show the connection to be most authoritatively established. Of course, then, Mr. Rice's theory of sanctification by mere water alone is one of the most baseless theories in Christendom. But I have yet remaining a fourteenth argument in support of this grand position: Peter tells in his first epistle, iii. 19: " By which also he went and preached unto the spirits in prison, which sometimes were disobedient, when once the long suffering of God waited in the days of Noah, while the ark was a preparing, wherein few, that is, eight souls, were saved by water. The like figure whereunto, even baptism, doth also now save us, (not the putting away of the filth of the flesh, but the answer of the good conscience toward God,) by the resurrection of Jesus Christ."

We began with Peter, who began the christian institution, and with Peter we shall end. From him we took our first argument, and from him we shall draw our fourteenth. His first precept in the new reign was, " Repent, and be baptized, every one of you, in the name of the Lord Jesus, not *because* your sins are forgiven you, but *for* the remission of sins." At the time this letter was written, Peter was an old man—probably had completed his threescore and ten years. He had observed the progress and operation of the gospel for some thirty years, or more. He opened the kingdom to the Jews, and afterwards to the Gentiles; he had seen its influences on both. In full view, then, of all the past history of christianity, and in bright anticipation of its ultimate and glorious triumph, he speaks to the brethren in Pontus, Galatia, Cappadocia, Asia, and Bythinia, as you have heard me read from the third chapter. He places baptism to the church in some correspondence with the ark to Noah, and the deluge. Noah had faith to go into the ark, and to commit himself to the flood, in the firm belief that God would bring him safely out of the deluge, and save him from destruction. Thus, immerged in a flood of water, when the fountains of the great deep were broken up, and the windows of heaven were opened, he was sustained by his faith in God's promise, and while the fleshly world of the ungodly perished, he escaped destruction. Now, says the apostle, baptism is a sort of antitype of this whole salvation. The like figure answering thereunto is baptism, by which, through water, we are saved, not, indeed, like the legal washings and bathings, which only sanctified to the cleansing of the flesh; not the washing away of the outward, natural, or legal filth of the flesh, but the answer of a good conscience toward God, (or the seeking of a good conscience,) by the resurrection of Jesus Christ from the dead. If, then, the Messiah says, "He that believeth, and is baptized, shall be *saved ;*" and if Peter says, "Baptism doth now save us," shall we not regard it as one of the great means of God's own appointment, for the sake of communicating to us an assurance of his love, through the blood of the everlasting covenant?

I have now given *fourteen* distinct and independent arguments in proof and illustration of this grand position. I am truly sorry that they have not been debated by my respondent. He seems exceedingly coy and prudent in coming into a close engagement upon all matters, but especially on this proposition. Not one of my arguments has yet been formally assailed. They stand now like one unbroken phalanx, side by side, in illustration and confirmation of my affirmation of the design of christain baptism. True, he has offered, in no very connected way, some objections and cavils, against several of them, but no argument has been assailed, no position canvassed—I am in full, and, indeed, in undisputed possession of my whole forces. In answer, however, to some things said here and elsewhere, against our connecting baptism and salvation, in almost any sense, and on the supposed interference between this doctrine of the assurance of remission through baptism and justification by faith, I shall also read a passage from "the *Christian System.*" It is found on page 258 :—

"In examining the New Testament, we find that a man is said to be '*justified by faith,*' Rom. v. 1; Gal. ii. 16, iii. 24. '*Justified freely by his grace,*' Rom. iii. 24; Tit. iii. 7. '*Justified by his blood,*' Rom. v. 9. '*Justified by works,*' James ii. 21. 24, 25. '*Justified in or by the name of the Lord Jesus,*' 1 Cor. vi. 11. '*Justified by Christ,*' Gal. ii. 16. '*Justified by knowledge,*' Isai. liii. 11. 'It is God that justifies,' Rom. iii. 33, viz. by these *seven* means—by Christ, his name, his blood, by knowledge, grace, faith, and by works. Are these all literal? Is there no room for interpretation here? He that selects *faith* out of seven, must either act arbitrarily, or show his reason; but the reason does not appear in the text. He must reason it out. Why, then, assume that faith *alone* is the reason of our justification? Why not assume that the *name* of the Lord is the great matter, seeing this name ' is the only name given under heaven by which any man can be saved;' and men, who believe, receive the '*remission of sins by his name,*' Acts x. 43; and especially because the name of Jesus, or of the Lord, is more frequently mentioned in the New Testament, in reference to all spiritual blessings, than any thing else!! Call all these *causes,* or *means* of justification; and what then? We have the grace of God for the *moving* cause, Jesus Christ for the *efficient* cause, his blood the *procuring* cause, knowledge the *disposing* cause, the name of the Lord the *immediate* cause, faith the *formal* cause, and works for the *concurring* cause.

For example: a gentleman on the sea-shore descried the wreck of a vessel at some distance from land, driving out into the ocean, and covered with a miserable and perishing sea-drenched crew. Moved by pure philanthropy, he sends his son with a boat to save them. When the boat arrives at the wreck, he invites them in, upon this condition, that they submit to his guidance. A number of the crew stretch out their arms, and seizing the boat with their hands, spring into it, take hold of the oars, and row to land, while some from cowardice, and others from some difficulty in coming at the boat, wait in expectation of a second trip; but before it returned, the wreck went to pieces, and they all perished. The *moving* cause of their salvation who escaped, was the good will of the gentleman on the shore; the son, who took the boat, was the *fficient* cause; the boat itself the *procuring* cause; the knowledge of their perishing condition and his invitation, the *disposing* cause; the seizing of the boat with their hands, and springing into it, the *immediate* cause; their consenting to his condition the *formal* cause; and their rowing to shore, under the guidance of his son, was the *concurring* cause of their salvation—Thus, men are justified or saved by grace, by Christ, by his blood, by faith, by knowledge, by the name of the Lord, and by works. But of the seven causes, three of which are purely instrumental, why choose *one* of the instrumental, and emphasize upon it, as the justifying or saving cause, to the exclusion of, or in preference to, the others? Every one, in its own place, is essentially necessary."

Such are our views, as often expressed on this subject.

We shall now attend to some things said on yesterday. Mr. Rice, you will remember, made one wholesale objection to my first seven arguments, viz. that they were unscriptural—they contradicted the Scriptures. Very easily said—but did he prove it? Did he select any one of them, analyze, and refute it? He took up Calvin, and showed you how I read authors, &c. Such was his refutation of my arguments. But he said, and asserted, and re-asserted, several things which, whether true or false, affect not the issue in any way whatever. What an edifying dissertation he gave us on "begotten and born, and born and begotten!" He said there were many spiritual benefits connected with being begotten, and with being born, and that it was indifferent which term we used on many occasions. Did that conflict with any thing I had said, or with any thing I have now read from the Christian System? Any one may have observed, that whether John says, a person is begotten or born of God, he speaks of him without any regard to any difference between these two states. He uses the phrase *characteristically*. It is two modes (if we were to translate them diversely,) of speaking of the same character. But in the original of John there is no difference. The change is according to the taste of the translator.

"He that believeth that Jesus is the Christ, is born of God;" and, of course, is begotten of God. And unless we speak very critically, whatever is true of him in the one figure, is also true of him in the other figure. These persons, however, of whom the apostle thus speaks, are all baptized persons—every one of them. He never supposes such a case as is often before our minds—a believing unbaptized man! Such a being could not have been found in the whole apostolic age. Faith is, indeed, the master principle of christianity. No one of this age, I presume, has either said or written more on this capital principle of our religion. It is vital, essential, and omnipotent in christianity. It removes mountains—it overcomes the world. It is the spring and fountain of a thousand pure and holy pleasures. It throws new charms over heaven, earth and sea. It makes the heavens more bright, and gives new beauties to the earth and all that it contains. It purifies the heart from all its unhallowed and polluting passions, and adorns human character with the most splendid virtues. It throws a bridge over the gulf of time past and of time to come, and connects both the past and the future with eternity. "It is the evidence of things not seen, and the confident expectation of things hoped for." It is the parent of all the christian graces, and is, itself, the offspring of heaven. No wonder, then, that men are said to be justified, sanctified, saved, &c. by faith. But the Westminster catechism says, by FAITH ALONE. At the word ALONE, we conscientiously demur.

The apostle James has said, a man is not justified by faith alone, and here we must go with the apostle against the creed. Mr. Rice exaggerates faith to depreciate baptism. I would give to both their proper position and influence in the christian religion.

But to resume the capital mistake in his theology. He contends that *hath* means actual possession. He that believeth *hath* eternal life. I say, in *grant*, in *promise*, within his reach, yet not invested with it. John the Baptist (John iii. 36) says, " He that believeth on the Son, hath everlasting life." While Mark says, "there is no one that has forsaken houses, lands, &c. for my sake, who shall not receive manifold more in the present time, and *in the world to come*, life everlasting." Can any one reconcile these sayings without admitting all that we contend for ? viz. that there is an *actual* possession, and a possession in *right*, or in grant. In the great day, the Messiah shall say to the righteous, "*inherit the kingdom* prepared for you before the foundation of the world." In Timothy, Paul says, " you may *lay hold* on eternal life." Here is a man of God exhorted by Paul, to *lay hold on* eternal life—and, indeed, the same apostle teaches, " that we are made heirs, *according to the hope of eternal life.*" Now, as I have before said, who can hope for what he has ! The conclusion is inevitable that, when we are said to be justified, sanctified, saved by faith, or to have eternal life, through believing, it does not mean that we actually have them now, or shall enjoy them hereafter, by mere faith alone, but in consequence of the efficiency of this principle displayed in the obedience of faith, or in submission to the authority and rule of the Lord.

Be it observed, however, with joyful attention, that when a child is born into any family, the privileges of the family are his in virtue of birth. True, his present or continuous enjoyment of them depends on his continuing in the family, and in being properly qualified to enjoy them. Thus a birth into the family of God entitles to very numerous, various, and glorious privileges. Like a king's son, he is born to a fine education, has a rich estate, and much glory and blessing in store. The child of God is entitled to the finest education. God is the author of three grand works, each of which contains many volumes. There are the volumes of nature, of providence, and of redemption. The Spirit of God is his preceptor in studying the volumes of redemption, and this gives him a more profound knowledge of all the others. He has many honorable relations. All the great, and noble, and honorable, and pure spirits, celestial and terrestrial, are his brethren and relatives. God is his father, Jesus, the supreme Judge, is his brother, and heaven and all its glories, are his inheritance. Truly, then, *he is rich in faith.*

But the question in debate is, does *mere birth* invest any one with all those hereditaments, privileges, honors, &c. or is not his arriving at full majority, at a manhood stature, through sanctification of the Spirit, as well as through the belief of the truth, by obeying, from the heart, the holy precepts of Christ's gospel, essential to the actual possession or enjoyment of all these immunities and honors ?—[*Time expired.*]

Friday, Nov. 24—12½ o'clock, P. M.

[MR. RICE'S SIXTH REPLY.]

MR. PRESIDENT—I discover that my friend has not forgotten the events of last week. My exposure of his translation, continues to haunt him. I have said not a word about his translation to-day, nor yesterday. Why, then, is he now bringing up again these old matters? Whilst discussing the mode of baptism, I did prove that his translation of a very important verse in the New Testament, is no translation, but a very great perversion of the original. Then was the time to have defended his translation, if he *could*. It is now too late. But he seems disposed to throw the responsibility of this gross mistranslation upon Dr. George Campbell. But has he not adopted it, and sent it forth to the world as his? Did he not make, in Dr. Campbell's translation, various emendations? Why, then, did he not rectify this most remarkable error?

I now learn, that when he claimed *catholic* authority in favor of his doctrine, he meant, not popish, but *universal* authority. Now, I deny that it is sustained by any such authority; and I call for the proof. It is not a little singular that he should commence a radical reformation, proclaiming all the world in error, and then discover that almost all are with him! I deny most positively, that his views of baptism in order to remission of sins, are sustained by universal authority.

I knew that I was touching a tender point, when I quoted one of the most prominent ministers of his church against him; but I cannot help that. In looking through the Millenial Harbinger, I saw that Dr. Fishback and Mr. Campbell had engaged in a protracted discussion of the very doctrine we are now debating; and that the doctor was decidedly opposed to his views. I paid some attention to his arguments, and discovered that Mr. Campbell did not answer them very satisfactorily; and I thought it might be well to give him some of those arguments to answer now. But, he says, this controversy with Dr. Fishback has nothing to do with the matter before us. He is very fond of quoting Calvin against Presbyterians; but so soon as I quote against him one of his strongest men, he declares, it has nothing to do with the subject before us!

Well, he is very *catholic* in his views. He says, his church does not compel all their ministry to adopt the same *opinions* and *speculations*. But are we now debating mere *opinions?* Is his doctrine of baptism, in order to remission of sins, an opinion or a speculation? If so, the gentleman is certainly running contrary to his own published principles; for he has maintained that no citizen of the kingdom of Christ has the right to propagate his *opinions*. But here he is, in a public debate, propagating his opinions! No; we are discussing doctrines—matters of faith—not speculations; and unless Mr. C. has recently succeeded in converting the doctor, they differ *toto cœlo*, not about speculations, but about doctrines.

But is Mr. C. really so catholic in his views and feelings? Would he allow me to preach in his church, unless I would agree to be immersed? I trow not. Yet how can he consistently exclude me, since he professes not to proscribe men for their opinions?

I will not charge my friend with courting popularity; but I will say, that he has, by some means, happened to adopt a course of conduct by which he has secured much greater popularity, than he ever could have gained, had he remained in the Presbyterian church.

But he is resolved to make me a *heretic*. He tells you, that in my exposition of Colossians ii. 10, 11, I have gone contrary to the Confession of Faith. But that is a book which he seems not to understand. Neither Paul nor the confession teaches the necessity of baptism in order to remission of sins. Under the old dispensation, as I have before said, water, the emblem of purification, was constantly associated with the Spirit and sanctification. So under the new, the ordinance of baptism is constantly connected with regeneration, which is called baptism. And Paul speaks of " the washing of regeneration," just as Ezekiel speaks of cleansing from moral pollution, by sprinkling clean water. The outward ordinance serves to illustrate the nature of the inward grace. So Peter tells us, it is not water-baptism that saves us—" not the putting away of the filth of the flesh, but the answer of a good conscience toward God"— not the outward baptism, but the inward grace, of which it is the sign or emblem.

The gentleman could not refer to this passage, without trying to make an argument against infant baptism. He brought up that subject yesterday; and to-day we have it again. I am quite sure he feels very much dissatisfied with his performances on this subject. He certainly would not recur to it again and again, if he believed that he had sustained himself.

I will now resume the train of argument against the doctrine of baptism in order to remission of sins. I have proved that this doctrine contradicts the express declarations of Christ, who said, without qualification, " He that believeth on the Son, *hath* everlasting life." The gentleman has attempted to evade the force of this declaration, by making the word ' *hath*' mean *may have*. To justify this most unauthorized perversion, he refers to scriptures which speak of eternal life as in the future, as the object of expectation and hope. But who does not know, that, so long as eternity endures, the righteous will be looking forward and anticipating increasing blessing and glory. If, then, we cannot possess eternal life, so long as we are looking forward, we can never possess it.

But it is worse than vain to attempt to escape the force of such language, presenting the same truth in such variety of forms. The Savior said to Martha, as she wept for her deceased brother, " He that believeth in me, though he were dead, yet shall he live: and whosoever liveth and believeth in me, shall never die;" John xi. 25, 26. The body may die, but the soul never will. Pardoned, sanctified, and saved, it will go onward and upward, ever enjoying the perfection of present felicity, and ever looking to future and greater glory.

But there is one passage which I quoted, to which I cannot arrest the attention of the gentleman, viz: " He that believeth on him *is not condemned;*" John iii. 18. According to his doctrine, many believers *are condemned.* The Savior says, they are not. Here is a flat contradiction. Paul, too, as I proved, teaches that every believer is justified— " justified by faith;" Rom. iii. I have reminded the gentleman of these passages repeatedly, but he cannot see them !

I have also proved his doctrine untrue by the indisputable facts, that those who are begotten, or born of God, whether baptized or not, do enjoy the remission of their sins. But he asks, why run away from the subject under discussion to the new birth? Because in his writings I discovered that he had relied very much on the new birth to sustain his views; for, with him, baptism is the new birth, and is designed to effect a change of state—a passing from condemnation to justification. I see, in his *Christianity Restored,* he has attempted, singularly enough, to illustrate his doctrine by representing naturalization in our country as a *birth.* The foreigner who emigrates from England to America, and is naturalized, he represents as *born of America!!!* And, as he who is born of America, enjoys the privileges of a citizen, so he, who is born of *water,* enjoys the privileges of the kingdom of Christ. Such an illustration, I presume, no one ever thought of using before; and the palpable absurdity of it, is evidence of the lameness of the doctrine. You see, then, I was not running from the subject under discussion, but running *into* it.

There are some remarkable peculiarities in the gentleman's theology. He teaches, that men are first *begotten without* the water, by the truth, and then *born of* water; and the water he represents as the *mother* of all christians ! ! ! The Scriptures teach us, that " Jerusalem, which is above, is the mother of us all ;" but they never do teach, that the water is our mother ! This is one of the peculiarities of Mr. Campbell's theology ! The inspired writers never speak of baptism as a birth, nor of water as the mother of believers. This fact, which is fatal to the gentleman's doctrine, I presume he will not answer.

I have proved, by a number of facts, that the new birth is not at all connected with baptism—that our Savior had no reference, particularly, to baptism, when he said, " Except a man be born of water and of the Spirit, he cannot enter into the kingdom of God." Mr. Campbell admits, that christian baptism was not instituted when the Savior uttered this language ; and how, I ask, can he prove, that he alluded to an ordinance not then in existence ? He may take it for granted, but he cannot furnish a particle of proof. And if he cannot, his doctrine goes by the board. Let the fact not be forgotten, that, when christian baptism was instituted, it was never called a *birth.* The expression, *born of God,* is intended to convey to our minds two important ideas, viz : 1 That the change denoted by it, constitutes us the children of God ; and 2. That it makes us, morally, like God—holy in heart. " That which is born of the flesh, is flesh ; and that which is born of the Spirit, is spirit."

I proved on yesterday, (and I will repeat the argument,) that every one who is *begotten* or *born* of God, enjoys the remission of sins. John, the apostle, says, " Whosoever believeth that Jesus is the Christ, is born of God." If the believer is born of God, he is a child ; and if a child, an heir of God, and a joint-heir with Christ. It will scarcely be denied, that the sins of all such are pardoned. But Mr. Campbell will not immerse a man till he professes to believe, that Jesus is the Christ; and, therefore, he cannot immerse him till he is born of God—is a child, and is in possession of the remission of sins. Consequently, his doctrine, which teaches, that sins are remitted in the act of being baptized, and not before, is untrue.

The gentleman has found justification in the Scriptures ascribed to *seven causes.* So he informs us; though it would not be difficult to prove, that the whole seven amount to some three or four. For example, who imagines, that justification in the name of Christ, and by Christ, are two distinct causes ? Is the *name* of Christ one thing, and Christ himself another ? But there is one fatal misfortune connected with this matter. It is this : BAPTISM IS NOT ONE OF THOSE SEVEN CAUSES, HIMSELF BEING JUDGE ! This fact being indisputable, I would not care, so far as this discussion is concerned, if justification were ascribed to forty causes. What are these seven causes ? They are, as enumerated by Mr. Campbell, the following: "by Christ, his name, his blood, by knowledge, grace, faith, and by works." Now where is baptism ? If his doctrine be true, baptism is one of the most important causes of justification. Yet, amongst all the causes to which he says it is ascribed, he cannot find it mentioned! If only baptism had been once mentioned as a cause of justification, how irresistibly it would have been urged by my friend ! But is it notmarvel-

33

lous to hear a man contending, most earnestly, that baptism is one of the most important causes of justification; and yet, when he himself enumerates all the causes mentioned in the Bible, and increases the number by making Christ one cause, his name another, and his blood a third, he cannot find baptism amongst them ! ! !

But he represents us as relying for justification and salvation on *faith alone*. We hold no such doctrine. Our confession does not say, that faith *alone* justifies men. It teaches, that they are justified on account of " the perfect obedience and full satisfaction of Christ, by God imputed to them, and *received by faith alone*." The meritorious ground of our justification, is the obedience of Christ unto death, even the death of the cross. The instrumental cause is faith, whereby the sinner, conscious of his helpless and guilty condition, receives and rests on Christ as his only Savior. Neither does our confession teach, that men can be justified and saved who do not live holy lives. Faith is the cause, of which good works are the necessary and uniform effect. Hence our confession teaches, that " Faith is not alone in the person justified, but is ever accompanied with all other saving graces, and is no dead faith; but worketh by love." As the *cause* cannot exist without producing its legitimate *effect*, so faith cannot exist in any mind without producing good works.

I will now resume the argument I was presenting when I sat down. I was proving, that the doctrine of Mr. C. ascribes to an external ordinance an unscriptural importance and efficacy. The one thing needful is, throughout the Scriptures, declared to be *vital piety*—the religion of the heart. No external ordinance, however important, was ever made essential to the remission of sins, or efficacious in securing that blessing. Circumcision, which was quite as important in the church under the former dispensation, as baptism now, was omitted, as I stated, during the forty years of the sojourn of the Israelites in the wilderness; and was then administered, on their arrival in the land of Canaan, to adults and infants. Besides, Paul has taught us, that it never was essential in order to remission of sins.

I was a little surprised to hear the gentleman proclaim his belief, that eternal life was not offered to the Jews—that their religion was a mere temporal affair. David prayed for remission of sins and for sanctification, (Psal. li.) and looked for eternal salvation. Abraham, by faith, " looked for a city which hath foundations, whose builder and maker is God." By faith, Moses " esteemed the *reproach of Christ* greater riches than the treasures in Egypt; for he had respect unto the recompense of the reward," (Heb. xi.) The ancient patriarchs and servants of God walked by faith, " died in faith," and were received up to glory.

But it was the capital error of the Jews, in the most corrupt period of their history, that they sought to be justified by their own righteousness; which they made to consist chiefly in their punctilious attention to external rites and forms. How often did the Savior and the apostles teach them the impossibility of securing justification by attending on any of those ordinances, or upon all of them. Never was it necessary for the Savior, whilst on earth, to rebuke the Jews for undervaluing external ordinances; but how frequently did he reprove them for attaching to them an undue importance and efficacy !

The Jewish law contained two principal classes of ordinances, *the bloody sacrifices* and the *washings*. These were, as Paul says, " a shadow of good things to come." The former pointed to the cross of

Christ, on which he should by one offering perfect them that are sanctified; the latter pointed to the work of the Holy Spirit in sanctifying the hearts of men.   The bloody sacrifices taught men their guilt and pointed them to the remedy, the blood of Christ; and the ablutions taught them their depravity and pointed them to the remedy, the Holy Spirit.

The Jews, in their blindness, lost sight of the promised Savior, the glorious substance, clung with the most perverse tenacity to the mere shadow, and fondly imagined, that the blood of bulls and of goats could atone for sin.   They also lost sight of the Holy Spirit and his agency in sanctifying the heart, and relied for purification upon external ablutions.   In their blind zeal they even added other ablutions to those divinely appointed, and incessantly washed the outside of the "cup and the platter," leaving the inside in its impurity.   They could not even sit down to eat when they came from the market or a public place, till they had washed their hands.   And not only were they most conscientious in their observance of the sacrifices and washings; but in regard to all external forms and ordinances, however unimportant, they were zealous in their observance.   The reproof uttered by our Savior, in view of this state of things, contains a principle which should never be lost sight of.   "Wo unto you, scribes and pharisees, hypocrites! for ye pay tithe of mint, and anise, and cummin, *and have omitted the weightier matters of the law, judgment, mercy, and faith*," Matt. xxiii. 23.

But this error was not peculiar to the Jews.   At a very early period in the history of the christian church, we find the same disposition developed.   It was not long until, losing sight of the true nature and design of the Lord's supper as a memorial of his sufferings, christians regarded the partaking of it as essential to salvation, and attached to it some mysterious efficacy in imparting grace.   Step by step they proceeded, until, having lost sight of the cross which it was intended ever to keep in full view, they deified the bread and the wine, and strangely imagined that the mystic words of the priest converted these elements into the body, blood, soul, and divinity of Christ!!   This was the perfection of human folly.   But baptism, the other sacrament, was almost equally perverted.   It was, at an early day, considered essential to salvation.   The Holy Spirit was supposed to sanctify the heart at the moment when baptism was administered; and those who died without baptism were supposed to be lost.   They proceeded even further, and, to impart greater virtue to the water, they consecrated it, and thus baptized with *holy water!*

This error has been common to human nature, in all ages, as the thousand forms and ceremonies of the various systems of pagan mythology demonstrate.

This, precisely, is the error into which Mr. Campbell has run.   Indeed he seems, in one respect, to have gone further into extremes, than the christians of the third and succeeding centuries.   They made external ordinances essential to salvation; but he makes the mode of an ordinance essential!   He not only insists that baptism is essential to secure remission of sin; but the water must be applied in a particular *mode*, or, according to his theology, it answers no purpose!   In this almost universal error of attaching unscriptural importance and efficacy to external rites, he has gone further than any one of whom I have heard or read.

To show the audience the wonderful efficacy he ascribes to baptism, I will read an extract from his debate with McCalla: (p. 137.)

"He appointed baptism to be, to every one that believed the record he has given of his Son, a formal pledge on his part of that believer's personal acquittal or pardon: so significant, and so expressive, that when the baptized believer rises out of the water, is born of water, enters the world a second time, HE ENTERS IT AS INNOCENT, AS CLEAN, AS UNSPOTTED, AS AN ANGEL. His conscience is purged from guilt, his body washed with pure water, even the washing of regeneration. He puts himself under the priesthood of Jesus, under his tuition and government. If afterwards he sins, through the weakness and corruption of human nature, or the temptation of the adversary, he, in the spirit of repentance, comes to his Advocate, confesses his fault, and obtains pardon."

I think it must be admitted, that he ascribes wonderful virtue to baptism! The last argument against this doctrine, which I shall now offer, is this: MR. CAMPBELL HIMSELF SAYS, IT IS NOT TRUE! This statement will doubtless surprise the audience; but nevertheless it is certain, that the gentleman himself has said, that the doctrine for which he is now contending is not true. I will prove this assertion by reading from his debate with McCalla: (p. 135.)

"The water of baptism, then, formally washes away our sins. The blood of Christ really washes away our sins. *Paul's sins were* REALLY *pardoned when he believed;* yet he had no solemn pledge of the fact, no formal acquittal, no formal purgation of his sins, until he washed them away in the water of baptism."

I could shake hands with my friend over this sentiment, and we might have something like *christian union.* What does he say? "Paul's sins were *really* pardoned, when he believed." This is all for which I am contending—that the sins of every individual are *really* pardoned, *when* he believes. I quoted Dr. Fishback, a little while ago, one of his right-hand men, in favor of this doctrine; and now I have Mr. Campbell himself on my side. It must be conceded, that I have the two most distinguished men in the gentleman's church sustaining the views for which I am contending. Now it is no part of my business to reconcile the doctrine here taught, with what he has elsewhere inculcated, or with what he is now inculcating. It is enough for me that he has said, that the doctrine for which he is now contending is not true! If he has since changed his views, and is disposed to retract what he has here published —very well. But so long as I have Mr. C. on my side, it will be admitted that, so far as this discussion is concerned, I am safe.

I will read again in the *Millenial Harbinger*, vol. iii. p. 304. The article was written in reply to Dr. Fishback, who was contending, that the remission of a man's sins is *not* suspended upon his being baptized. Mr. C. remarks: "You [Dr. F.] say, 'the essential point of difference between you and me is suggested in the following question; Is, or is not, the free favor of God, by which he justifies the believing sinner, or remits his sin, through the blood of Christ, suspended, according to the Gospel, upon his being baptized in water? You [Mr. Campbell] defend the affirmative, and I [Dr. F.] maintain the negative side of the question.' Now," remarks Mr. C., "let me tell you that *I maintain the negative too.* So we are both agreed! *Because, mark me closely, I do admit that a person who believes the Gospel, and cannot be immersed, may obtain remission.*"

This admission is fatal to the doctrine of baptism in order to remission of sins. I may believe the Gospel to-day, but may not have the opportunity to receive baptism before to-morrow, next week, or next month. Now am I under condemnation till to-morrow, next week, or next month? It is surely most undesirable to be under condemnation, even for a single night; because, during that time, the person is exposed to eternal death. Every one who truly believes in Christ, is disposed, at once, to obey every command, as he understands it. But suppose an individual mistakes something else for baptism, and believes that he has been baptized, when he has not; is he under condemnation because of this error? Mr. Campbell expresses the *opinion* that he is not. In the Millenial Harbinger, he expresses the opinion that there are some christians among " the sects." For this *charitable* (!) opinion, some of his zealous coadjutors found fault with him, as having, by expressing such an opinion, crippled their efforts in the laudable work of reformation. He reiterates the opinion, and writes as follows :

" In reply to this conscientious sister, I observe, that if there be no christians in the Protestant sects, there are certainly none among the Romanists, none among the Jews, Turks, pagans; and therefore no christians in the world except ourselves, or such of us as keep, or strive to keep, all the commandments of Jesus. Therefore, for many centuries there has been no church of Christ, no christians in the world; and the promises concerning the *everlasting* kingdom of Messiah have failed, and the *gates of hell have prevailed against his church!* This cannot be; and therefore there are christians among the sects.

But who is a christian? I answer, every one that believes in his heart that Jesus of Nazareth is the Messiah, the Son of God; repents of his sins, and obeys him in all things according to his measure of knowledge of his will. * * * *

I cannot, therefore, make any one duty the standard of christian state or character, not even immersion into the name of the Father, of the Son, and of the Holy Spirit, and in my heart regard all that have been sprinkled in infancy without their own knowledge and consent, as aliens from Christ and the well-grounded hope of heaven. ' Salvation was of the Jews,' acknowledged the Messiah; and yet he said of a foreigner, an alien from the commonwealth of Israel, a Syro-Phœnician, ' I have not found so great faith—no, not in Israel.'

Should I find a Pedo-baptist more intelligent in the christian Scriptures, more spiritually-minded and more devoted to the Lord than a Baptist, or one immersed on a profession of the ancient faith, I could not hesitate a moment in giving the preference of my heart to him that loveth most. Did I act otherwise, I would be a pure sectarian, a pharisee among christians. Still I will be asked, how do I know that any one loves my Master but by his obedience to his commandments? I answer, *in no other way.* But mark, I do not substitute obedience to one commandment, for universal, or even for general obedience. And should I see a sectarian Baptist or a Pedo-baptist more spiritually-minded, more generally conformed to the requisitions of the Messiah, than one who precisely acquiesces with me in the theory or practice of immersion as I teach, doubtless the former rather than the latter, would have my cordial approbation and love as a christian. So I judge, and so I feel. It is the image of Christ the christian looks for and loves; and this does not consist in being exact in a few items, but in general devotion to the whole truth as far as known.

With me mistakes of the understanding and errors of the affections are not to be confounded. They are as distant as the poles. An angel may mistake the meaning of a commandment, but he will obey it in the sense in which he understands it. John Bunyan and John Newton were very different persons, and had very different views of baptism, and of some other things; yet they were both disposed to obey, and to the extent of their knowledge did obey the Lord in every thing. * * * *

Now, unless I could prove that all who neglect the positive institutions

2 X

of Christ, and have substituted for them something else of human authority, do it knowingly, or, if not knowingly, are voluntarily ignorant of what is written, I could not, I dare not say that their mistakes are such as unchristianize all their professions."—*Mill. Harb. New Se.* vol. i. pp. 411, 412, 413.

John Bunyan and John Newton had very different views of baptism; and yet they were christians. This is quite orthodox. It is just saying that immersion is not essential to the remission of sins. Paul's sins were pardoned, he tells us, when he believed. So we believe. And we believe that all others will be pardoned, who believe in Jesus Christ. I have Mr. C. and Dr. Fishback with me to day; and as I am in so good company, I will just close here.—[*Time expired.*

Friday, Nov. 24—1 o'clock, P. M.
[MR. CAMPBELL'S SEVENTH ADDRESS.]

MR. PRESIDENT—If my friend, Mr. Rice, had thought more profoundly on the subjects submitted to his reflection, and on which he has been speaking, he would likely have discovered that there is not the least contradiction between my first and last views on the style of the apostle Paul. He does not, indeed, always speak in the same words. Mr. Rice has only demonstrated in these remarks, how much, on former occasions, he has misrepresented me. In the manner and in the matter of his objections and reasonings, he only certifies us of the truth, and confirms us in the justice of our conclusions.

In the beginning, he gave a wrong view of my sentiments as written and published, especially in some one or two points, to which I shall now call your attention. The gentleman, with great emphasis, expatiates on the seven causes of justification, exhibited in the extracts read from the Christian System. He says there are not so many. I have given chapter and verse for every one of them. He says, with a sort of dolorous sympathy, that not one of them alludes to baptism. We have the name of the Lord, and then we have the Lord himself, without the name. The highest authority in the universe is his name. What is the person of the hero, compared with the name of the victor? The name is sometimes a great deal more important than the person. No matter who is king, it is the name of the king that gives validity to the acts of the government. The name of the Lord is here mentioned. I did not quote the whole passage; but I will now read it. 1 Cor. vi. 11, "Such were some of you: but ye are washed, but ye are sanctified, but ye are justified in the name of the Lord Jesus, and by the Spirit of our God." Here we have washing, justification, and sanctification—and all of them collectively and severally represented as being alone, in the *name* of the Lord Jesus, and by the Spirit of our God. Evident, then, it is, that this washing is done in the name of the Lord, as well as that we are justified in his name. What other than the baptismal washing is performed in the name of the Lord? The apostle assigns adequate causes for this great change. The name of the Lord put upon any person by a divine warrant, is no ordinary matter; and the Spirit of the Lord given to any one, is competent to his victory over all iniquity. Were I to analyze and argue at length the two positions in this verse, as I understand them, we would probably find that we have the same two causes associated here, which we have already found four times connected, in this great work of pardon and renovation; for if we are immersed into the name of the Lord, we are justified by his name; and if we are sanctified by the

Spirit of our God, we are at once fitted for the high enjoyments of the christian rank and calling. I conceive, then, that we are represented here, as in other scriptures, as being justified by the name of the Lord, *believing in him*, in baptism; and that we are also sanctified by his Spirit. And, if so, does not baptism stand as high here as in the commission, according to Mark; and, also, in good keeping with Peter, on Pentecost, and in his first epistle?

With regard to the passage which has been so often quoted from John, I shall still notice it farther in its proper place. Indeed, it has been fully disposed of already, in the remarks offered on yesterday. My friend has intimated that I wished to evade it. This is only in harmony with his policy. When he wishes you to think he has a strong and convincing fact, or argument, he takes this method of gaining it credit. Have I not, however, given you, on this class of texts, something stronger than such insinuating assertions?—those, to you, are common now as household words?

I proceed to illustrate those passages read from the Debate with McCalla, and from the Harbinger. In order to dispense with the necessity and importance of baptism, the gentleman remarked, that as a man cannot baptize himself, it would be incongruous to suspend a matter so essentially necessary, upon the contingency of extrinsic help from another person. This, perhaps, to some weak minds, might assume the form of a solid objection to the value of the institution. A man cannot baptize himself, nor can he be baptized without an administrator and without water. Well, formidable though it appear, I am willing to meet it in all its wisdom and strength. I frankly admit the possibility of the contingency. Still, if there be any wisdom or potency in the objection drawn from it, it lies just as much in the way of my opponent, as in my way. It requires both water and an administrator with him. But the difference is in his favor, for he requires less water, and attaches much less consequence to the ordinance. That, however, avails nothing as to the real value of the objection. We will, therefore, select another case, in the importance of which we will equally agree—the sending of the gospel to the heathen. Now Mr. Rice believes, that a knowledge of the name of the Lord is essential to salvation; for where no vision is, the people perish. Now whether the people of remote countries shall ever hear the gospel, is made dependent upon the instrumentality of other persons than themselves. Some persons must be sent to them with the Bible—it must be translated into their tongues, and persons must be found to do it. Now in case of the failure of any of these contingencies, the salvation of the pagans is impossible. The question, then, arises: Is the Bible necessary to salvation, or the promulgation of the truths in it? Mr. Rice says, Yes. Well, then, let him reconcile this contingency first, before he demands of me to reconcile the one he has feigned on baptism. I say feigned; for while I have given him a real difficulty, on his principles, his is but a feigned difficulty on my principles. Because I do not make baptism absolutely essential to salvation in any case, while he makes the knowledge of Christ absolutely necessary in all cases. Let him adjust these matters at home, before he goes abroad with feigned difficulties!

There is nothing that does not depend upon contingencies of some sort: but according to our teaching, there is no one required to be baptized where baptism cannot be had. Baptism, where there is no faith, no water, no person to administer, was never demanded as an indispensable condition of salvation, by Him who has always enjoined upon man " mercy, rather than sacrifice."

Still, there have been matters of great moment suspended upon contingencies. A person who had committed a specified trespass, according to the law of Moses, who had in copartnery wronged the company, or who had violated a pledge, or taken away property feloniously, or by falsification, could not be pardoned only on certain conditions. He must make restitution of the principal, he must add twenty per cent., or one-fifth, to it : he must then find a priest, and an offering, and go to the priest, make confession of his sin, and have him to offer and intercede for him, or he could not obtain remission.

When Jesus said to the apostles, " Whose sins soever you retain are retained, and whose sins soever you remit are remitted to them," there was contingency in it; for they were not omnipresent, nor could they write or speak to the whole world. These are weak, very weak, objections, and as unreasonable as weak.

We must now hear Calvin. Mr. Rice has given you a specimen of my manner of quoting authorities. We shall now have a specimen of his, (to me *inimitable!*) art of mystification, and, as charity would have it, involuntary perversion. Calvin wrote every idea I have read you, and no one of ordinary candor, in my opinion, can misconceive it. A question may possibly arise in some minds, whether Calvin did not contradict himself. But that I have fairly and fully given you his words, there can be no doubt.

I will read a few extracts from book iv. vol. ii. indicative of the fact that he has spoken as plainly as I have done, on the subject of baptism for remission : (Book iv. chap. xv. sec. 5, 6, 7.)

" By baptism Christ has made us partakers of his death, in order that we may be engrafted into it. And as the scion derives substance and nourishment from the root on which it is engrafted ; so they, who receive baptism with the faith with which they ought to receive it, truly experience the efficacy of Christ's death in the mortification of the flesh, and also the energy of his resurrection in the vivification of the spirit."

The doctrine of John Calvin is the doctrine of the confession of faith. Observe the following extract :

" 6th. The last advantage which our faith receives from baptism, is the certain testimony it affords us, that we are not only engrafted into the life and death of Christ, but are so united as to be partakers of all his benefits."

This is all we contend for. Calvin saw the same design in John's baptism as in christian baptism.

" 7th. Hence also it is very certain that the ministry of John was precisely the same as that which was afterwards committed to the apostles. For their baptism was not different, though it was administered by different hands ; but the sameness of their doctrine shews their baptism to have been the same. John and the apostles agreed in the same doctrine : both baptized to repentance, both to remission of sins ; both baptized in the name of Christ, from whom repentance and remission of sins proceed."

This may be regarded as going too far in some particulars. Still it strikingly evinces his belief that all baptisms were for remission of sins. On John's baptism, as on the design of christian baptism, Mr. Rice repudiates Calvin. (Book iv. sec. 4. 11 :)

" I know the common opinion is, that remission of sins, which at our first regeneration we receive by baptism alone is afterwards received by repentance and the benefit of the keys. But the advocates of this opinion have fallen into an error, for want of considering that the power of the keys, of which they speak, is so dependent on baptism, that it cannot by any means be separated from it. It is true, that the sinner receives remission by the ministry of the church, but not without the preaching of the gospel. Now what is the nature of that preaching? That we are cleansed from our sins by the blood of Christ. What sign and testimony of that absolution is there, except baptism?

11th. We conclude, therefore, that we are baptized into the mortification of the flesh, which commences in us at baptism, which we pursue from day to day, and which will be perfected when we shall pass out of this life to the Lord."

We shall give you a little more of his remarks on the case of Cornelius than Mr. Rice gave you, that we may comprehend the apparent contradiction.

"15th. We may see this exemplified in Cornelius the centurion, who, after having received the remission of his sins and the visible graces of the Holy Spirit, was baptized: not with a view to obtain by baptism a more ample remission of sins, but a stronger exercise of faith, and an increase of confidence from that pledge. Perhaps it may be objected, why then did Ananias say to Paul, 'Arise, and be baptized, and wash away thy sin,' if sins are not washed away by the efficacy of baptism itself? I answer, we are said to receive or obtain that which our faith apprehends as presented to us by the Lord, whether at the time that he first declares it to us, or when by any subsequent testimony he affords us a more certain confirmation of it. Ananias, therefore, only intended to say to Paul, 'That thou mayest be assured that thy sins are forgiven, be baptized: for in baptism the Lord promises remission of sins; receive this, and be secure.' * * *

Nevertheless, from this sacrament, as from all others, we obtain nothing except what we receive by faith. If faith be wanting, it will be a testimony of our ingratitude, to accuse us before God, because we have not believed the promise given in the sacrament: but as baptism is a sign of our confession, we ought to testify by it, that our confidence is in the mercy of God, and our purity in the remission of sins, which is obtained for us by Jesus Christ; and that we enter into the church of God, in order to live in the same harmony of faith and charity, of one mind with all the faithful. This is what Paul meant when he said, that 'by one spirit we are all baptized into one body.'"

I agree with Calvin, as I understand him. We receive remission of sins in anticipation through faith, as Cornelius did; and with a clear assurance and solemn pledge through baptism. We must take all that Calvin has said on the subject, before we fully comprehend his meaning. I have therefore given a full outline of his whole views on the subject.

The case of Cornelius is urged, as a proof that I have either misconstrued or misstated Calvin's views of baptism for remission. But a careful examination of these extracts will only show that the gentleman is mistaken. Calvin repudiates the idea of receiving remission by the mere act of baptism without faith. His doctrine is, that through baptism we are said to receive that which our faith apprehends as presented to us by the Lord, "*whether at the time that he first declares it to us, or when by any subsequent testimony he affords us a more certain confirmation of it.*" Another extract corroborates this: (Book iv. chap. 15. sec. 17.)

"Now, since by the grace of God we have begun to repent, we accuse our blindness and hardness of heart for our long ingratitude to his great goodness. Yet we believe that the promise itself never expired; but on the contrary, we reason in the following manner: By baptism God promises remission of sins, and will certainly fulfill the promise to all believers: that

2 x 2

promise was offered to us in baptism; let us therefore embrace it by faith:
it was long dormant by reason of our unbelief: now then let us receive it
by faith."

His views of baptism extend still farther, as the following extract shows:

"Baptism is also attended with another advantage: it shews us our mortification in Christ, and our new life in him. For, as the apostle says, 'So
many of us as were baptized into Jesus Christ, were baptized into his death:
therefore we are buried with him by baptism into death, that we should
walk in newness of life.' In this passage he does not merely exhort us to
an imitation of Christ, as if he had said, that we are admonished by baptism, that after the example of his death we should die to sin, and that after
the example of his resurrection we should rise to righteousness; but he
goes considerably further, and teaches us that," &c.—*Calvin's Institutes*, vol.
ii. book ii. chap. xv. sec. 5.

Now, as I understand this, it substantially accords with the case read
from the Harbinger. I believe that when a person apprehends the gospel and embraces the Messiah in his soul, he has in anticipation received
the blessing. His mind finds peace in the Lord. "He rejoices with joy
unspeakable and full of glory." He anticipates the end of his faith—his
actual emancipation from sin. In his heart he dies unto sin, and by his
burial and resurrection with the Lord, he thus formally receives, what
was at first received by faith in anticipation.

There is no difficulty in reconciling Calvin with myself, any more than
with Paul, and the other New Testament writers. It is, however, nothing
to me, nor you, what Calvin's opinions were. Calvin, like other men,
had his errors and defects. He did not always select the most apposite
terms. I do not say that I have invariably used the words which I ought
to have used. This confession of faith has been amended, often amended,
in some points, and it yet needs other emendations. The gentleman said
I had not the concurrent assent of the universal church. I believe there
is not a proposition in the universe that can be proved in that sense of
universality. There is nothing absolutely universal. I never heard of
any opinion or tenet, approved by the unanimous vote of the church,
or of the whole family of man. I did not intend, sir, to speak of individual men, women and children; but when I spoke of the whole christian world, in terms of the most extensive universality, I meant all
parties, sects, and denominations, in the old world and in the new. I
have made my appeal to Greek fathers, Latin fathers, synods, councils,
special and œcumenical, and their creeds, to the rabbis and doctors of
ancient times, finally calling upon some of the more distinguished moderns, like Drs. Wall and Doddridge, to sustain my assertions, all of them
avowing, that John iii. 5, and Titus iii. 5, refer to baptism, and especially bearing testimony to the propriety of our interpretation of Acts
ii. 38. The church of England still avows the ancient faith. The creed
of St. Athanasius says, "We confess one baptism for the remission of
sins." The creed of Nice says, "We believe in one baptism for remission of sins." I am, if in error on this point, in good company, as Mr.
Rice would say. All the old creeds, the modern creeds, the ancient
fathers, the modern reformers, Luther and Calvin, and names the most
learned, the most honorable, the most venerable, the most admired, and
the most beloved, are all with me on this point. No one can assemble
such a host in support of any one dogma, proposition, doctrine, or tradition, as I can bring up in attestation of baptism for remission of sins.
But all this with me weighs nothing, not a feather, had I not Paul, and

James, and John, and Peter, the high functionaries and administrators of the kingdom of heaven.

As to what my friend says of outward, external ordinances, I need only remark, that I know of no such institutions of Christ. Prayer, praise, eating the supper, baptism, fasting, &c., are all alike bodily, mental, spiritual, outward and inward. Such language is that of Ashdod, and not of Canaan. I go for that religion with all my heart, and soul, and mind, and strength. Still, without the head, there can be no heart-religion. Without light there can be no love. If there be any externals in religion, I care nothing for them. It helps devotion to bow the knee, to stand up, to speak solemnly, to fast, to use words full of spiritual feeling. What act of religion so solemn as being buried with the Lord? What seizes the soul of man with such power, as the mighty, soul-subduing fact that we are entering into an everlasting covenant with the Supreme Divinity; vowing eternal faithfulness to the Messiah; putting on Christ as our wisdom, justification, sanctification, and redemption? What reflections touch the fountains of our moral sympathies with such awakenings, meltings, ecstasies, as these heaven-begotten emotions, rising within us when we personally rise with Jesus, and, in our affections, mount to heaven? How sweet the thought, too, that the Messiah himself led the way; that he put his body into the hands of John, and suffered him to accompany him into the mystic Jordan, and bury him there in solemn anticipation of his future interment in the bosom of his own earth.

If my friend, Mr. Rice, could speak experimentally on the subject of christian immersion, he would tell you that there is no action ever commanded of God of more solemn significance than holy baptism; that it operates powerfully upon those who are rightly exercised therein. What feeling like that of having the name of the Father, and of the Son, and of the Holy Spirit put upon a person by the authority of our Redeemer, Lawgiver and King? What singular associations spring up within us, when we feel ourselves enter into a relation that makes God our Father, Jesus our Savior, the Holy Spirit our Guest, Instructor and Guide; that connects with the hierarchies of heaven—its angels, authorities, principalities and powers; that emboldens us to draw near to God, having our hearts sprinkled from a guilty conscience, and our bodies bathed in the pure water of sanctification? No one could institute such an ordinance, filled with such honors, blessings, joys and transports, but Emanuel.

My friend still talks of what he has done. No doubt it is both necessary and expedient that he should do so. You will all judge of what I have done. But I will tell you, while he keeps talking thus, I am thinking of one saying of the Messiah, which always overwhelms me especially, when I think any one makes little of any of the commandments of the Lord. It is a saying of the Great King: "Whosoever shall break one of the least of these, my commandments, and shall teach men so, shall be of no esteem in the kingdom of heaven; but whosoever shall do and teach them, shall be of high esteem in the kingdom of heaven." Nothing is little that my Lord Messiah ever thought, said, commanded, or did. To stand up for him, and for his ordinances, and to plead the necessity of obeying to the letter, of honoring and magnifying him, of worshiping and adoring him, is my greatest honor, and my highest ambition. Heaven has yet revealed to me no higher honor, than to stand up for the honor of his commandments. I disclaim all merit; all claims of praise, honor or reward from him, I most cordially renounce. It is an act of mercy on his part to accept our purest offerings. Did we live the life of a Methusela, and devote all its hours to him, it would constitute no ground of boasting, no claim for his favor. We are saved by grace; still, our happiness and our honor are necessarily dependent upon our usefulness, our faithfulness to God, and our active and practical benevolence towards man. To walk by faith, is to walk with God. A heart and lip devoted to his will, is the highest style, dignity and happiness of man.—[*Time expired.*

Friday, Nov. 24—1½ o'clock, P. M.

[MR. RICE'S SEVENTH REPLY.]

MR. PRESIDENT—I wish, in commencing my reply, to read a brief extract from two of the gentleman's books, that you may be able to determine how far I have misrepresented him. I will read first from his debate with McCalla:

"The water of baptism, then, *formally* washes away our sins. *Paul's sins were* REALLY PARDONED *when he believed; yet he had no solemn pledge* of the fact, no *formal* acquittal, no *formal* purgation of his sins, until he washed them away in the water of baptism."

Let us compare with this his doctrine, as taught in the *Christian Baptist*, p. 422.

"That such was the universally received sense of immersion amongst the teachers and preachers of christianity, is most certain from express declaration and incident. For example: when Paul was immersed, it was declared and understood by the parties, *that all his previous sins were washed away in the act of immersion.*"

Again:

"What made the eunuch go on his way rejoicing? Was it because he had some difficult texts explained? Or was it because he had some distant hope or remote prospect of enjoying pardon and acceptance after death, or after the lapse of certain years of travail and of trial? No, indeed: he had found what thousands before him had experienced, peace with God, f om a conviction THAT HIS SINS HAD BEEN ACTUALLY FORGIVEN IN THE ACT OF IMMERSION. Indeed, the preaching of all the apostles, as well as all their writings, embrace this as a fact never to be called into question."

Now if any one can reconcile these doctrinal statements, he possesses more ingenuity than has fallen to me. In the debate with McCalla the gentleman said distinctly, that Paul's sins were *really pardoned when he believed.* In the Christian Baptist we learn, that they were washed away *in the act of immersion,* and that the sins of the eunuch were ACTUALLY FORGIVEN in the act of immersion! I cannot put these things together. I presume, however, that if Paul was *really* pardoned when he believed, he had evidence of that fact. If Mr. Campbell could ascertain it, (and he has asserted it,) certainly Paul himself might.

I will read again on the next page: "In the ancient gospel, it was first a belief in Jesus; next, immersion; then, forgiveness; then, peace with God; then, joy in the Holy Spirit." Now observe, in the ancient gospel we are told, it was first belief, then immersion, then forgiveness; but, in the debate with McCalla, Mr. C. tells us, in the case of Paul it was first faith, then real pardon, then immersion and *formal* pardon! I leave those who can, to reconcile these contradictory views. But as the gentleman is, in one statement of his views, precisely with me, I shall insist on keeping him on my side.

But he tells us, the confession of faith has been mended; and, therefore, he may be permitted to change his views. The confession consists of two parts: first, an outline of the doctrines of the Bible; secondly, a form of church government. The latter has been altered in some unimportant particulars; but the former has not, as the gentleman certainly ought to have known.

I have said, that God never made the remission of sins depend upon an act which a man cannot do for himself, but which must be performed by another. Suppose, for illustration, one of Mr. Campbell's New Testaments to be given to a man in Africa. He reads it, believes, and desires to obey it; but there is no one to immerse him, or, as it may often happen, not sufficient water in which to immerse him. Now if immersion is a prerequisite to the remission of sins, though his heart is right, though he is truly penitent and disposed to do his whole duty, he cannot be pardoned. He must live and die condemned, only because it was impossible that he should be immersed! Can any one believe, that such absurdities can belong to God's plan of salvation?

The gentleman has, indeed, expressed the opinion that the sins of such a person might be pardoned, and that he might be saved; but his opinion contradicts his doctrine; and if the latter be true, the former is false, and *vice versa*. He holds it to be a doctrine of revelation, that the remission of sins is secured only in immersion. Then let him point us to the place where God has made an exception to the general rule, and I will show him the passage which refutes his doctrine. His opinion and his doctrine cannot both be true, for in the Christian Baptist he asserts, that Peter made "*repentance, or reformation and immersion* EQUALLY NECESSARY TO FORGIVENESS;*" p. 417. Does he believe, that any adult will be pardoned and saved without *repentance*, or, as he calls it, *reformation?* I presume he does not. Then, if repentance and immersion are equally necessary, how can any be pardoned and saved without immersion? I repeat, his opinion or his doctrine must be abandoned. They cannot stand together.

But he tries to place me in a similar predicament. He says, that, according to my views, men must be ordained before they can preach; and many may be lost because their salvation depended on acts to be performed by others. I answer, the salvation of none depends on their hearing the Word *preached*. They can read the Bible, or hear it read, and thus become wise unto salvation. And those who have not the Bible, are accountable only for the light they have. God has never suspended the salvation of a soul upon an action which must be performed by another, and which circumstances may make it impossible to have performed. He whose heart is right, who believes in Jesus Christ, and is, consequently, disposed to obey his commandments, has the best assurance that his sins are remitted.

The gentleman has appealed to the Levitical law to sustain him. When he gives us the chapter and verse, which I hope he will do in his next speech, I will prove, that it affords him no support. [Mr. Campbell replied—6th chapter.] He says, it is in the 6th of Leviticus; and I say, when he reads it I will reply to it.

Mr. Campbell strangely attempts still to prove, that Calvin held the doctrine for which he is contending, and that he has not misrepresented him. Calvin says, "Baptism is a sign of initiation, by which we are admitted into the society of the church, in order that, being incorporated into Christ, we may be numbered among the children of God;" and he says, it secures to us three advantages : 1st. It is a symbol, or token, of our purification, &c. I deem it unnecessary again to read what I have already read in your hearing. I will, however, turn to the 4th section of the 15th chapter, which the gentleman read:

"I know the common opinion is, that remission of sins, which at our first regeneration we receive by baptism alone, is afterwards obtained by repentance and the benefit of the keys. But the advocates of this opinion have fallen into an error, for want of considering that the power of the keys, of which they speak, is so dependent upon baptism that it cannot by any means be separated from it," &c.

It is certainly remarkable, that the gentleman should have read as the real sentiments of Calvin, a statement he made of a popish error, which he immediately proceeded to refute ! Again, Calvin says:

"In this sense we are to understand what is said by Paul, that Christ sanctifies and cleanses the church ' with the washing of water ' by the word, (Eph. v. 26 ;) and in another place, that ' according to his mercy he saved us, by the washing of regeneration, and renewing of the Holy Ghost,' (Tit. iii. 5 ;) and by Peter, that ' baptism doth save us,' (1 Pet. iii. 21.) For it was not the intention of Paul to signify that our ablution and salvation are completed by the water, or that water contains in itself the virtue to purify, regenerate, and renew ; *nor did Peter mean that it was the cause of salvation, but only that the knowledge and assurance of it is received in this sacrament ;* which is sufficiently evident from the words they have used. For Paul connects together ' the word of life ' and ' the baptism of water ;' as if he had said, that one ablution and sanctification are announced to us by the gospel, and by baptism this message is confirmed. And Peter, after having said that baptism doth save us, immediately adds, that ' it is not the putting away the filth of the flesh, but the answer of a good conscience towards God ;' which proceeds from faith. But on the contrary, baptism promises us no other purification than by the sprinkling of the blood of Christ ; which is *emblematically represented by water on account of its resemblance to washing and cleansing.*"

Calvin speaks of baptism as an emblem of *sanctification* and as confirming to us the message of salvation. Mr. C. represents baptism as securing *justification.*

Again, speaking of the baptism of Cornelius, Calvin says—"We see this exemplified in Cornelius, the centurion, who, *after having received the remission of sins* and the visible graces of the Holy Spirit, was baptized ; *not with a view to obtain by baptism a more ample remission of his sins,* but a stronger exercise of faith, and an increase of confidence from that pledge." Observe, Calvin says distinctly, his sins were *first* remitted, and afterwards he received baptism. Could he possibly have employed language more flatly contradictory of the doctrine of Mr. Campbell? And why was he baptized? "Not with a view," says Calvin, "to obtain a more ample remission of his sins, but a stronger exercise of faith and an increase of confidence from that pledge." According to Calvin, Cornelius first believed and received the remission of sins and the gift of the Holy Ghost, and then received baptism for the purpose of strengthening his faith.

But let us hear Calvin once more. I read in his Commentary on Acts viii. 38, the passage so lengthily commented upon by Mr. Campbell:

"Tametsi in contextu verborum baptismus remissionem peccatorum hic præcedit, ordine tamen sequitur: quia nihil aliud est, quam bonorum, quæ per Christum consequimur, obsignatio, ut in conscientiis nostris rata sint." Although, in the arrangement of the words, baptism here *precedes* remission of sins, yet, in the order [of their occurrence] it *follows :* because it is nothing else than a seal of the blessings which we obtain through Christ, that they may be confirmed in our consciences.

According to Calvin, then, when Peter said, " Repent and be baptized for the remission of sins ;" although baptism is mentioned first, yet remission of sins is really first in the order of occurrence. Sins are first remitted, then baptism is administered. And he gives the reason why remission is properly first, viz : because baptism, so far from securing to us remission, is only a *seal* of the blessings we obtain through Christ. Such is the doctrine of Calvin. True or false, it is directly opposed to the doctrine of Mr. Campbell. I will cheerfully admit, that the whole world sustains him as fully as does Calvin.

I gave up Luther into his hands yesterday, not having particularly examined his views of the design of baptism; but I must take him back into our ranks to-day. I will read from his commentary on the epistle to the Galatians ii. 16.

" Here it is to be noted, that these three things, faith, Christ, acceptation or imputation, must be joined together. Faith taketh hold of Christ, and hath him present, and holdeth him inclosed, as the ring doth the precious stone. And whosoever shall be found having this confidence in Christ apprehended in the heart, him will God account righteous. This is the mean, and this is the merit, whereby we obtain the remission of sins and righteousness. Because thou believest in me, saith the Lord, and thy faith layeth hold upon Christ, whom I have freely given unto thee that he might be thy mediator and high-priest; therefore be thou justified and righteous. Wherefore God doth accept or account us as righteous, only for our faith in Christ."

Such is the doctrine of Luther, and such the doctrine for which I am contending. Justification, he teaches, is obtained by faith *only*, not by baptism. I will give you Wesley's doctrine on this subject, this evening, and will prove that he does not sustain Mr. Campbell.

He attempts to reconcile the contradictory doctrines he has published, by saying, that when an individual believes, he receives the remission of sins in *anticipation;* that his fears and distress subside, and he rejoices with joy unspeakable. But how his fears can subside, or how he can rejoice, when he is yet condemned and exposed to eternal ruin, I cannot imagine. I see no possible foundation for comfort in the condition of one whose sins are yet upon him. For Mr. Campbell has said—the unimmersed person, however his views of Christ may be changed, and his heart renewed, " is still unpardoned, unjustified, unsanctified, unreconciled, unadopted, and *lost to all christian life and enjoyment!"—Christ. Restored*, p. 196. What good has such a person received in *anticipation ?* How utterly inconsistent this declaration with that which I read from his debate with McCalla, in which he declared, that Paul's sins were *really pardoned when he believed!*

He would have you believe that his views are very *catholic*—not absolutely *universal;* but that all denominations agree with him on the subject. This I deny, and call for the evidence. He has told us, that our confession of faith teaches his doctrine, and that Calvin taught the same. I have proved that Calvin held just the doctrine for which I contend. That our confession teaches his views, I and all Presbyterians deny. Indeed, if a Presbyterian minister were known to preach such doctrine, he would soon cease to exercise the office of the ministry in our church.

It is true, our confession, in the article on baptism, quotes John iii. 5, Colossians ii. 10, 11, &c., because, as I have before remarked, under both the old and new dispensations water was religiously used, as an emblem of spiritual cleansing, or sanctification. But it is not true, that it says, that our Savior, in speaking of the new birth, referred to christian baptism; nor is it true, that either the framers of the confession, or Calvin, understood baptism, or the new birth, as effecting a change of *state*, as securing the remission of sins. By the new birth they understood a *change of heart*, or *regeneration*, of which water is the appointed emblem. But with Mr. Campbell, the new birth is not a change of heart, but a change of *state* from condemnation to justification. They did not adopt the views he entertains.

Neither did the old christian fathers teach his doctrine. Dr. Wall does not say they did. True, they used the word *regeneration* for baptism; but by regeneration they did not mean what Mr. C. means—merely a change of *state*, but a change of *heart*, which they believed to be effected in baptism, as well as consequent remission of sins. The fathers do not sustain him. He cannot prove that any of them taught his doctrine. If he can, I hope he will do so.

He says, he has no faith in *outward forms merely*. But it certainly is true that he has very strong faith in forms; for he teaches that an external ordinance, which an individual cannot administer to himself, is essential to the remission of sins, and, of course, to the salvation of the soul. It matters not, in his theology, how entirely changed the heart may be, how sincerely a man loves and trusts in Christ—all is vain and worthless without baptism, and even without *immersion!* Even a mistake about the *mode* of applying the water is fatal! I verily believe that the Jews, with all their zeal for external rites, and their confidence in their efficacy, would not have maintained that a man with a wicked heart could be saved. The gentleman seems to attach quite as much importance to baptism, as they did to circumcision, or to their various ablutions.

But that the audience may see how extremely he has magnified the importance of baptism, I will read a proposition which is very prominently stated, and argued at length in his *Christianity Restored*. It is this: " *That the Gospel has in it a command, and, as such, must be obeyed*," p. 196. *A* command, that is, *one* command! The Gospel has in it *one* command!! Now, I presume, he did not mean to say, that the Gospel has in it *only one* command; but certainly such language can mean nothing less, than that *the* command alluded to, is the *great* command in the Gospel, more important than any other. That command, Mr. C. tells us, is immersion, which, he says, " necessarily becomes the line of discrimination between the two states before described. On this side, and on that, mankind are in quite different states. On the one side they are pardoned, justified, sanctified, reconciled, adopted, and saved; on the other, they are in a state of condemnation." In this same book, as well as in the Millenial Harbinger, and other writings of the reformers, I find immersion called *obeying the Gospel, obedience of faith*, &c. When, in these writings, it is said, that persons have " *obeyed the Gospel*," or " made the good confession," I find that it is meant, that they have been *immersed!* Did the inspired writers ever say that the Gospel has in it *A* command? Did they ever represent being baptized as *obeying the Gospel*, as *the obedience of faith?* Never—not in a solitary instance!

But we are told by these modern theologians, that we must *obey* before we can be pardoned. This is true; but *believing* is as truly obedience to Christ, as being baptized. God commands men to believe and to repent; and those who do believe and repent, obey his commands as truly as when they receive baptism. It is not true, therefore, that the gospel is obeyed in nothing before baptism is received.   Yet, according to Mr. C.,*immersion* is the act of faith, by which alone persons can be pardoned !   This is what I consider ascribing an unscriptural importance and efficacy to an external ordinance.

The ordinances instituted by Christ are important in their place, but when removed from the place in the system of truth, which he has assigned them, and made to answer purposes for which they were never designed, the consequences must be ruinous.   This, as I have said, was one of the capital errors of the Jews.   The Savior often rebuked and condemned them, not for strict observance of divinely appointed ordinances, but for having substituted them for " the weightier matters of the law ;" for attaching to them undue importance, and ascribing to them an efficacy they did not possess.   The whole christian church, as I have before remarked, at an early day, was corrupted in the same way ; and vital piety was buried and almost extinguished under a multitude of forms and ceremonies.   Both baptism and the Lord's supper were perverted, so as to become a curse instead of a blessing.

In the close of this address, I am constrained to declare it as my clear and solemn conviction, that the views on this subject, published by Mr. Campbell, have fatally deceived thousands of souls.   They have been taught to believe, that in order to secure the remission of sins and acceptance with God, it was only necessary for them to believe that Jesus Christ is the Son of God, and to be immersed.   When they have made " the good confession," as it is called, and been plunged under the water, they are induced to believe, that their sins are actually pardoned, and that they are *saved.*   They go on through life, fondly dreaming that all is well, and that they are on their way to heaven.   Thus they are under a fatal delusion; for it is certain, if we regard the plainest declarations of God's Word, that their belief of the fact, that Christ is the Son of God, and being immersed, afford no evidence of remission of sins, or acceptance with God.   The doctrine, therefore, deludes many into the belief that they are safe, when in truth they are under the curse of God.   This belief that their sins are forgiven in the water, produces a feeling of security, and prevents all further investigation, and those who embrace it, are likely to die in the delusion.

I do not say, that all who have followed Mr. C., are thus fatally deceived; for I doubt not, many sincerely and truly pious persons have been led astray, without perceiving the dangerous character of the error, who yet look to the cross of Christ as the ground of their hope of pardon and acceptance.   But I do say, my solemn conviction is, that the tendency and, in thousands of instances, the effect of this doctrine is to induce persons to believe that they are pardoned and saved, when, in truth, they have not one scriptural evidence on which to base such belief.   They have been immersed, and they are told, that in being immersed they *obeyed the gospel,* and are consequently safe.   I am constrained to lift my voice against this soul-destroying doctrine, that finds evidence of pardon and acceptance with God in an external ordinance.—[*Time expired.*

Friday, Nov. 24—6 o'clock, P. M.
[MR. CAMPBELL'S EIGHTH ADDRESS.]

MR. PRESIDENT—It has been asserted and re-asserted that such passages as, " he that believeth is not condemned," and " he that believeth is passed from death to life," and " he that believeth hath eternal life,"

&c. conflict with, and refute the whole doctrine of baptism for the remission of sins. Mr. Rice urges them with such a vehemence as though he believed them to be invincible proofs, that a man may be safe from condemnation and ruin if he only believe, without obedience to the truth believed. For that is the case before us? When the Savior spoke of *him that believeth*, he did not mean a disobedient, ignorant, and lawless believer: one that said he had faith, but one who practically, really, sincerely believed his gospel. On many occasions, it is true, our Lord spake prospectively of his kingdom, as he did of his death, burial, and resurrection; and so I understand his discourse with Nicodemus. And then the phrase, " he that believeth," and such like, do neither indicate a mere act of the mind, nor a mere state of the mind; but an actual, practical recognition of the precepts addressed to belief. When, then, the Savior ascribes any good effect, any salutary or saving efficacy to faith, or to any other principle, he not only supposes it to be genuine, active, and operative; but that, also, it is associated with all other principles that lead to a practical acquiescence with the whole existing will of God as revealed.

To conclude this subject of faith, I will only add, that even on the subject of justification by faith, I am, in reference to baptism, in good company with John Calvin. I must read another short passage or two from the great Presbyterian reformer. The gentleman told you I had mistaken the drift of one passage read from Calvin. But he might have observed that I only began to read the wrong section, which was occasioned by a wrong marginal reference; and, therefore, I made no use of the passage. But you shall have an extract in direct harmony with my views, and also indicative of Calvin's own views of the connection between justification by faith, and baptism. He observes :—

" I know the common opinion is, that remission of sins, which at our first regeneration we receive by baptism alone, is afterwards obtained by repentance and the benefit of the keys."—*Calv. Inst.* vol. ii. b. iv. ch. 15, § 4.

" As if baptism itself were not a sacrament of repentance ; but if repentance be enjoined upon us as long as we live, the virtue of baptism ought to be extended to the same period. Wherefore it is evident that the faithful, whenever in any part of their lives they are distressed with a consciousness of their sins, may justly have recourse to the remembrance of baptism, in order to confirm themselves in the confidence of their interest in that one perpetual ablution which is enjoyed in the blood of Christ."—*Ibid.*

In the same section from which I have read these extracts, he further says :—

" It is true that the sinner receives remission by the ministry of the church, *but not without the preaching of the gospel.* Now what is the nature of that preaching—*that we are cleansed from our sins by the blood of Christ?* What sign and testimony of that ablution is there but baptism?"

Yes, I ask Mr. Rice, and every other Presbyterian, this question, which their own Calvin asked—" WHAT SIGN AND TESTIMONY OF THAT ABLUTION IS THERE BUT BAPTISM ?" This was the passage intended to be read. I have now given what I conceive a fair exhibit of the views of Calvin, on the proper province of faith and baptism, as connected in the remission of sins, through the blood of Christ.

To these testimonies given, from Luther and Calvin, I might add many such from Turrentine and from other continental reformers; but there is one man, who, above all others, stands next to Calvin; nay, indeed, in my esteem, above Calvin, both for learning and talents, and great mental independence. A greater luminary, *as a writer*, than Witsius, in the esteem of the best judges, has not arisen in the ranks of Protestant reformation. His reception in England by the people, the clergy, the archbishop of Canterbury, when sent upon a special mission, on a very important occasion, is said to have been of the most complimentary and flattering character enjoyed by any merely ecclesiastic character of that day. We shall now hear him for a few minutes speak for himself:—

Dr. Witsius, on the Economy of the Covenants, London, 1837, 2 vols. 8vo.—ii. vol. p. 429, says :—

" 18. The thing signified by baptism in general, is the reception into the covenant of grace, as administered under the New Testament."

Again on same page :

" Moreover, that reception into the covenant of grace imports two things: 1st. Communion with Christ and his mystical body, and consequently a participation of all his benefits. 2ndly. An engagement to incumbent duty. Both are signified and sealed by baptism. In respect to the former, we are said 'to be baptized into one body,' 1 Corinthians xii. 13; and 'saved by baptism,' Titus iii. 3, 5, 1 Peter iii. 21. With respect to the latter, baptism is called *sun eideeseos agathees eperoteema eis Theon*—'the answer of a good conscience towards God," 1 Pet. iii. 21.

Volume ii. pages 432, 433 :

" 26. First, therefore, the immersion into the water represents to us that tremendous abyss of divine justice, in which Christ was plunged for a time, in some measure, in consequence of his undertaking for our sins; as he complained under the type of David, Psalms lxix. 2 : 'I sink in deep mire, where there is no standing. I am come into deep waters, where the floods overflow me.' But more particularly, an immersion of this kind deprives us of the benefit of the light, and the other enjoyments of this world; so it is a very apt representation of the death of Christ. The continuing how short soever under the water, represents his burial, and the lowest degree of humiliation, when he was thought to be wholly cut off while in the grave, that was both sealed and guarded. The emersion or coming out of the water, gives us some resemblance of his resurrection or victory, obtained in his death, over death, which he vanquished within its inmost recesses, even the grave : all these particulars the apostle intimates in Rom. vi. 3, 4.

" 27. Moreover, baptism also signifies those blessings which believers obtain in Christ; and these are either present or future. Among the present, is fellowship in the death, burial, and resurrection of Christ; and the consequence of it, viz : the mortification and burying of our old man, and the raising of the new, by the efficacy of the blood and Spirit of Christ. For, the immersion into the water represents the death of the old man, even in such a manner that it can neither stand in judgment to our condemnation, nor exercise dominion over our bodies, that we should serve it in the lusts thereof. In the former respect, the death of the old man appertains to justification; in the latter to sanctification. The continuing under the water, represents the burying of the body of sin, whereby all hopes of a revival are cut off; so that after this, it is neither able to condemn nor rule over the elect. For, as in burying, the dead body, which is covered over with earth, is removed from the sight of men, and so weighed down by the earth thrown upon it, that should we suppose some life to remain in the buried person to be bestowed upon him anew by a miracle, yet it cannot fail to be stifled by the load of earth lying upon it, nor recover to any degree of permanence. In the same manner, when in baptism the person, sunk under the water, is for some time detained therein; this signifies and seals to us, that our sins are removed from the view of the divine justice, never to be imputed to our condemnation : or as Micah speaks, chap. vii. 19, ' he will subdue our iniquities, and cast all our sins into the depth of the sea ;' likewise, that the power of sin is so depressed and weakened, that it can no longer drive us at its pleasure, or hinder our salvation, or be able to resume the power which it has once lost, in order to bring us again under its dominion. The emersion out of the water is a symbol of the revival of the new man, after our sins are now sunk to a spiritual life by the resurrection of Christ. And this also the apostle declares, Rom. vi. 3—6, and Col. ii. 11, 12, where he intimates that our baptism is such a memorial of the things that happened to Christ, as at the same time to seal our communion with him in all these things, and our union as it were into one plant."

Vol. ii. page 434, § 31 :

" Thus far concerning the rites of immersion and emersion. Let us now consider the ablution or washing, which is the effect of the water applied to the body. In external baptism there is · the putting away the filth of the flesh,' 1 Peter iii. 21, which represents the ablution or washing away the filth of the soul contracted by sin ; Acts xxii. 16, ' Arise and be baptized, and wash away thy sins, calling on the name of the Lord.' But the filth of sin may be considered either with respect to the guilt, which is annexed to the filth or stain, and so it is removed by remission, which is a part of justification ; or with respect to the stain itself, or spiritual deformity and dissimilitude to the image of God, and so it is taken away by the grace of the sanctifying Sprit ; and both are sealed by baptism. Of the former Peter speaks, Acts ii. 38, ' Be baptized, every one of you, in the name of Jesus Christ, for the remission of sins.' Concerning the latter, Paul writes, Ephes. v. 25, 26, ' Christ loved the church, and gave himself for it ; that he might sanctify and cleanse it with the washing of water by the word.' And they are laid before us both together, 1 Cor. vi. 11, ' But ye are washed, but ye are sanctified, but ye are justified, in the name of the Lord Jesus, and by the Spirit of our God.' Ye are washed sacramentally in baptism, which washing is a symbol of the mystical washing : but the mystical washing comprehends both justification and sanctification, both which are performed in the name of the Lord Jesus,—that is, by the efficacy of his merits, and by the Spirit of our God, which effectually applies the merits of Christ to the elect."

Numerous passages might be read from this distinguished master in the Pedo-baptist Israel. From these two, however, his views may be pretty fairly estimated. The passages from John iii. and Titus iii., to which Mr. R. so often alludes, and which I have shown the Pedo-baptists almost universally refer to baptism, are not yet disposed of fully to his satisfaction. It is denied by him that baptism is ever called a "*birth*," and that these passages are so universally regarded as relating to baptism. I say again, that Dr. Wall, from whom he has taken so much argument on this occasion, says : " There is not one christian writer of any antiquity, in any language, but who understands the new birth of water, (John iii. 5,) as referring to baptism ; and, if it be not so understood, it is difficult to give any account how a person is born of water, any more than born of wood."—Vol. i. p. 110. Again, he says, after quoting Justin Martyr : " We see by him, that they understood John iii. 5, of water baptism, and so did *all the writers of those four hundred years*, NOT ONE MAN EXCEPTED."

Is not this clear and intelligible talk ?—who can misunderstand it ! " *Not one man excepted* " of all the writers of the first four hundred years. All proclaim the conviction that born of water means baptism ; and, indeed, the same host go for " *baptism for the remission of sins*," " *not one man excepted*." I say again, because of strangers present, that I quote these authorities, not to sustain my views, but to disprove those of my opponent. The Bible supports me; and those "fathers," to whom some people look with so much veneration, sustain us, and oppose them, in these two important particulars, as well as in some others. I could read you, from my Essay on Remission, (Christian System,) many such authorities, but as they are now common property, I will only add a few not quite so common.

I may add a few words from so great a man as John Wesley. I quoted him as a distinguished reformer in that treatise, affirming that, "baptism administered to real penitents, is both a *means* and a *seal* of pardon. Nor did God ordinarily, in the primitive church, bestow pardon on any, unless through this means." But I shall quote him again more at large, from another work than his commentary. I am sorry, indeed, that he uses the word *primitive* before church; as that would indicate that God forgave sins diversely in the *modern* church. This is an extract from a treatise on baptism, found in doctrinal tracts, published by order of the General Conference, New York, 1825.

" What are the *benefits* we receive by baptism? is the next point to be considered. And the first of these is, the washing away the guilt of original sin, by the application of the merits of Christ's death."—p. 4.

" By baptism we, who were ' by nature children of wrath,' are made the children of God. And this regeneration, which our church in so many places ascribes to baptism, is more than barely being admitted into the church, though commonly connected therewith; being ' grafted into the body of Christ's church, we are made the children of God by adoption and grace.' This is grounded on the plain words of our Lord, John iii. 5, ' Except a man be born again of water and of the Spirit, he cannot enter into kingdom of God.' By water then, as a mean, the water of baptism, we are regenerated or born again: whence it is also called by the apostle, ' the washing of regeneration.' Our church, therefore, ascribes no greater virtue to baptism, than Christ himself has done. Nor does she ascribe it to the outward washing, but to the inward grace, which added thereto makes it a sacrament. Herein a principle of grace is infused, which will not be wholly taken away, unless we quench the Holy Spirit of God by long continued wickedness."—p. 5.

Mr. Wesley (pp. 7, 8,) says:

" If infants are guilty of original sin, unless this be washed away by baptism, it cleaves to them." [And several other matters indicative of the obscurity of his mind on the subject.]

There is a singular eccentricity in the minds of Pedo-baptists on this subject. In this controversy they refuse a positive precept in one case, and build a positive institution in another, without any pretension of a positive precept. There is not in the king's English a more clear, definite and positive precept, than " Repent and be baptized, every one of you, in the name of the Lord Jesus, for the remission of sins." Can any one state a more explicit and intelligible positive precept than this one! Now when Pedo-baptists argue with us, you will occasionally ask for a positive precept. We give it in all cases requiring it. But when we produce one to them, they will not yield to it. We only ask them to give us a positive example—one single precedent of a domestic or an infant baptized on the faith of the household or parent; and promise to submit to it the moment it is offered. Yet they do not, because, indeed, they cannot, give one such case in the Bible. They ask subordination from us, when they produce what they call a fair inference; and will not yield to us, when we produce a *thus saith the Lord* in so many words. I began, the gentleman says, with "a thus saith the Lord," for all acts of worship; and we still continue to act upon that principle. In the midst of the most solemn scenes, since Jesus Christ left this earth, when the Holy Spirit was in Jerusalem, Peter uttered the oracle—"Repent and be baptized, every one of you;" (not formerly circumcised,) no, but every one in this house, circumcised or not, in heart or in body, and "be baptized for remission." Well, now, why will not the Pedobaptists give up and obey it!

But the gentleman demurs at our use of the phrase "obey the gospel." It is solemnly written by Paul, that "all shall be punished with an everlasting destruction from the presence of the Lord and the glory of his power, who obey not the Gospel." We neither believe nor teach that the phrase, "obedience of faith," means one single act; or that obeying the Gospel is one solitary deed. Certainly they do not "obey the Gospel," who do not obey the first precept; any more than they who obey the first, and afterwards apostatize. The Gospel calls for perpetual obedience, or a life of conformity to its pure and elevated piety and humanity. It is only to them, who, by a patient continuance in doing well, are seeking for glory, honor, and immortality, God will reward or bestow eternal life.

Still there is one act, the most solemn, significant, and sublime, which may emphatically be called obeying the Gospel—an act of homage the most profound, of devotion the most pure, of aspiration the most heavenly—when we confess the Lord, die on that confession to sin, and are buried into his death, and rise with him to newness of life. It is then the Sovereign of the universe says, "Thy sins be forgiven thee: go in peace."

Pardon is no quality of the mind, nor remission of sins a virtue. It is a sovereign act of favor on the part of the offended. "Justification is an act of God's free grace," as the old catechism says. It is no process; it is done in a moment—it is an act—a single act—a word—a volition. The persons to whom Peter spoke the precept, were believers. Their asking, "what shall we do?" was a confession of the facts alledged in the speech. Peter did not command them to believe—a proof that they had believed. Now I ask, how could he command believers to seek remission of sins, if pardon and faith were simultaneous? Nor did he say, "Be baptized, because your sins are forgiven you." The words used by our Lord in instituting the cup, This is my blood, shed for (not because of) the remission of sins. Why hold out the idea of baptism for the remission of sins, if the act was passed?! It might have been the intention of one or both parties to speak prospectively, but to speak of remission as past or present, entered not into the conceptions of either. Moreover there must be some reason for the act of pardon which did not exist before the moment that it passed. There is nothing done by God our Father without a proper reason.

Man desires, and God promises, an assurance of pardon. If any thing ought to be secured, this ought. If any covenant ought to be sealed, this most certainly has superlative claims. A covenant which involves one's present peace and his eternal destiny, ought to be made sure; solemnized and sealed in the most authoritative, formal, and sensible manner. For this, probably, among other sublime reasons, are we to be baptized into the name of the Father, and of the Son, and of the Holy Spirit. The terms of such a pardon should be clear and definite; they ought to be felt and understood in all their mysterious significance. The act of solemnization should be the most imposing in sacred grandeur; and the seal of confirmation no less than the sign manual of God's Spirit, and his own immutable promise and inviolable oath.

All men desire such a pledge in the direct ratios of their convictions of sin—of its deep, dark, and soul-ruining malignity. In the direct ratios of their apprehensions of the immaculate holiness, inflexible justice, and awful dignity of Him against whom it is committed, do they long for an acquittal, as evident and sure as the veracity of Him that cannot lie, can make it. It is, more or less, the desire of every awakened sinner, under heaven. Cornelius, too, and the best of the Jewish and gentile world, have sought it with a promptness, assiduity, and earnestness, equal to all their prospects and hopes of attaining it. The joy of pardon, of assured pardon, through the blood of the slain Lamb of God, is the purest, holiest, highest joy, that ever swelled the grateful heart of an adoring saint. It is, indeed, a joy unspeakable and full of glory.

I cannot think that He that swore to Abraham, and Isaac, and Jacob, could withhold from his children, raised up to him from Abraham's son and heir, a pledge of his love, as strong as that he gave the father of this illustrious and most honorable family.

The gentleman spoke of a delusion to which this doctrine is some way favorable. But he uttered it, as I thought, in terms unkind, uncharitable, and ambiguous. The delusion, so far as expressed, seemed to be that many concluded that in one act they had obeyed the gospel, and hence, that all was forever safe. I have never yet found any one who thought so. Such a case is possible—as possible as that thousands may imagine themselves to be "*ingrafted into Christ*," and "in covenant with God," in consequence of one drop of water put on their face while a sleeping babe, in the adorable name of the Almighty. We teach publicly and privately, that all the baptized must give all diligence to make their calling and election sure; must add to their faith courage, knowledge, temperance, patience, godliness, brotherly kindness, and philanthropy.

Persons, I again say, may be deluded under the best systems—under all systems. Possibly a few may be so deluded amongst us. But the question is, which system is most naturally and obviously tending that way—ours, or that which teaches thousands, millions, to regard themselves born, or initiated, into God's family, or sealed members of Christ's church—regenerated unto God, having received "a sign and seal of the covenant of grace of their ingrafting into Christ, of regeneration and the remission of sins," through the faith of a god-father, or an own father: one drop of water and the name of God, without any act, or deed, or word, or thought, or volition, or desire of their own? Whether such a system is more pregnant with delusion, or one that calls for personal knowledge, faith, repentance, and baptism, with all corresponding piety and humanity, I leave to you, sir, and this attentive and intelligent audience to decide.—[*Time expired.*

Friday, Nov. 24—6½ o'clock, P. M.

[MR. RICE'S EIGHTH REPLY.]

MR. PRESIDENT—Before proceeding to reply to my friend's last speech, I will read a few passages from the Confession of Faith:

"Baptism is a sacrament of the New Testament, ordained by Jesus Christ, not only for the solemn admission of the party baptized into the visible church, but also to be unto him a sign and seal of the covenant of grace, of his ingrafting into Christ, of regeneration, of remission of sins, and of his giving up unto God, through Jesus Christ, to walk in newness of life,"

&c. chap. xxviii. sec. 1.   Again, (sec. 5,) "Although it be a great sin to contemn or neglect this ordinance, yet grace and salvation are not so inseparably annexed unto it, as that no person can be regenerated or saved without it, or that all that are baptized are uudoubtedly regenerated."

Baptism, we are here taught, is an ordinance for the solemn admission of persons into the *visible church;* that it is a sign and seal of the covenant of grace, of ingrafting into Christ, of regeneration, of remission of sins, &c.   It is an outward sign of regeneration and of remission.   The confession does not say, that remission of sins is granted in the act of receiving baptism, and never before.   An instrument is first written, then sealed.   So a believer is first pardoned, and then receives the seal; or, more properly, the blessings promised in the covenant of grace, of which baptism is the seal, are enjoyed, when the conditions of the covenant are complied with.   The believer is pardoned and justified, so soon as he exercises faith in Christ.   Those baptized in infancy enjoy remission of sins, so soon as they, having come to responsible age, receive Christ as their Savior; and henceforth they enjoy all the spiritual blessings promised in the covenant of grace, sealed by christian baptism.   But Mr. Campbell holds, that remission of sins and justification are obtained in the act of receiving baptism, never before.   Now what says our confession on this subject?   "Justification is an act of God's free grace, wherein he pardoneth all our sins, and accepteth us as righteous in his sight, only for the righteousness of Christ imputed to us, and received by faith alone."—*Shorter Catechism.*   The confession does not say, we are justified by *faith alone,* as the gentleman intimates, but that we are justified for the righteousness of Christ imputed to us, and *received by faith alone.*   Yet it also says, "that faith is not alone in the person justified, but is ever accompanied with all other saving graces, and is no dead faith, but worketh by love," chap. xi.

Mr. Campbell tells us, that all this he learned when a child.   Certainly, if he did, he should have better remembered it, and have known, that the confession does not countenance the doctrine for which he contends.   He has quoted Mr. Wesley as having taught his doctrine of baptism, in order to the remission of sins.   It is possible that Wesley, who was an Episcopalian, wrote some things in the early part of his ministry, which savor of *baptismal regeneration;* but if he did, he certainly afterwards entertained very different sentiments.   I am not willing that the views of that great man shall be misrepresented, and made to favor dangerous errors.   If, then, he, in his youth, entertained on this subject erroneous views, and afterwards, upon more mature examination, renounced them, it is important that this should be known.   I will read an extract from his sermon on justification:—(Vol. i. p. 147.)

"Faith, therefore, is the *necessary* condition of justification: yea, and the *only necessary* condition thereof.   This is the second point carefully to be observed; that, the very moment God giveth faith, (for *it is the gift of God*) to the 'ungodly,' that 'worketh not,' that 'faith is counted to him for righteousness!'   He hath no righteousness at all, antecedent to this, not so much as negative righteousness, or innocence.   But 'faith is imputed to him for righteousness,' the very moment that he believeth.   Not that God (as was observed before) thinketh him to be what he is not.   But as 'he made Christ to sin for us,' that is, treated him as a sinner, punishing him for our sins; so he counteth us righteous, from the time we believe in him: that is, he doth not punish us for our sins, yea, treats us as though we were guiltless and righteous.   Surely the difficulty of assenting to the proposition, That faith is the *only condition* of justification, must arise from not understanding it. We mean thereby thus much, that it is the only thing that is immediately, indispensably, absolutely requisite, in order to pardon. As on the one hand, though a man should have every thing else without faith, yet he cannot be justified: so on the other, *though he be supposed to want every thing else, yet if he hath faith, he cannot but be justified.* For suppose a sinner of any kind or degree, in a full sense of his total ungodliness, of his utter inability to think, speak, or do good, and his absolute meetness for hell fire; suppose, I say, this sinner, helpless and hopeless, casts himself wholly on the mercy of God, in Christ, (which, indeed, he cannot do but by the grace of God,) *who can doubt but he is forgiven in that moment?*" &c

Such is the doctrine of John Wesley. I leave the audience to determine whether it is the doctrine for which Mr. Campbell contends.

He has certainly succeeded in proving, by Dr. Wall, that the ancient fathers used the word *regeneration* for baptism; but the misfortune is, that by regeneration they did not mean what he means. They believed that the heart was changed by the Holy Spirit at the time when baptism was administered, and, therefore, that remission of sins was then secured. This is not what he means by regeneration. But I am not concerned to go into an investigation of the opinions of those fathers; for though they were excellent witnesses as to matters of fact, I agree with Mr. Campbell in saying, they were rather poor theologians. He has told us, that with him their authority is worth little; and with me it is worth no more. The papists alone, I believe, feel bound to regard, as infallible, their "unanimous consent."

My friend discovers in Pedo-baptists a singular eccentricity. He says, they refuse to receive a *positive precept*—baptism in order to the remission of sins, and yet baptize infants without a positive precept. But this eccentricity entirely disappears when facts are known. I produced a positive precept for putting the children of believers into the church by the initiatory rite; and he was unable to find any thing like a precept for excluding them. This is a plain matter of fact.

But, is it true that we refuse a positive precept in regard to the design of baptism? No! our eccentricity consists in this: we refuse to take *Mr. Campbell's interpretation* of a positive precept. We refuse to interpret Peter's language as he interprets it. And have we not as good reason to charge him with refusing to regard a positive precept, because he differs from us as to its meaning, as he has to make a similar charge against us for differing from him, because we cannot acknowledge him infallible, and agree to see with his eyes?

I have a remark or two to make concerning *obeying the gospel.* Mr. Campbell says, the first act of subordination to Christ is called obedience to the gospel. But where in the New Testament is baptism called obedience to the gospel? The gentleman commenced his reformation with the avowed purpose of repudiating what he called "the language of Ashdod," and of speaking of Bible truths in Bible language—but you perceive, that when the language of the Bible does not suit him, he is quite willing to employ language of his own selection. Being baptized is never, in the Scriptures, called *obeying the gospel;* not an instance can be found of any such language. The very first command of the gospel, to all who hear it, is *to believe;* and the exercise of faith, and not being baptized, is the first act of subordination. Christ commands all to believe the gospel. Then when I do believe, do I not obey the gospel? He commands all to repent. When I repent, do I not obey the gospel? I obey the gospel in the act of believing and repenting; and if, as Mr. Campbell says, the first act of subordination to Christ secures remission of sins, it is certain that faith and repentance secure this blessing; and if so, his doctrine of the necessity of baptism, in order to remission, is false.

But he tells us, pardon is an act performed by God at a certain moment, and there must be some reason for performing that act, which did not previously exist.

What better reason can there be, than that the individual, under a deep sense of his guilt, falls into the arms of his compassionate Redeemer, and, like Peter, says—" Lord save, or I perish ?" If he receives Christ as his wisdom, righteousness, sanctification, and redemption, this is reason enough why his sins should be blotted out. But, says my friend, surely there ought to be a *seal* of remission. We contend that baptism is the sign and the seal; but we deny that it is the procuring cause of remission. What is the design of a seal ? An instrument admitted to record is just as valid as showing the intention of the parties before the seal is added, as afterwards; so a man's sins are pardoned when he believes, and the seal is applied afterwards. A seal is intended, not to give validity to the instrument, but to give it *notoriety*.

I did not say, that the members of Mr. C.'s church are taught, that they have nothing to do after baptism. I said, they are taught to believe that they were pardoned when they were immersed; and if it should turn out, as I solemnly believe it will, that such is not the truth, they are fatally deceived. They believe they are pardoned, when they are yet in their sins. This is the delusion of which I spoke. I am under a dangerous delusion, if I believe that I am pardoned, when in truth I am condemned.

My friend institutes a comparison between his teaching and ours, viz: whether his is more delusive than that of those who teach, that the sins of infants are remitted in baptism. We teach no such doctrine, as he ought to know. He says, he understands Presbyterianism. Now I make the unqualified assertion, that he cannot produce one respectable Presbyterian, in ancient or modern times, who ever taught, that infants had their sins remitted in the act of baptism. No child is taught so. I never saw a Presbyterian writer, nor heard a Presbyterian preacher who thus taught. If I knew a minister, in our church, who entertained such views, I should be prepared to table charges against him before his presbytery. I am sorry to discover that my friend knows so little of Presbyterianism.

As I have only one more speech upon this proposition, you will allow me now to give a brief recapitulation of the arguments. Let us place before our minds distinctly *the point in debate*. This is the more important, inasmuch as I believe it is impossible to determine, from what my friend has said, what he really believes. The question is not, whether one who contemns the ordinance, or wilfully refuses to be baptized, can be saved ? for he who deliberately refuses to obey any command of Christ, proves that he has not true faith or piety. Nor is the question, whether we can become members of the *visible church* without baptism ? for neither of us maintains that we can. Nor yet is it, whether baptism is a sign and seal of regeneration and of remission of sins ? This is admitted. But the question is this: whether a *penitent believer* is condemned till he is baptized, and is actually forgiven only in the act of being baptized ? This proposition my friend affirms, and I deny.

According to his doctrine, every man has his sins upon him through life and in death, if he has not submitted to baptism, and that administered by *immersion*. That this is his faith on the subject before us, I have proved by his own writings.

My *first* argument against this doctrine, is, that it flatly contradicts the plain and positive declarations of our Savior and the apostles. What says our Savior on this subject? " *He that believeth on him is not condemned.*" To this important passage, which of itself is an unanswerable refutation of his doctrine, I have not been able to arrest the attention of my friend; and I am afraid, he will not see it: I have again and again presented it before him, but he cannot see it. His doctrine (which directly contradicts the declaration of our Savior,) is—that he that believes *is* condemned, unless he have been immersed! He says, however, that faith is a principle in the heart—(he is getting quite orthodox)—that this faith would lead to obedienice, and thus, in obeying by being immersed, the sins of believers are remtted. But he has also said, that an *angel* might mistake the meaning of a command; and though a believer should sincerely desire to obey every command of Christ, and should fail to be immersed only through a mistake of the *head*, or the impossibility, under existing circumstances, of being immersed; this will not save him from eternal death. But the glorious Redeemer taught a very different doctrine. He said, Whosoever believes, is not condemned; every such person is justified. There is no qualification of the language; and it requires no criticism or comment—it cannot be misunderstood. Again: " He that believeth on the Son *hath* everlasting life." He now has life in actual possession. But see how variously the Savior expressed himself upon this subject! as if it were known to him, as certainly it was, that some would attempt to evade the force of his language. In John vi. 29, we read, " Jesus answered and said unto them, This is the work of God, that ye believe on him whom he hath sent." Again, 35th verse : "And Jesus said unto them, I am the bread of life : he that cometh to me shall never hunger; *and he that believeth on me shall never thirst.*" The conclusiveness of my argument depends not upon the word *hath*, in the passage " He that believeth on me *hath* everlasting life." The Savior varied his mode of expression, and said, "And he that believeth on me *shall never thirst.*" He shall receive abundantly the water of life. But Mr. C. teaches, that he that believeth shall thirst, unless he have also been immersed ! These plain, unequivocal and positive declarations of our Lord, will stand ¬qainst all the criticism the gentleman can bring to bear upon the subject. Our doctrine is fully sustained by more than one positive " Thus saith the Lord." He may appeal to all the critics and translators, but he cannot refute it.

My *second* argument is the fact, *that all who are* BEGOTTEN OF GOD, *do enjoy remission of sins.* The gentleman admits, that every believer, *before baptism*, is begotten of God; and John the apostle says—" Whosoever is born [or *begotten*, as Mr. C. would read it] of God doth not commit sin; for his seed remaineth in him : and he cannot sin, because he is born of God," (John iii. 9.) Every one who is begotten of God, has ceased to be a sinner, is holy in heart and in life. Are such persons condemned? But in the very next verse those begotten, are said to be *children of God*. " In this the children of God are manifest, and the children of the devil: whoever doeth not righteousness, is not of God," &c. But if they are children of God, they are " heirs, heirs of God, and joint-heirs with Christ," (Rom. viii. 17.) Their sins are remitted. Here we have no need of criticism on the word *eis*, or any other disputed term. The language is perfectly plain.

Again—"Every one that liveth is born [or begotten] of God, and *knoweth God*," (1 John iv. 7.) Compare this with the gospel by John, ch. xvii. 3, "This is life eternal, that they might *know* thee the only true God, and Jesus Christ whom thou hast sent." Every one who loves, is begotten of God, and *knows* God; and every one that *knows* God, has eternal life. His sins are remitted. Again—"Whoever is born of God *overcometh* the world; and this is the victory that overcometh the world, even our faith," (1 John v. 4.) What are the promises made to those who *overcome?* "To him that overcometh, will I give to set with me in my throne, even as I overcame, and am set down with my Father in his throne." "He that overcometh shall not be hurt of the second death," (See Rev. ii. and iii.) The sins of such persons are remitted. Again—"He that is begotten of God keepeth himself, and that wicked one toucheth him not," vs. 18. Look at all these plain and positive declarations concerning those who are *begotten* of God, and those glorious promises to them, and tell me, whether they do not enjoy remission of sins.

Once more—(1 John v. 1,) "Whosoever believeth that Jesus is the Christ is born [or begotten] of God : and every one that loveth him that begat, loveth him also that is begotten of him." Every believer is begotten of God, and is a child of God. Mr. C. will not immerse an individual until he professes to believe, that Jesus is the Christ; and if he does believe, John says, he is begotten of God, and, of course, enjoys all the blessings and promises just mentioned. Mr. Campbell cannot get him into the water, on his principles, until he is begotten of God, and consequently enjoys remission of sins. One such plain, unequivocal declaration of inspiration, is worth a thousand criticisms on *eis*, or any other disputed word.

My *third* argument is this : All who are *born* of God do enjoy the remission of sins; and the new birth is in no sense essentially connected with baptism. That all who are born of God, are pardoned, Mr. Campbell admits, as you will see by the following declaration in his *Christianity Restored*, p. 208.

"Those who are thus begotten and born of God, are children of God. It would be a monstrous supposition that such persons are not freed from their sins. *To be born of God, and born in sin, is inconceivable.* Remission of sins is as certainly granted to ' *the born of God*,' as life eternal and deliverance from corruption will be granted to the children of the resurrection, when born from the grave."

Now that baptism is not essential to the new birth, I have proved by a number of plain, incontrovertible facts : I. When the new birth is first spoken of, (John i. 11—13) water is not mentioned at all. Believers are said to have been "*born of God.*" Surely if water-baptism had been essential, it would have been alluded to, when the new birth is first mentioned.

II. When the conversation occurred between our Savior and Nicodemus, (John iii.) christian baptism had not been instituted. How, then, can it be proved, that our Savior had reference to an ordinance not then in existence? Certainly if he had such allusion, Nicodemus could not be expected to understand him. Moreover, by the same mode of argumentation adopted to prove, that the Savior referred to christian baptism, the papists have attempted to prove, that in John vi. he spoke of his supper, because he makes the eating of his flesh and the drinking of his blood essential to salvation; and thus they attempt to sustain the doctrine of transubstantiation.

III. My third fact is, that when christian baptism was instituted, it was never, by the inspired writers, called *a birth*. Not an instance of such a mode of expression can be found. Then it is fair to conclude, that it is not a birth.

IV. The reason given by our Savior why men must be born again, proves, that the new birth is a *change of heart*, wrought by the Holy Spirit, and not, as Mr. C. teaches, a *change of state* effected by baptism. What is the reason given? " For that which is born of the flesh is flesh; and that which is born of the Spirit is spirit," (John iii. 6.) The word *flesh*, when employed with reference to moral character, as in this passage, as I have proved, signifies *depravity*. The Savior's meaning, therefore, is—that by the natural birth we are like our parents—*sinful;* and by the spiritual birth we are like the Spirit—*holy.* The new birth is, therefore, a change from sinfulness to holiness, from the image of man, to the image of God, and not, as Mr. C. strangely imagines, a passing through water from a state of condemnation to a state of justification.

V. That the Savior had no reference to baptism as essential to the new birth, is evident from the fact that he reproved Nicodemus for not understanding the doctrine—"Art thou a master [teacher] of Israel, and knowest not these things?" This reproof shows, that the new birth is taught in the Old Testament, of which Nicodemus was a professed expounder, and which he ought therefore to have understood. Baptism in order to remission of sins is not there taught, but the doctrine of a regeneration by the Holy Spirit is. " A new heart also will I give you, and a new spirit will I put within you." It is, therefore, clear, that the new birth is a *change of heart*, not a *change of state*.

VI. The *mystery* connected with the new birth, proves that it is not a change of state effected by baptism. Nicodemus objected to the doctrine as mysterious. The Savior admitted that it is so, but proved that this is no valid objection against it; because even the blowing of the wind is equally mysterious—"The wind bloweth where it listeth; and thou hearest the sound thereof, but canst not tell whence it cometh or whither it goeth: so is every one that is born of the Spirit." Now, if the doctrine of Mr. C. be true, this illustration from the blowing of the wind is entirely inappropriate; for there is no mystery in the fact, (if it be a fact,) that God has said, he will pardon those who believe that Jesus is the Christ, and are immersed. It is one of the simplest things imaginable. The reference to the blowing of the wind, or, as Mr. Campbell strangely translates it, the *breathing of the Spirit*, is, therefore, out of place. But if the doctrine for which I contend is true, the allusion was most appropriate; for the operation of the Holy Spirit on the heart, is as mysterious as the blowing of the wind.

VII. It is a fact, that the inspired writers were constantly in the habit of connecting the emblem and the thing signified--the water and the Spirit. The Savior was speaking to a Jew who was familiar with all the ablutions of the law; and, therefore, he illustrated the nature of the new birth by reference to water, the emblem of purification.

VIII. That the new birth is a change of heart, and not a change of state, is proved by the scriptural evidence of persons having been born again—

2 Z

" For as many as are led by the Spirit of God, they are the sons of God," Rom. viii. 14. All who are led by the Spirit of God, whose hearts and lives conform to the gospel, are the children of God. The apostle does not say, they who have been *baptized* are the children of God. See, also, 1 John iii. 9, 10.

These plain, incontrovertible facts and arguments prove conclusively, that the new birth is a change of *heart* by the Spirit of God—not a change of *state*, effected by baptism. Consequently, when a man's heart is changed so that he loves God supremely, and believes in the Lord Jesus Christ, he is born of God, is a child of God, and an heir of eternal life; his sins are remitted, and he may approach God as his Father, and may rationally rejoice in the certain anticipation of the bliss of heaven.

My *fourth* argument against Mr. Campbell's doctrine is—that the language used by Peter in Acts ii. 38, does not teach the necessity of baptism in order to remission of sins. But I have not time now to proceed further.—[*Time expired.*

Mr. Campbell said, that he would not be able to get through with his argument in one speech of half an hour.

Mr. Rice. How much time will you need?

Mr. Campbell. Two half hour speeches will be sufficient.

Mr. Rice. Very well, sir.

Friday, Nov. 24—7 o'clock, P. M.
[MR. CAMPBELL'S NINTH ADDRESS.]

MR. PRESIDENT—My friend, Mr. Rice, and myself have not been taught in the same school, nor studied under the same masters. I commenced in the Presbyterian school, but he has continued longer in it than I did. One of the first discoveries I made, of real and abiding advantage to me, was the licentious manner in which they quote and apply the Scriptures in their pulpits, and in their books. I see they have not improved much since I left them, if Mr. Rice is a fair sample of the Presbyterians that now are. When I commenced preaching it was usual to quote, in a single sermon, almost a hundred texts of Scripture. Each head of discourse had its own list of authorities. In my youthful sallies I was accustomed to quote ten *texts*, as we called them, for one I now cite. There is no greater delusion than an array of verses, torn out of their respective contexts, and arranged in a new connection in support of some view or tenet, that was not before the mind of the inspired author, whose words we thus take without his consent, to illustrate or prove that which, were he present, he would most explicitly repudiate and disallow. The number of parallel texts, like synonymous words, is much smaller than, perhaps, any one of us would allow. There is some shade of difference, some little peculiarity, more striking and appreciable than the difference between consubstantiation and transubstantiation, both of which dogmata are sometimes proved by the same texts.

Mr. R. has quoted various passages in development of the phrases " begotten," and " born of God." His object was to shew the attributes of these subjects. Now, mark it well, as respects this debate, every one of those texts have been perverted and misapplied, for one fact, which all who think must perceive, viz. *that all those persons had been baptized* of whom the apostle spake. Hence the subject of John's proposition was one born both of water and of the Spirit, while the subject of Mr. Rice's proposition is one, as he conceives, born of the Spirit only; consequently his reasonings are most fallacious and deceitful. There was no such ecclesiastic personage in those days. To illustrate and confirm this we shall attend to John's discriminating mode of address. He says:

"I have written to you, little children, young men, and fathers. To you, little children, because your sins are forgiven you, on account of his name." If baptism had not, in those days, been regarded as a pledge of remission, in reason's name, how could John have said that the least in years, in the christian church, had their sins forgiven *on account of his name!!* No man can explain these words, but upon the admission of my premises. It is as if John said, you have only been baptized—you have just been born of water and Spirit. They had as yet formed no character, on account of which he could commend them. And to the next class: "I have written unto you, young men, because you are strong, and the Word of God abideth in you, and you have, [in the heat of youth and passion,] overcome the world." To the fathers he says, "I write unto you, fathers, because you have known·him [the Messiah] from the beginning." You still hold on your way and acknowledge him. If these views of this beautiful and instructive passage needs any other confirmation, you have it in the Hiphil or Hebrewistic form of the verb *know*, which is equivalent to *acknowledge*, or make known. I have written to you, little children, he says a second time, because you have *acknowledged* the Father—which, of course, all did in baptism. In a very wholesale way the gentleman makes quotations, and in this wholesale way do I dispose of them. The proof now given of the apostolic style in this case of being begotten and born, on which he has been occasionly entertaining us for two days, takes from him his whole premises, and exposes the perfect nudity of his position.

My friend has repeatedly objected to our mode of designating persons by representing them as having obeyed the gospel. I will only add on this subject, that in using it in this style, we are perfectly evangelical. In the apostolic age they were thus accustomed to speak of the baptized. How soon after Pentecost it got into use we may learn from the fact, that we have the conversion of the priests set forth in this language: "A great company of the priests became obedient to the faith." After the people left the priests, the priests followed them. They have seldom, in great companies, obeyed the truth, until deserted by the people. When the people are converted in great numbers, there is much reason to expect a large conversion of the clergy. Speaking of the gospel, Paul says, it is made known to all men, "for the obedience of faith;" and to the Romans, speaking of the unbelieving Jews, he says, "they have not obeyed the gospel," &c. But, of the brethren, he says, "you have obeyed from the heart that form of doctrine, [the gospel] delivered to you." We are then in good company, though not with Mr. Rice, in so speaking of the converted.

I have already said, perhaps, enough on the tendency of our respective systems towards delusion. The Scriptures say, "with the mouth confession is made unto salvation"—"with the heart man believes unto justification; but with the lips confession is made to salvation." Infants cannot confess to salvation, nor can they believe in the heart to justification. Paul never contrasts the head and the heart, as modern preachers do. He contrasts the *mouth* and the *heart*, which modern preachers do not. Now we ask for·both—a belief in the heart and a confession with the mouth, as necessary to salvation, in the ordinary dispensations of

Providence. This public oral confession is a very strong defence against imposition and delusion, compared with carrying in our bosoms sleeping infants to receive holy baptism, and to put on Christ. As many as were baptized into Christ in old times, had put on Christ. I have just as much reason to speak of the soul-ruining doctrines of Pedo-baptism, as he has to speak of the evil tendencies of mine.

Again: we assail not the passions. We address the understanding, the conscience, the affections. We assail the intellectual powers and moral feelings of our nature. Animal excitement, and all the fleshly appliances of the present age, we abjure. We regard every invention of that sort as human, and not divine—a new device in christianity. It was as perfect as the sun at first; and, like its Divne Author, " it is the same yesterday, to-day, and forever." Our system of conversion is in this point freer from delusion than any other known to me. Still I preach to all professors, " Examine yourselves, whether you be in the faith. Know you not that Christ is in you, except you be reprobate ?"

Touching the quotations from Mr. John Wesley, I presume they spake his sentiments when he wrote them. I desire not to tax the large and respectable denomination that has risen up under his auspices, with any views which they disallow. Both Messrs. Clark and Wesley have at times crossed their own paths, and each other's paths, very palpably, on this, as well as on some other points. The book from which those extracts were read, was printed not more than eighteen years ago, by authority of the denomination, and was then judged worthy of their patronage. Eighteen years, however, now-a-days produce great revolutions; for much light has gone forth into the land. Mr. Wesley, it will be remembered, has said on Paul's conversion, that " baptism is both a *means* and a *seal* of pardon," and that, in the primitive age, it was the ordinary way of receiving remission. John Wesley's mother, an admirable lady, said, " Sinners obtain remission by baptism, and christians by confession."

The references to Wall, on the use of the word *regeneration*, do not authorize Mr. Rice in saying, or in insinuating, that I have given any change or coloring whatever to his views touching the universality of baptism for remission, or as equivalent to " being born of water and of the Spirit," amongst all the ancients. I believe that almost all, if not absolutely all, the fathers, Greek and Latin, used regeneration and baptism as representative of the same action and event. I do not, however, approve the phraseology used by them on this subject. I call baptism " the washing of the new birth," rather than the new birth itself. So I think Paul most learnedly denominates it.

But our opponents have done us a great deal of injustice, in representing us as pleading for " *water regeneration*." They have endeavored to preach us down, and sing us down, and write us down, by holding us up to public reprobation, as advocates of a mere baptismal regeneration; but they have not succeeded, nor can they succeed, with any who will either hear us or read us on these subjects. No man believes more cordially, or teaches more fully, the necessity of a spiritual change of our affections—a change of heart—than I do. I have said a thousand times, that if a person were to be immersed twice seven times in the Jordan for the remission of his sins, or for the reception of the Holy Spirit, it would avail nothing more than wetting the face of a babe, unless his heart is changed by the word and Spirit of God. I have no confidence in any instrumentality, ordinance, means, or observance, unless the *heart is turned to God.* This is the fundamental, the capital point; but, with these, every other divine ordinance is essential for the spiritual enlargement, confirmation, and sanctification of the faithful.

Mr. Rice says I sometimes use the language of Ashdod. No doubt of it. When communicating with those who do not understand the language of Canaan, we must accommodate our style to their education. There is no scriptural authority for calling a change of heart, the new birth, or regeneration.

I doubt not that all the intelligent and conscientious, when their hearts are first turned to the Lord, unless deluded into the belief that they have been baptized, desire baptism. It is as natural for those who read the book, to desire baptism, as it was to the eunuch to exclaim, "See, here is water: what doth hinder my being baptized?" All whose hearts are touched from above, pant for baptism. They long for it—they desire it. It is only after they have been prevailed upon to believe that they have been baptized, that they can give up the anticipated pleasure. Many of them, too, give it up with reluctance; and I do know so much of human nature, and of the human heart, too, that no one sprinkled in perfect infancy, or who, on the testimony of some friend, believes he was, is ever so well satisfied, so perfectly pleased with himself and at rest, as he that on his own confession has voluntarily placed himself under the Lord by a baptism unto his death. A striking proof of this has occurred in death-bed scenes, in the numbers which I have seen and of which I have heard. No one has been found, as I believe, penitent or grieved in the immediate prospect of death, because he had been, on his own confession, buried with the Lord in baptism for the remission of his sins; but many of those who only believed that they had been sprinkled in infancy, on some other person's faith than their own, have died overwhelmed with unavailing penitence. Again I say, no death-bed penitent has ever lamented that he obeyed the Lord for himself.

I will, in reply to various vague generalities, which cannot be easily grouped under any one category, read a few passages, with a few remarks, from a name dear to many good Presbyterians in this city, not only inscribed upon a monumental church in the neighborhood, but embalmed in the memory of many yet living in the midst of us. I need scarcely add, I am about to read a few extracts from the Reverend James McCord. We shall commence with a passage on page 162.

"That is, in other words, if the testimony of Jesus Christ deserves consideration, there is no ordinary possibility of salvation without the limits of the church of God.

I know that the statement of such a sentiment is far from flattering to those who wish to be saved, but in a way and upon principles very different from those to which the page of inspiration points us. And I expect to be assailed at once with questions from all quarters—'What, then, will the heathen do?' 'What must become of many amiable and deserving people, who act in a way decidedly superior to many christian professors, although they are not of the church?' 'Why do you attach so much importance to mere externals, when every body knows that the essence of true religion consists in the dispositions of the heart?' We have not leisure to answer all these questions: nor do we deem an answer necessary."—*Last Appeal,* p. 162.

Is not this writer as uncharitable as a reformer? Complain not, my Presbyterian friends, of our uncharitableness, since one of your most gifted, and pious, and exemplary preachers, speaks as strongly and as uncom-

35   2 z 2

promisingly as any staunch reformer in the commonwealth of Kentucky. He tells you, that there is to you who have the Bible "no reasonable prospect of salvation but in connection with the church of Christ. There is," he adds, "no ordinary possibility of salvation without the precincts of the christian church." But let us hear him on baptism.

"You will not, therefore, deem it an unreasonable statement, that there is no ordinary possibility of salvation without the precincts of the christian church, if once we can clearly make it out to you, that the church is the great mean of effecting man's salvation.

This is not one of those questions that are only to be settled by long and difficult argument. It is a question of fact; and you will find the decision written as with a sunbeam in every page of Scripture. When the Savior gave commandment to his apostles to proclaim his great salvation to all people under heaven, what was the declaration that accompanied this commandment? 'He that believeth and is baptized shall be saved.' When those apostles made the first proof of their ministry, in the city of Jerusalem, on the memorable day of Pentecost, what was their answer to the agonized multitudes who felt convicted of the sin of crucifying God's own Messiah, and cried out in horror, 'Men and brethren, what shall we do?' 'Repent and be baptized every one of you, in the name of Jesus Christ, for the remission of sins, and ye shall receive the gift of the Holy Ghost.' This was their answer to the eager inquiry. When the apostles went abroad among the gentile nations, what other prescription did they ever give for attaining to God's salvation? 'Believe on the Lord Jesus Christ:' 'believe and be baptized:' 'the word is nigh thee, even in thy mouth and in thy heart—that if thou shalt confess with thy mouth the Lord Jesus, and shalt believe in thy heart that God hath raised him from the dead, thou shalt be saved. For with the heart man believeth unto righteousness; and with the mouth confession is made unto salvation.'"—*Last Appeal*, pp. 165, 166.

"And this is harshness! The God of immensity tenders you salvation; and you say you would gladly have it. But he tenders it in connection with that great society of which his own Messiah is the head and king; and you say you do not wish to be connected with his church. He tenders you his Spirit with the water of his baptism; and you say you had rather be saved without that baptism. He tenders you salvation, if you will submit to all his government, if you will wear his yoke, if you will learn of him; and you refuse to learn of him, you refuse to wear his yoke. You must be saved in your own way, not in God's way. You must be saved when it suits you to submit to his appointments, and not just when he invites you. And it is cruel in God's Messiah to withhold his great salvation from the little, pitiful, short-sighted, but self-sufficient being, who refuses to seek for it in the way he has directed? And it is harsh in me to tell you, that in acting thus perversely you trifle with your peace!"—pp. 170, 171.

"Incense, as we have already seen, is a symbol of the prayers of the saints. It is only in the true spiritual church that such prayers are offered; and they are symbolized by the incense burnt upon the golden altar in the holy place."—p. 184.

Could any one accustomed to hear our brethren speak, distinguish this address from those which they are often accustomed to hear from them in their discourses upon the gospel? He that could distinguish them, must have a more discriminating ear than I have. The second of the Acts, and the third of John, passed through his hands as diversely from the comments of Mr. Rice, as Mr. Rice's comments differ from ours.

But Mr. R. makes his grand defence of his interpretation of John iii. 5, on a very singular assumption, viz., that as christian baptism was not then instituted, our Savior could have no allusion to it. He could, then, during his whole ministry, have no allusion to anything not then actually existing, if the principle be sound. Our Lord spake, both in figure and without figure, prospectively of his death, burial, resurrection, kingdom, and cause in the world; and even ordained the supper prospectively. McCord, in his Last Appeal, reprobates these views of Mr. Rice, and corroborates mine.

But look for a moment at the style. *"You must be born again"*—as introductory to the kingdom of God. Again, and in the same discourse, he says, "the Son of Man *must be lifted up*," &c. Now Mr. Rice will admit, that "*must be*" in this case indicates what was then prospectively future: and why not admit that the same style, from the same speaker, and in the same conversation, may not also mean what was then prospectively future? In the original, the word and construction are identically the same, in verses 7 and 14. Evident, then, it is, as almost all truly learned men agree, that the whole discourse with Nicodemus was prospectively delivered. If time admitted, it were easy to give much more evidence of this sort. What I have stated, cannot easily be refuted. If Mr. R. however, will not hear the Westminster divines, and his friend Dr. Hall, he would not be persuaded though I gave a hundred other proofs.

I read these passages from Rev. McCord, not so much to corroborate either my views of John iii. 5, or Acts ii. 38, or of Mark xvi. 16, as to shew how exceedingly incongruous is the charge of uncharitable censoriousness, so frequently and so pertinaciously exhibited against us by our opponents. If Presbyterianism were to be redeemed from its humiliation in this commonwealth, by arraigning our piety or our benevolence—more vigorous and resolute attempts to represent us as opposed to a change of heart, or as so exclusive in our views and feelings, as to deny the possibility of salvation beyond our own communion—could not have been devised or prosecuted, than on the present occasion. To fasten these imputations upon us, rather than discuss the doctrinal issues between us, seems to be the great desideratum of my respondent. And to me the marvel is, that a denomination the most exclusive in all the community, if its standards are to be relied on, should presume to accuse us of views excessively exclusive, while seeking at other times to reproach us with the most indefinite latitudinarianism.

Indeed, McCord's views, before expressed, are but a development of one or two passages in the confession. I have time but for the two following:

" Others not elected, although they may be called by the ministry of the word, and may have some common operations of the Spirit, yet they never truly come to Christ, and therefore cannot be saved; much less *can men not professing the christian religion* be saved in any other way whatsoever, be they never so diligent to frame their lives according to the light of nature, and the law of that religion they do profess: and to assert and maintain that they may, is very pernicious and to be detested."—p. 65. sec. 4.

" The visible church, which is also catholic or universal under the gospel, (not confined unto one nation as before under the law,) consists of all those throughout the world that profess the true religion, together with their children; and is the kingdom of the Lord Jesus Christ, the chosen family of God, out of which there is no ordinary possibility of salvation."—p. 134. sec. 2.

This is, to say the least, quite as uncharitable as any thing we have said or written on the subject. Especially, as we know that those whose confession this is, pretend to regard and represent us in this community as not professing the true religion. Presbyterians, like my friend, of the true, genuine color, never change. They are all immutable. These sentiments, then, are essential to them all; and, of course, they can neither blame nor censure us, on the ground of uncharitableness.

I can neither advert to all the peculiar absurdities of the system I oppose, nor respond to every thing foreign to the question, deduced from my own writings or any other source, in the time allotted us; but I must notice the singular caprice that gives an ordinance to one because one of his parents is a professor, and withholds it from a child whose parents are more virtuous and benevolent than he, though not professors in their sense of the word—especially if they regard the ordinance of any salutary efficacy whatever.—[*Time expired.*

Friday, Nov. 24—7½ o'clock, P. M.
[MR. RICE'S NINTH REPLY.]

MR. PRESIDENT—The gentleman seems to abound in matter of one kind or another. I had expected to close the argument on this subject this morning; but, as on the mode of baptism, so on the *design*, he was so far from having proved his doctrine to his own satisfaction, that, at his request, I agreed to continue the discussion *two hours* this evening; and yet he calls for more time!!! Well, I have given him another speech, for I wish him to have full time to deliver himself on this whole subject. I desire it to be understood and known, that the *clergy* are not afraid of the light which he can throw around them; we are willing to meet his arguments in their undiminished strength.

He pretends, that the passages I quoted from the epistle of John, proving that all who are begotten of God, enjoy remission of sins, are all misapplied, because those things are spoken concerning *baptized persons*. It is truly astonishing, that any man should be willing to expose himself by assuming a position so perfectly untenable and absurd. No one who will read those passages, can doubt that John was giving general descriptions of christian character—pointing out the peculiar character of true christians. Let us, for a moment, examine those passages: "Whosoever is born of God doth not commit sin." The expression is absolutely universal, not limited to those immersed, or baptized. Again, verse 10: "In this the children of God are manifest, and the children of the devil." In what are they manifest? Not in the fact, that the one class have been baptized, and the other not, but in the fact, that the children of God *do righteousness and love their brethren.* All, therefore, who work righteousness, are the children of God, baptized or not. Again, 1 John iv. 7: "Beloved, let us love one another, for love is of God; and EVERY ONE THAT LOVETH is born of God, and knoweth God." Again, chap. v. 1: "WHOSOEVER believeth that Jesus is the Christ, is born of God; and EVERY ONE that loveth him that begat, loveth him also that is begotten of him." Now what shall we speak of the interpreter of God's word, who will gravely tell us, that these universal expressions are to be confined to those who had been *immersed?*

The expression ' *whosoever*,' and ' every one,' are as universal as any terms in any language can be. " *Whosoever* will, let him take the water of life freely." Yet Mr. Campbell, to sustain his cause, feels obliged to declare, that these expressions are to be limited to those who had been immersed! Sorely, indeed, must the cause be pressed, that cannot sustain itself, without resorting to perversions of God's word so glaring and so reckless!

I called on the gentleman to produce a passage of Scripture, which represents being baptized, as *obeying the gospel.* He refers us to Acts vi. 7: "And a great company of priests were obedient to the faith." And what has this passage to do with the question, whether being baptized is called obeying the gospel? Does he expect us to take it for granted, that baptism is meant, where it is not even distantly alluded to? The inspired historian says, the priests became obedient to the faith—but he says not a word about baptism. The gentleman asserted most boldly, the other day, that the promise in Galatians iii., referred to the land of Canaan, though Canaan is not mentioned in the whole epistle; and why should he not find baptism where it is not even hinted at?

He has found another passage in Rom. vi. 17: "But God be thanked that we were the servants of sin; but ye have obeyed from the heart that form of doctrine which was delivered you." Here, strange to tell, he thinks that to obey the form of doctrine delivered to them, though it is just the opposite of serving sin, is to be immersed! Obedience to the form of doctrine taught by Paul, is immersion; obedience to the faith is immersion; the name of the Lord refers to immersion; sanctification is immersion; every thing in the New Testament is immersion!! What a watery affair he would make the gospel!

By the way, he still keeps up the old song about infant baptism. Now if he is really suffering under the conviction of having been defeated in his war against infant baptism, we will give him another trial; but I am not disposed to discuss two subjects at once.

But he finds another passage in Rom. x. 10, where baptism is called obeying the gospel; it is this: "With the heart man believeth unto righteousness [that is, unto justification, which is obtained by faith]; and with the mouth confession is made unto salvation." Yes, *confession with the mouth* means immersion! Why, the question is not any longer, what passages speak of immersion, but where are any that do not!

Having read from Wesley's sermon on justification his real views, I leave Mr. Campbell to make what capital he can by claiming him. He must be in great need of arguments, or he would not drag in those whose views are precisely the opposite of his. Even Calvin cannot escape, although he said in so many words, that Cornelius first obtained remission of sins, and was afterwards baptized, "not with a view to obtain by baptism a more ample remission of sins;" and again, that baptism, though mentioned by Peter before remission, really succeeds it! After all, we are to believe, that Calvin agrees perfectly with Mr. Campbell, who maintains that remission of sins is actually obtained in baptism, not before! The gentleman tell us, he believes in a *change of heart*. We shall have occasion, in a short time, to inquire into his views on that subject. For the present, therefore, I pass it without particular remark.

Every believer, he informs us, will be immersed, unless beguiled by some one to believe that sprinkling is baptism. Who would not sympathize with such men as Calvin, Luther, Owen, Scott, and a multitude like them, who spent their lives in the prayerful study of the Scriptures, and, at last, were beguiled into the belief that sprinkling is baptism? They wished to know and do their duty; but somebody, it would seem, beguiled them. The Scriptures, we are told, do most clearly teach, that nothing but immersion is baptism; but such men as those, could not see it. They were beguiled!!! When I hear men uttering such sentiments, I am disposed to think, they prove very conclusively, that they have an exalted opinion of their own wisdom, and not much correct knowledge of human nature.

The gentleman says, he was a Presbyterian, till he was twenty-one years of age; and he imagines, that he understands the whole system of

Presbyterianism. Many young men, at that age, think themselves quite profound theologians. He retains the recollection of those youthful conceits; and seems still to think that he had, at that early period, made himself a rather uncommon divine! But I am constrained still very much to doubt, whether he ever knew much of Presbyterianism.

But he says, he has met with numbers who, on their death-beds, regretted that they had not been baptized on their own responsibility. This is indeed *news!* He is the first man I ever heard say, that he had met with even one case of the kind. I have visited the death-beds of a good many; and I am acquainted with many ministers who have been in the ministry longer than Mr. C. had lived, when he left the Presbyterian church, at twenty-one; and I have never heard from any of them of even one such case. Yet Mr. Campbell has met with numbers! Well, he has seen strange things, and met with singular people in this world!

He quotes McCord as saying, there is no ordinary possibility of salvation out of the church. I have no objection whatever to this doctrine. For he who refuses to become a member of the church of Christ, knowing that God has commanded him to do so, gives evidence, clear and decisive, that he has no true piety, and, of course, cannot be saved. But did McCord say, that the sins of believers are remitted only in baptism? He did not. The gentleman's running after helps so perfectly flimsy, shows how well he understands Presbyterianism, and how deeply he feels that his cause is sinking. These remarks are a sufficient answer to his comments on the language of our confession of faith.

As to the doctrine of election, if he really desires to discuss it, I will meet him at a proper time, and give him a fair opportunity to demolish it. I will not now be diverted from the subject before us; but if he wishes a discussion of that subject, he shall have it.

He still magnifies his *charity.* Let me give you some little evidence of the liberality and charity he exhibits: *Christianity Restored*, p. 240; "Infants, idiots, deaf and dumb persons, innocent pagans, wherever they can be found, *with all the pious Pedo-baptists*, we commend to the mercy of God." Again, an objection is presented and answered as follows: "But do not many of them [unimmersed persons] enjoy the present salvation of God?" Mr. C. answers, "How far they may be happy in the peace of God, and the hope of heaven, I presume not to say. And we know so much of human nature as to say, that he that *imagines* himself pardoned, will feel as happy as he that is really so. But one thing we do know, *that none can* RATIONALLY, *and with* CERTAINTY, *enjoy the peace of God, and the hope of heaven, but they who intelligently, and in full faith are born of water, or immersed for the remission of their sins.*"

The gentleman is quite charitable indeed, and pious too; for he commends pious Pedo-baptists, infants, idiots and pagans to the mercy of God! But he tells us, the pious Pedo-baptists cannot *rationally* and with *certainty* enjoy the hope of heaven! There is, it seems, no certainty that their sins are remitted. Like "his holiness," the pope, he is disposed to admit the possible salvation of the *incorrigibly ignorant!* The great ignorance of some may put them in a hopeful condition! If this is liberality and charity, he is welcome to the credit of it.

He has read to you some extracts from Witsius on the covenants. I subscribe very cordially to the views expressed by Witsius. He tells us, that baptism, as a seal of the covenant, binds those who receive it, to

a holy life—that it is a significant ordinance, pointing to spiritual blessings, the putting off the old man, spiritual resurrection, &c. But does
he say, as Mr. C. says, that the sins of the baptized *are actually remitted in the act of being baptized?* He does not—he believed no such
thing. The gentleman must be in trouble, or he would not attempt to
sustain himself by the authority of men whose views were the antipodes
of his, and whose writings are regarded in all our theological seminaries as
standard works. The simple truth is, there is just as great difference between his views and theirs, as there is between *actual* remission of sins,
and the *outward sign and seal of remission.*

I will now resume the recapitulation of the argument. I have proved,
that Mr. C.'s doctrine of baptism in order to remission of sins, flatly
contradicts the repeated, clear, and unequivocal declarations of Christ and
his apostles. I have proved it false by the fact, that all who are *begotten
of God* do enjoy remission of sins. The gentleman admits, that all who
believe are begotten of God—that they must be begotten before they are
baptized. But John the apostle teaches, that every one that is begotten
of God, does know God, overcome the world, and has the promise of
eternal life. They are, therefore, pardoned before he can get them into
the water.

I have disproved his doctrine also, from the fact, that all who are born
of God do enjoy remission of sins; and the new birth, as I have proved,
is not essentially connected with baptism, but is a change of heart. This
has been proved by a number of *facts* which he has not attempted to deny.
He has said, and reiterated, that the confession of faith makes John iii.
5, refer to baptism; and he charges me with abandoning the creed I
have solemnly adopted. But does the confession say, that this passage
means christian baptism? Not a word of it. In the chapter on baptism
it does refer to this passage, as illustrating the connection between the
emblem and the thing signified. But in the same chapter it refers to
Rom. iv. 2, "And he received the sign of circumcision, a seal of the
righteousness of the faith which he had—being yet uncircumcised," &c.
[Mr. Campbell. It is not in the same section.] I care not what section he read. He asserts, that the confession makes John iii. 5, refer to
baptism, because in the chapter on baptism this passage is quoted; but I
prove, that in the same chapter on baptism, the confession refers to Rom.
iv. 2, where the apostle is speaking of circumcision. So, according to
the gentleman's logic, the confession makes circumcision mean baptism!
The argument is as conclusive in the one case as in the other.

But, if he had been as familiar with Presbyterianism as he would have
us believe, he would have known, that in adopting the confession of faith
as containing the *system of doctrine* taught in the Scriptures, we do not
say, that every reference to Scripture is precisely appropriate. We adopt
its doctrines as true, but not every reference as correct. I fear the gentleman will find it necessary to go over his theological training again, before he will understand Presbyterianism.

It is, then, clear, that the new birth is not at all essentially connected
with baptism—that it is a change of heart; that, when the heart is renewed, the individual is born of God, is a child of God, and an heir to
the heavenly inheritance. *His sins are remitted.*

My *fourth* argument is, that the language of Peter, in Acts ii. 38,
does not teach the necessity of baptism in order to remission. Peter
said to the inquiring Jews, "Repent, and be baptized in the name of the

Lord Jesus for the remission of sins." Mr. Campbell has said in his *Christianity Restored*, that "immersion for the forgiveness of sins was *the command* addressed to these believers;" but this is a very great mistake. Peter commanded *repentance* and baptism. Now the question arises, whether repentance or baptism secures remission, or whether both are equally necessary. To determine this question, it becomes necessary to examine several other passages. We will suppose, for the sake of argument, that Peter meant to say, be baptized for or into *(eis)* the remission of sins. Does the word *eis*, translated *for*, mean *in order to?* Mr. Campbell affirms that it does. I admit, cheerfully, that it sometimes has this meaning, but such is by no means its uniform signification.

Let us, then, examine another passage in which we find a precisely similar expression; Matt. iii. 11, " I indeed baptize you with water into *(eis)* repentance." I asked the gentleman whether he believed, that John baptized the Jews in order that they might repent—be sorry for their sins? He says, no—but he baptized them *in order to* REFORMA-TION. But here he meets an insuperable difficulty, making John and Peter contradict each other. John, he says, baptized the Jews in order to reformation; and Peter commanded them first to reform, in order to receive baptism! Did John and Peter thus contradict each other? If they did not, Mr. Campbell's exposition of their language is certainly most erroneous. Our interpretation of their teaching makes them perfectly harmonize. John baptized the Jews *into* repentance. They came to him confessing their sins, and professing repentance; and into that professed repentance he baptized them. So on the day of Pentecost the converted Jews, hearing the offer of remission of sins through Jesus Christ, and professing to believe the proclamation and to receive Christ as their Savior, were baptized into this faith, received the sign and seal of that remission, obtained simply by faith.

But there is another insuperable difficulty in the way of Mr. C. If, as he says, the word translated *repentance* means *reformation*, and John said, I baptize you unto *reformation*, how are we to understand Peter's second discourse, in which he says—"*Reform* and be converted?" I have called on the gentleman to tell us, (but I apprehend, he never will do it,) what is the difference between *reformation* and *conversion?* In his translation he has it—"*reform* and be converted." I hope he will endeavor to tell us the difference between reformation and conversion. We wish to know, whether Peter said in effect, reform and be reformed; or, convert and be converted. Such are some of the insuperable difficulties attending the doctrine of Mr. C.

I have also presented for your consideration a *sixth* argument against his doctrine and against his interpretation of Peter's language, viz: Faith, repentance, and conversion mutually imply each other; and, therefore, remission of sins is promised indiscriminately to each of these graces. It is impossible that any one should have repentance—a change of mind—without conversion—a change of life; and it is impossible that there should be true faith without repentance and conversion. In a word, where there is repentance, there is faith; and where there is repentance and faith, there is conversion. These, then, like faith, hope, and charity, are uniformly found in the same heart. I have asked the gentleman, whether they can exist separately; and he pretends not to say, they can.

Then, inasmuch as faith, repentance, and conversion uniformly exist together, remission of sins may with perfect propriety be promised to either, or to all of them. Accordingly, we do in fact find the inspired writers promising remission to every penitent, to every converted person, to every believer. In the following passages, the remission of sins is promised to *repentance:* Luke xxiv. 46, "Thus it is written, and thus it behooved Christ to suffer, and to rise from the dead the third day, and that *repentance and remission of sins* should be preached in his name among all nations, beginning at Jerusalem." Again—Acts v. 31, "Him hath God exalted with his right hand, to be a prince and a Savior, for *to give repentance to Israel, and forgiveness of sins.*" Again—Acts xi. 18, "When they heard these things, they held their peace, and glorified God, saying, Then hath God also to the gentiles granted *repentance unto life.*" In each of these passages, repentance and remission of sins, or repentance and life, are connected together; so that every penitent may be assured that his sins are remitted. Remission of sins is also promised to *conversion.* Matt. xviii. 3, "Except ye be converted and become as little children, ye shall not enter into the kingdom of heaven." Every one, then, who is converted, will enjoy the blessings of God's kingdom.

The fact that repentance, faith and conversion, mutually imply each other, and are always found associated, explains the reason why remission of sins is promised indiscriminately to each of these graces. It also reconciles most fully the different directions given to inquiring minds by Peter and the other apostles. In Peter's first discourse (Acts ii.) he promised remission to those who repented. In his second, (Acts iii.) preaching to another company of inquirers, and, of course, telling them all the conditions of remission of sins, he said, "Repent *and be converted,* that your sins may be blotted out." Here baptism is not mentioned, nor is it necessarily implied in repentance and conversion, more than any other duty. Hence the conclusion is most obvious, that Peter did not regard baptism as a prerequisite to the remission of sins. The jailor (Acts xvi.) was commanded simply to believe, and on this one condition salvation was promised. It is, then, clear, that forgiveness of sins is promised indiscriminately to repentance, conversion, and faith ; but baptism is never mentioned as a prerequisite to remission.

When Peter preached to Cornelius, he said not a word about baptism in order to remission of sins. On the contrary, he declared in the most unqualified terms, "In every nation, he that feareth God and worketh righteousness, is accepted with him ;" and again—"To him give all the prophets witness, that through his name, whosoever believeth in him shall receive remission of sins," (verses 35, 43.) *Did the prophets testify, that remission of sins should be enjoyed through immersion?*

From the first discourse of Peter to the end of the New Testament, you cannot find one word about baptism *in order to* remission of sins. As John baptized into a profession of repentance for remission of sins ; so did Peter baptize into repentance and faith in Christ for remission ; and both John and Peter directed the faith of the baptized to Christ.

But Ananias' language to Paul is brought forward to sustain Mr. C. "Arise and be baptized, and wash away thy sins." But this language is fully explained by the fact stated and proved, that the inspired writers, both of the Old and of the New Testament, constantly connect together the *emblem* of sanctification with the *grace* of sanctification—water with the work of the Spirit. This fact affords a satisfactory explanation of all the passages of the New Testament, which have been supposed to favor the doctrine I am opposing.

My *seventh* argument against Mr. C.'s doctrine is this: If it be true, multitudes of the most pious and godly persons live and die condemned, and are forever lost. None but immersed persons, he most unequivocally teaches, can have rational evidence of remission. Sins, according to him, are remitted only in baptism. He does, indeed, express the opinion that some unimmersed persons, excluded from the kingdom of God here, may enter the kingdom of glory in heaven. But this opinion is perfectly absurd. The Scriptures no where teach, that any whose sins are not remitted in this life, will be pardoned in the next. I say, then, if Mr. Campbell's doctrine be true, *hell will be full of the most godly people who have lived on earth!*

We have often stood by the dying beds of those who, according to Mr. C.'s views, were never baptized; and we have witnessed their calmness in immediate view of death, the heavenly peace which passeth understanding, the joyful anticipation of speedily beholding their Redeemer's face without a veil to obscure his glory. We have seen them in this happy frame of mind, bid adieu to all they loved below, and sweetly fall asleep in Christ. But if Mr. C.'s doctrine be true, all this was delusion; for their sins were yet upon them, and their hopes were speedily blasted! This doctrine is most palpably contradictory of the Scriptures, which every where promise eternal life to all the *righteous*, and threaten destruction only to the wicked.

My *eighth* argument is—that Mr. C.'s doctrine ascribes an unscriptural importance and efficacy to an external ordinance. The Scriptures, as I have proved, every where declare, that the religion of the heart is the *one thing needful*, and the only thing essential to salvation. On this point I quoted a number of passages, to which the gentleman has attempted no reply. Circumcision was once delayed for forty years with the approbation of God, and, therefore, was never considered essential to salvation. Mr. Campbell has but fallen into the common error of human nature. The religion of all pagans consists chiefly in forms and ceremonies. The Jews lost sight of the cross of Christ, to which their bloody sacrifices pointed them, and clung to the mere shadow. They denied the agency of the Holy Spirit, of which their ablutions were but emblems, and fondly imagined that by their multiplied washings they might be acceptable to God. They were assiduous in cleansing the outside of the cup and the platter, leaving the inside polluted and defiled.

It is, I say, *the error of human nature.* Our Savior never found it necessary to reprove the Jews for undervaluing external rites; but often did he condemn them, for ascribing to them an efficacy they did not possess. The christian church was filled with corruption by the same error. The bread and the wine in the Lord's supper, designed to be a memorial of his death, were supposed to have attached to them some mysterious efficacy; the partaking of them was deemed necessary to salvation; and, finally, men, in the perfection of their folly, imagined that the bread and wine were actually changed into the body, blood, soul and divinity of Christ! They lost sight of the cross and the atonement; and their faith terminated on the mere symbols.

By a similar process and from a similar cause baptism began to be thought essential to salvation; then an efficacy was ascribed to it in securing the purification of the soul from sin; and to add to its virtue, water was consecrated, that the ordinance might be administered with *holy water.* Such is the progress Rome has made in making a Savior of external rites.

I have been surprised, in looking through Mr. Campbell's writings, to discover, how large a portion of the New Testament he makes to speak of immersion, and what efficacy he ascribes to it. In his debate with McCalla he declares, that the immersed believer comes up out of the water, *pure as an angel!* And in looking over his *Christianity Restored,* I happened to notice his remarks on Heb. x. 14, "For by one offering he hath perfected forever them that are sanctified," and I found him paraphrasing it thus: "By one offering up of himself, he has perfected the conscience of the *immersed* or *sanctified!*" p. 247. Yes—he has perfected forever the *immersed!!!* Sanctification means immersion, and indeed, with him, every thing seems to run into the water!—[*Time expired.*

Friday, Nov. 24—8 o'clock, P. M.
[MR. CAMPBELL'S TENTH ADDRESS.]

MR. PRESIDENT—This is my last address on this proposition, and having to touch upon numerous topics, I must, therefore, touch upon them lightly. Most of the important matters have been repeatedly adverted to, and are gone to record; therefore little need be said upon them. Whatever replies have been made to my regular arguments, if I have not adverted to them, it is because I have not noted them down, or supposed them to be worthy of any special attention. On this question, as generally before, we have had no real debate. The main points on which I relied, stated in my first speech, and in some of the others, are unreplied to, and some of them almost, if not altogether, unnoticed. My friend sometimes assumes to be facetious, and sometimes acrimonious; but in his last essay has addressed himself rather to your humor, than to your judgment or conscience. The following items have been repeatedly adverted to, or hinted at, during the investigation of this question

1. While we regard immersion, or christian baptism, as a wise, benevolent, and useful institution, we neither disparage, nor underrate, a new heart, repentance, or faith; nay, we teach with great clearness and definiteness, that unpreceded by faith and repentance, it is of no value whatsoever. These two constitute a change of heart, a mental conversion; for all believing penitents have a new heart, and are prepared for being born into the kingdom of God.

2. But in the second place, we insist upon the essential importance of baptism, as a divine institution, because Jesus Christ enacts no superfluities. In his religion there is not one ordinance that is not essential for some purpose; all-important to christian life, health, or usefulness. Not one of them, therefore, can with safety be dispensed with. Who, then, think you, acts more rationally; he that practically maintains faith, repentance, and baptism; or he that dispenses with any one of them, as, in his judgment, unnecessary or inexpedient? The strongest argument for any thing, and the best reason for doing any thing, is, that the Lord Jesus Christ has commanded it. A sound discretion, and a sound judgment, give to every thing its proper place, and no more. Neither faith, nor repentance, nor baptism, severally, nor altogether, are every thing in religion. But each one of them is indispensable, and no one of them can be a substitute for another. A person is not to be justified nor saved by faith alone. No man can trifle with baptism, so long as he remembers that Jesus said, "He that believeth, and is baptized, shall be saved." What God has joined together, let no man separate.

During the controversy on the design of baptism, up to this moment, we have not heard of any benefit whatever which it confers upon an infant. While I have been elaborating the important design of baptism, I had hoped that, if my opponent would not accede to my views on that subject, he would, at least, give us a clear numerical statement of the practical benefits resulting to his subjects of baptism. He has not been able to mention one benefit which baptism confers upon his true and proper subjects of it; for baptism, to an unconscious babe, imparts neither knowledge, nor faith, nor repentance, nor forgiveness, nor health, nor riches, nor long life, nor any good thing, temporal, spiritual, or eternal. In the name of common sense and reason, then, what has this controversy been about? If my friend triumphs, who has gained any thing? It recognizes a right; but then the *right* is there, whether recognized or not It is born in the church, and, therefore, baptism is not a door into any thing—and what are all church birthrights to it! They guaranty nothing. It is a grand superlative nullity. I do beseech and implore the gentleman to stand up to his task now, and tell us what are the advantages, benefits, and privileges of infant baptism? When he recounts them, fellow-citizens, mark them down, and ponder them well.

4. "Them that honor me," says Jesus, "I will honor." Now there is a pleasure, an ineffable pleasure, in obeying Jesus Christ. In magnifying his institutions we honor him, and we are honored; in magnifying them we cannot err. It was "his meat and his drink to do the will of him that sent him." One of the benefits of the institution is, that it affords a person a fine opportunity to honor the Lord. The more shame, reproach, and contumely, the better. And if there be none of these, then there is the pure, unalloyed joy of sincere personal consecration; of giving one's self away to the Lord; of entering into a solemn and everlasting covenant with the Lord. Millions of ages to come, there will be millions in paradise who will be delighted to revert to some river, or pool, or fountain, in which they put on Christ, and vowed eternal allegiance to him.

5. Mr. Rice says, many good and pious persons live, die, and go to hell, on my principles. On his own fallacious inferences, he should have said. This is, truly, an astonishing conclusion. It is, certainly, the result of a morbid state of the system. I should prescribe medicine, rather than argument, in this case. We send none to perdition but those who disbelieve and reject the gospel. And is it an unfavorable aspect of our religion, that it does not promise eternal life to those who disbelieve and disobey it!

No good—no religious, moral, or virtuous man, can perish through our views or principles. Our theory thunders terrors to none but the self-condemned. Human responsibility, in my views and doctrines, always depends upon, and is measured by, human ability. It is so, certainly, under the gospel. The man born blind will not be condemned for not seeing, nor the deaf for not hearing. The man who never heard the gospel, cannot disobey it; and he who, through any physical impossibility, is prevented from any ordinance, is no transgressor. It is only he who knows, and has power to do, his Master's will, that shall be punished for disobedience. None suffer, in our views, but those who are wilfully ignorant, or negligent of their duty. Natural ability, time, place, and circumstances, are all to be taken into the account; and none but those who sin against these, are, on our theory, to perish with an everlasting destruction, "from the presence of the Lord, and from the glory of his power." Infants dying, need neither faith, repentance, nor baptism, in order to their salvation, according to the Bible. They died in the first Adam, but the second Adam died for them, and they shall live with him.

6. Great men often believe great nonsense. St. Peter's church is filled with the busts of a thousand saints who were learned and pious teachers of transubstantiation, auricular confession, and purgatory ; who prayed to the Virgin Mary and to dead men. There are learned Protestants, and there are learned Papists, but the latter are more numerous than the former; consequently, neither learning, nor genius, nor talent, nor numbers, are tests of truth, or a proof that any tenet, custom, or tradition is canonical or useful.

7. Another particular observation in this summary which, I presume, you have made, and which I am sorry to be constrained to make, is the manner of proof adopted by Mr. Rice. He and I calculate very differently on the audience. I have been accustomed to give scriptural and rational proof of every proposition to those who wait on my ministrations ; but it appears that he is accustomed to *inform* his audience that he has proved his proposition, and seems to regard the phrases " IT IS SO " and " IT IS NOT SO," as most satisfactory evidence. Can any of you, my friends, recollect a proposition agreed upon, which he attempted to prove by any regular train of reasonings or facts ; or any one of mine, that has been assailed by him in any other way than by assertions and denials ? If you do, I must say I do not remember it.

8. I need not attempt a recapitulation of the arguments offered on this occasion. It would be to reiterate much of my first address, as well as portions of others. Of the fourteen arguments advanced on this subject, not one has been formally assailed. A few of them have been noticed in an allusive manner, but perhaps one half of them has not been even alluded to. Assumed contradictions in my writings and Mr. R.'s theory of the new birth, matters wholly foreign here, left but little time for the proper business of my respondent. I made the precepts and positive declarations of the New Testament, the basis of all my arguments. Several of them were direct precepts—each of them a formal " thus saith the Lord." The first of these, introduced by the Holy Spirit himself on the day of Pentecost, is itself alone sufficient, when all its circumstances are maturely considered. The solemn precept, obeyed by three thousand in one day, has itself alone satisfied many myriads now living and millions dead. And had it been proclaimed to all the world and been believed, would not the result have been the same ? Peter inseparably connected repentance and baptism, as necessary to a plenary remission of sin. It is still the same as at the beginning—the law has not been changed.

9. The Messiah himself, too, connected faith, baptism, and salvation together in the commission, as reported by John Mark. Is he not paramount authority ? What better guaranty than, "*He that believeth and is baptized shall be saved?*" Who can ask more. The heavens will fall before the Lord's word will fail. THUS SAITH THE LORD, "*He that believeth and is baptized shall be saved.*"

10. This is a saying for which Mr. R. has yet had no use. Peter's sayings and those of the Lord Jesus are not for one age, nation, or condition of men ; but for all nations, for all ages, for the human race. Jesus commanded this annunciation to be made *to every creature*—preach the same gospel to the four quarters of the world.

11. When Jesus sent Ananias to Saul of Tarsus, he also instructed

him to say to the anxious and inquiring Paul, "Arise and be baptized, and wash away thy sins, calling upon the name of the Lord." Does not this also indicate a clear fixedness of plan, a Divine uniformity in administering remission and salvation in the gospel age?

12. But take one more, and leave all the other arguments. Take the aged, venerable, authoritative Peter in the prospect of soon seeing the Lord. Peter, in his catholic epistle, does more than John the apostle. John only alludes to the subject of baptism, but Peter strongly maintains his pentecostal address. He says, speaking of Noah's salvation in water and by water, that we are saved in water and by water, as Noah in the ark was saved through the deluge. To which salvation, neither to the ark nor to the water alone, baptism corresponds as an antitype to a type, in saving those who enter the water as Noah entered the deluge, relying upon God's promises—thus seeking and obtaining the answer of a good conscience towards God; always the effect of remission, through faith in the resurrection of Jesus from the dead. He who cannot find a good foundation on such authorities as these, to name no other, is not to be reasoned with by moral arguments.

Neither Peter nor the Messiah was afraid of any unfavorable inferences from their use of the word *saved*. Some have wondered why our Lord did not place some of the social virtues immediately in association with faith, when he said, " He that believeth and——, &c., shall be saved." None of our opposing cotemporaries would have supplied the blank with the words " and is baptized." Peter, then, and his Master, sustain our use of this style of address, and authorize our conclusions also.

Should I err in following such authorities, I place between me and my Lawgiver and Judge the fact, that I stand behind all the apostles. What I say to my hearers, I have caught from the lips of those inspired pillars of the christian temple. When any one asks me *what he must do to be saved?* so soon as I ascertain his position, whether he be a believer, an unbeliever, or a penitent, I tender to him some one of the answers given by the authority of the Lord. I do not give the same answer to every inquirer, because the apostles did not. Their respective characters call for answers suited to them. To every believing querist, I give the answer that Peter gave on the ever-memorable Pentecost, believing that if the whole world had then been present, and joined in the same query, he would have given the same answer to all.

Men had better take care how they handle coals of fire. The word of God is not to be misapplied with impunity. Has he said, and shall he not do it? Has he spoken, and shall it not come to pass? The heavens and earth may pass away, but his word will never pass away. I should become a Presbyterian before to-morrow's dawn, if the book of God commanded me. My religion changed me once, and it would change me ten times, if I could only find one, " *thus saith the Lord*" for it. I set out to know the truth, the whole truth, and to obey it in all things. I have consecrated myself to its maintenance, and vowed to follow where it leads the way.

13. As to our *charity*—what an insulted word! As to our charity! Then, if charity consist in firmly and affectionately stating the truth to those who design to know it, we are most charitable. But, if charity mean flattery—saying to all, you are right—you are in the way to blessedness, whether or not, then are we most uncharitable, for we will not say so. And if charity mean hoping all things, I am willing to say, that

I do sincerely rejoice, that simple, honest mistakes, where they are not the result of corruption of heart, will not, in my opinion, preclude any Pedo-baptist from heaven, although on earth he should, through his mistakes, never enjoy the full reign of heaven in his soul. The Judge of all the earth will do right. I circumscribe not the Divine philanthropy—the Divine grace. I dare not say that there is no salvation in the church of Rome, or in that of Constantinople; though, certainly, Protestants do not regard them as churches builded upon the foundation of apostles and prophets, Jesus Christ being the chief corner-stone. In all the Protestant parties there are many excellent spirits, that mourn over the desolations of Zion—that love the gospel and its author most sincerely. My soul rejoices in the assurance that there are very many excellent spirits groaning under the weight of human tradition and error, who are looking for redemption from these misfortunes before a long time. I do not believe that pagans or infants will be condemned for not believing the gospel. Nay, my exposition of that document, given in this debate, confines it only to those who hear it. Still, I must say, that, in my full conviction, and assurance of faith, it is only the man who believes and obeys the original gospel, who repents of his sins, and is immersed for the remission of them, that can enter into the full and true enjoyment of the reign of God within the heart.

14. I said nothing on the subject of *election*, to call for any expression on the form of a challenge for the discussion of that question. The gentleman has, I think, enough on hand at present, without the burthen of Calvinian election. His proposition to debate that subject was wholly gratuitous and uncalled for.

15. There are yet one or two points that I shall touch very lightly. There is one good effect in christian baptism, on which I have not dwelt. It is its direct influence upon the baptized. It gives, indeed, a very strong impulse to the intelligent subject of it. He feels a solemn transition from one state to another. It is most solemnly impressive, inasmuch as he feels himself voluntarily putting on the Lord and Savior of the world; he feels himself partaking with the Savior in his death, burial and resurrection, and giving himself away to the Lord for time and for eternity—an event worthy of everlasting remembrance. It, therefore, greatly exercises the faith, hope, love and zeal of every intelligent and conscientious subject of it. I would not deprive my son, or my daughter, by my officiousness, from this most sublime pleasure, for all the honors, emoluments and privileges of the Roman hierarchy. I will teach them its meaning, its importance, its rich and liberal blessings; I will then leave it to themselves to act, to choose the time, and the place, and the circumstances. I will tell them of that preparation of heart necessary to a proper reception of it, and of the sweet peace, and joy, and love, which follow in its train, and then leave them to the Lord and themselves.

My time. almost expired, admonishes me to say a word upon the catholicity of our views. We have an eye single to the union of all christians on the old foundations. I would not hold an heretical or schismatical tenet for any consideration that could be presented to me. Now it so happens, that, although my very worthy friend, Mr. Rice, would represent me as most exclusive in my views and feelings; nay, as consigning to perdition all who are not immersed! I am, on the whole doctrine of baptism, action, subject, and design, much more catholic in every respect than he.

Suppose now, one great convention of the christian world had met to fix upon some basis of union and communion, and that they had agreed upon one single point, viz:—that whatever views were most generally believed, and first those that were universally believed, should be accepted and incorporated, instead of those believed by a minority.

Baptism comes before the convention: the question is first upon the action; a part vote for sprinkling, as valid baptism, a part for pouring, but all agree that immersion is valid baptism. It is, therefore, put down as *catholic*, and the other two as *sectarian*.

Next comes the subject of baptism: a part admit that an infant, without faith, is a proper subject, but only a part. But when the question is put, Is a professed, penitent believer, a proper subject, all the world says, Yes. This, then, is *catholic;* while an infant, as a subject, is sectarian.

Finally, the design of baptism is canvassed.

Some say it is a door into the church; others, a recognition that one is a member of the church; a third, that it is for the sake of christening, or giving a name. In none of these is there any approach to catholicity. But when its being for a "pledge of remission of sins, and of our ingrafting into Christ," is offered, the whole world, Greek, Roman, and all, unite in that view of it. This, then, is catholic, and the others sectarian.

Are we not, then, most catholic on this subject? Why not, then, sacrafice that which is so sectarian, and unite in one Lord, one faith, and one immersion?

Finally, fellow-citizens, it is the immediate duty of all who have not been immersed, to be immersed into the sacred name, for this richest of heaven's blessings, the privileges and immunities of the new kingdom and constitution. It is a matter, if neglected, sometimes of long and bitter repentance, but when submitted to in faith, it is never to be repented of. No one has yet said, on a dying bed, that he regretted his having been immersed, while thousands have repented at last, that they had not so honored the Lord. I have time only to add my unfeigned desires, that you may solemnly weigh all that you have heard on the present occasion, bring it all to the solemn and ultimate judge of all controversies, that holy Oracle, and speedily decide for yourselves, what you ought to do. It is all-important that you know the truth—that you obey the truth—and that you send it, with your commendations, to all your friends, neighbors, and fellow-citizens, and that this be done immediately. All of which I submit, with my kindest wishes, for your individual happiness, temporal and eternal. [*Time expired.*

Friday, Nov. 24—8½ o'clock, P. M.
[MR. RICE'S CONCLUDING REPLY.]

MR. PRESIDENT—It is one of the most difficult things imaginable to answer an *exhortation.* Indeed I do not know that it is necessary to answer the gentleman's exhortation to us, not to pervert the Bible. It was well enough, only very much out of place. Who claims the right to pervert the Bible, or to alter what God has said? His pathetic exhortation certainly implies, that every one is guilty of the awful sin of perverting the Bible, who ventures to demur to his interpretation of it. This, I presume, is not quite true. I think it within the bounds of possibility, that a man might differ from him on some important points, and yet be not guilty of wresting the Scriptures. I have preached so much against the infallibility of uninspired men, that I cannot now consent to place my friend, Mr. C., in St. Peter's chair. I denounce no man because he does not think precisely as I think, and teach just as I teach. "To his own Master he standeth or falleth." Nor do I intend to make an exhortation which would imply such a charge. On this occasion, I prefer argument to declamation.

Mr. Campbell commenced his speech by asking, which is the safer course, to take repentance, faith, and baptism, or to say that baptism is a matter of no importance? This question, if it has any pertinency, implies, that we regard it as a matter of indifference, whether persons submit to baptism or not. But does not every body know, that such is not the fact? What says our confession on this subject? "Although it be *a great sin* to contemn or neglect this ordinance, yet grace and salvation are not so inseparably annexed unto it, as that no person can be regenerated or saved without it," &c. Do we maintain, that it is a matter of indifference? Have I not repeatedly said, that the man who wilfully neglects the ordinance of baptism, proves thereby that he is destitute of piety, and cannot be saved? Why does the gentleman indulge in representations so contrary to our known views? What does he expect to gain by it?

Faith *alone*, he says, never secured pardon to any one. If by faith alone he means faith that produces no obedience, we hold to no such faith. Our confession, as I have proved, says, that faith is never alone, but is ever accompanied by other graces, and leads to good works. By faith we receive the Lord Jesus as our wisdom, righteousness, sanctification, and redemption; and repentance and conversion, as I have proved, universally accompany faith. "This is the victory that overcometh the world, even our faith." I have said nothing about faith *alone*, but faith that works by love, and leads to uniform obedience. I can conceive of no reason for such representations as the gentleman has made, unless it be, that he has no arguments to offer.

But on the subject of baptism, in order to the remission of sins, he breaks out in a pious strain, and tells us, that he cannot honor his Master too much by magnifying the value of his ordinances. True, he cannot honor Christ too much; and we are not at all sensible that we dishonor him, when we differ from Mr. C. concerning the relation baptism sustains to the plan of salvation.

Allow me to illustrate the force of his pious remarks. An architect is erecting a splendid building. The materials are all collected together; and the building is going up. One of the workmen insists on making a *pillar* of a piece of timber intended for a *rafter*. Another, better skilled in the science of architecture, remonstrates against this course; but his zealous fellow-laborer replies—'I cannot honor my employer too much. He is a wise and good man; and the more importance I give this piece of timber, the more I shall honor him.' The reasoning of the misguided architect would be just as good as that of my friend. We are trying to ascertain the place, in the temple of truth, which baptism was designed, by the Great Master, to occupy; but my pious friend is disposed to indulge his good feelings, and he exclaims—'Oh, I cannot honor my Master too much. The greater the importance and the efficacy we ascribe to it, the more we shall honor him!' Such appeals may work on the minds of the weak, but they are not argument, nor do they prove, that we honor our Savior by assigning to baptism a place he did not design it to occupy.

The gentleman tells us, he knows the strength and the weakness of

36

Presbyterianism. He may, on this occasion, have learned something of its *strength;* but I doubt whether he has discovered its *weakness.* I can scarcely bring myself to believe, that at the age of twenty-one he was so profound a theologian as he seems to imagine. Doubtless he thinks, that he knows the strength and the weakness of our cause; and doubtless he is mistaken. This is sufficiently evident, from the repeated and glaring misrepresentations of our doctrine he has made during this discussion.

He intimates, that for conscience' sake he gave up a very flattering religion. I will not charge him with being influenced by unworthy motives; but, most certainly, he has gained vastly more fame and applause, than he ever could have secured, had he become a Presbyterian minister. Whether he was seeking fame, is not for me to decide; but that he has adopted the very best plan to gain it, is certain. So that, as things have turned out, he cannot be considered a *martyr,* nor even accounted a sufferer by his change. As to his charity, of which he entertains a very exalted opinion, I will refer the audience to the opinion of his brother, Dr. Fishback, who pronounces his views, on this subject, more sectarian and illiberal, than entertained by any person known to him! His opinion is entitled to consideration; for he is not under the influence of unkind feelings toward Mr. C. If I had expressed such an opinion, you might, with some reason, suspect that it was the effect of prejudice; but, when it is expressed by an intimate friend, there is every reason to believe it to be well founded. I make against him no heavier charge, than his own *friends* prefer.

It is admitted, he has expressed the opinion that it is *possible* for some unimmersed persons to be saved; but it is certain that his doctrine and his opinion are contradictory—both cannot be true. His doctrine is, that baptism is necessary to the remission of sins; and his opinion is, that in many cases it is not necessary. The question then arises—*in what cases is baptism necessary,* since he admits it is not necessary in all? It would certainly be difficult to decide. I cannot reconcile his faith and his opinion; but I am now concerned only with the former.

Peter, the gentleman correctly supposes, would have preached to all the world the same doctrine he preached on the day of Pentecost. True: but he did not always or ever teach that baptism is necessary to remission of sins. I have said, and I think I have proved, that the Lord never did suspend the salvation of a soul upon an external ordinance. Ordinances are important in their place. They are designed to be means of grace—aids to lead to holiness of heart and life. But it will scarcely be denied, that persons may by the grace of God be sanctified without the privilege of participating in all the ordinances appointed for the edification of the church. And if the end be secured with a part of the means which might assist us, who shall say that the soul will be lost?

The gentleman's own friends have proclaimed him inconsistent in his different publications. Some time since, he expressed the opinion that there were some christians amongst " the sects." A zealous sister in his church was rather disturbed by this charitable announcement, and forthwith wrote to him for an explanation. He still adhered to his charitable view; whereupon a number of his friends found much fault with him, and charged him with having abandoned his former ground and weakened their efforts in the good cause of reformation. They continued to press him rather severely, and at last he was brought so nearly to what they deemed orthodoxy, that he only gave it as his *opinion* that the salvation of

unimmersed persons is *"possible,"* writing the word in *italics!* His
charity, which at first appeared somewhat expansive, dwindled down to
a mere point, a bare *possibility! ! !*

He says, he is not *accustomed* to make assertions without proof, and
expect the people to believe him. It was very important, indeed, that he
should inform the audience of this fact; for very many are of opinion,
that he has abounded in unproved assertions during this discussion. If
he had not informed them to the contrary, they would, in all probability,
have concluded that such is his general practice ; and indeed if it is not,
he has certainly done himself injustice on this occasion.

Another piece of information which was much needed, is, that I have
not answered one half of his arguments. I am quite certain that a large
number of intelligent persons really believed, that I had answered the whole
fourteen ; though I did not number them one, two, three, &c. But every
passage of Scripture on which he relied to prove his doctrine, I think I
have fairly examined, and have proved that it will not sustain his argument.

He has relied mainly on the language of Peter, (Acts ii. 38 ;) and I
have proved, as I think, that Peter did not teach that baptism is necessary
to the remission of sins. I maintain, that he preached the same conditions of remission in his second discourse, where baptism is not mentioned, as in his first; and the same to Cornelius as to those at Jerusalem.
The question is, not whether we shall believe Peter, but *what did Peter
say?* The gentleman seems disposed to make the impression, that we
are refusing to believe Peter's doctrine. What did Peter say? According to Mr. C.'s interpretation, he made baptism as necessary as repentance to remission of sins—necessary, of course, in all cases, for no exception is intimated. Then if we are to take Peter's doctrine, let us take
all that he taught. But this Mr. C. will not agree to do; for whilst his
interpretation of Peter's language makes baptism necessary to remission
in all cases, he now declares his belief, that it is necessary only in *some*
cases, and in others it is not !

I maintain that what God has declared without qualification to be necessary to salvation, is necessary in all cases. Mr. C. has said, that God
made repentance and immersion *equally necessary* to remission of sins.
But if immersion and repentance are equally necessary, how can he now
admit that the former is necessary only in *some* cases, and not in all ?
Moreover, in his debate with McCalla, as I have proved, he declared his
belief that Paul's sins were *really pardoned when he believed.* He does
not profess to have changed his views on this subject. He has admitted
every thing for which I am contending, and yet he says I am in the wrong,
and he in the right ! I cannot reconcile his sayings and doings. But I
quoted, amongst others, one passage of Scripture which is of itself, if there
were not another, a full and complete refutation of the gentleman's doctrine ; and I have not been able to get his attention to it, even to this good
hour. Indeed, I had but little hope that he would see it, for none are so
blind as he who will not see. The passage is this—" He that believeth
on him is not condemned."

He tells us, that he will place the apostles between him and the Judge,
when he shall account for the doctrines he has preached. Such language
may, perhaps, be an evidence of his sincerity in believing them ; but it is
no argument to prove them true.

He reiterates the declaration, that when John the apostle says,

" Whosoever believeth that Jesus is the Christ, is born of God," the
word *whosoever* must be confined to the members of the church; that is,
whosoever *in that church* believed! Let me read one passage in that
epistle, that you may judge of the correctness of this principle of interpretation. Chapter iii. 10: " In this the children of God are manifest,
and the children of the devil: whosoever doeth not righteousness is not of
God, neither he that loveth not his brother." That is, according to Mr.
C.'s interpretation, whosoever *of the immersed persons, members of the
church*, doeth not righteousness, is not of God! But we are not, according to him, to apply this language to any but church members! I am
truly surprised that any tolerable scholar should attempt to put such a
construction upon the plainest language. When I say, *whosoever* takes
arsenic will die, I do not mean persons in Kentucky or America simply,
but the whole human race. John was describing christian character, and
he said, whosoever of the human race believes that Jesus is the Christ,
is born of God. WHOSOEVER—why, it is the most comprehensive expression in any language. *And this is the only method he could devise,
to evade the force of the fact, that all who are begotten of God, baptized or not, are children of God, and enjoy remission of sins, and promise of eternal life ! ! !*

My friend, Mr. C., seems not to be able to see any advantage to be
derived from the ordinance of baptism, unless it be necessary to secure remission of sins. He might as well take the same position in regard to
the Lord's supper. I might ask him, of what use is the Lord's supper,
if remission of sins can be obtained before partaking of it? What is the
use of prayer, preaching, and other appointed means of grace? Much is
to be done for us, and by us, after our sins are forgiven, before we can
be prepared for heaven. Baptism, therefore, may and does answer important purposes, both to adults and to infants, though remission of sins
is not obtained in the act of receiving it. It is the seal of the covenant of
grace—a pledge to infant and adult, that so soon and so long as the
conditions of that covenant are complied with, remission of sins shall be
enjoyed. It is, then, a means of confirming and strengthening our faith.

I must now notice the *vote* proposed by the gentleman to prove the
catholicity of his principles. As he, the other day, engrossed three covenants in two; so, on this occasion he has engrossed the three subjects we
have discussed, in *one*. He tells us, if the question be put to all Christendom—Is pouring or sprinkling right?—many will vote in the negative;
but put the question—Is immersion right?—and all, he says, will say,
Yes. I do not think they would. I rather think that there are vast multitudes who would say, No, very decidedly. If the question were,
whether remission is *valid*, there might be a tolerably unanimous vote; for
many would vote that it is valid, who do not believe that it is the scriptural mode. But if they must vote whether it is *right or wrong*, they
will vote in the negative; and, if the gentleman would convince them that
the *mode* is essential to the validity of the ordinance, and then put the
question—Is immersion *valid?*—they will say, No.

Again, he puts the question, Is *adult* baptism right? All, as he truly
says, vote in the affirmative. But I do not like the form of the question.
Let us state it a little differently, thus: Is it right for believing parents to
neglect or refuse to have their children baptized? From east, west,
north and south, a thousand to one, they answer, No. The Greek church,
with ten thousand tongues, and almost all the christian churches on earth,

say, No. Put the question in the other form—Is it the duty of believing
parents to have their children baptized?—the same immense multitude
answer, Yes. Are we, then, to do violence to our judgment and our
conscience, to neglect or refuse to do what we believe God commands,
in order to bring about a union with the few who differ from us? Shall
the consciences of the thousand yield to the scruples of *one?* The question is not, whether adult baptism is right; but whether it is the solemn
duty of believing parents to give their children to God in the ordinance
of baptism? and on this question, we shall outvote the gentleman by an
overwhelming majority.

The third question was put as unfairly as the others. He would have
us vote, whether a baptized believer is pardoned. But let the question
be stated fairly. It is this: Is a penitent believer condemned until he is
immersed? The vote will be, ten thousand to one, against the gentleman.
Is the man forgiven, who is sincerely penitent, confesses and forsakes his
sins, and with an humble faith casts himself at the feet of Jesus, and, like
the publican, prays—" God be merciful to me a sinner?" Let this question be put to vote, and from east and west, north and south, all, with the
exception of a mere handfull, who profess to take the Bible as their infallible guide, will vote in the affirmative. Present the case of the man who
lies on his sick bed, and never can, or never will be immersed, but who
exercises an humble faith in Christ, as his wisdom, righteousness, sanctification, and redemption, and ask the christian world—those whose infallible guide is the word of God, whether the Scriptures contain a promise of salvation to such an individual? And again the almost unbroken
voice is in the affirmative.

And this decision, let it be noted, is not given as an *opinion,* but as
the clear and uniform teaching of the word of God. The hopes of such
an individual are based on promises too clear to be misunderstood; and
though he cannot, or believes he should not be immersed, he can safely
rest on those promises, and rejoice in his dying hour. Let the question
be fairly stated, and we are ready to take the vote. The gentleman, notwithstanding his remarkable *catholicity,* will be found in a very, very
small minority.

I have now given Mr. Campbell full time to bring forward all his arguments. I could have sustained the doctrine for which I contend, in a
shorter time. You have now heard him at length; and the plain *facts*
which I have presented, proving his doctrine unscriptural, are before you.
It certainly contradicts a large class of the plainest declarations of Christ
and his apostles; " HE THAT BELIEVETH ON HIM IS NOT CONDEMNED."
Every believer is pardoned and justified. Such is the language of our
Savior. It requires no criticism; it admits of but one interpretation.
Language cannot be plainer. The book of revelation is like the book of
nature. The most unlettered man can learn when to sow, what to sow,
and when to reap; and how to protect himself and his family from the in-
clemency of the season. So in the word of God, the conditions of pardon
and salvation are presented with so much simplicity and clearness, and
are so variously illustrated, that the wayfaring man, though unlearned,
need not err. When persons of common understanding, not blinded by
prejudice, read those plain declarations of our Savior, what do they understand him to mean? " He that believeth on him is not condemned."
" He that believeth on the Son, *hath* everlasting life." " He that believeth, shall never thirst." "He that believeth hath everlasting life, and

shall not come into condemnation, but is passed from death unto life.'' These, and a multitude of passages like them, are too plain to be misunderstood.   They directly contradict the doctrine, that baptism, especially *immersion*, is necessary in order to receive remission of sins.

The plain facts I have presented before you, sustained by a large number of scriptures, prove, conclusively, the erroneousness of the doctrine of Mr. Campbell.   The period is not distant when we, speakers and hearers, shall stand before the Judge of the living and the dead, to give account of our faith and our lives.   I desire you, my friends, to examine this subject, as for eternity.   Your eternal interests are as intimately connected with it, as mine.   I leave you to make your decision, whether the gentleman has proved, that baptism is necessary to secure the remission of sins—whether the penitent believer is condemned, until he is immersed !—[*Time expired.*

[END OF THE THIRD PROPOSITION.]

PROPOSITION FOURTH.

Baptism is to be Administered only by a Bishop or Ordained Presbyter. Mr. Rice affirms. Mr. Campbell denies.

[MR. RICE'S OPENING ADDRESS.]

MR. PRESIDENT—The proposition for discussion this morning, is the following: *Baptism is to be administered only by a bishop or ordained presbyter.* This I affirm, and Mr. Campbell denies.

In explanation of the proposition, allow me to state, that the terms *bishop* and *presbyter* we regard as two Scripture names for the same office. The word *episcopos*, translated bishop in the New Testament, signifies an overseer; and it seems to have been used to denote the ministerial office, because the presbyters or ministers of Christ are required to watch over the interests of his church and people. The proposition before us assumes, that presbyters and bishops hold the same office in the church.

The doctrine, then, for which I feel bound to contend, is—that the Scriptures authorize none but bishops or presbyters, properly ordained, to administer the ordinance of baptism. The audience perceive, at once, the precise point in debate. Mr. Campbell maintains, that every member of the church, male and female, young and old, has the right to administer this solemn and important ordinance. Against this latitudinarian doctrine I enter my protest, and offer my reasons.

As we have agreed to occupy but a single day in the discussion of this proposition, I design to present very briefly the arguments which appear to me to sustain the proposition I affirm.

The baptism of an individual, especially of an *adult*, on profession of his faith, I think it will be admitted, is an important event in his life; whether considered with reference to himself, or with reference to the interests of the church of Christ. Considered with reference to himself, it is important, for several reasons:

1. Baptism is an ordinance by which he who receives it, on profession of his faith, is recognized as a disciple of Christ, and admitted to a standing in his family. If he be a true christian, his spiritual interests are promoted by the reception of the ordinance; but if he be deceived, he is likely to be confirmed in his error. He persuades himself that he has obeyed an important command of the Savior. He is recognized by christians as a brother. His conscience ceases to warn him of his guilt and danger; his fears of future punishment subside; and he cherishes a delusive hope, perhaps, to the last moment of his life. Or, overborne by the temptations and unhallowed influences of the world, he turns again to his former course, and his conscience is "seared as with a hot iron." Such an individual has received an irreparable injury.

2. Baptism introduces the professed believer to privileges in the

church which, without true piety, he cannot enjoy or improve to his spiritual edification.   Attendance upon the ordinances of God's house with an impenitent, unbelieving, unrenewed heart, will involve him in guilt far more aggravated, than if he had remained in the world.   Of the Lord's supper, to which of course he approaches, it is said—"He that eateth and drinketh unworthily, eateth and drinketh condemnation to himself."   Equally true is it of all other privileges enjoyed by the church of Christ, that they prove a curse, not a blessing, to him who possesses not the spirit of the gospel.

3. As baptism introduces the professed believer to privileges which an unbeliever cannot improve; so it devolves upon him duties which none can discharge, but they who have been born again.   He sustains new relations to the church and to the world; out of these relations arise duties, the proper discharge of which is most important.   Not one of those duties can he discharge, unless he be a true disciple of Christ.   Consequently he is involved in the double guilt of partaking of ordinances he cannot improve, and of binding himself more solemnly to the duties he cannot perform.   He is greatly injured.

If we consider the baptism of a professed believer with reference to the interests of the church of Christ, it is an important matter.   For, 1st. The Head of the church requires that, as far as possible, it shall be kept pure—composed of worthy members.   He who, whilst an unbeliever, seeks and obtains admission into the church, not only involves himself in greater guilt, and exposes himself to an aggravated condemnation ; but he contributes in no small degree to draw upon it the frowns and the judgments of God.   The greatest caution which human wisdom can observe, will not preserve the church entirely free from unconverted communicants ; but so long as we remember, that one Achan in the camp of Israel drew upon the whole body the severe chastisements of God ; we cannot but feel, that it is alike the duty and the interest of the church to see to it, as far as possible, that her communicants shall be true believers.

2d. Baptism identifies the professed believer with the church.   He is regarded by the world as a christian ; and it is a fact, that the great majority of unconverted persons form their opinions of christianity, not so much from what they hear or read of its pure and sublime truths, as from what they see in the conduct of those who profess to have embraced it. They are expected in their daily conduct to illustrate the character and spirit of the gospel on which they profess to rely for salvation.   They who are acquainted with the state of things at the present day, must know, that no one cause so retards the progress of the gospel, as the ungodly lives of professors of religion.   Multitudes of men are disgusted with religion, and confirmed in infidelity, only or chiefly because they see many occupying a respectable stand as members in real or pretended churches of Christ, whose conduct is, in many respects, more exceptionable than that of multitudes who make no pretensions to religion.

These things being so, it will not be denied, that it is of the greatest moment to individuals, to the church, and to the world, that as far as possible the doors of the church be guarded, so as to exclude all unworthy persons.

In view of these incontrovertible truths, the importance of which we cannot now fully estimate, I emphatically ask, *Is it probable that the all-wise and benevolent Savior of men has given to the most ignorant, the most superstitious, and the most rash, as well as to the wisest, the most pious and prudent members of his church, the right to introduce to its fellowship just such characters as they may choose to baptize?* Can any one for a moment believe, that He, who regards the church as the apple of his eye, who has manifested his purpose to make it a pure church—a light of the world—has indeed put the keys of the kingdom into the hands of every individual who may have been admitted to its fellowship, however inexperienced, ignorant or rash? I might almost venture, without further argument, to pronounce the idea an impossibility.

What must inevitably result from granting such authority to every member of the church? Can it be otherwise, than that the church will be speedily filled with unworthy and ungodly persons, who cannot be excommunicated? A single rash, ignorant, or unworthy member, may baptize hundreds like himself, or still worse. These persons must be recognized as members of the church. Consequently its spirituality is gone; its light is extinguished; and the curse of God is upon it. Is it within the bounds of possibility, that our Savior, when he sent forth the apostles, so eminently qualified for their responsible work, to baptize and teach, did at the same time throw wide the doors of his church, and commit its purity, and even its existence, to the hands of every man, woman, and child, who might be recognized as a member of it?

Do civil governments proceed upon such principles? Have they not ever found it absolutely necessary to have officers properly appointed to perform every public duty. May every citizen of this commonwealth take it upon himself to act as sheriff, mayor, judge, or president, as he may think proper? Have not all civil governments found it necessary to have officers, whose qualifications are defined by their constitution and laws, appointed to discharge the duties appertaining to every department? How long would our government exist, if any citizen might, on his own responsibility, presume to act as sheriff, judge, president, &c.? How long would it be, till we should be involved in anarchy, war, and blood?

If civil governments cannot subsist without offices, and officers regularly appointed to discharge the duties connected with them, how can the kingdom of Christ on earth prosper, or even exist, if every member may, on his own responsibility, perform the duties connected with its most important offices? If the doctrine of Mr. Campbell be true, the church contains within itself the elements of its own destruction. The doctrine is, that every member of the church may administer baptism. A child of six or eight years of age may believe in Christ, and be admitted to membership in his church. Now for a moment contemplate the possible results of the doctrine of the gentleman. There is a little girl ten years of age, who has been baptized, and is a member of the church. She, according to this doctrine, has the right to baptize other little girls of ten, eight, or six years of age. And that little boy, of similar age, may baptize his comrades of the same age, or younger, as his *prudence* may dictate! The servant, who was baptized last sabbath, though profoundly ignorant of almost the alphabet of christianity, may, on the next sabbath, baptize as many of his fellow-servants as he can induce to say, they believe that Christ is the Son of God! All this and more may occur, according to the doctrine of my friend, without the violation of one law of the kingdom!!! The little girl, the boy, and the servant, have only exercised their inalienable rights. There is not only no law against what they have done, but the law of Christ authorizes it! What a spectacle the church of Christ would soon exhibit, if this doctrine should prevail!

Without any further direct appeal to the Scriptures, we may venture to say, it is incredible, absolutely incredible, that our Savior should have taught such a doctrine—that he should so unnecessarily have exposed his church to almost certain ruin.

But let us appeal directly to the law and the testimony. The commission given by our Savior to his apostles, confines both baptizing and preaching to them, and to those ordained after them, to the ministerial office. "Go ye, therefore, and teach all nations, baptizing them in the name of the Father, and of the Son, and of the Holy Ghost; teaching them to observe all things whatsoever I have commanded you: and lo, I am with you alway, even unto the end of the world. Amen."—*Matth.* xxviii. 19, 20.

This commission invested the apostles with the most important and responsible office ever conferred on any human being. They were authorized to ordain others properly qualified to the same office. Now, it is a principle universally recognized, that where an office is established, and certain specified duties annexed to it, no one but he who has been properly appointed to fill the office, can discharge any one of its duties. This principle is recognized by all civil governments. Suppose a private citizen—one of the wisest and most respectable, if you please, should undertake to act as sheriff for a few days; or suppose he should take the seat of the judge, even though, for the time being, vacant; what would be the consequences? Why, in the first place, all his acts would be pronounced *null* and *void*. No human being would be bound to regard them. In the second place, he would be punished as a violator of the laws of the land. Yet there is no law forbidding him, in so many words, to do what we suppose him to have done. The very fact, that such offices exist, and that particular duties are assigned to those who fill them, constitutes a prohibition of all other persons from interfering with those duties.

The same common-sense principle must be recognized in the kingdom of Jesus Christ. The sacred office of the ministry has been established by him, for the edification of the church. The qualifications of those who are to be invested with it, are detailed; and certain most important duties, on the proper discharge of which depend the purity and prosperity, if not the existence, of the church, are connected with the office, and enjoined most solemnly on those who fill it. Is it not, then, perfectly clear, according to the principle already stated and universally admitted, that the King of Zion intended to confine the discharge of those duties to the men who should fill the office? The very appointment of the office, and the solemn command to those invested with it, to baptize and preach, constitute a law against *lay-baptism*. And, as in civil government, so in the church of Christ, he who, without being invested with the office, presumes to exercise its functions, performs acts which are null and void, and makes himself a transgressor.

Will it be pretended, that the Savior was less wise in his legislation. or less careful to preserve the peace and purity of his church, than civil legislators; who guard against the evils of anarchy and oppression, by establishing offices and appointing men properly qualified to transact public duties? Unless the gentleman is prepared to cast upon him this imputation, he must abandon the doctrine, that every member of the church may of right administer the ordinance of baptism.

Let me here present distinctly the broad principle on which Mr. Campbell professes to have set out in his reformation. I hope that, on this occasion, he will be willing to act in conformity with it. I quote from the Christian System, p. 6:

"A deep and an abiding impression that the power, the consolations, and joys—the holiness and happiness of Christ's religion, were lost in the forms and ceremonies, in the speculations and conjectures, in the feuds and bickerings of sects and schisms, originated a project many years ago for uniting the sects, or rather the christians in all the sects, upon a clear and scriptural bond of union—*upon having a* ' THUS SAITH THE LORD,' *either in express terms, or in approved precedent, for every article of faith, and item of religious practice.*"

Now observe, the gentleman's reformation started upon the principle of having a "Thus saith the Lord" for every article of faith and every item of practice. I NOW CALL UPON HIM TO PRODUCE A "THUS SAITH THE LORD," FOR HIS DOCTRINE OF LAY-BAPTISM. Let me state fully his doctrine on this subject, as exhibited in the Milennial Harbinger, (vol. iii. pp. 236, 237.) Here I find some seven questions propounded by a correspondent, and answered by Mr. Campbell; one of which is as follows—"Are all immersed persons, male and female, to be so considered?" That is, are they legal administrators of baptism? Another is as follows—" Can an unimmersed person be so considered under any circumstances?" To these and other questions, Mr. C. replies as follows:

" *Answers to questions* 2, 3 *and* 4.—*There is no law in the christian Scriptures authorizing any one class of citizens in the christian kingdom to immerse, to the exclusion of any other class of citizens.* Apostles, evangelists, deacons, and unofficial persons, are all represented as immersing when occasion called for it. Paul, though not sent to immerse, yet did it when no other person was present. Philip immersed the eunuch; Ananias immersed Paul; Peter's deacons or attendants from Joppa immersed Cornelius and his friends. So that if we have no law enjoining it upon one or any class of citizens, we have examples so various and numerous as to teach us that any citizen in the kingdom is an acceptable administrator when circumstances call upon him. How far expediency may suggest the propriety of a congregation making it the duty of one or more persons to attend upon such as are to be introduced into the kingdom, is a question which a respect to circumstances may decide; but on the ground of scriptural authority, every male citizen in the kingdom is an acceptable and authorized administrator. As to female citizens immersing, we have no example of the sort on record. But as in the kingdom there is neither male nor female in the Lord, should any circumstance require it, there is no law or precedent which would condemn a sister for immersing a female were it to become necessary. Even the church of Rome, the most enslaved to priestly supremacy and official holiness, allowed females to baptize in certain cases. * *

But we might as rationally and as scripturally talk about a legal administrator of prayer, of praise, or of any religious service which one can render to, or perform for, another, as for baptism. Expediency, however, may in some circumstances decree that persons may be appointed by a congregation to preach and baptize."

According to the gentleman's doctrine, you perceive, that *females* have a right to administer baptism; and yet he acknowledges, that for this he cannot find a "Thus saith the Lord," nor a precedent in the New Testament! Even persons who never were baptized, he, in the same article, admits, may, in certain cases, administer the ordinance; though for such a practice he pretends not to find one word of authority in the Scriptures! Here we find in his writings, and of course in the practice he encourages, a most glaring departure from the fundamental principle of his reformation! The principle is, to have a " Thus saith the Lord," in so many words, for every item of faith and practice, or a clear and certain precedent. Yet here he advocates a doctrine, and authorizes a practice, for which he acknowledges himself unable to find in the Scriptures either precept or precedent!—a direct and palpable departure from his published principles.

I am not the first to discover the inconsistency, and to point out the danger of his doctrine on this subject, as you will see by a letter, from which I will read an extract, written by one of his correspondents, and published in the Millenial Harbinger, (vol. iii. pp. 473, 474.) The writer says :

" Now, if I understand you, you say, there is no law making it the duty of one to immerse, to the exclusion of others ; therefore, no disorder for any one in the kingdom to immerse : and it is also to be understood that every immersed person is in the kingdom. Let us now see the dilemma to which this would lead. And first, let it be noted that men, women, children, and servants, are understood to be in the kingdom. Men, women, children, and servants, are all then authorized to immerse ; yea, they are commanded to baptize, one as much as another, and this command is directly from the King himself. No disorder then for Jane, twelve years old, who was baptized yesterday, to baptize her schoolmate Mary, eleven years old, to-day ; and Mary, to-morrow, may, without disorder, baptize her little sister Judy, nine years old ; and the day following, Judy baptizes Harriet, six years old ; and Harriet baptizes all the little girls in the neighborhood, that she is able to manage, and that will say they believe in the heart, &c. All this is perfect order in the kingdom, if there is no law authorizing one class, to the exclusion of another, to immerse. I think it unnecessary to carry this matter further. We might adduce many more cases into which such an order, or rather disorder, would run. We will admit, that if every person, so soon as baptized, were filled with the spirit of wisdom and prudence, and the understanding of men, then there would be no such danger. But this is not the case ; nor is it likely ever to be so. As long as baptism is to be administered, as long as there are sinners to be converted and baptized, there will be found babes, young men, and old men, in experience, prudence and knowledge."

The writer of this letter, who signs himself *Barnabas*, is well spoken of by Mr. Campbell, and, I presume, is a member of his church. Still, with all his prejudice in favor of the gentleman, he could not but see the dreadful disorder and confusion which such a doctrine, carried out in practice, would introduce into the church With great propriety he remarks, that if every one became wise and prudent, as soon as baptized, such a principle might be tolerated. But little boys, girls, and servants, might take it into their heads, that it is a great thing to be engaged in making and baptizing converts ; and they can do so, according to Mr. Campbell, in perfect consistency with the law of Christ!

Should more prudent and considerate persons object to having the ordinance administered, and members introduced into the church, by such children, or by others equally ignorant and rash, they are prepared with a very conclusive answer. It is perfectly certain, they might say, and by all admitted, that it is the duty of some persons to baptize. Mr. Campbell teaches, that no one class of members of the church is authorized to do it, to the exclusion of others. Therefore, say they, it is as truly our duty as yours, to administer the ordinance. Consequently, every member of the church, old and young, ignorant and wise, boys, girls, and servants, may go to work, and immerse all around them who will submit to the operation!!! I now call on my friend Mr. C. to produce a "Thus saith the Lord," or a clear precedent for such a practice. If he can find the one or the other, it is contained in a portion of the New Testament which I have entirely overlooked.

It is not difficult to ascertain the cause of the adoption of principles and practices so unauthorized, and so ruinous to the church and to the souls of men. No one, taking the Bible as his only infallible guide, ever could have thought of adopting them. The gentleman is a great enemy of creeds. Yet, when he finds his system laboring under difficulties for which the Savior did not provide, he will make such additions as the exigency demands!

Where shall we look for the origin of the doctrine and the practice of *lay-baptism?* It originated in the unscriptural doctrine of *baptismal regeneration.* The belief became common, at an early period in the history of the church, that baptism is essential to salvation—that all who died unbaptized, would be lost. In consequence of this error, difficulties immediately arose; for, in multitudes of cases, ordained ministers could not be found to administer baptism to the dying. It became necessary, consequently, to provide for exigencies which, it would seem, our Savior never saw; for which, at any rate, he made no provision, and for the best of reasons, viz: they grew out of a doctrine which he never taught. It was, therefore, determined, that, in cases of urgent necessity, when a bishop or presbyter could not be obtained, the ordinance might be administered by *laymen.* It was thought better that a layman, in the absence of a minister, should be permitted to baptize, than that a soul should be lost. As yet, however, the church had not proceeded quite so far as my friend Mr. Campbell. They were not prepared to permit *all* the members of the church indiscriminately to baptize.

The false principle which they had adopted, however, soon carried them further. It was seen, that cases might, and did occur, in which *male* members could not be present; and the souls of many might be lost, for the lack of an external ordinance. Another step was taken, and *females* were authorized, in such cases, to baptize. This practice, however, for some time, met with opposition.

But even this extension of the privilege of administering the ordinance, did not entirely compass the object, for cases might occur, in which neither male nor female members of the church could be present. The church of Rome, therefore, in the boundlessness of her charity, decided, that baptism might be validly administered by unbaptized persons, and even by Jews, infidels and Turks, providing only that they intended to do what the church does! Such was the origin, and such is the history of this singularly absurd and injurious doctrine.

The same opinions which originally suggested the necessity of lay-baptism, I doubt not, have induced my friend, Mr. Campbell, to incorporate it in his creed.

He does not think it at all certain that persons can be saved without baptism. He desires, of course, to save as many as possible. A preaching brother cannot, at all times, be had to administer immersion. Sometimes it may occur, that a male member of the church cannot be obtained. He has been charitable enough, therefore, to believe and teach that *females* may baptize, and that it is the right of all members of the church, little and big, old and young. Still, the difficult cases were not all provided for. For example, there is a man who has repented, and believed, and desires baptism, but no person, who has been immersed, can be found to administer the ordinance to him. In such cases, my friend believes that an *unimmersed* person may officiate, and the baptism will be valid. With this last provision, however, he is not quite satisfied; yet it will answer.

The doctrine of Mr. Campbell on this point is precisely the doctrine of the church of Rome; and with him, as with "holy mother," it originated in another unscriptural tenet, viz: that the soul without baptism is in danger of being lost. Their common faith placed them in a common dilemma. They must either leave souls of even penitent believers in danger of being lost, because they could not receive an external ordinance, or they must authorize a practice, for which they could find neither precept nor example in the word of God. The principle on which it is based, is false. Our Savior did not authorize it. If the principle be not false, how, I ask, did it happen that He and his apostles never provided for these cases? Such emergencies must have occurred more frequently in the days of the apostles, than at the present time; for their doctrine spread rapidly, and there were but few ministers. How did it happen, then, that they gave no intimation that unordained persons, and even females, might validly baptize? Evidently no such difficulties were known to them. If the doctrine be true, it is most marvellous, that from the beginning to the end of the New Testament, we find not a trace of it. If such emergencies do really exist, it is passing strange that our Savior made no provision for them. My friend has been engaged in providing for emergencies which the Bible did not contemplate—endeavoring to remove difficulties the Savior never discovered. Yet he proclaims, *that the Bible, and the Bible alone, is the religion of Protestants!* Now I go for the Bible, and I am prepared to acquiesce in the administration of baptism by males and females, boys and girls, if he will give me a " Thus saith the Lord," for it.

In his reply to the letter, from which I read an extract, the gentleman states, that deacons and unofficial persons, in the apostolic age, administered baptism. I hope he will adduce some proof of the truth of this declaration. I have found no example of the administration of baptism by a deacon, or an unofficial person. There is, indeed, an example of a man baptizing who *had once been* a deacon, but was afterwards an *evangelist.* But, even if at the time he administered the ordinance, he was only a deacon, still he was an *officer* in the church of Christ. But I find not an instance in all the New Testament, in which deacons, or other unordained persons, ever baptized. If the gentleman can enlighten us on this subject, I hope he will not fail to do it. If he intends still to adhere to the fundamental principle of his reformation, every one must admit that he is bound either to abandon his doctrine, or produce a " Thus saith the Lord," in so many words, or a fair precedent, to sustain it. I am prepared to yield the question in a moment, if he will show me his authority.

And it behooves him more especially to be careful on this point; for he believes baptism necessary, in order to remission of sins. If I believed that all who are not validly baptized, are in danger of losing their souls, I should desire to be very certain, that I encouraged none to administer or to receive a baptism which is not scriptural. Convince me that a man is in danger of losing his soul, if he is not baptized, and I will be very careful whom I authorize or encourage to officiate in the administration of the ordinance. I would desire the authority to be as clear as language can make it. We know that an ordained minister has the right to baptize. To this all agree. But if you put the question to Protestant Christenrlom, whether laymen have the right, the almost unanimous decision will be, that they have not. Then, according to my friend's principles of *catholicity*, he must give it up. I never would, with my present views, unite with a body of professing christians, who permit all their members—even boys and girls—to introduce into the church whom they please. If the gentleman desires christian union, he will find it necessary to abandon this unscriptural doctrine : it will ever be a stumbling block : the great majority of Bible readers cannot be persuaded that baptism by a layman is christian baptism. He is certainly bound, on his own principles, to sustain his views, by a " Thus saith the Lord," or a fair and clear example, or abandon them.

I do not know that it is necessary to proceed farther with this argument. The doctrine for which I contend is so obviously correct, that it does not admit of much discussion, especially if we confine ourselves to the Bible. I know that my friend can find some authority for part of his practice, among the christian fathers of the third and following centuries, and that he can find some episcopal ministers who have favored lay-baptism; but both they and he must rely for support on *tradition*, not on the New Testament. They can find nothing there that even remotely hints at it. The whole difficulty, as before remarked, originated in embracing first an unscriptural doctrine, and then founding upon it an unscriptural practice. Thus one error leads to another, and that again to a third. He who tells a falsehood, finds it necessary to tell a second to conceal the first; and a third to reconcile the second. So it is with error : it is always inconsistent. The first step in the path of error, creates a difficulty ; then a second is introduced to remove it ; this makes the difficulty still greater, and a third becomes necessary, and so on *ad infinitum*. There is no telling where this downward course will terminate. False doctrines necessarily lead to unscriptural practices ; and both corrupt the church, and ruin the souls of men. My friend has embraced the erroneous doctrine, and is now defending the ruinous practice based upon it.

[Here Mr. R. sat down, having occupied but forty minutes of the sixty to which he was entitled.]

Saturday, Nov. 25—11 o'clock, A. M.
[MR. CAMPBELL'S FIRST REPLY.]

MR. PRESIDENT—Mr. Rice is quite generous this morning. He has kindly tendered me just twenty minutes of his hour ; rather, I presume, as a *bonus* than that I should assist him in proving his proposition. The affirmative does not suit my friend. He soon gets out of breath. To deny is easy, but to prove is hard : *hic labor hoc opus est.* Aye, this is the drudgery, this is the toil. The *onus probandi* is, to some minds, a burdensome affair ; especially when the case is knotty and rugged, as at present. It is rolling a large rock up a steep hill. He proposes to prove that the administrator of baptism must always be an ordained elder or bishop.

I did expect, however, the *form* of argument, the appearance of proof ; especially as this has long been a darling topic to the priesthood, to the clergy, descended in any way from the family and lineage of Gregory XVI. I need not tell you, my friends, that the failure has been as complete in argument, as in filling up his time. You have all heard the head and front of his proof, and you all can witness that he has not adduced one " *Thus saith the Lord;*" one precept or precedent from the Bible in proof of his proposition. That the gentleman should have spoken to you forty minutes without quoting one verse in proof of his position, is my first argument that the ground he assumes is untenable, wholly untenable. He has, in the most satisfactory way, disproved his proposition. He sought to fill up his time, and to amuse you, by reading various extracts from my correspondents and my writings. But it did not take. The amusement was all in his own imagination. Whoever read of a minor child baptizing a minor! It was too extravagant, even to amuse. He is creating a phantom, that he may destroy it. Our views have done no such mischief. I have, indeed, an easy task—nothing to do on this question; no arguments to repel, no facts to oppose. Still I must speak for an hour; and as I shall not find very much claiming my attention in what was said, I must draw upon my own resources. His observations were sometimes just. He said that baptism was important to the subject and to the church. It adds another to her members, and only such as the Lord approves should be admitted. Well, now, if such may be the dangers to the individual and the church, from an imprudent and unauthorized administrator; if both parties may suffer so much from an improper baptism, how does this reasoning bear upon the former questions of debate? How does it affect the infant and the church? The gentleman does not see where the logic strikes. He has wounded his own cause in this remark, more than he can aid this assumption of the clergy. He argues, that the mal-administration of baptism, on the part of some novice, may subject the person baptized to an eternal injury. Of course, that must arise from his ignorance and unbelief. What a wound has he thus inflicted on the whole Presbyterian church! Had I said, that it is possible, through the ignorance and unbelief of the subject, to subject him to an eternal detriment; I might have been accused of the want of charity. But when Mr. Rice thus admits the hazard to the individuals and the church from the baptism of improper subjects, does he not more than substantiate all that I have said against infant baptism, as corrupting to the church and injurious to the child? For can there be any person less qualified for baptism, than those wholly destitute of knowledge and of faith? In the report of additions made to the church of my friend last year, I observed three hundred and sixty-five infants were *discipled*. Were not they added without knowing anything at all of the meaning of the ordinance? And are they not consequently exposed to the danger and jeopardy of which he has been speaking? Now I contend, that inasmuch as the ordained elders of the church do thus injudiciously administer baptism, they are fully as dangerous to the church and to the individuals as those minors, concerning whom the gentleman drew so largely upon his imagination, who should, with all presumption, administer the ordinance to improper subjects. His argument, then, in this case, is doubly fatal: it is fatal to the cause of infant baptism, and fatal to the ordained eldership. But it will be said, the gentleman quoted one verse. Yes—but that verse was not to the point. He quoted a verse on which prelates depend for their glebes, and popes for their thrones. A verse, indeed, containing a commission to apostles, but mentioning neither bishop, elder, nor deacon; consequently, not pointing out any of their duties. The gentleman's logic in this case, resembles that of a captain, who, when asked for his commission, refers to that of a general. By what kind of logic does a captain's commission prove that he had to perform the duties of a general? Precisely so, our friend, Mr. Rice, when asked for a commission authorizing him, as a bishop, to baptize, throws down that of an apostle.

But I have said that the gentleman has not quoted a verse on the subject before him. We have no controversy about apostles, but we have about bishops, deacons, and private members. He must show, in all logic and in all law, a commission authorizing bishops or elders to baptize, before he asks for a commission for a deacon or private member to baptize. His loose declamations about civil officers, and the necessity of them, &c., is wholly inapposite and inconclusive here. They have commissions, and can show them. This apostolic commission, he very well knows, has been claimed by the popes; and Protestants have, in all times, opposed their pretensions. Now, every argument urged by them against the lordly pretensions of the pontiffs, equally bears against his assumption. They argue that apostles were a class of officers not designed nor needed to be continued; that their office and work was incommunicable, consequently intransmissible to successors. All Protestants agree that apostles neither had, nor could have successors. They derived their commission direct from heaven, and held it from the Lord in person. I presume and hope, that I shall not have to argue this question here; and yet it would seem as if Mr. R. holds his claim on apostolic grounds, offering, in proof, an apostolic commission. If he persists in this, we shall require of him to show that apostles *could* have successors; whether they were needed; and then, whether we have any possessed of plenipotentiary powers.

Some years ago, when matters were in their incipiency here, I delivered several discourses on the subject of this commission; setting forth the important fact—that in the commencement of all institutions, extraordinary ministers and agencies had been employed, because always necessary. Creation and providence are different works—essentially different, and fully represent what we mean. Moses and the apostles were creators of new institutions. But other classes of officers, priests, judges, ministers, of various orders and courses, preserve, manage and direct them. The creators have no successors—they cannot have. Their work is soon done. God created the present heavens and earth in six days; but how many agencies have been employed in preserving them during six thousand years?

Mr. Rice ought to have set the matter more clearly and logically before us. He ought to have shown us the different work and character of ambassadors, prime functionaries, ministers extraordinary, such as law-givers, apostles, and prophets, in contrast with the work and offices of ordinary ministers, such as bishops, evangelists, and deacons; calling them by scriptural names, and opening out their respective duties. Again, he ought to have shown the difference between what is requisite to the validity of ordinances, and what is merely necessary to the good order of christian communities; and then, perhaps, there would not only have been a clearer intelligence of the question in issue, but also, very probably, an agreement in all that is essential to the prosperity and happiness of the church. I may do this for him, perhaps, by reading an extract from a Presbyterian paper, the Protestant and Herald, of his own church, under date of October 26. It is a communication from a Mr. Smith. Under the caption of the "Ordination of Calvin," the question was, and yet is, whether John Calvin, one of the founders of Presbyterian power, was ever, himself, ordained to the office of an elder or bishop? a question, by the way, which seems highly doubtful—much more so than I had formerly been accustomed to think. After giving the views and doctrines of several Presbyterians on the subject of ordination, the writer goes on to show, that ordination does not confer validity on the adminis- tration of the ordinances and observances of the church; but is simply necessary to secure good order and decency in the observance of them. My text is in the following words: " Ordination by the imposition of hands, is not essential to the validity of church ordinances, but for the regularity and good order of the christian community." [We are sorry to say that we have lost the copy of the above newspaper, from which those extracts were read, and can therefore only give the substance, from our notes, as argued in the debate.] It is conceded, that whether Calvin was ordained or not, is entirely immaterial; that ordination is not neces- sary to give either efficacy or validity to any christian ordinance. It is only essential to having the ordinances duly kept, and properly attended to; and that, therefore, it is not a question at all affecting validity, but order and propriety of administration.

As we desire to furnish elements of thought for those who can think, and desire to think for themselves, I shall treat the audience to a more rich and valuable extract from the pen of the aforesaid good Dr. Carson, of Tubermore, Ireland; from whose learned Baptist pen, so profoundly immersed in Grecian lore and hoary antiquity, Mr. Rice has learned and quoted so much. Mr. Carson is a good, orthodox Baptist minister, whom I have seen and heard in my youthful days. He is the pastor of a country congregation of several hundred members, who practice weekly commu- nion, and, also, to some extent, free communion. He is a clear, argu- mentative, and vigorous speaker; more distinguished for acuteness and profoundness, than for eloquence. He is so orthodox as to be often called upon, on great occasions, such as anniversaries, pentecosts, and jubilees, by the Established Church, and by Dissenters of different com- munions. I believe he does not like me very well, because he took it into his head that I must be (from various evil reports) imbued with Uni- tarianism; but, on this point, I am just as orthodox as he is, and as ver- acious and unambiguous, also. He is, indeed, a paragon of orthodoxy; is sometimes annually sent for to preach in London and in Edinburgh. But here comes an extract from a jubilee sermon:

" *The duty of exertion to propagate the gospel extends to all christians without exception.* Every christian is a soldier, and every christian soldier must fight to put his Lord in possession of his rightful dominions. More is required of some than of others, but something is required of every one. The great body of christians may not be able to address public assemblies, but there is not one of them who may not tell his neighbor the way to heaven. Cannot the simplest man make known to others the ground on which he rests his own hope of salvation? If he knows the truth so as to be saved by it, he may declare it to others so as to save them. What can make it improper for an uneducated man to speak to his companions on the one thing needful? Can he speak to them on matters of worldly business, and can he not speak to them on the truth that saves the soul? Can he teach the mysteries of his trade, and can he not teach the way in which God's justice and mercy harmonize in the justification of the ungodly by faith in Christ Jesus?

Uneducated christians, even the poorest, have in private life more favora- ble opportunities of communicating the gospel to their associates, than the most learned and the most elevated in rank. The manners of the world make it difficult, if not impossible, to introduce the gospel into certain cir- cles. When the rich wish to preach the gospel, they must in general go to the poor They seldom have access to the ear of their own circle. Even the highest christian nobility will find their efforts impeded by innumerable obstacles in the forms of life in the upper ranks. When God designed that Cæsar and the mighty men of Rome should hear the gospel of Paul, he sent him as a prisoner to stand for his life before the emperor. Had Paul gone to Rome as a preacher, though he had been a Demosthenes, he might never have gained a hearing from Cæsar. Priests and princes would have represented him merely as a fanatic, and the ear of majesty might never have heard the gospel from his lips. In proportion to a man's elevation in rank is he shut out from the gospel; and in this respect the poor have the highest privileges. They hear and are saved, while the rich and the mighty perish without hearing it, though it may sound every where around them. How is this manifested and confirmed by town missionaries! The word of life can be sent into the hovels of vice, while the lordly palace, which has perhaps more need of it, must be passed by. The poor are always accessible, and the poorest christian may have, every day, opportunities of declaring the truth, from which the highest christian may be excluded. If the people about him are wicked, still he may find means to gain their ear about the value of the soul, and the redemption that is in Christ. The poorest and weakest member of a church may have access to innumerable persons from whom the pastor is entirely shut out, and will be heard when the pastor would give intolerable offence.

The deadly heresy which confines the preaching of the gospel to office conveyed by a certain succession, is an infernal machine for destroying the souls of men. It is one of the great artifices of Satan to spike the cannon on the gospel batteries. What can more effectually serve the kingdom of light? But it is as unscriptural as it is irrational. The scriptures know nothing of such a succession. It is the invention of the man of sin, calculated to extinguish the light, and promote the empire of darkness. And whatever may be the mode of conveying office, the preaching of the gospel, either publicly or privately, is not confined to office. Every christian has a right to preach the gospel, and according to his opportunities and his abilities it is his duty to preach it. This vile dogma of Oxford is self-evidently false. If the gospel is true, can there be any danger of sin in proclaiming its truths? If the gospel is salvation, and if God wills the salvation of men, can it be sinful to tell them of that which saves from hell? What would you think of a senator who should rise up in the British senate house, declaring that no watchmen ought to be employed in the city of London but those who have a regular succession from the watchmen who lived at the foundation of the city, and that, though the city were fired at innumerable points, no man had a right to cry, ' Fire! fire!' but the legal watchmen? It is only in religion that the effusions of folly and absurdity are dignified as wisdom."

I have read this pithy extract from the Millenial Harbinger, from which there are so many excellent things read you by my worthy friend—and in which there are many other good things to be read by others as well as he; and, I hope, for other purposes. The doctrine of the extract, my readers need not be told, is mine. I subscribe to it every word, and have long since, even in the days of the Christian Baptist, expressed them under other images.

That the *official grace* and *jus divinum* of the clergy, is a gratuitous assumption, I believe all sensible men of much intelligence very well know. I do certainly know it, and have long since exposed it: still I am a cordial friend of good order and of a christian ministry. As Mr. R. has preceded my way into political society, I will take a little excursion with him, and endeavor to illustrate my position, by a very intelligible comparison or two.

Man, in the state of nature, if any one ever saw him there, is a very free and sovereign kind of a dependent. He is as free as Ishmael, though the slave of a hundred wants and tyrannic passions; but, like the deer of the forest, he roams at large. At last, tired of his wanderings over nature's wilds, he courts society, and would fondly purchase it at some price. He is asked to surrender so many of his assumed natural and inalienable rights and liberties, for the sake of other advantages found in the fellowship and intercommunication of co-ordinate beings. He agrees to sell so many rights for so many privileges. The bargain is now closed, and is called a *constitution.* From the day it is signed, he uses those surrendered rights no more. To use those sold *rights,* would now be politically *wrong.* He has got for them a full price, and therefore they are no longer his. He still reserves the right of looking at the sun, of breathing the air, of eating and drinking earth's bounties, of walking on the earth, at least on the high-roads. He claims as much of mother earth as he can cover with his person, and never parts with the power of talking, nor sells the dear liberty of speech. But the law-giving power, with the power of judging and government, he has sold; and therefore, he can, of right, use these functions no more, unless they are granted to him by the persons with whom he has identified his fortunes.

From the moment the social compact political is formed, society being organized, its organs dispense all its special privileges according to law. Then no man takes upon himself any honor, office, or work, without a special call and appointment. Just so is it in the church.

When there is no church, but disciples of Christ scattered abroad, not organized, there can be no officers. When then any one desires baptism, any one to whom he applies may administer it. When a few brethren in one family, or neighborhood, organize themselves to meet once a week to shew forth the Lord's death, to read the Scriptures, sing and pray together, having no ordained officer among them, they appoint one of themselves, to break " the loaf of blessings," and to distribute " the cup of salvation." All this the New Testament, reason, common sense approve. But when societies are formed, christian communities created, and a church organization established by agreement; then, indeed, all offices are filled by the voice and ordination of the people. When that is accomplished, no one has a right, either inherent, natural, or divine, to discharge social duties, without a call and appointment from his compeers and associates. Do not Presbyterians, sensible, intelligent Presbyterians, assent to these views? I sincerely think they do. They have no faith in the doctrine of hereditary grace—of official power transmitted from age to age, through the leaky and crazy corporations of human bodies. Suppose a solitary Testament was borne on the wings of the wind to some savage island, filled with inhabitants. A first picks it up, reads, understands it, believes it. He communicates its intelligence to B, C, and D; they also receive it with joy. Presently, the hills and dales echo with the name of the Lord. They tell the glad tidings. Hundreds believe; they baptise them—consecrate them. They all decide that christianity is essentially a social system; that its tendency is to form a grand community—intelligent, pure, holy, happy, and co-extensive with humanity. Soon as they have organized and understood their calling, they elect and solemnly devote to the work by prayer and the imposition of the hands of a few, appointed by the many, A, B, C, and D, to the work of the ministry among them, in whatever departments of labor they may require. Henceforth all public social duties are performed by this ministry, whom practice makes more perfect in the work. These persons publicly preach, baptize, or preside in their assemblies, teach and govern, as the case may be.

I aim not at a perfect picture; I only give a sketch, a rude outline, that my views and my argument, or rather objection, to the position of Mr. R., may be appreciated. I do not say his arguments, but his position; for argument, or proof, from him I have not yet heard.

These views must be, perhaps they are already, approved by my Presbyterian friends. My regular readers will recognize them, as having been taught by me from my first visit to this commonwealth. They are held in various forms in the Christian Baptist. I am peculiarly gratified to say, that they are views very generally diffused throughout this great continent, and especially, to have recently read them from the pen of one of the greatest men of the age—and a very high functionary in the Episcopal church of England—no less a man than archbishop Whateley, of the province of Dublin; whose fame as a scholar is in all our colleges, and as a nervous, vigorous, and clear writer, has few superiors at the present time. I shall read a few pages from his recent work on the kingdom of Christ. I adopt it as a part of my argument, and commend it especially to my Episcopal and Presbyterian friends in Kentucky, and every where.

"Suppose, for instance, a number of emigrants, bound for some colony, to be shipwrecked on a desert island, such as afforded them means of subsistence, but precluded all reasonable hope of their quitting it: or suppose them to have taken refuge there as fugitives from intolerable oppression, or from a conquering enemy, (no uncommon case in ancient times): or to be the sole survivors of a pestilence or earthquake which had destroyed the rest of the nation: no one would maintain that these shipwrecked emigrants or fugitives were bound, or were permitted, to remain—themselves and their posterity—in a state of anarchy, on the ground of there being no one among them who could claim hereditary or other right to govern them. It would clearly be right, and wise, and necessary, that they should regard themselves as constituted, by the very circumstances of their position, a civil community; and should assemble to enact such laws, and appoint such magistrates, as they might judge most suitable to their circumstances. And obedience to those laws and governors, as soon as the constitution was settled, would become a moral duty to all the members of the community: and this, even though some of the enactments might appear, or might be (though not at variance with the immutable laws of morality, yet) considerably short of perfection. The king, or other magistrates thus appointed, would be legitimate rulers; and the laws framed by them, valid and binding. The precept of ' submitting to every ordinance of man, for the Lord's sake,' and of ' rendering to all, their due,' would apply in this case as completely as in respect of any civil community that exists."—*Whateley's Kingdom of Christ*, New York, 1843, 12mo. p. 193.

" But it would be absurd to maintain, that men placed in such a situation as has been here supposed are to be shut out, generation after generation, from the christian ordinances and the gospel covenant. Their circumstances would constitute them (as many as could be brought to agree in the essentials of faith and christian worship) a christian community; and would require them to do that which, if done *without* such necessity, would be schismatical. To make regulations for the church thus constituted, and to appoint as its ministers the fittest persons that could be found among them, and to celebrate the christian rites, would be a proceeding not productive, as in the other case, of division, but of union. And it would be a compliance—clearly pointed out to them by the providence which had placed them in that situation—with the manifest will of our Heavenly Master, that christians should live in a religious community, under such officers and such regulations as are essential to the existence of every community.

To say that christian ministers thus appointed would be, to all intents and purposes, real legitimate christian ministers, and that the ordinances of such a church would be no less valid and efficacious (supposing always that they are not in themselves superstitious and unscriptural) than those of any other church, is merely to say in other words that it would *be* a real christian church; possessing consequently, in common with *all communities* of whatever kind, the essential rights of a community to have officers and by-laws; and possessing also, in common with all *christian* communities, (*i. e.* churches) the especial sanction of our Lord, and his promise of ratifying ('binding in heaven') its enactments.

It really does seem not only absurd, but even impious, to represent it as the Lord's will, that persons who are believers in his gospel should, in consequence of the circumstances in which his Providence has placed them, condemn themselves and their posterity to live as heathens, instead of conforming as closely as those circumstances will allow to the institutions and directions of Christ and his apostles, by combining themselves into a christian society, regulated and conducted, in the best way they can, on gospel principles. And if such a society does enjoy the divine blessing and favor, it follows that its proceedings, its enactments, its officers, are legitimate and apostolical, as long as they are conformable to the principles which the apostles have laid down and recorded for our use: even as those (of whatever race 'after the flesh') who embraced and faithfully adhered to the gospel, were called by the apostle 'Abraham's seed,' and 'the Israel of God.'

The ministers of such a church as I have been supposing, would rightly claim 'apostolical succession,' because they would *rightfully hold the same office* which the apostles conferred on those 'elders whom they ordained in every city.' And it is impossible for any one of sound mind seriously to believe that the recognition of such claims, in a case like the one here supposed, affords a fair precedent for men who should wantonly secede from the church to which they had belonged, and take upon themselves to ordain ministers and form a new and independent church according to their own fancy."—p. 197.

I will yet read two other extracts: one showing that there is no certainty whatever in any pretended succession from the apostles. A layman may have baptized us all, for any thing which the rolls of time or the annals of the church can show. It is a proverb incontrovertibly true, "the stream can rise no higher than the fountain." Myriads of children, some of whom became priests and Levites, deacons and bishops, were sprinkled by private men and women, during hundreds of years, by the Romanists. There is not a man in Kentucky can trace his baptism back to any thing better than a lay origin, if archbishop Whateley told the truth.

"If, as has been above remarked, a man is taught that view of apostolical succession which makes every thing depend on the unbroken series between the apostles and the *individual* minister from whom each man receives the sacraments, or the individual bishop conferring ordination, (a fact which never can be ascertained with certainty,) and he is then presented with proofs, *not of this*, but of a different fact instead—the apostolical succession, *generally*, of the great body of the ministers of his church; and if he is taught to acquiesce with consolatory confidence in the regulations and ordinances of the church, not on such grounds as have been above laid down, but on the ground of their exact conformity to the model of the 'ancient church,' which exact conformity is in many cases more than can be satisfactorily proved, and in some can be easily *disproved;* the result of the attempt so to settle men's minds must be, with many, the most distressing doubt and perplexity. And others again, when taught to 'blend with Scripture,' as a portion of revelation, the traditions of the first three, or first four, or first seven, or fifteen centuries, may find it difficult to understand when, and where, and why they are to stop short abruptly in the application of the principles they have received: why, if one general council is to be admitted as having divine authority to bind the conscience and supersede private judgment, another is to be rejected by private judgment; and that too by the judgment of men who are not agreed with each other, or even with themselves, whether the council of Trent, for instance, is to be regarded as the beginning of the Romish apostasy, or as a promising omen of improvement in the church of Rome. That man must be strangely constituted, who can find consolatory security for his faith in such a guide; who can derive satisfactory confidence from the oracles of a Proteus!"—*King. of Christ*, p. 205.

" A member of the Anglican church, (I mean a sincere and thoroughly consistent member of it,) ought to feel a full conviction—and surely there are good grounds for that conviction—both that the reforms they introduced were no more than were loudly called for by a regard for gospel truth; and that the church, as constituted by them, does possess, in its regulations and its officers, ' apostolical succession,' in the sense in which it is essential that a christian community *should* possess it, viz. in being a regularly constituted christian society, framed in accordance with the fundamental principles taught by the apostles and their great Master.

Successors, in the apostolic office, the apostles have none. As *witnesses of the resurrection*, as *dispensers of miraculous gifts*, as inspired *oracles of divine revelation*, they have no successors. But as *members*, as *ministers*, as *governors* of christian communities, their successors are the regularly admitted members, the lawfully ordained ministers, the regular and recognized governors, of a regularly subsisting christian church; especially of a church which, conforming in fundamentals,—as I am persuaded ours does,—to gospel principles, claims and exercises no rights beyond those which have the clear sanction of our great Master, as being essentially implied in the very character of a community."—pp. 240, 241.

Here, then, is indisputable evidence from one of the most learned prelates of the Church of England, who is a fair exponent of the accumulated intelligence of that enlightened community—a community as well read in the true archeology of christianity as any church establishment in the world, that ordination descent from apostolic times is a mere figment of the human brain, and that no such doctrine is taught in the Bible. With archbishop Whateley, we say—" that a regularly constituted christian society, framed in accordance with the fundamental principles taught us by the apostles, and their great Master," has the only true, real apostolic succession of divine authenticity, and, therefore, we, as a christian community, have it.

Whenever, then, a christian community legitimately arises out of such circumstances, as already described, sanctioned by the New Testament— that is, holding the same doctrines and ordinances, customs and usages, when it appoints officers, and when they dispense ordinances, they are as divine and authoritative as any other officers and ordinances in any christian community on earth. This, we regard, as our true position as a community of churches—and all those passages read from our writings in their contextual meaning, do neither more nor less than set forth these views with a reference to christian society and its various circumstances.

Among the eccentricities of orthodoxy, I am called to notice one that is not among the least. Mr. Rice said something about graceless men, wicked knaves or hypocrites, that might baptize thousands under our system of operations. Well; exaggeration does better in poetry than in prose, and in florid and highly impassioned eloquence than in a frigid and dry logical analysis. But to afford the gentleman all the advantages of his hypothesis, admit some persons possessing true faith were baptized by graceless administrators; what then? Would official grace, his ecclesiastic authority, have made it any better? And more important still—would the faith, piety, and benefit of the subject, be either injured or annihilated by the character of the administrator!! But yet the eccentricity is not fully stated Ordained men, I mean in Mr. Rice's own views of ordination, are sometimes graceless men. And private members are sometimes men of unquestionable piety and moral worth. Now, suppose an unordained saint baptize A B, and an ordained reprobate baptize C D, why should the want of ordination on the part of the saint impair his act; and the want of piety on the part of the sinner, not impair his act? Is not that to place official grace above the true and real grace of God? Bring up the case before judge Orthodoxy, and he will decide for the official against the real grace of God, so far as the act of officiation is concerned; and hence many would rather take the eucharist loaf from the hands of a church dignitary, though evidently graceless, than from the hands of a saint of the purest excellence, on whose pate was not laid the hands of some prelate or presbytery. Protestants have sometimes said, that as christian ordinances receive not any virtue, neither do they lose any efficacy or spiritual benefit, from the hands of him that does administer them. So I teach.

With regard to the extracts read from the Millenial Harbinger, as usual, they are misapplied. The very commencement of them indicates that, viz: " *There is no law in the christian Scriptures authorizing any one* CLASS OF CITIZENS *in the christian kingdom to immerse to the exclusion of any other class of citizens.* Apostles, evangelists, deacons, and unofficial persons are all represented as immersing, when occasion called for it." Now, the question here is not about adults and minors—nor about males and females, but about *classes of persons.* It is not sexes nor ages, nor conditions, but classes of persons—apostles, evangelists, deacons, and unofficial persons. We affirm that there were no classes. We have given " *express precedents*" of all classes baptizing, and that is all our principles call for. Whether intentional or not, a person may read extracts so as not to give a fair representation of the views of a writer. We never, by word or action, sanctioned either females or minors as baptists. These come not under the head of those classes of which we were writing. We spoke of official classes. We have laymen, and deacons, deaconesses, elders, evangelists, pastors, besides apostles and prophets. There is no " Thus saith the Lord," in precept nor precedent, conferring baptism to, nor enjoining it upon, any one of these classes. Mr. Rice cannot shew a case, not one word or example of the sort, in the whole New Testament. I challenge him to produce one single verse, containing in it a clear, or even an obscure " *Thus saith the Lord.*" I predict he will not even make the attempt. He need not tell you it is not necessary, for it is, necessary; especially in the case of a bishop. That is essential to his affirmation.

I call upon Mr. Rice to furnish any precept in the New Testament authorizing or enjoining a *bishop* or an *elder* to baptize any one. I call upon him to produce an *example* of a bishop or an elder baptizing, *as such*, officially, if he pleases. He cannot do it. Now, the proposition which he has undertaken to sustain, calls for this. He affirms that an ordained bishop or elder has a right to administer the ordinance of baptism. He affirms more than that—for he undertakes to prove that only he has a right to baptize. If he cannot prove the first, certainly he cannot prove the second. Well, now, it lies upon him by every principle of logic, of reason, and of law to produce their commission. I will admit that such a commission will settle the matter, if it only says in effect—*Let the elders baptize.* I have said he can produce no example of any bishop baptizing any one as such; nor a precept so enjoining; and, therefore, it is impossible to prove that they only have a right to baptize. *I* care not about views of expediency, I go for law. But he delights in forming and displaying extreme cases of the extension or of the abuse of a principle. He will have boys baptizing men, and females baptizing females, as the result of a universal license. We, however, neither acknowledge nor grant such licenses. Yet I would like to put an extreme case:—Here is a father of fifty, with a son of fifteen, who have just escaped to a desert island from the wreck of a ship. They have carried with them a Bible. The son had been baptized and was a member of church one year before he was taken by his father to sea. The old gentleman had long been a sceptic. His misfortunes brought him to reflect, and called his attention to the Bible. His daily readings and the conversation and excellent demeanor of his son, overcame his scepticism. The Lord opened his mind, he believed the gospel, and became anxious to be baptized. After much deliberation and painful reflection upon his circumstances, he one day asked his son to accompany him to the sea-shore and baptize him. He did so. Was it wrong?

I am now prepared to say, in view of all the circumstances, that it was right, perfectly right. But now suppose any one should publish through this community that I taught that boys might baptize men, and sons their parents; and that I said that persons might be so appointed by churches; would that person do me justice or injustice? would he publish truth or falsehood? The principle involved in this case will one day condemn many for their very injurious calumnies and slanders, based on still more slender and unjustifiable grounds.

The case of Roger Williams and eleven others with him, was brought forward the other day. There was not an immersed believer in all Providence plantation, in all the district of country known to any of this little band of believers. The question with them was, "*What shall we do?* We all believe the gospel, we all desire to be baptized, but there is no one to baptize us. Shall we go or send one to England to be immersed, and await his return, or now immediately baptize each other and form a church?" They decided to obey the Lord promptly. One of the twelve immersed Roger Williams, then Williams immersed the eleven. So commenced American immersion! Well, now, I am such a radical, and yet I go as much for order as any man; I fearlessly give my opinion that they did right. Mr. Rice, probably, would have got up a mission, and despatched one of the company to Rome, or Constantinople, or London, and imported official grace! They obeyed common sense and the Bible, and left behind them a noble triumph of mental independence. Had the patriarch of Constantinople, or the pope of Rome, or his grace the archbishop of Canterbury, been present, or any other ecclesiastic in the world, and performed the service, it would, to say the least, have been no better done. But if asked, would such a course of things be orderly or christian-like, at this time, in this country? I decidedly say, No: it would be superlatively incongruous and disorderly.

Simpletons and odd fellows always argue from extreme cases. Supreme necessity gives law, and incontrollable circumstances must control us. Our method is, so far as known to me: churches appoint all their officers, their bishops, deacons, and evangelists. They authorize some one to be the *baptist* for the congregation. Sometimes, generally indeed, he is the evangelist, or an elder, or a deacon; he is, for the most part, some one of the ministry of the church. Comes it not, however, with an ill grace from Mr. R., to be fastidious about the administrator of baptism; coming as it does in room of circumcision? The gentleman adroitly converts all my allusions to the action or subject of baptism into a proof of my not being satisfied with the discussion of them. This is to prevent the proper use of them as illustrations, and, indeed, as part of the evidence of the design of baptism. I have not, however, exhausted any of these subjects by a great deal. Enough, indeed, has been said to meet the case and dispose of all that was alledged on the opposite side. Such, at least, is my opinion.

I will, then, recur to circumcision for an illustration of the case before us. The gentleman will have baptism in place of circumcision. Now, as Zipporah circumcised the son of Moses, and parents generally circumcised their children, why be so fastidious about the administrator of baptism? So complaisant am I, for the sake of argument, I will make another extreme case. Suppose two ladies in a foreign land, one a christian, the other not, should be sold into slavery among Turks, or pagans as barbarous as they. Their misfortunes soften the heart of the non-professor, and become a cause of her devotion to the Bible. She believes and repents. At her earnest solicitation her companion baptizes her, and she assumes the christian profession. Certainly Mr. Rice, with mother Zipporah in his eye, will not demur! I will not repudiate even this extreme case. I am of the opinion it was all right. But who thence infers, that I would license the sisters to baptize, does me no more justice than Mr. Rice.

These concessions are free-will offerings, uncalled for; but I desire to express more fully than on any previous occasion, my liberty in the gospel, and also my devotion to the most perfect good order in the christian community. I must then add, that those things, lawful and expedient in extreme cases, would, in my judgment, be both unlawful and inexpedient in our circumstances. Still, be it observed, *that the efficacy and salutary power of ordinances is in God and in the recipient, not in the human mediator.* The faith and preparation of heart, on the part of the recipient, is every thing; and the Lord's promises are to him directly, without any human instrumentality.

You will recollect that Mr. Rice read some extracts from Perrin, or some other historian, on the subject of succession, and made an attack upon the reputation of Mr. Jones, the Baptist historian, whose history of the Waldenses I commended some years ago, over whose shoulders the gentleman, in his friendship, hurled a javelin at me, for the sin of recommending said work, because it had traced up, or furnished a part of the train of succession of baptized churches, from the christian era to the present day. The work was first introduced and recommended to the community by elder Spencer Cone, of New York. I recommended, and still recommend it, not because of any particular respect for its author, nor from any indebtedness to the Baptists that introduced it: for neither Mr. Jones nor they have any claims upon my generosity whatever. It was then a tribute to truth, and to the oppressed cause of the only true baptism. But I did not happen to have the proper documents before me the other day, and could not at that time disprove the allegation.

This Mr. Jones is now charged by Mr. Rice, with a willful, perverse suppression of the truth, and thereby making Perrin bear testimony on the wrong side of the question.

Before attempting the defence of Mr. Jones from the aspersions thrown upon his reputation, the subject of a succession of churches practicing the christian ordinances, without any connection with the gospel establishment—themselves contending for views similar to those I am offering on this subject—demands a remark or two. I make these remarks.

In reference to the subject of succession as respects the question before us, let me be permitted to say, that since the days of bishop Sylvester till now, there have been immersed multitudes of persons not members of the church of Rome. They have been called by many names, such as Danites, Paulicians, Henricians, Novatians, Petrobrusians, Waldenses, Albigenses, &c., &c.—a mighty host of men, never under the direct influence of popery, who, in all ages, bore their firm and unwavering testimony against all its assumptions and pollutions. While the gentleman was telling you the other day, that, on our principles, the church was extinct for ages; many of you, with myself, were no doubt amazed at his inadvertence to those millions that opposed papal aggrandizement, and human tradition, down to the time of the reformation. Many have affirmed, that Luther and Calvin only translated the views of these witnesses into German and French, and sent them out in a new dress. They say that Savoy and other portions of Europe, long before Protestantism was born, had promulged and sustained all the cardinal truths, and more truth than was ever recognized by any Protestant throne or kingdom. Highly as I esteem the Protestant reformation, and the mighty men of that day, I esteem others more than they. These men originated nothing; but they concentrated and variously embodied and reproduced, in new and impressive forms, the tenets of Protestants, in fact, who had lived and died centuries before they were born. Still they were God's chosen vessels to accomplish at the proper time a mighty moral revolution, whose mighty sway and extended empire over the human mind and the destinies of the world, have not yet been fully appreciated.—[*Time expired.*

Saturday, Nov. 25—12 o'clock, M.
[MR. RICE'S SECOND ADDRESS.]

MR. PRESIDENT—Before entering upon the discussion of the subject under consideration, I wish to make a remark or two respecting Mr. Jones' history, which has been again brought up by my friend. In all the discussions in which I have engaged, I have met with nothing which has so much astonished me as the course now pursued by Mr. Campbell, in introducing Mr. Jones and his documents on the present occasion. As an apology for this singular conduct, he told you, that I read something from Jones on the doctrine of *succession*. This, however, is not the fact. I read not one word from Jones on this subject; not a word. Moreover, I have introduced nothing in my argument, to-day, concerning it. The gentleman might as well talk about the mountains in the moon, as about the doctrine of succession, in connection with the subject now under discussion. Nor have I read, in your hearing, any thing from Jones, on the question, whether baptism is to be administered only by an ordained minister. I read from Jones, a paragraph, to prove that in quoting Perrin's history, he left out what related to infant baptism, and inserted in its place, " baptism according to the primitive church." I have repeatedly expressed the conviction, that Mr. C. was dissatisfied with his efforts on the subject of infant baptism. Now, if he is anxious to discuss that subject again, let him say so, and let the necessary arrangements be made. I do protest against the introduction of the subject of infant baptism, whilst another, and totally different subject, is being discussed. I will discuss but one subject at a time. I really pity the cause that requires a man of the standing of my friend to violate our rules, by again introducing, and attempting to discuss a subject, after it has been disposed of. He must, indeed, be in an awful case, that he cannot get along without perpetually harping upon that subject. But, he says, he had not his books when the subject was under discussion. Why did he not have them? I trust the question of infant baptism, and of the faith of the Waldenses, will not be again introduced, until he is prepared to enter into arrangements for a new discussion of it. He asserts that there were anti-Pedo-baptists in all ages. If this were even true, what has it to do with the proposition now before us? I would tread the cause of Pedo-baptism under my feet, if I could not defend it without resorting to such means. If it will not bear fair and honorable discussion; if it cannot be sustained without the violation of the rules which I have bound myself to regard, I will abandon it forever. I will debate but one subject at a time; I will not allow myself to be diverted from the proposition before us, to a second debate, on a subject fully discussed several days since.

I will now resume the discussion. My friend says, that I have produced no passage of Scripture to sustain the proposition that baptism is to be administered only by a bishop or presbyter. The question in debate is not whether ordained ministers may baptize, but whether others, not ordained, are authorized to administer the ordinance? He does not deny that bishops or presbyters have the right to baptize; but he maintains, that all the members of the church have the same right. If they have, let it be proved; if my friend cannot find the Scripture authorizing them to baptize, it follows, of course, that lay-baptism is wholly without authority; and if without authority, it is not valid.

Again; the question is not, whether a regular succession from the apostles is essential to ordination; but whether private members of the church, persons admitted to be unordained, may administer baptism?

My friend says, as soon as a church is organized, it ought to appoint persons to administer the ordinance. This strikes me as being not exactly consistent with the sentiments set forth in his Harbinger; his language is as follows: " But we might as rationally, and as scripturally, talk about a legal administrator of prayer, of praise, or of any religious service which one can render to, and perform for, another, as for baptism. *Expediency, however, may, in some circumstances, decree that persons may be appointed by a congregation to preach and baptize.*"—Millen. Harb. vol. iii. p. 237. Does he here say that suitable persons *ought generally*, or *universally*, to be appointed to administer baptism? No. But he says expediency may, *in some circumstances*, require such a course. Is this the *general law* of which he was speaking?

He says, I misrepresented his views, as expressed in the Harbinger, where he states, that the administration of baptism is not confined to any *class* of citizens of the kingdom. But the difficulty is, that he contends that females have the right to baptize, and yet acknowledges that he finds neither precept nor example authorizing them to do so. This is not all. He maintains, in so many words, that "there is no law in the christian Scriptures, authorizing any one class of citizens in the christian kingdom to immerse, to the exclusion of any other class of citizens;" and that "there is neither male nor female in the Lord"—that consequently, a female may immerse a female, "were it to become necessary."

And now, I ask, who is to judge when circumstances require that females, or other unordained persons, shall baptize? Is the church to be called together, to determine this question? This is not pretended. Does it not, then, follow, that every one is to judge for himself? If a little girl thinks it right to baptize her little associates; or if a little boy thinks proper to baptize his play-fellows; or a servant, his fellow-servants; who, but themselves, is to judge of the circumstances? If the doctrine of Mr. Campbell be true, that every citizen of the kingdom, every church-member has the right to baptize—the license is, of necessity, universal. Each individual must act, in these matters of such momentous interest to the church, and to the eternal happiness of individuals, on his own responsibility.

But Mr. C. tells us, that no case has ever occurred, of minors undertaking to administer the ordinance of baptism. This may be true; but it is not because the doctrine he advocates, has prevented it; but because the people have had better sense than to carry it into practice. It is not the soundness of the doctrine that has prevented his church from being corrupted and disgraced by such disorders; but the fact, that common prudence has kept the members within narrower bounds than the faith he has inculcated. But when I have shown, that if the doctrine were fully carried out in practice, it would lead to results the most disastrous to the church, as well as to individuals, I have given evidence the most conclusive, that it cannot be of divine authority. It will not answer, to say that nobody has yet carried the practice as far as the doctrine authorizes; that does not prove that the doctrine is sound. I am looking at what would be the result, if it were fully carried out in practice, and showing that evil, and only evil, would result to the church. And Mr. Campbell attempts to evade the force of the argument, by saying, those disorders have not actually occurred!

The apostolical office, he tells us, is incommunicable; and the apostles had no successors. This is true, so far as the peculiar circumstances in which they were placed required extraordinary gifts and authority; but so far as baptizing and preaching are concerned, it is not true. It is admitted, that the apostles were ordained to baptize and teach; this, no one, with the Bible in his hand, can dispute. Nor can it be denied, that those who were ordained by them, were authorized to perform those duties. I do not say, that Timothy and Titus were, in every sense of the word, their *successors;* but that they were appointed to teach and baptize, none certainly will deny.

But I will not discuss the doctrine of the succession, because it is not the question before us. There are two questions confusedly introduced into the gentleman's speech. The first is, whether a regular line of succession from the apostles to the present day, is essential to the validity of *ordination;* and the second, whether a man must be *scripturally ordained,* before he is authorized to administer baptism. If you say, that a particular church, assembled for the purpose, has the right to ordain presbyters, I

3 D

will not oppose it now. If you maintain, that a man is lawfully ordained, when the members of the church set him apart to the ministerial office, so far as this debate is concerned, I will not call in question the correctness of your opinion. But the simple and only question now before us, and the only question I will now discuss, is, *whether a man, in order to baptize, must be scripturally ordained*. Now, all that my friend read from archbishop Whateley, was upon another subject—the doctrine of succession; and he might as well have read us a dissertation on the mountains of the moon, or the climate and productions of Africa. The archbishop is proving, that a regular succession from the apostles is not necessary to the validity of ordination, and that no man can trace such succession. It is not at all necessary for me to controvert his position. But does he maintain, that every citizen of the kingdom, every church-member, has a right to baptize? He does not say so. He supposes a company of christians cast upon an island, without an ordained minister, and desiring to enjoy the ordinances of God's house; and he contends, that ministers appointed by them are lawful ministers. I am not going to dispute the correctness of the position now, though I might on another occasion. The question before us, let me again say, is not *how* ministers are to be lawfully ordained, but whether, in order to administer baptism, they must be ordained *at all*. Concerning the question, whether individuals selected and set apart to the office of the ministry, by a company of christians on an island, would be validly ordained, I have nothing to say. But, whatever scriptural ordination may be, the question is, whether that is necessary, or essential to the proper and scriptural administration of baptism. Bishop Whateley is discussing one subject, and we are discussing another. Let us, then, keep distinctly in view, the subject in debate. My friend endeavors to confound these questions, but it is merely to conceal the weakness of his cause.

Mr. Smyth, from whose writings Mr. Campbell quoted an extract, is, like myself, comparatively a young man. We were in the theological seminary at the same time. I might, perhaps, not agree with every sentiment contained in the passage quoted. It is, however, of no service to Mr. Campbell's cause. Mr. Smyth expresses the opinion, that the mere ceremony of laying on hands is not essential to the office. There may be a question, whether the laying on of hands is necessary, or whether the mere selection of men to perform the duties of the office, is sufficient to constitute them ministers of the Gospel; but that question is not now before us.

Neither have I any thing to say about Mr. Carson's views of the doctrine of succession. His bare assertions, however, even if they related to the subject before us, I should not regard as authority. If he will produce the Scriptures in support of his views, I will weigh his arguments with candor; but when he gives his *opinion*, I am willing to let it go for what it is worth.

The gentleman is of opinion, that on the subject under discussion he and Presbyterians do not differ very materially. I believe, however, that they do differ from him *toto cœlo*. They will never admit, that all the members of the church, male and female, old and young, may, under any circumstances, administer the sacrament of baptism.

By way of illustrating his views, he refers to civil society, and says correctly, that in an unorganized state, individual rights are more extensive, than after the civil compact has been formed. In the former he may, of right, do many things which become unlawful, when he has become a member of an organized society. I am very much pleased with the illustration. And now, if you can find the period when the christian church was in an unorganized state, I will cheerfully admit, that there has been a time when unordained persons might baptize, as circumstances seemed to require. But the truth is, it never was in an unorganized state. Our Savior, at a very early period in the history of the world, organized his church; and from that day to this it never has been in an unorganized state; and consequently there never has been a time when laymen might baptize. I admit that my friend's church is unorganized; for he has informed us, that such is the fact. And he has been writing and laboring faithfully for two years past to get up an organization of some kind; but he has not yet succeeded. But *the church of Christ* is not unorganized. It has never been in an unorganized state. And as in an organized civil society no man may venture to discharge the functions of an office with which he has not been lawfully invested; so, for reasons far more important, can no man perform the duties of an office in Christ's church, which he has not been appointed to fill. It would be just as proper and as lawful for a man, on his own responsibility, to act as sheriff, judge, or president, as for one who is a private member of the church of Christ to officiate either in preaching or baptizing. It is just as right in the one case as in the other. Since the church has been organized, laws enacted, and the necessary officers appointed by the King himself, no individual has a right to perform the duties of an office with which he has not been invested.

With regard to the supposed case of persons cast upon an island, who might, by accident, find a copy of the New Testament; it is one of those improbable cases, which, so far as my information extends, has never occurred, and is never likely to occur. But should such a thing happen, it will then be quite time enough to take it into consideration.

Jesus Christ does not leave his people to the workings of blind chance. There is a providence over them, special as that which watches the falling of the little sparrow. It is not for us to imagine difficulties which in eighteen hundred years have never occurred, and in all probability never will occur, and undertake to legislate for them. The fact, that no provision seems to have been made by the all-wise Redeemer for such an exigency, should be considered a sufficient reason why we may not attempt it. The principles advocated by Whateley may be correct. He does not, however, advocate the doctrine of Mr. C., that every member of the church may baptize and preach, but only such as have been selected and set apart to that office. As before remarked, he was discussing a subject entirely different from that now before us.

Mr. Campbell considers it a singular paradox in our creed, that we admit the validity of baptism, administered by an unconverted minister, if he be properly ordained, and yet refuse to recognize it when administered by a pious but unordained man. I should suppose, that, to a man at all acquainted with the most common principles of government, there would appear to be nothing paradoxical in this. Every officer in our civil government ought to be an honest man. Yet if, after a man has been in office for years, it appears, that he was most dishonest and unworthy of the trust reposed in him, his official acts are as valid in law as if he had been an example of virtue. However unworthy he may be personally, he is *rectus in officio*—a lawfully appointed officer. But one of the most virtuous and worthy private citizens might perform the same official acts, and no one would recognize them as valid in law. This principle is absolutely essential to the order, if not to the very existence, of civil government; and, for reasons equally clear and no less important, it must be recognized and acted upon in ecclesiastical government.

I am not able to perceive wherein I either misconceived or misrepresented the gentleman in regard to the principles advocated by him in the Harbinger. He now seems disposed to confine the right of females, and other unofficial persons, to baptize, to *extreme cases*. But it is not so presented in the article from which I read an extract.

With the case of Roger Williams I am not, at present, concerned. I find nothing in the Scriptures to countenance the singular course pursued by him and his friends. I presume, he had been truly and validly baptized before. He became dissatisfied with his baptism; and this error placed him in the unpleasant predicament. Had he been satisfied with a scriptural baptism, he might have avoided both his difficulties and his absurdities.

But many persons in this audience, I doubt not, are astonished to find Mr. Campbell abandoning the very fundamental principle of his boasted reformation, which is—to have a "Thus saith the Lord," or a clear scriptural example for every article of faith, or item of practice. One of the prominent and most important articles of his faith is—that every member of the church, male and female, old and young, has the right to administer baptism. On this doctrine he encourages his people, as circumstances may require, to practice; and upon the truth of it, if his views of the design of baptism are correct, depends the salvation of souls. Has he produced a solitary passage of Scripture to sustain it? He has not. Yet it is with him a matter of *faith*. Where is the divine testimony on which it is founded? The gentleman has read extracts from the writings of archbishop Whateley, Thomas Smyth, D. D., and from somebody else. These are his authorities; but from the word of God he has given us neither precept nor example! Here is an article of his faith, on the truth of which depends the salvation of the soul, for which he is unable to produce even one precedent!! Thus is the fundamental principle of his reformation abandoned. I set a very low estimate upon a reformation, which is of a character so accommodating, that it will take the Scriptures when they sustain its principles, and abandon them when occasion requires.

But, strangely enough, the gentleman calls on me to produce a passage of Scripture which says, that none but a bishop or ordained presbyter may baptize. I doubt very much, whether you can find in our civil code a law forbidding any man, who is not a sheriff, to perform the duties belonging to that office. You may find a law which defines the duties of those who fill the office; and it is a principle of common sense and of common law, that no private citizen, nor any one not invested with that office, may interfere with its functions. So I have proved, that our Savior appointed twelve men to a high and responsible office; and that he authorized them to ordain others to the same office. The great duties required of these officers, were to *preach and baptize*. No other persons were ever commanded or authorized to do the one or the other. Here, then, is an office established in the church, provision made for the regular appointment of officers to fill it, and its duties clearly defined. These, according to the universally admitted principle just mentioned, no one, not regularly inducted into this office, can discharge the functions connected with it; and if any one, in his rashness, attempt it, his acts are null and void.

Yet the gentleman would have you believe, that I am bound to point to the Scripture, which, in so many words, forbids an unordained person to administer baptism! I assert, that a bishop or presbyter has the right to baptize. He admits it. Then, so far as my faith and my practice are concerned, I have nothing to prove. But he maintains, that *unordained persons*, and even *females*, may of right baptize. I call upon him to prove it. Surely it is but reasonable, that a man, especially one who boasts that he goes by the Bible, should prove the truth of that which he believes, and the lawfulness of his practice. But he wishes me to prove a *negative*, viz: that unordained persons, females, &c., have *not* the right to baptize! Why, he cannot find a passage in the Bible that, in so many words, forbids horse-racing, or card-playing. Yet he will admit, that I can prove both to be wrong. So I cannot produce a passage in the New Testament, that says, in so many words, that an unordained, or even an unbaptized person, shall not baptize; but I can prove by clear declarations of Scripture, that bishops or presbyters, and they only, were authorized to administer the ordinance; and that, so far as we can gain information from the inspired records, no others ever ventured to do it. Now if Mr. Campbell asserts, that unordained persons are authorized to baptize, it behooves him to adduce the proof. He admits the truth of all for which we contend, viz: that bishops or presbyters are authorized to baptize. Then, unless he can prove, that others have the same right, his doctrine must be abandoned; or if he still adheres to it, his reformation should, in consistency, be given up, for its fundamental principle is repudiated, and he is found in the ranks of those who substitute *tradition* for the Bible. Would it not be wiser in him to abandon this unscriptural tenet, than trample under foot his own principles? Is it indeed so very important for him to adhere to a doctrine and a practice for which he can find in the Bible not the slightest authority? Would it not be better for him, and better for his church, at once to abandon it?

He thinks it wise to change; and he tells us, he has very greatly changed his views. One more change, especially if it bring him nearer the Bible, will not hurt him. Let him bring this doctrine to the test— "to the law and to the testimony." I desire a "Thus saith the Lord" in support of it, and I must have it, or I shall still protest against it. At least, let us have a fair and clear precedent.

In reply to one of his correspondents, who made several inquiries on this important subject, he stated as a fact, that in the New Testament "Deacons, and unofficial persons, are all represented as immersing, when occasion called for it." I expected him to produce the evidence on which he founded this important assertion. I supposed that he would feel himself bound to bring forward the very passages; but, as yet, we have not been permitted to see even one of them! Alas! what is to become of that great truth in which he would appear so much to glory— *The Bible, and the Bible alone, is the religion of Protestants?*

The *ladies*, too, he believes, may baptize when circumstances require it; and each lady must, of course, determine for herself when circumstances do require her thus to officiate. For this item of his faith, the gentleman does not pretend to find either precept or precedent. Yet he believes it!

38   3 D 2

An unscriptural doctrine has given rise to these unscriptural and injurious practices. Better give up the doctrine; and the practices will, of course, be abandoned. According to our views, there is no necessity to provide for any cases for which the law of Christ does not provide. We do not believe, that penitent believers will be lost, even though they have not the opportunity to receive baptism. Consequently we have no occasion to call on the ladies and children to officiate in any case. "He that believeth on the Son, hath everlasting life." My friend, Mr. C., embraced one false doctrine; and to meet the difficulties growing out of this error, he embraced another, and upon these two errors based a most unscriptural practice. But alas! for his reformation; for it is unable to find precept or precedent for one of its most important doctrines.

Mr. Campbell says, I have given him considerable time, inasmuch as I occupied in my introductory speech but *forty minutes*. Well, I can spare him time. My doctrine and my practice on this subject he acknowledges to be scriptural. I can give him time to find and bring forward those scriptures which teach that laymen and women may baptize. I will give him as much time as can be deemed necessary, if he will produce *just one* passage of the kind.

I see no propriety in making long speeches, when my doctrine is admitted, and he produces no proof of the truth of his. It appears useless to reply to his quotations from archbishop Whateley and others, when they are discussing other subjects. It would be cruel, indeed, to continue warring against a man when he has no sword, no weapons, and can get none! I do not like to fight with a man in that condition. I think it is better to close the war. I cannot consent to contend with an unarmed man. When he can get a sword, I will again be with him; but I hope he will no longer rely on *human authority*. It is, indeed, most inconsistent in a man like Mr. C., who has waged a long and furious war against all bishops and presbyters, now to rely on them alone for support. *I will wait for the Scripture!*—[*Time expired.*

Saturday, Nov. 25—12¼ o'clock, P. M.
[MR. CAMPBELL'S SECOND REPLY.]

MR. PRESIDENT—I am sorely pressed sir! I am sorely pressed, fellow-citizens! I am grievously oppressed! Alas for me! alas for reformation! Such exclamations have become familiar as household words; you all understand them. When the gentleman has nothing to say, then I am just got into some dreadful predicament; when he has nothing to say, then my case is sure to be sorely pressed. Yes, my fellow-citizens, I am truly hard pressed; for to speak against nothing, is one of the hardest tasks that can be imposed on me.

If any one sees any relevancy in the remarks of my opponent to the question before us, I must envy him his powers of discrimination. I see nothing relevant—call it my obtusity, if you please—but I must say, that I see nothing at all relevant to the proposition.

In his first speech, he spoke forty minutes and sat down. Brought he one passage of Scripture that could be predicated of the subject of his proposition? Did he bring one verse, intimating that bishops and ordained ministers had a prescribed right to baptize? Is it not necessary to prove that they have a right to baptize, before we prove that none else have such a right? I said he could not produce one such text; and now you all see that my prediction was true; he did not, he could not, he has not brought the first word, declarative that bishops have a special right to baptize. All the passages of Scripture which I alledged, gave them the right to baptize, only in common with other persons; it was never associated with them, nor committed to them, *as bishops*. If other persons may baptize on particular occasions, and by the force of special circumstances, so may they; but as to an official and divine right, there is no evidence. Apostles baptized with all the authority of their high office, which gave them universal and supreme superintendence.

Mr. Rice, it seems, is resolved that I shall not defend Mr. Jones from the violent assault made upon his reputation the other day, in the presence of this great concourse. I do not introduce this subject because of any personal feeling, or by way of reprisal for his censures upon me, for recommending his history of the Waldenses. I do it as an act of justice to an injured man, and to an injured community. I have the documents to show, that the statements made here are a base aspersion of an unoffending man. But Mr. Rice refuses to hear them read. On him, then, be the responsibility. This matter has been inquired into, and refuted.

To return to our immediate subject. I was pleased to hear Mr. Rice admit, at last, that there was a perfectly organized society in the apostolic age. The apostles must then have had power to organize such a community. Now we have always contended, that christianity, being a moral positive institution—a special providence—it must have for all its essential provisions, the warrant of a divine precept—of a " Thus saith the Lord." What the apostles did as plenipotentiaries of the kingdom of heaven, is just as exemplary and authoritative as a divine command. To show that any thing was done in the presence of the apostles, with their approbation, is all-sufficient to warrant us to go and do likewise. When, then, any one claims official or special power, or privilege, we ask him for the authority—for a warrant from the ministers of the Great King.

As the gentleman admits every thing was done in good order in the apostolic church, and in conformity with the law of God, I need only show what that church did to obtain from him the concession that we may go and do likewise. I will, then, proceed to read a sketch of the way and manner things were done in the mother church, at Jerusalem, while all the apostles were yet living. After that the church in Jerusalem had increased to many thousands, a very fierce persecution arose : Stephen was slain, and all were dispersed, except the apostles. It reads in the following manner: Acts viii. 1 : " And at that time there was a great persecution against the church, which was at Jerusalem, and they were all scattered abroad throughout the regions of Judea and Samaria, except the apostles. And devout men carried Stephen to his burial, and made great lamentations over him. As for Saul, he made havoc of the church, entering into every house, and haling men and women, committed them to prison. Therefore, they that were scattered abroad went every where preaching the word."

Here, then, we have the church of so many thousands dispersed. Those scattered abroad, we are told, went every where through Judea and Samaria, preaching the word. Here, then we have a divine precedent. The historian gives us the history of one of these preachers, from whose career we may learn something of that of the others; his name was Philip : " Then Philip went down to the city of Samaria, and preached Christ unto them. And the people with one accord gave heed unto those things which Philip spake, hearing and seeing the miracles, which he did. And when they believed Philip preaching the things concerning the kingdom of God, and the name of the Lord Jesus, they were baptized, both men and women." He next gives the history of two distinguished persons—Simon Magus, and the Ethiopian eunuch. From these particular cases, we may learn much of the details of christianity. On account of the minute statements concerning the Samaritans, Simon and Philip, the eighth chapter of the Acts of Apostles is, to us, an invaluable document.

We have, then, the adventures and success of Philip detailed to the end of that chapter. The gospel was carried by him into Samaria; and was successfully preached to the Samaritans. Many of them heard, believed, and were baptized. The historian tells us, that many men and *women* were baptized. How particularly minute in detailing these, to us apparently very minor matters! It is evident, then, that the church in Jerusalem was not Presbyterian: for they licensed persons to preach, and withheld not from them the right to baptize. They may enlighten, and, as they say, convert the people, but must not baptize them. Philip baptized. No such licentiates were in the apostolic age. What a singular caprice of learned men! A preacher is licensed to go out into the wide world to preach the word; and, should he make a hundred converts in a day or a year, he has not power to baptize one of them! The apostolic commission was, " convert and baptize," according to him; and yet he asks for authority for these thousands to baptize. We have the adventures of only one of them given; and evident it is, that he both preached and baptized. What he did, we are compelled, by every principle of reason, to believe the others did. There were not two laws, two castes of preachers in those days. Philip's history is given, for one of two reasons: either because he was a very distinguished man among those preachers, or because of the important fact that the distinguished city of Samaria was visited, Simon the Sorcerer vanquished, and the arch-treasurer of queen Candaces' empire was converted. But those facts and incidents, which respect the *man* and his success, do not at all give him a new or different *office*. We still have preachers of different ranks of talent, honor, and usefulness; but they are all equal in office.

While we have these scriptural facts and documents before us, it may not be improper to note this fact also, that light is scattering over this land, and men in all parties begin to see it. Here is a book called " Bacon's Manual." It came from the east. Wise men come from the east, even in this country. Light has broken out even in New Haven. We shall read a few sentences:

" As to the persons by whom this ceremony of baptism was performed, I will say, in one word, that this, evidently, was deemed a matter of little consequence. Paul thought, that the ordinance of baptism was among the least of his duties as a minister of the gospel; 1 Cor. i. 14—17. I find nothing in the Bible, and nothing in what I have seen of the earliest christian writers, which implies that it was the peculiar duty, or the peculiar honor, of this or that officer, to administer baptism."—*Bacon's Manuel*, page 58.

" *The Lord's Supper.*—Where there were church officers, there the bishops presided over this, as over every other part of public worship. To preside over the church, at the Lord's table, belongs to their office, as obviously, as to preside over the prayers of the church, or over the public reading and expounding of the Scriptures, or over the debates of a meeting for church business. But where there were no officers, the organization of the church being, as at Corinth when Paul wrote his epistles, not yet completed;

there is no evidence that this commemoration of Christ was omitted, any more than prayers and singing.

Ordination was simply the public inauguration of a man to a particular work or office. It seems to have been done uniformly with prayer and the laying on of hands.

The imposition of hands is an ancient oriental form of benediction. Thus 'Jacob, when he was dying, blessed both the sons of Joseph.' Thus, little children were brought to Jesus in the days of his flesh, 'that he should put his hands on them and pray,' and after reproving his disciples for their interference, 'he laid his hands on them.' This benediction, this solemn commendation of the individual to the grace and blessing of God, is all that was meant by the imposition of hands in the inauguration of church officers, or, in the setting apart of a christian teacher to the sacred employment of preaching the gospel. The idea of any sacerdotal power, or divine virtue, transferred into the candidate, through the hands of the ordaining bishop or the presbytery, is a popish fancy, unworthy of an 'age of Bibles,' and unknown to the simplicity of the primitive times."—*Ib.* p. 59.

Thus speaks Leonard Bacon, pastor of the First Church in New Haven : second edition, New York, 1841. Without special call, or official designation, this gentleman argues, men holding private stations in the church may baptize, and not only that, but may also even dispense the supper—a matter, by some weak and superstitious minds, regarded as still more solemn and official. This is the doctrine of " the reformation," as Mr. R. denominates it. It is so, indeed. And it was the original and true doctrine of Protestantism ; and, better still, it is the true doctrine of the Scriptures, which has been asserted in every age, and received by all who have opposed the haughty pretensions of those who presumed to arrogate to themselves an exclusive right to mediate and negotiate between God and man. While we build only on apostles and prophets, we are pleased to see men of all parties opening their eyes to the primitive simplicity and high authority of the inspired Scriptures.

In the New Testament, we never read of any one waiting for an administrator, for the presence of an officer to dispense any ordinance whatever ; nor do we read of their ever sending abroad for any such functionaries. The most convenient person is always sent for as the operator. Witness the conversion and baptism of the apostle Paul. Not far from Damascus, in Syria, on the public highway, Paul saw the Lord, and believed his voice. He was led into the city. And who baptized the great apostle of the gentiles ? Surely they must send to Jerusalem for bishop James, a prince among the apostles !—or for Peter, the grand prelate and president of the whole college of apostles ! Nay, verily. There happened to be living in Damascus, just at that time, a " CERTAIN DISCIPLE," never before heard of, " named Ananias." We have no evidence that he was an official character of any sort ; and, consequently, that he *was*, is not to be assumed. Those who say that he was, must prove it. The Lord sent him to a certain place in Damascus, to inform this Saul of Tarsus, what to do for his own special salvation. The Lord had told him what to do for him as a witness and a minister ; but he did not preach to him the details of his own personal duties, under the Messiah's reign. This he left to some one who had received it from that Peter, to whom he solemnly and irrevocably had consigned the keys of the kingdom of heaven.

Now, as Paul's case was to be a remarkable one, this Ananias had a vision too, to dispose him to go to the house of one *Judas*, with whom Paul was then lodging. He was carefully directed to Straight Street, and to the house of Judas, and entering in, he found Paul yet blind. He laid his hands upon him in the name of the Lord, that he might receive his outward sight, and be inwardly filled with the holy Spirit. He then baptized him. "He received sight forthwith, and arose and was baptized." With such facts as these before us, why arraign our brethren, and censure them for following such examples as those already given? In censuring us, our friends censure the primitive church and the apostles themselves.

If Paul had been converted by any man according to the usage of that age, he would have been baptized by that man. But the Lord having taken the work entirely into his own hand, furnished a "*certain disciple* for administrator.

We must all admit, that matters were well understood at Jerusalem before the dispersion, and that the church there had been properly organized. Hence, their practice and example are all important to us. In that church, nor in any other, do we ever read of any special provision having been made for baptizing. This is a singular fact—a fact that ought to be, in this age of clerical pride and assumption, deeply engraved upon all minds—that neither in Jerusalem, nor in any church, city, or province, where christianity was planted in the days of the apostles, did there ever arise any question, or originate any law or precept, on the subject of an administrator of baptism nor of the holy supper. Even when specifying the qualifications of elders, or bishops, and deacons, and when assigning them their duties, the apostles never once mentioned any thing about the dispensation or administration of ordinances! There never arose any question on this subject, nor any difficulty calling for one line or word from any New Testament writer. Paul himself spent eighteen months in Corinth. "Many of the Corinthians hearing, believed and were baptized." Paul baptized but a very few of that immense multitude. Nor are we even informed who baptized any of them. Paul made others attend to this matter. He must have distributed it amongst others of inferior rank.

When Peter was sent by a Divine oracle from Joppa to Cesarea, to the house of the famous gentile centurion, Cornelius, to announce to him, his family, friends, and neighbors, the glad tidings; when, too, the Spirit of God was liberally, in his miraculous gifts, bestowed on that community, the apostle commanded others, who accompanied him, to baptize those gentiles. To change the style of Luke, the narrator, who preserves the third person; I say change it into the first—let Peter in his own person be heard, and it would read thus: Can any of you Jews, [six brethren, who accompanied him from Joppa;] can any of you forbid water, that these should be baptized as well as we? When no one responded, Peter said, In the name of the Lord, baptize them. In the third person it reads, "Then he commanded them to be baptized." Here, then, were neither bishops nor ministers; they were simply six brethren. They were not officials—there is no sort of evidence that they were. The presumption is, that they were not; and, of course, we cannot argue from them in any other light than that they were merely "six *brethren.*"

There is not, then, either in the case of the Samaritans, nor of the gentiles, nor even among the Jews, a single indication of any concern about the rank of an administrator of baptism or any other ordinance. Such questions were not then agitated, and of course the New Testament is wholly silent on the whole subject of official administrators of baptism, farther than we learn incidentally from the examples before us. I am singularly fortunate in being able to produce such instances of what, now-a-days, would be called lay-baptism, just under the eyes and direction of such churches, apostles, and prophets. It is wholly a work of supererogation. I am not required by any law of discussion to produce such evidence. But what should we have had to talk about in this case, if I had not found these documents. Mr. Rice has nothing to offer. He has been dipping buckets into empty wells and drawing nothing out. It is not any defect in his genius or invention. He has rather too much of that. It is the sterility, the barrenness of the soil.

Having, then, found no precept or precedent for episcopal or Presbyterian baptism; no authority for such classic and clerical administrations; but, on the contrary, having produced clear and indisputable cases of lay-baptism, under the inspection and by the authority of the Lord and his apostles; may we not regard the subject as clearly, satisfactorily and finally settled?

With regard to the good order of religious society, Mr. R. seems to represent us as having little or no regard for it. This is very far from fact. No one admires good order more than I, and no one, I think, is more ready to sacrifice his own opinions to obtain it. The beauty of the universe is its good order. A community without it must go to ruin. We are not, however, without church organization. We have hundreds of congregations, with their bishops and deacons, in as good order as, perhaps, any Presbyterian community in the commonwealth. But we have not any general system of organization, no system of general co-operation. This is, indeed, true. But, even in this respect we are now as all other societies have been in their incipiency. Presbyterian society was much longer than our whole existence in getting organized. They were so much perplexed and distracted about organization, that in the time of Knox there passed at one time eighteen years without a case of ordination by imposition of hands. The long reign of Elizabeth, and that of Edward VI., were spent in organizing, changing, and new-modifying that national institution called Episcopalianism. The Congregationalists, or Independents, were also in a transitive state for years. And Wesley's discipline and order was changed some seventeen times in his own life-time.

The apostles were not very precipitate in this work. It was upon the second tour of Paul and Barnabas, that they set things in order and ordained elders in every city. Paul left Timothy in Ephesus, not merely to keep the order established by Paul, but to set things in order as he had appointed him. The apostles were governed by circumstances, and had to wait for the developments of society. They did not enact nor legislate in anticipation, but in retrospection of difficulties and disorders.

We have been occasionally writing on order for many years. We have secured a good deal of it at many points, and still hope to secure it at more. The whole christian community should be perfectly organized and compacted together, and combine their energies and means in one grand system of redeeming man from ignorance, guilt, and bondage. But instead of mocking our efforts, as did certain persons of old the rebuilders of Jerusalem, our friends should rather commend us for what we have done, than censure us for what we have not done.

And here I am led to notice a statement of Mr. Rice that startled me no little. He says, that we have promulged a doctrine authorizing all

persons to baptize. He can produce no such document. It is a gross
—— I shall not name it. It is at least a misconception of his own. I
have already expressed myself fully on that point. We ought always to
assail the proper ground occupied by those we oppose, and not make for
them such arguments as we can easily refute. I do not demur to any
man assailing me through my own arguments, while I must always complain of his putting into my mouth propositions or aguments which I did
not use. Nor is it lawful to accuse me of maintaining the inferences
which Mr. Rice chooses to draw from my arguments. This is neither the
part of candor nor of moral rectitude. I will not consent to be responsible for his inferences, nor for those of any other man. I defend what I
have written, and not his inferences from it.—[*Time expired.*

Saturday, Nov. 25—1 *o'clock, P. M.*
[MR. RICE'S CLOSING ADDRESS.]

MR. PRESIDENT—I have a remark or two to make with regard to Jones'
history. I read it to the audience in connection with that of Perrin, for
the purpose of proving, that in quoting Perrin he threw out what his
author said of baptizing infants, and substituted in its place a statement
which was wholly different. The gentleman may apply to my conduct
in this matter what epithet he pleases; but I will, at any proper time,
meet him, and give him a fair opportunity of exposing it. I never shrink
from such responsibilities.

My friend, Mr. C., regrets (so he would have us think) to be obliged
to speak against nothing. When a man is called upon to produce a
" Thus saith the Lord" for his doctrines and practices, and is unable to
do it, I think a complaint that he has nothing to do, comes with a poor
grace from him. It looks very much as if he were speaking against the
Bible! I have been prepared to examine all his Bible authorities; but,
strange to tell, he has not produced one that is even plausible.

He maintains that there is no passage of Scripture authorizing bishops
to baptize, and calls on me to produce one. I will prove by Mr. Campbell himself, that every ordained presbyter is authorized to administer
baptism. I will read in the *Millenial Harbinger,* vol. iii. p. 475:—" No
person can be sent specially to baptize without preaching, NOR TO
PREACH WITHOUT BAPTIZING. But baptizing was the inferior of the two,
and, therefore, Paul says, in the *Hebrew idiom,* he was sent *to preach
rather than baptize.* This is precisely his meaning—nay, it is precisely
what he says, when his Jewish idiom is understood." The gentleman
has called on me to prove, that bishops are authorized to baptize; and
yet he has himself declared, that no one can be sent specially to preach
without baptizing!!! He must certainly have forgotten much that he
has written. I have very recently been looking through his writings, and
perhaps I have a more distinct recollection of many of them than he has.

I have not said, as he seems to intimate, that no particular church was
ever in an unorganized state. My remark was made distinctly concerning *the church of Christ.* I said, it has never been in an unorganized
state, so as to make it proper or lawful for private members to assume to
perform one of the functions of the ministerial office. Moreover, when
any particular church is to be organized, it should be done by properly
appointed officers.

But let us examine the Scriptures to which the gentleman has appealed
in support of his doctrine of lay-baptism. He refers to Acts viii. 4,

" Therefore they that were scattered abroad, went every where preaching the word." The word here rendered *preaching*, signifies telling good news; and it is admitted, that all christians have the right to tell to others the good news concerning salvation through Christ. As the christians at Jerusalem were scattered abroad by persecution, they went forth, telling their fellow-men these glad tidings. Such seems to be the meaning of the passage.

But if the gentleman insists that the word *euangelizomenoi*, translated preaching, means in this instance preaching in the official or technical sense of the word; he must admit, that the *women* as well as the men, became public preachers! This, I think, he will scarcely maintain. The inspired historian tells us, that the women as well as the men were scattered abroad, preaching; yet Mr. C. will confine the preaching to the men. Then how can he be sure, that it is not confined to *ordained* men? The word, however, does not mean preaching in the official sense, as I suppose, but telling the good news of salvation, as private christians may do.

But after all, there is not in this passage, nor in the connection, one word about *baptizing*. The question under discussion is, whether private members of the church may *baptize;* and to prove, that they have the authority, Mr. C. triumphantly adduces a passage in which there is not a syllable concerning baptism! It is one thing to inform an inquiring mind how he may be saved through Christ, and quite another to introduce him into the church of Christ, and thus afford him the opportunity, if he be an unworthy member, greatly to dishonor and injure the church and the cause of truth. The introduction of persons into the church by baptism, is no mere personal or private matter. One unworthy member can do more injury to the church and to the cause of Christ, than a dozen like him, who remain in the world. Hence our Savior was careful to whom he committed the keys of the kingdom. He did not authorize every member of the church who might choose to be officious, to initiate into the church whom he pleased.

The passage, I repeat, says not a word about baptizing—the only subject now before us. You perceive how the gentleman shifts and turns to save his unscriptural tenet. I call for a passage of Scripture to sustain his doctrine, that private members of the church may baptize; and he points us to one which speaks of persecuted christians wandering to and fro, and telling to their fellow-men the good news of salvation through Christ, but which says not a word about baptizing!

His next proof of lay-baptism is the fact, that Philip baptized the eunuch. But we have some information concerning Philip, which completely nullifies this argument. In Acts xxi. 8, we read as follows: "And the next day we that were of Paul's company departed, and came unto Cesarea; and we entered into the house *of Philip the* EVANGELIST, *which was one of the seven,* and abode with him." Philip was first elected and ordained to the office of deacon at Jerusalem, but afterwards became an *evangelist.* After receiving this last office it was, doubtless, that he went forth preaching and baptizing. There is not the least evidence that he was only a deacon when he baptized the eunuch. On the contrary, inasmuch as we know that he was ordained as an evangelist, the evidence is decidedly in favor of the opinion that he had received this office before he baptized the eunuch.

Mr. Campbell's third argument for lay-baptism is the fact, that Ananias baptized Paul; and he says, the *presumption* is, that he was not ordained to the office of the ministry. But does he know, that he was not ordained? Has he the slightest evidence on which to found the presumption, that he was not? This is an important question; for he cites Ananias as an instance in which an unordained man administered baptism; and he says, *in all probability* he was a private member. Has he the least evidence in the world on which to found such an opinion? He has not. Then what is his argument worth? Absolutely nothing.

His fourth argument in favor of lay-baptism is derived from the baptism of Cornelius and his family, (Acts x.) Certain brethren went with Peter to the house of Cornelius, and Mr. C. supposes, that some one of them, and not Peter, baptized him and his family. And he says, the *presumption* is, that they were unofficial persons. But on what evidence, I emphatically ask, is this presumption founded? I venture the assertion, that there is not the slightest evidence to support such a presumption. Some one or all of them may have been, and probably were ordained ministers of the gospel.

But the gentleman has appealed to these six brethren as proof positive, that unordained persons did administer baptism in the apostolic age. I ask, does he know, that they were unordained? He acknowledges that he does not. But he says, the *presumption* is, that they were unofficial persons. I reply, that there can be no presumption without some evidence. What evidence has he? None—absolutely none. Then, I again ask, what is his argument worth?

His Bible evidence in favor of the right of unordained males and females to baptize, has disappeared. He is not able to produce a " Thus saith the Lord," or a clear precedent to sustain it. Yet he has taught this doctrine, and encouraged thousands to practice accordingly; and although, according to his views, the salvation of the soul depends on the validity of baptism, he is now unable to sustain it by either precept or example from the Scriptures!

But he appeals to Leonard Bacon, of New Haven, as favoring his views. Dr. Bacon, if I am correctly informed, is, comparatively, a young man—a Congregationalist. I do not know, whether his reputation as a profound theologian would constitute him an *authority*. In the absence of all Scripture authority for lay-baptism, perhaps I ought not to attempt to rob him of this human authority. The gentleman is evidently in great difficulty; and he appeals to Dr. Bacon to help him out. He set out in his reformation on the safe principle of having for every article of faith, or item of practice, a " Thus saith the Lord," or a clear and certain precedent. In his present difficulties he finds, that he has not the Bible to sustain him; but he has got Leonard Bacon.—[A laugh.]

He tells us, that there is in the New Testament no law regulating the administration of baptism; and yet in his Harbinger we are told, as I have proved, that every man who was specially sent to preach, was also sent to baptize! Yet, strangely enough, he appeals to the fact, that Paul was not sent particularly to baptize, as evidence that the administration of baptism was not assigned to any particular class of persons! I rather think, however, that he has given a better reason than this, why Paul was not accustomed to baptize. In the Millenial Harbinger, (vol. ii. Extra, page 36,) he says—" He [Paul] was no *fisherman* like the twelve. He was not of that robust constitution. My bodily presence is weak, says he: and history gives him not size enough to baptize!" I know not to what *history* the gentleman had reference; but certainly the reason here assigned for his not being accustomed to baptize, is better than the one he now offers! Paul was not big enough to baptize!!! Then, indeed, it was very important he should have others to do it for him!

With regard to the organization of Mr. Campbell's church, I have nothing to say at present. That subject will be fully discussed under the proposition concerning creeds.

He charges me with a crime which he could not venture to name, for having said, that, according to his doctrine, every member of the church has the right to baptize. I am responsible for all the statements I make. I will prove the truth of the fact I stated, by Mr. Campbell himself! I will read in his *Christian System*, (p. 85,) " A christian is by profession a preacher of truth and righteousness, both by precept and example. *He may of right preach, baptize, and dispense the supper, as well as pray for all men, when circumstances demand it.*" Now who, I ask, is to determine when circumstances require a private member of the church to baptize? Has the gentleman's church ecclesiastical bodies by which the matter may be determined? He acknowledges that it has not. He wages an exterminating war against ecclesiastical courts. Each individual, therefore, must judge for himself or for herself, when he or she ought to administer baptism. For, as Mr. C. teaches, each may of right preach, baptize, &c., and none have authority to dictate to, or control him in the matter. Does not this completely sustain all that I have affirmed?

In the passage I read in the Harbinger, a short time since, he teaches that *females* may baptize, when circumstances require it; and yet he acknowledges, that he can find neither precept nor example to sustain him in the position. He even goes further, and maintains that an *unbaptized* person may, under certain circumstances, baptize. But who, I again ask, is to determine when circumstances do require such persons to venture upon a work so solemn and so responsible? There is no body, or court, to which the matter can be referred. The good lady, the little boy or girl, must determine, in any exigency, what is duty. This is the worst I have said of the gentleman's principles; and all this, as he must admit, is precisely according to the New Testament. It is so, if his doctrine is true.

As this is the last speech I shall make on this question, I must now, very briefly, sum up the argument.

The commission given by our Savior, I maintain, is a clear prohibition of lay-baptism. " Go ye," said he to the twelve, " and teach all nations, baptizing them in the name of the Father, and of the Son, and of the Holy Ghost; teaching them to observe all things whatsoever I have commanded you; and, lo, I am with you alway, even unto the end of the world, Amen." We know that the apostles were authorized and commanded to baptize and teach. But this is not all; the *promise extends to the end of time.* " Lo, I am with you alway, even unto the end of the world." It is, then, clear, that till the end of time, there is to be a class of men, solemnly invested with the ministerial office, whose business it shall be to preach the gospel, and to administer baptism. This cannot be successfully controverted.

But Mr. Campbell teaches, that not only bishops or presbyters, but private members, and even females, may of right baptize. I maintain, that this commission confines both preaching and baptizing to those who are clothed with the ministerial office. Here, you observe, we find a most important office, established in the church by Christ himself, designed to be perpetual. Twelve men, qualified for their responsible work by the King, are solemnly charged with the duties of the office; they are authorized and required to ordain others to engage in the same work; they are directed to look well to the character and the qualifications of those on whom they lay their hands, to whom they entrust the interests of the kingdom of God. As we read in the Acts of the Apostles, a brief history of their labors, we find them, in obedience to the authority of the Redeemer, ordaining other men to go forth and baptize, and to teach the mysteries of the kingdom.

But from the time when the commission was given, and the apostles inducted into their responsible office, we find not one instance of the administration of baptism by an unordained person. We do, indeed, read that baptism was administered, in some cases, by persons whose official character is not mentioned; but this fact proves nothing against the position I am maintaining, and nothing in favor of the doctrine of Mr. Campbell. For if I state, that an individual was baptized in one of our churches, on a certain day, it is wholly unnecessary for me to mention the fact, that the administrator was an ordained minister, because our views and our practice are generally known. For the same reason, it was not necessary that Luke, in writing the Acts of the Apostles, should, in recording a baptism, state that an ordained minister officiated; nor does his silence on this point, in any number of cases, afford the least ground of probability that those who administered the ordinance were private persons.

The fact, then, is, that the New Testament gives not a solitary instance in which baptism was administered by a person known to be unordained. There is neither precept nor precedent. Then Mr. Campbell is bound, according to the fundamental principle of his reformation, to abandon the doctrine, and the practice of lay-baptism.

In every government, civil and ecclesiastical, there must be offices established, and officers appointed to transact public business. And when particular duties are, by law, connected with a particular office, it is, as I have said, a principle universally admitted, that no individual, whatever his standing may be, can discharge the duties, until he is clothed with the office. Indeed, it is a principle, the necessity of which must be manifest to every one. For if every private individual may, on his own responsibility, transact public business, no government on earth, civil or ecclesiastical, can exist. Perfect anarchy must result in church and in state, from the adoption of such a principle. Whether, therefore, we regard the interests, present and future, of individuals, or the purity and peace of the church of Christ, and the honor of his cause, it is absolutely necessary that none but men properly qualified, and solemnly ordained to the ministerial office, should be permitted to administer the ordinance of baptism, and introduce persons to the fellowship of the church. Every one must see, that if each individual member may open the door, and admit into the church whom he pleases, consequences the most disastrous must follow.

The wisdom of the Redeemer is manifested by the fact, that he committed the work of teaching and baptizing to those who were qualified for the proper performance of it, and directed them to ordain others to the office, but to "lay hands suddenly on no man." There were most important reasons why he pursued this course. He intended not to have a church containing within itself the elements of its own destruction—leaving the male, the female, the young, the old, the rash, the superstitious, the ignorant, to throw wide its doors, and introduce just whom they might think proper.

It is a happy circumstance, that the doctrine of Mr. Campbell has not been fully and extensively carried out in practice. The preservation of his church, from " confusion worse confounded," is owing, he must admit, to the prudence and good sense which have prevented the members from acting in accordance with his doctrine, not to the soundness of the doctrine itself. If each member had undertaken to administer baptism, as, he says, each may of right do, the church, though now sufficiently involved in confusion, would have been in a condition far worse than it is.

I must here reply to one of the gentleman's arguments, which I forgot to notice in the proper place. He says, my objection to the right of females to baptize, comes with an ill grace from me, as a Pedo-baptist, since mothers, of olden time, circumcised their children. The Scriptures do not inform us that mothers had any such authority. The conduct of the wife of Moses is not approbated; and the temper she displayed on the occasion, does not evince that she was actuated by proper motives. There is not another example of the kind in the Bible. But God might have permitted unofficial persons to administer that ordinance under the old dispensation, and yet, when the church extended her boundaries over the earth, and was, of course, placed in circumstances greatly different, there would be reasons of greatest importance for confining the administration of the initiatory ordinance to men properly qualified, and set apart to the work. Under the old dispensation he did not say to the priests, or the prophets, " Go ye, and make disciples of all nations, *circumcising* them." Had such a commission been given, there would have been good reasons for confining the authority to circumcise to the prophets and the priests.

But under the new dispensation, the church was to lengthen her cords and strengthen her stakes. All nations were to be invited to participate in her privileges and blessings. The Savior then said to men qualified for the responsible work, " Go ye, and teach all nations, baptizing them in the name of the Father, and of the Son, and of the Holy Ghost." Thus he connected the work of baptizing and teaching, with the office of the ministry, and commanded those invested with the office, to discharge those duties, and to ordain others to the same work. He committed it to no private hands. There is, I repeat it, neither precept nor precedent in the Scriptures, authorizing any but bishops or presbyters to baptize ; and no private member dare attempt it, unless he, or she, is willing to trample under foot the authority of heaven.

Such are the views I entertain on this important subject; and such are some of the plain and obvious reasons by which they are sustained. I leave you, my friends, to determine, in view of your responsibility to Christ and his church, whether I have established the truth of the proposition, that *baptism is to be administered only by a bishop or presbyter, scripturally ordained.*—[*Time expired.*

Saturday, November 25—1½ *o'clock, P. M.*
[MR. CAMPBELL'S CLOSING REPLY.]

MR. PRESIDENT—The gentleman has, for once at least, sat down without telling us what he has done. You all see what he has not done. Notwithstanding the indisputable evidence of his failure, I will respond to what has been offered. Baptism is to be administered only by an ordained bishop or elder !! So he affirms : but where is the proof? His former speeches give us neither precept nor precedent. In my first reply, I once and again called for evidence; but I have called in vain. Finally, he gave an extract from the Millenial Harbinger. Now listen to his authority—vol. iii. p. 475:

"No person can be *sent* specially to baptize without preaching; nor to preach without baptizing. But baptizing was the inferior of the two, and therefore Paul says in the Hebrew idiom, he was sent to preach rather than to baptize. This is precisely his meaning—nay, it is precisely what he says, when his Jewish idiom is understood!"

Admit it all, does this prove that elders and bishops are sent abroad to preach as apostles?! And will it not also prove that all persons ordained or unordained, that preached, were accustomed to baptize?!

The Millenial Harbinger proves that Paul was not sent with special reference to baptize, but to preach. Was Paul a bishop?—a presbyter? Any proof short of proving Paul to have been an elder or a bishop, falls short of the proposition. As it is, it comes not within a thousand miles of the question. By the Harbinger, he cannot prove that Paul was a bishop or an elder of any church. He says he has read it more recently than I have. It is quite probable. Yet he has not found that in it. I wish the gentleman had read his Bible a little more. He confesses that I gave a good reason why Paul baptized but a few. Truth will sometimes force for itself an utterance. The gentleman, imperceptibly to himself, perhaps, has conceded that Paul practiced immersion: for surely he must admit that Paul had strength and size enough to sprinkle. Incidental arguments are generally both convincing and strong arguments. I will give another incidental argument. Paul said, he was not sent to baptize, but to preach. Baptizing, then, is inferior to preaching; yet Paul sometimes baptized. He baptized without a special commission, then? Was he right or wrong? We cannot choose the latter. He was right—was he not? Follows it not, then, that it is right to baptize without a commission—without a special license in some cases?! Paul, then, it seems, as any disciple may, on some occasions, baptized without a special commission. His case is then decidedly against Mr. Rice. The gentleman is out at every angle on this proposition. He now stands in an open field, in which there are no hiding places. What those skilled in the laws of debate may say, on hearing Mr. Rice plead, that he is not bound to prove that every one who baptized was a bishop, when proving that none but a bishop may baptize, I presume not to conjecture; but certainly they will smile at his calling upon me to prove that Philip was or was not a bishop, while he affirms that he was! I adduced several instances of persons baptizing, as well as Philip. How has he disposed of them? One of them was a very clear case, but he has not deigned to consider them. He admits, however, that all who preach, ought to baptize; and thinks it was so from the beginning. Why, then, license ministers to preach, and restrain them from baptizing?!

Acts, eighth chapter, as before shown, is an overwhelming instance of preaching and baptizing, without such licenses as are now deemed essential. The church in Jerusalem certainly amounted to many thousands before Stephen was slain. After that persecution, the church, with the exception of the apostles, was driven from the city. They continued at the metropolis. These dispersed brethren, we are told, "went every where preaching the word." That they baptized the converts, is most evident from the fact, that we are told of the baptism of the Samaritans, and of the eunuch, by one of them; and it is further evident from the concession of Mr. R., that, from the beginning, those who preached the gospel, baptized. But, says Mr. Rice, Philip *might* have been a bishop. Yes, *might have been!* And he adds, that we have reason to believe that he was an evangelist; but that he was an evangelist, specially so called, and appointed to the work, is yet to be proved. He might have been a bishop—he might have been an evangelist, &c. &c., is poor logic. Let us read the passage :—" And at that time there was a great persecution against the church which was in Jerusalem, and they were all scattered abroad through Judea and Samaria, except the apostles."—" They that were scattered abroad, went every where preaching the word ;" and Philip went down to Samaria, &c. It is, then, indisputably evident that they all preached and baptized their converts.

" But he might have been a bishop !" Well, let him prove that what *might have been*, actually *was*. Ananias might have been a bishop, too. All the persons named in the New Testament might have been any thing which partyism demands; but this species of logic, on this occasion, is wholly reprobate and inadmissible.

From the origin of baptism till now, no one superior to a disciple was called upon to administer it. The baptism of John was, indeed, from heaven, though some will have it, from men, and will have John to baptize as a Levite. Yet even this was administered by the disciples of Jesus—for "Jesus baptized not, but his disciples baptized." A community properly organized, will doubtless set apart some baptists, who will attend to this ordinance in a becoming manner, persons of discrimination, judgment, and responsibility of character.

The first gentile baptisms, it has been proved, and we now see it cannot be withstood, were performed by laymen. Peter took with him from Joppa to Cesarea " *six brethren.*" They had no official designation whatever. They were Jews by nation, and brethren by faith in Jesus Christ. These were commanded to baptize the first fruits of the gentile world. Unofficial persons, in the New Testament, are in distinction from those in office, usually called " brethren." Thus they stand forever stereotyped in the Jerusalem letters to the gentiles—" The apostles, elders, and brethren send greeting." Peter, then, and the six brethren, were the only baptized persons on the ground. Peter did not baptize, but *commanded* them to be baptized. The case is made out—and the negative side of the question sustained by arguments invincible—by facts indisputable.

The gentleman observes, there is no council to decide when circumstances make such baptists necessary *or* expedient. There is no need for such deliberations. The common sense of a community, and the good sense of aged and experienced brethren, will be a much safer palladium than ecclesiastic or synodical action. My general observation on this subject is, that any disciple or brother may baptize, only when circumstances require and authorize it. If the circumstances are mistaken, no very great danger may ensue; for, indeed, there is much less depending on the operation than any other circumstance, so far as the enjoyment of the blessing is regarded. We have not experienced much trouble or danger on that account, although the license has been carried farther by us, than any denomination in Christendom. It is now, indeed, much less frequent than formerly, and will become still less so, as we advance to a more complete organization. We cannot, then, in justice, be represented as teaching that every person, or any person, amongst us has a general right to administer baptism.

Mr. Rice takes pleasure to say and to reiterate it, that when he asserts any proposition or fact, he is always prepared to prove it. This is a fair and plausible saying. It sounds well. But the fact of its performance is better than the profession. How far it has been redeemed in this case, as well as on other occasions, you all perceive. What proof has been advanced on the present proposition? Does any one remember a verse in the Bible, or a fair and plausible inference? I do not.

The gentleman complains of my bringing books here to prove my views—and has frequently before complained of my reliance upon learned authorities, and upon numbers of witnesses, as if I were in those instances inconsistent with myself. He takes pleasure in the attempt to prove inconsistencies. Witness his readings from my writings. But how complete the failure, you have all doubtless observed. But do I use those books instead of the apostles? Do I rely upon the number or learning of my witnesses and vouchers? No. The Book of God is my magazine of arguments and proofs. I use these authorities to expose the nakedness of the land, and to show how empty the pretence of numbers and learning against us. He demurs at the testimony of Leonard Bacon, and would have you believe that I substitute him for the apostles. Who believes it? No one—not even Mr. Rice! Did I so use archbishop Whateley, or Mr. Smyth, or any one else? I only used these to show, that our views are not singular, and that light was breaking into his own church, or the Pedo-baptist societies upon these subjects, on account of which we have been so repudiated by such men as Mr. Rice.

The gentleman will, if possible, blur the face or the character of a witness whom he cannot at all dispose of. He is sometimes a young man, or he is on the wrong side, or some other demur. I was too young when I renounced Presbyterianism—yet some twenty-four years old! and Mr. Bacon is too young a man, though as old as my opponent! Strange logic. But when evidence is wanting for a proposition, it is politic to attempt to weaken the authorities on the other side, especially when their arguments cannot be at all encountered. But the embodiment of learning and good sense in the writings of these persons whom I adduce here, will obtain for them as much esteem and authority as I desire them to have. Mr. Bacon speaks with as much internal evidence of good sense, sound discretion, and intellectual endowment, as my opponent, or any other writer of his denomination in the country. Whateley is a giant intellect, and of attainments of the highest order.

Weak minds are the slaves of old times, and of old customs. They need the crutches of antiquity, and human authority. But men of vigorous minds ask, *what is truth?* not *who* says it. True, the lesser lights must yield to the superior. The moon will not contend with the sun, nor twilight with the risen day. But it is an evidence, to my mind at least, that a man has some intelligence, and some force of intellect, when he has so much mental independence as to think for himself.

Mr. Rice seems peculiarly fond of speaking of my church, or of "his friend's church." This is very well understood here. The gentleman knows, however, that I have no church, and claim no such thing. I am a member of Christ's church, and no more. I have presumed to lift up my voice for reformation, and multitudes have responded to it. But we are not our own church, nor our own people, but the Lord's. The authority we possess is not personal, nor official. It is the authority of the truth—the great truths elicited, or developed, in the current controversy, and reformation. Light has been elicited by the collision and co-operation of many minds; and it is gone forth, and going forth, with a power as irresistible as the light of God's sun.

We began at the right place, and at the right time—Jerusalem, and the descent of the Holy Spirit. One party begins at Rome, another at Constantinople, another at Geneva, Amsterdam, or Westminster, We begin at Jerusalem. Others began with Luther, with Calvin, or with Wesley. Some with this synod, and some with that. But we begin with the twelve apostles assembled in Jerusalem. We must, Mr. President, go beyond the reigns of king Henry VIII., prince Edward, and the mighty tyrant Elizabeth. We must, sir, go beyond St. Athanasius, St. Augustine, and the council of Nice. We must go up to Jerusalem and the holy twelve.

Bishop Purcell, as all the Catholic bishops, gloried in Rome, and in St. Peter. He has a line, or lineage, of bishops made out, from Peter to Gregory XVI., a splendid hoax, a golden dream. Those who have the idea of succession and hereditary grace in their heads, cannot dispense with it. So much of the pope as there is in every man's stomach, so much depends he upon this chain of so many links, not noticing how many wooden ones are interposed. Is not Rome the mother and mistress of all churches? exclaims the prelate—the learned prelate of Cincinnati! Was not Peter the first bishop of the imperial and eternal city? We say prove it, and we will believe it. But never was there a greater failure!! He could not prove that Peter was ever at Rome; and if he had—that he planted that church, and presided over it, is wholly out of the question. But we argued then as now, and triumphed then on this ground—and on this ground must always triumph, that Jerusalem is the mother of all true churches, and the mistress too, if we must have a MISTRESS rather than a LORD. We know that Peter was there, and set up the kingdom there, and that all the holy twelve were there, and that the first and last apostolic council was there; and letters patent issued thence in favor of all the gentile churches, and one grand act of incorporation emanated thence. To Jerusalem, then, we make our first and last appeal. Whenever Mr. Rice turns his eyes towards that ancient city, more ancient, by a thousand years, than Rome; more venerable, too, for a thousand reasons; he will give up his baptism—subject, action, design, and administrator, too. He will, indeed, allow a bishop to baptize a proper subject, but he will permit a deacon, too.

From Jerusalem sounded out the word of the Lord. It was the radiating centre of christianity. Great was the multitude of them that published it. The brethren from that point perambulated Judea, Samaria, Syria, &c. They preached the word every where, and every preacher occasionally baptized his own converts; even Paul himself sometimes immersed! What was right in those days, is still right. All persons, then, enlightened and gifted by God, may, by a *jure divino*, a right sacred and divine, proclaim the word when opportunity and circumstances present themselves, demanding it. He that persuades a sinner to come to the Lord, may also baptize him. For all of which we have the highest authority—the practice of the first church.

I am opposed to all innovations. Innovations, with me, are not the creations of last year, last century, nor of the last millenium. Innova-

39

tions are customs, usages, rites, doctrines that commenced one year after John wrote the word *amen* at the end of the Apocalypse. All have a right to read this book; to think, speak, and act for themselves. When they discover what the Lord would have them to do, they are not to confer with flesh and blood—with expediency, with worldly interests, honors, friends, relations, but to obey and honor the Lord that bought them.

The gentleman has given me so little to do, I shall only add—that I advocate good order, as well as abstract rights—and, while I have shown what circumstances authorize in some cases, what they have authorized on former occasions, I think that, in the present day, they authorize a very high regard to good order; and, as a general rule, call for particular persons for particular and special works and services.

But, fellow-citizens, we all do fade as a leaf—we are frail dust and ashes; our words soon pass away. They perish from our lips as the sound dies upon the ear. Our opinions are as light as air; but God's word has at all times firmly stood, and shall from age to age endure. "All flesh is grass," and the glory of man as the flower that fadeth away; "but the word of the Lord endureth forever." Bring all things, then, to its discriminating and solemn test; what accords with it receive, believe, and practice: what does not, reject as a human invention, and repudiate as a part of the doctrines and commandments of men.—[*Time expired.*

[END OF THE FOURTH PROPOSITION.]

PROPOSITION FIFTH.

In Conversion and Sanctification, the Spirit of God operates on Persons only through the Word. Mr. Campbell affirms. Mr. Rice denies.

Monday, Nov. 27—10 o'clock, A. M.

[MR. CAMPBELL'S OPENING ADDRESS.]

MR. PRESIDENT—The proposition to be discussed to-day, is admitted on all hands to be of transcendent importance to the christian. It is expressed in the following words :—*"In conversion and sanctification, the Spirit of God operates on persons only through the Word.*

Most controversies are mere logomachies—wars of words about words, and not about things. Perspicuity and precision in the definition of the terms of a proposition at the commencement, would have prevented more than half of all the debates ·in the world, and would have reduced the other half to less than half their size. Indeed, we yet need for daily use a much more simple and scriptural vocabulary, on the great subject of religion, as well as in some other departments of literature and science. The cumbrous, unwieldy, and badly assorted nomenclature of certain sciences, has, for centuries, retarded their progress. This is most unfortunately true in the intellectual and moral departments. Scholastic theology is greatly behind the age. The stale divinity of other times, refuses to reconsider its sense or its symbols. Hence the superabundance of the barbarous gibberish and miserable jargon yet extant in our creeds and systems of theoretic divinity. Some samples of these quaint vocables may be given in the discussion of the creed question.

Meantime, we have yet to learn how much perversion, not of language only, but of the mind also, has grown out of sectarian animosities and bickerings. The periodical hobbies of religious parties generate, like our political feuds, hosts of new terms ; and often change and modify the old ones, that even a well practiced politician, with Johnson, and Webster, and Richardson by his side, cannot now-a-days define either whig or tory, democrat or republican.

It is truly an interesting study to learn the new phraseology of religion, not only of religion in general, but of the different leading parties of the present church militant. An adept in this study could almost swear to a Romanist or a High-churchman, a Presbyterian or a Methodist, in the dark, if he only heard him speak for a single hour ; and that, too, without stating one of his peculiar dogmata. Certain words, like the *shibboleth* of the Ephraimites, invariably identify the religious tribe to which the speaker belongs.

In the midst of this babelism there is one fact, which it behooves me to state. I scarcely know how, indeed, to introduce it in this place ; and yet it is essential to a proper understanding of the whole subject before us. This fact is, that, in the strife of partyism, some Bible terms have been so appropriated to represent peculiar tenets and views which never occurred to their inspired authors ; that, were Paul now living amongst

611

us, he could not understand much of his own language. To this class belong the words regeneration, sanctification, and conversion.

With special reference to the discussion, and to the words of my proposition, I must, therefore, notice one capital blunder, which, if not now detected, might involve the subject before us in great obscurity. I cannot, however, much as I regret it, distinctly unfold my meaning in a single sentence. Allow me, then, to open it gradually to the apprehension of all.

The various conditions of man, as he was, as he now is, and as he shall hereafter be, as connected with Adam the first, and Adam the second, are set forth in Sacred Scripture, under various images and metaphors, each of which belongs exclusively to its own class, and is independent of every other one; requiring no addition nor subtraction of other images, from other classes, to complete or to unfold it. For example; the present condition of sinners, in Adam the first, is set forth under such metaphors as the following: dead, destroyed, lost, alienated, enemy, going astray, condemned in law, debtor, unclean, sold to sin, darkened, blind, &c. Each one of these has a class of opposite metaphors, of the same particular idea or figure. These metaphors, just now quoted, give rise to a corresponding class, indicative of his new condition in Adam the second, such as—quickened, made alive, born again, new created, saved, reconciled, friend, converted, illuminated, pardoned, redeemed, &c. The changing of these states is also set forth in suitable imagery; such as— regeneration, conversion, reconciliation, new creation, illumination, remission, adoption, redemption, salvation, &c. Now, the error to which I allude, primarily consists in not uniformly regarding each one of these as a *complete view* of man, in some one condition, or, in his whole condition in Adam the first, or in Adam the second; but in sometimes contemplating them as parts of one view, as fractions of one great whole, and, consequently, to be all added up to make out a full scriptural view of man, in Adam and in Christ, and of the transition from the one state to the other. From this wild confusion of metaphors—the indiscriminate use of certain leading terms, mere images it may be, our very best and most admired treatises on theology are not always exempt. Hence regeneration, conversion, justification, sanctification, &c. &c., are frequently represented as component parts of one process: whereas, any one of these, independent of the others, gives a full representation of the subject. Is a man regenerated? he is converted, justified, and sanctified. Is he sanctified? he is converted, justified and regenerated. With some system-builders, however, regeneration is an instantaneous act, between which and conversion there is a positive, substantive interval; next comes justification; and then, in some still future time, sanctification.

A foreigner, in becoming a citizen, is sometimes said to be naturalized, sometimes enfranchised, sometimes adopted, sometimes made a citizen. Now, what intelligent citizen regards these as parts of one process? Rather, who does not consider them as different metaphors, setting forth the same great change under various allusions to past and present circumstances? From such a statement, none but a simpleton would imagine that a foreigner was first naturalized, then enfranchised, then adopted, and finally made an American citizen: yet such a simpleton is that learned Rabbi, who represents a man, first regenerated, then converted, then justified, then sanctified, then saved.

Under any one of these images, various distinct acts of the mind, or of the whole person of an individual, may be necessary to the completion of the predicate concerning him. Thus, in regeneration or conversion, there may be included hearing, believing, repenting, and being baptized. These are connected as cause and effect, under a fixed administration or economy of salvation. So Paul asks, " How shall they call upon him in whom they have not believed ? How shall they believe in him of whom they have not heard ?—and how shall they hear without a preacher ?—and how shall they preach unless they be sent ?

The terms of my proposition will now be easily defined and apprehended. Conversion is a term denoting that whole moral or spiritual change, which is sometimes called sanctification, sometimes regeneration. These are not three changes, but one change indicated by these three terms, regeneration, conversion, sanctification. Whether we shall call it by one or the other of these, depends upon the metaphor we happen to have before us, in contemplating man as connected with the two Adams—the old or the new, the first or the second, the earthly or the heavenly. Is he dead in the first ?—then he is born again and alive in the second. Has he, like the prodigal son, strayed away in the first,—he returns, or is converted in the second. Is he unclean or polluted in the earthly Adam ?—he is sanctified in the heavenly. Is he lost in the first? —he is saved in the second. Is he destroyed and ruined in the first ?—he is created anew in the second Adam, the Lord from heaven.

If I am asked, why I admitted the terms conversion, sanctification, or regeneration into the proposition, I answer again, I could not help it. It would have been to debate the question, while settling the preliminaries. We must take the religious world as we have to take the natural or the political; that is, just as we find them, or as they find us. I seek to accomplish in this preamble, what ought to have been, but which could not be, accomplished, in settling the propositions. I therefore now, most distinctly and emphatically state, that with me, and in reference to this discussion, these terms, severally and collectively indicate a *moral*, a *spiritual*, and not a physical nor legal change.

A physical change has respect to the essence or form of the subject. A legal change, is a change as respects a legal sentence, or enactment. Hence pardon, remission, justification, have respect to law. But a moral or spiritual change, is a change of the moral state of the feelings, and of the soul. In contrast with a merely intellectual change—a change of views, it is called a change of the affections—a change of the heart. It is in this acceptation of the subject of my proposition, that I predicate of it, " The Spirit operates only through the Word."

The term *only* is, indeed, redundant ; because a moral change is effected only by motives, and motives are arguments ; and all the arguments ever used by the Holy Spirit, are found written in the book called the Word of Truth. Hence, the term *only* is equivalent to a denial of what I conceive to be the assumption of my respondent, viz : that the Spirit in regeneration, operates *sometimes* without the Word. *Only* is, therefore, by the force of circumstances, made to mean *always*. But, indeed, this is more a matter of form, than of any grave importance—inasmuch as the common admission of Protestants, and, I presume, of my opponent also, is, that the change of which we speak is a moral, or spiritual change.

If, then, I prove that conversion, or sanctification, is effected by the Word of Truth at all, I prove that it is a moral change, and, consequently, accomplished by the Holy Spirit, through the Word alone.

3 F

On the subject of spiritual influence, there are two extremes of doctrine. There is the *Word alone* system, and there is the *Spirit alone* system. I believe in neither. The former is the parent of a cold, lifeless rationalism and formality. The latter is, in some temperaments, the cause of a wild, irrepressible enthusiasm; and, in other cases, of a dark, melancholy despondency. With some, there is a sort of compound system, claiming both the Spirit and the Word—representing the naked Spirit of God operating upon the naked soul of man, without any argument, or motive, interposed in some mysterious and inexplicable way—incubating the soul, quickening, or making it spiritually alive, by a direct and immediate contact, without the intervention of one moral idea, or impression. But, after this creating act, there is the bringing to bear upon it the gospel revelation, called conversion. Hence, in this school, regeneration is the cause; and conversion, at some future time, the result of that abstract operation.

There yet remains another school, which never speculatively separates the Word and the Spirit; which, in every case of conversion, contemplates them as co-operating; or, which is the same thing, conceives of the Spirit of God as clothed with the gospel motives and arguments—enlightening, convincing, persuading sinners, and thus enabling them to flee from the wrath to come. In this school, conversion and regeneration are terms indicative of a moral or spiritual change—of a change accomplished through the arguments, the light, the love, the grace of God expressed and revealed, as well as approved by the supernatural attestations of the Holy Spirit. They believe, and teach, that it is the Spirit that quickens, and that the Word of God—the Living Word—is that incorruptible seed, which, when planted in the heart, vegetates, and germinates, and grows, and fructifies unto eternal life. They hold it to be unscriptural, irrational, unphilosophic, to discriminate between spiritual agency and instrumentality—between what the Word, *per se*, or the Spirit, *per se*, severally does; as though they were two independent, and wholly distinct powers, or influences. They object not to the co-operation of secondary causes; of various subordinate instrumentalities; the ministry of men; the ministry of angels; the doctrine of special providences; but, however, whenever the Word gets into the heart—the spiritual seed into the moral nature of man; it as naturally, as spontaneously grows there, as the sound, good corn, when deposited in the genial earth. It has life in it; and is, therefore, sublimely and divinely called "The Living and Effectual Word."

I prefer the comparisons of the Great Teacher. They are the most appropriate. We frequently err when handling these, because, in our quest of forbidden knowledge, we are disposed to carry them farther than he himself did. In the opening parable of the Gospel Age—a parable placed first in the synopsis of parables presented by Matthew, Mark, and Luke—he thus compares the Word of God to seed; and, with reference to that figure, he compares the human heart to soil, distributed into six varieties: the trodden pathway, the rocky field, the thorny cliff, the rich alluvian, the better, and the best of that. But we are not content with that beautiful and instructive representation of the philosophy of conversion. We must transcend these limits. We must explain the theory of vegetation. We must explain the theory of soils. We must even become spiritual geologists, and explore all the strata of mother earth; and even then, there yet remains an infinite series of whys and wherefores concerning all the reasons of things connected with these varieties. These speculations, and the conflicting theories to which they have given birth, we will and bequeath to the more curious and speculative, and will farther premise some things necessary to a proper opening of the argument.

Man, by his fall or apostasy from God, lost three things—union with God, original righteousness, and original holiness. In consequence of these tremendous losses he forfeited life, lost the right of inheriting the earth, and became subject to all the physical evils of this world. He is, therefore, with the earth on which he lives, doomed to destruction: meanwhile, a remedial system is introduced, originating in the free, sovereign, and unmerited favor of God; not, indeed, to restore man to an Eden lost—to an inheritance forfeited—to a life enjoyed before his alienation from his Divine Father and benefactor. This supremely glorious and transcendent scheme of Almighty love, contemplates a nearer, more intimate, and more sublime union with God, than that enjoyed in ancient paradise—a union, too, enduring as eternity—as indestructible as the divine essence. It bestows on man an everlasting righteousness, a perfect holiness, and an enduring blessedness in the presence of God for ever and ever.

To accomplish this a new manifestation of the Divinity became necessary. Hence the development of a plurality of existence in the Divine Nature. The God of the first chapter of Genesis is the Lord God of the second. Light advances as the pages of human history multiply, until we have God, the Word of God, and the Spirit of God clearly intimated in the law, the prophets, and the Psalms. But, it was not until the Sun of Righteousness arose—till the Word became incarnate and dwelt among us—till we beheld his glory as that of an only begotten of the Father, full of grace and truth; it was not till Jesus of Nazareth had finished the work of atonement on the hill of Calvary—till he had brought life and immortality to light, by his revival and resurrection from the sealed sepulchre of the Arimathean senator; it was not till he gave a commission to convert the whole world, that the development of the Father, and of the Son, and of the Holy Spirit was fully stated and completed. Since the descent of the Holy Spirit, on the birth-day of Christ's church—since the glorious immersion of the three thousand triumphs of the memorable Pentecost, the church has enjoyed the mysteries and sublime light of the Father, and of the Son, and of the Holy Spirit, as one Divinity, manifesting itself in these incomprehensible relations, in order to effect the complete recovery and perfect redemption of man from the guilt, the pollution, the power, and the punishment of sin.

No one, Mr. President, believes more firmly than I, and no one, I presume, endeavors to teach more distinctly and comprehensively than I, this mysterious, sublime, and incomprehensible plurality and unity in the Godhead. It is a relation that may be apprehended by all, though comprehended by none. It has its insuperable necessity in the present condition of the universe. Without it, no one can believe in, or be reconciled to, the remedial policy, as developed in the apostolic writings. And, sir, I have no more faith in any man's profession of religion, than I have in the sincerity of Mahomet, who does not believe in the Father, and in the Son, and in the Holy Spirit as co-operating in the illumination, pardon, and sanctification of fallen, sinful, and degraded man. While, then, I repudiate, with all my heart, the scholastic jargon of the Arian, Unitarian, and Trinitarian hypotheses, I stand up before heaven and earth in defence of the sacred style—in the fair, full and perfect comprehension of all its words and sentences, according to the canons of a sound, exegetical interpretation.

I would not, sir, value at the price of a single mill the religion of any man, as respects the grand affair of eternal life, whose religion is not begun, carried on, and completed by the personal agency of the Holy Spirit. Nay, sir, I esteem it the peculiar excellence and glory of our religion, that it is *spiritual;* that the soul of man is quickened, enlightened, sanctified and consoled by the indwelling presence of the Spirit of the eternal God. But, while avowing these my convictions, I have no more fellowship with those false and pernicious theories that confound the peculiar work of the Father with that of the Son, or with that of the Holy Spirit, or the work of any of these awful names with that of another; or which represents our illumination, conversion and sanctification as the work of the Spirit without the knowledge, belief and obedience of the gospel, as written by the holy apostles and evangelists, than I have with the author and finisher of the book of Mormon.

The revelation of Father, Son and Holy Spirit is not more clear and distinct than are the different offices assumed and performed by these glorious and ineffable Three in the present affairs of the universe. It is true, so far as unity of design and concurrence of action are contemplated, they co-operate in every work of creation, providence and redemption. Such is the concurrence expressed by the Messiah in these words—" My Father worketh hitherto, and I work"—"I and my Father are one"—" Whatsoever the Father doeth, the Son doeth likewise:" but not such a concurrence as annuls personality, impairs or interferes with the distinct offices of each in the salvation of man. For example: the Father sends his Son, and not the Son his Father. The Father provides a body and a soul for his Son, and not the Son for his Father. The Son offers up that body and soul for sin, and thus expiates it, which the Father does not, but accepts it. The Father and the Son send forth the Spirit, and not the Spirit either. The Spirit now advocates Christ's cause, and not Christ his own cause. The Holy Spirit now animates the church with his presence, and not Christ himself. He is the Head of the church, while the Spirit is the heart of it. The Father originates all, the Son executes all, the Spirit consummates all. Eternal volition, design and mission belong to the Father; reconciliation to the Son; sanctification to the Spirit. In each of these terms there are numerous terms and ideas of subordinate extent, to which we cannot now advert. At present, we consider the subject in its general character, and not in its particular details.

In the distribution of official agency, as it presents itself to our apprehension, with reference to the subject before us, we regard the benevolent design and plan of man's redemption, as originating in the bosom of our Divine Father; the atonement, or sacrificial ransom, as the peculiar work of the Messiah; and the advocacy of his cause, in accomplishing the conversion and sanctification of the world, the peculiar mission and office of the Holy Spirit. Thus, the Spirit is the author of the written Word, as much as Jesus Christ is the author of the blood of atonement. The atoning blood of the everlasting covenant, is not more peculiarly the blood of Jesus Christ, than is the Bible the immediate work of the Holy Spirit, inspired and dictated by him; "For holy men of old spake as they were moved by the Holy Spirit." Now, as Jesus, the Messiah, in the work of mediation, operates through his blood; so the Holy Spirit, in his official agency, operates through his Word and its ordinances. And thus we have arrived at the proper consideration of our proposition, to wit: In conversion and sanctification, the Holy Spirit operates only through the Word of Truth.

In how many other ways the Spirit of God may operate in nature, or in society, in the way of dreams, visions and miracles, comes not within the premises contained in our proposition. To what extent He may operate in suggestions, special providences, or in any other way, is neither affirmed nor denied in the proposition before us. It has respect to *conversion* and *sanctification* only. Whatever ground is fairly covered by these terms, belongs to this discussion. What lies not within these precincts, comes not legitimately into this debate.

I. Our *first* argument in proof of our proposition, shall be drawn from the *constitution of the human mind.*

That the human mind has a specific and well-defined constitution, is as evident, as that the body has a peculiar organization; or that the universe itself has one grand code of laws, which govern it. Our intellectual and moral constitution, as well as our physical, has its peculiar powers and capacities—not one of which is violated on the part of our Creator, in his remedial administration, any more than are our sensitive and animal faculties destroyed or violated by the physician, who rationally and benevolently aims at our restoration to health from some physical malady. No new faculties are imparted—no old faculty destroyed. They are neither more nor less in number; they are neither better nor worse in kind. Paul the apostle, and Saul of Tarsus, are the same person, so far as all the animal, intellectual and moral powers are concerned. His mental and physical temperament were just the same after, as before he became a christian. The Spirit of God, in effecting this great change, does not violate, metamorphose, or annihilate any power or faculty of the man, in making the saint. He merely receives new ideas, and new impressions, and undergoes a great moral, or spiritual change—so that he becomes alive wherein he was dead, and dead wherein he was formerly alive.

As the body or outward man has its peculiar organization, so has the mind. Both are organized in perfect adaptation to a world without us: the one to a world of sensible and material objects, the other to that world, and to a spiritual system also, with which it is to have perpetual intimacy and communion. But the mind is to commune with its Creator, and its Creator with it, through material as well as through spiritual nature: and for this purpose he has endowed it with faculties, and the body with senses favorable to these benevolent designs.

Now, as the body has to subsist upon material nature, and the mind upon the spiritual system, both are so organized and furnished as to secure and assimilate so much of both as are necessary for this end. Thus, for example, the body lives, moves, and has its being in the midst of matter from which it is to draw perpetual sustenance and comfort. For doing this, it is admirably fitted with an animal machinery, created for this purpose, without which animal life would immediately become extinct. The lungs are fitted for respiration, and the stomach is furnished with all the powers necessary to the reception, digestion, and assimilation of so much of material nature as is necessary to the heathful, vigorous and comfortable subsistence of the body. But nothing from without can afford it subsistence or comfort, but in harmony with this organization.

Man, then, has to live by breathing, eating, and drinking; and without these operations, nothing around him can afford him life and comfort.

Nothing of the bounties of nature can administer to his animal enjoyments in any other way. God, then, feeds and sustains man in perfect harmony with this organization. He neither dispenses with any of these powers nor violates them, in supporting physical life and comfort.

Precisely so is it in the spiritual system. The mind has its powers of receiving, assimilating, and enjoying whatever is suitable to itself, as the body with which it is furnished. While embodied, it has only its own proper faculties; but it has, also, organs and senses in the body, by and through which it communes with matter and with spirit, with God, and nature, and man; and through which they commune with it. It receives all the ideas of material nature by outward, bodily senses, without which it could not have one idea or impression of the external universe. A blind man has no idea of colors, nor a deaf man of sounds. Neither can any one give him an idea of them without those senses. Since the world began, every man sees by his eyes and hears by his ears. Whatever knowledge, therefore, is peculiar to any sense can never be acquired by another. If God give sight to the blind, or hearing to the deaf, he does it by restoring these senses: for, since the world began, no man has ever seen by his ears nor heard by his eyes.

So true it is, that all our ideas of the sensible universe are the result of sensation and reflection. All the knowledge we have of material nature, has been acquired by the exercise of our senses and of our reason upon those discoveries. With regard to the supernatural knowledge, or the knowledge of God, that comes wholly " by *faith*," and " faith " itself " comes by hearing." This aphorism is Divine. Faith is, therefore, a consequence of hearing, and hearing is the effect of speaking; for, hearing comes by the Word of God spoken, as much as faith itself comes by hearing. The intellectual and moral arrangement is, therefore—1. The word spoken; 2. hearing; 3. believing; 4. feeling; 5. doing. Such is the constitution of the human mind—a constitution divine and excellent, adapted to man's position in the universe. It is never violated in the moral government of God. Religious action is uniformly the effect of religious feeling: that is the effect of faith; that of hearing; and that of something spoken by God.

Now, as faith in God is the first principle—the soul-renewing principle of religion; as it is the regenerating, justifying, sanctifying principle; without it, it is impossible to be acceptable to God. With it, a man is a son of Abraham, a son of God; an heir apparent to eternal life—an everlasting kingdom.

And what is christian faith? It is a belief of testimony. It is a persuasion that God is true; that the gospel is divine; that God is love; that Christ's death is the sinner's life. It is trust in God. It is a reliance upon his truth, his faithfulness, his power. It is not merely a cold assent to truth, to testimony; but a cordial, joyful consent to it, and reception of it.

Still it is dependent on testimony. No testimony, no faith. The Spirit of God gave the testimony first. It bore witness to Jesus. It expected no faith without something to believe. Something to believe is always presented to faith; and that something must be heard before it can be believed; for, until it is heard, it is as though it were not—a nonentity. But it is not enough, that it be heard by the outward ear. God has given to man an inward, as well as an outward ear. The outward recognizes sounds only; the inward recognizes sense. Faith is, therefore, impossible without language; and, consequently, without the knowledge of language, and that language understood. It is neither necessary nor possible, without language—intelligible language. An infant cannot have faith; but it needs neither faith, nor regeneration, nor baptism. It was a figment of St. Augustine, adopted by Calvin, propagated in his Institutes, and adopted by his children.

These infant regenerators are lame in both limbs: in the right limb of faith, and in the left limb of philosophy. They move on crutches, and broken crutches, too. They have no philosophy of mind, or else they abandon it in all their theological embarrassments. They will have infants regenerated, and souls morally dead quickened by a direct impulse. The Spirit of God is supposed to incubate their souls—to descend upon them and work a grace in them—a faith without reason, without argument, without evidence, without intelligence, without perception, without fear, hope, love, confidence, or approbation.

The whole system of Calvinism, of Arminianism, is crazy just at this point. They build a world upon the back of a tortoise. They pile mountains upon an egg. They build palaces upon ice, and repose on couches of ether. They have not one clear idea on the subject of regeneration. It is to them a mystic mystery—a cabalistic word—a mere shibboleth. The philosophy of mind is converted into a heap of ruins. They have the Spirit of God operating without testimony—without apprehension or comprehension—without sense, susceptibility, or feeling: and all this for the sake of an incomprehensible, unintelligible, and worse than useless theory. I, therefore, *ex animo*, repudiate their whole theory of mystic influence, and metaphysical regeneration, as a vision of visions, a dream of dreams, at war with philosophy, with the philosophy of mind, with the Bible, with reason, with common sense, and with all christian experience.

II. Our *second* argument is deduced from the fact, that no living man has ever been heard of, and none can now be found, possessed of a single conception of christianity, of one spiritual thought, feeling, or emotion, where the Bible, or some tradition from it, has not been before him. Where the Bible has not been sent, or its traditions developed, there is not one single spiritual idea, word, or action. It is all midnight—a gloom profound—utter darkness. What stronger evidence can be adduced, than this most evident and indisputable fact? It weighs more than a thousand volumes of metaphysical speculations.

One would most rationally conclude, that if the Spirit of God did any where illuminate the human mind, or work into the heart the principle of faith previous to, and independent of, any knowledge of the Holy Scriptures, he would most probably do it in those portions of the earth, and amid those vast masses of human kind entirely destitute of the Word of Life; wholly ignorant of the " only name given under the whole heaven," by which any sinful man can be saved. If, then, he has never operated in this way, where the Bible has never gone, who can prove that he so operates here, where the Bible is enjoyed.

When, then, we reflect upon the melancholy fact so often pressed upon the attention of Christendom, by her missionaries to heathen lands, that not more than one-third of human kind enjoy the name of Jesus; that six-tenths or seven-tenths of mankind are wholly given up to the most stupid idolatries or delusions; that pagan darkness, and Mahometan impostures cover the fairest and largest portions of our earth, and ingulph the great majority of our race in the most debasing superstitions—in the grossest ignorance, sensuality, and vice; and that from these is withholden all spiritual and divine influence, of a regenerating and salutary character, so far as all documentary evidence avoucheth. If, then, indeed, the Spirit of the Bible, the Holy Spirit of our God, did, at all, travel out of the record, and work faith, or communicate intelligence, without verbal testimony, methinks this is the proper field. And there being no evidence of his having so done, is it not a fact as clear as revelation from heaven—clear as demonstration itself, that the illuminating, regenerating, converting, sanctifying influences of the Spirit of Wisdom and Revelation, are not antecedent to, nor independent of, the written oracles of that Spirit?

III. Our *third* argument is deduced from the fact, that no one professing to have been the subject of the illuminating, converting, and sanctifying operations of the Spirit of God, can ever express a single right conception or idea on the whole subject of spiritual things, not already found in the written word. We have been favored with numerous revelations of the experiences of the most spiritually minded and excellent christians of this our age. And on listening to them with the strictest attention, marking, with all our powers of discrimination, every idea, sentiment, and expression as uttered, I have never heard one suggestion containing the feeblest ray of light, which was not eighteen hundred years old, and already found in the Holy Scriptures—read of all men who choose to learn what the Spirit of God has said to saints and sinners. Evident then, it is, from this fact, which, I presume, I may also call an incontrovertible fact, that no light is communicated by the Holy Spirit, in regenerating and converting men; which is equivalent to saying, that " in conversion and sanctification the Spirit of God operates only through the Word of Truth."

IV. My *fourth* argument is derived from another fact, which calls for special consideration just at this point; to wit, *whatever is essential to regeneration in any case, is essential to it in all cases.* The change, called regeneration, is a specific change. It consists of certain elements, and is effected by a special agency. If it be a new heart given, a new life communicated, it is accomplished in all cases, as generation is, by the same agency and instrumentality. If, then, the Spirit of God, without faith, without the knowledge of the gospel, in any case regenerates an individual, he does so in all cases. But if faith in God, or a knowledge of Christ, is essential in one case, it is essential in every other case.

Now this being admitted, as I presume it will be, without farther argument or illustration, follows it not then, that neither the word of God, nor the gospel of Christ, neither preaching nor teaching, neither hearing nor believing, is necessary to regeneration, according to the doctrine of the Presbyterian church? inasmuch as that church believes and teaches that infants and pagans are regenerated, in some cases, without any instrumentality at all, but by the direct, naked, and abstract influence of the Spirit of God operating immediately upon their souls. As this is a most essential affair in this discussion, it is all-important that we deliver ourselves in the very words of the church, and especially in the creed of that branch of the church to which my respondent belongs.

" This effectual call is of God's free and especial grace alone; not from any thing at all foreseen in man: nor from any power or agency in the creature co-working with his special grace, *the creature being wholly pas-*

sive therein: being dead in sins and trespasses, until being quickened and renewed by the Holy Spirit, he is thereby enabled to answer this call, and to embrace the grace offered and contained in it; and that by no less power than that which raised up Christ from the dead. Elect infants, dying in infancy, are regenerated and saved by Christ through the Spirit, who worketh when, and where, and how he pleases: so also are all other elect persons, who are incapable of being outwardly called by the ministry of the word."

So speaks the *Confession*, chap. x. sec. 2, 3.

Now, I ask, of what use is the ministry of the Word in any case, so far as regeneration is concerned? This is a point on which I am peculiarly solicitous of illumination. Surely faith, and preaching, and the gospel ministry are all vain and useless in making a man a new creature, if dying infants and untaught pagans may be regenerated by the Spirit alone, without faith, knowledge, or any illumination whatever. Nay, indeed, if my position be true, and true it most assuredly is, that whatever is essential to regeneration in any case is essential in all cases, then, although we have three classes of subjects, to wit: elect infants, elect pagans, and elect gospel hearers, we have for them all one and the same species of regeneration. This is one of my reasons why I have charged my Presbyterian friends, on some occasions, of " making the Word of God of non-effect by their traditions;" and, therefore, I solicit such an exposition of this dogma as will set me right, if I err in this particular. As the confession reads, we have thus, in effecting the regeneration of an infant, the Spirit alone operating by a physical power, tantamount to that which raised up to life again, the dead body of the crucified Messiah.

Miracles, truly never cease on this hypothesis: inasmuch as the regeneration of every infant is a demonstration of a power as supernatural as the resurrection of the Messiah. Unfortunately, however, this power is not only never displayed to our conviction at the time, nor ever so displayed after the event as to become an object of perception, much less of sensible demonstration. If, indeed, as it sometimes happens in some branches of this school, regeneration is not regarded as another name for conversion and sanctification, but a previous work, then it will be important that we be enlightened on the question. How long the interval between regeneration and conversion, between regeneration and faith, and between regeneration and the dying infant's or pagan's exit? For if the interval should be such as to preclude the possibility of conversion and sanctification, we should have the startling fact promulged, that infants, and pagans too, dying regenerate, enter heaven without being converted! Another curious question will certainly arise here. Of what use is infant baptism, according to such a theory of regeneration? For, if elect infants are regenerated without knowledge, faith, repentance, or baptism, and if non-elect infants, though baptized, are not regenerated, why have such a war of words about a matter virtually worth nothing to the living or to the dead?

V. My *fifth* argument shall be deduced from the Holy Spirit's own method of addressing unconverted men; by signs addressed to the sense, and words to the understanding and affections. The Messiah himself, the seventy evangelists, and the twelve apostles were accomplished and fitted for their ministry to the world by such inspirations and accompanying powers as human nature and society, Jewish and pagan, then required, and I presume always will require. They were first sent to the lost sheep of the house of Israel; and afterwards the apostles were sent to the gentiles. Now, in seeking to regenerate and save the human family, they, divinely guided, uttered certain words, and accompanied them with certain miracles. These were the means supernaturally chosen and used. They were certainly apposite means; appropriate and fitted to the end proposed by the donor of this intelligence and power. He seems to have sought admission into the hearts of the people, by these glorious displays of divine power presented to the eye, and these words of grace addressed to the ear. They saw the sick healed, the leper cleansed, demons dispossessed and the dead raised; and, while seeing these solemn and significant arguments, they heard words of tenderness—words of pardon and of life spoken with a divine earnestness, with a heavenly sympathy and affection. Thus the Spirit sought to convert them. He used means, rational means; therefore, we argue, such means were necessary, and are still, in certain modifications of that same supernatural grandeur, necessary to conversion and sanctification. Signs, as Paul explains them, were necessary, not for believers, but for unbelievers. They were necessary to faith. The miracle opened the heart, the testimony of the Lord entered, and the Spirit of God with it; and the work of conversion was finished.

Now, may we not conclude that miracles and words are not a mere redundancy—a perfect superfluity? May we not regard them as essential means, employed by the Holy Spirit, in accomplishing his work? It is, perhaps, important also to say, that the proof of a proposition is always subordinate in rank to the proposition which it proves. The life is not in the miracle, but in that which the miracle proves. The grand proposition is, that Jesus is the Messiah, the Son of God, the Savior of the world. He that believes this proposition, is " begotten of God." It is the " incorruptible seed." It is the " living Word." It abideth forever. The church of the Messiah is built upon it. The promises, then, certainly justify the conclusion, that, in converting and sanctifying the world, the inspired apostles and evangelists used means of divine authority; and neither did depend upon, nor teach others to depend upon any agency from above, dispensing with such an instrumentality.

VI. Our *sixth* argument is derived from the name chosen by the Messiah, as the official designation of the Holy Spirit. He calls him the *Paracletos*, and that, too, with a special reference to his new mission. This term, occurring some five times in the apostolic writings, is, in the common version, translated both *comforter* and *advocate;* and, by Dr. Campbell, *monitor*. As an official name, I prefer *advocate* to either of the others. It is generic, and comprehends them both. An advocate may be a monitor, or a comforter; but a monitor, or a comforter, is not necessarily an *advocate*. Now, as the Spirit is to advocate Christ's cause, he must use means. Hence, when Jesus gives him the work of conviction, he furnishes him with suitable and competent arguments to effect the end of his mission. He was to convince the world of sin, righteousness and judgment. In accomplishing this, he was to argue from three topics, 1. The unbelief of the world; 2. Christ's reception in heaven; 3. The dethronement of his great adversary, the Prince of this world. Then the person, mission and character of the Messiah alone came into his pleadings. Jesus promised him the documents. And, indeed, the four evangelists are arranged upon the instruction given by the Messiah to his advocate. In converting men, the Spirit, the Holy Advocate, was to speak of Jesus. Hence, speaking of Jesus by the Spirit, is all that was necessary to the conversion of men. The official service and work thus assigned, the Holy Spirit is a standing evidence, that, in conversion and sanctification, he operates only through the Word. And, as it has been already shown, conversion is, in all cases, the same work, he operates in this department only by and through the Word, spoken or written; and neither physically nor metaphysically.

VII. Our *seventh* argument shall be deduced from the opening of the commission; from the gift of tongues, by which the Advocate commenced his operations. That the Messiah had a commission for convincing and converting the world, has been already shown. That he was to use arguments has been fully proved; that he was to speak and work also; that, by signs and miracles he accompanied the Word, and made it effectual. Now, that language is essential to the completion of the commission, is further proved from the great fact, that the first gift of the Holy Spirit, under the Messiah's commission, was the gift of tongues.

Language, not merely the various dialects of human speech, but language itself—not Hebrew, Greek and Roman—but that of which Hebrew, Greek and Roman are mere dialects, forms, or modes, is essential. He gave the first, and he gave the second. He made a glorious display of the use of language, of the need of tongues, in commencing his new work. He gave utterance; for utterance is his gift. So Paul to the Corinthians said, "You are enriched by him in all knowledge, and in all utterance." The day of Pentecost is the best comment on this whole subject of spiritual influence ever written. We have much use for it in this discussion. It is just as useful on the work of the Spirit, as on the genius and design of baptism.

It seldom occurs to us, that all Christendom—the living world, is now indebted for the very book that records the name, and embalms the memory of the Messiah, and for all that is known of the Holy Spirit—for the very language of the new covenant—for the gospel of the kingdom—and for every spiritual idea and conception of God, of heaven, of immortality, of our origin, nature, relations, obligations and destiny, to the immediate agency of this Spirit of all Wisdom and Revelation—to the gift of tongues, or of language. Yet, true to the letter it is, that "no one could say that Jesus is Lord, but by the Holy Spirit."

Some amongst us, through the ignorance that is in them on this grand theme, ascribe to the human mind the powers of the Holy Spirit. They represent the human mind as possessing some sort of innate power of originating spiritual ideas; to arrive at the knowledge of God by the mere contemplation of nature. They annihilate the doctrine of the fall; of human imbecility and depravity, and adorn human reason with a very splendid plagiarism, called natural religion. While at variance on almost every thing else, the mental philosopher and the Deist, the Romanist and the Protestant, the Calvinist and the Arminian admirably coalesce and harmonize in this self-congratulatory assumption. They say, that man can, by the feeble, glimmering rush-light of his own studies of nature, either descend from his *a priori*, or ascend from his *a posteriori* reasonings to God—to the apprehension of his very being and perfections; human responsibility, the soul's immortality, and a future state of rewards and punishments, without the Bible, and without the teaching of the Holy Spirit.

We have neither so studied nature nor learned the Bible. We subscribe to Paul's dogma, "The world by wisdom knew not God," and agree with him, that "it is by faith," and not by reason, "we know that the worlds were framed by the Word of God—so that things now seen existing did not formerly exist." We, indeed, ascribe all our ideas of spirit and of a spiritual system; our conceptions of God as creator—of creation itself, of providence, and of redemption, to one and the same Spirit, and to that *Logos* who, in one form or other, has been the prophet or the advocate of the Messiah and his cause, for some six thousand years.

We go yet further. We assign to the Spirit of all Wisdom and Revelation the origination of the spiritual language; perhaps, indeed, of all language. The most enlightened men, whether Pagans, Jews, or Christians, regard language as a divine revelation—even that large portion of it derived from sensible objects. The philosophers, from Plato down to Dr. Whitby, have claimed for the Supreme God this honor. They have refused it to either civilized or uncivilized man—to all conventional agreement. They have handled, with great effect, that plainest of propositions, that councils could not be convened; that if they had spontaneously arisen, no motions could have been made, no debates commenced nor conducted without the use of speech. Philosophers assume that men think in words, as well as communicate by them; or, at least, have some image of the thing, natural or artificial, or they cannot even think about it. The natural process, which can easily be made intelligible to all, is, that the *thing* is pre-existent, the *idea* of it next, and the *word* last. The line ascending is the word, the idea, the thing. The line descending is the thing, the idea, the word. Now, as the line descending is necessarily first, we must, especially in things spiritual, admit that the spiritual things could be communicated to man only by one that comprehends them, who had seen them, and who selected from the elements of that language first given to man, when he conversed face to face with God in Eden, the proper materials for words to communicate things spiritual. In strict accordance with this assumption, Moses teaches us that God conferred with Adam, and continued his lessons until Adam was able to give every creature around him a suitable name. That language commenced in this way all admit, from one fact, to wit: EVERY ONE SPEAKS THE LANGUAGE WHICH HE FIRST HEARS. This is his vernacular. A miracle is before us. The first man spoke without being spoken to; else God spoke to him. Either is a miracle: and of the two, the latter is of the easiest credence; and, indeed, it is to the faithful evidently true from the words of Moses. With Plato, then, I say, that God taught the primitive words, and from that, man manufactured the derivatives. With Newton, I say, God gave man reason and religion by giving him speech. With tradition, I say, that the god THATH of the Egyptians is the THEOS of the Bible, and the LOGOS of the New Testament. The LOGOS *incarnate* is the Messiah of christianity. Therefore, the Spirit of God, now the SPIRIT of the WORD, is the origin of all spiritual words and conceptions. With Paul, therefore, I say, "We speak spiritual things in spiritual words, or words which the Spirit teacheth, expressing spiritual things in spiritual words."

I will conclude in the language of the Hebrew poet: "It is God that teacheth man knowledge, and the inspiration of the Almighty giveth him understanding." "The entrance of thy Word giveth light: it giveth understanding to the simple." The very language, then, as well as the ideas that convert the soul, is spiritual. So that truly we may affirm, that in conversion, the Spirit of God operates upon a person only by and through the Word, and the ideas originated by himself. Of all which the first demonstration of the Spirit in fiery tongues, words, language, and signs, is a full and ample proof.—[*Time expired.*

Monday, Nov. 27—11 *o'clock, A. M.*
[MR. RICE'S FIRST REPLY.]

MR. PRESIDENT—There are two principal obstacles in the way of man's salvation. The one is, that he has broken the law of God, and is, therefore, condemned : the other is, that he possesses a depraved nature, and is, therefore, disqualified for the service of God and the happiness of heaven. There are, likewise, two great doctrines which especially characterize the gospel. The one is the atonement of Christ, by which we may be relieved from the curse of the law : the other is the work of the Spirit, by whose agency we may be sanctified and prepared for heaven. These doctrines constitute the two chief pillars in the temple of gospel truth ; and he who attempts to overturn the one or the other, does what he can to destroy the sacred edifice, and to expose the human race, helpless and hopeless, to the wrath of a just God.

The subject of discussion this morning is, therefore, as important as the immortal interests of the soul. Without the atonement of Christ, all must die in a state of condemnation ; and without the special agency of the Holy Spirit, all must die in depravity and be eternally lost.

In the discussion of a subject such as the one now before us, it is of the utmost importance that we understand distinctly the point in controversy. In this, as in his other introductory addresses, my friend, Mr. C., seems to have directed his efforts more to beauty of style and composition, than to the clear statement and defence of his faith. I venture the opinion, that no one individual in this large and intelligent audience, has been able to gather from the address he has just read to us, wherein we differ, or what is the point to be debated. If any one has been so happy as to have been enlightened concerning this important matter, I must award to him more ingenuity and discrimination than I possess. If time were allowed me, and I were capable of writing so handsome a discourse, I might afford the audience another hour's entertainment; and yet they would not know how far we agree in our views of this most important subject, nor wherein we differ.

The gentleman has said a number of things which are true, and a number of things which, I suppose, are not true. Indeed, I could but admire the number of topics he contrived to introduce in the course of an hour—sectarian phraseology, the Trinity, the parts of the work of salvation assigned to each of the Persons, the nature of matter and mind, infant baptism, the origin of language, &c. ! ! ! I cannot subscribe to much that he said with regard to theological systems and sectarian phraseology. With him, it seems, all churches are " *sects* " but his own ; and yet it would be difficult to find a denomination that is more accurately described by a correct definition of the word *sect*. He tells us, he can at any time know a Calvinist or an Arminian by his phraseology before he has heard him an hour. And I will say, that I can identify a modern reformer of his school in half the time ; not by his close adherence to Scripture phraseology, but by the *cant* of the sect. The exclusive claims of some of our modern sects to be *the church*, the *only true church*, savors more of the pride of Rome, than of the Spirit of the gospel. If, however, the gentleman can establish the high claims of his church, he will have accomplished an important work.

The proposition before us is in the following words :—"*In conversion and sanctification, the Holy Spirit operates on persons only through the Word of Truth.*"

The word *conversion*, as used in the Scriptures, in its most enlarged sense, expresses two important ideas, viz : 1st. a change of heart, and 2d. a change of conduct ; or a turning in heart and in life from sin to holiness, from the service of Satan to the service of God. The word signifies literally turning from one thing to another. When an individual who has been pursuing a certain course, turns to an opposite one, we naturally conclude that his mind is changed. Hence the word *conversion* came to signify both cause and effect—the change of heart, and the consequent change of conduct. In this sense it is used in Matt. xviii. 3 : " Except ye be converted, and become as little children, ye shall not enter into the kingdom of heaven."

The word *sanctification* is employed in the Scriptures, and by all accurate theological writers, not to signify something in its nature distinct from regeneration or conversion, but the progress of the gracious work of which regeneration is the commencement.

The difference between us, so far as this subject is concerned, is, in general terms, this : Mr. Campbell believes, that in the work of conversion and sanctification the Spirit operates ONLY *through the Truth*. I believe that the Holy Spirit operates through the truth where, in the nature of the case, the truth can be employed ; but I deny, that the Spirit operates ONLY through the truth. I would not have consented to discuss the proposition, if the word "*only*" had been omitted. For we believe and teach, that the Holy Spirit operates ordinarily through the truth, but not *only* through the truth.

That we may ascertain precisely the point in debate, it is important to inquire how far we agree. I remark, then, that we agree on the following points :

First. That the Holy Spirit dictated the Scriptures—that "holy men spake of old as they were moved by the Holy Ghost."

Secondly. That the Holy Spirit confirmed the truth of the Scriptures by miracles and prophecies.

Thirdly. That in the conversion and sanctification of those who are capable of receiving and understanding the Scriptures, the Spirit operates ordinarily through the truth. Thus far we are agreed. We differ on the following important points :

First. Mr. Campbell contends, that in conversion and sanctification the Spirit never operates without the truth, as the means of influencing the mind. I maintain, that in the case of those dying in infancy and idiocy, the Spirit operates without the truth.

Second. Mr. Campbell affirms, that in the conversion and sanctification of those capable of understanding the Word, the Spirit operates ONLY through the truth—that is, the Spirit dictated and confirmed the Word, and the Word, by its arguments and motives, converts and sanctifies the soul. I desire that this point may be very distinctly apprehended ; for it is of vital importance. Mr. Campbell teaches, that in conversion and sanctification, the Holy Spirit operates on the minds of men, just as *his spirit* operates on the minds of this audience ; or as the spirits of Demosthenes and Cicero operated on the minds of their auditors, or their readers, viz. by his words and arguments alone. As Mr. Campbell presents words and arguments to the minds of his hearers or readers, and those words and arguments exert an influence on them; so the Holy Spirit presents in the Scriptures arguments and motives; and by these alone does He operate on the human mind.

Such precisely is his doctrine on this vital subject. I regret that he did not, in his address, more distinctly present it. To prove to you, my friends, that I am not misrepresenting him, I will read several passages from his *Christianity Restored.*

" Because arguments are addressed to the understanding, will, and affections of men, they are called moral, inasmuch as their tendency is to form or change the habits, manners, or actions of men. Every spirit puts forth its moral power in words: that is, all the power it has over the views, habits, manners, or actions of men, is in the meaning and arrangement of its ideas expressed in words, or in significant signs addressed to the eye or ear. All the moral power of Cicero and Demosthenes was in their orations when spoken, and in the circumstances which gave them meaning; and whatever power these men have exercised over Greece and Rome since their death, is in their writings.

The tongue of the orator and the pen of the writer, though small instruments and of little physical power, are the two most powerful instruments in the world; because they are to the mind as the arms to the body—they are but the instruments of moral power. The strength is in what is spoken or written. *The argument is the power of the spirit of man; and the only power which one spirit can exert over another is its arguments.* How often do we see a whole congregation roused into certain actions, expressions of joy or sorrow, by the spirit of one man. Yet no person supposes that his spirit has literally deserted his body, and entered into every man and woman in the house, although it is often said he has filled them with his spirit. But how does that spirit, located in the head of yonder little man, fill all the thousands around him with joy or sadness, with fear and trembling, with zeal or indignation, as the case may be? How has it displayed such power over so many minds? *By words uttered by the tongue; by ideas communicated to the minds of the hearers.* In this way only can moral power be displayed.

From such premises we may say, that all the moral power which can be exerted on human beings, is, and must of necessity be, in the arguments addressed to them. No other power than moral power can operate on minds; and this power must always be clothed in words, addressed to the eye or ear. Thus we reason when revelation is altogether out of view. And when we think of the power of the Spirit of God exerted upon minds or human spirits, it is impossible for us to imagine, that that power can consist in any thing else but words or arguments. Thus, in the nature of things, we are prepared to expect verbal communications from the Spirit of God, if that Spirit operates at all upon our spirits. As the moral power of every man is in his arguments, so is the moral power of the Spirit of God in his arguments. Thus man still retains an image of his Creator: and from such analogy Paul reasons when he says, ' For the things of a man knows no man, save the spirit of a man which is in him; even so the things of God knows no man, save the Spirit of God.' And the analogy stops not here: for as he is said to resist another, whose arguments he understands and opposes; so are they said to resist the Holy Spirit, who always resist, or refuse to yield to his arguments."—pp. 348, 349.

" But to return. *As the spirit of man puts forth all its moral power, in the words which it fills with its ideas; so the Spirit of God puts forth all its converting and sanctifying power, in the words which it fills with its ideas.* Miracles cannot convert. They can only obtain a favorable hearing of the converting arguments. If they fail to obtain a favorable hearing, the arguments which they prove are impotent as an unknown tongue. If the Spirit of God has spoken all its arguments; or, if the New and Old Testament contain all the arguments which can be offered to reconcile man to God, and to purify them who are reconciled; then all the power of the Holy Spirit which can operate upon the human mind is spent; and he that is not sanctified and saved by these, cannot be saved by angels or spirits, human or divine. * * * *

We plead, *that all the converting power of the Holy Spirit is exhibited in the divine record.*"—pp. 350, 351.

These passages present, with great clearness, the views of Mr. C. on this important subject. He asserts, that in conversion and sanctification the Holy Spirit operates on the minds and hearts of men, only as the spirit of one man operates on the spirit of another. Nay, he even goes further, and denies, not only that the Spirit *does* operate except simply by words and arguments, but that he *can* exert any other influence over the human mind! In the Millenial Harbinger he has given us an exhibition of his doctrine, too clear to admit of any mistake as to his real sentiments. It is as follows:

"As all the influence which my spirit has exerted on other spirits, at home or abroad, has been by the stipulated signs of ideas, of spiritual operations, by my written or spoken word; so believe I that all the influence of God's good Spirit now felt in the way of conviction or consolation in the four quarters of the globe, is by the Word, written, read and heard; which is called the living oracles."—vol. vi. p. 356.

Thus you see, according to the gentleman's doctrine, the Spirit of God has no more power over the minds of men, than his spirit; except that He may present stronger arguments. That is, the only difference consists in the fact, that the Holy Spirit is a more powerful preacher than Mr. Campbell, though his operations are precisely of the same kind!!! Against this doctrine I enter my solemn protest.

We believe and teach, that in conversion and sanctification there is an influence of the Spirit in addition to that of the Word, and distinct from it—an influence, without which the arguments and motives of the gospel would never convert and sanctify one of Adam's ruined race. We further believe, that although the Word of God is employed as the instrument of conversion and sanctification, where it can be used; God has never confined himself to means and instrumentalities, where they cannot be employed. In all ordinary cases He has always clothed and fed men by the use of means; but when his people were journeying through the wilderness to the promised land, and could not obtain either food or raiment in the ordinary way, they were fed with manna from heaven; their thirst was quenched by water miraculously brought out of the rock, and their raiment was not permitted to wax old. When Elisha the prophet could no longer obtain food in the ordinary way, God sent a raven to bear it to him; and when the widow's cruse of oil was almost exhausted, it was miraculously replenished. So does He feed the soul with the bread of life, through means and instrumentalities when they are acessible, and without them when they are not.

But let it be remarked, that whilst we believe in an influence of the Spirit, in addition to the Word, and distinct from it, we do not believe that in conversion new *faculties* are created. The mind, both before and after conversion, possesses understanding, will, and affections. There is no creation of new faculties; but a change of the *moral nature*—a spiritual change—a change from sinfulness to holiness, and from the love and practice of sin to the love and service of God.

Nor do we maintain that in conversion and sanctification, the Holy Spirit reveals to the mind new truths not contained in the Scriptures. "For all Scripture is given by inspiration of God, and is profitable for doctrine, for reproof, for correction and instruction in righteousness : that the man of God may be perfect, thoroughly furnished unto all good works." The design of regeneration is not to reveal new truths, but to enable the sinner, who is blinded by his depravity, to see the truths of revelation in their beauty and excellency, and to incline him to embrace them, and to live accordingly. The difficulty is not, that God's revelation is not perfect, presenting every truth which is necessary to life and godliness; nor that its truths are *obscurely* taught; but that the hearts of men are "fully set in them to do evil"—that they "love darkness more than light"—that they are proud and rebellious, averse to the service of God, and to the plan of salvation which he has devised. The psalmist, David, sensible of his blindness to spiritual things, the glorious truths of revelation, offered this prayer : " Open thou mine eyes, that I may behold wondrous things out of thy law,"—Ps. cxix. 18. The law of God, the Holy Scriptures, he knew contained wonderful things ; but, in consequence of his sinful blindness, he did not behold them clearly and distinctly. He therefore prayed, not for an additional revelation, but for spiritual illumination, for sanctification, that the cause of his blindness being removed, he might see those things in their true nature; that, " with open face he might behold, as in a glass, the glory of the Lord."

This statement of the doctrine of divine influence, is a complete answer to the argument of Mr. Campbell, that those who profess to have been regenerated by the special influence of the Holy Spirit, have received no new ideas which are not contained in the Scriptures. Regeneration consists not in giving a new *revelation*, but a new *heart.*

In further elucidation of this subject, I remark, that the *modus operandi*, the manner in which the Spirit operates on the human heart, we do not pretend to comprehend. Nor is the mysteriousness of the influence, as to the mode of it, an objection against the doctrine. That God created mind and matter, is perfectly clear, and easily apprehended ; but *how* he created either the one or the other, none can understand. The fact, that the mind acts through the body, is clear ; but *how* it acts, no philosopher can explain. Nicodemus, the Jewish ruler, objected to this doctrine as mysterious, and the Savior replied, " The wind bloweth where it listeth ; and thou hearest the sound thereof, but canst not tell whence it cometh and whither it goeth ; so is every one that is born of the Spirit,"—John iii. We feel the blowing of the wind, and perceive its effects ; but *how* it blows, " whence it cometh, and whither it goeth," is a mystery. The Spirit renews the heart. We can realize the effects in ourselves, and see them in others ; but *how* He operates, we cannot comprehend. No man denies that the wind blows, because he cannot explain how it blows ; for he sees and feels the effects. The effects of the Spirit's agency are equally manifest. We see the wicked man turning from his wickedness, and delighting himself in the service of the Holy One of Heaven. We ascribe the marvellous effect to an adequate cause. That cause, the Scriptures teach us, is the Holy Spirit ; but the manner of his operation they do not explain, nor does it become us to inquire concerning it.

Again, I remark, the necessity of the special agency of the Spirit on the heart, in addition to the Word of Truth, does not arise from any lack of evidence that the Bible is a revelation from God. For, to every candid mind, who will weigh the evidence, it is not only conclusive, but overwhelming. Nor does it arise from any obscurity with which its instructions are conveyed; for the inspired pen-men wrote with inimitable simplicity. The great doctrines and duties of christianity are so clearly presented, and so variously illustrated, that all who are willing to know and obey the truth, must understand them. "The King's high-way" is made so plain, that "the way-faring man, though a fool, need not err therein." Nor does it arise from any defect in the *motives* presented in the gospel, to induce men to serve God: for they are high as heaven, deep as hell, vast as eternity, and melting as the dying agonies of the Son of God. Nor is a special divine influence necessary, because man is not a free moral agent; for he is as free as an angel to consider the motives placed before him, and to choose his own course. All that we mean, or can mean, by free moral agency, is, that men, looking at the motives which present themselves to their minds, voluntarily choose their own course. They do as they please—they are under no compulsion.

Why, then, it will be asked, is it necessary that there should be an influence of the Spirit, in addition to that of the Word, and distinct from it? The necessity arises simply from the depravity of the human heart—its pride, its love of sin, and its deep-rooted aversion to the character of God, to his pure law, and his soul-humbling gospel. To secure the perfect and perpetual obedience of the angels, it is enough that the will of God be made known to them; for they are holy—they love God with all their powers, and their fellow-beings as themselves. Their highest joy is derived from his service. They fly, swift as lightning, in obedience to his commands.

But such is not the character of man. He was created in the image of his Maker; but he is fallen—greatly fallen. The divine image has been defaced. The character of God, so glorious in the eyes of angels, has no attractions for him. Pride reigns in his heart. Angels prostrate themselves with adoring wonder and love, before the throne of God; but man is too proud to kneel before Jehovah. Angels find the perfect gratification of their pure affections, and the highest possible happiness, in the contemplation of the works and perfections of God, in communion with Him, and in his holy service. But man is fearfully degraded. He worships and serves the creature, and forgets the Creator. He loves earth, and its low and degrading pleasures. His affections are entwined around them. Appeals to his gratitude and to his interest, fail to withdraw them from earth, and fix them on heaven.

How shall we account for the widely different and opposite courses of conduct pursued by angels and men? Both are rational and accountable creatures, under the government of the same God, having the same motives to obedience. Why do they not see, feel, and act alike? The answer is plain. The angels are holy, and men are sinful—deeply depraved. Hence the necessity of a special divine influence, in addition to, and distinct from, the Word. *Motives* are sufficient to secure the obedience of angels; for they are holy; they are disposed to do their whole duty. Motives will not secure the obedience of men; for they are sinful; they are disposed to rebel. Consequently, if any of the human family love and serve God, it is because He "worketh in them to will and to do, of his good pleasure." If those who have entered upon his service, persevere to the end, it is because "He who began the good work in them, will perform it unto the day of Jesus Christ."

What are the effects of man's depravity, with regard to his reception of the gospel of Christ? The following are some of them:

1. Their minds, their affections, and their thoughts, are occupied with earthly objects; so that, like Gallio, they "care for none of these things." They cannot be induced to hear and to consider. The cares of the world, and the deceitfulness of riches, choke the word. "Israel doth not know; my people do not consider." They are unwilling to be taught the truths of revelation.

2. Others hear and think; but they are deeply averse to the soul-humbling doctrines of the cross, and its pure principles and precepts. "Man, through the pride of his countenance, will not seek after God." Desiring to take the world as their portion, they catch at every cavil against the truth of the Bible, and become infidels: or perverting its plain instructions, and seeking a broader way to heaven, they become heretics.

3. Others still, admitting the inspiration of the Scriptures, and the truth of the doctrines of the cross, are mere speculative believers; and loving the world and the things thereof, they reject the council of God against their own souls. They barter their immortal interests for the pursuits and pleasures of earth.

Such, briefly, are some of the effects of human depravity. It fills the mind with trifles, makes it averse to the truths of revelation, and to the service of God, and thus closes it against the appeals of the gospel of Christ.

In conversion and sanctification, this corruption of nature is to be subdued and eradicated. No individual, it is certain, will ever become a true christian, until he sees sin to be odious, and hates it; till he sees the character of God to be glorious, and loves it; till he perceives his lost condition, and the precise adaptation of the Gospel to secure his salvation, and cordially embraces it; in a word, till the service of God is his joy and his rejoicing. A radical moral change must be experienced, before the sinner will, or can, become a disciple of Christ.

That I have given a correct account of the character of man, I will now prove, by a number of plain declarations of Scripture. Indeed, it is scarcely necessary for me to enlarge on this branch of the subject: for we have just heard read, by Mr. Campbell, several passages of Scripture, which present a very dark picture of human nature. To those I will add several others. In John iii. 6, the Savior, giving the reason why the new birth is necessary, says: "For that which is born of the flesh is flesh; and that which is born of the Spirit is spirit." The meaning of this passage will be clear, if we can ascertain the meaning of the word *flesh*. This word has, in the Scriptures, several meanings; but when used with reference to moral character, it always signifies *depravity, sinfulness*. Thus it is used in Galatians v. 19—21, "Now the works of the flesh are manifest, which are these, adultery, fornication, uncleanness, lasciviousness, idolatry, witchcraft, hatred, variance, emulations, wrath, strife, seditions, heresies, envyings, murders, drunkenness, revilings, and such like." These are the works of the *flesh*, the legitimate products of man's corrupt nature, left to itself. Here we can be at no loss to understand the meaning of the word. It is the cause in man from which flow the dreadful evils here enumerated; it is his corrupt nature or disposition. And let it be remarked, no good is said to proceed from this nature; its fruits are "evil, and only evil, continually." In the same sense the word *flesh* is used in the Epistle to the Romans, viii. 1, 6, 8, 9, "There is, therefore, now no condemnation to them that are in Christ, who walk not after the flesh, but after the Spirit." "To walk after the *flesh* is to be wicked, to walk after the *Spirit* is to be holy." Again, "So then, they that are in the flesh cannot please God. But ye are not in the flesh, but in the Spirit, if so be that the Spirit of God dwell in you." They who are in the flesh cannot please God. It is evident, therefore, that there is nothing morally good in them ; for God is pleased with goodness where-ever he sees it. But who are in the flesh? All are in the flesh, unless the Spirit of God dwell in them. It is, then, perfectly clear, that the passage—" That which is born of the flesh is flesh,"—means, that by the natural birth all are depraved, entirely depraved ; for the flesh, as we have seen, produces nothing but evil.

The same doctrine is taught in Gen. viii. 21, "And the Lord smelled a sweet savor ; and the Lord said in his heart, I will not again curse the ground any more for man's sake ; for [or *though*] the imagination of his heart is evil from his youth." I do not read the description of man's character, as given in Genesis vi., because some have pretended, that it applied only to the corrupt generation then living ; and I desire to prove, that after the flood, when only Noah and his family remained on earth, the same doctrine was taught in the most unqualified terms—" The ima-gination of his heart, [the human heart] is evil from his youth." It is evil from the earliest period of his being.

The same doctrine is taught, in the strongest language, in Psalm li. 5 : " Behold, I was shapen in iniquity ; and in sin did my mother conceive me." Again, Psalm lviii. 3—5 : "The wicked are estranged from the womb ; they go astray as soon as they be born, speaking lies. Their poison is like the poison of a serpent ; they are like the deaf adder that stoppeth her ear ; which will not hearken to the voice of charmers, charming never so wisely." These passages teach the doctrine of the original and entire depravity of man from his birth, in language so clear and so strong, that comment is unnecessary.

The same exhibition of the character of man is made by the prophet Jeremiah, chap. xvii. 9, 10 : "The heart is deceitful above all things, and desperately wicked ; who can know it? I the Lord search the heart ; I try the reins, even to give every man according to his ways, and ac-cording to the fruit of his doings." Observe, he does not say the hearts of *some* men, or of some *classes* of men, are thus deceitful and desperate-ly wicked ; but THE HEART, using the most general expression in human language, without qualification. How dark is the picture—"deceitful above all things, and desperately wicked ;. who can know it !"

In the third chapter to the Romans, Paul gives an infallible description of man, as he is in heart and in life. "There is none righteous, no, not one ; there is none that understandeth, there is none that seeketh after God. They are all gone out of the way ; they are together become un-profitable ; there is none that doeth good, no, not one. Their throat is an open sepulchre ; with their tongues they have used deceit ; the poison of asps is under their lips ; whose mouth is full of cursing and bitterness. Their feet are swift to shed blood. Destruction and misery are in their ways ; and the way of peace have they not known. There is no fear of God before their eyes." Thus Paul presents the deep and total corrup-tion of man's nature. The description belongs not to one class, or to one nation, or to one age. He pronounces it a correct exhibition of the char-acter of both Jews and gentiles. All men do not actually commit all kinds of sin; nor do all proceed to the same length in any one course. But there are in man the seeds of all evil—a nature which, freed from restraint, and exposed to temptation, will run headlong into crimes of all kinds. Such is, in fact, the character of the human race, that John, the apostle, says, without qualification, "The whole world lieth in wickedness." 1 John v. 19.

In further confirmation of the doctrine of man's total depravity, if indeed the evidence can be increased, I will state an important fact, viz: *that all that is morally good in any man is by the Scriptures ascribed to a radical change of heart, of which God is the author.* Does any one do good works? Paul ascribes it to a new creation. "For we are his workmanship, created in Christ Jesus into good works, which God hath before ordained that we should walk in them," Eph. ii. 10. Does any one love God and his fellow-creatures? John says, "He that loveth *is born of God*," 1 John iv. 7. Does any one believe, that Jesus is the Christ? The same apostle says, he "is born of God," ch. v. 1. Since, then, all that is good in man is ascribed to a great change wrought in his heart by the Holy Spirit, and all that is evil is ascribed to his nature; it follows inevitably, that he is entirely corrupt.

Such being the character of men, it is impossible, till their hearts are renewed, that they shall love God, his law, or his gospel, or find pleasure in his service. The reason is this: No human being ever admired and loved a moral character just the opposite of his own. Both the judgment and the conscience of a wicked man may constrain him to acknowledge, that his virtuous neighbor is better than he; but he will not choose him as a companion, because of his purity of heart and life, nor find pleasure in his society. "The light shineth in darkness; and the darkness comprehendeth it not." Our Savior appeared amongst the Jews in all the perfection and loveliness of human nature and in the glory of divinity— "the glory as of the Only-begotten of the Father;" and yet they hated him, because his character was to theirs, as light to darkness. "For what fellowship hath righteousness with unrighteousness? and what communion hath light with darkness?" 2 Cor. vi. 14.

It is, then, perfectly clear, that every individual must experience a radical change in his moral character, before he ever will love God or embrace the gospel of Christ. But are the truths of revelation sufficient to effect this change? They are not. If a man has conceived a strong prejudice against his neighbor, through a mistaken view of his character and conduct, you may remove the prejudice by giving him correct information. Or if one man entertains unkind feelings towards another, only because of some peculiar circumstances in which they happen to be placed in relation to each other; a change of circumstances may produce a change of feelings—reconciliation may take place. Thus Joseph's brethren hated him, because they looked upon him as a successful rival in the affections of their father. But when the circumstances were changed, and, instead of regarding him as a rival, they looked up to him as a benefactor; their feelings were changed, and they were reconciled. But if a man hate the true character of his neighbor; if he dislike him, not viewed through erroneous information, but *as he really is;* the one or the other must greatly change, or they will never come together as friends. You cannot induce the man who hates the real character of his fellow-man, to love him, by presenting the hated qualities more distinctly to his view. The more distinctly he sees that which he dislikes, the stronger, of course, is his aversion to it. Suppose, for example, an individual has a most inveterate dislike to some particular *color*, red, if you please. Will you be able to make him admire it by placing it before his eyes in the clearest possible light? The color is the very thing he dislikes; and you present it to him in its scarlet hue with the hope of inducing him to admire it! Evidently until his *taste*, if I may so call it, is changed, no clearness of light through which it is seen, will cause him to admire it.

Let me apply the illustration. God is infinitely pure; his law is "holy, just, and good;" and his gospel is like its glorious author. The character of man is just the opposite. Consequently his aversion to God does not arise either from mistake, or from any unfavorable circumstances, which might be changed. He is sinful; God is infinitely pure; therefore there is in his heart a deep-rooted aversion to God. "The carnal mind is enmity against God." The word of God is compared to *light*. It is the medium through which we see the objects of revelation. Light is the medium through which you see objects around you. It presents to your view many things that please, and many that offend. Select, if you please, one of the objects to which you have the greatest aversion. Concentrate upon it as much light as possible, so that you distinctly see its every feature. Now let me ask, will this concentration of light upon an object to which you have the strongest aversion, cause you to admire and love it? You say, it will not. Light cannot change your feelings toward an object which you dislike. Either the object must change, or you must change before you will love it. Let your mind be changed; and the same light which before revealed its apparent deformity, will now reveal its beauty and loveliness.

So through the light of revelation we have presented to our minds the character of God, his law, his gospel, heaven and hell. This revelation presents these objects in their true character; but men, because of their depravity, feel a strong aversion to them. They are not averse to the character of God and the gospel of Christ *through mistake*, but they dislike these glorious objects in their real character. Now when a man whose heart is enmity to God in his true character, has that character presented to his mind by the light of Divine Truth; will the light cause him to admire and to love it? Or will he whose proud heart rises in rebellion against the pure and soul-humbling gospel, be induced to love and embrace it by having it very clearly presented to his view? Surely not. It is clear, then, that man must experience a radical moral renovation—must be greatly changed, or he never will love God and obey the gospel of Christ.

This I take to be correct philosophy, as well as correct theology. There is no mysticism and no abstruse speculation in it. It requires not the mind of a Newton, a Locke, or a Bacon to perceive its truth. It strikes the common sense of every reflecting mind; and it presents to view the reason why conversion and sanctification never can be secured, in the case of any one of our race, without an agency of the Holy Spirit in addition to the truth, and distinct from it.

Having thus briefly explained the doctrine for which I contend, and proved the necessity of a direct divine influence in conversion and sanctification, I wish now to offer some further arguments against the doctrine believed and taught by Mr. Campbell.

I. My first argument is this:—*It prescribes to the power of God over the human mind, an unreasonable and unscriptural limitation.* I can never subscribe to the doctrine, that God can exert over the human mind no more power than I, except that he may employ stronger arguments; that the Creator can influence men morally, only as they may be pleased to listen to his arguments. I can never consent to place the Holy Spirit on a perfect equality with man, except that he is a better preacher.

1st. The doctrine which thus limits the power of the Spirit, is *most unreasonable* as well as most *unscriptural.* God created man holy in the beginning, and he did it without words and arguments. Gen. i. 26, 27, "And God said, let us make man *in our image, after our likeness.* ——So God created man in his own image, in the image of God created he him." "Lo this only have I found, that God hath made man upright, but they have sought out many inventions." Now, if God could origi- nally create man holy, without words and arguments, who shall presume to assert that he *cannot* create him anew, and restore his lost image, with- out them; or that he has now no power over the human mind, beyond that of argument and motive? The gentleman may philosophise and speculate as much as he pleases, to prove that God has no more power over the heart of man than a fellow creature; but the simple fact now stated, that originally he made him upright without words or arguments, is abundantly sufficient to refute his theory.

As he created man holy, so can he new-create him. As he created Adam in his own image without words, so can he renew the infant mind, and prepare it for heaven, though it cannot receive the truth.

Mr. Campbell will not deny that God created man upright, since in his *Christian System* he has so taught: (pp, 26, 28.)

"Man, then, in his natural state, was not merely an animal, but an intel- lectual, moral, PURE, and HOLY being."

Again:

"God made man upright, but they sought out many inventions. Adam rebelled. The natural man became preternatural," &c.

If, then, God made man upright without words and arguments, exert- ing a moral influence over his mind without motives; who can prove, that now his power is limited to mere words and arguments?

It is admitted, that the light of revelation is necessary to call into exer- cise proper feelings and affections, and to prompt to a right course of conduct; for we cannot love an object of which we know nothing, nor obey a law concerning the requirements of which we are not informed. But whether the light will call into exercise such feelings, depends upon the moral character or state of the mind. The Jews beheld the miracles wrought by the Messiah in proof of his divinity and of his mission to save men; but such was the state of their minds, that they were either unconvinced or unwilling to become his followers. Thus Paul accounted for their blindness in reading the Old Testament, and yet rejecting the very truths which it most clearly revealed. "But their minds were blind- ed, for until this day remaineth the same veil untaken away in the read- ing of the Old Testament," 2 Cor. iii. 14.

The gentleman would make the impression on your minds, that accord- ing to our doctrine there is no need of the gospel at all. But this is not true. The light is necessary as the medium through which we may see the objects around us; but the light will not open the eyes of the blind. The sun may shine with noon-day brightness, but the blind man will be blind still; or if a man hate the light and shut his eyes against it, he will not see. This is not owing to any defect in the light, but to the defect in his eyes in the one case, and to hatred of light in the other. So the light of revealed truth is necessary to present to the mind the objects calculated to call into exercise holy affections; but whether the effect will be produced, depends upon the state of the heart. The fact, that men love darkness more than light, and turn from beholding it, argues no imperfection in the light.

The light is still necessary, though of itself it cannot cause the blind to see. The gospel is equally necessary, though of itself insufficient to renew and sanctify the depraved hearts of men. If a man were suddenly made as holy as an angel, he could not love God, unless he knew him; nor embrace the gospel, unless it were presented to him; nor do his work, unless it were made known to him; nor aspire to heaven, unless it were revealed to him. But when, by the Holy Spirit, the heart of the sinner has been renewed, he is filled with adoring gratitude, and with deep penitence, as the cross of Christ is presented to his view. He beholds an adaptation in the plan of salvation to his situation, which he never saw before; and a glory in the character of the blessed Redeemer, he never before beheld. In the beginning God made man upright; yet a revelation of himself and of his will, was absolutely necessary, that he might love and obey him. For similar reasons, the gospel is necessary, though alone it cannot purify man.

2d. That Mr. Campbell's doctrine prescribes an unreasonable and unscriptural limitation to the power of God over the human mind, is proved conclusively by *the fact, that God does, in the course of his providence, exert over the moral conduct of man, a controlling influence, which is not simply nor chiefly by words and arguments.* And if he can control them at all, without words and arguments, he can control them to any extent. This fact I will prove by several declarations of Scripture. Exod. xxxiv. 24. All the adult males of the Jews were required to go to Jerusalem thrice every year, to attend their three principal festivals. But how could they safely leave their families and their possessions exposed, as they must be, to the incursions of malignant enemies on their borders? To free their minds from apprehension, God gave them the following promise: "For I will cast out the nations before thee, and enlarge thy borders; neither shall any man desire thy land, when thou shalt go up to appear before the Lord." Does not this promise proclaim the truth, that God could and would exercise a controlling influence over the *desires* of the surrounding nations? He not only said, that they should not invade the territory of his people, but that they should not *desire* their land. Had he no power to control their desires? or did he restrain them by words and arguments?

Again, Prov. xxi. 1: "The king's heart is in the hand of the Lord: as the rivers of water, he turneth it whithersoever he will." Does Solomon mean that God turns the hearts of kings by *words and arguments?* Observe, the language is very emphatic—expressing the entire control which God can and does exercise over the hearts of kings. "He turneth it whithersoever he will, even as he turns the rivers of water." And if he can, and does thus completely turn the hearts of kings, can he not, and does he not also turn the hearts of others, not by words and arguments only? We cannot avoid seeing, that in this passage God claims to govern men by an influence far more powerful than mere motive.

The same truth is taught with equal clearness in Ezra vi. 22. The Jews, who had returned from captivity in Babylon, "kept the feast of unleavened bread seven days with joy: for the Lord had made them joyful, and turned the heart of the king of Assyria unto them, to strengthen their hands in the work of the house of God, the God of Israel." Here we have a very remarkable instance of the exertion of a divine influence over the moral conduct of a pagan king—a man who believed not in God's revelation, but was an idolater. He *turned* the proud heart of this king to his people, so that he aided them in the building of the temple at Jerusalem. Did he influence this king by words and arguments? Was this remarkable conduct of the king the effect of mere *motives?*

Again, chap. viii. 27, 28: "This Ezra went up from Babylon; and he was a ready scribe in the law of Moses, which the Lord God of Israel had given: and the king granted him all his request, according to the hand of the Lord his God upon him." Ezra having obtained a decree of the king, in favor of the work of building the temple, uttered the following language: "Blessed be the Lord God of our fathers, which hath put such a thing as this in the king's heart, to beautify the house of the Lord, which is in Jerusalem; and hath extended mercy unto me before the king and his counsellors, and before all the king's mighty princes." Ezra recognized the hand of the Lord in his success; a divine influence on the hearts of proud and ungodly idolaters; and he, therefore, offers thanks to God for this remarkable interposition. Was this an influence exerted by words and arguments? Did not God control the moral conduct of those men by another, and more powerful influence?

The same doctrine is illustrated and confirmed by Neh. i. 11. Nehemiah had heard of the deplorable condition of Jerusalem and its inhabitants; and he desired to go and rebuild the temple and the city. It was necessary to gain the consent of the king of Babylon; and, therefore, he prays—"O Lord, I beseech thee, let now thine ear be attentive to the prayer of thy servant, and to the prayer of thy servants, who desire to fear thy name; and prosper, I pray thee, thy servant this day, and grant him mercy in the sight of this man." Nehemiah prayed for what? That the Lord would so influence the mind of the king, that he would grant him his request. And his prayer was answered—"And the king granted me, according to the good hand of my God upon me."—chap. ii. 8.

These passages, and many others, prove, beyond controversy, that God can, and does exert upon the minds of men a controlling influence, distinct from words and arguments. Consequently the doctrine of Mr. Campbell, which denies that he does, or can exert any other moral influence than that of mere motives, is not true.

I will now offer a second argument against the gentleman's doctrine. By the way, I should have been disposed to follow him in his argument, if he had made any distinct statement of his doctrine, and attempted to prove it. But it cannot be expected that I should follow him in such a dissertation as that we have heard this morning; in which there is no clear and definite statement of the points at issue, and, of course, no clear and pointed argument. It has, therefore, become necessary for me to state his doctrine from his published works, and to advance arguments against it.

II. The argument I was about to offer, is this: *Mr. Campbell's doctrine necessarily involves the damnation of all infants and idiots.* I do not say, that he holds the doctrine of infant damnation; but I do say, that, to be consistent, he must hold it—for it follows, as a necessary consequence, if his doctrine concerning divine influence is true.

3 H

The gentleman, I must so far digress as to remark, is yet in trouble on the subject of infant baptism. He has brought it up again. I did suppose, that, after calling it up in almost every speech since the subject was disposed of, he had at last fully delivered himself upon it; but I was mistaken. If I understand his remarks correctly, he said, that all infants, baptized or not, are saved. Is he not aware, that no Presbyterian, Methodist, or evangelical Pedo-baptist baptizes infants for the purpose of saving them from hell, should they die in infancy? Many things in the plan of salvation we regard as useful, that are not absolutely essential to the salvation of the soul. We esteem it a precious privilege and a solemn duty to enter into covenant with God to train up our children in his nurture and admonition, and humbly to claim his promise to be a God to us and to our seed. God has commanded us to bring our children with us into the covenant and into the church; and we think it wise and useful to obey him. I hope the gentleman will now be satisfied; but if he still feels uneasy, he must still scatter his remarks about infant baptism through all his speeches to the close of the debate.

But to return. The gentleman's doctrine, I have said, necessarily involves the damnation of infants and idiots. This is an important argument; for more than one third of the human race die in infancy. And although I do not suppose, that his views will affect the safety of infants; still it is a subject which very deeply interests the feelings of every affectionate parent. It would indeed be difficult to induce them to believe, that infants, incapable of knowing right or wrong, are sent to hell.

It is a truth, clearly taught in Scripture and admitted by Mr. C., that infants and idiots are by nature depraved. Our Savior said—" That which is born of the flesh, is flesh." By the natural birth all are depraved. This, I say, Mr. Campbell admits. I will read an extract or two from his *Christian System*, where he has presented his views on this subject.

" This alarming and most strangely pregnant of all the facts in human history, proves that Adam was not only the common father, but the actual representative of all his children. * * * There is therefore a sin of our nature, as well as personal transgression. Some inappositely call the sin of our nature our ' original sin;' as if the sin of Adam was the personal offence of all his children. True indeed it is, our nature was corrupted by the fall of Adam before it was transmitted to us; and hence, that hereditary imbecility to do good, and that proneness to do evil, so universally apparent in all human beings. Let no man open his mouth against the transmission of a moral distemper, until he satisfactorily explain the fact, that the special characteristic vices of parents appear in their children as much as the color of their skin, their hair, or the contour of their faces. A disease in the moral constitution of man is as clearly transmissible as any physical taint, if there be any truth in history, biography, or human observation. Still man, with all his hereditary imbecility, is not under an invincible necessity to sin. Greatly prone to evil, easily seduced into transgression, he may or may not yield to passion· and seduction. Hence the differences we so often discover in the corruption and depravity of man. All inherit a fallen, consequently a sinful nature; though all are not equally depraved. * * * Condemned to natural death, and greatly fallen and depraved in our whole moral constitution though we certainly are, in consequence of the sin of Adam; still, because of the interposition of the second Adam, none are punished with everlasting destruction from the presence of the Lord, but those who actually and voluntarily sin against a dispensation of mercy under which they are placed."

This system is indeed quite orthodox; and since this is the gentleman's second confession of faith, we may hope that his third will bring him very nearly right! There is, then, he acknowledges, " a *sin of our nature*, as well as personal transgression;" there is " a disease in the moral constitution of man;" and he is " greatly fallen and depraved in his whole moral constitution." Now the question is—how are infants, thus fallen and depraved, to be saved? The gentleman, with singular inconsistency, admits their depravity, denies any divine influence by which they can be sanctified, and still expresses the opinion, that they may be saved!

Infants, it is admitted, are depraved. Then, concerning all that die in infancy, one of three things is necessarily true, viz: either they go to hell, or they go to heaven, *in their depravity;* or they are sanctified by the Spirit *without the truth.* But we know, that they cannot go to heaven in their depravity; we know, that they cannot be sanctified *through the truth*, which they cannot comprehend; and Mr. Campbell denies, that they can be sanctified *without the truth.* We are, therefore, forced to the horrible conclusion, if his doctrine be true, that they die in depravity, and are forever lost! With his *opinions* on this subject I have nothing to do. They directly contradict his *doctrine;* and, therefore, the one or the other is false. But here I will, for the present, close my argument.— [*Time expired.*

[MR. CAMPBELL'S SECOND ADDRESS.]

Monday, Nov. 27—12 o'clock, M.

MR. PRESIDENT—I have had reasons numerous and various, before to-day, to conclude that my zealous opponent has fallen upon a rather singular mode of conducting the defence of the dogmata of his party, and of assailing us. When the Presbyterians first proposed the discussion to me, it was distinctly stated and agreed upon, that we should severally maintain and defend the doctrines which we teach, in such words and propositions as we respectively preferred. The points selected were supposed to comprehend the points at issue. It was also always contemplated and understood on my part, that we should have an equal number of affirmatives and negatives, as our correspondence will exhibit, when examined from first to last. We have now had the experience of ten days, and upon an impartial retrospect of the past, and of the speech of this morning, I must say, that I have never before been placed exactly in the same circumstances. I have had some little experience in conducting popular discussions, and have had a considerable variety of opponents, some that sought always to lead, and some who preferred to follow; but I have never before found just such an opponent as my friend, Mr. Rice, one that will neither lead nor follow. [A laugh.] This is precisely the state of the case. He has conducted the discussion of two affirmatives. I did not wish to form an estimate of the man, his talents, or his policies, from his management of the first. But I have now all the data before me, which the present occasion will afford. He has done with his affirmative propositions. He is now, for the third time, on the negative.

On the first affirmative, I was curious to comprehend his resources, and to form a proper estimate of his powers of defence. After speaking nearly half an hour, he took out his watch, and during twenty minutes looked at it no less than five times. Finally, before his time expired, he asked the moderators if his time was not nearly expended. On learning that he had still a few minutes, he sat down. Thus toiled he under the *onus probandi* of an infant subject of baptism. On Saturday last, as most of you will remember, when his other affirmative was on hand, after various efforts in his opening speech, to advance into the merits of the question, after the fourth appeal to his tardy watch, he sat down at the end of forty minutes !

He looks to me, sir, for matter of argumentation. He is made for contradiction. I have then to furnish materials for both sides. Instead of responding to the proper issue, already formed, he seeks in my addresses new points from which to digress into new regions of negations ; that is to say, I must give him data out of which to excogitate new, adventitious, and foreign subjects—on which to wrangle in the way of digression. He endeavors to make me always affirm, even while on the negative side, that he may occupy a negative position as often as convenient.

Of all this I ought not, probably, to complain. It is the best, the very best mode of defence which his cause affords. I must, however, because of his boastful manner, expose the awkwardness of his position, and the barrenness of the soil which he occupies. He can do no better.

The gentleman knew that he had not one argument, not one precept, or precedent in the Bible in support of either of his affirmations. His hope, then, rested upon remote questions, far off inferences, involved reasonings, irrelevant or false issues and contingencies. And while I affirm and file off my arguments numerically, challenging investigation, why does he not, why can he not, respond to them as in duty bound, according to all the laws of disputation ? Has he then, sirs, at all responded to my opening speech on this grand proposition ? With all reasonable emphasis, I pronounced argument first, second, third, &c., in order to challenge his special attention. But I could not succeed. The gentleman is not to be moved in that way. I have then, sir, really and in truth, no opponent on this occasion. In a speech of one hour, he did not come up to one of my arguments, as though he felt it neither necessary or important formally to encounter them.

These arguments I introduced by a considerable preface, containing very important items of thought, and even of argument, as I supposed, demanding some notice. Even that, too, the gentleman found it most convenient to pass in a respectful silence. But he was pleased to say, that I do not state the issue, nor make out the difference between us. Did I not read the proposition ? Did I not distinctly affirm "That the Spirit of God *operates* in conversion and sanctification *only through the truth?*" This I solemnly affirm as my belief. This he denies. He maintains another proposition, viz : That the Spirit of God operates in conversion and sanctification, not only through the truth, *but sometimes without it.* The issue, then, was fairly stated and definitely made out. There is no necessity for expatiating much more on this subject. I submitted seven arguments in proof of the issue agreed upon. He has formally responded to none of them. In so doing I cannot but conclude that the argument, the real issue, is given up, and the gentleman *cannot* at all respond to my proof. This is my conscientious conviction. I may, then, either sit down, or proceed for the gratification of the audience, to state some other arguments and proofs. I opine the gentleman will never answer those now on hand ; indeed, I feel confident he cannot.

He has given us a few of the dry remains of some old harangues or lectures upon total depravity, which he may have preached around the country I know not how many times. This matter is wholly foreign to the subject. The question is not about total depravity. I believe man is depraved. He is proving a proposition, wide as the breadth of the heavens of the subject before us. I believe that God presides over all the works of his hands. But that is not the point of debate ; nor is the question about what God can or cannot do—whether or not he turns the hearts of kings and mortals, as the channels of the rivers or the seas are turned. Whether he disposes the hearts of men, without words, is not the question : for were it proved that he can move kings and princes, and men of all ranks and degrees, as I believe, without the Bible, and without words, that reaches not this issue at all. The question before us is about *sanctification*, about *conversion*. These are but sallies, feints, mock assaults, wholly alien to the issue. The question is, whether God *converts* men to Christ, or *sanctifies* christians, *without the truth of the Bible*. If I could now marvel at any course the gentleman might adopt, I would at his present singular attitude. Neither as affirmant or respondent will he keep to the Bible. I truly regret this truckling and catering to vulgar prejudices—this *ad captandum* rhetoric. When he will rise, he may tell you with a smile, " Well, I cannot please my friend, Mr. Campbell, nor do I expect to please him." Mighty logic, indeed ! Unanswerable argument, truly ! Alas !—as my friend would say—alas ! for the cause that depends upon such logical legerdemain !

While on this subject, I beg leave to expatiate for a moment on the scenes transpiring around us. I came here, at considerable sacrifice, to debate certain great principles with the elect representative of a respectable religious denomination, claiming the advantages of an elevated clerical character, and some antiquity in some of its tenets and forms. During ten days, I have carefully observed the management, the tactics and developments of my respondent and his party. I do not recollect on any occasion, certainly at no discussion of any great religious question, to have noticed so much homage and condescension to catch, if not to manufacture, public opinion—and to set on foot the opinion that Mr. R. had gained a glorious victory, in the cause of immersion at least. Touching this love of partizan triumph, I am aware that this is common to such occasions; but the means by which it is sought on the present occasion, really surpass every thing I have ever known or witnessed.

I was, indeed, expecting something of the kind ; but my anticipations have been greatly transcended. On arriving in this city, I asked a gentleman whom I now see standing in this audience, how many newspapers were published in this city, and by whom, and to what parties the editors belonged. Being informed on these points, the gentleman wished to know my reasons for making these inquiries. I responded, that I simply desired to know what facilities my Presbyterian friends might have for manufacturing public opinion. My experience led me to expect that efforts of this kind would be made ; for, in my debate with Mr. McCalla, past twenty years ago, that indefatigable party had spared no pains to propagate and circulate a glorious Pedo-baptist victory, and so continued for several days, until Pedo-baptism became so perfectly bald and naked, that none seemed disposed to do it homage. For at least two or three days, rumors were sent abroad all over the land, that Mr. McCalla had gloriously maintained the cause. A reverend gentleman, now in this assembly, one of the moderators of that discussion, on his return to Flemingsburgh, as I learn from good authority, very ingeniously explained the result of that discussion, very much to the credit of the party. The excited community, on hearing of his arrival, were anxious to hear his opinion as to the final result. Some of the elders of his church approaching him, said, "Well, sir, what of the debate?—how did it close?" " Why, sir," said he, " Campbell would prove that a *crow* was *white,* if you would listen to him." This sage remark saved the cause, at the expense of my reputation. It was the man that was defeated, and not the cause of infant baptism.

On the present occasion, I learn a more extended system has been got up. Runners spread the tidings abroad—letters are written to distant places ; even the Presbyterian press has proclaimed all over the land a glorious victory. To the old system more thoroughly carried out, has, in this age of the march of mind, been added a new invention. True, indeed, something like it in days of yore, seems to have occurred at Drury Lane and other London theatres, when some new actor was about to make his *debut.* In order to stimulate his energies, and to manufacture fame, a few friends were stationed in the galleries above, with a previous understanding when to clap, express their plaudits, and to encore his performances. As an improvement, I learn a laughing committee has been organized, with a clerical fugleman, at whose signal certain persons are to smile a little broad, and thus encourage my worthy friend ! I have, indeed, in these particulars, been somewhat disappointed. My Pedo-baptist friends have rather gone ahead of all my past experiences and expectations.

During the Roman Catholic discussion at Cincinnati, in 1836, I had a second lesson in this school of experience. A certain Protestant editor, who would at this day take rank among Puseyites of the first class, soon as the discussion began, set on foot a manufacturing of public opinion. He observed, very frankly, one day, that it was due to Protestantism that should not triumph over the bishop, on some of the questions at least; I for, said he, we ought all to know that our bishops stand or fall with those of the Roman hierarchy. " If Mr. Campbell destroys the succession, on what shall we hang our plea? our episcopacy goes by the board !" Still I was not prepared for all that I have seen, and read, and heard on this occasion. I had hoped the dignity of the discussion and the solemnity of the occasion would have prevented any thing of this sort.

For myself, I contend for truth, and not for victory without truth. My prayer is, that truth, immutable, eternal truth, may prevail. The occasion demands a calm, dignified, religious investigation of these grand principles. It is all-important that it should be so. We are getting up a book for the public, and we desire to give it to them without prejudice and without bribe. Our motto is, Read, think, judge, and decide every man for himself.

I did not come here to gain a triumph of that sort. I did not consider there were any laurels to be won, nor any honors to be gained in this field, nor from my present opponent. I presume no one of reflection thinks otherwise. I never felt more the dignity, grandeur, and power of truth than on the present occasion. She, standing erect, with lofty mien, and heaven-directed eye, deigns not to use any other arguments or to employ any other means than consience, religion, and the God of truth will sanction and approve. Her reliance is not on human passion, temporal interest, nor fleshly policies ; but on solid facts, substantial reasons, and dignified argumentation. Entering upon a new week and upon a new subject, I regard it due to myself, my brethren, the public, and the triumphing cause of Divine Truth, to offer this critique upon the past; that, if possible, we may redeem time and proceed in a manner more worthy of ourselves and the cause we advocate. To proceed, then, to the subject offered by Mr. Rice in his last speech.

Human depravity and special providence are not the topics on hand. The gentleman must reply to me or admit that he cannot. It is my duty now to lead, and his to follow, if he can. Meantime, I have nothing to defend, and nothing to do in further maintaining my position—it seems to be established. I will, therefore, make some remarks on the gentleman's use of my writings. I do not shrink from the discussion of any thing I have ever written on this subject. Yet it would be more than human, more than any mortal man has yet achieved, if, in twenty years' writing, and in issuing one magazine of forty-eight octavo pages every month, written both at home and abroad, in steamboats, hotels, and in the houses of my private friends and brethren; I should have so carefully, definitely, and congruously expressed myself on every occasion, on these much controverted subjects, as to furnish no occasion to our adversaries to extract a sentence or a passage which, when put into their crucible and mixed with other ingredients, might not be made to appear somewhat different from itself, and myself, and my other writings. To seal the lips of cavilling sectarians and captious priests, is a natural impossibility. The Great Teacher himself could not, at least he did not do it.

I state it as a fact somewhat curious, that for several years I have not looked over my first volumes; nor do I, when about to write upon a subject, feel it necessary to examine all that I have previously said about it. I am at no such pains to prevent contradictions, real or apparent. The secret is, I have, like the four cardinal points, certain grand principles clearly defined and solidly fixed in my own mind. These I cannot forget nor contradict. I can affirm, off-hand, what I have *not* written, if I cannot always say what I *have* written. I cannot contradict these fundamentals—they are sternly fixed in my mind. As the first principle of mathematics can never be forgotten, nor lost sight of, while the mind is master of itself; so the grand fundamental principles of christianity can never be forgotten by him who has once clearly apprehended and sincerely embraced them. We may not, however, always express ourselves with equal clearness and precision.

As respects the passages read from Christianity Restored, I will say that the gentleman has very greatly misrepresented me. I was explaining what is usually called *moral* power in contradistinction from *physical* power, or what some call *spiritual* power, as defined by some of our schoolmen. Physical force and the power of motives are very different things. Reasons, containing *motives*, constitute the elements and materials of all moral, *converting* or *sanctifying* power, so far as known to man. God's power is omnipotent, but it is consistent with himself and itself. The gospel, Paul says, is "*the power of God unto salvation.*" Hence the moral omnipotence of God is in the document called the gospel. God's moral power is infinitely superior to ours. *Yet all that power is in the gospel,* and this is all we mean by all the converting power being in the Word of God. God may employ other means, other power, if you please, in converting men; but nothing finally converts them but the light and love of God in the gospel.

Every word of God has life in it. If I might explain myself by one of the divine metaphors:—The seed, said Jesus, is *the Word of God.*

Now every grain of wheat, sound and good, has *life* in it; but it must be placed in a soil and under circumstances favorable to its development. It will not germinate nor grow but under those circumstances. Hence, when the Word of God is sown in the heart, it will grow and develop itself in all the fruits of righteousness and holiness. The question is not, *how* it is sown, *how it gets into the heart;* but the question is, as to the power developed and exhibited when there. Whenever the seed of the Word is planted in the moral constitution of man, I believe it will vegetate, grow, blossom, and fructify unto eternal life.

With Mr. Rice conversion and sanctification seem to be by the Spirit alone. If this be so in one case, it is so in all cases. This is one of my main arguments; for, as before affirmed, whatever will produce one ear of corn will produce an indefinite number; seeing that all that is essential in any one case, is essential, neither more nor less, in every other case. So observation and experience testify in all vegetable and animal products. Is it not so, also, in the spiritual? If the Bible is to be our only guide, that it is so, can be made most evident. It is thus that we use and apply those offensive words, that all the converting power of the Holy Spirit is in the Word. All the motives, arguments, and persuasions of the Holy Spirit are found in the record. He uses no other in the work of conversion, or in the work of sanctification. "Sanctify them through thy truth." "The law of the Lord is perfect, converting the soul." So far as *moral* influence is concerned there is none besides, none beyond this.

If there be any other moral or spiritual influence in the new creation of man, we call for the testimony and the definition of it. If the Lord converts, sanctifies, and saves an infant without the Word, the gospel of Christ—sanctification or conversion, then, is independent of the Word; and seeing it is so, the Word ceases to be *the means* of grace and of conversion. The fact that whatever is essential to one product, whether animal, vegetable, intellectual, moral or spiritual, is essential to every other result of the same kind, will one day explode this mystic, unintelligible, unscriptural jargon, which makes void and of non-effect the Word of the living God.

The doctrine which I oppose, so far as it is really believed and acted upon, neutralizes preaching, annuls the Bible, and perfectly annihilates human responsibility. I know of no doctrine more fatal. For if God, by some mysterious power, without light, knowledge, a new idea, view or reflection, touch the soul of A, B, or C, and make it holy by "infusing a holy principle," if he does this without any thought, motive, or argument, instantaneously and immediately, what comes of the doctrine of human responsibility! Of what use is preaching, or the name of the Lord Jesus, or any instrumentality whatever!! While, then, I believe and teach, and rejoice in the presence, and power, and positive influence of God's Spirit in the work of conversion and sanctification; I do repudiate a doctrine full of desolation—which makes man a mere machine, annihilates all rational liberty, destroys human responsibility, and makes the Word of God a mere superfluity, of no essential importance, of no salutary instrumentality in the great work of regeneration.—[*Time expired.*

Monday, Nov. 27—12½ o'clock, P. M.
[MR. RICE'S SECOND REPLY.]

MR. PRESIDENT—I have had some little experience in public debates; and I have uniformly observed, that when men find themselves pressed with arguments which they are conscious of being unable to answer, their effort is to induce the audience to believe that their opponents are saying absolutely nothing to the point. Such, as you are aware, has been the course pursued by my opponent from the commencement of this discussion. Fearful that the audience, in their simplicity, would believe that his arguments had been answered, and his doctrine overthrown, he has again and again most solemnly asseverated, as if divinely commissioned, that I had advanced not an argument, had said not one word bearing on the subject before us. Such are the means by which he vainly seeks, in his trouble, to save a sinking cause. Such are the means to which it is common for men to resort, when defending a bad cause.

But the gentleman has, at length, put forth his high decree, that Mr. Rice *must* follow him, or confess that he *cannot.* And it is now time for me to say to Mr. Campbell distinctly, that we have moderators, whose business it is to determine when I am out of order, to whose decisions I shall cheerfully submit; but that Mr. Campbell *cannot moderate me.* To his dictation I most assuredly will not submit.

His statements concerning my previous course in this discussion, are not true. I will not say, that he knows them to be untrue. I will not violate the rules of this discussion, and of common courtesy, as he has repeatedly done, by throwing out against him personal imputations; but I will say, he is mistaken.

Mr. Campbell. I submit to the Moderators whether I have violated the rules of this discussion.

Mr. Rice. I will, then, mention some of his expressions: "licentiousness of the tongue;"—"base aspersion," &c.

Mr. Campbell. If I say, an author has written a base aspersion, does this involve the moral character of my opponent?

Col. Speed Smith. I understood the expression, "base aspersion," to be used concerning the author read?

Mr. Rice. I read only two authors, Perrin and Jones. Perrin wrote a hundred years before Jones, and, therefore, could not have written against him a base aspersion. The charge was against myself.

Mr. Campbell. It was Faber to whom I referred, and not Perrin.

Mr. Rice. I have never seen any thing from Faber on this subject. I read the paragraph from Perrin, and compared Jones' quotation with the original; proving, that whilst he professed to quote Perrin, he omitted what related to infant baptism. The gentleman cannot escape.

When a man so accustomed to debate as Mr. Campbell, and so remarkable for his coolness and self-possession, displays so much temper, as the audience witnessed in his last speech, there is sad evidence that something is wrong. Men do not ordinarily lose their temper, when successful in argument. I will not now detain to reply to his singular assertions concerning my course in this discussion. I verily believe, that the sole cause of his trouble is, that I adhere too closely to the point. Every argument I have advanced bears directly on the subject in debate, unless when I am diverted from it, in pursuit of my opponent.

He, of course, expects you to believe, that he never wanders from the subject. Yet a part of his first speech was against infant baptism! The argument, I presume, would be this: Infants ought not to be baptized; therefore the Spirit, in conversion and sanctification, operates only through the truth!! He is always in order—precisely to the point! All this is very easily understood.

His statements concerning the debate with McCalla—the runners who proclaimed victory, &c., require proof. Moreover, the assertion that Mc-Calla was defeated, needs to be proved. I also desire some evidence that Mr. Burch, one of the moderators, made the remark charged upon him. I have the very best reason for asserting that it is not true. No doubt Mr. Campbell has been so informed; but when he makes statements that are to be stereotyped, and go forth to be read by thousands, he is solemnly bound to have his proof at hand. Who does not know, that thousands of rumors get afloat on such occasions, which have absolutely no foundation in truth? The gentleman really seems to have greedily swallowed all that his friends and his flatterers told him; and hence he found no difficulty in believing that every body ascribed to him a glorious victory.

But what has all this to do with the subject under discussion? Quite as much, no doubt, as his *ad captandum* closing speech on Saturday had to do with the administrator of baptism. To prove, of course, how closely he always adheres to the subject in debate, he gave us a long harangue about going for faith to Geneva, to Westminster, to Rome, &c.! So now he has given us a variety of statements, none of which are true, about my mode of conducting the discussion; the debate with McCalla; manufacturing public sentiment, &c.—all, of course, to prove, that in conversion and sanctification the Spirit operates only through the truth!!

In reading the gentleman's writings for the purpose of having his views distinctly before the audience, I was acting precisely in accordance with our written agreement, as the correspondence will show. I was not pleased with the wording of the proposition now under discussion; and I agreed to debate it with the distinct understanding and agreement on his part, that I would appeal to his writings in determining its true meaning. But I discover, that he is never so much out of temper, as when I read to the audience from his own works!

But the gentleman, in his excitement, told you, that I was delivering to you the dry remains of old harangues which had been delivered he knew not how often. This he asserts as a fact. Now, pray, how does he know? What are we to think of a man who will stand up and boldly assert facts, of the truth of which he cannot have evidence?

But he tells the audience, as usual, that his arguments have not been answered. Let us see whether they have or not. True, I did not choose to number them, one, two, three, &c.; but they have been effectually answered.

His first argument to prove, that there can be no divine influence on the human mind, except words and arguments, was based on his notion concerning its nature and constitution. This I was under no obligation to answer. If he will produce a "Thus saith the Lord" to sustain his doctrine, I will at once yield the point; but I am not concerned to answer a long metaphysical argument, based on what he conceives to be the constitution of the mind. He has professedly repudiated human philosophy, and taken the Bible alone as his guide; and yet, in the discussion of a scriptural doctrine, he hurries us immediately into the dark regions of metaphysical speculation! Does the Bible say, that such is the constitution of the human mind, that the Spirit of God can exert over it no moral influence, except by words and arguments? Mr. Campbell's philosophy says so; but where is the passage in God's word, that does so teach?

Now although I was under no obligation to answer such an argument, I did expose it by presenting the simple and indisputable fact, that originally God did create man holy, and that he did it without words and arguments. I also proved by the Scriptures, that God in his providence can and does exert a controlling influence over the moral conduct of men by his Spirit, and not simply or mainly by argument and motive. These simple and incontrovertible *Bible facts* demolish effectually his fine-spun metaphysical argument, written out with so much labor.

His second argument was, that there are among pagans, who have not the Bible, no spiritual ideas. This was answered by showing, that, according to our views, regeneration by the Holy Spirit is not designed to communicate new ideas, but to enlighten the mind by removing sin, the cause of its blindness, that it may see, in their true light, the truths contained in the Scriptures. The gentleman could not hear my reply.

His third argument was, that whatever is essential to regeneration in one case, is essential in all cases; and, therefore, if the Word of Truth is necessary in any case, it is necessary in all. This was fully answered by proving, that God has never limited himself in the bestowment of his blessings, to any particular means and instrumentalities. Ordinarily he has given his people food in the use of means; but when they have been placed in circumstances where means could not be employed, as in their journey through the wilderness, he has fed them without means. When the multitudes were with the Savior in a desert place, he gave them bread miraculously. So when infants are called from earth before they can be sanctified through the truth, they are sanctified without it. Surely if God would feed the bodies of his people without the ordinary means, he would not refuse to the soul of an infant the bread of life. The soul is worth infinitely more than the body, and eternal life than the temporal. Such was my reply to his third argument; and I regard it as perfectly conclusive.

His fourth argument was, that the Holy Spirit has addressed *words* and arguments to men. This is true; but does this fact prove, that in conversion and sanctification he operates *only* through the truth? He can easily prove, that ordinarily the Spirit operates through the truth; but he cannot prove, that he operates *only* through the truth. Yet this is precisely what he has undertaken to prove. His proof, therefore, falls very far short of his proposition.

His fifth argument was, that the Holy Spirit is called an *advocate*. . This is but a repetition of the other. But as an advocate, does he influence the mind only by words and arguments? The gentleman has not produced a passage of Scripture, which so teaches. He boasts, that for every article of his faith he has a "Thus saith the Lord." Has he, I ask you, my friends, produced one passage of Scripture that sustains his proposition? He has not, and he cannot. Yet he has heaped on me no slight reproach and abuse, because, as he pretends, I did not answer all his metaphysics!

Before proceeding farther in the regular course of argument, I must make a few remarks which I forgot at the proper time. The gentleman, in the recklessness of despair, has charged the Presbyterians of this community with attempting by unfair means to manufacture public sentiment against him. The charge is not true—not a word of truth in it.

If he believes what he has said, it only proves, that a man in trouble can persuade himself to believe the greatest absurdities. The truth is, my friends have been more than satisfied with the expression of public sentiment relative to this debate. So clear, so strong, so unanimous has been the verdict against him, by the crowds of intelligent persons of all classes, of different denominations and of no denomination, that they have had no temptation to seek to change it. I rejoice that such is the power of truth, that it and not Presbyterians, has made public sentiment what it is. I would not have it changed. I am more than satisfied.

But Mr. C. goes not for *victory*. I wish he would. I am anxious to see his gigantic powers brought fully to bear on the subject. It may be true, as he fretfully intimates, that he cannot gain very great fame by triumphing over one so feeble as your humble servant; but it is also true, that he may gain the more disgrace by failing, as he evidently has, to sustain himself. What opinion will the public form of the strength of his cause, when he, who would affect to look down with contempt upon men of ordinary powers, fails to sustain it. What must be thought of this boasted reformation, and of its invincible champion, when both sink under the feeble strokes of a mere pigmy!! It is truly cause for alarm, if, surrounded and sustained by almost an hundred of his preachers, and crowds of his people, who came to this place in the most confident expectation of a complete triumph, he cannot keep public sentiment from going strongly against him! Alas, for this vaunted reformation!

It would appear, if we are to believe the gentleman, that I misrepresented him by reading his own book. He says, he maintains, that MORAL power is exerted only by words and arguments; but he makes a distinction between *moral* power and purely *spiritual* power. I will again read from *Christianity Restored*, (pp. 347, 349,) and leave the audience to judge whether I misrepresented him.

"We have two sorts of power, physical and moral. By the former we operate upon matter; by the latter upon mind. To put matter in motion we use physical power, whether we call it animal or scientific power; to put mind in motion we use arguments, or motives addressed to the reason and nature of man. * * * Every spirit puts its moral power in words; that is, all the power it has over the views, habits, manners or actions of men, is in the meaning and arrangement of its ideas expressed in words, or significant signs addressed to the eye or ear."

Again:

"No other power than moral power can operate on minds; and this power must always be clothed in words addressed to the eye or ear. Thus we reason when revelation is altogether out of view. And when we think of the power of the Spirit of God exerted upon minds or human spirits, it is impossible for us to imagine that that power can consist in any thing else but words and arguments. Thus, in the nature of things, we are prepared to expect verbal communications from the Spirit of God, if that Spirit operates at all on our spirits. As the moral power of every man is in his arguments, so is the moral power of the Spirit of God in his arguments."

Now, observe, the gentleman tells us, we have only two kinds of power, viz. physical and *moral;* and he asserts, that no other power than *moral* power can operate on minds. He further affirms, that *every spirit* puts forth its moral power in *words;* that as the moral power of every man is in his arguments, so is the moral power of the Spirit of God in his arguments, which must be addressed to the eye or ear. I gave you the doctrine precisely as he has himself stated it. If he will say that he was in error when he wrote this book, we will certainly admit that he has the right to change; and since he is accustomed to change, it cannot injure him much. I once heard of a Dutchman and an Irishman who had been condemned to be hanged, and were in the same prison. The Irishman was greatly bewailing his fate. The Dutchman reproached him for his cowardice. Ah, said the Irishman, ye're *used* to it. Mr. C. is used to changing.

I must occasionally illustrate a point by an anecdote, since the gentleman has charged me with having a "a laughing committee" here; or they will have nothing to do. He has dealt out to this imaginary committee, which must be large, quite a lecture for their unworthy employment!

Let it be understood, that he has asserted, that *only moral* power can be exerted on mind, and that all the moral power of the Spirit must be put forth in words and arguments. He even goes so far as to say, that " if the Spirit of God has spoken all its arguments; or, if the New and Old Testaments contain all the arguments which can be offered to reconcile man to God, and to purify them who are reconciled, *then all the power of the Holy Spirit, which can operate upon the human mind, is* SPENT; and he that is not sanctified and saved by these, cannot be saved by angels or spirits, human or divine."—*Ib.* p. 350. If all the converting power of the Spirit is spent, there is, of course, no further influence that he can exert to save man.

The gentleman, either to illustrate or to prove his doctrine, told us that a grain of wheat or of corn, has life in it, and that when it is placed in the earth, it will grow; and so the Word of God, the seed, when it gets into man's moral nature, will bring forth fruit. But the wheat and the corn will not grow without the heat of the sun and rain; and man cannot create either the one or the other. I am pleased with the illustration; for the Scriptures teach, that though " Paul planteth, and Apollos watereth, God giveth the increase." In conversion and sanctification, there is a work for man and a work for God; and he who rejects God's part of the work, must be forever undone.

The gentleman objects to the doctrine for which we contend, that it makes the Word of God wholly unnecessary. Light cannot heal the eyes of the blind man, nor open the eyes of him who hates it. But is light therefore worthless? Light is the medium through which objects are seen; but if my eyes are diseased, the light, however brightly it may shine, cannot cause me to see. But let my eyes be healed, and then I can see by means of the light. As the light is absolutely necessary to vision, though it cannot cause the blind to see, so is the gospel necessary, though alone it cannot purify the depraved heart.

Again, Mr. Campbell objects that the doctrine of a special divine influence in conversion and sanctification, destroys the accountability of man. That this objection is wholly unfounded, is perfectly plain. Man is a free moral agent. In view of motives, he freely chooses and refuses. But his heart, as Solomon says, " is set in him to do evil." In the exercise of his freedom, he deliberately chooses to sin. Is he then a mere machine? But God works in him to will and to do—inclines him to turn from sin to holiness. Is his free agency thus destroyed? Cannot God incline the sinner to the path of righteousness, without interfering with his freedom and accountability? The gentleman would have us believe, that he never makes assertions without adducing the proof. I venture to say, that he cannot find a passage in the Bible, nor an acknowledged principle of mental philosophy, by which to sustain his objection.

3 I

When I closed my last speech, I was proving that Mr. Campbell's doctrine necessarily involves the damnation of infants and idiots. He admits their native depravity. He denies that they can be sanctified without the truth. We know that they cannot receive the truth; consequently they must die in their depravity; and wherever they may go, certain it is that they cannot go to heaven. He may express the opinion, that they may be saved, but his opinion contradicts his doctrine. There is no way of escaping the difficulty, but by abandoning the doctrine. He cannot answer the argument—it admits of no answer.

But the Scriptures clearly teach the necessity of regeneration in the case of infants, as well as of adults. Our Savior said to Nicodemus, "That which is born of the flesh is flesh; and that which is born of the Spirit is spirit,"—John iii. 6. Infants, it will be admitted, are born of the flesh; consequently they must be born of the Spirit, or they cannot enter into the kingdom of God. By the natural birth, they are sinful; by the spiritual birth, they become holy. But if, as Mr. C. teaches, infants cannot be born of the Spirit, they cannot be saved.

He complains, that I do not follow him in his train of remark, as the respondent should follow the affirmant. Whether I will follow him or not, depends very much on the course he takes. Every passage of Scripture which he may adduce in support of his doctrine, I will notice; but, in his metaphysical dissertations, I shall not feel bound to follow him.

III. My *third* argument against his doctrine is—that it contradicts the doctrine of human depravity, as taught in the Scriptures: for, if his doctrine is true, men sin only through ignorance or mistake. All that is necessary in order to convert and sanctify those, at least, who ever will be saved, is, according to Mr. C., simply to teach them the truth—to present before their minds words and arguments. Only teach them the truth, and they will turn and serve God, and go to heaven. Why, then, did they not sooner turn? Because they were laboring under mistaken notions. They had adopted erroneous views of the character of God, of his law, and his gospel! All that is necessary, therefore, according to this doctrine, is to correct their mistakes.

This doctrine, I say, is contrary to the Scriptures. Let us examine a few passages, which prove clearly, that men do not sin simply through mistake, but wilfully. Eccl. viii. 11: "Because sentence against an evil work is not executed speedily, therefore the heart of the sons of men is fully set in them to do evil." Ch. ix. 3: "Yea, also, the heart of the sons of men is full of evil, and madness is in their heart while they live, and after that they go to the dead." Ps. x. 4: "The wicked, through the pride of his countenance, will not seek after God: God is not in all his thoughts." The reception with which the gospel meets among men, is set forth in a parable by our Savior, in which he says, "And they all with one consent began to make excuse,"—Luke xiv. 18. Paul accounts for all the abominations of the heathens, by saying, "And even as they did not like to retain God in their knowledge, God gave them over to a reprobate mind," Rom. i. 28.

These scriptures and many others, teach most distinctly, that men sin, not because they are ignorant or are under mistaken impressions, but knowingly, wilfully, deliberately—that their actual transgressions flow from a corrupt and rebellious disposition. It is true, that men do fall into error; but it is not so much the error that causes them to sin, as it is sin that causes them to err. Paul, in his Epistle to the Romans, proves the depravity of the heathen, first, by their errors in belief, and secondly, by their immoralities in practice. The former affords as decided evidence of a sinful disposition as the latter. If a man stumble over every thing in his way in daylight, we know that he is blind. So if any man with the Bible in his hand, err fundamentally, we know that a sinful heart has blinded him.

The doctrine of Mr. C. makes men, at least those who will ever be saved, sin only through mistake. The Scriptures teach, that they sin knowingly, wilfully, and deliberately. His theory, therefore, contradicts the teaching of the Scriptures concerning human depravity. It is, therefore, false.

I fear I shall look at my watch too often for the comfort of my friend; but I do not like to commence a new argument, when my time is near out. So I will, for the present, close.

[Here Mr. Campbell arose and said: I beg the decision of the moderators upon the point, whether the respondent is not bound, according to the established usage of debate, to answer and respond to such matters as may be advanced by the affirmant.

One of the moderators then arose and remarked as follows: It is the most appropriate mode of procedure for the affirmant to open his ground of debate with such arguments as he may be able to adduce, and for the respondent to notice those grounds; but in his own way. The object of each is to prove his own position; but he must do it in his own mode. Men's minds are differently constituted. Their reasoning faculties run in different channels; and while one is making an argument, the other may suppose that he is evasive, and his remarks not appropriate: while the party replying may deem them perfectly so. All that we can decide is, whether or not the parties indulge in extraneous or irrelevant matter.

Mr. Campbell. Is it not usual for the respondent to reply in some way or other to the matter presented by the affirmant?

Moderator. It is certainly expected that he will notice the matter presented by the affirmant.

Another moderator remarked, that it had devolved upon him to offer a few words with reference to the course of procedure thus far. He had on several occasions observed the boundaries of good order to have been very nearly trodden upon; but it was always unpleasant, on such an occasion, to check the speaker; and, though he had been more than once upon the point of striking, when, by an explanation from the speaker the debate had been permitted to proceed. If he might be indulged in the suggestion, he would here intimate the propriety of avoiding, in future, every thing of a personal character: and he trusted that they would be able to get along without again touching so nearly upon the line.

The former moderator said, he would add another suggestion. He thought as if, generally, the debatants had conducted themselves with great propriety and decorum, which, to the moderators, had been highly gratifying. It could not be denied, however, that on some occasions there had been digressions from the true line of logical argumentation; and he would add, that these things would never do good, and that such matter would not look well in print. The propositions should alone be considered, and nothing but authorities and argument ought to be introduced into the discussion.

MR. FISHBACK said, as a friend, he would recommend the reading of the rules.

Mr. Campbell. Under these rules I have thought that my friend was out of order, in upbraiding me with the consequences of a doctrine which I do not teach. If I understood, he ascribes to my teaching the consequences of sending infants to hell; which I have ascribed to those cruel decrees.

Mr. Rice. I have stated, that I did not charge upon my friend with actually holding the doctrine of infant damnation.

Moderator. We cannot decide whether the argument is persuasive or conclusive. Mr. Rice has assumed and endeavored to disprove the doctrine advanced on the other side; and he has a right to try that argument and except to its absurdities. But whether he can maintain his ground, we are not prepared to decide.

Monday, Nov. 27—12½ o'clock, P. M.
[MR. CAMPBELL'S THIRD ADDRESS.]

MR. PRESIDENT—Sir: There are several small matters that require attention. Among these is the remark of Mr. Burch on the result of the McCalla debate, as to the conversion of a *black crow into a white one.*

Mr. Rice. Mr. Burch says he did not say so.

Mr. Campbell. Of course the gentleman means he did not remember his having said so. He could not testify in such a case. No man could testify in a case of this sort, after an interval of twenty years, what he did not say on such an occasion. One single good witness declaring that he heard him say so, would, in a court of evidence, set aside his want of recollection in the case, and would stand in law. A person's having no present recollection of what he said twenty years ago, is no proof that he did not say so. This is, indeed, a matter of very small moment—it is only the occasion that gives it any consequence.

Mr. Rice desires to know how I could say that he had been delivering the fragments of old harangues on total depravity. He seems to intimate that christian morality might be implicated in such a saying. I have satisfactory evidence of the fact from two sources. First, I have heard of his discourses on this subject round the country, in different places; and again, I have positive written evidence of the fact of his promulgation of these views in his controversy, in one of our periodicals, with president Shannon.

The remarks on the subject of my excitement, I will reserve to another occasion. I shall, then, proceed to the argument which closed my last speech.

If there be the slightest apparent relevency in the arguments of my opponent to any thing I have advanced, or to the true and proper issue before us, I hold myself in duty bound to respond to it. But when there are many things of the same class, it is not necessary to respond to them individually and severally. I will, in such case, select the strongest particular or incident introduced; and in disposing of that, as a matter of course, the others of that class are disposed of.

To illustrate and apply this observation, I must remind you that in my introductory address it is my aim to express, in a written form, the more cardinal principles, and classes of evidence and arguments relied on, as fixed points, to which at any time after, in the course of discussion, we may recur with certainty. In my opening address, therefore, I very formally propounded one invaluable principle or argument, in support of this thesis—that God has given to the human mind a certain constitution, as he has to the body of man, or to the universe; and that, whatever be the process of regeneration, conversion, or sanctification, it must, from the universal laws of the universe, be in perfect harmony with that constitution; hence no power or faculty of the human mind is changed or destroyed, in this great moral revolution of which we speak. A fact this, which, when duly appreciated, forever annihilates the system which I oppose. Mr. Rice gives evidence of its clearness and power. He felt it, and how does he seek to dispose of it? He tells us that God made man *holy* at first, and that he can do it again! He created Adam holy, and he may create others. This is, in reality, an admission of the unanswerable force of this argument. He therefore seeks to go beyond its dominions—beyond the present constitution of man, and affirms, that if God cannot violate his present constitution, he can do as he did before, make an original constitution or create him holy as he created Adam!! That is, he can create a new Adam out of the old Adam, as he created Adam out of the dust of the ground, &c.! Truly this is a triumph of no ordinary character. He commences a response by conceding my position, and asking for God the power to literally create a new man. But this is not the question before us. I admit that God could have created another Adam, and that he can now literally create a holy man; but it is not an original physical primordial creation, but a moral change, a moral renovation and creation of which we speak. It is not the origination of a new constitution, but a change of heart, a transformation moral that we are inquiring into.

Will the gentleman say that creation, providence, and redemption are the same process of divine power? Was not creation a miracle? Was there a previously existing constitution of the universe and of man? Did God make man after man's own previously existing constitution? Because God did at first give to man a constitution after his own image—follows it, therefore, that God will create for him a new constitution, now that he is fallen, and make him new by miracle?, And would not man be as perfect now as he was at first, according to this hypothesis? For when God made Adam holy, he was perfectly holy. Does God thus make christians perfectly holy? When these objections to his presumptive assumption are responded to, he shall have others.

Infants and adults are then created holy by the same direct and positive fiat, the same specific miracle that made Adam holy. Avaunt, then, all secondary causes, all ministerial means, all Bible preaching and moral argumentations! God makes infants, adults and pagans holy, by the same means that he made Adam holy; that is, by a miracle. With Mr. Rice every conversion is just as great a miracle as the creation of Adam; for recollect, his only escape from my argument is, that as God *could* and did give to Adam a holy constitution, so does he now give a holy constitution to infants, Pagans, Jews, and all other persons whom he pleases thus to create anew. Was there ever a more perfect fatalism than this? Every infant and adult now made holy is a miracle—a new and original demonstration of Omnipotence. Yet still the wonder is, that this new creation is not perfectly holy, inasmuch as all other works of God are perfect.

Now according to my introductory speech and fourth argument, I insist, that if one infant be regenerated, *without moral instrumentality*, all can; and if one perfect and complete regeneration, *without the Word* of God, can, in any case whatever, be consummated, then, in all other cases the Word is wholly unnecessary. For if I can produce one apple without a tree, or one ear of wheat without earth, then I can do it *ad infinitum.*

No living man, as I conceive, can in these points, refute my introductory address. I will insist that Mr. Rice explains to us why preach the word; why print Bibles; why send missionaries to foreign lands; why set on foot any human instrumentalities whatever, on the assumption that God makes men and infants holy, as he did Adam! I never objected to a spiritual religion. Nay, I love it,—I preach it,—I contend for it. I never would have jeopardized my reputation in questioning the popular notions of spiritual influence, but to aim a blow at the root of all fanaticism, and of a wild irrepressible enthusiasm. I believe not only in the Holy Spirit, but in a religion of which this Divine agent is both the substance, origin, cause, and reason. But, sir, in my humble opinion this metaphysical abstraction, this theological speculation, this electric, immedial operation, that makes an infant or a pagan holy in a moment, has been the most soul-ruining dogma ever invented, preached, or propagated. It has slain its tens of thousands. It has made sceptics, fanatics, despondents, and visionaries without number, and without limit.

These elect infants, elect pagans, elect idiots, on whom God acts when, where, and how he pleases, but makes them *holy* in a moment, without light, knowledge, faith, or love, (for though these may be called by them effects of the regeneration, the thing, the work, the operation itself, is anterior to them, above and independent of them, without any human agency whatever,) are figments of distempered brains, the creatures of religious romance, the offspring of a metaphysical delusion, for which there is no cure, but in the rational reading and study of the Book of God.

Mr. Rice seems, if I understand him, to have drunk deep into these muddy waters, and to have adopted the fable of infant regeneration as a choice of evils. His dilemma is, Infants are saved or lost. Not lost truly!—well then, they are saved. With, or without, regeneration! Without regeneration, is to him inadmissible, because then they would be saved in a state of wickedness. His theory is, therefore, adopted to get rid of a metaphysical difficulty. It owes its origin to a mystic knot which he cannot untie, and which he dares not cut. The regeneration of these infants is, then, not *moral*, but *physical*. Well, perhaps we may yet agree in their *physical regeneration*. I believe those dying infants, and with me they are all elect, are fitted for heaven by a physical regeneration, of which we shall hereafter speak. But in the mean time the question is lost, if we lose sight of the regeneration of which we now speak, and which is an essential part of the system we oppose.

What then, let me ask, is the philosophy of regeneration according to Mr. Rice? It is a change of heart. There we agree again. What sort of change?—not of the flesh, but of the spirit—a *change of the affections*, of the feelings *and sympathies of the soul*. Agreed!—a change so great that we love our former hates, and hate our former loves. We love God and our Savior supremely, and our brethren fervently. We hate Satan, falsehood, and sin. Hence comes the annihilation of his hypothesis—can an infant love or hate, without previous knowledge, faith or apprehension of things amiable and hateful!! No, says every man; where there is no light, no understanding, no intelligence, there can be no disposition at all, no moral feeling, no change of affections, no change of heart; consequently no infant moral or spiritual regeneration. It is impossible—it is inconceivable! No man can demonstrate, illustrate, or prove it. Whenever Mr. Rice can show that a man, a child, or an infant, can love what he never heard, saw, felt or thought of, and that he can love, fear, or eschew that of which he has no conception whatever, then, but not till then, can he offer one argument, reason, or evidence, of infant moral regeneration. Whenever he shows 'a man loving Jesus Christ, righteousness, and holiness, who has never heard of him—and hating Satan, sin, and impurity, who has never heard of them, then I will believe that he can find a dying infant, regenerated and sanctified in its spiritual and moral nature. Till then, I shall regard it as a mere phantasy, an idol, or chimera of the brain, and the whole doctrine growing out of it a miserable delusion.

But now with regard to our physical regeneration of infants, my faith is in the Lamb of God, who hath taken away the sin of the world. The atonement of the Messiah has made it compatible with God, with the honor of his throne and government, to save all those infants who die in Adam. He has made an ample provision for extending salvation from all the consequences of Adam's sin to whomsoever he will. Ever blessed be his adorable name! THE LAMB OF GOD HAS BORNE AWAY THE SIN OF THE WORLD. Infants then need that same kind of regeneration that Paul, and Peter, and James, and John, and all saints need—the entire destruction of this body of sin and death. The most perfect christian that I have seen, needs a regeneration to fit him for the immediate presence of God. The infant that falls asleep in its mother's bosom, and after a few short days breathes out its spirit gently there, needs no more change to fit it for Abraham's bosom, than that which the Spirit of God will effect in the resurrection of the dead, or in the transformation of the living saints at the time of his coming. Philosophy, reason, and faith, are alike silent on the subject of any infant regeneration before death. It is all theory—idle, empty, suicidal theory. Experience lifts her ten thousand voices against it. Whoever saw a child regenerated growing up from birth a pure and exemplary christian! Persons have been sanctified, that is, set apart to the Lord from their birth; but that any one was, in our sense of regeneration, changed in heart from birth, reason, revelation, experience, observation depose not; on this subject they are all as silent as death. While, then, I believe in the physical regeneration of infants after death, I repudiate their spiritual or moral regeneration in life, because unscriptural, irrational, and absurd.

This delusive doctrine operates very differently on two classes of subjects—the sanguine and vain, the imaginative and elate. Those of high self-esteem are often the victims of a conceit that they have been touched by a supernatural impulse, a sort of celestial electricity, which in a moment regenerated and gave them religion. Some of them tell right marvellous tales of mighty shocks of this sort. A lady of whom I recently heard, from a highly credible source, in describing her conversion, said, "The Holy Spirit went through her from head to foot, bursting off the nails from her fingers and toes." This was, truly, an extraordinary case; yet many of the same class, not so well marked, daily occur. These persons often live and die without any right conception of God, of his Son, or of his salvation—yet are they joyful, happy, riding on the clouds communing with spirits, and filled with rapture, which neither poetry nor philosophy can reveal. They carry with them through life, the notion that they were once truly regenerate, and, therefore, can never perish.

But there are some rather of a melancholy temperament; somewhat atrabilious and desponding. They are more rational, though less imagi-

native—they have little hope, and less self-esteem; but they feel their
need of this regeneration, without feeling that sensible touch Divine, which
instantly brings them out of nature's darkness and death into supernatural
light and life.   They are too rational to dream of it.   They are too sensible to imagine it; and sometimes they fall into a frightful melancholy,
which, in instances not a few, bereaves them of reason and sends them
into an asylum, where although surrounded with all that science and humanity can bestow, leaves them without the comforts and assistance
of relatives and friends, those best palliatives of mental alienation and
woe.

The gentleman has given us another exemplification of his freedom in
quoting Scriptures.   Paul may plant and Apollos water, but God gives the
increase.   His meaning is, Paul may plant the seed of religion in the
heart of A, B, and C, Apollos may water that seed, but God alone makes
it to grow.   I rejoice in the truth of the fact here stated, but I pronounce
the application of the passage to the point before us a gross misconception
and perversion of its meaning.   Paul may plant churches and Apollos
water churches, but God makes the churches grow.   So says the context—and so say I with all my heart.

I do not wish to lose time in expositions of the various sophisms of
false quotation and application of Scripture.   I do not even choose to defend my own writings from such illogical torture.   I should give no argument if I stopped to wrangle about all these misquotations and misap-
plications.   I only request those who choose to examine more accurately
these quotations, to read the whole contexts from which they are illegally
arrested.   The gentleman is very emphatic (for effect no doubt) in telling
you how often he calls my attention to certain matters, which but for his
manner of quoting them deserve no real regard, because irrelevant.   He
said the other day, he called my attention three times to a verse, and
finally affirmed that he could neither make me see or hear it, although I
had two or three times replied to it in common with its whole class.
And when it was for the third or fourth time replied to by me, what use
did the gentleman make of my reply ?   All those passages I have shewn,
like the oft repeated case of the thief on the cross, are misapplied, because they were spoken of things and persons as they were before the
gospel age commenced—before the christian ordinances were instituted or
the church began.   The thief indeed was saved without baptism; not
merely because there was no christian baptism then; for if there had, he
being converted as he was, and having no opportunity, would have been
saved without it, as all are who are providentially prevented from receiving it.   Scriptures are generally quoted wrong when applied to prove a
proposition not of the same species with that in the writer's mind.

The gentleman fights for victory, and he will have it in any and every
contingency whatever.   He has at proper intervals the mournful alas.
Alas! alas! for the reformation!   The unfeeling crowd, so perfectly destitute of sympathy, however, smile at his wailings!   He can hardly proceed under the dreadful weight of arguments on his side, and yet he cannot utter them.   For who has heard them!   I do not think it either
edifying or important to notice these matters, for any other reason than
to express my pleasure in reflecting upon the dignity of my cause and its
self-respect; that it needs not such ephemeral and political appliances to
sustain or commend it.

Mr. Rice may express all his conceptions of himself and his cause without any offence to me whatever. I presume that owing to his education he honestly thinks so; whether or not; I am obliged to so regard him, and I will so continue till the end. What is said here is to be read by all parties; and my only desire on that subject is that the book may be read impartially, and that the argument may be duly weighed on both sides. Let every man take up the book and read it as though it had fallen from heaven into his hands. Let him read it candidly, decide according to evidence and fact, and then let him act in perfect harmony with his convictions; and may the Lord bless him in so doing!—[*Time expired.*

Monday, Nov. 27—1½ o'clock, P. M.
[MR. RICE'S THIRD REPLY.]

MR. PRESIDENT—I have but a remark or two to make in reply to the singular logic of Mr. Campbell, concerning the alledged statement of Mr. Burch. No man, he would have us believe, can testify, that twenty years ago he did not make a certain statement! I presume Mr. Burch may very well know, he never did believe that Mr. C. triumphed over Mr. McCalla, and, therefore, that he never did make a statement which implied such an admission. He never believed that Mr. C. triumphed, and, consequently, never so said. The gentleman's *anonymous* evidence is worth absolutely nothing.

The gentleman attempts to justify his assertion, that I am delivering scraps of old harangues, by saying, that he has heard of my preaching on these subjects, and has seen, in my discussion with president Shannon, some of the same arguments I have advanced on this occasion. Why, I have read in his publications almost every thing he has advanced on this subject; and a considerable part of his closing speech, on Saturday, I heard almost verbatim some three years ago. Why, then, may I not charge him with delivering scraps of old harangues?

But he cannot so easily escape the difficulty into which his temper hurried him. For it is not true, that I have ever before discussed this subject just as I have done to-day. I have occasionally, it is true, discussed all these subjects, though not so thoroughly and extensively as now.

Regeneration, the gentleman says, must take place in harmony with the powers of the human mind. This is true. I have not said that in regeneration men are deprived of any of their faculties, or that new faculties are created. But he tells us, that creation is one thing, and the renewing the heart quite another; and he seems to consider the idea of creating holiness quite absurd. The doctrine of Mr. Campbell, as stated by himself, is,—that no other than *moral* power can be exerted on the human mind; and it must always be exerted by words and arguments. In refutation of this assumption, I stated the scripture fact, that God created man holy, and consequently there must have been a moral influence exerted, not by words or by arguments. We do not regard holiness as a distinct substance or essence. It is, however, true, that God created man with a holy heart or nature. How he did it I know not, nor does Mr. C. Inasmuch, then, as he understands not how that influence was exerted, which made man originally holy; he cannot possibly prove, that the Spirit may not now exert a moral influence, distinct from motives.

It is worthy of special remark, that Paul, in speaking of the sanctification of the human heart, uses the word *create*. "We are his workmanship, created in Christ Jesus unto good works," Eph. ii. 10. There is

42

not, in any language, a stronger word than the word *create*. Yet this word is employed, without qualification, in regard to the renewal of the human heart. If, then, this word does not express a direct divine influence, distinct from the word, and in addition to it, by what word, I ask, could the idea be expressed? God did not create the heavens and the earth by words and arguments; neither did he thus create the body or the soul of man. The very word *create* expresses the putting forth of divine power. Can it, then, be true, that God creates the heart anew by words and arguments? Is it not perfectly absurd to talk of creating by arguments? It is an abuse of language. God created man in his own image; and now, by the new creation he restores that image. In the latter, as in the former, there is an exertion of divine power; and in both the *modus operandi* is equally mysterious.

Mr. C. objects to the doctrine of special divine influence, that it makes every instance of conversion or regeneration a miracle. So it does, if we take his definition of a miracle; but if we take the definition given by all correct writers on the subject, regeneration is not a miracle. A miracle is a suspension of the laws of nature, by the immediate interposition of Divine power, of which men can take cognizance, for the purpose of confirming the truth of God's revelation. God sends rain; and in a time of dearth we pray for rain, not expecting God to work a miracle, and yet expecting him to put forth his power in answer to our prayers, so as to grant the desired blessing. Elisha prayed that it might not rain; and during the space of three years and a half it rained not. He prayed for rain, and it descended in torrents. In one sense, perhaps, these divine interpositions might be called miracles; but so far as man could see, the laws of nature were uninterrupted, both whilst the long drought continued, and when the rain descended. Properly speaking, therefore, there was, in this case, a divine interposition, but not a miracle.

So the Holy Spirit operates, though invisibly, on the hearts of all who are renewed. The change is wrought by supernatural power; but it is not a miracle because it is invisible, nor is it a suspension of the fixed laws of nature. The effects of the divine influence we do see. The man who, yesterday, delighted only in sin, to-day turns from his iniquities, and rejoices in the service of God. The effects are manifest; and common sense compels us to ascribe them to some adequate cause. The Bible teaches us, that the cause of the visible change is a new creation wrought by the Holy Spirit. "We are his workmanship, created in Christ Jesus unto good works."

Mr. Campbell objects again, that if, in one case, regeneration takes place without the Word, it must be so in all cases; and then, of what use is the Word? He has often told us, that it is far easier to *assert* than to *prove*. It is admitted, that regeneration is the same in all cases; but it is not admitted, that *the means employed* are, in all cases, the same. He asserts, that the same means must always be employed; but he cannot prove the truth of the assertion, either scripturally or philosophically. I know of no part of God's Word that teaches, that if God should sanctify a soul in one instance without the truth, because it cannot be employed, he must, of course, sanctify all others without the truth. God is a sovereign; and he works by means or without means, as his infinite wisdom directs.

But the gentleman asks, of what use is the Word, if regeneration can take place without it? If the question has any meaning, it is this: Of what use is the Word to *adults*, if infants, that cannot receive it, can be regenerated without it? This is a singular question. Or does he mean to ask, of what use is the Word to adults, if there is necessary a distinct divine influence? I presume if he had been in the camp of Israel, in the days of Joshua, he would have asked, why should the priests compass the walls of Jericho seven times, and blow rams' horns, since the walls will not fall without a direct interposition of divine power? The Lord commanded, and that is sufficient. Or, perhaps, he would have found fault with our Savior, because, in healing the eyes of the blind man, he used clay and spittle. He might ask, of what use are the clay and spittle, since they will not open his eyes without a direct exertion of divine power? Such is the logic of my friend. It is in vain to reason against *facts.* God has often employed means, when, without an immediate exertion of his power, they were wholly inadequate to accomplish the end. So he employs the Word ordinarily, though alone it is not adequate to effect the conversion and sanctification of men. Yet God has never confined himself to means and instrumentalities; and no man has the right to limit him where he has not limited himself.

The doctrine of special divine influence, Mr. Campbell believes, leads to a great deal of fanaticism; and he has told us an anecdote about some very fanatical woman. It is admitted, that there have been, and now are, many fanatics in the world; but his is quite as conclusive against the truth of christianity, as against the doctrine I am defending. Multitudes of those who have professed to be christians, have been, or now are fanatics; therefore, says the infidel, christianity leads to fanaticism, and, of course, it cannot be true. The infidel adopts Mr. Campbell's principle, and argues quite as conclusively as he. It is a trite remark, that the abuse of a doctrine, or of a principle, does not prove it false. Does the doctrine of special divine influence generally make fanatics of those who embrace it? There is not a body of people in this world, who are more free from fanaticism, than Presbyterians; and yet there are none who more firmly believe in the special agency of the Spirit, than they; nor any who more zealously contend for the constant use of *means*, in order to conversion and sanctification.

I could also tell an anecdote concerning a convert in Mr. C.'s church, that would be quite a match for the one he has related; but I could not do so, without treating this solemn subject with unbecoming levity.

The gentleman has at length produced one passage of Scripture in support of his doctrine. I am gratified to see him leaving his metaphysical speculations, which he has, indeed, long professed to repudiate, and entering upon this scripture proof. The passage is in John xvii. 17: "Sanctify them through thy truth: thy word is truth." It is really one of the most conclusive proofs of the truth of the doctrine I am advocating. Does not the Savior pray to his Father, to sanctify them? But if Mr. C.'s doctrine is true, why should he have prayed? He did not pray, that new truths, new arguments, might be revealed to his people. According to his doctrine, it was necessary only to give them the truth. But the Savior prayed to his Father to do something for them, and to do it by certain means—to exert on their minds a sanctifying influence distinct from the truth, but in connection with the truth.

Mr. Campbell asks, how can an infant be born of God, before it has any knowledge of God? There can be no disposition, he says, where there is no knowledge. I thought he had repudiated metaphysics; but really, he appears to rely upon his speculations more than upon the Bible.

But his philosophy is most unphilosophical and unscriptural. Who does not know, that there are a thousand things which we admire at first sight, and as many to which we feel a decided aversion? Does not this prove, that there may, and does, exist in the mind a disposition or inclination to love some objects, and to dislike others, even before we have any knowledge of them? There are dispositions existing in the mind, as well as tastes and appetites in the body, before the knowledge of the appropriate objects calls them into exercise. A child loves sweetness the first time it tastes it; and is charmed by music the first time it hears it. Why, then, may not the soul be in such a moral state, that when first it is made acquainted with the character of God, it will admire, love and adore him; or, that it will turn from him with strong aversion? There is neither sound theology, nor sound philosophy in the gentleman's objection.

But he is not willing to give up the salvation of infants; and he complains of me for urging the argument against his doctrine, that it necessarily involves the damnation of infants. He does not find fault with me for maintaining, that they are depraved; for, although he now denies that there can be moral disposition where there is no knowledge, he admits and teaches, that infants are by nature depraved!—that they have a proneness, a disposition to sin!! This being admitted, my argument against his doctrine is most certainly legitimate and conclusive. It is what logicians call the *reductio ad absurdum*—proving that it leads necessarily to results which he admits to be false and absurd. I was indeed surprised, that he thought it necessary to appeal to the moderators to protect his doctrine against the force of this argument.

He attempts, however, to escape from the difficulty by saying, that nothing more than the atonement of Christ is necessary to the salvation of infants. Does the blood of Christ purify the *heart?* The atonement secures the remission of sins; but does the Bible teach, that it takes away depravity? Why the very idea is absurd. There is not a word in the Bible to countenance such a notion. The difficulty still remains. Infants, as the gentleman admits, are depraved. How then shall they be sanctified and prepared for the enjoyments of a holy heaven? They cannot be sanctified through the truth; and Mr. C. asserts, that they cannot be sanctified without it. Therefore they must die in sin, and be forever lost! Such are the results to which his doctrine necessarily leads, whether he is willing consistently to carry it out or not.

There is nothing in the Bible, he tells us, that favors the idea of infant regeneration. He takes care, however, not to reply to the argument founded on John iii. 6, "For that which is born of the flesh is flesh; and that which is born of the Spirit is spirit." Infants are born of the flesh; and therefore they must be born of the Spirit; and if not born of the Spirit, they cannot enter into the kingdom of God—they must be lost. They cannot go to heaven in their depravity.

But, says the gentleman, adult believers must, at death, undergo as great a change in order to enter heaven, as infants need experience. For this assertion he can find no authority in the Bible; and it is vain for him on a subject such as we are now discussing, to give us either his opinions or his assertions. Death will produce on the mind no moral change, such as infants must experience before they can enter heaven.

It is, no doubt, true, as the gentleman says, that some persons who have believed in the doctrine of the special agency of the Spirit, have been melancholy, under the conviction that they were not serving God faithfully, or from other causes; but it cannot be proved, that the doctrine has any such tendency. On the contrary, thousands and tens of thousands have felt their hardened hearts melt under the blessed influences of the Spirit, have renewed their strength as they have waited on God in prayer, and have in their affections and joys mounted up as on the wings of an eagle, have run without weariness, and walked without fainting. "The Spirit itself," says Paul, "beareth witness with our spirit, that we are the children of God: and, if children, then heirs, heirs of God and joint-heirs with Christ." Convince the man who has become acquainted with his true character, that there is no such special influence of the Spirit—that he must prepare himself by his unaided exertions for heaven; and he will lie down in deep despair. He will never again entertain a hope that he can see God in peace, or enter into his rest. It is a holy heaven to which he desires to go; a holy God reigns there; holy angels worship around his glorious throne; and none but "the spirits of just men made perfect" can ever enter there. If, then, sinful man is left to prepare himself for such a heaven; well may he weep in despair.

In my last address I directed your attention to the language of Paul in 1 Cor. iii. 6, "I have planted, Apollos watered; but God gave the increase." But the gentleman says, Paul spoke of *planting churches.* There is no such expression in the connection. On what evidence, then, does he found the assertion? Paul was rebuking the Corinthian christians, because there were contentions among them, one saying, I am of Paul; another, I am of Apollos; and a third, I am of Cephas, and a fourth, I am of Christ. All this, he tells them, is most unwise as well as very sinful; for, says he, "who then is Paul, and who is Apollos, but ministers by whom ye believe, even as God gave to every man? I have planted, Apollos watered; but God gave the increase." Paul had planted the seed—had first preached the word in Corinth; Apollos had succeeded him with his eloquent exhortations; and God had by his Holy Spirit caused the seed to spring up and bring forth fruit.

But if Paul were speaking of planting a church (though this is not a scripture expression,) his meaning must be, that he had induced christians to remove from other parts to Corinth, and settle there. You may plant corn; but you must first have corn to plant. A church might be planted; but the members must be there before it could be planted. But Paul planted the seed, the word, and God blessed it to the conversion of many; Apollos preached and exhorted, and God blessed his labors to their growth in grace.

But if Paul could really plant a church, and Apollos could water it without any special divine influence; could they not keep it alive, and cause it to extend? Or what are we to understand by the declaration, that "God gave the increase?" The figure used by the apostle is both beautiful and striking; and the meaning cannot easily be misunderstood. Before you plant your seed, the ground must be prepared; and then the sun must shine, and the refreshing rains descend upon it. Man plants his seed and sometimes waters it; but there is no artificial sun to shine upon it. God must give the increase. So the ministers of Christ are to preach the word, to proclaim the glorious gospel to men, and look up to God for that divine influence, the outpouring of the Holy Spirit, which only can cause them to turn to God.

My friend cannot forget the past days of this discussion. He constantly calls up the subjects that have been disposed of. He says, that

3 K

on the third proposition he did answer my argument from John iii. 18—
" He that believeth on him is not condemned." I certainly did not hear
his answer. It must have been extremely brief. The truth is, it admits
of no answer. The obvious and only meaning is, that no believer, baptized or not, is condemned; but all believers are justified.

The last note I took of the gentleman's speech, relates to the charge
he had made, that great pains have been taken to bias the public sentiment,
to make the people believe, that he has failed to sustain himself. He
tells you, he has heard the fact from various quarters. I will not condescend to gather up floating reports, and state them here as facts for the
purpose of producing effect. When I state facts, and they are denied,
I will prove them. These reports, which would seem to have given him
so much trouble, are not only false and slanderous, but unspeakably ridiculous. Does the gentleman expect to make the impression, that the intelligent people who have come together from all parts of the country to
hear this debate, cannot judge for themselves, but will believe just what
Presbyterians tell them they must believe? This most ridiculous charge
I pronounce to be utterly false. There is not one word of truth in it.

I know not whether it is necessary for me to introduce any additional
arguments in favor of the doctrine for which I contend, until Mr. C. shall
have advanced something to sustain his proposition. I will, however,
quote a few passages of Scripture which clearly teach the doctrine of a
special divine agency in conversion and sanctification. Ezekiel xxxvi.
26, 27, "A new heart also will I give you, and a new spirit will I put
within you; and I will take away the stony heart out of your flesh, and
I will give you a heart of flesh. And I will put my Spirit within you,
and cause you to walk in my statutes, and ye shall keep my judgments
and do them." Does not God here proclaim himself the author of that
radical change of heart which causes men to turn from sin, and keep his
commandments? The passage is a promise and a prediction of the converting and sanctifying influences of the Spirit which should be exerted
upon the Jews in a future day. Does this language teach, that the Spirit
can exert on the heart no other moral power but that which is contained
in words and arguments? The Bible is, on all important points, a plain
book; and its obvious meaning is generally its true meaning. Now I
ask, what idea would this language convey to the mind of any one who has
no theory to support? When God says, I will give you a new heart,
would not such a person understand, that he would exert an influence
quite different from mere argument? I cheerfully leave every candid
hearer to determine, whether there is not here the promise of an influence of the Spirit in additton to the Word, and distinct from it.

The next passage I quote is Jer. xxxii. 37—" Behold, I will gather
them out of all countries whither I have driven them in mine anger, &c.,
and I will give them one heart and one way, that they may fear me forever, for the good of them and their children after them." Does the
prophet mean, that God would by *arguments* give to his people one
heart and one way? He promises to gather them from their wanderings,
and to exert such an influence on their minds, that with, one heart they
would turn from their sins to his service, and fear him forever. I ask
again, what idea would be conveyed by such language to the unsophisticated mind, to a plain honest man, who has no theory to support?
What is the obvious meaning of the language? I verily believe, that
there is not an intelligent man living who, on hearing this passage read,

would not, if he had no favorite theory to bias his judgment, understand it to teach the doctrine of a special divine influence distinct from mere words and arguments.—[*Time expired.*

Tuesday, Nov. 28—10 *o'clock, A. M.*
[MR. CAMPBELL'S FOURTH ADDRESS.]

MR. PRESIDENT—Before proceeding to the business of the day, I must make a few introductory remarks. In reference, then, to the incidents of yesterday I ought, perhaps, to advert to some of them which were not of so pleasant a character as usual. And, first, as to the incident in the after part of the day which called for an allusion to Mr. Burch. I did not, indeed, name that gentleman—Mr. Rice named him in your presence. My remarks could not in the least involve the moral character of that gentleman. I did not intend to impeach the moral character of Mr. Burch or any one else. It was, sir, I repeat, the most remote thing in my mind, to violate the feelings, unnecessarily, of any one present, much less the moral reputation of Mr. Burch. The fact stated I believed then, and I believe now, to be strictly true. But having ascertained, that Mr. Burch's feelings have been wounded, and a desire having been expressed that it should not go to record, I cheerfully consent that it be not published. I have no desire to put any thing on record which might at all tend to mar good feelings.*

As respects the imputation uttered on yesterday by Mr. Rice, that in some of my remarks touching the management of affairs here, I spake under excitement. If, by excitement, the gentleman means animal passion or anger, I cannot admit it. Exciting as have been some of the circumstances in which I have been placed in conducting this discussion, I have not allowed myself to yield to any temptation of that sort. If I appeared so to him or any one else, I certainly am not conscious of it. It must be because they thought I had provocation enough. It is with me a principle, confirmed by habit, on all occasions, especially one so solemn as the present, to hold in abeyance those passions which might be wrought up into effervescence. Knowing that the wrath of man worketh not the righteousness of God, I feel myself always admonished to avoid even the slightest appearance of it. I have, therefore, on no occasion of this sort, in all my life, been accused of any thing of this kind. Indeed, as the troubled water is generally muddy, and the calm gently flowing stream clear, excited passions are no way auxiliary to the ascertainment of truth, but rather of a contrary tendency. Mr. Rice is fully comprehended in this manœuvre.

I shall now proceed to the business of the day. The proposition before us is—"In conversion and sanctification the Spirit of God operates only through the Word of Truth," or *always* through the Word of Truth. Mr. Rice admits it *sometimes* so operates, but not always; sometimes operating without the Word of Truth. The proper difference between us is the difference between *sometimes* and *always*. That the Spirit of God does *operate* in both conversion and sanctification, we both admit. But I affirm and he denies that it operates *only* in that way. In sustaining the affirmative, my method has been to show that as these works of conversion and sanctification are specific works—works uniformly the same, as any of the products of the animal or vegetable king-

---

* Understanding from Mr. Rice, that Mr. Burch desired this incident to go to record, I have consented to the publication.   A. C.

doms, there must be uniformity in the operation. This the constitution of the human mind requires; and hence, whatever is in any one case essential to any one result, such as regeneration, is necessary in each and every other case whatever. So far we have reasoned on the inductive plan; these being the results of innumerable multitudes of facts, such as, no man can suggest an idea, or view, or feeling, of a moral or spiritual character, which has not been borrowed from the Bible; and again, the person destitute of that book, is destitute of all those ideas, impressions and sensations.

To these views Mr. R. has simply affirmed that there is no such uniformity; that it is not necessary. We call, but we call in vain, for an example of conversion by the Spirit alone, or where the Word was wholly unknown. Such a case, even were it plausibly alledged, would be entitled to very high consideration. He will not attempt such a case; he presumes upon no such evidence. His, then, is a position purely metaphysical, and belongs to the science of abstract speculative theology. It is wholly and forever insusceptible of any appreciable demonstration or proof. We have not only Bible declarations, but facts and analogies innumerable, on our side of the question. One of my axioms is, whatever is essential in one case is essential in every case. But as the gentleman has not met, and, I presume, will not meet me in debate on any one of these great positions, I shall proceed to a new argument, more intelligible to all minds, and more in support of these conclusions than any merely analogous or abstract reasonings could be. I open the New Testament at once and read as my

Eighth argument, 1 Peter i. 23, " Being born again, not of corruptible seed, but of incorruptible seed, by the Word of God which liveth and abideth forever." Now, as you all remember, our Lord himself compares his Word, or the Word of God, to seed planted or sown; and, under the parable of the sower, represents its various fortunes, and beautifully teaches the true philosophy of conversion in the fact, that the good ground is the man who "*receives the Word of God in an honest heart.*" Under both metaphors, drawn the one from the vegetable, the other from the animal kingdom; the Word of God is the seed, of which we are born again or renewed in heart and life. This Word of God liveth and abideth: for God lives and abides for ever.

1st. With regard to the essentiality of the seed. We all know that in the vegetable kingdom, without that there is no harvest, no fruit. And, as certain it is, that when the Word of God is not first sown in the heart, there can be no regeneration, or renewal of the spirit, and, consequently, no fruit brought forth unto eternal life. So the metaphors taken from the animal and vegetable kingdoms, teach the same lesson. But does not the mere fact that Peter says, that we are born again of incorruptible seed, declare that where this incorruptible seed is not, there can possibly be no birth! Unless, then, Mr. Rice can shew that it is just as true to say, we are born again, neither by corruptible nor incorruptible seed, without the Word of God,—this single passage settles this question forever, as I honestly conceive.

Is it necessary now to traverse the whole face of nature, to explore the whole kingdom of botany, to find a plant without a seed, in order to prove the proposition, *that every ear of corn comes from one grain of seed deposited in the earth?* No more is it essential to my argument, that I should first hear all the conversions in the world, before I conclude that there is one that originated without one word of God having been sown in the human heart. Will not all the world believe me, that if I prove in one case that without the specific seed,—corn, wheat, &c., we cannot have the crop, that it is true in all other cases, without a particular examination; and from every principle of analogy, if I prove the Word in one case of a new heart to be necessary, it needs not that I prove it to be so in every other heart, in every other case. The mere fact of calling the Gospel the incorruptible seed, is enough. Where that seed is not, the fruit of it cannot be.

The phrase, " the incorruptible seed" of any thing, indicates, in the ears of common sense, that it is essential to that thing; and if so, then who can be a christian without being born?—and who can be born but according to one uniform and immutable law? Now, in the theory of Mr. Rice, there is no uniformity; there is a plurality of ways of being born, which, to my mind, is most palpably at fault in every particular.

But I will adduce some other testimonies under this head of argument. We shall hear James the apostle, chapter i. 18: " Of his own will begat he us by the word of truth, that we should be a kind of first fruits of his creation." Hence the truth again appears as an instrument of regeneration. God's *will* is the origin of it; his *Spirit* the efficient *cause* of it; but the Word is the necessary *instrument* of it. *By the Word of Truth*, then, we are *begotten*, and not without it, according to James. We may add testimonies without increasing either authority or evidence; but, for the sake of illustration, if not for authority, we shall offer a few other testimonies to complete this particular argument. We shall hear Paul, as a *father*, speak to his sons in the faith in Corinth—1 Cor. iv. 15: "As my beloved *sons* I warn you: for though you have ten thousand instructors in Christ, yet have you not many fathers; for in Christ Jesus have I *begotten* you through the gospel." Paul regards the gospel just in the same attitude in which James represents it. The gospel is here the seed, the instrument of the conversion of the Corinthians.

But the whole oracle of God is unique on this subject. God " purifies the heart by faith," that is, *the truth believed*—not by believing as an act of the mind, but by the truth believed, which constitutes " *the faith.*" Paul also told the Thessalonians that God had, "from the beginning, chosen them to salvation through sanctification of the Spirit and belief of the truth." Here again the *belief of the truth* is the instrument of sanctification and salvation. I shall conclude this little summary of a portion of the direct and positive testimony of God, in proof of my grand position on the Holy Spirit's work of conversion and sanctification, by the testimony of the Messiah, in person: " Sanctify them through thy truth, O Father, for thy Word is the truth." Whether, then, we call the *truth* the *Word*, the *Word of God* the *gospel*, it is called the seed, the incorruptible seed of the new birth; by which a sinner is quickened, begotten, born, sanctified, purified, and saved. I regard this my eighth argument as a host in itself—nay, as the solemn, direct, and unequivocal declaration of God, in attestation of the entire truth and safety of the proposition concerning both conversion and sanctification. I wish Mr. Rice and the whole community to know, that I regard this argument, when fully canvassed and developed, as enough on this subject. I am willing to place the whole cause upon it.

I shall now go on to review some portions of Mr. R.'s speeches not yet noticed, which may by some be considered as constituting some objections to my former reasonings on the subject. The gentleman rallied with great zeal and warmth, upon the passage, " Paul planted and Apollos watered." He expressed some astonishment at my presuming to give such an interpretation, and I am just as much astonished at his pertinacity. It fully proves how much he is the slave of bad commentators. I have all good translators, commentators, and critics with me; but better still, I have got good Dr. Common Sense with me, and he will make it plain to all. Indeed, no really learned theologian thinks differently from me. But let us look to the context. The Word of God is not mentioned in the passage—as the gentleman said, Canaan was not found in the Epistle to the Galatians. Paul speaks of *men* and not of the *Word*. I planted you men in God's field or husbandry, and Apollos watered you, but God gave the increase, the growth. He presents the same persons under three distinct figures, in the same context, and connects with each an appropriate imagery. But we shall confine ourselves to two of them—the husbandry and the building. As a husbandry, Paul *planted* them; as a building, a temple, he laid *the foundation*. But if I must make it still plainer, I will then suppose it to be the Word. Well, then, Paul planted the Word in the people's heart; and Apollos watered it in their hearts; and God made it grow in their hearts. Paul, in this case, planted the Word by preaching the Word, and Apollos watered the Word by exhorting them through the Word; and God made it grow by his Spirit operating through the Word. Well, now Paul is placed in a most awkward attitude. He is converted into a school-boy confounding all laws and usages of the schools. He has Paul planting the Word by the Word! and Apollos watering the Word by the Word! Suppose we convert it into corn; then all the world will comprehend Paul's beautiful rhetoric. Paul planted corn by scattering corn in the fields—Apollos came along, and watered that corn, by scattering some of the same corn upon it ! !

But my friend superciliously asks—how can any one plant a church ? would you stick it in the ground ! ! Profoundly erudite objection ! How do men plant a colony of men ?—stick them in the ground ! ! Men have been said to plant churches and colonies from time immemorial ! The field or husbandry is the place where Paul figuratively planted men; and as living stones, he also builded them together, under another figure, " for an habitation of God through the Spirit." The apostle's rhetoric is classic, rich, and beautiful. As a *field*, Paul brought the Corinthians into it, and planted them in the nursery. Apollos came next, and refreshed them much by his exhortations ; and thus, through their joint labors, Corinthians became God's husbandry. I take pleasure in avowing my conviction that it is the blessing of God upon the labors of Paul and Apollos, that made these Corinthians grow. I do not labor this passage to oppose that idea ; but to expose this most licentious way of quoting the Scriptures, and forcing them into the sectarian service. The improvements in the science of hermeneutics will, I hope, move westwardly.

A favorite passage, which has been quoted oftener many times than any other text in the Bible, during this discussion, and for no reason that I can see, but because the word sprinkle—that blessed word *sprinkle*, is found in it, along with clean water—I must quote it once, out of courtesy: Eze. xxxvi. 25: " Then will I sprinkle clean water upon you, and ye shall be clean from all your filthiness; and from all your idols will I cleanse you." This is not literally water free from mud, but an allusion to the water mixed with ashes, which purified the unclean—a mere symbol here of the cleansing of the Jews. He says in verse 24: "For I will take you from among the heathen, and gather you out of all countries, and will bring you into your own land." Here there is an express declaration, that God would bring them back to their own land. "Then will I sprinkle clean water upon you, and ye shall be clean from all your filthiness, and from all your idols." It was to cleanse them from their idols by the water of purification. "A new heart also will I give you, and a new spirit will I put within you: and I will take away the stony heart out of your flesh, and I will give you a heart of flesh. And I will put my spirit within you, and cause you to walk in my statutes; and ye shall keep my judgments, and do them. And ye shall dwell in the land that I gave to your fathers; and ye shall be my people, and I will be your God." Now, with regard to this strong phrase—a new heart will I give you—suppose I should affirm, that men make their own hearts new? As he proves his positions, so would I prove it. Eze. xviii. 31: "Cast away from you all your transgressions, whereby ye have transgressed; and make you a new heart and a new spirit: for why will you die, O house of Israel." Here, I say, Israel is commanded to make for themselves a new heart; could I not prove that they were thus commanded by the sound of these words? My friend says, that God does *create* a clean heart. But in what sense? There is nothing to be gained by thus quoting scripture out of its proper connection. Paul says: "Be renewed in the spirit of your minds." I doubt not the propriety of both these forms of speech. The Lord does every thing that is good. He says: "I, the Lord, create light, and I create darkness; I create good, and I create evil; I, the Lord, do all these things." How does he do them—by his own immediate power? Certainly not. But by very various instruments—permits some, and appoints others, in various ways. He does not always create good and evil by the same means.

The word *create* does not only mean to make a thing out of original nonentity, but to change its relations, and sometimes only to new-modify it. In creating light, God does something. In creating darkness, he withholds something. In creating good, he imparts something. In creating evil, he withholds good. Men make to themselves a new heart; and God makes for them a new heart. He institutes the means, gives his Spirit, and they receive and obey the truth.

The gentleman, in an attempt to reply to the just objection that he makes conversion in every case a miracle equal to the resurrection of the Lord, went into the definition of a miracle, instead oi removing the difficulty, and asks what need of the instrumentality of angels in the world? We always admit that an angel's visit is a miracle. But what has that to do with the subject before us? I do not admire his definition of a miracle. I sometimes define it as "*A display of supernatural power in attestation of the truth of some proposition.*" That supernatural power may be either intellectual or physical: such as raising Lazarus, or foretelling the destruction of Jerusalem. But this is no place for such matters. God never squanders power unnecessarily. He never does by miracle what he can do without it. He works by secondary causes, unless some great emergency in the universe calls for the primary, original, creating power. God does not work without the laws of mind—nor change the laws of mind. He does not violate the constitution of the mind, nor give a man new powers, intellectual or moral, through any moral or supernatural change in this life. To work salvation, or a change of heart, without the laws of mind or contrary to the laws of mind, would be a miracle as great as the resurrection of Lazarus. And such I presume to be Mr. R.'s theory of regeneration—without knowledge, argument, faith, hope, or love; &c.; a direct, immediate operation of omnipotence upon the naked soul without any instrument between!!

The gentleman gave a singular definition of moral disposition. He made it a sort of animal instinct—for a child was disposed to love music! *Hunger* and *thirst* are also dispositions upon the same philosophy! And, sir, this was the answer given to a very important question, viz: If moral disposition be a part of regeneration, and if moral disposition be to love God and hate Satan; to love righteousness and hate iniquity—Query— Can an infant then be regenerated? Can it love or hate a being or a thing, concerning which it knows nothing more than a rock? Mr. R. cannot explain this difficulty, and it is fatal to his theory. If a child be regenerate, it must love holiness and hate iniquity; but this cannot be without knowledge—because in religion, as in every thing else, intellect pioneers the way, while the affections and the heart follow. We must see beauty before we can love it. We must see deformity before we can hate it. And, therefore, " the love of holiness and the hatred of sin" are impossible to an infant.—[*Time expired.*

Tuesday, Nov. 28—10½ *o'clock, A. M.*
[MR. RICE'S FOURTH REPLY.]

MR. PRESIDENT—Before proceeding to the discussion of the subject before us, I must briefly notice Mr. Campbell's statement concerning Mr. Burch, who was one of the moderators in the debate between him and Mr. McCalla. When he made the statement, on yesterday, about an opinion expressed by one of the moderators in that debate, there were present many who knew that Mr. Burch was alluded to. I wish now to say, that I am authorized by Mr. B. to deny most positively, that he ever expressed or entertained the opinion, that in that debate Mr. C. was victorious; and to state that, from that day to this, he has expressed precisely the opposite opinion. It is taking an unfair advantage of a man who, according to the rules of this discussion, cannot be permitted to reply, to prefer such charges.

The gentleman says, he has not spoken, at any time during the debate, under the influence of passion. I will not dispute the truth of his statement; but I must say, that he has said many things which would have been more excusable, if uttered under excitement, than if spoken deliberately.

It is of the first importance in this discussion, that we keep distinctly in view the point in debate. I stated it clearly on yesterday; but it has not been brought prominently to view in the speech of this morning. Indeed, I believe it would be utterly impossible to learn, from all the gentleman has said this morning, wherein we differ.

The main point in the debate is not whether the Spirit *always* operates through the truth. I was surprised to hear him read the proposition in this way—" *only* or *always*." I was not aware that the words *only* and *always* are synonymous. I presume that no dictionary can be found, that defines *only* to mean *always*. If you will substitute *always* for *only*, it will make a proposition radically different from that we are now discussing. What, then, are the points in regard to which we differ? 1st. We differ concerning the sanctification of infants and idiots. This, however, is not the only difference between us, nor the most important. For, 2nd. We differ widely concerning the influence of the Holy Spirit in the conversion and sanctification of *adults*.   Mr. Campbell contends, that the Spirit operates *only* through the truth.   I believe that the Spirit operates *ordinarily* through the truth, but not *only* through the truth.   The word *only*, in the proposition before us, is an emphatic and an important word.   He maintains, that the Spirit dictated the word, and confirmed it by miracles, and that the word, presented to the mind by any instrumentality, converts and sanctifies it.   That is, the Spirit, according to his doctrine, converts and sanctifies men, just as the spirit of Demosthenes and Cicero affected their hearers or readers ; and as the spirit of Mr. Campbell affects this audience !   He exerts on your minds no other influence than that exerted by his words and arguments.   Just so, according to his doctrine, the Spirit of God operates.

We believe and teach, that the Word is ordinarily employed in conversion and sanctification.   Yet there must be, and there is, an influence of the Spirit on the heart, in addition to the Word, and distinct from it ; and by this influence, especially, man is converted and sanctified.   This is, practically, the great point on which we differ.

As I have heretofore distinctly stated, we do not believe in a physical change of the faculties of the soul.   Mr. C.'s remarks about physical regeneration are, therefore, out of place.   Our confession of faith does not teach the doctrine, nor do we hold it.

He desires me to follow him in his train of argument.   I will now do so, as far as time will permit.   I have adduced against his doctrine some four distinct arguments, viz. 1. That it prescribes to the power of God over the human mind an unreasonable and an unscriptural limitation.   2. That it necessarily involves the damnation of infants and idiots.   3. That it contradicts the scripture doctrine of human depravity, making it arise from mere mistake ; whereas the Bible teaches, that men sin wilfully and deliberately.   4. I have quoted several passages of Scripture directly teaching the special agency of the Holy Spirit in conversion and sanctification.

I will now pay my respects to the gentleman's new arguments.   He refers us to Luke viii. 11, " The seed is the word of God ;" and to 1 Pet. i. 23.   Do these passages prove, that in conversion and sanctification the Spirit operates *only* through the truth ?   Do the seed of themselves produce the harvest.   Who ever heard of obtaining an abundant harvest only by seed ?   Does not the farmer first prepare his soil ?   He does not scatter his seed amongst thorns and weeds.   The human heart is like the unprepared earth ; and in the parable to which the gentleman referred, the seed that produced the harvest are said to be sown in " good ground"—in soil previously broken up and prepared.   But when the soil has been prepared, and the seed sown, the sun must shine, and the rain must descend, or there will be no harvest.   God has a most important agency in these things.   He only can cause the sun to shine, and the showers to refresh the earth.   In these things there is human agency, and there is divine agency.   So the servants of God sow the seed of life : but God prepares the hearts of men to receive it, and the Holy Spirit, like showers on the thirsty ground, causes it to spring up and bear fruit to the glory of God.   The argument from the passage under consideration is decidedly in favor of our views.   I prove my doctrine by the very arguments brought forward to overthrow it !

He has repeatedly asserted, if the word of God is employed in conversion and sanctification in one case, it must be necessary in all. But this is bare assertion. Let the gentleman prove it if he can. I should like to see him attempt to prove, that God has bound himself always to employ in this work the same means and instrumentalities. If he has thus limited himself, let the passage be produced; if he has not, who dares limit him?

The next argument used by Mr. C. is founded on James i. 18: "Of his own will begat he us with his Word of Truth." The argument is mine. I prove the doctrine of special divine influence by this very passage. Observe, it presents two influences exerted on man in regeneration—the agency of God who begets him, and the instrumentality of the truth through which he is begotten or renewed. Does James say, he begat us only by his Word? He does not. God begat us—he put forth power; and he did it in connection with his Word as the means. How, then, can it be said with truth, that the means or instrumentality did the whole work? James says, God did the work, and that he did it by the Word, not *only* by the Word. This is precisely the doctrine for which I am contending.

The next argument offered by Mr. C. is founded on the language of Paul in 1 Cor. iv. 15: "For in Christ Jesus I have begotten you through the gospel." There are commonly three agencies employed in the conversion and sanctification of the soul: 1st, the agency or influence of the Word; 2d, the agency of the minister who preaches it; and, 3d, the agency of the Holy Spirit on the heart, inducing men to receive the truth in the love of it, and to live according to its divine principles and precepts. There are some passages of Scripture which present particularly the agency of man; some which present the influence of the Word; and some which speak directly and clearly of the agency of the Holy Spirit. I believe in the importance of all these three. The special agency of the Spirit is taught as distinctly and as frequently as either of the others. It is unsafe, therefore, to reject any one of the three. We have not the right to do so.

I must now notice the remarks of the gentleman on 1 Cor. iii. 6: "I have planted, Apollos watered, but God gave the increase." He insists, that Paul speaks here of *planting the church.* Yet not a word is said about planting the church in the chapter, nor in the epistle. But he asks, if Paul planted the Word, how did Apollos water it? And I ask him, if Paul planted the church, how did Apollos water it? By preaching. He says, I make Apollos water the Word with the Word. But if there is any inconsistency, is he not equally guilty of it? He makes Paul plant the church by preaching the Word, and Apollos water it by preaching the Word; so that the planting and the watering are thus made to be the same operation. The truth is, Paul planted in the hearts of the people the seed of divine truth; God by his Holy Spirit caused the seed to grow; and then Apollos came and continued to proclaim the truth, in connection with which the Spirit still descended like refreshing showers on the parched earth, and brought the fruit to maturity.

That a special divine influence was exerted, is evident from the 5th verse: "Who then is Paul, and who is Apollos, but ministers by whom ye believed, *even as the Lord gave to every man?*" Does not the apostle here teach, that God inclined each one to believe, to receive the gospel.

But, says the gentleman, we talk of planting a colony or a city. [Mr. C.—I did not say *planting* a city, but *founding* a city.] Very well—I have nothing to do with the word *founding*. We are speaking of *planting*. When we speak of planting a tree, we mean removing it from one place and setting it in another. When men speak of planting a colony, they mean transferring people from one place, and establishing them in another. Did Paul transfer christians from Antioch and from other churches to Corinth? The Scriptures never speak of planting a church.

The gentleman is quite tired of hearing me quote Ezekiel, xxvi. 25, 26. True, I have had occasion frequently to quote it, for it presents the emblem of purification in connection with the work of the Spirit. I have referred to it as illustrating both the mode and the design of baptism; and I now have use for it in proof of the doctrine, that in conversion and sanctification there is an agency of the Spirit distinct from the truth. "A new heart also will I give you, and a new spirit will I put within you: and I will take away the stony heart out of your flesh, and I will give you an heart of flesh. And I will put my Spirit within you." Here God promises to give a new heart and a new spirit. How could language more fully teach the doctrine we hold? I have no occasion to say any thing more about the sprinkling of clean water. That part of the passage belongs to subjects that have been disposed of.

Mr. C. attempts to evade the force of this and other plain and unequivocal declarations of Scripture by telling you, that God commanded men to make themselves new hearts; and that Paul exhorted christians to be renewed in their minds.

And he says, he could thus prove, that men do renew their own hearts. So he perhaps could, if he could only prove, that men always do their duty. It is the duty of all men to love and serve God—to be holy; but the question is—Do they do it? God commands them to repent, believe, and be perfectly holy; but do they do so? But in the passage under consideration, God does not command men to do their duty; but he tells his people *what he will do.* " A new heart will I give you; and a new spirit will I put within you: and I will take away the stony heart out of your flesh. And I will put my Spirit within you, and cause you to walk in my statutes." Here we have most clearly exhibited the radical change of heart, and the consequent change of life, of which God is the glorious author. The cause must be bad, that leads a man to attempt to evade the force of language so perfectly unequivocal.

I rejoice to know, that in the Bible, as in the book of nature, the truths which are essential to the safety and happiness of men, are revealed in language so clear and so simple, that the uneducated as well as the wise may understand them. Not more certainly are we taught that God sends rain upon the thirsty earth, than that he pours out his Spirit upon the hearts of men; and he who can pray for the former, that his seed may produce an abundant harvest, may also pray with stronger faith for the latter, that he may bear the peaceable fruits of righteousness.

The gentleman repeats the assertion, that regeneration, according to our views, is a miracle. He admits, that it is not a miracle in the common acceptation of the word; but he chooses to use it in a new sense. If he chooses to say, that every event brought about by divine interposition, is a miracle, he must be permitted to do so; but such is not the meaning of the word as used in the Bible. Daily in the course of his providence, God puts forth his almighty power. If he does not, why should we pray for his protection? If all things are now governed by fixed laws, our prayers are worse than vain.

It is true, God does not directly interpose supernatural power without means, when means can be employed. But when an infant dies, that could not receive the Word, nor be sanctified through it, there is occasion for God to work without means. Mr. C. admits that infants are depraved; and therefore he must admit, that if they are not sanctified and prepared to enter heaven, they must be lost. And is not the soul of an infant of sufficient value to call for a divine influence without means to sanctify it? It is immortal; it will live through endless ages. It is worth more than the whole world. When such a spirit is called to leave the world, and is unfit for heaven; shall we be told, that God cannot sanctify it by his Spirit? that he cannot prepare it for the joys and glories of heaven?

The gentleman re-asserts his unphilosophical principle, that there can be no moral disposition, where there is no knowledge. A child, he says, cannot love God before it knows him. But it is absolutely certain, that the mind may be in such a state, that it will love some objects and feel an aversion to others on first sight. This is a fact known to every body. Thousands have experienced its truth; for they have loved or disliked persons and things the first moment they ever saw them. This love or aversion depends upon a previously existing character or state of mind.

Every thing has its nature. The lion, however young, has a lion's nature. All lions, in all climates and countries, manifest the same disposition, as soon as capable—proving that they possess a common nature. Plant two trees in the same soil; and let them be watered by the same stream; and one will produce sweet fruit, and the other bitter. They possess different natures. This very illustration is by the Savior applied to the subject now under discussion. He said, "make the tree good, and the fruit will be good." Make the heart pure, and the life will be pure. Again, he says—"A good man out of the good treasure of the heart bringeth forth good things; and an evil man out of the evil treasure, bringeth forth evil things," Matt. xii. 35. Such may be the moral disposition of a man's heart, that an object of compassion will in a moment call forth his sympathy and his benevolence. So may an infant possess a holy nature; so that when first it shall look upon God in heaven, it will love, adore, and worship him. This, I think, is perfectly clear to every one but my friend, Mr. C.

I think I have answered every argument he has offered; for I was careful to note them all. I will now adduce some further arguments in favor of a special agency of the Holy Spirit in conversion and sanctification.

The first passage I will read, is Ezekiel xi. 18, 19, which contains a prediction concerning the spiritual blessings which God would bestow upon the Jews: "And they shall come thither, and they shall take away all the detestable things thereof, and all the abominations thereof from thence. And I will give them one heart, and I will put a new spirit within you: and I will take the stony heart out of their flesh, and will give them an heart of flesh." Are we to understand by such language as this, that God intended at a future day simply to present the truth before their minds—the very truth which they now rejected? Or are we not plainly taught, that he purposed to exert upon their hearts such a spiritual influence, as would cause them to return to his service? The meaning of the passage is so perfectly plain, that no criticism can obscure it.

Again, I will read Isaiah liv. 3, "For I will pour water upon him that is thirsty, and floods upon the dry ground: I will pour my Spirit upon thy seed, and my blessings upon thine offspring; and they shall spring up as among the grass, as willows by the water courses." This is one of the precious promises made to the church in her affliction. The day was coming when the Lord would pour water upon the thirsty—would cause the influences of his Spirit to be abundantly enjoyed by his people and by their descendants. Here we have the emblem and the thing signified. This outpouring of the Spirit was to result in the conversion and sanctification of their seed.

Now compare this language with that employed by the prophet Joel, which was fulfilled on the day of Pentecost. "And it shall come to pass in the last days, (saith God,) I will pour out of my Spirit upon all flesh; and your sons and your daughters shall prophecy," &c. This language of Joel is admitted by all to denote a divine agency distinct from words and arguments. Then when Isaiah employs the very same expression—"I will pour my Spirit upon thy seed"—is it not clear, that he also speaks of an influence of the Spirit distinct from arguments? Mark, too, the happy results of this spiritual influence. The blessing of God was to descend upon their offspring; and they were to grow up spiritually as willows by the water-courses. They were to bring forth the peaceable fruits of righteousness.—[*Time expired.*

Tuesday, Nov. 28—11 *o'clock, A. M*
[MR. CAMPBELL'S FIFTH ADDRESS.]

MR. PRESIDENT—On yesterday morning, sir, I gave reasons why I sometimes read the word *always* for *only*—not as its grammatical import, but its contextual import in the proposition, as it relates to our respective views. Mr. Rice might, therefore, have saved his time for a more important purpose. The terms only and always, as before explained, have here an equivalent value; and, therefore, I lay no stress whatever upon any preference, except for sake of perspicuity.

The legitimate point of discussion in this proposition, is not whether the *Word operates*, but whether the *instrumentality* of the Word be necessary, according to the words, *only through the Word*. The gentleman is shifting the ground. I never said, nor wrote, that the Word was the original cause of man's salvation, nor even the efficient cause. I have never ranked it above the instrumental cause. All that has been offered by Mr. R. upon the subject, in any other view of the matter, is gratuitous and irrelevant. It is to change the proposition, and hide the point in his system, which I repudiate. The proposition is, in its own language, a refutation of all these iusinuations. It affirms that the Spirit of God *operates.* The question is not upon *operation,* but upon *instrumentality*—"only *through* the Word." This is the question to be debated here. If there be any controversy at all, this is just the point. If Mr. Rice will make the Word the uniform and universal instrument, he agrees with me. There is, then, no controversy about it. This is the true and real issue. Any other issue is false, feigned and deceptive. I have, during a protracted controversy for many years, given my views on physical, moral and spiritual influences; upon physical and metaphysical regeneration—but these are other questions than that now before us. What the Spirit of God *does,* is not the question; but by what *means* the Spirit of God *operates* in conversion and sanctification. The gentleman is seeking to get off from the question; still he perceives the real point, for he has offered arguments which have no relevancy, if that be not the point.

43   3 L

He argues against my views, because they "*limit the power of God.*" That is, of course, in confining the operation to the instrumentality of the Word. It *limits*, but does not *deny* the operation. He is right here. This is the issue, and the objection was made in a just view of it. Well, now, I meet the objection as a legitimate one. We shall try its merits. The Universalian says, the Unitarian, the Calvinist, and especially the Presbyterian, limits the power of God, because he makes salvation depend upon faith and a holy life. When Mr. Rice defends himself from that charge, his defence shall be mine from his charge of limitation. The Unitarian, too, talks against limiting the great God, in extending salvation beyond the precincts of Bible influence. But all this is idle talk. I do limit the power of God, only because he himself has limited it. God can only do by his power, what his wisdom and benevolence approve. He has no power beyond that, though almighty to do what these two perfections approbate. Therefore, "He cannot lie;" "He cannot deny himself." Therefore, he cannot make a wicked man happy; and, therefore, he can convert men only through the gospel. There are physical, as well as moral impossibilities. God cannot make two mountains without a valley. He cannot make light and darkness co-habit the same place at the same time. He cannot lie. This is another *ad captandum* argument. God can do many things he will not do. I say again, he can only do what is in harmony with all his perfections. There are, also, *moral* impossibilities. A virtuous and kind father could kill all his children, and yet he could not. He has physical, but not moral power. His arm could, but his heart could not; and, therefore, the moral sometimes triumphs over the physical. God can only save through the means his wisdom, justice and benevolence dictate.

But a second objection, pertinent to the true issue, is couched in the following terms: My doctrine "leads to infant damnation." That is, if the Spirit operates only through the Word, then infants cannot be saved, because they cannot understand, or believe the Word. Now if his views of faith and spiritual influence were correct, then the objection would lie against my affirmation, "*only through the Word.*" But his views being erroneous on these points, the objection is idle and impotent. These words, "infant damnation," are ugly words—and they come not so consistently from one who believes and teaches the confession. His creed divides infants into two classes—the *elect* and the "*non-elect.*" Of course, then, infant damnation is inevitable, if the confession be true. Now if we were to proportion the number of "*elect infants*," by the number of elect men, according to appearances, there would be a hundred non-elect, for one. And yet this gentleman upbraids my doctrine as objectionable, because it might, perchance, involve the possibility of infant damnation, when his own confession consigns an awful overwhelming majority of all infants to eternal perdition! Think not that I exaggerate the relative proportions. Look at the whole world! Pagans of all casts; Greek and Roman parties; Jews, Turks, Atheists, and all the reprobate Protestants! What disproportion between the good and the bad! It is as one to the hundred!

There is nothing more repulsive to the human mind, than the doctrine of infant damnation. It was the first item of Calvinistic faith, at which my infant soul revolted. I still remember my boyish reasonings on that tenet of elect and non-elect infants. I dared not to say, that it was absolutely false, seeing my creed and my ancestors recognized it. But, thought

I, can it be true? How can it be true? An infant is born, yet could not help it—it opened its eyes but once, and shut them forever—and went to everlasting anguish!!! That millions should be forced into existence, and forced out of it in a day, a month, a year, or some six or seven, and go down to everlasting agonies! My soul sickened at the thought!— and yet I had lived full fourteen years, before I presumed to utter to any mortal what my heart felt. I thank God, this doctrine of reprobate infants is not found any where but in the creed; and there they are found only in a minced form, by implication, in the words "elect infants."

There are various assertions and negations, and sometimes oft repeated, the only object of which, as it seems to me, is to call me off from the main issue. I should like to refer to all these matters, some of them several times repeated, if I had time, or if it were incumbent on me. We should lose nothing by a full examination of them all. Meantime, I am just reminded of the speculation on the word *holy*.

The gentleman's speculations on the word *holy*, and God's making man holy, and a holy house, &c. have not been full of light to my reason. Holiness is not a positive creation, an entity, a substantive existence, nor an attribute like wisdom, power, or goodness. It is a *relative* attribute. Were there no impurity there could be no holiness. In contrast with impurity, God, and angels, and saints, are holy beings. The gentleman's positions would apply as much to Eden and paradise as to man. He might say, God created Eden and paradise holy, as well as man. In that acceptation the universe was made holy. I must be permitted, though perhaps not in a way adapted to universal intelligence and acceptance, to offer a remark or two on man, tending to illustrate my position at least.

Man, with me, when contemplated in his whole person is a plural unit. He is one man, having a *body*, a *soul*, and a *spirit*. So both my philosophy and my Bible teach. Paul prayed for the Thessalonians that God would sanctify them wholly (*holoteleis*) their *body*, *soul*, and *spirit*. Their *pnuema, psuche, soma*. Not only have the Greeks these three names, but the Latins also. They had their *animus*, their *anima*, and their *corpus*. So had the Hebrews. So have the moderns, as we have —*body, soul, spirit*. The body is a mere organized material machine— the soul is the seat of all the passions and instincts of our nature, and is intimately connected with the blood. It is the animal life. The spirit is a purely intellectual principle, as intimately connected with the soul, as the soul with the blood, and the vital principle. Now the spirit, or intellectual principle in man, is not the seat of corruption, or of depravity abstractly, any more than the mere materials of human flesh. The understanding or intellect is indeed weakened, and sometimes perverted by the passions, the animal instincts and impulses. But the soul is the great seat of all those corrupting and debasing propensities and affections that involve the whole man in sin and misery. Man was not condemned for reasoning illogically; nor was he condemned because he was either hungry or thirsty, or had these appetites, but because captivated by his passions, he was led into actual rebellion. This is still the depravity of man. His spirit is enslaved to his passions and appetites. Its approvings and disapprovings are all more or less contaminated, biassed, and tinged by these rebellious elements, this "law of sin which is in his members." warring against the law of his mind, reason and conscience. Now these not being developed in infancy, any more than reason or conscience, places them under quite a different dispensation and destiny. Dying in that undeveloped state, they are not the subjects of condemnation eternal, never having disobeyed God, nor refused the gospel. They need not those operations of the Spirit of which the theory of Mr. Rice so often speaks, and with which it is so replete, all of which originated too in the brain of one Saint Augustine.

Hours might be consumed in the development of these principles; and without a full development, perhaps they ought not to be introduced. I have, indeed, spoken thus far, merely to show, that we have reason to repudiate the notion of the abstract, undefinable metaphysical regeneration of an infant, as essential to its salvation. It only needs, as before observed, a physical regeneration; a destruction of that body in which those seeds of passion and sinful appetites are so thickly sown, in consequence of the animal and sensitive having triumphed over the intellectual and moral man, and so entailing upon our race this natural proneness to evil. Hence the necessity of physical regeneration. The adult saint needs it as much as the infant. "That law, (or power) of sin," in the members, of which Paul complained—that "body of sin and death," under which he groaned, and which made him, in his own esteem, a "wretched man," must be *destroyed*. While "the inward man delighted in the law of God, he saw another law in his members, warring against that law of his mind, and bringing him into captivity to the law of sin, which was in his members." This will be destroyed in the saint before admission into heaven—and that is what I mean by physical regeneration; and this is destroyed before development in the dying infant, and, therefore, through the Lord Messiah; the RESURRECTION and the LIFE; the sin-atoning *Lamb of God;*—the SECOND ADAM—it slumbers in the bosom of its Father and its God, till the great regeneration of heaven and earth.

Mr. R. says, he believes not in physical regeneration. Why then believe in infant regeneration, without the moral means of the Word? Without a regeneration of the heart, he says, they cannot be saved; and that being without knowledge, faith, love, or hope, must be either physical or metaphysical, or both. I plead the physical regeneration of the body and animal soul, he the physical and immediate regeneration of the *spirit* while in the body. This, however, is all aside from the great question. It comes in by the way to illustrate or support the fact, that with him, regeneration is not according to my eighth argument, *through* the incorruptible seed of the Word, but *without* it. I will dismiss this episode by a quotation from Paul, Rom. v. "By one man's disobedience many were constituted sinners, so by one man's obedience shall many be constituted righteous;" and as death reigned, *before the law*, over them that had not sinned, as Adam did, by violating a positive precept; so grace will reign, by another man, over them that never obeyed a precept; who, by reason of their infancy, never on earth could discern between good and evil. So I opine, and in so thinking, I have much countenance, if not positive testimony, from my Father's Book. Our Savior's death has laid such a broad, strong, and enduring foundation, that the Divine Father of humanity can, with the most perfect propriety, so far as mortal vision can pierce, throw the arms of his sublime philanthropy around the dying millions of our race, whose only Son was in their flesh, and not only snatch them from the desolation of the grave, but also train them in the skies, as he does their parents on the earth, for the high beatitudes of an eternal fruition of Him that made and redeemed them from the earth.

Mr. Rice has not yet explained to us his views of faith. He has a regeneration without it; indeed, in all cases, I presume, a regeneration anterior to faith. Faith, as I perceive, is the effect of regeneration, not the cause, according to his theory. An holy principle is immediately infused, and then faith is a holy act of a holy soul, regenerated by immediate contact with the Divine Spirit. Hence his adult and infant regeneration are, if I understand him, alike physical, or without the Word of God. Faith or regeneration must be prior—a simultaneous existence is not supposable. With me, faith is first, and repentance, or a change of heart, next in the order of things—in the order of nature and causation. If regeneration be the cause of faith, anterior to faith, without faith, then again, of what use are all human instrumentalities, preaching, Bibles, &c.? I wonder, except to save appearances, why any one should be taught to read the Bible, or go to meeting, until he is born again. If regeneration is not within the control of any mortal instrumentality—if no means are to be used with reference to it, I ask, then, how do men make faith void, and the gospel of none effect? If the Bible be not a moral instrument in this matter, what kind of instrument is it?

With me every christian is a new man. His heart is changed. His soul is renewed in the image of God, " in knowledge, righteousness, and true holiness." God's Holy Spirit is the agent—his gospel is the instrument. Instrumental causes are not original nor procuring causes. Without the instrumental, however, it cannot be accomplished. No man can see without the instrument called an *eye*, or the instrument called *light*. Truth and faith are the grand means, or the conjoint means, of conversion and sanctification.

Mr. R. must again have up Paul and Apollos. It is a small matter—but he may have it again. I have not opened a commentator as an *authority* for my views in any case in the discussion, but I will read a few words from Henry confirmatory of them.

[Here Mr. C. read a passage from Henry, the copy of which is lost.]

I repose no confidence in Henry as a critic; but I do in McKnight, who paraphrases these words thus: "I have planted you in God's vineyard, others have watered you by giving you instruction; but God hath made you to grow." Henry, in his common sense view, very well agrees with McKnight. I know not how many critics agree with me, but I have the context.

Paul preached the Word, and Apollos watered the Word! A little better acquaintance with Paul and Apollos would relieve him from this strait. Paul was a powerful *reasoner*, and Apollos was an eloquent *exhorter*. Now, the reasoner is the strong man, and therefore grubs and plants. The exhorter follows him, and refreshes with his zeal, his ardor, his eloquence. They do well to go together. Two by two, let them go. One reasons, and one pleads. Sinners are converted, and saints are built up, and churches made to grow, by such joint-laborers in God's field. While the idea of a church is in our mind, the figure is apposite and beautiful. But substitute the Word, and it is destitute of consistency, propriety, and beauty. It is peculiarly unfortunate for the development of the great principles involved in these propositions, that I have no respondent. Eight arguments are now before us, without any response or closing upon any one, in the form of a direct issue. In my last, I brought the united testimony of Peter, Paul, and James, and of the Messiah himself, on the indispensible instrumentality of the Word. I gave all emphasis to the figure of *seed*, consecrated as it is by Jesus and the apostle Peter. It appears as though Mr. R. feared the figure and the argument deduced from it. He cannot but perceive, that if the Word be so compared to seed, with regard to the new creation, whether traced in its animal or vegetable associations, it is made essential to the product of a new man. Where that is not the offspring, the product cannot be. Our Savior carries the figure so far as to say, that if even the seed be sown in the heart, and the devil should take it away by any stratagem, then there is no change, no salvation. May I not then conclude that the gentleman's neglect to reply, is an indisputable evidence of his lack of ability to reply. Well, we shall expect to hear from him on the subject of physical regeneration, and especially on faith, as the cause or the effect of moral renovation. The gentleman has indeed said, the seed is not every thing! And so say we.

An acquaintance with Mr. Rice's manner of assertion, attack, and negation, makes it the more incumbent on me to keep the proper issue before you, fellow-citizens; and frequently to assert my views on the subject on which we have been most calumniated. Our reformation began in the conviction of the inadequacy of the corrupted forms of religion in popular use, to effect that thorough change of heart and life which the gospel contemplates as so essential to admission into heaven. You may have heard me say here, (and the whole country may have read it and heard it many a time,) that a seven-fold immersion in the river Jordan, or any other water, *without a previous change of heart, will avail nothing,* without a genuine faith and penitence. Nor would the most strict conformity to all the forms and usages of the most perfect church order; the most exact observance of all the ordinances, without personal faith, piety, and moral righteousness—without a new heart, hallowed lips, and a holy life, profit any man in reference to eternal salvation.

We are represented, because of the emphasis laid upon some ordinances, as though we made a savior of rites and ceremonies—as believing in water regeneration, and in the saving efficacy of immersion; and as looking no farther than to these outward bodily acts: all of which is just as far from the truth and from our views, as transubstantiation or purgatory. I have, indeed, no faith in conversion by the Word, without the Spirit; nor by the Spirit without the Word. The Spirit is ever present with the Word, in conversion and in sanctification. A change of heart is essential to a change of character, and both are essential to admission into the kingdom of God. "Without holiness no man shall enjoy God." Though as scrupulous as a Pharisee, in tithing, mint, anise, and cummin, and rigid to the letter in all observances, without those moral excellencies usually called righteousness and holiness, no man can be saved eternally: "for the unrighteous shall not enter the kingdom of God."—[*Time expired.*

Tuesday, Nov. 28—11½ o'clock, A. M.
[MR. RICE'S FIFTH REPLY.]

MR. PRESIDENT—I do not deny, that Mr. Campbell believes in the necessity of a change of heart; but the great difficulty is, that he rejects the only agency which can effect it. It is of little advantage for him to urge the necessity of such a change; so long as his doctrine makes it unattainable. He teaches, that without holiness no man shall see the face of God; but denies the only agency that can prepare him for the bliss of heaven.

I do not know what he means, when he says, the Spirit is always present with the Word; nor does he convey any definite information concerning his views, when he says, men are converted and sanctified by the Spirit and the Word. We desire to know what he means by these expressions. Does he mean, that in addition to the words and arguments contained in the Scriptures, there is an influence of the Spirit on the heart? If so, what are we contending about? But if I am to learn his views from his publications, he does not so believe. The manner in which he has illustrated his views on this subject, leaves no room to doubt what they are. The Holy Spirit, he has said, operates on the minds of men, just as the spirits of Demosthenes and Cicero operated on the minds of their hearers or readers. But, I ask, would there be any propriety in saying, that the spirits of Demosthenes and Cicero are always present with their writings? Who ever heard of such language being employed? If his illustration is not wholly deceptive, the Holy Spirit is with the Word in no other sense, than the spirits of those ancient orators are present with their writings which still are extant!

It is very important that we do not lose sight of the real difference between us. I will, therefore, again read a passage from his *Christianity Restored*, which I read on yesterday:

" Every spirit puts forth its moral power in words; that is, all the power it has over the views, habits, manners, or actions of men, is in the meaning and arrangement of its ideas expressed in words, or in significant signs addressed to the eye or ear. * * * * *The argument is the power of the spirit of man, and the only power which one spirit can exert over another is its arguments.*"

Observe, he says, only moral power can be exerted on minds; and every spirit puts forth the only power it can exert over others in words and arguments. The whole converting and sanctifying power of the Holy Spirit, he contends, is in the written Word. The Spirit dictated and confirmed the Word; and the Word accomplishes the whole work of conversion and sanctification. It is against this doctrine that I enter my solemn protest.

Mr. C. says, he holds, that the Word is only the *instrument* in conversion and sanctification. This, however, like his other statements, is entirely ambiguous; for the words of Demosthenes and Cicero were the instruments by which they sought to produce an effect on the minds of their hearers and readers. But he does not come out plainly and tell us, whether he believes in any influence of the Spirit distinct from the Word. Does the gentleman now believe in any such additional influence in conversion and sanctification; or does he still hold the doctrine taught in his publications? Does he retract his former views?

In our correspondence, so far as I had any thing to do with it, I was careful to have a perfect understanding, that I should have the right to explain the proposition by his published writings. To this he agreed; and I have read them. And most certainly he does deny any influence of the Holy Spirit in conversion and sanctification, except the mere force of words and arguments!

I am truly gratified, that the gentleman has brought forward the charge against us, of holding the doctrine of the damnation of infants; because it is believed by many who are unacquainted with our views. He says, our confession of faith teaches this doctrine. This is not correct. It is true that it speaks of elect infants—" Elect infants, dying in infancy, are regenerated and saved by Christ through the Spirit." Are all infants, dying in infancy, elect? All Presbyterians, who express an opinion on the subject, so believe. The expression, "elect infants," the gentleman seems to think, implies non-elect infants; but I call on him to produce one respectable Presbyterian author, who ever interpreted the confession of faith as he has. I never heard a Presbyterian minister, nor read a Presbyterian author who expressed the opinion, that infants dying in infancy are lost. Mr. Campbell boasts of his familiarity with the doctrines of our church. He, then, is the very man to make good this oft-repeated charge. I call for the proof.

So far as I know the sentiments of Presbyterians on this subject, they believe, that all that die in infancy are of the elect—are chosen of God to eternal life, and are sanctified by the Holy Spirit, and saved according to his eternal purpose. Infants do not die by accident. He whose providence extends to the falling of the sparrow, takes care of every human being; and we believe, that his purpose is to save those whom he calls from time before they are capable of knowing the truth.

But the gentleman has made the charge, that the Presbyterian church holds the doctrine of the damnation of infants; and now I demand the proof. What proportion of the human family are chosen to eternal life, our confession of faith does not profess to determine. The calculations of Mr. C., therefore, is an affair of his own, for which we are not responsible. The very worst that any candid man can say of our confession, so far as this subject is concerned, is, that it does not profess to determine whether all infants are saved. It gives not the least intimation that any are lost.

But the gentleman tells us that, when quite young, his mind was shocked at this doctrine. Is it not, then, most marvellous, that whilst his mind revolted at the imagined doctrine that *some* infants may be lost, he should have embraced a doctrine that makes it utterly impossible that any of those dying in infancy can be saved?! It was certainly a most singular effect of his early dislike of what he imagined to be the doctrine of our church!

I must say a word or two in reply to his remarks concerning the limiting of the power of God over the human mind. He says, he does limit the power of God, and that the Universalists complain of him for so doing; and he has specified two things which God cannot do, viz: he cannot lie, and he cannot make two hills without a valley! I was not aware that these things were the objects of *power*. Absurdities are not the objects of power. There is no objection to his speaking of the exertion of God's power as limited, where God has so spoken; but I call on him now to show us where, in the Bible, God has said that he cannot, or that he will not, exert on the human mind any power except through words and arguments. Or where has he said, that he cannot or will not sanctify the hearts of any of the human family without the Word! There is not such passage from Genesis to Revelation. And since God has not limited himself, who dares undertake to limit him?

Mr. C., let it be remembered, not only denies that God *does* exert on the human mind any other power than that of words or arguments; but he even goes so far as to assert, that he *cannot* operate except by the Truth!!! Where has God said that he *cannot?* Nowhere. How, then, can any man venture to say so?

I was quite pleased with the gentleman's last speech. For our cause it was the best he has made since the debate commenced, except that remarkable one on yesterday morning. His doctrine has driven him into absurdities so glaring, that all must see them. He asserts, that God did not create man *holy ;* and says, we might as well talk of making the garden of Eden holy ! Solomon said, " God made man *upright*, but he sought out many inventions." What is the meaning of the word *upright ?* What is the difference between uprightness and holiness ? If the gentleman chooses to charge Solomon with talking foolishly, let him do it. It is the language of Divine revelation.

Mr. C. says that there is no depravity in *intellect*—that it is all in our animal passions, which belong to the body. I was pleased to hear him advance this doctrine. Not that I desire to see any one run into dangerous error, but I am glad when false principles lead to such results as to prove to every one their erroneousness. The doctrine that depravity is in the body, not in the mind, is indeed quite ancient. The Manicheans held that matter is inherently evil, and that the soul is not depraved. Hence, they believed that to become holy, it was only necessary to afflict, starve, and emaciate the body ! If all sin is in the body, the sooner we get out of it the sooner we shall get clear of sin. If sin belongs to the body, let us get the body into a proper state, and all will be right !

But I understand that " sin is the transgression of the law," not that it consists in corruption of the body. The works of the flesh, as enumerated by Paul, are " Adultery, fornication, uncleanness, lasciviousness, *idolatry, witchcraft, hatred, variance, emulations, wrath, strife, seditions, heresies, envyings,* murders, drunkenness, revellings, and such like." By the word *flesh*, as I have repeatedly remarked, he means the depraved nature of the human mind, and these are its works. Yet Mr. C. tells you, that depravity is in the appetites and passions belonging to the body ! This is not only a contradiction of Paul, but of his own doctrine, as stated in his *Christian System*, where he says :

" Man, then, in his natural state, was not merely an animal, but an intellectual, moral, pure and holy being."—

Admitting and teaching that God created him holy. Again :

" There is, therefore, a sin of our nature, as well as personal transgression. Some inappositely call the sin of our nature our ' original sin ;' as if the sin of Adam was the personal offence of all his children. True indeed it is, our nature was corrupted by the fall of Adam before it was transmitted to us, and hence that hereditary imbecility to do do good, and that proneness to do evil, so universally apparent in all human beings. Let no man open his mouth against the transmission of a MORAL DISTEMPER, until he satisfactorily explain the fact, that the special characteristic vices of parents appear in their children, as much as the color of their skin, their hair, or the contour of their faces. A disease in the MORAL CONSTITUTION of man is as clearly transmissible as any physical taint, if there be any truth in history, biography, or human observation. * * * * All inherit a *fallen*, consequently a *sinful* nature ; though all are not equally depraved. * * * * Condemned to natural death, and greatly fallen and depraved IN OUR WHOLE MORAL CONSTITUTION though we certainly are, in consequence of the sin of Adam," &c.—chap. iv. sec. 4. pp. 29, 30.

Now, observe, he here distinctly states, that there is a *sin of our nature*, as well as personal transgression. Yet he has positively asserted, during this discussion, that there can be no *disposition*, where there is no knowledge ! In his last speech he located sin in the body ; but here he says, " let no man open his mouth against the transmission of a *moral distemper,* until he can satisfactorily explain the fact," &c. " A disease in *the moral constitution* of man is as clearly transmissible as any physical taint, if there be any truth in history, biography, or human observation !" And on the next page, " All inherit a *fallen,* therefore a *sinful* nature ;" or would he say, a *sinful body ?* Again, he represents man as depraved in his *whole moral constitution !* Ah, when a man, in order to sustain his tenets, is forced into such palpable contradictions, concerning subjects so clear, he must feel that his cause is hopeless !

A word about *physical regeneration.* He says, regeneration without means, as in case of infants, is physical regeneration. Let him prove it. He has asserted it, but the Bible does not so teach. I deny that the re-generation of a soul, without means, is physical; and an assertion is, I think, properly met by a denial.

Mr. C. says, I have not defined *regeneration.* I have explained *con-version* to mean a change of heart, followed by a change of life. The former is commonly called regeneration, and the latter conversion. Re-generation is a change of heart from sinfulness to holiness, and conse-quently from the love and practice of sin to the love and service of God. When the heart is renewed, man loves that Savior against whom hereto-fore it rose in enmity. He sees a divine beauty and loveliness where be-fore he saw, as it were, a root out of a dry ground. It is of this blessed work of the Spirit Paul speaks, when he says—" It is God that worketh in you to will and to do of his good pleasure." The heart is renewed by the Holy Spirit; and the result is, that the sinner wills and acts in obedience to God's commands.

The gentleman has read Henry's Commentary to prove, that in 1 Cor. iii. 6, Paul spoke of planting *a church.* I have not examined Henry on this passage; but I observed, that he read Henry's comment, not on the passage in dispute, but on the 10th verse, in which Paul says, " I as a wise master-builder have *laid the foundation !*" What was the founda-tion? It was Christ crucified—the doctrine of the cross. " Other foun-dation can no man lay than that is laid, which is Jesus Christ."

But I will admit, for the sake of argument, that Paul, when he used the word "*planted,*" meant planting the *church.* I see not how this can help the gentleman's argument. Paul planted the church, but God caus-ed it to grow—gave the increase. Paul planted it *instrumentally ;* God, by his Spirit, gave efficiency to the work. I have no objection, so far as this argument is concerned, to this interpretation. I will cheerfully admit that Paul planted the church instrumentally; but I also contend, that God caused it to grow—gave it life and increase. The gentleman, however, overlooked the 5th verse: " Who then is Paul, and who is Apollos, but ministers by whom ye believe, *even as the Lord gave to every man ?*" This passage speaks distinctly of a divine influence lead-ing the Corinthian christians to believe; but my friend did not see it!

He says, there was never a tree without a *seed ;* and hence he infers that no one was ever converted without the Word. This is running out figurative expressions, so as to make them contradict the plain teach-ing of the Bible. Gŏd at first created trees without seeds, and made all things without means. He fed the Israelites in the wilderness without means, because means could not be employed. The gentleman might as well deny that Elijah was fed by a raven, because persons are not com-monly thus supplied with food. God clothes and feeds men only in con-nection with means, when by the exertion of the power he has given them, the means can be used; but he has never confined himself to means. Nor has he ever said that he will, in no case, regenerate and sanctify without the written word.

I wish the audience distinctly to see the contradictory positions of the gentleman. Yesterday he assumed one position, and to-day the opposite. In my argument, showing that his doctrine necessarily involves the damnation of infants, I stated the fact, that infants are *depraved*. I stated, what all admit, that they cannot be sanctified *through the truth*. The conclusion, then, is unavoidable, that if they are not sanctified by the Spirit without the truth, they must, dying in infancy, either go to heaven in their depravity, or be forever lost. He admits their depravity, and therefore he is forced to admit, that if not sanctified without the truth, they go to heaven in unholiness, or to hell!

To escape the force of this argument, he told us, on yesterday, that only the atonement of Christ is necessary to save infants. But I replied, that the blood shed on the cross, does not change *the heart;* and that the difficulty in the way is, that they are *unholy*. Now, to escape the difficulty in which he is involved, he has located their depravity in the *body*. But this is not only absurd and unscriptural; but it is contradictory of his own writings on this very subject!

The difficulty, then, returns upon him with double force. If the doctrine taught in his *Christian System* is true, infants are depraved in their *whole moral constitution;* and, I ask, can beings thus depraved, dwell in the presence of the infinitely holy God? Who can believe it possible? The gentleman has contradicted himself more than once, and is now involved in the gross absurdity of maintaining the doctrine of *corporeal depravity!*

I, therefore, again urge against him the unanswerable argument, that his doctrine necessarily involves the damnation of all that die in infancy. The argument is a fair one—it is perfectly legitimate. It is what logicians call the *reductio ad absurdum*. He admits that the doctrine of infant damnation is both false and absurd. Consequently by proving that his doctrine necessarily involves this absurdity, I prove it untrue.

I will now bring forward some further Scripture evidence in favor of the doctrine of the special agency of the Spirit in conversion and sanctification; for I prefer to go by the Bible. I had supposed, from his former professions, that my friend, Mr. C., would do the same; but he has found it necessary to use a great deal of philosophy—quite an abundance of *metaphysics*. He seems to prefer these speculations to the Word of God.

I will read Ephesians ii. 1: "And you hath he quickened, who were dead in trespasses and sins." The word *quickened*, it is true, is not found in the original Greek, in the first verse; but it is in the fifth. "Even when we were dead in sins [God] hath *quickened* us together with Christ." The apostle represents men as dead in sin, and God as having quickened or made them alive. Did he quicken them with words and arguments? Did he reason with them, and exhort them to live? Surely this is not the meaning of the apostle. Jesus Christ stood at the grave of Lazarus, and said,—"Lazarus, come forth." Did he raise Lazarus from the dead merely by the words uttered, or by an exertion of almighty power accompanying the word? Every one admits, at once, that Lazarus was quickened by an immediate exertion of divine power. Precisely similar language is used with regard to regeneration. Men are dead; and God quickens them.

The next passage I read, is in the tenth verse of the same chapter, where the apostle proves, that men are not saved by good works: "For we are his workmanship, created in Christ Jesus unto good works, which God hath before ordained that we should walk in them." Now observe how it came to pass, that the Ephesian christians performed good works. God created them anew *unto* good works; their good works were all the result of a new creation, of which God was the author. Was this a creation by arguments? A creation by words and motives! The apostle used the very strongest term in any language, without qualification. And when the inspired writers selected the strongest language to express their ideas, and used it without qualification; we must take their words in their obvious and undiminished meaning. What word in the English, Hebrew, or Greek language could be selected, that would more unequivocally express the idea of a direct divine influence on the heart, than the word *create?* God directs his servants to use the strongest expressions on this subject, evidently knowing that there was no danger of their being misunderstood. We are, then, obliged to understand by this language a special divine influence, distinct from words and arguments, on the hearts of men. The language is too plain to require the aid of criticism to elicit its meaning, or to be obscured by plausible interpretations.— [*Time expired.*

Tuesday, Nov. 28—12 o'clock, M.
[MR. CAMPBELL'S SIXTH ADDRESS.]

MR. PRESIDENT—You perceive, sir, I doubt not, in common with this great assembly, that in the latitude and longitude of Mr. Rice's theory of response in debate, there is not a single point of theoretic or polemic theology that may not legitimately, or illegitimately, be brought into this discussion; and that, according to his interpretation of our rules of debate, we may touch at every point in the compass of the most extended ecclesiastic creed, in good keeping with the most strict construction of the proposition before us. Every thing, it seems, can interest Mr. R. and call forth some attention except the arguments on which I rely, and to which I challenge special attention. It is exceedingly painful to me to have to occupy so much time in the mere statement of what has been done, or left undone, by my respondent. But to pass on, from argument to argument, without any reply, or debate on the proper issue, and without a single notice of the failure or neglect on his part, would seem neither respectful to myself, nor to the audience. I exceedingly regret, sir, that I have so little to reply to, in the speech which we have just now heard. I have asked, not for the sake of asking a question with the appearance of something under it of great importance, as I have seen some persons do; but, sir, I have asked the gentleman for a single verse, Old Testament or New, that asserts *regeneration by the Spirit alone.* When adducing those of the most unambiguous and incontrovertible import, affirming regeneration through the instrumentality of the Word of God, I have not succeeded either in getting such a text, or in obtaining a response to those which I have presented.

His assumed leading objection to our views on the proposition in discussion is, that we rather make void the necessity of spiritual influence in our teachings of the christian religion; while our grand objection to his theory of spiritual influence, in the work of conversion, is, that it makes void the necessity of preaching the gospel, or reading the Bible. And while some affect to believe, that we take too many into the church on our terms of discipleship, we are of opinion that the opposite theory takes in too many that ought not to be admitted, both adults and infants, and that it keeps out of the christian profession, a great mass of intelligent and virtuous persons, many of them more worthy than some in the church, who are waiting for some miracle, some special impulse divine, which may at once renovate and rouse them into spiritual life and action; in the absence of which they dare not presume upon making the christian profession. To settle these matters, an appeal to the Scriptures, and to such reasonings as the Scriptures seem to sanction, has been instituted, and we have only to regret that it has not been followed up.

Notwithstanding the apparent absurdity of the thing, there are not a few who still regard something like physical impulses operating upon the soul, as a hammer in the hand of a smith operates upon the metal placed upon his anvil. Their notion, as far as we can gather it, is, that the Spirit of God comes into a personal contact with the spirit of a man, and either new-moulds or attempers, or changes, or imbues it with something from himself, which is sometimes called the infusion of a holy principle. And this seed or principle remains immutably and forever in that person, according to one theory, without any possibility of a failure of eternal life, but according to others, it may be lost forever. This divine touch is sometimes compared to that which reanimated the body of Lazarus, or raised to life the dead body of Jesus. The other theory is, that the Word or gospel of God is that type or medium, through which it sheds abroad in the human heart the love of God to man in the gift of his Son, and thus renews him in the moral image of his Redeemer, through an inward revelation of his grace and mercy in the heart.

Mr. Rice is greatly indebted to my writings. They supply him with something to read and to say, and give him an opportunity to play upon words. Every man of observation, however, understands the policy; and, therefore, it fails, as he does to establish any real discrepancy—and especially that he cannot get me into a mere logomachy. But once more I will enter my protest against his manner of quoting my writings. It is neither magnanimous, nor is it generous, nor is it fair. A man, with genius enough to be a mere quibbler, and that never had a very large capital, can figure away in great style in making Paul contradict James— and worse still, in making Paul contradict himself. The master quibblers in the science of doubting are inimitably astute in the art. Paul, says one, affirmed that " a man was justified by faith without works;" and James says, " a man is justified by works, and not by faith." Reconcile your two inspired apostles, if you can!! Again, continues he, Paul contradicted himself; for he said—" If you be circumcised, Christ shall profit you nothing." Yet he took his son Timothy, a christian man, who had been baptized also, and circumcised him, and sent him to preach Christ! What a consistent man was your Doctor Paul!!

I could find a hundred instances of this sort in the Bible, and spend a month with a sceptic arguing them. See what a file of newspapers, pamphlets, and Harbingers my friend has got around him! Does he dream of diverting me from the grand position into all these documents? I do not intend any such discussion. He may have that to himself, and I will attend to my business. I will give argument for argument, and document for document on the question before us ; but these hundred and one other topics the gentleman will please reserve for some other more favorable opportunity. As the gentleman affirms regeneration without

3 M

faith, he had better proceed to prove it by an induction of cases, and then I will examine them, if he cannot respond to me.

He represented me as saying, that all sin was in the body. I did not say so, nor any thing so importing. I have only said, that "sin works in our members," and that "in the flesh dwelleth no good thing," and that there is "a law working in the flesh and warring against the law of the mind, and bringing it into captivity to the law of sin, which is in the body"—and that, therefore, the seeds of sin and the roots of transgression are in the passions; and that the spirit is brought into captivity to the flesh—but there are the "sinful desires of the mind" as well as of the flesh, in consequence of this captivity. I said, that sin works through the body. Hence the greatest saint may, like Paul, long for the redemption of the body from sin and death. "Who shall deliver me from this body of sin and death? I thank God through Jesus Christ my Lord."

These reflections and associations led Paul to descant with great earnestness and grandeur upon the earnest expectation of the creature, and of the adoption, to wit: "the redemption of the body." I must take the pleasure of reading, with a passing remark, two or three sentences, Rom. viii. 19—21, "*The earnest expectation*" of our humbled body, "*the creature, waiteth*" in joyful hope "*for the manifestation*," the full development "*of the sons of God*" in their pure, sinless, and immortal bodies. "*For the creature*"—the mortal body—"*was made subject to vanity*"—dissolution—"*not willingly*," but it is reconciled to the grave "*by reason of him who has subjected it, in hope that the creature*"—the body—"*itself shall be delivered from the bondage of corruption into the glorious liberty of the sons of God*" at the resurrection. This is a portion of the glorious hope of every saint.

Now the dying infant is delivered from this body, sown with all these elements of sin, these "desires of the flesh," and the aged saint is also delivered from the same by death. This physical regeneration, *the birth of the spirit*, is essential to an entrance into the everlasting kingdom. But whence came this new designation—"*elect infants?*" It is not elect persons, nor elect men, but elect *infants*. There certainly were non-elect infants—not only non-elect men, but non-elect *infants*. Who taught this language? The creed and not the Bible! But we have been just now informed by a revelation made from the upper world through Mr. Rice, that all infants that die are "elect infants." If we had only a miracle we might believe in this new revelation. But what comes of the non-elect infants? They become non-elect men. Why then call them non-elect infants, as none of that kind can die? All non-elect infants are immortal infants! As infants they cannot die!! It is only above a year ago that this new revelation of elect infants, being all dying infants, first reached my ears. The Scotch Presbyterians never have been favored with this new revelation. I must again read this remarkable passage.

"3. Elect infants, dying in infancy, are regenerated and saved by Christ through the Spirit, who worketh when, and where, and how he pleaseth. So also are all other elect persons, who are incapable of being outwardly called by the ministry of the word."

The Westminster divines must have got into Mr. Rice's dilemma when they conceived this doctrine. They supposed but three conditions of the question. Infants dying were lost, or infants dying were saved; and if saved, they must be regenerated, because none can enter heaven but regenerated persons. They assumed the last, and made the doctrine to escape from the folly of the assumption! There are, then, three classes of elect persons to be regenerated by the Spirit without the Word. These are elect infants, elect pagans, and elect idiots. Of four classes of mankind, but one are regenerated through the Word. My friend will have three subjects of physical regeneration for my one. Will the gentleman say, that all these elect pagans are, like infants, in a state of irresponsibility? And if they are not, in what consists the parallelism? I heard of a lady who drank pretty deep into this new revelation. She became a monomaniac. She had a small family of infant children; and weary of the world herself, she thought it was best to make her own mind easy about her offspring, and to make their happiness secure. She accordingly rose up in the night and strangled them all. She gave this, on trial, as the only reason of her conduct. Of course, she was sent to the lunatic asylum.

I regret that my friend, Mr. Rice, could find so much time to discuss this matter rather than the question. I shall dismiss it with a single remark, viz: that it is but a flimsy and superficial covering for a very incredible and unchristian dogma. I would then advise its being expunged from the book altogether. Because, among other reasons, it had been more rational to have made the non-elect infants die; for then there would have been much more mercy than in this scheme. The elect would have lost nothing by living seventy years, but rather gained much by their good works; and the non-elect would have gained much too, in having no punishment to endure for actual transgressions; their only cause of regret would then be merely that they had been born. Thus dispose we of this branch of the philosophy of infant regeneration, *without* the Word.

The gentleman, in responding to my remarks upon the word *holy*, quoted a passage highly complimentary to his philological skill in interpreting language. As a proof that God created Adam holy, he says, "God made man *upright*, but they have sought out many inventions." Now the question is, are *holy* and *upright* synonymous terms? Does upright and holy mean the same? Mr. Rice, by the force of the quotation, makes a holy man an upright man, and an upright man is a holy man— still they are not at all equivalent. No man accustomed to criticism has ever argued, that because two epithets are applied to one man, the epithets must be one and the same in sense. Holiness means separation from sin. Sin must, therefore, previously exist before the term holiness could come into use. *Hagiosune* is derived from *hagee*, and that is a compound of two words—*a* privative, and *gee*, the earth. *Hagios*, holy, therefore, means *separate from the earth;* no earth, no separation from it. There is, then, a contrast in the word itself—unearthy, not earthy, separate from the earth. The very origin of the word *holy* intimates that there was something unclean before it, just as the word *unearthy* indicates there was something earthy before it. It is, therefore, good sense to say that God made man perfect, or in his own image. But the Bible does not say that God made man holy, and therefore I object to it in such an argument as this; although, in common free conversational style, I have no objection to say, that Adam was holy till he sinned.

The term holy is applied to the earth, to any thing at all separated to God's service or presence. Moses, said God, "take off your shoes, for you stand on holy ground." The Lord was there; that spot was separated to the presence of God. There is no moral quality in the word holy.

It indicates no moral attribute. It can, therefore, be applied to an altar, a temple, a camp, a vessel, the earth, or any thing sacred to the Lord. God is said to be *holy*, because he is separated from all impurity; infinitely separated from sin. " He is of purer eyes than to behold iniquity."

The argument, then, is, that God made Adam holy, and he makes an infant holy: the first by creation, the second by regeneration. And what means an holy infant? One regenerate, or one simply sanctified or separated to the Lord, as Samuel or John the Baptist was? If in that sense, the word is misapplied to regeneration; because these persons, like Jeremiah, are separated to the Lord or some special work. All persons and things called holy in the Bible, were specially set apart and separated to God in some peculiar way, or for some very special purpose. To apply this word as Mr. Rice has done, is, therefore, to mystify its proper meaning in the Scriptures, to confuse the sacred dialect, and to mislead us in our conceptions of Adam and his offspring. It is, therefore, an innovation not to be tolerated, but rather repudiated by all sensible and reflecting men.

I shall fill out my time with a few remarks on his definition of regeneration. He has at last given us a definition of this important word. But he has not yet answered the great question—whether is regeneration the cause or the effect of faith? Is regeneration the cause of faith or prior to faith; or is faith the effect of regeneration, or subsequent to it? Are they simultaneous? What connection between them? Is there any connection; and if any, what is it? I have brought up the subject in every form I can conceive of, to elicit from him such an expression as will facilitate our clear and satisfactory decision of this much and long litigated case.

He has, indeed, vouchsafed the following definition of regeneration: "It is a change of heart from a love of sin to a love of holiness." Whether it be an act, a process, or an effect, is not distinctly stated. Nothing but the heart is changed in regeneration. No such regeneration is found in the Bible. Persons are there spoken of as regenerated after their hearts are changed. His is scholastic regeneration. Be it so. We now understand him. Regeneration is, then, a change of heart from one love to another love. Now I believe in such a change, though I do not believe in calling it regeneration: for certainly regeneration in the New Testament is not that thing. *A regenerated person is a new creature.*

It is, then, but a *change* of disposition: for love is no more than an affection or disposition of the mind. There must, then, be a prior disposition; for, unless there be a disposition existing already, there can be no change of it. This is self-evident. Now, a disposition always presupposes an object. No person can think of a disposition, without conceiving of something to which the mind is turned or disposed. No one can possibly be disposed to an object of which he knows nothing. He must see in the object something to call forth his attention—to allure, attract, or some way draw out his affection or disposition towards it. Need I ask, how a person can love an object, or hate an object, of which he is perfectly ignorant?

But regeneration is a change of one disposition for another. Consequently there must be a change of objects to the mind. The mind must have in contrast two sorts of objects. It must contemplate them clearly, compare them accurately, discover a difference, a superior beauty and loveliness, before the disposition leaves the one and cleaves to the other.

Now, I ask—is an infant susceptible of all this discovery, contemplation, comparison, intelligence, preference and choice of objects? Can a child have any moral or immoral disposition, without an object? Can it have an object which it sees not, contemplates not, and cannot apprehend? Can it abandon one object and prefer another, without perception, comparison, and conclusion—without the power of reasoning and the possession of previous knowledge? I repeat it, sir, the gentleman's definition is fatal to his cause. It is without fact, without philosophy, without the Bible, and, therefore, cannot be assented to by any one of thought and reflection, whose mind has been called to the rational examination of the subject. Have we not, then, from his own definition, given a requiem to his speculation, and for ever sealed up his argument? When Mr. Rice disposes of this argument, we shall give him a few more. But, sir, he will never try.—[*Time expired.*

Tuesday, Nov. 28—12½ *o'clock, P.M.*
[MR. RICE'S SIXTH REPLY.]

MR. PRESIDENT—My friend calls on me to prove by the Scriptures, that the Spirit ever operates in conversion and sanctification, without the truth. He affirms, and has undertaken to prove, that the Spirit operates *only* through the truth. Has he produced a solitary passage that sustains his proposition? He has not, and he will not; for there is none such in the Bible. But he is in the affirmative. With what propriety, then, does he call on me to prove a negative? I might remain silent until he produces at least some show of argument from the Scriptures; for he professes to hold no article of faith, for which he cannot produce a "Thus saith the Lord." Where is his scripture-proof of the proposition now before us?

The Scriptures, as I have proved, speak of three agencies or influences, in the conversion and sanctification of men—the ministry, the Word, and the Holy Spirit. Mr. Campbell takes the ministry and the Word, but rejects the agency of the Spirit. I take all the three. This is the difference between us.

He says, he did not assert that all depravity is in the body. Yet, to prove that it has its seat in the body, he read to us the language of Paul to the Romans, chap. vii. 23 : "But I see another law in my members, warring against the law of my mind, and bringing me into captivity to the law of sin, which is in my members. O wretched man that I am! who shall deliver me from the body of this death?" But by his members, and the body of death, Paul did not mean his own body, but the corrupt propensities of his nature. He represents his remaining corruption as a dead body, which, in all its loathsomeness, he was carrying about with him. He desired most earnestly to be delivered, not from his natural body, but from his in-dwelling corruption.

The audience will remember my argument on this subject. I proved that the gentleman's doctrine necessarily involves the damnation of infants, because they are depraved, and he denies that they can be sanctified without the truth. I then understood him to say, that depravity is in the body, and, therefore, their souls might be saved. But now he has got the depravity back in the soul, and is involved in the old difficulty. The minds of infants, he admits, are depraved. How, then, can they be sanctified? Certainly not through the truth; and he denies that they can be sanctified by the Spirit, without the truth. Consequently, according to his doctrine, they die in their depravity, and are lost! There is no escape from the difficulty.

44　　　　　3 M 2

But Mr. C. says, that I am very unfair in quoting his writings; that he could read the writings of Paul, so as to make him apparently contradict himself. If any one attempt to prove that Paul contradicts himself, I am prepared to prove his perfect consistency. And if I have misrepresented Mr. Campbell, as he charges, he is the man, of all others, best qualified to correct the misrepresentation. Then let him do it. He is perfectly at liberty to produce his writings, and to prove, if he can, that I have misrepresented him. He conceded to me the right—as the correspondence will show—a right which I should have had without his consent—to read his writings in explanation of the proposition stated by himself; and now he is disposed to complain of me for doing it. I know it is distressing to him, but I cannot help it. I cannot possibly misunderstand his writings on this subject; for he states, with perfect clearness, that there are only two kinds of power—moral and physical. The former, which is exerted only by words and arguments, operating on mind; and the latter, on matter. In the book from which I read, his views are presented with entire clearness. I only wish he had stated them as clearly in this discussion. If he had come out with an open and fair presentation of his views, we should have known just where to find him. As at is, they are involved in mist and darkness impenetrable. Yet he is a man of remarkably clear intellect; but he is singularly inconsistent. At one time, he states his doctrines so clearly, as to admit of no doubt concerning them; and at another, he is dark as midnight, and it is impossible to ascertain what he believes.

I am happy, however, to have his books, from which we are able to ascertain precisely what he has taught, and to repel his charges of misrepresentation. If a man should, in a public discussion with me, read from a book of mine, and should not read enough fairly to represent me, I would read the remainder of the connection. Let Mr. C. do so.

He quotes Paul complaining that sin did work in his members, and that he carried about with him a *body of death;* and he tells us, the members are the corrupted passions seated in the body; and that Paul, when he came to die, needed a regeneration as much as do infants. I know of no system of philosophy that confines the *passions* to the body. We speak of the passion of hatred, or the passion of love. Some of the passions belong particularly to the body; others, to the mind. These two classes, Paul enumerates together, as the *works of the flesh.* (Gal. v. 19—21.) Anger, wrath, malice, hatred, envy, &c., belong to the mind. Paul found depravity in the mind. What he meant by the body of death, we may, perhaps, learn from chapter 6th, verse 6th, of the same epistle: " Knowing that our old man is crucified with him, that the body of sin might be destroyed, that henceforth we should not serve sin." The old man, or corrupt nature, is crucified; and the new man, or renewed nature, leads to a holy life. The same idea is conveyed, when he says, " They that are Christ's, have crucified the flesh with the affections and lusts."

The gentleman is now placed in this predicament; he must maintain the absurd doctrine, that depravity is only in the body, and not in the mind—and certainly his arguments look that way—and therefore infants, being pure when they leave the body, can go to heaven; or he must hold, that they die in their moral corruption, and are forever lost! There is no way to escape from these absurdities, but by abandoning his theory concerning spiritual influence. I cannot but believe it would be better to abandon his theory, than meet the consequences.

But he seeks to shield himself by charging our church with holding the doctrine of infant damnation. The expression "elect infants," used in our confession of faith, teaches no such thing. The word *elect* signifies *chosen from* or *out of;* and infants are chosen from the world, the human family. But he says, as there cannot be adults without infants, so there cannot be elect infants without non-elect infants. I was not aware that there could not be adults without infants. I know there have been adults without infants, and possibly there might be again. It is not true, that the word *elect*, applied to infants dying in infancy, implies that there are non-elect infants! Though he cannot prove the doctrine to be in our confession, he tells us he has heard it preached in good old Scotland. I was never in Scotland, nor can I know what strange things he may have heard there; but I again call on him to produce one respectable Presbyterian author, who has taught this doctrine. He has asserted, that the Presbyterian church holds the doctrine of infant damnation; and I demand the proof. Whenever I prefer a charge against his church, the proof shall be forthcoming when called for, and when he makes charges against my church, I shall certainly expect him to prove them. I hope he will not shrink from proving his assertions.

Concerning the doctrine of election I will only remark, that I am not disposed to mingle together things which are entirely distinct; I am, however, prepared to discuss this doctrine with him, whenever he chooses to enter into it properly; but I do not intend to permit him to divert the attention of the audience from the subject under consideration.

That infants are depraved, he admits. That they cannot be sanctified through the truth, we know. He denies that they can be sanctified without the truth. They must, therefore, die in sin, and be forever lost. I leave you, my friends, to determine whether a doctrine involving such consequences can be true.

Strangely enough, Mr. C. denies that God created man holy. I quoted the passage, "God made man upright." But now, for the first time in my life, I have heard it asserted, that the word *holy* does not express moral quality. When the heavenly hosts exclaim "holy, holy, holy, Lord God Almighty," do not they express moral quality? But the gentleman says, the word implies previous sinfulness. Angels are said to be holy, and God is holy. Does the word, in these cases, imply previous sin. If, however, the gentleman is disposed to be hypercritical about the word *holy*, I will take the word *upright*. "God made man upright." This word signifies, literally, standing erect or straight; and, as applied to denote moral qualities, it means conformity of God's law. He whose heart and life accord with that rule, is said to be an upright man.

The gentleman is now placed in the same difficulty from which he vainly sought to escape; for certain it is, that God made man *upright*, and that he did it not by words and arguments. If, then, God did, at first, create him upright, not by words or arguments, who shall say he cannot exert on his mind a divine influence, creating him anew unto good works? And if he can exert such an influence on the mind of an adult, who will deny that he can sanctify the infant?

He asks whether faith is the cause or the effect of regeneration. I am not disposed to be diverted from the proposition before us, to the discussion of other questions. The question now before us is—whether the Spirit of God operates only through the truth? Does the Bible say, the Spirit operates ONLY through the truth? It does not. But it does plainly teach, that infants must be regenerated, or born again. "For," said our Savior, "that which is born of the flesh is flesh, and that which is born of the Spirit is spirit." This is the reason why the new birth is absolutely necessary. But infants are born of the flesh; therefore they must be born of the Spirit. They cannot be regenerated through the truth; consequently they must be regenerated without it. This passage, therefore, teaches clearly the doctrine that regeneration may be, and is, effected by the Spirit without the truth.

But the gentleman returns to the position, that there can be no holiness without knowledge; and he asks—can an infant love holiness or hate sin, when it knows nothing of either? And I ask, can an infant love music before it has heard it? You say—no. But still there may be such a taste for music, that the moment when it first hears it, it will be charmed and delighted. So the heart of an infant may be so purified, that it will love and adore Jesus Christ so soon as it may be able to contemplate his character. Just here I will very briefly answer the gentleman's question concerning faith and regeneration, though I am under no obligation to do it. A dead man does not perform the acts which flow from life. He is first alive, and then he acts. Those who are spiritually dead, do not put forth the acts of spiritual life. They are first quickened, then they exercise true faith and love. Spiritual acts flow from spiritual life. This I take to be the doctrine of God's Word.

Having now paid due attention to the gentleman's speculations and arguments, I will invite the attention of the audience to some further Scripture evidences in favor of the special agency of the Holy Spirit in conversion and sanctification. I prefer to establish the doctrine for which I contend, by the clear testimony of the Bible.

I will read for your consideration Luke xxiv. 45, "Then opened he their understanding, that they might understand the Scriptures." The Savior, after his resurrection, appeared to his disciples, who as yet understood not the things concerning him, which are taught in the Old Testament. It is not said, that he opened their understandings *by* the Scriptures, but he opened their understandings, that they might understand the Scriptures. David felt his need of this divine illumination, when he prayed—"Open thou mine eyes, that I may behold wonderful things out of thy law," Ps. cxix. 18. There were wonderful things in God's Word; but because of his comparative blindness, he did not see them in all their divine excellency. These passages clearly teach the doctrine of the agency of the Holy Spirit in enlightening the minds of men.

The next passage I read is in, the epistle to Titus iii. 5, "Not by works of righteousness which we have done, but according to his mercy he saved us, by the washing of regeneration and renewing of the Holy Ghost, which he shed on us abundantly through Jesus Christ our Savior." We are saved by the *renewing* [making *anew*] of the Holy Spirit, which God shed *on us*. Does not this language teach with perfect clearness the doctrine of a direct divine influence on the heart? Or are we to understand by the Spirit being shed upon them, only their having the words and arguments contained in God's revelation? If such was the apostle's meaning, he certainly took a very singular method of expressing it. Let us compare with this the language employed in the Acts of the Apostles concerning the outpouring of the Spirit on the day of Pentecost: "I will pour out of my Spirit upon all flesh." Does not this language express an influence of the Spirit not exerted merely by words and arguments—a direct influence? All agree that it does. If, then, the pouring out of the Spirit expresses an influence distinct from mere words and arguments, does not the expression, " *shed upon*," mean the same thing. The expressions are very similar, and both evidently express a divine influence upon the minds of men, in addition to the truth, and distinct from it. Similar language is also used in regard to the descent of the Spirit on the family of Cornelius: " While Peter yet spake these words, the Holy Ghost *fell on* all them which heard the word," Acts x. 44. Was not this a direct influence of the Spirit? All admit that it was. If, then, the expression, *fell on*, expresses a direct divine agency, not by word or argument; does not the expression, *shed upon*, also express a special divine agency? It will not do to say, that one of these expressions has reference simply to the word, and the other to an influence distinct from the word. In employing this strong language without qualification, the apostles did not seem to feel the least apprehension, that their language would be understood to teach the necessity of an immediate agency of the Spirit in which they did not believe. We must, then, understand their language in its obvious sense.

I will now invite your attention to 1 Cor. ii. 14. I am acquainted with Mr. C.'s mode of commenting on this passage; and I bring it forward now, that he may have an opportunity of defending his interpretation of it, if he can. " But the natural man receiveth not the things of the Spirit of God; for they are foolishness unto him : neither can he know them, because they are spiritually discerned." The first question in order to ascertain the meaning of this passage, is concerning the expression, *natural man*. I understand the natural man to be man as he is by nature—unsanctified. That this is the correct explanation of the expression, is evident from the other instances in which the word *natural* is employed in the New Testament. Thus in 1 Cor. xv. 44, 45, "It is sown a *natural* body, it is raised a spiritual body. There is a *natural* body, and there is a spiritual body." The natural body here evidently is the body in its natural state, unchanged. The spiritual body is the body as it will be changed and refined at the resurrection. So the natural man means man as he is by nature, unrenewed. The word translated *natural* is also used by James iii. 15, " This wisdom descendeth not from above, but it is earthly, sensual, (Greek—*natural*,) devilish." Here the word *sensual* or *natural* evidently denotes moral corruption. The word is again found in the 19th verse of the epistle of Jude : " These be they who separate themselves, sensual, (Greek—*natural*,) having not the Spirit." The apostle is here speaking of " mockers in the last time, who should walk after their own ungodly lusts ;" and he says, they are *natural*, having not the Spirit.

These are all the instances in which the word translated *natural*, is used in the New Testament; and it is a fact, that in every instance where it is employed, with reference to moral character, it is used in a bad sense. When used with reference to the body, it denotes its natural state. It is, then, clear from the usage of the word, that, by the " natural man," Paul means man as he is by nature, sinful. The correctness of this interpretation is rendered certain by the connection. The natural man does not receive the things of the Spirit. Why? Because " they are *foolishness* to him." The meaning of this expression is made perfectly clear by the eighteenth verse of the first chapter : " For the preaching of the cross is to them that perish, foolishness ; but unto us which are saved, it is the power of

God." That is, they that perish see in the preaching of the cross, no wisdom, no adaptation of the plan of salvation to their condition, nothing attractive. It appears to them foolishness. So the natural man, like those who perish, receives not the gospel, the truths revealed by the Spirit; for they appear to him unmeaning, unwise, unlovely.

But if, as Mr. C. supposes, the natural man were simply a pagan, ignorant of divine revelation, the apostle would have said—The natural man receiveth not the things of the Spirit; for they are *not revealed* to him. But when he says, they are *foolishness* to him, we are compelled to understand that they have been presented to his mind, and that he sees in them no wisdom, nothing lovely or attractive to him; and therefore he rejects them; for a thing of which a man has never heard, cannot be said to be foolishness to him; and especially can it not be said, that he does not receive what was never presented to him, *because* it is foolishness to him.

By the natural man, then, we are to understand the *unrenewed* man, man as he is by nature. All such reject the gospel of Christ, "the things of the Spirit." Consequently the gospel alone is not sufficient to effect their conversion. They do not receive it—cannot understand it. Hence the absolute necessity of an agency of the Spirit, additional to the Truth, and distinct from it. They must experience such a change as will cause them to see wisdom, adaptation to their condition, beauty and attractiveness in the gospel. The spiritual or regenerated man, enlightened from above, admires and embraces the truths of divine revelation.

The next passage of Scripture to which I call your attention, is 1 Cor. i. 22—24 : " For the Jews require a sign, and the Greeks seek after wisdom; but we preach Christ crucified, unto the Jews a stumbling-block, and unto the Greeks foolishness; but unto them which are called both Jews and Greeks, Christ the power of God and the wisdom of God." Here you will observe the gospel was preached indiscriminately to Jews and Greeks, and both rejected it. There was, however, a third class, composed of both Jews and Greeks, to whom it was the power of God unto salvation. Those who received the gospel, and were converted and saved, are mentioned by the apostle as *" them which are called."* By this language he cannot mean the call of the Word, for all had this indiscriminately. It must be, then, an additional influence, an influence effectual in securing their conversion; for, to all such, the gospel was the power of God to salvation. By this call, then, we must understand the special agency of the Holy Spirit, not simply by words and arguments, calling them " out of darkness into his marvellous light." This passage establishes beyond controversy the doctrine for which we contend. That I have given the correct interpretation of it, would appear still more manifest, by comparing it with other passages in which the same apostle uses the word *called.*

I have time only to read one other passage in Hebrews viii. 10 : " For this is the covenant that I will make with the house of Israel after those days, saith the Lord; I will put my laws into their mind, and write them in their hearts: and I will be to them a God, and they shall be to me a people." This is a prophecy quoted by the apostle from Jeremiah. What does God promise to do? " I will put my laws into their mind, and write them in their hearts." Are we to understand by this, that he would influence them simply by words and arguments? They, at that time, had the Word of God before their minds—" line upon line, and precept upon precept." Inspired men were sent to reform, exhort, and warn them; but God declares his purpose, at a future day, to teach them effectually, to write his laws upon their hearts, and to cause all to know him, from the least to the greatest, and to walk in his statutes and do them. Does not this language most clearly and conclusively establish the doctrine that, in conversion and sanctification, the Spirit exerts on the human mind an influence in addition to that of the Word, and more powerful and efficacious? It is this agency only that can subdue the rebellious dispositions of men, melt their obdurate hearts, and cause them to love and serve Jesus Christ in sincerity and in truth.—[*Time expired.*

611

Tuesday, Nov. 28—1 o'clock, P. M.
[MR. CAMPBELL'S SEVENTH ADDRESS.]

MR. PRESIDENT—The gentleman has finally complied with my request. He has given an answer to so much of the question as concerns the priority of faith, or regeneration. He has clearly committed himself by avowing his conviction that regeneration, or a change of heart, is previous to faith. This is a point which I desired to elicit at an earlier period of this discussion. It would have saved time. We, however, thankfully accept it at this late hour. The gentleman backed it well with a liberal collection of scriptures. The only exception to his quotations is, that they happen not at all to pertain to the subject. He tries to shew that the Spirit operates through the Word. But that is not the question. We both professedly agree in that point. That the Spirit *operates*, is agreed on both sides. I hope the gentleman will not attempt to make another false issue here. He also admits that the Spirit *sometimes* operates through the Word. That is not the point to be proved. What, then, must I again ask, is the proposition? Is it not that " In conversion and sanctification the Spirit of God operates *only* through the Word?" He has proved that it operates through the Word. This I affirm. Has he come over? Or does he mean to use the scriptures that prove his operation *through* the Word, to prove his operation *without* the Word!! All scriptures, then, that prove that the Spirit of God operates through the Word, are irrelevant to his position, but relevant to mine, unless he comes fully over and affirms that it operates *only* through the Word.

I do not, indeed, think that the gentleman understands those portions of scripture right, else he could not have so quoted them. But it is not necessary now to make a commentary upon them. You will all understand that a passage of Scripture that proves the Holy Spirit operates *through* the Word, does not prove that he operates *without* the Word, or independent of it. It is with him, then, essentially necessary that a change of heart should precede faith. All men are dead. They must be quickened. True, all living men are dead to something. And a Pagan man, or a Jewish man, may be alive to his own theory, and dead to another. But the sophism seems to be, what rhetoricians sometimes call, killing the metaphor, or running it mad. Now a man that is metaphysically dead to one thing, is not literally dead to every thing else. There is still something alive in him, through which truth may find its way to his heart. His reason and conscience are not dead, although his heart may be. Paul says of a certain person—" She that liveth in pleasure, is dead while she lives." All this I have shewn in my opening speech, to which the gentleman has yet paid so little attention. Whenever any point or portion of Scripture is so interpreted, as to make another void, I

696 DEBATE ON THE

set it down, that it is most certainly misconstrued. Any theory, or view, of any passage which makes the preaching of the gospel of no use, that makes faith vain, or the Bible useless to that particular end, I hold to be infallibly wrong.

It is no new development. I have read it from the days of Thomas Boston till now. I presume the gentleman would make regeneration a miracle, a positive immediate act of Omnipotence, without any instrumentality at all. And I have drawn him out as large as life on that topic. *A change of heart is therefore before belief;* because the throng of the old modern school of self-ycleped orthodoxy stands in need of it. Whatever is before any thing, is without it. The cause may be without the effect, in one sense of the word cause, but the effect can in no sense be without the cause.

I say again, my voice never could have been raised upon the subject of spiritual influence, had not I seen in these extravagant forms, as I judge, it making void the Word of God, and the preaching of the gospel. I yet remember the singular impressions that sometimes accompanied my early readings of modern revivals. Many years since I read of a singular outpouring of the Spirit in New York. In a certain neighborhood, there were a thousand converts reported, as the result of a great outpouring of the Spirit. Of these thousand converts about one-third went to each of the three leading denominations in that neighborhood—Presbyterians, Methodists, Baptists. The first impression was—Did the Spirit of God thus at one outpouring make three hundred Presbyterians, Methodists, Baptists!! Strange operation! In old times he made them all christians; and of one heart and soul. I concluded there was some delusion in the affair: that man's spirit had likely as much to do in it, as the Spirit of God. Since that time I have been an observer of such occasions and reports, and suffice it to say, twenty-five years observation has greatly confirmed the first impression. Men and parties often make revivals, and now we have got a class of preachers, known by the title of "*revivalists*," men well disciplined in the art and mystery of obtaining outpourings of the Spirit.

But my standing proof of the great amount of deception practiced on such occasions, is the lamentable fact, that after the excitement ceases, and reason resumes her wonted dominion, the converts are about as unenlightened in the religion of the volume of God's own inspiration as before. Their feelings were moved, and their hearts quailed, or their affections were overcome by the scenes around them; yet still their minds were not enlightened, their spirits were not more elevated, nor their faith enlarged. In most instances, the converts are as ignorant of God and Christ, after, as before. Persons so converted, too, rarely love the Bible. They believe more in excitement than in the twelve apostles; and would rather listen to exciting speeches, than keep the commandments of God. Children love their proper parents more than others. Hence those born of great excitements, love them—born in storms and tempest of the soul, they have a great attachment to them. They feel more in debt to the revivalist than to the Bible; and they love him more ardently, and will obey him more joyfully and faithfully. They soon learn a few texts, and by these they prove every thing. A universal favorite is—" The Spirit bears witness with our spirits that we are the children of God." They reason from that within to prove that without, rather than from that without to prove that within. They prove the doctrine to be true by their feelings, and then they prove their feelings to be true by the doctrine. They reason in a most fallacious circle; and multitudes, it is to be feared, are deluded into fatal mistakes.

I heard the other day, indeed since the discussion commenced, that a preacher of some pretensions, and of some notoriety in this state—a man fond of conspicuity—in a recent discourse undertook to prove the resurrection of Christ to his audience by their feelings. He was himself suddenly transported into an ecstacy at the discovery of the new proof. He was, with Archimides, ready to say, *eureka*—I have found, I have found. He said, My friends, I have never heard it uttered, I have never read it in a book. It is to me a perfectly original argument, but really it appears to me the best I have ever heard. It is simple, and you can all apply it. Paul says, " If Christ be not risen faith is vain, preaching is vain; you are yet in your sins." Now follows it not, that when sins are pardoned, preaching is proved to be not in vain, and faith is demonstrated not to be in vain, and, consequently, Christ is risen from the dead. Now, brethren, I feel that my sins are pardoned, and you feel that your sins are pardoned; surely, then, neither our faith nor our preaching is vain. Hence we are infallibly certain, from our own hearts, that Jesus Christ rose from the dead! But suppose this sense, or feeling of forgiveness, is a delusion, what comes of the argument?!

In one word, if a spiritual illumination makes a Methodist, and a spiritual illumination makes a Baptist and a Congregationalist, it is not only a new light, a modern illumination, but it makes these parties of divine authority; and thus the Spirit is at war with itself in these different denominations. Here is A preaching against the Baptists by divine illumination, and here is B preaching against the Methodists by divine illumination, and here is C preaching against them both, and in favor of old-fashioned Presbyterianism, by the same divine illumination. Well, there are different ways to London, they say; and so there are to heaven, they argue!

But I will submit another case to these learned doctors. Of the numerous converts that joined a certain church, many have gone over to infidelity. They told of raptures, felt ecstacies, had their visions, and rejoiced in the assurance of pardoned sins. But now the Bible and religion are with them a mere delusion. They affirm it all to be a hoax. What now has become of their former illuminations? their visions and their ecstacies? They are all abandoned as a mere delusion. It is not denied that they once had those feelings, emotions, and transporting views. They still admit the fact of their former actual existence; but they were the results of a delusion? With their faith in the Bible, those pleasant dreams and fancies fled. No more light, nor spirit, nor inward witness. Now does not this prove, that there is no real foundation of confidence, no true hope in God, no real love of the truth, nor of the God of truth, in these phantasies! Had they been solid substantial evidences, would not their faith in them have remained when their faith in the testimony of prophets and apostles failed?

For these reasons, and not from any aversion to the doctrine of spiritual influence, do we repudiate the popular notions of getting religion, and of enjoying religion. We rejoice in the belief of the influence of the Spirit of God in the great work of our salvation from sin. We pray for larger measures of these divine influences. We desire them for the union of christians, and as an end to all these vain wranglings and controversies. No greater proof of the enjoyment of God's Spirit can be given, than an ardent devotion to all his oracles, and to the keeping of his commandments.

To return again to regeneration. Mr. R. has got the heart purified without faith, if I rightly understand him. The heart is renewed, changed, regenerated by the Spirit before faith; consequently faith is not necessary to the purification of the heart. There is much difference between our two systems. Mr. Rice has the heart purified before faith, I have the heart purified through faith. My reason for so believing is found in the fact that Peter said, God made no difference between Jew and Gentile, in that " HE PURIFIED THEIR HEARTS BY FAITH."

We are accustomed to regard the purification of the heart as the greatest of all things in religion. If, then, that be accomplished without faith, of what essential use is faith afterwards? If the greatest of all events is achieved without it, why may not the effects of that change be accomplished without it? Why do we preach the gospel to convert men, if, before they believe the gospel, and without the gospel, men are renewed and regenerated by the direct and immediate influence of God's Spirit? I would conclude, that if a man may be born of the Spirit without faith, he may also be saved without faith; and thus faith, from being the primary principle in religion, is anticipated and set aside by the Holy Spirit in the capital point of the renewal of the heart.

In the case of adults, for, with Mr. Rice regeneration is the same in all cases, we have a regenerated unbeliever; and if we could suppose an interval between regeneration and faith, as must be the case in all infants, then we have not only a regenerated unbeliever, but also the possibility, in the case of death, of such a one being saved without faith. Again, in the case of infants, the interval between regeneration and faith, may be an interval of years, for anything known to the contrary, and then we have the extraordinary case of an infant being a child of God, and living in the world without the knowledge of God, without Christ, and without hope!

I hope Mr. Rice will throw some light on this knotty subject, and if possible, reconcile these views of his church with those of the Bible, and the experiences and observations of a christian community. He has certainly been driven to a very high latitude, by adverse winds, when he has to assume that regeneration is wholly independent of faith, and always anterior to it—and thus, by one bold assumption, make void all the means of grace, and the utility of a christian ministry. But we shall wait for his expositions.

The gentleman, in his disquisitions upon holiness, still compares it to a taste. This is his only escape from the difficulties propounded in my last address. According to his church, holiness is set forth as the supreme love of God—or, " he is said to be holy, who loves the Lord with all his heart, and soul, and mind, and strength." A regenerated child possesses not this holiness—himself being judge. Neither has it a disposition towards God, for it has no knowledge of him. These concessions Mr. R. is obliged to make. The common sense of community requires them at his hand. But will it satisfy the intelligent, after having defined regeneration to be a change of heart, from the love of sin to the love of holiness, to be informed, that, instead of having this love of holiness, and hatred of sin, an infant has an undeveloped taste for them—something like a taste for music?!! But even this taste is an assumption. However, the gentleman does not even say it *has*, but a child "*might have* a taste for music." Still this *might have*, and *having* are different things. And inasmuch as the gentleman has not yet produced any child, nor any well-authenticated fact of any child having a taste for holiness, as having been charmed, as with music, on the first presentation of the subject, we must put it down as a complete failure on his part, to sustain his infant regeneration. He has truly toiled hard in this case, but certainly has not made out either the theory or the fact of *instinctive* holiness.

We have also had another dissertation on the word *holiness*. Any thing but the question on hand. Well, now, must I repeat that this term indicates no real substantial attribute, or virtue, but mere separation from all impurity?—or, if any one prefers it—*it is purity itself*. The tabernacle, and afterwards the temple, and all its functions, were *holy*. God's presence on earth or in heaven, makes all things holy, as did his presence in the mount with Moses. And even Mount Tabor, where Moses and Elias appeared to Jesus, is called the "Holy Mount," by Peter. The angels incessantly repeat this adorable conception of God; and thus represent him as infinitely, eternally and perfectly pure—removed from all contaminations. They say, "Holy, holy, holy is the Lord God Almighty!" But with them this is not merely a single attribute, but an ineffable conception of his infinite, awful, and glorious purity. In their eyes, it is his superlative beauty and loveliness. He is said to be of purer eyes than to behold iniquity; and the very heavens are represented as not clean in his sight.

But we are reminded, that *holiness* is a substantive requisite from christians; and that Jesus, the Messiah, is made unto us by God—"wisdom, righteousness, *holiness* and redemption." It is, therefore, important to understand it well, inasmuch as "without holiness, no man shall enjoy God." Jesus is not imputed to us for wisdom, righteousness, &c., but he is the author of these perfections in us. These terms comprehend much, and are indicative of very distinct conceptions and excellencies. Justice, or *righteousness*, has respect to positive duties and obligations to society. *Holiness*, or sanctification, a hatred of, and separation from all impurities; and *redemption* expresses our deliverance from death and the grave. We may, indeed, suppose it, as this term indicates, the consummation of salvation—that as it is the ultimate goal of man's aspirations, ("be you holy, for I am holy,") it must indicate the supreme of moral grandeur, and the perfection of moral excellence. But, in discussing the term philologically, it intimates no more than simple separation from sin, or any kind of legal or moral impurity. But we shall now proceed to a new argument on the *modus operandi*, or means of sanctification, which we shall call our ninth argument.

IX. It shall be based on the special commission given to Paul, as expounded by that given to the Messiah himself. And, therefore, we shall read that to the Messiah, as introductory to that presented to the apostle Paul. "I give thee," says Jehovah, "for a covenant of the people; for a light of the gentiles; to open the blind eyes; to bring out the prisoners from the prison, and them that sit in darkness out of the prison-house." "The Spirit of the Lord God is upon me; because the Lord has anointed me to preach good tidings to the meek; he hath sent me to bind up the broken-hearted, to proclaim liberty to the captives, and the opening of the prison to them that are bound; to proclaim the acceptable year of the Lord, and the day of vengeance of our God; to comfort all that mourn." Isaiah xlii. 6, 7; lxi. 1, 2. We shall now hear Paul relate his own, as he had it from the mouth of the Lord: "I have appeared unto thee for this purpose, to make thee a minister and a witness both of these things which thou hast seen, and of those things in the which I will appear unto thee. Delivering thee from the people and from the gentiles, unto whom now I send thee—to open their eyes, to turn them from darkness to light, and from the power of Satan unto God, that they may receive forgiveness of sins, and inheritance among them which are sanctified by faith, that is in me." Here, then, we have a full development in these grand commissions, of the manner and means employed in the wisdom and grace of God in converting and sanctifying the nations of the earth, through the mediation of the Messiah. The most conspicuous point, or the chief means stated, is—that God would use *light, knowledge, the gospel*, and that he would OPEN THE EYES of men—turning them from darkness to light, and from the kingdom and power of Satan to God. God, then, who commanded light to arise out of darkness, has used moral spiritual light—that is, revelation, the gospel—as the means of conversion and sanctification. Illumination is, therefore, an essential prerequisite to conversion and holiness. Without light there is no beauty; for in the dark, beauty and deformity are undistinguishable. Without light there is nothing amiable, because amiability requires the aid of light for its exposition, as much as beauty. The power of Satan is in *darkness;* the power of God is in *light.* God, therefore, works by light; and Satan by darkness. Hence, in Paul's commission, it reads, "Turn them from *darkness* to *light;*" and the consequence will be, "from the power of Satan to God;" and the ultimate effect will be remission of sins, and an inheritance among the sanctified. After the study of these, and many such similar documents, found in the Bible, I confess I am wholly unable to conceive of a religion without knowledge, without faith, without an apprehension, an intellectual, as well as a cordial reception, of the gospel of Christ. I repudiate, therefore, with my whole heart, this notion of infant, idiot and pagan regeneration—this speculative conversion, without light, knowledge, faith, hope or love. It makes void the whole moral machinery of the Bible, the christian ministry, and the commission of the Holy Spirit. It is no advocate of Christ; it is no comforter of the soul, on the hypothesis of infant, and pagan, and idiot regeneration.

But again, what is orthodoxy worth on Mr. Rice's hypothesis? what is it better than heterodoxy? *In not one single point.* Persons are regenerated without any doctrine, good, bad, or indifferent. It is a work that depends on nothing but the special, direct, and immediate impulse, or impression of the Spirit upon the naked soul of an infant, a pagan, or a gospel hearer. This rage for orthodoxy is madness upon his hypothesis. Why this crusade against us on the part of my friend? We can do no harm, if his theory of conversion and sanctification be true! All that the Spirit regenerates live for ever according to him! Consequently they cannot be injured; *and none else can be saved.* In what a singular attitude stands he before this community and the universe, if his notions of regeneration are worth any thing! The gentleman will not, because he cannot, explain his zeal for orthodoxy on his principles. If the Spirit descends from heaven on a person, and by a direct touch regenerates him without faith, without knowledge, or preparation of any sort, what can sound doctrine and sound preaching avail? Mr. Rice's theory is a moral paralysis to the tongue and to the heart of a preacher. It is to the hearers a moral stupor, a spiritual lethargy.

There are *no means* of regeneration at all on his assumption. I wish I could say, with an emphasis that would seal it upon the heart forever, if Mr. Rice's theory be any thing but a mental hallucination, there are no means of conversion or sanctification—no means whatever of regeneration. I ask him what are the *means?* Can he name them? He cannot. Prayer, preaching, reading, all ordinances, are useless. Man, with him, is born again before he believes. He is as passive in the new birth as in the first birth. There were no motives, no volitions, no previous impulses of the soul in his first; nor are there any in his second birth. He runs the two metaphors of *birth* and *death* into a fatal paralysis.

Are you prepared, fellow-citizens of the nineteenth century—are you prepared to receive a doctrine of regeneration, that at one fell swoop, annihilates all means of grace whatsoever?—that makes faith, preaching, praying, reading, &c. altogether vain! This has been, in my esteem for many years, the most false delusion. I saw the doctrine of metaphysical and romantic regeneration leading just to this point. This is its natural *Ultima Thule* issue. If it always ends not here with you, it is only because you cannot, or do not understand it. Well did the Messiah say, of certain Rabbis, you make void the Word of God by your traditions.

I do, sir, most sincerely regard the Spirit of God as the author of every spiritual and noble desire in the human heart; the author of every pious affection, of every holy aspiration of our souls. His mysterious but certain power, is in, and with the gospel, and he makes it the power of God to salvation to every one that believes it. He sanctifies us through the truth. He works in us by it to will and do of his good pleasure. He is the Spirit of grace, because he is the Spirit of truth.

Much has been said, and whispered, and gossiped, concerning my heterodoxy. But, sir, allow me to compliment myself—I am, in all the great and weighty matters of religion, more orthodox than any of my impugners. I speak it not boastingly, sir, but in declaration of my general views of all gospel truths. I do not believe, sir, most sincerely, that there is any of those gentlemen that oppose us, more radically and universally orthodox on all these great subjects of evangelical faith, piety, and morality, than we.—[*Time expired.*]

Tuesday, Nov. 28—1½ *o'clock, P. M.*
[MR. RICE'S SEVENTH REPLY.]

Mr. President—I do not remember ever to have seen a man who pretended to religion of any kind, who did not consider himself rather more orthodox than others. This is a common weakness of human nature. It displays itself everywhere, and especially in men who imagine themselves to be great reformers, and believe all but themselves in serious error. If it be true, as my friend evidently thinks, that of all the world he only, and those who agree with him, are in the light, whilst all Christendom grope in midnight darkness; it follows, as a necessary consequence, that he is one of the most orthodox men! There can be no doubt about it.

We might, perhaps, excuse the other remarks the gentleman has so repeatedly made, concerning the doctrine of Presbyterians, which he professes perfectly to understand; but when he charges our church with holding the doctrine of infant damnation, we have the right to expect him to produce at least one Presbyterian author who has taught it. I have challenged him to produce even one, and he has not done it; nor has he

3 N 2

been able to prove that it is countenanced by our confession of faith. I deny that our church holds the doctrine. He has made the charge, and *once more I demand the proof*. I had supposed him to be a man who had so much experence in public discussions, that he would be prepared, at once, when he stated facts, to prove them. But it is not so. Very far otherwise.

I will now proceed to respond to his remarks and arguments, if, indeed, he has offered arguments, to prove the proposition he affirms. Let me ask you, my friends, has he produced one passage of Scripture that says, the Spirit operates in conversion and sanctification *only* through the truth? What passage has he quoted? Do you remember one? I certainly did not hear one quoted. Yet the gentleman boasts that he, more than all other men, confines his faith within the lids of the Bible.

He says, I have been proving only that the Spirit does *operate*, and this he admits. Such, however, is not the fact. I have been proving that the Spirit does not operate *only* through the truth, but that in conversion and sanctification there is an influence of the Spirit, an addition to the Word, and distinct from it. This doctrine he, in his writings and discussions, has positively denied. I like to see a man march up boldly and fearlessly to the defence of his published principles, or openly and candidly retract them. He has very repeatedly taught and published, that *only moral power* can be exerted on mind, and moral power can be exerted *only by words and arguments*, addressed to the eye or ear. Yet from what we have heard from him on this occasion, no one would imagine that he had ever believed such a doctrine. I do desire to see him come up and openly defend his published doctrines, or retract them. I have been proving that in the conversion and sanctification of adults, there is, 1st, the instrumentality of the Word; and, 2nd, a distinct agency of the Holy Spirit, for which the pious are accustomed to pray—an influence effectually renewing and sanctifying the soul. This latter agency Mr. C. denies. This is the most important point in regard to which we differ; and I am resolved to keep it prominently before the audience.

The gentleman has asserted, that a number of his arguments remain unnoticed. If there are such, I have entirely missed them; and I do not know how it could have happened, for I have taken full notes of his speeches. If there are any that remain unanswered, I hope he will mention them.

He has informed us how he was led to adopt his present views. He heard of the Spirit being poured out in divers places, and the result was, that so many Baptists, so many Methodists, and so many Presbyterians were made; and he concluded, that if all this had been the work of the Spirit, it would have been more *unique*. Really I had supposed, that he professed to have been led to the adoption of his views simply by a calm and unprejudiced examination of the Bible; but it appears that I was mistaken. He now informs us, that his faith in the special agency of the Spirit was shaken, if not destroyed, by hearing that the Spirit was poured out in this, that, and the other place. Verily I see nothing in this to shake the faith of a believer in the truth of the Scriptures. What is the language of the Bible on this subject? On the day of Pentecost the prophecy of Joel began to be fulfilled, in which he said, "It shall come to pass in the last days, (saith God,) I will *pour out* of my Spirit upon *all flesh*," &c. And Paul says, God saves us "by the washing of regeneration and renewing of the Holy Ghost, which he *shed on us abundantly*, through Jesus Christ." I cannot envy the feelings of the man who can speak slightingly of the very language of the Bible. If Paul, and Peter, and Joel were in error, I am willing to err with them.

But he says, if the Spirit had converted all those Baptists, Presbyterians, and Methodists, they would all have been alike. I see no absurdity or inconsistency in believing, that the Spirit of God may renew the hearts of several hundred persons, and that some of them might become Baptists, others Presbyterians, and others Methodists. I believe, that in all these, and other evangelical denominations, there are vast numbers who, with garments washed in the blood of the Lamb, will stand in the presence of God, where there is fullness of joy forever. I have never taken the ground that the Presbyterian church constitutes the whole family of God on earth, and that all other churches are synagogues of Satan! The gentleman cannot believe that the Spirit of God would make Methodists, Episcopalians, Baptists, and Presbyterians. But, I ask, has he not repeatedly published his belief that there are christians among "the sects;" christians, of course, converted by the Holy Spirit?

But he says, the work, if it were the work of the Spirit, would be more *unique;* those converted would be in their views more alike. Is the work unique in his own church, where he holds that disciples are made on principles truly apostolic? Do he and his brethren agree with each other in their views? I can point to a preacher of high standing in his church, who, for a length of time after joining his church and being recognized as a minister, believed in the doctrine of universal salvation! I can point to another prominent preacher in his church, who denies that man has a *soul,* and contends most zealously that in the Scriptures the word *soul* means *breath!!!* Why is not the work of the Spirit unique in his church? If this be a fair test of the work of God, and Mr. C. professes to think it is, his church is the very last place in this wide world where we could expect to find it; for in it, as he himself has informed us, *all sorts of doctrines have been preached by all sorts of men!!!* If the uniqueness of the work be the ground on which we are to form a judgment of its character, he would better have said nothing on the subject.

He has told you an anecdote illustrative of the fanaticism to which our doctrine leads, and I like to hear anecdotes occasionally. He told you of a certain preacher who adopted a very singular method of proving the doctrine of the resurrection; and he argues, even gravely, that those who are said to have experienced the special influences of the Spirit, are quite as ignorant of the Word of God as before. Well, I must tell an anecdote to match his. I hope my "laughing committee" are all present. [Laughing.] A young man not far from Lexington had been immersed into the church of my friend, where, we are to suppose, converts are made in the right way. After his immersion he, as is rather common in certain quarters, was somewhat wise in his own conceit, and anxious to make converts to his new views. He soon got into a discussion with some persons older and better informed than himself, who quoted against his doctrine a passage from the Old Testament. Not being quite prepared to meet the argument, he replied, "I care nothing about that—the Old Testament was written before the flood." [A laugh.] I doubt whether he was even so well taught as the gentleman's preacher. Indeed, it admits of very serious doubt, whether, as a general thing, his people, in the knowledge of the Scriptures, can justly claim any superiority over others.

But as further evidence that the doctrine for which we contend is not true, Mr. C. tells you, that he has known many who professed to be converted by the Spirit, who afterwards apostatized and became infidels. Does he know whether in the days of the apostles there were any cases of the kind? Were there not many who seemed to run well for a time, and then turned to the beggarly elements of the world? Perhaps the apostles did not preach as they should? Certainly they employed language very much like that we use on this subject. This circumstance may, perhaps, account for the fact that many apostatized!! I should like to inquire of my friend, whether any who have become members of his church, and who appeared zealous for a time, have afterwards apostatized? I think he will admit that many such cases have occurred, and that they became worse than before their professed conversion. One of his preachers, as I remarked several days since, stated, that he knew churches to which, some little time since, large accessions had been made, that were now almost dead. It is not wise in my friend to use arguments that, if at all sound, will ruin his own cause. The same class of arguments might be urged with equal conclusiveness against christianity itself. At any rate, his argument, if it proves any thing, affords conclusive evidence that he himself preaches false doctrine.

But it is a principle universally acknowledged, that the abuse of a doctrine is no valid argument against it. If men delude themselves, or are deluded by others into the belief that they have experienced a change of heart, when in truth they have not; is this to be urged against the fact, that all true conversions are effected by the special agency of the Spirit? Another objection urged by Mr. C. is, that according to our doctrine regeneration precedes faith. Suppose the matter to be just as he has represented it, he is reasoning as decidedly against the apostle John as against us. John says, "Whosoever believeth that Jesus is the Christ, is born of God," 1 John v. 1. According to the apostle, every believer is born of God, is regenerated. Regeneration is the *cause* of which faith is an *effect*. The fact that an individual believes, is proof that he is regenerated. Paul, too, represents men as "dead in trespasses and sins," and God as quickening them, Eph. ii. 1—5. If my friend had lived in those days, and had entertained his present views, I cannot but think he would have disapproved of Paul's theology. For certainly a dead man cannot put forth acts, as one who is alive. And he would have exposed the ridiculous absurdity of preaching to men who are dead! Faith is certainly the act of a being who is spiritually alive, and he must be quickened before he exercises faith.

But, says Mr. C., this doctrine makes faith and the preaching of the Word wholly unnecessary and useless. There is a passage in Paul's defence before Agrippa, that completely refutes this objection. "King Agrippa," exclaimed Paul, "believest thou the prophets? I know that thou believest," Acts xxvi. 27. Was Agrippa a pious man? Had he the faith that overcomes the world? He had faith, but not the faith that secures salvation. He believed the truth of divine revelation; but he did not approve and embrace it. In this sense multitudes believe. They doubt not the inspiration of the Scriptures, nor that they teach the great and essential doctrines and duties of christianity; but they do not love and embrace the gospel. Evangelical faith works by love, and leads to good works.

The kind of faith exercised by Agrippa, though it could not secure justification and eternal life, is not useless. It induces men to hear the Word, to read it, to think of it; and God may, through the truth, renew and sanctify them. This faith precedes regeneration; but the faith that works by love and overcomes the world, is consequent upon regeneration. He who is induced to embrace fundamental error, is not likely ever to be converted; for God does not sanctify through error. But he who theoretically believes the truth, may be converted and sanctified by the Spirit through the truth.

As to the objection, that this doctrine makes the preaching of the Word unnecessary, it has not the least foundation. God is pleased to work by means, when they can be employed. And not only does he employ means where they are wholly inefficient without the exertion of his power; but he has employed such means as had not the least tendency to produce the desired effect. Our Savior used clay and spittle in opening the eyes of a blind man. According to the logic of Mr. C., it was wholly unnecessary and unwise to use such means. He would ask, why use means that will not produce the effect? God has been pleased to say, that he will convert and sanctify the heart through the truth, though the truth alone cannot convert and sanctify; and who shall say, it is unwise? The gentleman's whole difficulty arises from an entire misapprehension of our views.

He tells us, he has known persons who professed to have been regenerated one day, and yet they did not believe for many days afterwards! I am obliged to admit, that he has found more singular people in this world, than any man I have ever known! I, of course, cannot dispute the truth of his statement; but I have never heard of persons entertaining such notions. Just as rationally might you talk of a man being alive several days without breathing. The moment when there is life, there are the actions that flow from it. Lazarus was no sooner made alive, than he breathed. So soon as there is in the soul spiritual life, it manifests itself by spiritual acts. He who is regenerated, believes, loves and obeys God. Such is the simple truth on this subject. It is God's truth.

The gentleman tells you, that I have reduced holiness to mere *instinct*. And he asks, how can there be holiness, which is love to God, where there is no knowledge of God? How can an infant be holy, when it cannot know God? In reply, I say, every thing possesses what we call *nature*. Our Savior said—" A good man out of the good treasure of the heart, bringeth forth good things; and an evil man out of the evil treasure, bringeth forth evil things," Matt. xii. 35. Here the heart or moral nature of man is represented as a treasure, fountain or source from which flow all his good and all his evil actions. If the heart be impure, it will prompt to conduct of the same character. There is something in a fruit-tree which we call its nature, which causes it to produce fruit of a particular kind. Two trees may grow in the same soil, be watered by the same stream, and warmed by the same sun; and yet they will produce different kinds of fruit. Common sense leads us to ascribe these different effects to causes equally different. The circumstances being the same, we conclude, that the causes are in the trees; and we say, they have different *natures*. The chemist cannot analyze the trees, and point out what we call their *nature;* yet common sense forces us to admit its existence.

No less certain is it, that men may and do possess a nature or disposition, prior to their acts and choices, which is sinful or holy. It was in illustration of this very principle, that our Savior said—" Make the tree good, and his fruit good; or else make the tree corrupt and his fruit corrupt: for the tree is known by his fruit," Matt. xii. 33. Of two men, who are living under the government of the same God, and enjoying the

45

same gospel privileges, one loves, adores, and serves God ; and the other knowingly, wilfully, and deliberately rebels against him. You call the one a good man—a holy man, and the other an unholy—a wicked man. Common sense compels us to believe, that the actions of the one flow from a pure source—a holy nature, and those of the other, from an unholy nature. The cause exists before the effect ; and these different natures or dispositions exist before the actions to which they prompt. There may, then, be in the mind of an infant the disposition which will induce it to love and serve God, or the opposite disposition, which will induce it to rebel against him, so soon as capable of knowing him. There is in this nothing more unphilosophical, than that there should be a disposition to love music. If I were to assert, that there can be no such thing before the person has heard music; how could he prove the contrary ? He asserts, that there can be no disposition to love God, where there is no knowledge of him. To prove this he can produce no acknowledged principle of philosophy ; and, as I have proved, it is directly contradictory of the Bible. I will not give up plain and positive declarations of the Word of God for his unphilosophical speculations.

In reply to the gentleman's charge, that our church holds the doctrine of infant damnation, I gave the common interpretation of the language of our confession of faith. This interpretation, he says, he never heard until recently. Well, I verily believe, there are a great many things in this world of which he has never heard; for it is a notorious fact, that the interpretation I gave of the language of our book, is the one universally given by Presbyterians.

All the gentleman's learned criticisms on the word *holy*, even if they were correct, could not help him out of the difficulty, arising from his limiting the power of God over the human mind. The word *holy*, he says, does not express *moral quality*. Suppose we admit it. I have proved, that God originally made man *upright ;* and all we desire, is to have him made upright again. If God made him upright once, he is able to make him so again. Mr. C. says, God *cannot* exert on the human mind any moral power, except by words : I say he can.

The word *holy*, when applied to moral character, as it is constantly in the Bible, does not mean simply separation from all impurity. A log of wood might be separated from all impurity ; but it would still not be holy. The word expresses most clearly moral purity. But I will not spend time in such criticisms.

My friend has brought forward one more passage of Scripture to sustain his doctrine. We occasionally induce him to leave his metaphysics, and enter the Bible. He quotes Acts xxvi. 18, where we are told that God sent Paul to the gentiles, " to open their eyes, and to turn them from darkness to light, and from the power of Satan unto God." But here a very important question arises, viz : Was Paul sent to do this work by *the Word only?* The passage does not say so. Paul had a certain work to do. He was sent to preach the unsearchable riches of Christ. But God had also a work to do. So Paul taught the Ephesians. They were dead in trespasses and in sins, and God quickened them, Eph ii. 1—5. I should like to hear the gentleman explain that passage, so as to make it consistent with his faith. He has brought forward several passages ; but, unfortunately, they all, when properly understood, refute his doctrine, and establish ours.

He says, he cannot conceive of a religion that begins in darkness—in mere blind feeling. Neither can I. But I can conceive that God may "call men out of darkness into his marvellous light," (1 Pet. ii. 9,) that he may open their eyes and renew their hearts, causing them to love the light; for, our Savior said, "This is the condemnation, that light is come into the world; and men love darkness more than light." For this pure light David prayed: "Open mine eyes, that I may behold wonderful things out of thy law." The Word was before his mind; but he prayed that God would grant him more purity of heart, that he might better understand it, and appreciate more fully its glorious truths. Such is the religion in which we believe.

I have now gone through the whole catalogue of my friend's arguments. I do not consider them very strong. I believe he quoted but one text of Scripture. I will now very briefly present one more argument, in proof of the doctrine that the Spirit operates, not through the truth *only*. The Scriptures teach that God *gives repentance*. Christ was exalted a prince and a Savior, "for to give repentance unto Israel, and remission of sins," Acts v. 31. Can any one believe that God gives both remission and repentance, merely by the preaching of the Word? The obvious meaning of the apostle is, that he inclines men by his blessed Spirit, to repent, that he may grant to them remission of sins." So again, in Acts xi. 18: "Then hath God also to the gentiles *granted repentance* unto life." Now, what is meant but that God granted the gentiles the gracious influence of his Holy Spirit, and thus induced them to repent? The grace of God brought them to repentance; but going to God brought them also to repentance. I have one more passage, 2 Tim. ii. 25, 26: "In meekness, instructing those that oppose themselves; if God peradventure will give them repentance to the acknowledging of the truth: and that they may recover themselves out of the snare of the devil, who are taken captive by him at his will." The truth is before them. They have heard it; but will not receive it. Now, here God is said to give them repentance, or a change of mind, to the acknowledgment of the truth. I ask any man, if this language does not mean something additional to the mere influence of the Word? They had heard the truth, but it failed to lead them to repentance; and now God exerts in their minds a more effectual agency. We do not see how it was possible for the Savior and the apostles to have taught more plainly the doctrine of a special agency of the Spirit, in addition to the Word? I defy any one to teach it in stronger language. If the Bible does not teach the operation of the Spirit, distinct from the Word, I defy mortal man to teach it by any language. When the apostles used the strongest language, without qualification, did they not wish it to be understood according to its obvious import? It is, then, clear that they taught that the Spirit operates not only through the Truth, but in addition to it. They all taught it, and took delight in it. It is one of the chief pillars in the Temple of Truth; and he who denies it, leaves man to perish without hope. But I will close for the present.—[*Time expired.*

Wednesday, Nov. 29—10 *o'clock, A. M.*
[MR. CAMPBELL'S EIGHTH ADDRESS.]

MR. PRESIDENT—It is all-important in every debate, especially in this one, that the proper issue be kept distinctly and definitely before the minds of the debatants and of the auditors. There is no question of more sublime comprehension, of more awful grandeur, or of more transcendent importance, than the question of spiritual and Divine influence. *Like* the vital principle, however, it is the most sublimated, and in its naked and abstract form, the most unapproachable of all the entities of creation. It is, indeed, the vital principle of religion, and, therefore, the most incomprehensible, though the most real and substantive existence in the universe. The question before us involves the value of the Bible, and all its ordinances—the gospel, its ministry, and all that mortals have comprehended under that most precious conception called *the means of grace.* I feel that I am discussing the value of the Bible, the gospel, the church, the ministry, while endeavoring to know what the converting and sanctifying power and influence of God's Spirit is. Let us, then, fix our minds upon the precise points expressed in the proposition before us. *"In conversion and sanctification the Spirit of God operates on persons only through the truth."*

There is no debate upon spiritual operations. They are of an abstract nature and quality. It is not possible for a man to conceive of spiritual operations. The fact of the operation is as evident as gravity, but who can explain it? No man can form a single conception of any spiritual influence or operation. Who can grasp the idea of a spirit? Who can apprehend its nature, its identity, its form, its person, or its modes of living, moving, and operating! We can neither have a consistent idea of a spirit nor of any of its operations. That the Spirit of God operates on the human understanding and heart is just as certain as that man has an understanding and affections. Our spirit is allied to the spiritual system, to the Great Spirit. God can commune, and does commune with man, and man with God.

It is the glory of our religion that it is spiritual and divine, and that as man has both a body and a spirit, his religion also has both. This question has respect rather to the means and to the effect of the operation, nad not to the operation itself. Times without number have I declared that the Scriptures are but an instrument, an embodiment in speech of spiritual power, and like all other instruments, this instrument is adapted to some end. Without that instrument the end proposed by it cannot be obtained.

Now, does the Spirit operate through the instrument, or without it, in the ordinary work of conversion and sanctification? This is the question in its present form. This question involves various other questions. No question either in nature, religion, or society, is properly insular. These are all perfect systems, and, therefore, there is not one insular or independent truth in any one, nor all of them. Not a particle of the universe, not an atom of our planet is independent of other atoms and principles. Nor is there an isolated verse, nor an independent period in the Bible. Those atoms of the universe, those particles of our planet, and those verses of our Bible, are to be contemplated with reference to the whole. Little minds sport with particles, great minds with systems.

Mr. Rice has quoted some passages of Scripture. But have they been quoted as proverbs, or as parts of great contexts? I do not believe that any one passage, read you by my friend, has any thing specially to do with the question before us. I might throw into a speech thirty verses, and make thirty assertions, and prove nothing, only that I intended to employ some one else, some other mind than my own, for not one of the thirty may come within a thousand miles of the real issue. My manner is to notice every thing relied upon as proof of the proposition on hand; not every thing, however, that may be offered on various other matters. That would be the work of months and not of weeks. I will, so far as I have recollection or memoranda, allude to some of the proofs offered, to show that the Spirit operates in conversion without the Word. These are supposed to be against my views. I have proved that it operates through the Word, and my proofs are in the main unassailed. Mr. R.'s plan is to prove a proposition the contrary of our stipulated proposition. He seeks to prove that the Spirit operates without the Word from such passages as the following: Luke xxiv. 45.

" Then opened he their understanding, that they might understand the Scriptures." In the first place it is irrelevant, because this has no respect to regeneration nor conversion ; nor does it speak particularly of sanctification. Again, it was *Jesus* and not the *Spirit*. They were disciples and not sinners. " To open the understanding " is also explained in the context, verse 32. Thus the subject of the operation is explained in these words ; " Did not our hearts burn within us, while he talked with us, and while he opened to us the Scriptures ?" To open the Scriptures to the understanding, is the meaning of the Hebrewistic phrase, " open the understanding to understand the Scriptures." Their hearts burned not by the abstract spirit, but through the talk—" while he talked with us." So dispose we of this passage. Was the opening previous to, and independent of the speaking of the Word ?!

Another proof text was 1 Cor. ii. 14: " The natural man receiveth not the things of the Spirit of God, for they are foolishness to him ; neither can he know them, because they are spiritually discerned." The natural man is here contrasted with the spiritual man. The word is sometimes rendered physical, natural, animal, sensual. Natural is the most common. It is four times natural, and twice sensual in the common version. McKnight prefers the animal man, and he is high authority in Scotland, and I learn, of high authority in the theological school at Princeton. Some of the professors there, I am told, speak of him in much admiration. The animal man, then, in the context, means the " *wise man according to the flesh*,"—in contrast with the spiritual man, *wise according to the Spirit*.

A sensual man is a man merely of sense ; but it has come to signify one enslaved to sense. Now such a man, who has no other guide than sense, cannot receive the things of the Spirit of God. " *The things of the Spirit*" can only be discerned by him that is spiritual—one that is enlightened by the Spirit. But the things of the Spirit are revealed things—and, therefore, the discernment of revealed things is very different from the discernment of nothing—as in the case of infants, pagans, idiots, &c. supposed to be regenerated without having the things of the Spirit discerned at all. The text, therefore, comes not within a thousand miles of the subject on hand.

I object, however, altogether to the theological appropriation of this term. Our gospel-hearers are not Paul's *natural* men—and, therefore, it is the sophism of equivocation, or of an ambiguous term, of which all are guilty, who use this word as equivalent, to the citizens of Kentucky who read the Bible. We have no natural men in that sense, nor in the proper sense of that word. Adam was a *natural* man ; we, as his mere offspring, are *preternatural* men, and under Christ we hope to rise to be *supernatural men.*

I object to much of the nomenclature of modern theology. We have drawn too much on the paganized vocabulary of Rome. Neither Jewish,

3 O

Christian, nor Pagan, but a mongrel dialect is the jargon of the present age. Nature and grace are from the same God—twin sisters of the same divine family. But man has strayed away from God and nature, and has become a preternatural being. From this miserable condition God proposes, in his glorious philanthropy, to redeem man and to make him supernatural through Christ, the second Adam, the Lord from heaven. God made man upright, and while he remained in nature, that is, in his natural or original state, he had not a passion, appetite, or instinct which he might not most religiously gratify. But now his soul is harrassed with the tumult of a thousand passions, lusts, appetites, and elements that war against his soul. If there were no sin in human nature, there could be none in obeying all its passions. Sceptics are deceived, always deceived, and fatally deceived, in their reasonings from Mr. Rice's premises. Like him, they suppose man to be in the state of nature; and, therefore, think it no crime to gratify their passions. Their reasoning is just, but their premises are false, and their conclusion is a fatal error.

We have had numerous allusions and references to Titus iii. 5. The gentleman can find in the phrase, "renewing of the Holy Spirit," no proof of a proposition contrary to mine. The renewing of the Holy Spirit is in the second birth connected with other means. He has saved us through the washing of the new birth, and the renewing of the Holy Spirit. This renewing of the Spirit is not immediate, nor exclusive of other means; it being associated with a washing, and a shedding forth of the Spirit through Jesus Christ our Savior.

The gentleman has more than once called upon me to read something from some of my books contrary to what he has read. Being here in person, I prefer speaking on these subjects *viva voce*, to reading my views already published. Besides, I have no time to debate a hundred questions, growing out of his designs, of which I am now apprized. The gentleman may read from them when he is hard pressed for matter. I perceive this is his principal use of them. For me, when my present resources are exhausted, I may turn in and debate with him on those writings. I have another reason; I do not find just such passages as suit all the topics that occur. Yet, as a matter of complaisance, I will furnish the gentleman with one or two extracts, if he will ask me for no more: (*Christian System*, p. 66.)

"Some will ask, has not this gift been conferred on us to make us christians? True indeed, no man can say that Jesus is Lord but by the Holy Spirit. As observed in its proper place, the Spirit of God is the perfecter and finisher of all divine works. 'The Spirit of God moved upon the waters;' 'the hand of the Lord has made me; the Spirit of the Almighty has given me life;' 'by his Spirit he has garnished the heavens; his hand has formed the crooked serpent'—the milky way; 'the Spirit descended upon him;' 'God himself bare the apostles witness, by divers miracles and gifts of the Holy Spirit, according to his will;' 'holy men of old spake as they were moved by the Holy Spirit;' 'when the Spirit of truth, the Advocate, is come, he will convict the world of sin, because they believe not on me, and of justification, because I go to my Father;' 'God was manifest in the flesh, and justified by the Spirit.'

Now we cannot separate the Spirit and word of God, and ascribe so much power to the one and so much to the other: for so did not the apostles. Whatever the word does, the Spirit does; and whatever the Spirit does in the work of converting men, the word does. We neither believe nor teach abstract Spirit, nor abstract word; but word and Spirit, and Spirit and word."

Again : (pp. 277, 278.)

" ' He has saved us,' says the apostle Paul, ' by the bath of regeneration, and *the renewing of the Holy Spirit*, which he poured on us richly through Jesus Christ our Savior ; that being justified by his favor, [in the bath of regeneration,] we might be made heirs according to the hope of eternal life.' Thus, and not by works of righteousness, he has saved us. Consequently being born of the Spirit, or the renewing of the Holy Spirit, is as necessary as the bath of regeneration to the salvation of the soul, and to the enjoyment of the hope of heaven, of which the apostle speaks. Into the kingdom of which we are born of water, the Holy Spirit is as the atmosphere in the kingdom of nature : we mean, that the influences of the Holy Spirit are as necessary to the *new life*, as the atmosphere is to our animal life in the kingdom of nature. All that is done in us before regeneration, God our Father effects by *the word*, or the gospel as dictated or confirmed by his Holy Spirit. But after we are thus begotten and born by the Spirit of God —after our new birth, the Holy Spirit is shed on us richly through Jesus Christ our Savior ; of which the peace of mind, the love, the joy, and the hope of the regenerate is full proof : for these are amongst the fruits of that Holy Spirit of promise of which we speak."

Many other such passages might be read from our numerous writings on this subject. But this, as a specimen, may perhaps suffice to gratify my friend.

The gentleman also relies upon the new covenant in proof of his proposition. Of the four provisions of the new institution, only one of them applies to this subject. The first is—" I will put my laws into their mind, and write them upon their heart." Now in every covenant there are parties—the covenanter and the covenantees. God is the covenanter, and christians the covenantees. " With the house of Israel, (not according to the flesh, but according to the Spirit,) I will make a new covenant." Now what bearing has this on the question before us ? Were the covenantees infants, pagans, idiots, unconverted men ? ! If not, the passage is wholly misapplied, because brought to prove a subject wholly different from that in the mind of the Spirit. We are debating about the work of the Spirit on conversion, and in that discussion a question has arisen about regeneration, and the question on that subject is—are persons regenerated by the Spirit without the Word ? This position the gentleman is now seeking to prove, and this is one of his proofs. Having shown its entire impertinence to the subject, we shall attend to another point.

Mr. Rice, from some remarks made in some of my essays, in illustration of the converting power in the divine Word, on the influences which the writings of Demosthenes and Cicero have exerted upon the world, has sought to institute a comparison for me—to make me say, that, as all the moral or argumentative power of Demosthenes and Cicero is in their writings, so all God's moral power is in his Word. So far so good ; but the gentleman goes a little farther, and would not allow the case to terminate there, but supposed me to assign no other power or presence to the Spirit of God than to the spirit and personal influence of those ancient orators. I am prepared to say, that, so far as moral power is concerned, the arguments and motives of the Spirit of God are all set forth in the New Institution, in all their perfection ; and that this power cannot be increased. Nay, I argue, that if the Spirit of God were again to descend, as on Pentecost, and in the person of a new legate from heaven, should plead with the human race, touching their condition and destiny under God's philanthropy and active benevolence ; when he had set forth, in all their amplitude, all the facts and promises in the universe on this subject,

he would then, at the close of the effort, have not increased one grain
the amount of the moral momentum and influence of the gospel. He
would not then have increased, in the least, its converting power. For
if the story is all told now, and if God veraciously and sincerely asks,
what more could be done than what I have done for my vineyard, then
there is no possibility of accumulating the power by any other means;
but whether the ever-living and ever-present Spirit of our God may not
through that truth, in ways unknown to mortals, affect the soul of man,
by fixing the attention upon it, or removing, providentially, obstructions,
&c., is neither affirmed nor denied in that comparison, nor in the circumstances that called it forth. And this having been spoken with special
reference to the fanaticism and wild enthusiasm of the age, in certain cases
of pretended new light and new-converting power, ought to have been
construed accordingly. But this method of torturing men's words by
putting them on the partizan rack, and dislocating every joint, works as
pervertingly on them as on the Word of God. Whenever all the gospel
argument is comprehended, all the moral power of God is exhausted;
for beyond that he has never displayed any to any man, and he that hears
not Moses and the prophets, Christ and his apostles, would not be persuaded though one rose from the dead.

The gentleman has more than once asked me for proof that the Spirit
operates *only* through the Word; and avows that unless I shew him
some text that exactly affirms that, he will not believe. Well, I gave him
in my proposition on the design of baptism the very words in the book,
with the mere supplement *past*, to which he did not demur, and then he
would not believe. And I verily believe if I gave him every word in one
verse, he would be for construing it in a different sense. But this is a
new mode of argumentation, by which he could not prove one article in
his creed; for not one of them is found in the identical words of the book.
Nor could we prove any proposition not found verbatim in the Bible.
But I have proved *only* through the Word. By shewing first, that the
Spirit does regenerate and sanctify through the Word—and, in the same
place, by that great law of the physical and moral universe, that whatever
is necessary to any given result, is always necessary. Also, by various
other considerations and arguments, yet unnoticed by him. Did I not,
on yesterday, demonstrate on his own definition of regeneration, the utter
impossibility of infant regeneration? and yet he has neither retracted nor
defended the definition. Surely he ought to do the one or the other.

At the commencement of this discussion he clearly stated that the Spirit
does sometimes operate on adults through the Word. Had it not been
for idiots, pagans, and infants, he would, no doubt, have said *only* through
the Word. He has since admitted that on adults he operates *generally*
through the Word. It was some time before he gave us a definition of
regeneration; and still longer before he informed us, whether faith or regeneration were prior, or which was the cause of the other. Finally, he
informed us that regeneration preceded faith, therefore both infants and
adults are regenerated without faith, and prior to faith. Without perceiving, and, I am confident, without intending it, he has thus indisputably proved my fourth argument, which, you will remember, says—
*Whatever is essential to regeneration in one case, is essential in
all cases.* For having been brought to concede—namely: that regeneration is prior to faith; thus making adults the subject of regeneration without belief, and infants as a matter of course, because incapa-

ble of belief; we have obtained from him the admission of my fourth argument. Again, we have proved to his own satisfaction that the Spirit generally operates through the Word on adults, and in some cases *only* through the Word; follows it not, then, that according to our fourth argument, regeneration must be through the Word, and therefore infant regeneration is impossible. In any view of the matter, then, I may say, without the fear of successful contradiction from any quarter, that Mr. Rice has given us the data for his own refutation, and now stands self-refuted for the reasons now assigned. This subject is still susceptible of farther illustration, but my time being almost expired, I shall only add a few words on the plan of the Bible as developing its theory of regeneration.

The Old and New Testaments are arranged upon the same grand plan. They present a record of facts well documented and proved. The first five books of both Testaments are historical. The historical and the didactic go together. The fact, first, the testimony concerning it, and then the development of it. There is one grand arrangement of revelation, adapted to the constitution and philosophy of man. The order of things is simple, because it is rational. The connection is first, *fact*—next, *testimony* concerning that fact—that something said or done;—then *faith*, or the belief of that testimony;—after that, *feeling*—in harmony with whatever is believed—joyful or sorrowful, good or bad;—and in the last place, *action*—a course of conduct corresponding with that feeling. This is not only the rational, but it is the fixed and necessary and immutable arrangement of things producing faith and growing out of it. It is no arbitrary division—no conventional arrangement. It must be so while man is a being that walks by faith, and while faith is the belief of testimony. These five words—fact, testimony, faith, feeling, action—set forth the economy of the Bible,—and are the grand links in that Divine chain that give to the facts of revelation their influence on the soul of man. The thing done or spoken by God, or man, called the *fact*, passes into the testimony, and the *testimony* passes into *faith*, and the fact, in that faith, passes into corresponding *feeling*, and then it is made living and efficient in the *action*. Now this being the immutable order of things, and regeneration being the offspring of the Word of God believed, it is impossible that any one, incapable of understanding the fact, of believing the testimony, of exercising faith, of possessing moral feeling, and of correspondent action, can be regenerated.—[*Time expired.*]

Wednesday, Nov. 29—10½ *o'clock, A. M.*
[MR. RICE'S EIGHTH REPLY.]
MR. PRESIDENT—I intend that, throughout this discussion, the precise points in debate shall be kept distinctly in view. Mr. C. says, he admits that in conversion and sanctification the Spirit does operate, and that the Word is only the *instrument.* I inquired of him, on yesterday, what he meant by this language? Whether he holds that there is any operation of the Spirit distinct from the Word? or whether he believes only, that the Spirit dictated the Word and confirmed it by miracle, and now the Word converts and sanctifies? To this important question I received no answer. If he believes the Spirit to be the *agent* in this work, he must put forth some power; for there cannot be an *agent* without an *action.* If, then, his language means any thing, it must be, that at the moment when the soul is converted, the Spirit of God exerts converting power, performs an act which produces this result. I wished

3 o 2

to be informed, whether he believes that the Spirit exerts an influence distinct from the Word; but he would not answer the question.

He told us also, that the Spirit is always present with the Word. I asked him what he meant by this language; but I received no answer! I discover plainly, that the audience are not to see the real point at issue, unless I constantly keep it before them; and this I am resolved to do.

The great question, is not whether ordinarily the Spirit operates through the truth; but whether the only influence exerted in conversion and sanctification, is that of words and arguments—whether the Spirit of God operates on the hearts of men only as Mr. C.'s spirit operates on the minds of this audience? This is the question—I use the gentleman's own illustration. We are not debating the question, by what *instrumentality* the Spirit converts and sanctifies men; but what is the work which the Spirit does? We hold, that in the case of infants and idiots, inasmuch as instrumentality cannot be employed, sanctification takes place without the truth. In the case of adults we hold, that there is not only the influence of words and arguments, but a distinct influence of the Spirit, opening the eyes and purifying the heart. This Mr. C. denies.

The gentleman has a clear head. I wonder at the confusion in which he keeps his real sentiments. On some subjects he delivers himself with great clearness; and on the one before us he has *written* clearly. Yet this is the third day we have been on this proposition; and I must say, that more fog and mist I never did see thrown around any subject!

Let me now give you a specimen of the manner in which my biblical friend expounds Scripture. He professes to be a very biblical man. In proof of a divine influence in addition to the Word, I quoted Luke xxiv. 45: "Then opened he their understandings, that they might understand the Scriptures." The inspired writer, you observe, does not say, he opened their understandings *in order that* they might understand the Scriptures. What is the gentleman's reply? He turns to the 27th verse—"And beginning at Moses and all the prophets, he expounded unto them in all the scriptures, the things concerning himself." Now according to his principles of interpretation, expounding the Scriptures and opening their understandings that they might understand them, are the same thing! Why, you might expound the Scriptures to persons by the hour, and yet they might have no correct understanding of them; but if you had power to open their understandings, the whole difficulty would be at once removed. Remove the causes of their blindness, and they will see clearly. So did David pray—"Open thou mine eyes, that I may behold wondrous things out of thy law." Did he not pray for a divine influence on his mind, opening his understanding? It is vain to attempt to evade the force of language so perfectly plain. It will not do to say, that to open the understanding and to open the Scriptures, are phrases meaning the same thing.

To prove the necessity of the special work of the Spirit on the heart, I quoted 1 Cor. ii. 14: "The natural man receiveth not the things of the Spirit; for they are foolishness to him: neither can he know them, because they are spiritually discerned." The gentleman appeals to McKnight, who translates the phrase "*animal man*." And he tells us, he has somewhere heard, that the professors in the Princeton theological seminary have placed McKnight at the head of critical commentators. This may be true; but I should prefer to have some proof of the fact. But let us take his translation. Now the question is, who is the *animal man?* Mr. C. says he is the pagan without a divine revelation to guide him. But the fact is, the word translated *natural* or *animal*, has not this meaning in one instance in the New Testament. It is used in 1 Cor. xv. 44, 45, to distinguish the natural body from the *spiritual* body. The natural body, we know, means the body as it is by nature, unchanged. " It is sown (or buried) a natural body." The spiritual body means the body as it will be changed at the resurrection. So the natural man means man as he is by nature—depraved; and the spiritual man is the man renewed by the Holy Spirit.

The same word, as I have already stated, is used by James, who describes the wisdom which is not from above, as " earthly, *sensual*, [Gr. *natural*,] devilish." In this passage the word is used with reference to moral character, and it certainly expresses the idea of depravity. It is also used by Jude, v. 19, where he describes the wicked thus : " These be they who separate themselves, sensual, [Gr. *natural*,] having not the Spirit." The wicked, who have not the Spirit, are described as natural or sensual. On the use of the word in these passages, the gentleman forgot to make even a passing remark. The usage of the New Testament, in regard to this word, leaves no room to doubt what is its meaning. The natural man certainly is man in his native depravity. Mr. C. objects to the use of the word *natural*, as applied to man in his depravity, because by nature he was not depraved. He, therefore, uses the word *preternatural*. But he seems not to remember, that in making this objection he is finding fault with the language of inspiration. In the epistle to the Ephesians, Paul says, men are " by *nature* the children of wrath," ch. ii. 3. The word here used is *phusis*, the literal and uniform meaning of which is *nature*. If Paul thus uses the word *nature*, I may be excused for following his example !

But Mr. C. was careful not to notice the succeeding part of the verse under discussion. Why does not the natural man receive the things of the Spirit? Because, says Paul, " *they are* FOOLISHNESS *unto him*." The meaning of this language, as I proved, is made perfectly clear by ch. i. 18, " The preaching of the cross is to them that perish, foolishness ; but unto us which are saved, it is the power of God." That is, when they hear the Gospel preached, it is to them foolishness ; they see in it no wisdom, no adaptation to their condition, nothing attractive ; and therefore they reject it. So to " the natural man" the things of the Spirit, the truths of the Gospel, are foolishness, and he rejects them. But if Mr. C.'s interpretation be correct, the passage should read thus : The animal man receiveth not the things of the Spirit, *for they are not* REVEALED *to him!*

It is now perfectly clear, that " the natural man" is the *unrenewed man ;* and since unrenewed men do not receive, but uniformly reject the gospel ; it follows, inevitably, that the special influence of the Holy Spirit, in addition to the Word, is absolutely necessary to their conversion and sanctification. Consequently, in every case of conversion, such a divine influence is actually exerted.

To show you how much I have misrepresented him, the gentleman read a paragraph or two from his *Christian System.* I am pleased to see him read his publications ; and I am quite disposed to aid him in presenting them before you. On page 66 he read as follows : " Some will ask, has not this gift [of the Spirit] been conferred on us to make us christians ? True, indeed, no man can say that Jesus is Lord, but by the

Holy Spirit. As observed in its proper place, the Spirit of God is the perfecter and finisher of all divine works. ' The Spirit moved upon the waters,' " &c. But the difficulty is, that in this whole paragraph he says not one word concerning an influence of the Spirit upon the heart, in conversion! He quotes several passages, as follows: " The hand of the Lord has made me, the Spirit of the Almighty has given me life ;" " By his Spirit he has garnished the heavens, his hand has formed the crooked serpent;" " The Spirit descended upon him; God himself bore the apostles witness, by divers miracles and gifts of the Holy Spirit, according to his will." Not one of these passages, nor any one quoted by him, has the slightest reference to a change of the heart by the Holy Spirit.

He also read on the next page: " Now we cannot separate the Spirit and the Word of God, and ascribe so much power to the one and so much to the other; for so did not the apostles. Whatever the Word does, the Spirit does; and whatever the Spirit does, in the work of converting men, the Word does. We neither believe nor teach abstract Spirit nor abstract Word—but Word and Spirit, and Spirit and Word." All this is perfectly ambiguous. For if the Spirit dictated and confirmed the Word, and the Word converts and sanctifies men; it is true, in a sense, that the Spirit does the work. *But does Mr. C. hold to an influence of the Spirit in conversion, distinct from the Word?* On this point these paragraphs give us no light. Let me read on the 277th page of his *Christianity Restored*. Perhaps we shall here gain some information. He says:

" But this pouring out of the influences, this renewing of the Holy Spirit, is as necessary as the bath of regeneration to the salvation of the soul, and to the enjoyment of the hope of heaven, of which the apostle speaks. In the kingdom into which we are born of water, the Holy Spirit is as the atmosphere in the kingdom of nature : we mean, that the influences of the Holy Spirit are as necessary to the new life, as the atmosphere is to our animal life in the kingdom of nature. All that is done in us before regeneration, God our Father effects by the word, or the gospel as dictated and confirmed by his Holy Spirit. But after we are thus begotten and born by the Spirit of God—after our new birth, the Holy Spirit is shed on us richly through Jesus Christ our Savior ; of which the peace of mind, the love, the joy, and the hope of the regenerate is full proof: for these are amongst the fruits of that Holy Spirit of promise, of which we speak."

On this passage I make two or three remarks. 1. " This pouring out of the influences, this renewing of the Holy Spirit," he says, " is *as necessary as* the birth of regeneration [immersion] to the salvation of the soul, and to the enjoyment of the hope of heaven." The influences of the Spirit only *as necessary* to salvation, as *immersion*—not more so !!! 2. Observe, he says—" All that is done in us before regeneration [immersion] God our Father effects *by the Word, or the gospel as dictated and confirmed by his Holy Spirit.*" Here we have a denial as clear and as strong as language can make it, of any influence in conversion, except that of the Word as dictated and confirmed by the Spirit. This is the most important point about which we differ, and which I desire the audience not to lose sight of. 3. As my friend is fond of asking questions, I wish to ask him—WHAT KIND OF INFLUENCE DOES THE SPIRIT EXERT ON THE MINDS OF IMMERSED BELIEVERS ? This is a very important question. He has said in his publications—that there are but two kinds of power—*moral and physical.* He has also said, that the only power that can be exerted on mind, is moral power; and he has said, that " every spirit puts forth its moral power in words,"—that " all the power it has over the views, habits, manners or actions of men, is in the meaning and arrangement of its ideas expressed in words ; or in significant signs addressed to the eye or ear." Now I am particularly anxious to know what kind of influence the Spirit does exert on the minds of believers, after they are immersed. Is it *physical* power? My friend will say— no. Is it *spiritual* power—neither physical nor moral ? He will say—no. Is it a moral influence which sanctifies the heart? If so, it must be an influence simply and only of the Word. Will the gentleman enlighten us on this subject ? We wish to know something about this influence which is not physical, nor moral, nor any thing else !

I was pleased to hear him, for once, come out and express with some clearness his real sentiments. The Spirit of God, he tells us, produces moral effects *only by arguments ;* that when all his arguments and motives are brought to bear on the mind, his moral power is *exhausted.* This is precisely what I read on yesterday from his Christianity Restored. What more moral power could Demosthenes or Cicero exert on their hearers or readers, after they had put forth all their arguments ? So it appears, according to this doctrine, that the Holy Spirit has no more power over the minds and hearts of men than had those ancient orators, except that he may reason more powerfully ! ! ! So he teaches in his *Christianity Restored:* (pp. 348, 349.)

" Because arguments are addressed to the understanding, will, and affections of men, they are called moral, inasmuch as their tendency is to form or change the habits, manners, or actions of men. Every spirit puts forth its moral power in words ; that is, all the power it has over the views, habits, manners, or actions of men, is in the meaning and arrangement of its ideas expressed in words, or in significant signs addressed to the eye or ear. All the moral power of Cicero and Demosthenes was in their orations when spoken, and in the circumstances which gave them meaning ; and whatever power these men have exercised over Greece and Rome since their death, is in their writings. * * * *

From such premises we may say, that all the moral power which can be exerted on human beings, is, and must of necessity be, in the arguments addressed to them. No other power than moral power can operate on minds ; and this power must always be clothed in words, addressed to the eye or ear. Thus we reason when revelation is altogether out of view. And when we think of the power of the Spirit of God exerted upon minds or human spirits, it is impossible for us to imagine, that that power can consist in any thing else but words or arguments. Thus, in the nature of things, we are prepared to expect verbal communications from the Spirit of God, if that Spirit operates at all upon our spirits. *As the moral power of every man is in his arguments, so is the moral power of the Spirit of God in his arguments.*"

This limiting of the power of God, I have said, is both unscriptural and unreasonable. God originally created man *upright.* He exerted on him an influence, not by words and arguments, which made him holy. Who shall venture, in view of this fact, to say, he cannot now exert an influence which will renew his sinful nature ?

The gentleman asks, what can the Spirit do, after all his arguments have been put forth? Will he inform us, how the devil tempts men to sin ? He acknowledges, that the devil has access to the minds of men, and exerts a moral influence, not by words and arguments addressed to the eye or ear; yet he cannot tell us how that influence is exerted. If, then, we do not know how good or evil spirits can exert an influence on

our minds; is it not most presumptuous in any man to assert, that the
Holy Spirit *cannot* exert a moral or spiritual influence except by words
and arguments addressed to the eye or ear? Shall we venture to say,
that the devil has more power over the human mind, than God?!!

Let all this false philosophy go to the winds, and give us the Bible.
The gentleman is attempting to prove, that in conversion and sanctification the Spirit operates on persons *only through the truth*. If there is
a passage in the Bible that expresses such a sentiment, let us have it. I
desire to see the passage, if it is in the Bible. If it is not, he would better abandon his doctrine.

But he says, the proposition he affirmed on the design of baptism, was,
with the exception of one word, precisely the language of the Bible, and
yet I was not satisfied with it. The difficulty was, that I was not satisfied with *his interpretation* of the language of the Bible, because it flatly
contradicted many of the plainest declarations of Christ and the apostles!
The gentleman has a remarkable tact at representing all men who differ
from him, as fighting against the Scriptures. I verily do not believe, that
he is infallible; and believing him fallible, I must venture to differ from him.

He has given you, my friends, some important information this morning, viz: that on yesterday I gave up the whole question! I venture to
say, that not an individual in the house, except himself, discovered that I
had done so. It was, therefore, particularly important that *he* should
make the announcement! But how did I give up the question? By admitting, that generally the Spirit operates through the truth. So says
Mr. C. Let me repeat the substance of my remarks on this point, and
the audience will judge whether I gave it up. I stated distinctly, that the
Scriptures speak of two kinds of faith, very different in their character
King Agrippa had the one, and Paul had the other. Paul, in his defence,
thus addressed the king: "King Agrippa, believest thou the prophets? I
know that thou believest." Yet Agrippa was not a christian, but only
almost persuaded to be a christian. It is evident to every man's common sense, that you may believe a thing to be true, and yet be perfectly
indifferent concerning it. "Gallio cared for none of these things." You
may be constrained by clear evidence to believe a truth, and yet most
earnestly wish it were not a truth. Thousands believe the Bible to be a
divine revelation, and yet are wholly indifferent to its sublime truths.
Their minds are occupied with other subjects, and their time employed in
worldly pursuits. One goes to his farm, another to his merchandize;
and each says, "I pray thee, have me excused." There are others who
are constrained to admit the truth of the Bible, but are deeply averse to its
doctrines and precepts. "The devils believe and tremble."

This faith, though it leads the soul not immediately to Christ, is yet
important; because it causes men to hear and to think, that their consciences may be reached, and that God may regenerate and sanctify them
through the truth. Thus they may be induced to embrace the gospel,
which before they both believed and hated; or to the appeals of which
they were indifferent. The faith of Agrippa is the faith which precedes
regeneration; and the faith of Paul is the effect of it. The faith of Paul
worked by love, and overcame the world. This is the faith of which
John speaks, as an effect of the new birth: "Whosoever believeth that
Jesus is the Christ, is born of God." *I should be pleased to know, whether
Mr. C. ascribes to faith any moral quality;* or whether he supposes
that men believe in Christ, just as they believe that there was such a man

as Cæsar, and as they believe what he relates of his wars. Is not faith the cordial reception of Christ as our Savior? I did not give up the question.

I have offered a considerable number of arguments, to which my friend has attempted no reply. He has pursued his usual course. He says they are *irrelevant*. This is the easiest way in the world to answer arguments. If a man finds them unanswerable, he can say they are all irrelevant! To prove that in conversion and sanctification there is an agency of the Spirit, distinct from the Word, I quoted such passages as the following: " I will pour out my Spirit upon thy seed." "A new heart also will I give you, and a new spirit will I put within you." " I will give them one heart and one mind," &c. They are all irrelevant, says the gentleman. Such is his answer; though every one can see that they bear directly and most conclusively on the point at issue; for they teach in the clearest manner, that men repent and believe, because God sheds upon them his Holy Spirit.

My time is so nearly out, that I will not now introduce another argument.—[*Time expired.*

Wednesday, Nov. 29—11 o'clock, A. M.
[MR. CAMPBELL'S NINTH ADDRESS.]

MR. PRESIDENT—More than half the time occupied by my friend has been devoted to the consideration of passages of Scripture more or less animadverted on before. He deems them of great importance, and I am willing that he should think so. But as I deem them no way relevant to our position in the question, I shall hasten, in the first place, to state some other arguments; reserving for farther notice of these to circumstances. His remarks on spiritual operations, when further explained, may, perhaps, be comprehended. As yet, however, to me they are not comprehensible. I will answer his interrogations when they are more definitely set forth. Let him explain his *distinct* power. I cannot comprehend his theory of an abstract power. If he say superadded power, I wish to know of what character it is: physical or moral? I can readily conceive of various means being employed to secure the attention of persons to impress the subject on the mind, and of means used providentially to remove obstructions; but to talk of superadded power, of a distinct power, without any definition of the nature and character of it, seems not in the least to enlighten us. If I see a man take an axe and fell a tree, I call the axe the instrument, and I say, whatever power he puts forth in felling the tree is put forth through the axe. Not one chip is removed without it. This illustrates so much of the subject as pertains to *instrumentality*. I am at a loss to understand his additional power. I see but the man and the axe, and the tree falls. That the Spirit *operates* through the instrumentality of the Word I doubt not; but if asked to explain the *modus operandi*, I confess my inability. The fact of the power I admit, but the *how* it works I presume not to comprehend. If Mr. Rice will set it forth, I will cheerfully avow my assent or dissent, as the case may be; for I keep no secrets on that subject, or any other, connected with man's salvation. I candidly consider, that the gentleman has, however, conceded the real issue. He has got a regeneration without true faith, but now seems to have need of a pretended faith, or some sort of an indescribable, partial, imperfect faith as a prerequisite. He has a faith before, and a faith after regeneration. But this seems not to meet the case, nor relieve him from the dilemma. His indefinable, previous faith is just no faith at all; and, therefore, his true doctrine is regeneration without faith, and consequently without any human instrumentality. A faith that does not renew the heart, is a species of infidelity. His infant and adult, his pagan and idiot, regeneration are therefore all of one sort; all special miracles without any instrumentality whatever. He has, indeed, as before shown, admitted my fourth argument; and, according to it, as regeneration is in one case, it is in all cases. Whatever means are necessary to produce one ear of corn, are necessary to the production of every other ear of corn. So in all well regulated states, whatever is necessary to constitute one foreigner a citizen, is necessary to the naturalization of every other foreigner. We shall, then, till otherwise informed, regard this case as settled.

On my side of this question, I have only to prove that the seed is essential to the fruit, and on this, I presume, amplification is not called for. When, however, Mr. Rice again brings up this same view, I may amplify still farther. Till then, I will not spend time in expatiating on principles so well established, so universally admitted. Neither need I dwell upon the peculiar arrangement of the Scriptures, on the principle submitted at the close of my last address. It is true, that I intend it to be the basis of a branch of the evidence adduced, in confirmation of the views given. Our feelings are properly called our active powers. Now, in religion, they are properly dependent on our faith—no true faith, no true feeling. That again depends not merely upon the testimony being good and valid, but upon our appreciation of it. No one can believe testimony which he does not understand; hence, if either the testimony of God, or the facts contained in the Bible, have any thing to do with renewing or purifying the heart, there can be no renewal without a previous belief.

But I hasten to state another argument, which shall obtain the rank of my tenth argument, in proof of the proposition. It is expressed in the following words:

X. *Whatever influence is ascribed to the Word of God in the sacred Scriptures, is also ascribed to the Spirit of God.* Or in other words, what the Spirit of God is at one time, and in one place, said to do, is at some other time or in some other place, ascribed to the Word of God. Hence I argue that they do not operate separately, but in all cases conjointly. We shall give an induction of a number of cases in exemplification of the fact. Are we said to be *enlightened* by the Spirit of God? We are told in another place, " The commandment of the Lord is pure, enlightening the eyes." Again, " The entrance of thy word giveth light, and makes the simple wise." Are we said to be converted by the Spirit of God? we hear the prophet David say, "The law of the Lord is perfect, converting the soul." Are we said to be sanctified through the Spirit of God? we hear our Lord praying to his Father, " Sanctify them through thy truth, thy Word is the truth." Are we said to be quickened by the Spirit of God? the same is ascribed to the Word of God. David says, " Thy Word, O Lord, hath quickened me,"—" Stay me with thy precepts, thy statutes quicken me." This is one of the strongest expressions.

In other forms of speech, the same effects and influence are ascribed to both. Paul, in one context, says, " Be filled with the Spirit;" and when again speaking of the same subject, in another, he says, " Let the Word of Christ dwell in you richly." In both cases the precepts are to be fulfilled in the same way, " teaching and admonishing one another in psalms and hymns and spiritual songs, making melody in your hearts to the Lord." " The Spirit," says Paul to Timothy, " speaketh expressly that in the latter day some shall depart from the faith." Again, "Know ye, in the last days perilous times shall come." Again, Paul says he has sanctified the church and cleansed it with " a bath of water and the Word." In another instance he says, he hath saved us " with the washing of regeneration and renewal of the Holy Spirit." Are we said to be " born of the Spirit?" we are also said to be born again, or " regenerated by the Word of God." I might trace this matter much further, but I presume, as we have touched upon the most important items, we have found such an induction as will satisfy the most scrupulous. Unless questioned, I shall then affirm it as a conclusion fairly drawn, that whatever effects or influences connected with conversion and sanctification are, in one portion of Scripture, assigned to the Word, are ascribed also to the Spirit; and so interchangeably throughont both Testaments. Whence we conclude, that the Spirit and Word of God are not separate and distinct kinds of power—the one superadded to the other, but both acting conjointly and simultaneously in the work of sanctification and salvation.

As Mr. Rice would seem to argue for two substantive powers, essentially distinct from each other, I do hope he will be at pains to explain to us the peculiar discriminating characteristics or attributes of each.

XI. My eleventh argument is deduced from the important fact, that resisting the Word of God, and resisting the Spirit of God, are shown to be the same thing, by very clear and explicit testimonies: such as Stephen, the proto-martyr, when filled with the Holy Spirit, and, indeed, speaking as the Holy Spirit gave him utterance, in the presence of the sanhedrim, said, " You uncircumcised in heart and ears, as your fathers did, so do you. *You do always resist the Holy Spirit.*" What proof does he alledge? He adds, " As your fathers did, so do you," (resist.) " Which of the prophets did they not persecute?" This, then, is his proof. In persecuting the prophets, they resisted the Holy Spirit; because the words spoken by the prophets, were suggested by the Spirit. We are said to resist a person, when we resist his word. When, then, any one resists the words of the prophets or the apostles, he is said by inspired men *to resist* the Holy Spirit. This important fact should be more frequently insisted on than it is. Men should be taught, that in resisting the words spoken by apostles and prophets, they are, in truth, resisting the Holy Spirit, by whom they uttered those words. May we not, then, consistently say, with Stephen, that when men resist the prophets and apostles in their writings, and will not submit to their teachings, they are resisting the Holy Spirit? This being admitted, follows it not again, that the Spirit of God operates through the truth; and that we are not to suppose that in conversion and sanctification, they do not act separately and distinctly from each other?

A still more impressive instance of this kind, we find in the book of Nehemiah. In his admirable prayer, preserved in the ninth chapter, he has two very remarkable expressions; one in the 20th and one in the 29th verse. In the former, when speaking of the instructions given the Jews by Moses, he said, " Thou gavest also thy good Spirit to instruct them;" and in the latter, he says, " Many years didst thou forbear them, and testifiedst against them by thy SPIRIT in thy prophets, yet would they not hear." Here, then, we are taught that God, by his Spirit in Moses, instructed the Jews by his good Spirit, and that in testifying to them by the prophets, God was testifying to them by his Holy Spirit. We are, then, still more fully confirmed in the conclusion that the Spirit of God operates through his Word, and only through his Word, in conversion and sanctification; and that the Word and Spirit of God, in those spiritual and moral changes and influences of which we now speak, are never to be regarded as operating apart; that whatever is done by the Word of God, is done by the Spirit of God; and whatever is done by the Spirit, is done through the Truth—and certainly he can through that instrument operate most powerfully on the spirit of man, as all christians experience, and the saints of all time exhibit.

Notwithstanding the pains taken in my opening speech on this subjec, to indicate the different offices assigned to the Father, and the Son, and the Holy Spirit, in the work of salvation, it seems, from some of the quotations offered by Mr. Rice, that he indiscriminately assigns to any one of them the work peculiarly and exclusively assigned to another. Seeing this so often done by others, and presuming that it might occur here, I remonstrated against it as both illogical and unscriptural. How often is the passage, Matt. xvi. 17, "Flesh and blood hath not revealed this to you, Peter, but my Father, who is in heaven," quoted, with a special reference to the work of the Holy Spirit. The system-makers and system-mongers, almost to a man, press this passage into their service. They prove by it a special revelation to Peter by the Holy Spirit: to all of which I have no objection whatever, so far as either the possibility or practicability of making original suggestions to Peter, on this or any other subject, is concerned. But I plead for the proper application and interpretation of the Scriptures, much more than for the particular import of a single text, however important that text may be.

It was the *Father*, and not the *Spirit*, of whom Jesus here speaks. It was "*my Father who is in heaven,*" that revealed this fact to you, Peter, that I am the Son of God, and the Christ of God. The fact, as stated, too, is very plain. God spake out from heaven, after the Messiah's baptism, and revealed who he was. He also indicated him by the Spirit descending in the form of a dove, and lighting upon his head. This being done very publicly, and reported in Jerusalem, as we learn from John, chapter v., "Peter must have heard and believed," whether at the Jordan when it happened, or not. Thus it was that the Father revealed, and in person introduced, his Son. Peter, in common with some others, believed it.

I said in the commencement of this discussion, that I did not affirm nor deny as to any other operations of the Spirit, save in conversion and sanctification. What he may do in the way of suggestions or impressions, by direct communication of original ideas, or in bringing things to remembrance long since forgotten, I presume not to discuss. I believe he has exerted, and can exert, such influences. Nor do I say what influence he may exert, or cause to be exerted, in bringing men's minds to consider these matters; but I confine my reasonings and proofs to *conversion* and *sanctification*. I wish Mr. Rice, when he next quotes John iii. 5, would give us the predicate of "So is every one born of the Spirit." What means the word *so?*

XII. My twelfth argument is deduced from the fact—that God created nothing without his Word. "He said, let there be light, and there was light." "By faith," says Paul, "we know that the worlds were framed by the Word of God." All the details of the six days show that, "God

made all things by the Word of his power." Of course, then, we have
no idea of any new creation or regeneration without the Word of God.
Mr. Rice has taken it for granted, that God made man holy at first without his Word. But this is a mere assumption. It is an overwhelming
fact, that God does nothing in creation nor redemption without his Word.
His creative power has always been embodied in that sublime instrument.
Nay, it is the sword of the Spirit. Still, there was *through that Word*
an almighty power put forth, and still there is both in conversion and
sanctification God works mightily in the human heart by his Word.
The heart of the King's enemies are mightily broken by it. Hence, faith
comes by hearing, and hearing by the Word of God.

Indeed, there is much of this wisdom of God apparent in the fact that
he has chosen the term *Logos* to represent the author and founder of
the christian faith, in his antecedent state of existence. And hence,
John represents Jesus Christ himself as the *Word of God incarnate.*
" Now the *Word* was made flesh," or became flesh, " and dwelt amongst
us." This is a mysterious name. He had a name given him which no
one can comprehend. His name is the WORD OF GOD. Now, as Jesus
Christ was " once God manifest in Word," and now God manifest
in flesh, we have reason to regard *the Word of God* as an embodiment
of his wisdom and power. This, however, is spoken with a reference to
the gospel Word ; for Jesus Christ is both the wisdom and the *power* of
God, and so is his gospel ; because containing this development. It is
the wisdom and power of God unto salvation, to every one that believes it.

It was not, however, in creating light alone that God employed his
Word. Every work of creation is represented as the product of his
Word. He said, " Let there be a firmament in the midst of the waters,"
and it was so. Again, " Let the dry land appear," and it was so. " Let
the earth bring forth grass," and it was so. And last of all, " Let us
make man in our image, after our likeness, and let them have dominion.
So God created man." God, therefore, made man in his own image
by his Word, and he now restores him to that same image, by his Word
of power. Thus we have all the authority of the Bible with us in our
views of spiritual and divine influence. A spiritual, or moral, or creative
power, without the Word of God, is a phantom, a mere speculation. It
receives no countenance from the Bible.

The gentleman said something about false premises. It will come up
in its own time. If he would follow my argument in the usual way of
response, it would prevent many such assertions. These matters would
then come up in their proper place, as well as in their proper time.

The Lord has embodied his will in his Word. Now the will of God
is another form of his power. Divine volition is divine power. The
Word of God is the *fiat* of God. " *Let there be,*" is a mere volition
expressed. Indeed, we may go further, and say, that the Word of the
Lord, is the Lord himself. The word of a king, is the king himself, so
far as authority or power is considered. As the Lord Jesus is the Word
of God incarnate, so is his Word an embodiment of his power. For, as
Solomon says, " Where the word of a king is, there is power;" there is
the power of the king himself. The Word of God is, then, the actual
power of God. God is a consuming fire, and his " Word is as fire, and
as a hammer that breaketh the rock to pieces." It should not, therefore,
be thought strange, that the Word of God, and the Spirit of God, are
sometimes represented as equi-potent—as equivalent. Indeed, in all

those passages that represent the Word and Spirit of God as being the causes of the same effects, this equivalency is clearly implied. Hence, while Peter says, "By the Word of God the heavens were of old," Job says, "By his Spirit he has garnished the heavens."

Can any one imagine what power could have been superadded to the Word of God, that created light, that made the heavens and the earth, that made man upright or *holy*, as Mr. R. says! Let him explain what that power could have been, which was distinct from, and attached to, or that accompanied that *word* by which all things were created and made. Explain that *accompanying* power, and I will explain the *accompanying* spiritual or superadded power in the case of regeneration! You cannot break a man down by physical power. You cannot soften and subdue the heart, as you grind a rock to pieces. A superadded power beyond motive, is inconceivable to any mind accustomed to think accurately upon spiritual and mental operations. The heart of man is to be subdued, melted, purified from all its hatred of God and enmity, by *love ;* by developments of grace, and not by any conceivable influence of a different nature. His love is poured out into our hearts, says Paul, by the Holy Spirit that is given to us.

Men had better be careful how they speak of, and how they treat, the word of God. It will stand forever. Till the heavens pass away, not one word shall fail. Mountains, by the wasting hand of time, may crumble down to dust—oceans may recede from their ancient limits—the heavens and the earth may pass away—but God's word shall never, never pass away. It is God's mighty moral lever, by which he raises man from earth to heaven. It is his almighty, awful, sublime and gracious will, embodied in such a medium as can enter the secret chambers of the human heart and conscience, and there stand up for God, and confound the sinner in his presence. The love of God is all enveloped in it, and that is the great secret of its charm—the mystery of its power to save. It is love, and love alone, that can reconcile the heart of man to God. Now love is a matter of intelligence—a matter that is to be told, heard, believed, and received by faith. "The power of God to salvation," is the persuasive power of infinite and eternal love, and not the compulsive and subduing power of any force superadded to it. The promise of eternal life is itself a power of mighty magnitude. So are all the promises that enter into the christian hope. These are almighty impulses, when understood and believed, upon the veracity and faithfulness of God.

But there yet remains another argument, of the inductive kind, which adapts itself to all minds, which I may, in my next address, offer to your consideration. We shall have an examination of every case of conversion reported in the Bible history of the primitive church, down to the end of the inspired record. Meantime, I must attend to some texts of Scripture advanced by Mr. Rice, to show that repentance is the gift of God. But who denies it? He has quoted three texts upon this subject. Two of the three speak of the grant of repentance and remission of sins, in the sense of the gospel. And one of them, the last, speaks of one opposing the truth. They are the following: "He," the Messiah, "is exalted a Prince and a Savior, to grant repentance to Israel, and the forgiveness of sins ;"—a dispensation of mercy. The second is, "Then has God *also* granted unto the gentiles repentance unto life." He has also extended salvation to the gentiles upon the same principles of repentance given to the Jews. And, in the case of an opponent, says Paul, "Instruct him meekly;" that if he have not hardened himself against the truth, God may, peradventure, extend to him the advantage of repentance.—[*Time expired.*

Wednesday, Nov. 29—11½ *o'clock, A. M.*
[MR. RICE'S NINTH REPLY.]

MR. PRESIDENT—I was very much gratified to hear the illustration of the work of the Spirit introduced by the gentleman at the commence-ment of his last argument. It is this: An individual takes an axe and cuts down a tree. All the power he exerts is through the axe. Now I wish to know, whether the man does not, at the time he is cutting the tree, put forth power? Is this not the fact? Then if the illustration be appropriate, it follows, that at the time when a man is converted, the Spirit of God must put forth power in some form—by some direct act; and that is precisely what my friend denies. For he contends, as I proved in my last speech, that before immersion no other influence is ex-erted on the mind, but that of the Word. To make the illustration suit his doctrine, the axe must cut the tree till it is almost ready to fall, and then the man must take hold of it, and complete the work! I think I can give a much more correct and striking illustration of his doctrine, than the one he has given. A certain man made and tempered the axe; the axe cut the tree; and therefore the maker of the axe might be said to have cut it. So the Spirit of God dictated and confirmed the Word; the Word converts men; and in this sense the Spirit converts them. Just as the man who made and tempered the axe might be said to do what the axe does, so the Spirit who dictated and confirmed the Word, may be said to do what the Word does. Or, a certain man made a gun; and the gun, in the hands of some other person, shot a man. Then the maker of the gun is chargeable with having killed the person who was shot with it! These illustrations are precisely in point; and if my friend can gain any thing to his cause by them he shall be welcome to them. But in the cutting of the tree there must be an agency distinct from the axe, which is the instrument. The man who employs the axe as the instrument, must, at the time, put forth power; or the instrument can accomplish ab-solutely nothing. Now the question before us is, whether conversion is effected *by the truth alone;* or whether the Spirit puts forth its power in addition to the influence of the Word? The gentleman's illustration proves our doctrine conclusively.

I have not admitted, nor will I admit, that in regeneration or conver-sion, God's mode of proceeding is, in all cases, the same. The Bible does not teach, that God always produces this change by the same instru-mentality. Mr. C. has not produced a passage which sustains his asser-tion. I have said, and I repeat it, where God has not limited himself, no man dares attempt to limit him. Ordinarily he works by means; but he has not said, that he will never work without means. When his people were journeying in the wilderness, where food could not be procured by means, h? gave them manna for food; and if he fed the bodies of the children of Israel without means, may he not save the souls of infants without means?

There is not a text in the whole Bible which says, that the Lord *can-not* sanctify the heart without the intervention of the Word. Nor is there one which says, he *will not.* Yet my friend has ventured to say, that he *will not,* and that he *cannot!* In his Christianity Restored he says, if all the reasons and arguments by which men can be converted,

3 P 2

are contained in the Old and New Testaments, the power of the Holy
Spirit is *spent*—that he will not, and that he cannot do more. The Bible says neither one nor the other. And if it be true, either that he cannot, or that he will not, exert a sanctifying agency in any case without
the truth, all infants must go to perdition. The argument is one that cannot be answered.

The gentleman has repeatedly contradicted himself, since this subject
has been before us. You will remember, that on the first day of this discussion, he told us, that nothing more is necessary to secure the salvation
of infants, than the atonement of Christ. I replied, that the atonement
cannot change the heart. On yesterday he told us, that depravity was
seated in the body, not in the mind, and therefore infants need no change
to fit them for heaven, but the separation of the soul from the body. Now
he seems to have it in the mind. So he is still involved in the old difficulty, and has left infants and idiots without the possibility of being
saved !

The gentleman excuses himself for having been so constantly involved in
the mists of metaphysics, by telling you, that he is following me. Did you
hear his first speech ? It was one of the most metaphysical discourses I
ever heard. There was scarcely a passage of Scripture in it. Now he
is following me ! I did not introduce these philosophical or unphilosophical speculations. He introduced them, and I followed him partially.
On this, as on all other religious subjects, I am perfectly satisfied with
the plain instructions of the Bible—a book which I love infinitely more
than his philosophy.

In his last speech he gave us what he considers the philosophy of the
Bible concerning conversion and sanctification. It is this : first, fact—
then testimony—then faith—then feeling—then action. Now, there is a
very serious difficulty about this philosophy. For when a fact is proved,
and the people are constrained to believe it true, their feelings are of different and even opposite characters. One approves, another disapproves ; one
loves, another hates. So it is in regard to the Bible. All men by nature
are opposed to it. When convinced that it is a revelation from God, and
informed concerning its contents, they do not approve and embrace them ;
nor will they, until their hearts are renewed. And if ever they are to be
induced to love God, the Spirit must so purify their hearts, that they will
no longer love darkness more than light ; that they will see the odiousness of sin, the beauty of holiness, and the glory of the divine perfections.
There must be a radical change ; for no human being ever loved a moral
character, which is the opposite of his own. This difficulty completely
overturns all the gentleman's philosophy. It will answer him no purpose. His fact, his testimony, his faith, may all exist, and yet the right
kind of *feeling*—the great thing, after all, may be wanting,

I will now briefly reply to his arguments drawn from the Scriptures.
He says, whatever influence is ascribed to the Spirit, in the Bible, is also
ascribed to the Word. If the Spirit enlightens, the Word also enlightens :
if the Spirit converts, the Word converts. By this argument he expects
to prove, that when the Scriptures speak of the operations of the Spirit,
the written Word is meant—that when the Word operates on the heart,
the Spirit is said to operate. By this mode of reasoning I could establish
some very singular propositions. I could prove, that, when the Lord
Jesus opened the eyes of the blind man, the light caused him to see.
What would you think, if I should thence infer, that he opened his eyes

by means of light?! It is true, the psalmist says, " The entrance of thy Word giveth light;" but if my eyes are diseased, the light cannot heal them. This is the work of the great Physician. When he put forth his power and healed the eyes of the blind man, then the light broke in, and he could see. In one sense it is true, that the light caused him to see. In another and most important sense, the Savior, and not the light, gave him vision. There was a divine power exerted, which was entirely distinct from the light. So in one sense it is true, that the Word of God causes the spiritually blind to see; but in another and most important sense, the Holy Spirit opens their eyes, effects their conversion.

In the Acts of the Apostles, (ch. xxvi.) it is said, that Paul was sent *to open* the eyes of the blind. Now, by adopting the logic of Mr. Campbell, I could prove by this passage, that whatever influence is ascribed to the Word, is ascribed also to Paul; and from this fact I would reach the conclusion that in conversion and sanctification the Spirit operates only through *human instrumentality!* I could also prove conclusively, that, if conversion is ascribed to the Spirit, it is also ascribed to Paul and other preachers of the gospel; for James the apostle says—" Brethren, if any of you do err from the truth, and one *convert* him, let him know, that he which CONVERTETH the sinner from the error of his way, shall save a soul from death, &c. Now does the Spirit of God convert sinners? So does Paul—so do other preachers. Therefore, (and the conclusion is precisely as legitimate as that by which the gentleman proved that the Spirit operates only through the truth)—therefore, in conversion and sanctification the Spirit never operates, except through a preacher. Such is the reasoning of my worthy friend.

The truth is, that conversion and sanctification are commonly effected by three distinct agencies: the agency of the Word; the agency of the man who presents it, and the agency of the Spirit, which is taught as distinctly as the others, and is represented as more important—causing men to receive the truth in the love of it, and to obey it. I believe in all the three. God does not confine the operations of his grace in converting men to the instrumentality of the living preacher. My friend will agree, that some have been converted by reading the Word, without a preacher. Sometimes all the three are employed—the preacher, the Word, and the Spirit; sometimes only two; and sometimes only one, as in the case of infants, where it is impossible that either the Word or the ministry can be employed.

The fact that the Word is said to convert men, does not prove that the Spirit does not sanctify infants without the Word; nor that conversion is ever effected simply by the influence of the Word. I might say with truth, that the blowing of the rams' horns prostrated the walls of Jericho; for they would not have fallen, if the horns had not been blown. But it would be folly to say, that the blowing of the horns was the power by which alone they were made to fall. Christ opened the eyes of the man born blind, by the use of spittle and clay: but if I were to affirm, that his eyes were opened *only* by spittle and clay, I should speak most unwisely. So the gentleman's argument will not bear one moment's careful examination. It is absolutely worthless.

Mr. C. told us, a few days ago, that according to a correct principle of language, the definition of a word, if substituted for it, will make good sense. Now let us try his doctrine by this principle. He says, that when the agency of the Spirit is spoken of, the Word is meant. Let us try it—" He saved us by the washing of regeneration and the renewing of his *Word*, which he shed on us abundantly," &c.! Now, did the apostle mean, that he shed his *Word* on men abundantly through Jesus Christ? Again—" I will pour out *my Word* upon your seed!" Is this the idea the prophet intended to convey? Again—" I will take away the stony heart out of your flesh." That is, I will reason, talk, argue with you! Is this the meaning of the prophet? The fact is, there are passages of Scripture which teach, that conversion and sanctification are effected by the instrumentality of the Word; but not by the Word *only*. There are others that recognize the agency of man; but not his agency *only*. The agency of the Spirit is the only agency which is declared to be absolutely necessary in all cases. The ministry is sometimes necessary, and so is the Word; because God has appointed these as the ordinary means through which the blessings of his salvation shall be conveyed to men. But neither of these is always necessary. The agency of the Spirit is absolutely essential in all cases; because, as all men and all infants are " born of the flesh," and are, therefore, carnal; so all must be born of the Spirit.

Great errors, the gentleman seems to think, grow out of *systems* of theology; and he would have you believe, that he is quite opposed to system-making. Do you see that book? [Pointing to the CHRISTIAN SYSTEM.] Who is the author of it? My friend. If he is not a system-maker, he has not told the truth; for he calls this book " The Christian System," and he says those who make systems, are system-makers. I think he is in very good company; but I hope he does not claim the exclusive privilege of making systems. Certainly he should allow others to make systems, at least occasionally. " Christianity Restored" was his first system, and the " Christian System" his second. If he can make two systems, he should, at least, permit us to make one.

Another argument urged by Mr. C. is, that God never made any thing *without a word;* and he tells us that God created the world by a word. But I assert that he never created any thing only by a word. If we were to admit, that in the work of creation he did literally speak words, this would only prove, that when he spoke he exerted Almighty power to produce the result. So the word of God is used ordinarily in conversion. But there is also a divine influence exerted on the heart, in addition to the Word, and distinct from it.

But what is the truth in regard to creation by words? The inspired writers, to express most strikingly the infinite ease with which God created all things, represented him as speaking, and it was done—as commanding, and it stood fast. He had but to speak, and the universe sprang into being at his bidding! But will the gentleman say, that he created all things *by words and arguments?* Has he not told us that words and arguments could only exert a moral power? Did God create the soul of man by arguments? He is confounding things as dissimilar as light and darkness. What connection is there between creation and argument? If he will prove that God created man by argument and motive, I will admit, that the same influence may renew him in the image of God. Christ raised Lazarus from the dead by words, but not by words *only*. When he said " Lazarus, come forth," he exerted an omnipotent power.

In the original creation of man, God exerted immediate power. He created nothing by words. So in creating man anew, in restoring his divine image to his soul, there is an agency of the Spirit, in addition to the Word, and distinct from it. How absurd, then, the gentleman's argument from the works of creation, to prove, that in conversion and sanctification the Spirit operates on the mind simply by words and motives! Strange logic, indeed!

My friend will alarm us, if he cannot convince us. He says, men had better take care how they trifle with the word of God. And I would say, that he had better take care how he speaks of the Holy Spirit. In the Millenial Harbinger, (vol. ii. p. 211,) he uses this language: "Some Holy Ghost is the soul of every popular sermon, and the essential point in every evangelical creed." I must confess I was shocked when I cast my eye on this sentence. I know the gentleman does not admire the English word Ghost, but he is perfectly aware that these words are used as the name of the third person in the adorable Trinity. I have heard similar language from men less intelligent, but I could not have supposed that he would allow himself to utter, or to write, such an expression. Since he has done so, I cannot help thinking that the warning he has given, does not come well from him. I have never heard any professor of religion speak of the word of God as he has spoken of the Holy Spirit.

I will now proceed to offer some additional arguments against the doctrine taught by Mr. Campbell. The first that I will offer is this: his doctrine makes it both useless and improper to pray for the conversion of men. I know, he will not deny, that it is the duty and the privilege of christians to pray, that God would convert sinners; for we have both precept and example authorizing and requiring it. Paul said concerning himself—"My heart's desire and prayer to God for Israel is, that they might be saved;" Rom. x. 1. And he directed, that "supplications, prayers, intercessions, and giving of thanks, be made for all men;" 1 Tim. ii. 1. But whilst the duty is perfectly clear, if we regard either precept or precedent, or both, the doctrine of Mr. C. makes it wholly unnecessary, if not improper. This objection did not originate with me, or perhaps it might be supposed to be founded in a misconception of his views. It has occurred to his own friends and followers, as a very serious difficulty. I will read part of a letter written to him by a gentleman who is a member of his church, and published in the *Millenial Harbinger*, (vol. ii. p. 469,) in which the objection is strongly stated.

"Without any further preface or apology, I will come at once to the object I had in addressing you at this time, and that is, to ask your opinion whether it be lawful, according to the will of God as revealed to us, to pray for our unconverted friends—that is, to ask God to convert them to the christian religion? If it be true, as you affirm, (and which I am not prepared to controvert,) that the righteousness of a christian is a righteousness by faith in Jesus as the Messiah; that that faith comes alone by hearing or reading the testimony concerning Jesus; and that we have no right to expect any influence superinducing the mind to faith, or even causing the sinner to examine this testimony, or place himself in circumstances for the light of divine truth to shine upon his mind; I say, upon the supposition that these things are so, what right has any one to expect that God will answer his prayers in the behalf of his unconverted friends? Ever since I have felt the importance of divine things, I have felt the most anxious solicitude for many of my relatives and friends who on their part manifested the greatest indifference to these matters, and have often tried to pray for them too, that God would cause them to submit themselves to Jesus as the only Savior of sinners: but whether these prayers were in accordance to the word of our Divine Master, I confess I am somewhat at a loss to say. When we pray, we are told to pray in faith; and in order that we may pray

in faith, as I understand, we should pray for such things as our Heavenly
Father has authorized us to expect at his hands, and no other. Now if the
Divine Being exercises no other influence over the minds of men than that
influence which is derived to them through the words he has spoken to men,
and we cannot prevail upon wicked men to give attention to those words,
the question is, are we authorized to expect that God will answer our requests in the behalf of such an one? Here is my difficulty, and it has long
been a difficulty with me; and I find it is no less so with many of my friends
and your friends. If you have opportunity to write me a private letter on
this subject, I will esteem it as a singular favor: or if you consider the subject of enough importance, you can, if you please, furnish us an essay upon
it through the Harbinger. Very affectionately,   WILL. Z. THOMSON."

The difficulty, it appears, had presented itself, not to the mind of some
one individual of a speculative character, but to many of Mr. C.'s friends,
who were familiar with his writings. In view of his denial of the agency
of the Spirit in conversion, they ask, whether it is right that they should
pray to God to convert their unbelieving friends, and whether they have
any right to expect God to answer such prayers? In his reply to this
letter Mr. C. gave not the slightest intimation that the writer had misconceived his views of the agency of the Spirit; and yet he states them
precisely as I have stated them.

Now if this doctrine be true, I ask emphatically, where is the propriety of praying for the unconverted? Have we a promise from God, that
he will answer such prayers? If this doctrine be true, we have not; for
the Spirit has dictated and confirmed the Word of Truth, and no influence will or can be exerted, in addition to the Word, to cause the wicked
to turn to God. If, then, no special divine influence is promised, or can
be exerted to cause men to repent and believe, why should we pray for
it? And how can we pray in faith?

This I regard as a most important matter; for it is as truly a part of
the plan of Infinite Wisdom to convert men in answer to prayer, as by
the instrumentality of the preached gospel. It is, moreover, one of the
consolations of many an afflicted father and mother, that they can pray
in faith for the conversion of their children, when far away, exposed to
the temptations and unhallowed influences of a wicked world. Could
you approach their closet, where they have retired to commune with
God, and to pour the desires and the sorrows of their hearts into his ear;
you might hear them plead with an irresistible eloquence, that by his
Holy Spirit he would convince their children of sin, of righteousness and
of judgment; that he would turn their feet from the paths of folly and sin
unto his testimonies. How many ten thousand such prayers are incessantly ascending from the hearts of God's faithful children for those who
are dear to them, and for a sin-ruined world! But if this doctrine be true,
those prayers are all in vain. Not one of them ever was, or ever can be
heard. We must bid the weeping father and mother, and the heart-broken
wife, to pray no more for those whose salvation is almost as dear to them
as their own. Then let all prayers for the unconverted cease. Let it be
known, that God has done for them all he will do, or can do; and if they
are not converted by reading or hearing the Word, they must perish! If
this doctrine be true, why did the apostles give themselves to *prayer* and
the preaching of the Word? Why did Paul pray, that Israel might be
saved? Why should we pray for the success of the gospel? Shall we
bow down and implore God to do what we believe he never will do?

The difficulty stops not here. It makes prayer for believers equally vain—at least so far as regards their sanctification. For although the gentleman says, the Spirit is poured out on those who are immersed; it does not exert a sanctifying influence. In the proposition under discussion the ground is taken, that in sanctification, as well as in conversion, the Spirit operates *only* through the truth. Why, then, should christians pray for themselves and for each other, that they may be sanctified? Paul prayed for the Philippian christians, because he was confident, that he who had begun a good work in them, would perform it until the day of Jesus Christ; Philip. i. 6. He prayed for the Ephesians, that they might be strengthened with might by his Spirit in the inner man. The apostles once prayed to the Savior, "Lord, increase our faith." Did they desire an additional revelation or other miracles? Or did they desire, that he would take away the cause of their unbelief—their depravity? A certain man came and desired the Savior to heal his son. He asked him, Believest thou that I can do this? He answered, with tears, "Lord, I believe; help thou mine unbelief." He also said to Peter, on a certain occasion—"Simon, Satan hath desired to have thee, that he may sift thee as wheat; but I have prayed for thee, that thy faith fail not." Here we have examples of prayers offered, for a divine influence to strengthen faith and to sanctify the heart.

I turn your attention to one more example of this kind. David, under a deep sense of the corruption of his heart, prayed—"Create in me a clean heart, O God, and renew a right spirit within me;" Ps. li. 10. Now, I ask, would not every unprejudiced mind understand the Psalmist to pray, that God would exert a purifying influence on his heart? Did he believe, that all the converting and sanctifying power of the Spirit is in the Word? Multitudes of similar passages are found in the Scriptures. I have brought forward several where prayer was offered and answered for a supernatural influence to be exerted on the hearts of the wicked. In a word, the Scriptures teach with perfect clearness, from Genesis to Revelation, that the Spirit of God can, and does exert a controling, converting, enlightening, and sanctifying influence on the hearts of men, not by words and arguments simply, but more powerful and efficacious.—[*Time expired.*

Wednesday, Nov. 29—12 *o'clock, M.*
[MR. CAMPBELL'S TENTH ADDRESS.]

Mr. President—I am now so well acquainted with my friend, Mr. R., as to know when he feels himself grievously pressed and oppressed. He has not responded to any of those all-important questions and difficulties, propounded to him as growing out of his assumptions. What light has been thrown upon the subject of that power, abstract and superadded, of which he speaks so much? Has he not passed the matter in perfect silence? May I not, with propriety, say, it is an indescribable power— wholly unintelligible—since the gentleman himself can give no account of it? I repeat once more, that whenever the gentleman describes his metaphysical abstract power, superadded to the Word, I will affirm, or deny, in the most definite manner. I believe in a substantive influence of the Spirit of God through the truth, upon the conscience, the understanding and the affections.

He appears to approve of the figure of the wood-chopper and his axe. But in his remarks, he seems to have forgotten, that on his theory, the wood-chopper has to cut the tree down without the axe. Or, if he should use the axe in any case at all, he must superadd some power without the

axe, beyond the axe, and wholly extra its instrumentality!! Figures are
not to be used for any other purpose than they are proposed. I do not
make this one represent the Word of God in any other particular, than its
mere instrumentality. He had no time to explain how his infant is cut
off the stock of depravity, without one stroke of the axe. But he had time
to hold up this book [The Christian System,] as my confession of faith.
He ought, in these precious moments, to avoid things extraneous, and refer
that subject to the creed-question. I shall then show who makes creeds,
and binds them, as heavy burdens, upon men's shoulders.

His dissertation upon power is inapplicable to the subject before us. I
might, on his own principles, ask him why he prays for the salvation of
any person, seeing he believes and teaches, that the number of the elect is
so definite and fixed, that it can neither be increased nor diminished one
single individual!! Is that not, by his own showing, labor in vain? The
means and the end are both so foreordained, that without the one, the other
cannot be, either in salvation or condemnation. Hence, all the powers of
the universe cannot add one to either the saved, or the condemned.

Fellow-citizens, from all the premises before my mind, I conclude, that
the Spirit of Truth—that omnipresent, animating Spirit of our God—
whose sword or instrument this book is, is always present in the work of
conversion, and through this truth changes the sinner's affections, and
draws out his soul to God. It is, therefore, doing us an act of the greatest
injustice, to represent us as comparing the Bible to the writings of any
dead or absent man, in this point of comparison. In some points of view,
all books are alike; but in other points of view, they are exceedingly dissimilar. In comparison of all other books, the Bible is superlatively a
book *sui generis.* Its author not only ever lives, but is ever present in it,
and with it, *operating through it, by it,* and *with it,* upon saints and sinners. The gentleman talks upon themes he does not comprehend. Abstract spiritual operations in nature, and in redemption, are wholly beyond
his ken. Were he to speak to the day of eternity, he cannot communicate one distinct idea on the subject.

The singular course of my opponent has constrained me to quote, and
comment on numerous passages of Scripture, no way connected with our
topics of discussion. But he will have it so; and, therefore, we must occasionally launch into matters somewhat remote and recondite. He relies much upon such passages as—"The wind bloweth where it listeth;
and thou hearest the sound thereof, but canst not tell whence it cometh, or
whither it goeth. So is every one that is born of the Spirit." He seems
to glory in the mystery of his regeneration, because he cannot explain it.
His main argument is—it is a mystery, and we cannot understand it;
therefore, my doctrine is true! I asked him to explain the predicate of
the last proposition. The words were—"*So is every one that is born
of the Spirit.*" But has he done it? No. He cannot, I predict, explain
the word *so.* The subject of the proposition is,—*Every one that is
born of the Spirit*—is compared to what? So *what?* That is the
question he cannot answer!! He has mistaken the point of comparison.
To him, indeed, it is a mystery. I call for the predicate of the proposition; and then we shall canvass the whole matter.

When I sat down, I was expatiating on some other of my respondent's
proof-texts—the passages concerning the grant of repentance to Jews and
gentiles, by him that is exalted a *Prince* and a *Savior.* I shall illustrate
the view, which I partially expressed at the close of my last address.

Suppose the people of any country had all been destitute of the right of suffrage—living under an absolute despotism, in consequence of some great political disaster. Meantime, some great prince interposes in their behalf, invades the country, overcomes the tyrant, and, when in authority over the people, grants to the whole state the right of suffrage—would it be just to say, that he had, by some special, personal, direct approach to every man, constrained, or specially induced him to go to the polls and vote? That, indeed, he might do. But the question is, not whether he might, or might not do so, but whether the language imports that he does so! True, Jesus Christ has been exalted a PRINCE and a SAVIOR, to grant to Israel, and afterwards to the gentiles, repentance unto life and remission of sins. Does that mean he makes a personal appeal to every one, or to any one in particular?—or, that he has opened a way in which all, if they please, may obtain the benefits of repentance, and remission of sins? I do not say, that other scriptures may teach this doctrine. But the question is—do the passages Mr. Rice has quoted, prove that point at all? I affirm the clear conviction they do not. But let every man judge for himself. It is one thing indeed to confer a right upon a people; but whether they shall use it, is quite another question. An opponent may so oppose the truth, as to make it questionable whether, on repentance, God would forgive him—whether God would grant him the benefits of repentance. Thus says Paul, in meekness instructing them that oppose themselves, if God peradventure might grant them repentance (the advantages of repentance,) to eternal life. I am not controverting the fact, but I am controverting the appositeness of the gentleman's quotations, and that extreme latitudinarianism, in which he indulges. To grant a right, and to compel to use it, are very different ideas. God confers the rights, and thus opens the way for our voluntary acceptance of them. We rejoice in the glorious fact, that God has granted repentance unto life to the whole gentile world. Philology peremptorily forbids any other interpretation of this passage. It is not to believing gentiles, or to a few gentiles, but in contrast with the Jews. They said, "Then hath God *also to the gentiles* granted repentance unto life." Repentance unto life is, then, bestowed on all the nations to which the gospel is preached; and whosoever will, may come and possess its advantages. To interpret this according to my opponent's scheme —that is, to make it respect a few individuals, specially called and constrained to come in, is to rob the gentile world of one of the richest charters ever expressed in human speech. I thank my God, that Jesus Christ has been exalted a "PRINCE and a SAVIOR," to grant repentance unto life, not unto Israel only, but TO THE GENTILES ALSO. Mr. Rice's freedom with this statute, robs us of our rights, for the sake of a speculative assumption.

As great injustice is done me by Mr. Rice, in sometimes changing this position of *only* in the proposition, I do not maintain that a person is converted by the Word only. I say that, "In conversion, &c., the Spirit operates only through the Word;" not that a person is converted by the Word only. The latter excludes the Spirit altogether, which is directly in contradiction of the ground assumed in my opening speech. We are only converted through the Word; only we are converted through the Word; and we are converted through the Word only, are three very different propositions. The gentleman ought to place the word *only* where it stands in the proposition.

The gentleman has again introduced the subject of infant damnation.

3 Q

I am sorry to spend time on such an ungracious theme; but as my reputation is somewhat involved in what was said yesterday, I must show that I have not misconstrued the doctrines preached, and interpretations of Scripture given on this subject, by the good Old Scotch Presbyterians. I am indeed pleased to see that Mr. Rice is ashamed of it, and has taxed his ingenuity to find a new way of expounding the elect infants of the creed. His interpretation is ingenious—apparently so, however, because it does not read elect *persons*, but elect *infants*.

All infants that die are elect infants! A happy conception truly! But a fair construction of the confession will not authorize it. I first heard the gloss last year. But neither the founders of Calvinism on the continent, nor the Westminster divines, so understood this matter, as my reading and recollection fully justify. I shall read a few passages on this subject; and first, one from Calvin's Institutes. I have both the Latin original and Calvin's own French translation of the passage. I wonder not that Calvin, to quote his own words, calls it, Decretum quidem horribile, fateor; which professor Norton renders as follows: "I ask again, how it has come to pass, that the fall of Adam has involved so many nations with their infant children in eternal death, and this without remedy, but because such was the will of God? It is a dreadful decree, I confess." Knowing that Allen has translated it, softening it down, I give the following from other authorities:

[Translated from the Latin.]—"I ask, again, whence has it happened, that the fall of Adam has involved so many nations together with their infant children in eternal death without remedy, unless that it has so pleased God?—A horrible decree indeed, I confess."

[From the French.]—"I ask them again, whence it has come to pass, that the fall of Adam has involved with him so many nations with their infants, unless that it has thus pleased God?—I confess, that this decree ought to shock us."

But Calvin, besides this passage quoted from his Institutes, (lib. 3, c. 23, § 7,) in speaking of the errors of Servetus, says: "In the meantime, certain salvation is said [by Servetus] to await all at the final judgment, exept those who have brought upon themselves the punishment of eternal death, by their personal sins; (*propriis sceleribus;*) from which it is also inferred that all who are taken from life while INFANTS AND YOUNG CHILDREN, are exempt from eternal death, although they are elsewhere called accursed," Tract. Theo. Refut. Error Mich. Serveti. This was one of Servetus's errors, according to Calvin. Servetus would have all infants saved that died; but Calvin thought this a great error, because there were of these same infants called accursed. Augustine, in condemning the doctrine of Pelagius, says, "We affirm that they (infants) will not be saved and have eternal life, except they be baptized in Christ;" and much more to the same effect.

Turretin, the chief of Calvinistic writers, teaches the same doctrine in the clearest manner. He is of high authority at Princeton, and has stood on my shelf for thirty years. He says:

"The ancient Pelagians, who having followed as their master Pelagius the Briton, denied original sin in all its parts, contending that the sin of Adam hurt nobody but himself, or if it should be said to have injured any body else, that it was through example or imitation, not by propagation. Not unlike them are the Remonstrants, who in their apology pronounced certain, whatever Augustine and others may have determined to the contrary, that God will appoint, and that he, on account of *original sin,* so called, with justice can appoint NO ETERNAL TORMENTS to INFANTS, of whatever lot or descent, dying without actual and personal sins; holding that their opinion, viz. that any infants will be appointed to *eternal torments* is opposed to the divine goodness and right reason; nay, that it is uncertain whether the preponderance is in favor of the absurdity or its cruelty."

Here, then, is an explicit declaration from a Calvinist of the highest authority, that God can, in justice, appoint infants to eternal torments. Indeed I can quote distinguished Calvinists in considerable numbers, in proof that infant damnation on account of original sin, was the doctrine of a portion of the Protestant Reformation, of the Synod of Dort, and of the Westminster Assembly. But I am sorry to have been compelled to bring up a doctrine of this sort on this occasion; and certainly would not, had Mr. Rice not compelled me to it. But when I undertake to prove any thing, I do prove it, and can prove it.

One man may be said to convert another, as Paul begat the Corinthians, through the gospel, and was spiritually their father. But Mr. Rice says, then they may be said to do all other things akin to conversion— quicken, save, &c. That is not a fair inference. It is so far fetched and so gross as not to entangle any one—no one can believe it. But it seems I committed a great sin in his eyes, in speaking of the *Holy Ghosts* of several systems—the alledged chimeras of modern theories. Be it understood, then, that I never use the word, "Holy Ghost," with disrespect; although I think the term ought to be changed into "*Holy Spirit.*" Time was, when it was a very proper term. I have shown, somewhere within the last seven years, that our Saxon forefathers used the word *ghost* as equivalent to our word *guest*, and properly enough called our spirits *guests*, while in our bodies—regarding the body as a house or tabernacle, and the spirit as a *guest* or *ghost*. I was, some years since, much struck with the fact, that we have not in the common English Bible, the word *Holy Ghost* in the Old Testament at all, but *Holy Spirit:* and, in the same version, we have Holy Ghost most frequently, though not exclusively, in the New. Tyndale, I presume, was the cause of this, in the New Testament; for in many points, nay, in most points, Tyndale was followed by James' translators. The question arose in my mind, why Tyndale did so, and the answer occurred in this way : the Spirit of God was promised in the Old Testament to be the *guest* of the christian church—that, as in a temple, it was to reside in it; hence, the Spirit of the Old Testament having become the guest of the New, Tyndale introduced Holy Ghost for the Holy Spirit of the previous age. With us, however, ghost has degenerated into the representative of a disembodied spirit, the spirit of a dead man. Hence, I think it is bad taste to call the living Spirit of the living God, a Holy Ghost, according to our modern usage.

While, then, the new theories of modern times about spiritual influence is, indeed, more ghostly than spiritual, they may, with more propriety than we, use the term Holy Ghost; and as all parties have not one theory, more than one faith, I see no more impropriety in speaking of *Holy Ghosts*, more than of two faiths, two Lords, two Spirits, two baptisms, which I believe are universally tolerated. Still if I am, by so doing, chargeable with disrespect for either the name or the persons that use it, I should not patronize it at all. For my own part I prefer, and almost universally use, the name *Holy Spirit.*

The theories of spiritual influence are as variable as the winds, and fires, and floods of the earth. With some it is the baptism of fire, with others it is a mighty rushing wind, and with some it is water. Some read " born of the Spirit, even born of the water"—thereby making water and Spirit identical. The sin against the Holy Spirit, as explained by our Savior, consists in *speaking against* the works of the Spirit, ascribing his miracles to satanic influence—a sin which cannot, in this his view, be committed now. It was not a sin of thought, a general action; but a sin of the *tongue*, accompanied with a cordial malice.

Mr. R. would make me almost, if not altogether, guilty of the sin and error of Manicheism, because of my remarks upon the law of sin in the fleshly members. I must now, according to him, have translated all sin from the mind into the flesh. Hence he quotes envy, and hatred, and pride, &c. as antagonizing with my views. And yet, while I give to the mind sinful views and desires, may I not ask him whence come envy, and pride, and hatred? Do they not generally come from the flesh? Do they not spring from our worldly and fleshly associations, from our carnal and temporal interests? The mind is enslaved to the body. Our intellectual powers are all placed under tribute to some fleshly and earthly objects. Hence hatred, variance, strife, emulation, fraud, &c. come almost exclusively from our competitions about securing so much of earth's and time's favors, as gratify our fleshly lusts and pleasures. Whence, then, come these sinful desires but from the flesh? Still I am very far from saying that sin is wholly and exclusively confined to the flesh. But all the elements of sin are there. Through " this body of sin and death," as Paul calls it, sin " works in our members to bring forth fruit unto death." The mind is, indeed, made to participate in all these fleshly lusts that war against our souls; " for the flesh lusteth against the Spirit, and the Spirit against the flesh, so that we cannot do the things that we would."

We must also revert to the word *holy.* I objected merely to his use of the word, and not to the word, nor the thing. He represented the heart as being made *holy* by an immediate *fiat.* God made man holy, as he created him. To-day he has added " not by the word only." Did I say, in my speech, *by the word only?* That is a wrong issue. His argument was, that God made man without a word. Mine was, that he did not. He has changed his position, and got up a new issue. I argue that God created nothing without a word. But it was so inapplicable! In his view, I presume it was, because fatal to his assumption. No one can form a single conception of naked power. It is bad philosophy to descant upon it, as well as bad theology.

Still, *holiness* is not of the nature of a distinct, separate, and substantive attribute, as wisdom, power, goodness. And yet it is not an attribute of God, as eternity, infinity, immutability; because it is relative to impurity. It is an attribute, or perfection, in contrast with sin and impurity. In classifying the Divine perfections, I usually distribute them into four classes; three which nature developes—wisdom, power, and goodness; three which the law developes—justice, truth, and holiness; three which the gospel developes—mercy, condescension, and love; and three attributes of all these, viz. eternity, immutability, and infinity. These apply to all the others. Hence God our Father is eternally, immutably, and infinitely just, wise, good, powerful, &c. These three last are perfections of perfections Purity has been preferred to holiness by some writers, because a more clear and distinct conception to most minds than the term holiness. It is indeed, as before observed, the supreme excellence and majesty of God; and in the esteem of the higher order of intelligence, it is a generic exponent of all his adorable perfections. Hence, in their most sublime anthems and ecstacies, this word is the consecrated symbol of their highest admiration.

I now proceed to the argument proposed at the close of my last speech. It is to be deduced from that inestimable document called the "Acts of the Apostles;" a document of the highest value to the church. It is worth all the ecclesiastic histories of all nations and languages, because it is authentic and authoritative; and because it gives just such a development of things, as reveals christianity to us in all its practical details. We see the apostles in the field of labor, carrying out their commission; and also the particular lessons Christ and the Holy Spirit taught them! I have much use for the Scriptures of truth in this argument, and will use them very freely.

The argument I now propose is simply this: I will show that all the reported conversions, detailed in that book as occurring for some thirty years after the ascension, are represented as having been *through* what the persons SAW performed, and heard said, from the original witnesses and heralds of the resurrection of the Messiah. I wish to adduce every case on record, and show from them all, that these conversions were in accordance with our proposition. And certainly, if Mr. Rice cannot produce a single case in which conversion was accomplished without the Word, or Gospel testimony being presented and heard, he will have most signally failed in sustaining his negation of this proposition.—[*Time expired.*

Wednesday, Nov. 20—12½ o'clock, P. M.

[MR. RICE'S TENTH REPLY.]

MR. PRESIDENT—I shall be prepared to pay due attention to my friend, when he comes to speak of making systems and binding them upon the consciences of men; and I expect to prove, that he is quite as liable to the charge, as are those whom he denounces. I am truly anxious to reach that subject.

The gentleman has failed to make any answer whatever to my argument against his doctrine, that it makes prayer, especially for unbelievers, unnecessary and improper. Does he deny it, or attempt to prove, that the objection is not valid? Not a word of it. He makes no attempt to prove, that his doctrine is at all consistent with prayer. But he says, I am in the same predicament, because I believe in the doctrine of election. Suppose this were true; would he be the better for having me in company with him in his errors? If the doctrine of election were the subject under discussion, I would promptly meet and refute his charge, not by showing, that he is involved in the same difficulty, but by proving the objection not to be well founded. I should have no fears in meeting the gentleman on that subject. If we were discussing the doctrine of election, I would turn to his "Christian System," and prove, that he himself teaches, that the purposes of God are eternal, and that "the whole affair of man's redemption, even to the preparation of the eternal abodes of the righteous, was arranged ere time was born." This might pass for tolerable Calvinism.

He tells us, the Spirit of God is always present with his Word. I have asked, and now ask again, what does he mean by this language? It is easy, and not uncommon for men to use expressions which convey no definite idea either to their own minds, or to those of their hearers. In his writings he has so clearly stated and illustrated his views, as to leave no room to doubt what he really believes. He has said distinctly, that no power but moral power can be exerted on minds; and that moral power can be exerted only by words and arguments. He has declared his belief, that when the Spirit of God had dictated and confirmed the Scriptures, all his converting and sanctifying power was SPENT. Perhaps I can explain in what sense he supposes the Spirit to be present and to operate with the Word. As Mr. Campbell's spirit is present with the ideas he has published in his Harbinger, operating on the minds of his readers; so, in the same sense the Spirit of God is present with the Scriptures. I use his own illustration. Such being his meaning, does he believe in any other agency in conversion and sanctification, than that of the Word dictated and confirmed by the Holy Spirit?

It is not necessary for me now to enter into any discussion of the passage in John iii., "The wind bloweth where it listeth," &c. I quoted it while we were discussing the design of baptism, and since simply to prove, that the new birth is, in some sense, mysterious. I was proving the erroneousness of Mr. C.'s doctrine, by showing, that, according to the Bible, there is a mystery connected with the new birth; but according to his views, there was no mystery about it.

How the Spirit operates on the heart in conversion and sanctification I profess not to understand. And since Mr. C. cannot explain how Satan exerts an influence on the human mind; I am certainly not bound to explain how the Spirit operates in conversion. Indeed we cannot explain the *how* of any one fact in nature. No wonder, then, if the agency of the Spirit is mysterious.

The gentleman has made an attempt to answer some of my arguments. I am gratified that he made the effort. I wish to see him march up to the question boldly, and expose my arguments, if he can. I proved the doctrine of the special influence of the Spirit by the fact, that God is said to *give repentance.* Paul directs Timothy in meekness to "instruct those that oppose themselves; if God peradventure will give them repentance to the acknowledging of the truth," 2 Tim. ii. 25. This argument the gentleman attempts to answer by an illustration. Suppose, says he, certain persons for a time deprived of the right of suffrage, and again having this right restored; he who restored the right, would be said to give them the right of suffrage, but would not force them to exercise it. This is indeed a most singular illustration. Did Paul say, instruct those who oppose themselves, if peradventure God will give them *the right*, the *privilege* to repent? Does Luke say, Christ is exalted a Prince and a Savior to give men *the right* to repent? Really I was not aware, that any human being had ever been deprived of the right to repent! Nor did I know, that God had ever refused to look with compassion on the broken heart and contrite spirit. Men have always had the right, and it has always been their duty to repent. Consequently we find nothing in the Scriptures about granting men the right, the privilege! This is one of the many absurdities into which the gentleman's erroneous doctrines forces him. The language of inspiration is—"Then hath God also to the gentiles granted repentance [not the right to repent] unto life," Acts xi. 18. Instruct them "if peradventure God will grant them repentance to the acknowledging of the truth." But to make these passages accord with Mr. C.'s theology, we must allow him to introduce the word *right* or *privilege*, before repentance! If I may be permitted thus to interpolate or expunge words from the Bible, I can make it teach any thing, even the greatest absurdity. But the Scriptures declare, that God does grant unto men repentance to the acknowledging of the truth, repentance unto life—that he does exert upon their minds a divine influence, leading them to repent and turn from sin to God.

I proved the doctrine of a special divine influence also by Luke xxiv. 45—" Then opened he their understandings, that they might understand the Scriptures." The gentleman replied, that this passage is irrelevant, because Christ, not the Holy Spirit, opened their understandings. Strange reply ! Christ is represented as working many miracles, and he is said to have wrought them by the Spirit of God, Matt. xii. 28. The Spirit is said to be shed on us abundantly through Jesus Christ, Tit. iii. 5. It is by virtue of his atoning sacrifice and intercession, that the Holy Spirit is poured out upon the hearts of men. By his blessed Spirit, therefore, he opened the understandings of his disciples, that they might understand the Scriptures.

The gentleman makes a criticism on the difference between the phrases —through the Word only, and only through the Word. I am not concerned to answer it. I was not pleased, as he knows, with the proposition as it is worded, because I believed it left room for quibbling ; and I would not have consented to debate it, but with the distinct and express understanding that I should interpret it by his publications on the subject. I have proved that in his Christianity Restored, he says, there are only two kinds of power, moral and physical ; that only moral power can operate on the the human mind ; and that all moral power is in words and arguments. Let the gentleman either come out candidly and say, that he was in error when he wrote the books from which I have quoted ; or come up to the defence of his published doctrines. It does not look well for a man to attempt to conceal the truth in this way.

He seems to regret the necessity that is laid upon him to speak of the doctrine of infant damnation, as held by Presbyterians ! I am truly glad that the subject has been brought up on this occasion ; for Mr. C. is the very man to prove upon us this stale charge, if it can be proved. On yesterday he professed to find it in our confession of faith. He now acknowledges that it is not there ; but he says Calvin taught it. I deny that Calvin ever taught it. If he did, I have failed to find it in his writings.

Now what is the doctrine taught by Calvin in the passage quoted ? Does he teach that infants are actually lost ? He does not. He contends that in consequence of the fall of Adam, all his posterity, infants and adults, are in a state of condemnation, and are exposed to the wrath of God ; and that, had no remedy been provided, all must have perished. He does not say that any infant actually perishes, but that all are exposed to ruin in consequence of the fall, and must have perished had no remedy been provided. The gentleman might have proved, with equal conclusiveness, that according to Calvin, all nations, adults as well as infants, do actually perish forever; for he speaks not of infants only, but of both adults and infants—of the whole race.

Is it true that the gentleman's reformation cannot sustain itself without such caricatures and gross misrepresentations of the doctrines of others ? No man has more frequently complained of being misrepresented than Mr. C., and no man living has done greater injustice to others, living and dead.

Calvin did not teach the doctrine he has charged upon him. But he quotes Augustine as teaching it. Was Augustine a Presbyterian ? The gentleman is attempting to prove that the Presbyterian church holds the doctrine of infant damnation, and, to establish the charge, he quotes Augustine!!! But he quotes Turretin too. Was Turretin a member of the Presbyterian church? But I will subscribe to the doctrine of Turretin. He opposes the sentiments of those who say, that it would be unjust in God to exclude infants from heaven—that he is bound in justice to save them. He holds, not that infants are actually lost, but that their salvation is of *grace*, not of *justice*. Zanchius was also quoted. Was he a Presbyterian? This author, in speaking of infants, uses the Latin word *damno;* but Mr. C. certainly knows that this word means simply to *condemn*. The doctrine of Zanchius, as that of Calvin and Turretin, seems clearly to be, that all the human race, in consequence of the sin of Adam, are involved in a common condemnation, from which they can be saved only by the grace of God in Christ.

But this doctrine, as Mr. C. ought to know, is not peculiar to those who are called Calvinists. It is taught with great clearness and force by Rev. Richard Watson, in his Theological Institutes; which, if I mistake not, is regarded as a kind of text book by our Methodist brethren. He, as well as Presbyterians, teaches, that in consequence of the sin of Adam, the human race are all, old and young, justly exposed to the wrath of God; and that all who are saved, are saved by *grace*. The gentleman has repeatedly boasted of his thorough acquaintance with Presbyterianism. I will not charge him with willful misrepresentation of the doctrines of the Presbyterian church; but I will say, that you can scarcely find an old Presbyterian lady, who does not know that our church never did teach or hold the doctrine he has charged upon her. Charity, then, requires us to suppose that his knowledge of Presbyterianism is very limited. He certainly is not half so well informed concerning these matters, as he professes to be.

He attempted to prove, that the Spirit operates in conversion and sanctification *only* through the truth, by the fact, that whatever the Spirit is represented as doing, the Word is also said to do—that if the Spirit converts men, the Word converts them. I replied, that by the same logic, I could prove, that the Spirit operates only through human instrumentality; because Paul was sent to *convert* the gentiles, and ministers of the gospel are said to convert men. The argument, therefore, would prove as conclusively, that the Spirit never converted a person without human instrumentality—that he operates *only* through the living minister, as that he never converts and sanctifies without the truth, or that he operates *only* through the truth. But the gentleman seeks to escape from the difficulty by saying, Paul was not sent to *quicken* men. Paul was to open their eyes and to turn them from darkness to light, and from the power of Satan to God. Could this be done without their being quickened, or made spiritually alive? Paul said to the Corinthians—"In Christ Jesus I have begotten you through the gospel;" 1 Cor. iv. 15. Can a person be begotten, and not quickened? There is no way in which he can escape. His argument proves as conclusively, that the Spirit operates only through human instrumentality, as that he operates only through the truth.

I think it unnecessary to press the gentleman much further with the absurdity of locating all depravity in man's animal nature. It is perfectly certain, without argument, that anger, wrath, malice, hatred, are passions which belong to the mind; that have no necessary connection with the body. The mind can hate as malignantly out of the body as in it. There is no truth in his philosophy. It is *profoundly absurd*. Nor is there one word in the Bible to countenance it.

I see neither pertinency nor meaning in all the gentleman has said about the word *holy*. On yesterday, he told us, strangely enough, that it did not express *moral quality*. I did not choose, because it was wholly unnecessary, to spend time disputing about a word. I, therefore, quoted the passage—"God made man *upright*." The word *upright* is admitted to express moral quality. If, then, God originally made man upright, not by words and arguments, it follows, that he can do it again—that his power over the human mind is not confined to mere motives. But, says Mr. C., God did not make man upright without a *word;* but he said, "Let us make man," &c. Were these words addressed to man? Did they create him in whole or in part? Did they exert even the slightest influence? No—man was created in the image of God by an immediate exertion of his omnipotent power. A word never created anything. If, then, God did originally exert on man such a power, as made him holy or upright, not by words; who shall dare say, he cannot restore his image to the soul, either through the Word or without it? The Word of God is not able, of itself, to overcome the enmity of the human heart, and to inspire it with supreme love to God.

I wish now to present the remaining arguments which I had purposed to offer, and then to give a brief and condensed view of the ground over which we have passed. I have said, that Mr. C.'s doctrine prescribes to the power of God an unreasonable and unscriptural limitation; and this I have proved by the facts—that originally God created man holy, and that he does exert a controling influence over his moral conduct, not merely or chiefly by words and arguments. I will now prove, that God can, and that he does exert on the human mind a converting and sanctifying power, distinct from the Word, by the inspired accounts of the first revivals. In the second chapter of the Acts of the Apostles, we learn, that on the day of Pentecost three thousand souls were converted. Men who went to the temple in all their pride, unbelief, love of sin, and hatred of the truth, were on that day converted, became penitent believers, were filled with hatred of sin and love to God, and were added to the church. This was a most remarkable event. The change wrought in their minds was *sudden*. They went to the temple loving sin and hating the truth. They left it hating sin and rejoicing in Christ. The change was *radical* and *thorough*. The things they hated one hour before, they now supremely loved. They beheld in the Savior a beauty and a glory they had never before discovered; and in the plan of salvation they saw an adaptation to their real condition and necessities which they had never discovered. They trusted, loved, praised, and worshiped the Redeemer of men. The change was *permanent*. From that hour to the hour of their death they proved by their lives, that they were *new creatures*. Through reproach and persecutions, even unto death, they held out faithfully. They counted not their lives dear. They suffered joyfully the spoiling of their goods, knowing that through Christ they had the assurance of a heavenly inheritance.

Now let me ask any reflecting man, how do you account for this sudden, radical, permanent change in the hearts and lives of those persons? Was it effected by the *miracles* they witnessed? Miracles, Mr. C. admits, cannot convert men. They can only arrest their attention, and convince them of the truth; but they cannot change the heart. The question is, what caused these wicked men so suddenly and so ardently to love the truth which they had hated? What caused them to see in sin an odiousness they had not before seen, and in holiness a beauty they had never before perceived? Why did they now find their highest happiness in that service from which hitherto they had turned with aversion and disgust? Was this astonishing revolution in their dispositions, views and feelings, effected by Peter's arguments? Many of them had doubtless heard the preaching of Him who spake as never man spake; and they were not thus affected. Thousands had heard the gracious words which constantly fell from his lips; but no discourse of his ever produced effects such as we are now contemplating. Besides, it is a fact, proved by universal observation, that if the characters of bad men are changed by arguments and motives, the change is very gradual. They do not readily subdue passions long indulged, and attain to the possession of opposite virtues. Such changes, even if ever effected merely by motives, are the work of months, if not of years. But the work we are now contemplating, was effected in a day, even in an hour; for when the Lord works, a moment is as good as a year. Suddenly the three thousand had new hearts, new views, new feelings, new sorrows, new joys. They were new creatures. Old things had passed away, and, behold, all things were new!

Here we learn why it was, that the apostle's preaching was attended with so much greater success than that of the Savior. He wrought stupendous miracles, and spake with an eloquence which no human orator could ever rival; but the Holy Spirit was not so abundantly poured out before his ascension to heaven, as after. Can any one, not blinded by a false theory, doubt, that on the day of Pentecost the Holy Spirit exerted on the minds and hearts of the three thousand a power distinct from the Word, and more efficacious?

Another argument in favor of the doctrine of a special agency of the Spirit, an argument which, as it appears to me, has great weight, is this: *The contrary doctrine leaves man in a hopeless condition.* Heaven is a holy place. An infinitely holy God reigns there; and holy angels bow around his throne. God has taught us that nothing impure can enter into the holy city; that none from earth but " the spirits of just men made perfect " can approach his presence. Men are deeply depraved. Even the most godly groan under indwelling corruption. Tell them, that they must, by their own exertions, in view of the motives of the gospel, prepare themselves to see God; and they will be down and weep in despair. A man is suddenly called to die, and to appear before his Judge. He may be a pious man; but he is conscious of being very imperfect. What assurance can he have, that he is pure enough to be admitted to stand in the presence of God? What distressing apprehensions must fill his mind. How gloomy must be his future prospects. But let him hear the language of Paul: "Being confident of this very thing, that he which hath begun a good work in you will perform it until the day of Jesus Christ," Phil. i. 6. Cheered by such a promise, the humble believer, though conscious of great imperfection, feels his fears subside, and his hopes rise. If God has undertaken the work, it will be well done. He is assured, that Christ will present his happy spirit before his Father, " without spot or wrinkle." He knows, he will soon behold his face in righteousness. Never will I give up this soul-cheering doctrine, and those great and precious promises founded upon it.   Living and dying I hope to experience their fulfillment.

This doctrine is the hope of our guilty and polluted race.   God will pour out his Spirit on all flesh.   In answer to the prayers of the faithful, it shall descend as showers on the thirsty earth, and shall cause the wilderness and the solitary place to be glad, and the desert to blossom as the rose.

I must present one more argument.   It is this : the great mass—the overwhelming majority of the readers of the Bible, in all ages, have understood it to teach the doctrine for which I am contending.   This fact cannot be denied.   Now Mr. C. agrees with me, that on all important points of faith and duty the Bible is a plain book, easily understood. It was designed to be read and understood by the unlearned as well as the wise.   Ask all who have made that blessed book their study, how they understand it on this subject; and with wonderful unanimity they declare their firm belief, that it teaches, that in conversion and sanctification, there is a divine and efficacious influence of the Spirit, distinct from the Word.   This influence, in connection with the cross of Christ, is the ground of their hope.   For it they pray, day and night; and in the witness of the Spirit, that they are the children of God they rejoice.

If the doctrine of Mr. C. is indeed true, the fact I have just stated, is most unaccountable.   How shall we account for the fact, that the whole christian world have misunderstood the Bible on this vital point?   Is its teaching plain ? and yet almost all have misunderstood it !   If Mr. C. so thinks, he of all men should, in consistency, believe most firmly in the doctrine of *total depravity*.   How else can he account for the amazing blindness of almost all the readers of the Bible ?   Indeed I know not whether we should more wonder at the blindness and stupidity of all Christendom, or at the superior illumination of Mr. C. and those who agree with him !   How it has happened that they, whilst denying all supernatural illumination, have gained so much greater light than all others, I cannot comprehend.

I trust the time will never come, when I shall feel myself constrained to differ in regard to any fundamental doctrine of christianity, from the overwhelming majority of the wise and the good.   Were I to entertain such views, I should greatly suspect myself of being under some blinding influence.   We need not, however, appeal to the views of even the wisest and best.   On this vital subject, the language of inspiration is clear and full.   It leaves no room to doubt that God has promised to save us, by the washing of regeneration and renewing of the Holy Ghost, shed upon us abundantly through Jesus Christ.

I have now offered as many arguments as I designed to present on this topic—not all that I could offer.   It is not my plan to confuse your minds by a great multiplicity of arguments, but to present a few that are clear, striking, and conclusive.

I will now commence a brief review of the ground over which I have traveled.   What have been the precise points in debate ?   I have said, that my opponent and myself agree, that the Holy Spirit dictated and confirmed the Scriptures.   We agree, also, that ordinarily the Spirit operates, in some sense, through the Word.

Mr. C. contends, that the Spirit never operates without the truth.   I contend, that in the case of infants and idiots, he does.   Mr. C. believes, that in the conversion and sanctification of adults, the Spirit operates *only* through the truth—that he dictated and confirmed the Word, and the Word converts and sanctifies. I maintain, that, in addition to the Word, and distinct from it, there is an influence of the Spirit on the heart, without which the Word would never convert and sanctify any human being.

Let me repeat a few explanations, that I may not be misunderstood. I do not hold, that in regeneration, there is a change of the physical nature of the mind, but a change of the dispositions and affections of the heart. Nor do I hold that in regeneration any new revelation is made—any new ideas given which are not taught in the Scriptures; but such a change of heart as enables the renewed soul to see the beauty and excellency of the things there revealed. "Open mine eyes," prayed David, "that I may read wonderful things out of thy law."

Again. The *modus operandi*, the manner in which the Spirit operates on the heart, I do not profess to understand. The fact that he does operate, is clear; the *mode* is mysterious. That God created man, is certain; *how* he created him is mysterious. How spirits communicate their thoughts to each other, or to the mind of man, I do not comprehend. We pry not into things beyond our comprehension.

The necessity of the special influence of the Spirit, I have said, does not arise from any lack of *evidence* that the Scriptures are true; for the evidence is convincing and overwhelming. Nor does it arise from any *obscurity* in the manner of presenting the truths taught in the Bible; for they are presented with remarkable simplicity and clearness. Nor does it arise from the fact that men are not perfectly free agents; for they are. The necessity of the divine influence arises from the deep, the total depravity of human nature; the aversion of the unsanctified heart to the holy character of God, to his pure law, and his soul-humbling gospel. "This is the condemnation," said our Savior, "that light is come into the world: and men loved darkness more than light, because their deeds were evil." The Word of God alone cannot change their hearts, so that they will hate darkness and love light—turn from sin and follow holiness.

The effects of this depravity are, that the affections of men are placed on forbidden objects; their minds are pre-occupied with worldly plans and desires; and they refuse to hear the Word; or, hearing, they reject or pervert its divine teachings and become infidels or heretics; or, being speculative believers, they live without Christ and without God in the world.—[*Time expired.*

Wednesday, Nov. 29—1 o'clock, P. M.

[MR. CAMPBELL'S CLOSING ADDRESS.]

MR. PRESIDENT—I have but thirty minutes to close the argument, unless I should be indulged with a few more. I am sorry to see Mr. Rice so positive in his assertions and contradictions respecting the readings and comments on Calvin. He has not given a correct translation of Calvin's Latin, according to the copy now before me. I have read other translations of it, besides my own, and I have also read Calvin's own French translation of the passage in dispute. I will read an interpretation of it by Jeremiah Taylor:—

"If we are guilty of Adam's sin by the decree of God, by his choice and constitution that it should be so, as Mr. Calvin and Dr. Twiss (that I may name no more for that side) do expressly teach, it follows that God is the author of our sin, so that I may use Mr. Calvin's words—'How is it that so many nations with their children should be involved in the fall without remedy, but because God would have it so; and if that be the matter, then

to God, as the cause, must that sin and *that condemnation* be ascribed.' "—
Jere. Taylor's Works, Heb. ed. vol. ix. p. 322; quoted by the Christ. Ex-
aminer, Boston, 1828.

Now if the gentleman desires to contest the matter farther, I now inform him that I shall be forthcoming under the next question on creeds.
At present we must close this present argument, and reserve what we have
farther to say on the "horrible decree," till the next question, under
which it will be quite as suitable as here. I will sustain the ground
which I occupy by ample authority.

His allusions to repentance unto life and remission, are more for appearance than from any new ideas or new arguments. I have shewn
it to be not individual and personal, but commensurate with the Gentile
world—a rich and glorious tender to all the nations of the earth. A
matter alike unexpected by Jew or Gentile. The question stands as I left
it in my last address.

The letter from brother Thomson on the subject of prayer, read from
the Millenial Harbinger by Mr. Rice, was introduced for effect, and especially to hide his own retreat from the difficulty propounded to him on
that very same subject. Why did he not read my answer to it? That
would have set the matter in its proper attitude before you. My time
will not allow me to read such disquisitions and comment on them.
They are not called for. There are few who can comprehend the reasons
of things. The best philosophy of prayer is, that God has granted the
privilege, enjoined the duty, and given a promise. We, therefore, violate no decree, and sin against no revelation in praying for all men. I
believe, practice, and preach the necessity and propriety of praying for
the salvation of our children, families, friends, &c. as much as I believe,
preach, or practice any point of domestic and social duties and privileges.
If I were to follow Mr. Rice into all these digressions into my writings,
we should have scores of questions in discussion.

He says there is a certain power displayed in conversion, and so say I.
And does it not come with as good a grace from me as from him? But
he says he goes for a power beyond the naked Word, and that, too, an
accompanying power. Well, the word *accompanying* explains not the
nature of that power, and for that I have asked more than once, but I have
asked in vain. He can neither expound what the "*accompanying power*" is, or can be, nor how it operates; and, therefore, whether or not we
agree, I could not say. I believe the Spirit accompanies the Word, is always present with the Word, and actually and personally works through
it upon the moral nature of man, but not without it. I presume not to
speculate upon the nature of this power, nor the mode of operation. I
believe the Holy Spirit sheds abroad in our hearts the love of God, and
dwells in all the faithful; that it sanctifies them through the truth; that
"it works in them to will and do," and that it comforts them in all their
afflictions.

But the Spirit of God does not thus enter into the wicked. When it
fell from heaven on Pentecost, it fell only on the one hundred and
twenty, and not upon the promiscuous assembly. For the multitude, after the Spirit's *descent*, did still upbraid the disciples with drunkenness.
Those who first received it that day, preached by it to the audience. The
thousands who heard, *were pierced to the heart*, and yet had not received
the Spirit. They believed, and were in an agony of fear and terror, but yet
had not received the Spirit. They asked what they should do, and yet

had not received it. Peter commanded them to "Repent and be baptized, every one of you, for the remission of sins, and *you shall receive* the gift of the Holy Spirit." Of course, then, they had not yet received that gift. They, however, *gladly received his word, and were baptized.* We have, then, the first three thousand converts regenerated by gladly receiving the Word and baptism. This is a strong fact for the first one in my *fourteenth* argument.

The *second* fact of conversion is found, Acts iv., and the question is, how were they regenerated? We shall read the passage. "Now that many of them which HEARD THE WORD believed, and the number of the men was about *five thousand.*" We are now morally certain that these five thousand were converted by the Spirit only through the Word. We have already eight thousand examples of our allegation, and not one instance of one converted without the Word.

Our *third* exemplification is found, Acts v. 14: "And believers were the more added to the Lord, multitudes of both men and women." Women are here mentioned as well as men. We have, then, got multitudes of both sexes to add, in proof that the Spirit converted these, not without the Word, but by what they saw and heard.

We shall find a *fourth* example, Acts viii. 5, 6, 12. Philip went to Samaria and preached Christ to them. "And when they believed Philip preaching the things concerning the Kingdom of God and the name of the Lord Jesus, they were baptized, both men and women." So the Samaritans were regenerated by the Holy Spirit through faith in the Word, which Philip preached.

A *fifth* example is found in the eunuch. "If thou believest with all thy heart, thou mayest." He said: "I believe that Jesus Christ is the Son of God." Then he, too, was born of the water, and converted, not without the Word.

Paul furnishes a *sixth* case. When he had fallen to the ground, he heard "a voice saying to him, Saul, Saul, why persecuteth thou me— I am Jesus whom thou persecutest." His case is certainly one of indisputable certainty. He both saw, heard, and believed, and was baptized.

Eneas furnishes a *seventh* case. And Peter said to him, "Eneas, Jesus Christ maketh thee whole—arise and make thy bed."

The citizens of Lydda and Saron furnish the *eigth* case. Of them we read—"All that dwelt in Lydda and Saron saw Eneas" made whole by Peter, and *they "turned to the Lord."* The people of Lydda and Saron were converted by what they *saw* and *heard.* Conversion here, too, was not by the Spirit alone.

The inhabitants of Joppa furnish the *ninth* case. On Peter's visit, and the revival of Dorcas, through his preaching, many believed in the Lord. So that Peter tarried there many days.

Cornelius and his friends, furnish the *tenth* case. That is so notorious, it needs only to be named. Peter told the words of salvation, and the Spirit miraculously sustained him. So that he, also, and his friends, were regenerated, through both the Word and the Spirit.

The Antiochans constitute the *eleventh* case. Common preachers, exiles from Jerusalem, came to Antioch, Phenice and Cypress. The hand of the Lord was with them. They spake unto the Grecians, preaching the Lord Jesus, and a great number believed and turned unto the Lord. See also Acts xiii. 43—48.

Sergius Paulus, deputy governor of Paphos, gives us the *twelfth* case. When he saw Paul strike Elymas, the sorcerer, blind; and heard Paul preach, he believed, being astonished at the doctrine of the Lord.

Lydia constitutes the *thirteenth* case. Lydia, a pious lady, *a worshiper of God*, whose heart the Lord had formerly touched, attended to Paul's preaching, *believed*, and was baptized.

The Philippian jailor heard Paul; he and all his house believed in God, and were filled with joy. This is the *fourteenth* special case.

Dionysius, the Areopagite of Athens, Lady Damaris and others with them, heard Paul, believed, and clave unto him and the Lord. These noble Athenians constitute the *fifteenth* case.

Crispus, the chief ruler of the Corinthian synagogue, and all his family, hearing Paul, believed on the Lord. This is the *sixteenth* case.

The Corinthians constitute the *seventeenth* example. Many of the Corinthians hearing, believed, and were baptized. The whole story is here beautifully told in the three words, "hearing, believing, and being baptized."

The Ephesians constitute the *eighteenth* case. Many of them hearing Paul, believed, came and confessed their deeds, burned fifty thousand pieces of silver worth of books; "so mightily grew the word of the Lord, and prevailed."

To these I may add the cripple at Lystra, as a *nineteenth* case; the people of Iconium as a *twentieth*—"To whom Paul *so* spake, that a multitude believed;" and as the *twenty-first* example, the noble Bereans, "who searched the Scriptures daily, therefore many of them believed." Here are twenty-one clear and distinct cases recorded in one book, containing, in all, probably not less than from thirty to fifty thousand persons; in every one of which they *heard, believed,* and were *baptized.* So that, as far as sacred history goes, the Spirit of God never did operate in conversion without the Word.

Now I ask Mr. Rice to bring forward one single case of any one being converted to the Lord without the Word being first heard and believed! If the salvation of the world depended on it, he could not give it. It is, then, so far as the New Testament deposeth, idle, and worse than idle, to talk about sanctification or conversion, without the Word and Spirit of God. They are always united in the great work. No one is converted by the Word alone, nor by the Spirit alone.

Having then surveyed the premises, and heard the arguments and objections from the other side, I proceed, with great haste, to place in a miniature view the whole argument before you. I. The first of this series of thirteen arguments was drawn from the constitution of the human mind, intellectual and moral. It was shown that the human mind, like the human body, has a specific constitution, which is never to be violated. In no instance does God, in the government of the universe, violate the laws and constitution which he has given, in effecting the ordinary objects of his providence, moral government, or in the scheme of redemption. He always addresses himself to man in harmony with his constitution: first addessing his understanding, then his conscience, then his affections. Miracles only excepted, he has never violated the powers given to man. He gives no new powers, annihilates no old powers, but takes the human constitution as he made it; and by enlightening the understanding, and renewing the heart by the gospel, effects, through his Holy Spirit, that grand moral change which constitutes a new moral creation.

II. Our second argument was deduced from the fact, that from the earliest antiquity till now, there never has been found a human being in any country or age, possessed of one spiritual idea, impression, or feeling, where some portion of the Word or revelation of God had not been spoken to him, or read by him. So that it appears, in fact, indisputable, that the Spirit of God rather follows, and in no case precedes, the progress or arrival of his Word. We have the history of man, in the four quarters of the world, in attestation of this most significant and momentous fact.

III. By an induction of many cases of personal experience, from observation, and, I may add, by a general concession, it appears, that amongst christians the most gifted and enlightened, not one idea can be suggested from the most gifted, the most eminently illuminated with spiritual light and intelligence—not one idea can be expressed, not taken from the Holy Scriptures. Not one thought, idea, or impression, truly spiritual, can be heard from any man in Christendom, not borrowed from that Holy Book, directly or indirectly. These two matter-of-fact arguments, on almost any other subject, would be deemed all-sufficient.

IV. My fourth argument consisted in the avowal and development of that great law of mind, and of all organic existences, animal or vegetable, viz. that whatever is essential to the production of any specific result, is necessary in all cases. Whatever is essential to the production of any one effect, or offspring, vegetable or animal; any one result, intellectual or moral, is always and invariably necessary to the consummation of the same results. Therefore whatever is essential to the conversion of one individual, is essential to the conversion of every other individual. It need not be urged that the same order and arrangement of things is necessary, because that is not implied as always essential; but so much of order, arrangement, and circumstances, as are essential to the production of one ear of corn, are uniformly and invariably necessary. Just so in the new birth. When called to assert and maintain any fact, we are not obliged to explain the whole nature, reasons, and contingencies thereof— I am only obliged to establish the fact itself. Natural birth is always the same thing. *So is the spiritual.* Baptism is always the same thing. Mr. Rice, without knowing it or designing it, was constrained to come to this result. While, in fact, seeking to oppose it, he came to the very same conclusion. He first argued for infant regeneration without faith; he then sought to have believers regenerated in some way different, but ultimately he asserted that regeneration was also before faith in adults, and thus, by the force of the universal law, he came to my grand conclusion, *that whatever is necessary to the new birth, or regeneration, in one case, is necessary in all other cases.* And so that point is decided.

V. My fifth argument is deduced from the name, Advocate, given to the Holy Spirit by the Messiah, as his *official designation*, in conducting the work of conversion, convincing the world of sin, righteousness, and judgment. He was, then, to use words in pleading this cause; hence it is a moral argument, and a change effected by motives.

VI. My sixth argument is drawn from the commission given to this Advocate in pleading his cause. He was to convince the world of sin, righteousness, and judgment, by certain means. The Messiah prescribes the topics. He furnishes the arguments, and states them to the disciples in advance. The first topic is—"*because they believe not in me;*" the second—"*because I go to my Father, and you see me no more;*" the third is—"*because the Prince of the world is cast out.*" In this way, then, the work was to be conducted, and it has been conducted. And so proceeded the apostles through their whole ministry. All useful and successful pleaders, in all ages, have been obliged to adopt this course. And while the human constitution remains as it now is, the same course must be essentially and substantially pursued.

VII. My seventh argument is founded on that most significant and sublime fact, that the first gift the Spirit of God bestowed on the apostles was the *gift of tongues.* What could have been more apposite to teach, that the Spirit of God was to operate through the Word, than, as prefatory to the work, first of all giving to its pleaders the gift of tongues? that by the machinery of words, he might accomplish his glorious work of regenerating the world. These seven arguments I distinctly stated in my first address on this subject. To some of these there was no reply whatever made. To none of them was a direct and formal refutation attempted. I regard them as I did at first, not only as unassailed but unassailable.

VIII. My eighth argument was composed of the direct and explicit testimony of the apostles, affirming regeneration and conversion through the Word of God, as the seed or principle of the new life. The instrumentality of the Word was asserted by James as the will or ordinance of God. We had the united testimony of two apostles directly and positively affirming the very issue in our proposition. James affirming, that of his own will begat he us BY, *not without*, the Word of Truth. And Peter saying, "We are born again," or according to McKnight, "We are regenerated, or having regenerated us, not by corruptible, but through," not without, "the incorruptible seed of the Word of God, which liveth and abideth forever." Here is as clear an indication of the instrumentality of the Word as can be expressed in human language. To explain these passages away is impossible, and you see how my opponent has evaded them. Paul, also, in various forms of speech, gives us similar views of the instrumentality of the Word. He told the Corinthians that he himself had "begotten them through the gospel." Thus making the gospel the indispensable instrument of regeneration. Peter, indeed, asserted before all the apostles in the convention at Jerusalem, that God purifies the heart by faith. But it was reserved to these latter times to assume and teach, that God purifies the heart without faith, before faith, and independent of the Word of God.

IX. I elicited a ninth argument from the commission given to the Messiah, as reported in Isaiah, and from the commission given to Paul from the Messiah in person, with respect to the conversion of the gentiles. This commission is reported by Paul himself in his speech before king Agrippa, Acts xxvi. These commissions show the arrangement of means in reference to conversion, remission and sanctification, in the Divine mind, purpose and plan. Illumination through the gospel is always first. The apostle was sent to "open the eyes" of the nations. He was "to turn them from darkness to light, and from the power of Satan unto God, in order to their forgiveness and participation of an inheritance amongst those *sanctified through faith.*"

X. My tenth argument consisted of those scriptures which show that whatever is ascribed to the Holy Spirit in the work of salvation, is also ascribed to the *Word;* and that what is ascribed to the *Word*, is also ascribed to the *Spirit.* The gentleman has not found a single exception to it. Are persons said to be enlightened, quickened, converted, sanctified, regenerated, comforted, &c., by the Word? they are also in some other scriptures said to be so by the Spirit; and vice versa. This agent and instrument were so inseparably connected in the minds of the apostles and prophets, that they could not conceive of the one without the other, in any operation or effect connected with the salvation of man.

XI. My eleventh argument was deduced from the fact, that those who resisted the Word of God, or the persons that spoke it, are said to resist the Spirit of God. By not giving ear to the prophets that spoke by the Spirit, they resisted the Spirit. The Sanhedrim of the Jews, who resisted the words spoken by Stephen and by the twelve apostles, are represented by him as resisting the Holy Spirit. His words are—"As your fathers did, so do you always resist the Holy Spirit. Which of the prophets have not your fathers persecuted? and they have slain them that showed before the coming of the JUST ONE, of whom you have now been the betrayers and murderers."

XII. A twelfth argument was deduced from another important fact: that the strivings of the prophets by their words, are represented as the strivings of the Holy Spirit. Thus spoke Nehemiah, "thou sendest thy good Spirit to instruct them," through Moses, "and thou testifiedst against them by thy SPIRIT, in thy prophets, yet would they not give ear." Thus, in the Divine Word, the Spirit and the Word of God, and those who spoke it by the immediate authority of God, are so perfectly identified, that every thing that is said to be done *by*, *to*, *for*, or *against* the one is said to be done *to*, *by*, *for*, or *against* the other. So that we may still say, that those who hear not Moses nor the prophets, would not be persuaded, though one rose from the dead! God still strives with men by his Spirit, and they still resist his Spirit, in and through the Word spoken by prophets and apostles. "*Let every one hear what the Spirit saith to the churches.*"

XIII. My thirteenth argument consists in that most sublime and impressive fact, that God no where has operated without his *Word*, either in the old creation or in the new. In nature and in grace, God operates not without his Word. *He never has wrought without means.* He has, so far as earth's annals reach, and as the rolls of eternity have been opened to our view, never done any thing without an instrumentality. The naked Spirit of God never has operated upon the naked spirit of man, so far as all science, all revelation teach. Abstract spiritual operations is a pure metaphysical dream. There is nothing to favor such a conceit in nature, providence or grace. God broke the awful stillness of eternity with his own creative voice. HE SPOKE, *before any thing was done*. Speech, or language, or a word, is the original and sublime instrumentality of all divine operations. God said, LET THERE BE LIGHT, and light was born. Does not the Bible say, "By faith we understand that the worlds were framed *by the Word of God*," so that the things that were made, were not made of things that did formerly exist. They were made out of the Word of God. All things having been created by the Word of God. Most evident it is, that his Word is the *all creative instrument*. Without it was not any thing made that now exists. Of course, then, if persons were to be created anew in Christ Jesus, without the Word of God, it would be a perfect anomaly, something wholly new in the history of the universe. If God operated upon absolute nonentity, and then upon inert matter, by his Word, and if his Spirit thus brooded on old chaos, what tongue of man can prove that in the new creation, he regenerates, renews, re-creates and sanctifies man without his Word!! It never can be done, Mr. President. It is not only out of the power of Mr. Rice, but every other living man to show, that God moves at all in the affairs of redemption, but through his Word. God's Spirit and Word operated conjointly on ancient chaos, and they still operate together on the chaos of the human heart in its sins. Read Psalm xxix. 3—9; Psalm xxxiii. 6—9. So my *fourteenth* argument details.

I am sorry that my time is always too short for the full development of the great elements of things, and mighty evidences of truth found in these propositions. I have arranged, however, such amount of facts and evidences as, I humbly think, never can be set aside by the ingenuity of mortal man. I am willing to commit these *fourteen* arguments to the world, fearless of the consequences. I think the case is a clear one, and one upon which we may say we have line upon line, and precept upon precept. We have certainly the law and the prophets.

In conclusion, then, I must say, that we have been much reproached and slandered on this theme. It is not from any aversion to preaching the Holy Spirit, (for we do efficaciously preach it,) that I have been constrained to take this ground, so offensive to some, and which has been made, in many instances, to retard the great and growing cause of reformation which we plead. I believe and teach the inspiration of the Spirit, the influences and effects of the Spirit of God in the hearts of all christians, men and women. The man who represents me as opposed to a spiritual religion and to the operations, converting and sanctifying, of the Holy Spirit, does me the highest injustice, and blasphemes my good name in a way he must answer for to a higher tribunal. I have been long endeavoring to draw the proper lines between a wild enthusiasm and the true Spirit of our God—between what is spiritual and animal in some of the present forms of christianity; and to save my contemporaries from a religion of blind impulses, animal excitements, and new revelations, by which I most sincerely believe vast multitudes are deluded to everlasting ruin. With Paul, and with me, there is but one body and but one Spirit, as there is but one hope of our calling—as there is but one God and Father of us all.—[*Time expired.*

Wednesday, Nov. 29—1¼ *o'clock, P. M.*
[MR. RICE'S CLOSING REPLY.]

MR. PRESIDENT—I see not what advantage the gentleman expects to gain by attempting to blacken the character of Calvin—a man who was a blessing to the world, and who has long since gone to his rest. He says, I have not a correct translation of Calvin's Institutes. I have one of the very best that has been made. But there are present in this large audience many scholars, who understand the Latin language. I was waiting to hear him read to us the original. He certainly cannot expect us to take his bare assertion in matters of this kind.

He emphasized the expression *horrible decree.* Yet I presume, he knows perfectly well, that the Latin word *horribilis* is not precisely synonymous with the English word *horrible*, derived from it. Calvin used it in the sense of *awful.* But, as I have already remarked, if Mr. C.'s interpretation of Calvin were correct, it would prove, not that he held that some infants are lost, but that all nations, infants and adults, believers and unbelievers, perish without remedy; for he includes them all! Yet every one knows, that he held no such doctrine. I will read from Calvin one passage which may throw some light on this subject. It is in the chapter on baptism.

"The mischievous consequences of that ill-stated notion, that baptism is necessary to salvation, are overlooked by persons in general, and therefore they are less cautious; for the reception of an opinion, that all who happen to'die without baptism are lost, makes our condition worse than that of the ancient people, as though the grace of God were more restricted now than it was under the law; it leads to the conclusion, that Christ came not to fulfill the promises, but to abolish them; since the promise which, at that time, was of itself sufficiently efficacious to insure salvation before the eighth day, would have no validity now without the assistance of the sign."
—book iv. chap. xv. sec. 20.

Calvin here contends, that it is unnecessary for lay-men to baptize a child that is likely to die; because its salvation is secure without baptism. He never taught the doctrine the gentleman has charged upon him. The charge has been often made, but, I believe, never proved. If any passage can be found in his works that does teach the doctrine, I wish to see it produced.

Mr. C. still vainly strives to evade the force of the argument for a special divine influence, founded on the fact, that God is said to grant or give repentance. He says, God granted repentance, not to individuals, but to the *whole gentile world!* The Bible does not say so. Peter had related to his brethren at Jerusalem the conversion of the family of Cornelius, a single gentile family. When they heard the history of this interesting event, "they glorified God, saying, Then hath God also to the gentiles granted repentance unto life;" Acts xi. 18. Did they say, God hath granted to the gentiles *the privilege* of repenting? Had they not always this privilege? Was it ever refused to them? Was it not always their *duty* to repent? But the language of Paul to Timothy places the matter beyond cavil or objection—"In meekness instructing those that oppose themselves; if God peradventure will give them repentance to the acknowledging of the truth;" 2 Tim. ii. 25. The gentleman says, God had given repentance to the whole gentile world; but Paul directs Timothy in meekness to instruct a certain class of wicked persons, if peradventure God *will* grant them repentance; so that they will acknowledge the truth. It is worse than vain to attempt to destroy the force of language so perfectly clear.

One of my most conclusive arguments against Mr. C.'s doctrine, is—that it makes prayer for unconverted persons, as well as for the sanctification of believers, both unavailing and improper. To prove that this insurmountable difficulty had occurred to his own friends, as well as to me, I read a letter from a member of his church, published in the Harbinger. How does he answer it? Why, he says, I ought to have read his answer to the letter. It would have required rather more time than I have to spare; for of all men he excels in going round and round a difficulty which he feels himself incapable of meeting. Besides, it is my business to present arguments against his doctrine, and his to answer them. But he would have you believe, that when I present an argument against his views, I am bound, if he have written anything on the subject, to read his answer!!! This is truly a singular demand.

I repeat the argument. If his doctrine be true, there is absolutely no propriety in praying. Why should we, and how can we, pray for blessings, which we verily believe, God will never grant? He says, he prays for the conversion of sinners. When he enters the pulpit, he stands before the congregation, and prays that God will convert the unbelieving portion of it; and then he opens the Bible, and tells them, that God *will not* convert them—that the Spirit has dictated and confirmed the Word, and they must be converted and sanctified by it, or be lost!!! If his doctrine be true, what are his prayers worth? But he says, he prays for the conversion of sinners. It is a happy thing when, as it sometimes happens, a man's *heart* keeps in the path of duty, when his *head* would lead him from it. The better feelings of the heart do not always yield to the frigid speculations of the head. I am happy to hear, that he still prays that God would convert sinners, even though he tells them he will not do it!

I wish now to notice the list of some eight arguments, on which the gentleman has principally relied, to prove that the Spirit operates only through the truth.

1. The first was from the nature of the human mind—an argument purely metaphysical. But that God can, and does, exert a moral influence on the mind, distinct from words and arguments, was proved by the facts, that he created man upright, and that in protecting his church and people, the Bible teaches us, that he has exerted a controling influence over the moral conduct of wicked men, not by words and arguments.

2. His second argument was, that there are no spiritual ideas where the Word of God is not possessed. This assertion he cannot prove. I have no objection, however, to admitting it; for the design of regeneration is not to make a new revelation, but to change the heart, and cause the sinner to understand and embrace the truths of the Bible. This argument, therefore, is worthless. It bears not upon the doctrine for which I contend.

3. Again, he argues, that whatever is necessary to regeneration in one case, is necessary in all cases; and, consequently, if the Word be necessary at all, regeneration cannot occur without it, in any case. But the Bible says no such thing. God has never said, that he will employ the same instrumentality in all cases. Sometimes, as I have proved, the living ministry is employed in converting men; and, at other times, it is not. This bold assertion, therefore, is without proof, and is contrary to fact.

4. His next argument is, that the Holy Spirit is called an *Advocate.* But does this name prove, that the Spirit, in converting and sanctifying men, employs no other influence, than that of words and arguments? Most certainly it does not.

5. On the day of Pentecost, he tells us, the first miraculous gift was that of *tongues* or *languages;* and the Spirit did employ words. Does the fact, that God ordinarily employs the instrumentality of the truth in converting men, prove that he *always* employs it—or, that he does not exert any other influence on their minds? Certainly it does not. These assertions, founded on such facts, are not worth a straw. The premises and the conclusion are the poles apart.

6. His next argument is, that believers are said to have been *begotten by the Word.* But God is said to beget them. So then, God is the agent, and the Word the instrument. Does this prove, that he exerts no other influence but that of the Word? The conclusion follows not from the premises. The expression, " purifying their hearts by faith," it would not be difficult to prove, militates not against the doctrine of special divine influence.

7. Naked Spirit, he asserts, never operates on naked spirit. This is

48

mere assertion. How can the gentleman prove it true? Does he know
how one spirit influences another? Can he inform us how Satan can
tempt men? Does he understand it? What are such unproved assertions
worth?

But he says, he does not pretend to know how the Spirit operates. He
has tried to tell us both how he *can*, and how he *cannot* operate. I will
not misrepresent him. I will, therefore, keep his language before your
minds. Let me once more read from his *Christianity Restored*, (p. 350):

" But to return. *As the spirit of man puts forth all its moral power, in
the words which it fills with its ideas; so the Spirit of God puts forth all its
converting and sanctifying power, in the words which it fills with its ideas.*
Miracles cannot convert. They can only obtain a favorable hearing of the
converting arguments. If they fail to obtain a favorable hearing, the arguments which they prove are impotent as an unknown tongue. If the Spirit
of God has spoken all its arguments; or, if the New and Old Testament
contain all the arguments which can be offered to reconcile man to God,
and to purify them who are reconciled; *then all the power of the Holy Spirit
which can operate upon the human mind is* SPENT, *and he that is not sanctified and saved by these, cannot be saved by angels or spirits, human or
divine.*"

The gentleman could not have employed language more clear and definite. He puts the Holy Spirit, in regard to conversion and sanctification,
on a perfect equality with man, except so far as he may present more
powerful motives than man. In the most definite terms, he denies any
influence of the Spirit, other than that of his words and arguments. I
hold, that the Word is ordinarily used, but not always; and that when it
is used, there is also an influence of the Spirit distinct from it, renewing
the heart, and inclining the sinner to receive the truth in the love of it.

In reply to my argument from the conversions on the day of Pentecost,
Mr. C. says, those persons were converted, not without the Word. But
did he prove that the three thousand were converted simply by the Word?
He did not, and he cannot. The apostles gave themselves not only to
preaching, but to prayer, Acts vi. 4. Why did they pray? Because
they knew that the Word alone could not convert men. They therefore
prayed for the efficacious influences of the Holy Spirit. The very fact,
that they connected prayer with preaching, proves conclusively that they
believed the special and immediate agency of the Spirit necessary. The
argument is conclusive.

But suppose I should admit, that the Spirit operates on adults, only
through the truth; would it follow, that the same is true of infants? I
can easily prove, that adults are saved by faith, never without it; but does
it follow that infants must believe, or be damned? According to the gentleman's logic it would; for he contends, that whatever is essential in one
case, is essential in all cases. Neither reason nor Scripture will permit
us to assume the principle, that what is said of adults is applicable to infants. Mr. C. denies that infants are regenerated by the Spirit. So he
leaves them to die in sin and be lost.

I will now resume the recapitulation of my argument. The necessity
of the agency of the Spirit on the hearts of men, I have said, arises simply from their deep depravity. I have proved by a large number of passages of Scripture, that man by nature is destitute of holiness, and inclined only to sin; that he is born of the flesh and is carnal; that his
thoughts are evil from his youth; that he is conceived in sin, and goes
astray from his very birth; that his heart is deceitful above all things and

desperately wicked, &c. &c. I have also stated and proved the fact, that whatever is truly good in any man, is in the Scriptures ascribed to a radical change wrought in his heart by God. This most important fact, Mr. C. has not denied. Man being thus totally depraved, estranged from God, I have proved, that he never will, and never can love God, until he shall have experienced a radical moral renovation—a change which cannot be effected simply by the Word of God.

I have offered several arguments against the doctrine taught by Mr. C., and in favor of the doctrine of a special divine influence in conversion and sanctification.

I. My first argument against his doctrine was—that it prescribes to the power of God over the human mind, an unreasonable and unscriptural limitation. This I proved by two plain facts, viz: 1st. God made man holy, upright, without words or arguments. In what manner he did it, we know not; but most certainly the fact that such a power was exerted, proves that God can sanctify the soul either through the truth, or without it. 2d. I proved by several passages of Scripture, that he claims and has exercised a controling influence over the moral conduct of men by an influence more powerful than mere motives. And if he can consistently control their moral feelings and conduct at all, without argument and motive; can he not exert such an influence as will lead them to Christ? To this argument Mr. C, has attempted no reply.

II. My second argument was—that the doctrine of Mr. C. necessarily involves the damnation of infants and idiots. He admits that they are depraved, that they "inherit a *sinful* nature," that they are "greatly fallen and depraved in their whole moral constitution." This being true, one of three consequences must follow, viz: 1st. they go to hell; or, 2d. they go to heaven in their depravity ; or, 3rd. they are sanctified by the Spirit, without the Word. He will not say, they go to hell; nor will he pretend that they go to heaven in their depravity. The conclusion is, therefore, inevitable, that they are sanctified by the Spirit without the Word. This is our doctrine ; and it is the doctrine of the Bible. Our Savior taught that all must be born again, because " that which is born of the flesh is flesh"—is carnal; and therefore it must be born of the Spirit. You have seen how the gentleman writhed under this argument, and to what absurdities and contradictions he has been driven to evade its force. I leave you, my friends, to determine whether it is more accordant with reason and Scripture, that infants should be sanctified by the Spirit without the truth, or that they should be for ever lost.

III. My third argument was—that the doctrine of Mr. C. contradicts the teaching of the Scriptures, concerning the depravity of man. They teach that men sin knowingly, willfully and deliberately ; that their hearts are fully set in them to do evil. According to his doctrine, they sin only through mistake or error ; and all that is necessary to convert them, is to give them correct information. To this argument he has not even attempted to reply. He has said not one word concerning it—not a word.

IV. My fourth argument was, that a large number of passages of Scripture directly and most clearly teach, that in conversion and sanctification, the Spirit of God exerts an influence powerful and efficacious, in addition to the Word, and distinct from it. "I will give them one heart and one way, that they may fear me forever, for the good of them and their children after them," Jer. xxxii. 39. Does this language mean that God would reason with them? No. The time was coming, when he would take the work into his own hands; and then his people would have one heart and one way. Again, "I will pour out water upon him that is thirsty, and floods upon the dry ground: I will pour my Spirit upon thy seed, and my blessing upon thine offspring; and they shall spring up as among the grass, as willows by the water-courses," Isaiah xliv. 3. Such are the blessed results, when the Spirit of God moves upon the hearts of men. Again, "A new heart also will I give you, and a new spirit will I put within you; and I will take away the stony heart out of your flesh, and I will give you an heart of flesh. And I will put my Spirit within you," &c. Ezekiel xxxvi. 26. I need not repeat other passages, quoted from the Old Testament. To the most of them, the gentleman has attempted no reply.

In the New Testament, we find declarations equally strong in proof of our doctrine. Thus in Eph. ii. 10, Paul says, "We are his workmanship, created in Christ Jesus unto good works, which God hath before ordained, that we should walk in them." I endeavored to prevail on the gentleman to notice this text, but could not succeed. The word *create* is the strongest word in any language; and the apostle uses it without qualification, to express that change which is wrought in man by the Spirit, and which results in his doing good works.

Again, in the same chapter, the apostle represents man as dead in trespasses and in sins, and as being quickened by the power of God. Was a dead man ever made alive by words or arguments? Jesus stood at the grave of Lazarus and said, "Lazarus, come forth;" but at that moment he exerted an almighty power to quicken him. So when God speaks to the sinner, who is spiritually dead, his Spirit breathes into his soul spiritual life—exerts an influence which causes him to embrace Christ as his Savior, and rejoice in his service.

In the epistle to Titus, the apostle says, God saves us "by the washing of regeneration and renewing of the Holy Ghost, which he shed on us abundantly through Jesus Christ," chap. iii. 5. And I have proved, that in every instance where the expressions "poured out," "shed upon," &c. occur, an immediate divine influence, distinct from the Word, is intended. When the Spirit *fell upon* Cornelius and his family, Mr. C. admits there was an immediate agency of the Spirit, entirely distinct from the Word; but when the same kind of expression is used concerning conversion and sanctification, he denies that any special and distinct agency is intended!

These and a number of other passages I have read, to most of which no answer has been attempted, prove conclusively, that in conversion and sanctification there is an agency of the Spirit, distinct from the Word, renewing the heart and inclining it to the service of God. Most certainly such is the obvious meaning of these scriptures; and they will bear no other interpretation.

V. My fifth argument was, that God is represented as giving repentance unto life—as granting repentance to the acknowledging of the truth. *Faith*, too, is declared to be the effect of regeneration. "Whosoever believeth that Jesus is the Christ, is born of God:" 1 John v. 1. So in 1 Cor. iii. 5, Paul says, "Who then is Paul, and who is Apollos, but ministers by whom ye believe, *even as God gave to every man*." This passage I could not possibly induce Mr. Campbell to see! There are many others that teach most clearly, that repentance, faith, and every grace, are the result of a change of heart, of which God is the author—all of which establish the doctrine for which I contend.

VI. My sixth argument was, that the doctrine of Mr. C. makes prayer for the unconverted, and even for the sanctification of believers, wholly useless and improper. Why should we ask God to convert men, and then preach to them, that he never purposed to convert any man, woman or child, by any other influence than that of arguments, presented before their minds? Some of the followers of the gentleman are quite consistent. I have observed, that in their public prayers, they rarely ever ask God to convert sinners. If I believed as they do, I might reason with men; but I should never think of praying to God, to cause them to turn and live. And why pray at all?—for Mr. C. teaches, that both conversion and sanctification are to be obtained by reading or hearing the Word, and by this only. If Paul believed this doctrine, why did he pray for the Ephesian christians, that they might be "strengthened with might in the inner man by his Spirit?" Paul believed in the special agency of the Spirit, and therefore prayed. This doctrine has been, and still is, the consolation of thousands of the followers of Christ, who regard it as one of their highest privileges, to pray for the conversion and salvation of dear friends, who are far away, or whose hearts are callous to the appeals of divine truth.

VII. My seventh argument was—that the conversions on the day of Pentecost and afterwards, prove a divine influence distinct from the Word. On that memorable day three thousand souls were suddenly converted to God. With repentance for their sins and faith in Jesus Christ, they entered his church, and, to the day of their death, delighted in his service. Arguments and motives never produced in the minds of men such a revolution in an hour. "It was the Lord's work, and marvellous in our eyes." Thousands and tens of thousands have since experienced the same happy change. And even in these last days we are permitted to witness the fulfillment of God's promise to pour out his Spirit on all flesh. We often see a general religious interest gradually pervading a town or neighborhood, where no extraordinary efforts have been made to arrest the attention of the people. Christians become more prayerful. The unconverted pause and consider. They go to the house of God which they had seldom entered, and hear with fixed attention the melting appeals of divine truth. The solemnity increases. The most careless become thoughtful. The proud are humbled. The most hopeless are reclaimed. They come "as clouds and as doves to their windows." Many are added to the church of God, and continue to adorn the doctrine of Christ by a godly life. Who can believe, that results like these are the effect of mere argument and motive? No—it is the Lord's work. His Spirit is poured out as showers on the thirsty ground.

VIII. My last argument is—that the overwhelming majority of all the readers of the Bible, in all ages, have understood it to teach the doctrine for which I contend. From Methodists, Baptists, Episcopalians, and others, we differ in some things; but we meet at the cross of Christ. We hold the doctrine of human depravity and the absolute necessity of the special agency of the Holy Spirit in order to effect the conversion and sanctification of men. We can bow together around the mercy-seat, and unitedly pray to God, that his Word may run and be glorified—that men may be convinced and converted, and that believers may be sanctified.

Indeed so clearly is this doctrine taught in the Scriptures, that few have been found to deny it. Is the Bible a plain book? My friend admits that it is; and if it is, he is certainly in error; for the overwhelming

3 S

mass of the wise and the good are against him. If his doctrine be true, we must conclude, that the Bible is one of the most obscure books ever written; for few indeed have been able to understand it on this vital point.

But I must bring my remarks to a close. I do rejoice and bless God, that in the defence of this fundamental doctrine of christianity, I am sustained by so large a portion of those who profess to take the Bible as their only infallible guide. On this hallowed ground we meet, sensible of our need of divine aid in our preparation for heaven, and confident that in answer to our united prayers, he who began the good work in us, will perform it unto the day of Jesus Christ.

Here, too, we find our encouragement to go forth and preach the gospel which is " not after man." If I believed that no other influence but that of words and arguments would be exerted on the minds of men, I should have no heart to preach another sermon. I possess no eloquence that can melt the hardened hearts of men ; no power to open their eyes and turn them from darkness to light, and from the power of Satan to God. My encouragement to preach the unsearchable riches of Christ is found in the promise—that God will pour out his Spirit on all flesh, and will cause the wilderness and the solitary place to be glad, and the desert to bud and blossom as the rose.

Convince me, that no such agency is promised, and I will weep for myself and for my race. There is no hope for man if this doctrine be not true. He is not, and never will be, pure enough to see God. Let me exhort those who have been induced to reject it, to a careful re-examination of the whole subject. If ninety-nine hundredths of the pious readers of the Bible were against me on a point so vital, I would examine again and again. I should greatly fear, that I had fatally erred, and that, depending on my own efforts with only motives before me, I should fail of preparation for heaven.

May God, in his infinite mercy, guide you and me into the knowledge of all truth ; and may we be sanctified and fitted for the enjoyments of heaven by his Holy Spirit.—[*Time expired.*

[END OF THE FIFTH PROPOSITION.]

PROPOSITION SIXTH.

Human Creeds, as Bonds of Union and Communion, are necessarily Heretical and Schismatical. Mr. Campbell affirms. Mr. Rice denies.

Thursday, Nov. 30—10 o'clock, A. M.
[MR. CAMPBELL'S OPENING ADDRESS.]

MR. PRESIDENT—Modern christianity, like astronomy, geology, or geography, has its technical terms and definitions. So had ancient, and so had primitive christianity; for between primitive and ancient and modern christianity there are as well defined lines and bounderies as between Virginia, Kentucky, and Ohio. The primitive christians had one, and but one faith, written out for them by apostles and prophets: we have it in one volume, usually called the New Testament. The ancients, in some three or four centuries, set on foot several creed manufactories, called synods and councils, ecumenical and particular.

Three of their choicest productions have escaped the ravages of time, and are still extant under the names of the Apostles' Creed, the Nicene, and the Athanasian. The first and the last of these, all the world now admits are not the works of the names they bear. They are religious impositions practiced upon the credulity of less favored ages than the present. Still they indicate fewer aberrations from the Scriptures of truth, than those modern affairs, excogitated and fashioned at Trent, at Augsburgh, at Dort, and at Westminster.

Between those last mentioned and the first, there is as great a difference as there is between the artificial grandeur of imperial Rome, at the zenith of her glory, and that Rome that Romulus built. And between the Nicene formula of faith and the gospel according to Matthew or John, there is such a difference as usually appears between a young man, in the very prime and vigor of youth, and one of our finest Parisian anatomical preparations.

Creeds bear the impress and character of their natal age, as does the human face bear upon its lines and shades the years it has seen and felt. They are exponents of the christian improvement and civilization of their respective eras. The Apostles' creed, or that of Nice, or that attributed to Athanasius, would be as much in good keeping with this our day, as a continental almanac, published by Ben Franklin in the days of Peter Porcupine, would suit the present year of grace, at the meridian of Lexington.

In the days of the apostles there was something called "*the faith*," "the form of sound words," "the truth," "the gospel," which was to them something more than our summaries, called creeds and confessions of faith.

These summaries were first called *symbols*, and afterwards *creeds*. The former term is of Grecian, the latter of Roman origin and authority. The Greek, *sumbolon*, properly signifies a *mark*, *note*, or *sign*. It was used by some Greeks to denote a military sign. So Herodian uses it.

759

St. Cyprian is the first that used the term to indicate an epitome or abridgment of the christian faith—and was sometimes understood to mean, the distinguishing mark and character of a christian. The confession made at baptism was called the symbol of the candidate. This, probably, was the origin of the ecclesiastic use of the word. They were, according to some, called symbols because the makers of them acted in councils and synods, and each one threw in some article or articles, and the whole collection of these several offerings was called, etymologically, a *symbol*. So our most learned ecclesiastics understand the matter. Dupin, vol. i. p. 37, Dublin Ed. A. D. 1723.

In the third century, it is said, there were as many symbols as authors. I find them in Irenæus, Tertullian, St. Cyprian, &c., confined, indeed, to about the same number of articles, and generally to some of the same topics found in the apostles' creed: none of them, however, propounded as a term of communion; none of them made either the covenant or constitution of any particular church, much less of the churches in particular districts. On the whole, then, we remark that synods and symbols are Greek, councils and creeds are Roman. The antiquity of the oldest creed now extant is no more than Papal; and its catholicity lies between the Vandals and the Sicilians, between the Euxine and the western ocean. A Grecian *symbol* had some truth and some philosophy on its side; but a Roman creed had neither. The reasons are, the Greek symbol was a compound of christian truths, a summary or synopsis of prominent facts, of which the document called the apostles' creed is a fair specimen. But the Roman creeds, like those of Trent, Augsburgh, and Westminster, are not portraitures of ancient truths or facts, so much as records of modern opinions and inferences concerning them. There was some use for a heart, as well as a head, on the part of those who approved the symbols: but the moderns have no use for the heart, having imposed all the labor upon the brains, in acknowledging their tests of orthodoxy. As a matter of curiosity and for future reference, I shall here read the apostles' creed.

" I believe in God the Father Almighty, maker of heaven and earth: and in Jesus Christ, his only Son our Lord; who was conceived by the Holy Ghost, born of the Virgin Mary, suffered under Pontius Pilate, was crucified, dead and buried; he descended into hell; the third day he rose from the dead; he ascended into heaven, and sitteth on the right hand of God the Father Almighty; from thence he shall come to judge the quick and the dead. I believe in the holy Ghost; the holy catholic church; the communion of saints; the forgiveness of sins; the resurrection of the body, and the life everlasting. Amen."

And the Nicene creed:

" I believe in one God the Father Almighty, maker of heaven and earth, and of all things visible and invisible: and in one Lord Jesus Christ, the only-begotten Son of God, begotten of his Father before all worlds; God of God, Light of Light, very God of very God, begotten, not made, being of one substance with the Father, by whom all things were made; who for us men, and for our salvation, came down from heaven, and was incarnate by the Holy Ghost of the Virgin Mary, and was made man, and was crucified also for us under Pontius Pilate. He suffered and was buried, and the third day he rose again, according to the Scriptures, and ascended into heaven, and sitteth on the right hand of the Father; and he shall come again, with glory, to judge both the quick and the dead; whose kingdom shall have no end. And I believe in the Holy Ghost, the Lord and giver of life, who proceedeth from the Father and the Son; who with the Father and the Son together is worshiped and glorified, who spake by the prophets. And I believe one catholic and apostolic church. I acknowledge one baptism for the remission of sins; and I look for the resurrection of the dead, and the life of the world to come. Amen."

We shall next present the creed usually called the creed of St. Athanasius:

"Whosoever will be saved, before all things it is necessary that he hold the catholic faith; which faith except every one do keep whole and undefiled, without doubt he shall perish everlastingly. And the catholic faith is this: That we worship One God in Trinity, and Trinity in Unity; neither confounding the persons, nor dividing the substance. For there is one Person of the Father, another of the Son, and another of the Holy Ghost: but the Godhead of the Father, of the Son, and of the Holy Ghost, is all one; the glory equal, the majesty co-eternal. Such as the Father is, such is the Son, and such is the Holy Ghost; the Father uncreate, the Son uncreate, and the Holy Ghost uncreate; the Father incomprehensible, the Son incomprehensible, and the Holy Ghost incomprehensible; the Father eternal, the Son eternal, and the Holy Ghost eternal: and yet they are not three eternals, but one eternal; as also there are not three incomprehensibles, nor three uncreated, but one uncreated, and one incomprehensible. So likewise the Father is Almighty, the Son Almighty, and the Holy Ghost Almighty: and yet they are not three Almighties, but one Almighty. So the Father is God, the Son is God, and the Holy Ghost is God: and yet there are not three Gods, but one God. So likewise the Father is Lord, the Son Lord, and the Holy Ghost Lord: and yet not three Lords, but one Lord. For like as we are compelled by the christian verity to acknowledge every Person by himself to be God and Lord, so are we forbidden by the catholic religion to say, there be three Gods, or three Lords.

The Father is made of none, neither created, nor begotten. The Son is of the Father alone, not made, nor created, but begotten. The Holy Ghost is of the Father and of the Son, neither made, nor created, nor begotten, but proceeding. So there is one Father, not three Fathers; one Son, not three Sons; one Holy Ghost, not three Holy Ghosts. And in this Trinity none is afore or after the other, none is greater or less than the other; but the whole three Persons are co-eternal together, and co-equal. So that in all things, as is aforesaid, the Unity in Trinity and the Trinity in Unity is to be worshiped. He therefore that will be saved, must thus think of the Trinity.

Furthermore, it is necessary to everlasting salvation, that he also believe rightly the incarnation of our Lord Jesus Christ. For the right faith is, that we believe and confess that our Lord Jesus Christ, the Son of God, is God and man; God of the substance of the Father, begotten before the worlds, and man of the substance of his mother, born in the world; perfect God, and perfect man; of a reasonable soul and human flesh subsisting; equal to the Father as touching his Godhead, and inferior to the Father as touching his manhood. Who, although he be God and man, yet he is not two, but one Christ; one, not by conversion of the Godhead into flesh, but by taking of the manhood into God; one altogether, not by confusion of substance, but by unity of person: for as the reasonable soul and flesh is one man, so God and man is one Christ. Who suffered for our salvation, descended into hell, rose again the third day from the dead, he ascended into heaven, he sitteth on the right hand of the Father God Almighty: from whence he shall come to judge the quick and the dead. At whose coming all men shall rise again with their bodies, and shall give account of their own works; and they that have done good shall go into life everlasting, and they that have done evil into everlasting fire.

This is the catholic faith; which except a man believe faithfully, he cannot be saved. Glory be to the Father," &c.

Concerning the Athanasian creed, Waddington, fellow of Trinity college, Cambridge, says:

"The sublime truths which it contains are not expressed in the language of Holy Scripture; nor could they possibly have been so expressed, since the inspired writers were not studious minutely to expound inscrutable mysteries. Neither can it plead any sanctity from high antiquity, or even traditional authority; since it was composed many centuries after the time of the apostles, in a very corrupt age of a corrupt church, and composed in so much obscurity, that the very pen from which it proceeded is not certainly known to us. The inventions of men, when they have been associated for ages with the exercise of religion, should indeed be touched with respect and discretion; but it is a dangerous error to treat them as inviolable, and it is something worse than error to confound them in holiness and reverence with the words and things of God."—p. 193.

Ecclesiastic creeds and the faith apostolic are just as diverse as inference and premise, as fallibility and infallibility, as human reason and divine wisdom. When, then, we use the word *creed* in this discussion, we do not mean the truth nor the faith, the law nor the gospel, the apostles' writings, or those of the prophets. Nor do we mean our simple belief of the testimony of God. We all have a belief and a knowledge of christian doctrine; but this belief or knowledge is not what is indicated by a creed. A creed or confession of faith is an ecclesiastic document— the mind and will of some synod or council possessing authority—as a term of communion, by which persons and opinions are to be tested, approbated, or reprobated.

The documents, therefore, which constitute the subject of our proposition, are such as the Thirty-nine Articles; the Westminster Creed, with all its numerous and various emendations, to that of the present year; the Baptist Confession of Faith in all its varieties; the creed of Pope Pius and the Council of Trent, or the Methodistic Discipline, amended and improved some two and twenty times.

All creeds and confessions become the constitution of churches. The persons called a church or community are said to be builded upon them. They generally, indeed, assume that the creed itself is builded on the Bible, and the church on both. The Bible is, then, the subterraneous basis, or that portion of the foundation buried under ground. The creed is that visible, above-ground part of the basis, and on which the church immediately rests, and from which it receives its name. This assumption of a Bible sub-basis, is, however, but a mere illusion. Take, for illustration, the high-church and low-church Episcopal, the Presbyterian, the Methodist and the Baptist, to go no farther. These all are said to be builded on the Bible; but between them and the Bible is interposed the creed from which they receive their name. The Bible, then, is to all the sects in Christendom what the earth is to London, the basis on which the several palaces, castles, and dwellings rest. The earth, however, is the foundation of none of them, in correct language. No one would think of calling the earth the foundation of Westminster Abbey, Windsor Palace, or the old Parliament House. No more can I call the Bible the foundation of the Episcopal, Presbyterian, Methodist, and Baptist churches, or any one of the scores of communities that pretend to build on it. Contemplated as buildings, creeds are their proper foundations. Contemplated as *bodies*, they are their constitutions.

They are, therefore, the basis of the parties. As many creeds, so many parties; Cæsar's maxim fitly illustrates their history. "Money," said he, " will raise soldiers, and soldiers will raise money." Thus creeds will make parties, and parties will make creeds; so the matter has operated from the day of their birth till now. From these general definitions and remarks introductory, we shall therefore proceed to the proof of our proposition.

ARGUMENT I. *That creeds are necessarily heretical, is argued, first, from the fact that they are human and fallible productions.*

They are called *human,* not merely because they are the production of human effort, but because they are also the offspring of human authority. No one can, in reason and truth, assign to them a divine authority; because no man can produce any precept or divine warrant for their manufacture. No apostle, prophet, or evangelist gave any authority to any church, community, or council, to furnish such a document.

Now, in order to give them any other than human authority, four things are necessary. 1st. A divine precept commanding the thing to be done. 2d. A selection of persons by whom it must be executed. 3d. A time fixed or extended, during which the work is to be accomplished; and, 4th. A command to the christian communities to receive and use them for the ends and uses for which they were created. In the absence of this divine arrangement and enactment, they must be contemplated as a presumptuous interference with the legislative prerogative of Zion's Lawgiver and King—as a daring attempt to intrude into his peculiar office, who has all authority in heaven and earth committed to him for the government of his church. It is offering strange fire on God's altar, and burning incense uncommanded by him whose right it is to ordain his own worship. It is in fact a reproach, an indignity, offered to his living oracles, and to the competency and fidelity of his ambassadors and plenipotentiaries, to the world and to the church.

Who, in a controversy with an apostle or a saint, could answer the following interrogations? Did not the Messiah see the end from the beginning? Did not he anticipate all that has happened on earth since his ascension into heaven? Did not his servant Paul forewarn us of a most important and widely extended apostasy? Did he not say that the time would come when they would not endure sound doctrine, but should accumulate teachers for themselves, having itching ears? that they should turn away their ears from the truth, and be turned unto fables? Did he not know the devices of Satan to annoy his heritage, and to seduce his servants into the paths of schism and alienation, and thus set them at variance with one another? And had he, in his wisdom and benevolence, thought that to prevent all this, a symbol or b of summary of true faith or true doctrine, clearly and strongly set forth, was necessary or expedient; had he not the residue of the Spirit, and agents in abundance to accomplish his wishes? If, then, with all these premises in his eye, and all the details of two thousand years as clearly seen in the future as they are now in the past, he provided the documents which we have, and gave them in charge, to be kept without addition or subtraction till he return; why should any one presume to obtrude his opinions and notions upon him, and make his views of expediency a reason why he should set forth on his own responsibility, or in conjunction with others, his equals and co-ordinates, a synopsis or digest of God's revelations, selecting for it such views and portions of God's own book as, in his finite, feeble and fallible judgment, partially and imperfectly enlightened, he might judge expedient to form a system of belief—a rule of practice for a christian community?

The setting up of calves at Bethel and Dan by Jeroboam, the son of Nebat, who made Israel to sin, seems to me to be only a mere exaggeration of the principle involved in such a device. And such, too, was the golden symbol manufactured by Aaron out of Egyptian gold, to go before Israel in the absence of Moses. Had the Lord thought a miniature of the Bible, an image of the whole revelation, a proper basis for church union and communion, Paul was the man, or Peter, or James, or John, or all of them together, to give us the sum of the matter, and command all men to regard it as the covenant or constitution of Christ's church in general, and of each congregation in particular—and then we would have an authoritative creed, a divine rule of faith, by which to receive and reject all mankind.

His not having done it is the best argument in the world why it should not be attempted by mortal and fallible man; and if I am asked for other reasons why, so far as I can apprehend them they shall be forthcoming at a proper time and place. Meantime, the point to which these remarks and reasonings tend, must be distinctly stated. Do they not, then, lead to the conclusion, that all these covenants are human, wholly human, in conception, design, and execution? and, consequently, as the stream can rise no higher than the fountain, they are fallible, weak, and imperfect documents—not of such dimensions, texture, and solidity, as to be either the foundation or constitution of Christ's glorious church, redeemed by his blood and sanctified by his Spirit. It is building a golden palace upon the grass, a divine temple upon reeds and rushes.

But where the necessary schismatical tendency of thes documents? I answer, the very attempt to create such a thing immediately divides into parties those who before were one. A affirms his conviction, that the attempt is impious. B argues, that it is expedient to keep out error and secure union amongst those that are now of one opinion. But A responds, we are not required to be, because we cannot be, of one opinion; and so far from the project creating unity of opinion, already it forms two opinions—one concerning the impiety, and the other touching the expediency of the affair. The proposition to create and to adopt is, therefore, essentially heretical and divisive; and, when the proposition is adopted, two parties, before in embryo by the proposition, are now by the resolution actually and formally in existence. The reason of all this is, perhaps, not yet fully developed. It lies, indeed, hid in the fallibility of human nature.

We, sooner or later, all discover, that between the fallible and the infallible there is a gulf, into which the universe might be hurled without at all reducing the chasm. Finites and fallibles are weak authorities when heaven and immortality are at stake. And the moment that B propounds his synopsis with the slightest air of authority, in the way of exacting obedience or acknowledgment, that moment there is something in human nature that whispers in A, who is this brother B? A fallible like myself! A great man he may be; but he is fond of his own opinion, and prides himself upon his superiority. I will not lay a victim upon his altar nor burn incense at his shrine; I, too, am a man, and will yield to none the right to dictate to me—God alone is infallible. His word is the only unerring rule of truth. I will cut myself off from the society of B, or any one like him, who claims for his private judgment the respect and homage due only to the well authenticated precepts and statutes of the Eternal King.

We all, on reflection, feel the want of the authority of certain truths while reading our creeds and confessions, and hence that perpetual restlessness and mutation manifest on all the pages of their history, from the days of Arius, the schismatic, down to the present time. A document that has authority, proper authority with men, must be superhuman, super-angelic, supernatural—it must be the word of God; where that fails to awe or allure into a holy acquiescence, there is a manifest want of piety and all the essential elements of christian character; and while such persons may make a church by themselves, Christ's church wants them not, and has made no arrangement to retain them. The parson may desire to retain such for their money; the flock may wish to retain them for their worldly respectability; but as the Messiah would not receive them into heaven, he will not sanction any arrangement made to retain them in his church on earth.

II. Creeds, then, are necessarily heretical, not only on this account; but, in the *second place*—they strain out the nats and swallow the camels; nay, worse, they rack off the pure wine of the church and retain the lees. It is a striking demonstration of man's slowness to learn, that a fact so palpable as this, that creeds have always been roots of bitterness, apples of discord, and either causes or occasions of driving out the good and retaining the bad, should have, since the days of the council of Nice, been passing before the eyes of the whole church militant, and yet unobserved and unappreciated by the great majority of professors; at least not so practically observed as to have induced them to take away these stumbling blocks out of the way of the people.

And what more natural, even *a priori*, than that the hypocritical, designing and wicked would subscribe, when their pride, or their passions, or their temporal interests made a place in a popular community an advantage, or an honor to them? Or, that the conscientious, upright, and scrupulously virtuous, would hesitate, demur and refuse to admit a tenet, or a rule of action resting, in their opinion, upon mere human authority; and not only that, but in their judgment, impinging, contravening, or making void a divine precept or arrangement. I say, what truth lies more upon the surface of things? What law of human nature is more clearly imprinted in more legible characters upon the very face of society, than this one? and how few, comparatively, seem to have profitably attended to it. For what do all the pages of ecclesiastical history reveal? What do the voluminous records, not merely of the dark ages, but of all ages, disclose on these premises? That human creeds have made more heretics than christians; more parties than reformations; more martyrs than saints; more wars than peace; more hatred than love; more death than life; that they have killed or driven out all the apostles, prophets and reformers of the church and of the world. The Messiah himself, one of their victims, spoke a volume in one sentence against creeds and church covenants—and the most severely true and caustic sentence he ever uttered; it is superlatively laconic and pithy: " *It cannot be that a prophet perish out of Jerusalem!* O Jerusalem! O Jerusalem! that stonest the prophets, and killest them that God hath sent to you!" Need I ask, what means Jerusalem in this connection? Stands it not for the church authorities, with their doctrinal and perceptive traditions, against which he so often inveighed? It was an established creed, and a generation of vipers, in the form of devout pharisees, and skillful and learned rabbis and scribes, that constituted that fearful desolating power that crucified the Messiah.

Pontius Pilate only obeyed the established priesthood; he only executed the sentence of the church-courts. They said, they had *a law* (a creed—a discipline,) by which he must die. That law, or creed, was the decision of their councils—precisely in the form of our creeds. This fact itself, methinks, is enough. It is a monumental fact, on which is inscribed the melancholy but true character of all such institutes.

Need we, indeed, any other proof of our proposition, than the stern, incontrovertible fact, that all the world's greatest benefactors—apostles, prophets and reformers—have been declared heretics and schismatics—reprobated, and cast out of synagogues and churches, through the native, direct and immediate influence and operation of these documents? Can any man afford one instance of any community building upon the Bible alone, upon the apostles and prophets, without any other creed or directory than the written Word of God—ever so doing, ever repudiating, or injuring in character, in person or property, any saint or distinguished man, any minister of mercy, any benefactor of our race? Let him name the church; let him name the man. But if I am asked, in return, to name those who have been so maltreated by creed-mongers, creed-makers and creed-advocates, I shall begin with Jesus Christ himself, and end not with the Wickliffs, the Jeromes, the Husses, the Luthers, the Calvins, the Rogerses, the Bunyans—but with those now living, whose characters have been immolated at the shrine of orthodoxy, and their names cast out as evil, because they prefer the commandments of God to the doctrines and traditions of men.

We must, however, still advert to the fact of their power to retain the lees, while they rack off into new vessels the good wine of the kingdom. The case of Arius himself, is both a full illustration and proof of what I mean.

The Nicene creed, as all the world knows, owed its origin to the opinions of Arius. Even the first great council, with the great Constantine at its head, had probably never assembled at Nice, or any where else, but for this bold and daring genius. Had Alexander, bishop of Alexandria, when he failed to convince his presbyter, Arius, of the impropriety of his speculations on the divine nature of the Messiah, not called a council of his clergy, and passed certain decrees upon the speculation, and excommunicated Arius, because of his dissent from their phraseology—Arius would not have been driven to Palestine, and there made a party to his views, which, by the assistance of Eusebius, bishop of Nicomedia, soon spread over all the empire. The spread of this greatly agitated the church; and the great Constantine undertook to gather the bishops of the world to Nice, and legislate the Arians into the church or out of the empire. Athanasius and the Arians finally split on the difference between an *i* and an *o;* between *homoousios* and *homoiuosios*. The *homoousios* was decreed orthodox, and the *homoiuosios* heterodox—and the line of the two great parties were drawn. Arius was dubbed *heretic*, and Athanasius *saint;* and so it reads for fifteen hundred years. Athanasius became bishop of the great church of Alexandria, and Arius wandered a heretic through Illyricum for some three or four years. Recalled, at length, by the same fickle Constantine, and asked to subscribe the creed of Nice—made to repudiate his heresy, he, for the sake of bread and board in the church, subscribed the same creed; and had he not died one day too soon, he had doubtless been received into full communion by the bishop of Constantinople—the emperor having so commanded.

After the death of Constantine, his son Constantius, and his court, sided with the Arians—different emperors took different sides. Valentinian supported Athanasianism in the west, and Valens, his own brother, supported Arianism in the east half of the empire. Hence orthodoxy at Rome was heterodoxy at Constantinople, and *vice versa.* The bishop of Rome finally became infallible, and fixed Athanasianism at Rome, where it has continued ever since; while the other half, that is, the African and Eastern churches, supported Arianism, in some form or other, down to *semi-demi-Arianism;* and finally, it became so sublimated, that the metaphysical doctors, through the finest spectacles, have long since failed to comprehend or appreciate the difference. Here, then, we have a fair exposition of all that we maintain on this question. This being a sort of prototype of all heretical creeds, it may serve as a standing text—and its history, as the common history of the thousand speculative doctrines, creeds and parties in ancient and modern Christendom.

It is important that the tendency of creeds to the corruption of the church, by admitting the evil and rejecting the good, should be kept prominently before the mind of those who desire correct and salutary conclusions on this most interesting subject. If it be a fact, that such is their tendency, it ought to be distinctly stated, fully proved and deeply impressed on the public mind. Let us, then, look again at this case of the celebrated Arius, so early occurring and so famous in the annals of the church, and compare it with some illustrious cases nearer our own times. The fact that Arius, within some four years, subscribed the Nicene creed, which in his heart he despised—the identical creed which was conceived and consummated in order to his exclusion and that of his party—for the sake of a respite from persecution and a place in the church, is itself, methinks, a full exposition of their inutility and evil tendency. Men of no principle may thus be expected to subscribe at the dictation of those in power, or at the demands of pride, passion or interest; while the honorable, and those of tender conscience, will rather be excommunicated than yield to the temptation. We shall moreover allude to two very notorious and well authenticated facts in the history of Puritanism and Presbyterianism, from which I am sorry to observe our Presbyterian friends have not profited more. There was the sacramental test act, during the reign of Elizabeth, which compelled all dissenters to take the sacrament once a year in the established church, a device to detect the Romanist party in England. But it was as oppressive to puritans as to papists. The infidels and non-religionists, together with many Romanists, to secure or retain their interests, annually partook. But the pious and conscientious dissenters left the country or suffered political disabilities, rather than eat the supper to show that they were not papists or enemies of the establishment. Again, under the act of conformity to certain prayers, rules and ceremonies, requiring subscription on or before St. Bartholomew's day, August, 1662; what multitudes suffered in a similar way! while the vascillating, temporizing, who had no conscience, turned the affair to good account. No less than two thousand pious non-conformist ministers resigned their livings rather than violate their consciences. Thus a mighty host of the very best ministers in the realm were ejected to make room for more pliant tools. Neale says more than 1500 men of loose morals, together with a troop of young men from the universities and divinity halls, without either piety or experience, filled their places; and no doubt by their time serving spirit greatly lowered the standard of piety and virtue all over the kingdom. These acts of uniformity, courts of high commission, star-chamber courts, test acts and creeds, are but various modifications of the same principle. Hence, the history of the operation of any of them, under circumstances favorable to its full development, is the history of them all.

III. While this view of the subject is before us, we must more formally advert to their proscriptive and persecuting bearings and tendencies. It is a startling fact, that all ecclesiastic persecutions, ancient and modern, are connected with the introduction, modification, transformation, or administration of creeds. Think not, Mr. President, that I am about to relate the tales of woe, to invoke the ghosts of slain legions of saints and martyrs, to disclose the dark and horrible massacres of inquisitorial tribunals through the long dark night of papal ascendency. No, sir, far be it from the happy scenes which now surround us in this favored land, the blest abode of rational and religious freedom, in which the sword has not yet learned to serve at the altar—in which we have no established priesthood, no court religion, no royal creed, no lords spiritual, no vicar of Christ, no vicegerent of heaven's eternal King—no auto de fes—no te deums—no holocausts—no whole burnt offerings of slaughtered heretics. No—thanks to the God of all justice, of all mercy, and of all truth! that we sit under our own vines and fig-trees—that we worship God according to the Bible, or our own interpretation of it, without the anathemas, the inquisitions, the pains, the terrors of incarnate demons, in the form of holy fathers and apostolic successors.

But, in the illustration and confirmation of our position, we are obliged to glance at the operation of creeds and tests of communion amongst our good Protestant dissenters—Puritans of the Protestant faith who swarm around the *sacred fires*—the sacerdotal robes and vestment—the religious habits of the famous Hooper of refusal memory, consecrated more by his glorious martyrdom under Mary of bloody memory, than by his *pro tempore* refusal of the sacerdotal appendages of papal robes in the form of Aaronic habits. This great man's stern and unbending integrity was the first occasion, rather than an actual cause, of our own glorious revolution. He was, indeed, the grand prototype of that noble race of mighty men, the patriarchs of civil liberty—the original fathers of the illustrious sisterhood of American republics. Two months before his being burnt at Gloucester, February 9th, 1555, not yet three centuries ago, he wrote to Bullinger: "We resolutely despise fire and sword for the cause of Christ; we know in whom we have believed, and are sure we have committed our souls to him in well doing! We are the Lord's; let him do with us as seemeth good in his sight." Such was the man, Mr. President, who, with the immortal Rogers, of Smithfield memory, roasted in the fire of papal cruelty, gave the first grand impulse to the cause of liberty, civil and religious. At their smouldering embers was lit the torch of American liberty. From their altar was borne across the seas the sacred fire that has warmed and illuminated the new world, and given to us our free and liberal institutions. So much good—negative, it is true, as respects this cause—so much good, however, have proscriptive creeds and acts of uniformity done to our happy country, and to the human race. But that I may not be supposed to give any false coloring, either from my views or my feelings, to the sayings and doings of my Episcopal, Puritanical, and Presbyterian friends, in adducing them as examples of the schismatic spirit of their creeds, I shall allow the candid, impartial, and justly celebrated Daniel Neale, who died a little more than one century ago, not to tell the whole story, but to give a mere passing notice of the operation of creeds, even in the more generous hands of Protestant dissenters.

" *That* UNIFORMITY *of sentiments in religion is not to be attained among christians; nor will a* COMPREHENSION *within an establishment be of service to the cause of truth and liberty without a* TOLERATION *of all our dutiful subjects.* Wise and good men, after their most diligent searches after truth, have seen things in a different light; which is not to be avoided as long as they have liberty to judge for themselves. If *Christ* had appointed an infallible judge upon earth, or men were to be determined by an implicit faith in their superiors, there would be an end of such differences; but all the engines of human policy that have been set at work to obtain it have hitherto failed of success. Subscriptions, and a variety of oaths and other tests, having occasioned great mischiefs to the church; by these means men of weak morals and ambitious views have been raised to the highest preferments, while others of stricter virtue and superior talents have been neglected and laid aside; and *power* has been lodged in the hands of those who have used it in an unchristian manner, to force men to an agreement in sounds and outward appearances, contrary to the true conviction and sense of their minds: and thus a lasting reproach has been brought on the christian name, and on the genuine principles of a protestant church.

All parties of christians when in power have been guilty of persecution for conscience' sake. The annals of the church are a most melancholy demonstration of this truth. Let the reader call to mind the bloody proceedings of the *popish bishops* in queen Mary's reign, and the account that has been given of the *Star Chamber* and *High Commission Court* in later times; what number of useful ministers have been sequestered, imprisoned, and their families reduced to poverty and disgrace, for refusing to wear a *white surplice,* or to comply with a *few indifferent ceremonies!* What havoc did the Presbyterians make with their covenant uniformity, their *jure divino* discipline, and their rigid prohibition of reading the old service book! And though the Independents had a better notion of the rights of conscience, how defective was their instrument of government under *Cromwell!* how arbitrary the proceedings of their triers! how narrow their list of fundamentals! and how severe their restraints of the press! And though the rigorous proceedings of the Puritans of this age did by no means rival those of the prelates before and after the civil wars, yet they are so many species of persecution, and not to be justified even by the confusion of the times in which they were acted.

It is unsafe and dangerous to entrust any sort of clergy with the power of the sword; for our Savior's kingdom is not of this world,—' *If it were,*' says he, ' *then would my servants fight, but now is my kingdom not from hence.*' The church and state should stand on a distinct basis, and their jurisdiction be agreeable to the nature of their crimes; those of the church *purely spiritual,* and those of the state *purely civil.*

Reformation of religion, or a redress of grievances in the church, has not in fact arisen from the clergy. I would not be thought to reflect upon that *venerable* order, which is of great usefulness and deserved honor when the ends of its institution are pursued. But so strange has been the infatuation, so enchanting the lust of dominion and the charms of riches and honor, that the propagation of piety and virtue has been very much neglected, and little else thought of but how they might rise higher in the authority and grandeur of this world, and fortify their strong holds against all that should attack them. In the dawn of the *reformation,* the clergy maintained the *pope's supremacy* against the king till they were cast in *præmunire.* In the reign of *queen Elizabeth,* there was but one of the whole bench who would join in the consecration of a *protestant bishop.* And when the reformation was established, how cruelly did those protestant bishops, who themselves had suffered for religion, vex the *Puritans* because they could not

49 3 T

come up to their standard! How unfriendly did they behave at the Hampton-court *conference!* at the restoration of king Charles II, and at the late revolution of *king William* and *queen Mary!* when the most solemn promises were broken, and the most hopeful opportunity of accommodating differences among protestants lost by the perverseness of the clergy towards those very men who had saved them from ruin. So little ground is there to hope for an union among christians, or the propagation of truth, peace and charity from *councils, synods, general assemblies,* or *convocations of the clergy* of any sort whatsoever!"—[*Time expired.*]

Thursday, Nov. 30—11 *o'clock, A. M.*
[MR. RICE'S FIRST REPLY.]

MR. PRESIDENT—I agree with my friend, Mr. C., that the union of all the disciples of Christ is an object greatly to be desired. I go for christian union on scriptural principles, as zealously as he; and so do evangelical denominations generally, so far as I know. We differ not concerning the importance of the object, but concerning the proper method of securing it. He has adopted a plan which he supposes will prove successful. We regard it as unscriptural and dangerous to the cause of truth and righteousness. We think there is a better plan, by which ultimately the object will be attained.

I do not purpose to answer every thing contained in his labored essay; for much the larger part of it did not bear upon the question, whether human creeds, as bonds of union and communion, are necessarily heretical and schismatical. Those remarks which relate to the proposition before us, will be noticed.

With those churches that use creeds, the Bible, he tells us, is the *subterranean foundation*, while their creed is the foundation above ground; so that "the sects," as he calls all churches but his own, have two foundations. Well, there is comfort in the fact, that the Bible is really under us. No church will sink, that has the Bible as its foundation, even though it be subterranean. In building, it is important to dig deep and lay under ground a solid foundation. I was pleased to hear the gentleman admit, that we have the Bible under us; for if it is, we cannot sink—our foundation stands firm. But is he not in the same predicament in which he would place us? His Christian Baptist, Christianity Restored, Christian System and other writings, contain his creed—the foundation above ground. Unfortunately, I think, the Bible is not quite under him. The difference between his church and "the sects," is this: The notions and opinions of each individual in his church, form their foundation, and therefore there is no unity of faith; whilst each of "the sects" have a common faith, a common bond of union. This being the case, I am unable to see wherein he has ground of boasting, unless it be, that his church has a greater number of foundations than any other.

One of his arguments to prove human creeds necessarily heretical and schismatical, is—that there is in the Bible no command to make a creed. But there is no command to make a "Christian System," as he has done, and to write and publish any thing on religious subjects. Are we to conclude, that every thing is unlawful, that is not in the Scriptures directly commanded? If so, the gentleman has seriously erred in making his various publications. But I contend, that "where there is no law, there is no transgression." Let him prove, then, that we are forbidden to have a creed.

Another argument urged is—that creeds are *fallible.* But his writings are also fallible; and yet they are sent forth to exert an influence on multitudes of immortal minds. If we are forbidden to have a fallible creed, how can he venture to induce his fellow-creatures, whose salvation depends on their receiving the truth, to believe his fallible teachings?

But, he says, creeds make more heretics than christians; that the attempt to impose our opinions on others creates schisms. Yet strange as it may seem, he is doing the very thing which he has so strongly condemned! No man living has excommunicated so many christians as he. This charge I will prove, not by his enemies, but by his friends. Barton W. Stone, now a minister in Mr. C.'s church, speaking of the reformers, says: "Should they make their own peculiar views of immersion a term of fellowship, it will be impossible for them to repel, successfully, the imputation of being sectarians, and of having an authoritative creed (though not written) of one article at least, which is formed of their opinions of truth; and this short creed would exclude more christians from union, than any creed with which I am acquainted." To this Mr. Campbell replied—"I agree with the Christian Messenger, [Stone's paper] that there will be more christians (calling all Christendom christians) excluded by insisting on this command—'Be immersed,' &c. than by any creed in Christendom." *Millen. Harb.* v. i. pp. 370, 372. Now, let me ask, do those christians who refuse to be immersed, reject the Bible as their only infallible guide? Or do they only refuse to be bound by Mr. Campbell's opinion of what it teaches? They do not understand the Savior to have commanded immersion. Yet for the crime of refusing to adopt his opinion concerning the mode of administering an external ordinance, he excludes more christians, so far as he can exclude them, than any creed in Christendom!!!

I will read an extract from a letter of another of Mr. Campbell's brethren—one who is engaged with him in this discussion. I allude to Dr. Fishback. With regard to the *design* of baptism he states *five* different opinions, entertained by different persons and denominations. The fourth is, that sins are remitted only in the act of immersion, and that all are in their sins, notwithstanding their repentance and faith, until they are actually baptized for the remission of their sins. This he gives as Mr. Campbell's doctrine, and remarks—

"But of all the five opinions stated, the fourth one is the most exclusive, sectarian, and uncharitable; and, if fostered, cannot fail to drive from the affections and fellowship of those who entertain it all who differ from them, as being in their sins, however otherwise pious and godly.—*Millen. Harb.* vol. ii. p. 509.

Thus it is evident, that whilst the gentleman declaims so eloquently against the schismatical tendency of creeds, and in favor of christian union, he is himself denouncing and excommunicating the whole of Christendom, as being in Babylon, as using the language of Ashdod, because they will not adopt his opinion on some one or two points. It is true, his own brethren being witnesses, that he has a creed, though not written, more exclusive and sectarian than any sect in Christendom!!

But creeds, he says, cause persecution; and he descanted eloquently on the persecution suffered by Arius, in the fourth century. Let the gentleman give us some little evidence, that creeds do originate persecution. If he will prove that they have any such tendency, I will immediately abandon the defence of them. *But have those who had no written creed, never persecuted?* For if they have, (and who does not know it?) it is certain that persecution does not originate in creeds. That it is wrong to *force* men to adopt any creed, written or unwritten, I maintain as earnestly as Mr. C. But facts prove, beyond contradiction, that churches, having no written creed, may be, and are, as exclusive and as sectarian as any other, and as much disposed to force their opinions on others. The gentleman's own church affords us evidence conclusive of the truth of this remark; for without a written creed they have excommunicated more christians than any creed in Christendom! There is not another Protestant denomination so exclusive as they!

But in order to discuss this subject satisfactorily, we must understand the precise point in debate. And let me here remark, that opposition to creeds was the starting point in Mr. C.'s reformation. It is the more important, therefore, that we examine the principle carefully; for if he set out on false principles, the course of conduct based upon those principles is, of course, wrong. I will read an extract or two from his *Christian System*, for which I may have use hereafter: (pp. 8, 9.)

" The principle which was inscribed upon our banners when we withdrew from the ranks of the sects, was, Faith in Jesus as the true Messiah, and obedience to him as our Law-giver and King, the only *test* of christian character, and the *only* bond of christian union, communion, and co-operation, irrespective of all creeds, opinions, commandments and traditions of men. *   *   *   * Unitarians, for example, have warred against human creeds, because those creeds taught Trinitarianism. Arminians, too, have been hostile to creeds, because those creeds supported Calvinism. It has indeed been alledged, that all schismatics, good and bad, since the days of John Wickliffe, and long before, have opposed creeds of human invention, because those creeds opposed them. But so far as this controversy resembles them in its opposition to creeds, it is to be distinguished from them in this all-essential attribute, viz. *that our opposition to creeds arose from a conviction, that whether the opinions in them were true or false, they were hostile to the union, peace, harmony, purity and joy of christians, and adverse to the conversion of the world to Jesus Christ.*"

But my charitable friend did not stop with condemning the use of creeds, as tending to hinder the union of christians, and the progress of the gospel. He has denounced and excommunicated all those churches and individuals who have perpetrated the awful crime of making a creed! Since, then, the using of a written creed is made a damning sin, it is the more important that we inquire into the merits of the question. To show you the high ground taken by the gentleman, on this subject, I will read a brief extract from the *Christian Baptist*, (pp. 4, 23.)

" Besides, to convert the heathen to the popular christianity of these times would be an object of no great consequence, as the popular christians themselves, for the most part, require to be converted to the christianity of the New Testament."

Again:

" The worshiping establishments now in operation throughout Christendom, increased and cemented by their respective voluminous confessions of faith, and their ecclesiastical constitutions, *are not churches of Jesus Christ, but the legitimate daughters of that mother of harlots, the church of Rome!*"

Again, I will read in the *Millenial Harbinger*, vol. iii. p. 362. Here we have a sort of doctrinal catechism. I will read question 168, and the answer:

" *Q.* And what of the apostasy—do you place all the sects in the apostasy?

A. Yes; all religious sects who have any human bond of union; all who rally under any articles of confederation, other than the apostles' doctrine, and who refuse to yield all homage to the ancient order of things."

All, it seems, who are guilty of the heinous crime of using a creed, are apostates from the church of Christ and from christianity! I have read these extracts, my friends, that you may know the exclusiveness of the doctrine of my charitable friend. Surely it behooves us to examine into this subject, and ascertain whether writing and adopting a creed is, indeed, a crime of such magnitude as he pretends—a crime which amounts to apostasy, and excludes from the church and from heaven.

The question now before us, is not whether the Nicene or the Athanasian creed, the Westminster confession, or any other creed now in existence, is good or bad, true or false. It is admitted, that there may be, as there have been, erroneous creeds—creeds teaching false doctrines; and it is not denied that a bad creed will do injury, as will error, no matter in what way it may be inculcated. But the question before us is not whether any particular creed is true or false, *but whether it is lawful and expedient to have any creed—whether creeds are necessarily heretical and schismatical.* This being the question, and the only question before us, you at once see the irrelevancy of all that my friend read to us concerning the Nicene and Athanasian creeds.

To determine whether the using of a creed is lawful or unlawful, whether it tends necessarily to schism and heresy, it is necessary to inquire, what is the design of creeds, as used by Protestant christians? They are designed to answer several purposes, which I will proceed to state.

I. A creed is intended to be a public declaration of the great doctrines and truths which we, as a body, understand the Bible to teach. It is not a *substitute* for the Bible, nor an *addition* to it. The Westminister confession (which I mention as an example, not as in this respect differing from others,) commences with a declaration, that the Bible, and the Bible alone, contains the whole revelation of God, designed to be a rule of faith and of life for his people.

"The whole counsel of God, concerning all things necessary for his own glory, man's salvation, faith, and life, is either expressly set down in Scripture, or by good and necessary consequence may be deduced from Scripture: unto which nothing at any time is to be added, whether by new revelation of the Spirit, or tradition of men."

The confession, you see, at the very outset, declares, that the Bible teaches every doctrine necessary to be believed, and prescribes every duty to be performed in order to salvation, to which nothing is, at any time, to be added, either by new revelation, or traditions of men. Then this creed is not a substitute for the Bible, nor an addition to it. Other creeds, adopted by evangelical denominations, take the same ground. Viewing creeds, then, not as substitutes for, or additions to, the Bible, but as public declarations of what those adopting them understand the Bible to teach, we may inquire, whether they tend to produce heresy and schism.

Now let me here state an important fact, viz: It is impossible to know any thing of a man's faith, from the mere fact of his saying, that he takes the Bible alone as his infallible guide. When you hear an individual make this declaration, I ask, do you know any thing definitely concerning his faith—what particular doctrines he believes? You do not. The difficulty arises not from any obscurity in which the doctrines of the Bible are involved, for its fundamental truths especially are taught with remarkable clearness, and very variously illustrated. The difficulty arises from the fact, that men, professing to be guided in their faith and practice by the Bible, have perverted its language, and employed it in a great va-

3 T 2

riety of senses.   When men, therefore, use Scripture phraseology, it is
by no means certain, that they use it in the sense in which it was employed by the inspired writers.   For example, the time was, when the
expression " Son of God," had a clear and well-defined meaning.   It
was then universally understood to express the proper divinity of Christ.
When he said to the Jews—" My Father worketh hitherto, and I work,"
we are told, " the Jews sought the more to kill him, because he not only
had broken the Sabbath, but said also that God was his Father, *making*
himself equal with God,"—John v. 17, 18.   But now the Arian, who
makes Christ only a super-angelic creature, and the Socinian, who makes
him a mere man, still use the Scripture language, " Son of God ;" but by
it they mean something infinitely different from what the inspired writers
meant.   The difficulty arises not from any indefiniteness in the expression as used by the inspired writers ; for they evidently used it to express
the underived divinity of Christ.   But erring men have given to the language of inspiration new meanings ; and hence it happens, that whilst the
Arian, the Socinian, and the Trinitarian, all profess to take the Bible alone
as their infallible guide ; they differ infinitely in their interpretation of its
language on this vital subject.   You cannot, therefore, know the faith of
any man by the fact that he professes to take the Bible as his rule of
faith and practice.

The very great importance of each denomination of professing christians giving a public declaration of the principal doctrines and truths they
understand the Scriptures to teach, will appear from two or three considerations.

1st. Persons desiring to enjoy membership in the church of Christ,
can learn the views we, as a body, entertain, compare them with the Bible—the only rule of faith—and determine whether they can conscientiously unite and co-operate with us.   No prudent man will become a
member of any society, of any kind, until he knows what are their principles.   Much less will any considerate man unite himself with any body
of professing christians, until he is well satisfied, that, as a body, they
hold and teach the fundamental doctrines and truths of christianity.   In
his selection of a church, not only are his usefulness and his comfort involved ; but by it his children, and his children's children, are to have their
faith moulded, and their destiny determined.   Never does a man take a
step more solemn in its character, or more momentous in its results, than
when he identifies himself and his family with a particular body of professing christians.   If there be any one act of his life which ought to be
preceded by most careful and prayerful examination, this is the act.   The
interests, present and future, of those most dear to him, and to whom he
is under obligations the most solemn, require him to be assured before
connecting himself and them with any church, that that church holds and
teaches the truth.

Now suppose a man with his family to arrive in this country from
England.   He desires to become a member of the church of Christ.   He
finds a number of bodies claiming to constitute a part of that church, and
several, (of which the church of my friend Mr. C. is one,) claiming to
be *the* church.   The deeply interesting question arises, with which of
these bodies can he, consulting his duty, his usefulness, his happiness,
and the present and eternal interest of his family, unite himself.   Before
he can determine, he wishes to know, and it is absolutely essential that
he should know, how they severally understand the Bible—what are the

doctrines they understand it to teach. If he thinks of becoming a member of any one of them, he desires first to compare their views with the Word of God. He can take our confession of faith and very soon ascertain what Presbyterians understand the Bible to teach; and he can carefully compare their doctrines with that blessed Book, and determine, in view of all his responsibilities, whether he can co-operate with us. And he may learn from the creeds of the Methodists, Episcopalians and others, what are their views. Thus he may be able to take a position in which he and his family can be happy and useful.

But whither, I emphatically ask, in this world would such a man go to ascertain the doctrines of this modern reformation? Where could he ascertain what Mr. Campbell's church, as a body, understand the Bible to teach? I have said publicly, on another occasion, that there is absolutely no source from which such information can be gained. The statement has been by some of his brethren pronounced slanderous. I now make it in the presence of Mr. Campbell, that he may disprove it, if he can; and I call on him to enlighten us on this subject. I may ascertain what he as an individual believes; but what his church as a body believes, I cannot possibly be informed; nor can any man living, unless he could hear every one of the preachers and members declare their sentiments. Hence no considerate man, as it appears to me, can become a member of that church. He who does so, if he love the truth, may soon have occasion to repent his imprudent step.

2d. A second important purpose answered by creeds, is this: other christian communities can, by an examination of our creed, for example, determine whether they can recognize us as constituting a part of the family of God, and how far they can co-operate with us. I take it as granted, that every true christian desires to know and recognize all the disciples of Christ, and, so far as he consistently can, to co-operate with them in promoting his cause. Other denominations of christians can, by an examination of our creed, very soon determine whether they can acknowledge the Presbyterian church, as a part of Christ's church. So when we wish to determine whether we can acknowledge the Methodist, the Baptist, or the Episcopal church, we can examine their creed, and ascertain what they understand the Scriptures to teach. On examining their articles of faith we see, that on some points we differ from them; but we also see, that on the fundamental doctrines of the gospel we are agreed —that we stand, side by side, on the same immovable foundation. We can, therefore, own them as brethren in the Lord, and rejoice in their success in spreading abroad the saving knowledge of Christ.

But how can any denomination of christians determine to recognize Mr. Campbell's church? Aye, here is the difficulty. One man preaches one kind of doctrine, and another the opposite; and thus they are involved in endless contradiction. Even their leader, Mr. C., notwithstanding his strong partialities, is constrained to acknowledge and declare, that in it all sorts of doctrine have been preached by almost all sorts of men! It is impossible to ascertain what, as a church, they do believe. The very least, therefore, that any evangelical denomination can say, is, that they do not know them, and cannot acknowledge -them.

3d. A third purpose answered by a creed, is—that it becomes an important means of instruction to members of the church. Our confession contains a clear and distinct statement of the principal doctrines and duties of christianity, with suitable reference to the word of God as supporting them.

4th. A creed is an important means of correcting misrepresentations and slanders concerning the faith of the church. No body of professing christians is willing to lie under misrepresentations, to have their character blackened, and the minds of the people prejudiced against them, by being charged with holding and teaching doctrines they abhor. But a church with no creed cannot but be misrepresented. No man has complained more of misrepresentations and slanders of his church than Mr. C. Yet how can it be otherwise than that all kinds of doctrine will be charged upon them, since he himself declares, that they do in fact preach all kinds of doctrine? Indeed one can scarcely charge the church with holding any one tenet, without slandering or misrepresenting some of its members; for, *as a body*, they believe scarcely any thing! You hear one of their preachers to-day preach a certain set of doctrines; and another individual hears another preach doctrines widely different, if not directly contrary. You state what you have heard preached; and you are charged with slander by some one who heard the other individual.

But if men misrepresent our doctrines, as they often do, our confession of faith is a standing refutation of their false statements. If they charge us with believing the doctrine of infant damnation, we refute and expose the charge by reference to our book.

To these purposes answered by a creed, Mr. Campbell cannot object. I venture to assert, that he himself would not unite with any body of professing christians on their mere declaration that they go by the Bible, without further inquiries or explanations. He would desire some particular information concerning their faith. Even the Shakers, I believe, profess to receive the New Testament as their infallible guide. I remember once to have read a letter from a Shaker female to her mother, and I found it filled with quotations from the New Testament most strangely misapplied. All errorists profess to find their faith in the Bible.

A Mr. Jones, of England, wrote to Mr. Campbell, inquiring particularly concerning his faith and the faith of his church on a number of points. Mr. C. replied at considerable length, giving a detailed account of the items of their belief. Why did he not say to Mr. Jones—'we go by the Bible; read it and you will find our faith?' But although he denounces all creeds and professes to go by the Bible alone, he thought it necessary particularly to write out and send his creed to Jones, and his friends, over the water! And in turn he inquired of Jones concerning the faith of those with whom he was associated. If any one wishes to know what Presbyterians believe, we refer him to our confession; and when we find others subscribing to that book, we can form some definite idea, if they are honest men, what they understand the Scriptures to teach. But Mr. Campbell, to remove the very difficulties I have suggested, has published a kind of creed, which he calls "The Christian System." That you may understand for what purposes he published this work, I will read an extract on pages 10, 11.

"Having paid a very candid and considerate regard to all that has been offered against these principles, as well as having been admonished from the extremes into which some of our friends and brethren have carried some points, I undertake this work with a deep sense of its necessity, and with much anticipation of its utility, in exhibiting a concentrated view of the whole ground we occupy—of rectifying some extremes—of furnishing new means of defence to those engaged in contending with this generation for primitive christianity."

He undertook this work with a deep sense of its *necessity*, and anticipating much good that it would do by giving a concentrated view of the whole ground he and his church occupy! Does not the Bible exhibit with sufficient clearness the views they entertain? No. And he wished to rectify some extremes. Could not the Bible rectify them? But last, though not least, he wished to furnish new means of defence to his preachers. No doubt, they greatly needed means of defence; but how he, on his principles, could so think, I do not understand. Does he not contend, that the Bible, without any creed or any other help, furnishes abundant means of defence against error?

The Christian System is not adopted by the gentleman's church; for it is a creed which they could not honestly adopt. And here is the difficulty attending it. It professes to give "a concentrated view of the whole ground" his church occupies, of the principles they hold. But what evidence have we, that, as a body, they adopt these principles? I know that many of his leading preachers do reject some of the most important doctrines here stated. If I were to charge them with holding such views, they would consider themselves very much misrepresented. The church, as a body, does not hold them. Many are further from the truth. This System would induce us to believe, that Mr. C. is returning to Babylon.

But these private creeds are absolutely worthless. They do not give the information desired concerning the faith of the church. I have recently seen two or three little creeds, in the *Christian Journal*, a paper published in Harrodsburgh, each professing to give an outline of what the gentleman's church, or some portion of it, holds; but they differ most seriously from each other. In one, I find the doctrine of *total depravity;* and in the other it is entirely omitted. Some of the most prominent preachers in the church do not believe it. We have truly quite a variety of published statements of doctrine, coming from leading men in this reformation; but who can tell what the church, as a body, believes? If they consider themselves often misrepresented, they should remember, that if men say any thing concerning their faith, they can scarcely avoid misrepresenting some of them. How, I ask, can any considerate man unite himself, and connect the destinies of his family, with a body of people whose faith he never can ascertain, because there is no unity and no means of certain information concerning it?

II. The second general purpose answered by a creed is, that *it is a standard of ministerial qualification, as well as of the qualifications of other church officers.* A minister of the gospel, Paul says, must be "apt to teach," 1 Tim. iii. 2. He must be one who "holds fast the faithful word, as he hath been taught, that he may be able by sound doctrine both to exhort and convince the gainsayers," Tit. i. 9. Other passages of the same character might be quoted, were it necessary.

Mr. Campbell will not deny that some qualifications are necessary to the work of the ministry. He will admit, that the man who undertakes to preach the gospel, ought to possess some education, to be able to teach. Men will not patronize a teacher of a little country school, until they have some evidence that he understands the branches he proposes to teach. Unspeakably more important is it, that he who undertakes to expound the Word of God to immortal minds, should be "apt to teach." And the church is most solemnly bound to know, that he possesses the necessary qualifications, before she ordains him to the work.

Again, Mr. C. will not deny, that the candidate of the ministerial office should give evidence of his personal purity and of his soundness in the faith. If he be not truly pious, whatever talents and learning he may possess, he cannot preach the gospel. If he be not sound in the faith—if he hold dangerous error, he will mislead and ruin multitudes. The gentleman will not deny the necessity of these qualifications; nor will he deny that it is both the duty and the interest of the church, as far as possible, to see to it that none enter upon the responsible work, who are destitute of them; for " whether one member suffers, all the members suffer with it." Every unworthy minister is a terrible curse to the body with which he is connected.

Now observe, God has made it the solemn duty of the church to secure, as far as possible, ministers possessing these qualifications. He has prescribed no particular method of ascertaining the qualifications of individuals seeking the office. No passage of Scripture can be produced requiring any one method to be pursued. Then it follows, that he has left the church to secure the object in whatever way may be deemed wisest or most expedient. This, I presume, cannot be denied.

The Presbyterians have deemed it wise to draw up an outline of the doctrines and truths they understand the Scriptures to teach, and to require all who seek the office of the ministry at their hands, to state distinctly whether they so understand them. We have also agreed on what we regard as a proper standard of literary and scientific attainments, that our ministers, being sound in the faith and suitably educated, may be " workmen that need not be ashamed." Our regard for the cause of Christ and for the eternal interests of men, as well as our solemn responsibility to God, forbid us to allow men to go forth with our sanction, until we have ascertained, as far as possible, whether they have the qualifications required by the Head of the church.

Quacks in medicine kill the body. Quacks in theology kill the soul. If it is wise in our legislatures to forbid men to practice medicine, until duly qualified, surely it is wise in the church to refuse to invest men with the office of the ministry, until they are properly prepared for its solemn duties. Paul admonished Timothy to " lay hands suddenly on no man" —not to place in the sacred office " a novice, lest, being lifted up with pride, he fall into the condemnation of the devil."

The uniformity of our standard of ministerial qualifications, begets confidence and preserves harmony throughout our church. If a Presbyterian minister from the east or the far west visit our churches, we are not afraid, that, if invited to preach in our pulpits, he will inculcate dangerous and destructive error. We know his faith. True, we may be deceived by hypocrites. Our creeds are not expected entirely to shield us from such imposition.

Nor is this all. Creeds, so far from creating schism, tend to draw evangelical denominations more closely together. In examining the creeds of our Methodist, Baptist, Episcopal or Congregational brethren, we discover that on some points we differ from them; but we also see, that as to the fundamental doctrines of the gospel, we agree. We can, therefore, preach and pray together, and aid each other in the good work. I can sincerely thank God, that the labors of the Wesleyan Methodists have been blessed to the conversion of thousands of blinded pagans, in the islands of the South Sea; that the Baptists have successfully proclaimed the gospel in Burmah; and that other evangelical denominations are engaged in the same glorious work. I bid them God speed. Some time since, I read with deep interest an account of a meeting of a number of missionaries, of several evangelical denominations, at Jerusalem, for the purpose of consulting how they might most successfully promote the cause of truth and righteousness in that dark region. They knew well each others' views of divine truth by means of their several creeds, and were thereby prepared to co-operate in the general cause.

Not long since, two denominations of Presbyterians were united in one ecclesiastical organization, and formed the General Assembly of the Presbyterian church in Ireland. They had a creed, by which they could ascertain each others' views; and, finding themselves on common ground, they became united in one body. And I understand, there is now a plan on foot, for the purpose of uniting two very respectable denominations in our country. I mean the German Reformed and the Dutch Reformed churches.

III. The adoption of our confession of faith, let it be distinctly understood, is not required as a condition of membership in our church. In order to obtain membership, we require persons to receive the fundamental doctrines of the gospel, and to give satisfactory evidence of possessing true piety. It is not expected, that before entering the church, persons who have been converted, will examine a system of truth so extensive as that contained in our confession. We do not expect the pupil to be as well instructed as his teacher.

Now I ask my friend, Mr. C., where in the Bible he can find a law forbidding creeds for these purposes? There are two principles taught in the Scriptures, of which we should never lose sight: 1st. We may not do what the Bible forbids; and, 2d. We may not condemn what the Bible does not condemn. If there is in the Bible a passage which condemns the use of creeds for the purposes I have mentioned, let it be produced. If there is not, by what authority does Mr. C. condemn as apostates, all christians who have a creed? Most assuredly, if he cannot find a "Thus saith the Lord," to sustain him in his sweeping denunciations, he and his church stand in a most unenviable attitude. They have condemned those whom God has not condemned. They have excommunicated multitudes whom he owns as his children, because they have ventured to do what he never did forbid. "Judge not, that ye be not judged."

Again, *I ask, what is the standard of ministerial qualification in Mr. Campbell's church?* By the way, I do not speak *his* church in an invidious sense, as he seems to imagine. I often speak of the Presbyterian church as *my* church; and of Kentucky as *my* native state. But I am particularly anxious to know what is the standard of ministerial qualification in his church. What education is required of those who desire to become public teachers? What knowledge of the Scriptures—what soundness in the faith is required? What truths are they required to believe and teach, when they go forth under the sanction of the church? I press these questions the more earnestly, because we are to regard this as *the model church*—as THE church—the very best and most successful effort in this nineteenth century, "to restore the ancient order of things." Is there in the gentleman's church, any uniform standard of education? There is not! Is any particular acquaintance with the Scriptures—any theological training required? None!! Is there any standard as to soundness in the faith? None whatever!!!

What is the consequence of this state of things? All sorts of men may preach, and do preach all sorts of doctrine. No wonder—the door is wide open. And who does not know, that if all *may* preach, the most rash, self-conceited, ignorant persons *will* preach? Such men will, to a great extent, be your preachers; whilst those better qualified, but more modest, will shrink from the responsibility.

.Concerning CHRISTIAN UNION let me repeat, we are most decidedly in favor of it. This is a theme on which my friend Mr. C. has long declaimed. And where is the christian whose heart does not respond to every appeal in favor of the union of the disciples of Christ? BUT WHAT IS CHRISTIAN UNION? We go for it not in *name*, but in *fact*. Let us inquire what is the union of which the inspired writers speak. Paul, in the Epistle to the Ephesians, thus speaks concerning it: "And he gave some, apostles; and some, prophets; and some, evangelists; and some, pastors and teachers; for the perfecting of the saints, for the work of the ministry, for the edifying of the body of Christ: till we all come in the unity of the faith, and of the knowledge of the Son of God, unto a perfect man, unto the measure of the stature of the fullness of Christ:" chapter iv. 11—13.

What is the union of which the apostle speaks? It is the *unity of the faith, and of the knowledge of the Son of God*. The oneness of which the Bible speaks, does not consist in having the same name, or in sustaining the same ecclesiastical relation. A thousand persons may be thrown together in the same church, and yet there may be no real unity, and no true union amongst them. They may all profess to be guided by the Bible, but their views may be so discordant, that they are not one in any good sense. Bible unity consists in having the same faith, knowing and receiving the same great doctrines and truths, as taught in the Scriptures; and no union without this is desirable or attainable. If any man can devise a plan by which a closer union of this kind can be secured, I will promote it with all my heart. But I do not believe in the plan of throwing all christians into one ecclesiastical organization, so long as they differ on some important points of doctrine and order.

The different families in this city are now living in harmony and friendship. They enjoy each other's society, and afford mutual assistance, as circumstances require; and, in one important sense, they constitute one community. But throw them all into one house, and they would quarrel in less than twenty-four hours. [A laugh.] They have different ways of doing divers things, and they would be constantly coming in collision. So it is with the different evangelical denominations. They can now cordially co-operate in many benevolent enterprises, and rejoice in each others' success in doing good. But bring us all together in one organization, with our different views of minor matters, and difficulties must almost immediately arise. When they all see alike, there will be no difficulty in prevailing on them to unite in one body, as the two denominations in Ireland have done. Till then, they can labor in the cause of Christ more harmoniously and more efficiently in their separate organizations, than if thrown into one body.

Mr. Campbell has undertaken to prove, that human creeds, as bonds of union and communion, are necessarily heretical and schismatical. In addition to the arguments already offered on the negative of this proposition, I wish to state and prove one important fact, viz. *There is more heresy and more schism in those churches that have no creeds, than in most of those that have creeds.* The gentleman contends that creeds produce heresy and schism; but if I prove that these evils abound more where there are no creeds, than where there are, it will follow that he has ascribed effects to a wrong cause. If a physician should contend, that a certain malignant fever is caused by a particular climate, and it were proved that the same fever does, in fact, prevail in a very different climate; it would follow, that he had entirely mistaken the cause. When a man ascribes an effect to a certain cause, if I can prove that the effect exists where the cause is not found, the conclusion is inevitable, that he has not found the true cause.

Now I assert, and am prepared to prove, that there is more real schism, and more heresy, in the church of which Mr. C. is a member, than can be found in any Protestant church that has a creed. This church is the latest edition of a no-creed church, and, he will say, the very best. I am willing so to take it. I will now proceed to prove the truth of my statement. If I make it appear that heresy and schism abound in his church, the conclusion will follow, that creeds are not the cause of these evils.

1. *It is a fact, that his church necessarily admits to its communion errorists of almost every grade.* But he tells us, his church goes by the Bible. Do they go by the Bible, *as Mr. C. understands it?* No—for then he would be pope; and he professes to be a bitter enemy of all popes. Do they go by the Bible, *as each little church understands it?* No—for then every little church, of a dozen members, would be constituted an infallible council. Do they go by the Bible, *as each individual understands it for himself?* This must be the way.

Then, I ask, is not Mr. C.'s church obliged to receive to its fellowship every individual who professes to take the Bible as his rule of faith and practice? The church is not to interpret the Bible for him. Now suppose I should renounce my creed, and seek to become a member of the gentleman's church—would they receive me? I say to them I have no written creed—I go by the Bible, and I claim the right of membership in the church. They are solemnly bound to receive me, or renounce their fundamental principle. How can they exclude the Arian, the Socinian, the Universalist, or any errorist who may choose to enter the church? They all profess to take the Bible as their infallible guide. The Universalist, for example, can say, that he has no written creed—that he goes by the Bible alone. The door into the church is wide enough to admit him. You cannot reject him without a palpable abandonment of your fundamental principle, that every man is to take the Bible simply as he understands it. I will prove, in due time, that the gentleman's church has a creed—a short one indeed, but one of the most exclusive in the world.

I will now prove, that their foundation is broad enough for all to stand upon—that they cannot exclude any individual who professes to take the Bible alone as his rule of faith and life. They must even admit the Pedobaptist, or abandon their principle; for he professes to go by the Book. I will read in *Christianity Restored*, pp. 118, 119.

"But the grandeur, sublimity, and beauty of the foundation of hope, and of ecclesiastical or social union, established by the Author and Founder of christianity, consisted in this, that *the belief of one fact*, and that upon the best evidence in the world, is all that is requisite, as far as faith goes, to salvation. The belief of this *one fact*, and submission to *one institution* expressive of it, is all that is required of Heaven to admission into the church. A christian, as defined, not by Dr. Johnson, nor any creed-maker, but by one taught from Heaven, is one that believes this one fact, and has submitted to one institution, and whose deportment accords with the morality and virtue of the great Prophet. The one fact is expressed in a single propo-

3 U

sition, that Jesus the Nazarene is the Messiah. The evidence upon which it is to be believed is the testimony of twelve men, confirmed by prophecy, miracles and spiritual gifts. The one institution is baptism into the name of the Father, and of the Son, and of the Holy Spirit. Every such person is a disciple, in the fullest sense of the word, the moment he has believed this one fact."—[*Time expired.*

Thursday, Nov. 30—12 *o'clock, M.*
[MR. CAMPBELL'S SECOND ADDRESS.]

MR. PRESIDENT—A person, in only one half hour, can make more points than could be discussed in a year. Nay, sir, a child can propose more questions in five minutes than a philosopher could answer in an age. The speech which you have just heard, is a most singular compound, difficult to refer to any one head or classification; but, fortunately, it was most self-refutable and suicidal. The drift and scope of the first half of it was to prove me to be one of the most exclusive men in the world. He spent almost half his time in showing the detailed evidences of my superlative exclusiveness: but the remainder of it was, indeed, not in the most complimentary way, yet still it was decidedly in favor of my remarkable inclusiveness and latitudinarianism. So that our exclusive inclusiveness was made to stand out before you in very bold dimensions. Strange conceptions. We exclude all and receive all—mentally at least. We manage, however, this peculiar exclusiveness of theory so as to make it the most inclusive of any other system in operation in this community. We must, then, attend, if not to all, to as many, at least, as possible of these points of evidence by which Mr. Rice would sustain these grievous imputations and aspersions, for arguments no one will call them.

He commenced by telling you how many books I have written, and this, of course, is his first argument in defence of creeds. Now, in point of logic, this argument is refuted by one fact, viz: that of all these books not one has ever been used as a confession of faith by any congregation, or community, in the world. If I had, then, written a hundred volumes, they would not, in the aggregate, nor in the detail, count any thing at all as an offset against this little book, called the Westminster Confession of Faith, for one reason that a child may comprehend: no individual, no society amongst us either so contemplates them, or uses them, in theory or in practice. On yesterday, holding up this volume—the "*Christian System in reference to the union of christians,*" &c.—by way of response, he would have you believe, that we regarded it as a creed, or some such thing. I must, then, pause a moment on this, his first argument for creeds. Does not the gentleman comprehend the difference between writing a book on any religious question, and making that book a creed, a test by which to try the principles of men, in order to church or ministerial fellowship? If Mr. Rice comprehends the difference, to what influence, then, are we to assign his attempt to place this book before you in such an attitude?

But, as it is always fair and honorable, in discussion, to answer an argument in the very same logic and rhetoric by which it is assailed, I ask, if writing a book on any religious subject be making a creed, then how many creeds have the Presbyterians in their church?!! How many hundred to one, or how many thousand to one, have they against us? Who can count the number of folios, quartos, octavos, and duodecimos issued from the Presbyterian press, and published by its doctors, its learned rabbins, ministers, laymen, on every question in theology—didactic, speculative, polemic, pragmatic, practical, &c. How many magazines, reviews, repositories, and periodicals are annually still teeming from their presses! Are these all creeds and confessions of faith? If not, then, in logic, in truth, and in candor, why so represent my few unpretending volumes? I have too much respect for your good sense, my fellow-citizens—I have too much respect for my own intellectual standing in this community, than to argue such a point before you. I think it is more than sufficient to state the fact, and submit the case thus formally to your own deliberate reflections and decision! We all write books, and will continue, if not Solomons, like king Solomon, to write many books; for he says, of many books there is no *end*. I presume *in number* he meant; and true it is, also, of many books there is no *point*. But time will do with most of our books as it did with those of even Solomon the wise—send them to oblivion.

We are not, then, to be impugned for writing a book; nor are our arguments against creeds to be met with the fact, that we have written a volume, or various volumes, upon the religious and moral questions that agitate and disturb society. All professors, Catholic and Protestant, distinguish between writing a book and making a creed. We cannot be assailed on this point but by a train of reasoning that would reprobate all Catholic, all Protestant Christendom, in all ages and in all nations. He that does not, or cannot, appreciate the difference between making a doctrinal standard, to measure candidates for admission into christian churches, and a book explanatory of our views of any thing in the Bible, or out of it, is not to be reasoned with on any subject.

But the gentleman has pronounced a compliment on the confession. Remark the drift of his words—men read the Bible and mistake its meaning—misconstrue, overstrain, and pervert its language. Take, for example, says he, the phrase, "*Son of God.*" This phrase is now so well defined in the creeds, that it is a test of orthodoxy! Handsome compliment truly! Uninspired men traced, ascertained, and fixed for ever the exact meaning of the phrase, "*Son of God,*" so that now they can keep out hosts of heretics and heresiarchs, who, through the loose, unguarded, and vague style of inspired men, had, before the invention of these safeguards of truth, crept into the church! How comes it to pass, that uninspired men have views so much clearer, definite, and unambiguous, than those guided and inspired by the Holy Spirit, and are able to express them in terms so much more apposite than did the holy twelve?! Does not Mr. R. believe, that holy men spake as they were moved by the Holy Spirit? Now if John Calvin, or the Westminster divines, can speak more learnedly, more intelligibly, more definitely, than the inspired oracles of God's Spirit, what is the value of inspiration? The less inspiration the better!

Desultory must be my notices of such a defence of creeds as you have heard. The gentleman's next argument in favor of creeds is my uncharitableness. Well, I am pleased with this argument. He must be expert at it; for I am told, it has been one of his standing topics for several years. It will give me an opportunity of meeting the charge with one well versed in the subject, profoundly read, and erudite on this theme. He has not studied my writings to much profit, if he still regards me as most exclusively uncharitable. Well, what is the true state of the case? We all see, that Christendom is, at present, in a disturbed, agitated, dis-

located condition—cut up, or frittered down into sects and parties innumerable, wholly unwarranted by right reason, pure religion, the Bible,
the God of the Bible.   Before the high, and holy, and puissant intelligences of earth and heaven, this state of things is most intolerable.   I
have, for some five and twenty years, regarded human creeds as both the
cause and the effect of partyism, and the main perpetuating causes of
schism, and, therefore, have remonstrated and inveighed against them.
Not, like many who oppose creeds, because they have first opposed their
peculiar tenets; we opposed them on their own demerits, not because
they opposed us.   In this particular at least, if not on other accounts,
we differ from the great majority of those who oppose them—because
old parties were sustained by them, because they made new parties,
and because they were roots of bitterness and apples of discord, we
opposed them.

In lieu of them all, we tendered the book that God gave us.   We regard the Lord Jesus Christ as King, Lord, Lawgiver, and Prophet of the
church, and well qualified by the power of the Holy Spirit, to give us all
a perfect volume—one in substance and in form exactly adapted, as he
would have it, for just such a family as the great family of man ; if we
believe that the Lord Jesus was wiser and more benevolent than all his
followers, in their united wisdom and benevolence ; and that he both
could and would give them such a book as they needed.   It is both the
light of salvation and the bond of union amongst the saved.   We abjure
creeds, simply as substitutes, directly or indirectly substitutes, for the book
of inspiration.   In other respects, we have no objection whatever to any
people publishing their tenets, or views, or practices to the world.   I have
no more objections to writing my opinions than I have to speaking them.
But, mark it well, it is the making of such compends of views, in the
ecclesiastic sense, *creeds* (that is, *terms of communion or bonds of union*)
—I say again, as ecclesiastic documents, as terms of exclusion and reception of members, we abjure them.   Calling them creeds, is, indeed, a grand
misnomer.   They have been, in days of yore, collects of speculations, by
which in numerous instances to ferret out heretics and slaughter inno-
cents—tests of orthodoxy, which in no country a person can safely, so
far as respects his person, his reputation or his property, publicly oppose.
They have, in ages of proscription and tyranny, for the single sin of non-
conformity, slaughtered their millions.   On these accounts, as causes of
oppression to scrupulous consciences ; as sources of alienation and es-
trangement amongst good men ; as tests to proscribe and oppress, to persecute and to destroy, we solemnly abjure them, regardless of their contents, whether orthodox or heterodox.   Our sin, in the eyes of all devoted to them, is, that we substitute for them the new covenant as our
church covenant, and the apostolic writings as our *christian* creed, believing all things in the law and in the prophets.

We preach, in the words of that book, the gospel, as promulged by the
apostles in Jerusalem.   We use, in all important matters, the exact words
of inspiration.   We command all men to believe, repent and bring forth
fruits worthy of reformation.   We enjoin the same good works commanded by the Lord and by his apostles.   We receive men of all denominations under heaven—of all sects and parties, who will make the good
confession, on which Jesus Christ builded his church.   We propound
that confession of the faith in the identical words of inspiration ; so that
they who avow it, express a divine faith, and build upon a consecrated

foundation—a well tried corner stone. On a candid and sincere confession of this faith, we immerse all persons, and then present them with God's own book as their book of faith, piety, and morality. This is our most obnoxious offence against the partyism of this age.

On this ground many of us have stood for many years. We have fully tested this principle. Men, formerly of all persuasions, and of all denominations and prejudices, have been baptized on this good confession, and have united in one community. Among them are found those who had been Romanists, Episcopalians, Presbyterians, Methodists, Baptists, Restorationists, Quakers, Arians, Unitarians, &c., &c. We have one faith, one Lord, one baptism, but various opinions. These, when left to vegetate, without annoyance, if erroneous, wither and die. We find much philosophy in one of Paul's precepts, somewhat mistranslated, "Receive one another without regard to differences of opinion." We, indeed, receive to our communion persons of other denominations who will take upon them the responsibility of their participating with us. We do, indeed, in our affections and in our practice, receive all christians, all who give evidence of their faith in the Messiah, and of their attachment to his person, character, and will.

Our charities are, then, more extensive than those of my opponent. We have not so many dogmas in our creed. All these persons, of so many and so contradictory opinions, weekly meet around our Lord's table in hundreds of churches all over the land. Our bond of union is, faith in the slain Messiah, in his death for our sins, and his resurrection for our justification. Therefore, we acknowledge nothing among us but Christ, and him crucified. We do not talk of old opinions—we desire to be absorbed in the Lord Messiah, as made unto us "wisdom, righteousness, sanctification, and redemption."

Our doctrine is catholic, very catholic—not Roman Catholic, nor Greek Catholic—but simply catholic. All admit the New Testament and its ordinances, the seven unities of Paul. We are so exclusive, however, that we say to every one, without the fold, you must repent and be baptized for the remission of your sins, if you would enjoy the fullness of the blessing of the gospel of Christ. Still we do not so make conditions of ultimate salvation out of the conditions of church membership. We are not now descanting upon the conditions of salvation among the antediluvians, the Jews, the pagans, infants, and those otherwise incapable of hearing, believing, and obeying the gospel. Mr. Rice has told us what is necessary to a church on earth. We extend our views much farther. We stand on ground much more catholic and charitable; embracing, without regard to so many diversities of opinion, all who sincerely believe in the Messiah, and are willing to be governed by his precepts.

After all the gentleman has said of his confession of faith, it is very far from a scriptural, plain, and intelligible exhibition of christian doctrine. I could satisfy Presbyterian clergymen themselves that there is no formulary of faith more obscure, or difficult of definite and clear apprehension, than the creed and catechism of Westminster. In proof of this, I appeal to the divisions it has made during the two centuries of its existence. It was a document made by divines and politicians—a state expedient, with which no church of Christ, no professed body of christians, had any thing to do. It was political in its conception, political in its execution, and political in its spirit and design. It was as political in its day, as were our articles of state confederation in their day and generation; and got up

50 3 u 2

for a purpose as similar as any two great conventional affairs could be, at the distance of two centuries, and of four thousand miles.

With all the boasted plainness and clearness of that document, its most learned ministers interpret both it and the Bible as diversely as Mr. Rice and myself. I will select an instance, by way of illustration, from the subject of debate on yesterday, and show him how one of the most distinguished Presbyterian preachers in the valley of the Mississippi, understands the doctrine of the Bible and the confession on that question. The doctrine which I have set forth here on the present occasion is the doctrine of the confession on spiritual influence, if the elder Dr. Beecher is a competent judge of this doctrine: the doctrine which I have taught here, not the doctrine reprobated in my opponent's last speech yesterday evening, as mine; for the doctrine he assigned to me then and there is not my doctrine at all, as my own addresses will show to every candid mind. But my own doctrine, set forth in this discussion, is the doctrine of the Presbyterian church, if Mr. Beecher be right, and the Westminster confession be an intelligible document; and here now is the proof of it in the Doctor's own words:

"*Dr. Beecher.*—I hold that God operates on matter by his direct omnipotence; and that he operates on mind by the gospel, and by the whole amount of moral means, which he applies to it, called in Scripture the word, the truth, &c. But Dr. Wilson asks, is it to be endured that any man should say that God will exclude himself from immediate, direct operation on mind in regeneration? Why that will be just as he chooses. He will not, unless it so seems good in his sight; and if it does, he will. The question is whether he *does*, and we are to bring no *a priori* conclusions to that question. To the word and to the testimony. What does *God* say? Dr. Wilson says, that I hold God *cannot* directly operate on the human mind; and he is awfully horrified that such an idea should ever have been advanced. But I did not say any such thing, and never have said it. * *

I did not say that God *cannot* act on the human mind directly; nor have I ever said that he does so act. I said that no such thing could be advanced philosophically and theoretically as God acting by means and not by means at the same time. I was only interpreting what God says about it. I never said that it was *impossible* for him to do what he would, by direct agency. But I *did* say, that if he does it directly, then he does not do it *mediately*. If he does it by naked omnipotence, then he does not do it by the word as an instrument: for the two things are inconsistent. No doubt God can do either. But he chooses to do one, and not the other. To settle which this is, I go not to philosophy and speculation, but to the word of God. If there is any heresy in my opinions on this subject, it is the heresy of the confession of faith. My faith is in that position which both the confession and the catechisms lay down. I advance no theory about it. I stand upon the language of the confession. If that is not with me, then I must fall. All I say is, that direct action without an instrument, and action by the truth, are not the same thing, and cannot co-exist. If a man levels a tree by pushing it down with his naked hand, then he does not level the tree by chopping it down with an axe. Now the confession and the word of God say that God converts men by the truth. Here I beg leave to offer, in corroboration of my view, the opinion of Matthew Henry, in his Commentary on James i. 18:

' *Of his own will begat he us with the word of truth.*—Here let us take notice, 1. A true christian is a creature begotten anew. * * * 2. The original of this good work is here declared: it is of God's own will; not by our skill or power, not from any good foreseen in us, or done by us, but purely from the goodwill and grace of God. 3. The means whereby this is effected are pointed out: the word of truth, that is, the gospel; as St. Paul expresses it more plainly, 1 Cor. iv. 15, *I have begotten you to Jesus Christ through the gospel.* This gospel is indeed a word of truth, or else it could never produce such zeal, such lasting, such great and noble effects. We may rely upon it, and venture our immortal souls upon it.'"

I affirm, if I know the meaning of words, that the doctrine and inter-pretations of Dr. Beecher, as set forth in this extract, backed by Matthew Henry, is precisely what I have been endeavoring to set forth for the last three days. Have I not said that the question was, whether *with* or *without the truth;* whether *mediately* or *immediately;* whether *directly* or through an *instrument*, the Spirit operates upon the sinner in conver-sion, and the saint in sanctification? I say, it is either the one or the other. So says Dr. Beecher. I say, it is either mediately or immedi-ately. So says the Doctor. I say, it is mediately, or through an instru-ment, or through the Word. So says the Doctor. We are perfectly agreed in all these points. Do you think, sir, that Dr. Beecher does not under-stand the confession? If not, what is this confession worth? But if there be heresy in me, it is in the confession too, if Dr. Beecher is right. Either, then, the confession is an obscure book, or it teaches the doctrine which I teach.

Mr. Rice asks me for authority. Authority for what—for his having a creed other than the Bible? Let him bring his own authority! I have precepts authorizing me to contend for *the faith* formerly delivered to the saints. Let him bring a *Thus saith the Lord*, in support of his assertions. But he asks for a precept against creeds. The gentleman has changed since the other day. He said, there was no precept against promiscuous dancing—against games of chance. Why, then, ask me for a precept against creeds? *Tempora mutantur, et nos mutamur in illis.* We change principles with books—tenets with times, as some might translate it. There is no precept against duelling, horse-racing, theatres, &c.—and shall we ask for a precept *against* creeds! He knows the proof lies upon the affirmant. He feels the lack of divine authority. He can bring no authority for making a creed. Whenever he attempts, we will demon-strate his failure. I presume he will not try.

The gentleman talks of quacks in medicine, and quacks in theology. I admit there are such, many such. We have learned quacks, too. I am opposed to learned, as well as to unlearned quacks. I presume, even the pope of Rome, in his esteem, is a learned quack—else why pretend to infallibility? Many of his prelates, too, are learned quacks. If they are not, they are true expositors of the Bible; and if they be—alas, for the Bible!

Mr. Rice asks another question: What is our standard of orthodoxy—of ministerial orthodoxy or attainments? I could, perhaps, satisfy the gentleman's laudable curiosity by telling him some of our practice. When we baptize a Presbyterian, or any other of the Pedo-baptist family of churches, we simply add to his old stock of knowledge on hand, all that he confesses in his baptism, and all that he sees new in our order of wor-ship. If he should have a tongue to speak, and a character worthy of being a proclaimer of the truth, we send him out into the vineyard. The other evening, for example, we baptized a Pedo-baptist minister, of repu-table education and character—a graduate of Union college, New York, and of the theological seminary at Gettysburgh, Pennsylvania. We only require such a brother to add to his former biblical attainments the new ideas acquired, and then go and spread them abroad through the length

and breadth of the land. We commend to him the New Testament especially as our creed, and advise him to take Moses and the prophets as pioneers to the christian institution; and as he grows in knowledge, teach it,
that his profiting may appear to all.

I confess, in our widely extended connection, we have many sent out
too soon—not properly qualified. But in this respect, we are no worse
than were the Lutherans and Calvinists of former times. I can tell a long
story about their proceedings, and their difficulties, errors and blunders,
during their incipiency. There is the elementary state, and the transition
state in society, as well as the matured and perfected state. Every thing
cannot be done in a few days. Years were occupied in the experiments
of Presbyterians, Lutherans and English Episcopalians. The Presbyterians in Scotland were not able to form a synod till 1560, if I remember
right. And then a synod was somewhat different from what it is now.
Indeed, the General Assembly in this community have changed as much
within thirty years, as our own community.—[*Time expired.*

Thursday, Nov. 30—12½ o'clock, P. M.
[MR. RICE'S SECOND REPLY.]

MR. PRESIDENT—I expected, in the discussion of this subject, to propound to my friend some questions that would prove troublesome, and
rather difficult to answer. He must, however, allow me to ask a few now
and then.

He would have you think, that I made a very suicidal speech; but not
another individual in the house, I venture to say, made the discovery.
How was it suicidal? Why, he says, I proved his church to be more
exclusive than any other, and more inclusive. I did, indeed, not only
assert, but I proved, that it is more exclusive than any other. I proved
it, not by enemies, but by prominent men in his own church—Dr. Fishback and Barton W. Stone. But I also proved, he says, that it includes
every body; and this was my inconsistency. I proved, that according to
the fundamental principles of his reformation, he is bound to receive all,
good and bad, who profess to take the Bible as their infallible guide; and
that, in his exclusiveness, he is most inconsistent with his own principles.
His foundation is broad enough to receive all; but in practice he excludes
multitudes of the most godly christians. The inconsistency was not in
my speech, but in his principles and his conduct.

The writing of a book, he says, is not the same thing as making a creed.
This is true; but he attempted to prove it wrong to make a creed, because
there is no command to do it. It is, then, wrong to do any thing we are
not commanded to do. But there is no command to write and publish a
book; and, therefore, according to this mode of reasoning, it is wrong to
do it. He contended, that it is wrong to make a creed, because human
creeds are *fallible.* I turned his own logic against himself; for if it is
wrong to make a fallible creed to influence the minds of men, it is also
wrong to write a fallible book, and publish it. There is no difference as
to the principle; for men are no more bound to adopt my creed, than to
believe my book.

The gentleman tells you, I said that the Bible does not determine the
meaning of the expression "Son of God;" but the confession of faith
does. This is a misrepresentation of the most singular character. I said
nothing that could be tortured into such a sentiment. I am constrained
to think, that, from some cause or other, he hears very imperfectly. In

deed, his hearing has appeared to be bad for some time. What did I say?
I said very distinctly, that there was a time when the expression "Son
of God," had a clear and well-defined meaning—that in the Bible it is
evidently used to signify the underived divinity of Christ; and to prove
it I quoted John v. 18, where it is said, that when he called God his Father,
the Jews were anxious to stone him, because they understood him to
make himself equal with God. The gentleman, strangely enough, has
represented me as saying precisely the opposite of what I did say! I further said, that since the days of the apostles, men have used this expression, which was once perfectly definite in its meaning, in so great a variety of senses, that we do not know, without an explanation, what they
mean by it. The Trinitarian understands it to express the divinity of our
Savior; but the Socinian, who makes him a mere man, still uses the expression—"Son of God." Its meaning, as it is used in the Bible, is
clear; but as used by many men, it is not so. Certainly the gentleman
hears badly; there must be something the matter.

The Bible, he says, is a very plain book—so plain in its teaching, that no
one can present its truths more plainly. If it is, why has he written so
much for the purpose of explaining it? He will certainly admit, that the
doctrines of the Bible may be made as clear in a creed, as he can make
them in his books. If, then, creeds cannot make them plainer, his publications cannot; and, therefore, they should never have been made! I
admit, that on all important points the Bible teaches with great simplicity
and plainness; but yet the Savior deemed it wise to have men qualified
and appointed to expound it. The Bible is plain; but men's heads are
not clear. Sin blinds them; and hence the fact cannot be denied, that it
is impossible to know what a man believes concerning Christ, from the
circumstance of his calling him the Son of God.

The schism in the church, caused by the Arian heresy, the gentleman
has represented as caused by the Nicene creed. This is a great mistake.
The schism existed, in fact, before the creed was made. Arius had denied the divinity of Christ, and had gained many adherents. He and his
followers had rejected some of the fundamental doctrines of the gospel, and
could no longer be considered as belonging to the church of Christ. The
creed formed at Nice had the effect of separating those who robbed Christ
of his glory, from those who "honored the Son even as they honored the
Father." If this was a schism, it was a most desirable one. When men
deny the divinity of our Savior, and rob him of his glory by making him
a mere creature, it is time that they should be separated from the body
of believers. We can hold no communion with such persons. Such
was the division caused by the Nicene creed.

Mr. Campbell gravely tells us, that the head and front of his offending,
is—that he believes the New Testament to be the best book in the world,
and opposes the substitution of creeds for the Bible. Now he knows,
that no Protestant ever censured him for opposing the substituting of
creeds for the Bible; and no Protestant denomination ever desired to do
any such thing. I know of no church but the Romish, that does substitute a creed for the Bible.

Persecutions, he tells us, are caused by creeds. It is vain to reason
against *fact*. By whom, I ask, was civil and religious liberty established, and the rights of conscience secured in this country? The blood
of Presbyterians flowed freely in the defence of these sacred rights; and
Presbyterian ministers stood prominent as the most zealous and unflinch-

ing friends of liberty, civil and religious. In the day of the mighty struggle for freedom, this reformation was not born. The victory was won, and this country was free long before it was heard of. It has come into existence and been permitted to extend its influence under the protection of that liberty which was bought with the blood of those who subscribed to creeds. Now in the enjoyment of that liberty, it boasts of its zeal in freedom's cause, and denounces those who sacrificed their all in this world to gain it. Such a course shows how far men will often presume upon the ignorance and credulity of the people.

I have said, it is impossible to know what men believe by the mere fact that they profess to receive the Bible as their rule of faith—that all classes of errorists, Arians, Socinians, Universalists, and even Shakers and Mormons, profess great regard for the Bible. But, says Mr. C., we teach men just as the New Testament does, that they must believe and be baptized. No—this is not quite correct. He and his friends teach men, not to be baptized, but to be *immersed*. And herein they do most glaringly depart from their own principles. For, they tell us, they have no creed but the New Testament, and that they allow every one to interpret that book for himself. And they do, in other points, adhere to their principles. They allow men to form their own opinions concerning the character and work of Christ, the work of the Spirit, &c.—but on that one subject, immersion, they take the liberty of thinking for us. They will receive no one, unless on that subject he thinks just as they think. He must believe, that baptism is immersion. They say virtually, 'You may think for yourself on all other subjects; but let us think for you on this.' But I say, if I am to think for myself at all, let me form my own opinion on all subjects. If you are to think for me; why, do all my thinking and save me the trouble !

My friend says, he does not disturb men on account of their opinions; that the best way to destroy erroneous opinions, is to let them alone. Then why does he not let infant baptism alone? Why does he wage an exterminating war against baptism by pouring and sprinkling? If error will die when it is let alone; why does he oppose these errors, as he considers them? He has some very singular philosophy on this subject. Some erroneous opinions, he seems to think, will die, if not disturbed; whilst others must be killed !

I was truly astonished to hear the gentleman say, that he would cheerfully admit a Presbyterian or an Episcopalian to commune with him at the Lord's table. In his Millenial Harbinger he has said precisely the opposite. Mr. Jones, of England, of whom I have spoken before, wrote to Mr. Campbell, asking information on this very point—that is, whether the church with which he is connected, admitted unimmersed persons to commune. I will read an extract from Mr. C.'s reply,—(*Millen. Harb.* vol. vi. pp. 18, 19 :)

" Your third question is, ' *Do any of your churches admit unbaptized persons to communion; a practice that is becoming very prevalent in this country ?*' NOT ONE, AS FAR AS KNOWN TO ME. I am at a loss to understand on what principle—by what law, precedent or license, any congregation founded upon the apostles and prophets, Jesus Christ being the chief corner stone, could dispense with the practice of the primitive church—with the commandment of the Lord, and the authority of his apostles. Does not this look like making void the word or commandment of God by human tradition? I know not how I could exhort one professor to ' arise and be baptized,' as Ananias commanded Saul, and at the same time receive another into the congregation without it. Nay, why not dispense with it altogether, and be consistent? If I felt myself authorized to dispense with it in one case, I know not why I might not dispense with it in every case, and thus wholly annul the institution of Jesus Christ. But this is said only with respect to the authority by which it is done. Viewed in relation to the meaning and design of the institution, it assumes a still more inexplicable mysteriousness. Does christian immersion mean any thing to a believer? Is it the sign, or pledge, or means of any spiritual blessing? Is it the demand, or seeking, or answer of a good conscience? Has it any thing to do with the understanding, the conscience, the state, or character of a man? And if so, what is it? If he be as happy in himself, and as acceptable to God without it as with it, is it not an unmeaning ceremony? * * * *

The Baptist churches in England must, on this point, assume the Methodistic and Cumberland Presbyterian ground in America. In this accommodating age, many of these preachers have given up their own conscience to the proselyte. They say, we will sprinkle you with water, or we will pour water upon you, or we will immerse you in water, or we will lay a moist finger on your forehead; and we will do it in the name or by the authority of the Lord."

Now is it not passing strange, that Mr. C. should tell us, that he is well pleased to have Methodists, Presbyterians and others commune with him at the Lord's table, and yet that he should have told Mr. Jones, of England, and published it in his Harbinger, that he and his churches admit no such persons to commune with them!!! Well, he goes for changing. He says, wise men change. I am happy to find him changing his ground, as we are to suppose he is now doing, and embracing more liberal principles! I presume, of course, he will not deny, that when he wrote to Jones, he was most decidedly opposed to permitting unimmersed persons to commune with him. So far, so good. Great efforts have been made recently to excite odium against the Presbyterian church, because we are not willing to have our members commune with the reformers; but here we find Mr. C. himself making decided opposition to such inter-communion!

The Westminster confession, the gentleman says, has made quite a number of parties. I deny it; and when he thinks proper to produce his proof, I shall be prepared to meet it. He thinks, he can convince even Presbyterian clergymen of its evil tendencies. I very much doubt it. Indeed, as I have had occasion repeatedly to say, I even doubt whether he is very familiar with its principles. Certainly he is not, if we are to judge by what we have heard from him during this discussion.

The gentleman has considerable skill in the management of his cause. Some days after the question of infant baptism had been disposed of, and when my books on that subject were not present, he brought up Mr. Jones and the opinions of the Waldenses, relating exclusively to that subject. And now he reads to us Dr. Beecher's book on a subject the discussion of which was closed on yesterday! I am perfectly willing, that he shall in this way proclaim his own defeat. I know, that no sensible man will injure himself by thus introducing again subjects that have been disposed of, unless he is dreadfully pressed.

Dr. Beecher, I presume, does not teach the doctrine advocated by Mr. C. Indeed he himself seems very reluctant now to teach it; for he keeps it involved in mist and darkness. At one time he seems to admit an influence of the Spirit distinct from the Word, in conversion and sanctification. At another, he labors to prove, that words and arguments do the whole work. But does Beecher say, that men can be converted by words and arguments? Unless he has recently changed his ground, he does not. I think, if he were present, he would consider himself misrepresented. The gentleman must be permitted to discuss the propositions which have been disposed of, until he is satisfied.

He seems to regard me as very inconsistent in calling on him to produce a passage of Scripture that condemns creeds; for he says, I am in the *affirmative.* I was not aware of that fact. Did not he make the introductory speech this morning? I was in the negative when the discussion of this proposition commenced. How, then, has the gentleman placed me in the affirmative? This strikes me as a new mode of debating. I am in the affirmative; and Mr. C. is the affirmant! He affirms that human creeds, as bonds of union and communion, are necessarily heretical and schismatical. This I deny. There must be something the matter with my friend's head. It is evidently becoming muddy [a laugh.] He does not seem to know exactly where he is; only that he is somewhere in the neighborhood. [Continued laughter.]

It is quite proper, on this proposition, that he should be in the affirmative. If a man condemn and excommunicate me for any course of conduct I may choose to adopt; I have the right to ask him to be kind enough to show me the law. I have the right to do any thing that the Word of God does not forbid. The different churches were moving on with a tolerable degree of harmony, each denomination having its creed; and Mr. C. rose up and denounced the whole of them as apostates—as guilty of the most heinous crime. We request him to please to prove his charges. He excommunicates us, because we have a creed. I ask him where has God forbidden us to have a creed? I am under no obligation to produce scripture *authorizing* the use of creeds; for "where there is no law, there is no transgression." There is a passage that says— " Judge not, that ye be not judged."

He says, I cannot find a passage that, in so many words, condemns playing at cards, horse-racing, and the like. If I cannot find the law which really condemns these things, I will cease to condemn them. I ask not for a passage of Scripture which, in so many words, condemns creeds; but I desire one which by any fair construction condemns them. I will agree to admit horse-racers and gamblers into the church, if I cannot find a law in the Bible condemning these practices. He has not produced one text, which, by any fair construction, condemns the use of creeds; and he cannot produce one. To illustrate the obvious truth, that those who preach the gospel should possess some education, piety and soundness in the faith, I remarked, that quacks in medicine kill the body —quacks in theology kill the soul. Aye, says my friend, there are *learned* quacks, as well as ignorant ones. But did I speak of the necessity of learning alone? Can he find a man learned, pious and sound in the faith, who is a quack in theology? Such a character was never known.

I have asked the gentleman, what is the standard of ministerial qualifications in his church; but I have received no answer. He does not deny, that the church is bound to see to it; that those who enter the ministry, shall possess some education, true piety, and soundness in the faith— " holding fast the form of sound words." I ask him, what is the standard in his church? He cannot tell me! They have none!! No literary or scientific training, no education, is required. And as to soundness in the faith, their ministers must profess to believe, that Christ is the Son of God, and that baptism is immersion!

Pedo-baptist ministers who join that church, he says, are not questioned about their opinions, but are exhorted to preach the gospel. I presume, they are not troubled with many converts of this character. There always have been some cases of apostasy—some, too, who are unwilling to give up all religion, but are tired of the narrow way. They generally find a broader road.

But let us test the liberality of the gentleman's church. Suppose I should become a member of it, and on next Sabbath should preach a strongly Calvinistic discourse; I wonder whether it would not create a difficulty. My doctrines, I incline to think, would make a noise. My friend would not permit me to preach what I believe, unless it came at least in the neighborhood of his faith. There is really quite as much tyranny amongst the reformers, as amongst "the sects" they so liberally denounce.

Mr. Campbell. Mention a case.

Mr. Rice. I will—a Dr. Thomas, of Virginia, a prominent preacher in the gentleman's church, contended that men have no souls—that they are constituted of body, blood, and breath—that the word *soul*, in the Scripture, means *breath*—and that infants, idiots, pagans and Pedo-baptists, are annihilated. My friend opposed his doctrines; but the Doctor insisted, that he had received his training in Ireland and Scotland, where the people believe in ghosts and witches, and that, although a great reformer, he was not quite reformed. Mr. C., at length, refused to hold christian fellowship with him, and called on the church of which he was a member, to excommunicate him. Now this man professed to take the Bible as his only guide. He believed, that Christ is the Son of God, and was zealous for immersion. How, then, could Mr. C. exclude him, without a violation of the principles on which he had been admitted?

The gentleman cannot deny, that his church is troubled with very serious disorders; but he says, similar evils attended the Reformation of the 16th century. The circumstances attending the commencement of that reformation were widely different from those which existed when Mr. Campbell became a reformer. Then the people had, for centuries, been almost wholly ignorant of the Bible. They could not read it, and were not even permitted to possess it. Even multitudes of the clergy could not write their own names. Amongst people ignorant of the Bible, and degraded by a miserable superstition, Calvin and Luther, and their fellow-laborers, began their glorious work. No wonder, then, that many, when freed from the restraints and the degrading slavery of superstition and clerical domination, turned their liberty to licentiousness, and ran into excesses. No wonder, that some time was required to secure order and harmony in the churches. But the reformers of the 16th century never did allow all sorts of doctrine to be preached by almost all sorts of men in their churches. They did not open the door wide enough for every thing to enter. Yet if they had done so, they would have been more excusable in that day, than Mr. C. and his church are in doing so now.

Mr. Campbell commenced his reformation in an enlightened age, and in a country where the Bible is known and read. He has undertaken radically to reform those who have been reading the Bible from their infancy. And now when his new church is overrun with errors of all grades, and involved in great confusion, he attempts to apologize for it by telling us, there were disorders in the 16th century when light first began to dawn upon the midnight darkness!!! There is a vast difference

3 X

in the circumstances attending these two reformations. And if, within some fifteen years, the gentleman's church has been filled with confusion and trouble; it is not likely that he will ever succeed in securing order and harmony. The teacher who has disorder in his school during the first month, will have it to end of the session. If he begin with loose reins, he will not easily take them up afterwards.

Mr. C. has commenced with loose reins—very loose; and now he cannot secure order. He has been laboring for some two or three years to get some kind of organization; but the state of things is no better than before; and, I venture to say, it never will be.

But he says, Presbyterianism has very much changed within thirty years. I deny that it has. Let him prove it. When I state facts concerning his church, I hold myself bound to prove them. I deny, that our doctrines have been changed in thirty, fifty, or one hundred years.

Mr. Campbell. Presbyterians have changed.

Mr. Rice. Neither the one nor the other.—[*Time expired.*

Thursday, Nov. 30—1 *o'clock, P. M.*
[MR. CAMPBELL'S THIRD ADDRESS.]

MR. PRESIDENT—The gentleman complains of my hearing. His memory, sir, is much more at fault than my hearing. He would have you to know, as a matter of great importance, that books are fallible, and creeds are fallible, and that there is no command to write a book; nor to read one, I presume; and there is no command to write a creed, and so all books and creeds are equally without Divine authority! This is another of the gentleman's false issues. It is not the point in controversy. We have no debate about the right or authority, human or Divine, for writing or reading any sort of book. Nor do we debate about the propriety of giving, in manuscript or in print, an exhibit of all our views of religion or of the Bible. These, at present, would all be false or feigned issues, and introduced to mystify the subject. The issue is about the USE we may make of a book as a creed; or whether we may found a church on an instrument, made up of our own selections from the Bible, or of our own inferences, opinions, and views of expediency, &c. I argue that no man has, *from the Lord,* any such power; that no people have any right, warrant, or authority, from the Lord, to do so. The gentleman would make me equal with himself, by asking me for Divine authority to build on the Book alone. I have, for him, some authority, some positive precepts, which we shall present to him in due time. I need not remind you, fellow-citizens, of my friend's *manner.* You all understand him. Whenever he begins to deplore my want of authority, weakness, &c., he is then without an argument, and without any other means of entertaining you. I need not henceforth notice this very familiar species of logic and rhetoric.

He has told you of the good deeds of Presbyterians in the cause of human liberty, as another argument in proof of the Divine authority of creeds. I did not say any thing on that subject. I did not say that they were unwilling to shed their blood in civil wars. He would seem to draw invidious comparisons. If to fight in revolutionary wars be a christian virtue, neither he nor we are worthy of any invidious comparison with those who did, except in one point, that we were not born quite so soon as they. For the great crime that we, reformers, were not born a hundred years ago, we must plead guilty. But as this is a political affair,

I know not by which of our rules of discussion it has found access here. But this much I must say; that those who concur with us in our views of Bible interpretation, creeds, and church organization, were the patrons and promulgers of the principles that originated our political institutions; and infused into the mother country, and into this, the true doctrines of civil liberty. I will read from this little book a few sentences confirmatory of our views, written by the greatest patron and advocate of civil and religious liberty in the world! The author of the essay on toleration; the immortal philosopher and christian, John Locke, the author of the first American constitution ever ferried over the waves that part us from the father-land. It was he, as I have somewhere learned in former years, that wrote the constitution and bill of rights for North Carolina. But I must let you hear what the philosopher says on the question now before us.

"But since men are solicitous about the true church, I would only ask them, here by the way, if it be not more agreeable to the church of Christ to make the conditions of her communion to consist in such things, and such things only, as the Holy Spirit has in the Holy Scriptures declared, in express words, to be necessary for salvation; I ask, I say, whether this be not more agreeable to the church of Christ, than for men to impose their own inventions and interpretations upon others, as if they were of divine authority; and to establish by ecclesiastical laws, as absolutely necessary to the profession of christianity, such things as the Holy Scriptures do either not mention, or at least not expressly command? Whosoever requires those things in order to ecclesiastical communion, which Christ does not require in order to life eternal, he may perhaps indeed constitute a society accommodated to his own opinions and his own advantage; but how that can be called the church of Christ, which is established upon laws that are not his, and which excludes such persons from its communion as he will one day receive into the kingdom of heaven, I understand not. But this being not a proper place to inquire into the mark of the true church, I will only mind those that contend so earnestly for the decrees of their own society, and that cry out continually, the church! the church! with as much noise, and perhaps upon the same principle, as the Ephesian silversmiths did for their Diana; this, I say, I desire to mind them of, that the gospel frequently declares that the true disciples of Christ must suffer persecution; but that the church of Christ should persecute others, and force others by fire and sword to embrace her faith and doctrine, I could never yet find in any of the books of the New Testament.

The end of a religious society, as has already been said, is the public worship of God, and by means thereof the acqui 'tion of eternal life. All discipline ought therefore to tend to that end, and all ecclesiastical laws to be thereunto confined."—*A Letter concerning Toleration, by John Locke, Esq.*, Paisley, 1790.

I am obliged to Mr. Rice for calling forth this document. It is worth more than the size of this volume in pure gold. Such are the views of the man that taught England and the founders of our republics, the true principles of civil and religious liberty. I ask every person of reflection in this community, whether this great philosopher and politician has not expressed our identical views in the extract read. No man can understand civil liberty, who does not understand religious liberty—the rights of conscience.

An observation of some consequence was made by Mr. Rice, and I am glad to hear one from him of that sort. He did not, however, give you a correct definition of our views of confessions of faith. We do not say, that creeds and confessions of faith are the causes of all errors and heresies.

I have never so taught any where. Our proposition does not say, that they are the cause of *all* heresy—very different from it. I could much wish, that Mr. Rice had learned to distinguish more clearly. I teach, that parties are older than *written* creeds; that there were persons who made divisions, before there were *written* creeds. Satan was the first sectary that ever lived. He made a party. He is the prime *heresiarch*, and the author of the oldest schism in the universe. I could trace through two centuries before Arius and the council of Nice, other causes for parties than creeds. But it is important to know, that whatever causes operated to produce divisions, the great source of all ecclesiastical division was the dogmatical opinions of churches and synods. These preserved the strife; consolidated and perpetuated the enterprize, which, but for them, had soon spent its strength and given up the ghost!

Although councils and synods brought forth *written creeds* at last, there was no document of that sort, before the end of the first quarter of the fourth century. The Nicene document was the first document of the kind embalmed on the pages of ancient history. Its simplicity and brevity, in the midst of its profound obscurity, is a good index of the age which gave it birth. The dispute between Alexander the orthodox, and Arius the heterodox, was indeed prior to the creed. Yet had it not been for the *political* views and interference of the great Constantine, and his three hundred and eighteen bishops, Arianism would, like all the previous feuds, have lived its day and died. But the emperor and his party must make a great noise in the world, and he must give himself an ecclesiastic renown, and so they wrought up the silly dogmata of the bishop and his presbyter into an everlasting document of schism and partyism.

The vagaries of these moon-struck theologians were now embodied into a permanent form, had a habitation and a name, and started on their career of schism and blood. The sword—the CHRISTIAN SWORD of proscription, was now, for the first time, manufactured; and the trumpet of a new kind of war was moulded, cast and polished at Nice. Had the bishops treated the incomprehensible nothing with indifference in their ecclesiastic functions, the echo of Arianism had never reached us. It would have perished with the costumes of the age, and would not have inflicted upon the world and the church so many grievous calamities, and such an enduring disgrace!

From that day commenced the reign of creeds. If there be any one portion of human history, which more than another exhibits the weakness of the human understanding, and the corruptions of the human heart, it is the history of creeds and their operations. But as I have not time to tell much of this story, I will let you hear how the idols grew, and the worshipers increased, by reading a few lines from Hilary, bishop of Poictiers:

"Hilary, bishop of Poictiers, in Aquitania, who flourished in the *fourth* century, 'blames Constantius, the emperor, for the variety and contrariety of those creeds that were made after the council of Nice,' and says to him: 'You feign yourself to be a christian, and you are the enemy of Jesus Christ; you are become Anti-christ, and have begun his work: you intrude into the office of procuring new creeds to be made, and you live like a pagan.' He also says: 'It is a thing equally deplorable and dangerous, that there are *as many creeds* as there are opinions among men, as many doctrines as inclinations, and as many sources of blasphemy as there are faults among us; BECAUSE WE MAKE CREEDS ARBITRARILY, AND EXPLAIN THEM AS ARBITRARILY. And as there is but one faith, so there is but one only God, one Lord, and one baptism. We renounce this one faith, when we make so *many different creeds;* and that diversity is the reason why we have *no true faith* among us. We cannot be ignorant, that SINCE THE COUNCIL OF NICE, we have done nothing but make CREEDS. And while we fight against WORDS, litigate about new questions, dispute about equivocal TERMS, complain of authors, that every one may make HIS OWN PARTY triumph, while we cannot AGREE; while we anathematize one another, there is hardly *one* that adheres to JESUS CHRIST. What change was there not in the creed LAST YEAR! The first council ordained a silence on the *homoousion;* the second established it, and would have us speak; the third excuses the fathers of the council, and pretends they took the word *ousia* simply; the fourth condemns them, instead of excusing them. With respect to the likeness of the Son of God to the Father, which is the faith of our deplorable times, they dispute whether he is like in whole or in part. These are rare folks to unravel the secrets of heaven. Nevertheless it is for these CREEDS, about invisible mysteries, that we calumniate one another, not for our belief in God. We make creeds every year; nay, every moon we repent of what we have done; we defend those that repent, we anathematize those that we defended. So that we condemn either the doctrine of others in ourselves, or our own in that of others; and, reciprocally tearing one another to pieces, we have been the cause of each other's ruin.' "

We must turn again to the case of Arius, and draw from it a lesson. Here we read in plain terms the deplorable consequences of one false step in conducting ecclesiastic affairs. It ought to be an everlasting monument. The history of the Arian creed, and its wars, political and ecclesiastical, would fill many volumes. The reformation, of which I have been for many years one of the humble advocates, has derived important advantages from the history of such developments of human nature. We long since learned the lesson, that to draw a well-defined boundary between *faith* and *opinion,* and, while we earnestly contend for *the faith,* to allow perfect freedom of *opinion,* and of the expression of opinion, is the true philosophy of church union, and the sovereign antidote against heresy. Hence, in our communion at this moment, we have as strong Calvinists and as strong Arminians, as any, I presume, in this house—certainly many that have been such. Yet we go hand in hand, in one faith, one hope, and in all christian union and co-operation in the great cause of personal sanctification and human redemption. It is a pleasure to see such persons holding in abeyance their former opinions, conclusions and reasonings; the result of an early education and the effects of youthful associations; sacrificing all their ancient predilections and partialities, for the sake of the pure and holy principles of a religion that was fully and perfectly taught and developed before the age of Luther, of Calvin, or of any of the reformers, of popery or any other superstition, living or dead. They see not those specks, while heaven's bright sun of righteousness and truth shines into their souls in all its glorious effulgence.

It is not the object of our efforts to make men think alike on a thousand themes. Let men think as they please on any matters of human opinion, and upon " doctrines of religion," provided only they hold THE HEAD Christ, and keep his commandments. I have learned, not only the theory, but the fact—that if you wish opinionism to cease or to subside, you must not call up and debate every thing that men think or say. You may debate any thing into consequence, or you may, by a dignified silence, waste it into oblivion. I have known innumerable instances of persons outliving their opinions, and erroneous reasonings, and even sometimes forgetting the modes of reasoning by which they had embraced and maintained them. This was the natural result of the philosophy of letting them alone. In this way, they came to be of one mind in all points in which unity of thought is desirable, in order to unity of worship and of action. We have had as much experience in the operation of these principles, having observed them longer than perhaps any of our contemporaries. I feel myself authorized to say, that there are many persons in our communion who, within ten or fifteen years, have attained to more unanimity and uniformity of thinking, speaking and acting upon all the great elements of christianity, than is usually found in the members of any other community in the country. I do not think, after all, that you, sir, could find so much uniformity of sentiment, covering so many former opinions and doctrines, in so many degrees of latitude, and amongst so many persons, as already are united in the ranks of reformation. This we regard as a matter so well proved and documented amongst us, that it has already all the certainty of a moral demonstration.

Mr. Rice would, as usual, have me calling upon Dr. Beecher for proof of my doctrine, or for help in sustaining it. Did I call upon Dr. Beecher's opinions to corroborate mine, or to show that his views of the Westminster creed and mine are the same? Or was it to show that such was the obscurity of the creed, that men believing it and teaching it, have come to conclusions as diverse as are my views of regeneration and those of Mr. Rice? Did I not show that Dr. Beecher's views of regeneration through the truth and mine are the same; and that, too, while he advocates the creed as teaching them? This is the proper view of that case. It is, therefore, without evidence to argue that Paul, James, and John are less definite and intelligible than the Westminster divines. I envy no man the possession of such a talent for making capital in this way out of any thing, or every thing, or nothing, as suits his embarrassments.

The gentleman has introduced an extract from my correspondence with Mr. Jones of London, touching upon communion, which demands an observation or two. I have more respect for his understanding than to think that Mr. Rice does not comprehend this subject better. The English Baptists very generally practice open communion, as they call it. They invite persons unbaptized to participate with them at the Lord's table. Now, the difference between them and our brethren, in cases where such persons occasionally commune with them, is this: They do not invite them, *as such*, to commune in the supper; but some of them sometimes say, that "the table is the *Lord's* and not theirs; and that, though they cannot invite any to partake of it, but those visibly and ostensibly, by their own baptism, the Lord's people, still, not presuming to say that those only are the Lord's people, in this day of division, we debar no consistent professor of the faith of any party, who, *upon his own responsibility*, chooses to partake with us. Thus we throw the responsibility upon him, while the English Baptists, in many instances, take it upon themselves. I argue not the merits of this question here. I only exhibit it, in evidence that our liberality, as it is called, goes beyond the most strict sects of the Pedo-baptists—beyond the party represented by my opponent.

Indeed, there is nothing strictly sectarian in our views. There is no opinionism in our system of operations. The facts we believe are admitted; the ordinances we practice are admitted; the piety and the morality we inculcate, are admitted—universally admitted, by all Christendom

There are none excluded from our communities but those who deny the faith, those immoral or unrighteous, and those who are schismatics.

These three classes are by divine authority to be severed from the faithful. The schismatic is excluded, not for his opinion, but for the unrighteous use he makes of it.

The gentleman rather ludicrously speaks of our tyrannizing over those who differ from us—that is, for repudiating such persons as one Dr. Thomas, of whom he speaks, who, in his *medico*-theological speculations has made a grand discovery that men have no other souls than atmospheric air—that the soul of a man dwells neither in his head, nor in his heart, but in his lungs; and, consequently, giving up the ghost is only giving up his last soul, or last inspiration. Well, if that be tyranny, I have deeds of tyranny to relate that would make the whole affair of tyranny a matter of amusement, rather than of grave reprehension. We know whom to exclude. Amongst them, however, are none for any particular mode of interpreting the Scripture; but *for the use made of their interpretation of it.* Morality lies in that, and not in the different ways of reading and interpreting a verse. We are told positively who shall not inherit the kingdom of God, and such should not dwell in any church.

Who ever thought of a church like Noah's ark—filled with beasts, clean and unclean? Is it tyrannical to exclude a drunkard, a railer, or a schismatic? Are we tyrannical because we exact of those who teach the christian religion, that they should teach the things commanded, and not contradict the views of apostles and prophets—nor set on foot a system of operations contrary to the express Word of God?

The gentleman says that Presbyterianism has not changed. What, then, have Presbyterians been doing in their general assemblies and synods in all the world for the last thirty years? Is there no change in doctrine, or administration of any kind? If Presbyterians have not changed, what means this mighty movement? and all these new and old school notions, debates, strifes, and divisions! Mr. Rice, I presume, belongs to the old school, dyed in the wool, and of course he does not, nay, indeed, *he* cannot, change. The reason why he cannot plead for a more just and generous exposition of the confessional exponent of the Bible, is his belief that the old school does not err, cannot err; for they are the true blue of Calvinism, which he affirms cannot change. A true old school Presbyterian, if not infallible, is indeed in an awkward posture; he cannot change. But is it not a singular theory? The confession explains the Bible, and yet the confession cannot be explained by those who are sworn to teach it; for they explain it differently.

What is this Presbyterian controversy about? Both parties go for the same confession. But the old school says the new school erroneously interpret it; and the new school replies that the old school never did understand it. The thirty-nine new articles, all the speculative world believe to be Calvinistic. Yet most of those who teach them are Arminians. The Earl of Chatham once truly said of the Church of England in his day, that "she had Calvinistic articles, Arminian clergy, and a popish liturgy." A just but severe compliment to creeds—a just expose of their power to preserve a ministry of one faith, or of one system of interpretation. Elizabeth made the doctrinal part popular in her reign, and the majority believed with the Queen; but since then, while the outworks of the establishment are the same, the doctrine and the spirit of that day are fled.

Report says, the new school Presbyterians are for *mediate* influence,

the old for *immediate*. I hope you will excuse me for adverting to it;
and not take the allusion in proof that I am dissatisfied with the debate on
spiritual influence, and give me another challenge.   Well, the difference
between *im* and no *im* in the words *mediate* and *immediate* is as valid as
the *i* and the *o* difference in the Nicene, to justify the war between the
old and the new school Presbyterians.   There is, indeed, a very great difference between immediate and mediate influence—the one brings naked
spirits together, the other places the Bible revelations, or the gospel, between.   I hope Mr. Rice will explain to us what he understands is the
immutability of Presbyterianism.   There is some new spirit abroad in
the Presbyterian church.   What can it be?—[*Time expired.*

Thursday, Nov. 30—1½ *o'clock, A. M.*
[MR. RICE'S THIRD REPLY.]

MR. PRESIDENT.—My friend, Mr. C., goes against making creeds and
enforcing them on the consciences of men. I am not aware, that Presbyterians, Methodists, or any Protestant denomination, claim authority to
force or impose their creed on any one. It is a matter of free choice
with every individual, whether he will become a member of our church,
or some other. If on comparing our creed with the Scriptures, he regards it as supported by them, and, therefore, chooses our church; there
is no violence offered to his conscience. On the contrary, he acts precisely according to its dictates. In order to sustain his proposition the
gentleman seems to consider it necessary to oppose principles which we
do not hold, principles which we condemn as decidedly and as strongly
as he does. So far as force has been employed in any case to induce persons to adopt a creed, we condemn it. But Mr. C. also goes against
substituting creeds for the Bible. So do we; and so do all evangelical
denominations. His great reformation, therefore, commenced with waging
an exterminating war against errors that did not exist.

He charges me with having indulged in invidious comparisons in my
remarks concerning those who were instruments in the hands of God of
securing to our country civil and religious liberty. So far as the revolutionary struggle was concerned, I could not institute a comparison between two things, one of which did not then exist. His reformation is
a beardless youth about sixteen years of age! I said, it had not been
heard of in those days of trial, and that it should be modest in boasting
of its zeal for liberty before it is tried. This, I presume, is not invidious.

I do not object to the views of Mr. Locke, as expressed in the extract
read by Mr. C. He is opposed to requiring of men what the Scriptures
do not require. So am I; and so are all Presbyterians and other evangelical churches. We do not wish to require of any human being, as a
condition of membership, what the Scriptures do not require. He is
opposed to excluding from our christian fellowship those whom we expect to meet in heaven. So am I. I plead for communing with those
who hold the fundamental doctrines of the gospel.

But the gentleman seemed not to see, that the sentiments of Locke
condemn his practice. Locke was opposed to excluding from our communion those we expect to meet in heaven. Yet Mr. C. excludes many
whom he expects to meet there. [Mr. Campbell denies the assertion.]
The gentleman calls all churches but his own, " sects," and represents
them as constituting Babylon—the apostasy. Yet he professes to believe, that there are christians among " the sects," as I will prove from

his Harbinger. [Mr. Campbell. Have we excluded them?] I will answer his question presently, when I come to speak of his letter to Jones.

He says, he does not contend, that creeds are the cause of all heresy and division. Let him prove, that they do at all cause either heresy or schism. He does not maintain simply, that *erroneous* creeds produce heresy and schism, but that *all* creeds necessarily produce these evils. Even a *true* creed, according to his logic, is necessarily heretical and schismatical; and that creeds are the great cause of divisions. All we desire, is to have this proved.

If there had been no creed formed against Arianism, he says, it would have died. This is *assertion*. We desire the proof. There not only is no certain evidence, that such would have been the result of leaving that heresy unopposed; but there is no probability of it. Weeds grow without cultivation. The earth produces them spontaneously. So does error flourish in the human heart. The seeds of error there find a soil in which they grow luxuriantly. He says, let error alone, and it will die. The Scriptures do not teach, nor do they direct us to let error alone. On the contrary, Paul says, "A little leaven leaveneth the whole lump." He and Paul seem to have come to opposite conclusions on this subject.

He declaims earnestly against forcing opinions upon men. Yet some of his own friends—prominent ministers in his church, have said and published, that he does enforce his opinions, so as to exclude multitudes of the most pious persons! It does not look well for a man to declaim against his own practice—to condemn others for what he himself is doing.

The extract he read from Hilary may be well enough. But the question before us, as I have before stated, is not whether any particular creed is good or bad, true or false; but whether the making of a creed—a true creed—involves the sins of heresy and schism. There is one important point concerning which I desire some information. The gentleman appears to attach great importance to a distinction he makes between *faith* and *opinion*. I DESIRE TO KNOW WHERE FAITH ENDS, AND OPINION BEGINS. I wish information on this subject particularly; because, unless I greatly err, Mr. Campbell's church are constantly acting in violation of their own principles in relation to it.

He says, they have amongst them both Calvinists and Arminians; I am constrained to doubt whether they have any real Calvinists; for a true Calvinist believes firmly, that the doctrines, called Calvinistic, are taught in the Bible, and he, of course, considers himself solemnly bound to propagate them. Such an one is not likely to become a member of a church that will not permit him quietly to preach what he believes to be God's revealed truth. Nor would a conscientious Arminian unite himself with a church, where he could not preach what he believes. Doubtless there are men who will bind themselves to keep back part of the truth, as they understand it; but I do not admire their principles nor their conscientiousness.

Mr. C. says, he quoted Dr. Beecher on the work of the Spirit, to show how different are his views of the confession of faith from mine. Yet he was careful to state, very emphatically, that Dr. B. agreed with him on that subject! He will take the opportunity, as often as possible, to slip in something in the way of argument on the subjects already disposed of. But we are not discussing the question, whether Dr. B. and I agree

51

in the interpretation of the confession of faith; nor whether the Westminster confession presents its doctrine clearly; but whether it is lawful for us to have a creed at all. The quotation from Beecher, therefore, was out of place.

Mr. Campbell attempts to make capital of the fact, that the old and new school Presbyterians differ in their interpretations of the confession of faith. If we are to judge from what he has said on the subject, he certainly does not understand it. I have had occasion to examine the differences between them quite extensively. The difference is not so much concerning the obvious meaning of the book, as concerning the degree of strictness with which it should be adopted. The old school have been disposed to require a more strict adoption of the particular doctrines of the confession, than the new school. The latter were disposed to adopt it only "for substance of doctrine;" the former believe, that such an adoption opened the way for the introduction of serious errors. This has been, so far as the present subject is concerned, the principal ground of controversy; not what the obvious language of the confession of faith teaches, but with what degree of strictness it should be adopted. The new school brethren, I doubt not, would consider themselves misrepresented, if charged with holding, that conversion is effected not by an immediate agency of the Spirit. So far as I know, they would, as a body, deny the charge. This is a subject, however, which I am not disposed now to discuss, as it bears not on the point at issue.

It would seem, from the remarks of the gentleman, that there is in his church great unanimity in their views of divine truth. And yet, he himself has published the fact, that they have "all sorts of doctrine preached by almost all sorts of men." I know they all meet in the water, but no where else! On all other doctrinal points each, it would appear, thinks for himself.

I will now attend to the gentleman's statements about admitting unimmersed persons to communicate with him, and will answer his question propounded a few minutes since. He attempts to reconcile the statement made here with that made to Jones, of England, by saying, that his church does not *invite* unimmersed persons to commune with them; but if they come on their own responsibility, they do not debar them. Let me again read Mr. Jones's question and his reply—(*Millen. Harb.* vol. vi. p. 18.) "*Do any of your churches* ADMIT *unbaptized persons to communion; a practice that is becoming very prevalent in this country?*" Observe, the question is not, does your church INVITE, but do they ADMIT such persons to communion? To this question Mr. C. replies— "NOT ONE, AS FAR AS KNOWN TO ME"!?! The gentleman has certainly given accounts of the principles and the practice of his church, which are directly contradictory. He has told Jones, and the people in England, that they do not *admit* unimmersed persons to communion; that it is decidedly wrong to admit them; and he has told us to-day, that they do admit them, and are well pleased to have them come! If he can reconcile these opposite statements, let him do it. When I see over a door "*No admittance,*" I understand, distinctly, that I am not to enter.

He asserts, that every item of faith and practice, as held by his church, is *catholic.* This is a great mistake. Do all agree that immersion is the only apostolic, or christian baptism? Not one in a thousand has admitted it. This tenet, then, is far, very far, from being catholic.

He justifies himself in attempting to exclude Dr. Thomas, the materialist, by telling us he never plead for a church like Noah's ark—that his church requires men to teach, as did the apostles. That is right. But the question is, how can he, on his principles, exclude any errorist? Who is to judge whether an individual preaches, as did the apostles? Is Mr. Campbell to be the judge? Then he is pope. Is the man himself to judge? Then you cannot exclude him. Is the church, of which he is a member, to judge? Then they are to be for him a kind of creed. Yes— according to the principles on which the gentleman and his church proceed, any little church of a dozen members, or a smaller number, males and females, girls, boys, and servants, are to set in judgment on the orthodoxy or heterodoxy of a minister of the gospel, who happens to have his membership among them! They may gravely decide, that he is not teaching as did the apostles, and excommunicate him for heresy. He is thus deprived of a standing in the church; his character is injured; his usefulness destroyed; and he has no remedy!

One, amongst many important differences between Mr. C.'s church and ours, is—that in his, a man even of the highest standing may be deprived of his dearest rights and privileges by half-a-dozen uninformed or prejudiced persons; whilst in ours, the humblest member cannot be finally deprived of his standing until, if he choose to appeal, the voice of the whole church has decided on his case. With us, the strongest possible protection is thrown around the reputation and the privileges of every member, and especially of every minister. The gentleman's church affords no such protection. No man has any more assurance that his character will not be injured, and his privileges taken from him, than is found in the wisdom and piety of the members of the church, perhaps of a dozen members, to which he belongs. Dr. Thomas contended, that he was teaching the doctrines taught by the apostles. Mr. Campbell decided that he was not, and called on his church to excommunicate him, because he differed in his interpretations of the Bible from him! But, according to his principles, how could he attempt to exclude Thomas? He solemnly declared, that he took the Bible as his only infallible guide, and eschewed all creeds.

I will now proceed to offer some further arguments, showing that creeds are not necessarily heretical and schismatical. I have already stated the important fact, that in Mr. Campbell's church, by which all creeds are repudiated, there is more heresy, and more schism, than in any Protestant church that has a creed. The door into it is wide enough to admit all who profess to believe that Jesus Christ is the Son of God, and are willing to be immersed. Not only Calvinists and Arminians, some of whom the gentleman boasts of having, but Arians, Socinians, Universalists, &c. &c. may enter. His foundation is broad enough for them all to stand on. There is no error held by any who bear the christian name, that may not find a lodging-place in this *reformed* church, except that of sprinkling and baptizing infants! And even Pedo-baptists cannot be excluded, without the most flagrant violation of the fundamental principles of this reformation. To prove to you, my friends, that I am not misrepresenting the gentleman's principles, I will read an extract or two from his *Christianity Restored*, (pp. 122, 123:)

" I will now show how they cannot make a sect of us. We will acknowledge all as christians who acknowledge the gospel facts, and obey Jesus Christ. But, says one, will you receive a Unitarian? No; nor a Trinitarian. We will have neither Unitarians nor Trinitarians. How can this be? Systems make Unitarians and Trinitarians. Renounce the system, and you renounce its creatures. But the creatures of other systems now exist, and some of them will come in your way : how will you dispose of them? 1 answer, we will unmake them. Again, I am asked, how will you unmake them? I answer, by laying no emphasis upon their opinions.

What is a Unitarian? One who contends that Jesus Christ is not the Son of God. Such a one has denied the faith, and therefore we reject him. But, says a Trinitarian, many Unitarians acknowledge that Jesus Christ is the Son of God in a sense of their own. Admit it. Then, I ask, how do you know they have a sense of their own? intuitively, or by their words? Not intuitively, but by their words. And what are these words? are they Bible words? If they are, we cannot object to them : if they are not, we will not hear them, or, what is the same thing, we will not discuss them at all. If he will ascribe to Jesus all Bible attributes, names, works, and worship, we will not fight with him about scholastic words. But if he will not ascribe to him every thing that the first christians ascribed, and worship and adore him as the first christians did, we will reject him ; not because of his private opinions, but because he refuses to honor Jesus as the first converts did, and withholds from him the titles and honors which God and his apostles have bestowed upon him.

In like manner we will deal with a Trinitarian. If he will ascribe to the Father, Son, and Holy Spirit, all that the first believers ascribed, and nothing more, we will receive him. But we will not allow him to apply scholastic and barbarous epithets to the Father, the Son, or the Holy Spirit. If he will dogmatize and become a factionist, we will reject him ; not because of his opinions, but because of his attempting to make a faction, or to lord it over God's heritage."

Concerning these sentiments I have several remarks to make.

1st. Mr. C. says, he will receive a Unitarian into his church, if he will ascribe to Jesus all Bible attributes, names, works, and worship ; but if he will not ascribe to him all that the first christians ascribed, and worship and adore him as the first christians did, he will reject him. Now let me ask, who is to determine whether the Unitarian worships and adores Jesus Christ as the first christians did? Is Mr. C. to judge? Then you make him pope. Is each little church to judge? Then you make each church an infallible council to determine what its members shall believe, and how they shall worship Christ. Is each individual to judge for himself? Then each will decide that he does worship and adore Jesus as the first christians did. So it all amounts to nothing—the Unitarian, of whatever grade, must be received.

2d. But the gentleman says, he will deal in like manner with the Trinitarian. He, too, must ascribe to the Father, Son, and Holy Spirit, all that the first christians ascribed, and no more. Who, I again ask, is to judge in this case? But here I find something truly remarkable. He says—" we will not allow him [the Trinitarian] to apply scholastic and barbarous epithets to the Father, the Son, and the Holy Spirit." Who is to decide what epithets are barbarous and scholastic? Where has the Bible authorized Mr. Campbell or his church to excommunicate a man for using, in reference to the Trinity, any words he may choose, that convey no false idea? By what authority does the gentleman say, we shall not use such words as he may choose to call scholastic or barbarous? If here is not a most remarkable exhibition of latitudinarianism and tyranny, I know not what these terms mean! Men are left to judge for themselves, so far as the doctrines of the Bible are concerned; but they are to be excommunicated for using certain words which God has never forbidden them to use ! ! !

But let me read a little further.

" And will you receive a Universalist too? No ; not as a Universalist.

If a man, professing Universalist opinions, should apply for admission, we will receive him, if he will consent to use and apply all the Bible phrases in their plain reference to the future state of men and angels. We will not hearken to those questions which gender strife, nor discuss them at all. If any person say such is his private opinion, let him have it as his private opinion, but lay no stress upon it; and if it be a wrong private opinion, it will die a natural death much sooner than if you attempt to kill it."

The gentleman tells us, he will receive a Universalist; but he will not receive him *as a Universalist.* Well, he is a Universalist and nothing else. He will not receive him *as what he is;* of course he will receive him *as what he is not!* To illustrate the idea, you propose to sell a sheep to a man. He tells you, he will not buy him *as a sheep;* but call it a *horse,* and I will take it! I never read this paragraph without being reminded of a certain man of olden time, who had the singular fortune to be both a duke and a bishop. One day an acquaintance heard him using profane language, and said to him with much surprise—" Do you, a *bishop,* swear?" " O," replied the dignitary, " I do not swear *as a bishop:* I swear *as a duke."* " But," replied his quizzical friend, " when the devil comes for the duke, what will become of the bishop?" [A laugh.] If the doctrine of the Universalist should be fundamentally erroneous, let me ask, when the devil comes for the Universalist, what will become of the reformer? [Continued laughter.]

But my friend Mr. C. is quite strict just here. He will receive a man professing Universalist opinions, only on condition that " he will consent to use and apply all the Bible phrases in their plain reference to the future state of men and angels." Of course, according to this doctrine, a man may be a Universalist, and yet use all the Bible phrases in their plain and obvious reference to future punishment!!! But let me ask again, who is to determine whether the Universalist does so use them? All Universalists profess to use the Bible words and phrases in their plain and obvious sense. Now suppose one of your reformed preachers should, on next Sabbath, preach the Universalist doctrine. You call him before the church to try him for heresy. You ask him—' Do you use these Bible phrases and words in their plain reference to the future state of men and angels?' He says—' I do.' Now what can you do with him? You must let him alone! He will preach the same doctrine again on the next Sabbath. What will you do? How can the gentleman, on his principles, exclude him? I assert, that, without an entire abandonment of his principles he cannot exclude him. Mr. Campbell must be made pope; or each little church, an infallible council to determine men's faith; or errorists of all grades must be allowed to be members and ministers amongst them. For the principle is—that each individual is to go by the Bible, not as Mr. C. or the church understands it, but as he understands it for himself. Then his church must be a Noah's ark—full of beasts, clean and unclean, especially the latter! He cannot prevent it. All sorts of doctrine will be, as they have been, preached by all sorts of men. His door is wide enough to admit all; and his foundation broad enough to afford them room to stand.

Now let me ask, did Jesus Christ establish his church on such principles? No—his truth he regarded as more precious than gold, yea, than much fine gold; and his church was to be the light of the world. Never did he establish it on such principles as would admit to its communion or to its ministry all sorts of men and all kinds of doctrine.—[*Time expired.*

3 Y

Friday, Dec. 1—10 o'clock, A. M.
[MR. CAMPBELL'S FOURTH ADDRESS.]

MR. PRESIDENT—In recapitulating the details of yesterday, we must first state the proposition, and then the principal arguments and topics of debate. The proposition in debate now is,—*Human creeds, as bonds of union and terms of communion, are necessarily heretical and schismatical.* That they are so, was argued in our introductory address from the fact that they are human and fallible productions. It was shown that they were wholly *human* expedients from two prominent facts; 1st. That there were no persons commanded to make them; and, 2d. That no church was commanded to receive them, both of which would be essential to their authority. That they are human and fallible, and wanting in authority, tending to division in feelings—producing alienation in heart, and in their overt fruits and results ultimating in schism and all its tremendous train of evil consequences, was argued from various other topics, but especially from their actual fruits and effects, as shown in their history from the beginning till now. The history of the operation of any expedient is generally found to be the best exposition of the wisdom of its inventor. Tried by this test, a very prolific topic, both of argument and illustration, it appeared that their tendency to partyism and heresy has been amply developed in the fact, *that they have always retained the corrupt members of the community*—the pliant, temporizing, and worldly professors, while in innumerable instances, excluding those of tender conscience, the virtuous uncompromising and faithful worshipers of God. Various subordinate topics, of which we cannot now speak particularly, have been introduced, both in development and confirmation of these statements. We now immediately proceed to the consideration of objections offered by Mr. Rice.

Rather in extenuation of their evil tendencies, than as an argument in their favor, it was alledged by him, that they were not generally enforced upon the whole community;—that they are enforced only on certain persons in reference to particular places, offices, or obligations. As to his meaning of *enforcement,* I know nothing. The term must be used ecclesiastically, in some restricted and special sense. We should like to have it explained. They are so far enforced as to become instruments of excommunication to all those who publicly dissent from their dogmata. They make a person worthy of excommunication, because of an opinion, or a dissent from certain doctrines; when these opinions and doctrines are publicly avowed. Such, certainly, has been their operation in times past, and such is now their operation in some communities. I own, indeed, that in some societies they are almost a dead letter. They are more nominal than real. The spirit of the age holds them in abeyance. Light has gone forth into the land; and therefore they cannot be enforced as in former times. Still they are occasionally enforced, and that so far as to excommunicate men from christian churches, so called, because of difference of opinion, though their faith be sound and their lives virtuous. This is what I mean by enforcing them ecclesiastically. We have this term, however, authoritatively explained in the confession, in chap. 30, one of the mutable sections of the constitution of the Presbyterian church:

"I. The Lord Jesus, as king and head of the church, has therein appointed a government, in the hand of church officers, distinct from the civil magistrate.

II. To these officers the keys of the kingdom of heaven are committed; by virtue whereof they have power respectively to retain and remit sins, to shut that kingdom against the impenitent both by the word and censures, and to open it unto penitent sinners by the ministry of the gospel, and by absolution from censures, as occasion shall require."

This is the highest species of power spiritual that I know any thing of. It is chartered by the confession and maintained by all the ecclesiastical courts of the church. And so infallibly are the Scriptures explained in the confession, that they are very seldom quoted in the public courts of that church. This custom is so tenaciously adhered to, that sometimes in the longest and most important trials, not one verse is quoted. Even in the excision of a minister, a congregation, or a synod, the confession is quoted, argued, and relied on for authority, without a single reference to a text in the Bible. The creed, and the practice under it, as indicated in this thirtieth chapter, exhibit the highest assumptions of power claimed by any community in the country.

There is a way of extenuating matters, and hiding them from our own eyes, as well as from those of others. But, with all the relaxing and liberalizing views of the age, in this land of free, and liberal, and enlightened institutions, confessions of faith are still heretical and schismatical. And that, too, not merely among the less enlightened, but of those who claim to be amongst the most enlightened of our community. How has the creed—the pure, definite, perspicuous and excellent Westminster creed—wrought in this community within our own time—within the memory, not of the old men, but of the young men of this community? After some ten or twelve years debating in the synods, and in the general assemblies of this same Presbyterian community, upon the true meaning and interpretation of the Westminster creed, what was the issue? Did it prove conservative or heretical? Did it unite, harmonize and cement in one holy communion, this educated and well-organized brotherhood? Tell it not in Gath!—publish it not in Askelon! It only excommunicated some *sixty thousand brethren*, and *five hundred ministers!!!*

These, too, were not infant members; they were not minors; but actual, *bona fide* communicants, with all their household members! Is not this alone a full demonstration of our proposition, that creeds are *heretical* and *schismatical?*

The meaning of the creed—the interpretation of the symbol, was the sole cause of this tremendous disruption—of this new denomination of Presbyterians. I put one solemn and weighty question to every conscientious man in our community: If a creed, such as this innocent and unassuming document, has power to cut off sixty thousand persons by one single stroke, what more puissant cause of schism and division could be created and sustained by any tribunal known to our laws and customs? At present I can, indeed, expatiate no farther on this subject. I shall, however, read farther from this document, illustrative of the powers of this instrument to preserve unity:—(Beecher's Trial.)

" In respect to the right of private interpretation in the first instance, I presume I must have misunderstood my brother Wilson, when he says, the confession is not to be explained. That is popery. The papists have no right of private judgment. They must believe as the pope and council believe, and may believe no otherwise. They are forbidden to exercise their own understanding, and must receive words and doctrines in the sense prescribed and prepared for them. I cannot suppose my brother so holds; but that when he subscribes the confession, he subscribes to what, at the time,

he understands to be its meaning. Who else is to judge for him? Is the
pope to be called in? Is he to ask a general council what the confession
means? Does he not look at it with his own eyes, and interpret it with
his own understanding? But as I understand my brother, he insists that
there is to be no explanation; but that every expression of doctrinal sentiment is to be placed side by side with the confession, and measured by it:
just as you would put two tables side by side to see if they are of the same
size. You are to try the sermon and the confession by the ear, and see if
they sound alike. If they do not, the sermon is heretical, and the author
a heretic. Can this be his meaning? * * * *

In joining the Presbyterian church, each individual member, unless he
comes in as an ignoramus, without knowing what he professes, does explain
her standards for himself. He must do it, and he has a right to do it, unless his joining the church means nothing and professes nothing. If it does
mean any thing, it must mean what he intends it to mean: and of this he
must, in the first instance be himself the judge. * * * *

I say, that each minister and each member has as good a right to his own
exposition of the common standard as another has. * * I have as good
a right to call you a heretic, because your exposition of the confession does
not agree with my view of it, as you have to call me a heretic, because my
understanding of the confession does not agree with yours. You say that I
am a heretic according to the plain and obvious meaning of our standards.
But your 'plain and obvious meaning,' is not my 'plain and obvious meaning;' and who is to be umpire between us? The constitution has provided
one. * * * *

Dr. Wilson says the Bible is not to be explained by Presbyterians in
their controversies with each other, because its meaning is explained in the
creeds. And he has before insisted that the creed is not to be explained.
What then, I pray, is to be explained? He and I are not to explain the
Bible. Why? Because he and I agree in receiving the confession of faith.
But we must by no means explain how we understand the confession. How
then, I ask again, is any thing to be understood between us? Are we only
to hear the sound thump on our ears, and attach no meaning to it? And
how shall we know that we attach the same meaning to it, if we must not
explain? I do not doubt that Dr. Wilson has some meaning about the matter which he has not expressed; but it ought to have been expressed."

Such is the power of the confession to preserve unity, and to prevent
discords amongst brethren. If it ever has operated more advantageously,
I have been misinformed in the records of the past.

The gentleman complains that our foundation is too broad—too liberal.
It is indeed broad, liberal and strong. If it were not so, it would not be a
christian foundation. Christianity is a liberal institution. It was conceived in view of the ruin of a world. God looked upon, not the thousand
millions of one age, but upon the untold millions of all ages. And he
looked, with the inconceivable compassion of a Divine Father, rich in
mercy, and plenteous in redemption. He laid help for us on the shoulder
of a Divine Man, "who meted out heaven with a span, comprehended the
dust of the earth in a measure, weighed the mountains in scales, and the
hills in a balance;" the Great Philanthropist—whose wide charities and
tender compassions embrace all ages, all races, all generations of men.
He knows no difference of castes, ranks, dignities. Before his eyes, kings
and their subjects—the nobles of the earth and their slaves—the tyrants
and their vassals, lose all their differences. Their circumstantial grandeur, and their circumstantial meanness are as nothing. He looks upon
them all as men—fallen, ruined men. He made one splendid sacrifice for
all; and has commanded his gospel to be preached from pole to pole—and

from Jerusalem to the uttermost parts of the earth. He bids all nations, languages and tribes of men a hearty welcome to the rich provisions of his bounteous table, made large enough, and well supplied with the richest provisions of his unwasting fullness. Surely, then, that ought to be a large house, on a broad foundation, that has in it a table for saved men of every nation under heaven.

He has commanded a simple story to be told, levelled to the apprehension of all. It is expressed in plain, clear and forcible terms. The great cardinal principles upon which the kingdom rests, are made intelligible to all; and every one who sincerely believes these, and is baptized, is, without any other instrument, creed, covenant or bond, entitled to the rank and immunities of the city of God, the spiritual Jerusalem, the residence of the Great King. This is precisely our foundation. Strong or weak, broad or narrow, it is commensurate with the christian charter. It embraces all that believe in Jesus as the Christ of all nations, sects and parties, and makes them all one in Christ Jesus.

Another objection noted on my brief: Mr. Rice objects to my issue in the case of Arius. I re-affirm the conviction, that had Arius been treated as a *man*—as a human being—and his opinions left to find their own level, we should have never heard of him or them. Nine times in ten, mere opinion, when let alone, will die a natural death, or lead an inoffensive life. But if you want an opinion to live, gain power, make a party, and descend to after times, call a council, get up a debate, assemble the orators, and keep it for a few years before the public mind, and then you secure a party. I say, call no council, make no decrees, excite not human passions. Such are my convictions, and in them I am sustained by some of the wisest and best men who have spoken on the Nicene controversy. Had the subject been let alone—*ecclesiastically* alone—it would not have outlived the age which gave it birth.

But, sir, be it emphatically spoken, that letting it alone *ecclesiastically*, and *doing nothing*, are very different things. Mr. Rice intimated that my policy is the letting alone policy. He dehorts against letting errors alone. I do not so argue. It is *opinions*, and not *ordinances* nor *faith*, I let alone. We may let some things alone in one sense, and not let them alone in another sense. There is a difference between suing a man at law, and letting the difficulty alone.

The gentleman has drawn a distinction between the old school and the new school of the Presbyterian church. The old school go for strict construction, literal construction, and the new school, of course, go for a free, liberal translation of the creed. But that is not just the whole. The substance is different. They have the essential, and non-essential parts of the creed; and, in truth, with the two parties, there are two creeds, made out of one book, taken in two senses. At all events, Mr. Rice must admit the book is quite obscure, or they have not clear heads.

But how often have you heard the saying quoted by Mr. Rice, that "all sorts of doctrine, by all sorts of men, are preached amongst us." This is one of his standing texts, taken from the Millenial Harbinger. Well, it is not exactly quoted. There is one word of much limitation left out, "*almost* all sorts of men." In saying this, I follow an illustrious example. Paul, in his day, was just thus plain and candid. He gave specifications of almost all sorts of doctrine, preached even while he yet lived. Some preached that the resurrection was actually passed, and had overthrown the faith of some. Some were, for the sake of filthy lucre,

3 y 2

preaching what they ought not. Some preached that the world was immediately coming to an end; some said the law of Moses and circumcis. ion should be observed by gentile converts, &c.; and Paul sent it all over the world, and for all ages too. We are then a good deal like our great apostle, and a little like the primitive church, too, in this particular! Mr. R. could not, were he and I both to try, find as great a variety amongst us, of character, preachers, and doctrine, as I can find in the New Testament, complained of by Paul and his associates. So that the argument is as strong against Paul and the primitive church, as against myself and my brethren.

He has repeated a passage from Mr. Jones' correspondence with me. I repeat it, also, that there is not now, and certainly there was not when that was written, any thing amongst us, strictly and literally construed, like that which Mr. Jones had in his eye in England, when that was strictly and literally construed. We have *no open communion* with us, and they in England have. That principle is not at all recognized amongst us. In England there are large communities of free communion Baptists, who admit Pedo-baptists as freely as they do the baptized: we have no such custom amongst us. There may be ten or one hundred congregations amongst us, that have made that matter a question: the great majority, as far as I know, have not. A few cases, such as I have before described, have occurred, and I have witnessed them with some degree of satisfaction.

Among other curious arguments and objections against creeds, the gentleman has asked, how we get people out of the church. He says there is no way of getting them out. We are not like the Jews, who had no way of getting folks out of their church but by killing them. We, notwithstanding Mr. Rice could not see the door, have some way of getting them out. Every church that has a door into it, has also one out of it. We let them in by the BOOK, and put them out by the BOOK. God has given us instructions in our *creed book* how to manage these matters. Was there ever any creed so much slandered and opposed as ours, and by the clergy too?—or any community more calumniated than ours? Is the Bible so defective as to give no laws for the reception and exclusion of members? If they are not in the Bible, how got they into the creed? If any one would stand up and preach amongst us, that Jesus Christ had not been buried, or that he rose not from the dead, we should find a door large enough for his ejection; and for all schismatics and unrighteous persons, we have quite a large and easy egress.

Mr. R. says there is more heresy amongst those who have no creed, than amongst those who have. Let him prove it, or make an effort, and I will reply. As yet, he has made no such effort, and I presume will not.

He reads from my books, and if the gentleman would always read a little more, I should be still more obliged to him. Whenenever he reads any thing from them, of such doubtful or difficult meaning, as to require either explanation or defence, he will find me always forthcoming. Should I be convicted of any error, I shall not only be willing to retract, but thankful to him who in a good spirit points it out. Mr. Rice is not likely to gain that honor.

Those desirous of examining the passages read, will generally find that the connection, or the replies made to those correspondents, will meet all the artificial difficulties and apparent incongruities created by my worthy opponent. Some passages read on yesterday were made to appear most vulnerable. Those touching the receiving of persons, supposed to be very erroneous and heretical, demand a remark or two.

The question, for example, would you receive a Universalist—a Unitarian? We respond, not *as such*. Nor would we receive a Trinitarian, *as such*. With the New Testament in our hands, we know nothing of Calvinist, Arminian, Unitarian, Arian, &c. We ask the question, do you believe that Jesus of Nazareth is the Messiah, the Son of God? If any man cordially respond—Yes, we baptize him. We ask, on that subject, no farther questions. But suppose I doubted his faith, or his intelligence in the object of Christ's death, either before or after his baptism. I ask the question, do you believe Jesus died *for our sins*, and rose *for our justification?* He says, *No*—perseveringly says, *No*. I repudiate him as not believing the gospel facts in their proper meaning. But does he say unequivocally, *Yes*, I suspicion, I judge him not. So long as he loves and honors the Messiah, by keeping his precepts, so long I love and honor him as a christian brother. But if any one equivocates on any of these questions of fact, we simply say, he disbelieves the testimony of God, or what is in effect the same, does he not understand it; so of the Universalian, the Presbyterian, the Methodist.

In this sectarian age, good men are found labelled with these symbols of human weakness and human folly. We can neither justify nor condemn a man for his unfortunate education, for his peculiar organization, or his eccentric opinions. Treat him rationally, treat him humanely, and in a christian-like manner, and all these opinions will evaporate, or die within him. Receive him not as a Calvinist, a Papist, a Baptist, or a Universalist; receive him as a *man* and as a *christian*. Show him that you receive him in the name of the Lord, upon his faith, his hope, and love, and you will soon allure him from his false opinions, if he have any. But repudiate and excommunicate him for an opinion, you wed him to it; he feels the attachment of a martyr to that in which there is no value, but in his suffering for it. It has cost him something, and he will not part with it for nothing.

There was a remark made yesterday, about one amongst us who had been a Universalist preacher, approved now for many years on account of his christian doctrine and christian demeanor. He had a companion and fellow-soldier in the cause of Universalianism, who was immersed into the original gospel. We laid no stress upon their former theory. They had confessed the ancient faith, and were immersed into it; and I, for one, said that they ought now to preach Christ, and abandon the proclamation of any of these opinions; and on a pledge to do so—to proclaim that " Christ died for our sins," and " that he that believed and was baptized, should be saved, and that he that believeth not shall be damned." On this agreement I gave them my hand and my brotherhood. I said, let these opinions alone; they will certainly die, if you preach the gospel, and talk no more about them. The prediction has been verified to the letter. So perfectly just our reasoning on this subject, that they have long since said these opinions have been dissipated, they know not whither, and the very arguments that sustained them, have fled with them. I once more repeat it—let those opinions alone. Preach faith, piety, morality, and the opinions contrary to these will, as the vapors of the morning before the rising sun, pass away.

I have yet some other arguments to offer on the proposition, though it appears I have already submitted too many for my opponent. I reserve one or two arguments for a whole speech, and will, for that half hour, attend to no objections. Meantime, as my minutes are almost numbered, I shall offer a short argument from a high source. It is an apostolic precept; one that, in my judgment, positively inhibits all these documents called creeds. Paul says to Timothy, "hold fast the form of sound words, which thou hast heard of me in faith and love, which is in Christ Jesus;" 2 Tim. i. 13. We all understand the difference between the *form* and the *substance* of a thing. It is *form* that makes this a desk; the substance is wood, and common to many other things in this house. These pews are all of the same material, and so is the floor of the church. But it is form that gives to each its name, its use, its character. To contend for the *form*, then, is to contend for the thing itself. In this case, if you have the form, you have the thing. Sometimes, if you have the form you have the substance—and this is a case of that sort. At other times you may have the substance without the form. The word *hupotuposis*, found here, and only on another occasion in the New Testament, is a term that indicates pattern, example. Paul uses it in the first epistle, saying "that Jesus Christ had set him forth as a *pattern*, or *precedent*, to all that should hereafter believe on him, to life everlasting." The same idea is suggested, when Moses was commanded to make all things after the *pattern* shown to him on the mount. We are, in the same sense, commanded to hold fast the exact FORM of *sound words* delivered by the apostles. Paul did not say, hold fast the substance, or a synopsis, or summary of sound doctrine; but, said he, "hold fast *the form of sound words* which I have given you," &c.—[*Time expired.*]

Friday, Dec. 1—10½ *o'clock, A. M.*

[MR. RICE'S FOURTH REPLY.]

MR. PRESIDENT—My friend, Mr. C., has undertaken to prove, that human creeds are *necessarily* heretical and schismatical—that wherever they exist, they necessarily produce heresy and schism. As poison necessarily produces disease and death, when received into the stomach; so, according to Mr. C., creeds, wherever used, produce heresy and schism in the church. Do facts sustain him in his position? They, on the contrary, prove it untrue; for creeds do exist, and have long existed, without causing either heresy or schism.

In making a creed, we state in writing the principal truths which we understand the Bible to teach. Now let me ask Mr. C.—can we not understand what the Bible teaches? He will admit that we can. Then if we do understand what it teaches, and commit it to writing, have we not a true creed—a creed in exact accordance with the word of God? All say, we have. Yet this true creed, this creed which is in precise agreement with God's written word, if Mr. C.'s doctrine be true, necessarily produces heresy and schism. But if the truths of the Bible, when embodied in a creed, necessarily produce heresy and schism; the Bible itself must be necessarily heretical and schismatical!!!

Creeds, says the gentleman, produce divisions. Will he deny, that there have been a number of divisions in his own church?—divisions, I mean, in particular churches? For there are many particular churches scattered over the country; but they have no general organization—are wholly independent of each other; and, therefore, they cannot properly be considered one ecclesiastical body, any more than fifty independent political bodies can be called one civil government. But in these little democracies there has been division after division, with angry feelings, bickerings and confusion. I have very recently received some pamphlets giving a deplorable exhibition of the state of things in some of them. These churches have no creeds; but they have lamentable divisions. If, then, we do in fact find divisions and strife, where there are no creeds, is it not evident, that the mere fact, that such evils sometimes exist in churches having creeds, does not at all prove, that they are caused by creeds? The evil effects are found, where the cause to which Mr. C. ascribes them does not exist.

It is absolutely essential to the support of the gentleman's proposition, that he prove, not only that there have been divisions where creeds were used, but that he produce clear evidence, *that they were caused by creeds.* This he has not attempted to prove. He has declaimed abundantly about schisms, divisions and strifes; but let him prove, that creeds do produce them. It is absolutely necessary that he shall do this. Till he makes this point clear he has proved nothing.

He represents us as *enforcing* our views upon the consciences of men. We do no such thing. No one joins our church, but as a matter of choice. All have the opportunity of comparing our doctrines with the Bible, and of determining for themselves whether those doctrines are true, and whether they can be happy with us. But he charges us with excommunicating, for opinion's sake, pious and godly people. I deny that we do any such thing. Let the charge be proved. We do suspend and excommunicate persons for denying the fundamental doctrines of the gospel, as well as for unchristian conduct. If a member of our church denies the doctrine of the Divinity of Christ, we exclude him; because the rejection of this doctrine is in effect the rejection of the gospel. But, as I have before distinctly stated, the adoption of our confession of faith never was a condition of membership in our church. We have many members who have not had time and opportunity to examine it. We do not expect the pupil, on entering the school, to be as well instructed as the teacher. We never excommunicate persons for errors not generally considered by evangelical churches to be *fundamental.*

The gentleman read from the Confession of Faith, the following passage concerning "the power of the keys:"

"To these officers the keys of the kingdom of heaven are committed; by virtue whereof they have power respectively to retain and remit sins, to shut that kingdom against the impenitent, both by the word and censures; and to open it unto penitent sinners, by the ministry of the gospel, and by absolution from censures, as occasion shall require."—chap. 30.

Now what is the meaning of the phrase—"kingdom of heaven?" It is the church of Christ. What are the keys? The authority to open and shut the door—to receive into the church those who give evidence of possessing the scriptural qualifications, exclude unworthy members, and to preach the gospel, offering salvation to all. Presbyterians never claimed authority literally to pardon or condemn men—to admit them into heaven or to exclude them from it. Where now is the claim of high power of which the gentleman speaks?

Let me now inquire of him how things are managed in his church. Does not every church in his connection claim and exercise the same authority? Do they not vote persons in, and vote them out of the church sometimes by wholesale? Every little church of a dozen or half a dozen members, claims as high authority as was ever claimed by the general assembly of the Presbyterian church! Declamation against claims of exorbitant power come with an ill grace from Mr. C.; for he and his little churches exercise the power of the keys with a vengeance. The difference between us is—that in our church the most obscure member cannot be deprived of his privileges, until the general assembly has decided on his case, if he is pleased to bring it before them. In that body, composed of representatives from the whole church, little neighborhood jealousies and party feelings cannot prejudice his cause. But how is it in the gentleman's church? In any particular church a few influential or intriguing persons, or families, may gain over to their notions a majority of the members; and, if they choose, they may excommunicate any minority, however respectable; and though ever so unjustly deprived of their rights, they can appeal to no higher tribunal under heaven! Which of these churches, I emphatically ask, affords the greatest security against the arbitrary exercise of power? In which are the rights of private members and of ministers best protected?

The gentleman repeats the assertion, that our confession of faith has been changed; and he specifies the article concerning the authority of the civil magistrate in matters of religion. But he ought to have known, that our church never did adopt that article. When the Westminster confession was adopted by the Presbyterian church in the United States, it was expressly excepted. It is not true, therefore, that we have changed our doctrines.

But he tells us, that he has rarely heard the Scriptures quoted in the meetings in the ecclesiastical courts of the Presbyterian church. The reason, I presume, is—that he has rarely attended their meetings, and knows very little about their proceedings. I never in my life attended one of our church courts, when any important question was discussed, without hearing appeals constantly made to the Word of God as the only infallible rule of faith and of practice. It is true, we do not consider it necessary to discuss anew every subject as often as we are called to act upon it. We have, on mature examination, agreed that the confession of faith contains the system of doctrine taught in the Scriptures, and that its principles of church government are agreeable to the inspired Word. We, therefore, often proceed upon these admitted principles. I presume, the gentleman himself would scarcely think it necessary in one of his churches to enter into protracted arguments to prove, that immersion is necessary in order to admission to membership; or that an individual baptized by sprinkling would not be admitted.

My friend Mr. C. has been for years an editor and a reformer, and, as we have a right to conclude, has carefully noted passing events. Yet it is rather strange—that concerning some of the most important of them, he is very imperfectly informed. How happened it, he asks, that, a few years since, sixty thousand members and ministers were excommunicated from the Presbyterian church? I answer, such an event never did happen. Many years ago a plan of union was adopted by the general assembly of the Presbyterian church and the Congregational association of Vermont, the design of which was to unite Presbyterians and Congregationalists, in destitute settlements, where neither was strong enough to sustain themselves alone. In process of time many churches were thus organized, and also presbyteries and synods. The provisions of the plan were such, that Congregationalists might exercise a controling influence on our church courts, without being themselves subject to our laws and regulations. In 1837, our general assemby, seeing great evil arising from this state of things, resolved, that only Presbyterians could be permitted to belong to our church, and to vote in our ecclesiastical courts. Those bodies formed on the aforesaid plan being thus excluded from our church, many ministers and churches, dissatisfied with the action of the assembly, withdrew. *None of them, however, were excommunicated.* We still acknowledge them as christian brethren, and as churches of Christ. We have never pronounced them heretics; for they have not rejected the fundamental doctrines of christianity.

But what caused this division? *It was not caused by the fact of our having a creed, but by our failing to adhere to its wise provisions and regulations.* Still no real Presbyterian was designed to be excluded from our church; nor were others excommunicated nor ecclesiastically censured. We simply resolved, that those who take part in the government of our church, must submit to be governed.

The gentleman says, I complain of his church for being too *liberal;* and he informs us, that christianity is a liberal thing. He is mistaken. I do not complain that they are too liberal, or that they are liberal at all. I find fault with their *latitudinarian* principles and practice; and, let me say, there is a very great difference between *latitudinarianism* and *liberality.* I find fault with his church, because it is too much like Noah's ark: it has a door wide enough, and a platform broad enough, to receive error of every grade. It compromises God's glorious truth. Our Savior laid no such foundation, and taught no such principles.

We require those who seek membership in our church to profess their faith in the fundamental doctrines of christianity. But what, I ask, are the fundamental doctrines required to be received in order to membership in Mr. C.'s church? What are the cardinal principles of which he speaks? Will he please to enlighten us on this subject?

He has, once and again, asserted, that if Arianism had been let alone *ecclesiastically,* it would speedily have died. All we ask of him, is to prove that such errors, if not disturbed, will die. I am curious to know how he has ascertained that such would be the result of letting them alone.

Once more, he has brought up that troublesome question about his admitting unimmersed persons to communion. He says, he does not *invite* them; but if they come on their own responsibility, he will not debar them. But Mr. Jones asked him, do you ADMIT them? Mr. C. replied, we do not admit them. When I see over a door "no admittance," I understand distinctly, that I am not to enter there. After all, what is the amount of the gentleman's liberality, of which he has so much boasted? Why, if unimmersed persons will go and commune with him without an invitation, he will not refuse to let them do it. If they enter his tabernacle, he will not drive them out! Or, more properly, he does not admit them, as he said to Jones; and yet he does admit them!!!

Well, I am happy to find him becoming more liberal. He is even now more liberal, it would seem, than his churches; for they, he says, have not adopted the plan of admitting unimmersed persons to commune. It is to be hoped, however, they will be influenced by his good example. But ought he not to write to England, and let his friends there know, that he has changed his opinion since he wrote to them on this subject?

I have said and proved, that the gentleman cannot exclude from his

church any errorist of any grade without violating the fundamental principles of his reformation. He evidently feels the difficulty. But he says,
if they should go against the Bible, they exclude them. But I ask again,
if you bring a man before the church, charged with preaching dangerous
error, who is to judge whether the doctrines he has propagated are contrary to the Scriptures? Is Mr. Campbell to be the judge? No; for
then he would be instead of a creed. Is the church of which he is a
member to judge? Certainly not; and for the same reason. Is the individual to decide in his own case? Then, of course, he is clear. The
gentleman cannot exclude him without abandoning his published principles.

Observe, Mr. C. teaches, that no church has the right to require as a
condition of membership any thing more than the professed belief that
Christ is the Son of God, and immersion. When a man applies for membership, he is asked, whether he believes that Jesus Christ is the Son of
God. On answering this one question in the affirmative, and submitting
to immersion, he is a member in good and regular standing. Now, Dr.
Thomas, the Materialist, professed firmly to believe that Jesus Christ is
the Son of God; and so zealous was he for immersion, in order to remission of sins, that he actually immersed again those who came to him from
the Baptists. He had not violated either of the conditions on which he
entered the church. He still professed to take the Bible as his only guide.
He contended, that he was not teaching error; but Mr. C. said he was,
and called on his church to exclude him. In doing so, however, he disregarded his own principles.

He will receive a Unitarian into his church, he tells us, if he will take
the words of Scripture relative to the character and works of Christ, in
their *fair construction*. Here we meet the old difficulty. *Who is to determine what is the fair construction?* Every man will say, that he
does take the fair construction. Is Mr. C. to judge? Or is the church
to judge? Or is each individual to judge for himself? One of your
preachers, for example, is found preaching that Jesus Christ is a creature,
and that he died only as a martyr. You table charges against him; and
he appears before the church. They ask him—"Do you believe that
Jesus Christ is the Son of God?" He answers in the affirmative. They
ask him again—"Do you believe that he bore our sins in his own body
on the tree?" He answers affirmatively. You are forced to acquit him.
But, next Sabbath, he again preaches the same doctrine. You try him
again, and with the same result. How, I ask again, can Mr. C. exclude
such a man? I say, he can do it only by a flagrant departure from his
own principles.

Whether I have produced contradictions in Mr. Campbell's writings I
cheerfully leave the audience to judge. He expresses the hope that I
will read much more from them. If it will be any comfort to him, I assure him that I expect to abound in quotations from his books.

The gentleman has a singular method of destroying error. He tells
us of a man, once a Universalist preacher, who has not only forgotten his
former doctrine, but does not even remember the arguments by which he
defended it. Only let Universalism alone, he says, and it will die a natural death. Well, if he would let creeds alone, perhaps they would die
too. And if he and his friends would not disturb Pedo-baptism, would
not it also die? If one error will die by being let alone, why not another? The gentleman has been engaged most assiduously and zealously

for thirty years, laboring to destroy what he considers errors; and now he has made the remarkable discovery, that some of the very worst of them will die soonest by being let alone! I very much wish, that he would inform us what particular errors will die by being neglected, and which it is necessary to destroy by opposition; for I have no wish to spend time and strength in making war upon errors that will die sooner if not disturbed.

Universalism, which he has been so willing to admit into his church, is in its tendency one of the most demoralizing errors that has cursed the world. An old and shrewd German black smith once heard a Universalist preach in his neighborhood. He became restless under the sermon; and so soon as the congregation was dismissed, he approached the preacher and said to him—"If dis doctrine bees true, be sure you must not preach it any more." "Why not?" inquired the preacher. "Because," said the Dutchman, "one of my neighbors has already stole one half my smit tools; and if he does find dis out, he will have all de rest." The Dutchman saw the tendency of the doctrine. Yet this is one of the errors Mr. C. is willing to allow to place in his church till it will die! I am not disposed to treat it so leniently. It may do great mischief before its death.

Mr. Campbell has, at last, given us his law prohibiting creeds. It is Paul's exhortation to Timothy—"Hold fast the form of sound words." That is, take the Bible just as it is. We do so take it, and hold it fast. But does this scripture forbid us to write down what we understand the form of sound words to mean? The gentleman has himself published a book of some size, called "The Christian System." This book is divided off into chapters and sections just as our creed; and in each chapter it professedly explains some doctrine taught in that "form of sound words." If a single individual may write a book, expounding the doctrine of sound words, as he understands it; I cannot see why a body of professing christians who agree in their views, might not be permitted to do the same thing. This argument certainly will not prove, that "creeds are necessarily heretical and schismatical." The gentleman must look for another. I have called on him to produce a solitary passage that directly or indirectly forbids the use of creeds. Where is there one?

I wish now to make some farther remarks on Mr. Campbell's plan of receiving Universalists. I have proved, that, according to his principles, Unitarians of any grade, Arians or Socinians, Universalists and errorists of every grade, may become members of his church; and I now assert, that they may be *preachers* as well as members. This I will prove by Mr. C. himself—

"A christian is by profession a preacher of truth and righteousness, both by precept and example. He may of right preach, baptize, and dispense the supper, as well as pray for all men, when circumstances demand it."— *Christian System*, p. 85.

This is not mere *theory* with Mr. Campbell. He has shown his faith by his works, as I will prove from the Millenial Harbinger, vol. i. p. 147. Mr. Raines, now of Paris, formerly a Universalist preacher, was, some years since, immersed by the reformers. He appeared at the Mahoning association. Some of the brethren were not quite prepared to receive him as a preacher among them. Mr. Raines stated distinctly that he still held Universalist sentiments, which quite alarmed some of the fraternity. Whereupon the difficulty was, by Mr. C.'s influence, settled in the following manner:

" Whether he held these views as matters of faith, or as pure matters of opinion, was then propounded to him. He avowed them to be, in his judgment, matters of opinion, and not matters of faith ; and, in reply to another question, averred that he would not teach them, believing them to be matters of opinion, and not the gospel of Jesus Christ. Although a majority of the brethren were satisfied, still a number were not reconciled to this decision. It was repeatedly urged that it mattered not what his private opinions were on this subject, provided he regarded them only as matters of opinion, and held them as private property."

I have a few remarks to make on this singular proceeding, only part of which I shall have time to make at present. Mr. Raines, of whom I do not intend to speak disrespectfully, was a preacher of Universalism—a doctrine which is admitted to be erroneous and demoralizing. He was received as a preacher in Mr. C.'s church, without any change in his sentiments. He distinctly stated, that they were not changed ; that he still believed that all men would be saved. But, though his belief was unchanged, he consented to give it a new name. Hitherto he had held Universalism as a *doctrine*—a matter of *faith*. He now agreed to call it an *opinion ;* and it became at once perfectly harmless ! Arsenic, if you call it *poison*, will kill you ; but call it *food*, and it will become nourishing ! So Universalism, if you call it *faith*, is ruinous ; but only name it *opinion*, and all is well ! ! !

I have called on the gentleman to tell us the precise difference between *faith* and *opinion*—where faith ends, and opinion begins. I am particularly desirous of definite information on this point ; and I insist that Mr. Campbell should afford it, because I have propounded the question to more than one of the proclaimers in his church, and they could not answer it. I incline to think, that in their theology, it is a distinction without a difference. Here we find the old error still held under a new name ; and the name seems to possess a charm that destroys all its evil effects ! Perhaps the giving it a new name, caused the gentleman to forget the arguments by which he was accustomed to defend it ! We need information on this subject.—[*Time expired.*

Friday, Dec. 1—11 o'clock, A. M.
[MR. CAMPBELL'S FIFTH ADDRESS.]

MR. PRESIDENT—Before I sat down, I promised a consecutive argument, or two, that should occupy half an hour, without turning aside to notice objections. Before doing this, I must add a few remarks to the argument introduced at the close of my last speech. I had just placed before you a divine precept, authoritatively commanding the holding fast of the inspired form of sound words, delivered by the apostles. Now, a confession of faith is not " *the form of sound words*," but only the form of the construction put upon them by uninspired men. Nothing is more latitudinarian than the word substance, if I might exemplify by the last two discourses of Mr. Rice. This notion of holding fast the *substance* is a perfect delusion ; and more especially, when we hold fast that substance through a printed book, called a confession of faith, or a summary of christian doctrine. In all such cases, we have two summaries, two confessions, and two forms of the constructive sense of Paul's form of sound words. We have first the written form—the printed confession ; we have, again, our mental form of that confession—that is, our ideas of the ideas expressed in the book. Our views of the Bible on this mode of procedure, are but *our views of certain men's views of the Bible.* This is a demonstrable fact. Here is Paul's form of sound words. There is the confession, or the form of construction of the sense of Paul's form of sound words; and, in my mind, are my views, or the mental form of the confession. The Bible is the first form; the confession the second form; and my own views of the last book, the third form of the same idea. There is the form; the Bible; there is a view of that form; the confession; and there is my view of the confession—which is to me the influential form. Nothing, then, is more slily deceptive; and yet, when canvassed to the bottom, nothing is more glaringly delusive, than to represent a confession as a final expression, or our own individual expression of our views of the Bible. When you tell your views of the Bible to A, he forms his views of your words and interpretations, and then, through these, he comes to certain conclusions concerning the book. But his conclusion is the third version of the matter, and not the second. You may imagine that it is the same in substance with the second; but suppose it were—it is a *new* form. Some say to us, you have your views of the Bible, and the Bible too—and, therefore, you have a confession of faith. Grant it, then, for the sake of argument, and follows it not, that he has two confessions—the written one, and the mental one?

In Scotland, the *Burgher* and the *Anti-burgher* Presbyterians wrote their testimony, expressive of some of their views of the confession. Now have they not, *being founded on this testimony*, a different foundation from other Presbyterians? and if so, they are a distinct community. So are the Presbyterians built upon the confession, different from those builded on the Bible. Should Mr. Rice write his views, and some one write his views of Mr. Rice's views, and another write his views of the reviewer's views, what would be the color of the mind that receives the last, compared with the mind that received the first? As various often his, who listens to the creeds and catechisms explanatory of the Bible. I prefer the fountain to the muddy stream; and, therefore, take the original document, and place my mind directly upon it.

Along with this precept from Paul, I must plead one from Jude: "Contend earnestly for the faith once delivered to the saints." Jude wrote his short and comprehensive epistle near the close of the apostolic age. He saw an approaching defection, and enjoined, in these words, an antidote against the early workings of the mystery of iniquity. He saw the efforts to introduce new things by the converted Jews and pagans, incorporated in the christian family, and in the midst of these efforts wrote his epistle. Such a precept, emanating from such circumstances, is equivalent to a positive prohibition of every thing but *the faith*, the truth, the identical words commended by apostles and prophets, as the foundation of the christian temple, and the constitution of the christian church. The gentleman asks for precepts authorizing the book alone!!

Mr. Rice has told us, indeed, that the confession of faith is not *the constitution* of the Presbyterian church. But, with its form of discipline and church government, it *is* the identical constitution of the Presbyterian church. And, with these words before me, allow me to introduce another view of the subject.

In this universe, there are numerous and various constitutions, both celestial and terrestrial. But of all these documents and things called constitutions, there are three, of which God is himself the author and the finisher. He has bestowed on man, and probably on angels, too, the right of making for themselves a sort of bye-law constitution, in reference to their social intercommunications. But neither to angel nor to man, has he given the liberty of making a constitution for the universe, a constitution for the human body, nor a constitution for the church of God.

Good and valid reasons can be given, why man should not have been entrusted with the draft of a constitution for the universe, and why he should not have been permitted to form a constitution for his own body. All will find in his utter incompetency, many good reasons why he should not have been entrusted with such an undertaking. To my mind he is just as incompetent to perform the last, as either of the other two. Had any man a tolerably distinct and accurate view of the mystical body of Christ—of that mysterious and sublime institution, the church of the living God, he would feel himself as wholly inadequate to the task of forming for it a constitution as he, physically, intellectually, and morally is, for his own body or the whole universe of God.

The church, the true church, of the true Redeemer, is a glorious institution; and hence it was decreed before the christian age began, and foretold by one of Israel's sweetest and most seraphic bards, the evangelical Isaiah: " Unto us a child is born; unto us a son is given, and the government shall be on his shoulder, and his name shall be called *Wonderful, Counsellor*, the Mighty God, the *Founder of the Everlasting Age*, the Prince of Peace." He is then, the Wonderful Founder of the gospel institution, the Everlasting Age. The noblest and most august titles in the universe surround his mitre and his crown! Among these is one, to us, of ineffable interest, " *the* AUTHOR *and the founder of* THE FAITH." " Of man's miraculous mistakes, this bears the palm"—that he should presume to draft a constitution for the church of Jesus Christ! He could as easily make one for the hierarchies of heaven, or for the universe of God.

When the Messiah began to prepare himself for this glorious work divine, the Holy Spirit was given to him without measure. All knowledge, wisdom, eloquence and power, were bestowed upon him as the human and divine head of this mighty assembly of saints. What a community the christian family is—spread over the whole earth in some periods of its history, and commensurate with all time, embracing all lands, languages and nations; all ranks and degrees of men—the learned and the rude, the sage and the child; all varieties of man—the noblest and most gifted of earth's mightiest spirits, the giant intellects of humanity! To make for such an association a constitution?—what a task! Had a council of the heavens been called; had Gabriel, Raphael, Uriel, and all the sons of light and celestial fire been convened to deliberate for an age, they could not have made a constitution for Christ's church. They could not have sketched a system, even had it been adopted to the letter, that could have united, cemented, coalesced, and harmonized, in everlasting peace and amity, a society like that of which we speak. Hence the Lord Messiah was made " *the covenant*" and the leader, the lawgiver, the author and the finisher of the christian constitution. On that, and that alone, can the church be built. Take that constitution, then, and make it the basis, the only basis of a christian society. Let his oracles, decisions, and government be first, last, and midst, the alpha and the omega; then all christians of all nations, ages, and conditions, can form one grand, holy, and happy community.

We have made an experiment under circumstances not the most propitious, in the midst of many conflicting and rival institutions, to lay again the same well tried old corner-stone—the primitive confession on which the church was built—the stone which the Master laid at Cæsarea Philippi, on which to build his church, in first commending it to the notice of the world, promising most solemnly to build his church of all nations and ages upon it. The experiment for the time has been most successful. Probably not less than two hundred thousand persons of all the creeds, and parties, and various associations around us; persons of all sorts and varieties of mind, education, and circumstances in Christendom, as well as those from the ranks of scepticism, in its various forms, have united in making the same confession, and have associated upon the same grand fundamental constitutional principles. They are found, too, in all the states of this immense union and its territories. They are found in the Canadas, and in all northern America. They are found in England, Ireland, Scotland, and Wales; and, without any other bond of union than the new and everlasting constitution, signed, sealed, and delivered by the Lord Jesus, through his holy apostles. United in this, and builded on this foundation, we still maintain unity of spirit in the bonds of peace. Still, Mr. Rice expresses his astonishment that we should hang together at all, asking, meantime, how we keep out heretics and offenders! His imagination at one time, has us excluding whole masses; at another time, not able to induce one to enter. Now, we cannot take in one; again, we cannot exclude one!

And what is the character of all these communities? I presume I will have credit, even with our adversaries themselves, in saying that they are, as congregations, at full par value, in all proper points of comparison, with the same number of persons and communities; whether in London, Edinburgh, New York, Philadelphia, or in this city. They will compare with other denominations in good sense, in a fair reputation for medium talent and learning; for staid, good habits, and all the social virtues. Now, we argue, that if so many persons of all those varieties, before mentioned, can meet, unite and co-operate in faith, hope and love, on this foundation, under this new constitution; all the world—all who know, believe, and love the same Savior, might. It is broad enough and strong enough for them all. What other demonstrations of its practicability and adequacy can be demanded? And, if any one ask the reason of all this success and co-operation, I present the charter, the confession of our faith, the creed, the constitution, if you please, under which we are incorporated. The strength, however, of the whole edifice, is in its foundation; and the still more interior secret of the strength of our system is, that IT IS DIVINE. It is the foundation which *God* has laid in Zion. It is not both divine and human. It is wholly divine.

Does any one ask me, what it is? I wish I had a summer's day and my wonted strength, to develop its glorious features to your view. A full revelation of it would disarm our opponents, and take from them more than half their arguments. I tell you, my fellow-citizens, the christian faith is quite a simple, but most comprehensive and potent document. The five books of Moses, together with the prophets, compose the Jew's religion. The christian believes all these too, and studies them well; but christianity was born after Christ. There were Jews and gentiles innumerable before Christ was born. But we speak not of the Jewish nor of the patriarchal ages. The Harbinger had done his work. He prepared a people for the Lord, and introduced the sublime and glorious age of Messiah the Prince—but christianity is more than John preached. The principles of christianity, like the grand laws of nature, are simple and few, but omnipotent to all the ends of its author. What sublime and awful wonders are revealed in heaven to the eye of the philosopher, by the operation of the centripetal and centrifugal forces! Silently and unobtrusively these laws, for ages, have swayed creation's ample bounds, kept the universe to its place, and guided all the mighty masses in their unmeasured circuits of miles unnumbered, through all the fields of occupied space. That regularity, harmony, beauty, and beneficence spread over those empyreal regions, where the march of revolving worlds overwhelms the adoring saint, and fills his soul with admiration of the Divine author of the universe—all spring from, and are the mysterious result of, the happy combination of these two stupendous principles.

So is it in our most holy faith. There are but two grand principles in christianity—two laws revealed and developed, whose combination produces similar harmony, beauty, and loveliness in the world of mind as in the world of matter. But, leaving the development of these for the present, I must at once declare the simplicity of this divine constitution of remedial mercy. It has but three grand ideas peculiar to itself; and these all concern the King. I am sorry that this mysterious and sublime simplicity does not appear to those who set about making constitutions for Christ's kindom. This confession of omnipotent moral power, because the offspring of infinite wisdom and benevolence, must be learned from one passage, Matt. xvi. " Who am I, do men say ?" We must advance one step farther—who am I, do *you* say ? Peter, in one momentous period, expressed the whole affair—Thou art the Messiah, the Son of the Living God. The *two* ideas expressed, concern the *person* of the Messiah and his *office*. The one implied, concerns his *character;* for it was through his character, as developed, that Peter recognized his person and his Messiahship. Now let us take off the shoes from off our feet, for we stand on holy ground; and let us hear him unfold to Peter his intentions—" Blessed art thou Simon, son of Jonas! Flesh and blood has not revealed this unto thee, but my Father who is in heaven. And I say unto thee, thou art Peter, (a stone,) and on this rock *I will build* my *church*, and the gates of hell, (hades,) shall not prevail against it." It will stand forever. " I will give unto thee, (thyself alone, Peter,) the keys of the kingdom of heaven, (my church,) and whose sins soever you remit, they are remitted; and whose sins soever you retain, they shall be retained." Here, then, is the whole revelation of the mystery of the christian constitution—the full confession of the christian faith. All that is peculiar to christianity is found in these words; not merely in embryo, but in a clearly expressed outline. A clear perception, and a cordial belief of these two facts will make any man a christian. He may carry them out in their vast dimensions and glorious developments, to all eternity. He may ponder upon them until his spirit is transformed into the image of God; until he shines in more than angelic brightness, in all the purity and beauty of heavenly love. Man glorified in heaven, gifted with immortality, and rapt in the ecstacies of infinite and eternal blessedness, is but the mere result of a proper apprehension of, and conformity to, this confession. I am always overwhelmed with astonishment in observing how this document has been disparaged and set at nought by our builders of churches. It seems still to be a " stone of stumbling and a rock of offence." Yet Jesus calls it the *rock*. It is in the figure of a church or a temple, the foundation, *the rock*. When all societies build on this one foundation, and on it only, then shall there be unity of faith, of affection, and of co-operation; but never, never till then. Every other foundation is sand. Hence they have all wasted away. Innumerable parties have perished from the earth; and so will all the present, built on any other foundation than this rock.

I again say, that every denomination built on any other foundation than this rock—on this simple confession of faith in the fair, just, and well defined meaning of its words, will as certainly perish from the earth as man does. They may have much truth in their systems, but they have so much mortality with it, that perish they must as sects, parties, and denominations. Their doom is written—"Dust thou art, and unto dust thou shalt return." They may pass through many changes in the progress of decomposition; for the Presbyterians of the 16th and 17th centuries are not just those of the 18th and 19th, as the sequel may yet show.

Whenever any man discovers this rock, and is willing to build on it alone; whenever he sees its firmness, its strength, and is willing to place himself upon it for time and for eternity, and on it alone, I say to him— Give me your hand, brother, you must come out and pass through the ceremony of naturalization; you must be born of water as well as of the Spirit, and enter into the new and everlasting covenant; you must assume the name of the Father, of the Son, and of the Holy Spirit. On that simple confession with the lips, that he believes in his heart this glorious truth, he is, by the authority of the heavens, constituted a christian; and he that treats him unkindly, treats his Lord and Master so. Other foundation can no man lay, that will endure; nor any one which, while it does endure, can receive the family of God.

We can neither in reason nor in conscience, ask this person to subscribe twenty-five, thirty-three, or thirty-nine articles. He is but a newborn child. We expect him to *grow*. We will not put him upon the iron bedstead of Procrustes and stretch him up to thirty-nine articles. We will place him in the cradle of maternal kindness, and feed him with the sincere milk of the Word, that he may grow thereby. Nor will we, at any time, say to him, Brother, you must never grow beyond the *thirty-ninth* article. If you go to the *fortieth*, we will cut you down or send you adrift. If hou live three-score years and ten, remember, you must never think of the fortieth article. You must subscribe them all now at your birth; and subscribe no more at your death. If you should attain to the knowledge, the gifts, and the graces of the sweet psalmist of Israel, you must never think of transcending those nine and thirty, or those three and thirty articles of belief.

My objection to these documents is not merely that they are summaries; but that they are summaries made ready to our hands, by the aids of orthodoxy—hereditaments of ancestral acquisition. God designed no summary. He could have made one by Paul, or all of the apostles, but he would not have such a thing. He intended us all to commune with him through his blessed, soul-illuminating, sanctifying, saving truth. He would have us dig in the mines of knowledge, for ourselves. He would have us become intellectually and morally rich, by our own labors. He would have us to apply our minds to the truth, as we place an instrument on a stone, to sharpen and polish it. By pressing that instrument, and holding it for a long time on that stone, by continual attrition, it becomes bright and sharp. So by the continual attrition of the word of God upon our hearts, and by the Spirit of our God upon our spirits, they become more discriminating in the things of God, as well as shine with the brightness and beauty of holiness. I never knew any one converted or sanctified by reading one of these summaries. These confessions of faith have been long in the world. Has any one been converted by them? Among all the published reports of converted persons, by numerous and various instrumentalities, I never knew of man, woman, or child, having been converted by reading articles of faith, or books of discipline.

But they have been roots of bitterness, causes of division; have made numerous sects, and preserved and upheld those that, but for them, had long since perished from the earth. They are unsanctified documents. Pardon me for saying, they are unholy things. They were not made by the authority of God, but in contravention of it; and in opposition to his own confession, given in the sixteenth chapter of Matthew. They are opposed, without intending it, to the last oracle we have heard from heaven, from the holy mount—"This is my Son, the beloved, in whom I delight; HEAR HIM." Moses and Elijah came from heaven to do him honor. They laid their commissions at his feet. Heaven recalled them, and left him with us, as the Messenger of the everlasting covenant, with the solemn and final precept, HEAR HIM.

It has been hearing him that has made the prophets of Greece, and Rome, and Geneva, and Westminster, children in my eyes. I once looked up to them; but thank my Lord, I now look down upon them, not in contempt for them, but as teachers of no authority with me. Over me they have no more authority than the dreams of my childhood, or the fancy sketches of our modern poets. I stand upon higher, holier, stronger ground, than upon such a paper platform as they have reared.

This, sir, is the constitution of the Presbyterian church—this volume in my hand, manufactured two hundred years ago, and from time to time amended in some points. Such documents men *can* make. For such churches they can make constitutions. But, sir, this book is not the constitution of *Christ's* church. They call these *"branch"* churches, branches of Christ's church. But these are words not found in the Bible. Jesus Christ has not said one word about these *branch* institutions. It is, then, from the very name itself, heretical and schismatical. It makes a branch. The Methodists, and Baptists, &c., are branches too, made by such heretical substitutes for, or appendages to, the christian Scriptures. The more our brethren in these branch institutions are ensnared and captivated by such designations, and fallacious titles, the more are they false to the great catholic, all-absorbing, and soul-redeeming principles. The very fact, that this document is the constitution of this denomination, makes it both heretical and schismatical; for it is not a constitution of Christ's body, it is a rival of it. Such, then, is the argument which I would draw, and which I would delight to fill up, on the fact and figure of the constitution of Christ's church. The sum of the whole matter, then, is this—we have a divine constitution for the whole kingdom of Jesus Christ, adapted to the genius of humanity, the circumstances of the human race, the churches' relations to worlds unseen, to the whole universe of God; and hence every other one is essentially and perpetually heretical and schismatical.

Hence, then, we are not only commanded to hold fast the form of sound words, but to "*contend earnestly for the* FAITH, once delivered to the saints." I have shewn that this faith is that of which Jesus Christ is both the *author* and the *finisher;* consequently, he is neither the author nor the finisher of the Westminster, nor of any other confession in the world. So place we ourselves before this community, and in this attitude I desire to place myself before earth and heaven; as now contending for that faith, and that faith only, delivered by the great Functionary of the universe to us, fallen men, by the holy apostles and prophets.—[*Time expired.*

Friday, Dec. 1—11½ *o'clock, A. M.*

[MR. RICE'S FIFTH REPLY.]

MR. PRESIDENT.—I think my friend, Mr. Campbell, is rising to-day in his powers of declamation and exhortation—both of which are useful in their proper place. There was, however, one great misfortune attending his last speech, which, by the way, was quite handsomely delivered. The whole foundation will be swept away by the correction of a strange error into which he has fallen. I will attend to that matter presently.

He seems really to believe, that we cannot "hold fast the form of sound words," if we venture to commit to writing what we understand the Scriptures to teach! The moment we write what we understand to be the meaning of that form of sound words, we have abandoned it!! Yet Mr. C. can write and publish in his Christian System what he understands it to teach, and still hold it fast! He claims the right to do what the whole Presbyterian church does not attempt; and that which, when done by us, amounts to apostasy and deserves excommunication, becomes perfectly harmless, when done by him! We greatly sin, if we, as a body, agree in our views of the Bible, and commit them to writing, requiring our ministers to teach them; but Mr. C. can write what he pleases, and it is no sin! I have long known, that Presbyterian sins were, in certain quarters, considered the greatest of all sins. Many things which in them are unpardonable, are in others quite venial. But I call for the passage of Scripture that condemns the use of creeds.

The Westminster confession, he says, must be very obscure, because in Scotland they have written explanations of it, and even explanations of explanations. Let us have the proof. When I state facts, I prove them; and I shall expect him to do the same. Let us have the documents; and they shall be attended to. I have not seen any of the explanations of explanations. I hope he will let us see one of them.

But, says Mr. C., why not go to the fountain head, the Bible, for our faith? Did you ever hear a Presbyterian minister preach, who did not urge his hearers to go to the fountain head? Do not our ministers universally preach the general reading of the Scriptures, as the only rule of faith? I venture to assert, that at this day, notwithstanding all the eloquent declamations of Mr. C. and his friends concerning the excellence of the Bible, Presbyterians are more accustomed to read and study it, than his church. An agent for the Bible Society has stated, that in his journeyings to and fro, he has found many families connected with it, without a Bible! Very few Presbyterian families, if any, can be found in such a situation. You may find them destitute of the conveniences and even of the necessaries of life; but rarely indeed can you find them without a Bible. There is not on earth a body of professing christians who read it more, or more constantly urge others to read, or prize it more highly as the "lamp to their feet and the light to their path," than Presbyterians.

And where, let me ask, can the gentleman find a class of men who have more zealously promoted the circulation of the Scriptures, without note or comment, at home and abroad, in civilized and in pagan lands, than the clergy of the Presbyterian church. Or where can be found a body of people who have more generally or more liberally contributed of their means to give the Bible to the destitute? And what has been the course pursued by Mr. C. and his church in relation to the efforts to cirlate the Scriptures without note or comment? For years he stood up in opposition to all Bible societies, and did as much as any other man to cripple their operations. I am truly pleased to learn, that his views, so strangely wrong, have become changed on this subject. But what have his people done toward the circulation of the Bible, of which he speaks in terms so exalted? He has himself published the fact, that they have done almost nothing ; that very few of them have given any thing to this noble and philanthropic cause ! Is it not most marvelous, that the very people who profess to be more zealous than all others for the Bible, and the Bible alone, have either opposed, or done little or nothing to promote its general circulation ; whilst the very churches, clergy and people, Presbyterians and others, whom they condemn as establishing creeds for the Bible—as making the Word of God of non-effect by their traditions—as afraid of the light—are zealously and liberally contributing time, talents and money in placing the Bible, without note or comment, in the hands of all the human family ? ! These facts are worth more, infinitely more, to place this subject in its true light, than all the pretty declamations of the gentleman since the commencement of the debate. We show our faith by our works. Let our friends do the same.

The gentleman has found a second passage of Scripture which, as he supposes, prohibits the use of creeds. It is in the epistle of Jude— "Earnestly contend for the faith which was once delivered to the saints." The faith once delivered to the saints consists of the doctrines and truths taught in the Scriptures. For these, Presbyterians do contend earnestly. But does Jude forbid us to write out a brief outline of these truths, and to say to all men—thus we understand the Bible? The gentleman has not ventured to deny the fact stated in my first speech, that you cannot know in detail what any man believes, from the fact, that he professes to have no other creed but the Bible. This difficulty arises not from any obscurity attending the instructions of the inspired writers, but from the indisputable fact that men have perverted its language, attaching to it ideas never intended to be communicated by them. The gentleman's farfetched inference from Jude's language, is wholly illegitimate.

I now come to sweep away the foundation on which my friend's beautiful speech—the best he has made—was based. There are three things, he tells us, for which men cannot make constitutions—the universe, man, and the church. Presbyterians, he would have you believe, have had the presumption to attempt to make a *constitution* for the church of Christ. Now, the truth is, *the confession of faith is not the constitution of the Presbyterian church.* The word *constitution*, it is true, is used in various senses ; and in one sense the confession of faith may be called the constitution of our church. But, in the sense of original legislation, we do not admit, that it is *the constitution.* We hold, that the Bible is *the* constitution of the Presbyterian church. We hold no doctrine nor principle as obligatory, which we do not believe to be inculcated in the Sacred Word. The confession of faith itself affords the best refutation of the gentleman's charge. I will read in our Form of Government, chap. i. sec. 7 :

" That all church power, whether exercised by the body in general, or in the way of representation by delegated authority, IS ONLY MINISTERIAL AND DECLARATIVE; *that is to say*, that the Holy Scriptures are the ONLY RULE OF FAITH AND MANNERS; *that no church judicatory ought to pretend to make laws to bind the conscience, in virtue of their own authority;* and that all their decisions should be founded upon THE RECORDED WILL OF GOD. Now though it will be easily admitted, that all synods and councils may err, through the frailty inseparable from humanity; yet there is much greater danger from THE USURPED CLAIM OF MAKING LAWS, than from the right of judging upon laws already made, and COMMON TO ALL WHO PROFESS THE GOSPEL; although this right, as necessity requires in the present state, be lodged with fallible men."

Here, you observe, is an explicit declaration, that all church power is simply *ministerial* and *declarative*, not *legislative*—that the Holy Scriptures are the only rule of faith and manners. Here is a distinct renunciation of all power to *make laws* to bind the consciences of men, and a declaration, as strong as language can make it, that church courts must found all their decisions on the Word of God—that, instead of *usurping* the claim to make laws, they can only judge according to the laws of the Bible, which are common to all who profess the gospel.

Now what becomes of the gentleman's charge, that the Presbyterians have attempted TO MAKE A CONSTITUTION for the church of Christ? What have they done? They have given in a few chapters a brief statement of the great doctrines and principles of church government taught in the Bible, and especially in the New Testament, and they have referred to the chapter and verse in the Bible which, as they believe, sustains every article and every important principle. How essentially different this from usurping legislative power, and attempting to make a constitution for the church! So the gentleman's beautiful speech evaporates.

But we are not the only people, in these latter days, who might be charged with making constitutions for the church. The gentleman himself, notwithstanding his eloquent declamation, has actually tried his hand at this work! If we were to judge by what he has said during this discussion, we should believe, that no man on earth confines himself, in his faith and practice, so closely to the Bible as he. He goes by THE BOOK. Yet he has been telling his people, for two years past, that their church is unorganized, overrun with ruinous error, and likely to be rent in pieces; and that they must get up an organization. For the purpose of securing this important object, he submitted to them a *constitution*, which I will read. For the sake of illustrating his principles, he supposes a number of churches in the island of Guernsey, in council assembled, and about to form an organization, with the following constitution: (*Millen. Harb., New Series*, Vol. vii. No. 2, pp. 85, 86.)

" 1st. That they should act as one body, regarding all the existing congregations of the island, and any others that might be formed by their instrumentality or that of others laboring under their auspices, and thus connected with them, as constituent and component communities of one body; but holding in their private capacities, as christian familes, certain reserved and untransferrable rights, duties and privileges, which are individual and private, and not to be interfered with by the body *as such*. [Amongst these they enumerated the election and appointment of their congregational officers: That each church should have its own eldership and deaconate, and at least one *president elder*, whose whole time shall be sacred to the calls and supervision of the church; for which services he shall be supported by the brethrèn, so far as his needs require and their abilities allow.]

2nd. That every individual community shall respect the private acts and rights of every other community, and not at all interfere with them.

3rd. That in all cases where public officers, such as messengers of any public character, and especially evangelists, who are to be regarded as officers of the whole body, *a concurrence of a plurality of churches by their officers* be regarded as necessary, if not to empower them to discharge official duties in a single congregation, at least necessary to give them general acceptance, and to constitute them public and responsible agents of the whole body.

4th. That when any community shall have any case of great difficulty beyond its ability satisfactorily to dispose of, reference may be had to other communities for a council or committee to assist in such case ; whose decision shall be final,—an end of all farther litigation or debate on the premises.

5th. That whenever any great question of finance, as the means of successfully prosecuting any public object, or any other event of great public interest shall require it, a special general meeting of messengers from all the congregations shall be called by the person who presided at the last general meeting ; and that the eldership and deaconates of all the congregations, or so many of them as can attend, shall always be at least a portion of the messengers who attend on such occasions.

6th. Finally, that all the public duties of the christian church shall be attended to as though it were, what it is in fact, *one body*, under the Head— the Messiah ; and, therefore, arrangements and provisions shall be always made in general meetings for the most faithful, prompt and satisfactory discharge of all these duties.

The above outline is offered to the examination of the brethren, as embracing much, if not every thing, that, in our judgment, is wanting to a complete and perfect organization. We shall be happy to receive any substantial objections to it from our brethren, and shall give them a faithful, patient, and full consideration.   A. C."

Here I find a plan of organization—a CONSTITUTION containing six articles, offered to the gentleman's church for their adoption, in order to a complete organization. And, which is remarkable, there is in this constitution not one reference to the Scriptures! Now I had thought that the gentleman gloried in the fact that the New Testament is their constitution, the all-sufficient constitution of his church. But what do I see here? A constitution of six articles, without one reference to the New Testament—a constitution to which he intimates some additions may be necessary !!! On this constitution of six articles, and such as may be added, his church is to be organized! He is declaiming against "the sects" in general and the Presbyterians in particular, for having done the very thing he is now attempting to do, though in a very imperfect manner! He abuses all constitutions of churches made by man, and yet seeks to make one! If the New Testament is his constitution, as he pretends, why does he not go by it? Why offer these six articles to the churches as necessary to a complete organization? When a man's conduct is directly at war with his words, or when he is found at different times advocating principles, the most contradictory, and condemning in others what he allows in himself, we cannot but see that something is wrong—radically wrong.

But, after all, the evil is — that Mr. Campbell's brethren have not agreed to receive his constitution, and his church yet remains in its unorganized and confused state.

The gentleman has again made quite an imposing exhibition of the numbers who have united with his church—about two hundred thousand persons. So many have, from time to time, joined his church ; but how many have apostatized, he does not inform us. Many, as I have proved since the commencement of this debate, have turned again to the world or to "the sects." It is not exactly fair to count all who have become members, without *discounting* those who have turned back.

I am more than doubtful whether there is ground of boasting or of argument in the fact, that Mr. C. has succeeded in collecting such a multitude of men and women of all kinds in one unorganized mass, with all kinds of notions and opinions. He has told us, that in his church he has Calvinists (and one of his prominent preachers has attempted to prove, that Calvinism is tantamount to Atheism) and Arminians; and has Unitarians, Universalists, Materialists—all sorts of men preaching all kinds of doctrine, and of course, all sorts of members. It is of such an unorganized, incoherent, confused multitude, that the gentleman boasts! In his vain attempt to organize them in one body he has offered them a constitution, consisting of *six articles*, and not a text of Scripture! They have not received it, and, I presume, they never will.

Error, he has truly said, often gains converts more rapidly than truth; and yet he boasts of his rapid increase of numbers, as evidence conclusive that his principles are correct! His argument would prove the Mormons right. I do not institute a comparison between the Mormons and the gentleman's church; but certainly, they have increased more rapidly. They commenced their operations only a few years ago; and now see what multitudes of converts they have made, and how much more complete and efficient their organization, than that of his church. Amongst them, we hear of no clashing in doctrine or in practice; and only occasionally of an apostate. If, then, the argument turns on the rapid increase of numbers irrespective of their religious views and character, it proves too much for my friend. Sidney Rigdon, formerly one of his most popular preachers, and his right-hand man in the debate with McCalla, has sworn allegiance to Joe Smith, and now looks back with compassion on his *quondam* friend and leader, as yet in Babylon. Sidney has finally reached the point of perfect unity of faith, and fancies that he walks the streets of the New Jerusalem! The gentleman's argument proves too much.

It is indeed true, that Peter made a good confession, when he said— "Thou art the Christ, the Son of the living God;" and it is true, that it embraces two great points—the character and office of Christ. But what is that character? He is God as well as man. He "thought it not robbery to be equal with God." Mr. C., I believe, professes to believe in the true and proper Divinity of Christ. But if we ask Barton W. Stone, a prominent preacher in the same church, concerning his character, he will tell us, that the Son of God existed before the creation of the world, *but not from eternity;* and consequently he makes him only an exalted *creature.* If Mr. C. believes in the Divinity of Christ, there is an infinite difference between his faith and that of Mr. Stone. There is no comparison between finite and infinite, between the most exalted creature and the eternal God. Both these gentlemen call Christ the Son of God; and both profess to build on THE ROCK; but if Mr. C. is on the *rock*, Mr. Stone is on the *sand*. Yet they are both in the same church!

Again. What is the *office* of Christ, the second point embraced in Peter's confession? If I understand Mr. C., he believes, that Christ bore the punishment due to our sins on the cross. But if we ask Mr. Stone, he will tell us, that Christ suffered only that by being made acquainted with what he endured, the hearts of wicked men might relent,

4 A

and that they might be induced to turn to God. He denies, that Christ bore the punishment due to our sins. This amounts to a denial of the most important part of his work. There is an infinite difference between the faith of Messrs. Stone and Campbell concerning the character and work of Christ. Yet both are on THE ROCK!!! Now let me ask emphatically, what kind of a church is this, made up of materials so discordant, embodying differences so radical?

It is true, as Mr. C. says, that his creed is a short one. All he requires is, that persons desiring to enter the church, say they believe that Christ is the Son of God. He inquires not whether they understand the language they adopt, or what meaning they attach to it. The Arian, who makes the Savior an exalted creature, and the Socinian, who makes him a mere man, alike profess to believe the proposition; and both are received as christian brethren; though both deny both the true character and the work of Christ, and rob him of his glory! Of what use are words, unless they convey definite ideas? Of what advantage is it for a person to say, " I believe that Christ is the Son of God;" unless he understands what ideas the inspired writer intended to convey by these words? He who rejects the *true meaning* of Bible words and phrases, rejects the Bible. Unless, then, we ask men what they understand by the language of Scripture, we must receive the Arian, the Socinian, *every body.*

After all, the gentleman's creed is not *always* so short. It is sometimes short, and sometimes long. He says, he asks those who apply for membership, only to profess to believe that Christ is the Son of God. But ask a Pedo-baptist that question—" Do you believe that Christ is the Son of God?" He will answer, Yes. Now will the gentleman receive him? No—he must have a confession from him about his faith in immersion, and about the baptism of infants. Thus it will become tolerably long!

But it is doubtful whether there is much uniformity either in faith or practice in the churches of the reformers; for it appears, that they are entirely independent of each other. My worthy friend, Dr. Fishback, in a letter to the Synod of Kentucky, gave a brief confession of faith, or statement of the faith of the church that worships in this building; in which he remarks as follows:

" Permit me, however, to say, that the church [in Lexington] is independent in her constitution and government of all other churches, and sustains no connection with any church or denomination of christians, that authorizes them to make a creed for her, or which subjects her to their legislation or government, or that makes her responsible for any error that may be imputed to them."—*Christian Journal*, Oct. 28, 1843.

Here we have a church actually independent of all others, in no sense accountable to any for its errors, nor in any degree responsible for the doctrines of others. If the other churches are equally independent of each other, they do not constitute one body, but are just so many perfectly independent democracies, no one of which is responsible for any thing believed or done by the others. Such is the boasted reformation of the nineteenth century!

The gentleman professes to eschew all creeds; but he says, he is willing at any time, to give his views of the meaning of the Scriptures. But why should he give them? Are not his views well expressed by the inspired writers? Why not refer all who wish to know his views, to the New Testament? His sentiments and his conduct are strangely contradictory.

As an argument against creeds, the gentleman says, he never heard of any one converted by reading a confession of faith. He seems to forget, that a great many important and interesting things happen in this world, of which he never hears. A brother has just informed me that a lady in his congregation had her attention turned to the subject of religion by reading the Westminster confession, who recently died in the triumphs of faith. She doubtless read the Scriptures, which are abundantly quoted in that excellent book; for I suppose, that two-thirds of the doctrinal part of it consists of quotations from the Bible. But did he ever hear of any one being coverted by reading his " Christian System?" I certainly never did. Creeds are not designed particularly to effect the conversion of the wicked; nor is his Christian System. He tells us, that it is designed to give a condensed statement of the doctrines of his church, to rectify certain extremes, and to furnish means of defence to his preachers. (page 10.)

Mr. C. speaks quite slightingly of our church—claiming only to be *a branch* of the church of Christ. He and Gregory XVI. both claim for their respective communities the high honor of being THE *church!* These claims no doubt, are equally valid. But I rejoice that the Presbyterian church has ever recognized as brethren all who hold the fundamental doctrines of the gospel. And let me remark, all such are nearer to us in their faith, than the leading men in Mr. C.'s reformation are to each other—much more. He has repeatedly magnified his charity and liberality, since the commencement of this discussion; but now look at it. His church is THE *church.* So says Gregory, as he sets in St. Peter's chair!

I will now offer a few more remarks concerning the reception of the Universalist preacher into Mr. C.'s church. He was received, as I stated, without a change of sentiment; only his former *faith* he agreed to call an *opinion*. The Bible teaches with perfect plainness, that the wicked shall be eternally punished. Mr. Raines' *opinion* was, that the doctrine of the Bible was not true. Again—If he believed that all will be saved, he must have believed that this doctrine is taught in the Bible. How then could he call it an *opinion?* Did the inspired writers propagate mere opinions? Here we have an exhibition of their *christian union.* Mr. Campbell's faith was—that the wicked would be eternally punished; and Mr. Raines' *opinion* was, that Mr. C.'s *faith* was not true! Yet, although Mr. Raines' opinion contradicted Mr. Campbell's faith, we are to believe that their faith was precisely the same!

But Mr. Raines, as a preacher of the gospel, was bound to declare to men the " whole counsel of God." His opinion was, that the Bible teaches Universalism. How, then, could he promise not to preach it? How could he lend himself to keep back a part of what he believed to be the truth of the Bible? And is this the plan of christian union devised by Mr. C.? Does he require men, as a condition of being proclaimers in his church, to promise not to preach truths they conscientiously believe to be taught in the Scriptures? Never, so long as life lasts, will I promise any man, or body of men, that I will not preach the whole truth; nor will I have any thing to do with a plan of union which requires me to disregard the conviction of my conscience.—[*Time expired.*

Friday, Dec. 1—1½ *o'clock, P. M.*
[MR. CAMPBELL'S SIXTH ADDRESS.]

MR. PRESIDENT—I regret, sir, to have to discuss so many frivolous matters; when, however, small things become great, by the force of circumstances, or great things small, it becomes more necessary to attend to them. An infinitely small issue is now being made on the subject of publishing books—a singular issue, growing out of the proposition before us! I have published a book called "the Christian System, in Reference to the Union of Christians," &c.; and the Presbyterian church has published a book called "THE CONSTITUTION *of the Presbyterian Church in the United States of America,*" &c. The one, on my part, is offered to the world as a matter alike addressed to every human being—obligatory on no one—the offspring of one mind, without any previous understanding or agreement. And here is the constitution of the Presbyterian church, published and ratified by the general assembly, at their sessions in May, 1821, and *amended* in 1833!! Need I do more than read the titles of the two books? The whole matter is irrelevant. According to the laws of the land, and the freedom of the press, every man may publish what he pleases. But, sir, the matter before us is not the *publication* of a book, but the *use* made of it when published. Did I make any book that I have published a bond of union—a constitution for our church—then, indeed, I would be justly censurable by all the intelligences, celestial and terrestrial. Heaven and earth would condemn me. Strange that a person of so much intellectual sagacity, can so confound things in his mind, as to compare matters in their use and application, as opposite as the zenith and nadir— as ourselves and our antipodes.

The next great matter, was my reference to different expositions and books, on the doctrines of the confession of faith, made symbols of by new Presbyterian associations. Has not Mr. Rice read of the questions and debates, which resulted in the formation of three new kinds of Presbyterians in Scotland, two of which are still existing here. I allude to the Burgher and Anti-burgher churches, and to the Relief Presbyterians, peculiar to Scotland. The Burghers are known in this country as *Unionists;* and the Anti-burghers as *Seceders.* I presumed my friend was conversant with their various publications, acts and testimonies against each other. Surely, the gentleman does not expect me to carry with me a library for his information—or, does he plead ignorance of matters so public and notorious, to consume time in discussing them? I have heard all these parties preach, and am acquainted with much of their history, but cannot waste time in edifying him on these subjects.

But thus my friend, Mr. Rice, would escape from the charge of making a rent in the American Presbyterian church, by the excommunication of only sixty thousand good orderly professors, and five hundred pastors. But they did not *cast them* out! I presume he means, they did not open the door and *unguibus et pedibus,* violently seize and lead them out. They politely showed them the door, and invited them to walk out; and that for sensible and sensitive men is a hint sufficiently operative. Assuredly he will not argue, that the sixty thousand drove out the majority. I repeat, that this innocent and harmless document, called "the constitution of the Presbyterian church," only cast out, at one impulse, some sixty thousand members of as fair moral, intellectual, and literary reputation, as those who excluded them, by making terms of submission to which they could not succomb. When I see a Lord's table spread and furnished with the memorials of a Savior's love, and hear the members of the same community say to their brethren—on certain conditions you may partake with us to-day ;—on reflecting upon the past, we now say to you, that on these terms only can we recognize and treat you as worthy participants here. When again these terms and conditions are mere interpretations of the constitution of the Presbyterian church, may we not say, that the minority are driven out of the church upon grounds of interpretation, when they are thus refused a crumb of bread but upon the principle of conformity ? So I understand the new scheme in the Presbyterian church. But still, to call them christians and brethren, only makes the matter worse. It is indeed acknowledging the sin while committing it. To admit them to be actual, bona fide, members of Christ's church, and then refuse them a brother's blessing, a right to eat at the family table, is much more provoking to heaven and earth than to cast them out as heathen men and publicans.

When Mr. Rice affirmed that there was no such document as the " constitution of the Presbyterian church," and, in reply, I read the title page of the book in my hand, which reads—" The Constitution of the Presbyterian Church," &c., he seizes, by way of offset, a number of the Millenial Harbinger, and, holding it before you, reads some overtures by way of illustrating a principle—a few resolutions offered in a parabolic scene—and, with an air of profound wisdom, presumes that these resolutions, relative to a system of co-operation among particular communities, already in existence, is just such a thing as the constitution of the Presbyterian church ! Mr. Rice says there is no such book as the Constitution of the Presbyterian Church of the United States of America. How shall I dispose of such an opponent, who presumes to deny the very title page in my hand, printed in capitals !

But here are two Presbyterian ministers, over the signatures of Calvin and Philo, arguing, in the Protestant and Herald, the grave question, whether the constitution of the Presbyterian church has in it any principle or law authorizing its amendment. The one affirming, that in the constitution there is no redeeming, recuperative principle ; that, if it take sick, a doctor need not be called, for it cannot be mended. The other admitting its liability to disease, and the possibility of a remedy—bnt then so far off, and so difficult of application, that it might almost as well have been without it. It was, indeed, wisely decided, that the constitution may endure, inasmuch as the principle of self-preservation and of recuperation is in it, whether or not it can, if ever, be applied. It is, however, conceded on all hands, that it *is* the constitution of the Presbyterian church, and that it has in it the principle and power of self-preservation, and even of improvement ; that the principle has been formerly applied, and that it worked well, and that it is in the bounds of possibility that it may be applied again, should circumstances so require.

Mr. Rice endeavors to relieve himself, by showing that I am in the mud, if he be in the mire. Well, two wrongs will not make one right, as the adage goes. And suppose I, in proposing resolutions, relative to a system of co-operation, (no faith nor morality being in the question,) had erred, will that excuse his making a *confession of faith*, a form of church government, and of church discipline—an entire *constitution* for Christ's kingdom, as he imagines, a politico-ecclesiastic constitution, as it may be denominated ? !

This, however, is the first time that I have heard it assumed, that if one

53

profess to believe in the Bible, he must never offer a single resolution on any subject whatever, concerning any temporal or circumstantial office connected with the operations of christian benevolence, or any other subject, calling for the co-operation of the whole community. I do not ascribe these modes of reasoning to the obtusity of Mr. Rice, but to his too great perspicacity. He sees but too keenly the tendency or course of an argument or fact, and sets out to meet it in advance. In arguing against manufacturing a *creed*, that is *faith*, no one says that resolutions, and records, and exhibits, written and printed, may not be given to the church or the world. This is a morbid state of feeling to which no sensible man, of sound judgment and discretion, is ever subjected. We are discussing creeds, terms and conditions of communion; constitutions of churches made by men—and not the printing of books, tracts, or newspapers—I offer to any community, rules of decorum, of co-operation, in any matter, in the form of resolutions. They may receive, reject, amend, &c.; but out of these they never can, while memory reigns, and language retains its meaning, form a creed. These pretend to no authority, usurp no power, affect not conscience. But according to Mr. Rice, a single resolution offered, is tantamount to forming a creed! Such is his logic on this occasion. But we charge upon him the maintenance of a human constitution for Christ's church!!!

I regret to condescend to a species of logic unworthy of so grave an occasion, and of so dignified a theme, as the constitution of Christ's church. When Scripture, reason, history, and even the faculty of invention, fail to furnish Mr. R. with something to say in favor of the utility of creeds, he turns in to upbraid us with Mormonism and Sidney Rigdon. And what has Sidney Rigdon or Mormonism to do with our creed question? Mormonism has a creed, and Rigdon is an apostate from our society. Can the gentleman, from these two facts, draw an argument in favor of creeds? But Mormons have increased, and we have increased, and Presbyterians have increased—and if *increase* proves us right, it proves all right. We, indeed, neither argue from increase nor decrease, that any proposition of a moral or religious character, is true. I neither appeal to antiquity, nor to numbers, nor to sincerity, as tests of truth. But there was something more than all this in the allusion to Rigdon and Mormonism. But is it an argument against us as a denomination, that Rigdon was once a member of our church? Then is it not an argument against Presbyterianism, that Kentucky Shakerism, and its founders, went out of the bosom of that community? I mention this as a mere sample of the ease with which reprisals of that category can be made every where; for, from the days of Simon Magus till now, apostates have emanated from the best societies. I did not expect to have such rhetoric to dispose of, on this grave subject. I did expect a more manly, dignified, and rational argument and opposition than this. But so long as Mr. R. has nothing better to offer, perhaps we ought to blame the cause, rather than its advocate.

It seems as though we did not use the term *church* alike. The term is used by us as it is commonly used by Congregationalists. By Mr. R. it is used as Presbyterians generally use it. We speak of particular churches or congregations—the church at Rome, Lexington, Paris, Frankfort, &c. the churches of Kentucky, not the *church* of Kentucky. We cannot discuss all these matters. In modern times we read of the church of England, the church of Scotland, &c.; in old times, the churches of Judea, the churches of Galatia. &c. We have neither national, provincial, nor sectarian church. We have many *churches*, but no *church*. Nor do we desire a church, in that sense of the word. It is true, the apostles speak of the church, not, however, of the church of any nation, but of Christ. These parochial institutions called churches, built upon such constitutions as we have been discussing, are rivals of each other, and rivals, in the aggregate, of the churches builded on Christ's constitution.

If there be on earth a society that could admit of all the orderly and obedient disciples of the Messiah, that is just such an institution as the Messiah built, and it is just such a one as he would recognize were he now to re-return to the earth. Whatever society, then, has a constitution commensurate with all the children of God, who are visibly and manifestly following the Lord in obedience, that society is apostolic and Divine, and no other one. Can any one think, were the Lord to revisit this world just now, that he would recognize any of the numerous churches of the nations as his, built upon the policies, opinions and rivalries of earth! Would he call any one his, who has taken another name? I repeat it, if there be on earth a community that he would recognize as his, it would be that single community that builds precisely upon the foundation which he himself projected at Cesarea Philippi; and on which the apostles builded the societies, called churches, in the old cities and provinces of the Roman empire. He has bound himself by every law in this new constitution to do so. He might, indeed, have reason to upbraid some, yea, very many, of the Laodicean sin of lukewarmness, still he would recognize them as on the right foundation.

Mr. Rice seems to take pleasure in his supposed ingenious dissertations upon the alledged discrepancy between our opinions and our doctrine, and in setting them in array against each other. This is of that species of logic in which he most abounds, usually addressed to the supposed prejudices, or want of discrimination of the audience. It is called *ad captandum*, because it would seem to be designed to inveigle, or catch the unthinking and the unwary. He perfectly comprehends, as I suppose, why we affirm, that sects among christians are wholly inadmissible ; wholly unauthorized, and obnoxious to the indignation of heaven. He understands why christians may, in the aggregate, be a sect, in contrast with Jews and pagans, and, on that account, be most acceptable to the Lord ; while any schism, sect or party amongst them is intolerable. I say, with Paul, " After the way which they call a sect, (a heresy,) so worship I the God of my fathers, believing all things in the law, and in the prophets." Yet that same Paul could not endure the appearance of a sect among the Corinthians—" While one says, I am of Paul; and another, I am of Apollos ; and another, I am of Cephas; and another, I am of Christ : are you not *carnal* and *walk as men?*" A sect amongst christians, in Paul's eyes, was a solecism, an intolerable incongruity.

Now these sects are all founded on *opinions*, and not on *faith*. Every society in Christendom admits the same faith, or builds on all the same grand evangelical facts ; though, indeed, by their opinions and traditions, some of them have made the faith of God of none effect. But having written so largely on the difference between faith, knowledge and opinion, I deem it unnecessary, on this occasion, to descant upon them. For the sake of some, however, who may not have read or examined this subject, I will make a remark or two. With us, then, faith is *testimony believed ;* knowledge is our own *experience ;* and opinion is *probable inference.* Whenever we have clear, well authenticated testimony, we have faith ;

and this faith is always in the ratio of the testimony we have, or in our apprehension of its truth and certainty. Our personal acquaintance with men and things constitutes our knowledge; of which, different individuals, according to their discrimination and capacity, have various proportions. But, in the absence of our own personal acquaintance, observation and experience, and in the absence of good and well authenticated testimony, we have mere *opinion*. So I define and use these terms. Some of our dictionaries are not clear, in marking their respective boundaries. But all men have a right to define in what sense they use leading and important terms, as signs of their own ideas. If I may explain by a single example, I will say, I *believe* that Julius Cæsar was assassinated in the Roman senate-house, at the statue of Pompey; I *know* that the sun is the source of our light and heat; and I am *of opinion*, that Saturn is inhabited.

Now, as diverse in religion as in nature, are these terms and their associations. In religion, we have one Lord, one faith, one baptism, one body, one spirit, one hope, and one God and Father. But we have many opinions. The church, then, may have opinions by thousands, while her faith is limited to the inspired testimony of apostles and prophets: where that testimony begins and ends, faith begins and ends. In faith, then, all christians may be one; though of diverse knowledge and of numerous opinions. In faith we must be one, for there is but one christian faith; while, in opinions, we may differ. Hence we are commanded to receive one another, without regard to differences of opinion, Rom. xv. 1, 2.

The grand error in Presbyterianism is, that it seems never to recognize where faith ends, and where opinion begins; nay, it very often confounds faith and opinion, and lays full as much emphasis upon right opinions, as upon right faith; and, in some instances, places opinion above faith. Our faith, then, and our opinions, do not clash, for *we never have both faith and opinion on the same subject*.

Mr. Rice has made some allusions to a document written by Dr. Fishback. It is, however, in my opinion, so distorted that no one can be imposed on by his remarks. The whole connection shows it to be so. I do not know what view he has of church foundations; but permit me to say, that each of our communities is, in every thing concerning itself, perfectly independent of every other congregation in the world. All our communities build, indeed, on one and the same foundation—Apostolic and Divine—but they have their own by-laws and arrangements, and in these they are independent of each other. None of them sustain any ecclesiastical connection with any other church, or connection, or set of christians who authorize or use any formula of faith, called a creed.

We are, my fellow-citizens, what is called *Congregational* communities. Every one of our congregations regards itself as a church of Jesus Christ: having over them no other government under Christ but their own immediate eldership. They are amenable to no foreign court, called a classic presbytery, synod, or general or national assembly, conference, or council, local or œcumenical. We believe that wherever two or three are assembled in any one place, Jesus the Lord of christians, the King of saints, is there; and he is no more than present, if he ever be present at all—he is no more than present in a synod or general assembly. We have the King and his Statute Book in our congregations. Why, then, should we go abroad for either the one or the other?

As respects civil authorities, there ought to be inferior and superior courts. But with us, we have the same Judge always upon the bench.

We do not commence our suits in the cellar, and then ascend to the middle story, and then to the upper story of Christ's house. Few men see the absurdities of carrying up doctrinal points in controversy and cases of conscience, as they try civil or criminal pleas, because the whole matter of ecclesiastical politics is hid in the mists and fogs of theological maxims, causes and precedents. There is no end of the appeal system, if once you transcend a single committee of umpires. When you commence in the *court* system, you must ascend, step by step, till you find a pope, a vicegerent, a demi-god. There is even in questions of *miney and thiney*, more safety at home than abroad. The parties and the circumstances can be better appreciated, and justice secured, somewhere nigher home than at Rome or Constantinople. I am now prepared for another argument. I may probably occupy the remainder of this address and the whole of my next, without any special reply to Mr. *Rice*. Indeed, there is little or nothing in all these little matters, advanced by him, bearing upon the main issue before us. I value them only as affording me an opportunity to define our position.

But here comes a notice from a brother, requesting it to be stated that, in some allusions made to him by Mr. Rice, he has been misrepresented, as having said that Calvinism is Atheism. He solemnly denies ever having so said, or so believed; and it is but an act of justice due him to state thus publicly, as he has been publicly assailed, that he disavows the allegation as wholly unfounded on fact. As he cannot speak for himself here, in his own person, I judge I am authorized to say this much for him.

Before, then, I sit down, I shall affirm another argument in support of my position against human creeds. I prove them heretical from the fact that, during the whole period of the churches' unity—say from 150 to 200 years after Christ—they had no written documents of any authority whatever, but the inspired documents. Ask Mosheim, Du Pin, Waddington, &c., and they will tell you, that before creeds were, unity was; after them, divisions and sects and parties were. The reasons why, are given *in extenso* by Waddington, and Mosheim, and Neander, and others. I shall give one extract from Waddington—the Episcopalian Waddington:—

" The first christians used no written creed: the confession of faith, which was held necessary to salvation, was delivered to children or converts by word of mouth, and entrusted to their memory. Moreover, in the several independent churches, the rule of faith was liable to some slight changes, according to the opinion and discretion of the bishop presiding in each. Hence it arose, that when the creeds of those numerous communities came at length to be written and compared together, they were found to contain some variations. This was natural and necessary. But when we add that those variations were for the most part merely verbal, and in no instance involved any question of essential importance, we advance a truth which will seem strange to those who are familiar with the angry disputations of later ages. But the fact is easily accounted for. The earliest pastors of the church drew their belief from the Scripture itself, as delivered to them by writing or preaching, and they were contented to express that belief in the language of Scripture. They were not curious to investigate that which is not clearly revealed, but they adhered faithfully to that which they *knew* to be true; therefore their variations were without schism, and their differences without acrimony. The creed which was first adopted, and that perhaps in the very earliest age, by the church of Rome, was that which is now called the apostles' creed; and it was the general opinion, from the fourth century downwards, that it was actually the production of those blessed persons, assembled for that purpose. Our evidence is not sufficient to establish that fact, and some writers very confidently reject it. But there is reasonable ground for our assurance that the form of faith, which we still repeat and inculcate, was in use and honor in the very early propagation of our religion."—*Waddington's Church History*, pp. 45, 46.

The same view of the matter is reported by Mosheim, and the more modern German historians, Neander, Geseller, &c. When they came to baptism, they all made the same confession, and were builded together upon the same foundation; and having only the apostolic writings, easily maintained unity of spirit by the bonds of peace. They had no formula of doctrine as yet, other than the apostolic formula, which we still have in the living oracles of the New Testament. I presume it is always a safe argument, that the same cause will always produce the same effect. If, then, we take the divinely authenticated and authorized creed of the sacred writings, and allow for differences of opinion, not properly called the faith, we might all unite on the same foundation, and enjoy the same peace and harmony. We are making the same experiment now, and so far it proves itself to be as divinely effectual, as in the first and second centuries. It has been tried in different nations, and works well both in the old world and in the new. From the history of former times, and from our own experience, as well as from the doctrines delivered in the book, we have the fullest assurance of its perfect adaptation to society, and of its ultimate triumph over all rival systems in the world. The church was once united and happy on the apostolic writings, and it will be so again.—[*Time expired.*

Friday, Dec. 1—12½ *o'clock, P. M.*
[MR. RICE'S SIXTH REPLY.]

MR. PRESIDENT—It is a happy thing for the cause of my friend, Mr. C., that he does not feel bound to enlighten us on the subject of church history. I called for some proof of his assertion, that in Scotland it had been deemed necessary to write not only explanations of the confession of faith, but explanations of explanations; but he does not feel bound to give it. It is one of the easiest things imaginable to make assertions, and to prove them, as the gentleman does, by saying—every body knows it!

He has undertaken to prove, not only that creeds are unlawful, but that they are necessarily heretical and schismatical. I have stated distinctly the design of a creed. It is a public declaration of the principal doctrines and truths which we understand the Bible to teach, made in order that those who desire membership in the church of Christ, may compare it with the Bible, and determine whether they can conscientiously and cordially unite with us. And it is a standard of ministerial qualifications, that the church may, with uniformity, require those who seek the office of the ministry, or who are to be ruling elders or deacons, to possess the scriptural character and attainments. Where is the law against a creed for such purposes? We are now near the close of the second day's discussion on this proposition; and yet we have had not a passage produced, that even looks that way.

To prove, that creeds produce schisms, Mr. C. mentions the Burghers and anti-Burghers of Scotland. It is true, they divided; but the question is—*did the creed cause the schism?* We have heard of the Burghers and Anti-burghers; and we have also heard of divisions in Mr. C.'s church. Now it is absolutely necessary for him, if he would sustain his proposition, not only to prove, that there have been schisms, but that they were caused by creeds—that they necessarily result from the mere fact of having a human creed of any kind. There has recently been a division in the church of Scotland; but it was not caused by their confession of faith, but by a difficulty growing out of their political relations as an established church.

Concerning the Burghers and Anti-burghers, I will read a short article in the Encyclopædia of Religious Knowledge.

"BURGHERS. A numerous and respectable class of seceders from the church of Scotland, originally connected with the Associate Presbytery; but some difference arising about the lawfulness of the Burgess oath, a separation took place in 1739, and those who refused the oath were called Anti-burghers; but as these sects have been lately happily united, it is not now necessary to enter into the merits of the dispute."

Now if, as Mr. C. takes for granted, their creed caused the division, I presume it is fair to conclude that it also healed it. It is, indeed, somewhat remarkable that it should have operated in opposite ways. It divided them, it would seem, and afterwards united them! Certainly creeds cannot necessarily be heretical and schismatical; or when they were once divided, their creed would have kept them separate. If the gentleman can prove, that creeds have caused division, I can prove, by evidence quite as conclusive, that they have brought together individuals and bodies that, but for them, would never have united.

Mr. C. still harps upon the alledged fact, that the new school were cut off from our church. Has he forgotten his efforts to have Dr. Thomas, one of his most gifted preachers, excommunicated, because he differed from him? It is true, he did afterwards most inconsistently become reconciled to the Doctor, without any change having taken place in his views. Still he did what he could to exclude him.

It is a principle universally recognized in all well organized governments, civil and ecclesiastical, that those who enjoy common rights and privileges, must sustain common responsibilities. It would be a strange proceeding in the congress of these United States to permit representatives from the Canadas to become members of that body, and to deliberate and vote, and then to return and be subject to their own laws, not to those they had aided in making for us. Could such a thing be tolerated? Suppose several members of this church in Lexington should go to Bethany, Va., and claim the right to deliberate and vote in the business proceedings of Mr. C.'s particular church; would he permit it? Would he not request them to return home, and attend to their own affairs? And what would he think of them, if they should charge him with having excommunicated them? And mark the fact—there is this day as close a union between those churches and ministers, whom he represents as having been excommunicated, and our church, as there is between Mr. C.'s church, at Bethany, and the church in Lexington; or as there is between the hundreds of particular churches claimed by the gentleman.

The church in Lexington, as Dr. Fishback has informed us, is "independent in her constitution and government of all other churches," and sustains no responsibility to any other churches, that makes it accountable either for their legislation or for their errors. The government of the United States is independent of all other civil governments. Would it, then, be true to say, the government of the United States, and that of England, constitute one political body? No more do the thousand particular churches scattered over this country, which are claimed by Mr.

C., constitute one ecclesiastical body. He acknowledges the church in
Lexington as a church of Christ, and its members as christian brethren.
So do we acknowledge the new school churches and their members and
ministers as christian brethren. The decision of our general assembly
amounted to this—that none could be permitted to vote in our ecclesiastical bodies, who would not submit to our laws; that if they were Presbyterians in name, and in privileges and rights, they must be Presbyterians in fact and in their responsibilities. But the gentleman has said, they
were excommunicated. This is not true. No ecclesiastical censure was
passed upon those synods which, as bodies, were excluded from a standing in our church. We simply said to them—do your business in your
own way; and we will do ours. Would not Mr. C. say the same thing
to members of the church in Lexington, should they attempt to exert a
controling influence in the church at Bethany? Why does he blame us
and denounce our creed, because we acted on a principle recognized by
himself and by all men?

The gentleman, to prove the charge against Presbyterians of attempting to *make a constitution* for the church of Christ, triumphantly exhibited before the audience the title-page of our confession of faith—" THE
CONSTITUTION OF THE PRESBYTERIAN CHURCH," &c. I anticipated his
course; and whilst he was preparing his paper, I turned to some remarks
of his in the Millenial Harbinger, (New Series, vol. ii. p. 471,) concerning
his *Christianity Restored*. He says, " I have long intended to apologize
for the title of the book called ' Christianity Restored;' and intend, on a
new edition of it, which is now called for, to find a shorter and more appropriate name for the cover, as well as the title-page." He acknowledges that the title-page of his book is faulty, and conveys an erroneous
idea. Now I have just as good a right to charge on him the sentiment
expressed by his title-page, as he has to charge on us what he supposes to
be expressed on ours. The general assembly, I presume, did not determine, precisely, what the title-page should be, but left that matter to
the publishing committee.

But, for argument sake, I will admit that, strictly and properly, the
confession of faith may be called the constitution of the Presbyterian
church; but, I say, it is not a constitution of our *manufacture*. The
framers of that book collected into a small space, and arranged systematically, the doctrines taught, and the principles of church government inculcated throughout the Bible; for every article of faith, and for every
important principle of action, they have referred to the chapter and verse
where it is taught. To *make a constitution*, is to originate something
which did not before exist. To collect together, in chapters and sections,
existing laws, admitted to be as binding before, as after their being thus
arranged, is an entirely different matter. The former, as our confession
says, would be *usurpation;* the latter is lawful and right. The former
we did not do; the latter we did.

But Dr. Fishback, in his confession, says, the church in Lexington is
" independent in her *constitution* and government, of all other churches;"
and it certainly embraces one very important doctrine, to which many of
them would by no means subscribe. I mean the doctrine of *total hereditary depravity*. He says:

" Her whole system of religion is contained in the Old and New Testaments, which comprehend, as we understand the Scriptures, the original
creation of man in the image and likeness of God; his fall and the loss of

that image, together with the loss of union and communion with God ; and that by sin man became involved in pollution and death ; as by it all his posterity have begun to exist out of fellowship with God, and have come into the world without the knowledge or love of Him, and without power, moral or natural, to relieve themselves from that state of ignorance, carnality, and death.   This is what we call *total depravity*, (and which I would call "*hereditary depravity :*") all that makes man to differ from this state for the better, is owing to the interposition and effect of divine grace and mercy."

This doctrine, which forms a permanent part of the creed of the church in Lexington, is pronounced by Mr. Raines, one of Mr. Campbell's chosen committee, *a libel on human nature!* Whilst discussing the design of baptism, I read an extract from an article written by Dr. Fishback, and published in the Harbinger, showing that the Doctor does not believe in Mr. C.'s doctrine of baptism in order to remission of sins—that he pronounces it an exclusive and sectarian dogma ! Here we have a most striking exhibition of the unity of faith amongst the leading ministers in the gentleman's church ! Mr. Campbell, Dr. Fishback, and Mr. Raines— three of this committee of war, contradict and denounce some of the most prominent points in each other's creed !

But I proved that, whilst Mr. C. is denouncing Presbyterians and other denominations, for attempting to make a constitution for the church, he is laboring to accomplish the very same thing! What is his reply? He says, that offering a series of resolutions is a very different thing from making a constitution.   When a man offers a series of resolutions, embodying principles designed to be the basis of the organization of a body, civil and ecclesiastical, he does what he can to form a constitution. If Mr. C. has not succeeded in making a constitution for his churches, the fault is not his.   He has done all that he can.   He has drafted the resolutions, the articles, and offered them for the consideration and adoption of the churches.   The only reason of his failure is the fact, that they have not been willing to adopt his constitution.

But why did he offer those articles to the churches ?   If his people believed what he taught them, how could they adopt them ?   He has taught them to glory in having the New Testament as their only constitution. Now he teaches them principles precisely opposite, and urges them to adopt his constitution ! ! !

The gentleman appears to be rather in an ill humor at the remarks I made concerning the rapid increase of members in his churches.   He tells you, he desires sound argument—he is not willing to turn aside for every trifle.   The audience know perfectly well, that I was only replying to an *ad captandum* argument which he had urged.   He boasted of the unprecedented increase of his numbers.   I replied, that he had himself said, that error often travels faster, and gains more converts, than truth ; that the Mormons have increased in numbers faster than his churches ; and that if we were to judge of the goodness of a cause by the rapid increase of converts, the weight of argument would be against him.   He now tells us, this is all irrelevant ; and he desires that I would not answer his popular appeals !   At one time he charges me with not following him ; and at another, he complains of my pressing upon him too closely.   I cannot please him.

But he asks, whence came the Shakers ?   And he would have you believe, that our creed made them.   I answer, they were *great reformers.* Like Mr. C., they gained a wonderful amount of *new light,* and denounced

4 B

all the world as groping in midnight darkness, blind-folded by a designing clergy. One part of these reformers, called New Lights, headed by Barton W. Stone, who discovered that Jesus Christ was only a *creature*, are now quite orthodox members of Mr. C.'s church! About the year 1801, they proclaimed that the Millenium had commenced—that the true light had gone forth among the people! And so far as I can judge, their claim to be reformers, and to constitute *the* church, was about as valid as that of my friend, Mr. C. Some of those who denied the old and tried doctrines of the Presbyterian church, and gloried in their new light, reformed rather too much, and became dancing Shakers! .The work of reformation is sometimes hazardous. *Reform* is the watchword of every demagogue and of every fanatic.

Mr. Campbell is confident, that if our Savior were to visit the earth, he would not acknowledge a church that has *a wrong name*. His churches have found it somewhat difficult to determine, whether they would be called *Disciples* or *Christians*. I believe, however, they have pretty generally agreed on the latter. We are told, that the followers of Christ were first called Christians at Antioch; but whether the name was assumed by themselves, or given them in reproach by their enemies, is a mooted question. I do not say, that *names* are wholly unimportant; but I have learned, as well from the history of the past, as from occurrences in our day, that the more destitute persons are of that which commands the approbation or the respect of men, the more solicitous they are about the *name*. Persons who claim descent from noble families, but retain in their character few or no traces of nobility, rarely neglect an opportunity of speaking of their ancestry. Papists, who possess less of true catholicity than any people on earth, are most offended, if you refuse to call them *Catholic*. The less men have of a desirable *thing*, the more noise they make about the *name*. It is a universal weakness of human nature. The Savior and his apostles attached great importance to *things*, not to *names*.

But the Presbyterian church has a scriptural name—a name certainly given by inspiration. In the New Testament we read both of Presbyters and Presbyteries; we do not find the word *Reformer*—a name to which our friends do not seriously object—applied to Christ's disciples. Now what is a Presbyterian church, but a church having Presbyters and Presbyteries? We have a Bible name. So far, then, we are up with our friends!

My friend Mr. C. manifests some impatience at my calling on him to define the boundaries between *faith* and *opinion*. He tells you, that I know the difference perfectly well. I desired him to tell us the difference, because I intended to prove, so soon as he did so, that he and his church have practically disregarded their own principles on this subject. He has given us his explanation. He says, where there is *testimony*, there is faith; where there is no testimony, there is no faith. Every point, then, concerning which the Scriptures give us testimony, is a matter of *faith*, not of *opinion*. Now let me ask the gentleman, do the Scriptures give us testimony concerning the future state of the wicked—whether they are to be finally saved or eternally lost? He admits that they do; and in a long discussion with a Universalist, he proved it. This, therefore, is a matter of *faith*. How, then, I emphatically ask, could he receive Mr. Raines, who did not believe this article of faith, but was avowedly a Universalist in sentiment? And how could he consistently call on him to state whether he held Universalism as a matter of *faith*, or only as an *opinion?* How could he receive him, when he declared his disbelief of this cardinal doctrine of the Bible? He goes for agreement in *faith*, liberty in *opinion;* and yet he receives a man as a preacher of the gospel, who avows his disbelief of a very important doctrine, concerning which the Scriptures very distinctly testify! Is this union in faith?

Again—Do the Scriptures give us testimony concerning the character of Christ—whether he is a *creature*, or God equal with the Father? The gentleman admits that they do give us clear testimony on this point. Then, according to his principles, it is a matter of *faith*, not of *opinion*, How, then, could he unite with Barton W. Stone, who boldly denies the true and proper divinity of the Son of God? As I have before remarked, between the published faith of Mr. Campbell, and of Mr. Stone, on this cardinal doctrine, there is an infinite difference—a difference as great as between the words *finite* and *infinite*—*creature* and *creator*. The one makes him a creature; the other believes him to be the mighty God. What an immeasurable difference between the foundations on which they professedly build! Here is a difference vast as eternity between these two gentlemen, concerning a point of *faith*—one of the most important points presented in the Bible. Yet they have united in one church—professedly having one *Lord*, one *faith*, one *baptism!* Now I ask you, my friends, what sort of christian union is this?

My friend, Mr. C., tells us, that in his church they do not carry up appeals from one court to another. He may now consider this an excellence in his church government; but our civil government, the very best in the world, is managed on very different principles. I presume no intelligent citizen of these United States would be willing to give up his right of appeal. All consider their rights better secured by the right of appeal from the county court to the court of appeals. And Mr. C. himself, though he formerly occupied different ground, has recently been contending for the right of appeal. I will read a brief extract from the Millenial Harbinger, (New Series. vol. v. p. 54,) hoping to read more on this point hereafter:

"The right of prayer is not more natural, nor necessary, than the right of appeal. There is no government, or state, or family, that can subsist without it. It was a part of every religious institution before the christian.; and if it be no part of it, it is a perfect anomaly in all social institutions."

The right of appeal is here declared to be both clear and absolutely necessary to the existence of the church; but the difficulty in the gentleman's church—the insuperable difficulty, is, that there is no ecclesiastical tribunal to which their members, when suffering injustice, can appeal. To what body can they appeal? We have church courts from the session, composed of the pastor and elders of a particular church, to the general assembly of the whole church. His church has none. They enjoy not the right of appeal, though as clear as the right of prayer, and essential to the existence of the church! What would be the condition of our country, if the right of appeal were admitted; and yet there were no courts above that of the magistrate? In Mr. C.'s church, there is a difference of opinion on this important subject—some contending earnestly for the right of appeal, as clearly scriptural, and others denying it altogether. Hence they are not likely very soon to have any thing of the nature of courts of appeal; though Mr. C. considers the right essential to the very existence of the church.

Dr. Pinkerton, the gentleman says, denies having said that Calvinism is atheistic. If he will give a copy of his letter to me, containing a challenge to a public discussion, I will prove that one of the points he undertook to establish, was, that the confession of faith teaches what is *tantamount to Atheism*. And if Calvinism is *tantamount* to Atheism, pray what is the difference between it and Atheism? How much better is it than Atheism? I would not give a farthing for the difference. I am not in the habit of stating facts which I am not prepared to prove.

I must now notice another argument of the gentleman, against creeds. He states that, during the first two hundred years of the christian era, there was no written creed. To this argument I reply:—

1st. During those two hundred years, the church, as he told you the other day, was overrun with errors of all kinds. Nay, he asserted that almost all the errors of popery originated during that period. Though I do not admit it was so corrupt as he has represented it, it is certain that many injurious errors had marred its beauty and impaired its strength. Thus we see how the church prospered without creeds. Now, for more than two hundred years, the Presbyterian church has preserved her soundness of faith and purity of practice. She is not by any means so corrupt as the church had become at the close of the second century. She is as pure as when she threw off the shackles of popery, and took the Bible alone as her infallible guide. Without a creed, she would doubtless have long since been overrun with errors of all kinds. We may, therefore, learn, from the early corruption of the church, how important it is to have a scriptural creed. The argument is in our favor.

2d. For a length of time after the apostolic age, the language of the Scriptures, as used by professing christians, retained in a good degree its definiteness of meaning. But as the distance from the apostles became greater, and errorists multiplied, new ideas came to be commonly attached to the language of inspiration; and it became impossible, as it confessedly now is, to know a man's faith by the mere fact of his using Bible words and phrases. It was necessary, therefore, that the church should be more watchful. John said—"Try the spirits whether they are of God, because many false prophets are gone out into the world;" 1 John iv. 1. Errorists used the language of the Scriptures. Therefore the plan was adopted of agreeing upon something like an outline of the doctrines and truths of the Scriptures—of inquiring of those who desired to enter the ministry, whether they so understood them. So do we. This is a sufficient reply to the argument.

Let me now close my remarks on the reception of Universalists into Mr. C.'s church. Mr. Raines, when received, distinctly stated, that he still held Universalist sentiments. He agreed to hold them as *opinions*, and not to propagate them. Yet, according to Mr. C., the Scriptures give clear and positive testimony against this opinion of Mr. Raines. Of course, the doctrine of the eternal punishment of the wicked is a matter of *faith*, not of *opinion*.

But Mr. Raines was going to preach the gospel; and, consequently, he was most solemnly bound to keep back nothing—"to declare the whole counsel of God." But how was it possible for him to do this, when he held an opinion which he now admits, and Mr. C. then believed, to be in direct contradiction to the apostolic doctrine? In a discourse of his, in the *Christian Preacher*, he says:

" It is my intention to endeavor to prove, laconically and positively, that

Universalism is not only not a doctrine of the New Testament, but that it is most palpably contradicted by many testimonies found in the Christian Scriptures. And in order to do this, I will in the first place prove, that there are three distinct classes of salvation taught in the New Testament, and that the fundamental assumptions of Universalists, on which Universalism is predicated, are in direct contradiction to the apostolic doctrine relative to these salvations."

Mr. Raines held a doctrine which he agreed to call an *opinion;* but which, as he now admits, is flatly contradictory of the doctrine of the apostles. Yet he was received by Mr. C. as having with him and his churches the *one faith!* The church of Rome manages this matter better. She also makes a distinction between faith and opinion; but she determines the boundaries between them thus: All the points on which her councils can agree, are called *doctrines;* and those concerning which they differ, are *opinions.*

I need not now stay to prove, that B. W. Stone and his followers are Unitarians. My friend, I think, will not deny it. If he does, I will immediately prove it. Unitarians deny the Divinity of Christ. It matters not whether they be high Arians, or low Socinians; they equally rob him of his glory. The Scriptures require all men to " honor the Son even as they honor the Father;" John v. 23. Can a Unitarian do this? If he believes him to be a creature, will he not honor, or rather dishonor, him as a creature? I care not for the difference between Arianism and Socinianism. There is an infinite distance between the most exalted finite being and the infinite and eternal God. Both Arianism and Socinianism rob Christ of all his glory. The Bible knows nothing of christian union with persons holding sentiments so erroneous, so dishonoring to God, and so fatal to the hopes of men.—[*Time expired.*

Friday, Dec. 1—1½ *o'clock, P. M*
[MR. CAMPBELL'S SEVENTH ADDRESS.]

MR. PRESIDENT—It is sometimes expedient and necessary to carry the war into Carthage, and try what sort of a defence the Carthaginians can make at home. From the assaults made upon us, and the defence of creeds, you might imagine that the Westminster confession produced the most perfect harmony of views, and the most cordial attachment amongst all its members—that it was a palladium, a sovereign shield against error, heresy, and schism. Well now, is such the fact? Are they who subscribed it perfectly united in opinion, and in an affectionate and holy cooperation? Nothing is more contrary to fact than such an assumption! I have some little acquaintance with a few distinguished men of that denomination, and I am acquainted with many of their writers, (being a constant subscriber to some of their most popular and authoritative works.) I therefore speak advisedly on this subject. I shall quote one of their most distinguished men who, before he left them and joined the Episcopalians, occupied a very high place in the esteem of the denomination. I allude to Andrew Wylie, D. D., president of the college at Bloomington, Indiana. I have had some acquaintance with this gentleman for thirty years; having been my neighbor, while president, first of Jefferson, and then of Washington college, Pennsylvania, both of them under Presbyterian influence. This gentleman, a few years since, published a tract on creeds; in which he says, he never knew a Presbyterian minister, who believed all the Westminster confession of faith, taking the words in their fair

4 B 2

constructive sense. So speaks one of the most gifted men, whose ancestry, for I know not how long back, were strict Calvinists, of the old Presbyterian order.

Perhaps not one minister in one hundred of that denomination, believes all that book, called the Westminster Creed—the constitution of the Presbyterian church. Now, if they, notwithstanding all these differences of opinion and modes of interpretation, can still unite and co-operate in one community, why may not those who take the Bible, and yet do not agree in all their opinions, co-operate in one society?

But, of those who concur with Dr. Wylie, I must quote some others. Hear a few words from Dr. Bishop's Plea for United Christian Action. The Doctor says:

"To what extent diversity of opinion as to doctrines exists among the ministers of the Presbyterian church of the present generation, very few, I am persuaded, are prepared to say with any degree of exactness. But were we to compare the present state of opinion with what is known to have been the state of opinion among the divines of a former generation, who are now admitted to have been orthodox, the result likely would be, that we are not more divided on any of the leading doctrines of the Westminister confession of faith, than the fathers of that age themselves were. Baxter and Owen, for instance, are readily appealed to by almost every minister of the Presbyterian church, as standards of correct theological opinion; and yet these men have given very different explanations of some of the most important doctrines of the Westminister confession; and neither of these men went in all things with the assembly. Nor have we any reason to believe that the divines of the assembly themselves, in their final vote upon the most of the articles in the confession, were agreed upon any other principle, than the principle of compromise. An approximation towards unity of opinion as to the best modes of expressing our individual views of divine truth, is all that ever can be obtained in our adherence to a public creed."—*Beecher's Trial*, p, 18.

But who is it that has read Neale's history of the Puritans, that does not know that even the authors and finishers of the Westminster faith, delivered two hundred years ago to the British parliament, did not themselves believe it? Perhaps, amongst them all, the whole of it was believed; while not one man believed it all. It was adopted, item per item; some dissenting here, and some dissenting there, while for each there was a majority in the detail; and upon the final vote in the aggregate, a majority for all, upon the principle of compromise. Hence the confession was never signed by the men who made it!

But it may be said, that while the authors of that document, and those who subscribed to it, differ as to their opinions on various points within it, still they love one another and co-operate in a christian spirit, while maintaining and teaching the grand doctrines of the book. Very far from it! I will give a specimen from a book that I hold in my hand, in which are found many savory morsels of this sort. It is Dr. Beecher's trial. His good brother, Dr. Wilson, of Cincinnati, in a very fraternal way, commends his reverend brother Beecher as being addicted to the sins of falsification and hypocrisy. These are but two of six grievous charges brought against Dr. Beecher by his good brother Wilson, as follows:

IV. Specification: "I charge Dr. Beecher with the sin of *slander :* viz., In belying the whole church of God, by bringing odium on all who sincerely receive the standards of the Presbyterian church," &c., &c., &c.

VI. Specification: "I charge Dr. Beecher with the sin of *hypocrisy ;* I mean dissimulation in important religious matters:" "In entering the Presbyterian church, without adopting her standards," &c., &c.

As this is no very pleasant task imposed on me, I will make as little do as possible. I merely design to show how these bonds of union and communion work in the details of ecclesiastic co-operation, and how much they promote brotherly kindness and charity.

But we are represented as having in our community persons who hold and teach very different doctrines on important subjects; such as total depravity, Unitarianism, &c. Suppose this were the fact, we are only neighborlike, it would appear. But the gentleman has not proved this yet. He speaks, indeed, of different views of the phrase " *total depravity*," as found amongst some of us. But this is a question of the schools, and not found in our confession of faith at all; and therefore some of our preachers have, it would seem, spoken irreverently of this doctrine of the schools, and without any fear of the clergy before their eyes. One says it is total, and another says it is not *total*. One speaks of its totality as respects the *whole man*, in all his parts, body, soul, and spirit; another as respects its *degrees:* one affirming that persons may grow worse in one sense; another, that they are, in another sense, so depraved at first, that they cannot deteriorate, &c., &c. Some of our brethren, too, accuse the Presbyterians of denying the doctrine of total depravity; because they assign to fallen man the power of acquiring the knowledge of God, without revelation, &c., &c. All this may suit very well, to show off signs of conflict between our theory and practice; but it is, so far as our principles are implicated, wholly unimportant and irrelevant. It is, I say, unimportant; because one speaks of total depravity as in the confession; another of total depravity as in the Bible: and both discuss the doctrine only as an index of theological opinions amongst the sects; while all agree, that man is fallen and depraved, and without the interposition of the Messiah and the Holy Spirit, cannot be saved.

But Unitarianism is also preached amongst us. So says Mr. Rice. If so, I know it not. For my part, I know and acknowledge no man as a brother, preaching Unitarianism amongst us. I say again, that I neither know of any such person, nor do I acknowledge any such person as a fellow-laborer with me. I must have the case made out—fully made out before it is tried. We have, indeed, in our communion, persons who have been Unitarians, Roman Catholics, Presbyterians, Episcopalians, Methodists, Deists, sceptics, &c. But that *they are such now*, is not true. And should any one accuse us of holding communion with those who teach Romanism, Methodism, Unitarianism, or scepticism, we charge him with bringing against us a railing accusation.

But the gentleman flings out in broad cast his calumnies, rather than his arguments, and endeavors to merge the whole question of creeds in attempts to arraign our profession, and our efforts at reformation. He has just now read a short passage out of this book, a notice of the union of the Burghers and of the Anti-burghers—and alledges either as a fact or an argument, rather as both, that as they were separated by the confession of faith, they have been united and reconciled by it. I presume that I know the history of that matter a little better than his author or himself. It was not the confession that has brought them together. But so far as they have been brought together, it was the *Regium donum*, this royal bounty, or *bonus*, that accomplished it. Some thirty-five years ago, it was proposed by the government of England, in order to loyalize the dissenters from the by law-established creed and government church, to confer upon them some annuity, or sum of money, to be distributed amongst the congregations, on condition that they would be reconciled to each other, and unite as one denomination. And as these two bodies of Presbyterians could not obtain the Regium donum in any other way, after some considerable sparring, they made such legal approaches to each other, as secured the royal salary. But that it extended no farther, is apparent from the fact, that where there was no bounty, there was no union; for in this country, the same two denominations, here known as Unionists and Seceders, are not yet united. The union was effected no farther than the Regium donum was concerned. It was the sole cause, and the whole extent of that union. Some conscientious ministers held out against it, some two or three of both denominations. But they got no guineas. Till finally besieged into acquiescence, they all, with one exception, took the *bonus*, and then politically united. So much for the gentleman's confession of faith having re-united the Burghers and Anti-burghers of Scotland and Ireland!!

The gentleman is not yet satisfied with his former attempts at defence from the denial of the Westminster confession, as the constitution of the Presbyterian church in the United States. He will balance the account by a critique on the outside cover title of this volume, called "Christianity Restored." That is not the title affixed by me on any book written by me. The book-binder's label on the cover, and the author's title page, are very different facts, in reason and in law. That is no sort of offset; and, certainly, there is not the same excuse and explanation with reference to the constitution of the Presbyterian church. Because, in the proceedings of the supreme courts of that church, it is frequently so denominated—I say, that the general assembly itself has so denominated it in its various enactments upon the subject. The synods and councils of that church do not, as before said, call the confession of faith, or a portion of it, the constitution of the Presbyterian church; but the forms of discipline and government, together with the confession, form the constitution of the Presbyterian church of North America. It is so regarded and universally received. Destroy this constitution, and the Presbyterian church is no more. That such is the constitution of the Presbyterian church, Mr. Rice, however adverse to the disclosure of the fact, cannot possibly escape from it.

We sometimes condemn christians for going a begging to the world—to Satan's kingdom, to raise means and facilities for supporting the church of God. But the Presbyterian church has greatly transcended any other denomination in this particular—that they get the constitution of their church from the world—from a political government. If there be any world beyond the church, or any kingdom of Satan in the world, then, indeed, their constitution came from that department. I ask the question, who made this book? The answer is, the Westminster assembly. And who were the Westminster assembly? The answer is—a body of one hundred and twenty men, elected, summoned, convened, arranged, directed and paid by the parliament of England. There were put into it, as a component part of it, ten lords, twenty commoners. No council, church, or association ecclesiastic, elected, appointed or commissioned any one to have any thing to do in it. The parliament had its own political views and designs, and it elected just such persons as it regarded favorable to these policies and designs. Of the whole number of clergy selected, scarcely more than sixty were in regular attendance. The parliament not only set a guard over them in the ten lords and twenty commoners, but they would not allow them to choose their own speaker or chairman. When they met, they had not the selection of a single topic, nor the discussion of a single subject left to their discretion. All was prescribed to them by their pay-masters in parliament. They were told when and where to begin, and where to stop. They gave them for a commencement, the thirty-nine articles to masticate and digest. They spent ten long weeks in debate upon some fifteen of these. They laid aside that subject and took up another, when parliament bade them. But, after some one thousand and ten sessions, at four shillings sterling per diem, they drew out their splendid constitution of the Presbyterian church—though, even then, parliament would not disperse nor adjourn them—for the truth is, they neither adjourned themselves, nor were adjourned according to law. After a change of government, or the restoration of Charles, each man returned quietly home to his own place. The gentleman says, it has not been much amended; at least, he so considers it. Of course, then, his church has got its constitution from the celebrated Rump parliament, as it was afterwards most scientifically called.

That it was made by men in the flesh, and of the flesh, not like our constitution, will appear still more evident from an examination of the spirit infused into the old Presbyterians, who first adopted it. In their history we shall clearly see how it operated. It is true, that some Episcopalians were summoned, and some Independents, and some Erastians. But only one bishop attended, I think, for one day. Five Independents, indeed, continued almost all the time. But two Erastians were present, (and the great Selden, the greatest man in that body, was one of them,) because the parliament that dictated to them and controlled them were Erastians, whose distinguishing maxim was: That there was no Divine right for any kind of church government; that whatever form the state enacted was best; and that, therefore, it was a state affair, and ecclesiastically indifferent. I am glad to see a new work, recently from the American press, giving an account of these matters in part, with which I found it necessary, in the commencement of our efforts against these human inventions many years ago, to make myself familiar.

I have said, that neither the Episcopalians nor Independents had much to do in furnishing these documents; and, therefore, we must look to Presbyterians to understand the spirit of the constitution of that society. That it was heretical, schismatical and, withal, proscriptive, even to persecution, I am constrained to show, in support of my thesis.

In the ratio of their power, the majority of that assembly and the clergy in London, and round the county, who sympathized with them in doctrine, associated to proscribe, and did for a time succeed in prohibiting the reading of the liturgy of the English church; and, indeed, by statutory law, inhibited it in all public assemblies. Not content with this, Neale says, vol. iii. p. 291:

"The Presbyterian ministers, despairing of success with the commons, instead of yielding to the times, resolved to apply to the house of lords, who received them civilly, and promised to take their request into consideration; but no advances being made in two months, they were out of all patience, and determined to renew their application; and to give it the greater weight, prevailed with the lord mayor and court of aldermen, to join with them in presenting an address, which they did, January 16—"For a speedy settlement of church government, according to the covenant, and that no toleration might be given to popery, prelacy, superstition, heresy, profaneness, or any thing contrary to sound doctrine, and that all private assemblies might be restrained." The lords thanked them for their zeal, and recommended it to the city magistrates to suppress all such unlawful assemblies; but the houses were not to be moved as yet by such disagreeable importunity; however, this laid the foundation of those jealousies and misunderstandings between the city and parliament, which in the end proved the ruin of the Presbyterian cause."

Matters were still carried farther. They went against toleration, as a sin not to be endured. They represent it as a sort of Pandora's box, pregnant with all errors and sins. Neale says, vol. iii. pp. 386, 387:

"The last error they witness against, and in which all agree, is called "*the error of toleration*, patronizing and promoting all other errors, heresies and blasphemies whatsoever, under the grossly abused notion of liberty of conscience;" and here they complain as a very great grievance, 'That men should have liberty to worship God in that way and manner as shall appear to them most agreeable to the word of God; and no man be punished or discountenanced by authority for the same; and, that an enforced uniformity of religion throughout a nation or state confounds the civil and religious, and denies the very principles of christianity and civility.'"

Again and still worse: I must read another extract from Neale; and I shall give no other comment on it than what that candid and impartial historian himself gives by way of preamble to it in the words following, to wit: pp. 483, 484.

"To return to the parliament, which was now recruited with such *Presbyterian* members as had absconded, or deserted their stations, while the army was quartered in the neighborhood of the city; these gentlemen, finding they had the superiority in the house, resumed their courage; and took the opportunity of discovering their principles and spirit, in passing such a law against heretics as is hardly to be paralleled among Protestants. It had been laid aside by the influence of the army for above nine months, till May 1st, when it was voted that all ordinances concerning church government referred to committees, be brought in and debated; and that *the ordinance concerning blasphemy and heresy* be now determined, which was done accordingly. This was one of the most shocking laws I have met with in restraint of religious liberty, and shows that the governing *Presbyterians* would have made a terrible use of their power had they been supported by the sword of the civil magistrate. The ordinance is dated May 2nd, 1648, and ordains, "That all persons who shall willingly maintain, publish or defend, by preaching or writing, the following heresies, with obstinacy, shall, upon complaint and proof, by the oaths of two witnesses, before two justices of the peace, or confession of the party, be committed to prison, without bail or mainprize, till the next jail delivery; and in case the indictment shall then be found, and the party upon his trial shall not abjure his said error, and his defence and maintenance of the same, he shall suffer the pains of death, as in case of felony, without benefit of clergy; and if he recant or abjure, he shall remain in prison till he find sureties that he will not maintain the said heresies or errors any more; but if he relapse, and is convicted a second time, he shall suffer death as before.

The heresies or errors are these following eight, of which I only mention the 7th & 8th.

7th. The denying that the Holy Scriptures of the Old and New Testaments are the word of God.

8th. The denying of the resurrection of the dead, and a future judgment."

Such was that love of civil liberty and toleration infused into the good old orthodox Presbyterians, who, as my friend Mr. R. says, never changed, and who have always been distinguished for their love of liberty! I do not think, indeed, that these men would attempt such things now. They have read Locke on Toleration, and the spirit of the age has dispossessed the demon of partizan zeal to a very great extent; at least, it has taken away the horn of his power. The papal see itself, in the day of its glorious power, went no farther in black-letter, than did the creed-party in the day of their strength. The parties were then in power, and they forgot right. The truth of this reason is incontrovertible; it is a part of English history, and found in the rolls of her parliamentary acts.

Other points of error were punished by other penalties not quite so severe.

"The ordinance proceeds to specify some other errors of less demerit, and says: That whosoever shall maintain or defend them shall, upon conviction by the oaths of two witnesses, or by his own confession before two justices of peace, be ordered to renounce the said error or errors in the public congregation of the parish from whence the complaint comes, or where the offence was committed, and in case of refusal he shall be committed to prison till he find sureties that he shall not publish or maintain the said error or errors any more. The errors are these following:—being sixteen in number, of which I only mention the 11th, because it respects one of our propositions.

11th. That the baptism of infants is unlawful and void.; and that such persons ought to be baptized again. "

Various other passages are marked here, to the same effect. I will read them if necessary. I only, however, desire a clear and full sample— a mere proof of my position. That human creeds are heretical and schismatical is clearly evinced, I should judge, is fully demonstrated by these effects before us. Such demonstrations are not, indeed, confined to Presbyterians. The Episcopalians also took a hand in this game. Baptists were persecuted, even unto death, in some periods of their reign. In England every proscriptive edict, in some six months after its passage, was imported into New England or Virginia, and re-enacted here under similar pains and penalties. I am sorry to find, in some of the antique specimens of Virginia Episcopal proscription, the following statute enacted against the poor old Baptists of the Old Dominion:

"*Copy of a Law found in Henning's Statutes at large, vol. 2, page 165, Dec. 1662, 14th Charles II.*

"ARTICLE III.—Against persons that refuse to have their children baptized.

" Whereas many schismatical persons, out of their averseness to the orthodox established religion, or out of the new fangled conceits of their own hereticall inventions, refuse to have their children baptized:

Be it therefore enacted by the authority aforesaid, That all persons that, in contempt of the divine sacrament of baptism, shall refuse, when they may carry their child to a lawful minister in that county, to have them baptized, shall be amerced two thousand pounds of tobacco—halfe to the informer and half to the publique. "

This goes to prove, that the Presbyterian creed is not the only one that has, on both sides of the Atlantic, been schismatical, proscriptive, and heretical, in the highest degree. Could Mr. Rice reconcile these acts of Presbyterians with the love of civil liberty and equal rights, of which he has spoken, he ought to do it. But whether he does or not, I must again express my conviction that they would not now, as a denomination, if even they had the power which they once had, but which they never can hereafter regain, do as their fathers did. Many of them, in my acquaintance, love liberty, and are willing to extend it to others, as well as to enjoy it themselves.

Touching the word tantamount, in allusion to a subject before-mention

ed, may not one say that a certain principle of Calvinism is tantamount
to paganism or heathenism, without incurring the charge of having said
that Calvinism is atheism or heathenism, &c.?—[*Time expired.*

Friday, Dec. 1—1½ o'clock, P. M.
[MR. RICE'S SEVENTH REPLY.]

MR. PRESIDENT—The gentleman tells us, that Dr. Wiley has said,
that he never saw a Presbyterian who believed the whole of the confession of faith. I have seen many that believe it. When men become
dissatisfied with their church, and abandon it, they very frequently justify themselves by making charges which they cannot prove. Such, we
have reason to believe, was the fact in regard to Dr. W. Dr. Bishop's
remark bears not on the subject before us. We do not pretend to think
precisely alike on every point in theology. Our confession of faith contains an outline of the system of truth taught in the Scriptures, and we
believe it. But in Mr. C.'s church I have found Unitarians, Universalists, and Materialists. Can he find, in the Presbyterian church, any such
differences, concerning the essentials of christianity? I defy him to find
any thing of the kind. Still, he says, there are differences, and the authors of the confession did not believe it. Let him state them definitely,
and I will give them due attention.

I have nothing to say concerning Dr. Wilson's charges against Dr.
Beecher. It has nothing to do with the lawfulness of creeds. Dr. Beecher might be guilty of the charges, and still professedly receive the confession of faith. Whether such was the fact, I pretend not to decide. But
if arguments of this kind had any thing to do with the question before us,
I could produce documents which would bear somewhat severely upon
Mr. Campbell. I have a pamphlet recently published by a Mr. McVay,
who has been for years a preacher in this reformed church, in which he
prefers, against Mr. C. and Mr. Smith, his friend, very serious charges.
I will balance the charges of Dr. Wilson against Dr. Beecher, with the
charges of McVay against Mr. Campbell, and, so far as the lawfulness
of creeds is concerned, the one will weigh as much as the other—for neither has any thing to do with it. The old adage has wisdom in it—
"Those who live in glass houses, should not throw stones."

The gentleman makes a vain effort to reconcile the doctrine of Mr.
Raines and Dr. Fishback. Mr. Raines, he says, pronounces the doctrine
of total depravity, as taught in the confession of faith, a libel on human
nature, but not the doctrine as held by Dr. Fishback. Let us compare
Dr. F.'s views of total depravity, with those presented in the confession.

"The original creation of man in the image and likeness of God; his
fall, and the loss of that image, together with the loss of union and communion with God; and that by sin man became involved in pollution and
death; as by it all his posterity have begun to exist out of fellowship with
God, and have come into the world without the knowledge or love of him,
and without power, moral or natural, to relieve themselves from that state
of ignorance, casualty, and death. This is what we call *total depravity,*
(and which I would call *"hereditary depravity:"*) all that makes man to differ from this state for the better, is owing to the interposition and effect of
divine grace and mercy."

This is the Doctor's creed. It is extremely orthodox; for it denies to
man all ability, natural or moral, to relieve himself from his ignorance,
pollution, carnality, and death. Let us now read the passage from our
confession, so positively denounced by Mr. Raines:

" The sinfulness of that estate whereunto men fall, consisteth in the guilt of Adam's first sin, the want of that righteousness wherein he was created, and the corruption of his nature, whereby he is utterly indisposed, disabled and made opposite to all that is spiritually good, and wholly inclined to all evil, and that continually."

I should like to see the gentleman point out the difference on this point, between Dr. Fishback's creed and ours. Now hear what Mr. Raines says on this subject: "*This doctrine is a libel on human nature, of the grossest kind.*" Here is christian union and unity of faith for you!

The gentleman says, there are no persons amongst his people, preaching Unitarianism and Universalism; but he does not deny, that there are many who *believe* these ruinous errors. If he can induce them so to compromise matters with their consciences, as that they will refuse or neglect to preach what they believe to be taught in the Bible, and can secure union by such means, I am willing that his reformation shall have the full credit of it. They believe those doctrines; but they are required to call them *opinions*, and to keep them to themselves. Mr. Stone, though a decided Unitarian, dares not preach Unitarianism! So it would seem. I would leave the society of all men, before I would promise not to preach truths which I conscientiously believe to be taught in the word of God; for all its doctrines are profitable, and every faithful minister is solemnly bound to declare the whole counsel of God to men. If there is union in a body of men composed of materials so utterly discordant, most assuredly it is not *christian union.*

I have said, there is infinite difference between the faith of Messrs. Stone and Campbell. I wish now to prove the truth of this statement. In an article from the pen of Mr. Stone, published in the Christian Baptist, the writer takes Mr. C. to task, for having published something indicating a belief in the Divinity of Christ. Having presented *seven* arguments against this doctrine, he remarks:

" If these observations be true, will it not follow indirectly, that the Word (*di hon,*) *by whom* all things were made, was not the only true God, but a person that existed with the only true God before creation began; not from eternity, else he must be the only true God; but long before the reign of Augustus Cæsar?" p. 379.

Mr. Stone denies that Christ is the only true God, or *that he existed from eternity.* Consequently there must have been a period when he began to exist. And since he could not have been the author of his own existence, he must have been a *creature.*

Those gentlemen differ no less on the subject of the *atonement*—the very foundation of the gospel. Mr. C. contends, that Christ did bear the punishment of our sins in his cross; and Mr. Stone denies it. The views entertained by Mr. Stone on this subject are thus presented by him in a discussion with Mr. Campbell: (*Millenial Harbinger, New Series,* vol. v. pp. 63, 64.)

" How the death of Christ bears away our sins, or takes them away, I will endeavor to illustrate by a figure. In the early settlement of Kentucky, a colony resided on the border of that country, continually exposed to the bloody incursions of the Indians. In this colony was a man of marked benevolence and goodness: he was wealthy, and had a care over all, that none should want the necessaries of life. He had a son, the very image of himself. Among them also lived a man of opposite character—of marked malevolence and wickedness. He hated this good man and his son, and endeavored to injure them in their persons, property, and character, though of their beneficence he shared in common with others. A banditti of Indians passed by, and apprehended this wicked man, and hurried him off to the wilderness. The good man with pain and sorrow heard the news : he called his son and told the distressing situation of his neighbor. My son, will you at the exposure or sacrifice of your own life, rescue him? I go, father ; and instantly started—found the trace—rapidly pursued, and overtook them. He saw the trembling wretch bound to a tree, and the pile of wood around him ready to burn him, and the Indians preparing to dance to his shrieks and cries. The son rushes to the tree, cuts with his tomahawk the cords that bound him : in an instant the man flees and evades the torture. But the son is apprehended and burnt.

The wicked man now sees the great love and goodness of the father and of the son. He is convinced of his sins against them, and repents ; he hates his sins, and his hatred to the good man and his son is slain, taken away— he is reconciled. He feels constrained to go to the father, confess his sins, and plead forgiveness. He goes weeping, humbly confessing his sins, and asks forgiveness. I forgive you, said the father joyfully, well knowing when he gave his son that nothing else could save the poor man, destroy his enmity, and reconcile him. Surely it was the love and goodness of the father and his son, and this love seen in the death of the son, that effected this great change in the man—that brought him to repentance, and consequently to forgiveness.

Now what effects did the death of the son produce in the father? Did it produce in him love, favor, or good-will to the wicked man? No : these were in him before. Did it dispose or make him more willing to pardon him? No : he was always willing to pardon him whenever he repented or came within the sphere of forgiveness. It had no direct effect on the father ; it directly affected the wicked man to a change and repentance ; it indirectly effected pleasure and joy in the father at the change and repentance indirectly effected in the man by the death of his son.

The application to our heavenly Father and to his Son is easy, and shows how repentance, forgiveness, redemption, sanctification, and the bearing away of sin, are effected by love to the believing obedient soul. This figure is introduced only to show what principle leads to repentance and forgiveness—the goodness of God."

In reference to this subject, Mr. C. remarks, in one of his replies to Mr. Stone :—

"*Brother Stone*—WE are discussing the greatest question in the world-- *For what did the Messiah die?*" p. 253.

On page 538, of the same volume, having copied into the Harbinger an article from the Messenger, Mr. Stone's paper, in which he proposes to close the discussion, Mr. Campbell thus remarks :—

"Since the above was written, I have had the painful intelligence that Elder Stone has been stricken with the palsy, and is not likely to recover. From recent accounts, indeed, it is probable that ere now he has passed the Jordan and gone to rest. Under all the circumstances, I conceive it inexpedient to prosecute the subject farther at present. The discussion, on my part, was undertaken with a reference to two points: The first, the transcendent importance of the question itself—For what did Christ die? The second, a very general misconception and consequent misrepresentation of our views of it. I did, I confess, expect that brother Stone would have more fully and satisfactorily relieved himself and the cause of reformation from the imputation of some of our opponents on the subject of Unitarianism in its sectarian acceptation. In this respect, though measurably disappointed, I am persuaded it will not be without advantage to the cause of reformation, that so much has been written on the subject in the way of discussion—with one, too, who had spent so many years in debates and discussions on that or some kindred branch of the same subject."

I have read these extracts to show how fundamentally the two most prominent men in this reform church differ from each other on two of the most important doctrines of the gospel—the character and the work of Christ. In regard to both, my friend Mr. C. admits, that we have Scripture testimony, clear and strong. Both are, then, matters of *faith*, not of *opinion*. In their faith concerning them, they differ radically; and yet they are united in the same church, and profess to have the one faith! In such union I have no confidence; and to it the Bible gives not the least countenance.

The clergy, the gentleman says, will unite if you give them *money*. I presume he ought to know by what motives he is influenced in his religious career; and we know how very natural it is for men to judge others by themselves—to suppose others to be under the influence which controls them. When a man makes such charges against others, without the slightest evidence of their truth, we are constrained to suspect, that he knows something experimentally on the subject. I pretend not to sit in judgment on the motives of Mr. C.; but it is a remarkable fact, if I am correctly informed, that he has, by his various labors and offices, accumulated more wealth than any one of the *venal clergy*, as he considers them. I venture to assert, that there is not in this country a Presbyterian minister who has, by his ministerial labors, accumulated the one-tenth part as much as has Mr. Campbell. And yet he has not failed to denounce *the clergy* as a most corrupt and venal set of men!!!

Destroy the confession of faith, says Mr. C., and you cannot find the Presbyterian church. We could find a body still of quite as much consistency, far more harmonious in its views, than his own church. There are hundreds of little independent democracies scattered through the country, wholly independent of each other in government and in doctrine, which are claimed by him as constituting his church. If our confession were destroyed, we should still have a much more homogenous and united body.

The Westminster confession, he says, was a political invention, gotten up for political purposes. It is true, the parliament of England did appoint a large number of learned and godly men to prepare a creed according to the Word of God; and they, after long and prayerful deliberation, drew up the Westminster confession. It is also true, that our Bible was translated by order of King James. If, then, we are to denounce the confession, because its framers were called together by political men, we must, for the same reason, denounce our translation of the Bible! The argument is as conclusive in the one case, as in the other. But when I have compared the confession with the Word of God, and found it to state, with remarkable clearness and correctness, its great doctrines and truths, I am not disposed either to denounce or to reject it, because the Westminster assembly of divines was controlled by parliament.

The gentleman has labored to make the impression, that creeds in general, and the Westminster confession in particular, are *persecuting* in their character and tendency. It is true, that in the day in which the Westminster assembly met, few men understood the rights of conscience. I am not prepared, however, to admit the correctness of all that Mr. Neale has written concerning Presbyterians. He was a zealous Congregationalist, and, of course, somewhat under the influence of his feelings. I cheerfully admit, that there were some Presbyterians who did not fully understand the rights of conscience; but in this respect they were by no means peculiar. It was the error of the age. All were, more or less, under its influence. BUT WAS THIS ERROR CAUSED BY CREEDS? Mr. C. has told us, that he does not believe that Presbyterians would now persecute. Yet they have their creed still, which, he says, is the cause of persecution!

It is true, that Mr. C.'s church has never literally persecuted men unto death; but it is also true, that it has never had the opportunity to persecute. It is yet quite a *beardless youth*—only about sixteen years old! It does not look well in a youth in his *teens* to denounce older persons, and to boast what he would do, when he has never been tried. I do not charge the reformers with a disposition to persecute; but I think it out of place, that they should boast before they are tried.

I have proved, that there are in Mr. C.'s church, Universalists and Unitarians. I will now prove, that there are Materialists—men who deny that man has a soul. Dr. Thomas, formerly of Virginia, since of Illinois, one of Mr. C.'s gifted preachers, published a paper called the *Gospel Advocate*, in which he set forth and zealously defended the doctrine, that man is composed of body, blood, and *breath*—that the word *soul*, in the Scriptures, means *breath*—that the righteous sleep in their graves till the resurrection—and pagans, infants, and idiots, are annihilated! I will not take time to prove these facts, unless they are called in question.

Mr. C. opposed these notions of the Doctor; but he refused to hearken to the voice from Bethany. At length he held a public discussion with one of our ministers, in which he defeated these heresies, and was about to publish it in a book. Mr. C. then renounced fellowship with him, and called on his church to excommunicate him. This, of course, was not schismatical! It was done quite ecclesiastically!! All that Mr. C. deemed necessary, was to renounce and denounce him!

Thus things went on for a time; when the two' gentlemen met, and held a public discussion of three days; and, neither of them being convinced, they became reconciled, and agreed to co-operate in the good cause of reformation. So brother Campbell and brother Thomas went forth to enlighten the people, by preaching the gospel!! [Mr. Campbell here denied that they went forth together, and called for proof.] I will read the account of their reconciliation, and agreement to co-operate, as copied from Dr. Thomas' paper into the Millenial Harbinger, New Series, vol. iii. pp. 74, 75.

"We, the undersigned brethren, in free consultation, met at the house of brother John Tinsley Jeter, at Paineville; and after frankly comparing our views, unanimously agreed upon the resolution subjoined, and submitted the same for the consideration of brethren Campbell and Thomas; and brother Thomas agreeing to abide the same, all difficulties were adjusted, and perfect harmony and co-operation mutually agreed upon between them.

Resolved, That whereas certain things believed and propagated by Dr. Thomas, in relation to the mortality of man, the resurrection of the dead, and the final destiny of the wicked, having given offence to many brethren, and being likely to produce a division amongst us; and believing the said views to be of no practical benefit, we recommend to brother Thomas to discontinue the discussion of the same, unless in his defence when misrepresented.

Signed by—Wm. A. Stone, Thomas E. Jeter, et als. The resolution being agreed upon by the brethren, brother C. and myself were requested to appear before them. The result of their deliberations was reported to us; we acquiesced in the recommendation after a few words of mutual explanation; and having recognized our christian fraternity, the brethren gave in their names to brother Stone to be appended in the order affixed.

Paineville, Amelia, Va., Nov. 15th, 1838."

Here we have the reconciliation and agreement to co-operate. But the gentleman says, they did not *travel the same road together!* No: Dr. Thomas remained in Virginia, and still maintained his old sentiments. If any thing could prove that a man has no soul, it would be the fact that he held such doctrines as those held by this reform preacher! Dr. Thomas held sentiments which are subversive of all religion; and yet he was recognized by Mr. Campbell as a brother and a minister of the gospel; and they go forth co-operating in the work of preaching the gospel, and "restoring the ancient order of things!!!" And to this day, Thomas, if he has not of his own accord abandoned the church, continues to hold the rank and office of a preacher.

Here is christian union with a witness. Trinitarians, Unitarians, and Materialists, all preaching the gospel together! Why, then, should the gentleman attempt to exclude any thing from such a church? For it is scarcely possible that any should wander farther from the truth than some of these.

But in the gentleman's committee, selected to aid him in this debate, we have an illustration of the unity in faith of his church. Mr. Campbell holds, and has labored faithfully to prove, the doctrine of baptism, in order to the remission of sins. Dr. Fishback denies it. Dr. F. holds the doctrine of *total hereditary depravity.* Mr. Campbell and Mr. Shannon deny it; and Mr. Raines says, "it is a libel on human nature of the grossest kind." Mr. Shannon believes, that the Scriptures are adequate to the conversion of men, without any superadded spiritual influence. Mr. Raines says he does not believe it! So they go. Here we have a most edifying illustration of what the gentleman calls christian union. The very committee who have come up to war against Presbyterians and "the sects," are forced to contradict each other, and to differ radically in regard to the most important doctrines of the gospel! May we ever be preserved from such union! The inspired writers know nothing of it. It has no countenance from the Word of God.

And mark it!—This is the latest and best edition of a church without a creed! Let us gain from Mr. Campbell some further information concerning its present state and prospects. I know he would not slander his own church. Doubtless his strong partialities would prevent him from seeing and exposing many existing evils. We will hear his testimony:

"But there is a still more delicate and responsible species of communion, sometimes called ministerial communion, on the proper exercise of which most essentially depends the character, dignity and success of the christian ministry, to which we more especially invite the attention of our brethren. I lay it down as a maxim not to be questioned, that where there is christian communion of any sort, special or common, there must be an amenability of the participants to some common tribunal, and a mutual responsibility to watch over, and nourish, and comfort one another.

Suppose, then, (but indeed we have not to suppose such a case; for it too often happens,) that numerous communities, each upon its own responsibility and its own discretion, sends abroad public ministers of the Word, without proper regard to the character and attainments of such public functionaries; and that, in their various and extensive peregrinations, they visit the churches and commune with them; will it not follow that, either directly or indirectly, such evangelists and missionaries are responsible to those churches, and to be as subject to reproof, admonition, and general supervision as they are entitled to the aids, encouragement, and christian hospitalities of the congregations they visit? But is it so amongst us? Are all our public men of such a character, call and mission, as we approve? Or are not some of them their own messengers, or the apostles of irresponsible communities—without piety, moral character or intelligence worthy of the countenance, esteem, support or affection of the christian communities? And shall we commune with them and recognize them as ministers of Christ, or the messengers and evangelists of his church, merely because they had either the vanity, self-esteem, or boldness to assume an office and a character which neither the church on earth nor in heaven awards to them?!

The cause of reformation has suffered more from this portion of its pretended friends than from all its enemies put together. This state of things is indeed generally attendant on the incipiency of all public and social institutions. *But we have had a very large portion of this unhappy and mischievous influence to contend with. Every sort of doctrine has been proclaimed by almost all sorts of preachers, under the broad banners and with the supposed sanction of the begun reformation.* We are glad to follow, rather than to lead public opinion amongst ourselves on this subject. Experience teaches with effect, what theory could not accomplish."—*Mill. Harb.* vol. vi. No. 2, pp. 63, 64.

Mr. Campbell says there must be mutual accountability, where there is christian communion of any sort; but Mr. Fishback seems to go for strict independency. But I will read more of this to-morrow.—[*Time expired.*

Saturday, Dec. 2—10 o'clock, A. M.
[MR. CAMPBELL'S EIGHTH ADDRESS.]

MR. PRESIDENT—Having so often spoken of the Westminster in such high terms of admiration as, upon the whole, with all its faults, one of the best creeds in Christendom; and having read so much from it already, I shall voluntarily read but one other extract; which I do for the sake of giving it conspicuity, and for the sake of commending it to the especial consideration of my Presbyterian friends, and especially of my friend, Mr. Rice, as constituting one of my main arguments against creeds:

"9. The infallible rule of interpretation of Scripture, is the Scripture itself; and therefore, when there is a question about the true and full sense of any scripture, (which is not manifold, but one,) it may be searched and known by other places that speak more clearly.

10. The Supreme Judge, by whom all controversies of religion are to be determined, and all decrees of councils, opinions of ancient writers, doctrines of men, and private spirits, are to be examined, and in whose sentence we are to rest, can be no other but the Holy Spirit speaking in the Scripture."—*Confession of Faith,* chap. i. sec. 9, 10, p. 14.

In the course of my remarks and responses to the allegations brought forward by my friend, some matters transpired yesterday of a very important character, respecting what is here called "*the constitution of the Presbyterian church.*" Mr. R. would represent me as exonerating the confession of his church from that persecuting spirit which characterized the framers of it, and the parliamentary acts which enforced it; alledging, moreover, that it has lost its persecuting spirit. That is not the interpretation I put upon it, nor is it the true one. I believe the same document, under favorable circumstances, would still operate in the same way. The people and the spirit of the age have changed, but the spirit and body of the confession is still the same. I wish it to be distinctly understood, that my opinion is, that the same document in a society of the same, or of a similar character, would produce the same effects now as then. I ascribe the change not to the document, nor to the party, but to the spirit of the age, and the superior light that has gone forth into the land. The spirit of a sectary is naturally and necessarily an intolerant spirit, and the creed is the great means of cherishing, developing, and maturing it. Hence we say, the persecution is in the document, when we ought rather to say, it is in the man that solemnly subscribes and obliges himself to believe and teach it.

Light, spiritual and divine, is not to be confined by the landmarks and boundaries of human legislation. No legislative ordinances, no human enactments, can restrain the rising of the sun or the free communication of its animating and salutary influences. No more can ecclesiastical canons, or the penal statutes of kings or priests, shut out from our eyes the direct and reflex light of Bible truth, which is now pouring forth its benign influences upon the whole social system in this our favored land— in this our happy age. The blighting influences, of which we have been complaining, are, therefore, not so much to be feared now, as in days of yore. Sectarianism has, indeed, been cherished by this document, and is still kept alive by it in many hearts, that else had melted, under the genial influences of gospel grace, and overflowed in all the holy sympathies and tender affections of christian benevolence. It affords me no pleasure to have to go into details of facts explanatory of the melancholy reflection, that still the old leven works, and that the spirit which party creeds infuse, is wholly alien from the kind and generous spirit that breathes in the holy faith, once delivered to the saints. Sorry indeed I am, that the course pursued by my friend yesterday compels me again to advert to this ungrateful theme.

The gentleman is making rather a licentious use of my writings. He brings up matters wholly extraneous of our agreement by correspondence, and not authorized by our rules. In any matters, relevant to the matter on hand, I am pleased to hear so much of them transferred into this discussion ; but to read what has been said against us by our opponents, and matters entirely remote from the question on hand, is rather unauthorized either by usage or by agreement. What has the document read, concerning Dr. Thomas or his views, to do with the subject before us ? Do we fraternize with persons denying the resurrection of all the dead, or that there is a spirit in man ? I do not. The agreement was made, and so far as I assented to it, was entered into, upon the concessions made by Dr. Thomas, and the opinion then entertained by me, that he was himself really grieved in spirit for his course; and had also resolved, from conviction of its folly and inutility, to abandon it altogether. I trusted that he had seen how unfounded were his views, and so informed my friends, whose hopes of his future course were not so sanguine as my own. It has, indeed, since appeared that he has not abandoned them ; and, in violation of that agreement, has gone on to promulge them, both by word and writing.

I cannot honor such a mode of warfare as that pursued against our principles, by calling it legitimate argumentation. There is much of the *non causa pro causa* in it, of the substitution of false causes, and of false effects. It is indeed possible by assuming for facts, things that never happened, and by reasoning from them either in the way of illustration or confirmation of our assumptions, to make a shew of reason and of evidence, when there is neither the one nor the other.

But if the gentleman is determined to go into the private details of such incidents, by way of oppugning us, I must shew what the tendency and practice of his church and principles have been in matters of this sort.

He is only ministering to me superior weapons against himself. I must, therefore, again illustrate the mutual complaisance and reciprocal esteem of Presbyterian doctors for one another, in a letter from Rev. Dr. Miller, of Princeton, as introduced into Beecher's trial and acquittal. We have a character of Presbyterian ministers, living in holy communion, that startles me, not a little, to see printed in a Presbyterian book. " Dr. Miller's letter," says Dr. Wilson, of Cincinnati, page 82, " is truly characteristic. It exhibits the urbanity of Dr. Miller to the life. It proves the courtesy and kindness of that distinguished man, who wrote letters to Presbyterians *proving that some of our ministers* were guilty *of offences in the church as heinous as* SWINDLING, FORGERY, and PERJURY in civil society, and at the same time *protesting against a separation from such* men"!!! With how good a grace a reproof comes from such a quarter for our winking at doctrinal errors!! Is not the above an effectual reply to all such imputations? If such be the men, matured and perfected, under a matured and perfected system, now almost two centuries old; and, if they are by its operation constrained to keep, not only members, but MINISTERS, of such character as depicted by these pious and exemplary doctors, are we to be upbraided by them for having some bold youthful speculators, upon some untaught questions!! What are these opinions, compared with crimes as base as " swindling, forgery, and perjury?"

We reprobate these opinions and speculations, and regard those as schismatics and heretics who seek to propagate them. There is no society on earth, all of whose members can be perfectly approbated. If principles are thus to be tested, no arguments could sustain any cause. Even in the apostolic age, the conduct of every christian professor could not be approbated.

But we must have at least two witnesses to the truth, in attestation of the operation of the creed system—I mean its whole operation in doors, on the faith, union, harmony, and brotherly kindness of the creed system. I am obliged to go into this matter fully once for all.

" *Preamble and resolutions adopted by the church of Harmony, December the* 3*d,* 1840.—Determined to preserve the *spirit* and *principles* of our standards, as well as the *name* of Presbyterianism, at a called meeting on the 3d of December, 1840, well attended, the members present unanimously subscribed the underwritten *document.*

" The members of the church of Harmony, having met for the purpose of deliberating upon the alarming posture of affairs in our ecclesiastical connection, after mature reflection, and after solemnly invoking Divine counsel, adopted the following preamble and resolutions:

WE have viewed with deep regret the spirit of encroachment upon what we conceive to be our rights, as members of the old school Presbyterian church. We have been pained to witness, since the unparalleled stretch of power by the general assembly in the sessions of '37 and '38, that the spirit of which we complain has been so actively and injuriously at work: That our *ecclesiastical courts*, in place of being as bulwarks, set up for the protection of our religious privileges, and for the defence of the Gospel, have been converted into engines of oppression Have repeatedly disregarded the claims of justice—violated the constitution of our church—and exhibited feelings at variance with the religion of Christ, and in conformity to the carnal policy of men, seeking rather to promote the purposes of party than the glory of God."

Observe, that those Presbyterian congregations are taught to regard the confession as " *the constitution* of their church." Why should they thus so denominate the book, at this time, if they were not accustomed, in all their courts, so to denominate it?

In proof of what we assert, we would refer, say they,

" I. To the *deposition and excommunication of the Versailles session*—a sentence inflicted WITHOUT TRIAL, and through an exertion of *usurped power, not to be borne by the citizens of a free country*."

"Usurped power, not to be borne by the citizens of a free country." Now, if Presbyterians can, "*without trial*," thus "usurp power" not to be endured, even themselves being judges, "by the citizens of a free country," for the sake of sustaining the creed and the *form of government*, have we, in the least, exaggerated the tendency of the system of human creed government, in representing it as necessarily proscriptive, tyrannical, and schismatical? Nothing is always tyrannical. No despotism is forever active. Even the papal tyranny itself sometimes sleeps. It is only occasionally that the most iron despotism lays upon its subject the rod of its anger. Occasion must call it forth into action. It is then, and only then, when roused into action, that all its power and tendencies are fully developed.

"II. We refer to the *ground assumed* by the leading men in synod, *when that case was taken up by appeal*—viz. That presbytery had the right to cut off the session without trial ; and that synod might proceed in a similar manner against presbytery, if circumstances made it necessary.

III. We refer to the *public, repeated and undisputed assertion* of one of the leading men in our church, "*that the dominant party felt themselves bound to protect their minorities*"—a principle at war with the genius and spirit of our institution ; and which acted out, has led to a series of judicial investigations the *most partial, and we would add, the most disgraceful ever placed upon the records of any court in our country, either civil or ecclesiastical.*"

"*Judicial investigations, the most partial* and, as we believe, the most *disgraceful* ever placed upon the records of any court in our country, *either civil or ecclesiastical!*" If the Presbyterians themselves so speak of their own government, of the acts of their own beloved ministry, and of the bearings of their own system, may we not use this document in full illustration and development of the truth of our positions on this question ?

"IV. We refer to the *trial and suspension of the Rev.* J. C. STILES,—a proceeding, in our view, attended with circumstances of unexampled contempt of every rule of decorum, and in violation of the constitution, laws and usages of the Presbyterian church.

1st. Because the mind of the religious community, a few weeks before the trial came on, was poisoned by a scandalous publication from the pen of the Rev. Mr. Rice, editor of the Protestant and Herald—whose gross misstatements and perversions of fact tended to prejudice the cause of the accused, and served to stimulate presbytery to a deed, which may be regarded as the consummation of intemperate zeal and party violence."

I am not the only person, then, that accuses my friend, Mr. Rice, with " gross perversions of fact," and " gross misstatements too." His zeal for the old-fashioned and immutable Presbyterianism, without any evil intention on his part, betrays him into such a course of action, as his brethren feel themselves, at times, authorized, according to their views, to call " gross perversions of fact," and "gross misstatements of fact."

" 2d. Because, according to their own decision in reference to the Versailles session, *presbytery had no jurisdiction in the case*—presenting themselves and acting in the *fourfold capacity of prosecutors, judges, witnesses and jurymen*."

Presbytery, it seems, then, in the judgment of Presbyterians themselves, can act in the fourfold capacity of prosecutors, judges, witnesses, and jury ! I have always heard this objection to the courts of that community, in such cases. It is one of the standing objections to the operations of the system, so far back as the records of its proceedings have reached us.

" 3d. Because the verdict was *contrary to evidence ;* as the only charge proved against him was the public discussion of the Reform measures ; in which he stands justified by the *free* constitution of our church.

4th. Because they did not grant him the *right of appeal* from their first sentence, of which, according to our book of discipline, he might avail himself at any time within ten days : but immediately proceeded to pronounce a higher degree of censure, and suspend him from all the functions of the gospel ministry—they say, for " CONTUMACY "—because he " refuses to submit " "*now*" to a "decision" declared *above.*

In view of these facts, therefore,

Resolved, I. That the members of the Harmony church do avow it as our solemn belief, that the *high handed measures* of our ecclesiastical courts, have inflicted a deep wound upon the cause of religion in our land :—that their attempts to repress *freedom of discussion* is a *blow* aimed at our *republican* institutions; and that were we to submit *any longer* to these assumed powers, we should consider ourselves as *standing in the attitude of foes to human liberty.*"

Here, then, is " the *solemn belief*" of the members of the Harmony church, that a new institution ought to be got up; that they would be "*foes to liberty*" if they should any longer submit to " *attempts to repress freedom of discussion,*" and " to blows aimed at our republican institutions.'' Yet Mr. Rice would have us believe that the love of liberty, of freedom of debate, and of free institutions, were of the very spirit and essence of Presbyterianism !

This may serve as a specimen of the operations of Presbyterians in the United States, for some few years past, especially since the commencement of the distinctions between new and old school in that denomination.

" II. *Resolved,* That we disclaim all connection with the *old school Presbyterian church ;* and that we consider it an imperious duty, at the present crisis, to *form a distinct presbytery*—with a view, at some future period, of connecting ourselves with a Western and Southern Presbyterian church, provided such an one can be organized free from the taint of abolitionism.

III. *Resolved,* That the session of the Harmony church attend the convention to meet on the 18th of this month at Lexington, to represent and attend to the interest of this church.''

I will only add to this chapter of details of the creed system a single incident which quite recently occurred during, and in the last session, of the synod of Kentucky, in this very city. A worthy brother minister, the Rev. Mr. Preston, of the Presbyterian church, had, during this last year, presumed "*to break the loaf*" some once or twice with our brethren at Georgetown. Having been arraigned before presbytery for this great offence, from whose decision he appealed to synod, his case came up in order at last session. While it was before synod, and in course of trial, a venerable and worthy gentleman of many years experience in the ministry, arose, and among other very acceptable words, said, that he had never heard these people (reformers) preach, nor would he allow his children to hear them preach. He judged it a profanation of the sabbath to hear them ; and that, " so long as he was able to wear a blue stocking, he never would hear them.'' Yet he could denounce them as guilty of heresy and profanation. All this was said in the city of Lexington, in the year of grace, eighteen hundred and forty-three. Go, sir, not to Westminster, but to Rome, and ask, what proscriptive and denunciatory measures—what haughtier pretensions to infallibility, could have emanated from the genius of popery itself! But the synod presented the following resolution:

[A copy of the resolution could not be obtained by the reporters.]

The synod sustained the views of the presbytery, and the gentleman withdrew from its jurisdiction. I shall not expatiate on this trial. There is one point in it to which, however, I must advert. It is the fact, that when this conscientious and independent brother was arraigned for trial, being seized with hemoptysis, and unable to speak, he was not allowed a single day to prepare for the investigation of his case. Since the days of the Star Chamber and High Court of Commission, during the reign of Elizabeth, I doubt whether any thing so small as this affair, was treated more in the spirit of those days of ecclesiastic tyranny and domination.

Here, then, is an intelligent and useful member of the church, and minister of religion, set aside merely for the sin of celebrating the Lord's supper with a people whom the synod thought proper to denounce as holding errors. They seem to have forgotten that they themselves had all been denounced by other synods and councils, as reprobate in doctrine and unworthy of the name of christians. Orthodoxy is, indeed, very arbitrary and whimsical in its decisions. To-day it reprobates what it commended yesterday, and will to-morrow reprobate what it approves to-day. Power and numbers consecrate every thing: hence, while parties are weak and struggling into power, they are always erroneous and heretical by those in authority; but when they triumph over their rivals, the sin of heterodoxy no more adheres to them.

I blame the system, not the men. These creeds have always operated in this way. It is in this view of the subject, in contrast with those who hold the Book alone, that we pronounce them to be of schismatical tendency, and ultimating in tyranny and oppression.

Had I time to accomplish it this morning, I should glance at the whole history of the practical operations of the Westminster creed, from its origin till now. But that is at present out of the question. I shall, therefore, only glance at its actual effects in this western country; almost exclusively, indeed, in this commonwealth, in the memory of one generation. Only one class of Presbyterians were here at the commencement of the present century. In 1803, did not the oppression of some of its technical abstractions on Trinity, cause the disseverance and disruption of the denomination? Arianism, or Unitarianism, as Mr. Rice calls it, was the result of the agony of that day. The whole Springfield presbytery was severed from the denomination, a part of it turning Arian, and another part terminating in Shakerism. I call these results by the names which the people of that day imposed on them. An abstract, dogmatic and erroneous nomenclature, gave birth to these new forms, by whatever name they should be called. Indeed, this unscriptural vocabulary, this metaphysical jargon, has been the occasion of much the larger part of all the strife and partyism of Protestantism. Think only of the unscriptural terms, 'Eternal Son,' 'eternal generation,' 'eternal procession,' 'eternal justification,' 'Trinity,' 'Triune God,' 'con-substantial,' 'co-eternal,' &c. &c. Here are terms and phrases no inspired man ever used, and no sane man ever understood. These wild abstrusities beget a speculative habit; and men, with a little conceit, and a little philosophic pride, getting into controversy on these mystic points, soon generate feuds; and, if they are only a little self-willed and conscientious, a new sect or party will be the result. Latitudinarian comments, and new modes of construction, gave birth to those two American parties, called " Newlights," and " Shakers."

Extremes beget each other. Only contemplate the fanaticism of the Shakers, growing out of a Presbyterian education. They supposed themselves moved by the *Holy* Spirit, in some new, direct or immediate way ; and, therefore, commenced howling, barking, leaping, jerking, and other spasmodic operations. No pagan fanaticism ever did transcend some of the scenes said to have been transacted at the commencement of the present century, in this good commonwealth, under the reaction of the creed-system. A latitudinarianism of interpretation, of thinking, speaking, acting, rarely equalled, never surpassed, was the genuine revulsionary operation of the then reigning system, upon that peculiar class of mind subjected to those influences. Like combustion, fanaticism cannot be developed, without the proper materials and circumstances.

I am not speaking of the Scotch Cameronians, the good old solemn league and covenant Covenanters, nor of other English, Scotch and Irish Presbyterians—I am speaking of the Kentucky Presbyterians of the present century. And whence came the Cumberlanders—the Presbyterians on the Kentucky and Tennessee sides of that sacred river? Was it not the oppression of the creed, in some of its doctrinal and disciplinary parts?

Was it not the high ground taken by some, and the efforts to impose their views and constructions upon others? The same causes, operating upon different minds, on particular subjects, generally terminate in the formation of some new denomination, and that, too, upon some particular point or points. This new denomination, if I am rightly informed, now nearly equals the old Presbyterians in the same districts of country. When to these you add the late general schism, which is not confined to Kentucky or Tennessee, but which extends over all the states, where Presbyterianism exists, and count the sixty thousand new-school neucleus and the old school, we have four schisms in forty years ; or rather, for one old Presbyterian church we have, through the instrumentality of one party and its creed, no less than five communities. Has not the Westminster wrought well in the way of increase of parties in this valley ? ! A fruitful mother of discords truly ! ! This is a proof, strong and clear, within the memory of the living men around us. Contemplate Shakerism, New-lightism, Cumberland Presbyterianism, New-schoolism and Old-schoolism, and what a powerful argument to sustain my position, that human creeds are *heretical* and *schismatical!* It was the creeds and their interpretation that caused all this discord and strife. Every one of these parties began about something within the creed. How, in reason's name, can these facts be disposed of ! !

Many things in the development of social life, I verily believe and teach, ought to be let alone. When men indulge in speculations, so long as they do not presume to propagate them, better to let them alone. What would Mr. Rice have done with such persons as Dr. Thomas? What would our Westminster divines have done with Elder B. W. Stone? They would, according to their construction of his opinions, certainly have either cut off his head or hanged him by the statute read from Neale. I do not say the Kentucky Presbyterians would now do this. I speak of their fathers, about the year 1648. I read you on yesterday an act which said that Unitarians should " die without benefit of clergy." Under that statute, it would have gone equally hard with the Materialist. But as the

Savior said he came not to destroy men's lives, but to save them; so we prefer to save men's lives by the gospel rather than to destroy them. Hence I sought to save some of those speculators, until my friends supposed I almost sympathized with their opinions. I cheerfully say, I do not approve of all that Barton W. Stone has written and said, yet I believe our society has been, and is pursuing a most salutary and redeeming policy. Whither has fled the Newlightism of former days? How long will its speculations be remembered, that floated on the winds of thirty years?!

Presbyterians, and all the other parties in the field, could not dispose of it, till the pleaders for the reformation arose in the length and breadth of the land. They have indeed disposed of it in such a way, as to lead the honest and candid into more scriptural and consistent views and practices, and to paralyze and silence the uncandid declaimers upon these speculations.

New generations will now grow up under new influences. The offspring of those persons propagating erroneous speculations, will grow up under new influences. The Bible and its facts, and new associations, will make of them a new people. They will rally round the banners of the original institutions of Christ. They will place themselves upon the naked book of God alone. If they err and do wrong, the Bible will set them right again. They may go wrong for a time, but they are in the safe-keeping of apostles and prophets, while at school with the Great Teacher and the holy Twelve. These teachers, should they err, will set them right again. I believe we have done a good work, for which even the Presbyterians should thank us, in removing out of their way what *they* could not; and for correcting errors growing out of their own misinterpretations of the Directory of God, which, with all their learning, ability and zeal, *they failed to vanquish!*—[*Time expired.*

Saturday, Dec. 2—10½ *o'clock, A. M.*
[MR. RICE'S EIGHTH REPLY.]

MR. PRESIDENT—My friend, Mr. C., who would seem to know intuitively what errors will die, if let alone, and which must be killed; also sees with no less clearness, that under certain circumstances, the Westminster confession would lead to persecution. Will he please to put his finger on one passage or sentiment in it, that even distantly looks towards persecution? From the first chapter to the last, there is not one that contains an illiberal or persecuting tenet. I deny that it ever did, in any age, induce any man or class of men to persecute. No creed produces persecution, unless it embodies persecuting principles.

It would be as unwise, and as decidedly wrong, to attempt to force men, by civil penalties, to embrace the Bible, as to compel them to receive a creed; and both have been, at different times, attempted. Our Savior was condemned to death *by an appeal to the Bible,* not to a human creed. The Jews appealed to the law of Moses against blasphemy, and said to Pilate, " We have a law, and by our law he ought to die, because he made himself the Son of God," John xix. 7. Never were there more malignant persecutions than have been carried on in the name of the Bible, without a human creed. The infidel might as plausibly maintain, that christianity itself persecutes, as Mr. C. that creeds are necessarily intolerant. Had the Anabaptists of Germany a written creed? They had not. Yet where, in the history of the christian church, can you find a

more fanatical and intolerant sect than they? The infidels of France had
no creed, but where, in the history of man, can you find such a scene of
diabolical persecution, as characterized "the reign of terror"—the period
of the revolution?

If, then, it be true, that in different ages and nations men have persecuted, in the name of the Bible, without a creed, and even without a religious belief of any kind; who can believe in the philosophy of my friend,
when he makes creeds the cause of persecution? There is no error more
common amongst men, than that of ascribing effects to wrong causes.
Each party, political and religious, is disposed to attribute existing or apprehended evils to causes which they dislike. In their judgments they
are often controlled by prejudices, contrary alike to philosophy and to
fact. The gentleman says, creeds lead to persecution. Let him, if he
can, prove, or give even the slightest evidence, that a creed not embodying persecuting principles, leads to persecution. If men hold intolerant
opinions, they will persecute, whether those opinions are committed to
writing or not.

The gentleman has repeatedly expressed his particular gratification at
my reading so much from his various publications. Then, again, he
complains bitterly, as if I were doing him serious injustice. This morning he tells you, that he never gave me the right to read his books on
every subject. I ask him no favors on this matter. I have the right to
read any thing he or any one else has written, bearing on the subjects under discussion. He has the right to quote the confession of faith, or any
author he may fancy. I have the same right; and, therefore, do not ask
his permission to read any or all of his books, as I may choose. He
may complain if he will. I know he feels unpleasantly at having the
contradictions and absurdities of his books exposed; but I cannot help it.

I was not a little surprised to hear Mr. Campbell say, that he thought
Dr. Thomas, the Materialist, had abandoned his errors. I will again read
from the Millenial Harbinger, that we may see whether there was the
slightest foundation for such an opinion:

"We, the undersigned brethren, in free consultation, met at the house of
brother John Tinsley Jeter, at Paineville; and after frankly comparing our
views, unanimously agreed upon the resolution subjoined, and submitted
the same for the consideration of brethren Campbell and Thomas; and brother Thomas agreeing to abide the same, all difficulties were adjusted, and
perfect harmony and co-operation mutually agreed upon between them.

Resolved, That whereas certain things *believed and propagated by Dr.
Thomas*, in relation to the mortality of man, the resurrection of the dead,
and the final destiny of the wicked, having given offence to many brethren,
and being likely to produce a division amongst us, and believing the said
views to be of no *practical* benefit, we recommend to brother Thomas to
discontinue the discussion of the same, *unless in his defence when misrepresented*." Signed by some twenty-four persons.

This is the document; and you observe that, so far from confessing
and abandoning his errors, Dr. Thomas expressly retained the right to
discuss them *in his defence, when misrepresented*. If, afterwards, there
were mutual explanations, in which he retracted his errors, why was not
the paper altered by striking out the part which granted him the right to
defend them? I prefer to take the document itself, which concedes the
right, and in connection with which, he declared positively that his views
remained unaltered. Dr. Thomas has been, for a number of years, advocating those errors; and, if I am correctly informed, is yet a member and

a preacher in Mr. C.'s church. Certainly he is, unless he has voluntarily withdrawn.

The gentleman seems to be quite pained by the necessity of referring to certain personal difficulties between several ministers, which have nothing whatever to do with the subject in hand. How he feels about such matters now, I pretend not to know; but I do know that his Christian Baptist abounds with just such attempts to injure the reputation of the clergy of all denominations. Dr. Miller, he informs us, charged certain men, formerly in our church, with dishonesty, in adopting our confession of faith. This may all be true, and yet creeds may not be heretical and schismatical. Creeds are not designed to detect dishonest men. I presume the gentleman will not deny, that men may be dishonest in professing to receive the Bible as their only infallible guide.

But what is the difference between Mr. Campbell's church and ours, with regard to errorists and unworthy men? As in the time of the apostles, some crept in unawares, so now, some dishonest men may gain admittance into our church. But in his, are found Arians, Socinians, Universalists, Materialists, who have entered *in perfect consistency with the principles of the church.* The door is wide enough to receive them, and the foundation broad enough for them to stand on. My friend Mr. C. says, he will receive Unitarians and Universalists. It is one thing for errorists to gain admittance to a church under the garb of a false profession, and quite another for them to be received, whilst avowing their erroneous faith. [Mr. Campbell. I never said so.] The gentleman now says, he has never said that he would receive a Unitarian or a Universalist! I will prove that he has said he will receive them, if they will use the Bible words, and hold their errors as *opinions.* I will read in his *Christianity Restored*, (pp. 122, 123:)

"I will now show how they cannot make a sect of us. We will acknowledge all as christians who acknowledge the gospel facts, and obey Jesus Christ. But, says one, will you receive a Unitarian? No; nor a Trinitarian. We will have neither Unitarians nor Trinitarians. How can this, be! Systems make Unitarians and Trinitarians. Renounce the system, and you renounce its creatures.

But the creatures of other systems now exist, and some of them will come in your way. How will you dispose of them? I answer, We will unmake them. Again I am asked, How will you unmake them? I answer, By laying no emphasis upon their opinions.

What is a Unitarian? One who contends that Jesus-Christ is not the Son of God. Such a one has denied the faith, and therefore we reject him. But, says a Trinitarian, many Unitarians acknowledge that Jesus Christ is the Son of God in a sense of their own. Admit it. Then I ask, How do you know they have a sense of their own? Intuitively, or by their words? Not intuitively, but by their words. And what are these words? Are they Bible words? If they are, we cannot object to them—if they are not, we will not hear them; or, what is the same thing, we will not discuss them at all. If he will ascribe to Jesus all Bible attributes, names, works, and worship, we will not fight with him about scholastic words: but if he will not ascribe to him every thing that the first christians ascribed, and worship and adore him as the first christians did, we will reject him, not because of his private opinions, but because he refuses to honor Jesus as the first converts did, and withholds from him the titles and honors which God and his apostles have bestowed upon him.

In like manner we will deal with a Trinitarian. If he will ascribe to the Father, Son, and Holy Spirit, all that the first believers ascribed, and nothing more, we will receive him—but we will not allow him to apply scholastic and barbarous epithets to the Father, the Son, or the Holy Spirit. If he will dogmatize and become a factionist, we reject him—not because of his opinions, but because of his attempting to make a faction, or to lord it over God's heritage.

And will you receive a Universalist too? No; not as a Universalist. If a man, professing Universalist opinions, should apply for admission, we will receive him, if he will consent to use and apply all the Bible phrases in their plain reference to the future state of men and angels. We will not hearken to those questions which gender strife, nor discuss them at all. If a person say such is his private opinion, let him have it as his private opinion; but lay no stress upon it: and if it be a wrong private opinion, it will die a natural death much sooner than if you attempt to kill it."

If the Universalist says, he holds his errors as private opinions, the gentleman says, he will receive him, and let him hold them still. This is precisely what I have asserted.

I think he ought to have felt unpleasantly, when he read a document passed by a new school church in this vicinity. What had it to do with the question, whether creeds are heretical and schismatical? Absolutely nothing. But it contains some personal imputations against myself, thrown out under the excitement arising from the suspension of a minister to whom they were attached; and therefore it was, that he read it! If I were inclined to return evil for evil, I would read the pamphlet I hold in my hand, published by a Mr. McVay, one of the preachers in his church, preferring against Mr. C. very serious charges. It contains a number of certificates, signed by respectable persons. This document would be a fair match for the Harmony paper. But my cause requires no such defence.

In regard to Mr. Preston's case, various false statements have been published in the Harrodsburg Christian Journal, by certain anonymous writers. The gentleman, by way of showing the intolerance of the synod of Kentucky, states that Mr. Preston, though in bad health, was not allowed a day to prepare his defence. The facts of the case are these: Mr. Preston had two or three times communed with the reformers—at which conduct some of his brethren were grieved. He came before the presbytery, and asked their opinion of his conduct. He had not been arraigned—and was not called before that body to answer to charges preferred against him. He stated the fact, that he had communed with a church known not to be acknowledged by ours, and asked their opinion. They were prepared to give it; and, after hearing his reasons, they said to him—"We think your conduct is highly censurable." He appealed to synod. That body heard him fully in defence of his conduct, and then expressed the same opinion. He was not excommunicated nor suspended. This is all. If the gentleman can prove us intolerant by such evidences, he is most welcome to do so.

But, to cap the climax, and to prove unanswerably how much Presbyterians are bent on persecution, the gentleman told you, that there is living in this city a Presbyterian minister who said, he had not heard these reformers preach, and did not wish to hear them. I supposed, that in this free country, a man had a right to hear, or refuse to hear, whom he pleased, without being justly chargeable with intolerance. But I now learn, that all who think they can better employ their time, than by going to hear Mr. C. or his preachers, are to be branded as persecutors! It is, indeed, a singular species of persecution, which consists in letting men alone! I think it within the bounds of possibility, that the minister alluded to has *read* enough concerning the principles of this new reformation, to determine that he may spend his sabbaths more profitably than by seeking edification from that quarter.

But Mr. C. boasts of his liberality. Yet when a gentleman in England inquired of him, whether his churches *admit* unimmersed persons to communion, he answered in the most unqualified terms—" Not one of them, as far as known to me." Presbyterians are chargeable with a persecuting spirit, if they refuse to allow their members to commune with the reformers ; but the reformers are quite charitable in refusing to permit any unimmersed person to commune with them !!!

My friend has often displayed the extent of his charity and liberality in bold relief. A specimen of the kind is found in his Christian Baptist, (p. 23.)

" Thirdly, the worshiping establishments now in operation throughout Christendom, increased and cemented by their respective voluminous confessions of faith, and their ecclesiastical constitutions, are not churches of Jesus Christ, but the legitimate daughters of that Mother of Harlots, the church of Rome."

Let me give another specimen from the Millenial Harbinger, (vol. i. p. 349.)

" This respectable sect, [Presbyterians,] respectable not so much for its humility, spirituality, and piety ; but respectable for its numbers, its wealth, and learning ; for its ancient foundation, being only the *second* daughter of the second marriage of the kings of the earth with MISTRESS ROMA BABYLONA, now in her third century, is annually publishing to the world, how illy she is adapted to our government, to the salvation of this community, temporally, spiritually, or eternally, to the spread and progress of the christian religion," &c.

Thus he speaks of Presbyterians ; and yet he tells you now, that he is quite willing to have those children of Mistress Roma Babylona commune with him !!!

The gentleman sometimes hints remotely at the question before us. Creeds, he says, produced Arianism, and Shakerism, howlings, barkings, &c., in our own country. Did not Arius teach his heresies; and did they not rapidly spread through the church before a creed was adopted ? How, then, could the creed have produced it ? Did the effect exist before the cause ? And how did the creed produce Shakers ? How did it make people howl and bark ? I am really curious to understand the philosophy of this matter. It is true that the Shakers carried their *reformation* rather too far for my friend; but still they were reformers. One of the advantages secured to our church by our creed is, that we are enabled, with some despatch, to get rid of all such errorists. We desire not to have in our communion, men who reject the fundamental principles of the gospel, however respectable in character or in numbers. But did the *ism* of my friend produce the Materialism of Dr. Thomas, or the partyism of McVay ? Let him answer the question ; and he will refute his charges against our creed.

But he asks, what would the old Presbyterian fathers have done with Dr. Thomas ? Certainly they would not have retained him in their communion. But I do not admit that Presbyterians in England and Scotland were inclined, generally, to persecute. There doubtless were some of all parties who did not understand the rights of conscience, and who desired a church establishment. But that Presbyterians were in favor of killing those who differed from them, is not true. Presbyterians did not constitute the parliament, to whose persecuting laws the gentleman has referred.   Whether there was any considerable number of Presbyterians in that parliament, I know not.   Anabaptists, and others, have violently persecuted without a creed.   How, then, can it be made appear, that the intolerance of any age or country, was caused by the existence of creeds?

The gentleman has now informed us of one great good growing out of his reformation.   But for it, he says, there would have been in the West a body of Unitarians for a hundred years to come!   If it is any credit to his reformation, that it has embraced in its bosom multitudes who rob Christ of his glory, by denying his divinity; and the sinner of hope, by denying his atonement; he is most welcome to it!   His foundation is broad enough for all such; but the Bible knows nothing of such compromises of the truth, to effect union with those who deny the Lord that bought them.

I will now proceed to give some further development of the true character and condition of Mr. C.'s church, by reading a few extracts which I commenced on yesterday afternoon; (Millenial Harbinger, vol. vi., No. 6, pp. 243, 244:)

"How few public preachers and teachers at this day are there, that need not to be ashamed of their aptitude to discriminate and apply the holy oracles!   Ought not many to blush who presume to speak by a divine call specially to them addressed, for their ignorance of all the laws of language, the force of words, the logical point in an argument, the meaning of the sacred style, and their inaptitude to expound and apply the word of truth!   How many ought to blush for their irreverent manner of speaking in the divine presence—their vapid and most irreligious way of pronouncing the divine names and attributes—their profanation of the privilege of prayer in the most undevout style of addressing God, and of speaking to him merely for the sake of speaking to men—correcting what they deem popular errors, and eulogizing kindred spirits, while addressing the awful throne of God!   The times are sadly out of joint in all these respects.   Public prayers are sometimes mere sermons preached to God—critiques on doctrine, satires on rival dogmas, protracted efforts at saying something commendable, random attempts to be eloquent, monotonous gibberish, empty, loud, and vehement vociferations.   For all this insolence to heaven, and for all these lamentable defects, we have neither jurisdiction nor tribunal!   We certainly have not, if every individual may send himself and authorize his own acts; or if a small, weak, irresponsible community may send out whom it pleases into the world.   The cause of reformation would ere now have overrun the whole community, but for two causes.   One is, the great masses of neglected new converts, who are not taught the christian religion in scriptural churches, and who consequently lose confidence in themselves, return to the world, or remain dry and barren branches in the mystic vine.   The other is a class of unsent, unaccomplished, uneducated advocates, who plead it; amongst whom, too, have been found a number of persons of immoral character, who have assumed the profession as a cloak of covetousness—as means of imposing themselves on the unsuspecting and benevolent. * * * * * *
We have bled at every pore through the lacerations of many such.   And had not our cause possessed more than mortal strength—had it not been of celestial origin and divine power, it had long since been prostrate through traitors, pretenders, incompetent disciplinarians, and impotent administrators."

What a picture this of the preachers and members of this boasted church—the latest and best edition of a no-creed church!   The evils are not exaggerated.   The picture is drawn by the gentleman himself; and we know that he would not slander his own church. He says—"We have bled at every pore through the lacerations of many such"—that is, of their own preachers!   Why, if I were to see a man bleeding at every pore, I should be sure that he would die, if the doctor did not speedily come to his relief. And if he were thus bleeding from self-inflicted wounds, I should certainly think, that he ought to be confined in a straight-jacket! But if I were told, that he was the only sane and healthy man in that community, I should regard it as a horrible place. I should make a speedy retreat from amongst them. But let me read a little further on page 245.

" But we have not yet laid open the great defects of our evangelical ministry. There are the belligerent theorists, whose special care it is, in every sermon, or on all public occasions, to disinter the remains of some fallen or decayed system, exhibit its bones and putrid remains, and then to bury it again with all the honors of an ecclesiastic war; and, in contrast with it, to unfold the charms of a wiser and better theory. Alas! what pranks are played on earth, in the presence of mourning angels, by those whose undertaking it is to persuade sinners to turn to God and live forever!

Another portion of our more gifted and ingenious cohorts have addicted themselves to the enviable task of public censors of the senior theologians. Boys in their *teens*, or youths who, for years to come, would not have been permitted to lay a shoulder of mutton on God's ancient altar, are now gravely and learnedly exposing the errors of Luther, Calvin, Wesley, the synods of Dort, Westminster and Trent, *cum multis alliis*, with as much self-approbation and secret relish as the most exquisite sensualist devours a favorite dish when his appetite is stimulated with the pickles of Macenas and a fast of full twelve hours. These are the wild beasts of our Ephesus, with whom it is more difficult to conflict than with those with whom Paul fought at the capital of Asia. Yet these are workmen who are never ashamed, but always glory in their success in what they call preaching the gospel of peace.

Of these profanations of the evangelical office, and of these flagrant aberrations from good sense, good taste, and approved models, the more intelligent and pious communities are always complaining; but without perceiving that they have the power of preventing the evil. They flatter themselves that Time, the great teacher, innovater, and reformer, will, of his own accord, correct these evils. But will it save the multitudes that are fatally injured in the meantime while the experiment is in progress! And has the Lord commissioned Time and Experiment as his reforming agents?"

Such is the account of the present state and prospects of his church, given by the gentleman himself. Again, he says, "Every sort of doctrine has been proclaimed by almost all sorts of preachers, under the broad banner and with the supposed sanction of the begun reformation;" (Mil. Harb. vol. vi. No. 2, p. 64.) If the leading man in the church feels constrained to portray its condition in such language, how dark would be the picture drawn, in its true colors, by an impartial hand! Who would desire to enter such a church? Who could regard it, with all its errors and its confusion, as " the pillar and ground of the truth?" Let me remain among " the sects" where such men are not tolerated, and where such errors are not cherished to the ruin, present and eternal, of multitudes.

Another argument I shall urge against the gentleman's plan of christian union, is, *that he has felt constrained radically to change his ground since he commenced his reformation, and is now advocating the very principles he once boldly denounced!* In the beginning of his career he denounced all denominations for doing precisely what he is now himself doing. He began with taking the New Testament as the only constitution of the churches. Now he is offering them, and urging upon them, several articles, written by himself, as the basis of a general organization! Many of his friends and followers have been alarmed at the progress he seems to be making towards "Babylon;" and well they may be.—[*Time expired.*

Saturday, Dec. 2—11 o'clock, A. M.

[MR. CAMPBELL'S NINTH ADDRESS.]

MR. PRESIDENT—Mr. Rice, it seems, has left the argument, and is determined to proceed in his begun course of calumniating the community with which I stand connected. He will not provoke me to reply to such calumnies, in any other way than I have already done. I have shown that the apostle Paul said full as much against his brethren, as I have ever said against mine; nay, much more than I have yet said. I have given a few examples of the manner in which he inveighed against some whom he himself had converted from Judaism and Paganism to Christ. Every society has to contend with unprofitable and unworthy members. Of all the churches in Galatia, Paul said more than I have ever said of all the churches in Kentucky, or of any one state of this Union. Of them, Paul said—"*I stand in doubt of you,* lest I have bestowed upon you labor in vain."—"Am I become your enemy because I tell you the truth?"—"I call God to witness, that you would, at one time, have plucked out your eyes, and have given them to me." Any one disposed to calumniate Paul and his labors, from his own writings, would have had a fine opportunity from his letter to the Galatians, as well as from those to Timothy and the Corinthians.

But it is not only of the dereliction of these churches that great apostle complains. He says not only "Demas has forsaken me," but "all in Asia have forsaken me." "I pray God not to lay this sin to their charge." Mr. Rice, had he been in Paul's place, would not have told over these apostasies and obliquities of his brethren. He would have concealed them. He would not have published their imperfections as I have done. Stood he in the same relations to community, he would not, as I still do, expose the frailties and errors of those associated with him. Which of us seems, in these specifications, to walk more after the example of Paul? I feel myself in duty bound to remonstrate against the errors of my brethren, as against the errors of other men—nay, more. I may have, indeed, said of them things more severe than I should have said. Still, I glory in the fact, that my prejudices and partialities have not hid their frailties from my eyes, nor sealed my lips in reproving them. Mr. R. confers upon me an honor of which I am proud, really proud. He honors my candor, my impartiality, and my love of truth. I shall, then, always persevere in this course of reproving defects in friend or opponent. We have reformed, and are reforming, and still will reform. We have placed before ourselves and brethren a very high standard of perfection, and to this we must still direct our eyes. I hope the very censures of our ardent and devoted friend, Mr. Rice, will still admonish us to ascend still higher in our aspirations after christian excellence.

I have been endeavoring to relieve my Presbyterian friends from the imputation, that those deeds of intolerance and persecution which history records against their fathers, were the workings of their system, rather than of any personal or ancestral depravity of nature; that the system, and not the people, was to blame for it. This is, indeed, my real conviction. But he will not let the creed have it. He admits that they have done those deeds; and, as one endorsed by Presbyterians, he can do no less than admit it. Neale is candid, honest, and impartial. He was recommended to my early readings, by some of the best Presbyterians I have ever known. Not only he, however, but all our historians, and religious dictionaries and encyclopœdias, attest the fact, that all creeds, since that of Nice and saint Athanasius, have been baptized in blood. The Bible and its friends have killed no person. Martyrologists say that creeds have made in various forms, and in all time, their *fifty millions* of martyrs. Christians do not kill christians. Never, never! Jesus said, "All who take the sword, shall perish with the sword." Doubtless in defence of religion.

The gentleman says, the Anabaptists persecuted! That has been often said. But what have we to do with the Anabaptists? It is, indeed, one of the brightest glories of the Baptists, the pure immersionists, that they have never shed one drop of blood in defence of their creed or practice. I am not speaking of the Munster fanatics—but I speak of those properly called Baptists, in contrast with the Pedo-baptists. I know the gentleman will tell you that they never had it in their power. Roger Williams and his colony might have done it. Persecutions might have been introduced into Rhode Island, as easily as into Connecticut or Massachusetts. But the founders of those colonies were of different views. I have said the confession has been changed, altered, and improved, in some particulars. The article on the power of the civil magistrate has, indeed, been much improved in our American Westminster confession. It does not now, as formerly, authorize the sword to serve at the altar. It does not now constrain any man to lift up his hand and swear, by high heaven, that he will "extirpate popery and prelacy by all civil pains;" as did the solemn league and covenant. You have read the history of the holy and bloody wars of orthodoxy for forty years; and did I not read the solemn decree of the men who made that creed?

It is indeed possible that it might be the men and not the principles. I have known some men that would never persecute others on any account, or in any way. The milk of human kindness flowed too freely though their veins. No system, the most intolerant, could make them cruel. Still I opine, it was their *principles*, and not the peculiarity of a bilious or atrabilious temperament. The spirit, the very genius of a human bond of union, a human standard, around which the human affections are taught to revolve, is as certainly exclusive as there is self-love in man, and a love for one's own opinions. When men, under the influence of a creed, oral or written, can pass a law to hang men for an opinion, for a theory or a doctrine, there must be an attachment to opinions of a very morbid and predominating character. To imprison one for immersing or refusing to sprinkle an applicant, certainly evinces not only the fact of the previous existence of an opinion favorable to sprinkling, but of an undue attachment to it, and it moreover exhibits a theory of human nature, of civil rights, of rational liberty, wholly incompatible with our views of justice, reason, and conscience.

I have before said, that I am under no necessity whatever, in my own defence, to take this view of the subject, in the maintenance of my position on the use and tendency of human tests of orthodoxy. I take this ground on principles of respect for my Presbyterian contemporaries, to relieve them as *men* from the *spirit of the system.* They have caught the spirit of the age, of our free institutions, and they cannot think or act as their fathers did. There is too much Bible reading in this land, and intercommunication with other denominations, with men of piety and elevated conceptions of human rights, and liberty of thought, of speech, of conscience and of action. I do not think that the people are now so intolerant. I will therefore blame the system rather than the people.

Still, Mr. Rice will excuse the creed rather than the men. I blame the system, but he blames the men. It is true that men made the law to punish heretics and the heterodox with death; and that these men had those principles within them before the statute which they had just enacted. But these men were themselves the creatures of other systems of the same kind which they had now ordained. It was then the system that made them pass such laws. I do not, as I before said, think that the men of this age, the Presbyterians around me, would persecute any of us to death. Light has become too strong, and public opinion has been revolutionized, and one of the most dangerous articles in the creed has been reformed. Still there is a species of newspaper defamation, of pulpit and synodical calumny, of religious neighborhood gossiping, that murders men's reputation, slays their usefulness, and as effectually, in certain regions, restrains their influence, as would banishment or imprisonment. By turning over to the article on persecution, in that encyclopœdia lying beside him, the gentleman will find enough on that subject to satisfy any reasonable man, that I have not exaggerated the matter at all;—and that although we have not persecutions of the first class, we still have of all the subordinate ranks enough to sustain our position, that creeds are still schismatical and heretical.

This being the last day of our discussion, I am resolved to confine myself to such topics as directly illustrate and establish the proposition. I did not, through this discussion, nor do I now, respond to every thing the gentleman has introduced. I have already given my reasons why I am not only not obliged to do it, but why it ought not to be done. I answer every thing that I remember of consequence, or in any direct way affecting the proposition.

On this subject I have used no stronger terms than have the Presbyterians themselves. One of their correspondents in this commonwealth, as I learn from those who read it in the denominational press, calls his own church "*a stripling of Rome*." All indeed are striplings of Rome who are not purified from her errors. Between England and Rome they were wont to say, there was but a paper wall. If so, between England and Scotland there is a still thinner paper wall. If the establishment of England be the first in descent, that of Scotland may be regarded as the second in descent from the mother and mistress church, and as possessing a little of the body and the spirit of the old queen.

I do, indeed, believe, that so long as persons become members of a church without their own personal responsibility, while natural generation, without personal regeneration, makes members, we must have a community carnal, intolerant, and proscriptive. I have often said so, I have so written, and I still believe it. It has ever been so. All the ecclesiastic persecutions have, as before shown, emanated from such communities. But I have other points on which I must offer a few connected remarks. And first, we invite your attention to an historical glance at schism.

I said yesterday, or the day before, that Satan was the first *sectary* in the universe, and that the first schism occurred in heaven. The Messiah informs us that Satan "*abode not in the truth*." He departed from it and became a liar and a deceiver. That truth was doubtless a revelation of good things to come in some of the other dominions of God. But so it was, the lofty seraph did not choose to acquiesce in it. He became disaffected towards it, apostatized, and became a heretic and heresiarch. For this, he and all who rallied around the new principle of disloyalty, were exiled from heaven. This was a tremendous heresy and fall. On discord bent, the great schismatic plotted the severance of man from God's covenant of life. The ruin of our race was fully plotted, the scheme matured, and inexperienced Eve was selected for his victim. He succeeded. He turned away her ear from God's word, substituted a commentary upon it which made it void; and she, *believing the lie*, put forth her hand and plucked down ruin upon herself and all her children. This was the second schism.

After a full development of this sad catastrophe and a judgment held, God, in the fullness of his philanthropy, set on foot a remedial system. He promised a victorious Redeemer, and set up a sacrificial institution. Adam and Eve brought up their family under that dispensation. They had their altar, their victims, their sabbath, and their family worship. Cain and Abel, their eldest sons, followed their example, and each one brought his offerings to the Lord. Abel believed the promised *Lamb of God*, and brought from his flock a *sin-offering*. Cain, regardless of the necessity of a Mediator, and a bloody victim, brought merely his *thank-offering*, the first fruits of his harvest. Having disdained the remedial system, God disdained him, and would not receive his offering by such token of his regard as he had shewn to that of Abel. Cain's proud and unbelieving heart was filled with rage, and turned away from God and his own brother. They went into a debate—Cain's anger was kindled into a rage, and, incensed with pride and envy, he rose up against Abel and slew him. He left his father's house, became a vagabond or wanderer, and roamed abroad to the land afterwards called Nod, and there set up an institution of his own. Thus commenced the second schism in the family of man. Cain is a full developed schismatic now, and how like the grand apostate! He became a liar and a murderer. Falsehood, heresy, schism and persecution seem to commence and travel together in one sad league of ruin. Virtue, alas! piety itself, becomes obnoxious to the wrath of the schismatic! "Wherefore slew he him?" said John, "because his own works were evil, and his brother's righteous." We must not pause here. We must pursue the history of schism farther.

Marriage was a divine institution. And equal matches, as respected piety and faith, have always been the law of heaven. A wiser and a holier institution is not inscribed upon the rolls of time. But from that covenant too, man apostatized, and polygamy and unequal matches commenced in the time of Seth. This consummated the wickedness of the old world, and God fixed a day for its destruction. The intermarriage of "the sons of God" with "the daughters of men" made the cup of antediluvian impurity overflow, and one tremendous deluge destroyed the whole race, one family alone excepted. But though a world is drowned, and only one family saved, still in it are all the seeds of human depravity, and the remembrance of the sins of a former world.

God makes a new covenant with Noah and his offspring—of which one is selected as the root of blessings to the new world. Time rolled on, and families are formed and multiplied. A distribution of the earth was about being made; and, it seems, the whole family of man engaged themselves in the plains of Shinar, in constructing one new bond of union, in raising up one tower to heaven, in opposition to divine revelation from God. The Lord descends; in the style of metaphor, the Lord descends —frowns upon their toils—divides their speech, and sets them all adrift; scattering them according to their families, their nations and languages. This was the schism of schisms.

God had said that he would bless Shem—that he would enlarge Japhet, and curse Canaan, for reasons which, to his wisdom, were all just, righteous and merciful. Shem was, however, made the depository of the promises of the world's redemption. The Lord God of Shem is the Benefactor of our world; and our eyes are directed to him as the hope of the race.

From this family God raised up, called and separated, Abraham ; made him the father of nations, and of the Messiah ; cut him off from all the world by circumcision, making him a pilgrim for life. He gave him new promises, and confirmed with him " the covenant concerning the Messiah." Time advanced. Four hundred years of discipline and various misfortunes, fitted his posterity for a new dispensation. The Lord sent Moses, and led them out of Egypt—conducted them into the desert—made of them a wonderful nation—supported them by miracle for forty years, and threw such a hedge around them as, methinks, ought to have kept them a separate and distinct people, pious and devout above all people, and for all generations. But, to preserve unity, he gave them but one mediator, one grand national covenant, one altar, one law, one tabernacle, one high priest, and one common inheritance ; all of which was given to them in one book—the book of the covenant, or constitution of Israel.

A strong foundation was thus laid to preserve unity of faith, feeling, and action in this one grand national family. Time rolled on through four centuries of judges, until the age of kings came—until, in the days of Solomon the wise, the nation gained its zenith glory, and still preserved its ancient institutions, all of which were firmly established by this great prince in one august temple, the most magnificent building ever erected by the hand of man. Judah reigned. David, the son of Jesse, was its first king ; Solomon the second; and then came the weak, and foolish, and tyrannical Rehoboam. Then came the great schism in the symbolic and picturesque nation—the many-tongued schism, replete with much instruction to all the world. It is the grand national schism, whose whole history is not yet fully written. For the sin of David, God rent the kingdom in part from the house of David, and gave almost ten tribes to Jeroboam the son of Nebat, " who made Israel *to sin.*"

This cunning and potent rival of Rehoboam, from motives profoundly political, machinated a grand schism in the established worship, in order to produce an abiding schism in the affections of the people. He reasoned thus: So long as the people worship at one altar, through one priesthood, and in one temple, they will naturally coalesce again in one commonwealth and serve one king. Such was the philosophy of Jeroboam, and all history has proved it true. He therefore made new places of worship, on the plea of convenience and expediency ; and had two golden calves cast and finished ; one for Bethel, sacred from the days of Jacob ; and one for Dan, at a convenient distance. Instead, then, of going up to one altar, one temple and one high priest, to worship God and commune with their brethren, they heretically set up for themselves—and thus alienation and strife commenced. Again we see, on a larger scale, and for a longer continuance, falsehood, heresy, schism and persecution, marching in copartnery through the land of Israel, until, in one rencounter, *more than a million of warriors are slain in a single day!*

This was the era of *state religion;* and it was the era of *false gods, false altars and false worship.* Golden calves are easily converted into idols ; and mercenary priests will serve at their altars, under the smiles of an approving monarch. But what was the consequence? The kings of Israel were a wicked dynasty, and the people, though in tribes almost four to one, in some two centuries were reduced to slavery, and carried out of their own country, and never since have been gathered. So ended the schism of Jeroboam, and those who with him united around the schismatic altars that he had reared.

The land of Canaan and the sceptre continued, with the true altar and temple, in the families of Judah and Benjamin, though a small number of tribes worshiped there ; and although often chastised for their follies, they were never abandoned till the Messiah came and set up his institution among them.

Let us now collect these facts and views together, and give them their true and proper significance and emphasis. We have seen in all these schisms, from that of Satan down to that of Jeroboam, the true nature, character and consequences of schism. When we have before us the victims of all these several schisms grouped together ; Satan and his angels —Cain and his posterity, down to the deluge—the Babel builders and their nameless misfortunes—the national schism of Israel and all its untold calamities—methinks, we have a lesson, the clearest, the most forcible, and the most appalling that could be given to mortal man. He that doubts the connection between schism, rebellion, persecution and murder, is not to be rationally convinced by human power. Christianity contemplates the obliteration of all these schisms. It contemplates the completion of one great family, gathered out of all families ; built upon one grand foundation, having one temple, one altar, one law, one faith, one high priest, one spirit, one inheritance. *Every thing in it is unity and community.* It contemplates one nation, out of all nations ; one people, out of all people; one Book, one law, one Savior, one worship, one Judge and one heaven, as the only means of rescuing man, and saving him from the numerous and various misfortunes and calamities, that one grand schism has entailed upon our world, for thousands of years past, and for an eternity to come.

Now, in tracing out this glorious scheme of Heaven, we discover that God has been consolidating and harmonizing our race upon one faith and one hope ; upon a few simple, well-defined, and strong principles ; and that he has regarded as treasonable every defection from them, stamping upon every apostasy the clearest, broadest, and most enduring marks of his fiercest indignation. In every age ignorance, cruelty, and persecution have followed in the train of schism ; so that we doubt not, could any one trace all human miseries to one common and prolific fountain, that fountain would be religious discords.

Hence we infer that those modes of exhibiting and teaching christianity, and those modes only, which accord with these important and fundamental views—which seek to discover to man the true centre of attraction, to reconcile man to his God and to his fellow-men, by obliterating and annihilating every cause of division, every source of discord—are most acceptable to God, most sanctifying to the church, and most persuasive and

4 E

converting as respects the world. Some grand fundamental principle, harmonizing all human hearts, uniting all souls, and preventing all rivalries, jealousies, and envyings, must be projected, in order to this glorious consummation.

That grand principle, whatever it be, must possess the sanction of divine authority. It must have more to commend it than the mere rationality, beauty, and simplicity of the scheme. It must have a paramount, a Divine authority. Nothing addressed to human genius, to fancy, to imagination, to mere reason, will ever command the admiration or acquiescence, or the conscience, or the love of man. God in Christ must be perceived, regarded, and felt as the author of any scheme or system that contemplates the union, harmony, and co-operation of all the christian profession. It must have the awful, sublime, and adorable sanction of the King eternal, immortal, and invisible, to it. It must have his sign manual, and the seal of supernatural power and grandeur.

The fact that all synods, councils, and convocations are, by Protestants, acknowledged to have erred, will forever stain the pride of all their boasted glory, impair their authority, and convert their wisdom into folly. Whenever the time comes for the one fold, the one shepherd, and the one holy and beloved brotherhood, to combine all their energies in the holy cause, they will as certainly reprobate all human devices, and rally on the identical ground originally consecrated by the feet of all the apostles. If, then, there is to be any millenium, any thousand years of triumphant christianity before the Lord comes, these systems must all be abjured, and men must place the church exactly on the ground, the identical ground, on which she stood at the beginning. This was my first, and it is my present capital objecion to all partizan schemes, that they are not made for man, but for one class; not for all ages, but for one age; not for all countries and climes, but for some one latitude of humanity. They are not adapted nor framed for the human race. Now, the New Testament is just that very sort of document; and it is the only one that ever was, or is, or evermore shall be. It can make of discordant sects what it once made of Jews and Gentiles, one new man, slaying the enmity and making peace.

Christianity, allow me to reiterate it again and again, in all its pristine characteristics, is directly and supremely adapted to the genius of human nature; not to the people of one quarter of the world, of one race, or of one age, but to all quarters of the globe, to all races of men, and to all the ages of time. It takes hold of man with the grasp of omnipotence, because it contemplates him at once in the light of his whole destiny, as he was, as he is, and as he must hereafter be. Its philosophy of happiness is the subordination of all our passions, of all our desires, and all our volitions, to the will, and pleasure, and dictation of Jesus the Messiah. It proposes a glorious leader, a mighty and triumphant prince, as our chief, as our captain and commander; whose charms and accomplishments are so grand and fascinating, as to attract the admiring eyes and enraptured hearts of the true aristocracy and nobility of the universe.

Men must have a leader. The genius of humanity calls for it. Christians cannot have a human leader. They must have a *Divine leader*. Leaders, rather than creeds, make parties and keep them. So Paul understood the matter when he said, " One says, I am of Paul, and I of Apollos, and I of Cephas, and I of Christ," &c. Satan made a party in heaven; Cain made a party; Nimrod made a party; Cæsar made a party, as well as Jeroboam, son of Nebat, who made Israel to sin. Leaders are first in making parties, and creeds are second. Attachment to the man generally precedes attachment to the principles—the leader while he lives, and his principles and views when he is dead. There is much more truth in the adage " *Men and not principles*," than in that which says, " *Principles and not men.*" I presume he is the wise man who goes for both " *Principles and men.*"

We would not presume, on such an occasion, to give the history of attachments to human leaders, originating the present parties. But this we may say, that if any one will be at the pains to read the history of creeds and councils, with this idea in his mind, he will find that, nine times in ten, in the history of the church, and often in the state, attachments to men's persons precede attachments to abstract principles. True, indeed, that principles and their parties are so often identified, that we more frequently contemplate them together than apart: so it comes to pass, that one says, I am of Calvin, and I of Luther, and I of Wesley, and I of Christ.

Seeing, then, that things are so, and have worked so, in all the records of the past, we have long since resolved to guard against schism, and all the causes and occasions thereof, by calling no man on earth master, or father, or leader; and by acknowledging one teacher, the Messiah—one another as brethren in him. United in him, we stand for ever; alienated from him, we fall into everlasting ruin.—[*Time expired.*

*Saturday, Dec. 2—*11½ *o'clock, A. M.*
[MR. RICE'S NINTH REPLY.]

MR. PRESIDENT—It is true, that Paul complained of false brethren gaining admittance into the church in his day, and leading many astray. But there is one very great difference between the church of my friend, Mr. C., and Paul's church. If errorists and unworthy men entered Paul's church, *they were obliged to creep in unawares;* but Mr. C. receives them, when they openly avow their errors, provided only that they will call them *opinions.* They need practice no concealment in order to enter his church. He has a door wide enough to admit them with all their errors. Such was not Paul's church; and such were not Paul's principles. There is, therefore, no similarity between the two.

I am willing to award to the gentleman due credit for his candor in exposing the condition of his church; but I am not sure, however, that he was not rather more influenced by a desire to alarm them, and thus to induce them to come into his measures, than by his extraordinary candor. He could prevail on them to organize on his constitution, instead of the New Testament, only by showing them, that they were on the borders of anarchy and ruin! He thinks, that if I had been in his place, I would have concealed these evils. However that might be, I incline to the opinion, that he would better have followed the advice given to one of his brethren, who had divulged the state of things in a particular church. The church numbered about *two hundred* members. A very respectable old gentleman, one of its members, in conversation with one of our ministers, happened to express the opinion, that of the two hundred, perhaps *twenty-five* or *thirty*, judging by their lives and conversation, were truly pious. He was arraigned and tried for slandering the brethren. But on his trial he said, his mind was changed since he made the remark and his opinion was, that there were not more than *four* or *five* who were pious! Finding him not inclined to retract, the preacher said to him— " Well, brother, if you think thus badly of us, don't tell our enemies. If general Jackson had told Packenham his weak points, he'd never have gained the battle of New Orleans. Brother, don't tell Packenham." The gentleman has told Packenham his weak points, and he cannot wonder if they are noticed.

Neale, he says, is endorsed by Presbyterians, and is placed in the hands of candidates for the ministry. Hume's history of England is often placed in the hands of young men; but we do not endorse all that he has written. Neale's is a valuable history; but we do not endorse every thing he wrote. His judgment was doubtless sometimes swayed by prejudices.

The fact is—Presbyterianism was never actually established by law in England; and, therefore, Presbyterians had not the power to persecute. Yet the gentleman says, persecuting laws were enacted by the very men who made the Westminster confession. This is not correct. The confession was drafted by a body of learned and godly ministers, called together by parliament. They were not members of parliament. When they had agreed upon a confession of faith, embracing an outline of the doctrines and truths of the Bible, their work was done. The objectionable laws, of which the gentleman has spoken, were not made by them.

The gentleman does not deny, that the Anabaptists persecuted, and were guilty of many acts of violence, though they had no creed; but he says, *pure* immersionists never persecuted. This may be true. It is also true, that those whom he calls pure immersionists, never had the opportunity to persecute. Whether they would have persecuted, if power had been in their hands, or whether their sufferings had taught them to respect the rights of conscience, I pretend not to determine. It is enough, however, as an offset to the gentleman's argument, to prove the fact, that some of the most terrible persecutors have been men without a written creed. No creed ever led to persecution, unless it embraced persecuting tenets. I have called on the gentleman to point out one intolerant principle in our confession. He has not attempted it. Its principles are of precisely the opposite character; *so that no one who truly embraces them, can persecute.*

Mr. C. charges us with persecuting his church by misrepresentation and slander—the only way, he says, in which men in this country can persecute. If misrepresenting and caricaturing the principles of men be persecution, then is he the greatest persecutor of the age! He has published against the clergy, of all denominations, multitudes of charges which are not true, and which, therefore, he cannot possibly prove. I do not say, that he knew them to be false; but I do say, they are not true. And, so far as our church is concerned, he is the less excusable, because we have a creed which presents clearly our principles, and with which he professes to be familiar. But in his church he has told us, that all sorts of doctrine have been preached by almost all kinds of men. I can scarcely think it possible to slander a body of people who have amongst them persons holding all sorts of doctrine; for, though it might be slandering some of them to charge them with holding almost any one doctrine, yet, since all sorts are held by one or another among them, we cannot but represent some of them correctly. By the way, I desire to see the Presbyterian paper, referred to by the gentleman, which represents our church as a *stripling of Rome,*

Pedobaptism, (the old subject again,) the gentleman says, brings a great deal of *carnality* into the church. I should think that such men as Dr. Thomas, the Materialist, would cause his church to abound in carnality; for he makes men nothing but carnality, except their *breath!* Yet he and his followers and adherents have for years remained in connection with Mr. C.'s church! But, as I have before remarked, I am prepared, at any time, to compare churches with him, both as to soundness of faith and purity of life.

Mr. C. has been laboring to prove, that human creeds are necessarily heretical and schismatical. His course of argument in his last speech was truly singular. He commenced in heaven with Satan, the first heresiarch and schismatic. But did Satan prepare a creed, and induce the angels to adopt it? If not, how does this case of schism prove that creeds are necessarily heretical and schismatical?

The second schism mentioned by the gentleman, was in the family of Adam. Here Cain was the schismatic; but had he a written creed? He was also a persecutor; but, so far as my information extends, Cain had no creed. If my friend has ascertained that he had a creed, the argument will be pertinent; but if he has not, it is against him.

The third schism, he tells us, was at the tower of Babel, where God confused their tongues, and the people were scattered abroad. Was this schism caused by a written creed? No: the Lord confused their language. According to the philosophy of Mr. C., the most effectual means of separating them, would have been to give them a creed.

Some have supposed that their language was confused, not by causing them to use words not before known, but by confusing their minds in regard to the meaning of the words before employed; so that, if one called for a brick, another would bring him a trowel. If he called for a trowel, a hammer was brought. Thus they used the same words, but gave them entirely different meanings. Whether the confusion was caused in this way, I pretend not to decide; but, seeing the endless confusion in Mr. C.'s church, caused precisely in this way, I am the more inclined to think the theory correct. Thus all, for example, call our Savior "the Son of God;" but this language one understands to teach that he is God, equal with the Father; another, that he is a super-angelic creature; and a third, that he is a good man. All use the same language, but attach to it different and even opposite meanings! This looks very much like Babel.

The next schism mentioned by the gentleman, was that caused by the apostasy of the ten tribes of the Jews under Jeroboam. Did Jeroboam write a creed, and compel them to adopt it? Here we have another great schism where there was no human creed. Mr. Campbell commenced with the rebellion in heaven, and mentioned every important schism that occurred amongst the people of God during four thousand years; *and not one of them was caused by a creed!* Yet his object was to prove, that human creeds are necessarily heretical and schismatical. But instead of this, he proved conclusively that there have been many schisms, where there were no creeds. How, then, I ask, does it appear that the schisms in the christian church were caused by creeds? The gentleman has proved just the opposite of what he intended, viz: that heresies and schisms are to be ascribed, not to creeds, but to other causes.

He says, the Savior gave his church but *one faith.* What does he mean by one faith? They who have one faith, of course believe the same important and essential truths. In his church, one believes in a Sa-

vior, who is " the mighty God;" another, in a Savior who is only a creature. One honors the Son, even as he honors the Father; another honors, or dishonors, him as a creature. One believes that he died to
atone for our sins; another, that he died to cause men to repent. One believes, that the wicked will be turned into hell, and punished forever; another, that they will be taken to heaven, and made forever happy. Have all
these *one faith*? Far, very far, from it. Yet this is the unity in the gentleman's church!!! I can prove, and I will do it before this discussion
closes, that the different evangelical denominations have more unity of faith
—are nearer together, than these modern reformers are to each other.

Partyism, says the gentleman, arises from attachment to *some chief*
or *leader*. He never said a truer thing. But if partyism comes from
attachment to a chief, it is not caused by creeds. The Westminster confession was not made by a chief. We are, it is true, sometimes called
Calvinists; but although we believe that Calvin was a great and good
man, whose views of divine truth were generally correct, we have never
adopted his Institutes as our creed, nor do we believe all that he taught.
For example, he contended that John's baptism was christian baptism,
but Presbyterians believe no such thing. We have no chief.

In the days of the apostles there was no human creed, and yet there
were parties formed. One was of Paul, another of Apollos, a third of
Cephas, and a fourth of Christ. The gentleman has almost saved me the
trouble of offering further arguments against his proposition. He began
in heaven, and gave us some account of all the important schisms down
to the christian era; and it appeared, that no one of them was caused by
a creed. Yet his object was to prove, that human creeds are necessarily
heretical and schismatical.

I will now offer another argument to prove, that the principles advocated by Mr. C. are wrong. It is this: *He has himself radically changed
his ground, since he commenced his reformation.* He began with maintaining, that the New Testament is abundantly sufficient to guide the
churches in faith and practice, without any articles of faith, or rules of
church government, drawn up by men. Yet, as I have proved, he has
actually drafted a constitution of some six articles, and offered it to his
churches, as a basis of a general organization! The churches have not
received it; and many consider him, in offering such a constitution, as
palpably inconsistent with his published principles. If time permitted, I
should like to read several extracts from the Christian Baptist, (pp. 25,
73, 531,) where the gentleman contends, " that every such society [indi-
vidual church] with its bishops and deacons, is the highest tribunal on
earth to which an individual christian can appeal; that whosoever will
not hear it, has no other tribunal to which he can look for redress."
" That an individual church, or congregation of Christ's disciples, is the
only ecclesiastical body recognized in the New Testament—is the highest
court of Christ on earth:" " that wherever they [the churches] form a
quorum, and call for the business of the churches, they are a popish calf,
or *muley*, or a harmless stag, or something akin to the old grand beast
with seven heads and ten horns:" " that every christian community must
settle its own troubles—NO APPEAL FROM ONE CONGREGATION TO ANO-
THER." Yet, in the Millenial Harbinger, he contends most earnestly,
that the right of prayer is not more natural, nor necessary, nor expedient,
than the right of appeal;" that " there is no government, or state, or family, that can subsist without it;" that " every church that departs from

the faith, or from the discipline of Christ's kingdom, or that unrighteously or unwisely administers its affairs to the great detriment of individual members, a particular congregation, or the whole church of Christ, must be tried by some tribunal;" that "if any one or more of these churches err from the faith, or from the discipline, or from a just, impartial, and christian administration, they are amenable to the rest, and will be judged some way or other, and disallowed."—(New Series, vol. v. pp. 38—47.) This is approximating the true principles of church order. But whilst individuals, in his churches, may claim the right of appeal, *there is no tribunal to which they can appeal.* Our church has a very great advantage over his. We claim the right of appeal, and there are tribunals regularly constituted, to which every member may appeal; and no minister or private member can be finally excluded from our church, until the general assembly of the whole church has heard, and decided upon his case, if he choose to bring it before them. Thus the rights and immunities of individuals, and of particular churches, are as completely protected, as in the nature of things they can be. The difference between Mr. C. and us is, that he admits the right and the absolute necessity of appeals, but cannot exercise that right; we claim the right, and have an organization that secures the exercise of it.

I desire, now, to present one more argument very distinctly. It is this: *After all the gentleman's declamation against creeds, his churches actually have a creed.* They have not adopted the constitution he offered them, but still they have a creed. It is short—containing *two articles*, the substance of which is—1st. That immersion only is baptism; 2nd. That infant baptism is not to be tolerated. They will receive no one into the church who has not been immersed, and they will not permit their members to have their children baptized.

But in having such a creed they are most inconsistent with their own principles. They have proclaimed to the world, that they go by the New Testament alone; that they pretend not to judge of men's opinions; that they require those who wish to unite with them, only to say, that they believe Christ to be the Son of God, and are willing to be baptized. They do not profess to take the New Testament, as Mr. Campbell interprets it; nor as each little church interprets it; but as each individual understands it. Now, suppose I should take the gentleman upon his own principles, and apply for membership in his church. He would ask me, 'Do you believe that Jesus Christ is the Son of God?' I answer in the affirmative. He would ask again, 'Are you willing to be baptized?' I answer, I have been baptized. Will he receive me? He will not. He demands that I shall be *immersed.* But I understand the Scriptures to authorize the administration of baptism by pouring or sprinkling; and I solemnly believe, that I have been scripturally baptized. But Mr. C. and his friends say, 'We understand the New Testament to require *immersion;'* and they positively refuse me admittance into their church, unless I will take their opinion concerning this matter. I must be baptized again to accommodate them. Now, I ask, are they not seeking to impose on me their opinions? Are they not making their opinions a term of membership in the church? Does not their creed operate as effectually to exclude believers from their communion, as any other creed on earth?

Again, I wish to have my children baptized. They tell me I cannot be permitted to do so. But I understand the Bible to require it. They tell me, they do not so understand it; and I must go by their interpretation. Do they not again make their opinion concerning the meaning of the Scriptures, a term of communion?

Now, observe how much greater importance is attached by Mr. C. to external ordinances, than to the fundamental truths of christianity. Even the *mode of applying the water* in baptism is made more important than the true character and work of Christ. Here comes a man asking admission into his church, and declaring his opinion that Christ is not equal with the Father—that he did not exist from eternity. So believes Barton W. Stone: yet they receive this man as a christian brother, if he will be immersed, and will not have his children baptized! The same individual declares his belief, that Christ died only to cause men to repent, not to meet the demands of God's broken law. Still they receive him. Another comes and declares his belief in the doctrines of Universalism. They will take him, if he will call his error an opinion, and will not propagate it!

Now, I ask any thinking man to say, whether the mode of applying the water in baptism is more important than the character and work of the Son of God. Mr. C. will not admit a man into his church without immersion, even though he would call his views concerning sprinkling an *opinion;* but he will receive those whose opinion is—that Christ is a creature!!! He will allow those to enter his church, who rob Christ of all his glory; but he will not receive one who would diminish, in the slightest degree, the quantity of water to be used in baptism! He will permit men to enter his church, who deny that Christ bore the punishment due to our sins; and affirm, that he died only that, by witnessing or hearing of his sufferings, men's hearts might be melted and brought to repentance. He will permit them to take away the glorious foundation laid in Zion, on which the church stands; but he will not allow me to diminish aught from the quantity of water in baptism!

Is it true that God has revealed so much more clearly the mode of baptism, than the true character and work of his Son, that men may deny the latter with impunity, but must hold the former on pain of excommunication? Has he not distinctly and emphatically required " that all men should honor the Son, even as they honor the Father?" And has he not added, " He that honoreth not the Son honoreth not the Father which hath sent him?" John v. 23. But does not the gentleman make it more important that men should be *immersed*, than that they should honor the Son of God, as he has commanded, and trust in his glorious work of atonement, as it is exhibited in the Scriptures?

Again, Mr. C. will receive into his church those who avow their belief, that the wicked, as well as the righteous, will go to heaven. Is it possible that the mode of baptism by immersion is so much more clearly revealed, than the eternal punishment of the wicked, that we may safely deny the latter, but must hold the former, or be excluded from God's kingdom?

Does not the gentleman and his friends attach wonderful importance to an external ordinance, and a strange insignificancy to the character and work of the glorious Redeemer? Is this the faith taught in the Bible? Do the inspired writers so exalt the mode of baptism? Do they so disregard the character and work of the Son of God—the foundation laid in Zion? Is a union founded on such views truly *christian union?*

I will offer but one more argument against the proposition, that human creeds are necessarily heretical and schismatical. It is this: *There is more real christian union amongst Presbyterians, Methodists, Cumber-*

land Presbyterians, Congregationalists, Baptists, and other evangelical denominations, than there is among these modern reformers. These denominations, I mean to say, have more unity of faith—are much nearer to each other in their views of the great doctrines of christianity, than the reformers are to each other. If the time shall ever come, when the Methodists, or any one of these denominations, will deny that Christ is God equal with the Father; or that he bore the punishment due our sins; or when they will admit to their communion and their ministry men avowing such opinions, we will bid them a final adieu. We will never again acknowledge them as christian brethren, or hold christian fellowship with them. There is an infinite distance between the most exalted finite being and the infinite and eternal God. There can be no comparison between *finite* and *infinite;* between *creature* and *Creator.* How can two persons, whose faith is infinitely different—who build on foundations as unlike as the creature and the Creator—walk together? How can it be said with truth, that they have " one Lord, one faith, one baptism?" How can they be said to receive the same gospel? No—should any one of these denominations so exalt the mere mode of an ordinance, or the ordinance itself, and so disregard the character and work of Christ, we will never again acknowledge them.

With them all we agree in the essential doctrines of christianity. They believe in the fall and total depravity of man; and so do we. They believe in the doctrine of the Trinity, and in the divinity of Christ, and the personality and divinity of the Holy Spirit; and so do we. They believe that Christ died for our sins, bearing them in his own body on the cross; and so do we. They believe that regeneration by the special agency of the Holy Spirit, is absolutely essential to salvation; and so do we. They believe in the resurrection of the body, and eternal rewards and punishments; and so do we. They call on men to believe, repent and obey all God's commands; and so do we. These denominations differ on some points of doctrine and church order; but they agree in holding the great doctrines of the gospel, which are essential to a compliance with the conditions of salvation.

Every system of truth has its fundamental principles, which are essential to it; and minor points, in regard to which those holding the same system, may differ. The Newtonian philosophy has its fundamental principles, which are believed by all who hold the system. But there are many points connected with it, concerning which they do differ. This is true, also, of the sublime system of truth revealed in the Scriptures. Every truth is important in its place; but the knowledge and belief of every truth is not essential to salvation. Evangelical denominations are united in holding every doctrine which the Scriptures make essential to a compliance with the conditions of salvation. They can, therefore, pray together, and rejoice in each others' success in extending the knowledge of Christ and his glorious gospel; and they can truly thank God, that they are united in their efforts to make known to the heathen " the unsearchable riches of Christ ."

The real difference between Mr. Campbell's church and the evangelical denominations, so far as christian union is concerned, is this: He and his churches have union in *name,* and radical disunion in *fact.* We have different denominational *names,* but union in *fact.* We have " unity of faith,"—they, unity in name. There is, I repeat it, vastly more real christian union—union in faith—amongst the evangelical denominations, than amongst the reformers themselves. We are actually nearer together, than they are to each other. We agree in faith more nearly with Methodists, Baptists, Episcopalians and other evangelical denominations, than Dr. Fishback with Mr. Campbell. Mr. C. believes, and has labored to prove, that baptism is necessary in order to remission of sins. Dr. F. denies it. Dr. Fishback avows his belief in the doctrine of total hereditary depravity. Mr. Campbell denies it. [Mr. C. It is not so.] I will read an extract from his *Christian System*, that the audience may judge whether it is so, (pp. 29, 30:)

"Still man, with all his hereditary imbecility, is not under an invincible necessity to sin. Greatly prone to evil, easily seduced into transgression, *he may or he may not yield to passion and seduction.* Hence the difference we so often discover in the corruption and depravity of man. All inherit a *fallen,* consequently a *sinful* nature; *though all are not equally depraved.* Thus we find the degrees of sinfulness and depravity are very different in different persons."

Dr. Fishback says, all men are so totally depraved, *that they have no power, either natural or moral,* to avoid sinning, or to help themselves out of their deplorable condition!

Here are Mr. Campbell and his committee of four prominent preachers, who have come up to war against us; and yet it is a fact, as I have fully proved, that they differ from each other more, concerning the great doctrines of the gospel, than we differ from the Methodists, the old Baptists, or any other evangelical denomination! We are nearer to each of those bodies, than these gentlemen are to each other! We are infinitely nearer to each other, than Mr. C. professes to be to B. W. Stone, or to any of his members who deny the divinity of Christ, or the eternal punishment of the wicked. Yet the gentleman calls on us to give up our union, which is *real,* for theirs, which is *merely nominal!* Call not on us to abandon our creeds, which serve to show us how near we are to each other, and to promote christian confidence and co-operation, to enter a body, where the most important truths of christianity are compromised and sacrificed for a name; where, in the awful name of God, all sorts of men are preaching all sorts of doctrine. Alas! for such christian union! I have formed a far higher opinion of christian union. I rejoice in believing, that the church of Christ is really and truly ONE; that all of whom it is composed, do hold the head, Jesus Christ, and do maintain all the fundamental doctrines of the Bible. They have *one faith;* they build on the same foundation, and constitute one spiritual temple.—[*Time expired.*

Saturday, Dec. 2—12 o'clock, M.
[MR. CAMPBELL'S TENTH ADDRESS.]

MR. PRESIDENT—It is, sir, a painful task to have to respond to such a speech as you have just heard. For many years, sir, I have been accustomed to hear addresses upon all sorts of subjects, and from almost all sorts of men; but such a tissue of misrepresentation and abuse, from any one professing piety, I have not heard in all my life, so far as my present recollections testify. It is too, sir, to be called an argument!! Argument!!! If this be logic, argument, rhetoric, religion, or morality, I confess I know not the meaning of those words. If this be a fair, honorable, and christian discussion of principles—of great sectional divisions of thought and language, I do acknowledge myself to be unacquainted with the signs of ideas and the elements of things literary or moral. I will, however, sir, in my usual calmness, endeavor to make a few remarks upon the more prominent topics of abuse.

The gentleman commenced by telling you of his views of the difference between the reformation for which we plead, and the character of the primitive church; alledging, that while certain errorist and improper persons crept in among them unawares, we, knowingly, willingly, and designedly, take them in openly! That is to say—that when immoral persons, and those avowedly erroneous in the grand fundamental points of religious faith, present themselves for admission, we receive them, as Universalists, Arians, Unitarians, &c. &c. only on condition that they will be immersed! I ask, is not this the impression the gentleman would make upon your minds; are not these the views he seeks to communicate to your understandings in the speech which you have just now heard! As truly, as honestly, he might say, we open our churches to Mahometans, Mormons, and infidels! Yes, sir, there would be just as much truth in the one imputation as in the other. His allegation, sir, to speak in the mildest terms, is without fact, without authority, without any sort of evidence—written, spoken, or published, by any man belonging to our community. We disclaim the whole as imputations most unjust and ungenerous—as the distorted imaginations of his own bewildered head.

It is one of the distinguishing characteristics of our pleadings for reformation, that our press has always been open to our enemies. From the 4th day of July, 1823, till now, I have conducted a printing press which has issued a volume every year, and a number every month, without a single failure; and, sir, those volumes are filled with communications from our enemies, to speak in sectarian style, as from our friends. I believe, sir, mine is the only press in this nation that has systematically and undeviatingly given both sides on every question, and opened its pages to all sorts of opponents—Romanists, Protestants, infidel or sectarian, provided only he paid a decent regard to the laws of grammar and politeness. I believe, sir, I may go farther and say, that my periodical was the first and the only religious periodical in the world which has pursued that course. They were, in those days, all pledged to some creed or party—all one sided. I have been shut out of all their pages. They dared not to admit my essays. They feared to let their readers hear from me on those subjects which they were inculcating. To those very persons that shut us out, we have tendered them page for page, line for line, word for word in our volumes. Some of them have accepted, some of them have declined. We have then, sir, nothing secret, nothing clandestine. We have called for investigation, for documents, arguments, and evidence. On our pages all parties have been heard and responded to, so that our constant readers are the most intelligent persons in the religious world. They know both sides. What, may I ask, is the augury of this? Does it omen the fear of light, or the love of darkness? Indicates it the fear of man, or the consciousness of truth and its eternal strength? Is this the way that conscious error or weakness intrude themselves upon the public ear? No, sir. No, fellow-citizens, you know it is not. You cannot, with all your various and multifarious modes of thinking, imagine a course more creditable, more just, more candid, more honorable before heaven and earth than the course I have pursued, for the last twenty years, in conducting this great discussion of principles. We impute to no man, to no party, principles that they disavow. We fearlessly open and avow our own. We say to every man—hear, examine, judge, and decide for yourself. Every distinguishing principle of this reformation has passed through an ordeal of the most fiery discrimination. And, sir, as soon will the arm of mortal arrest the rising sun, or stop the planets in their course, as any mind stay the progress of truths that have been so clearly spoken by prophets and apostles, and that have passed through such a burning furnace unscathed and unimpaired.

What you have just heard from my opponent is not true. It is a fabrication—the whole of it, sir. I have never received a Unitarian, nor a Universalist, *as such*, knowing them to be such in the common acceptation. It

is easy to put a false gloss upon any thing, even sometimes without designing it. A fool's cap may be put upon the head of a wise man. It is easy
to be witty, too, without much wisdom, and to arraign opinion against
faith, and faith against opinion. We, however, have no such contrast nor
difficulty, because we never have both faith and opinion on the same
subject.

Should I hear a man say, that he thinks all men will ultimately be holy
and happy, I respond, the Scriptures do not say so. The Scriptures positively say—"They that know not God, and obey not the gospel, shall be
punished with an everlasting destruction from the presence of the Lord and
the glory of his power." He says, I admit all that; I believe it will
be just so with the wicked, but I do not think it will be eternal, absolute
duration without end. Well, your *think so* and your faith may be at variance; but the word of the Lord must be acknowledged and taught, and
only on that ground can I fraternize with you. Suppose, then, he accede to
this proposition, and thus renounce the inculcation and *belief* of that opinion, is he a Universalist? Mr. Rice has used and eulogized saint *Origen*,
and some other saints who, like him, abjured eternal misery. Does he not
know, that Origen, his own learned, eloquent saint Origen, was of the opinion
just now quoted! Among the ancient fathers, Greek and Latin, and amongst
the moderns, I could bring up many scores of them, in full communion with
the orthodox, as Sabellian, as Universalian as any of the persons ever were
to whom allusions have been just made, if time and prudence would authorize the digression. But I neither choose nor need to run that race. The
gentleman knows, that many of our greatest and best men have taught and
practiced upon this principle, and sometimes actually entertained the
very tenets which both he and I reprobate as unscriptural and dangerous.
It is, sir, all for effect the gentleman thus manœuvres.

But, sir, I feel myself standing in the midst of a great community. I
disdain any thing and every thing but fair, manly, candid and honorable
discussion. I know how this community already feels, and will feel, upon
this subject, when it is all laid before them. I have had no respondent.
We have never met in the field of fair debate, of fair and manly discussion
and argument. Not a point has been canvassed in a way like debate, except a portion of the first question on *baptizo*. I was frequently admonished that I must come here prepared for another sort of work and defence,
than that implied in those propositions; that I should need other weapons
than logic, and the Bible, and good sense. I could not yield to it, believing
that the self-respect of those who selected Mr. Rice for their champion,
would not dishonor their profession before the face of all men, saints and
sinners. I begin to see there was some truth in the prediction. I proposed to meet any honorable antagonist selected by the denomination on
fair logical, scriptural ground, believing that our views had not yet been
fairly heard in much of this community. Many thousands have had their
ears turned away from us by the most gross and palpable misrepresentations. The gentleman cannot secure his hold upon many of this class but
by misrepresenting our real views and practices. I once said to a Presbyterian minister, my neighbor in Virginia, who I thought occasionally misrepresented me: Sir, I learn that you have proposed to preach a few sermons to your people on infant baptism. "Yes, sir;" said he, "the times
seem to require it." Well, said I, do they not all believe that doctrine?
"O yes, O yes; they all believe it," he rejoined. Well, said I, we have a
church here that does not believe it, and you would likely do more good
by preaching a few sermons to them on the subject; and in the mean time,
while you occupy our desk, I will occupy yours, if you please; and in a
neighborly way deliver as many discourses to your people on believer's
baptism. "Ah, sir," said he, "I do not think that would suit just quite
so well."

No, Mr. President, that course does not suit quite so well. But, sir, it always suits me very well. I will freely make exchanges of this sort any where, every where. We are not afraid that our brethren either read or hear the other side of this or any other question.

A person may so often, and for so long a time, misrepresent the views of another, as to mistake his own misrepresentations for the truth itself. It is in this way, and only in this view of the subject, that I can excuse much that has been said, and more that has been insinuated, on the present occasion. Nay, this state of mind, when perfected, condemns in advance of evidence. For example :—It came in my way the other day to advert to the fact that a respectable minister of the Lutheran Reformed church, on the weight of the evidence adduced on the subject of immersion, was so fully convinced of the truth as candidly and promptly to obey and honor the Lord, by being immersed into his death. How, let me ask, did the gentleman advert to this fact? In substance he said :—" Aye, there are many persons now-a-days, who, tired of the narrow way of truth, prefer the broader and smoother way of going to destruction !" Is not this the fair construction of his remarks on that event? Such was the charitable construction put upon the character of a gentleman and a minister, concerning whose moral character he knew just nothing at all. Now I ask, was it comely, was it honorable, was it christian-like, and worthy of the standing of Mr. Rice with this community, to thus arraign, before an immense assembly, the motives, and to reprobate the character, of an unoffending, a conscientious and highly respectable christian minister; whose credentials and standing are just as respectable as that of Mr. Rice or any other minister of his age in this assembly! It was well for this intrepid, conscientious, and exemplary brother, that he happens to have at his command honorable testimonials, both from Union college, New York, and from the theological seminary at Gettysburgh, Pennsylvania, and of his connections ecclesiastic in this state up to the present hour. Yet no sooner is this fact announced here than the sectarian breath of invidious misrepresentation would blast his fair reputation, and consign him to the society of those who apostatized from the way of righteousness into the much frequented path of ruin !! " Yes," says Mr. Rice, " there are many who are seeking a broad and easy way to ruin !"

And still worse, in the next sentence of this defamatory speech, the gentleman has said, we cannot be misrepresented in this latitude and in this age. Fellow-citizens, do you know your neighbors and your fellow-citizens, with whom you daily converse? Look around you ; can you accord with such calumnies as these? Have you not lived long enough with us to know that our views, our principles, and our proceedings can be misrepresented—most wantonly and perversely misrepresented? There are few men, that a truthful man would say, on proper reflection, cannot be misrepresented. Have you not heard them much misrepresented on the present occasion? When shall this savage warfare against us have an end? Are there no boundaries, no limits, to the tongue or to the pen? If we are thus to be perpetually maligned and opposed by such weapons, and such means, we desire to know it. I did not expect such gross misrepresentations of views, and tenets, and persons, and practices!

In his allusions to my remarks on schism, the gentleman knows he is not within a thousand miles of the point. I was defining schism by the facts and documents which the Bible furnishes. I was developing its workings by the details of those most fearful schisms, of such tremendous results and consequences, as to involve innumerable masses of intelligence in all manner of wretchedness, temporal, spiritual, and eternal. Our Savior has informed us, that Satan apostatized from the truth. This is a clear indication that there was truth propounded ; that Satan was once in that truth ; that he proposed something else, and united upon that with other spirits ; and thus made a party, which, when consummated by some overt act of disloyalty, caused his excommunication from the heavens. This was, in-

4 F

deed, the original schism, and in every great point of analogy, comes up to the ecclesiastic schisms, in consequence of creeds, oral or written. Creeds are nuncupative, as well as written. Hence they have made divisions before any of them was formally written out. Their being written is only necessary to give them permanency, and more extended sway. They are, however, as powerful to divide before, as after written. The creed system was just as well developed in the first, and in the last, of that series of ancient schisms, as it was at Nice, or Rome, or Constantinople, under the christian dispensation. In Jeroboam's time, the established creed had the golden calves of Bethel, and of Dan, and a priesthood ordained by law, as its symbol. It was a *rival* principle against the one Divine ritual, high priest and Mediator That is the great point in them all, the essential and characteristic point—THEY ARE RIVAL SYSTEMS. I care not whether the articles be one or one hundred. They are, one and all, in essence and form, *rival* institutions. This great fact the gentleman seems to have forgotten, or overlooked. Every schism, from that of Satan down to New Testament times, and since, has been a rival institution to the one set up by God; and, therefore, they are all the same in essence, spirit, and tendency; obnoxious to the displeasure of heaven, and injurious to the peace and prosperity of Zion.

Our Savior was himself a great reformer; certainly the greatest that ever lived. " He came to his own and they received him not." Still, he went to the synagogue, and, as long as he lived, conformed to the usages and customs that were established in the nation and in the synagogue. I have ventured to say, that he was a regular reader in the synagogue of Nazareth. He went into the synagogue of Nazareth, and, *as his manner was*, stood up for to read. I need not say to this audience how he inveighed against the scribes, pharisees, and ecclesiastics, as we would call them, of that day. Did he, on account of the diverse theories of that age, abandon the temple or the synagogue, or any of the existing religious institutions? Did he not sit and worship in the same synagogue with Pharisee, and Sadducee, and Herodian? He did not, so far as they had any worship, or public institution of religion, abstain from them on account of those different and discordant theories. Although he sometimes severely inveighed against those same pharisees, scribes, and rulers, who sat in Moses' chair, he nevertheless frequented the ordinances, visited the synagogues, and commanded the people to listen to those men who sat on Moses' seat.

It is true he gathered around him a company of friends and disciples; but both he and they conformed to the Jewish institutions down to the moment of the last supper. His party was never regarded as a sect or a schism, during his life; neither were the disciples of John. In those days they did not make unity of opinion, nor oneness of theory the bond of union. A new institution they did, indeed, establish upon new principles, under a new, an entirely new dispensation of things.

My time will not allow me to do more than notice a few of the more prominent points in the last speech. A volume of such declamations may, indeed, be replied to in a few specifications. I should be glad, however, to expatiate upon them, severally, in detail. Meanwhile I have but one half hour more to speak, and as I have yet another new argument to offer, I shall in the first place, attend to it.

According to Mr. Rice, creeds are more needed and more used, as standards by which to measure the teachers, and as a test of ministerial communion, than for the common or private members of a church. Suppose, then, an Arminian minister sue for admission into the Presbyterian church, to become a member of that church, will they receive him and retain him, though sound in every thing but the single theory of Arminianism? This question answered, and we shall find a new proof that creeds, even as tests of ministerial communion and co-operation, are necessarily heretical and schismatical. If Presbyterianism has not changed, or the people called Presbyterians have not changed, and if the creed be not schismatical, will **Mr. Rice** explain to us how five hundred churches and sixty thousand members have been separated from the general assembly! Was not Arminian doctrine among the exciting, and moving, and efficient causes of this schism?

Some might imagine that such is the benevolence, and liberality, and christian charity of Presbyterians, that they would gladly unite with Methodists, Baptists, Episcopalians, &c. Why can they not unite first among themselves!? They would not, indeed, exclude those persons, if they will sit still and be silent. But preachers will not be silent; they must speak, and they must speak out their Arminianism, and their peculiarities; and the consequence will be, they will make a party. Then, indeed, the creed will be brought to bear upon them, and they will be cast out, as have been all other ministers, in all past time, down to the late five hundred non-conformists. I do hope the gentleman will attempt to show that the creed is not necessarily heretical in this case.

The gentleman, in his warmth and impassioned style, says I have written a thousand things that are not true. This is easily said. He might as well have said ten thousand; and then I could balance the account, by saying he had *said* ten thousand things that were not true, and that would be quite as logical a refutation!

Among other strange things, and new arguments urged by the gentleman, is the intelligence given us that there is much union and unanimity between Presbyterians, Methodists, Baptists, &c. Well, in truth I sincerely wish that all the Pedo-baptists would unite. I have often said, that they ought all to have united long ago. I think we are likely to be instrumental in uniting all these Pedo-baptist parties in one grand co-operation; and that, perhaps, upon a principle very like that which united Herod and Pontius Pilate, in days of yore. I say again, the whole Pedo-baptist denomination should form one great Pedo-baptist union. What is the use of ten kinds of Presbyterians, such as we now have in England, Scotland, and the United States? I earnestly desire that all these parties should amalgamate, coalesce, and be one; and that all the Baptists of all the earth would also unite and make one great party. Then we should have but two ecclesiastic armies in the field. Between them, then, the battle and the war would be; and that settled, the profession would be one and undivided; and is not that a consummation most devoutly to be wished?

And why can they not unite? They occasionally do unite. They make a truce of ten or twenty days, for the sake of great effect upon the community. They cry out, union and co-operation, for the sake of one grand campaign. They go into the field of action with a well understood stipulation, that they are not to preach their peculiarities during the truce; and at the end of the battle, they agree to divide the spoil, in as equal shares as the peculiar tastes of the new converts will admit. If this can be done in all godly sincerity and in all conscientiousness, for ten days, why not for a hundred—for a thousand—for life?

But, if all these parties unite in opposing us, we shall really become the greatest of reformers. If we, with no creed but the Bible, unite them all in one human creed, we will even then have done a great work. I think, indeed, that this is quite as practicable as to put us down. Nay, they will all unite before that point is gained. The more they oppose us, if we may reason from the past, the better. That system has been tried, and we are well pleased with the result. No combination can harm us. The elasticity of our principles and our efforts, will always be in the direct ratio of confederated opposition. For the sake of the truth, then, I desire union among ourselves, and union against us. We have eternal truths in charge—they cannot be overcome. Men may kick against the goads, but they will spill their own blood. They may fight against the Rock of Ages; but they will be broken to pieces. What millions of millions of mighty billows have dashed upon the rock of Gibraltar and yet it stands unshaken! What fierce tempests have burst upon its summit, and yet it stands unbroken! What mighty thunders have rolled over it, and lightnings played around it, and yet it is unscathed! So stands the man of truth, upon the rock of truth, while trusting in the God of truth, undaunted, unappalled, unconquered. So stand we, in the midst of this savage warfare, which to-day you have heard and seen, as strong, as sanguine, as confident, as when we first began—nay, much more so. We have heard the concentrated acquisitions of the whole party in opposition. This but reveals our strength, and stimulates our exertions. A thousand volumes of such abuse would only inspire more zeal, and invigorate our efforts in a cause of so much promise, and of so much honor to God and man. I am pleased to hear all that can be said against us. I hope that where there is any justice in the remarks, and even in the reproaches offered, that we shall all profit from them. If any of you, brethren, have given occasion to the adversary to speak reproachfully, you will, no doubt, stand admonished and corrected. Truth is truth, though an enemy say it; and sometimes we are indebted more to our enemies than to our friends.

Our principles, however imperfectly carried out, are now, I sincerely think, shown to be insuperable, invulnerable. They have long and often been assailed; but, like the pure gold, they have always came out of the furnace with brighter lustre. You have seen by what means they are now assailed—and that neither Scripture, nor reason, nor argument, can be offered against them.

Truth, my friends, holy truth, stands upon the Rock of Ages. It lifts its head above the clouds—above the stars. It communes with God. It holds sweet converse with the hierarchs around the throne of the Eternal King; with those elders, sons of light, and with the spirits of the mighty dead. It is the bright effluence of the bright essence of the uncreated mind. God spoke, and Truth was born. Its days are the years of God. Embodied in the Word of God, it came down from heaven and became incarnate. It is, therefore, immortal, and cannot be killed. It will survive all its foes, and stand erect when every idol falls. No one knows its gigantic strength. It has been often cast down, but never destroyed. For ages past, it has been gathering strength and preparing for a mightier conflict yet, than time records. It needs no fleshly wisdom, nor worldly policy, to give it power or gain it victory. It is itself redeeming, soul-redeeming, and disenthralling. It has passed through fire, and flood, and tempest, and is as fresh, as fair, as beautiful, and as puissant, as ever. I feel myself peculiarly happy in being permitted, in being honored, to stand up for it, when most insulted and disparaged by its professed friends. He that defends it, feels the strength of mountains, as though girded with the everlasting hills. It gives him more than mortal strength, and enlarges his benevolence wide as humanity itself.

I am sorry that I have been so much disappointed in the promise of an honorable, high-minded, and dignified investigation of its great principles. But, though assailed with unbecoming rudeness, it cannot be destroyed. It is self-preserving and recuperative. Conceived in the bosom of everlasting love, its aspirations are to its native heaven. Light and fire, earth's purest elements, are but the shadows of its glory. The tongues of lambent flame that sat upon the heads of the apostles, were but indicative of its irradiating and consuming potency. But its language is that of love, of purity, and peace. It reviles not again. Hence, those holy men that heaven commissioned to promulge and to defend it, spake it in love, and in meekness, while their lips were hallowed, and their tongues were touched with live coals from the altar of Jehovah.—*Time expired.*

Saturday, Dec. 2—12½ o'clock, P. M.

[MR. RICE'S TENTH REPLY.]

MR. PRESIDENT—I have observed, from the commencement of this discussion, how much better my friend, Mr. Campbell, succeeds in declamation and exhortation, than in argumentation. The very best speeches he has made, are those in which he has ceased to argue the question before us, and delivered eulogies on truth in general. Truth, we all admit, is, in value, above all price; and we believe and teach, that it is mighty, and will prevail. But the question is, *what is truth?* Mr. C., in all his declamations, assumes that it is with him; but we also profess to hold and to love the truth. But what, I ask, have these pretty eulogies on truth to do with the question, whether human creeds are necessarily heretical and schismatical? I admire the beauty of the gentleman's speech; but the logic of it is, indeed, poor. It has no bearing on the only point at issue. We want *argument*, as well as pretty speeches, handsomely delivered. He seemed about to commence an argument, but flew off at a tangent, and soared aloft amid the sublimities of truth in general.

His starting point was indeed sufficiently low. He began by telling, as usual, how painful it is to respond to such a speech, as you had heard, a tissue of abuse and misrepresentation. I say again to the gentleman, that he cannot excite me. I never have been excited in debate; and he will utterly fail to throw me off my guard. He is at liberty, therefore, in his closing speech, to say just what he pleases. A dozen such epithets as he has repeatedly used, will fall powerless as empty air.

He denies receiving Universalists into his church. Well, whenever he denies a fact which I state, I will certainly prove it true. I read, on yesterday, from one of his own books, a declaration, that he would receive Universalists, if they would agree to hold their errors as opinions, and not propagate them; and I proved from the Millenial Harbinger that he had actually received a Universalist preacher, Mr. Raines, who declared that on that subject, his sentiments remained unchanged. What is Universalism? It is the belief that all men, righteous and wicked, will be saved. Against this doctrine, Mr. C. has contended zealously; yet he received a man as a preacher of the gospel, who declared openly his belief of it. I will here take occasion to read Mr. Raines' statement concerning his position and belief, when received into Mr. C.'s church: (Mill. Harbinger, vol. i. p. 390:

"At the Mahoning Association, about five months after my immersion, I was publicly questioned relative to my sentiments; and from a bench on which I stood, I did not hesitate to declare to the whole congregation, that it was still my opinion that all men would finally become holy and happy. This fact can be proved by scores of witnesses."

This is an extract of a letter from Mr. Raines; and he informs us that, when questioned concerning his views, he did not hesitate to declare to the whole congregation, that it was still my opinion, that all men would finally become holy and happy—that he was still a Universalist in sentiment; yet Mr. C. charges me with slandering him, when I state this incontrovertible fact!

In regard to Barton W. Stone, I desired him either to admit or deny that he is a Unitarian. Let me again read an extract from a letter of Mr. Stone to Mr. Campbell, in which he condemns Mr. C.'s apparently Trinitarian notion, and avows openly his Unitarian faith; (Chris. Bap., p. 379:)

"If these observations be true, will it not follow undeniably, that the *Word* (di'hou) by whom all things were made, was not the only true God, but a person that existed with the only true God before creation began; not from eternity, else he must be the only true God; but long before the reign of Augustus Cæsar?"

Mr. Stone, you observe, positively denies that Christ is the only true God, or that he existed *from eternity.* But if he existed not from eternity, there was a period when he began to exist. Did he then create himself? This, no one believes. Then he was created by God, and is as truly a dependent creature as any angel in heaven! Mr. Stone, therefore, makes the Savior a *creature.* I care not whether he considers him a super-angelic creature or a mere man. The difference is not worth contending about; for there is an infinite distance between the most exalted creature and the infinite Jehovah. These Universalists and Unitarians have been received into the gentleman's church with open arms; and yet he says, I abuse him and his church, when I state, and prove from his own books, these incontrovertible facts!!!

To show his great love of truth, and his impartiality in giving to all a fair hearing, he states that he has opened his columns to free discussion; but that the editors of the "sectarian" papers have refused him a hearing in their columns. Reformers, who originate new notions, or revive old ones, I believe, are generally anxious to engage in controversy; and, for the sake of getting their notions into other papers, are willing to open their own to discussion. But editors generally, I presume, were not particularly interested in the gentleman's discoveries; and their readers, satisfied with the faith they had, did not wish to see them. They might, therefore, with propriety, decline filling their columns with such discussions; even though they were not afraid of the light. Recently, however, you have had the opportunity of seeing a written discussion between myself and the President of Bacon college, which was published in the Presbyterian paper.

But I think the gentleman must, in all candor admit, now and hereafter, that "the clergy" are not so much afraid of the light, as he had imagined. If they had been, you would not have seen me on this occasion, as the opponent of the champion of this reformation—a man of no inconsiderable learning and talent—one of the first debaters of the day—who has been, for *thirty years*, debating the precise points embraced in this discussion. When I was in a country school, learning the first rudiments of an English education, he was becoming known as a reformer and a man of war! I am happy, on this occasion, to give to the public evidence the most conclusive, that we fear not the light, nor tremble to meet the champion of this reformation of the 19th century! I am one amongst a thousand. He is the leader, and is admitted to be the strongest man connected with his church. Yet we feared not the contest.

But he says, his friends told him he needed not argument to meet me, but something of a very different character. He seems, indeed, to have believed what they told him, if we are to judge by the amount of argument compared with *something else*, which he has abundantly employed. I have always observed that men, when sinking under the weight of arguments they cannot answer, are likely to resort to the means of defence adopted by the gentleman; but I do not remember to have seen any one descend to such abuse, so long as he had any thing in the shape of arguments to offer. He seems, indeed, to have been, from the beginning, anticipating a defeat; for he told us the other day, that on reaching Lexington, he had made particular inquiries concerning the editors of the city. He was quite apprehensive that they would give out a bad report of his success. I made no inquiries of the kind, perhaps because I did not expect to be defeated; and I supposed that the editors were gentlemen, and would publish nothing contrary to fact. Finding no danger to be apprehended from the editors, his imagination filled the city with men under Presbyterian influence, running to and fro, manufacturing public sentiment, and cheating the people out of their wits!!! All this may pass for what it is worth. It is understood.

Another evidence of his magnanimity and love of truth, is found in the fact, which he stated, that he had insisted on a Pedo-baptist minister preaching in his pulpit, on infant baptism. We care not to go into his pulpit; but we are happy to have the privilege of meeting him here, where he is under no restraint from the rules of courtesy, but is fully at liberty to expose our arguments, if he can.

But the gentleman is quite offended at my remarks in allusion to a young Lutheran preacher he has immersed. The case, I knew, was brought up for effect; and therefore I stated, what we all know to be a fact, that there is a class of roving preachers who go from church to church, as they may find inducements. With these floating gentry, changes are easily made. Their *principles* are not in their way. But it is but right that it should be known, that this gentleman has not been converted by the power of Mr. C.'s arguments on this occasion; for he himself stated, an evening or two since in a sermon, that he had for some time entertained his present views. So I learn from the very best authority.

But the gentleman deprecates this *savage warfare*, which consists, in part, in stating important facts, and proving them from his own writings. Yet he has long been accustomed to charge upon the clergy of all denominations, the most heinous crimes, without one particle of evidence. Did you not hear him, on yesterday, attributing to them the basest principles? Did he not assert, that, *for money*, they would compromise or abandon their principles, and unite in one body? It is perfectly right in his eyes, that he should be permitted to abound in such unproved charges; but it is out of the question that I should state *facts*, and prove them by his own writings! Let me give you another specimen of the mode of dealing adopted by the gentleman. In his Christian Baptist, (pp. 166—168,) I find an infidel publication, entitled *"The third Epistle of Peter, to the Preachers and Rulers of Congregations.—A Looking-glass for the Clergy."* This publication, the work of some scoffing infidel, is headed by Mr. C. with the following remarks:

"One of the best proofs that a prophecy is what it purports to be, is its exact fulfillment. If this rule be adopted in relation to the "Third Epistle of Peter," there can be no doubt that it was written in the true spirit of prophecy. We thought it worthy of being preserved, and therefore have given it a place in this work.—*Ed. C. B.*"

I read from this document a single extract, as follows:

"'In all your gettings,' get money! Now, therefore, when you go forth on your ministerial journey, go where there are silver and gold, and where each man will pay according to his measure. For, verily I say, you must get your reward.

"Go you not forth as those that have been sent, 'without two coats, without gold or silver, or brass in their purses; without scrip for their journey, or shoes, or staves;' but go you forth in the good things of the world.

"And when you shall hear of a church that is vacant, and has no one to preach therein, then be that a call to you, and be you mindful of the call, and take you charge of the flock thereof and of the fleece thereof, even of the golden fleece.

"And when you shall have fleeced your flock, and shall know of another call, and if the flock be greater, or rather if the fleece be greater, then greater be also to you the call. Then shall you leave your old flock, and of the new flock shall you take the charge."

This is but a specimen of this miserable document, which the gentleman dignifies as a prophecy which has been actually fulfilled. He thinks nothing of making, against the ministers of the Gospel, of all denominations, charges like these. I have frequently observed, that those persons who are most fond of throwing out "railing accusations" against others, are most impatient when the truth is told concerning themselves.

Christ, the gentleman says, was a great reformer. It is true. But he never did admit to his church those who denied his Divinity and his atonement. Moreover, he excommunicated the whole Jewish nation, who refused to receive him in his true character, and thus he made what the Jews called a great *schism*. And they charged the schism upon christianity about as correctly as the gentleman has charged certain other schisms upon creeds, and confessions of faith.

He asks, whether the Presbyterian church would retain, in its communion, an Arminian preacher. We differ on several points from our Methodist brethren; and whilst we can sincerely acknowledge them as christian brethren, and their ministers as christian ministers; and whilst we can occasionally preach with them, we, and they, believe, that we can labor more harmoniously in different organizations, than if thrown into one body. It would not be wise to have these United States thrown into one consolidated government. It is much better, under existing circumstances, that each state shall have its own constitution and peculiar laws; while the whole forms but one general government. Perhaps Mr. C. would think it wise to have all the state constitutions abolished. The twelve tribes of Israel journeyed together in great harmony towards the promised land, yet each retained its distinct organization and its appointed place. So the different denominations of christians, so long as there are differences in some important points, will co-operate in the general cause more harmoniously, by retaining each its separate organization.

But the gentleman thinks he has succeeded in producing among "the sects" a new kind of union—a union between Presbyterians and Methodists, and others, which heretofore has not existed. So far back as my acquaintance with Presbyterianism, in this country, extends, our church has always acknowledged the denominations called *evangelical*, as constituting a part of the church of Christ. It is true, we cannot unite with Unitarians, Universalists, and such gross errorists, and all profess to preach the same gospel. It is the peculiarity of Mr. C.'s church, that it can unite things diametrically opposite, and have men preach the gospel, who deny its fundamental doctrine. This, however, is not *christian union*.

Having now duly noticed all the small matters which constituted the gentleman's speech, I wish, in the way of recapitulation, to present before your minds the whole ground over which I have traveled in the discussion of the question before us.

Let us remember distinctly the point at issue. The question before us is not, whether any particular creed is good or bad, true or false; nor is it, whether we have the right to force our opinions upon others. We all agree that we have no right to attempt to compel men to receive either the Bible or a creed. "God alone," says our confession, "is Lord of the conscience." In matters of religion, every individual must judge for himself, being responsible for his opinions and views only to God. Persecution in every form is abominable. This, then, is not the question.

But the question is, *whether human creeds are necessarily heretical and schismatical*—whether it is at all lawful to have a creed. This is an important question—especially so in Mr. C.'s theology; for the using of a creed, according to his views, amounts to *apostasy;* and he excommunicates and denounces all bodies of christians who perpetrate the awful crime of making a creed—of committing to writing an outline of what they understand the Bible to teach, and holding this epitome as a creed!

To determine whether creeds are necessarily heretical and schismatical; whether they are lawful or unlawful, I stated distinctly what purposes they are designed to answer.

I. They are not designed to be a *substitute* for the Bible, nor an *addition* to it. Our confession of faith commences with declaring that, "The whole counsel of God, concerning all things necessary for his own glory, man's salvation, faith and life, is either expressly set down in Scripture, or by good and necessary consequence may be deduced from Scripture; unto which nothing at any time is to be added, whether by new revelations of the Spirit, or traditions of men,"—that "the Holy Scriptures are the only rule of faith and manners."

II. Creeds are designed to be a public declaration of the principal doctrines and truths, which those who adopt them understand the Scriptures to teach. I have stated the fact, which Mr. C. has not denied, that it is impossible to know what a man believes, by the mere fact that he professes to take the Bible as his only infallible guide. Not because the Bible is either *obscure* or *contradictory*, but because men have perverted its language, and attached to it various contradictory and absurd meanings. The phrase "Son of God," as used in the Book, has a clear and definite meaning. It is intended to express the true and proper Divinity of Christ. But the Arians and

Socinians use it in a sense infinitely different. If, then, it be true, that we cannot know a man's faith by the fact that he professes to go by the Bible, it becomes very important that every denomination of professing christians should give a public declaration of the doctrines which they understand the Bible to teach.

1. It is necessary for the reformation of those who desire to become members of the church of Christ. I have said, and I repeat it, that no prudent man will join any society of people, and more especially a religious society, until he is acquainted with their principles; until he knows what are the great doctrines which they understand the Scriptures to teach. This information any one can give concerning the Presbyterian, the Methodist and other churches, by examining their creeds. Every one has thus the opportunity, not only of knowing what we teach, but of comparing our doctrines with the Word of God—the infallible standard, that he may determine whether he can conscientiously unite with us.

2. Creeds are also important for the information of other christian communities. All true christians desire to know and acknowledge all Christ's disciples; and, so far as they can, to co-operate with them in promoting the common cause. The question then arises: *Shall we recognize as christian brethren, as a church of Christ, a certain body of professing christians?* We cannot determine to acknowledge them, until we know their principles—until we know how they understand the Scriptures. The respective creeds of the different denominations afford the desired information. They show how near they are to each other in their views, and wherein they differ. They can thus determine whether they can recognize each other as christians, and how far they can harmoniously co-operate.

3. These public declarations of our faith also afford important information and instruction to members of the church; and serve to correct misrepresentations of our doctrines.

Can the gentleman offer any valid objection to a creed for these purposes? I asked him, in my first speech on this proposition, whether he would become a member of any church on their declaration, that they take the Bible as their infallible guide, without inquiring further into their principles. He gave me no answer.

I have also asked him, and I now repeat the question—*to what source of information would he direct a man who desired to know how his church, as a body, understood the Bible?* Would he direct him to the Bible? All profess to go by the Bible; but the inquirer wishes to know what his church, as a body, understands the Bible to teach. When this question was propounded to him by a man in England, he did not direct him to the Bible, but gave him a detailed account of his faith. Will the gentleman please to tell us where such an inquirer as I have supposed, would gain the desired information?

I know very well where I may ascertain what Mr. Campbell teaches; but where I can be informed what his church, as a body, teaches, I confess I do not know. Here we see his strange inconsistency. He has published his "Christian System," as he says, for the purpose, among other things, of "exhibiting a connected view of the whole ground we [reformers] occupy." Why did he not direct those who wish to know their whole ground, to the Bible? This would not answer. He felt constrained to make a public declaration of their faith.

But here is the difficulty attending this Christian System. It entirely fails to give the needed information. It informs the public what Mr. C. believes and teaches; but does his church, as a body, believe just as he does? *They do not.* Many differ from him on very important points. Then, I ask again, where shall we ascertain what his church, as a body, understand the Bible to teach? Is there any source of information on this important point?

III. Creeds, I have said, are designed to be a standard of ministerial qualification, as well as of the qualifications of other officers in the church.

57

The gentleman does not deny that those who become preachers of the gospel, ought to possess some qualifications. He does not deny that they are required to have some education ; that the Bible requires that they "hold fast the faithful word." He will not deny that they should give satisfactory evidence of possessing true piety ; nor will he deny that all churches are solemnly bound, and that it is their true interest, to see to it, that only those properly qualified, enter the ministry.

Now, it is a fact which I have stated, and which he has not denied, that the Scriptures, whilst they require the church to ascertain the qualifications of those who seek to enter the ministry, prescribe no particular method by which this should be done. We are, therefore, left free to select the method which may seem to us most wise, and best adapted to secure the object. Our church has deemed it wise to draw up and publish an outline of the system of divine truth, which we understand the Bible to teach, and by means of this creed to secure throughout the church some good degree of uniformity, not only in the faith, but in other qualifications for the ministerial office. Our responsibility to God, and our regard for the interests of the church and of the souls of men, alike forbid us to ordain and send forth as preachers of the gospel, men of whose soundness in the faith we are not satisfied, or who have not such qualifications as will make them "apt to teach." Quacks in medicine kill the body : quacks in theology kill the soul!

IV. Creeds, I have said, are not designed to be a condition of membership in the church. The pupil, on entering the school, is not expected to be as well instructed as his teachers. We require those who desire to enter our church, sincerely and intelligently to adopt the fundamental doctrines of christianity, and to give satisfactory evidence of possessing true piety. According to the Scriptures, there are certain qualifications necessary to membership in the church ; and other stronger qualifications to enter the ministry.

Now, I ask, where in the Bible is there a solitary passage that forbids the use of creeds for these purposes ? The gentleman has not produced one, and he cannot. I ask not for a text that says, in so many words, creeds are unlawful ; but I call for one which *by any fair construction* condemns them. He and his friends insist, that all who use creeds, are *apostates*, and are to be excommunicated. It behooves him, then, to produce the law against them.

He has told us, that there is in the Bible no command to make a creed. But is every thing unlawful, which is not directly commanded in the Bible ? Is everything not specially commanded, necessarily heretical and schismatical ?

He has said, that creeds are *fallible*. But is every thing unlawful that is fallible ? Then it is wrong to have fallible teachers. If we act upon the principle, that whatever is fallible, is unlawful, let us give up all fallible things. If the precept is sound in one case, it is so in all.

He has said, that making a fallible creed tends directly to produce schism. But I can prove, that the publishing of books, which were not creeds, has often caused schisms, even as extensive and mischievous as any ever produced by a creed. The truth is, schisms and heresies have generally originated with such publications, not with creeds. Creeds may *embody* error, but they cannot *originate* it.

He has said, creeds lead to persecution ; but I have stated, and proved, that some of the most abominable persecutions the world has ever witnessed, were instigated by those who had no written creeds. Such were the persecutions suffered by our Savior and his apostles, and by the primitive christians.

He has urged against creeds Paul's exhortation to Timothy, to "hold fast the *form* of sound words." But we take the Bible just as it is. We, however, take the liberty to say, and to write, what we understand the Bible to teach. Let the gentleman prove, if he can, that this is inconsistent with holding the form of sound words.

He brings forward the exhortation of Jude, to christians, to contend for the faith once delivered to the saints; but he cannot possibly prove, that when we hold and contend for the truths of the Bible, we do not contend for *the faith.*

He has told us, it is not lawful to make a *constitution* for the church. My reply is—that we have not *made* a constitution, but have only collected and arranged in a few chapters, the doctrines and principles of church order, taught in the Bible. This he cannot prove to be unlawful. How, then, does this objection prove, that creeds are necessarily heretical and schismatical?

He has said, there was no creed for the first two centuries of the christian era. But I have stated, and he has admitted, that during that time the church was overrun with error. Does not this fact rather prove the necessity of a creed clearly defining the doctrines of the Bible, and guarding against the admission of errorists into the bosom of the church?

I defy the gentleman to point to an instance in which a creed has produced a schism in a church; or in which a creed not containing intolerant principles ever produced persecutions. We have had our attention directed to a number of schisms, and a number of persecutions; but it is yet to be proved, that creeds produced either the one or the other.

In the commencement of the discussion of this proposition I pressed on the gentleman a question which I wish once more very distinctly to present, viz.: *What is the standard of ministerial qualifications in Mr. Campbell's church, as to education, soundness in the faith, and personal piety?*— [*Time expired.*

Saturday, Dec. 2—1 o'clock, P. M.

[MR. CAMPBELL'S CLOSING ADDRESS.]

Mr. President—I regret to see so little regard to truth and decorum manifested in reference to the gentleman immersed the other evening, whose case happened to be alluded to. It seems as though his very virtues were to be converted into faults, by the scowls of sectarianism. I did not know, till this moment, that he was in the house, to hear this most unjustifiable attack upon his reputation. He has just sent up to me the following note, which I beg leave to read:

" I never said, that I had not changed my course on the subject of infant baptism, since I have been here. Many of the sentiments held by the advocates of the reformation, I have long held and taught; but, on the subject of infant baptism, I have changed my course since I have been here, and in consequence of this debate. WM. R. MCCHESNEY."

I do hope, that a brother of such reputation in the community, and in a very respectable portion of the church militant, will be allowed to follow out his convictions of truth and duty, without being thus wantonly assailed.

The gentleman has given me a few things to note. He has adverted to the *regium donum* bond of union amongst Burgher and Anti-burgher Presbyterians. It is true that I made a remark, in reply to his remark, upon the powers of the confession to heal divisions, and to unite belligerent parties; upon its powers of consolidation, and harmonizing of discordant and disaffected brethren; and, by a fact of which he seemed to be ignorant, shewed that money had done what he supposed the Westminster creed had done! He does not seem thankful for the information; nevertheless, I will give him a little more on the subject. The Burghers, or Unionists, of America, were the most numerous party of the two, and most interested in the affair. They moved first, and sent off three ministerial delegates to wait on the parliament, to secure for the two parties, now united, (especially because neither could be gifted without the other,) the royal bounty. I remember, for it happened in my youth, to have heard them say, the Burghers were most active and most avaricious in the affair; and after they succeeded in getting the bounty, did not please the others with a fair division of the spoil. It so happened, however, in the course of divine Providence, that in about the space of one year, the whole three delegates died, without once having drawn their quota! Some of the disaffected hesitated not to call it a judgment from heaven upon them, for their dereliction of principle, and their unbecoming cupidity in managing the affair. The confession of faith had nothing to do with their union. It was *gold*, sir, and not *faith*, that harmonized them. I know, indeed, there are some few men who cannot be bought or sold. The gentleman's remarks, both upon myself and concerning others, were as uncalled for as they were inaccurate and invidious. I do not say, that all the priests or clergy were mercenary. Still, however, although there are some ministers that a mountain of gold could not buy over to an opinion, or an ignoble deed, the majority could be bought for a much less sum, as all history and all time have written. It is lamentably true, that venality has been the standing frailty of the priesthood in all ages. Hence, as the majority rules, I still opine, that if the whole community would withhold their *regium donum* until all the parties in this commonwealth, or any other, would unite; in a very few years they would be all of one heart and soul, in pleading a common cause. I do not wish to swell the union party, however, by such an acquisition, and am pleased to think that the friends of union will not be entrammeled with any such alliance.

To return to my last argument. When asked whether he would retain an Arminian preacher in his church, Mr. Rice, as you all saw, evaded the question; and taking the manner of his answer and the answer together, it is very obvious to you all that he would not retain him. The creed, indeed, calls for his expulsion, and Mr. Rice goes for the creed. Well, now, this excluded Arminian preacher (I mean excluded from the Presbyterian church,) will not be silent, when turned out. His opinions are now more sacred. He has been wedded to them by persecution, as he will call it. He promulges them, and makes a party. Are not these creeds, Mr. Rice himself being judge, heretical and schismatical? Every one, in this case, can see it. *And in this way all the Protestant parties began.*

If Mr. Rice's system is true, it is much older than he is. But not so much as you might suppose. He must have lived in the time of reformation. It must have occurred to him as well as to you, and to all persons that think that this boasted union and co-operation, of which he sometimes speaks, for the last ten or twelve years, is quite a new thing. Some think it is a good omen of the millenium. But the fact is, that it is an opposition union—a union got up to oppose us. It is a sort of holy alliance against a cause, for which they are too weak in detail. I repeat my wishes, that they may still more closely unite, and that they may in truth harmonize forever. We shall then have been instruments of harmony, and of much good.

Had I time, I could give you some amusing speculations of these saints, Origen, Augustine, Tertullian and Cyprian, by way of an offset to those figments detailed by my friend. But I have but a few minutes, and can employ them better.

I shall now give you a rapid sketch of the prominent arguments and points submitted in the development and confirmation of this proposition. I call them *arguments*, because used as such, though, because of the broad cast miscellanies of my friend, they were neither counted out, nor so formally discussed as I could have desired. Still, the half of them is more than enough for my purposes.

I beg your special attention to this grand preliminary fact so often stated, but not respected by Mr. Rice, that *written creeds* were the causes of all schism, or of all persecution. I never thought it, said it, or wrote it. They are the cause of much sectarian schism, when oral, and when written. Indeed, oral or noncupative creeds were the causes of persecutions and schisms before the era of written creeds, as we have shown. Alcohol has slain its millions, but it is not the only cause of death. Again, when I speak of creeds, I speak of them as *ecclesiastic* documents, set up as explained in my first lecture.

I. My first argument was, that they are without any Divine authority whatever. God commanded no one to make them, no one to write them, and no church to receive them. This argument has not been answered by any fact or example indicative of any such authority. And did Mr. Rice talk for an age he could not find one—not one *Thus saith the Lord*, for any synopsis, formula, or precedent of the sort. Had the apostles put any thing of the sort at the close of the volume, it would have been a satire upon the whole book. It would have been a sort of *labor-saving machinery* which the book does not sanction, or it would have been a sort of acknowledgment that the book was not well adapted in the aggregate to the wants of society. God intended that it should cost much personal labor, much reading, thinking, praying, searching, meditating, conversing about it. He intended to keep the mind of man much in company with himself, by giving him a book which he might read for a thousand years, and still find something new. I have sometimes said that a fortune left to a child is the greatest misfortune that can befall it. It almost universally proves itself to be so. Whatever lifts a young man's mind above the employment of his own energies—robs him of the employment and enjoyment of himself, and lets him down to ennui, or uselessness, or dissipation, or premature ruin. But hereditary orthodoxy is still a greater misfortune. That often ruins a man in his best interests, and always prevents him the pleasure of searching for the truth, of musing, reflecting, and acting for himself.

II. Creeds have often operated, and their tendency in time of defection is, to cast out the good, the intelligent, the pure, and to retain those of a contrary opinion. They are great strainers, which retain the lees and rack off the pure wine. They killed our Savior, the apostles, and prophets, the saints and the non-conformists of all the ages, since the days of Daniel the prophet.

III. They have generally been proscriptive and overbearing. This needs no demonstration.

IV. They are treasonable attempts to dethrone the liege king, lawgiver and prophet of the church. We are divinely commanded to *hear him.* He is the supreme head of all authority and power, and " *the Author and the Finisher of the faith.*" He must, then, regard all other authors of faith as rivals of his, else why substitute a fallible for an infallible!

V. Creeds are divinely prohibited by several precepts, such as—"Hold fast the form of sound words, which you have heard from me," says Paul to Timothy. Again, says Jude—"Contend earnestly for the faith formerly delivered to the saints."—"Hold fast the traditions which you have heard from us, whether by word or by our epistle." So Paul commands the Thessalonians; "This is my beloved Son, *hear him,*" &c. &c. These and such like passages, by enjoining the sacred Scriptures upon us, as the documents to be held fast in form, earnestly contended for, and submitted to, clearly inhibit all rivals, substitutes, summaries, and so forth. If they command to hear, Christ forbids a rival Lord; so does the command to hold fast the form of words, the traditions, the faith delived once for all to the saints.

VI. We desire to lay much emphasis upon this important fact, that the interval from the death of the apostles to the year two hundred, the purest, and most harmonious, united, prosperous and happy period of the church, had no creed whatever but the apostolic writings. It is admitted that there were plain declarations of faith made at baptism, but nothing formal or exed, either oral or written, for two hundred years. It is also admitted, that in the third century, men began to have oral creeds, and controversies about ordinances and observances, and that, therefore, before written creeds were issued, the very formulas discussed and commended began to produce heresies and divisions before the grand Nicene development. If Dr. Miller and Dr. Mosheim, Waddington, and many other such are right, the purest period of christianity was when they had the book and the book only. No creeds no parties, is as true as one faith one baptism.

VII. They necessarily become constitutions of churches, and as such, embody and perpetuate the elements of schism, from generation to generation. A society built upon a religious controversy is a sort of a commemorative institution, cherishing in the minds of those in succeeding ages those ancient animosities, and making them love and hate artificially and irrationally. In that point of view, the principle of attachment is not Christ, but an opinion.

VIII. As constitutions of churches, they are unfriendly to that growth in christian knowledge, and the development of the social excellencies of our profession, which, in the apostolic age, were presented by the voice of inspiration, as the paramount objects of christian attainment. By attaching the mind to the party shibboleths, they detach it from a free and unrestrained consecration of itself to the whole truth of God's book. They continually confine the mind to a certain range of tenets and principles, which have ac quired an undue and contingent importance; giving to thirty-nine or thirty three points a fictitious importance, and thus, in a certain sense, oblitera ting the proper distinctions between children, young men and fathers, in the christian church.

IX. They are unfavorable to spirituality. By presenting truth in the cold, anatomical, formulary outlines of speculative propriety, they call for a merely intellectual effort of the understanding, and touch not the moral feelings of the heart. Hence no one can be converted or sanctified through them. They are the mere mummies of the life-inspiring truths of the Bible, which breathe with living efficacy and the warmth of Divine love upon the soul. No one ever fell in love with a skeleton, however just its proportions, or however perfect its organization; and no one ever will fall in love with the anatomical abstractions of a creed.

X. They falsely assumed to be a proper exponent of Scripture doctrine; and to be plainer and more intelligible than the Bible. This is as derogatory to the honor of the Bible, as it is false in philosophy and fact. They are the veriest jargon of abstract terms, compared with the clear, intelligible and admirable simplicity and beauty of the christian and divine writings. Take the word *election*, or the phrase *Son of God*, as explained in the creed, and in the Bible, and can any one imagine a greater contrast in all that is plain, intelligible and beautiful? Is not the Spirit of God the Spirit of eloquence, of clear conceptions, and of appropriate, beautiful and sublime language? I would not believe an angel, if he stood before me, and presumed to improve the diction of the apostles and prophets. The Spirit of the living God is the Spirit of revelation, of all wisdom and utterance. We are always infinitely more safe under its guidance, than under that of any man.

XI. They have been peculiarly hostile to reformation, by ejecting godly and intelligent ministers of religion. This has ever marked their progress, from the days of the apostles till now. *All the great reformers of the world have been excommunicated persons.* No eminent religious reformer has ever been permitted to exercise his ministry in the church in which he commenced. They have always been cast out of synagogues, rejected and disallowed by the leaders of the people, and by their creeds.

XII. They are wholly superfluous and redundant, so far as the detection of either error or errorists is implicated. The greatest plea for them has always been their importance and utility, as the means of detecting heretics and heresy But this is wholly an assumption, without the authority of reason or of fact. The seven Asiatic epistles, addressed by the Lord to those ancient and renowned societies, are a thorough refutation of this pretence. To one of these societies the Lord says, " Thou hast tried them which say they are apostles and are not, and hast proved them liars," &c. If, then, pretenders of the highest grade were detected and repudiated by churches possessing only parts of the New Testament, without the help of creeds, who will say, that we, now-a-days, cannot try persons by the Bible, detect their aberrations, and inflict upon them proper punishment?

XIII. But finally, (as we cannot now fully make out all the points that came up in the course of the discussion,) they are obstacles, great obstacles, in the way of uniting christians. No man thinks that the world will ever be converted to Episcopalianism, Presbyterianism or Methodism, &c. &c.

All these denominations are the creatures of the apostasy. Christianity was before them all, and it will survive them all. *They must all perish.* Take from each of them its peculiarities, and christianity remains, so far as they possess parts of it. What all sects have in common may be christianity; but what they have in particular most certainly is not. They have all been long enough in the field to try their powers. They never can do more than they have done. They have prayed for revivals, and they make them, and have had them. They have changed their tactics as often as Laban changed the wages of Jacob. They have proved their entire inadequacy to satisfy the wants of humanity—their utter incompetency to convert the world. They are not suited to the genius of human nature, and must give place to something that is. That popular something is the pure and uncorrupt catholicity of original christianity, in letter and spirit, as inscribed upon these pages. These partizan institutions, built upon peculiar phrenological developments of human nature, must give way to the whole genius of human nature. We want a broader, deeper, higher, purer, more spiritual christianity than any of them. The world wants it, and christians pray for it!

Has not Presbyterianism been in this state since its commencement, some sixty years at least? Has not Episcopacy urged its plea for almost the same time? And what have they done? Presbyterianism, with all its experience, learning and powerful organization, its well-disciplined corps of officers, its seventy-five or eighty ministers, has now some eight thousand communicants; and the Episcopalians, with their learned and excellent bishop, and some twenty ministers, have something less than one thousand *bona fide* communicants. And what is our position? In something less than twenty years, with all our want of organization, experience, concerted action and concentrated enterprize, we have at this time some forty thousand members! How can this be explained, but upon the fact, that the original gospel adapts itself to the whole genius of human nature—while these peculiar casts of tenets, adapted to special developments of the human mind, are not in harmony with the wants and wishes of our common nature?

If the sects would sheathe forever the sword of partizan strife; if they would make one great *auto da fe* of all their creeds and shibboleths; if they would make one grand burnt-offering of their schismatical constitutions, and cast forever to the moles and the bats their ancient and apocryphal traditions, and then unite on the apostolic and divine institutions, the christian religion might be sent to the farthest domicil of man in less than a single age—in less than the life of one man.

Protestant England and Protestant America have, at their disposal, all the means necessary to send the gospel from pole to pole, and from the Thames or the Euphrates to the ends of the earth. They have men enough; genius, learning, talent, ships, books, money, enterprize, zeal, adequate to such a splendid scheme; if they would, in christian faith and purity, unite in one holy effort, on the book of God, to humanize, civilize, and evangelize all the brotherhood of man. The unholy warfare of this age is international, inter-sectional, inter-partizan. All the artillery—intellectual, moral, physical, is expended upon the little citadels, fortifications, and towers of partyism. It is a barbarous, uncivil, savage warfare against our own religion, against ourselves, against the common Savior, against the whole family of man.

For all these reasons, I pray for the annihilation of partyism, and of every thing that, directly or indirectly, tends to keep it up; and instead of these human devices, of which I have so often spoken, these ordinances and traditions of men, I plead for the Bible, and nothing but the Bible, as the standard and rule of all our personal and social duties; our bond of union, our terms of communion, the directory and formulary of our whole church relations—faith, discipline, and government.

Upon my memoranda of items deferred, I find a note on the subject of the Peshito-Syriac version of the New Testament. It is a matter of no great consequence at this time: yet it is worthy of record, with special reference to the use made of it on the first proposition. I had, during the time of that discussion, an indistinct impression that, inasmuch as the whole apocalypse was wanting in that version, with some passages in the gospel history, and some of the epistles, that Mr. Rice was mistaken in quoting it as the Peshito version of the passage in debate. Since, having been favored with the loan of his copy, I have examined it, and find that, as I conjectured, it is not the Peshito version, but a version made up from different sources, having borrowed the apocalypse, and the epistles of Peter and John, that are wanting in the Peshito, from some other source.

I find, also, some other matters noted for consideration, but time will not allow me to notice, out of a considerable variety, more than one or two. Of things unnoticed, there is nothing of essential importance. My answers to most of them would be, that they could either be retorted upon my opponent, or shown to be irrelevant. For example—Mr. Rice represents our communities, and their neighbors, as ignorant of our views, because they can find no authoritative exhibit of them; and that it is rather a leap in the dark for any one to join our societies, without something more than the Bible and the fugitive words of a preacher. Of course, the gentleman would represent it as quite different in his church. But if Dr. Wylie never found one Presbyterian, in thirty years, that believed it all—what then? If not one in twenty ever reads it at all; and if, of those who do read it, not one in fifty comprehends it all; and if not one in a hundred believes it all—wherein do they excel? If my own observations and acquaintance might be regarded as a safe data of comparison, my deliberate opinion is, that our brethren know more of each other's views, than Presbyterians know of each other's views—and the world around us know more of our views, in detail, than they know of those of the Presbyterians. Such, I say, are my convictions. But every man, in this case, will, of course, think and judge for himself.

But, my fellow-citizens, there is one point that cannot be too deeply impressed upon your minds—that the union of christians is essential to the conversion of the world, both at home and abroad. Now, as creeds foster, and keep alive, and transmit these parties, on this single account alone, they seem to me altogether worthy of a cordial reprobation. Where there is no contention, the fire of strife goeth out; and where there is nothing to contend about, contention itself ceases. Remove, then, these causes of contention; take God's own book; bear with diversities of opinion in things not revealed; and, as Paul says, "Let us walk by the same rule, let us mind the same thing;" and, to paraphrase his words, "if in any thing you be of different opinions, God will reveal this unto you:" for in this way only, could he invoke peace on them, and on the Israel of God.

You might, methinks, infer the utter impossibility of either converting or improving the world under the present aspects of Christendom. I have known Lexington and its vicinity for twenty years, and am of opinion that it was as nearly converted then as now. The same may be said of this whole commonwealth. Yet you have been praying for union, and for the conversion of the world, and have been getting up all manner of excitements for this purpose, during this period. Something is radically wrong. Why have not your prayers been answered, and your efforts blessed? Does not the Lord say that he desires all men to come to repentance, and to the acknowledgment of the truth, and to be saved! You are straitened and restrained in yourselves, and not by the Lord. He promises to open the heavens, and to pour out a blessing large as your desires, provided only you will obey him. Let us unite upon the ancient foundation. Let us cast away our idols, our human inventions, and meet around one common altar, and there bow our knees together in cordial union and co-operation; then the gospel will resume its ancient spirit and power, spread its holy influences far and wide, and bless your children, and your children's children, through many generations. In this way you will bequeath to them the richest inheritance, and embalm your memory in their grateful admiration and esteem.

Do you not see, how unavailing are all your domestic and foreign missionary efforts? How many lives have been sacrificed! How much treasure has been expended! and how little has been done!! You tell me that thousands have been converted; that many pagans have been brought into the christian profession. I might give you all you claim, and still prove that nothing has been done—that nothing can be done, worthy of the cause, while you are all divided at home. I will undertake to prove, from your most authentic statistics, that your divisions annually make more sceptics at home, than your missionaries convert abroad. Were you to claim for your missionary labors, during the last forty years, one hundred thousand genuine converts from amongst the heathen, think you, that amongst the "dedicated offspring" of the Protestant parties in America, to say nothing of Great Britain and the world, not more than one hundred thousand have gone over to infidelity!! Yes, more than twice as many are annually lost at home, through your divisions, than are saved abroad by all your exertions. Hold not up the word of promise to your ears; apply not the flattering unction to your souls, that the world is to be converted while your hearts are full of error, heresy, and schism. It cannot be. It is impossible. Jesus made the union of christians essential to the salvation of the world: "I pray," said he, "that all who believe on me may be one—that the world may believe that thou hast sent me"—that the world may be converted. Was Jesus mistaken!! Certainly he was, if you are right in thinking the world may be converted, whether you are united or not—whether you are one or divided.

The land is full of infidelity. Your schools, your colleges, are full of scepticism. The great majority of your educated men are infidels; some open and acknowledged—many only show it by keeping out of your churches. The reason is, the gospel is blasphemed by the discords, the variance, the hatred, and the strife engendered by your partyism. Abandon your sectarianism, meet on the holy Scriptures, and bear with one another's infirmities, and then pray for a blessing on your labors, and the Lord will pour out his Spirit upon you, and his blessing upon your offspring; and you "shall grow up as among the grass, and as willows by the water-courses."

Brethren, you have heard a discussion of sixteen days. You have engaged in the great work of reformation, personal, domestic, and ecclesiastic. You have now heard all the exceptions, cavils, and objections that, after much preparation and elaborate research, can be alledged against our cause, by a denomination whose means and abilities are equal to any other in the country. I need not tell you how impotent the strongest efforts are to assail any of our grand positions. Of all this you are perfectly competent to decide for yourselves. But let us now renew our strength, our ardor, our zeal, and our efforts against all partyism, and in support of the apostolic institutions—*the faith once delivered to the saints.* I never felt the truth more strong nor error more weak than now. We have commenced at the right place. The Acts of the Apostles—the three first chapters of that book, give us the pure beginning of our religion, and how unassailable we are there you all feel. To this great work I, in common with many of you, have been long devoted. In the retrospection of the past, we have much to be grateful for—"hitherto has the Lord helped us." In anticipation of the future we have much to hope.

Fellow-citizens—If there be truth in the Bible—and if there be not truth there, there is no truth anywhere—then is this matter supremely worthy of your candid, concentrated, and most devout examination. Your responsibilities are great, because your opportunities are equal to those of any people in the world. May I importune your impartial examination and decision on the testimony and evidence now in your possession? You are to judge for yourselves, and to act out a character in which your eternal destiny is involved.

I cannot sit down without expressing my admiration of the patient and long protracted attention of this immense assemblage, and of the general decorum and most exemplary behavior of an audience so numerous, so various, and so much interested in the mighty issues of the occasion; nor without commending you all to the blessing of the God of Abraham, of Isaac, and of Jacob, tendered to the nations through his beloved Son; may you all be enriched with that blessing now, henceforth, and forever!

[Addressing the moderators, Mr. Campbell said:]

Gentlemen, allow me to tender to you my sincere thanks for the very patient, impartial, and dignified manner in which you have presided over this discussion.—[*Time expired.*

Saturday, Dec. 2—1½ o'clock, P. M
[MR. RICE'S CLOSING REPLY.]

MR. PRESIDENT—I have but a single remark to make in relation to the individual whose name has been introduced by Mr. Campbell, as a convert to his views. Written statements have just been handed me by *five* highly respectable gentlemen, who went to hear that gentleman's sermon; and they all state, that they understood him distinctly to say, that nothing he had heard during this discussion had changed his views. It is, indeed, a very small matter. His opinion would weigh very little in the scale of public sentiment, concerning the merits of the debate.

Concerning the *regium donum*, causing the Burghers and Anti-burghers to unite, the gentleman has made a statement which, I presume, he would find it difficult to prove. He added, however, the general charge against the ministers in this country, that they are so destitute of honesty, that they would compromise their principles for money. He now says, it is a *common saying*, that the clergy are the most venal set of men on earth. It may be a common saying in certain quarters; but it is a base slander, no matter by whom it may be uttered. It is admitted that there have been, and that there are now, many unworthy men who profess to be ministers of the gospel; but the charge is preferred against them as a *class;* and, as thus made, I pronounce it false.

The gentleman presents what he considers a strong, matter-of-fact argument, to prove that creeds make *sects*, viz: that Presbyterians will not retain an Arminian preacher; and, therefore, men holding Arminian sentiments must form a sect. The Bible speaks not of all christians being united in one society, and having one *name;* but of their having one faith, holding the same great doctrines of divine revelation. The churches may possess all that is essential to the unity of faith, and yet so far differ as to render it expedient that they be ranged in different organizations. Even Paul and Barnabas once disagreed, concerning a question of expediency; " and the contention was so sharp between them, that they departed asunder one from the other," each taking the man he preferred as his companion. Still, they belonged to the same church. With our Methodist brethren, we agree as to all that is essential to the existence of the church, and the salvation of the soul. The fact that we so far differ, in some points, as to make it expedient to have different organizations, does not prove that we are not on the same foundation laid in Zion; or that we belong not to the same church. The great camp-meetings of which he speaks, had nothing to do with our union with evangelical denominations. Long before the gentleman's reformation was born, Presbyterians recognized the Methodists, Baptists, and other evangelical denominations, as component parts of the church catholic.

Origen, and some other of the christian ministers of the third and following centuries, it is admitted, fell into some serious errors. They lived in an age of prevailing superstition. The fact that they may have been pious, notwithstanding their errors, is no reason why men holding such errors should now be permitted to enter the ministry. But, as the gentleman did not specify the errors to which he alluded, a more particular reply is unnecessary.

He says, he has not contended that creeds are the cause of *all schism.* But has he produced one instance in which a creed has caused any schism? He has referred to not an instance, in which I cannot prove that the schism was produced by other causes. He has, therefore, failed to prove that creeds are necessarily heretical and schismatical.

He has told us that there is no command to make a creed; and that, if the apostles had appended a creed to the Bible, it would have proved it imperfect—that it is not sufficiently plain to be understood. And so does every sermon he preaches, and every page he writes. If the meaning of the Bible is as plain as it can be made, why does he attempt to explain it? The argument, *if we were to admit that creeds were designed to explain the Scriptures*, would be as conclusive against preaching and publishing explanations of them, as against making creeds.

Hereditary orthodoxy the gentleman considers a great evil. But I should consider hereditary *heterodoxy* an evil of much greater magnitude. If it is an evil to be taught from infancy to believe the *truth*, it is, to say the least, a much greater evil to be taught dangerous and destructive error. The catechism, he thinks, has done immense mischief. Does he not teach his children what he believes to be true? He is a singular father, if he does not. He certainly expounds to them the meaning of the Scriptures as he understands them. We do no more. Why, then, does he condemn us for doing just what he does? If he insists that we ought to change our views, we say the same concerning his. Some persons are opposed to giving children any religious instruction, that when they arrive at years of discretion, they may, without prejudice or previous bias, form their religious views for themselves. They reason quite as conclusively as does Mr. Campbell. His reasoning, if it be worth any thing, would prove conclusively that parents should give their children no religious instruction of any kind.

The gentleman has asserted and reasserted, that creeds cause persecution; but he has not proved, nor can he prove, that any creed not inculcating intolerant principles ever did cause persecution.

Nor can he prove his assertion, that the using of creeds is rebellion against Christ. He has asserted it, but he has produced not the slightest proof of its truth. There is no law in the Bible which can be construed to prohibit christians committing to writing an outline of the doctrines they understand the Bible to teach, for the purposes creeds are designed to answer.

Mr. C. asserts, that where there are no creeds, there are no parties. This is a great mistake. He has told us of a schism in heaven, another in Adam's family, and another at the tower of Babel, and several others, where there were no creeds.

Creeds, he says, become constitutions of churches. This objection has been fully refuted. But he affirms, that they are unfavorable to growth in knowledge. I am perfectly willing to test the validity of this objection by comparing the numbers of the churches that have creeds, with those of his church, as to their knowledge of the Scriptures, or of other subjects. I am disposed to institute the comparison, and let the facts speak for themselves. Stern facts prove his objection utterly unfounded.

Another objection he urges against creeds, is—that they are cold and lifeless, and are, therefore, unfavorable to *spirituality*. I do not understand the philosophy of this objection. I am unable to see why the truths of the Bible, when written in a book called a Confession of Faith, should become cold and lifeless. Again, I am willing to compare the churches that have creeds with Mr. C.'s church; and if we cannot show quite as large a proportion of eminently spiritual persons, as his church, we will abandon creeds. Let facts answer the objection.

He objects to creeds also, that they falsely assume to be exponents of the Bible. Not a whit more falsely than every sermon he preaches, and every page he writes. Let facts and his own practice answer the objection.

He has told you, that I have often said, that the phrase *Son of God* is not so well explained in the Bible, as in the confession of faith. I have said no such thing, but precisely the opposite. I have said, that as used in the Bible its meaning is clear and definite; but, as used by men of various classes and characters, it is not so. When a man professes to believe, that Christ is the Son of God, it is necessary to inquire of him how he understands this language; because men do employ it in senses infinitely different and opposite. Therefore, until he explains the sense in which he understands it, you know nothing of his real faith.

Another objection urged by Mr. C. against creeds, is—that they eject *conscientious ministers*. When a man in his church perseveres in preaching Universalism, does not he say, that he will exclude him? And does he deny, that a man may feel conscientiously bound to preach Universalism, or Unitarianism, or even Deism? Yet he professes to exclude all such, notwithstanding their conscientiousness. The objection, therefore, lies with all its force against his own principles.

The seven Asiatic churches, he says, excluded false professors without a creed. True; but did not John the apostle write seven epistles to them, directing and commanding them to exclude these errorists? If there were now inspired men living in the church, there might be no need of creeds; but the days of inspiration are passed.

He objects to creeds, because so long as they exist, the church cannot be united. But it is a fact, that in Ireland two denominations having a creed have been united, and now constitute the general assembly of the Presbyterian church in Ireland. In Scotland, the Burghers and Anti-burghers have become united. By their respective creeds the different denominations are enabled to compare views, and ascertain how near they are together, and whether they can unite and harmoniously co-operate. The tendency of creeds, therefore, is not to separate, but to unite those who agree in sentiment.

Mr. Campbell purposes to destroy all creeds; but what plan of union does he propose? He calls on us to unite with him and his gospel church. On what conditions are we to unite? We must unite *in the water!* He will meet us at no other point. We must adopt his *opinion* concerning immersion. We may differ from him on many other most important points; but we must, on this point, think as he thinks. He has the most exclusive creed on earth. So say B. W. Stone and Dr. Fishback. He objects to creeds, that they exclude from the church conscientious ministers. Are not Pedobaptists as conscientious as others? Yet they are all excluded by his creed!

He calls on us to unite; but he will not allow us to unite with him, unless we will adopt his opinions concerning the mode and subjects of baptism. He says to us, 'You have been baptized, as you think the Scriptures direct; but now please to be baptized in our way, and we will unite most harmoniously!' That is, in plain English, if all christians will consent to adopt Mr. C.'s notions, and join his church, he will unite with them most cordially!!! Why not all be Presbyterians! We believe that we are on the Scriptural foundation; and if the gentleman and his churches will become true Presbyterians, we shall be most happy to receive them. I might declaim, in this way, as plausibly as Mr. Campbell has done; but, after all, it is mere declamation. There is no argument in it.

He tells you how little Presbyterians are doing to convert men to christianity. But if we are to believe his statement, his numbers are greater than ours. Let me inquire, then, what are his churches doing? Have they any missionaries who have gone to preach to the heathen "the unsearchable riches of Christ?" Not one, so far as I am informed! Much importance as the gentleman and his friends attach to the Word of God, they have sent not an individual to make it known to the benighted heathen! Indeed, Mr. C. has stood up in opposition to missionary societies, and he has not labored without effect; for an individual in Mason county, Kentucky, whose letter is published in the Christian Baptist, wrote to him, saying—"Your paper has well nigh stopped missionary operations in this state,"—(p. 144.) Such has been the effect of Mr. C.'s principles. Presbyterians, though according to his statement not so numerous as his followers, have their missionaries in heathen lands, preaching to them the word of life. Other denominations have likewise their missionary operations. Now, who are doing most to extend to all men the knowledge of the gospel; those who have creeds, or those who reject them? I had occasion to state, on yesterday, that the gentleman complains of his people, that they do little or nothing to promote the general circulation of the Scriptures, either at home or abroad. Presbyterians, it is true, come far short of doing their duty; still they are liberal and active in this truly benevolent enterprize. Let facts speak on these subjects. They proclaim in language that cannot be misunderstood, and with an amount of ardor that cannot be resisted, the great superiority of the churches that have creeds over the no-creed church of my friend.

I was not surprised, (for no unfairness in debate, on the part of the gentleman, can now surprise me,) that he again introduced the mode of baptism, disposed of almost two weeks since, and made an attempt to relieve himself from the difficulty into which he was thrown, in connection with the old Peshito-Syriac version of the New Testament. He asserted most positively, not only in the discussion on the mode of baptism, but in his publications, that no translator, ancient or modern, ever did translate the word *bapto*, or *baptizo*, to *sprinkle* or *pour*. I proved, indisputably, that the Syriac, the Ethiopic, and the Vulgate, three of the most ancient and valuable versions, do translate *bapto*, to sprinkle, in Rev. xix. 13; and that Origen, the most learned of the Greek fathers, in giving the sense of this passage, substituted *rantizo*, to sprinkle, for *bapto*. The gentleman could not deny these facts. But now, at the very close of the discussion, he gets the Syriac Testament, and'attempts, even at this late hour, to escape from his difficulties, by telling the audience that the apocalypse is not in the old Peshito-Syriac version.

Now let me state a few facts. It is a fact, that the learned immersionist, Dr. Gale, quotes this very passage, and states, that the old Peshito-Syriac version here uses a word signifying to *sprinkle;* and he asserts, that it is so ancient, that it is almost of as high authority as the original. And here, he argues, there was a different reading. It was in reading his reflections on Wall's history of Infant Baptism, that my attention was turned to this fact.

Mr. Campbell. Dr. Gale does not say that it was the Peshito version.*

It is a fact, that Mr. Carson, the gentleman's judicious and profound critic, did not know that the translator had not all the authority given it by Gale, though he deemed that there was every evidence of a different reading.

The book I hold in my hand is the old Peshito-Syriac version of the New Testament—the oldest translation in the world, and one of the best. I have the edition published by Schaaf & Linsden, two eminent critics. At what time the translation of the apocalypse was made, I do not know; neither does Mr. C. It is, however, considered as of high authority by the ablest critics. The fact, that instead of *bapto*, the word in the original Greek, the Syriac has a word signifying to *sprinkle*, the gentleman does not deny. Nor does he deny, that both the Ethiopic and Vulgate translations also have words signifying to sprinkle, and that Origen did, in giving the sense of the passage, substitute *rantizo* for *bapto*. These indisputable facts prove most conclusively, that the assertion he has repeatedly published, that *bapto* is never translated to sprinkle, is not true. I hope the gentleman is now satisfied—as he has been permitted once more to violate the rules of this discussion, by introducing subjects after they have been disposed of.

He asserts, that there is not one Presbyterian minister in every score who believes the confession of faith. How DOES HE KNOW? He appeals to Dr. Wiley, who became disaffected and left our church. But such charges made against ministers of the gospel, require proof. [Mr. C. I did not say *preachers*.] I have stated, that we do not require the adoption of the confession of faith, as a condition of membership in our church. We do not expect the pupil, before entering the school, to be as well instructed as the teacher. The teacher we require to possess proper qualifications for his re-

---

* Mr. Campbell and Mr. Rice now agree to quote the identical words of Dr. Gale, for the benefit of the reader; as follows:—"I have likewise observed, that the *Syriac and Ethiopic* versions, which for their antiquity must be thought almost as valuable and authentic as the original itself, render the passage by words which signify *to sprinkle*."

sponsible work; and the private member we expect to grow in knowledge. I have, however, met with but few Presbyterians, who do not believe the doctrines of our confession of faith. Yet we do not excommunicate those who may have doubts concerning some of the less essential parts.

The gentleman has once more told you, that I denied that our Savior was buried. I denied no such thing. I said he was not put down into the earth, so that the plunging of a person into the water would resemble his burial.

Having now fully answered his speech, I will resume the recapitulation of my argument. I have said, that creeds are not designed to be either a substitute for the Bible, nor an addition to it; that they are designed to be a public declaration of the principal doctrines and truths which we understand the Bible to teach; so that those who desire membership in the church may be put in possession of the necessary information concerning our views; that other christian communities may know how to treat us; that our members may gain instruction, and that slanders and misrepresentations may be repelled and exposed.

I have again and again asked the gentleman, to what source of information he would direct those who desire to know what his church, as a body, understands the Bible to teach—but I could not induce him to answer the question. [Mr. C. I would direct them to the Bible.] He says, he would direct them to the Bible, to ascertain how his church understands the Bible! Yet when Mr. Jones, of England, wrote to him, and inquired what he understood the Bible to teach, he did not direct him to the Bible, but gave him a detailed account of his faith! Why did he treat Mr. Jones so much better than he treats others?

But all persons who make any pretensions to religion, profess to take the Bible as their guide—the Arians, Socinians, Universalists, and even the Shakers! They, however, attach widely different meanings to the language of the Scriptures. The gentleman's directions, therefore, would not give the information sought. A prudent and conscientious man will not unite himself to a church, until he knows what they understand the Scriptures to teach. Where, I again ask, can such a man gain the desired information concerning Mr. C.'s church? To this question I cannot get an answer. I have pressed it the more earnestly, because I have been charged with slandering his church, when I have said, that there is no source from which any one can learn what, as a body, they understand the Bible to teach. I, therefore, repeated the assertion in his presence, and called on him to disprove it if he could. He has not done so.

Another most important question I have asked, and asked in vain, is: What is the standard of ministerial qualification in his church, as to education, personal piety and soundness in the faith? What do they require of those whom they send forth to mould the faith of immortal spirits? Men are not employed to teach even a common school, unless they give evidence of possessing some suitable qualifications. Yet here is a church, claiming to be *the* church, that permits all sorts of doctrine to be preached by all sorts of men! It is not denied, that the Bible requires those who enter the ministry to possess important qualifications; but this church has no standard, and no uniformity in practice. A little church of a dozen members, or even a smaller number, may ordain and send forth preachers, to ruin the souls of multitudes by their errors! I leave you, my friends, to determine whether those churches that have a scriptural standard of ministerial qualification, or those that have none, are more faithfully discharging their solemn duties to the Head of the church, and the souls of men.

I have disproved the gentleman's proposition that creeds are necessarily heretical and schismatical, by the fact that there is more heresy and more schism in the churches that have no creeds, than in those that have them. I have taken Mr. Campbell's church as the latest and best edition of a no-creed church. Into this church, errorists of all grades may enter; and from it they cannot be excluded, without a departure from the fundamental principles they have adopted.

I. Mr. C. contends, that when persons desire membership in the church, we have no right to ask them more than two questions, viz: 1st. Do you believe that Jesus Christ is the Son of God? 2d. Are you willing to be baptized? If they answer these questions in the affirmative, he holds, that they are to be admitted without further inquiry. Now, we know that errorists of all grades will answer these affirmatively; consequently the door is open for them all to enter.

II. Mr. C. has said that he will receive into his church persons who hold Universalist and Unitarian sentiments; and I have proved, by his own publication, that he has, in fact, received such. But, mark the strange mixture of latitudinarianism and tyranny in his principles. He will receive a Unitarian or a Trinitarian; but he says, they shall not be permitted to apply to the Father, the Son, and the Holy Spirit, "scholastic and barbarous epithets." That is, they are not to use language which he choses to call scholastic and barbarous. But where has God forbidden men to use any words which convey not erroneous sentiments? By what authority does Mr. C. undertake to dictate to men what words they may use to express their ideas?

This is not all. He will receive a Universalist, for example, only on condition that he will hold his faith as an *opinion*, and abstain from all attempts to propagate it. But how can any conscientious man be reduced to promise not to propagate truths which he honestly believes to be taught in the Bible? Yet he must sacrifice his conscience, or he will not be received!

Mr. C., as I have proved, received into his church B. W. Stone, though he openly denies the Divinity and the atonement of Christ; and he received Dr. Thomas, though he denied that men have souls! Mr. Stone and Mr. Campbell differ infinitely in their faith—the one denying the Divinity of Christ, and the other asserting it; the one denying the atonement of Christ, and the other contending for it. Still they united!

Mr. C. makes an important difference between *faith* and *opinion*. I called on him to inform us precisely where faith ends and opinion begins. He told us, that when we have the testimony of the Scriptures concerning any point, it is a matter of faith. I then proved that he had disregarded his own principles; for he admits that we have clear testimony concerning the character and work of Christ, and yet he has received those who deny both. He admits that we have testimony concerning the eternal punishment of the wicked; and yet he has received those who deny it. He contends that we have testimony concerning the *design* of baptism; and yet he has received a prominent man who denies his doctrine on this subject!

III. I have read the testimony of Mr. C. concerning the present state of his church; and from it we learn that they have all sorts of doctrine preached by almost all sorts of men; and that it is bleeding at every pore by the lacerations of its own preachers and teachers!—and worse still, they have no way of preventing such disorders!! Yet this is the *model church* of the nineteenth century! This church receives into its capacious bosom errorists of all grades, if only they will be immersed and give up infant baptism.

IV. Mr. C., after all, has a creed—a most exclusive creed. He requires all to adopt his opinion concerning the mode of baptism. All must be immersed. He will allow them to think as they please concerning the character of the Son of God and his glorious work; or concerning the eternal state of the wicked; but they must be *immersed!* Thus you perceive that the gentleman attaches more importance to the mode of an external ordinance, than to the fundamental doctrines of the gospel!!

V. I have proved that there is more real christian union among "the sects," as the gentleman calls them, than amongst the reformers themselves. We differ not from Methodists, Baptists, Congregationalists, or any evangelical denomination, half so widely as Mr. Stone differs from Mr. Campbell; or as Messrs. Campbell, Fishback, Raines and Shannon, differ from each other!

VI. I have proved that Mr. C. has radically changed his ground on this subject; and is now advocating principles of church government which he once decidedly condemned.

The argument on this subject is now closed. I ask you, my friends, in view of all you have heard, has Mr. C. succeeded in proving that all who use a creed are guilty of heresy and schism? Has he proved that they are apostates from Christ, and rebels against him, and that they are worthy of excommunication from his family? Decide for yourselves, for you are as deeply interested as I. HAS HE PROVED HIS PROPOSITION, THAT HUMAN CREEDS ARE NECESSARILY HERETICAL AND SCHISMATICAL?

My friends, throughout this discussion I have defended doctrines which I solemnly believe to be taught in God's holy word. I have sought to sustain them by arguments, which, in my judgment, demonstrate their truth. We shall all, ere long, stand before the judgment seat of Christ, that we may answer for our faith and our practice. Then it becomes us to search for the truth, as for hidden treasures, and to prize it more than gold—yea, than much fine gold.

I solemnly believe that my friend, Mr. Campbell, is in error, seriously in error. Thousands of men, wiser than I, believe the same. It is for you to determine, so far as your duty and your interests are concerned, whether his doctrines are sustained by the word of God.

If there is a man living who could overthrow our doctrines, and establish those for which he has contended, he is the man. That he is a man of talents, and of considerable learning, all admit. He has been a man of war from his youth. For thirty years he has made himself thoroughly acquainted with the subjects we have discussed. He has for his opponent one, who, as he has more than once intimated, is greatly his inferior in talent and learning; so much so, that he could gain no new laurels by vanquishing him. Now has he sustained any one of his propositions? Has he gained a victory on a single proposition? To what conclusion must this intelligent audience come, after seeing the mighty chieftain falling under the blows of one so much his inferior.

I have the right, in view of his claim to superiority, to ascribe the success which has attended my efforts, in this discussion, to the strength of my cause. Even a weak man may, under the banner of truth, urge a successful war against a giant, who has not the truth to sustain him.

I will not make this discussion a *personal matter*. I am the enemy of no man. Boldly and fearlessly I must and will defend what I believe to be God's precious truth; but I am not the personal enemy of Mr. Campbell. I will yet be on terms of friendship with him, if he will permit me. I would not designedly or unnecessarily wound his feelings, or the feelings of others. I close this discussion with the kindest feelings towards my opponent and his friends. My prayer is, that God, in his mercy, will hasten the day, when true christian union—unity of the faith and in the knowledge of the Son of God, may universally prevail; when all the disciples of Christ shall be more nearly alike, and shall be able, more harmoniously and efficiently to co-operate in spreading over the earth the knowledge of the glorious Gospel; when they will present to the powers of darkness an unbroken phalanx. May all who bear the christian name, build on the Rock of Ages, that they may be able to stand, when the earth shall be shaken to its centre.

Gentlemen Moderators—I return to you my sincere thanks for your kindness and patience, in consenting to occupy so much of your time in attending upon our investigations, and for the dignified and impartial manner in which you have presided over this debate. May God, of his mercy, bestow upon you his richest blessings; and may you, having enjoyed the honors our country has conferred, and may yet confer upon you, attain to the unspeakably higher honor of being owned as children of God, and heirs of eternal felicity.—[*Time expired.*

[Elder Jacob Creath then arose, and pronounced the following benediction·]
Father of all our mercies! God of all consolation and favor! We pray that thy blessing may rest upon us all, and upon all those, in every place, who, with us, love and fear the Lord. Amen.